AMERICA'S
GOD AND COUNTRY
Encyclopedia Of Quotations

AMERICA'S
GOD AND COUNTRY
Encyclopedia Of Quotations

An Invaluable Resource
Highlighting America's Noble Heritage
Profound Quotes From Founding Fathers,
Presidents, Statesmen, Scientists,
Constitutions, Court Decisions ...

WILLIAM J. FEDERER

AMERISEARCH, INC.

P.O. Box 20163, St. Louis, MO 63123, 1-888-USA-WORD, www.amerisearch.net

ISBN 1-880563-09-6 (hard)
ISBN 1-880563-05-3 (paper)
CD ROM American Quotations (software)

Conditions of Use

Photographs, Illustrations and Other Credits

Front cover photograph: "The Declaration of Independence" (1786-1794) painted by John Trumbull. Reproduced by permission from the Architect of the United States Capitol. For more information, see entry in Chapter D, entitled "The Declaration of Independence," dated July 2, 1776.

Back cover photograph: "The First Prayer in Congress," September 7, 1774 in Carpenter's Hall, Philadelphia, by T.H. Matheson (c. 1848). Courtesy Library of Congress. For more information, see entry in Chapter C, entitled "Continental Congress," dated September 7, 1774.

Unless otherwise indicated, photographs and illustrations are reproduced by permission from *Dictionary of American Portraits, 0* 1967 by Dover Publications, Inc.; *The American Revolution: A Picture Sourcebook 0* 1975 by Dover Publications, Inc.; and other books from the Dover Pictorial Archive, by Dover Publications, Inc. Other illustrations are reproduced by permission from the Graphic Products Corporation.

Special acknowledgment is given to Karen Morgan, founder; People of the Past Historical Dramatizations; P.O. Box 426; Cortland, OH 44410; (216) 638-8606.

Library of Congress Cataloging-in-Publication Data

America's God and country: encyclopedia of quotations / [compiled by]
    William J. Federer.
        P. cm.
        "An invaluable reference highlighting America's noble heritage, for use in speeches, papers, debates, essays, editorials, civic addresses
        Includes bibliographical references and index.
        ISBN 1-880563-09-6: (alk. paper)
        ISBN 1-880563-05-3 (pbk.) : (alk. paper)

    1. Quotations, American--Encyclopedias.   I. Federer, William J. (William Joseph), 1957-

    PN608LA625 1999
    081--dc2O   93-11967 CIP

To my

beautiful,

lovely, faithful wife, Sue,

whose support made this book possible

and to our wonderful, precious children,

Jessica, Gabriel, Melody & Michael,

and to our children's children,

and to our children's

children's

children,

and...

Contents

Index of Entries

Courtesy Illustrations and Photographs

Appearing in alphabetical order by subject on the following pages, these illustrations are reproduced by courtesy of the sources listed below:

A
John Adams, 141, 559, Courtesy Independence National Historical Park

B
1st Lord Baltimore, George Calvert, 34, 419, Courtesy Enoch Pratt Free Library
2nd Lord Baltimore, Cecilius Calvert, 34, 419, Courtesy Enoch Pratt Free Library
Phineas Taylor Barnum, 37, Courtesy Loan Collection of Sterling Seeley, Barnum Museum
Richard Bassett, 38, Courtesy Historical Society of Delaware
Katherine Lee Bates, 39, Courtesy Mrs. Dorothy Burgess
Lyman Beecher, 43, Courtesy Library of Congress, Brady-Handy Collection
Jeremiah Sullivan Black, 51, Courtesy Library of Congress, Brady-Handy Collection
John Brown, 77, Courtesy Library of Congress, Brady-Handy Collection
William Cullen Bryant, 78, Courtesy New-York Historical Society
Benjamin Franklin Butler, 84, Courtesy Library of Congress, Brady-Handy Collection

C
Cecilius Calvert, 2nd Baron Baltimore, 34, 419, Courtesy Enoch Pratt Free Library
George Calvert, 1st Baron Baltimore, 34, 419, Courtesy Enoch Pratt Free Library
George Washington Carver, 93, Courtesy Tuskegee Institute
Salmon Portland Chase, 100, 172, Courtesy National Archives, Brady Collection
Christopher Columbus, 113, 306, Courtesy Eric Schaal
Calvin Coolidge, 180, Courtesy Library of Congress
Mrs. Calvin Coolidge (nee Grace Anne Goodhue), 181, Courtesy Forbes Library

D
John Dickinson, 211, Courtesy Independence National Historical Park
Jonathan Dickinson, 494, 520, 703, Courtesy Princeton University Archives
Pierre Samuel du Pont de Nemours, 221, Courtesy E.I. du Pont de Nemours & Co., Inc.

E
Dwight David Eisenhower, 225, Courtesy Library of Congress
Mrs. Dwight David Eisenhower (nee Mamie Geneva Doud), 227, Courtesy White House Collection

F
Henry Ford, 94, Courtesy Automobile Manufacturers Association, Inc.
Benjamin Franklin, 246, Courtesy Independence National Historical Park
Mrs. Benjamin Franklin (nee Deborah Read), 247, Courtesy American Philosophical Society

G
James Abram Garfield, 256, Courtesy National Archives, Brady Collection
Ulysses Simpson Grant, 265, 366, Courtesy Peter A. Fuley & Son
Mrs. Ulysses Simpson Grant (nee Julia Dent), 265, Courtesy Library of Congress
Simon Greenleaf, 267, Courtesy Library of Congress

H
Alexander Hamilton, 274, 395, Courtesy Independence National Historical Park

Warren Gamaliel Harding, 278, Courtesy Library of Congress
Benjamin Harrison, 279, Courtesy Benjamin H. Walker
William Henry Harrison, 279, Courtesy Metropolitan Museum of Art, Stokes-Hawes Collection
Nathaniel Hawthorne, 283, Courtesy National Archives, Brady Collection
John Milton Hay, 284, Courtesy Brown University Library, John Hay Collection
Rutherford Birchard Hayes, 286, Courtesy Library of Congress, Brady-Handy Collection
Patrick Henry, 287, Courtesy Colonial Williamsburg
Herbert Clark Hoover, 295, Courtesy Library of Congress

J
Andrew Jackson, 307, 310, Courtesy Metropolitan Museum of Art, Dick Fund
Thomas Jefferson, 322, 397 Courtesy Princeton University
Thomas Jefferson, 327, 666, Courtesy Bowdoin College Museum of Art
Lyndon Baines Johnson, 335, Courtesy Library of Congress
William Samuel Johnson, 337, Courtesy Columbiana Collection, Columbia University

K
Howard Atwood Kelly, 343, Courtesy New York Academy of Medicine
John Fitzgerald Kennedy, 346, Courtesy The White House

L
Henry Lee, 363, 635, Courtesy Independence National Historical Park
Richard Henry Lee, 362, Courtesy Independence National Historical Park
Robert Edward Lee, 363, Courtesy Library of Congress, Brady-Handy Collection
Sir Lionel Luckhoo, 404, Courtesy Sir Lionel Luckhoo

M
John Marshall, 417, Courtesy Virginia Museum of Fine Arts, The Glasgow Fund
Mayflower replica at Plymouth Bay, Massachusetts, 435, Courtesy Margaret J. Kinney
William Holmes McGuffey, 439, Courtesy Ohio University
James McHenry, 442, Courtesy Independence National Historical Park
Minuteman Monument at Lexington, Massachusetts, 60, 427, Courtesy Margaret J. Kinney
John Peter Muhlenberg, 460, 641 Courtesy Independence National Historical Park

P
Matthew Calbraith Perry, 509, Courtesy New-York Historical Society

R
Edmund Jennings Randolph, 152, 249, 526, Courtesy Virginia State Library
M.G. "Pat" Robertson, 535, Courtesy Christian Broadcasting Network, Inc.
Franklin Delano Roosevelt, 537, Courtesy Franklin D. Roosevelt Library
Franklin Delano Roosevelt, 538, Courtesy Library of Congress

S
Benjamin Silliman, 562, 709, Courtesy Burndy Library
Richard Stockton, 573, Courtesy Independence National Historical Park
William Ashley "Billy" Sunday, 578, Courtesy New-York Historical Society

T
William Howard Taft, 579, Courtesy Library of Congress
Charles Thomson, 139, Courtesy Independence National Historical Park
Harry S. Truman, 588, Courtesy Harry S. Truman Library

V
Martin Van Buren, 621, Courtesy U.S. Department of State

W
George Washington, 490, 643, Courtesy Henry Francis du Pont Winterthur Museum
George Washington, 644, Courtesy Washington and Lee University
Daniel Webster, 668, Courtesy New-York Historical Society
James Wilson, 696, Courtesy Independence National Historical Park
Woodrow Wilson, 697, Courtesy New-York Historical Society
John Witherspoon, 702, Courtesy Independence National Historical Park

Y
Elihu Yale, 707, Courtesy Yale University

A

School District of Abington Township, Pennsylvania (prior to 1963), endorsed the public school policy stating:

> Each school...shall be opened by the reading, without comment, of a chapter in the Holy Bible....Participation in the opening exercises...is voluntary. The student reading the verses from the Bible may select the passages and read from any version he chooses....There are no prefatory statements, no questions asked or solicited, no comments or explanations made and no interpretations given at or during the exercises. The students and parents are advised that the student may absent himself from the classroom or, should he elect to remain, not participate in the exercises.[1]

⁊

Lord Acton (1843-1902), whose given name was John Emerich Edward Dalberg Acton, was an English historian of great renown. He served as Regius Professor of Modern History at Cambridge University and as editor of the massive *Cambridge Modern History*. In 1877, Lord Acton declared, concerning liberty:

> That great political idea, sanctifying freedom and consecrating it to God, teaching men to treasure the liberties of others as their own, and to defend them for the love of justice and charity more than as a claim of right, has been the soul of what is great and good in the progress of the last two hundred years.[2]

In a letter to Bishop Mandell Creighton, dated April 5, 1881, Lord Acton wrote:

All power tends to corrupt and absolute power corrupts absolutely.[3]

ᴥ

Abigail Adams (1744-1818), was the wife of John Adams, the 2nd President of the United States of America, and the mother of 6th President, John Quincy Adams. At the age of 20, she married John Adams and they had five children. She strongly supported her husband's career. Her letters and memoirs are now considered major historical documents revealing life during the Revolutionary era.

Abigail Adams

On October 16, 1774, just prior to the outbreak of war with Great Britain, Abigail wrote to John Adams from their home in Braintree:

> I dare not express to you, at three hundred miles distance, how ardently I long for your return....And whether the end will be tragical, Heaven only knows. You cannot be, I know, nor do I wish to see you, an inactive spectator; but if the sword be drawn, I bid adieu to all domestic felicity, and look forward to that country where there are neither wars nor rumors of war, in a firm belief that through the mercy of its King we shall both rejoice there together...
>
> Your most affectionate,
> Abigail Adams.[4]

On June 18, 1775, in the midst of the conflict with Britain, Abigail Adams wrote to her husband, John:

> The race is not to the swift, nor the battle to the strong; but the God of Israel is He that giveth strength and power unto His people. Trust in Him at all times, ye people, pour out your hearts before Him; God is a refuge for us.
>
> Charlestown is laid in ashes. The battle began upon our entrenchments upon Bunker's Hill, Saturday morning about 3 o'clock, and has not ceased yet, and it is now three o'clock Sabbath afternoon. It is expected they will come out over the Neck tonight, and a dreadful battle must ensue. Almighty God, cover the heads of our countrymen, and be a shield to our dear friends...
>
> Abigail Adams.[5]

On Sunday, September 16, 1775, Abigail wrote to John Adams of her trust in God:

> I set myself down to write with a heart depressed with the melancholy scenes around me. My letter will be only a bill of mortality; though thanks be to the Being who restraineth the pestilence, that it has not yet proved mortal to any of our family, though we live in daily expectation that Patty will not continue many hours....
>
> And unto Him who mounts the whirlwind and directs the storm, I will cheerfully leave the ordering of my lot and whether adverse or prosperous days should be my future portion, I will trust in His right Hand to lead me safely through, and after a short rotation of events, fix me in a state immutable and happy....Adieu! I need not say how sincerely I am your affectionate
>
> Abigail Adams.[6]

Near the time of November 5, 1775, Abigail wrote to her friend, Mercy Warren:

> A patriot without religion in my estimation is as great a paradox as an honest Man without the fear of God. Is it possible that he whom no moral obligations bind, can have any real Good Will towards Men? Can he be a patriot who, by an openly vicious conduct, is undermining the very bonds of Society?...The Scriptures tell us "righteousness exalteth a Nation."[7]

On June 20, 1776, Abigail Adams wrote to reassure her husband, John, in Philadelphia:

> I feel no anxiety at the large armament designed against us. The remarkable interpositions of heaven in our favor cannot be too gratefully acknowledged. He who fed the Israelites in the wilderness, who clothes the lilies of the field and who feeds the young ravens when they cry, will not forsake a people engaged in so right a cause, if we remember His loving kindness.[8]

On March 20, 1780, Abigail Adams wrote to her son, John Quincy Adams:

> The only sure and permanent foundation of virtue is religion. Let

this important truth be engraven upon your heart....Justice, humanity and benevolence are the duties you owe to society in general. To your Country the same duties are incumbent upon you with the additional obligation of sacrificing ease, pleasure, wealth and life itself for its defense and security.[9]

On February 8, 1797, Abigail wrote to her husband, John, at the occasion of his election as the 2nd President of the United States:

You have this day to declare yourself head of a nation. "And now, O Lord, my God, Thou hast made thy servant ruler over the people. Give unto him an understanding heart, that he may know how to go out and come in before this great people; that he may discern between good and bad. For who is able to judge this thy so great a people?" were the words of a royal Sovereign; and not less applicable to him who is invested with the Chief Magistracy of a nation, though he wear not a crown, nor robes of royalty....

Though personally absent...my petitions to Heaven are that "the things which make for peace may not be hidden from your eyes."...That you may be enabled to discharge them with honor to yourself, with justice and impartiality to your country, and with satisfaction to this great people, shall be the daily prayer of your

Abigail Adams.[10]

૨▲

✓ John Adams (1735-1826), was the 2nd President of the United States of America and the first president to live in the White House. He had also served as the Vice-President for eight years under President George Washington. The Library of Congress and the Department of the Navy were established under his presidency.

John Adams

A graduate of Harvard, John Adams became a member of the Continental Congress and a signer of the Declaration of Independence. He is distinguished for having personally urged Thomas Jefferson to write the Declaration, as well as for having recommended George Washington as the Commander-in-Chief of the Continental Army. He was the main author of the Constitution of Massachusetts in 1780.

John Adams was the U.S. Minister to France, and, along with John Jay and Benjamin Franklin, helped negotiate the treaty with Great Britain ending the Revolutionary War. Later he was U.S. Minister to Britain. During this time he greatly influenced the American states to ratify the Constitution by writing a three-volume work entitled, *A Defense of the Constitutions of the Government of the United States.*

In his diary entry dated February 22, 1756, John Adams wrote:

> Suppose a nation in some distant region should take the Bible for their only law book, and every member should regulate his conduct by the precepts there exhibited! Every member would be obliged in conscience, to temperance, frugality, and industry; to justice, kindness, and charity towards his fellow men; and to piety, love, and reverence toward Almighty God....What a Eutopia, what a Paradise would this region be.[11]

John Adams wrote in his notes for *A Dissertation on the Canon and Feudal Law*, February of 1765:

> I always consider the settlement of America with reverence and wonder, as the opening of a grand scene and design in Providence for the illumination of the ignorant, and the emancipation of the slavish part of mankind all over the earth.[12]

In his diary, Sunday, February 9, 1772, John Adams wrote:

> "If I would go to Hell for an eternal moment or so, I might be knighted"—Shakespeare.
>
> By a courtier I mean one who applies himself to the passions and prejudices, the follies and vices of great men in order to obtain their smiles, esteem and patronage, and consequently their favours and preferments....
> A Master requires of all who seek his favour an implicit resignation to his will and humor, and these require that he be soothed, flattered, and assisted in his vices and follies, perhaps the blackest crimes that men can commit. The first thought of this will produce in a mind...a soliloquy, something like my [Shakespeare] motto—as if he should say—The Minister of State or the Governor would promote my interest,

would advance me to places of honour and profit, would raise me to titles and dignities that will be perpetuated in my family, in a word would make the fortune of me and my posterity forever, if I would but comply with his desires and become his instruments to promote his measures....

We see every day that our imaginations are so strong and our reason so weak, the charms of wealth and power are so enchanting, and the belief of future punishments so faint that men find ways to persuade themselves to believe any absurdity, to submit to any prostitution, rather than forego their wishes and desires. Their reason becomes at last an eloquent advocate on the side of their passions, and [they] bring themselves to believe that black is white, that vice is virtue, that folly is wisdom and eternity a moment....

I dread the consequences. [A master] requires of me such compliances, such horrid crimes, such a sacrifice of my honour, my conscience, my friends, my country, my God, as the Scriptures inform us must be punished with nothing less than Hell fire, eternal torment. And this is so unequal a price to pay for the honours and emoluments in the power of a minister or Governor, that I cannot prevail upon myself to think of it. The duration of future punishment terrifies me. If I could but deceive myself so far as to think eternity a moment only, I could comply and be promoted.[13]

On July 4, 1774, John Adams wrote to his wife, Abigail, from Patten's at Arundel:

We went to meeting at Wells and had the pleasure of hearing my friend upon "Be not partakers in other men's sins. Keep yourselves pure."

...We...took our horses to the meeting in the afternoon and heard the minister again upon "Seek first the kingdom of God and his righteousness, and all these things shall be added unto you." There is great pleasure in hearing sermons so serious, so clear, so sensible and instructive as these...[14]

On September 7, 1774, John Adams wrote to his wife, Abigail, describing the effects of the prayer which opened the first session of the Continental Congress:

When the Congress met, Mr. Cushing made a motion that it should be opened with Prayer. It was opposed by Mr. Jay of New York, and Mr. Rutledge of South Carolina because we were so divided in religious sentiments, some Episcopalians, some Quakers, some Anabaptists, some Presbyterians, and some Congregationalists, that we could not join in the same act of worship.

Mr. Samuel Adams arose and said that he was no bigot, and could hear a Prayer from any gentleman of Piety and virtue, who was at the same time a friend to his Country. He was a stranger in Philadelphia, but had heard that Mr. Duche' deserved that character and therefore he moved that Mr. Duche', an Episcopal clergyman might be desired to read Prayers to Congress tomorrow morning.

The motion was seconded, and passed in the affirmative. Mr. Randolph, our president, vailed on Mr. Duche', and received for answer, that if his health would permit, he certainly would.[15]

Accordingly, next morning [the Rev. Mr. Duche'] appeared with his clerk and in his pontificals, and read several prayers in the established form, and read the collect for the seventh day of September, which was the thirty-fifth Psalm. You must remember, this was the next morning after we heard the horrible rumor of the cannonade of Boston.

I never saw a greater effect upon an audience. It seemed as if heaven had ordained that Psalm to be read on that morning. After this, Mr. Duche', unexpectedly to everybody, struck out into an extemporary prayer, which filled the bosom of every man present. I must confess, I never heard a better prayer, or one so well pronounced.

Episcopalian as he is, Dr. Cooper himself [Adams' personal pastor] never prayed with such fervor, such ardor, such earnestness and pathos, and in language so elegant and sublime, for America, for the Congress, for the province of Massachusetts Bay, and especially the town of Boston. It has had an excellent effect upon everybody here. I must beg you to read that Psalm.[16]

On October 9, 1774, John Adams wrote from Philadelphia to his wife, Abigail:

> This day I went to Dr. Allison's meeting in the afternoon, and heard the Dr. Francis Allison...give a good discourse upon the Lord's Supper....
>
> I had rather go to Church. We have better sermons, better prayers, better speakers, softer, sweeter music, and genteeler company. And I must confess that the Episcopal church is quite as agreeable to my taste as the Presbyterian....I like the Congregational way best, next to that the Independent...[17]

In 1774, John Adams wrote a commentary entitled, *Novanglus:*

A History of the Dispute with America, from its Origin, in 1754, to the Present Time. In it, Adams admonished the clergy to speak out regarding public errors, saying:

> It is the duty of the clergy to accommodate their discourses to the times, to preach against such sins as are most prevalent, and recommend such virtues as are most wanted. For example, if exorbitant ambition and venality are predominant, ought they not to warn their hearers against those vices? If public spirit is much wanted, should they not inculcate this great virtue? If the rights and duties of Christian magistrates and subjects are disputed, should they not explain them, show their nature, ends, limitations, and restrictions, how much soever it may move the gall of Massachusetts.[18]

On June 21, 1776, John Adams wrote:

> Statesmen, my dear Sir, may plan and speculate for liberty, but it is Religion and Morality alone, which can establish the Principles upon which Freedom can securely stand.
> The only foundation of a free Constitution is pure Virtue, and if this cannot be inspired into our People in a greater Measure, than they have it now, they may change their Rulers and the forms of Government, but they will not obtain a lasting liberty.[19]

In contemplating the effect that separation from England would mean to him personally, John Adams wrote:

> If it be the pleasure of Heaven that my country shall require the poor offering of my life, the victim shall be ready, at the appointed hour of sacrifice, come when that hour may. But while I do live, let me have a country, and that a free country![20]

On July 1, 1776, John Adams spoke profoundly at the Continental Congress to the delegates from the Thirteen Colonies:

> Before God, I believe the hour has come. My judgement approves this measure, and my whole heart is in it. All that I have, and all that I am, and all that I hope in this life, I am now ready here to stake upon it. And I leave off as I began, that live or die, survive or perish, I am for the Declaration. It is my living sentiment, and by the blessing of God

it shall be my dying sentiment. Independence now, and Independence for ever![21]

On July 3, 1776, the day following Congress' approval of the Declaration of Independence, John Adams wrote to his wife, Abigail, regarding the gravity of the decision:

It is the will of heaven that the two countries should be sundered forever. It may be the will of heaven that America shall suffer calamities still more wasting and distresses yet more dreadful. If this is to be the case, it will have this good effect, at least: it will inspire us with many virtues which we have not, and correct many errors, follies and vices, which threaten to disturb, dishonor and destroy us...The furnace of affliction produces refinements in states, as well as individuals.[22]

On July 3, 1776, John Adams wrote again to his wife, Abigail, reflecting on what he had shared in Congress and, with prophetic insight, declaring the importance of that day:

The second day of July, 1776, will be the most memorable epoch in the history of America. I am apt to believe that it will be celebrated by succeeding generations as the great anniversary Festival. It ought to be commemorated, as the Day of Deliverance, by solemn acts of devotion to God Almighty. It ought to be solemnized with pomp and parade, with shows, games, sports, guns, bells, bonfires and illuminations, from one end of this continent to the other, from this time forward forever.

You will think me transported with enthusiasm, but I am not. I am well aware of the toil and blood and treasure that it will cost to maintain this Declaration, and support and defend these States. Yet through all the gloom I can see the rays of ravishing light and glory. I can see that the end is worth more than all the means; that posterity will triumph in that day's transaction, even though we [may regret] it, which I trust in God we shall not.[23]

On June 2, 1778, John Adams made this journal entry while in Paris:

In vain are Schools, Academies, and Universities instituted, if loose Principles and licentious habits are impressed upon Children in their earliest years....The Vices and Examples of the Parents cannot be concealed from the Children. How is it possible that Children can have any just Sense of the sacred Obligations of Morality or Religion if, from their earliest Infancy, they learn their Mothers live in habitual Infidelity to their fathers, and their fathers in as constant Infidelity to their Mothers?[24]

In concern for his sons, John Adams advised his wife, Abigail, to:

Let them revere nothing but Religion, Morality and Liberty.[25]

John Adams, in a letter written from Holland on July 12, 1782, twice referred to politics as:

A divine science.[26]

In retorting Thomas Paine's assertions, John Adams stated in his diary, July 26, 1796:

The Christian religion is, above all the Religions that ever prevailed or existed in ancient or modern times, the religion of Wisdom, Virtue, Equity, and Humanity. Let the Blackguard Paine say what he will; it is Resignation to God, it is Goodness itself to Man.[27]

On March 4, 1797, in his Inaugural Address, President John Adams declared:

And may that Being who is supreme over all, the Patron of Order, the Fountain of Justice, and the Protector in all ages of the world of virtuous liberty, continue His blessings upon this nation.[28]

On October 11, 1798, President John Adams stated in his address to the military:

We have no government armed with power capable of contending with human passions unbridled by morality and religion. Avarice, ambition, revenge, or gallantry, would break the strongest cords of our Constitution as a whale goes through a net. Our Constitution was made only for a moral and religious people. It is wholly inadequate to the government of any other.[29]

On March 6, 1799, President John Adams called for a *National Fast Day:*

> As no truth is more clearly taught in the Volume of Inspiration, nor any more fully demonstrated by the experience of all ages, than that a deep sense and a due acknowledgment of the growing providence of a Supreme Being and of the accountableness of men to Him as the searcher of hearts and righteous distributer of rewards and punishments are conducive equally to the happiness of individuals and to the well-being of communities....
>
> I have thought proper to recommend, and I hereby recommend accordingly, that Thursday, the twenty-fifth day of April next, be observed throughout the United States of America as a day of solemn humiliation, fasting, and prayer;
>
> that the citizens on that day abstain, as far as may be, from their secular occupation, and devote the time to the sacred duties of religion, in public and in private;
>
> that they call to mind our numerous offenses against the most high God, confess them before Him with the sincerest penitence, implore his pardoning mercy, through the Great Mediator and Redeemer, for our past transgressions, and that through the grace of His Holy Spirit, we may be disposed and enabled to yield a more suitable obedience to his righteous requisitions in time to come; that He would interpose to arrest the progress of that impiety and licentiousness in principle and practice so offensive to Himself and so ruinous to mankind;
>
> that He would make us deeply sensible that "righteousness exalteth a nation but sin is a reproach to any people" (Proverbs 14:34).[30]

On November 2, 1800, John Adams became the first president to move into the White House. As he was writing a letter to his wife, he composed a beautiful prayer, which was later engraved upon the mantel in the state dining room:

John Adams

> I pray Heaven to bestow THE BEST OF BLESSINGS ON THIS HOUSE and All that shall

hereafter Inhabit it, May none but Honest and Wise Men ever rule under This Roof.[31]

In a letter to Judge F.A. Van der Kemp, February 16, 1809, John Adams wrote:

✓The Hebrews have done more to civilize men than any other nation....[God] ordered the Jews to preserve and propagate to all mankind the doctrine of a supreme, intelligent, wise, almighty sovereign of the universe....[which is] to be the great essential principle of morality, and consequently all civilization.[32]✓

On August 28, 1811, John Adams wrote:

Religion and virtue are the only foundations, not only of republicanism and of all free government, but of social felicity under all governments and in all the combinations of human society.[33]

In a letter to Mr. Warren, John Adams expounded:

[This] Form of Government...is productive of every Thing which is great and excellent among Men. But its Principles are as easily destroyed, as human nature is corrupted....A Government is only to be supported by pure Religion or Austere Morals. Private, and public Virtue is the only Foundation of Republics.[34]

On June 28, 1813, in a letter to Thomas Jefferson, John Adams wrote:

The general principles, on which the Fathers achieved independence, were the only Principles in which that beautiful Assembly of young Gentlemen could Unite....And what were these general Principles? I answer, the general Principles of Christianity, in which all these Sects were United: And the general Principles of English and American Liberty, in which all those young Men United, and which had United all Parties in America, in Majorities sufficient to assert and maintain her Independence.

Now I will avow, that I then believe, and now believe, that those general Principles of Christianity, are as eternal and immutable, as the Existence and Attributes of God; and that those Principles of Liberty, are as unalterable as human Nature and our terrestrial, mundane System.[35]

In a letter to Thomas Jefferson, John Adams wrote:

Have you ever found in history, one single example of a Nation thoroughly corrupted that was afterwards restored to virtue?...And without virtue, there can be no political liberty....Will you tell me how to prevent riches from becoming the effects of temperance and industry?

Will you tell me how to prevent luxury from producing effeminacy, intoxication, extravagance, vice and folly?...I believe no effort in favour of virtue is lost...[36]

In a letter to Thomas Jefferson, December 25, 1813, John Adams wrote:

I have examined all religions, as well as my narrow sphere, my straightened means, and my busy life, would allow; and the result is that the Bible is the best Book in the world. It contains more philosophy than all the libraries I have seen.[37]

In writing to Thomas Jefferson, June 20, 1815, John Adams explained:

The question before the human race is, whether the God of nature shall govern the world by His own laws...[38]

In a letter dated November 4, 1816, John Adams wrote to Thomas Jefferson:

The Ten Commandments and the Sermon on the Mount contain my religion...[39]

In a letter to Judge F.A. Van der Kemp, December 27, 1816, John Adams wrote:

As I understand the Christian religion, it was, and is, a revelation.[40]

On April 19, 1817, John Adams wrote in a letter to Thomas Jefferson:

> √ Without religion, this world would be something not fit to be mentioned in polite company.
> ...The most abandoned scoundrel that ever existed, never yet wholly extinguished his Conscience and while Conscience remains, there is some religion.[41] √

On October 7, 1818, John Adams wrote, telling Thomas Jefferson of his wife's impending death:

> ⌄ Now, sir, for my griefs! The dear partner of my life for 54 years as a wife and for many more as a lover, now lies in extremis, forbidden to speak or to be spoken to...If human life is a bubble, no matter how soon it breaks, if it is, as I firmly believe, an immortal existence, we ought patiently to wait the instructions of the great Teacher.
> I am, Sir, your deeply afflicted friend,
> John Adams[42] √

John Adams wrote:

> √ That you and I shall meet in a better world I have no doubt than we now exist on the same globe; if my reason did not convince me of this, Cicero's Dream of Scipio, and his Essay on Friendship and Old Age would have been sufficient for that purpose. But Jesus taught us that a future state is a social state, when He promised to prepare places in His Father's house of many mansions, for His disciples.[43] √

John Adams and Thomas Jefferson were on opposite sides of several major political issues, and many times engaged in heated debates. John Adams, the 2nd President, was succeeded in office by Thomas Jefferson. So strong were his feelings against Jefferson at the time, that Adams even left Washington, D.C., to avoid being at Jefferson's Inauguration.

Later in life, though, the two became the best of friends. Their correspondence reveals, not only their faith, but also their friendship. John Adams and Thomas Jefferson both died on the same day, July 4, 1826, exactly 50 years after they had signed the

Declaration of Independence. Once a hardened political opponent of Jefferson's, John Adams' last words were:

> ✓ Thank God, Jefferson lives![44] ✓

☙

John Quincy Adams (1767-1848), was the 6th President of the United States and son of John Adams, the 2nd President. When he was 11, John Quincy Adams' mother, Abigail Adams, sent him to be with his father who was serving as the U.S. Minister in France. He became so adept that, in three years at the age of 14, he received the Congressional appointment to the Court of Catherine the Great in Russia.

John Quincy Adams

He was a U.S. Senator; U.S. Minister to France; and U.S. Minister to Britain, where he negotiated the Treaty of Ghent, ending the War of 1812. He was Secretary of State for President James Monroe and in that position obtained Florida (1819) and promulgated the *Monroe Doctrine.*

John Quincy Adams, one of the few Presidents to re-enter politics after having served as President, became a Congressman in 1831 and adamantly opposed slavery. Nicknamed the "Hell-Hound of Slavery," he singlehandedly led the fight to lift the *Gag Rule* which had prohibited discussion of the slavery issue in Congress. When asked why he never seemed discouraged or depressed over championing such an unpopular fight, John Quincy Adams replied:

> ✓ Duty is ours; results are God's.[45] ✓

In September of 1811, John Quincy Adams wrote a letter to his son from St. Petersburg, Russia, while serving for the second time as an ambassador to that country:

> ✓ My dear Son:
> In your letter of the 18th January to your mother, you mentioned

---

that you read to your aunt a chapter in the Bible or a section of Doddridge's Annotations every evening.

This information gave me real pleasure; for so great is my veneration for the Bible, and so strong my belief, that when duly read and meditated on, it is of all books in the world, that which contributes most to make men good, wise, and happy—that the earlier my children begin to read it, the more steadily they pursue the practice of reading it throughout their lives, the more lively and confident will be my hopes that they will prove useful citizens of their country, respectable members of society, and a real blessing to their parents....

I have myself, for many years, made it a practice to read through the Bible once every year....

My custom is, to read four to five chapters every morning immediately after rising from my bed. It employs about an hour of my time....

It is essential, my son, in order that you may go through life with comfort to yourself, and usefulness to your fellow-creatures, that you should form and adopt certain rules or principles, for the government of your own conduct and temper....

It is in the Bible, you must learn them, and from the Bible how to practice them. Those duties are to God, to your fellow-creatures, and to yourself. "Thou shalt love the Lord thy God, with all thy heart, and with all thy soul, and with all thy mind, and with all thy strength, and thy neighbor as thy self." On these two commandments, Jesus Christ expressly says, "hang all the law and the prophets"; that is to say, the whole purpose of Divine Revelation is to inculcate them efficaciously upon the minds of men....

Let us, then, search the Scriptures....The Bible contains the revelation of the will of God. It contains the history of the creation of the world, and of mankind; and afterward the history of one peculiar nation, certainly the most extraordinary nation that has ever appeared upon the earth.

It contains a system of religion, and of morality, which we may examine upon its own merits, independent of the sanction it receives from being the Word of God....

I shall number separately those letters that I mean to write you upon the subject of the Bible....I wish that hereafter they may be useful to your brothers and sisters, as well as to you.

As you will receive them as a token of affection for you, during my absence....From your affectionate Father,

John Quincy Adams[46]

On December 31, 1812, John Quincy Adams penned this entry in his diary:

✓ I offer to a merciful God at the close of this year my humble tribute of gratitude for the blessings with which He has, in the course of it, favored me and those dear to me....

My endeavors to quell the rebellion of the heart have been sincere, and have been assisted with the blessing from above. As I advance in life, its evils multiply, and the instances of mortality become more frequent and approach nearer to myself. The greater is the need for fortitude to encounter the woes that flesh is heir to, and of religion to support pains for which there is no other remedy.[47] ✓

After negotiating the Treaty of Ghent, on December 24, 1814, John Quincy Adams wrote several times from London regarding the false doctrines which were being promulgated among the intellectuals back in Boston:

I perceive that the Trinitarians and the Unitarians in Boston are sparring together....Most of the Boston Unitarians are my particular friends, but I never thought much of the eloquence or the theology of Priestly. His *Socrates and Jesus Compared* is a wretched performance. Socrates and Jesus! A farthing candle and the sun! I pray you to read Massilon's sermon on the divinity of Christ, and then the whole New Testament, after which be a Socinian if you can.[48]

I find in the New Testament, Jesus Christ accosted in His own presence by one of His disciples as God, without disclaiming the appellation. I see Him explicitly declared by at least two other of the Apostles to be God, expressly and repeatedly announced, not only as having existed before the worlds, but as the Creator of the worlds without beginning of days or end of years. I see Him named in the great prophecy of Isaiah concerning him to be the mighty God!...

The texts are too numerous, they are from parts of the Scriptures too diversified, they are sometimes connected by too strong a chain of argument, and the inferences from them are, to my mind, too direct and irresistible, to admit of the explanations which the Unitarians sometimes attempt to give them, or the evasions by which, at others, they endeavor to escape from them.[49]

You ask me what Bible I take as the standard of my faith—the Hebrew, the Samaritan, the old English translation, or what? I answer, the Bible containing the Sermon on the Mount—any Bible that I can...understand. The New Testament I have repeatedly read in the original Greek, in the Latin, in the Geneva Protestant, in Sacy's

Catholic French translations, in Luther's German translation, in the common English Protestant, and in the Douay Catholic translations.

I take any one of them for my standard of faith. ...But the Sermon on the Mount commands me to lay up for myself treasures, not upon earth, but in Heaven. My hopes of a future life are all founded upon the Gospel of Christ .... You think it blasphemous that the omnipotent Creator could be crucified. God is a spirit. The spirit was not crucified. The body of Jesus of Nazareth was crucified.

The Spirit, whether external or created, was beyond the reach of the cross. You see, my orthodoxy grows on me, and I still unite with you in the doctrine of toleration and benevolence. [50]

John Wingate Thorton, in his book *The Pulpit of the American Revolution,* 1860, wrote:

The highest glory of the American Revolution , said John Quincy Adams, was this: it connected, in one indissoluble bond, the principles of civil government with the principles of Christianity. [51]

On July 4, 1821, John Quincy Adams stated:

√ From the day of the Declaration ... they (the American people) were bound by the laws of God, which they all, and by the laws of The Gospel, which they nearly all, acknowledge as the rules of their conduct. [52] √

On July 4, 1837, in a speech celebrating the 61st Anniversary of the signing of the Declaration, John Quincy Adams proclaimed to the inhabitants of the Town of Newburyport:

Why is it that, next to the birthday of the Savior of the World, your most joyous and most venerated festival returns on this day.

Is it not that, in the chain of human events, the birthday of the nation is indissolubly linked with the birthday of the Savior? That it forms a leading event in the Progress of the Gospel dispensation?

Is it not that the Declaration of Independence first organized the social compact on the foundation of the Redeemer's mission upon earth?

That it laid the cornerstone of human government upon the first precepts of Christianity and gave to the world the first irrevocable pledge of the fulfillment of the prophecies announced directly from Heaven at the birth of the Saviour and predicted by the greatest of the Hebrew prophets 600 years before. [53]

In 1838, in a speech before Congress, John Quincy Adams spoke:

Sir, I might go through the whole of the sacred history of the Jews to the advent of our Saviour and find innumerable examples of women who not only took an active part in politics of their times, but who are held up with honor to posterity for doing so. Our Savior himself, while on earth, performed that most stupendous miracle, of raising of Lazarus from the dead, at the petition of a woman.[54]

In his diary which he kept meticulously, John Quincy Adams made note of his church attendance:

There is scarcely a Sunday passes [that I don't] hear something of which a pointed application to my own situation and circumstances occurs to my thoughts. It is often consolation, support, encouragement—sometimes warning and admonition, sometimes keen and trying remembrance of deep distress. The lines [of the Isaac Watts hymn sung that Sunday] are of the cheering kind.[55]

John Quincy Adams revealed his convictions and philosophy in the following quotations:

The first and almost the only Book deserving of universal attention is the Bible.[56]

I speak as a man of the world to men of the world; and I say to you, Search the Scriptures! The Bible is the book of all others, to be read at all ages, and in all conditions of human life; not to be read once or twice or thrice through, and then laid aside, but to be read in small portions of one or two chapters every day, and never to be intermitted, unless by some overruling necessity.[57]

In what light soever we regard the Bible, whether with reference to revelation, to history, or to morality, it is an invaluable and inexhaustible mine of knowledge and virtue.[58]

It is no slight testimonial, both to the merit and worth of Christianity, that in all ages since its promulgation the great mass of those who have risen to eminence by their profound wisdom and integrity have recognized and reverenced Jesus of Nazareth as the Son of the living God.[59] ✓

✓ Posterity—you will never know how much it has cost my generation to preserve your freedom. I hope you will make good use of it.[60] ✓

On February 27, 1844, at the age of 77, John Quincy Adams was not only a U.S. Congressman, but also the chairman of the American Bible Society. In addressing that organization, he proclaimed:

✓ I deem myself fortunate in having the opportunity, at a stage of a long life drawing rapidly to its close, to bear at this place, the capital of our National Union, in the Hall of representatives of the North American people, in the chair of the presiding officer of the assembly representing the whole people, the personification of the great and mighty nation—to bear my solemn testimonial of reverence and gratitude to that book of books, the Holy Bible....

The Bible carries with it the history of the creation, the fall and redemption of man, and discloses to him, in the infant born at Bethlehem, the Legislator and Saviour of the world.[61] ✓

On December 3, 1844, after nearly eight years of anti-slavery effort, John Quincy Adams' motion succeeded to rescind the infamous *Gag Rule,* which had forbidden the discussion of slavery in the Congress. His recognition as a national hero came after a long, lonely and unpopular struggle against powerful slavery interests. He wrote in his diary:

✓ Blessed, forever blessed, be the name of God![62] ✓

On July 11, 1846, his 80th birthday, John Quincy Adams entered in his diary:

✓ I enter upon my eightieth year, with thanksgiving to God for all the blessings and mercies which His providence has bestowed upon me throughout a life extended now to the longest term allotted to the life of man; with supplication for the continuance of those blessings and mercies to me and mine, as long as it shall suit the dispensations of His wise providence, and for resignation to His will when my appointed time shall come.[63]

In an article in *The Churchman,* John Quincy Adams wrote:

There are two prayers that I love to say—the first is the Lord's Prayer, and because the Lord taught it; and the other is what seems to be a child's prayer: "Now I lay me down to sleep," and I love to say that because it suits me. I have been repeating it every night for many years past, and I say it yet, and I expect to say it my last night on earth if I am conscious. But I have added a few words more to the prayer so as to express my trust in Christ, and also to acknowledge what I ask, for I ask as a favor, and not because I deserve it. This is it:

"Now I lay me down to sleep,
I pray the Lord my soul to keep;
If I should die before I wake,
I pray the Lord my soul to take;
For Jesus' sake. Amen."[64]

Near the end of his life, John Quincy Adams made these entries in his diary:

May I never cease to be grateful for the numberless blessings received through life at His hands, never repine at what He has denied, never murmur at the dispensations of Providence, and implore His forgiveness for all the errors and delinquencies of my life![65]

Providence, has showered blessings upon me profusely. But they have been blessings unforseen and unsought. *Non nobis, Domine, non nobis, sed nomini tuo do gloriam.* [Not to us, Lord, not to us, but to your name be the glory.][66]

❧

Samuel Adams (1722-1803), was known as the "Father of the American Revolution." Along with his cousin John Adams, Samuel Adams labored over 20 years as a patriot and leader. He instigated the Boston Tea Party, signed the Declaration of Independence,

Samuel Adams

called for the first Continental Congress and served as a member of Congress until 1781.

He helped draft the Massachusetts Constitution, and served as Lieutenant Governor under Governor John Hancock. He later became the Governor of Massachusetts.

Samuel Adams formed the Committees of Correspondence, which were largely responsible for the unity and cohesion of the Colonists preceding the Revolution. The original Committee, formed in Boston, had three goals: (1) to delineate the rights of Colonists as men, (2) to detail how these rights had been violated, (3) to publicize these rights and the violations thereof throughout the Colonies. His reports were spread like fire through the towns and parishes, many times by an early *pony express* system. His work, *The Rights of the Colonists*, was circulated in 1772:

> The right to freedom being the gift of the Almighty...
> The rights of the colonists as Christians...may be best understood by reading and carefully studying the institution of The Great Law Giver and Head of the Christian Church, which are to be found clearly written and promulgated in the New Testament.[67]

On September 6, 1774, the second day of the Continental Congress, Samuel Adams proposed that the session be opened with prayer, in spite of the various Christian sects represented:

The colonists delivered important news on handbills by pony express.

> Christian men, who had come together for solemn deliberation in the hour of their extremity, to say there was so wide a difference in their

religious belief that they could not, as one man, bow the knee in prayer to the Almighty, whose advice and assistance they hoped to obtain. [68]

As the Declaration of Independence was being signed, 1776, Samuel Adams declared:

We have this day restored the Sovereign to Whom all men ought to be obedient. He reigns in heaven and from the rising to the setting of the sun, let His kingdom come. [69]

In a letter to James Warren, February 12, 1779, Samuel Adams wrote:

A general dissolution of principles and manners will more surely overthrow the liberties of America than the whole force of the common enemy. While the people are virtuous they cannot be subdued; but when they lose their virtue they will be ready to surrender their liberties to the first external or internal invader.... If virtue and knowledge are diffused among the people, they will never be enslaved. This will be their great security. [70]

Samuel Adams stated:

Neither the wisest constitution nor the wisest laws will secure the liberty and happiness of a people whose manners are universally corrupt. [71]

He therefore is the truest friend to the liberty of his country who tries most to promote its virtue, and who, so far as his power and influence extend, will not suffer a man to be chosen into any office of power and trust who is not a wise and virtuous man .... The sum of all is, if we would most truly enjoy this gift of Heaven, let us become a Virtuous people. [72]

On October 4,1790, Samuel Adams wrote to his cousin John Adams, who was then Vice-President of the United States:

Let divines and philosophers, statesmen and patriots, unite their endeavors to renovate the age, by impressing the minds of men with the importance of educating their little boys and girls, of inculcating in the minds of youth the fear and love of the Deity and universal philanthropy, and, in subordination to these great principles, the love of their country; of instructing them in the art of self-government without which they never can act a wise part in the government of societies, great or small; in short, of leading them in the study and practice of the exalted virtues of the Christian system.[73]

On October 18, 1790, John Adams wrote in reply concerning these issues, stating:

You and I agree.[74]

In 1794, Governor Samuel Adams of Massachusetts, having just risen from Lieutenant Governor upon the death of Governor John Hancock, addressed the state legislature:

✓ In the supposed state of nature, all men are equally bound by the laws of nature, or to speak more properly, the laws of the Creator:— They are imprinted by the finger of God on the heart of man. Thou shall do no injury to thy neighbor, is the voice of nature and reason, and it is confirmed by written revelation.[75] ✓

Samuel Adams declared:

I conceive we cannot better express ourselves than by humbly supplicating the Supreme Ruler of the world....
that the confusions that are and have been among the nations may be overruled by the promoting and speedily bringing in the holy and happy period when the kingdoms of our Lord and Saviour Jesus Christ may be everywhere established, and the people willingly bow to the sceptre of Him who is the Prince of Peace.[76]

In addressing the young man whom his daughter intended to marry, Samuel Adams remarked:

I could say a thousand things to you, if I had leisure. I could dwell on the importance of piety and religion, of industry and frugality, of prudence, economy, regularity and even Government, all of which are essential to the well being of a family. But I have not time. I cannot however help repeating piety, because I think it indispensable. Religion in a family is at once its brightest ornament and its best security.[77]

Samuel Adams wrote in his *Will:*

√ Principally, and first of all, I resign my soul to the Almighty Being who gave it, and my body I commit to the dust, relying on the merits of Jesus Christ for the pardon of my sins.[78] ✓

ॐ

Robert Aitken (1734-1802), on January 21, 1781, as publisher of *The Pennsylvania Magazine*, petitioned Congress for permission to print Bibles, since there was a shortage of Bibles in America due to the Revolutionary War interrupting trade with England. The Continental Congress, September 10, 1782, in response to this shortage of Bibles, approved and recommended to the people that *The Holy Bible* be printed by Robert Aitken of Philadelphia. This first American Bible was to be "a neat edition of the Holy Scriptures for the use of schools":[79]

> Whereupon, Resolved, That the United States in Congress assembled...recommend this edition of the Bible to the inhabitants of the United States, and hereby authorize [Robert Aitken] to publish this recommendation in the manner he shall think proper.[80]

ॐ

Alabama Courts 1983, in the case of *Jaffree v. Board of School Commissioners of Mobile County*, 544 F. Supp. 1104 (S. D. Ala. 1983), Judge Brevard Hand quoted from the nineteenth-century United States Supreme Court Justice Joseph Story, who succinctly clarified the original meaning of the First Amendment:

> The real object of the First Amendment was not to countenance, much less to advance Mohammedanism, or Judaism, or infidelity, by prostrating Christianity, but to exclude all rivalry among Christian sects [denominations] and to prevent any national ecclesiastical patronage of the national government.[81]

ॐ

Ethan Allen (1738-1789), was an American Revolutionary War leader and Commander of the Green Mountain Boys. On the morning of May 10, 1775, in a surprise attack, Allen's troops surrounded Fort Ticonderoga on Lake Champlain. Ethan Allen demanded that Captain de la Place surrender the fort instantly. The bewildered captain asked in whose name and in whose authority Allen was making such a demand. Ethan Allen responded:

> In the Name of the Great Jehovah and the Continental Congress.[82]

૨ઌ

Fisher Ames (1758-1808), was a Congressman from Massachusetts in the First Session of the Congress of the United States when the Bill of Rights was formulated. It was Fisher Ames who, on August 20, 1789, suggested the wording of the First Amendment, which was adopted by the House:

Fisher Ames

> Congress shall make no law establishing religion, or to prevent the free exercise thereof, or to infringe the rights of conscience.[83]

Fisher Ames shared his beliefs concerning education:

> Should not the Bible regain the place it once held as a schoolbook? Its morals are pure, its examples are captivating and noble.... The reverence for the sacred book that is thus early impressed lasts long; and, probably, if not impressed in infancy, never takes firm hold of the mind.... In no Book is there so good English, so pure and so elegant, and by teaching all the same they will speak alike, and the Bible will justly remain the standard of language as well as of faith.[84]

On September 20, 1789, in an article published in *Palladium* magazine, Fisher Ames stated:

> We have a dangerous trend beginning to take place in our education. We're starting to put more and more textbooks into our schools.... We've become accustomed of late of putting little books into the hands of children containing fables and moral lessons.... We are spending less time in the classroom on the Bible, which should be the principal text in our schools.... The Bible states these great moral lessons better than any other manmade book.[85]

Proclamation of Amnesty 1863, included in President Abraham Lincoln's reconstruction plans for the south, contained a statement to be sworn to by those receiving pardon for activities during the Civil War:

> I, _____ _____, do solemnly swear, in presence of Almighty God, that I will henceforth faithfully support, protect, and defend the Constitution of the United States and the Union of the States thereunder....So help me God.[86]

Andre Marie Ampere (1775-1836), was a French electrician and scientific writer who discovered the relationship between magnetism and electricity, and defined a unit to measure the strength of an electric current. (Amperes equals volts divided by ohms.) Ampere wrote on a piece of paper before his death:

> Believe in God, in His providence, in a future life, in the recompense of the good; in the punishment of the wicked; in the sublimity and truth of the doctrines of Christ, in a revelation of this doctrine by a special divine inspiration for the salvation of the human race.[87]

Hans Christian Andersen (1805-1875), was a Danish novelist and story-writer, who authored many fairy tales, including *The Ugly Duckling*, *The Emperor's New Clothes* and *The Tinder Box*. In his autobiography, entitled *The Fairy Tale of My Life*, 1855, Hans Christian Andersen wrote:

> Depressed in spirit, I took up my Bible, which lay before me, for an oracle; opened it, pointed blindly at a place, and read: "O Israel, thou hast destroyed thyself; but in Me is thine help." (*Hosea.*) Yes, Father, I am weak, but Thou lookest into my heart and wilt be my help.
> Here also (Copenhagen) I obtained a place, after I had given seven pieces. The different periods of my life passed before me. I knelt down upon the stage and repeated our Lord's Prayer, just at the spot where I now sit amongst the first and distinguished men. Humility and

prayer unto God for strength to deserve happiness, filled my heart. May He always enable me to preserve these feelings.[88]

Hans Christian Andersen wrote what has become one of Denmark's best-known carols, entitled "Barn (Child) Jesus":

Child Jesus came to earth this day,
To save us sinners dying
And cradled in the straw and hay
The Holy One is lying.
The star shines down the child to greet,
The lowing oxen kiss his feet.
Hallelujah, Hallelujah, Child Jesus!

Take courage, Soul so weak and worn,
Thy sorrows have departed.
A Child in David's town is born,
To heal the broken hearted.
Then let us haste this child to find
And children be in heart and mind.
Hallelujah, Hallelujah, Child Jesus![89]

&

Henry Bowen Anthony

Henry Bowen Anthony (1815-1884), was a United States Senator, who, on January 9, 1872, delivered a eulogy of Roger Williams in Congress:

He knew, for God, whose prophet he was, revealed it to him, that the great principles for which he contended, and for which he suffered, founded in the eternal fitness of things, would endure forever. He did not inquire if his name would survive a generation. In his vision of the future he saw mankind emancipated from...the blindness of bigotry, from the cruelties of intolerance. He saw the nations walking forth into the liberty wherewith Christ had made them free.[90]

&

Motto of The State of Arizona 1912 (originally adopted in 1863), states:

√ Ditat Deus (God Enriches)[91] √

૱

Constitution of the State of Arkansas 1874, stated:

Preamble. We the people of Arkansas, grateful to Almighty God for the privilege of choosing and forming our own government...[92]

૱

Arkansas Supreme Court 1905, was quoted by Supreme Court Justice David J. Brewer in his lecture, entitled, "The United States a Christian Nation." The opinion rendered in the case of *Shover v. The State*, 10 English, 263, included:

This system of religion (Christianity) is recognized as constituting a part and parcel of the common law.[93]

૱

John Armstrong (1758-1843), was a Congressman, a United States Senator, a diplomat and a general. He expressed:

Nor is this spiritual and moral disease to be healed by a better education, a few external, transient thoughts. It requires the hand of the great Physician, the Lord Jesus Christ, by His Holy Spirit, and belief of the truth renewing the state of the mind and disposition of the heart as

John Armstrong

well, thereby leading the soul from a sense of fear of the wrath of God, the penalty of this broken law, and helpless in itself, to flee to the merits of Jesus, that only refuge or foundation which God hath laid in His Church, and who was made sin for us (that is, a sin-offering), that all "believers be made the righteousness of God by Him."[94]

૱

Chester Alan Arthur (1829-1886), was the 21st President of the United States of America, 1881-1885. The son of a Baptist preacher

in New York State, Chester Arthur graduated from college at the age of 18. He then became a lawyer and earned publicity for his strong anti-slavery efforts. Once he helped six slaves win freedom.

During the Civil War, Arthur served as the Quartermaster General for the State of New York. He was elected the Vice-President of the United States of America in 1881, and assumed the highest office when President Garfield died. Earning the nickname of Gentleman Boss for his success in running an honest government, Arthur's term spanned the period when international time zones were set, New York and Chicago were connected by telephone lines, and bank robber Jesse James was killed.

President Chester A. Arthur proclaimed:

> Heaven save us.[95]

&

Articles of Confederation November 15, 1777, proposed by the Continental Congress, constituted the government in America prior to the writing of the United States Constitution. It was signed July 9, 1778, and finally ratified by the states March 1, 1781:

> Whereas the delegates of the United States of America in Congress assembled did on the fifteenth day of November in the Year of Our Lord one thousand seven hundred and seventy seven, and in the second year of the independence of America agree on certain Articles of Confederation and perpetual union between the States...[96]

> And whereas it has pleased the Great Governor of the World to incline the hearts of the Legislatures we respectively represent in Congress, to approve of, and to authorize us to ratify the said Articles of Confederation and perpetual union.[97]

&

B

Johann Sebastian Bach (1685-1750), a famous German composer, was considered the "master of masters" because of his inspiring musical compositions. Bach composed a cantata which expressed the fervency of his faith in Christ's atoning work on the cross, entitled:

> Jesus, Meine Freude. (Jesus, My Joy!)[1]

Other great works displaying his faith include *Passion According to St. Matthew* and *Passion According to St. John*.

In expressing his conviction concerning the purpose of music, Johann Sebastian Bach asserted:

> The aim and final end of all music should be none other than the glory of God and the refreshment of the soul. If heed is not paid to this, it is not true music but a diabolical bawling and twanging.[2]

ॐ

Sir Francis Bacon (1561-1626), the Baron Verulam, Viscount St. Albans, was an English philosopher, essayist, courtier, jurist and statesman. As Lord Chancellor of England, Bacon was significantly responsible for the formulation and acceptance of the *scientific method*, which stressed gathering data from experimentation and induction rather than through the practice of philosophical deduction promulgated by Aristotle. Francis Bacon was responsible for helping to found the Royal Society of London. He wrote:

There are two books laid before us to study, to prevent our falling into error; first, the volume of Scriptures, which reveal the will of God; then the volume of the Creatures, which express His power.[3]

There never was found, in any age of the world, either philosophy, or sect, or religion, or law, or discipline, which did so highly exalt the good of the community, and increase private and particular good as the holy Christian faith. Hence, it clearly appears that it was one and the same God that gave the Christian law to men, who gave the laws of nature to the creatures.[4]

In his work, *The Advancement of Learning, Book II*, Sir Francis Bacon expressed:

But men must know that in this theater of man's life it is reserved only for God and the angels to be lookers on.[5]

All good moral philosophy is but the handmaid to religion.[6]

In his treatise entitled, *Of Atheism*, Sir Francis Bacon declared:

A little philosophy inclineth man's mind to atheism, but depth in philosophy bringeth men's minds about to religion.[7]

Sir Francis Bacon, as recorded in the *Literary and Religious Works of Francis Bacon, Volume II*, stated:

I believe that the Word of God, whereby His will is revealed, continued in revelation and tradition with Moses; and that the Scriptures were from Moses' time to the time of the Apostles and Evangelists; in whose ages, after the coming of the Holy Ghost, the teacher of all truth, the book of Scripture was shut and closed, so as to receive no new addition, and the Church hath no power after the Scriptures to teach or command anything contrary to the written word.
I believe that Jesus, the Lord, became in the flesh a sacrificer and a sacrifice for sin; a satisfaction and price paid to the justice of God; a meriter of Glory and the Kingdom; a pattern of all righteousness; a preacher of the Word, which Himself was; a finisher of the ceremonies; a cornerstone to remove the separation between Jew and Gentile; an intercessor for the Church; a Lord of nature in his miracles; a conqueror of death and the power of darkness in His resurrection;

and that He fulfilled the whole counsel of God; performing all His sacred offices, and anointing on earth, accomplishing the whole work of the redemption and restitution of man to a state superior to the angels, whereas the state of man by creation was inferior; and reconciled and established all things according to the eternal will of the Father.[8]

In 1626, Sir Francis Bacon wrote in his *Will:*

I bequeath my soul to God....My body to be buried obscurely. For my name and memory, I leave it to men's charitable speeches, and to foreign nations, and the next age.[9]

ख

Abraham Baldwin (1754-1807), was a signer of the Constitution of the United States, member of Congress, U.S. Senator, statesman, lawyer and educator.

*Abraham
Baldwin*

He graduated from Yale University and, in 1781, was offered the professorship of divinity there. He served as chaplain in the Continental Army during the Revolutionary War and later studied law. In 1783 he was admitted to the bar, elected to the state assembly, and later chosen as a representative from Georgia to the Constitutional Convention.

He was founder and first President of the University of Georgia, and through his far-sighted efforts, he secured for the university 40,000 acres of land. His expertise in law and ministry was manifest in his writing of the *Charter of the College of Georgia*:

As it is the distinguishing happiness of free governments that civil order should be the result of choice and not of necessity, and the common wishes of the people become the laws of the land, their public prosperity and even existence very much depend upon suitably forming the minds and morals of their citizens.

When the minds of the people in general are viciously disposed and unprincipled, and their conduct disorderly, a free government will be attended with greater confusions and evils more horrid than the wild, uncultivated state of nature.

It can only be happy when the public principles and opinions are properly directed, and their manners regulated.

This is an influence beyond the reach of laws and punishments, and can be claimed only by religion and education.

It should therefore be among the first objects of those who wish well to the national prosperity to encourage and support the principles of religion and morality, and early to place the youth under the forming hand of society, that by instruction they may be molded to the love of virtue and good order.

Sending them abroad to other countries for their education will not answer these purposes, is too humiliating an acknowledgement of the ignorance or inferiority of our own, and will always be the cause of so great foreign attachments that upon principles of policy it is inadmissible.[10]

&

Stanley Baldwin (1867-1947), the 1st Earl Baldwin of Bewdley, was the British Prime Minister during the periods 1923-24, 1924-29 and 1935-37. He stated:

(The Holy Bible is not only great but high explosive literature. It works in strange ways and no living man can tell or know how that book in its journeyings through the world has started an individual soul 10,000 different places into a new life, a new belief, a new conception and a new faith.[11]

&

2nd Lord
Baltimore
Cecilius Calvert

Lord Baltimore Cecilius Calvert (1605-1675), the Second Lord Baltimore, was the founder of the Colony of Maryland, named in honor of Queen Henrietta Maria. In 1632 he received the *Charter of Maryland* from King Charles I. (It had originally been issued to his father, George Calvert, First Lord Baltimore, who was the

1st Lord
Baltimore
George Calvert

Secretary of State for King James I; however, George Calvert died

before he could embark.) The *Charter of Maryland* declared:

> Our well beloved and right trusty subject Coecilius Calvert, Baron of Baltimore...being animated with a laudable, and pious Zeal for extending the Christian Religion...hath humbly besought Leave of Us that he may transport...a numerous Colony of the English Nation, to a certain Region...having no Knowledge of the Divine Being.[12]

On March 25, 1634, Leonard Calvert (1606-1647), the younger brother of Lord Baltimore Cecilius Calvert, arrived in the Chesapeake Bay area with two ships, the *Ark* and the *Dove*. Instated by his brother to lead the first expedition and to function as governor, Leonard Calvert, along with over 230 emigrants, founded the first capital, named St. Mary's City. One of the colonists, Father White, described their arrival:

> We celebrated mass....This had never been done before in this part of the world. After we had completed, we took on our shoulders a great cross, which we had hewn out of a tree, and advancing in order to the appointed place, with the assistance of the Governor and his associates...we erected a trophy to Christ the Savior.[13]

This newly chartered colony was founded initially as a refuge for persecuted Catholics, but then in 1649 the famous *Toleration Act* was issued which gave Christians of all denominations religious liberty. The form of oath prescribed in Governor Stone's time avouched:

> I do further swear that I will not myself, nor any other person, directly or indirectly, trouble, molest, or discountenance any person whatever, in the said province, professing to believe in Jesus Christ.[14]

A vote passed by the Assembly in eulogy of Leonard Calvert three years after his death, stated:

> Great and manifold are the benefits wherewith Almighty God hath blessed this colony, first brought and landed within the province of Maryland, at your lordship's charge, and continued by your care and industry, in the happy restitution of a blessed peace unto us, being lately wasted by a miserable dissension and unhappy war.

But more estimable are the blessings poured on this province, in planting Christianity among a people that knew not God, nor had heard of Christ. All which, we recognize and acknowledge to be done and performed, next under God, by your lordship's pious intention towards the advancement and propagation of the Christian religion, and the peace and happiness of this colony and province.[15]

George Bancroft

George Bancroft (1800-1891), a famous historian, diplomat and educator, served as the Secretary of the Navy under President Polk. Under his direction, the United States Naval Academy at Annapolis was established. He also served as U.S. Minister to Great Britain and Germany.

In 1834, he published the first volume of his ten-volume *History of the United States*. This was the first comprehensive history of America written from its beginnings to the ratification of the Constitution. For more than 50 years it was the best-known and most widely read history of America.

In his *History of the United States, Volume I*, George Bancroft explained:

Puritanism had exalted the laity....For him the wonderful counsels of the Almighty had appointed a Saviour; for him the laws of nature had been compelled and consulted, the heavens had opened, the earth had quaked, the Sun had veiled his face, and Christ had died and risen again.[16]

From his address entitled, *The Progress of Mankind,* published in his work *Literary and Historical Miscellanies,* George Bancroft declared:

For the regeneration of the world it was requisite that the Divine Being should enter the abodes and hearts of men and dwell there; that a belief in Him should be received which would include all truth respecting His essence; that He should be known, not as a distant Providence of boundless power and uncertain and inactive will, but as

God present in the flesh....

Amid the deep sorrows of humanity during the sad conflict which was protracted during centuries for the overthrow of the past and the reconstruction of society, the consciousness of an incarnate God carried peace into the bosom of humanity....

This doctrine once communicated to man, was not to be eradicated. It spread as widely, as swiftly, and as silently as the light, and the idea of GOD WITH US dwelt and dwells in every system of thought that can pretend to vitality; in every oppressed people, whose struggles to be free have the promise of success; in every soul that sighs for redemption.[17]

ϩ

Phineas Taylor Barnum (1810-1891), the well-known exhibitor and philanthropist, was the originator of *The Greatest Show of Earth*. He expounded:

Phineas Taylor Barnum

Christ was sent into the world by our kind Father in Heaven to teach that "God is Love"; that love is the fulfilling of the law; and turn us away from our transgressions by showing us that the "way of the transgressor is hard," and always will be hard as long as we transgress; but charity, unselfishness, and a godly life is filled with joy and peace—that at the last the Almighty Father, being Almighty, and being our Father, will bring about immediate harmony.

The old Bible I believe to be as correct a history as could have been formed in remote ages—containing accounts of various lives and experiences by which we ought to profit. The New Testament abounds in testimony of the undying love of our Saviour for all, and especially for the poor, the unfortunate, and the erring. His mission was to teach them, and to save them from their sins by reconciling them to their Heavenly Father, and not reconciling Him to His created beings, for He was never unreconciled.[18]

ϩ

Frederic Auguste Bartholdi(1834-1904), was the renowned French sculptor who designed and constructed *The Statue of Liberty*. Given by the nation of France to the United States, July 4, 1884,

Frederic Auguste Bartholdi

The Statue of Liberty has become a symbol of freedom throughout the world. The largest of its kind, the statue weighs 450,000 pounds and stands 305 feet above the base of the pedestal. It is supported by a steel structure built by Gustave Eiffel. Frederic Auguste Bartholdi wrote:

The statue was born for this place which inspired its conception. May God be pleased to bless my efforts and my work, and to crown it with success, the duration and the moral influence which it ought to have.[19]

ช

Bruce Barton (1886-1967), an influential American advertising executive, author and politician, stated:

Voltaire spoke of the Bible as a short-lived book. He said that within a hundred years it would pass from common use. Not many people read Voltaire today, but his house has been packed with Bibles as a depot of a Bible society.[20]

The Bible rose to the place it now occupies because it deserved to rise to that place, and not because God sent anybody with a box of tricks to prove its divine authority.[21]

ช

Richard Bassett (1745-1815), one of the signers of the Constitution of the United States, was also instrumental in leading his state of Delaware to be the first to ratify the United States Constitution. In addition, he was a U.S. Senator, Governor of Delaware, Chief Justice of the Supreme Court of Delaware, Captain in the Revolutionary War, lawyer and planter. He helped write the Constitution of the State of Delaware and was appointed by President John Adams as a U.S. Circuit Court Judge.

Richard Bassett

Richard Bassett converted to Methodism during the Revolutionary War and became close personal friends with Francis Asbury, the famous circuit-riding preacher. Richard Bassett personally contributed half the cost of building the First Methodist Church in Dover.[22] He freed his slaves and then paid them as hired labor. On his way to the Methodist campmeetings, many times on his own plantation, he would ride joyfully with his former slaves, sharing the enthusiasm of their singing as they went.[23]

Major William Pierce of Georgia, the only delegate to the Constitutional Convention who recorded character sketches of each of the delegates, described Richard Bassett as:

> A religious enthusiast, lately turned Methodist, who serves his country because it is the will of the people that he should do so. He is a man of plain sense, and has modesty enough to hold his tongue. He is a gentlemanly man, and is in high estimation among Methodists.[24]

Richard Bassett participated in the writing of the Constitution of the State of Delaware, which states:

> *Article XXII* Every person who shall be chosen a member of either house, or appointed to any office or place of trust...shall...make and subscribe the following declaration, to wit: "I, _____, do profess faith in God the Father, and in Jesus Christ His only Son, and in the Holy Ghost, one God, blessed for evermore; and I do acknowledge the holy scriptures of the Old and New Testament to be given by divine inspiration."[25]

ᔍ

Katherine Lee Bates (1859-1929), was an American educator and poet. In 1892, she wrote the famous patriotic song *America the Beautiful* after seeing the inspiring view from atop Pike's Peak in Colorado. So popular was this song that it almost became the United States National Anthem in 1920:

Katherine Lee Bates

O Beautiful for Spacious Skies,
For Amber Waves of Grain,
For Purple Mountain Majesties
Above the Fruited Plain!

America! America!
God Shed His Grace on Thee
And Crowned Thy Good with Brotherhood
From Sea to Shining Sea!

O Beautiful for Pilgrims Feet,
Whose Stern Impassioned Stress
A Thoroughfare for Freedom Beat
Across the Wilderness!

America! America!
God Mend Thy Every Flaw,
Confirm Thy Soul in Self-Control
Thy Liberty in Law!

O Beautiful for Heros Proved
In Liberating Strife,
Who More Than Self Their Country Loved,
And Mercy More Than Life!

America! America!
May God Thy Gold Refine
Till All Success Be Nobleness
And Every Gain Divine!

O Beautiful for Patriots Dream
That Sees Beyond the Years
Thine Alabaster Cities Gleam
Undimmed by Human Tears!

America! America!
God Shed His Grace On Thee
And Crown Thy Good With Brotherhood
From Sea to Shining Sea![26]

&

Richard Baxter (1615-1691), was an English nonconformist chaplain and scholar, who, in 1681, wrote *Poetical Fragments—Love Breathing Thanks and Praise.* In it, he declared:

> I preached as never sure to preach again,
> And as a dying man to dying men.[27]

ता

Gunning Bedford (1747-1812), one of the signers of the Constitution of the United States of America, was the delegate from Delaware to the Constitutional Convention, where he played a considerable part in the Federal Convention.[28] He was later appointed by President Washington to the First Federal District Court in 1789.

Gunning Bedford

Bedford attended Princeton University, where he and James Madison shared a room. While there, he studied under the formative influence of John Witherspoon, one of the nation's premier theologians and legal scholars.[29]

As a delegate from the State of Delaware, he would have complied with the requirements for office as stipulated by his state's constitution, which included:

> *Article XXII* Every person who shall be chosen a member of either house, or appointed to any office or place of trust...shall...make and subscribe the following declaration, to wit: "I, _____, do profess faith in God the Father, and in Jesus Christ His only Son, and in the Holy Ghost, one God, blessed for evermore; and I do acknowledge the holy scriptures of the Old and New Testament to be given by divine inspiration."[30]

ता

Henry Ward Beecher (1813-1887), a famous American editor, abolitionist and clergyman, powerfully influenced the country. He was the son of the famous New England theologian Lyman Beecher and brother of Harriet Beecher Stowe, the famous novelist and reformer who wrote the book *Uncle Tom's Cabin.*

Henry Ward Beecher

Over 2,500 people flocked to hear him each week at the Plymouth Church of Brooklyn, New York. He increasingly used his pulpit to denounce civil corruption, support women's suffrage (the right to vote), and preach against slavery:[31]

Sink the Bible to the bottom of the ocean, and still man's obligations to God would be unchanged. He would have the same path to tread, only his lamp and his guide would be gone; the same voyage to make, but his chart and compass would be overboard.[32]

If a man cannot be a Christian in the place where he is, he cannot be a Christian anywhere.[33]

A Christian is nothing but a sinful man who has put himself to school to Christ for the honest purpose of becoming better.[34]

Christianity works while infidelity talks. She feeds the hungry, clothes the naked, visits and cheers the sick, and seeks the lost, while infidelity abuses her and babbles nonsense and profanity. "By their fruits ye shall know them."[35]

There's not much practical Christianity in the man who lives on better terms with angels and seraphs, than with his children, servants, and neighbors.[36]

"I can forgive but I cannot forget" is only another way of saying "I cannot forgive."[37]

The Bible is God's chart for you to steer by, to keep you from the bottom of the sea, and to show you where the harbor is, and how to reach it without running on the rocks or bars.[38]

૨**ન**

Lyman Beecher (1775-1863), was a renowned Presbyterian clergyman in New England. He preached in Boston and Cincinnati, where he later became President of Lane Theological Seminary.

He was the father of both Henry Ward Beecher, one of the most eloquent preachers of his time, and Harriet Beecher Stowe, author of the book *Uncle Tom's Cabin*, which greatly precipitated the abolition of slavery.

In 1831, Lyman Beecher wrote in the newspaper, *The Spirit of the Pilgrims:*

Lyman Beecher

> The government of God is the only government which will hold society, against depravity within and temptation without; and this it must do by the force of its own law written upon the heart.
>
> This is that unity of the Spirit and that bond of peace which can alone perpetuate national purity and tranquility—that law of universal and impartial love by which alone nations can be kept back from ruin. There is no safety for republics but in self-government, under the influence of a holy heart, swayed by the government of God.[39]

Lyman Beecher wrote in his autobiography:

> The enemy employs influential friends of Christ to wound one another, and to propagate distrust, alienation, and acrimony....
>
> The strength of the Church depends upon our concentrated action....
>
> Whatever, therefore, propagates suspicion and distrust among brethren who have long acted together, paralyzes their power....
>
> Of this, the great enemy of the Church is perfectly aware, and has never failed, when the concentration of forces against him had become too formidable for direct resistance, to ease himself of his adversaries by dividing them.[40]

Lyman Beecher commented concerning his life:

> I was made for action. The Lord drove me, but I was ready. I have always been going at full speed...harnessed to the Chariot of Christ, whose wheels of fire have rolled onward, high and dreadful to His foes and glorious to His friends![41]

❧

Ludwig van Beethoven (1770-1827), was a Prussian composer

who ranks among the greatest in history. He was a contemporary of Mozart and Haydn. Beethoven began losing his hearing at the age of 28 and eventually became totally deaf. Incredibly, though, he continued writing music, creating some of the greatest symphonies, concertos, sonatas, string quartets and choral masterpieces that the world has ever known. Beethoven wrote:

> Today happens to be the Lord's Day, so I will quote you something from my Bible: "See that ye love one another as I have loved you."[42]

> No friend have I. I must live by myself alone; but I know well that God is nearer to me than others in my art, so I will walk fearlessly with Him. I have always known and understood Him.[43]

ے

George Eugene Belknap (1832-1903), held the distinguished positions in the United States Navy of Commodore, 1885, and Rear Admiral, 1889. He declared:

> No nation can materially enlarge her borders and rise to great ascendancy except on the basis of Christianity and its revealed Word. In such ferment of unrest, such tumult of change, the old religions will surely give way to the power of the Cross.
> The Light of the World will irradiate those fair lands. The utterly indifferent temperature of the Chinese conduces to this ambition of Japan, and so surely as she accomplishes her lofty ambition, so surely will the Cross of our Saviour be uplifted over it all in all the significance of its power.[44]

> As an eye-witness, I assert it to be a fact beyond contradiction that there is not an official, or any other person, from emperors, down to the lowest coolies in China and Japan, who are not indebted every day to the work of our American Missionaries.[45]

ے

Charles Bell (1774-1842), a great anatomist and surgeon, was professor of Comparative Anatomy at the Royal College of Surgeons in England and author of numerous volumes. The title of one of his most famous treatises was:

> The Hand; Its Mechanism and Vital Endowments, and Evincing
> Design, and Illustrating the Power, Wisdom, and Goodness of God.[46]

ᵄ

Francis Bellamy (1856-1931), was a minister from Boston, who was ordained in the Baptist Church of Little Falls, New York. He was a member of the staff of *The Youth's Companion,* which first published his *Pledge of Allegiance* on September 8, 1892. At the dedication of the 1892 Chicago World's Fair on October 12, 1892, public-school children first recited the *Pledge of Allegiance* during the National School Celebration on the 400th anniversary of Columbus' discovery of America.

On June 14, 1954, by a Joint Resolution of Congress, 243 (Public Law 83-396), the words "under God" were added to the *Pledge of Allegiance* from Abraham Lincoln's famous Gettysburg Address, "...that this nation, under God, shall have a new birth...."[47] (The *Pledge* was initially adopted by the 79th Congress on December 28, 1945, as Public Law 287.) President Eisenhower signed the pledge into law:

> I pledge allegiance to the flag of the United States of America and
> to the Republic for which it stands, one Nation under God, indivisible,
> with liberty and justice for all.[48]

President Eisenhower gave his support to the Congressional Act, which added the phrase "under God" to the *Pledge of Allegiance,* saying:

> In this way we are reaffirming the transcendence of religious faith
> in America's heritage and future; in this way we shall constantly
> strengthen those spiritual weapons which forever will be our country's
> most powerful resource in peace and war.[49]

President Eisenhower then stood on the steps of the Capitol Building and recited the *Pledge of Allegiance* for the first time with the phrase, "one Nation under God."[50]

#&

George Bennard (1873-1958), wrote the famous hymn *The Old Rugged Cross* in 1913, which included:

> I will cling to the old rugged cross,
> And exchange it some day for a crown.[51]

#&

Sir Risdon Bennett (1809-1891), was the President of the Royal Society of Physicians. In 1890, Sir Risdon Bennett wrote in the *Report of the Christian Evidence Society:*

> ✓ It has been truly said that "the real evidence of Christianity is in its power." And how can we look around the world and fail to see proof of this power wherever the Gospel is known, among all races of mankind, all classes of society, all ranks of intellect. What is there comparable to the religion of Jesus Christ in promoting the happiness and welfare of mankind? The full influence of its power, even as regards the present life, we have indeed yet to see; and we can but faintly appreciate the inestimable light as shed on the life to come, the full glory of which has yet to be revealed.[52] ✓

#&

William W. Bennett, who in 1877 published his remarkable documentary *A Narrative of the Great Revival Which Prevailed in the Southern Armies*, was a chaplain in Robert E. Lee's Army of Northern Virginia during the Civil War. He also headed the *Methodist Soldiers' Tract Association.* Concerning the conversions in the Confederate ranks, Chaplain Bennett wrote:

> ✓ Up to January, 1865, it was estimated that nearly 150,000 soldiers had been converted during the progress of the war, and it was believed that fully one-third of all the soldiers in the field were praying men, and members of some branch of the Christian Church.[53] ✓

> In the army of General Lee, while it lay on the upper Rappahannock, the revival flame swept through every corps, division, brigade, and regiment. [One chaplain explained]:

"The whole army is a vast field, ready and ripe to the harvest....The susceptibility of the soldiers to the gospel is wonderful, and, doubtful as the remark may appear, the military camp is most favorable to the work of revival. The soldiers, with the simplicity of little children, listen to and embrace the truth. Already over two thousand have professed conversion, and two thousand more are penitent....

Oh, it is affecting to see the soldiers crowd and press about the preacher for want of tracts, etc., he has to distribute, and it is sad to see hundreds retiring without being supplied!"[54]

[Another minister wrote]: "The cold, mud, and rain, have produced great suffering and sickness among the troops; for we have been entirely without shelter in very exposed positions....In our field hospital we have over 350 sick....

I never saw men who were better prepared to receive religious instruction and advice....The dying begged for our prayers and our songs. Every evening we would gather around the wounded and sing and pray with them. Many wounded, who had hitherto led wicked lives, became entirely changed....

One young Tennessean, James Scott, of the 32d Tennessee,... continually begged us to sing for him and to pray with him. He earnestly desired to see his mother before he died, which was not permitted, as she was in the enemy's lines, and he died rejoicing in the grace of God."[55]

After the *Battle of Cross Keys*, a soldier recounted to Chaplain Bennett his observation of General Stonewall Jackson:

I saw something today which affected me more than anything I ever saw or read on religion. While the battle was raging and the bullets were flying, Jackson rode by, calm as if he were at home, but his head was raised toward heaven, and his lips were moving evidently in prayer.[56]

Chaplain Bennett took the dying words of T.S. Chandler of the 6th South Carolina Regiment:

Tell my mother that I am lying without hope of recovery....My hope is in Christ, for whose sake I hope to be saved. Tell her that she and my brother cannot see me again on earth, but they can meet me in heaven....I know I am going there.[57]

In the spring of 1865, there was almost a continual revival among General Robert E. Lee's ranks. Chaplain Bennett records a resolution adopted by five brigades of the Georgia troops:

> That we hereby acknowledge the sinfulness of our past conduct as a just and sufficient ground for the displeasure of Almighty God; and that, earnestly repenting of our sins, we are determined, by His grace, to amend our lives for the future; and, in earnest supplication to God, through the mediation of His Son, Jesus Christ, we implore the forgiveness of our sins and seek the Divine favor and protection. [58]

Arthur Christopher Benson (1862-1925), was a well-known English educator and author, who, in 1902, wrote *Land of Hope and Glory:*

> Land of hope and glory, mother of the free,
> How shall we extol thee, who are born of thee?
> Wider still and wider shall thy bounds be set;
> God, who made thee mighty, make thee mightier yet. [59]

Irving Berlin (1888-1989), was the Russian-born American songwriter, who, in 1938, wrote the famous American patriotic song *God Bless America:*

> God Bless America, Land that I Love,
> Stand Beside Her, and Guide Her,
> Through the Night, with the Light From Above,
> From the Mountains, to the Prairies,
> To the Oceans White with Foam,
> God Bless America, My Home Sweet Home,
> God Bless America, My Home Sweet Home! [60]

The Holy Bible was found to have directly contributed to 34% of all quotes by the Founding Fathers. This was discovered after reviewing 15,000 items from the Founding Fathers (including newspaper articles, pamphlets, books, monographs, etc.) The other main sources that the Founders quoted include: Montesquieu, Blackstone, Locke, Pufendorf, etc., who themselves took 60% of their quotes directly from the Bible. Direct and indirect quotes combined reveal that the majority of quotes of the Founding Fathers are derived from the Bible.[61] ✓

Studies show the majority of Founding Fathers' quotes are derived from the Bible

ᴥ

Jean Baptiste Lemoyne, Sieur de Bienville

Jean Baptiste Lemoyne, SIEUR DE Bienville (1680-1768), the Colonial Governor of Louisiana and founder of New Orleans, wrote in his *Will*:

✓ In the name of the Father, etc. Persuaded, as I am, of the necessity of death, and the uncertainty of the hour, I wish, before it arrives, to put my affairs in order. First, I consign my soul to God...I implore the mercy of God and Jesus Christ, my Saviour.[62] ✓

ᴥ

John Armor Bingham (1815-1900), was a U.S. Congressman, 1855-1863 and 1865-1873. He served as the Judge Advocate at the trial of President Abraham Lincoln's assassin and as one of the managers of President Andrew Johnson's impeachment trial. John Armor Bingham was also the U.S. Minister to Japan, 1873-1885. He stated:

✓ I was instructed in early youth by precept and example of my father and mother. I hereby became convinced of the truth of Christ's teaching, and of the inspiration of the Holy Scriptures. My convictions on this subject must suffice for me; I will not surrender them to any man.

I do not hesitate to say, however, as a strong belief of mine, that Christ, by His living and His dying and His reappearance after crucifixion brought life and immortality to light. It seems to me not to be a question that the Christ of the New Testament lived and will live forevermore.

My inner consciousness teaches me that in His discourse on the Mount He is chiefly revealed to be more than a man, and that He was and is Divine.[63]

ॐ

Otto Eduard Leopold von Bismarck (1815-1898), the Prussian Chancellor who was responsible for uniting the German people, declared:

Would to God that, apart from what is known in the world, I had no other sins upon my soul, for which I only hope to be forgiven by trusting in the blood of Christ.

I know not whence I should derive my sense of duty if not from God. Orders and titles have no charm for me; I firmly believe in a life after death...

To my steadfast faith alone do I owe the power of resisting all manner of absurdities which I have seen displayed throughout the past ten years. Deprive me of my faith, and you rob me of my Fatherland. Were I not a staunch Christian, did I not stand upon the miraculous basis of religion, you would never have possessed a Federal Chancellor in my person.[64]

In a speech to the Reichstag, February 6, 1888, Chancellor Otto von Bismarck stated:

We Germans fear God, but nothing else in the world.[65]

In describing Otto von Bismarck, the Chancellor of the newly united German Empire, President James Garfield stated:

I am struck with the fact that Bismarck, the great statesman of Germany, probably the foremost man in Europe today, stated as an unquestioned principle, that the support, the defense, and propagation of the Christian Gospel is the central object of the German government.[66]

ॐ

Hugo La Fayette Black (1886-1971), a United States Supreme Court Justice, wrote in a 1962 decision:

> Indeed, as late as the time of the Revolutionary War, there were established churches in at least eight of the thirteen former colonies and established religions in at least four of the other five.[67]

&

Jeremiah Sullivan Black (1810-1883), the United States Attorney General under President James Buchanan, in August, 1881, wrote in the *North American Review:*

Jeremiah Sullivan Black

> As a matter of fact, Jesus Christ died that sinners might be reconciled to God, and in that sense He died for them; that is, to furnish them with the means of averting Divine justice, which their crimes had provoked.
>
> A man who, by any contrivance, causes his own offense to be visited on the head of an innocent person is unspeakably depraved. But are Christians guilty of this baseness, because they accept the blessings of an institution which their great Benefactor died to establish?
>
> Loyalty to the King who erected a most magnificent government for us at the cost of His life—fidelity to the Master who bought us with His blood—is not the fraudulent substitution in place of the criminal.[68]

&

Sir William Blackstone (1723-1780), was the renowned English jurist who played a leading role in forming the basis of law in America. Blackstone lectured at Oxford, and from 1765 to 1770 published his highly influential work, *Commentaries on the Laws of England*, which by 1775 had sold more copies in America than in England.

His *Commentaries*, which were universally accepted in America, set the foundation for great legal minds such as Chief Justice John Marshall.[69] When scholars examined nearly 15,000 items written by the Founding Fathers from 1760 to 1805 (including books, newspapers articles, monographs, pamphlets, etc.), they found that Sir William Blackstone was quoted more than any other author except one.[70]

James Madison, the "Chief Architect of the Constitution," endorsed Blackstone, saying:

> I very cheerfully express my approbation of the proposed edition of Blackstone's Commentaries.[71]

Blackstone expressed the presuppositional base for law:

> Man, considered as a creature, must necessarily be subject to the laws of his Creator, for he is entirely a dependent being....And, consequently, as man depends absolutely upon his Maker for everything, it is necessary that he should in all points conform to his Maker's will...this will of his Maker is called the law of nature.[72]

> These laws laid down by God are the eternal immutable laws of good and evil....This law of nature dictated by God himself, is of course superior in obligation to any other. It is binding over all the globe, in all countries, and at all times: no human laws are of any validity if contrary to this...[73]

> The doctrines thus delivered we call the revealed or divine law, and they are to be found only in the holy scriptures...[and] are found upon comparison to be really part of the original law of nature. Upon these two foundations, the law of nature and the law of revelation, depend all human laws; that is to say, no human laws should be suffered to contradict these.[74]

> Blasphemy against the Almighty is denying his being or providence, or uttering contumelious reproaches on our Savior Christ. It is punished, at common law by fine and imprisonment, for Christianity is part of the laws of the land.[75]

> If [the legislature] will positively enact a thing to be done, the judges are not at liberty to reject it, for that were to set the judicial power above that of the legislature, which would be subversive of all government.[76]

> To deny the possibility, nay, actual existence, of witchcraft and sorcery, is at once to contradict the revealed Word of God in various passages both of the Old and New Testament.[77]

The preservation of Christianity as a national religion is abstracted from its own intrinsic truth, of the utmost consequence to the civil state, which a single instance will sufficiently demonstrate.

The belief of a future state of rewards and punishments, the entertaining just ideas of the main attributes of the Supreme Being, and a firm persuasion that He superintends and will finally compensate every action in human life (all which are revealed in the doctrines of our Savior, Christ), these are the grand foundations of all judicial oaths, which call God to witness the truth of those facts which perhaps may be only known to Him and the party attesting;

all moral evidences, therefore, all confidence in human veracity, must be weakened by apostasy, and overthrown by total infidelity.

Wherefore, all affronts to Christianity, or endeavors to depreciate its efficacy, in those who have once professed it, are highly deserving of censure.[78]

James Gillespie Blaine

James Gillespie Blaine (1830-1893), was the Secretary of State under Presidents James Garfield and Benjamin Harrison, and the Speaker of the House and a Congressman for 20 years. In *Columbus and Columbia, a Pictorial History of the Man and the Nation*, the Honorable Blaine wrote:

No proverb ever supplanted the patience of Job or the wisdom of Solomon....Moses has never been surpassed in statesmanship.

A scientific theology is pointing out the footprints of the Creator to common sense. The brotherhood of man, the Fatherhood of God, is becoming the corner-stone of religion, as revealed in Christ, and as clearly traced in human history.[79]

John Blair (1732-1800), a signer of the Constitution of the United States (being only 33 years old at the time), was elected to Virginia's Supreme Court of Appeals, and in 1798 was appointed by President George Washington as a Justice on the United States Supreme Court. John Blair was also active in the Episcopal church in Williamsburg, Virginia.

John Blair

A letter to his sister, at the time of her husband's death, gives evidence of John Blair's principles:

> With much grief of my own and real sympathy for yours, I sit down to write you a Letter of Condolence on as great a Loss as could have befallen you...but an event no way contingent but absolutely certain itself it being appointed for all men once to die....

Let us seek for comfort where alone it may be found, let us learn a dutiful acquiescence in whatsoever proceeds from that Great Being from whom we ourselves proceeded and who being the sole Author of all our enjoyments has an undoubted Right to withdraw them in his own good time and whose Goodness so conspicuous in his General Providence may be as eminent for aught we know though not so plainly discerned even when He deals to us the bitter cup of Affliction.

We may all profit in the School of Adversity if we will but make a proper use of its Sacred Lessons. If in this life only we had hope it would indeed be harder to acquire a due serenity of mind upon the loss of a beloved Friend.

If he were absolutely extinct, to forget him would be perhaps necessary to our Peace of Mind. But now as our Holy Religion teaches we may contemplate him translated to a better Life and ineffably enjoying all that variety of Bliss which Eye hath not seen nor Ear heard nor the Heart conceived.

May the Celestial vision forever preserve you from the Gloominess of Grief and reconcile you to all the Dispensations of Him who cannot err. My situation both with Respect to my Family and Fortune (all being in the Power of the Enemy and much in their possession) is bad enough. But I trust for a happy issue and for power to bear all His appointments as I ought.[80]

❧

Edward William Bok (1863-1930), a Dutch-born American journalist and editor of *The Ladies' Home Journal*, wrote in the September 1894 issue of that popular magazine:

There are myriads of people on this earth who believe in the divinity of Christ; people of

Edward William Bok

the finest minds and the greatest learning. It is not a mark of intelligence to question divine things. The divinity of Christ is a question of the heart. No one who studies the Life of Christ can fail to believe that in Him the world had a Being unlike any other man, and His own teachings, His own words, His own life are the best proofs of his Divinity. [81]

&

Frank Borman (1928-   ), Commander of the Apollo VIII spacecraft, which was the first manned ship to orbit the moon, shared this message on December 24,1968, by remote television up-link as he looked at the earth from 240,000 miles away:

> In the beginning God created the heaven and the earth. And the earth was without form, and void; and darkness was upon the face of the deep. And the Spirit of God moved upon the face of the waters. And God said, Let there be light; and there was light... And God saw that it was good. [82]

&

Boston, Massachusetts, 1765, was the place where the famous Congregational Minister Jonathan Mayhew, of West Church, gave a patriotic sermon which reflected the Colonists' feelings toward King George III's hated Stamp Act:

Jonathan Mayhew

> The king is as much bound by his oath not to infringe the legal rights of the people, as the people are bound to yield subjection to him. From whence it follows that as soon as the prince sets himself above the law, he loses the king in the tyrant. He does, to all intents and purposes, un-king himself. [83]

&

Boston Gazette September 1768, carried an article which read:

> If an army should be sent to reduce us to slavery, we will put our

lives in our hands and cry to the Judge of all the earth....Behold, how they come to cast us out of this possession which Thou hast given us to inherit. Help us, Lord, our God, for we rest on Thee, and in Thy name we go against this multitude.[84]

🍃

The Boston Tea Party

December 16, 1773, followed just three years after the Boston Massacre, where five Americans were killed by British soldiers who commandeered their homes. The British then began imposing on the Colonies taxation, which eventually became unbearable.

The Boston Tea Party

Early in the year of 1773, the men of Marlborough, Massachusetts, declared unanimously:

The Boston Massacre

Death is more eligible than slavery. A free-born people are not required by the religion of Jesus Christ to submit to tyranny, but may make use of such power as God has given them to recover and support their laws and liberties...[We] implore the Ruler above the skies, that He would make bare His arm in defense of His Church and people, and let Israel go.[85]

The Colonists in Boston responded to the intolerable taxes imposed by the British. A band of citizens, disguised as Indians, threw the cargo of 342 chests of tea from a British East India

The British blockade of Boston Harbor

Company ship into the Boston Harbor.

In 1774, the Parliament of Great Britain decided to blockade the Boston harbor by passing the *Boston Port Bill*, thus destroying

The Boston Tea Party took place on December 16, 1773, when Bostonians, disguised as Indians, boarded three British ships and threw overboard chests of tea in protest of Britain's attempt to tax American tea consumption.

all trade and effectively starving the inhabitants of the city.

The Committee of Correspondence sent word of their plight to the rest of the Colonies, who responded by calling for a *Day of Fasting and Prayer* on June 1, 1774, (the day the blockade would begin). This was done in order:

> ...to seek divine direction and aid.[86]

The towns, cities and surrounding Colonies began sending their support. In August, 1774, William Prescott led the men of Pepperell, Massachusetts, to deliver many loads of rye. He wrote to the men of Boston:

> We heartily sympathize with you, and are always ready to do all in our power for your support, comfort and relief; knowing that Providence has placed you where you must stand the first shock. We consider we are all embarked in [the same boat] and must sink or swim together. We think if we submit to these regulations, all is gone.
>
> Our forefathers passed the vast Atlantic, spent their blood and treasure, that they might enjoy their liberties, both civil and religious, and transmit them to their posterity....Now if we should give them up, can our children rise up and call us blessed?....
>
> Let us all be of one heart, and stand fast in the liberty wherewith Christ has made us free; and may he, of his infinite mercy grant us deliverance out of all our troubles."[87]

The inhabitants of Boston responded to this encouraging support by declaring:

> The Christian sympathy and generosity of our friends through the Continent cannot fail to inspire the inhabitants of this town with patience, resignation, and firmness, while we trust in the Supreme Ruler of the universe, that he will graciously hear our cries, and in his time free us from our present bondage and make us rejoice in his great salvation.[88]

Josiah Quincy

Josiah Quincy, the American orator of freedom, voiced the Colonists' sentiments in 1774:

> Blandishments will not fascinate us, nor will threats of a "halter" intimidate. For, under God, we are determined that wheresoever, whensoever,

or howsoever we shall be called to make our exit, we will die free men.[89]

The Colonists grew in their resilience and confidence in God, to the point where one Crown-appointed Governor wrote of the condition to the Board of Trade back in England:

If you ask an American, who is his master? He will tell you he has none, nor any governor but Jesus Christ.[90]

The cry, *"No King but King Jesus!"* sounded across the Colonies.

The Committees of Correspondence soon began sounding the cry across the Colonies:

No King but King Jesus![91]

As a result of this crisis, the Colonies joined together in Philadelphia for the first Continental Congress on September 5, 1774.[92] (See *Continental Congress.*)

October 22, 1774, the Provincial Congress of Massachusetts, which met in Boston, began to voice their serious concerns, as President John Hancock declared:

We think it is incumbent upon this people to humble themselves before God on account of their sins, for He hath been pleased in His righteous judgement to suffer a great calamity to befall us, as the present controversy between Great Britain and the Colonies. [And] also to implore the Divine Blessing upon us, that by the assistance of His grace, we may be enabled to reform whatever is amiss among us, that so God may be pleased to continue to us the blessings we enjoy, and remove the tokens of His displeasure, by causing harmony and union to be restored between Great Britain and the Colonies.[93]

In 1774, the Provincial Congress of Massachusetts addressed the inhabitants of Massachusetts Bay:

Resistance to tyranny becomes the Christian and social duty of each individual....Continue steadfast, and with a proper sense of your dependence on God, nobly defend those rights which heaven gave, and no man ought to take from us.[94]

In 1774, the Provincial Congress of Massachusetts reorganized the Massachusetts militia, providing that over one-third of all new regiments be made up of "Minutemen." The minutemen, known as such because they would be ready to fight at a minute's notice, would drill as citizen soldiers on the parade ground, then

go to the church to hear exhortation and prayer. Many times the deacon of the church, or even the pastor, would lead the drill. They proclaimed, "Our cause is just" and believed it was their Christian duty to defend it.[95] The Provincial Congress of Massachusetts charged the minutemen:

You...are placed by Providence in the post of honor, because it is the post of danger....The eyes not only of North America and the whole British Empire, but of all Europe, are upon you. Let us be, therefore, altogether solicitous that no disorderly behavior, nothing unbecoming our characters as Americans, as citizens and Christians, be justly chargeable to us.[96]

Minuteman, a historical monument stands at Lexington, Massachusetts.

≈

Elias Boudinot (1740-1821), was the Founding Father who held the position of President of the Continental Congress in 1783. He later became the U.S. Congressman from New Jersey. He was renowned for being the founder and President of the American Bible Society. Elias Boudinot stated:

Elias Boudinot

"Thou shalt love thy neighbor as thyself"—Let it then (as workmanship of the same Divine hand) be our peculiar constant care and vigilant attention to inculcate this sacred principle, and to hand it down to posterity....Good government generally begins in the family, and if the moral character of a people once degenerate, their political character must soon follow.[97]

ॐ

Professor Louis Bounoure March 8, 1984, was quoted in *The Advocate* publication. His statement carried considerable credence, as he had been the President of the Biological Society of Strasbourg, Director of the Strasbourg Zoological Museum, and later Director at the French National Centre of Scientific Research. Professor Bounoure declared:

Evolutionism is a fairy tale for grown-ups. This theory has helped nothing in the progress of science. It is useless.[98]

ॐ

Robert Boyle (1626-1691), who was known as the "Father of Modern Chemistry," was one of the founders of the Royal Society of London. His contributions in physics and chemistry are significant, including the discovery of the basic law of gas dynamics, relating gas pressures to temperature and volume. Devoting much of his time to propagating the gospel, he wrote the *Boyle Lectures* in the field of apologetics for proving the Christian religion. Robert Boyle stated:

Our Saviour would love at no less rate than death; and from the supereminent height of glory, stooped and debased Himself to the sufferance of the extremest of indignities, and sunk himself to the bottom of abjectness, to exalt our condition to the contrary extreme.[99]

In his work entitled *Some Considerations Touching the Style of the Holy Scriptures*, Robert Boyle wrote:

The Books of Scripture illustrate and expound each other; as in the mariner's compass, the needle's extremity, though it seems to point purposely to the north, doth yet at the same time discover both east and west, as distant as they are from it and each other, so do some texts of Scripture guide us to the intelligence of others, for which they are widely distant in the Bible.[100]

ঽ৯

√ ***William Bradford*** (1590-1657), the leader of the Pilgrims, was elected as Governor of the Plymouth Colony in 1621, and reelected every year until his death in 1657, except for five years in which he declined. In Bradford's history, *Of Plymouth Plantation*, he traced the events that led to the Pilgrims' departure from England:

It is well knowne unto ye godly and judicious how since ye first breaking out of ye lighte of ye gospell in our Honourable Nation of England, (which was ye first of nations whom ye Lord adorned ther with, after the grosse darkness...which had covered and overspread ye Christian world), what warrs and oppossissions ever since, Satan, hath raised, maintained, and continued against the Saints, from time to time, in one sort or other.

Some times by bloody death and cruell torments; other whiles imprisonments, banishments, and other hard usages; as being loath his kingdom should goe downe, and trueth prevaile, and ye churches of God reverte to their anciente puritie and recover their primative order, libertie, and bewtie.

But when he could not prevaile by these means againste the maine trueths of ye gospell, but that they began to take rootting in many places, being watered by ye blooud of ye martires, and blessed from heaven with a gracious encrease; he then begane to take him to his anciente strategeme used of old against the first Christians.

That when by ye bloody and barbarous persecutions of ye heathen Emperours, he could not stop and subvert the course of ye gospell, but that it speedily overspred with a wonderfull celeritie the then best known parts...ye professours themselves, (working upon their pride and ambition, with other corrupte passions incident to all mortall men, yea to ye saints themselves in some measure), by which woefull effects followed; as not only bitter contentions, and hartburnings, schismes, with other horrible confusions, but Satan tooke occasion and advantage therby to foyst in a number of vile...cannons and decrees, which have since been as snares to many poore and peacable souls even to this day.

So as in ye anciente times, the persecutions by ye heathen and their Emperours, was not greater than of the Christians one against another....[101]

In 1607, as a result of the terrible religious persecution—which brought harm to their persons, reputations, families, and livelihoods—the Pilgrims departed from their home country of England for Holland. Governor Bradford recorded the farewell:

> Being thus constrained to leave their native soyle and countrie, their lands and livings, and all their friends and famillier acquantance....to goe into a countrie they knew not (but by hearsay) wher they must learne a new language, and get their livings they knew not how, it being a dear place, and subject to the miseries of war, it was by many thought an adventure almost desperate, a case intolerable, and a miserie worse than death....
>
> But these things did not dismay them (though they did sometimes trouble them) for their desires were sett on ye ways of God and to enjoye His ordinances; but they rested in His providence, and knew whom they had believed....[102]

In describing the Pilgrims' covenant to establish their church, William Bradford wrote:

> They shook off this yoke of antichristian bondage, and as the Lord's free people, joined themselves by a covenant of the Lord into a church estate in the fellowship of the gospel, to walk in all His ways, made known unto them, according to their best endeavours, whatsoever it should cost them, the Lord assisting them.[103]

In 1618, the Pilgrims' Church of Leyden in Holland sent seven Articles to the Counsel of England for consideration in the decision as to whether the Pilgrims would be allowed to settle in Virginia. The Articles included:

> *Article III* The King's Majesty we acknowledge for Supreme Governor in his Dominion...but in all things obedience is due unto him if the thing commanded be not against God's Word....
>
> *Article VII* And lastly, we desire to give unto all Superiors due honor to preserve the unity of the Spirit, with all who fear God, to have peace with all men what in us lieth, and wherein we err to be instructed by any.

Subscribed by John Robinson and William Brewster.[104]

In their letter to Edwin Sandys in London, John Robinson and William Brewster explained that the Pilgrims were:

> ...Knit together as a body in a most strict and sacred bond and covenant of the Lord, of the violation whereof we make great conscience, and by virtue whereof we do hold ourselves straitly tied to all care of each other's good, and of the whole by every one and so mutually.[105]

In 1620, after having lived in Holland for 12 years, Governor William Bradford described the Pilgrims' departure from Holland to England, where they would board the ship bound for America. Out of 103 Pilgrims who left, 51 died in the first terrible winter in the New World:

> So being ready to departe, they had a day of solleme humiliation, their pastor taking his texte from Ezra 8:21: "And ther at ye river, by Ahava, I proclaimed a fast, that we might humble ourselves before our God and seeke of Him a right way for us, and for our Children, and for our substance."
>
> ...The rest of the time was spent in powering out prairs to ye Lord with greate fervencie, mixed with abundance of tears. And ye time being come that they must departe, they were accompanied with most of their brethren out of ye citie, unto a towne sundrie miles off called Delfes-Haven, wher the ship lay ready to receive them....
>
> ...they knew they were pilgrimes (Hebrews 12), but lift their eyes to ye heavens, their dearest cuntrie, and quieted their spirits...
>
> What could now sustaine them but ye spirite of God and His grace? May not and ought not the children of these fathers rightly say: Our fathers were Englishmen which came over this great ocean, and were ready to perish in this wilderness; (Deuteronomy 26:5, 7) but they cried unto ye Lord, and He heard their voyce, and looked on their adversitie, etc.
>
> Let them therefore praise ye Lord, because He is good, and His mercies endure for ever. (107 Psalm: v. 1, 2, 4, 5, 8) Yea let them which have been redeemed of ye Lord, show how He hath delivered them from ye hand of ye oppressour.
>
> When they wandered in ye deserte wilderness out of ye way, and found no citie to dwell in, both hungrie, and thirstie, their sowle was overwhelmed in them. Let them confess before ye Lord His loving kindness, and His wonderful works before ye sons of men.[106]

Having been blown off course from their intended landing in Virginia by a terrible storm, the Pilgrims landed at Cape Cod on November 11, 1620. William Bradford recounted the landing in *Of Plymouth Plantation:*

> Being thus arrived in a good harbor, and brought safe to land, they fell upon their knees and blessed the God of Heaven who had brought them over the vast and furious ocean, and delivered them from all the perils and miseries thereof, again to set their feet on the firm and stable earth, their proper element.[107]

Little did the Pilgrims know that if they had landed there a few years earlier, they would have been massacred by the Patuxet, one of the fiercest Indian tribes on the American coast. The tribe, however, had been completely destroyed by a plague in 1617, although historians do not know why.

Governor William Bradford and the leaders on the *Mayflower* signed the *Mayflower Compact* on November 11, 1620, before setting foot on dry land. This was America's first great constitutional document:

> ✓ In ye name of God, Amen. We whose names are underwriten, the loyall subjects of our dread soveraigne Lord, King James, by ye grace of God, of Great Britaine, France, & Ireland king, defender of ye faith, etc., having undertaken, for ye glorie of God, and advancemente of ye Christian faith, and honour of our king & countrie, a voyage to plant ye first colonie in ye Northerne parts of Virginia,
>
> doe by these presents solemnly & mutually in ye presence of God, and one of another, covenant & combine our selves togeather into a civill body politick, for our better ordering & preservation & furtherance of ye ends aforesaid;
>
> and by vertue hearof to enacte, constitute, and frame such just & equall lawes, ordinances, acts, constitutions & offices, from time to time, as shall be thought most meete & convenient for ye generall good of ye Colonie, unto which we promise all due submission and obedience.
>
> In witnes wherof we have hereunder subscribed our names at Cap-Codd ye 11. of November, in ye year of ye raigne of our soveraigne lord, King James, of England, France, & Ireland ye eighteenth, and by Scotland ye fiftie fourth. Ano:Dom. 1620.[108]

In March of 1621, as recorded in Governor Bradford's *Of*

Plymouth Plantation, Squanto joined the Pilgrims:

> About the 16th of March [1621], a certain Indian came boldly amongst them and spoke to them in broken English....His name was Samoset. He told them also of another Indian whose name was Squanto, a native of this place, who had been in England and could speak better English than himself...
>
> [A]bout four or five days after, came...the aforesaid Squanto...[He] continued with them and was their interpreter and was a special instrument sent of God for their good beyond their expectation. He showed them how to plant corn, where to take fish and other commodities, and guided them to unknown places, and never left them till he died.
>
> He was a native of these parts, and had been one of the few survivors of the plague hereabouts. He was carried away with others by one Hunt, a captain of a ship, who intended to sell them for slaves in Spain; but he got away for England, and was received by a merchant in London, and employed in Newfoundland and other parts, and lastly brought into these parts by a Captain Dermer.[109]

On November 29, 1623, three years after the Pilgrims' arrival and two years after the first Thanksgiving, Governor William Bradford made an official proclamation for a day of Thanksgiving:

> To all ye Pilgrims:
>
> In as much as the great Father has given us this year an abundant harvest of Indian corn, wheat, peas, beans, squashes, and garden vegetable, and has made the forests to abound with game and the sea with fish and clams, and inasmuch as he has protected us from the ravages of the savages, has spared us from pestilence and disease, has granted us freedom to worship God according to the dictates of our own conscience;
>
> now I, your magistrate, do proclaim that all ye Pilgrims, with your wives and ye little ones, do gather at ye meeting house, on ye hill, between the hours of 9 and 12 in the day time, on Thursday, November ye 29th, of the year of our Lord one thousand six hundred and twenty-three, and the third year since ye Pilgrims landed on ye Pilgrim Rock, there to listen to ye pastor and render thanksgiving to ye Almighty God for all His blessings. William Bradford, Ye Governor of Ye Colony.[110]

In 1647, Bradford wrote in his famous historical work, *Of Plymouth Plantation:*[111]

Last and not least, they cherished a great hope and inward zeal of laying good foundations, or at least making some ways toward it, for the propagation and advance of the gospel of the kingdom of Christ in the remote parts of the world, even though they should be but stepping stones to others in the performance of so great a work. [112]

Thus out of small beginnings greater things have been produced by His hand that made all things of nothing, and gives being to all things that are; and, as one small candle may light a thousand, so the light here kindled hath shone unto many, yea in some sort to our whole nation; let the glorious name of Jehovah have all the praise. [113]

Toward the end of his life, William Bradford wrote in *Of Plymouth Plantation:*

Though I am growne aged, yet I have had a longing desire, to see with my own eyes, something of the most ancient language, and holy tongue, in which the Law, and oracles of God were writ; and in which God, and angels, spoke to the holy patriarchs, of old time; and what names were given to things, from the creation.

And though I cannot attaine to much herein, yet I am refreshed, to have seen some glimpse hereof; (as Moses saw the Land of Canaan afarr off) my aime and desire is, to see how the words, and phrases lye in the holy texte; and to dicerne somewhat of the same for my owne contente. [114]

Inscribed on Governor William Bradford's grave at Burial Hill in Plymouth, Massachusetts, are the remarks:

Under this stone rests the ashes of William Bradford, a zealous Puritan, and sincere Christian Governor of Plymouth Colony from 1621 to 1657, (the year he died) aged 69, except 5 years, which he declined.

Let the right hand of the Lord awake. (Inscribed in Hebrew)

What our fathers with so much difficulty attained do not basely relinquish. (Inscribed in Latin). [115]

❧

Omar Bradley (1893-1981), one of the most popular generals of

World War II, commanded the Second Army Corps in North Africa throughout the Tunisian and Sicilian campaigns. He was later given command of the United States Ground Forces for the invasion of France, and then in August of 1944 he commanded the Twelfth Army Group in France and Germany. Appointed to the position of Joint Chiefs of Staff in 1949, Omar Bradley was promoted to the rank of General of the Army before he retired in 1953. In his address on Armistice Day, 1948, General Bradley stated:

> We have grasped the mystery of the atom and rejected the Sermon on the Mount....
>
> The world has achieved brilliance without conscience. Ours is a world of nuclear giants and ethical infants.[116]

ᴣ⧏

Wernher Magnus Maximillan von Braun (1912-1977), known as the "Father of the American Space Program," was the director of NASA and the U.S. guided missile program. He earned a Ph.D. from the University of Berlin, and went on to develop the famed V-2 rocket during World War II. In 1945, he emigrated from Germany to the United States; and in 1955, became a citizen. Wernher von Braun, one of the top space scientists in the world, stated:

> In this age of space flight, when we use the modern tools of science to advance into new regions of human activity, the Bible—this grandiose, stirring history of the gradual revelation and unfolding of the moral law—remains in every way an up-to-date book.
>
> Our knowledge and use of the laws of nature that enable us to fly to the Moon also enable us to destroy our home planet with the atom bomb. Science itself does not address the question whether we should use the power at our disposal for good or for evil.
>
> The guidelines of what we ought to do are furnished in the moral law of God. It is no longer enough that we pray that God may be with us on our side. We must learn to pray that we may be on God's side.[117]

Wernher von Braun gave the following statement in the foreword to his *Anthology on the creation and design exhibited in nature:*

Manned space flight is an amazing achievement, but it has opened for mankind thus far only a tiny door for viewing the awesome reaches of space. An outlook through this peephole at the vast mysteries of the universe should only confirm our belief in the certainty of its Creator.

I find it as difficult to understand a scientist who does not acknowledge the presence of a superior rationality behind the existence of the universe as it is to comprehend a theologian who would deny the advance of science.[118]

In May of 1974, Wernher von Braun, in a published article, stated:

One cannot be exposed to the law and order of the universe without concluding that there must be design and purpose behind it all....The better we understand the intricacies of the universe and all it harbors, the more reason we have found to marvel at the inherent design upon which it is based...

To be forced to believe only one conclusion—that everything in the universe happened by chance—would violate the very objectivity of science itself....What random process could produce the brains of a man or the system of the human eye?...

They (evolutionists) challenge science to prove the existence of God. But must we really light a candle to see the sun?...They say they cannot visualize a Designer. Well, can a physicist visualize an electron?...What strange rationale makes some physicists accept the inconceivable electron as real while refusing to accept the reality of a Designer on the ground that they cannot conceive Him?...

It is in scientific honesty that I endorse the presentation of alternative theories for the origin of the universe, life and man in the science classroom. It would be an error to overlook the possibility that the universe was planned rather than happening by chance.[119]

෨

David Brearly (1745-1790), was a signer of the Constitution of the United States of America. He also served as a Colonel in the Revolutionary Army, was appointed Federal Judge in New Jersey by President George Washington and served as Chief Justice of the Supreme Court of New Jersey.

He attended Princeton College, where he was under the instruction of the Reverend John Witherspoon, one of the nation's premier theologians and legal experts. He was admitted to the bar in 1767 and was so outspoken for the cause of liberty that he was arrested for "high treason" against Britain. David Brearly was also active in many areas of religion; he was:

> .... A warden of St. Michael's Church ....a compiler of the *Protestant Episcopal Prayer Book* and a delegate to the Episcopal General Convention in 1786. [120]

David Brearly

🙠

David Josiah Brewer (1837-1910), a justice of the United State Supreme Court, gave the court's opinion in the 1892 case of *Church of the Holy Trinity v. United States,* (143 U.S. 457-458, 465-471, 36 L ed 226):

> No purpose of action against religion can be imputed to any legislation, state or national, because this is a religious people. This is historically true. From the discovery of this continent to the present hour, there is a single voice making this affirmation.

David Josiah Brewer

The commission to Christopher Columbus .... [recited] that it is hoped that by God's assistance some of the continents and islands in the ocean will be discovered...

The first colonial grant made to Sir Walter Raleigh in 1584 .... and the grant authorizing him to enact statutes for the government of the proposed colony provided that they be not against the true Christian faith...

The first charter of Virginia, granted by King James I in 1606 .... commenced the grant in these words: "...in propagating of Christian Religion to such People as yet live in Darkness..."

Language of similar import may be found in the subsequent charters of that colony .... in 1609 and 1611; and the same is true of the various charters granted to the other colonies. In language more or less emphatic is the establishment of the Christian religion declared to be one of the purposes of the grant. The celebrated compact made by the Pilgrims in the Mayflower, 1620, recites: "Having undertaken for the Glory of God, and advancement of the Christian faith... a voyage to plant the first colony in the northern parts of Virginia....

The fundamental orders of Connecticut, under which a provisional government was instituted in 1638-1639, commence with this declaration:

"....And well knowing where a people are gathered together the word of God requires that to maintain the peace and union .... there should be an orderly and decent government established according to God .... to maintain and preserve the liberty and purity of the gospel of our Lord Jesus which we now profess .... of the said gospel [which] is now practiced amongst us."

In the charter of privileges granted by William Penn to the province of Pennsylvania, in 1701, it is recited:

"....no people can be truly happy, though under the greatest enjoyment of civil liberties, if abridged of .... their religious profession and worship..."

Coming nearer to the present time, the Declaration of Independence recognizes the presence of the Divine in human affairs in these words:

We hold these truths to be self-evident, that all men are created equal, that they are endowed by their Creator with certain unalienable Rights .... appealing to the Supreme Judge of the world for the rectitude of our intentions .... And for the support of this Declaration, with firm reliance on the Protection of Divine Providence, we mutually pledge to each other our Lives, our Fortunes, and our sacred Honor.

... We find everywhere a clear recognition of the same truth .... because of a general recognition of this truth, the question has seldom been presented to the courts...

There is no dissonance in these declarations. There is a universal language pervading them all, having one meaning; they affirm and reaffirm that this is a religious nation. These are not individual sayings, declarations of private persons: they are organic utterances; they speak the voice of the entire people.

While because of a general recognition of this truth the question has seldom been presented to the courts, yet we find that in *Updegraph v. The Commonwealth,* it was decided that,

Christianity, general Christianity, is, and always has been, a part of the common law .... not Christianity with an established church .... but Christianity with liberty of conscience to all men.

And in *The People v. Ruggles,* Chancellor Kent, the great commentator on American law, speaking as Chief Justice of the Supreme Court of New York, said:

The people of this State, in common with the people of this country, profess the general doctrines of Christianity, as the rule of their faith and practice .... We are a Christian people, and the morality of the country is deeply engrafted upon Christianity, and not upon the doctrines or worship of those imposters.

And in the famous case of *Vidal v. Girard's Executors,* this Court...

observed: "It is also said, and truly, that the Christian religion is a part of the common law..."

If we pass beyond these matters to a view of American life as expressed by its laws, its business, its customs and its society, we find everywhere a clear recognition of the same truth. Among other matters note the following: The form of oath universally prevailing, concluding with an appeal to the Almighty; the custom of opening sessions of all deliberative bodies and most conventions with prayer; the prefatory words of all wills, "In the name of God, amen"; the laws respecting the observance of the Sabbath, with the general cessation of all secular business, and the closing of courts, legislatures, and other similar public assemblies on that day; the churches and church organizations which abound in every city, town and hamlet; the multitude of charitable organizations existing everywhere under Christian auspices; the gigantic missionary associations, with general support, and aiming to establish Christian missions in every quarter of the globe.

These, and many other matters which might be noticed, add a volume of unofficial declarations to the mass of organic utterances that this is a Christian nation .... We find everywhere a clear recognition of the same truth. [121]

The happiness of a people and the good order and preservation of civil government essentially depend upon piety, religion and morality. [122]

Religion, morality, and knowledge [are] necessary to good government, the preservation of liberty, and the happiness of mankind. [122]

A commentary on *Church of the Holy Trinity v. US* summerized:

Our laws and our institutions must necessarily be based upon and embody the teachings of the Redeemer of mankind. It is impossible that it should be otherwise; and in this sense and to this extent our civilization and our institutions are emphatically Christian. [123]

Associate justice David Josiah Brewer wrote:

I Believe in Jesus Christ as the great Helper, Comforter and Saviour of humanity, and the Holy Bible as bearing to us the story of his mission, the rules of duty, the revelation of Eternal Life, and also the conditions under which the attainment of that life are possible.

No Book contains more truths, or is more worthy of confidence than the Bible; none brings more joy to the sorrowing, more strength to the weak, or more stimulus to the nobly ambitious; none makes life sweeter, or death easier or less sad. [124]

≈

Sir David Brewster (1781-1868), was the Scottish physicist who, in 1817, patented his invention of the kaleidoscope. He founded the science of optical mineralogy, involving light polarization, and was a founder and President of the British Association for the Advancement of Science. Sir David Brewster stated:

> I shall see Jesus, and that will be grand!...Oh, is it not sad that all are not contented with the beautiful simple plan of salvation—Jesus Christ only—who has done so much for us.
>
> "Notwithstanding his talents!" That disgusts me: merit for a man to bow his intellect to the Cross! Why, what can the highest intellect on earth do but to bow to God's Word and God's mind thankfully?
>
> When I find a doctrine plainly stated in the Bible, that is enough, God knows. I can depend on God's Word. We should not expect in this world to be free from things obscure to us, and beyond our ability to explain....
>
> To believe in the Lord Jesus Christ is to live; I trust Him and enjoy His peace.[125]

≈

George Nixon Briggs (1796-1861), was the Governor of Massachusetts; a U.S. Congressman for six successive terms; and a philanthropist. In May of 1850, while President of the American Baptist Missionary Union, he addressed the missionaries in Buffalo:

> You go to an embassy compared with which all the embassies of men dwindle into insignificance. You go forth as ambassadors of Christ. You go to crumble idols—to convey light to benighted minds—to kindle love to God in the souls of ungodly men.
>
> Who can overestimate the qualifications necessary for such work? The fervent, effectual prayer shall ascend to the mercy seat for you.
>
> You shall never see the day when your brethren who sent you out shall turn their backs on you; but look higher, the Saviour has told you, "Lo, I am with you always, even unto the end of the world." The Almighty Friend will always be at your side to sustain you.[126]

≈

Rupert Brooke (1887-1915), was an English poet famous for writing verse with vivid beauty. A graduate of Cambridge University, he traveled in Germany, America, the South Seas and the Aegean Sea. His well-read sonnets include *1914* and *The Great Lover*. In his poem *Peace*, Rupert Brooke wrote:

> Now, God be thanked, Who has matched us with His hour,
> And caught our youth, and wakened us from sleeping.[127]

æ

John Brooks (1752-1825), a physician who became the Governor of Massachusetts, stated:

> I look back upon my humble life with humility. I am sensible of many imperfections that cling to me. I know that the present is neither the season nor the place to begin the preparation for death.
>
> Our whole life is given us for this great object, and the work of preparation should be early commenced, and be never relaxed till the end of our days. To God I can appeal that it has been my humble endeavor to serve Him with sincerity; and wherein I have failed, I trust in His grace to forgive.
>
> I now rest my soul on the mercy of the adorable Creator, through the only mediation of His Son, our Lord.[128]

æ

Phillips Brooks (1835-1893), was one of the best-known American writers and speakers of his time. He attended Harvard while James Russell Lowell, Oliver Wendell Holmes and Henry Wadsworth Longfellow taught there. He pastored in Philadelphia before becoming the rector of Trinity Church in Boston, and later the bishop of the Protestant Episcopal Church in Massachusetts. In 1867, he wrote one of his famous songs, *O Little Town of Bethlehem*:

> O little town of Bethlehem!
> How still we see thee lie;
> Above thy deep and dreamless sleep
> The silent stars go by;

Yet in thy dark streets shineth
The everlasting Light;
The hopes and fears of all the years
Are met in thee tonight.[129]

Phillips Brooks, in his sermon *Going Up to Jerusalem* wrote:

✓ Do not pray for easy lives. Pray to be stronger men! Do not pray for tasks equal to your powers. Pray for powers equal to your tasks.[130] ✓

ಎ

Jacob Broom (1752-1810), in addition to being a signer of the Constitution of the United States of America, was also a banker, entrepreneur, farmer, merchant and surveyor. Jacob Broom was described in the *Official Papers of Delaware,* written in 1909, as follows:

A fair example of the product of a sturdy, energetic, sagacious ancestry and evangelical Swedish orthodoxy, co-operating amid the trying environments of a struggling colony in an undeveloped land....
He lived in one of the potential crises of history, in which and for which the sublime visions and words of prophets and apostles had developed and inspired a stalwart manhood....
As it is an accepted fact that "the foundation of all permanent prosperity is a right regard for the Divine Being", it is proper to say that Jacob Broom was a God-fearing man.[131] ⌴

As a delegate from the State of Delaware, he would have complied with the requirements for office as stipulated by his state's constitution, which included:

✓ *Article XXII* Every person who shall be chosen a member of either house, or appointed to any office or place of trust...shall...make and subscribe the following declaration, to wit: "I, _____, do profess faith in God the Father, and in Jesus Christ His only Son, and in the Holy Ghost, one God, blessed for evermore; and I do acknowledge the holy scriptures of the Old and New Testament to be given by divine inspiration."[132] ✓

In a letter to his son, then a senior at Princeton College, Jacob

Broom wrote in 1794:

> Do not be so much flattered as to relax in your application; do not forget to be a Christian. I have said much to you on this head, and I hope an indelible impression is made.[133]

ᨠ

William Bross (1813-1890), was a journalist and the editor of the *Chicago Tribune*. In an interview, William Bross gave his reply to three questions inquiring how he attained success:

> **1.** What maxims have had a strong influence on your life, and helped to your success?:
> The Proverbs of Solomon and other Scriptures. They were quoted a thousand times by my honored father, and caused an effort to do my duty each day, under a constant sense of obligation to my Saviour and fellow man.

> **2.** What do you consider essential elements of success for a young man entering upon such a profession as yours?:
> Sterling, unflinching integrity in all matters, public and private. Let everyone do his whole duty, both to God and man. Let him follow earnestly the teachings of the Scriptures and eschew infidelity in all its forms.

> **3.** What, in your observation, have been the chief causes of the numerous failures in the life of business and professional men?:
> Want of integrity, careless of the truth, reckless in thought and expression, lack of trust in God, and a disregard of the teachings of His Holy Word, bad company, and bad morals in any of their many phases.[134]

ᨠ

John Brown (1800-1859), was an abolitionist, reformer and northern martyr. In his efforts to free the slaves, he opened his barn in Pennsylvania as a station on the Underground Railroad, and even lived in a black community for a time. He also took extreme steps, most notably the killing of settlers who believed individuals had the choice of enslaving a human life, and the seizing of the government arsenal at Harper's Ferry, Virginia. He was captured, sentenced, and on December 2, 1859, he was hanged. Labeled insane by some, he was called Saint John the Just by Louisa May Alcott, the author of *Little Women*.

At the end of a church service, in which the murder of the abolitionist publisher Elijah Lovejoy was recounted, John Brown stood up in the back of the church and declared:

John Brown

Here, before God, in the presence of these witnesses, I consecrate my life to the destruction of slavery. [135]

In a letter John Brown wrote:

I commend you all to Him "whose mercy endureth forever," to the God of my fathers, "whose I am, and whom I serve." "He will never leave you nor forsake you." Finally, my dearly beloved, be of good comfort!

Be sure to remember and follow my advice, and my example, too, so far as it has been consistent with the holy religion of Jesus Christ, in which I remain a most firm and humble believer.

Never forget the poor, nor think anything in them to be lost in you, even though they may be black as Ebedmelech, the Ethiopian eunuch, who cared for Jeremiah in the pit of the dungeon; or as black as the one to whom Philip preached Christ. [136]

&

Joseph Emerson Brown (1821-1894), a U.S. Senator and Governor of Georgia for four terms, replied to a letter inquiring as to his beliefs, by stating:

In reply to your letter asking a few lines as to my opinion of Christ and the Bible, I have to state with pleasure that I believe the Holy Bible is the inspired Word of God, and contains the only true rule of faith and practice. I believe that Jesus Christ is the Son of God, the Sovereign of the universe, and the Saviour of all who believe in Him. [137]

&

Robert Browning (1812-1889), an English poet, whose famous works include *Pauline, My Last Duchess,* and *The Ring and the Book,* wrote:

> Grow old along with me. The best is yet to be; the last of life, for which the first was made. Our times are in His hands who saith, "A whole I planned, youth shows but half. Trust God; see all, nor be afraid."[138]

In *The Guardian Angel,* 1842, Robert Browning wrote:

> O world, as God has made it! All is beauty.[139]

Robert Browning wrote in *Instans Tyrannus*, 1845:

> Just my vengeance complete,
> The man sprang to his feet,
> Stood erect, caught at God's skirts, and prayed!
> —So, I was afraid![140]

William Cullen Bryant

William Cullen Bryant (1794-1878), known as the "Father of American Poets," became very popular for his poetry, which included such titles as: *Thanatopsis, To a Waterfowl, The Death of the Flowers* and *To the Fringed Gentian.* For 50 years, he was the editor in chief of the *New York Evening Post.* William Cullen Bryant wrote:

The sacredness of the Bible awes me, and I approach it with the same sort of reverential feeling that an ancient Hebrew might be supposed to feel who was about to touch the ark of God with unhallowed hands.[141]

> The very men who, in the pride of their investigations into the secrets of the internal world, turn a look of scorn upon the Christian system of belief, are not aware how much of the peace and order of society, how much the happiness of households, and the purest of those who are the dearest to them, are owing to the influence of that religion extending beyond their sphere....

√ In my view, the life, the teachings, the labors, and the sufferings of the blessed Jesus, there can be no admiration too profound, no love of which the human heart is capable too warm, no gratitude too earnest and deep of which He is justly the object.[142]

ॐ

James Buchanan (1791-1868), the 15th President of the United States of America, had previously served as Secretary of State for President James K. Polk. He had also been a U.S. Congressman, a U.S. Senator, and a Minister to Great Britain under President Franklin Pierce. He was the only bachelor President; his fiancée died when he was a young man. In his Inaugural Address, March 4, 1857, President James Buchanan petitioned:

James Buchanan

√ In entering upon this great office I must humbly invoke the God of our fathers for wisdom and firmness to execute its high and responsible duties.[143]

On February 29, 1844, James Buchanan wrote a letter to his brother from Washington:

I am a believer; but not with that degree of firmness of faith calculated to exercise a controlling influence on my conduct. I ought constantly to pray, "Help Thou my unbelief." I trust that the Almighty Father, through the merits and atonement of His Son, will yet vouchsafe to me a clearer and stronger faith than I possess.[144]

Nearing the end of his life, James Buchanan wrote:

√ We are both at a period of life when it is our duty to relax our grasp on the world fast receding, and fix our thoughts, desires, and affections on One who knows no change. I trust in God that, through the merits and atonement of His Son, we may both be prepared for the inevitable change.[145]

ॐ

Peter Bulkeley (1583-1659), the Puritan leader who founded the city of Concord, Massachusetts, stated in 1651:

Peter Bulkeley

> We are as a city set upon a hill, in the open view of all the earth....We profess ourselves to be a people in covenant with God, and therefore...the Lord our God...will cry shame upon us if we walk contrary to the covenant which we have promised to walk in. If we open the mouths of men against our profession, by reason of the scandalousness of our lives, we (of all men) shall have the greater sin.[146]

&

John Bunyan (1628-1688), the renowned English author, in 1678, wrote the classic *Pilgrim's Progress*. This famous allegory of a Christian's life has been translated into over 100 languages and, after the Bible, has held the position as the world's best seller for hundreds of years. John Bunyan, born in Bedford, England, was a poor, unskilled tinker who was imprisoned for 12 years for preaching without a license. It was during this time that he did much of his writing, while supporting his family by making shoelaces. In the *Shepherd Boy's Song*, John Bunyan wrote:

> My sword I give to him that shall succeed me in my pilgrimage, and my courage and skill to him that can get it. My marks and scars I carry with me, to be a witness for me, that I have fought His battles who now will be my rewarder.[147]

&

Warren Earl Burger (1907-   ), the Chief Justice of the Supreme Court, who, on July 5, 1983, delivered the court's opinion in regard to chaplains opening the Legislative sessions with prayer:

> The men who wrote the First Amendment religion clause did not view paid legislative chaplains and opening prayers as a violation of that amendment...the practice of opening sessions with prayer has continued without interruption ever since that early session of Congress.[148]

It can hardly be thought that in the same week the members of the first Congress voted to appoint and pay a chaplain for each House and also voted to approved the draft of the First Amendment...(that) they intended to forbid what they had just declared acceptable.[149]

√ [Chaplains and prayer] are deeply embedded in the history and tradition of this country.[150]

In a 1984 opinion, Chief Justice Warren Burger upheld that the city of Pawtucket, R.I., did not violate the Constitution by displaying a Nativity scene. Noting that presidential orders and proclamations from Congress have designated Christmas as a national holiday in religious terms since 1789, he wrote:

√ There is an unbroken history of official acknowledgement by all three branches of government of the role of religion in American life....The Constitution does not require a complete separation of church and state. It affirmatively mandates accommodation, not merely tolerance, of all religions and forbids hostility towards any.[151]

ૐ

Edmund Burke (1729-1797), was an outstanding orator, author and leader in Great Britain during the time of the Revolutionary War. On March 22, 1775, in his *Second Speech on the Conciliation with America—The Thirteen Resolutions*, Edmund Burke addressed Parliament, saying:

Edmund Burke

Religion, always a principle of energy, in this new people is no way worn out or impaired; and their mode of professing it is also one main cause of this free spirit.

The people are Protestants; and of that kind which is the most adverse to all implicit submission of mind and opinion. This is a persuasion not only favorable to Liberty, but built upon it.

All Protestantism, even the most cold and passive, is a sort of dissent. But the religion most prevalent in our Northern Colonies is a refinement on the principle of resistance; it is the dissidence of dissent, and the protestantism of the Protestant religion.[152]

Freedom and not servitude is the cure of anarchy; as religion, and not atheism, is the true remedy for superstition.[153]

I have been told by an eminent bookseller, that in no branch of his business, after tracts of popular devotion, were so many books as those on law exported to the Plantations [Colonies].[154]

In *The Works and Correspondence of the Right Honorable Edmund Burke, Volume VI,* Edmund Burke stated:

The Scripture is no one summary of doctrines regularly digested, in which a man could not mistake his way; it is a most remarkable, but most multifarious, collection of the records of the Divine economy; a collection of an infinite variety of theology, history, prophecy, psalmody, morality, allegory, legislation, carried through different books, by different authors, at different ages, for different ends and purposes.[155]

In his work *Reflections on the Revolution in France,* Edmund Burke wrote in 1790:

People will not look forward to posterity who never look backward to their ancestors.[156]

On May 28, 1794, in the *Impeachment of Warren Hastings,* Edmund Burke stated:

There is but one law for all, namely, that law which governs all law, the law of our Creator, the law of humanity, justice, equity—the law of nature, and of nations.[157]

On January 9, 1795, in a letter to William Smith, Edmund Burke made this famous statement:

All that is necessary for evil to triumph is for good men to do nothing.[158]

In 1797, in his *Letters on a Regicide Peace,* Edmund Burke wrote:

The blood of man should never be shed but to redeem the blood of man. It is well shed for our family, for our friends, for our God, for our country, for our kind. The rest is vanity; the rest is crime.[159]

Edmund Burke wrote:

What is liberty without wisdom and without virtue? It is the greatest of all possible evils; for it is folly, vice, and madness, without restraint.

Men are qualified for civil liberty in exact proportion to their disposition to put moral chains upon their own appetites....

Society cannot exist, unless a controlling power upon will and appetite be placed somewhere; and the less of it there is within, the more there must be without.

It is ordained in the eternal constitution of things, that men of intemperate minds cannot be free. Their passions forge their fetters.[160]

Edmund Burke resigned himself, stating:

First, according to the ancient, good, and laudable custom, of which my heart and understanding recognize the propriety, I bequeath my soul to God, hoping for His mercy through the only merits of our Lord and Saviour Jesus Christ.[161]

&

George Herbert Walker Bush (1924-   ), the 41st President of the United States of America, on May 3, 1990, declared a *National Day of Prayer:*

The great faith that led our Nation's Founding Fathers to pursue this bold experience in self-government has sustained us in uncertain and perilous times; it has given us strength and inspiration to this very day.

Like them, we do very well to recall our "firm reliance on the protection of Divine Providence," to give thanks for the freedom and prosperity this Nation enjoys, and to pray for continued help and guidance from our wise and loving Creator.[162]

President George Bush, 1992, in his *National Day of Prayer Proclamation* declared:

Whatever our individual religious convictions may be, each of us is invited to join in this National Day of Prayer. Indeed, although we may find our own words to express it, each of us can echo this timeless prayer of Solomon, the ancient king who prayed for, and received, the gift of wisdom:

The Lord our God be with us, as He was with our fathers; may He not leave us or forsake us; so that He may incline our hearts to Him, to walk in all His ways...that all the peoples of the earth may know that the Lord is God; there is no other.[163]

Benjamin Franklin Butler

Benjamin Franklin Butler (1795-1858), was the United States Attorney General, 1833-1838, under President Andrew Jackson. He served as the U.S. Secretary of War, 1836-1837, and as the U.S. Attorney for the Southern District of New York, 1838-1848. In addition to serving in the New York State Legislature, Butler was the head of the electoral college of New York in 1845. In an address at Alexandria, D.C., Benjamin Franklin Butler stated in 1834:

He is truly happy, whatever may be his temporal condition, who can call God his Father in the full assurance of faith and hope. And amid all his trials, conflicts, and doubts, the feeblest Christian is still comparatively happy; because cheered by the hope...that the hour is coming when he shall be delivered from "this body of sin and death" and in the vision of his Redeemer...and felicity of angels.

Not only does the Bible inculcate, with sanctions of the highest import, a system of the purest morality, but in the person and character of our Blessed Saviour it exhibits a tangible illustration of that system.

In Him we have set before us—what, till the publication of the Gospel, the world had never seen—a model of feeling and action, adapted to all times, places, and circumstances; and combining so much of wisdom, benevolence, and holiness, that none can fathom its sublimity; and yet, presented in a form so simple, that even a child may be made to understand and taught to love it.[164]

Robert C. Byrd (1918-   ), on June 27, 1962, as a United States Senator from West Virginia, delivered a message in Congress just two days after the Supreme Court declared prayer in schools unconstitutional:

✓ Inasmuch as our greatest leaders have shown no doubt about God's proper place in the American birthright, can we, in our day, dare do less?...

In no other place in the United States are there so many, and such varied official evidences of deep and abiding faith in God on the part of Government as there are in Washington....

Every session of the House and the Senate begins with prayer. Each house has its own chaplain.

The Eighty-third Congress set aside a small room in the Capitol, just off the rotunda, for the private prayer and meditation of members of Congress. The room is always open when Congress is in session, but it is not open to the public. The room's focal point is a stained glass window showing George Washington kneeling in prayer. Behind him is etched these words from Psalm 16:1: "Preserve me, O God, for in Thee do I put my trust."

Inside the rotunda is a picture of the Pilgrims about to embark from Holland on the sister ship of the *Mayflower,* the *Speedwell.* The ship's revered chaplain, Brewster, who later joined the *Mayflower,* has open on his lap the Bible. Very clear are the words, "the New Testament according to our Lord and Savior, Jesus Christ." On the sail is the motto of the Pilgrims, "In God We Trust, God With Us."

The phrase, "In God We Trust," appears opposite the President of the Senate, who is the Vice-President of the United States. The same phrase, in large words inscribed in the marble, backdrops the Speaker of the House of Representatives.

Above the head of the Chief Justice of the Supreme Court are the Ten Commandments, with the great American eagle protecting them. Moses is included among the great lawgivers in Herman A MacNeil's marble sculpture group on the east front. The crier who opens each session closes with the words, "God save the United States and this Honorable Court."

Engraved on the metal on the top of the Washington Monument are the words: "Praise be to God." Lining the walls of the stairwell are such biblical phrases as "Search the Scriptures," "Holiness to the Lord," "Train up a child in the way he should go, and when he is old he will not depart from it."

Numerous quotations from Scripture can be found within its [the Library of Congress] walls. One reminds each American of his responsibility to his Maker: "What doth the Lord require of thee, but to do justly and love mercy and walk humbly with thy God"(Micah 6:8).

Another in the lawmaker's library preserves the Psalmist's

acknowledgment that all nature reflects the order and beauty of the Creator, "The heavens declare the glory of God, and the firmament showeth His handiwork" (Psalm 19:1). And still another reference: "The light shineth in darkness, and the darkness comprehendeth it not" (John 1:5).[165]

√ Millions have stood in the Lincoln Memorial and gazed up at the statue of the great Abraham Lincoln. The sculptor who chiseled the features of Lincoln in granite all but seems to make Lincoln speak his own words inscribed into the walls.

"...That this Nation, under God, shall have a new birth of freedom, and that government of the people, by the people, for the people, shall not perish from the earth."

At the opposite end, on the north wall, his Second Inaugural Address alludes to "God," the "Bible," "providence," "the Almighty," and "divine attributes."

It then continues:

As was said 3000 years ago, so it still must be said, "The judgements of the Lord are true and righteous altogether."

On the south banks of Washington's Tidal Basin, Thomas Jefferson still speaks:

"God who gave us life gave us liberty. Can the liberties of a nation be secure when we have removed a conviction that these liberties are the gift of God? Indeed I tremble for my country when I reflect that God is just, that his justice cannot sleep forever."

[These words of Jefferson are] a forceful and explicit warning that to remove God from this country will destroy it.[166]

❧

$\checkmark$ *C*

John Caldwell Calhoun (1782-1850), served as a Congressman and Senator from South Carolina. He was the Secretary of War under President James Monroe; Secretary of State under President John Tyler; and Vice-President under Presidents John Quincy Adams and Andrew Jackson. He was a prominent supporter of "states rights," and in 1850, the year he died, he gave his last speech to the Senate regarding the Civil War that lay ahead:

> The cords that bind the States together are not only many, but various in character....The strongest of those of a spiritual and ecclesiastical nature, consisted in the unity of the great religious denominations, all of which originally embraced the whole Union. All these denominations, with the exception, perhaps, of the Catholics, were organized very much upon the principle of our political institutions.
>
> Beginning with smaller meetings, corresponding with the political divisions of the country, their organization terminated in one great central assemblage, corresponding very much with the character of Congress. At these meetings the principal clergymen and lay members of the respective denominations, from all parts of the Union, met to transact business relating to their common concerns.
>
> It was not confined to what appertained to the doctrines and discipline of the respective denominations, but extended to plans for disseminating the Bible, establishing missions, distributing tracts, and of establishing presses for the publications of tracts, newspapers, and periodicals, with a view of diffusing religious information, and for the support of their respective doctrines and creeds.
>
> All this combined contributed greatly to strengthen the bonds of the Union. The ties which held each denomination together formed a strong cord to hold the whole Union together; but, powerful as they were, they have not been able to resist the explosive effect of slavery agitation...[1]

&

California Supreme Court 1980, in the case of *Devin Walker v. First Orthodox Presbyterian Church*, 760-028.9, gave its opinion:

> Freedom of religion is so fundamental to American history that it must be preserved even at the expense of other rights which have become institutionalized by the Democratic process.[2]

&

Thomas Carlyle (1795-1881), was a famous Scottish essayist and historian whose works were controversial yet highly praised. His books include *The Life of Schiller*, 1826; *The French Revolution*, 1837; *On Heros and Hero Worship*, 1840. He also translated Goethe's works from German into English. Thomas Carlyle wrote:

> The Bible is the truest utterance that ever came by alphabetic letters from the soul of man, through which, as through a window divinely opened, all men can look into the stillness of eternity, and discern in glimpses their far-distant, long-forgotten home.[3]

> I call the Book of Job, apart from all the theories about it, one of the grandest things ever written with the pen.[4]

In his *Miscellaneous Papers*, Thomas Carlyle wrote:

> The Hebrew Bible, is it not before all things true as no other book ever was or will be?[5]

In his essays *Corn-Law Rhymes*, Carlyle wrote:

> In the poorest cottage are books: is one Book wherein, for several thousand of years, the spirit of man has found light, and nourishment, and an interpreting response to whatever is deepest in him.[6]

In his *Critical and Miscellaneous Essays*, 1827, Carlyle wrote:

> The Bible itself has, in all changes of theory about it, this as its highest distinction: that it is the truest of all books. The Book springs, every word of it, from the intensest convictions, from the very heart's

core, of those who penned it; and has not that been a successful Book? Did all the Paternoster Rows of the world ever hear of one so successful?[7]

In 1827, Thomas Carlyle wrote in *The State of German Literature:*

> The three great elements of modern civilization: gunpowder, printing, and the Protestant religion.[8]

In Book III, Chapter III of his *Sartor Resartus,* written in 1833-1834, Thomas Carlyle wrote:

> If thou ask to what height man has carried it, look to our divinest symbol: Jesus of Nazareth, and His life, and His biography, and what followed therefrom. Higher has the human thought never reached; this is Christianity and Christendom—a symbol of quite perennial, infinite character, whose significance will ever demand to be anew inquired into and anew made manifest.[9]

In Book II, Chapter 9 of *Sartor Resartus,* he wrote:

> Love not Pleasure; love God.[10]

੨੨

William Bliss Carman (1861-1929), was the preeminent lyric poet of Canada. A distant relative of Ralph Waldo Emerson, Carman became well known as a magazine writer, as the editor of the *New York Independent,* and as the editor of the *Oxford Book of American Verse.* His first volume, *Low Tide on Grand Pre,* was published in 1893, followed by the books of verse: *Songs of Vagabondia, A Winter Holiday, Pipes of Pan,* and *Ballads of Lost Haven.* In his work, *Vestigia,* William Bliss Carman wrote:

> I took a day to search for God,
> And found Him not. But as I trod
> By rocky ledge, through woods untamed,
> Just where one scarlet lily flamed,
> I saw His footprint in the sod.[11]

੨੨

Colony of Carolina 1650, was originally named "Carolana" or "Charles' land," after King Charles I of England. Originally part of Virginia, it had been granted to Sir Robert Heath in 1629.

(Virginia was named after the "Virgin Queen" Elizabeth I by Sir Walter Raleigh, who explored the area and attempted to found a settlement on Roanoke Island, April 9, 1585. On August 13, 1587, the members of the colony converted the Indian Manteo, and he was baptized into the Christian faith. That same month the first child was born in America, and she was baptized Virginia Dare. The Roanoke Colony was unsuccessful and later became known as the "Lost Colony."[12])

It wasn't until the 1650s that English colonists began to settle the area permanently. The first governor, William Sayle, was a Nonconformist and allowed religious toleration to all denominations: Calvinists and Baptists from England and parts of New England, Huguenots (French Protestants), Episcopalians, Scotch-Irish Presbyterians, Lutherans, German Reformed, Moravians, etc.[13]

Of the many Christians who began to settle in North Carolina beginning in 1653, the Quaker missionaries were among the most notable, with even George Fox, the founder of Quakerism, preaching there. At a later date, the Quaker family of Daniel Boone, along with other Quaker families, pioneered the Yadkin River Valley along the North Carolina frontier. The first Baptist congregation was formed there in 1727, and was followed later by the Methodist congregations, who recognized Negro ministers and preached strongly against slavery.[14]

NORTH CAROLINA

Seal of North Carolina

ੲ

Charter of Carolina 1663, was granted by King Charles II to Sir William Berkeley and the seven other lord proprietors (initially granted by King Charles I to Sir Robert Heath in 1629). It stated:

Being excited with a laudable and pious zeal for the propagation of the Christian faith....[they] have humbly besought leave of us...to transport and make an ample colony...unto a certain country...in the parts of America not yet cultivated or planted, and only inhabited by some barbarous people, who have no knowledge of Almighty God.[15]

 है

Fundamental Constitutions of the Carolinas

1663, was drawn up by the famous philosopher, John Locke, at the request of Sir William Berkeley and the seven other lord proprietors of the colony.[16] It stated:

SOUTH CAROLINA

No man shall be permitted to be a freeman of Carolina, or to have any estate of habitation within it that doth not acknowledge a God, and that God is publicly and solemnly to be worshiped.[17]

Seal of South Carolina

 है

James Earl "Jimmy" Carter (1924-   ), the 39th President of the United States of America, spoke in his Inaugural Address, January 20, 1977, saying:

Here before me is the Bible used in the inauguration of our first President in 1789, and I have just taken the oath of office on the Bible my mother gave me just a few years ago, opened to the timeless admonition from the ancient prophet Micah: "He hath showed thee, O man, what is good; and what does the Lord require of thee, but to do justly, and to love mercy, and to walk humbly with thy God"(Micah 6:2).[18]

On March 16, 1976, in an interview with Robert L. Turner, Jimmy Carter explained:

We believe that the first time we're born, as children, it's human life given to us; and when we accept Jesus as our Savior, it's a new life. That's what "born again" means.[19]

 है

Robert "King" Carter (1663-1732), was the Governor of the Virginia Colony, as approved by King George II in July of 1726, having previously served as Lieutenant Commander of the counties of Lancaster and Northumberland since 1715. He was President of the Council, a Member of the House of Burgesses at Jamestown, the Colonial Treasurer, as well as the Speaker of the House and Chairman of the powerful *Committee of Propriations and Grievances.*

Robert "King" Carter

Robert "King" Carter was one of the most significant figures during the period of America's founding, acting as rector of William and Mary College, and owning property consisting of 300,000 acres of land. He was the father of Anne Hill Carter, who was married to the famous Revolutionary War hero, Light Horse Harry Lee. Their son was Robert E. Lee.

Robert Carter's son, John, had gone to England to study, but instead had squandered his time and money. After accumulating numerous debts, the young Carter repented. On July 22, 1720, Robert Carter wrote to Mr. Perry, his son's guardian in England:

> My son, I find, upon the stool of repentance. It will be well he will come to his senses at last....He begs of me to forget his past extravagances, and desires I may not insist upon a particular account from him, and that he will give me no more occasion of future complaints. Upon these terms I am willing....Thus you see I am no stranger to the story of the Gospel.[20]

On July 23, 1720, Robert Carter wrote to his son John in England:

> Dear Son John:
> May Heaven keep you fixed to this resolution without wavering. It will prove a cordial to your heart all the days of your life. Upon these hopes I shall pass over what's past....Pray take a little more care of your brothers in England. The rest is to beg God's blessing upon you.[21]

Robert Carter built Christ Church in Lancaster County, Virginia, where he served as a vestryman. He is buried in the churchyard; his epitaph reads:

Robert Carter, Esq., an honorable man, who exalted his high birth by noble endowments and pure morals. He sustained the College of William and Mary in the most trying times. He was Governor, Speaker of the House and Treasurer...he built and endowed at his own expense, this sacred edifice, a lasting monument of his piety to God.[22]

&

Peter Cartwright (1785-1872), was a Methodist circuit-riding preacher who was one of the most famous evangelists and planters of new churches in the West. Peter Cartwright preached nearly 15,000 sermons and baptized almost 10,000 converts. In 1824 he left Kentucky and Tennessee, because of his disdain for slavery, and moved to Illinois, where he ran for Congress. He lost his bid for Congress in 1846 to Abraham Lincoln.[23] In recalling his own conversion, Peter Cartwright shared:

Peter Cartwright

> I went with weeping multitudes and bowed before the preaching stand, and earnestly prayed for mercy. In the midst of a solemn struggle of soul, an impression was made upon my mind, as though a voice said to me: "Thy sins are all forgiven thee."[24]

&

George Washington Carver (1864-1943), an agricultural chemist of international fame, introduced hundreds of uses for the peanut, soybean, pecan and sweet potato. This revolutionized the economy of the South since these crops replenished the soil, which had become depleted through years of cotton growth.

After his mother was kidnapped when he was an infant, George Washington Carver was raised by Uncle Moses and Aunt Sue Carver. Being of poor health as a child, he spent much time around the house and in the woods. He later went to school

George Washington Carver

in Neosho, Missouri, then in Kansas. He graduated from Iowa State College of Agriculture and Mechanical Arts. George Washington Carver was also an accomplished artist; one of his paintings, *The Yucca,* received an Honorable Mention at the 1893 Chicago World's Fair.

Booker Taliaferro Washington

In 1896 he gave up his faculty position at Iowa State College of Agriculture to join Booker T. Washington, President of the newly founded Tuskegee Institute in Alabama. He made many medical contributions, including Penol and a cure for infantile paralysis.

His discoveries from the peanut (over 300), the sweet potato (over 118), as well as from the soybean, etc., included cosmetics, face powder, lotion, shaving cream, vinegar, cold cream, printer's ink, salad oil, rubbing oil, instant coffee, leather stains from mahogany to blue, synthetic tapioca and egg yolk, flour, paints, non-toxic colors (from which crayons were eventually created).

Henry Ford became personal friends with Dr. Carver, being fascinated with his method of deriving rubber from milkweed. Mr. Ford tried many times to get Dr. Carver to join him in business, but Carver was committed to helping his people and the South. Mr. Ford built a duplicate of Dr. Carver's birthplace at his *Dearborn Village,* and built a school for children named *George Washington Carver School.*

Henry Ford

George Washington Carver was visited at Tuskegee Institute by Vice-President Calvin Coolidge, and by President Franklin D. Roosevelt. He became a confidant and advisor to leaders and scientists from all over the world, ranging from Thomas Edison to Mahatma Gandhi. (Edison had also offered him a position with a six-figure income, but Carver turned it down).

In the summer of 1920, the Young Men's Christian Association of Blue Ridge, North Carolina, invited Professor Carver to speak at their summer school for the southern states. Dr. Willis D.

Weatherford, President of Blue Ridge, introduced Professor Carver as the speaker. Carver, with his high voice, surprised the audience as he exclaimed humorously:

> I always look forward to introductions as opportunities to learn something about myself....

He continued:

> Years ago I went into my laboratory and said, "Dear Mr. Creator, please tell me what the universe was made for?"
>
> The Great Creator answered, "You want to know too much for that little mind of yours. Ask for something more your size, little man."
>
> Then I asked. "Please, Mr. Creator, tell me what man was made for?"
>
> Again the Great Creator replied, "You are still asking too much. Cut down on the extent and improve the intent."
>
> So then I asked, "Please, Mr. Creator, will you tell me why the peanut was made?"
>
> "That's better, but even then it's infinite. What do you want to know about the peanut?"
>
> "Mr. Creator, can I make milk out of the peanut?"
>
> "What kind of milk do you want? Good Jersey milk or just plain boarding house milk?"
>
> "Good Jersey milk."
>
> And then the Great Creator taught me to take the peanut apart and put it together again. And out of the process have come forth all these products![25]

Among the numerous products displayed was a bottle of *good Jersey milk*. (Three-and-a-half ounces of peanuts produced one pint of rich milk or one quart of boardinghouse blue john!)[26]

In 1921, George Washington Carver accepted the invitation to address the United States Senate Ways and Means Committee in Washington, D.C., concerning the potential uses of the peanut and other new crops to improve the economy of the South. Initially given only ten minutes to speak, he instantly enthralled the committee so much that the Chairman said, "Go ahead Brother. Your time is unlimited!"

Carver spoke for one hour and forty-five minutes. At the end of his address, the Chairman of the Committee asked:

> "Dr. Carver, how did you learn all of these things?"
> Carver answered:
> "From an old book"
> "What book?" asked the Senator.
> Carver replied, "The Bible."
> The Senator inquired, "Does the Bible tell about peanuts?"
> "No, Sir" Dr. Carver replied, "But it tells about the God who made
> the peanut. I asked Him to show me what to do with the peanut, and
> He did."[27]

George Washington Carver named his laboratory *God's Little Workshop* and never took any scientific textbooks into it; he merely asked God how to perform his experiments.

On November 19, 1924, having accepted the invitation of the Women's Board of Domestic Missions to speak in New York City's Marble Collegiate Church, Dr. Carver declared before the 500 people assembled:

> God is going to reveal to us things He never revealed before if we
> put our hands in His. No books ever go into my laboratory. The thing
> I am to do and the way of doing it are revealed to me. I never have to
> grope for methods. The method is revealed to me the moment I am
> inspired to create something new. Without God to draw aside the
> curtain I would be helpless.[28]

He would lock the door behind him when he went into his laboratory, as he confided:

> Only alone can I draw close enough to God to discover His
> secrets.[29]

George Washington Carver had developed a lifelong friendship with Jim Hardwick from the Virginia Polytechnic Institute. (Jim's brother, Harry Hardwick, had become the head football coach of the U.S. Naval Academy.) During one of Jim Hardwick's visits to *Tuskegee Institute* in 1928, he asked Dr. Carver to share some of his observations about God. George Washington Carver responded:

As a very small boy exploring the almost virgin woods of the old Carver place, I had the impression someone had just been there ahead of me. Things were so orderly, so clean, so harmoniously beautiful. A few years later in this same woods I was to understand the meaning of this boyish impression. Because I was practically overwhelmed with the sense of some Great Presence. Not only had someone been there. Someone was there....

Years later when I read in the Scriptures, "In Him we live and move and have our being," I knew what the writer meant. Never since have I been without this consciousness of the Creator speaking to me....The out of doors has been to me more and more a great cathedral in which God could be continuously spoken to and heard from....

Man, who needed a purpose, a mission, to keep him alive, had one. He could be...God's co-worker....

My attitude toward life was also my attitude toward science. Jesus said one must be born again, must become as a little child. He must let no laziness, no fear, no stubbornness keep him from his duty.

If he were born again he would see life from such a plane he would have the energy not to be impeded in his duty by these various sidetrackers and inhibitions. My work, my life, must be in the spirit of a little child seeking only to know the truth and follow it.

My purpose alone must be God's purpose—to increase the welfare and happiness of His people. Nature will not permit a vacuum. It will be filled with something.

Human need is really a great spiritual vacuum which God seeks to fill...

With one hand in the hand of a fellow man in need and the other in the hand of Christ, He could get across the vacuum and I became an agent. Then the passage, "I can do all things through Christ which strengtheneth me," came to have real meaning.

As I worked on projects which fulfilled a real human need forces were working through me which amazed me. I would often go to sleep with an apparently insoluble problem. When I woke the answer was there.

Why, then, should we who believe in Christ be so surprised at what God can do with a willing man in a laboratory? Some things must be baffling to the critic who has never been born again.

By nature I am a conserver. I have found nature to be a conserver. Nothing is wasted or permanently lost in nature. Things change their form, but they do not cease to exist.

After I leave this world I do not believe I am through. God would be a bigger fool than even a man if he did not conserve what seems to be the most important thing he has yet done in the universe. This kind of reasoning may aid the young.

When you get your grip on the last rung of the ladder and look over the wall as I am now doing you don't need their proofs. You see. You know you will not die.[30]

In 1939, George Washington Carver was awarded the Roosevelt Medal, with the declaration:

To a scientist humbly seeking the guidance of God and a liberator to men of the white race as well as the black.[31]

George Washington Carver remarked:

The secret of my success? It is simple. It is found in the Bible, "In all thy ways acknowledge Him and He shall direct thy paths."[32]

Lewis Cass

Lewis Cass (1782-1866), was an American soldier, lawyer, politician and diplomat. After serving in the War of 1812, he became the Governor-General of the Territory of Michigan, where he made treaties with the Indians, organized townships and built roads. He was a United States Senator, Secretary of State under President James Buchanan and the Democratic Candidate for the Presidency in 1848. Lewis Cass stated:

Independent of its connection with human destiny hereafter, the fate of republican government is indissolubly bound up with the fate of the Christian religion, and a people who reject its holy faith will find themselves the slaves of their own evil passions and of arbitrary power.[33]

In a letter from Washington, dated 1846, Lewis Cass wrote:

God, in His providence, has given us a Book of His revealed will to be with us at the commencement of our career in this life and at its termination; and to accompany us during all chances and changes of this trying and fitful progress, to control the passions, to enlighten the judgment, to guide the conscience, to teach us what we ought to do here, and what we shall be hereafter.[34]

On December 14, 1852, Lewis Cass gave the obituary address for Daniel Webster in the United States Senate:

> And beyond all this he died in the faith of the Christian—humble, but hopeful—adding another to the long list of eminent men who have searched the Gospel of Jesus Christ, and have found it to be the word and the will of God.[35]

> "How are the mighty fallen!" we may yet exclaim, when reft of our great and wisest; but they fall to rise again from death to life, when such quickening faith in the mercy of God and in the sacrifice of the Redeemer comes to shed upon them its happy influence this side of the grave and beyond it.[36]

૨એ

(Jay David) Whittaker Chambers (1901-1961), was an American journalist who had formerly been a Communist agent but recanted and defected to the West. He stated:

> Freedom is a need of the soul, and nothing else. It is in striving toward God that the soul strives continually after a condition of freedom. God alone is the inciter and guarantor of freedom. He is the only guarantor.
> External freedom is only an aspect of interior freedom. Political freedom, as the Western world has known it, is only a political reading of the Bible. Religion and freedom are indivisible. Without freedom the soul dies. Without the soul there is no justification for freedom.[37]

> Humanism is not new. It is, in fact, man's second oldest faith. Its promise was whispered in the first days of the Creation under the Tree of the Knowledge of Good and Evil: "Ye shall be as gods."[38]

૨એ

Salmon Portland Chase (1808-1873), the U.S. Secretary of the Treasury under President Abraham Lincoln, also served as the Governor of Ohio, a U.S. Senator and was appointed by President

Lincoln as Chief Justice of the Supreme Court. He was a strong opponent of slavery, defending so many escaped slaves when he first started practicing law that he was given the nickname "Attorney-General of Fugitive Slaves."

On November 20, 1861, Secretary of the Treasury Salmon Portland Chase wrote to the Director of the Mint in Philadelphia:

Salmon Portland Chase

> Dear Sir,
>
> No nation can be strong except in the strength of God or safe except in His defense. The trust of our people in God should be declared on our national coins.
>
> You will cause a device to be prepared without unnecessary delay with a motto expressing in the fewest and tersest words possible this national recognition.
>
> Yours truly,
> (Sgd). S.P. Chase[39]

On December 9, 1863, Secretary of the Treasury S.P. Chase wrote again to the Director of the Mint, James Pollock:

> I approve your mottos, only suggesting that on that with the Washington obverse, the motto should begin with the word "Our," so as to read:
> "Our God and our Country." And on that with the shield, it should be changed so as to read: "In God We Trust."[40]

On March 3, 1865, the Congress of the United States of America approved the Treasury Secretary Salmon Portland Chase's instruction to the U.S. mint to prepare a "device" to inscribe U.S. coins with the motto:

> In God We Trust[41]

Salmon Portland Chase declared:

> Give me solid and substantial religion; give me an humble, gentle lover of God and man; a man full of mercy and good fruits, without partiality and without hypocrisy; a man laying himself out in the works of faith, the patience of hope, the labor of love. Let my soul be

with those Christians, wheresoever they are, and whatsoever opinion they are of.[42]

When shall I be thoroughly imbued with a humble, self-denying, holy spirit? O Lord, my Saviour, do Thou assist and teach me!...

Today I rose too late; attended private and family prayers; afterwards read several chapters in Leviticus, having again began to read the Scriptures in course, intending to read the Old Testament in private, and the New with the family. It is my deliberate opinion that all the writings of all moral and political writers do not contain so much practical wisdom, whether applicable to state or persons.[43]

᠘

Samuel Chase

Samuel Chase (1741-1811), who was appointed a Justice on the United States Supreme Court by George Washington, was also a signer of the Declaration of Independence and later served as the Chief Justice of the State of Maryland. In the case of *Runkel v. Winemiller*, 1799, Justice Chase gave the court's opinion:

Religion is of general and public concern, and on its support depend, in great measure, the peace and good order of government, the safety and happiness of the people.

By our form of government, the Christian religion is the established religion; and all sects and denominations of Christians are placed upon the same equal footing, and are equally entitled to protection in their religious liberty.[44]

In 1799, a dispute arose over whether Thomas M'Creery, an Irish emigrant, had in fact become naturalized as an American citizen and thereby able to leave an estate to a relative still living in Ireland. The court decided in M'Creery's favor based on a certificate executed before Justice Chase:

Thomas M'Creery, in order to become...naturalized according to the Act of Assembly...on the 30th of September, 1795, took the oath...before the Honorable Samuel Chase, Esquire, then being the Chief Judge of the State of Maryland...and did then and there receive

from the said Chief Judge, a certificate thereof...:
"Maryland; I, Samuel Chase, Chief Judge of the State of Maryland,
do hereby certify all whom it may concern, that...personally appeared
before me Thomas M'Creery, and did repeat and subscribe a declaration
of his belief in the Christian Religion, and take the oath required by the
Act of Assembly of this State, entitled, *An Act for Naturalization.*"[45]

ﻬ

Francois René de Chateaubriand (1768-1848), was a famous
French writer who helped begin the literary style known as
Romanticism, which emphasized man's emotion in a rather
flowery style. In 1802, writing on his conversion to Christianity in
Le Genie du Christianisme, Chateaubriand declared:

J'ai pleure' et j'ai cru. (I wept and I believed.)[46]

ﻬ

Geoffrey Chaucer (1340-1400), was known as the "Father of English
Poetry." Honored as an English poet-laureate, Geoffrey Chaucer
wrote with vividness, charm and humor, demonstrating his
dramatic ability. In extracts from *The Canterbury Tales,* created in
1387, Chaucer wrote:

Who folwith Cristes Gospel and His lord
But we, that humble ben, and chast, and pore,
Workers of Goddes Word, not auditours.
                    —*The Sompnoures Tale*[47]

O cause first of our confusioun,
Till Crist had bought us with His blood agayn!
Loketh, how dere, schortly for to sayn,
Abought was first this cursed felonye;
Corrupt was al this world for glutonye.
Adam our fader, and his wfy also,
Fro Paradys to labour and to wo
Were dryven for that vice, it is no drede.
For whils that Adam fasted, as I rede,
He was in Paradys, and when that he
Eet of the fruyt defendit of a tre,
He was cast out to wo and into peyne.

Now for the love of Crist that for us dyde,
Levith youre othis, borthe gret and smale.
 —*The Pardoneres Tale*[47]

But Cristes loore and his apostles twelve
He taughte, but first he folwed it hymselve.[48]

For in the sterres, clearer than is glass,
Is written, God woot, whoso koude it reade,
The deeth of every man.[49]

Sathan, that evere us waiteth to bigile.[50]

ða

John Cheever (1912-1982), an American author, wrote in *The Wapshot Chronicle*, 1957:

Fear tastes like a rusty knife and do not let her into your house.
Courage tastes of blood. Stand up straight. Admire the world. Relish
the love of a gentle woman. Trust in the Lord.[51]

ða

Gilbert Keith Chesterton (1874-1936), was one of the most powerful and original of the modern British poets and novelists. His fondness of paradox is seen in his great works: *Heretics; Orthodoxy; Outline of Sanity; All Is Grist;* and *All I Survey*. In *English Men of Letters*, Chesterton wrote very enlightening sketches about both Browning and Dickens. In *What's Wrong with the World*, 1910, Gilbert Keith Chesterton wrote:

The Christian ideal has not been tried and found wanting; it has
been found difficult and left untried.[52]

ða

Charles Chiniquy (1809-1899), a famous Catholic priest in Canada, became known as the "Apostle of Temperance of Canada." In 1851, he brought 7,500 French Canadians into Illinois to found the French Colony of St. Anne. The church he built, at 334 S. St. Louis

Avenue, in St. Anne, Illinois, still stands. Late in life he was befriended by Abraham Lincoln. He wrote of his experience after studying the Scripture:

> It seemed that God was far away, but He was very near. Suddenly the thought entered my mind: "You have your Gospel; read it, and you will find the light." On my knees, and with trembling hand, I opened the book. Not I, but God opened it, for my eyes fell on I Cor. 7:23: "You have been bought with a price; do not become the slaves of men."
>
> With these words the light came to me, and for the first time I saw the great mystery of salvation, as much as man can see it. I said to myself, "Jesus has bought me. Then, if Jesus has bought me, He has saved me. I am saved! Jesus is my God! All the works of God are perfect! I am, then, perfectly saved—Jesus could not save me by half. I am saved by the blood of the Lamb. I am saved by the death of Jesus...."
>
> I then felt such a joy, such a peace, that the angels of God could not be more happy than I was....
>
> It was thus I found the Light and the great mystery of our salvation, which is so simple and so beautiful, so sublime and so grand.[53]

❧

Rufus Choate (1799-1859), was a powerful lawyer, Congressman, and U.S. Senator. Before he was six years old, Rufus had become so familiar with *Pilgrim's Progress* as to repeat from memory large portions of it. He was extremely fond of the Bible.[54] Choate was famous for his definition of a lawyer's vacation as "the space between a question to a witness and his answer." Rufus Choate declared:

Rufus Choate

No lawyer can afford to be ignorant of the Bible.[55]

❧

Agatha Christie (1891-1975), was an acclaimed British author of popular detective fiction, and a playwright. She wrote *Murder on the Orient Express, The Murder of Roger Ackroyd, The Mousetrap,*

Curtain and *The Mysterious Affair at Styles.* She created the well-known fictional detectives, Miss Jane Marple and Hercule Poirot. In *An Autobiography,* published in 1977 after her death, Agatha Christie wrote in Part III, *Growing Up:*

> If you love, you will suffer, and if you do not love, you do not know the meaning of a Christian life.[56]

&

Sir Winston Leonard Spencer Churchill (1874-1965), was the British statesman who led Great Britain through World War II. The direct descendant of the 1st Duke of Marlborough, he served as a correspondent in the Boer War and joined Parliament in 1900. After holding several positions, he rejoined the army in World War I and served in France. Later he was reelected, becoming the Chancellor of the Exchequer, First Lord of the Admiralty and finally the Prime Minister. Sir Winston Churchill, in addition to being a remarkable orator, was an acclaimed author, receiving the Nobel Prize for Literature in 1953.

On June 16, 1941, in a radio broadcast to America, on receiving the honorary degree of Doctor of Laws from the University of Rochester, New York, Sir Winston Churchill replied:

> The destiny of mankind is not decided by material computation. When great causes are on the move in the world...we learn that we are spirits, not animals, and that something is going on in space and time, and beyond space and time...[57]

On October 29, 1941, in an address at Harrow School, Churchill admonished:

> Never give in, never give in, never, never, never, never—in nothing, great or small, large or petty—never give in except to convictions of honor and good sense....
>
> Do not let us speak of darker days; let us speak rather of sterner days. These are not dark days: these are great days—the greatest days our country has ever lived; and we must all thank God that we have been allowed, each of us according to our stations, to play a part in

making these days memorable in the history of our race.[58]

On December 30, 1941, in a speech to the Canadian Senate and House of Commons in Ottawa, Sir Winston Churchill declared:

> We have to win that world for our children....We have to win it by our sacrifices. We have not won it yet. The crisis is upon us....In this strange, terrible world war there is a place for everyone, man and woman, old and young, hale and halt; service in a thousand forms is open....The mine, the factory, the dockyard, the salt sea waves, the fields to till, the home, the hospital, the chair of the scientist, the pulpit of the preacher—from the highest to the humblest tasks, all are equal honor; all have their part to play.[59]

ⵣ

Tom Campbell Clark (1899-1977), was an Associate Justice of the United States Supreme Court, having been appointed by President Harry S. Truman. Both he and his son, Ramsey Clark, held the post of U.S. Attorney General. Justice Tom Campbell Clark stated:

> The Founding Fathers believed devoutly that there was a God and that the unalienable rights of man were rooted—not in the state, nor the legislature, nor in any other human power—but in God alone.[60]

ⵣ

Cassius Marcellus Clay (1810-1903), served as a statesman and as a diplomat to Russia under both President Abraham Lincoln and President Ulysses S. Grant. He was a strong opponent of slavery and greatly involved in the abolitionist movement. Cassius Marcellus Clay declared:

Cassius Marcellus Clay

> The Bible, the record of Divine Revelation, is the one Book of religion and morals. Of all religious systems the Christian is most in unison with the law of God and the needs of man. The spirit of God inspires all living things. Jesus Christ is the leading inspiration, and is, therefore Divine.[61]

ॐ

Henry Clay (1777-1852), was a powerful U.S. Senator who also served as a Congressman. He was elected Speaker of the House six times, and for nearly 40 years was a leading American statesman. Clay was part of the "Great Triumvirate," with Daniel Webster and John Calhoun, which dominated Congress during the early to mid-1800s. Known as *The Great Compromiser*, Clay was able to keep the North and the South together as the Union for many years. Although he was a Presidential Candidate several times, Clay never was elected.

Henry Clay

In 1839, when he was about to give a speech in which he would declare himself against slavery, one of his friends warned him that this would ruin his chances to become President. To this, Henry Clay gave his famous reply:

> I would rather be right than President.[62]

From a speech to the Kentucky Colonization Society, at Frankfort, 1829, Henry Clay proclaimed:

> Eighteen hundred years have rolled away since the Son of God, our blessed Redeemer, offered Himself on Mount Calvary for the salvation of our species; and more than half of mankind still continue to deny His Divine mission and the truth of His sacred Word....
>
> When we shall, as soon we must, be translated from this into another form of existence, is the hope presumptuous that we shall behold the common Father of the whites and blacks, the great Ruler of the Universe, cast his all-seeing eye upon civilized and regenerated Africa, its cultivated fields, its coasts studded with numerous cities, adorned with towering temples dedicated to the pure religion of his redeeming son?[63]

In a conversation with Congressman John C. Breckinridge, Henry Clay declared:

> The vanity of the world, and its insufficiency to satisfy the soul of

man, has been long a settled conviction of my mind. Man's inability to secure by his own merits the approbation of God, I feel to be true. I trust in the atonement of the Saviour of mercy, as the ground of my acceptance and of my hope of salvation.[64]

Henry Clay confided with Congressman Venable:

I am not afraid to die, sir; I have hope, faith, and some confidence; I have an abiding trust in the merits and mediation of our Saviour.[65]

Stephen Grover Cleveland (1837-1908), served as both the 22nd and 24th President of the United States, the Governor of New York and the Mayor of Buffalo. In his Inaugural Address on March 4, 1885, President Cleveland stated:

Grover Cleveland

And let us not trust to human effort alone, but humbly acknowledge the power and goodness of Almighty God who presides over the destiny of nations, and who has at all times been revealed in our country's history, let us invoke His aid and His blessings upon our labors....I know there is a Supreme Being who rules the affairs of men.[66]

Charles W. Skelton reported President Grover Cleveland's response to a conflict with the Indians:

At the close of the Mohonk Conference, our Committee went to President Cleveland to petition him regarding certain methods. He said that he sympathized with our plans and ideas; "but," he continued, "gentlemen, you may do all you can at Mohonk; I may do all I can here in the White House, and Congress may do all it can over there, but," (and he then turned and picked up a Bible on his desk,) "gentlemen, after all, that Book has got to settle the Indian Problem."[67]

In *The Writings and Speeches of Grover Cleveland*, Stephen Grover Cleveland declared:

The citizen is a better business man if he is a Christian gentleman, and, surely, business is not the less prosperous and successful if conducted on Christian principles....

All must admit that the reception of the teachings of Christ results in the purest patriotism, in the most scrupulous fidelity to public trust, and in the best type of citizenship.

Those who manage the affairs of government are by this means reminded that the law of God demands that they should be courageously true to the interests of the people, and that the Ruler of the Universe will require of them a strict account of their stewardship.

The teachings of both human and Divine law thus merging into one word, duty, form the only union of Church and state that a civil and religious government can recognize.[68]

🙵

Francis Marion Cockrell (1834-1915), a U.S. Senator from Missouri for five consecutive terms, from 1875 to 1910, declared in 1875:

> Christianity is a reality, not an appearance. Were it a myth devised by cunning impostors, it would have come to naught before this. It has done more to fraternize the races than all human systems of religion together. The Bible is supreme over all books. Beside it there is none other. Its Divine truths meet the wants of a world-wide humanity.[69]

🙵

Samuel Taylor Coleridge (1772-1834), was a famous English poet, philosopher and critic. His works, which began the "Romantic period" of English literature, include *Kubla Khan*, 1797; *The Rime of the Ancient Mariner*, 1797-98; and *Christabel*, 1797-1800. He stated:

> I know the Bible is inspired because it finds me at greater depths of my being than any other book.[70]

> Is it fitting to run Jesus Christ in a silly parallel with Socrates—the Being whom thousands of millions of intellectual creatures, of whom I am a humble unit, take to be their Redeemer—with an Athenian philosopher, of whom we know nothing except his glorification in Plato and Socrates?[71]

In 1798, writing in his famous work *The Rime of the Ancient Mariner*, Samuel Taylor Coleridge composed the lines:

> He prayeth best who loveth best
> All things both great and small;
> For the dear God who loveth us,
> He made and loveth all.[72]

In an autographed letter to Mr. Colson, kept in the Wellesley College Library, Coleridge wrote:

> But, above all things, I entreat you, my dear Colson, to preserve your faith in Christ. It is my wealth in poverty, my joy in sorrow, my peace amid tumult. For all the evil I have committed, I have found it to be so. I can smile with pity at the infidel whose vanity makes him dream that I should barter such a blessing for the few subtleties from the school of the cold-blooded sophists.[73]

As recorded in *Studies in Poetry and Philosophy*, Coleridge wrote:

> I receive, with full and grateful faith, the assurance of Revelation, that the Word, which is from eternity with God, and is God, assumed human nature, in order to redeem me and all mankind from our connate corruption. I believe that the assumption of humanity by the Son of God was revealed to us by the Word made flesh, and manifested to us in Jesus Christ, and that His miraculous birth, His agony, His crucifixion, resurrection and ascension were all both symbols of redemption and necessary parts of that awful process.[74]

ॐ

Schuyler Colfax

Schuyler Colfax (1823-1885), the Vice-President under Ulysses S. Grant, also served seven terms as a U.S. Congressman and was Speaker of the House from 1863-1869; he founded the *Daughters of Rebekah*. Schuyler Colfax said:

> Man derives his greatest happiness not by that which he does for himself, but by what he accomplishes for others. This is a sad world at best—a world of sorrow, of suffering, of injustice, and falsification; men stab those whom they hate with the stiletto of slander, but it is for the followers of our Lord to improve it, and to make it more as Christ would have it. The most precious crown of fame

that a human being can ask is to kneel at the bar of God and hear the beautiful words, "Well done, good and faithful servant."[75]

Just fifty years ago this fall, in a large city by the seashore, nearly a thousand miles from here, a lady, whose husband was dead, took her little boy by the hand, and led him to the Sabbath-school.

For thirty years afterwards he was a scholar or a teacher of the Sabbath-school, and he has never forgotten those instructions of youth. The lady who took her little boy to that Sunday-school is now in a happier land, but the boy is still living.

That lady was my beloved mother, who is with her Father and Saviour in heaven, and that little boy was myself. Today I come to this school with my little boy, and his mother with us, that we may place his imperfect steps in the path in which my mother placed my little feet half a century ago.[76]

ôæ

Samuel Colgate

Samuel Colgate (1822-1897), the son of William Colgate, expanded his father's soap business into one of the largest establishments of its kind in the world. Samuel Colgate's father, William, was noted for giving at least a tenth of his net yearly earnings to charities, and was an organizer of both the American Bible Society and the American and Foreign Bible Society. Samuel Colgate was a benefactor and trustee of Madison University in Hamilton, N.Y., which was renamed in 1890 to Colgate University. Being an influential American manufacturer and philanthropist, Samuel Colgate avouched:

The only spiritual light in the world comes through Jesus Christ and the inspired Book; redemption and forgiveness of sin alone through Christ. Without His presence and the teachings of the Bible we would be enshrouded in moral darkness and despair.

The condition of those nations without a Christ, contrasted with those where Christ is accepted, reveals so marked a difference that no arguments are needed. It is an object-lesson so plain that it can be seen and understood by all. May "the earth be full of the knowledge of the Lord, as the waters cover the sea."[77]

ôæ

Alfred Holt Colquitt (1824-1894), was a U.S. Senator, the Governor of Georgia, as well as being an orator and statesman. On December 7, 1887, in Washington, Alfred Holt Colquitt remarked at the Evangelical Alliance:

> I believe it is the mission of the ministers today, and of Christian laymen in this land, to go out into the fields and highways and meet the enemies that are seeking to place barriers in the way of Christian civilization—to meet the foe as he comes.
>
> Religion and politics ought to be wedded like a loving pair. The spirit of our Master, who preached peace, should preside at our diplomatic councils. The love of our neighbor and of our friends— these should be the bases, not only of our Christianity and our patriotism, but of our daily politics.
>
> I like to hear learned sermons and magnificent discourses— appeals purely to the intellect—abstract and abstruse ideas, and all that. But looking at the masses of mankind, and reviewing from the standpoint which I occupy, it is clear to me that there is a mission given to every lover of Christ to stand forth as the propagator of that religion which tempers the politics and statesmanship of this country.[78]

&

Chuck W. Colson (1931-   ), a former White House aid, has since become a nationally known speaker and author. In 1981, serving as the director of Prison Fellowship, Chuck Colson explained:

> Imprisonment as a primary means of criminal punishment is a relatively modern concept. It was turned to as a humane alternative to the older patterns of harsh physical penalties for nearly all crimes. Quakers introduced the concept in Pennsylvania.
>
> The first American prison was established in Philadelphia when the Walnut Street Jail was converted into a series of solitary cells where offenders were kept in solitary confinement. The theory was that they would become "penitents," confessing their crimes before God and thereby gaining a spiritual rehabilitation. Hence, the name "penitentiary"— as a place for penitents.[79]

&

Columbia University 1754, was founded originally as Kings College in New York, named after King George II. It grew to become one of the most influential universities in America.

Its seal consists of a seated woman with the Hebrew Tetragrammaton name of God, *YHVH*, written above her head. The Latin motto inscribed across the top is Psalm 36:10, "In Thy light we see light." In alluding to Psalm 27:1, the Hebrew phrase *Uri El* ("God is my light") is written on a ribbon and under the woman's feet the scripture is inscribed, "I PET.II.1-2," an admonishment to desire the pure milk of God's Word.[80]

Christopher Columbus (1451-1506), after seven years of trying to convince the monarchs of Europe to finance his expedition, won the support of Queen Isabella of Castille and King Ferdinand of Aragon. Columbus set sail on August 3, 1492, and, after the longest voyage ever made out of sight of land, discovered the New World on October 12, 1492. In his *Libro de las profecias (Book of Prophecies)*, Columbus wrote:

Christopher Columbus

At a very early age I began to sail upon the ocean. For more than forty years, I have sailed everywhere that people go.

I prayed to the most merciful Lord about my heart's great desire, and He gave me the spirit and the intelligence for the task: seafaring, astronomy, geometry, arithmetic, skill in drafting spherical maps and placing correctly the cities, rivers, mountains and ports. I also studied cosmology, history, chronology and philosophy.

It was the Lord who put into my mind (I could feel His hand upon me) the fact that it would be possible to sail from here to the Indies. All who heard of my project rejected it with laughter, ridiculing me.

There is no question that the inspiration was from the Holy Spirit, because he comforted me with rays of marvelous illumination from the Holy Scriptures, a strong and clear testimony from the 44 books of the Old Testament, from the four Gospels, and from the 23 Epistles of the blessed Apostles, encouraging me continually to press forward, and without ceasing for a moment they now encourage me to make haste.

Our Lord Jesus desired to perform a very obvious miracle in the voyage to the Indies, to comfort me and the whole people of God. I spent seven years in the royal court, discussing the matter with many persons of great reputation and wisdom in all the arts; and in the end they concluded that it was all foolishness, so they gave it up.

But since things generally came to pass that were predicted by our Savior Jesus Christ, we should also believe that this particular prophecy will come to pass. In support of this, I offer the gospel text, Matt. 24:25, in which Jesus said that all things would pass away, but not his marvelous Word. He affirmed that it was necessary that all things be fulfilled that were prophesied by himself and by the prophets.

I said that I would state my reasons: I hold alone to the sacred and Holy Scriptures, and to the interpretations of prophecy given by certain devout persons.

It is possible that those who see this book will accuse me of being unlearned in literature, of being a layman and a sailor. I reply with the words of Matt. 11:25: "Lord, because thou hast hid these things from the wise and prudent, and hath revealed them unto babes."

The Holy Scripture testifies in the Old Testament by our Redeemer Jesus Christ, that the world must come to an end. The signs of when this must happen are given by Matthew, Mark and Luke. The prophets also predicted many things about it.

Our Redeemer Jesus Christ said that before the end of the world, all things must come to pass that had been written by the prophets.

The prophets wrote in various ways. Isaiah is the one most praised by Jerome, Augustine, and by the other theologians. They all say that Isaiah was not only a prophet, but an evangelist as well. Isaiah goes into great detail in describing future events and in calling all people to our holy catholic faith. Most of the prophecies of Holy Scripture have been fulfilled already...

I am a most unworthy sinner, but I have cried out to the Lord for grace and mercy, and they have covered me completely. I have found the sweetest consolations since I made it my whole purpose to enjoy His marvelous presence.

For the execution of the journey to the Indies I did not make use of intelligence, mathematics or maps. It is simply the fulfillment of what Isaiah had prophesied. All this is what I desire to write down for you in this book.

No one should fear to undertake any task in the name of our Savior, if it is just and if the intention is purely for His holy service. The working out of all things has been assigned to each person by our Lord, but it all happens according to His sovereign will even though He gives advice.

He lacks nothing that it is in the power of men to give him. Oh what a gracious Lord, who desires that people should perform for Him those things for which He holds Himself responsible! Day and night moment by moment, everyone should express to Him their most devoted gratitude.

I said that some of the prophecies remained yet to be fulfilled. These are great and wonderful things for the earth, and the signs are that the Lord is hastening the end. The fact that the gospel must still be preached to so many lands in such a short time, this is what convinces me.[81]

Queen Isabella's commission to Columbus recited:

*Isabel I
(Isabella the
Catholic)*

> It is hoped that by God's assistance some of the continents and islands in the ocean will be discovered[82]....for the glory of God.[83]

On August 3, 1492, every crew member gave his last confession and received Holy Communion. Then, according to Bartolomé de Las Casas:

> [Columbus] received the very holy sacrament of the Eucharist on the very day that he entered upon the sea; and in the name of Jesus ordered the sails to be set and left the harbor of Palos for the river of Saltes and the Ocean Sea with three equipped caravels, giving the commencement to the First Voyage and Discovery of the Indies.[84]

In the typical custom of the age, each day a young sailor would announce the day by singing out:

> Blessed be the light of day
> And the Holy Cross, we say;
> and the Lord of Veritie
> And the Holy Trinity.
> Blessed be th' immortal soul
> And the Lord who keeps it whole,
> Blessed be the light of day
> And He who sends the night away.[85]

Then the sailors would recite the "Pater Noster" (Our Father) and the "Ave Maria," followed by:

> God give us good days, good voyage, good passage to the ship, sir captain and master and good company, so let there be a good voyage;

many good days may God grant your graces, gentlemen of the afterguard and gentlemen forward.[86]

The hourglass, which was turned on the half-hour, marked the time, accompanied by the young sailor proclaiming:

> Blessed be the hour our Lord was born,
> St. Mary who bore Him,
> and St. John who baptized Him.[87]

In 1492 Columbus opened the journal of his first voyage across the Atlantic by addressing King Ferdinand and Queen Isabel:

> In the Name of Our Lord Jesus Christ,
> Because, most Christian and very Exalted, Excellent and mighty Princes, King and Queen of the Spains and of the Islands of the Sea, our Lord and Lady, in this present year 1492, after Your Highnesses had made an end to the war with the Moors who ruled in Europe, and had concluded the war in the very great City of Granada, where in the present year, on the second day of the month of January, I saw the Royal Standards of Your Highnesses placed by force of arms on the towers of the Alhambra (which is the citadel of the said city),
> And I saw the Moorish King come forth to the gates of the city and kiss the Royal Hands of Your Highnesses and the Prince of my Lord, and soon after in that same month, through information that I had given to Your Highnesses concerning the lands of India, and of a Prince who is called Gran Can [Grand Khan], which is to say in our vernacular "King of Kings," how many times he and his predecessors had sent to Rome to seek doctors in our Holy Faith to instruct him therein, and that never had the Holy Father provided them, and thus so many people were lost through lapsing into idolatries and receiving doctrines of perdition;
> And Your Highnesses, as Catholic Christians and Princes devoted to the Holy Christian Faith and the propagators thereof, and enemies of the sect of Mahomet and of all idolatries and heresies, resolved to send me, Christopher Columbus, to the said regions of India, to see the said princes and peoples and lands and the dispositions of them and of all, and the manner in which may be undertaken their conversion to our Holy Faith, and ordained that I should not go by land (the usual way) to the Orient, but by the route of the Occident, by which no one to this day knows for sure that anyone has gone....[88]

Bartolomé de Las Casas, (1474-1566), called "the Apostle of the Indies," was one of the first Christian missionaries to America. As the first priest ordained in the New World, he became known for his devotion to the oppressed and enslaved natives. In addition to knowing Columbus personally, Bartolomé's father and uncle were shipmates and colonists under Columbus. Bartolomé de Las Casas copied Columbus' original *Journal of the First Voyage (El Libro de la Primera Navegacion)* into an abstract, in which is recounted:

October 8, 1492. "Thanks be to God," says the Admiral; "the air is soft as in April in Seville, and it is a pleasure to be in it, so fragrant it is."

October 10, 1492. Here the people could stand it no longer and complained of the long voyage; but the Admiral cheered them as best he could, holding out good hope of the advantages they would have. He added that it was useless to complain, he had come [to go] to the Indies, and so had to continue it until he found them, with the help of Our Lord.

October 12, 1492. At two hours after midnight appeared the land, at a distance of 2 leagues. They handed all sails and set the *treo,* which is the mainsail without bonnets, and lay-to, waiting for daylight Friday, when they arrived at an island of the Bahamas that was called in the Indians' tongue Guanahani' [San Salvador]....
So that they might be well-disposed towards us, for I knew that they were a people to be delivered and converted to our Holy Faith rather by love than by force, I gave to some red caps and to others glass beads, which they hung around their necks, and many other things of slight value. At this they were greatly pleased and became so entirely our friends that it was a wonder to see....I believe that they would easily be made Christians, for it seemed to me that they had no religion of their own. Our Lord willing, when I depart, I shall bring back six of them to your Highnesses, that they may learn to talk our language.

October 16, 1492. I don't recognize in them any religion, and I believe that they very promptly would turn Christians, for they are of very good understanding.

October 28, 1492. The Admiral says that he never beheld so fair a thing: trees all along the river, beautiful and green, and different from ours, with flowers and fruits each according to their kind, many birds and little birds which sing very sweetly.

November 6, 1492. I maintain, Most Serene Princes, that if they had access to devout religious persons knowing the language, they would all turn Christian, and so I hope in Our Lord that Your Highnesses will do something about it with much care, in order to turn to the Church so numerous a folk, and to convert them as you have destroyed those who would not seek to confess the Father, Son and Holy Ghost. And after your days (for we are all mortal) you will leave your realms in a very tranquil state, and free from heresy and wickedness, and will be well received before the eternal Creator, to whom I pray to grant you long life and great increase of many realms and lordships, and both will and disposition to increase the holy Christian religion, as hitherto you have done.

November 27, 1492. But now, please our Lord, I shall see the most that I may, and little by little I shall come, to understand and know, and I will have this language taught to people of my household, because I see that all so far have one language. And afterwards the benefits will be known, and it will be endeavored to have these folk Christians, for that will easily be done, since they have no religion; nor are they idolaters....And I say that Your Highness ought not to consent that any foreigner does business or sets foot here, except Christian Catholics, since this was the end and the beginning of the enterprise, that it should be for the enhancement and glory of the Christian religion, nor should anyone who is not a good Christian come to these parts.

December 12, 1492. [Columbus raised a great cross at the entrance of the harbor of Moustique Bay on the northwest coast of the island of Hispaniola] as a sign that Your Highnesses hold the country for yours, and principally for a sign of Jesus Christ Our Lord, and honor of Christianity.

December 16, 1492. Because they [the Arawak tribe], are the best people in the world and above all the gentlest, I have much hope in Our Lord that Your Highnesses will make them all Christians, and they will be all yours, as for yours I hold them.

December 22, 1492. The Admiral ordered the lord to be given some things, and he and all his folk rested in great contentment, believing truly that they had come from the sky, and to see the Christians they held themselves very fortunate.

December 24, 1492. Your Highnesses may believe that in all the world there can be no better or gentler people. Your Highnesses should feel great joy, because presently they will be Christians, and instructed in the good manners of your realms; for a better people there cannot be on earth, and both people and land are in such quantity that I don't know how to write it.[89]

The first island Columbus landed on, he christened San Salvador, meaning "Holy Saviour." Then as he knelt, he prayed:

O Lord, Almighty and everlasting God, by Thy holy Word Thou hast created the heaven, and the earth, and the sea; blessed and glorified be Thy Name, and praised be Thy Majesty, which hath deigned to use us, Thy humble servants, that Thy holy Name may be proclaimed in this second part of the earth.[90]

As they landed on each island, Columbus had his men erect a large wooden cross:

As a token of Jesus Christ our Lord, and in honor of the Christian faith.[91]

According to Columbus' personal log, his purpose in seeking "undiscovered worlds" was to:

...bring the Gospel of Jesus Christ to the heathens.[92] [And]

...bring the Word of God to unknown coastlands.[93]

The *Santa Maria* ran aground on Christmas eve, December 24, 1492, and the ship had to be abandoned. On the Island of Haiti, Columbus left 40 men in a settlement named La Navidad, meaning "The Nativity." He promised to return the next year.

On January 13, 1493, Columbus described in his journal their first encounter with the cannibalistic tribe of the Canibs, or Caribs, from which *Caribbean* originates. (The English word *cannibal* is derived from the Spanish word *caribe*, which means "piranha.")

Seeing them [the Caribs] running towards them, the Christians...gave an Indian a great slash on the buttocks, and wounded another in the breast with an arrow. Seeing that they could gain little, although the Christians were not more than seven, they [the Caribs] 50 and more, began to flee, until not one remained, one leaving his arrows here, and another his bow there. The Christians would have killed many of them, it is said, if the pilot who went with them as their captain had not prevented it. The Christians returned to the caravel with their boat, and when the Admiral knew of it he said that on the one hand he was sorry and on the other not, since they would have fear of the Christians, because without doubt, says he, the folk there are bad actors (as one says), and he believed that they were Caribs, and ate men...[94]

On February 15, 1493, on his return trip from having discovered America, Christopher Columbus wrote to King Ferdinand and Queen Isabella, and to Luis de Sant Angel, Treasurer of Aragon, from on board the ship *Caravel*, anchored off the Canary Islands:

To the first island which I found I gave the name San Salvador [Holy Savior], in recognition of His Heavenly Majesty, who marvelously hath given all this; the Indians call it Guanahani....

I forbade that they should be given things so worthless as pieces of broken crockery and broken glass, and lace points, although when they were able to get them, they thought they had the best jewel in the world; thus it was learned that a sailor for a lace point received gold to the weight of two and a half castellanos, and others much more for other things which were worth much less; yea, for new blancas, for them they would give all that they had, although it might be two or three castellanos' weight of gold or an arroba or two of spun cotton; they even took pieces of the broken hoops of the wine casks and, like animals, gave what they had, so that it seemed to me wrong and I forbade it, and I gave them a thousand good, pleasing things which I had brought, in order that they might be fond of us, and furthermore might become Christians and be inclined to the love and service of Their Highnesses and of the whole Castilian nation [Spain], and try to help us and to give us of the things which they have in abundance and which are necessary to us.

And they know neither sect nor idolatry, with the exception that all believe that the source of all power and goodness is the sky, and they believe very firmly that I, with these ships and people, came from the sky, and in this belief they everywhere received me, after they had overcome their fear.

And this does not result from their being ignorant (for they are of a very keen intelligence and men who navigate all those seas, so that it is wondrous the good account they give of everything), but because they have never seen people clothed or ships like ours....

Praise be to our eternal God, our Lord, who gives to all those who walk in His ways victory over all things which seem impossible; of which this is signally one, for, although others have spoken or written concerning these countries, it was all conjecture, as no one could say that he had seen them—it amounting only to this, that those who heard listened the more, and regarded the matter rather as a fable than anything else.

But our Redeemer has granted this victory to our illustrious King and Queen and their kingdoms, which have acquired great fame by an event of such high importance, in which all Christendom ought to rejoice, and which it ought to celebrate with great festivals and the offering of solemn thanks to the Holy Trinity with many sincere prayers, both for the great exaltation which may accrue to them in turning so many nations to our holy faith, and also for the temporal benefits which will bring great refreshment and gain, not only to Spain, but to all Christians.

Done on board the Caravel, off the Canary Islands, on the fifteenth day of February, Fourteen hundred and ninety-three. At your orders,
The Admiral.[95]

On March 15, 1493, Columbus wrote in his journal:

Of this voyage, I observe...that it has miraculously been shown, as may be understood by this writing, by the many signal miracles that He has shown on the voyage, and for me, who for so great a time was in the court of Your Highnesses with the opposition and against the opinion of so many high personages of your household, who were all against me, alleging this undertaking to be folly, which I hope in Our Lord will be to the greater glory of Christianity, which to some slight extent already has happened.[96]

In 1493, Columbus wrote a letter to Gabriel Sanchez, Spain's General Treasurer:

That which the unaided intellect of man could not compass, the spirit of God has granted to human exertions, for God is wont to hear the prayers of His servants who love His precepts even to the performance of apparent impossibilities. Therefore, let the king and queen, our princes and their most happy kingdoms, and all the other provinces of Christendom, render thanks to our Lord and Saviour Jesus Christ....[97]

Columbus viewed himself as:

Servant...of the Most High Saviour, Christ, the Son of Mary.[98]

Queen Isabella informed the Pope of Columbus' attempt:

To bear the light of Christ west to the heathen undiscovered lands.[99]

On April 9, 1493, Columbus wrote to the King and Queen about plans for a second voyage. He recommended that approximately 2,000 colonists accompany him to settle three or four villages, according the custom of Spain, each with its own notary and magistrate, and that:

There be a church and abbots or friars to administer the sacraments, perform divine worship, and convert the natives.[100]

✓On May 29, 1493, King Ferdinand and Queen Isabel granted Columbus' request for a second voyage, pronouncing:

It hath pleased God, Our Lord, in His abundant mercy to reveal the said Islands and Mainland to the King and Queen, our Lords, by the diligence of the Don Christopher Columbus, their Admiral, Viceroy and Governor thereof, who hath reported it to Their Highnesses that he knew the people he found residing therein to be very ripe to be converted to our Holy Catholic Faith, since they have neither dogma nor doctrine; wherefore it hath pleased and greatly pleaseth Their Highnesses (since in all matters it is meet that their principal concern be for the service of God, Our Lord, and the enhancement of Our Holy Catholic Faith); wherefore, desiring the augmentation and increase of our Holy Catholic Faith, Their Highnesses charge and direct the said Admiral, Viceroy and Governor that by all ways and means he strive and endeavor to win over the inhabitants of the said Islands and Mainland to be converted to our Holy Catholic Faith....

[Priest and clerics will be sent] to see that they be carefully taught the principles of Our Holy Faith....

[The Admiral should] force and compel all those who sail therein as well as all others who are to go out from here later on, that they treat the said Indians very well and lovingly and abstain from doing them any injury, arranging that both people hold much conversation and intimacy, each serving the others to the best of their ability. Moreover,

the said Admiral shall graciously present them with things from the
merchandise of Their Highnesses which he is carrying for barter, and
honor them much; and if some person or persons should maltreat the
said Indians in any manner whatsoever, the said Admiral, as Viceroy
and Governor of Their Highnesses, shall punish them severely by the
virtue of the authority vested in him by Their Majesties for this
purpose...[101]

On September 25, 1493, Columbus set sail from Cadiz, Spain,
with 1,200 colonists and 17 ships. They landed in the Indies on
November 3, 1493, where Columbus continued his discovery of
the islands of Dominica, Mariagalante, Todos los Santos and St.
Maria de Guadalupe.

In returning to the settlement of La Navidad on the island of
Haiti, where he had left the 40 men from the wrecked *Santa Maria*,
Columbus' worst fears were realized. The Caribs had attacked the
fort and had killed all his men. Thereafter, Columbus had to resist
a growing apprehension amongst the colonists, who previously
had anticipated only the marvelous conditions reported from the
first voyage.

In 1495, Michele de Cuneo, a young Italian nobleman who had
accompanied Columbus on this second voyage, recounted in a
letter further evidence of the cannibalistic Caribs who inhabited
the islands:

> In that island [St. Maria de Guadalupe] we took twelve very
> beautiful and very fat women from 15 to 16 years old, together with
> two boys of the same age. These had the genital organ cut to the belly;
> and this we thought had been done in order to prevent them from
> meddling with their wives or maybe to fatten them up and later eat
> them. These boys and girls had been taken by the above mentioned
> Caribs; and we sent them to Spain to the King, as a sample....
>
> The Caribs whenever they catch these Indians eat them as we
> would eat kids [goats] and they say that a boy's flesh tastes better than
> that of a woman. Of this human flesh they are very greedy, so that to
> eat of that flesh they stay out of their country for six, eight, or even ten
> years before they repatriate; and they stay so long, whenever they go,
> that they depopulate the islands....
>
> We went to the temple of those Caribs, in which we found two
> wooden statues, arranged so that they look like a Pieta. We were told
> that whenever someone's father is sick, the son goes to the temple and

tells the idol that his father is ill and the idol says whether he should live or not; and he stays there until the idol answers yes or no. If he says no, the son goes home, cuts his father's head off and then cooks it; I don't believe they eat it but truly when it is white they place it in the above-mentioned temple; and this they do only to the lords. That idol is called Seyti....

According to what we have seen in all the islands where we have been, both the Indians and the Caribs are largely sodomites, not knowing (I believe) whether they are acting right or wrong. We have judged that this accursed vice may have come to the Indians from those Caribs; because these, as I said before, are wilder men and when conquering and eating those Indians, for spite they may also have committed that extreme offence, which proceeding thence may have been transmitted from one to the other.[102]

Dr. Diego Alvarez Chanca, the chief physician on Columbus' second voyage, described with disgust their encounter with the Caribs:

We inquired of the women who were prisoners of the inhabitants what sort of people these islanders were and they replied, "Caribs." As soon as they learned that we abhor such kind of people because of their evil practice of eating human flesh, they felt delighted...

They told us that the Carib men use them with such cruelty as would scarcely be believed; and that they eat the children which they bear them, only bringing up those whom they have by their native wives. Such of their male enemies, as they can take away alive, they bring here to their homes to make a feast of them and those who are killed in battle they eat up after the fighting is over.

They declare that the flesh of man is good to eat that nothing can compare with it in the world; and this is quite evident, for the human bones we found in the houses, everything that could be gnawed had already been gnawed so that nothing remained but what was too hard to eat; in one of the houses we found a man's neck cooking in a pot...

In their wars of the inhabitants of the neighboring islands these people capture as many of the women as they can, especially those who are young and handsome and keep them as body servants and concubines; and so great a number do they carry off that in fifty houses we entered no man was found but all were women. Of that large number of captive females more than twenty handsome woman came away voluntarily with us.

When the Caribs take away boys as prisoners of war they remove their organs, fatten them until they grow up and then, when they wish to make a great feast, they kill and eat them, for they say the flesh of women and youngsters is not good to eat. Three boys thus mutilated came fleeing to us when we visited the houses.[103]

Columbus, after establishing the settlements of Isabella and Santo Domingo on the island of Hispaniola, proceeded to explore for five months, leaving the colony under poor supervision. Supplies in the colonies began to diminish, tropical diseases were spreading, and the colonists grew discontent. By the time the next fleet left for Spain, 200 colonists, most in bad health, left with it. Their complaints resulted in a royal investigation in October of 1495, much to the outrage of Columbus. In March 1496, Columbus left for Spain to defend himself.

Six years after the discovery of the New World, Columbus' concern for the spiritual welfare of the native people was still of primary importance. In his famous mayorazgo, *Testament of Founding Hereditary Family Estate,* dated Thursday, February 22, 1498, he stated:

> Also I order to said Don Diego, my son, or to him who will inherit said mayorazgo, that he shall help to maintain and sustain on the Island of Espanola four good teachers of the holy theology with the intention to convert to our holy religion all those people in the Indias, and when it pleases God that the income of the mayorazgo will increase, that then also be increased the number of such devoted persons who will help all these people to become Christians. And may he not worry about the money that it will be necessary to spend for the purpose...[104]

On May 30, 1498, Columbus left from Spain on his third voyage with six ships. He decided that the first new land he discovered would be named in honor of the Trinity. Sighting an island off the coast of Venezuela, which coincidentally had three peaks, he gave it the name Trinidad; it has retained the name to this day.

On October 18, 1498, Christopher Columbus wrote to his Sovereigns, Queen Isabel and King Ferdinand:

Your Highnesses have an Other World here, by which our holy faith can be to greatly advanced and from which such great wealth can be drawn.[105]

Columbus had sent the first nugget of gold back to his son, Don Diego, to deliver to Queen Isabel of Spain, with the instructions:

To return it to her (Queen Isabel) so that she may see the miracle of the Lord and remember to whom she ought to thank for it.[106]

When Columbus finally arrived at the island of Hispaniola, he was greeted by the scene of a revolt, due to the disease and privation on the island. His brothers Bartholomew and Don Diego, who had been left in authority, were helpless to put it down. Himself being in bad health, Columbus conceded to the demands of the distraught colonists and gave them two ships to return home. In the midst of despair, Columbus wrote:

The day after Christmas Day, 1499, all having left me, I was attacked by the Indians...and was placed in such extremity that fleeing death, I took to sea in a small caravel. Then Our Lord aided me, saying, "Man of little faith, do not fear, I am with thee." And he dispersed my enemies, and showed me how I might fulfill my vows. Unhappy sinner that I am, to have placed all my hopes in the things of this world![107]

Due to the turbulent reports they had received, King Ferdinand and Queen Isabel appointed Francisco de Bobadilla as Governor of the Indies in the place of Columbus. He arrived in Hispaniola on August 23, 1500, arrested Columbus and his brothers, put them in chains and sent them back to Cadiz, Spain.

In October of 1500, during the most humiliating moment of his life, Columbus wrote to a friend and confidante of the Queen, Dona Juana de Torres:

Hope in Him who created all men sustaineth me: His succor hath always been very near. At another time, not long ago, when I was in great distress, He helped me up with his right hand, saying, "O man of little faith, arise, for it is I; fear not."

I came with such cordial affection to serve these princes, and I have served them with unheard of and unseen devotion. Of the New Heaven and Earth which Our Lord made, as St. John writes in the Apocalypse, after he had spoken it by the mouth of Isaiah, He made me the messenger thereof and showed me where to go.

...I undertook a new voyage to the New Heaven and World which hitherto had been hidden. And if, like the rest of the Indies, this is not held in high esteem over there; this is no wonder, since it came to light through my exertions.

The Holy Spirit inspired St. Peter and, with him, the others of the Twelve, and they all struggled in this world, and many were their labors and their hardships; in the end they triumphed over all....

They judge me there as a governor who had gone to Sicily or to a city or town under a regular government, where laws can be observed in toto without fear of losing all; and I am suffering grave injury. I should be judged as a captain who went from Spain to the Indies...where by divine will I have placed under the sovereignty of the King and Queen our Lords, an Other World, whereby Spain, which was reckoned poor, is become the richest of countries.

I ought to be judged as a captain, who for so long a time, up to the present day, hath borne arms without laying them down for an hour, and by knights of the sword and not by [men of] letters, unless they were Greeks or Romans or others of modern times, of whom there are so many and so noble in Spain; for otherwise I am greatly aggrieved, since in the Indies there is neither a town nor settlement.[108]

When the King and Queen saw Columbus, they immediately ordered his chains removed, restored the property Bobadilla had confiscated, restored the one-tenth of the revenues which he had been promised, and restored to him the title, "Admiral of the Ocean Sea," although they realized he could not continue to govern the Indies. Bobadilla, who had previously chained Columbus, was removed as governor, although his actions were not condemned. In an ironic turn of events, during his fourth voyage, Columbus warned the governor of Hispaniola of an impending hurricane. His counsel was spurned and 24 ships were sunk, killing 500 people, among whom was Bobadilla.

Columbus always loved to apply the Sacred Scriptures to his own life and adventures.[109] That religious elements played a great part in Columbus' thoughts and actions is evident from all his writings. It may be surprising that his concept of sailing west to reach the Indies was less the result of geographical theories than of his faith in certain biblical texts—specifically the Book of Isaiah.[110] In his book, *Libro de las profecias (Book of Prophecies)*, written around 1501, between his third and fourth voyages, Columbus cited the following Scripture passages:

> The LORD reigneth, let the earth rejoice; let the multitude of isles be glad thereof (Psalm 97:1).

> Sing unto the LORD a new song, and His praise from the ends of the earth, ye that go down to the sea, and all that is therein; the isles, and the inhabitants thereof (Isaiah 42:10).

> Listen, O isles, unto Me; and hearken, ye people from far; The Lord hath called me from the womb; from the bowels of my mother hath he made mention of my name (Isaiah 49:1).

> I will also give thee for a light to the Gentiles, that thou mayest be my salvation unto the end of the earth (Isaiah 49:6).

> My righteousness is near; My salvation is gone forth...The isles shall wait upon Me, and on Mine arm shall they trust (Isaiah 51:5).

> Surely the isles wait for me, and the ships of Tarshish first, to bring thy sons from far, their silver and their gold with them, unto the name of the Lord thy God, and to the Holy One of Israel, because he hath glorified thee (Isaiah 60:9).

> I am sought of them that asked not for Me; I am found of them that sought Me not; I said, Behold Me, behold Me, unto a nation that was not called by My name (Isaiah 65:1).

> Go ye therefore, and teach all nations, baptizing them in the name of the Father and of the Son and of the Holy Ghost: Teaching them to observe all things whatsoever I have commanded you: And, lo, I am with you always, even unto the end of the world (Matthew 28:19,20).

> But ye shall receive power after that the Holy Ghost is come upon you; and you shall be witnesses unto me both in Jerusalem, and in all Judea, and in Samaria, and unto the uttermost part of the earth (Acts 1:8).[111]

In May of 1502, Christopher Columbus, along with his brother Bartholomew and son Don Ferdinand (who was 13 years old), set sail on his fourth voyage. With the express purpose of finding Asia, they explored the coasts of Cuba, Honduras, Nicaragua and Costa Rica. Sailing along the coast of Panama, Columbus did not realize how close he was to discovering the Pacific Ocean.

His health failing, Columbus had a makeshift cabin built on deck so he could direct the crew and observe the ocean. With worm-eaten planks in his ship, they became stranded on the coast of Jamaica for over a year (June 25, 1503, to June 29, 1504).

On July 7, 1503, while shipwrecked and in pain, Christopher Columbus related his many afflictions in his *Lettera Rarissima to the Sovereigns* from Jamaica, not knowing whether anyone would read his letter:

> In January the mouth of the river became obstructed. In April, the vessels were all worm-eaten, and I could not keep them above water. At this time the river cut a channel, by which I brought out three empty ships with considerable difficulty. The boats went back into the river for salt and water. The sea rose high and furious and would not let them out again.
>
> The Indians were many and united and attacked them and in the end killed them. My brother and all the rest of the people were living on board a vessel which lay inside. I was outside very much alone, on this rude coast, with a high fever and very fatigued. There was no hope of escape. In this state, I climbed painfully to the highest part of the ship and cried out for help with a fearful voice, weeping, to Your Highnesses' war captains, in every direction; but none replied. At length, groaning with exhaustion, I fell asleep, and heard a compassionate voice saying,
>
> "O fool, and slow to believe and serve thy God, the God of every man! What more did He do for Moses or for David his servant than for thee? From thy birth He hath ever held thee in special charge. When He saw thee at man's estate, marvelously did He cause thy name to resound over the earth.
>
> "The Indies, so rich a portion of the world, He gave thee for thine own, and thou has divided them as it has pleased thee. Of those barriers of the Ocean Sea, which were closed with such mighty chains, He hath given thee the keys. Thou was obeyed in so many lands, and thou hast won noble fame from Christendom. What more did He do

for the people of Israel, when he carried them out of Egypt; or for David, whom from a shepherd He raised to be king over Judea?

"Turn thou to Him and acknowledge thy faults; His mercy is infinite; thine old age shall not hinder thee from performing mighty deeds, for many and vast heritages He holdeth. Abraham was past 100 when he begat Isaac, and Sarah was no young girl. Thou criest out for succor with a doubting heart.

"Reflect, who has afflicted thee so grievously and so often, God or the world? The privileges and promises which God bestows, he doth not revoke; nor doth He say, after having received service, that this was not His intention, and that it is to be understood differently. Nor doth He mete out suffering to make a show of His might.

"Whatever He promises He fulfills with interest; that is His way. Thus I have told thee what thy Creator hath done for thee and what He doth for all men. He hath now revealed a portion of the rewards for so many toils and dangers thou hast borne in the service of others."[112]

Continuing in his letter, Columbus recounted his many previous trials:

The tempest was terrible and separated me from my [other] vessels that night, putting everyone of them in desperate straits, with nothing to look forward to but death. Each was certain the others had been destroyed. What man ever born, not excepting Job, who would not have died of despair, when in such weather seeking safety for my son, my brother, shipmates, and myself, we were forbidden [access to] the land and the harbors which I, by God's will and sweating blood, had won for Spain?...

I was taken prisoner and thrown with two brothers into a ship, weighed down with irons, stripped of my clothing, cruelly treated, and without being called before a court of justice for a hearing!...

I began my service [to you] at twenty-eight, and I now have not a single hair on my head that is not white. My body is infirm, and all that was left to me and to my brothers, even to our coats, was taken and sold, [without hearing or trial] to my great dishonor and injury....

Because of the very sincere intentions I have always had in serving your Majesties (Queen Isabel and King Ferdinand) and the most unmerited affronts I have suffered, I cannot remain silent much as I might wish to do. As I have said, I am now worn out.

Heretofore I have wept for others; may Heaven now have pity upon me and may the earth weep for me! In things temporal I have not even a farthing for the offering; and as to spiritual things, I have stayed here in the Indies in the manner I have described; isolated in this sorrow, ill, daily awaiting death, and surrounded by a horde of savages and enemies of ours, and so far removed from the holy sacraments of the holy church that my soul would be forgotten by it if it were to depart from my body.

Let those who have charity, justice and truth weep for me! I did not come on this voyage for gain, honor or wealth, that is certain; for then the hope of all such things was dead. I came to Your Highnesses with honest purpose and sincere zeal; and I do not lie.

I humbly beseech your Highnesses that if it please God to take me from this place, you will have the goodness to arrange for me to go to Rome and on other holy pilgrimages. May the Holy Trinity guard your life and exalt your high station! Christ-bearer.[113]

In his work, *Libro de las profecias (Book of Prophecies)*, Christopher Columbus wrote:

My hope in the One who created us all sustains me: He is an ever present help in trouble....When I was extremely depressed, He raised me with His right hand, saying, "O man of little faith, get up, it is I; do not be afraid."[114]

Christopher Columbus' real name, as early history books disclose, was Cristobal Colon. He encased his signature in a triangular pattern, with the beautiful names *El Shaddai* ("Almighty God") and *Adonai* ("Lord God") abbreviated, written above his signature, *Christopher Ferens* ("Christ Bearer"): *X.p.o. Ferens* was meant to represent Columbus as the cross-bearer or Christ-bearer:

.S.	(*El Shaddai*—"Almighty God")
.S. A.S.	(*El Shaddai, Adonai*—"Lord God"—*El Shaddai*)
X M Y	("Jesus, Mary, Joseph")
: *X.p.o. Ferens.*[115]	("Christ-bearer")

Ferdinand Columbus, the son of Christopher, wrote in the biography of his father, *The Life of the Admiral Christopher Columbus*, an explanation of the meaning of his name:

So the surname of Colon [Italian form of Columbus] which he revived was a fitting one, because in Greek it means "member," and by his proper name Christopher, men might know that he was a member of Christ, by Whom he was sent for the salvation of those people.

And if we give his name its Latin form, which is Christophorus Colonus, we may say that just as St. Christopher is reported to have gotten that name because he carried Christ over deep waters with great danger to himself, and just as he conveyed over people whom no other could have carried, so the Admiral Christophorus Colonus, asking Christ's aid and protection in that perilous pass, crossed over with his company that the Indian nations might become dwellers in the triumphant Church of Heaven.

There is reason to believe that many souls that Satan expected to catch because they had not passed through the waters of baptism were by the Admiral made dwellers in the eternal glory of Paradise....

The Admiral was a well built man of more than average statute, the face long, the cheeks somewhat high, his body neither fat nor lean. He had an aquiline nose and light-colored eyes; his complexion too was light and tending to bright red. In his youth his hair was blonde, but when he reached the age of thirty, it all turned white.

In eating and drinking, and in adornment of his person, he was very moderate and modest. He was affable in conversation with strangers and very pleasant to the members of his household, though with a certain gravity. He was so strict in matters of religion that for fasting and saying prayers he might have been taken for a member of a religious order.

He was so great an enemy of swearing and blasphemy that I give my word I never heard him utter any other oath than "by St. Ferdinand!" and when he grew very angry with someone, his rebuke was to say "God take you!" for doing or saying that.

If he had to write anything, he always began by writing these words: IESUS cum MARIA sit nobis in via. And so fine was his hand that he might have earned his bread by that skill alone.[116]

Bartolomé de Las Casas, (1474-1566), the priest who was called "the Apostle of the Indies" because of his commitment to the oppressed and enslaved natives, not only knew Columbus personally, but his father and uncle were shipmates and colonists under the Admiral as well. In his *Historie de las Indias*, Bartolomé de Las Casas described Christopher Columbus:

In matters of the Christian religion, without doubt he was a Catholic and of great devotion, for in everything he did and said or sought to begin, he always interposed "In the name of the Holy Trinity I will do this," or "launch this" or "this will come to pass."

In whatever letter or other thing he wrote, he put at the head

"Jesus and Mary be with us on the way," and of these writings of his in his own hand I have plenty now in my possession. His oath was sometimes "I swear by San Fernando;" when he sought to affirm something of great importance in his letters on oath, especially in writing to the Sovereigns, he said, "I swear that this is true."

He observed the fasts of the Church most faithfully, confessed and made communion often, read the canonical offices like a churchman or member of a religious order, hated blasphemy and profane swearing...seemed very grateful to God for benefits received from the divine hand, wherefore, as in the proverb, he hourly admitted that God had conferred upon him great mercies, as upon David...

He was extraordinarily zealous for the divine service; he desired and was eager for the conversion of these people [native Americans], and that in every region the faith of Jesus Christ be planted and enhanced. And he was especially affected and devoted to the idea that God should deem him worthy of aiding somewhat in recovering the Holy Sepulchre...

He was a gentleman of great force of spirit, of lofty thoughts, naturally inclined (from what we may gather of his life, deeds, writings and conversation) to undertake worthy deeds and signal enterprises; patient and long-suffering (as later shall appear), and a forgiver of injuries, and wished nothing more than that those who offended against him should recognize their errors, and that the delinquents be reconciled with him; most constant and endowed with forbearance in the hardships and adversities which were always occurring and which were incredible and infinite; ever holding great confidence in divine providence.

And verily, from what I have heard from him and from my own father, who was with him when he returned to colonize Hispaniola in 1493, and from others who accompanied and served him, he held and always kept on terms of intimate fidelity and devotion to the Sovereigns.[117]

On November 7, 1504, Columbus returned from his fourth and last voyage. Weakened in his flesh, he suffered from gout, arthritis and feverish deliriums. Just 19 days later, his heart was further saddened by the news of Queen Isabella's death. Over the next few years, Columbus occupied himself securing his house and obtaining positions for his descendants.

On May 20, 1506, he took a sudden turn for the worse. He called to his bedside his brother Diego, and sons Ferdinand and Diego, as well as his loyal captains. Christopher Columbus, as recorded by his son Ferdinand, uttered as his last words the last words of Christ:

> In manus tuas, Domine, commendo spiritum meum. (Into your hands, Father, I commend my soul.)[118]

≈

Congress of Massachusetts, Provincial October 22, 1774, concurred with the declaration of its President, John Hancock:

> We think it is incumbent upon this people to humble themselves before God on account of their sins, for He hath been pleased in His righteous judgement to suffer a great calamity to befall us, as the present controversy between Great Britain and the Colonies. [And] also to implore the Divine Blessing upon us, that by the assistance of His grace, we may be enabled to reform whatever is amiss among us, that so God may be pleased to continue to us the blessings we enjoy, and remove the tokens of His displeasure, by causing harmony and union to be restored between Great Britain and these Colonies.[119]

≈

MASSACHUSETTS.

Seal of Massachusetts

Congress of Massachusetts, Provincial 1774, resolved:

> Resistance to tyranny becomes the Christian and social duty of each individual....Continue steadfast, and with a proper sense of your dependence on God, nobly defend those rights which heaven gave, and no man ought to take from us.[120]

≈

Congress of Massachusetts, Provincial 1774, reorganized the Massachusetts militia, providing that over one-third of all new regiments be made up of "Minutemen." The minutemen, known as such because they would be ready to fight at a minute's notice, would drill as citizen soldiers on the parade ground, then go to

the church to hear exhortation and prayer. Many times the deacon of the church, or even the pastor, would lead the drill. They proclaimed, "Our cause is just" and believed it was their Christian duty to defend it.[121] The Provincial Congress of Massachusetts charged the minutemen:

> You...are placed by Providence in the post of honor, because it is the post of danger....The eyes not only of North America and the whole British Empire, but of all Europe, are upon you. Let us be, therefore, altogether solicitous that no disorderly behavior, nothing unbecoming our characters as Americans, as citizens and Christians, be justly chargeable to us.[122]

છે

Continental Congress September 6, 1774, made their first official act a call for prayer, as recorded in the *Journals of the Continental*

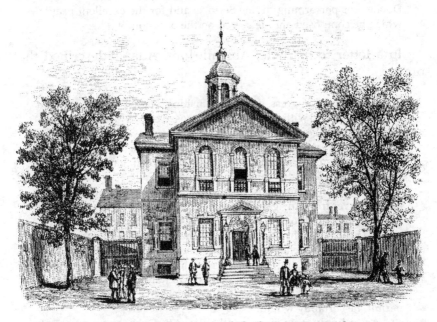

Carpenter's Hall, Philadelphia, site of the first Continental Congress in September, 1774.

Congress, after just receiving the news that the British troops had attacked Boston:

> Tuesday, September 6, 1774. Resolved, That the Rev. Mr. Duché be desired to open the Congress tomorrow morning with prayers, at the Carpenter's Hall, at 9 o'clock.[123]

Jacob Duché

Continental Congress September 7, 1774, as recorded in the *Journals of the Continental Congress,* invited Rev. Mr. Duché to open the first Congress in Carpenter's Hall, Philadelphia, with prayer:

> Wednesday, September 7, 1774, 9 o'clock a.m. Agreeable to the resolve of yesterday, the meeting was opened with prayers by the Rev. Mr. Duché. Voted, That the thanks of Congress be given to Mr. Duché...for performing divine Service, and for the excellent prayer, which he composed and delivered on the occasion.[124]

In a letter to his wife, Abigail, John Adams described that prayer:

> When the Congress met, Mr. Cushing made a motion that it should be opened with Prayer. It was opposed by Mr. Jay of New York, and Mr. Rutledge of South Carolina because we were so divided in religious sentiments, some Episcopalians, some Quakers, some Anabaptists, some Presbyterians, and some Congregationalists, that we could not join in the same act of worship.
>
> Mr. Samuel Adams arose and said that he was no bigot, and could hear a Prayer from any gentleman of Piety and virtue, who was at the same time a friend to his Country. He was a stranger in Philadelphia, but had heard that Mr. Duché deserved that character and therefore he moved that Mr. Duché, an Episcopal clergyman might be desired to read Prayers to Congress tomorrow morning. The motion was seconded, and passed in the affirmative. Mr. Randolph, our president, vailed on Mr. Duché, and received for answer, that if his health would permit, he certainly would.[125]
>
> Accordingly, next morning [the Rev. Mr. Duché] appeared with his clerk and in his pontificals, and read several prayers in the established form, and read the collect for the seventh day of September,

which was the thirty-fifth Psalm. You must remember, this was the next morning after we heard the horrible rumor of the cannonade of Boston.

I never saw a greater effect upon an audience. It seem as if heaven had ordained that Psalm to be read on that morning. After this, Mr. Duché, unexpectedly to every body, struck out into an extemporary prayer, which filled the bosom of every man present. I must confess, I never heard a better prayer, or one so well pronounced.

Episcopalian as he is, Dr. Cooper himself [Adams' personal pastor] never prayed with such fervor, such ardor, such earnestness and pathos, and in language so elegant and sublime, for America, for the Congress, for the province of Massachusetts Bay, and especially the town of Boston. It has had an excellent effect upon everybody here. I must beg you to read that Psalm."[126]

The 35th Psalm, the Psalter for the seventh day of September, was read by Rev. Mr. Duché in the first Continental Congress. It begins:

Plead my cause, Oh, Lord, with them that strive with me, fight against them that fight against me. Take hold of buckler and shield, and rise up for my help. Draw also the spear and the battle-axe to meet those who pursue me; Say to my soul, "I am your salvation." Let those be ashamed and dishonored who seek my life; Let those be turned back and humiliated who devise evil against me.[127]

The First Prayer in Congress, offered extemporaneously by Rev. Mr. Duché in Carpenter's Hall, Philadelphia, on September 7, 1774:

Be Thou present O God of Wisdom and direct the counsel of this Honorable Assembly; enable them to settle all things on the best and surest foundations; that the scene of blood may be speedily closed; that Order, Harmony and Peace may be effectually restored, and the Truth and Justice, Religion and Piety, prevail and flourish among the people.

Preserve the health of their bodies, and the vigor of their minds, shower down on them, and the millions they here represent, such temporal Blessings as Thou seest expedient for them in this world, and crown them with everlasting Glory in the world to come. All this we ask in the name and through the merits of Jesus Christ, Thy Son and our Saviour, Amen.[128]

"The First Prayer in Congress," painted by T.H. Matheson (c. 1848), was uttered on September 7, 1774 in Carpenter's Hall, Philadelphia.

The Library of Congress, from the collected reports of the various patriots, recorded on a famous historical placard the effect of that first prayer upon Congress:

> Washington was kneeling there, and Henry, Randolph, Rutledge, Lee, and Jay, and by their side there stood, bowed in reverence, the Puritan Patriots of New England, who at that moment had reason to believe that an armed soldiery was wasting their humble households. It was believed that Boston had been bombarded and destroyed.
>
> They prayed fervently "for America, for Congress, for the Province of Massachusetts Bay, and especially for the town of Boston," and who can realize the emotion with which they turned imploringly to Heaven for Divine interposition and—"It was enough" says Mr. Adams, "to melt a heart of stone. I saw the tears gush into the eyes of the old, grave, Pacific Quakers of Philadelphia."[129]

Continental Congress September 1774, passed the Articles of Association, as recorded by the Secretary of Congress, Charles Thomson, in the *Journals of Congress.* It stated:

Charles Thomson

> *Article* X That the late Act of Parliament for establishing...the French Laws in that extensive country now called Quebec, is dangerous in an extreme degree to the Protestant Religion and to the civil rights and liberties of all America; and therefore as men and protestant Christians, we are indispensably obliged to take all proper measures for our security.[130]

Continental Congress June 12, 1775, less than two months after "the shot heard 'round the world" was fired at Concord, issued a call for all citizens to fast and pray and confess their sins that the Lord God might bless the land:

Lexington, 11 miles northwest of Boston, was on the road that the British troops took to capture the arms depot at Concord.

> And it is recommended to Christians, of all denominations, to assemble for public worship, and to abstain from servile labour and recreations on said day.[131]

Continental Congress July 6, 1775, passed *The Declaration of the Causes and Necessity of Taking Up Arms,* which concluded:

In June 1775, the Second Continental Congress, sitting in Philadelphia, appointed George Washington as Commander-in-Chief of "the forces raised and to be raised in defence of American Liberty."

With a humble confidence in the mercies of the Supreme and impartial God and ruler of the universe, we most devoutly implore His divine goodness to protect us happily through this great conflict, and to dispose our adversaries to reconciliation on reasonable terms, and thereby to relieve the empire from the calamities of civil war.[132]

❧

Continental Congress July 19, 1775, as recorded in the *Journals of Congress*, resolved:

Agreed, The Congress meet here to Morrow morning, at half after 9 o'clock, in order to attend divine service at Mr. Duché's Church; and that in the afternoon they meet here to go from this place and attend divine service at Doctr Allison's church.[133]

❧

Continental Congress March 16, 1776, appointed a day of fasting and prayer for the Colonies:

> The Congress....Desirous...to have people of all ranks and degrees duly impressed with a solemn sense of God's superintending providence, and of their duty, devoutly to rely...on his aid and direction...
>
> Do earnestly recommend Friday, the 17th day of May be observed by the colonies as a day of humiliation, fasting, and prayer; that we may, with united hearts, confess and bewail our manifold sins and transgressions, and, by sincere repentance and amendment of life, appease God's righteous displeasure, and, through the merits and mediation of Jesus Christ, obtain this pardon and forgiveness.[134]

ﾞﾑ

Continental Congress July 1, 1776, heard John Adams declare his intentions to the delegates from the Thirteen Colonies:

John Adams

> Before God, I believe the hour has come. My judgement approves this measure, and my whole heart is in it. All that I have, and all that I am, and all that I hope in this life, I am now ready here to stake upon it. And I leave off as I began, that live or die, survive or perish, I am for the Declaration. It is my living sentiment, and by the blessing of God it shall be my dying sentiment. Independence now, and Independence for ever![135]

ﾞﾑ

Continental Congress July 2, 1776, approved the wording for the Declaration of Independence. On July 4, 1776, delegates of the Continental Congress voted to accept it. On July 8, 1776, the Declaration was read publicly for the first time outside of Independence Hall in Philadelphia, accompanied by the ringing of the Liberty Bell. On July 19, Congress ordered it engrossed in script on parchment and on August 2, 1776, the members of Congress signed the parchment copy:

The Declaration of Independence.
Congress passed the resolution calling for independence on July 2, 1776.
On July 4, the formal Declaration was adopted.
This illustration reproduces the formal Declaration engrossed on parchment,
probably by Timothy Matlack of Philadelphia, and signed by most members of
Congress on August 2, 1776.

When in the Course of human events, it becomes necessary for one people to dissolve the political bands which have connected them with another, and to assume among the powers of the earth, the separate and equal station to which the Laws of Nature and of Nature's God entitles them...

We hold these truths to be self-evident, that all men are created equal. That they are endowed by their Creator with certain inalienable rights, that among these are life, liberty and the pursuit of happiness...

We, Therefore, the Representatives of the United States of America, in General Congress, Assembled, appealing to the Supreme Judge of the world for the rectitude of our intentions...

And for the support of this Declaration, with a firm reliance on the protection of Divine Providence, we mutually pledge to each other our Lives, our Fortunes, and our sacred Honor.[136]

After each of the delegates had signed the Declaration of Independence, Samuel Adams declared:

We have this day restored the Sovereign to Whom all men ought to be obedient. He reigns in heaven and from the rising to the setting of the sun, let His kingdom come.[137]

за

Continental Congress July 3, 1776, recorded John Adams' proclamation:

The second day of July, 1776, will be the most memorable epoch in the history of America, to be celebrated by succeeding generations as the great anniversary festival, commemorated as the day of deliverance by solemn acts of devotion to God Almighty from one end of the Continent to the other, from this time forward forevermore.[138]

On July 3, 1776, the day after Congress approved the wording of the Declaration of Independence, John Adams wrote to his wife, Abigail, reflecting on what he had shared in Congress and, with prophetic insight, declaring the importance of that day:

I am apt to believe that it will be celebrated by succeeding generations as the great anniversary Festival. It ought to be commemorated, as the Day of Deliverance, by solemn acts of devotion to God Almighty. It ought to be solemnized with pomp and parade, with shows, games, sports, guns, bells, bonfires and illuminations, from one end of this continent to the other, from this time forward forever.

You will think me transported with enthusiasm, but I am not. I am well aware of the toil and blood and treasure that it will cost to maintain this Declaration, and support and defend these States. Yet through all the gloom I can see the rays of ravishing light and glory. I can see that the end is worth more than all the means; that posterity will triumph in that day's transaction, even though we [may regret] it, which I trust in God we shall not.[139]

The 56 signers of the Declaration of Independence paid a tremendous price for our freedom: 5 were arrested by the British as traitors, 12 had their homes looted and burned by the enemy, 17 lost their fortunes, 2 lost sons in the Continental Army and 9 fought and died during the Revolutionary War.[140]

ea

Continental Congress July 8, 1776, for the first time read the Declaration of Independence publicly, as the famous "Liberty Bell" was rung. Congress then established a three-man committee, consisting of Thomas Jefferson, John Adams and Benjamin Franklin, for the purpose of designing a great seal for the United States.

Benjamin Franklin's suggestions for a seal and motto, characterizing the spirit of this new nation, were:

Moses lifting up his wand, and dividing the red sea, and pharaoh in his chariot overwhelmed with the waters. This motto: "Rebellion to tyrants is obedience to God."[141]

Thomas Jefferson proposed:

The children of Israel in the wilderness, led by a cloud by day, and a pillar of fire by night.[142]

ea

John Nixon, a member of the Philadelphia Committee of Safety, gave the first public reading of the Declaration of Independence from the steps of Independence Hall.

Continental Congress July 9, 1776, on the day following the first public reading of the Declaration of Independence in Philadelphia and the ringing of the "Liberty Bell," moved to establish prayer as a daily part of this new nation:

> Resolved, That the Rev. Mr. J. Duché be appointed chaplain to Congress, and that he be desired to attend every morning at 9 o'clock.[143]

❧

Continental Congress July 9, 1776, authorized the Continental Army to provide chaplains for their troops. On that same day, General George Washington, the Commander-in-Chief of the Continental Army, issued the order to appoint chaplains to every regiment.[144]

In his first general order to his troops, General George Washington called on:

> Every officer and man...to live, and act, as becomes a Christian Soldier defending the dearest Rights and Liberties of his country.[145]

ૐ

Continental Congress September 11, 1777, approved and recommended to the people that 20,000 copies of *The Holy Bible* be imported from other sources. This was in response to the shortage of

General George Washington and troops

Bibles in America caused by the Revolutionary War interrupting trade with England. The Chaplain of Congress, Patrick Allison, brought the matter to the attention of Congress, who assigned it to a special Congressional Committee, which reported:

> The use of the Bible is so universal and its importance so great that your committee refers the above to the consideration of Congress, and if Congress shall not think it expedient to order the importation of types and paper, the Committee recommends that Congress will order the Committee of Commerce to import 20,000 Bibles from Holland, Scotland, or elsewhere, into the different parts of the States of the Union.
>
> Whereupon it was resolved accordingly to direct said Committee of Commerce to import 20,000 copies of the Bible.[146]

ૐ

Continental Congress November 1, 1777, issued The *First National Proclamation of Thanksgiving* to all colonies, as a result of their victory at Saratoga:

Forasmuch as it is the indispensable duty of all men to adore the superintending Providence of Almighty God; to acknowledge with gratitude their obligation to Him for benefits received and to implore such further blessing as they stand in need of; and it having pleased Him in His abundant mercy not only to continue to us the innumerable bounties of His common Providence...to smile upon us as in the prosecution of a just and necessary war for the defense and establishment of our unalienable rights and liberties...

It is therefore recommended to the legislative or executive powers of these United States, to set apart Thursday, the eighteenth day of December next, for the solemn thanksgiving and praise:

That with one heart and one voice the good people may express the grateful feelings of their hearts, and consecrate themselves to the service of their Divine Benefactor; and that together with their sincere acknowledgements and offerings, they may join the penitent confession of their manifold sins, whereby they had forfeited every favour, and their humble and earnest supplication that it may please God, through the merits of Jesus Christ, mercifully to forgive and blot them out of remembrance;

That it may please Him graciously to afford His blessings on the governments of these states respectively, and prosper the public council of the whole; to inspire our commanders both by land and sea, and all under them, with that wisdom and fortitude which may render them fit instruments, under the Providence of Almighty God, to secure for these United States, the greatest of all human blessings, independence and peace;

That it may please Him, to prosper the trade and manufactures of the people, and the labour of the husbandman, that our land may yet yield its increase; to take school and seminaries of education, so necessary for cultivating the principles of true liberty, virtue and piety, under His nurturing hand, and to prosper the means of religion for the promotion and enlargement of that kingdom which consisteth "in righteous, peace and joy in the Holy Ghost."

And it is further recommended, that servile labour, and such recreation as, though at other times innocent, may be unbecoming the purpose of this appointment, be omitted on so solemn an occasion.[147]

ès

Continental Congress November 15, 1777, proposed and signed the Articles of Confederation, which constituted the government in America prior to the writing of the Constitution. It was finally ratified by the states March 1, 1781:

...on the fifteenth day of November in the year of our Lord one thousand seven hundred and seventy seven.[148]

And whereas it has pleased the Great Governor of the world to incline the hearts of the Legislatures we respectively represent in Congress,

The Convention was held at the State House in Philadelphia.

to approve of, and to authorize us to ratify the said articles of confederation and perpetual union.[149]

સ

Continental Congress October 18, 1780, issued a *Proclamation for a Day of Public Thanksgiving and Prayer*. This came after the revealing of and subsequent deliverance from Benedict Arnold's plot to betray General George Washington and his troops to the British:

> Whereas it hath pleased Almighty God, the Father of all mercies, amidst the vicissitudes and calamities of war, to bestow blessings on the people of these states, which call for their devout and thankful acknowledgements, more especially in the late remarkable interposition of his watchful providence, in the rescuing the person of our Commander-in-Chief and the army from imminent dangers, at the moment when treason was ripened for execution....
>
> It is therefore recommended to the several states...a day of public thanksgiving and prayer, that all the people may assemble on that day to celebrate the praises of our Divine Benefactor; to confess our unworthiness of the least of his favours, and to offer our fervent supplications to the God of all grace...to cause the knowledge of Christianity to spread over all the earth.[150]

સ

[The Articles of Confederation of the United States of America were ratified on March 1, 1781, and constituted the nation's form of government until March 4, 1789. See *Articles of Confederation*.]

૨**

Congress of the Confederation September 10, 1782, in response to the need for Bibles which again arose, granted approval to print "a neat edition of the Holy Scriptures for the use of schools." The printing was contracted to Robert Aitken of Philadelphia, a bookseller and the publisher of *The Pennsylvania Magazine*, who had previously petitioned Congress on January 21, 1781. This edition has come to be known as the *Bible of the Revolution*. The following Endorsement of Congress was printed on its front page.[151]

> Whereupon, Resolved, That the United States in Congress assembled...recommend this edition of the Bible to the inhabitants of the United States, and hereby authorize [Robert Aitken] to publish this recommendation in the manner he shall think proper.[152]

૨**

Congress of the Confederation 1783, ratified a peace treaty with Great Britain at the close of the Revolutionary War. The treaty began:

> In the name of the Most Holy and Undivided Trinity. It having pleased the Divine Providence to dispose the hearts of the most serene and most potent Prince George the Third, by the Grace of God, King of Great Britain, France, and Ireland, Defender of the Faith,...and of the United States of America, to forget all past misunderstandings and differences....[153]

૨**

Congress of the Confederation 1787, passed an act in which special lands were designated:

> ...for the sole use of Christian Indians and the Moravian Brethren missionaries, for civilizing the Indians and promoting Christianity.[154]

[This act was extended three times during Thomas Jefferson's presidency.]

❧

Constitutional Convention   May 14, 1787, began at the State House (Independence Hall) for the purpose of revising the Articles of Confederation and formulating the Constitution. George Washington, who had been unanimously elected as President of the Convention, rose during the Convention and admonished the delegates:

> If to please the people, we offer what we ourselves disapprove, how can we afterward defend our work? Let us raise a standard to which the wise and the honest can repair; the event is in the Hand of God![155]

❧

Constitutional Convention   June 28, 1787, Thursday, was embroiled in a bitter debate over how each state was to be represented in the new government. The hostile feelings created by the smaller states being pitted against the larger states was so bitter that some delegates actually left the Convention.

Benjamin Franklin, being the President (Governor) of Pennsylvania, hosted the rest of the 55 delegates attending the Convention. Being the senior member of the convention, at 81 years of age, he commanded the respect of all present, and, as recorded in James Madison's detailed records, he arose to address the Congress in this moment of crisis:

Benjamin Franklin

> Mr. President, the small progress we have made after four or five weeks close attendance & continual reasonings with each other—our different sentiments on almost every question, several of the last producing as many noes as ayes, is methinks a melancholy proof of the imperfection of the Human Understanding.
>
> We indeed seem to feel our own want of political wisdom, since we have been running about in search of it. We have gone back to

ancient history for models of government, and examined the different forms of those Republics, which, having been formed with the seeds of their own dissolution, now no longer exist. And we have viewed Modern States all round Europe, but find none of their Constitutions suitable to our circumstances.

In this situation of this Assembly, groping as it were in the dark to find political truth, and scarce able to distinguish it when presented to us, how has it happened, Sir, that we have not hitherto once thought of humbly applying to the Father of lights to illuminate our understanding?

In the beginning of the Contest with Great Britain, when we were sensible of danger we had daily prayer in this room for the Divine protection. —Our prayers, Sir, were heard, and they were graciously answered. All of us who were engaged in the struggle must have observed frequent instances of a superintending providence in our favor.

To that kind providence we owe this happy opportunity of consulting in peace on the means of establishing our future national felicity. And have we now forgotten that powerful Friend? or do we imagine we no longer need His assistance?

I have lived, Sir, a long time, and the longer I live, the more convincing proofs I see of this truth—that God Governs in the affairs of men. And if a sparrow cannot fall to the ground without His notice, is it probable that an empire can rise without His aid?

We have been assured, Sir, in the Sacred Writings, that "except the Lord build the House, they labor in vain that build it." I firmly believe this; and I also believe that without his concurring aid we shall succeed in this political building no better than the Builders of Babel: We shall be divided by our partial local interests; our projects will be confounded, and we ourselves shall become a reproach and bye word down to future ages. And what is worse, mankind may hereafter from this unfortunate instance, despair of establishing Governments by Human wisdom and leave it to chance, war and conquest.

I therefore beg leave to move—that henceforth prayers imploring the assistance of Heaven, and its blessing on our deliberations, be held in this Assembly every morning before we proceed to business, and that one or more of the clergy of this city be requested to officiate in that service.[156]

Jonathan Dayton

Jonathan Dayton, delegate from New Jersey, reported the reaction of Congress to Dr. Franklin's rebuke:

The Doctor sat down; and never did I behold a countenance at once so dignified and delighted as was that of Washington at the close of the address; nor were the members of the convention generally less affected. The words of the venerable Franklin fell upon our ears with a weight and authority, even greater than we may suppose an oracle to have had in a Roman senate![157]

Following the historical address, James Madison moved,[158] seconded by Roger Sherman of Connecticut,[159] that Dr. Franklin's appeal for prayer be enacted. Edmund Jennings Randolph of Virginia further moved:

James Madison

Roger Sherman

That a sermon be preached at the request of the convention on the 4th of July, the anniversary of Independence; and thenceforward prayers be used in ye Convention every morning.[160]

[Of note is the fact that prayers have opened both houses of Congress ever since.][161]

The clergy of the city responded to this request and effected a profound change in the convention, when they reconvened on July 2, 1787, as noted in Jonathan Dayton's records:

We assembled again; and...every unfriendly feeling had been expelled, and a spirit of conciliation had been cultivated.[162]

On July 4th, the entire Convention assembled in the Reformed Calvinistic Church, according to the proposal by Edmund Jennings Randolph of Virginia, and heard a sermon by Rev. William Rogers. His prayer was a reflection of the hearts of all the delegates following the convicting admonition of Dr. Franklin:

We fervently recommend to the fatherly notice...our federal convention...Favor them, from day to day, with thy inspiring presence; be their

Edmund Jennings Randolph

wisdom and strength; enable them to devise such measures as may prove happy instruments in healing all divisions and prove the good of the great whole;...that the United States of America may form one example of a free and virtuous government....

May we...continue, under the influence of republican virtue, to partake of all the blessings of cultivated and Christian society.[163]

ᴥ

Congress of the Confederation July 13, 1787, passed "An Ordinance for the Government of the Territory of the United States, North-West of the River Ohio," later shortened to the Northwest Ordinance. (This ordinance was later passed by the United States Congress, and signed into law by President George Washington, August 4, 1789, just as the First Amendment was being formulated):

> *Article III* Religion, morality, and knowledge being necessary to good government and the happiness of mankind, schools and the means of education shall be forever encouraged.[164]

ᴥ

Constitutional Convention

September 17, 1787, called for a vote on the new Constitution. Thirty-nine of the fifty-five delegates at the Constitutional Convention signed the Constitution. By June 21, 1788, nine of the states had ratified it, establishing the Constitution. All of the states had completed ratification by January 10, 1791.[165]

The Convention was held at the State House in Philadelphia.

Virtually all of the 55 writers and signers of the United States Constitution of 1787, were members of Christian denominations: 29 were Anglicans, 16 to 18 were Calvinists, 2 were Methodists, 2 were Lutherans, 2 were Roman Catholic, 1 lapsed Quaker and sometimes Anglican, and 1 open Deist—Dr. Franklin who attended every kind of Christian worship, called for public prayer, and contributed to all denominations.[166]

*The Constitution
of The United States Of America*

We the people of the United States, in order to form a more perfect union, establish justice, insure domestic tranquility, provide for the common defense, promote the general welfare, and secure the Blessings of Liberty to ourselves and our posterity, do ordain and establish this Constitution for the United States of America.[167]

Article I, Section 7, Paragraph 2: If any bill shall not be returned by the President within ten Days (Sundays excepted)....[168]

Done in Convention, by the unanimous consent of the States present, the seventeenth day of September, in the year of our LORD one thousand seven hundred and eighty seven.[169]

[See *Congress of the United States*, January 19, 1853.]

Congress of the United States of America April 27, 1789, passed a resolution in the Senate, and two days later in the House, giving instructions with regard to the Inauguration of George Washington as the first President of the United States:

Resolved, That after the oath shall have been administered to the President, he, attended by the Vice President, and the members of the Senate, and House of Representatives, proceed to St. Paul's Chapel, to hear divine service, to be performed by the Chaplain of Congress already appointed.[170]

George Washington

The *Annals of Congress* give a record of the events on April 30, 1789, following President George Washington's Inauguration:

The President, the Vice-President, the Senate, and House of Representatives, &c., then proceeded to St. Paul's Chapel, where divine service was performed by the Chaplains of Congress.[171]

A week prior to the Inauguration, April 23, 1789, the schedule

Enroute to his Inauguration in New York in 1789, George Washington enjoyed a triumphant reception in Trenton, the scene of one of his greatest victories.

of events for that special day was published in the newspaper, *Daily Advertiser:*

> On the morning of the day on which our illustrious President will be invested with his office, the bells will ring at nine o'clock, when the people may go up and in a solemn manner commit the new Government, with its important train of consequences, to the holy protection and blessings of the Most High. An early hour is prudently fixed for this peculiar act of devotion, and it is designed wholly for prayer.[172]

&

Congress of the United States of America April 30, 1789, was addressed by President George Washington in his famous Inaugural Speech to Both Houses of Congress. He had just taken the oath of office on the balcony of Federal Hall in New York City, with his hand upon a Bible opened to Deuteronomy, chapter 28. Embarrassed by the thunderous ovation which followed the Inauguration ceremony, the pealing church bells and the roaring of artillery, he went inside to deliver his address to Congress:[173]

> Such being the impressions under which I have, in obedience to the public summons, repaired to the present station, it would be peculiarly improper to omit, in this first official act, my fervent supplications to that Almighty Being who rules over the universe, who presides in the councils of nations and whose providential aids can supply every human defect;
>
> that His benediction may consecrate to the liberties and happiness of the people of the United States a Government instituted by themselves for these essential purposes; and may enable every instrument employed in its administration to execute with success, the functions allotted to his charge.
>
> In tendering this homage to the Great Author of every public and private good, I assure myself that it expresses your sentiments not less than my own; nor those of my fellow-citizens at large, less than either.
>
> No people can be bound to acknowledge and adore the Invisible Hand which conducts the affairs of men more than the people of the United States. Every step by which they have advanced to the character of an independent nation seems to have been distinguished by some token of providential agency.
>
> And in the important revolution just accomplished, in the system of their United government, the tranquil deliberations and voluntary

On April 29, 1789, George Washington was inaugurated as President at Federal Hall, New York.

consent of so many distinct communities, from which the event has resulted, can not be compared with the means by which most governments have been established, without some return of pious gratitude, along with an humble anticipation of the future blessings which the past seem to presage.

These reflections, arising out of the present crisis, have forced themselves too strongly on my mind to be suppressed. You will join with me I trust in thinking, that there are none under the influence of which the proceedings of a new and free Government can more auspiciously commence.

We ought to be no less persuaded that the propitious smiles of Heaven can never be expected on a nation that disregards the eternal rules of order and right which Heaven itself has ordained; and since the preservation of the sacred fire of liberty and the destiny of the republican model of government are justly considered as deeply, perhaps finally, staked on the experiment....[174]

&

Congress of the United States of America May 1, 1789, approved in the House of Representatives to elect Rev. William Linn, a Dutch Reformed minister in New York City, as its chaplain and then appropriated $500.00 from the Federal treasury to pay his salary. The Right Reverend Bishop Samuel Provost was elected and publicly paid to be the chaplain of the Senate. Both the House and the Senate have continued to regularly open every session with prayer.[175]

ᥤᴥ

Congress of the United States of America August 4, 1789, repassed the Northwest Ordinance; it had been previously passed under the Articles of Confederation. The *United States Annotated Code*, in establishing requirements for those territories seeking statehood, lists the Northwest Ordinance as one of the most significant governmental instruments, along with the Articles of Confederation, the Declaration of Independence and the Constitution.

George Washington

President George Washington signed it into law on August 7, 1789, during the same period of time in which the First Amendment was being formulated:

> *Article III* Religion, morality, and knowledge, being necessary to good government and the happiness of mankind, schools and the means of education shall forever be encouraged.[176]

ᥤᴥ

Congress of the United States of America September 25, 1789, voted on the final version of the first ten amendments to the Constitution, known as the Bill of Rights. The First Amendment states:

> Congress shall make no law respecting the establishment of religion, or prohibiting the free exercise thereof.[177]

The initial draft of the First Amendment was made by James Madison on June 8, 1789. His wording was:

> The civil rights of none shall be abridged on account of religious belief or worship, nor shall any national religion be established, nor shall the full and equal rights of conscience be in any manner, or on any

pretext, infringed.[178]

Following much discussion, the House Select Committee, on August 15, 1789, proposed the revised wording:

> No religion shall be established by law, nor shall the equal rights of conscience be infringed.[179]

Peter Sylvester, Representative of New York, objected to the Select Committee's version as:

> It might be thought to have a tendency to abolish religion altogether.[180]

James Madison then proposed the insertion of the word "national" before religion, but this was not accepted. Madison's interpretation of the wording was:

> That Congress should not establish a religion, and enforce the legal worship of it by law, nor compel men to worship God in any manner contrary to their conscience.[181]

Congressman Benjamin Huntington, son of the prestigious governor of Connecticut, protested that:

> The words might be taken in such latitude as to be extremely hurtful to the cause of religion.[182]

Congressman Huntington then suggested that:

> The amendment be made in such a way as to secure the rights of religion, but not to patronize those who professed no religion at all.[183]

Roger Sherman

Roger Sherman did not even want an amendment, realizing that the federal government was not to have any say in what was under the individual states' jurisdictions.

James Madison realized that Congressman Benjamin Huntington:

...apprehended the meaning of the words to be, that Congress should not establish a religion and enforce the legal observation of it by law, nor compel men to worship God in any manner contrary to their conscience.[184]

Madison then responded agreeably to Congressman Huntington and Congressman Sylvester, that he:

...believes that the people feared one sect might obtain a preeminence, or two [Congregational and Anglican] combine and establish a religion to which they would compel others to conform.[185]

On August 15, 1789, Samuel Livermore of New Hampshire proposed the wording:

Congress shall make no laws touching religion, or infringing the rights of conscience.[186]

The House agreed and accepted the first five words of this version.

On August 20, 1789, Fisher Ames of Massachusetts introduced the language:

Congress shall make no law establishing religion, or to prevent the free exercise thereof, or to infringe the rights of conscience.[187]

This proposal was accepted by the House, which then sent it to the Senate for discussion. On September 3, 1789, the Senate proposed several versions in succession:

Congress shall not make any law infringing the rights of conscience, or establishing any religious sect or society.[188]

Congress shall make no law establishing any particular denomination of religion in preference to another, or prohibiting the free exercise thereof, nor shall the rights of conscience be infringed.[189]

Congress shall make no law establishing one religious society in preference to others, or to infringe on the rights of conscience.[190]

The version accepted by the Senate at the end of the day, September 3, 1789 was:

> Congress shall make no law establishing religion, or prohibiting the free exercise thereof.[191]

On September 9, 1789, the Senate agreed on the version:

> Congress shall make no law establishing articles of faith or a mode of worship, or prohibiting the free exercise of religion.[192]

This proposal was then sent to a joint committee of both the House and the Senate to reconcile the differences. The final wording agreed upon was:

> Congress shall make no law respecting an establishment of religion, or prohibiting the free exercise thereof.[193]

On December 15, 1791, The Bill of Rights was finally ratified by the states. This was a declaration of what the federal government could *not* do, leaving the States free within the controls of their own constitutions.

The First Amendment in its entirety, states:

> Congress shall make no law respecting an establishment of religion, or prohibiting the free exercise thereof; or abridging the freedom of speech, or of the press; or the right of the people peaceably to assemble, and to petition the Government for a redress of grievances.

The Second Amendment states:

> A well regulated Militia, being necessary to the security of a free state, the right of the people to keep and bear Arms, shall not be infringed.

The Third Amendment states:

> No soldier shall, in time of peace be quartered in any house, without the consent of the owner, nor in time of war, but in a manner to be prescribed by law.

The Fourth Amendment states:

The right of the people to be secure in their persons, houses, papers, and effects, against unreasonable searches and seizures, shall not be violated, and no Warrants shall issue, but upon probable cause, supported by Oath or affirmation, and particularly describing the place to be searched, and the persons or things to be seized.

The Fifth Amendment states:

No person shall be held to answer for a capital, or otherwise infamous crime, unless on a presentment or indictment of a Grand Jury, except in cases arising in the land or naval forces, or in the Militia, when in actual service in time of War or public danger; nor shall any person be subject for the same offence to be twice put in jeopardy of life or limb; nor be compelled in any criminal case to be a witness against himself, nor be deprived of life, liberty, or property, without due process of law; nor shall private property be taken for public use without just compensation.

The Sixth Amendment states:

In all criminal prosecutions, the accused shall enjoy the right to a speedy and public trial, by an impartial jury of the State and district wherein the crime shall have been committed, which district shall have been previously ascertained by law, and to be informed of the nature and cause of the accusation; to be confronted with the witnesses against him; to have compulsory process for obtaining Witnesses in his favor, and to have the assistance of counsel for his defense.

The Seventh Amendment states:

In Suits at common law, where the value in controversy shall exceed twenty dollars, the right of trial by jury shall be preserved, and no fact tried by a jury, shall be otherwise reexamined in any Court of the United States, than according to the rules of common law.

The Eighth Amendment states:

Excessive bail shall not be required, nor excessive fines imposed, nor cruel and unusual punishments inflicted.

The Ninth Amendment states:

> The enumeration in the Constitution, of certain rights, shall not be construed to deny or disparage others retained by the people.

The Tenth Amendment states:

> The powers not delegated to the United States by the Constitution, nor prohibited by it to the States, are reserved to the States respectively, or to the people.[194]

❧

Congress of the United States of America September 25, 1789, unanimously approved a resolution asking President George Washington to proclaim a *National Day of Thanksgiving:*

> Friday, September 25, [1789]. Day of Thanksgiving. Resolved. That a joint committee of both Houses be directed to wait upon the President of the United States to request that he recommend to the people of the United States a day of public thanksgiving and prayer, to be observed by acknowledging, with grateful hearts, the many signal favors of Almighty God, especially by affording them an opportunity peaceably to establish a constitution of government for their safety and happiness.[195]

George Washington

The Journals of Congress, documenting the discussions of Congress in regard to this proclamation, recorded the comments of Mr. Roger Sherman of Connecticut:

> Mr. Sherman justified the practice of Thanksgiving, on any signal event, not only as a laudable one in itself, but as warranted by a number of precedents in Holy Writ: for instance, the solemn thanksgivings and rejoicings which took place in the time of Solomon, after the building of the temple, was a case in point. This example, he thought, worthy of Christian imitation on the present occasion.[196]

Roger Sherman

President George Washington, on October 3, 1789, from the city of New York, proclaimed a *National Day of Thanksgiving:*

> Whereas it is the duty of all nations to acknowledge the providence of Almighty God, to obey His will, to be grateful for his benefits, and humbly to implore His protection and favor....
>
> Now, therefore, I do recommend and assign Thursday, the twenty-sixth day of November next, to be devoted by the people of these United States...
>
> that we then may all unite unto him our sincere and humble thanks for His kind care and protection of the people of this country previous to their becoming a nation; for the signal and manifold mercies and the favorable interpositions of His providence in the course and conclusion of the late war;

George Washington's Inauguration, Federal Hall, New York.

for the great degree of tranquility, union, and plenty which we have since enjoyed; for the peaceable and rational manner in which we have been enabled to establish constitutions of government for our safety and happiness, and particularly the national one now lately instituted; for the civil and religious liberty with which we are blessed....

And also that we may then unite in most humbly offering our prayers and supplications to the great Lord and Ruler of Nations, and beseech Him to pardon our national and other transgressions...to promote the knowledge and practice of the true religion and virtue....

Given under my hand, at the city of New York, the 3rd of October, A.D. 1789.

Go Washington.[197]

ᴈᴀ

Congress of the United States of America January 1, 1795, heard President George Washington give his renowned *National Thanksgiving Proclamation*, which declared Thursday, the 19th of February, 1795, as a National Day of Thanksgiving. In it he stated:

Our duty as a people, with devout reverence and affectionate gratitude, to acknowledge our many and great obligations to Almighty God, and implore Him to continue and confirm the blessings we experienced.[198]

ᴈᴀ

Congress of the United States of America April 30, 1802, during the administration of President Thomas Jefferson, passed *The Enabling Act for Ohio*, which required the government being formed in that territory to be such as was:

Thomas Jefferson

...not repugnant to the [Northwest Ordinance].[199]

The Northwest Ordinance stated:

Article III Religion, morality, and knowledge, being necessary to good government and the happiness of mankind, schools and the means of education shall forever be encouraged.[200]

ᶾᶏ

Outacity,
Cherokee Indian
Chief

Congress of the United States of America
December 3, 1803, ratified *A Treaty Between the United States and the Kaskaskia Tribe of Indians.* This treaty, which had been recommended by President Thomas Jefferson, included the annual support of a Catholic missionary priest of $100, to be paid out of the Federal treasury. At a later date two other treaties with similar provisions were made: the *Treaty with the Wyandots etc.,* in 1805 and the *Treaty with the Cherokees* in 1806.[201]

ᶾᶏ

Congress of the United States of America June 4, 1805, during Thomas Jefferson's presidency, drafted a *Treaty of Peace and Amity with Tripoli,* ratified April 12, 1806. Congress deleted from the previous June 7, 1797 treaty, an unauthorized phrase that the United States "is not, in any sense founded on the Christian religion..."[202] (an insertion intended to clarify that the American government was not like the Mohammedan, Buddhist, or Hindu countries, where the government controls the religious life of its people).

Of note is the fact that this phrase is also not found in the Arabic version of the 1797 treaty,[203] and appears to have been an unauthorized insertion by Joel Barlow, the American consul at Algiers who oversaw the translation process from Arabic to English. The original Arabic translation of the treaty contains the following wording:

> Glory be to God! Declaration of the third article. We have agreed that if American Christians are traveling with a nation that is at war with the well-preserved Tripoli, and he [evidently the Tripolitan] takes [prisoners] from the Christian enemies and from the American Christians with whom we are at peace, then sets them free; neither he nor his goods shall be taken....Praise be to God!...May God strengthen [the Pasha of Tripoli], and the Americans....May God make it all

permanent love and a good conclusion between us....by His grace and favor, amen![204]

&

Congress of the United States of America April 13, 1816, during the administration of President James Madison, passed *The Enabling Act for Indiana*, which required the government being formed in that territory to be such as was:

...not repugnant to the [Northwest Ordinance].[205]

The Northwest Ordinance stated:

Article III Religion, morality, and knowledge, being necessary to good government and the happiness of mankind, schools and the means of education shall forever be encouraged.[206]

&

Congress of the United States of America March 1, 1817, during the administration of President James Monroe, passed *The Enabling Act for Mississippi*, which required the government being formed in that territory to be such as was:

...not repugnant to the principles of the [Northwest Ordinance].[207]

The Northwest Ordinance stated:

Article III Religion, morality, and knowledge, being necessary to good government and the happiness of mankind, schools and the means of education shall forever be encouraged.[208]

&

Congress of the United States of America 1822, ratified in both the House and Senate of the United States, along with Great Britain and Ireland, the *Convention for Indemnity under Award of Emperor of Russia as to the True Construction of the First Article of the*

Treaty of December 24, 1814. It begins with these words:

> In the name of the Most Holy and Indivisible Trinity.[209]

&

Congress of the United States of America 1838, passed the Act designating:

> Chaplains...are to perform the double service of clergymen and schoolmaster.[210]

[Referred to by the *House Judiciary Committee report of 1854.*]

&

Congress of the United States of America January 19, 1853, as part of a Congressional investigation, records the report of Mr. Badger of the Senate Judiciary Committee:

> The [First Amendment] clause speaks of "an establishment of religion." What is meant by that expression? It referred, without doubt, to that establishment which existed in the mother-country ...endowment at the public expense, peculiar privileges to its members, or disadvantages or penalties upon those who should reject its doctrines or belong to other communions,—such law would be a "law respecting an establishment of religion..."
>
> They intended, by this amendment, to prohibit "an establishment of religion" such as the English Church presented, or any thing like it. But they had no fear or jealousy of religion itself, nor did they wish to see us an irreligious people....
>
> They did not intend to spread over all the public authorities and the whole public action of the nation the dead and revolting spectacle of atheistic apathy. Not so had the battles of the Revolution been fought and the deliberations of the Revolutionary Congress been conducted.[211]

> In the law, Sunday is a "dies non;"....The executive departments, the public establishments, are all closed on Sundays; on that day neither House of Congress sits....
>
> Sunday, the Christian Sabbath, recognized and respected by all

the departments of the Government....[212]

Here is a recognition by law, and by universal usage, not only of a Sabbath, but of the Christian Sabbath, in exclusion of the Jewish or Mohammedan Sabbath....the recognition of the Christian Sabbath [by the Constitution] is complete and perfect.[213]

We are a Christian people...not because the law demands it, not to gain exclusive benefits or to avoid legal disabilities, but from choice and education; and in a land thus universally Christian, what is to be expected, what desired, but that we shall pay due regard to Christianity.[214]

❧

Congress of the United States of America March 27, 1854, received the report of Mr. Meacham of the House Committee on the Judiciary:

What is an establishment of religion? It must have a creed, defining what a man must believe; it must have rites and ordinances, which believers must observe; it must have ministers of defined qualifications, to teach the doctrines and administer the rites; it must have tests for the submissive and penalties for the non-conformist. There never was as established religion without all these....

At the adoption of the Constitution...every State...provided as regularly for the support of the Church as for the support of the Government....

Down to the Revolution, every colony did sustain religion in some form. It was deemed peculiarly proper that the religion of liberty should be upheld by a free people.

Had the people, during the Revolution, had a suspicion of any attempt to war against Christianity, that Revolution would have been strangled in its cradle.

At the time of the adoption of the Constitution and the amendments, the universal sentiment was that Christianity should be encouraged, not any one sect [denomination]. Any attempt to level and discard all religion would have been viewed with universal indignation. The object was not to substitute Judaism or Mohammedanism, or infidelity, but to prevent rivalry among the [Christian] sects to the exclusion of others.

It [Christianity] must be considered as the foundation on which the whole structure rests. Laws will not have permanence or power without the sanction of religious sentiment,—without a firm belief that there is a Power above us that will reward our virtues and punish our vices.

In this age there can be no substitute for Christianity: that, in its general principles, is the great conservative element on which we must rely for the purity and permanence of free institutions. That was the religion of the founders of the republic, and they expected it to remain the religion of their descendants. There is a great and very prevalent error on this subject in the opinion that those who organized this Government did not legislate on religion.[215]

᠗

Congress of the United States of America May 1854, passed a resolution in the House which declared:

The great vital and conservative element in our system is the belief of our people in the pure doctrines and divine truths of the gospel of Jesus Christ.[216]

᠗

Congress of the United States of America March 3, 1863, passed this resolution in the United States Senate:

Resolved, That devoutly recognizing the supreme authority and just government of Almighty God in all the affairs of men and nations, and sincerely believing that no people, however great in numbers and resources, or however strong in the justness of their cause, can prosper without His favor, and at the same time deploring the national offenses which have provoked His righteous judgment, yet encouraged in this day of trouble by the assurance of His Word, to seek Him for succor according to His appointed way, through Jesus Christ, the Senate of the United States does hereby request the President of the United States, by his proclamation, to designate and set apart a day for national prayer and humiliation.[217]

√On March 30, 1863, President Abraham Lincoln issued a historic *Proclamation Appointing a National Fast Day:*

Whereas, the Senate of the United States devoutly recognizing the

Supreme Authority and just Government of Almighty God in all the affairs of men and of nations, has, by a resolution, requested the President to designate and set apart a day for national prayer and humiliation:

And whereas, it is the duty of nations as well as of men to own their dependence upon the overruling power of God, to confess their sins and transgressions in humble sorrow yet with assured hope that genuine repentance will lead to mercy and pardon, and to recognize the sublime truth, announced in the Holy Scriptures and proven by all history: that those nations only are blessed whose God is the Lord:

And, insomuch as we know that, by His divine law, nations like individuals are subjected to punishments and chastisement in this world, may we not justly fear that the awful calamity of civil war, which now desolates the land may be but a punishment inflicted upon us for our presumptuous sins to the needful end of our national reformation as a whole people?

We have been the recipients of the choicest bounties of Heaven. We have been preserved these many years in peace and prosperity. We have grown in numbers, wealth and power as no other nation has ever grown.

But we have forgotten God. We have forgotten the gracious Hand which preserved us in peace, and multiplied and enriched and strengthened us; and we have vainly imagined, in the deceitfulness of our hearts, that all these blessings were produced by some superior wisdom and virtue of our own.

Intoxicated with unbroken success, we have become too self-sufficient to feel the necessity of redeeming and preserving grace, too proud to pray to the God that made us!

It behooves us then to humble ourselves before the offended Power, to confess our national sins and to pray for clemency and forgiveness.

Now, therefore, in compliance with the request and fully concurring in the view of the Senate, I do, by this my proclamation, designate and set apart Thursday, the 30th day of April, 1863, as a day of national humiliation, fasting and prayer.

And I do hereby request all the people to abstain on that day from their ordinary secular pursuits, and to unite, at their several places of public worship and their respective homes, in keeping the day holy to the Lord and devoted to the humble discharge of the religious duties proper to that solemn occasion.

All this being done, in sincerity and truth, let us then rest humbly in the hope authorized by the Divine teachings, that the united cry of the nation will be heard on high and answered with blessing no less than the pardon of our national sins and the restoration of our now divided and suffering country to its former happy condition of unity and peace.

In witness whereof, I have hereunto set my hand and caused the seal of the United States to be affixed. By the President: Abraham Lincoln.[218]

&

Congress of the United States of America October 3, 1863, passed an Act of Congress designating an annual *National Day of Thanksgiving*, as proclaimed by President Abraham Lincoln:

I do, therefore, invite my fellow citizens in every part of the United States...to set apart and observe the last Thursday of November next as a day of Thanksgiving and Praise to our beneficent Father who dwelleth in the heavens....[it is] announced in the Holy Scriptures and proven by all history, that those nations are blessed whose God is the Lord....It has seemed to me fit and proper that God should be solemnly, reverently and gratefully acknowledged, as with one heart and one voice, by the whole American people.[219]

&

Congress of the United States of America March 3, 1865, approved Salmon Portland Chase's instruction to the U.S. mint. As the Secretary of the Treasury under Abraham Lincoln, Chase instructed the mint to prepare a "device" to inscribe U.S. coins with the motto:

In God We Trust[220]

Salmon Portland Chase

&

Congress of the United States of America March 3, 1931, adopted *The Star Spangled Banner* as the National Anthem (36 U.S.C. Sec.170). This anthem was written by Francis Scott Key, September 14, 1814, at the Battle of Fort McHenry during the War of 1812. The fourth verse is as follows:

O! thus be it ever when free men shall stand

Between their loved home and the war's desolation;
Blest with vict'ry and peace, may the Heav'n-rescued land
Praise the Pow'r that hath made and preserved us a nation!
Then conquer we must, when our cause it is just;
And this be our motto, "In God is our trust!"
And the star spangled banner in triumph shall wave
O'er the land of the free and the home of the brave![221]

Congress of the Unites States of America June 14, 1954, approved the Joint Resolution 243 (Public Law 83-396), which added the words "under God" to the *Pledge of Allegiance.* (The *Pledge* was initially adopted by the 79th Congress on December 28, 1945, as Public Law 287.) On June 14, 1954, President Eisenhower signed it into law:

I pledge allegiance to the flag of the United States of America and to the Republic for which it stands, one Nation under God, indivisible, with liberty and justice for all.[222]

The *Pledge of Allegiance* was written in 1892 by a Baptist minister from Boston named Francis Bellamy, who was ordained in the Baptist Church of Little Falls, New York. He was a member of the staff of *The Youth's Companion,* which first published the Pledge on September 8, 1892. At the dedication of the 1892 Chicago World's Fair on October 12, 1892, public-school children first recited the *Pledge of Allegiance* during the National School Celebration on the 400th anniversary of Columbus' discovery of America. The words "under God" were taken from Abraham Lincoln's famous Gettysburg Address, "...that this nation, under God, shall have a new birth...."[223]

On June 14, 1954, President Eisenhower gave his support to the Congressional Act, which added the phrase "under God" to the *Pledge of Allegiance,* by signing it into law, saying:

In this way we are reaffirming the transcendence of religious faith in America's heritage and future; in this way we shall constantly strengthen those spiritual weapons which forever will be our country's most powerful resource in peace and war.[224]

President Eisenhower then stood on the steps of the Capitol Building and recited the *Pledge of Allegiance* with the phrase "one Nation under God" for the first time.[225]

❧

Congress of the United States of America 1954, approved in both the Senate and House of Representatives of the 83rd Congress, a joint resolution calling for the establishment of:

A room with facilities for prayer and meditation for the use of Members of the Senate and House of Representatives.[226]

This small room in the Capitol, just off the rotunda, is always open when Congress is in session. It is for the private prayer and meditation of members of Congress, and is not open to the public.

An open Bible is upon an altar, and located above it is the focal point of the room, which is a stained glass window showing George Washington kneeling in prayer. Behind him are etched these words from Psalm 16:1: "Preserve me, O God; for in thee do I put my trust."

Of note is that every session of the House and the Senate begins with prayer; each house has its own chaplain. Each President also concludes his oath of office, having his hand upon an open Bible, with the words, "So help me God."

Inside the rotunda is the figure of the crucified Christ, as well as a picture of the Pilgrims about to embark from Holland on the sister ship of the *Mayflower*, the *Speedwell*. The ship's revered chaplain, Brewster, who later joined the *Mayflower*, has open on his lap the Bible. On the walls of the Capitol dome very clearly are the words, "The New Testament according to our Lord and Savior Jesus Christ." On the sail is the motto of the Pilgrims, "In God We Trust, God With Us."

The phrase, "In God We Trust," appears opposite the President of the Senate, who is the Vice-President of the United States. The same phrase, in large words inscribed in the marble, backdrops the Speaker of the House of Representatives.

On the Great Seal of the United States, the phrase *Annuit Coeptis* is inscribed, which means, "[God] has smiled on our undertaking." Under the Seal, the phrase from Lincoln's famous Gettysburg Address is engraved, "This nation under God."

The Dirksen Office Building has the words "IN GOD WE TRUST" inscribed in bronze relief.[227]

&

Congress of the United States of America July 20, 1956, by Joint Resolution, adopted Rep. Charles E. Bennett's (FL) bill providing that the official national motto of the United States of America be:

> In God We Trust[228]

&

Congress of the United States of America 1977, ratified Public Law 77-379, in which the President officially proclaims the fourth Thursday of every November:

> A National Day of Thanksgiving.[229]

&

Congress of the United States of America October 4, 1982, in a Joint Resolution of the 97th Congress, signed by President Reagan, declared 1983 the "Year of the Bible," Public Law 97-280:

> WHEREAS the Bible, the Word of God, has made a unique contribution in shaping the United States as a distinctive and blessed nation and people; WHEREAS deeply held religious convictions springing from the Holy Scriptures led to the early settlement of our Nation; WHEREAS Biblical teachings inspired concepts of civil government that are contained in our Declaration of Independence and Constitution of the United States...NOW, THEREFORE, be it Resolved...to designate 1983 as a national "Year of the Bible" in recognition of both the formative influence the Bible has been for our Nation, and our national need to study and apply the teachings of the Holy Scriptures.[230]

[See *Year of the Bible*, 1983.]

⁂

Congress of the United States of America August 11, 1984, by a Senate vote of 88-11 and a House vote of 337-77, voted the Equal Access Act into law. The Supreme Court upheld it by a vote of 8-1 in the *Westside Community Schools v. Mergens* case in 1990. Section 4071 (20 U.S.C. §§ 4071-74) explains that denial of equal access is prohibited:

> Sec. 4071. (a) It shall be unlawful for any public secondary school which receives Federal financial assistance and which has a limited open forum to deny equal access or a fair opportunity to, or discriminate against, any students who wish to conduct a meeting within that limited open forum on the basis of the religious, political, philosophical, or other content of the speech at such meeting.[231]

⁂

Congress of the United States of America January 25, 1988, by a Joint Resolution of the 100th Congress, declared the first Thursday of each May to be recognized as a *National Day of Prayer*.

PUBLIC LAW 100-307—MAY 5, 1988
One Hundredth Congress of the United States of America
AT THE SECOND SESSION
Begun and held at the City of Washington on Monday, the twenty-fifth day of January, one thousand nine hundred and eighty-eight
AN ACT
To provide for setting aside the first Thursday in May as the date on which the National Day of Prayer is celebrated.

Be it enacted by the Senate and House of Representatives of the United States of America in Congress assembled, That the joint resolution entitled "Joint Resolution to provide for setting aside an appropriate day as a National Day of Prayer," approved April 17, 1952 (Public Law 82-324; 66 Stat. 64), is amended by striking "a suitable day each year, other than a Sunday," and inserting in lieu thereof "the first Thursday in May in each year."

Speaker of the House of Representatives   May 5, 1988
President of the Senate Pro Tempore   Ronald Reagan[232]

❧

Fundamental Orders (Constitution) of Connecticut January 14, 1639, was the first constitution written in America, instituting a provisional government and later serving as the model for the United States Constitution.[233] It was penned by Roger Ludlow in 1638, after he heard a sermon by Thomas Hooker, the famous Puritan minister, who, along with his congregation, help to found Connecticut. So important was this work that Connecticut became known as "The Constitution State."[234] The committee framing the orders was charged to make the laws:

CONNECTICUT.

Seal of Connecticut

> As near the law of God as they can be.[235]

The Connecticut towns of Hartford, Wethersfield and Windsor adopted the Constitution, January 14, 1639. The Preamble stated:

> Forasmuch as it has pleased the Almighty God by the wise disposition of His divine providence so to order and dispose of things that we the inhabitants and residents of Windsor, Hartford and Wethersfield and now cohabiting and dwelling in and upon the River Connecticut and the lands thereunto adjoining;
>
> and well knowing when a people are gathered together the Word of God requires, that to meinteine the peace and union of such a people, there should bee an orderly and decent government established according to God, to order and dispose of the affairs of all the people at all seasons as occasion shall require;
>
> do therefore associate and conjoin ourselves to be as one public State or Commonwealth, and do, for ourselves and our successors and such as shall be adjoined to us at any time hereafter, enter into Combination and Confederation together, to meinteine and presearve the libberty and purity of the Gospell of our Lord Jesus which we now professe...
>
> Which, according to the truth of the said Gospell, is now practised amongst us; as allso, in our civill affaires to be guided and governed according to such lawes, rules, orders, and decrees.[236]

In 1639 at Quinipiack (New Haven), Connecticut, the first

example of a written constitution, constituting a government and defining its powers, was composed as a distinct organic act. The articles which made up this constitution included:

✓   *Article I* That the Scriptures hold forth a perfect rule for the direction and government of all men in all duties which they are to perform to God and men, as well in families and commonwealths as in matters of the church.

Article II That as in matters which concern the gathering and ordering of a church, so likewise in all public offices which concern civil order,—as the choice of magistrates and officers, making and repealing laws, dividing allotments of inheritance, and all things of like nature,—they would all be governed by those rules which the Scripture held forth to them.

Article III That all those who had desired to be received free planters had settled in the plantation with a purpose, resolution, and desire that they might be admitted into church fellowship according to Christ.

Article IV That all the free planters held themselves bound to establish such civil order as might best conduce to the securing of the purity and peace of the ordinance to themselves, and their posterity according to God.[237]

Following the adoption of the Constitution, Rev. Mr. Davenport solemnly charged the governor of the Colony, quoting from Deuteronomy 1:16-17:

And I charge your judges at that time, saying, Hear the causes between your brethren, and judge righteously between every man and his brother, and the stranger that is with him. Ye shall not be afraid of the face of man; for the judgment is God's: and the cause that is too hard for you, bring it unto me, and I will hear it.[238]

‎ð‎

General Court of Connecticut 1639, established under the Constitution of Connecticut, issued the order:

That God's word should be the only rule for ordering the affairs of government in this commonwealth.[239]

‎ð‎

Colony of Connecticut 1647, along with the Colony of Massachusetts passed the *Old Deluder Satan Law* to prevent illiteracy and to prevent the abuse of power over a population ignorant of Scriptures, as had been the case in Europe. The law stated:

> It being one chiefe project of that old deluder, Sathan, to keepe men from the knowledge of the scriptures, as in former time....
> It is therefore ordered...[that] after the Lord hath increased [the settlement] to the number of fifty howshoulders, [they] shall forthwith appoint one within theire towne, to teach all such children as shall resorte to him, to write and read....
> And it is further ordered, that where any towne shall increase to the number of one hundred families or howshoulders, they shall sett up a grammar schoole for the university.[240]

&

The Constitution of the State of Connecticut 1776, stated:

> The People of this State...by the Providence of God...hath the sole and exclusive right of governing themselves as a free, sovereign, and independent State...and forasmuch as the free fruition of such liberties and privileges as humanity, civility, and Christianity call for, as is due to every man in his place and proportion...hath ever been, and will be the tranquility and stability of Churches and Commonwealth; and the denial thereof, the disturbances, if not the ruin of both.[241] (until 1818)

&

The State of Connecticut 1785-1786, enacted in the Legislature the arrangement for the sale of the Western Reserve Lands, which included a provision that there should be reserved in each township: 500 acres for the gospel, 500 acres for schools and 240 acres:

> To be granted in fee simple to the first gospel minister who shall settle in such town.[242]

&

The Constitution of the United States September 17, 1787, reads:

> We the people of the United States, in order to...secure the Blessings of Liberty to ourselves and our posterity...[243]

Article I, Section 7, Paragraph 2: If any bill shall not be returned by the President within ten Days (Sundays excepted)...[244]

Done in Convention, by the unanimous consent of the States present, the seventeenth day of September, in the year of our Lord one thousand seven hundred and eighty seven.[245]

[Of note is the fact that virtually all of the 55 writers and signers of the United States Constitution of 1787, were members of Christian denominations: 29 were Anglicans, 16 to 18 were Calvinists, 2 were Methodists, 2 were Lutherans, 2 were Roman Catholic, 1 lapsed Quaker and sometimes Anglican, and 1 open Deist—Dr. Franklin who attended every kind of Christian worship, called for public prayer, and contributed to all denominations.][246]

&

(John) Calvin Coolidge (1872-1933), was the 30th President of the United States of America, during the era known as the "Roaring Twenties," from 1923 until 1929. He held many political offices, first being the mayor of Northhampton, then he was elected to the state senate, followed by lieutenant governor and, in 1918, he became the governor of Massachusetts. He gained popularity by refusing to allow the police to join unions and go on strike, which would jeopardize public security. Calvin Coolidge was elected Vice-President under Warren G. Harding in the election of 1921.

Calvin Coolidge

On Memorial Day, May 31, 1923, Calvin Coolidge, then Vice-President under President Harding, stated in his message entitled "The Destiny of America":

If there be a destiny, it is of no avail for us unless we work with it. The ways of Providence will be of no advantage to us unless we proceed in the same direction. If we perceive a destiny in America, if we believe that Providence has been the guide, our own success, our own salvation require that we should act and serve in harmony and obedience....

They were intent upon establishing a Christian commonwealth in accordance with the principle of self-government. They were an inspired body of men. It has been said that God sifted the nations that He might send choice grain into the wilderness....Who can fail to see in it the hand of destiny? Who can doubt that it has been guided by a Divine Providence?[247]

August 3, 1923, upon receiving the news that President Warren G. Harding had died, Vice-President Coolidge, who was visiting his family, was immediately sworn in as President. The official who gave the oath was his father, who happened to be the Justice of the Peace in that township. On August 4, 1923, President Coolidge issued a Proclamation of a National Day of Mourning and Prayer:

Mrs. Calvin Coolidge (nee Grace Anne Goodhue)

To bow down in submission to the will of Almighty God.[248]

In his Inaugural address, March 4, 1925, President Calvin Coolidge stated:

America seeks no empires built on blood and force. No ambition, no temptation, lures her to thought of foreign dominion. The legions which she sends forth are armed, not with the sword, but with the Cross. The higher state to which she seeks the allegiance of all mankind is not human, but of Divine origin. She cherishes no purpose, save to merit the favor of Almighty God.[249]

In September of 1923, President Coolidge wrote to the Right Rev. James E. Freeman:

The strength of our country is the strength of its religious convictions.[250]

Calvin Coolidge stated:

The foundations of our society and our government rest so much on the teachings of the Bible that it would be difficult to support them if faith in these teachings would cease to be practically universal in our country.[251]

❧

City of Coppell, Texas April 27, 1993, passed the following resolution:

RESOLUTION NO. 042793.1

A RESOLUTION URGING THAT PRAYER BE RETURNED TO THE PUBLIC SCHOOLS AND THAT CITIES ACROSS THE STATE OF TEXAS JOIN IN AN EFFORT TO REINSTATE PRAYER IN THE PUBLIC SCHOOLS BY PASSING SIMILAR RESOLUTIONS AND UNITING IN A GRASS ROOTS MOVEMENT FOR THAT PURPOSE.

WHEREAS, the Constitution of the United States Article (1) states "Congress shall make no law respecting an establishment of religion, or prohibiting the free exercise thereof..."

WHEREAS, our nation was founded upon the many different religious beliefs and ideals of settlers from other countries; and

WHEREAS, our nation was founded on the freedom OF RELIGION and was not founded on the freedom FROM RELIGION; and

WHEREAS, through time court decisions and certain interest groups have contributed to the deterioration of those religious beliefs and ideals to the extent that prayer has been banned from the public school system; and

WHEREAS, public schools are in a unique position to influence and guide the lives of this nation's youth; and

WHEREAS, the City Council strongly believes that reinstitution of prayer in the public schools will move this nation toward those religious ideals and beliefs upon which this nation was founded; and

WHEREAS, the City Council urges all cities across this State to join in an effort to reinstate prayer in the public schools by passing similar resolutions and uniting in a "grass roots" movement for that purpose;

NOW THEREFORE, BE IT RESOLVED BY THE CITY COUNCIL OF THE CITY OF COPPELL, TEXAS:

Section 1. That the City Council of the City of Coppell, Texas strongly urges that prayer be returned to the public school systems of this nation and invites all cities across this State to join in an effort to reinstate prayer in the public schools by passing similar resolutions and uniting in a grass roots movement for that purpose.

DULY PASSED AND APPROVED by the City Council of the City of Coppell, Texas on this the 27th day of April, 1993.

THE CITY OF COPPELL, TEXAS
By *Mark Wolfe, Mayor*
ATTEST:
Linda Grau, Assistant City Secretary.[252]

ða.

Hernando Cortez (1485-1547), was the Spanish explorer who conquered Mexico. In 1504, at the age of nineteen, Cortez came to the island of Hispaniola and was given a land grant by Governor Diego Columbus, Christopher Columbus' son. After establishing himself as a wealthy hidalgo, Cortez joined Diego Velasquez in the conquest of Cuba in 1511. There he became a gentleman farmer and alcalde (town mayor.) In 1518, Governor Velasquez commissioned Cortez, along with Captain Pedro de Alvarado, to lead an expedition to the Yucatan in Mexico.

On February 10, 1519, before embarking for Mexico, Cortez addressed his force of approximately 500 men, supplied with sixteen horses and ten cannons, saying:

> Soldiers of Spain, we are standing upon the verge of the greatest adventure ever undertaken by so small a body of men. We now leave the known world behind us: from this time forth we plunge into a region never before trodden by men of our race or religion. The hazards of this adventure I shall not dwell upon; they are well estimated by the bravest among you.
>
> But I speak now of the immortal glory you will bring to Spanish arms, and to yourselves, the successful accomplishment of the mission before us. The shores we shall storm are lined with teeming millions of savages, unfriendly if not openly hostile.
>
> We have only our swords and our good right arms to protect us against their overwhelming numbers. Therefore let not childish strife or inner dissension weaken the front we must present to the enemy. If we go as united as we go courageously, we have nothing to fear, nothing to lose....
>
> We are on a crusade. We are marching as Christians into a land of infidels. We seek not only to subdue boundless territory in the name of our Emperor Don Carlos, but to win millions of unsalvaged souls to the True Faith....
>
> Let us therefore enter upon our labors, so auspiciously begun, and in the name of our God and our Emperor carry them joyously, confidently to a triumphant conclusion.[253]

Shortly after landing, on July 10, 1519, Hernando Cortez sent his *First Dispatch* to Queen Juana and her son, Charles V, from the city he founded, named Vera Cruz (City of the True Cross). In the dispatch, he stated:

> It seems most credible that our Lord God has purposefully allowed
> these lands [Mexico] to be discovered...so that Your Majesties may be
> fruitful and deserving in His sight by causing these barbaric tribes to
> be enlightened and brought to the faith by Your hand.[254]

Cortez then ordered his ships sunk in the harbor, causing his
men to realize they either had to be victorious or die. In an era of
Crusades to free the Holy Land from the Muslims, and his own
country having just driven the last of the heathen Mohammedans
from Granada, less than thirty years prior, Cortez led his troops
inland as Crusaders in a Holy cause. (Coincidentally, this was the
exactly same time the Reformation was beginning in Europe
through Martin Luther.)

Cortez came to free a nation from barbaric pagan cannibalism.
His troops soon met with one horrendous sight after another:
human hearts that had been cut out of living prisoners found
nailed to temple walls; pyramid style temples covered with
human blood; bodies of men and boys without arms or legs;
human skulls stacked on poles; hundreds of thousands of human
skulls regularly arranged in piles; gnawed human bones piled in
houses and streets; wooden houses, built with gratings, jammed
full of captives being fattened up for sacrifice; pagan priests
matted with dried human blood, covered with the stench of
carrion, practicing sodomy; humans sacrificed on pagan altars
and then rolled down temple steps where frenzied hoards ate
their bodies; devotees eating the fresh carcasses of those who
were sacrificed; roasted human arms, legs and heads; warriors
eating the corpses of those they slew in battle, etc....[255]

This was a result of their religion; they believed that all the
universe was one and that people were just a part of the universe.
They believed that the Sun god needed human blood to live and
that the Aztecs were responsible to feed him the blood he needed
daily.

As the Spanish troops went from town to town, the Indian
tribes were elated that they would be set free from the Aztec rule.
Cortez would immediately free the captives awaiting sacrifice,

break the idols, roll them down the temple steps, then erect a cross and preach Christ unto them. Francisco Lopez de Gomara, Cortez' personal secretary and chaplain, reported one such instance in Cozumel:

> So Jeronimo de Aguilar preached to them about salvation, and, either because of what he told them, or because of the beginning they had already made, they were pleased to have their idols cast down, and they even assisted at it, breaking into small pieces what they had formerly held sacred. And soon our Spaniards had left not a whole idol standing, and in each chapel they set up a Cross or the image of Our Lady, whom all the islanders worshipped with prayer and great devotion....
>
> They begged Cortez to leave someone behind to teach them to believe in the God of the Christians; but he did not dare consent, for fear they might kill the preacher, and also because he had few priests and friars with him. And in this he did wrong, in view of their earnest request and supplications.[256]

After defeating the Tabascan tribe, Cortez preached to them through the interpretation of Jeronimo de Aguilar, a Catholic priest who had been shipwrecked on Yucatan eight years earlier and had learned the language. As reported by Gomara:

> Cortez told them of their blindness and great vanity in worshipping many gods and making sacrifices of human blood to them, and in thinking that those images, being mute and soulless, made by the Indians with their own hands, were capable of doing good or harm. He then told them of a single God, Creator of Heaven and earth and men, whom the Christians worshiped and served, and whom all men should worship and serve.
>
> In short, after he had explained the Mysteries to them, and how the Son of God had suffered on the Cross, they accepted it and broke up their idols. Thus it was that with great reverence, before a large concourse of Indians, and with many tears on the part of the Spaniards, a Cross was erected in the temple of Potonchan, and our men first, kneeling, kissed and worshiped it, and after them the Indians.[257]

Meeting resistance with the Cempoallan tribe, before they finally relented, one of Cortez' men suggested accommodating them for the time being. Cortez adamantly replied:

How can we ever accomplish anything worth doing for the honour of God if we do not first abolish these sacrifices made to idols?[258]

Cortez and his men fought numerous battles against insurmountable odds. His small band repeatedly fought victoriously against the deadly spears, arrows and ambushes of the murderous tribes. Cortez' success depended upon the Indian tribes who fought alongside as he championed their cause of freedom from the bloody Aztecs and their quotas of sacrificed prisoners. In giving battle instructions to his troops, Cortez exhorted:

> Sirs, let us follow our banner which bears the sign of the Holy Cross, and through it we shall conquer![259]

When ambassadors from Montezuma arrived bearing gifts, Cortez took the opportunity to preach to them through an interpreter.

Bernal Diaz del Castillo, a soldier who served with Cortez, recorded the scene:

> When Tendile and Pitalpitoque [Montezuma's ambassadors] saw us thus kneeling, as they were very intelligent, they asked what was the reason that we humbled ourselves before a tree cut in that particular way. As Cortez heard this remark he said to the Padre de la Merced who was present: "It is a good opportunity, father, as we have good material at hand, to explain through our interpreters matters touching our holy faith."
>
> And then he delivered a discourse to the Caciques so fitting to the occasion that no good theologian could have bettered it.
>
> After telling them that we were Christians and relating all matters pertaining to our holy religion, he told them that their idols were not good but evil things which would take flight at the presence of the sign of the cross, for on a similar cross the Lord of Heaven and earth and all created things suffered passion and death; that it is He whom we adore and in whom we believe, our true God, Jesus Christ, who had been willing to suffer and die in order to save the whole human race; that the third day He rose again and is now in heaven; and that by Him we shall all be judged.
>
> Cortez said many other things very well expressed, which they would report them to their prince Montezuma. Cortez also told them

that one of the objects for which our great Emperor had sent us to their country was to abolish human sacrifices and the other evil rites which they practised...[260]

Upon reaching Mexico city, Montezuma asked Cortez if he was the god Quetzalcoatl, who was predicted to return from the east, as a white man with a beard and blue eyes, to stamp out human sacrifice and deliver the oppressed.
Cortez replied:

It was true that we came from where the sun rose, and were the vassals and servants of a great Prince called the Emperor Don Carlos, who held beneath his sway many and great princes, and that the Emperor having heard of him and what a great prince he was, had sent us to these parts to see him, and to beg them to become Christians, the same as our Emperor and all of us, so that his soul and those of all his vassals might be saved.[261]

Montezuma was in awe of Cortez and his men, primarily because of the signs and portents that had ominously foretold Quetzalcoatl's return and the end of the Aztec empire, such as: the water of the lake around Mexico City boiling over due to volcanic eruption, the sky being lit with northern lights, comets, earthquakes, the temple of the sun god catching fire, the king's sister revived from her grave and saying strange beings would enter the country and ruin it, an eerie wailing noise at night, etc....[262] According to soldier Bernal Diaz del Castillo's account, Cortez discoursed with Montezuma further:

We told them we were Christians and worshipped one true and only God, named Jesus Christ, who suffered death and passion to save us, and we told them that a cross (when they asked why we worshipped it) was a sign of the other Cross on which our Lord God was crucified for our salvation; and that the death and passion which he suffered was for the salvation of the whole human race, which was lost, and that this our God rose on the third day and is now in heaven, and it is He who made the heavens and the earth, the sea and the sands, and created all the things that are in the world, and He sends the rain and the dew, and nothing happens in the world without His holy will.
That we believe in Him and worship Him; but that those whom they look upon as gods are not so, but are devils, which are worse, and

they could see that they were evil and of little worth, for where we had set up crosses such as those his ambassadors had seen, they dared not appear before them, through fear of them, and that as time went on they would notice this....

He explained to him very clearly about creation of the world, and how we are all brothers, sons of one father and one mother who were called Adam and Eve, and how such a brother as our great Emperor, grieving for the perdition of so many souls, such as those which their idols were leading to Hell, where they burn in living flames, had sent us, so that after what he [Montezuma] had now heard he would put a stop to it and they would no longer adore these Idols or sacrifice Indian men and women to them, for we were all brethren, nor should they commit sodomy or thefts.

He also told them that, in the course of time, our Lord and King would send some men among us who lead very holy lives, much better than we do, who will explain to them all about it, for at present we merely came to give them due warning. And so he prayed him to do what he was asked and carry it into effect.[263]

After that, Montezuma showed Cortez and his men their temples. There was a theatre made of human skulls and mortar, wherein Gonzalo de Umbria counted 136,000 skulls, which included those in the steps and on poles. A tower was made of skulls too numerous to count. There were obsidian knives, stone altars, black-robed priests with hair matted down with human blood, idols with basins for human blood, walls and steps covered with human blood and gore, an idol made out of seeds kneaded and ground with the blood of virgins and babies, pits where the human bodies were thrown after people had eaten off the arms and legs, etc....

Bernal Diaz del Castillo records Cortez' comments to Montezuma after viewing all the horrible sights:

> Our Captain said to Montezuma through our interpreter, half laughing: "Señor Montezuma, I do not understand how such a great Prince and wise man as you are has not come to the conclusion, in your mind, that these idols of yours are not gods, but evil things that are called devils, and so that you may know it and all your priests may see it clearly, do me the favour to approve of my placing a cross here on the top of this tower...."[264]

Soon after, Cortez placed Montezuma under house arrest in his own palace, destroyed the pagan idols and caused a great uproar in the city. Montezuma, who had developed a friendship with Cortez, tried to quell the rage but was pelted with rocks by his own people. Deeply depressed and feeling a seemingly providential loss of control over his empire and his life, Montezuma died. Bernal Diaz del Castillo recalled the Spaniards' response:

> Cortez wept for him, and all of us Captains and soldiers, and there was no man among us who knew him and was intimate with him, who did not bemoan him as though he were our father, and it is not to be wondered at, considering how good he was. [265]

Cortez fought against overwhelming odds to make his way out of the city, although with great loss to his ranks. He battled thousands of Aztecs in his campaign to get back to the coast.

After several months of recovery, Cortez decided to mount a final attack on Mexico City. On December 26, 1520, Cortez addressed his force of 540 soldiers and 40 cavalry, who were armed with 80 crossbows and nine muskets, saying:

> My brothers, I give many thanks to Jesus Christ to see you now cured of your wounds and free from sickness. I am glad to find you armed and eager to return to Mexico [City] to avenge the deaths of your comrades and recover that great city. This, I trust in God, we shall soon do, because we have with us Tlazcala and many other provinces, and because you are who you are, and the enemies the same as they have been, and we shall do so for the Christian Faith that we proclaim...
>
> The principal reason for our coming to these parts is to glorify and preach the Faith of Jesus Christ....
>
> We cast down their idols, put a stop to their sacrificing and eating of men, and began to convert the Indians during the few days we were in Mexico.
>
> It is not fitting that we abandon all that good that we began, rather, we should go wherever our Faith and the sins of our enemies call us.
>
> They, indeed, deserve a great whipping and punishment, because, if you remember, the people of the city, not satisfied with killing an infinite number of men, women, and children in sacrifices to their

gods (devils, rather), eat them afterward, a cruel thing, abhorrent to God and punished by Him, and one which all good men, especially Christians, abominate, forbid, and chastise.

Moreover, without penalty or shame, they commit that accursed sin because of which five cities, along with Sodom, were burned and destroyed.

Well, then, what greater or better reward could one desire here on earth than to uproot these evils and plant the Faith among such cruel men, by proclaiming the Holy Gospel?

Let us go, then, and serve God, honor our nation, magnify our King, and enrich ourselves, for the conquest of Mexico is all these things. Tomorrow, with the help of God, we shall begin.[266]

Inscribed on Hernando Cortez' coat of arms was:

Judicium Domini apprehendit eos, et fortitudo ejus corroboravit bracchium meum. (The judgement of the Lord overtook them; His might strengthened my arm.)[267]

&

John Cotton (1584-1652), a Puritan scholar and clergyman, was perhaps the most influential leader in shaping the destiny of Puritan New England. Principles stated in his sermons were frequently practiced by civil authorities immediately. In 1636, Rev. John Cotton delineated a code of laws, in which he included the phrase:

John Cotton

the Law of Nature, delivered by God.[268]

He ended his work with the scripture reference, Isaiah 33:22:

The Lord is our Judge.
The Lord is our Law-giver.
The Lord is our King, He will save us.[269]

In reflection on the human tendency to be corrupted by power, Rev. John Cotton wrote:

Let all the world learn to give mortall men no greater power than they are content they shall use, for use it they will: and unless they be better taught of God, they will use it ever and anon....

For whatever transcendent power is given, will certainly over-run those that give it, and those that receive it: there is a straine in a mans heart that will sometime or other runne out to excesse, unlesse the Lord restraine it, but it is not good to venture it: It is necessary therefore, that all power that is on earth be limited, Church-power or other...

It is counted a matter of danger to the State to limit Prerogatives; but it is a further danger, not to have them limited: They will be like a Tempest, if they be not limited: A Prince himselfe cannot tell where hee will confine himselfe, nor can the people tell....

√It is therefore fit for every man to be studious of the bounds which the Lord hath set: and for the People, in whom fundamentally all power lyes, to give as much power as God in his word gives to men:

And it is meet that Magistrates in the commonwealth, and so Officers in Churches should desire to know the utmost bounds of their own power, and it is safe for both:

All intrenchment upon the bounds which God hath not given, they are not enlargements, but burdens and snares: They will certainly lead the spirit of a man out of his way sooner or later.

It is wholesome and safe to be dealt withall as God deales with the vast Sea; Hitherto shalt thou come, but there shalt thou stay thy proud waves: and therefore if they be but banks of simple sand, they will be good enough to check the vast roaring Sea.[270]

John Cotton declared:

What He hath planted, He will maintain. Every plantation His right hand hath not planted shall be rooted up, but His own plantation shall prosper and flourish.

When He promiseth peace and safety, what enemies shall be able to make the promise of God of none effect? Neglect not wall and bulwarks and fortifications for your own defense, but ever let the name of the Lord be your strong tower, and the word of His promise, the rock of your refuge.

His word that made heaven and earth will not fail, till heaven and earth be no more....If God make a covenant to be a God to thee and thine, then it is thy part to see to it that thy children and servants be God's people.[271]

As the Massachusetts Bay Colony grew, churches were built and towns sprang up around them. Inevitably, though, some people stopped going to church. John Cotton remarked:

But when men thus depart, God usually...[entertains] them with such restless agitations that they are driven to repent of their former rashness, and many times return to the church from which they had broken away.[272]

ّ◆

William Cowper (1731-1800), was a famous English poet who pioneered the English Romantic movement. His works include: *Table Talk; Truth; Expostulations; On Receipt of My Mother's Picture;* and *The Castaway.* His most renowned work, published in 1785, was *The Task,* which included his best-known poem, "The Diverting History of John Gilpin." He also completed a translation of Homer. In 1779, William Cowper published *The Olney Hymns,* which include: "Oh! for a Closer Walk with God," "There Is a Fountain Filled with Blood," and "God Moves in a Mysterious Way."

In his work, *The Task,* 1785, William Cowper composed the poem, "Winter Walk at Noon":

> Nature is but a name for an effect,
> Whose cause is God.[273]

ّ◆

Samuel Sullivan Cox (1824-1889), was a Congressman, lawyer, diplomat, journalist and popular speaker. In the work *Memorial Addresses,* published by the United States Congress in 1890, Samuel Sullivan Cox's address to Congress is recorded:

Samuel Sullivan Cox

> I believe in the religion which was taught and exemplified in the life of the Nazarene, and I never fail to bear testimony to the ennobling and purifying influence of the Christian religion....
> There was a poignancy in my heart when I saw the old church, where I so often worshipped, razed to the ground. Was it not there I attended my first Sunday-school? There it was that I learned my Bible verses, and received my red and blue tickets for proficiency. There it was that I accomplished the memorable task of reciting all of St. Paul

to the Romans....

Those early memories were cut in durable stone. Tarnished by worldliness, dusted with the activities of life, they have pursued me through the various vicissitudes of professional, literary, and political life.

They became the nucleus of studies in college; the very coat of mail in the struggles against selfishness and skepticism; in fine, they prefigured and preordained my choice of spiritual belief against the delusive sophistries of new philosophies and mere material science.

They have enabled me, in following and studying the physical advancement of the past century, to perceive in all the atoms, forms, and forces of nature and the phenomena of mind, the truth and benignity of the great scheme of human redemption, which is founded on the veracity of Christ, and becomes, with lapsing years, more beautiful with the white radiance of an ennobling spirituality.[274]

ða

Richard Crashaw (1613-1649), was an English *Metaphysical poet*, known for using striking figures of speech. Associated with John Donne, and a contemporary of both John Bunyan and John Milton, Richard Crashaw wrote, in 1652, his *Hymn of the Nativity:*

> Poor world (said I) what wilt thou do
> To entertain this starry stranger?
> Is this the best thou canst bestow?
> A cold, and not too cleanly, manger?
> Contend, ye powers of heav'n and earth,
> To fit a bed for this huge birth.[275]

ða

Oliver Cromwell (1599-1658), held the title of Lord-Protector of the English Commonwealth. Parliament, at one point, offered him the title of King of England, but he refused. He was a strong supporter of religious freedom, and at one time even considered emigrating to the Puritan Colony in America.

During the Civil War in England, his cavalry was the most-powerful and best-drilled regiment in England, earning the reputation of "Ironsides." He chose soldiers for their religious enthusiasm as well as for their military forcefulness, and he did not lose a single battle.

The persecuted Christian movement known as the Society of Friends, or Quakers, grew rapidly in England during Cromwell's rule; even William Penn, founder of Pennsylvania, became a Quaker. George Fox, founder of the Society of Friends, befriended Cromwell. When the Puritan movement within the Anglican Church split into the Presbyterian and Independent, Cromwell became an Independent. On August 3, 1650, in his *Letter to the General Assembly of the Church of Scotland,* Oliver Cromwell wrote:

> I beseech you, in the bowels of Christ, think it possible you may be mistaken.[276]

On September 12, 1654, in a message to Parliament, Cromwell asserted:

> Necessity hath no law. Feigned necessities, imaginary necessities...are the greatest cozenage that men can put upon the Providence of God, and make pretenses to break rules by.[277]

Oliver Cromwell prayed:

> Lord, though wretched and miserable, I am in covenant with Thee through grace, and I will come unto Thee for my people....
> Make the name of Christ glorious in the world. Teach those who look too much on Thy instruments to depend on Thyself more. Pardon such as desire to trample on the dust of a poor worm, for they are Thine too, and pardon the folly of this short prayer, for Jesus Christ, His Sake.[278]

&

William Thomas Cummings (1903-1944), was a chaplain in the U.S. Army at the beginning of World War II. He was eventually captured by the Japanese and died when his unmarked ship was sunk en route from the Philippines to Japan. While serving with the American troops in defending the Philippines, Father Cummings gave a stirring field sermon at Bataan in 1942, declaring:

> There are no atheists in the foxholes.[279]

&

D

The Dallas High Schools September, 1946, published a *Bible Study Course—New Testament, Bulletin No. 170.* It was authorized by the Board of Education, April 23, 1946, and printed in The Dallas Public Schools Printshop, Dallas, Texas:

> Foreword....the Dallas public schools allowed one-half credit toward high-school graduation for the successful completion of a general survey course in the Bible, given in the churches and Sunday schools of the city. In 1939, it was decided to provide separate courses in the Old and the New Testaments, each course carrying one-half unit of credit toward high-school graduation.
>
> E.B. Comstock,
> Assistant Superintendent
> in Charge of High Schools[1]

INTRODUCTION
REGULATIONS GOVERNING
NEW TESTAMENT STUDY COURSE

1. Classes may be organized by any Sunday school or church or any other religious organization for the purpose of studying the Bible in their respective organizations with a view to obtaining high-school credit. Successful completion of the course gives one-half unit credit toward high-school graduation.

2. An application blank, giving necessary information about the class, must be filled out and filed with the Assistant Superintendent in charge of Dallas High Schools.

3. There must be a minimum of forty class periods of 90 minutes net teaching time; or sixty 60-minute periods, net time; or eighty 45-minute periods, net time. In no case will fewer than forty different class sessions be accepted.

4. The text used is the NEW TESTAMENT STUDY COURSE, a

syllabus published by the authority of the Dallas Board of Education for use in Bible Study credit classes.

5....9.²

MINIMUM REQUIREMENTS
(NEW TESTAMENT)

The course is itself a "minimum course," since teachers are expected to supplement rather than subtract from the topics included. The following summary requirements are listed for purpose of emphasis and review:

1. Ability to name and classify the books of the Bible (common classifications).

2. General knowledge of the New Testament as outlined in the course of study. Reading of the entire New Testament is required.

3. Ability to reproduce the memory passages indicated in connection with the lessons and given in full in the appendix.

4....10.³

APPENDIX
REQUIRED MEMORY VERSES
(for review purposes)

(Pupils should be able to reproduce from memory each of the following quotations when given the accompanying lead, the book, chapter, and verse reference.)

LESSON I.
1. The pre-existence of Christ:
In the beginning was the Word, and the Word was with God, and the Word was God....All things were made by him; and without him was not anything made that was made....And the Word was made flesh, and dwelt among us, (and we beheld his glory, the glory as of the only begotten of the Father,) full of grace and truth. (John 1:1, 3, 14)

LESSON II.
2. Jesus to the devil in the wilderness:
It is written, Man shall not live by bread alone, but by every word that proceedeth out of the mouth of God....It is written again, Thou shalt not tempt the Lord thy God....Get thee hence, Satan: for it is written, Thou shalt worship the Lord thy God, and him only shalt thou serve. (Matthew 4:4, 7, 10)

LESSON III.
    3. The purpose of Christ's coming:
For God so loved the world that he gave his only begotten Son, that whosoever believeth in him should not perish, but have eternal life. (John 3:16)

LESSON IV....LESSON XLV.[4]

❪

Charles Anderson Dana (1819-1897), was an American newspaper journalist and the editor-in-chief of the *New York Sun*, under whose management it grew to become one of the largest newspapers in the country. He also served as Assistant Secretary of War during the Civil War. Charles Dana wrote:

Charles Anderson Dana

    I believe in Christianity; that it is the religion taught to men by God Himself in Person on earth. I also believe the Bible to be a Divine revelation. Christianity is not comparable with any other religion. It is the religion which came from God's own lips, and therefore the only true religion. The incarnation is a fact, and Christianity is based on revealed truth.
    There are some books that are absolutely indispensable to the kind of education that we are contemplating, and to the profession that we are now considering; and of all these, the most indispensable, the most useful, the one whose knowledge is most effective, is the Bible.
    There is no Book from which more valuable lessons can be learned. I am considering it now as a manual of utility, or professional preparation, and professional use for a journalist.
    There is no Book whose style is more suggestive and more instructive, from which you learn more directly that sublime simplicity which never exaggerates, which recounts the greatest event with solemnity, of course, but without sentimentality or affection, none which you open with such confidence and lay down with such reverence; there is no Book like the Bible.
    When you get into a controversy and want exactly the right answer, when you are looking for an expression, what is there that closes a dispute like a verse from the Bible? What is it that sets up the

right principle for you, which pleads for a policy, for a cause, so much as the right passage of the Holy Scripture? [5]

ﺰ

James Dwight Dana (1813-1895), was a famous American geologist and Yale professor, succeeding the renowned Professor Silliman. He was the president of the Geological Society of America, as well as the American Association for the Advancement of Science. James Dana became the editor-in-chief of *The American Journal of Science* and was the author of numerous books on mineralogy and geology, including *System of Mineralogy and Manual of Geology.* James Dana stated:

James Dwight
Dana

> That grand old Book of God still stands; and this old earth, the more its leaves are turned over and pondered, the more it will sustain and illustrate the Sacred Word. [6]

ﺰ

Charles Robert Darwin (1809-1882), was a British naturalist who propounded a theory of origins known as evolution. In his work, *Origin of Species,* 1859, Darwin wrote:

> To suppose that the eye with all its inimitable contrivances for adjusting the focus to different distances, for admitting different amounts of light, and for the correction of spherical and chromatic aberration, could have been formed by natural selection, seems, I freely confess, absurd in the highest degree. [7]

> Why then is not every geological formation and every stratum full of such intermediate links? Geology assuredly does not reveal any such finely graduated organic chain; and this, perhaps, is the most obvious and serious objection which can be urged against the theory. [8]

> For I am well aware that scarcely a single point is discussed in this volume on which facts cannot be adduced, often apparently leading to

conclusions directly opposite to those at which I arrived.[9]

There is a grandeur in this view of life, with its several powers, having been originally breathed by the Creator into a few forms or into one.[10]

Reflecting on his work near the end of his life, Charles Darwin confessed:

I was a young man with unformed ideas. I threw out queries, suggestions, wondering all the time over everything; and to my astonishment the ideas took like wildfire. People made a religion of them.[11]

Being bedridden many months before his death, Darwin was often found reading. When one visitor asked what it was he was studying, he replied:

Hebrews, still Hebrews. "The Royal Book," I call it.[12]

After speaking on "the holiness of God" and "the grandeur of this Book,"[13] Darwin declared:

Christ Jesus and his salvation. Is not that the best theme?[14]

ᴢᴀ

Jonathan
Dayton

Jonathan Dayton (1760-1824), one of the signers of the Constitution of the United States, was a delegate from New Jersey, a U.S. Senator and the Speaker of the House. The city of Dayton, Ohio, was named after him.

On June 28, 1787, at the Constitutional Convention in Philadelphia, Jonathan Dayton wrote down the effects on Congress of Dr. Benjamin Franklin's monumental speech calling for Congress to be opened with prayer every day:

The Doctor sat down; and never did I behold a countenance at once so dignified and delighted as was that of Washington at the close of the address; nor were the members of the convention generally less affected. The words of the venerable Franklin fell upon our ears with a weight and authority, even greater that we may suppose an oracle to have had in a Roman senate![15]

ᵹ

The Declaration of Independence July 2, 1776, was approved in wording by the Continental Congress. On July 4, 1776, the delegates voted to accept it and declare America's independence from Great Britain. On July 8, 1776, the Declaration was read in public for the first time, outside Independence Hall, Philadelphia, accompanied by the ringing of the Liberty Bell. On July 19, Congress ordered it engrossed in script on parchment, and on August 2, 1776, the members of Congress signed the parchment copy:

> When in the Course of human events, it becomes necessary for one people to dissolve the political bands which have connected them with another, and to assume among the powers of the earth, the separate and equal station to which the Laws of Nature and of Nature's God entitles them...
>
> We hold these truths to be self-evident, that all men are created equal. That they are endowed by their Creator with certain inalienable Rights, that among these are Life...
>
> We, Therefore, the Representatives of the United States of America, in General Congress, Assembled, appealing to the Supreme Judge of the world for the rectitude of our intentions...
>
> And for the support of this Declaration, with a firm reliance on the protection of Divine Providence, we mutually pledge to each other our Lives, our Fortunes, and our sacred Honor.[16]

On July 3, 1776, the day following the approval by Congress of the Declaration of Independence, John Adams wrote to his wife, Abigail:

> I am apt to believe that it will be celebrated by succeeding generations as the great anniversary Festival. It ought to be commemorated, as the day of deliverance, by solemn acts of devotion to God Almighty.[17]

"The Signing of the Declaration of Independence"
This engraving after John Trumbull's painting (which appears on the
front cover of this book), portrays the presentation of the Declaration
to the Congress by the committee which prepared it.

As the parchment copy of the Declaration of Independence was being signed by the members of the Continental Congress, August 2, 1776, Samuel Adams declared:

> We have this day restored the Sovereign to Whom all men ought to be obedient. He reigns in heaven and from the rising to the setting of the sun, let His kingdom come.[18]

❧

Daniel Defoe (1660-1731), was the renowned English novelist who authored the world famous novel, *Robinson Crusoe,* published in 1719. In volume III of *A Selection from the Works of Daniel Defoe,* he declared:

> In what glorious colors do the Scriptures, upon all occasions,

represent these two hand-in-hand graces, faith and repentance? There is not one mention of faith in the whole Scriptures but what is recommended in some way or other to our admiration, and to our practice; it is the foundation and the top-stone of all religion, the right hand to lead, and the left hand to support, in the whole journey of the Christian, even through this world, and into the next; in a word, it is the sum and substance of the Gospel foundation.[19]

How incongruous is it to the decoration of the government, that a man should be punished for drunkenness and set in stocks for swearing, but shall have liberty to deny the God of Heaven, and dispute against the very sum and substance of the Christian doctrine; shall banter the Scripture, and make ballads of the Pentateuch; turn all the principles of religion, the salvation of the soul, the death of our Saviour, and the revelation of the Gospel into ridicule. And shall we pretend to reformation of manners, and suppressing immoralities, while such as this is the general mixture of conversation?

If a man talk against the government, or speak scurrilously of the King, he is led to the old Bailey, and from thence to the pillory, or whipping-post, and it should be so; but he may speak treason against the Majesty of Heaven, deny the Godhead of the Redeemer, and make a jest of the Holy Ghost, and thus affront the Power we all adore, and yet with impunity.[20]

In his first great work, *The True Born Englishman,* a satirical poem written in 1701, Daniel Defoe quipped:

> Whenever God erects a house of prayer
> The devil always builds a chapel there;
> And 'twill be found, upon examination,
> The latter has the largest congregation.[21]

~

DeKalb County Community School District (prior to 1967), endorsed this poem to be recited in its kindergarten classes:

> We thank you for the flowers so sweet; We thank you for the food we eat; We thank you for the birds that sing; We thank you for everything.[22]

~

DELAWARE

Seal of Delaware

The Constitution of the State of Delaware 1776, stated:

Article XXII Every person who shall be chosen a member of either house, or appointed to any office or place of trust...shall...make and subscribe the following declaration, to wit: "I, _____, do profess faith in God the Father, and in Jesus Christ His only Son, and in the Holy Ghost, one God, blessed for evermore; I do acknowledge the holy scriptures of the Old and New Testament to be given by divine inspiration."[23] (until 1792)

Delaware's Constitution also stated:

[It is] the duty of all men frequently to assemble together for the public worship of the Author of the Universe....[although] no man ought to be compelled to attend any religious worship.[24]

༄

Denver Post January 20, 1905, reported this revealing article:

Remarkable Outburst of Gospel Sentiment....Noonday Meetings Draw Congregations Unprecedented in Numbers.

For two hours at midday all Denver was held in a spell....The marts of trade were deserted between noon and two o'clock this afternoon, and all worldly affairs were forgotten, and the entire city was given over to meditation of higher things. The Spirit of the Almighty pervaded every nook.

Going to and coming from the great meetings, the thousands of men and women radiated this Spirit which filled them, and the clear Colorado sunshine was made brighter by the reflected glow of the light of God shining from happy faces.

Seldom has such a remarkable sight been witnessed—an entire great city, in the middle of a busy weekday, bowing before the throne of heaven and asking and receiving the blessings of the King of the Universe.[25]

༄

Alexis de Tocqueville (1805-1859), was a famous French statesman, historian and social philosopher. Beginning in 1831, he and Gustave de Beaumont toured the country of America for the purpose of observing the American people and their institutions. His two-part work, which was published in 1835 and 1840, was entitled *Democracy in America*. It has been described as "the most comprehensive and penetrating analysis of the relationship between character and society in America that has ever been written."[26] In it he related:

Upon my arrival in the United States the religious aspect of the country was the first thing that struck my attention; and the longer I stayed there, the more I perceived the great political consequences resulting from this new state of things.

In France I had almost always seen the spirit of religion and the spirit of freedom marching in opposite directions. But in America I found they were intimately united and that they reigned in common over the same country.[27]

Religion in America...must be regarded as the foremost of the political institutions of that country; for if it does not impart a taste for freedom, it facilitates the use of it. Indeed, it is in this same point of view that the inhabitants of the United States themselves look upon religious belief.

I do not know whether all Americans have a sincere faith in their religion—for who can search the human heart?—But I am certain that they hold it to be indispensable to the maintenance of republican institutions. This opinion is not peculiar to a class of citizens or a party, but it belongs to the whole nation and to every rank of society.[28]

The sects that exist in the United States are innumerable. They all differ in respect to the worship which is due to the Creator; but they all agree in respect to the duties which are due from man to man.

Each sect adores the Deity in its own peculiar manner, but all sects preach the same moral law in the name of God....

Moreover, all the sects of the United States are comprised within the great unity of Christianity, and Christian morality is everywhere the same.[29]

In the United States the sovereign authority is religious,...there is no country in the world where the Christian religion retains a greater influence over the souls of men than in America, and there can be no greater proof of its utility and of its conformity to human nature than that its influence is powerfully felt over the most enlightened and free nation of the earth. [30]

In the United States, if a political character attacks a sect [denomination], this may not prevent even the partisans of that very sect, from supporting him; but if he attacks all the sects together [Christianity], every one abandons him and he remains alone. [31]

I do not question that the great austerity of manners that is observable in the United States arises, in the first instance, from religious faith.... its influence over the mind of woman is supreme, and women are the protectors of morals. There is certainly no country in the world where the tie of marriage is more respected than in America or where conjugal happiness is more highly or worthily appreciated. [32]

In the United States the influence of religion is not confined to the manners, but it extends to the intelligence of the people.... Christianity, therefore reigns without obstacle, by universal consent; the consequence is, as I have before observed, that every principle of the moral world is fixed and determinate. [33]

The safeguard of morality is religion, and morality is the best security of law as well as the surest pledge of freedom. [34]

The Americans combine the notions of Christianity and of liberty so intimately in their minds, that it is impossible to make them conceive the one without the other. [35]

Christianity is the companion of liberty in all its conflicts-the cradle of its infancy, and the divine source of its claims. [36]

They brought with them... a form of Christianity, which I cannot better describe, than by styling it a democratic and republican religion.... From the earliest settlement of the emigrants, politics and religion contracted an alliance which has never been dissolved. [37]

The Christian nations of our age seem to me to present a most alarming spectacle; the impulse which is bearing them along is so strong that it cannot be stopped, but it is not yet so rapid that it cannot be guided: their fate is in their hands; yet a little while and it may be no longer. [38]

Alexis de Tocqueville wrote that he found in America:

An ostensible respect for Christian morality and virtue. [39]... [and that] almost all education is intrusted to the clergy. [40]

Alexis de Tocqueville is attributed with the observation:

I sought for the key to the greatness and genius of America in her harbors...; in her fertile fields and boundless forests; in her rich mines and vast world commerce; in her public school system and institutions of learning. I sought for it in her democratic Congress and in her matchless Constitution.

Not until I went into the churches of America and heard her pulpits flame with righteousness did I understand the secret of her genius and power.

America is great because America is good, and if America ever ceases to be good, America will cease to be great. [41]

In August of 1831, while traveling through Chester County in New York, Alexis de Tocqueville had the opportunity to observe a court case. He wrote:

While I was in America, a witness, who happened to be called at the assizes of the county of Chester (state of New York), declared that he did not believe in the existence of God or in the immortality of the soul. The judge refused to admit his evidence, on the ground that the witness had destroyed beforehand all confidence of the court in what he was about to say. The newspapers related the fact without any further comment. *The New York Spectator* of August 23d, 1831, relates the fact in the following terms:

"The court of common pleas of Chester county (New York), a few days since rejected a witness who declared his disbelief in the existence of God. The presiding judge remarked, that he had not before been aware that there was a man living who did not believe in the existence of God; that this belief constituted the sanction of all testimony in a court of justice: and that he knew of no case in a Christian country, where a witness had been permitted to testify without such belief." [42]

෨

Charles Dickens (1812-1870), was a distinguished English author, whose works include: *Pickwick Papers, 1837; Oliver Twist, 1838; David Copperfield, 1849-50; Great Expectations, 1860-61; Tale of Two*

Cities, 1859; and the favorite, *A Christmas Carol,* 1843. Charles Dickens remarked:

> The New Testament is the very best book that ever was or ever will be known in the world.[43]

Perhaps the most touching moment in Charles Dickens' famous novel, *A Christmas Carol,* which sold 6,000 copies the first day, was Tiny Tim's line:

> God bless us every one.[44]

Charles Dickens remarked:

> I love little children, and it is not a slight thing when they, who are fresh from God, love us.[45]

In 1849, 21 years before his death, Charles Dickens wrote a work expressly for his children, of which he and his wife, Catherine, had ten. Entitled *The Life of Our Lord,* the work included the miraculous events surrounding Jesus' birth, His miracle ministry, His death on the cross and His resurrection. The work, written without thought of publication, was left in the possession of his sister-in-law, Miss Georgia Hogarth. At her death in 1917, it came into the possession of his son, Sir Henry Fielding Dickens, who made provision in his *Will* for it to be published. In March of 1934, Marie Dickens proceeded to have it published, in serial form, by the Associated Newspapers, Ltd., of London. In it, Charles Dickens expressed:

> My dear children, I am very anxious that you should know something about the History of Jesus Christ. For everybody ought to know about Him. No one ever lived, who was so good, so kind, so gentle, and so sorry for all people who did wrong, or were in anyway ill or miserable, as he was. And he is now in Heaven, where we hope to go, and to meet each other after we are dead, and there be happy always together, you never can think what a good place Heaven is, without knowing who he was and what he did....[46]

When the Star stopped, the wise men went in, and saw the Child with Mary his Mother....

John said, "Why should I baptize you, who are so much better than I!" Jesus Christ made answer, "Suffer it to be so now." So John baptized him. And when he was baptized, the sky opened, and a beautiful bird like a dove came flying down, and the voice of God, speaking up in Heaven, was heard to say, "This is my beloved son, in whom I am well pleased!"...

When he came out of the Wilderness, he began to cure sick people by only laying his hand upon them; for God had given him power to heal the sick, and to give sight to the blind, and to do many wonderful and solemn things of which I shall tell you more bye and bye, and which are called "The Miracles" of Christ. I wish you would remember that word, because I shall use it again, and I should like you to know that it means something which is very wonderful and which could not be done without God's leave and assistance....

Jesus turned this water into wine, by only lifting up his hand....

For God had given Jesus Christ the power to do such wonders; and he did them, that people might know he was not a common man, and might believe what he taught them, and also believe that God had sent him; and many people, hearing this, and hearing that he cured the sick, did begin to believe in him....

He stopped, and went into Simon Peter's boat, and asked him if he had caught many fish. Peter said No; though they had worked all night with their nets, they had caught nothing. Christ said, "let down the net again." They did so; and it was immediately so full of fish, that it required the strength of many men (who came and helped them) to lift it out of the water, and even then it was very hard to do. This was another of the miracles of Jesus Christ....

This Leper fell at the feet of Jesus Christ, and said "Lord! If thou wilt, thou cans't make me well!" Jesus, always full of compassion, stretched out his hand, and said "I will! Be thou well!" And his disease went away, immediately, and he was cured....

Jesus, full of pity, said "Arise! Take up thy bed, and go to thine own home!" And the man rose up and went away quite well; blessing him, and thanking God....

Then Jesus Christ, glad that the Centurion believed in him so truly, said "Be it so!" And the servant became well, from that moment....

Then he commanded the room to be cleared of the people that were in it, and going to the dead child, took her by the hand, and she rose up quite well, as if she had been only asleep. Oh what a sight it must have been to see her parents clasp her in their arms, and kiss her, and thank God, and Jesus Christ his Son, for such great Mercy!...

For they brought sick people out into the streets and roads

through which he passed, and cried out to him to touch them, and when he did, they became well....

The bearers of the bier standing still, he walked up to it and touched it with his hand, and said "Young Man! Arise." The dead man, coming to life again at the sound of the Saviour's voice, rose up and began to speak....

Jesus, coming near him, perceived that he was torn by an Evil Spirit, and cast the madness out of him, and into a herd of swine....

Our Saviour said to him, "take up thy bed and go away." And he went away, quite well....

Jesus ordered the stone to be rolled away, which was done. Then, after casting up his eyes, and thanking God, he said, in a loud and solemn voice, "Lazarus, come forth!" and the dead man, Lazarus, restored to life, came out among the people, and went home with his sisters. At this sight, so awful and affecting, many of the people there, believed that Christ was indeed the Son of God, come to instruct and save mankind....

Pilate was troubled in his mind to hear them so clamorous against Jesus Christ. His wife, too, had dreamed all night about it, and sent to him upon the Judgement Seat saying "Have nothing to do with that just man!"...

Bearing his cross, upon his shoulder, like the commonest and most wicked criminal, our blessed Saviour, Jesus Christ, surrounded by the persecuting crowd, went out of Jerusalem to a place called in the Hebrew language, Golgotha....

And crying "Father! Into thy hands I commend my Spirit!"—died. Then, there was a dreadful earthquake; and the great wall of the Temple, cracked; and the rocks were rent asunder. The guards, terrified at these sights, said to each other, "Surely this was the Son of God!"...

When that morning began to dawn, Mary Magdalene and the other Mary, and some other women, came to the Sepulchre, with some more spices which they had prepared. As they were saying to each other, "How shall we roll away the stone?" the earth trembled and shook, and an angel, descending from Heaven, rolled it back, and then sat resting on it. His countenance was like lightning, and his garments were white as snow....

As she gave this answer, she turned round, and saw Jesus standing behind her...Jesus pronounced her name, "Mary." Then she knew him, and starting, exclaimed "Master!"...

When they all three sat down to supper, he took some bread, and blessed it, and broke it....Looking on him in wonder they found that his face was changed before them, and that it was Christ himself; and as they looked on him, he disappeared....

While they were speaking, Jesus suddenly stood in the midst of all the company, and said "Peace be unto ye!" Seeing that they were greatly frightened, he shewed them his hands and feet, and invited them to touch Him; and, to encourage them and give them time to recover themselves, he ate a piece of broiled fish and a piece of honeycomb before them all....

And conducting his disciples at last, out of Jerusalem as far as Bethany, he blessed them, and ascended in a cloud to Heaven, and took His place at the right hand of God....

Two white-robed angels appeared among them, and told them that as they had seen Christ ascend to Heaven, so He would, one day, come descending from it, to judge the World....

When Christ was seen no more, the Apostles began to teach the People as He had commanded them....And through the power He had given them they healed the sick, and gave sight to the Blind, and speech to the Dumb, and Hearing to the Deaf....

They took the name of Christians from Our Saviour Christ, and carried Crosses as their sign, because on a Cross He had suffered Death....

So thousands upon thousands of Christians sprung up and taught the people and were cruelly killed, and were succeeded by other Christians, until the Religion gradually became the great religion of the World.

The End.[47]

In a letter to his youngest son, Edward, Charles Dickens wrote:

Try to do to others as you would like to have them do to you; and do not be discouraged if they fail sometimes. It is much better for you that they should fail in obeying the greatest rule laid down by our Saviour than that you should.

I have put a New Testament among your books for the very same reasons, and with the very same hopes, that made me write an easy account of it for you when you were a child, because it is the best Book that ever was or ever will be known in the world; and because it teaches you the best lessons by which any human creature who tries to be truthful and faithful to duty can possibly be guided.[48]

In a letter to his daughter, Charles Dickens wrote:

As your brothers have gone away, one by one, I have written to each such words as I am writing to you, and have entreated them all to guide themselves by this Book, putting aside the interpretations of men. You will remember that you have never at home been wearied about religious observances or mere formalities. I have always been anxious not to weary my children with such things before they were old enough to form opinions respecting them.

You will, therefore, understand the better that I now most solemnly impress upon you the truth and beauty of the Christian religion as it came from Jesus Christ Himself, and the impossibility of your going far wrong if you humbly and heartily respect it. Only one thing more on this head: The more we are in earnest as to feeling it, the less we are disposed to hold forth about it.

Never abandon the wholesome practice of saying your own private prayers night and morning. I have never abandoned it myself, and I know the comfort of it.[49]

Charles Dickens wrote in his *Will*:

I commit my soul to the mercy of God through our Lord and Saviour Jesus Christ, and I exhort my children to try and guide themselves by the teachings of the New Testament in its broad spirit, and to put no faith in any man's narrow construction of its letter here or there.[50]

John Dickinson

John Dickinson (1732-1808), a signer of the Constitution of the United States of America, was also a member of the Continental Congress and the writer of the first draft of The Articles of Confederation. He served as the President of the Supreme Executive Council of Pennsylvania, in addition to being an accomplished lawyer, planter and state legislator.

He was the founder of Dickinson College in Carlisle, Pennsylvania, in 1773, and known for giving generously to the Friends (Quakers) in Philadelphia for their educational pursuits.

Dickinson wrote persuasive letters regarding the soundness of Christian evidences and the authority of Scripture.[51] He campaigned for the passage of the Constitution by writing a series of letters which he signed "Fabius." This greatly contributed to Delaware and Pennsylvania being the first two states to ratify the Constitution.

John Dickinson is best remembered as "The Penman of the Revolution." His popular pamphlets gained wide circulation and became very influential in the cause of freedom. Some of his most famous ones were: *Petition to the King*, 1771; *The Declaration and Resolves of the First Continental Congress*, 1774; and *The Declaration of the cause of taking up arms*, 1775. His most stirring pamphlet was his *Letter from a Farmer in Pennsylvania:*

> But while Divine Providence, that gave me existence in a land of freedom, permits my head to think, my lips to speak, and my hand to move, I shall so highly and gratefully value the blessing received as to take care that my silence and inactivity shall not give my implied assent to my act, degrading my brethren and myself from the birthright, wherewith heaven itself "hath made us free."...
>
> I pray GOD that he may be pleased to inspire you and your posterity, to the latest ages, with a spirit of which I have an idea, that I find a difficulty to express.

John Dickinson's pamphlet "Letter from a Farmer in Pennsylvania" was instrumental in stirring the colonists to the cause of freedom.

I express it in the best manner I can, I mean a spirit that shall so guide you that it will be impossible to determine whether an American's character is most distinguishable for his loyalty to his Sovereign, his duty to his mother country, his love of freedom, or his affection for his native soil....

But, above all, let us implore the protection of that infinitely good and gracious Being [Proverbs 8:15] "by whom kings reign, and princes decree justice...."

A communication of her rights in general, and particularly of that great one, the foundation of all the rest—that their property, acquired with so much pain and hazard, should be disposed of by none but themselves—or to use the beautiful and emphatic language of the sacred scriptures [Micah 4:4] "that they should sit every man under his vine, and under his fig-tree, and NONE SHOULD MAKE THEM AFRAID...."

But whatever kind of minister he is, that attempts to innovate a single iota in the privileges of these colonies, him I hope you will undauntedly oppose; and that you will never suffer yourselves to be cheated or frightened into any unworthy obsequiousness.

On such emergencies you may surely, without presumption, believe that ALMIGHTY GOD himself will look upon your righteous contest with gracious approbation.[52]

In the Continental Congress of 1776, John Dickinson courageously bid farewell to the government of England:

The happiness of these Colonies has been, during the whole course of this fatal controversy, our first wish; their reconciliation with Great Britain our next: ardently have we prayed for the accomplishment of both.

But if we must renounce the one or the other, we humbly trust in the mercies of the Supreme Governor of the universe that we shall not stand condemned before His throne if our choice is determined by that law of self-preservation which his Divine wisdom has seen fit to implant in the hearts of His creatures.[53]

John Dickinson met with the other delegates from Pennsylvania less than two months before the Declaration of Independence was signed to suggest requirements for the members of the Convention to subscribe to before being seated. One of the recommended stipulations was the following declaration:

> I do profess faith in God the Father, and in Jesus Christ his Eternal Son the true God, and in the Holy Spirit, one God blessed for evermore; and I do acknowledge the Holy Scriptures of the Old and New Testaments to be given by Divine inspiration.[54]

In 1768, John Dickinson wrote in *The Liberty Song:*

> Then join hand in hand, brave Americans all!
> By uniting we stand, by dividing we fall![55]

ਣਾ

Thomas Dilworth in 1740, published his schoolbook, the *New Guide to the English Tongue,* in England. Benefitting from his experience as a distinguished educator and textbook writer, Thomas Dilworth's book grew in popularity, until, by 1765, it was universally adopted by all the New England schools in America. This book, which contained spelling, reading and grammar lessons, was "adorned with proper Scriptures." Its first lesson, comprised of words three letters long or less, went as such:

> No Man may put off the Law of God.
> The Way of God is no ill Way.
> My Joy is in God all the Day.
> A bad Man is a Foe to God.[56]

Noah Webster, known as the "Schoolmaster to America," used only Dilworth's book and the Bible in his earliest school. Thomas Dilworth said he wanted to:

> [Rescue] poor creatures from the Slavery of Sin and Satan by setting "the word of God for a Lantern to our feet and a Light to our Paths."[57]

Noah Webster

ਣਾ

Benjamin Disraeli (1804-1881), the 1st Earl of Beaconsfield, held the position of British Prime Minister in 1868, and again from 1874 to 1880. An accomplished author and diplomat, Benjamin Disraeli wrote:

The time will come when countless myriads will find music in the songs of Zion and solace in the parables of Galilee....The pupil of Moses may ask himself whether all the princes of the House of David have done so much for the Jews as the Prince who was crucified?[58]

૨&

Dr. James C. Dobson (1936-   ), is the founder and president of Focus on the Family, which produces a nationally syndicated radio program heard daily on over 2500 stations. He served for 14 years as an Associate Clinical Professor of Pediatrics at the University of Southern California School of Medicine, and served for 17 years on the Attending Staff of Children's Hospital of Los Angeles.

Dr. James Dobson's books include: *Hide and Seek, Self-Esteem for the Child*, 1974; *What Wives Wish Their Husbands Knew About Women*, 1975; *Preparing for Adolescence*, 1978; *The Strong-Willed Child*, 1978; *Love Must Be Tough*, 1983; and the best seller *Dare to Discipline*, 1970 (revised and updated in 1993), which has sold over 2 million copies. His film series, "Focus on the Family," has been seen by over 70 million people, being rivaled in success only by his later series, "Turn Your Heart Toward Home."

In 1980 Dr. Dobson was commended by President Carter for serving on the Task Force for the White House Conferences on the Family. In 1982 he was appointed by President Reagan to the National Advisory Commission for Juvenile Justice and Delinquency Prevention. He served as chairman of the United States Army Task Force on Families, was appointed to Attorney General Edwin Meese's Commission on Pornography in 1985, and served on the Attorney General's Advisory Board on Missing and Exploited Children in 1987.

In his January 1994 "Focus on the Family" newsletter, Dr. James Dobson concluded:

Can there be any doubt, hearing these echoes from the culture, that a great Civil War of Values is being waged in the Western nations, or that radical anti-family forces are making dramatic alterations in the way we think and act? I've seen that upheaval coming for almost a decade, but it is now evident to anyone who watches the evening television. The family is not simply disintegrating from natural forces and pressures. Its demise is being orchestrated at the highest levels of government, and by radical special-interest groups.

Am I concerned by these recent trends? Yes, the pattern of events reveals a society in dramatic decline. Indeed, the value system that has served us so well for 217 years may not survive the next decade. But before we throw in the towel, we need to look at numerous encouraging developments taking place simultaneously. There have been some exciting occurrences in the past year that may eventually lead to a better day. Let me share a few of those bright spots in what is otherwise a dismal scene:

High on the list of good news from 1993 is the prayer movement that is spreading across North America. What Marshall Foster calls "a quiet revolution" is occurring in thousands of churches and denominations....Dick Eastman's "Schools of Prayer" are experiencing similar enthusiastic acceptance.

Yet another burgeoning prayer effort is spearheaded by Dr. Joe Aldrich of Northwest Renewal Ministries. *Christianity Today* said this: "[They have] tapped into a thirst for prayer in a region known for its high proportion of unchurched citizens....Associate Jerry Dirks said, "We are seeing an amazing, divinely implanted hunger for God unlike anything we've seen."

The National Day of Prayer, headed by my wife, Shirley, is also experiencing an unprecedented response. Forty-nine of the 50 state governors issued prayer proclamations last year (Gov. Lowell Weicker of Connecticut was the lone exception). Celebrations were held in cities and communities all across America. So far this year, the requests for materials and advice are running far ahead of last season. "There is obviously a new awareness," said Shirley, "that prayer is the *only* answer to our terrible social problems."

Undoubtedly reflecting the same spiritual hunger, the Promise Keepers phenomenon has become one of the most exciting developments in the history of Christendom. Never has there been anything quite like it. When I was conducting family conferences 20 years ago, husbands typically attended because their wives asked (or insisted) that they do so. But last summer in Boulder, Colo., 50,000 men jammed Folson Field to worship, sing, learn and share in Christian fellowship. They came from every continent on earth, investing their vacations and often limited resources to draw nearer to God. And this was only the beginning. Similar events are scheduled next summer in Portland, Los Angeles, Boise, Boulder, Dallas and Indianapolis. (For information, write Promise Keepers, P.O. Box 18376, Boulder, CO 80308.)

Equally encouraging is the spiritual revival occurring within today's generation of students. Genuine faith is alive and well among these courageous kids who dare to defend their beliefs in a godless and often hostile environment. Huge numbers gathered around their school flags to pray last September in a program called "See You at the Pole." George Barna, of Barna Research Group, estimated that more than a million students participated nationwide.

There is more good news to share. In a scientific poll commissioned by the Family Research Council, Americans were asked if they would rather live in a community "that strongly upholds traditional family values" or a community "that is very tolerant of non-traditional life-styles." The findings were released in December, showing that citizens favored traditional values by a margin of 76 percent to 19 percent. Common sense is still alive and well in the population at large.

So what is going on here? How can such wholesome developments occur in the midst of almost unprecedented wickedness? Isn't that what the Scripture teaches us? Romans 5:20 says, "But where sin abounded, grace did much more abound." It is true today. As culture moves away from its Judeo-Christian roots, more and more people appear to recognize the devastation of sin and are turning to the Good News of the gospel.

This means as the long night of paganism descends on Western nations, we as believers are afforded an even greater opportunity to share the faith that burns within us. Therefore, we must not yield to discouragement, even when everything we cherish appears to be eroding. God is in control, and He can bring triumph out of tragedy.[59]

ða

John Donne (1572-1631), the chaplain to King James I in 1615, was considered one of England's greatest poets. Educated at Oxford and Cambridge, his works have been an inspiration to many writers. The line from his *Devotions upon Emergent Occasions*, 1624, "...send not to know for whom the bell tolls: it tolls for thee," inspired Ernest Hemingway's famous novel, *For Whom the Bell Tolls*, 1940. John Donne wrote:

> No man is an island, entire of itself; every man is a piece of the continent, a part of the main; if a clod be washed away by the sea, Europe is the less, as well as if a promontory were, as well as if a manor of thy friends or of thine own were; any man's death diminishes me, because I am involved in mankind; and therefore never send to know for whom the bell tolls; it tolls for thee.[60]

John Donne wrote in his *Holy Sonnets, no.14:*

> Batter my heart, three-personed God; for you
> As yet but knock, breathe, shine, and seek to mend.[61]

In his sermon before the Earl of Carlisle, delivered in the autumn of 1622, John Donne admonished:

> What gnashing is not a comfort, what gnawing of the worm is not a tickling, what torment is not a marriage bed to this damnation, to be secluded eternally, eternally, eternally from the sight of God?[62]

On Christmas day, 1625, John Donne declared:

> Now God comes to thee, not as in the dawning of the day, not as in the bud of the spring, but as the sun at noon to illustrate all shadows, as the sheaves in harvest, to fill all penuries, all occasions invite his mercies, and all times are his seasons.[63]

On December 12, 1626, at the funeral of Sir William Cokayne, John Donne proclaimed:

> I throw myself down in my chamber, and I call in and invite God and his angels thither, and when they are there, I neglect God and his angels, for the noise of a fly, for the rattling of a coach, for the whining of a door.[64]

&

Fedor Mikhailovich Dostoevski (1821-1881), was a famous Russian writer, ranking with Tolstoi as a master of the psychological novel. Having been sentenced by the czar to ten years of hard labor in Siberia, as a result of his revolutionary involvement, Dostoevski wrote with great ability on the human spirit and suffering. His most famous works include *Crime and Punishment,* 1866; *The Idiot,* 1868-69; *The Possessed,* 1869-72; in addition to *The House of the Dead; Insulted and the Injured;* and *Memoirs from Underground.* In his work, *Brothers Karamazov,* written 1879-1880, Dostoevski wrote:

> If you were to destroy in mankind the belief in immortality, not only love but every living force maintaining the life of the world would at once be dried up.[65]

⟐

William Orville Douglas (1898-1980), was a Justice of the United States Supreme Court. In the 1952 case of *Zorach v. Clauson*, 343 US 306 307 313, Justice Douglas asserted:

> The First Amendment, however, does not say that in every respect there shall be a separation of Church and State. Rather, it studiously defines the manner, the specific ways, in which there shall be no concert or union or dependency one on the other.
> That is the common sense of the matter. Otherwise the state and religion would be aliens to each other—hostile, suspicious, and even unfriendly....
> Municipalities would not be permitted to render police or fire protection to religious groups. Policemen who helped parishioners into their places of worship would violate the Constitution.
> Prayers in our legislative halls; the appeals to the Almighty in the messages of the Chief Executive; the proclamation making Thanksgiving Day a holiday; "so help me God" in our courtroom oaths—
> these and all other references to the Almighty that run through our laws, our public rituals, our ceremonies, would be flouting the First Amendment.
> We are a religious people and our institutions presuppose a Supreme Being....No constitutional requirement makes it necessary for government to be hostile to religion and to throw its weight against the efforts to widen the scope of religious influence. The government must remain neutral when it comes to competition between sects...
> A fastidious atheist or agnostic could even object to the supplication with which the Court opens each session: "God save the United States and this Honorable Court.[66]

⟐

Frederick Douglass (1817-1895), a former slave, became a commanding abolitionist and spokesman for all slaves. Thousands of people were brought out of their indifferent attitude toward the value of human life by his powerful orations exposing the silent scream of the slaves. Many were deeply moved away from the opinion that it was a person's choice whether or not to enslave another person, and multitudes began supporting the right to life for all humans, regardless of their race or circumstances.
Frederick Douglass included this story in retelling his

conversion:

> I loved all mankind, slaveholder not excepted, though I abhorred slavery more than ever. I saw the world in a new light....I gathered scattered pages of the Bible from the filthy street gutters, and washed and dried them, that in moments of leisure I might get a word or two of wisdom from them.[67]

In the *Narrative of the Life of Frederick Douglass*, 1845, he wrote in chapter 2:

> Every tone [of the songs of the slaves] was a testimony against slavery, and a prayer to God for deliverance from chains.[68]

᷒

Jacob Duché (1738-1798), was the Anglican clergyman, who, at the request of the Continental Congress, opened the first session of Congress with prayer. As recorded in the *Journals of the Continental Congress*, the first official act of Congress, immediately upon receiving the news that British troops had attacked Boston, was to open in prayer:

Jacob Duché

> Tuesday, September 6, 1774. Resolved, That the Rev. Mr. Duché be desired to open the Congress tomorrow morning with prayers, at the Carpenter's Hall, at 9 o'clock.[69]

The 35th Psalm, the Psalter for the seventh day of September, which was read by Rev. Mr. Duché in the first Continental Congress, begins:

> Plead my cause, Oh, Lord, with them that strive with me, fight against them that fight against me. Take hold of buckler and shield, and rise up for my help. Draw also the spear and the battle-axe to meet those who pursue me; Say to my soul, "I am your salvation." Let those be ashamed and dishonored who seek my life; Let those be turned back and humiliated who devise evil against me.[70]

Rev. Mr. Duché, in Carpenter's Hall, Philadelphia, proceeded extemporaneously to offer the *First Prayer in Congress* on September 7, 1774:

> Be Thou present, O God of Wisdom, and direct the counsel of this Honorable Assembly; enable them to settle all things on the best and surest foundations; that the scene of blood may be speedily closed; that Order, Harmony and Peace may be effectually restored, and that Truth and Justice, Religion and Piety, prevail and flourish among the people.
>
> Preserve the health of their bodies, and the vigor of their minds, shower down on them, and the millions they here represent, such temporal Blessings as Thou seest expedient for them in this world, and crown them with everlasting Glory in the world to come. All this we ask in the name and through the merits of Jesus Christ, Thy Son and our Saviour, Amen.[71]

The *Journals of Congress* record Congress' appreciation to Rev. Mr. Duché:

> Wednesday, September 7, 1774, 9 o'clock a.m. Agreeable to the resolve of yesterday, the meeting was opened with prayers by the Rev. Mr. Duché. Voted, That the thanks of Congress be given to Mr. Duché...for performing divine Service, and for the excellent prayer, which he composed and delivered on the occasion.[72]

❧

Pierre Samuel du Pont de Nemours (1739-1817), a French-born American economist and politician, along with his son, Eleuthere Irenee, founded the E.I. du Pont de Nemours & Company in 1802 near Wilmington, Delaware. They began to produce a higher quality gunpowder which caused their company, especially after the War of 1812, to grow rapidly, eventually becoming the industrial giant of du Pont Industries.

Pierre Samuel du Pont de Nemours

Thomas Jefferson had commissioned du Pont de Nemours to survey and report on the status of American education in the early 1800's. He reported:

> Most young Americans...can read, write and cipher. Not more

than four in a thousand are unable to write legibly....

In America, a great number of people read the Bible, and all the people read a newspaper. The fathers read aloud to their children while breakfast is being prepared—a task which occupies the mothers for three-quarters of an hour every morning....

It is because of this kind of education that the Americans of the United States...have the advantage of having a larger proportion of moderately well-informed men.[73]

Timothy Dwight (1752-1817), the president of Yale, was an influential author and educator. He was the grandson of Jonathan Edwards, the famous New England minister and president of Princeton. It was during his presidency at Yale that a powerful revival ensued at the New Haven campus with a large percentage of the class, not only professing Christ, but entering the ministry.

Timothy Dwight On July 4th, 1798, President Dwight declared:

Religion and liberty are the meat and the drink of the body politic. Withdraw one of them and it languishes, consumes, and dies...Without religion we may possibly retain the freedom of savages, bears, and wolves, but not the freedom of New England. If our religion were gone, our state of society would perish with it, and nothing would be left.[74]

Timothy Dwight stated:

Where there is no religion, there is no morality....With the loss of religion...the ultimate foundation of confidence is blown up; and the security of life, liberty and property are buried in ruins.[75]

The Bible is a window in this prison of hope, through which we look into eternity.[76]

Perhaps no one who has persisted in his efforts to gain eternal life was ever finally deserted by the Spirit of grace.[77]

E

Jonathan Edwards (1703-1758), the third president of Princeton University (formerly called the College of New Jersey), was a great American religious leader whose preaching began the revival known as the "Great Awakening." This great movement of faith swept the American Colonies, helping to unite them prior to the Revolutionary War.

Jonathan Edwards

He married Sarah Pierrepont in 1727 and together they committed to raise their eleven children in the respect of God. Their success as parents was revealed in a study done in 1900, showing that their descendants included 13 college presidents, 65 professors, 30 judges, 100 lawyers, a dean of a prestigious law school, 80 public office holders, nearly 100 missionaries, 3 mayors of large cities, 3 governors, 3 United States Senators, 1 comptroller of the United States Treasury and 1 Vice-President of the United States.[1] In his *Narrative of Surprising Conversions,* Jonathan Edwards wrote:

> And then it was, in the latter part of December, that the Spirit of God began extraordinarily to...work amongst us. There were, very suddenly, one after another, five or six persons who were, to all appearance, savingly converted, and some of them wrought upon in a very remarkable manner.
>
> Particularly I was surprised with the relation of a young woman, who had been one of the greatest company-keepers in the whole town. When she came to me, I had never heard that she was become in any ways serious, but by the conversation I had with her, it appeared to me that what she gave an account of was a glorious work of God's infinite power and sovereign grace, and that God had given her a new heart,

truly broken and sanctified....

God made it, I suppose, the greatest occasion of awakening to others, of anything that ever came to pass in the town. I have had abundant opportunity to know the effect it had, by my private conversation with many. The news of it seemed to be almost like a flash of lighting upon the hearts of young people all over the town, and upon many others....

Presently upon this, a great and earnest concern about the great things of religion and the eternal world became universal in all parts of the town and among persons of all degrees and all ages. The noise of the dry bones waxed louder and louder....

Those that were wont to be the vainest and loosest, and those that had been the most disposed to think and speak slightly of vital and experimental religion, were not generally subject to great awakenings. And the work of conversion was carried on in a most astonishing manner and increased more and more; souls did, as it were, come by flocks to Jesus Christ....

This work of God, as it was carried on and the number of true saints multiplied, soon made a glorious alteration in the town, so that in the spring and summer following, Anno 1735, the town seemed to be full of the presence of God.

It never was so full of love, nor so full of joy...there were remarkable tokens of God's presence in almost every house. It was a time of joy in families on the account of salvation's being brought unto them, parents rejoicing over their children as new born, and husbands over their wives, and wives over their husbands.

The goings of God were then seen in His sanctuary, God's day was a delight and His tabernacles were amiable. Our public assembles were then beautiful; the congregation was alive in God's service, everyone earnestly intent on the public worship, every hearer eager to drink the words of the minister as they came from his mouth.

The assembly in general were, from time to time, in tears while the word was preached, some weeping with sorrow and distress, others with joy and love, others with pity and concern for their neighbors.

There were many instances of persons that came from abroad, on visits or on business...[who] partook of that shower of divine blessing that God rained down here and went home rejoicing. Till at length the same work began to appear and prevail in several other towns in the country.

In the month of March, the people of South Hadley began to be seized with a deep concern about the things of religion, which very soon became universal...About the same time, it began to break forth in the west part of Suffield...and it soon spread into all parts of the town. It next appeared at Sunderland...

About the same time it began to appear in a part of Deerfield...Hatfield...West Springfield...Long Meadow...Endfield... Westfield...Northfield...In every place, God brought His saving blessings with Him, and His Word, attended with Spirit...returned not void.[2]

Jonathan Edwards exclaimed:

There is no leveler like Christianity, but it levels by lifting all who receive it to the lofty table-land of a true character and of undying hope both for this world and the next.[3]

ð

Albert Einstein (1879-1955), the famous German-born American theoretical physicist, developed the theory of relativity, which was the basis for the application of atomic energy. In 1921, Albert Einstein was the recipient of the Nobel Prize, and in 1952 he was offered the position of President of Israel, but turned it down. Albert Einstein stated:

God Almighty does not throw dice.[4]

Another of Albert Einstein's statements, inscribed in Fine Hall at Princeton University, reads:

Raffiniert ist der Herr Gott, aber Boshaft ist er nicht." (God is clever, but not dishonest.)[5]

ð

Dwight David Eisenhower(1890-1969), the 34th President of the United States, was also the Supreme Commander of Allied Forces during World War II. On the night of July 10, 1943, General Eisenhower observed the armada of 3000 naval ships that he had ordered to battle, sailing from Malta to the shores of Sicily. He saluted his men, then bowed his head in prayer.

Dwight David Eisenhower

To the officer next to him he commented:

> There comes a time when you've used your brains, your training, your technical skill, and the die is cast and the events are in the hands of God, and there you have to leave them.[6]

On June 14, 1954, President Eisenhower supported and signed into law the Congressional Act, Joint Resolution 243, which added the phrase "under God" to the *Pledge of Allegiance:*

> In this way we are reaffirming the transcendence of religious faith in America's heritage and future; in this way we shall constantly strengthen those spiritual weapons which forever will be our country's most powerful resource in peace and war.[7]

President Eisenhower then stood on the steps of the Capitol Building and recited the *Pledge of Allegiance* with the phrase "one Nation under God" for the first time:[8]

> I pledge allegiance to the flag of the United States of America, and to the Republic for which it stands, one nation, under God, indivisible, with liberty and justice for all.[9]

(The *Pledge of Allegiance* was first written in 1892 by a Baptist minister from Boston named Francis Bellamy, who was ordained in the Baptist Church of Little Falls, New York. He was a member of the staff of *The Youth's Companion,* which first published the Pledge on September 8, 1892. At the dedication of the 1892 Chicago World's Fair on October 12, 1892, public-school children first recited the *Pledge of Allegiance* during the National School Celebration on the 400th anniversary of Columbus' discovery of America. The words "under God" were taken from Abraham Lincoln's famous Gettysburg Address, "...that this nation, under God, shall have a new birth....")[10]

In 1954, President Dwight David Eisenhower, said:

> The purpose of a devout and united people was set forth in the pages of The Bible...(1) to live in freedom (2) to work in a prosperous land...and (3) to obey the commandments of God....This Biblical story

*Mrs. Dwight
David
Eisenhower
(nee Mamie
Geneva Doud)*

of the Promised land inspired the founders of America. It continues to inspire us....[11]

In his Inaugural Address, January 21, 1957, President Dwight D. Eisenhower exclaimed:

Before all else, we seek upon our common labor as a nation, the blessings of Almighty God. And the hopes in our hearts fashion the deepest prayers of our whole people.[12]

Dwight D. Eisenhower stated:

The spirit of man is more important than mere physical strength, and the spiritual fiber of a nation than its wealth.[13]

The Bible is endorsed by the ages. Our civilization is built upon its words. In no other book is there such a collection of inspired wisdom, reality, and hope.[14]

ॐ

John Eliot (1604-1690), called "The Apostle to the Indians," was the first minister to teach Christianity to the Indians of New England. A graduate of Cambridge, he traveled to Boston in 1631, where he became a teacher and pastor. A young Indian who had converted from paganism to Christianity helped Eliot learn various Indian dialects. John Eliot was responsible for having written the first Indian translation of the Bible, and the first Indian grammar book. In addition, he established 3,600 Indians into over a dozen self-governing communities. In his work, *The Christian Commonwealth*, 1659, which was a draft of a plan of government for the Natick Indian community, Eliot explained that:

[It is not for man] to search humane Polities and Platformes of Government, contrived by the wisdom of man; but as the Lord hath carried on their works for them, so they ought to go unto the Lord and enquire at the Word of his mouth, what Platforme of Government he hath therein commanded; and humble themselves to embrace that as the best...[The] written Word of God is the perfect System or Frame of Laws, to guide all the Moral actions of man, either towards God or man.[15]

In 1640, John Eliot, along with Richard Mather and Thomas Welch, printed the very first book in the colonies. Using the first printing press in the American colonies, located in Cambridge, Massachusetts, this book became the approved hymnal of the Massachusetts Bay Colony. Known as the *Bay Psalm Book,* it was entitled:

THE WHOLE BOOKE OF PSALMES faithfully TRANSLATED into ENGLISH Metre, Whereunto is prefixed a discourse declaring not only the lawfulness, but also the necessity of the heavenly Ordinances of singing Scripture Psalmes in the Churches of God.[16]

ೆ

Queen Elizabeth I (1533-1603), the Queen of England from 1558 to 1603, answered the question at her Coronation as to the presence of Christ in the Sacrament, by saying:

Christ was the Word that spake it,
He took the bread and brake it,
And what that Word did make it,
I do believe and take it.[17]

Queen Elizabeth I asserted:

I am your Queen. I will never be by violence constrained to do anything. I thank God I am endued with such qualities that if I were turned out of the Realm in my petticoat I were able to live in any place in Christendom.[18]

Queen Elizabeth I (Elizabeth Tudor; the "Virgin Queen")

In 1601, Queen Elizabeth gave *The Golden Speech,* saying:

Though God hath raised me high, yet this I count the glory of my crown: that I have reigned with your loves.[19]

Queen Elizabeth I spoke to her ladies regarding her epitaph, saying:

I am no lover of pompous title, but only desire that my name may be recorded in a line or two, which shall briefly express my name, my virginity, the years of my reign, the reformation of religion under it, and my preservation of peace.[20]

&

(Henry) Havelock Ellis (1859-1939), an English psychologist and author, wrote in his work, *The Dance of Life*, published 1923:

The Promised Land always lies on the other side of a wilderness.[21]

&

Ralph Waldo Emerson (1803-1882), was the famous American poet who wrote the *Concord Hymn*, 1836. This poem made famous the Revolutionary War battle at Concord, Massachusetts, with the phrase "the shot heard around the world." Ralph Waldo Emerson acknowledged:

All I have seen has taught me to trust the Creator for all I have not seen.[22]

&

Magnus Eriksson II(1316-1374), as king of Norway, Sweden and Skaane, commissioned an Icelandic judge named Paul Knudsen to lead an expedition to Greenland in 1354:

Magnus, by the grace of God, King of Norway, Sweden and Skaane, sends to all men who see or hear this letter good health and happiness.

We desire to make known to you that you [Paul Knudsen] is to take the men who shall do in the knarr [royal vessel]; whether they be named or not named,...from my bodyguard, and also from among the retainers of other men, whom you may wish to take on the voyage who are best qualified to accompany him, whether as officers or men.

We ask that you accept this our command with a right good will for the cause, inasmuch as we do it for the honor of God, and for the sake of our soul, and for the sake of our predecessors who in Greenland established Christianity and have maintained it until this time, and we will not let it perish in our days.

Know this for truth, that whoever defies this our command shall meet with our serious displeasure and receive full punishment.

Executed in Bergen, Monday after Simon and Judah's Day in the six and thirtieth year of our rule [1354]. By Orm Ostenson, our regent, sealed.[23]

Edward Everett (1794-1865), an American diplomat, educator, orator and clergyman, was Governor of Massachusetts, U.S. Minister to Britain, Secretary of State under President Fillmore, and a U.S. Senator. He also was the president of Harvard and spoke at Gettysburg with President Lincoln. Edward Everett stated:

Edward Everett

All the distinctive features and superiority of our republican institutions are derived from the teachings of Scripture.[24]

In an address at the opening of the Dudley Observatory in Albany, New York, Edward Everett remarked:

I do not wonder at the superstition of the ancient magicians, who, in the morning of the world, went up to the hilltops of Central Asia, and, ignorant of the true God, adored the most glorious work of his hand.

But I am filled with amazement, when I am told, that, in this enlightened age and in the heart of the Christian world, there are persons who can witness this daily manifestation of the power and wisdom of the Creator, and yet say in their hearts, There is no God.[25]

Johannes Ewald (1743-1781), was a famous Danish lyric poet. Among his great dramas were *Balder's Death* and *The Fisher*, which contains the Danish national song, "King Christian Stood by the Lofty Mast." Johannes Ewald conceded:

In this little book (the New Testament), is contained all the wisdom of the world.[26]

F

Henri Jean Fabre (1823-1915), considered the "Father of Modern Entomology," was a famous biologist who pioneered unprecedented studies of insects in their habitats. He also authored numerous popular textbooks, including *Souvenirs entomologigues,* 1879-1907. Henri Jean Fabre, who was a personal friend of Louis Pasteur, asserted concerning God:

> Without Him I understand nothing; without Him all is darkness....Every period had its manias. I regard Atheism as a mania. It is the malady of the age. You could take my skin from me more easily than my faith in God.[1]

&

Michael Faraday (1791-1867), an English chemist and naturalist, was one of the greatest physicists of all time. In 1833, he was honored as professor of chemistry at the prestigious Royal Institute. He pioneered the liquefaction of gases and discovered benzene, which is used in aniline dyes, perfumes, and high explosives.

Michael Faraday's most famous scientific contributions include the discovery of electrolysis, electromagnetic induction, the concept of magnetic lines of force, and the invention of the first electrical generator in 1831. Michael Faraday avowed:

> It is permitted to the Christian to think of death; he is even represented as praying that God would teach him to number his days. Words are given him: "Thanks be unto God, who giveth us the victory through our Lord Jesus Christ." And though the thought of death

brings the thought of judgment, it also brings to the Christian the thought of Him who died, who rose again for the justification of those who believe in Him.[2]

The Christian who is taught by God (by His Word and Holy Spirit) finds his guide in the Word of God, and commits the keeping of his soul in the hands of God. He looks for no assurance beyond what the Word of God can give him; and if his mind is troubled by the cares and fears which may assail him, he can go nowhere but to the throne of grace and to Scripture.

No outward manifestation can give either instruction or assurance to him, nor can any outward opposition or trouble diminish his confidence for Christ crucified, to the Jews a stumbling block and to the Greeks foolishness; but to them who are called, Christ the power of God and the wisdom of God. The Christian religion is a revelation, and that revelation is the Word of God.[3]

❧

David Glasgow Farragut (1801-1870), was promoted to an Admiral in the U.S. Navy in 1866, after having served as its first Rear Admiral, a rank he earned in 1862 by capturing New Orleans during the Civil War. He helped General Ulysses S. Grant capture Vicksburg in 1863, and then took command of a fleet to capture Mobile, Alabama, in 1864. Through tremendous fire, Farragut bravely forced his way into Mobile Bay, which was filled with mines (torpedoes), roaring his now famous phrase, "Damn the torpedoes. Full steam ahead!"

David Glasgow Farragut

In the *Life and Letters of Admiral D.G. Farragut,* written by his son, Loyall Farragut, Admiral David Glasgow Farragut declared that:

He never felt so near his Master as he did when in a storm, knowing that on his skill depended the safety of so many lives.[4]

When David Glasgow Farragut was dangerously ill in Chicago,

he called for a clergyman to come and pray to the Lord with him, saying:

He must be my pilot now![5]

&

The Federalist Papers (1787-1788), were a series of articles explaining the need for, and urging the ratification of, the United States Constitution by the individual State governments. Published in New York newspapers, these articles were written by Alexander Hamilton, James Madison and John Jay under the pen name of "Publius." Without the powerful arguments presented in *The Federalist Papers*, the Constitution most likely would not have been ratified.

John Jay

Federalist Paper No. 47: When the legislative and executive powers are united in the same person or body, there can be no liberty, because apprehensions may arise lest the same monarch or senate should enact tyrannical laws, to execute them in a tyrannical manner. Were the power of judging joined with the legislative, the life and liberty of the subject would then be the legislator. Were it joined to the executive power, the judge might behave with all the violence of an oppressor.[6]

James Madison

Federalist Paper No. 51 (Madison): In republican government, the legislative authority necessarily predominates.[7]

Federalist Paper No. 81 (Hamilton): In the first place, there is not a syllable in the plan under consideration which directly empowers the national courts to construe the laws according to the spirit of the Constitution.[8]

Alexander Hamilton

Henry Fielding (1707-1754), was an English playwright and novelist, whose greatest novels include *Joseph Andrews*, 1742; *Jonathan Wild*, 1743; *Tom Jones*, 1749; *Amelia*, 1752; and *Journal of a Voyage to Lisbon*, written shortly before his death. In *Joseph Andrew*, book III, chapter 5, Henry Fielding stated:

> Public schools are the nurseries of all vice and immorality.[9]

James Thomas Fields (1817-1881), in *The Captain's Daughter; or The Ballad of the Tempest*, written in 1858, penned this famous line:

> But his little daughter whispered,
> As she took his icy hand,
> Isn't God upon the ocean,
> Just the same as on the land?[10]

Charles
Grandison
Finney

Charles Grandison Finney (1792-1875), one of the greatest American preachers in the early 19th century, was an educator, author and the president of Oberlin College in Ohio. He believed that every human life was valuable and strongly supported giving freedom to the slaves. His college was a busy station on the Underground Railroad, which secretly brought slaves to freedom. Under Charles Finney's direction as president, Oberlin College was the first university in America to award college degrees to women and to blacks. His college graduated Mary Jane Patterson, the first black woman ever to receive a bachelor's degree in the United States.

His famous *Lectures on Revivals*, 1835, had a powerful impact in England, profoundly affecting George Williams, who went on to found the Young Men's Christian Association (YMCA), 1844, and inspiring William and Catherine Booth, who founded The Salvation Army, 1865.

Charles G. Finney helped form the Benevolent Empire, a great network of volunteer societies organized to aid in solving social problems. Among them were the American Board of Commissioners for Foreign Missions, 1810; American Bible Society, 1816; American Sunday School Union, 1817; American Tract Society, 1826; American Home Mission Society, 1826; and American Temperance Society, 1826. By 1834, the budget of these organizations was almost as large as the federal budget of that time. Charles Finney said concerning the Kingdom of God:

> Every member must work or quit. No honorary members.[11]

Charles Finney declared:

> The church must take right ground in regards to politics....The time has come for Christians to vote for honest men, and take consistent ground in politics or the Lord will curse them...
>
> God cannot sustain this free and blessed country, which we love and pray for, unless the Church will take right ground. Politics are a part of a religion in such a country as this, and Christians must do their duty to their country as a part of their duty to God...
>
> God will bless or curse this nation according to the course Christians take in politics.[12]

ða

The First Amendment December 15, 1791, was added to the Constitution of the United States of America, along with nine other amendments, which together compose *The Bill of Rights*. The First Amendment reads:

> Congress shall make no law respecting an establishment of religion, or prohibiting the free exercise thereof; or abridging the freedom of speech, or of the press; or the right of the people peaceably to assemble, and to petition the Government for a redress of grievances.[13]

(See also "Congress of the United States.")

&

St. Johns River Settlement, Florida June 30, 1564, was established
by Rene de Laudonniere, who led a group of French Huguenots
(Protestants from France) to colonize and build Fort Caroline near
present-day Jacksonville, Florida. Rene de Laudonniere recorded:

> We sang a psalm of Thanksgiving unto God, beseeching Him that
> it would please Him to continue His accustomed goodness towards
> us.[14]

&

Gerald Rudolph Ford (1913-), became the 38th President of the
United States, after replacing Vice-President Spiro Agnew who
resigned, and then President Richard Nixon who also resigned.
He is the only person to succeed to that office without being
elected. Upon assuming office on August 9, 1974, President
Gerald Ford entreated:

> I ask you to confirm me as your president with your prayers....God
> helping me, I will not let you down.[15]

President Gerald Ford, on December 5, 1974, upheld that:

Without God there could be no American form of government, nor an American way of life. Recognition of the Supreme Being is the first—the most basic—expression of Americanism. Thus the founding fathers of America saw it, and thus with God's help, it will continue to be.[16]

ๅ

Kirk Fordice (1934-   ), as Governor of Mississippi, affirmed in November, 1992, that:

America is a Christian nation.[17]

As quoted in *The New York Times*, November 18, 1992, Governor Kirk Fordice illuminated:

The less we emphasize the Christian religion the further we fall into the abyss of poor character and chaos in the United States of America.[18]

ๅ

Howell M. Forgy (1908-1983), the chaplain on a cruiser during the time of the Japanese attack on Pearl Harbor, encouraged the men as they were handling the ammunition on December 7, 1941:

Praise the Lord and pass the ammunition.[19]

ๅ

Henry Emerson Fosdick (1878-1969), one of the best-known ministers of his day, pastored the First Presbyterian Church in New York City, and, later, the Park Avenue Baptist Church also in New York City. He wrote numerous famous works, including: *The Meaning of Prayer, Twelve Tests of Character, The Manhood of the Master, On Being a Real Person,* and *On Being Fit to Live.* In 1920, he wrote *The Meaning of Service,* in which he stated:

The Sea of Galilee and the Dead Sea are made of the same water.

It flows down, clear and cool, from the heights of Hermon and the roots of the cedars of Lebanon. The Sea of Galilee makes beauty of it, for the Sea of Galilee has an outlet. It gets to give. It gathers in its riches that it may pour them out again to fertilize the Jordan plain. But the Dead Sea with the same water makes horror. For the Dead Sea has no outlet. It gets to keep.[20]

❧

George Fox (1624-1691), was the founder of the Society of Friends, or "Quakers." He ministered in England, Ireland, Scotland, Holland, North America and the West Indies, often being imprisoned for his beliefs. Fox was a close friend of William Penn's, another famous Quaker and the founder of the colony of Pennsylvania. Penn traveled and preached with George Fox, himself being imprisoned three times for his faith, once in the Tower of London for eight months. In 1694, George Fox wrote in his journal:

> The Lord showed me, so that I did see clearly, that he did not dwell in these temples which men had commanded and set up, but in people's hearts...his people were his temple, and he dwelt in them....
> When the Lord sent me forth into the world, He forbade me to put off my hat to any, high or low....
> Justice Bennet of Derby, was the first that called us Quakers, because I bid them tremble at the word of the Lord. This was in the year 1650....
> He [Oliver Cromwell] said: "I see there is a people risen, that I cannot win either with gifts, honors, offices or places; but all other sects and people I can.[21]

❧

Anne Frank (1929-1945), a Dutch Jewish diarist, wrote a telling narrative of her life in Holland during the Nazi occupation. In *The Diary of a Young Girl*, dated March 7, 1944, Anne Frank wrote:

> Whoever is happy will make others happy too. He who has courage and faith will never perish in misery![22]

❧

Benjamin Franklin

Benjamin Franklin(1706-1790), one of America's most instrumental statesmen, was also an author, scientist and printer. He served as a diplomat to France and England; was the President (Governor) of Pennsylvania; founded the University of Pennsylvania; signed the Declaration of Independence, the Articles of Confederation and the Constitution. Benjamin Franklin was the 15th of 17 children and, because his father's profession of candle-making did not provide enough funds for a formal education, he began his apprenticeship as a printer at the age of 12. Benjamin Franklin initially gained wide acclaim as a literary genius through the annual publication of his book, *Poor Richard's Almanac* (from 1732-1757). This work contained innumerable proverbs, such as:

> God heals, and the doctor takes the fees.[23]

> God helps them that help themselves. (June 1736)[24]

> Work as if you were to live 100 years; pray as if you were to die tomorrow. (May 1757)[25]

In addition to having taught himself five languages, he became known as "the Newton of his Age." He made important discoveries in electricity, coining the terms "positive and negative charges," "conductor," "condenser," "battery," and "electric shock." He invented the lightning rod, which earned him the Royal Society's Copley Medal and honorary degrees from Harvard and Yale Universities in 1753. He also invented the Franklin stove, the rocking chair, bi-focal glasses, in addition to numerous scientific discoveries. He organized the first postal system in America, the first volunteer fire department, a circulating public library, a city police force and the lighting of streets.

Franklin was responsible for bringing France into the Revolutionary War on the side of the Colonies, which proved to be of vital importance to the cause of independence. He also went to Paris in August 1781 to negotiate the *Treaty of Paris,* which ended the War with the British on September 3, 1783. The terms of this treaty were described as "so advantageous to the Colonies that it has been called the greatest achievement in the history of American diplomacy."[26]

In 1748, as Pennsylvania's Governor, Benjamin Franklin proposed Pennsylvania's first Fast Day:

> It is the duty of mankind on all suitable occasions to acknowledge their dependence on the Divine Being...[that] Almighty God would mercifully interpose and still the rage of war among the nations...[and that] He would take this province under His protection, confound the designs and defeat the attempts of its enemies, and unite our hearts and strengthen our hands in every undertaking that may be for the public good, and for our defence and security in this time of danger.[27]

On August 23, 1750, from Philadelphia, Benjamin Franklin wrote to Dr. Samuel Johnson, the first President of King's College (now Columbia University) regarding the education of youth:

> I think with you, that nothing is of more importance for the public weal, than to form and train up youth in wisdom and virtue....I think also, general virtue is more probably to be expected and obtained from the education of youth, than from the exhortation of adult persons; bad habits and vices of the mind being, like diseases of the body, more easily prevented than cured.
>
> I think, moreover, that talents for the education of youth are the gift of God; and that he on whom they are bestowed, whenever a way is opened for the use of them, is as strongly called as if he heard a voice from heaven.[28]

On June 6, 1753, Benjamin Franklin wrote from Philadelphia to Joseph Huey:

> I can only show my gratitude for these mercies from God, by a readiness to help his other children and my brethren. For I do not think that thanks and compliments, though repeated weekly, can discharge our real obligations to each other, and much less those to our Creator.
>
> You will see in this my notion of good works, that I am far from expecting to merit heaven by them. By heaven we understand a state of happiness, infinite in degree, and eternal in duration. I can do nothing to deserve such rewards....Even the mixed, imperfect pleasures we enjoy in this world, are rather from God's goodness than our merit;

how much more such happiness of heaven!

For my part I have not the vanity to think I deserve it...but content myself in submitting to the will and disposal of that God who made me, who has hitherto preserved and blessed me, and in whose fatherly goodness I may well confide, that he will never make me miserable; and that even the afflictions I may at any time suffer shall tend to my benefit.

The faith you mention has certainly its use in the world. I do not desire to see it diminished, nor would I endeavor to lessen it in any man. But I wish it were more productive of good works, than I have generally seen it; I mean real good works; works of kindness, charity, mercy, and public spirit; not holiday-keeping, sermon-reading or hearing; performing church ceremonies, or making long prayers, filled with flatteries and compliments...

The worship of God is a duty; the hearing and reading of sermons may be useful; but, if men rest in hearing and praying, as too many do, it is as if a tree should value itself on being watered and putting forth leaves, though it never produce any fruit.[29]

Benjamin Franklin founded the Pennsylvania Hospital in 1751. In documenting the undertaking, Franklin recorded *Some Account of the Pennsylvania Hospital from its first rise, to the beginning of the fifth month, called May 1754.* In it he writes:

It would be a neglect of that justice which is due to the physicians and surgeons of this hospital, not to acknowledge that their care and skill, and their punctual and regular attendance, under the Divine Blessing, has been a principal means of advancing this charity to the flourishing state in which we have now the pleasure to view it.

Relying on the continuance of the Favour of Heaven, upon the future endeavors of all who may be concerned in the management of the institution, for its further advancement, we close this account with the abstract of a sermon, preached before the Governors...[30]

The inscription which Benjamin Franklin composed for the cornerstone reads:

In the year of Christ, 1755:...This building, by the bounty of the Government and of many private persons, was piously founded, for the relief of the sick and miserable. May the God of mercies bless the undertaking![31]

In 1757, Benjamin Franklin wrote an essay, entitled *The Ways to Wealth*, while sailing to England to serve as Colonial Agent. In it he writes:

> This doctrine, my friends, is reason and wisdom; but after all, do not depend too much upon your own industry, and frugality, and prudence, though excellent things, for they may all be blasted without the blessing of Heaven; and therefore, ask that blessing humbly, and be not uncharitable to those that at the present seem to want [lack] it, but comfort and help them. Remember, Job suffered, and was afterwards prosperous.[32]

In his *Autobiography*, published in complete form in 1868, Franklin mentions a small book that he carried with him all the time. In it was a list of 13 virtues that he had chosen as his lifetime goals:

1) Temperance:...drink not to elevation.
2) Silence:...avoid trifling conversation.
3) Order: Let all your things have their places...
4) Resolution:...perform without fail what you resolve.
5) Frugality:...i.e. waste nothing.
6) Industry: Lose no time; be always employ'd...
7) Sincerity: Use no hurtful deceit; think innocently...
8) Justice: Wrong none by doing injuries...
9) Moderation: Avoid extremes; forbear resenting...
10) Cleanliness: Tolerate no uncleanliness in body...
11) Tranquility: Be not disturbed at trifles...
12) Chastity:
13) Humility: Imitate Jesus...[33]

Benjamin Franklin wrote in his *Autobiography* this prayer that he prayed every day:

> O powerful goodness! Bountiful Father! Merciful Guide! Increase in me that wisdom which discovers my truest interest. Strengthen my resolution to perform what that wisdom dictates. Accept my kind offices to thy other children as the only return in my power for thy continual favours to me.[34]

In his *Autobiography*, Benjamin Franklin commented on his

religious views:

I had been religiously educated as a Presbyterian; and though some of the dogmas of that persuasion, such as the *eternal decrees of God, election, reprobation, etc.*, appeared to me unintelligible, others doubtful, and I early absented myself from the public assemblies of the sect, Sunday being my studying day, I was never without religious principles.

I never doubted, for instance, the existence of the Deity; that he made the world, and governed it by his Providence; that the most acceptable service of God was the doing good to man; that our souls are immortal; and that all crime will be punished, and virtue rewarded, either here or hereafter. These I esteemed the essentials of every religion; and, being to be found in all the religions we had in our country, I respected them all, though with different degrees of respect, as I found them more or less mixed with other articles, which without any tendency to inspire, promote, or confirm morality, served principally to divide us, and make us unfriendly to one another.

This respect of all...induced me to avoid all discourse that might tend to lessen the good opinion another might have of his own religion; and as our province increased in people, and new places of worship were continually wanted, and generally erected by voluntary contribution, my mite for such purpose, whatever might be the sect, was never refused.

Though I seldom attended any public worship, I had still an opinion of its propriety, and of its utility when rightly conducted, and I regularly paid my annual subscription for the support of the only Presbyterian minister or meeting we had in Philadelphia. He used to visit me sometimes as a friend, and admonish me to attend his administration.[35]

In his *Maxims and Morals*, Benjamin Franklin wrote many lessons, of which are the following:

Search others for their virtues, thy self for thy vices.

Keep your eyes open before marriage, half shut afterwards.

My father convinced me that nothing was useful which was not honest.

Freedom is not a gift bestowed upon us by other men, but a

right that belongs to us by the laws of God and nature.

Virtue alone is sufficient to make a man great, glorious and happy.

Let the fair sex be assured that I shall always treat them and their affairs with the utmost decency and respect.

Self-denial is really the highest self-gratification.

Beware of little expenses.

Remember Job suffered and was afterwards prosperous.

I never doubted the existence of the Deity, that he made the world, and governed it by His Providence.

The event God only knows.

Good wives and good plantations are made by good husbands.

Hope and faith may be more firmly grounded upon Charity than Charity upon hope and faith.

Virtue is not secure until its practice has become habitual.

Nothing is so likely to make a man's fortune as virtue.

Without virtue man can have no happiness.

The pleasures of this world are rather from God's goodness than our own merit.

Contrary habits must be broken, and good ones acquired and established, before we can have any dependence on a steady, uniform rectitude of conduct.

Let no pleasure tempt thee, no profit allure thee, no ambition corrupt thee, no example sway thee, no persuasion move thee to do anything which thou knowest to be evil; so thou shalt live jollily, for a good conscience is a continual Christmas.[36]

Benjamin Franklin was a very close friend of George Whitefield's, the famous preacher of the Great Awakening. In his *Autobiography*, Franklin wrote about attending Whitefield's crusades at the Philadelphia Courthouse steps. He noted over 30,000 people were present, and that Whitefield's voice could be heard nearly a mile away.

Benjamin Franklin became very appreciative of the preaching of George Whitefield, even to the extent of printing many of his sermons and journals.

So great was the response of the Colonies to Whitefield's preaching of the gospel, that the churches were not able to hold the people. Benjamin Franklin built a grand auditorium for the sole purpose of having his friend George Whitefield preach in it when he came to Pennsylvania.

After the crusades, Franklin donated the auditorium to be the first building of the University of Pennsylvania. A bronze statue of George Whitefield still stands in front, commemorating the Great Awakening Revivals in the colonies prior to the Revolutionary War.

Noting the effects of Whitefield's ministry and of the Christian influence on city life, Franklin wrote in his autobiography:

> It was wonderful to see the change soon made in the manners of our inhabitants. From being thoughtless or indifferent about religion, it seemed as if all the world were growing religious, so that one could not walk thro' the town in an evening without hearing psalms sung in different families of every street.[37]

In 1752, Benjamin Franklin received a letter from his friend George Whitefield:

> My Dear Doctor....I find that you grow more and more famous in the learned world.[38]

In 1764, Benjamin Franklin wrote to George Whitefield, ending the letter with this salutation:

> Your frequently repeated Wishes and Prayers for my Eternal as well as temporal Happiness are very obliging. I can only thank you for them, and offer you mine in return.[39]

In 1769, George Whitefield wrote to Benjamin Franklin on the night before his last trip to America. In this last surviving letter, Whitefield shares his desire that both he and Franklin would:

> Be in that happy number of those who is the midst of the tremendous final blaze shall cry Amen. [40]

In the last letter Benjamin Franklin wrote to George Whitefield, Franklin revealed:

> Life, like a dramatic piece, should... finish handsomely. Being now in the last act, I began to cast about for something fit to end with.... I sometimes wish, that you and I were jointly employ'd by the Crown to settle a colony on the Ohio... to settle in that fine country a strong body of religious and industrious people!... Might it not greatly facilitate the introduction of pure religion among the heathen, if we could, by such a colony, show them a better sample of Christians than they commonly see in our Indian traders? [41]

Benjamin Franklin, in July of 1776, was appointed part of a committee to draft a seal for the newly united states which would characterize the spirit of the nation. He proposed:

> Moses lifting up his wand, and dividing the red sea, and pharaoh in his chariot overwhelmed with the waters. This motto: "Rebellion to tyrants is obedience to God. [42]

Benjamin Franklin

In a letter to the French ministry, March 1778, Benjamin Franklin is attributed with writing:

> Whoever shall introduce into public affairs the principles of primitive Christianity will change the face of the world. [43]

Benjamin Franklin stated:

> A Bible and a newspaper in every house, a good school in every district-all studied and appreciated as they merit-are the principal support of virtue, morality, and civil liberty. [44]

In his pamphlet entitled *Information to Those Who Would Remove to America*, written to Europeans who were considering the move to America or intending to send their young people to seek their fortune in this land of opportunity, Benjamin Franklin wrote:

> Hence bad examples to youth are more rare in America, which must be a comfortable consideration to parents. To this may be truly added, that serious religion, under its various denominations, is not only tolerated, but respected and practised.
>
> Atheism is unknown there; Infidelity rare and secret; so that persons may live to a great age in that country without having their piety shocked by meeting with either an Atheist or an Infidel.
>
> And the Divine Being seems to have manifested his approbation of the mutual forbearance and kindness with which the different sects treat each other; by the remarkable prosperity with which he has been pleased to favor the whole country.[45]

In a letter to Robert R. Livingston, 1784, Benjamin Franklin wrote:

Robert R. Livingston

> I am now entering on my 78th year....If I live to see this peace concluded, I shall beg leave to remind the Congress of their promise, then to dismiss me. I shall be happy to sing with old Simeon, "Now lettest thou thy servant depart in peace, for mine eyes have seen thy salvation."[46]

Mrs. Benjamin Franklin (nee Deborah Read)

In a letter dated April 17, 1787, Benjamin Franklin expounded:

> Only a virtuous people are capable of freedom. As nations become corrupt and vicious, they have more need of masters.[47]

On Thursday, June 28, 1787, Benjamin Franklin delivered a powerful speech to the Constitutional Convention, which was embroiled in a bitter debate over how each state was to be represented in the new government. The hostile feelings, created by the smaller states being pitted against the larger states, was so bitter that some delegates actually left the Convention.

Benjamin Franklin, being the President (Governor) of Pennsylvania, hosted the rest of the 55 delegates attending the Convention. Being the senior member of the convention at 81 years of age, he commanded the respect of all present, and, as recorded in James Madison's detailed records, he rose to speak in this moment of crisis:

Mr. President:

The small progress we have made after four or five weeks close attendance & continual reasonings with each other—our different sentiments on almost every question, several of the last producing as many noes as ayes, is methinks a melancholy proof of the imperfection of the Human Understanding.

We indeed seem to feel our own want of political wisdom, since we have been running about in search of it. We have gone back to ancient history for models of government, and examined the different forms of those Republics which, having been formed with the seeds of their own dissolution, now no longer exist. And we have viewed Modern States all round Europe, but find none of their Constitutions suitable to our circumstances.

In this situation of this Assembly, groping as it were in the dark to find political truth, and scarce able to distinguish it when presented to us, how has it happened, Sir, that we have not hitherto once thought of humbly applying to the Father of lights to illuminate our understanding?

In the beginning of the Contest with G. Britain, when we were sensible of danger, we had daily prayer in this room for Divine protection.—Our prayers, Sir, were heard, & they were graciously answered. All of us who were engaged in the struggle must have observed frequent instances of a superintending Providence in our favor.

To that kind Providence we owe this happy opportunity of consulting in peace on the means of establishing our future national felicity. And have we now forgotten that powerful Friend? or do we imagine we no longer need His assistance?

I have lived, Sir, a long time, and the longer I live, the more convincing proofs I see of this truth—that God Governs in the affairs of men. And if a sparrow cannot fall to the ground without His notice, is it probable that an empire can rise without His aid?

We have been assured, Sir, in the Sacred Writings, that "except the Lord build the House, they labor in vain that build it." I firmly believe this; and I also believe that without his concurring aid we shall succeed in this political building no better than the Builders of Babel: We shall be divided by our partial local interests; our projects will be confounded, and we ourselves shall become a reproach and bye word down to future ages.

And what is worse, mankind may hereafter from this unfortunate instance, despair of establishing Governments by Human wisdom and leave it to chance, war and conquest.

I therefore beg leave to move—that henceforth prayers imploring the assistance of Heaven, and its blessing on our deliberations, be held in this Assembly every morning before we proceed to business, and that one or more of the clergy of this city be requested to officiate in that service.[48]

The response of the convention to this speech of Benjamin Franklin was reported by Jonathan Dayton, the delegate from New Jersey:

Jonathan Dayton

> The Doctor sat down; and never did I behold a countenance at once so dignified and delighted as was that of Washington at the close of the address; nor were the members of the convention generally less affected. The words of the venerable Franklin fell upon our ears with a weight and authority, even greater than we may suppose an oracle to have had in a Roman senate![49]

Edmund Jennings Randolph

Following Franklin's historical address, James Madison moved,[50] seconded by Roger Sherman of Connecticut,[51] that Dr. Franklin's appeal for prayer be enacted. Edmund Jennings Randolph of Virginia further moved:

> That a sermon be preached at the request of the convention on the 4th of July, the anniversary of Independence; & thenceforward prayers be used in ye Convention every morning.[52]

[Of note is the fact that prayers have opened both houses of Congress ever since.][53]

The clergy of the city responded to this request and effected a profound change in the convention when they reconvened on July 2, 1787, as noted in Jonathan Dayton's records:

> We assembled again; and...every unfriendly feeling had been expelled, and a spirit of conciliation had been cultivated.[54]

On July 4th, the entire Convention assembled in the Reformed Calvinistic Church, according to the proposal by Edmund Jennings Randolph of Virginia, and heard a sermon by Rev. William Rogers. His prayer reflected the hearts of the delegates following Franklin's admonition:

> We fervently recommend to the fatherly notice...our federal convention...Favor them, from day to day, with thy inspiring presence; be their wisdom and strength; enable them to devise such measures as may prove happy instruments in healing all divisions and prove the good of the great whole;...that the United States of America may form one example of a free and virtuous government...
>
> May we...continue, under the influence of republican virtue, to partake of all the blessings of cultivated and Christian society.[55]

As an ambassador of the United States, Benjamin Franklin was at a dinner of foreign dignitaries in Versailles. The minister of Great Britain proposed a toast to King George III, likening him to the sun. The French minister, in like kind, proposed a toast to King Louis XVI, comparing him with the moon. Benjamin Franklin stood up and toasted:

> George Washington, Commander of the American armies, who, like Joshua of old, commanded the sun and the moon to stand still, and they obeyed him.[56]

On March 9, 1790, Benjamin Franklin wrote to Ezra Stiles, President of Yale University:

> Here is my Creed. I believe in one God, the Creator of the Universe. That He governs it by His Providence. That He ought to be worshipped.
>
> That the most acceptable service we render to Him is in doing good to His other Children. That the soul of Man is immortal, and will

be treated with Justice in another Life respecting its conduct in this. These I take to be the fundamental points in all sound Religion, and I regard them as you do in whatever Sect I meet with them.

As to Jesus of Nazareth, my Opinion of whom you particularly desire, I think the System of Morals and his Religion, as he left them to us, is the best the World ever saw, or is likely to see.[57]

Benjamin Franklin wrote in his *Articles of Belief and Acts of Religion:*

It is that particular wise and good God, who is the Author and Owner of our system, that I propose for the Object of my praise and adoration.

For I conceive that He has in Himself some of those passions He has planted in us, and that, since He has given us reason whereby we are capable of observing His wisdom in the Creation, He is not above caring for us, being pleas'd with our praise, and offended when we slight Him, or neglect His Glory.

I conceive for many reasons that He is a good Being, and as I should be happy to have so wise, good and powerful a Being my Friend, let me consider in what Manner I shall make myself most acceptable to Him.[58]

Being mindful that before I address the Deity my soul ought to be calm and serene, free from passion and perturbation, or otherwise elevated with rational joy and pleasure, I ought to use a countenance that expresses a filial respect, mixed with a kind of smiling that signifies inward joy and satisfaction and admiration.[59]

O Creator, O Father, I believe that Thou are Good, and Thou art pleas'd with the pleasure of Thy children.

Praised be Thy Name forever.

By Thy Power hast thou made the glorious Sun, with his attending worlds; from the energy of Thy mighty Will they first received their prodigious motion, and by Thy Wisdom hast Thou prescribed the wondrous laws by which they move.

Praised be Thy Name forever.

By Thy Wisdom hast thou formed all things, Thou hast created man, bestowing life and reason, and plac'd him in dignity superior to Thy other earthly Creatures.

Praised be Thy Name forever.

Thy Wisdom, Thy Power, and Thy GOODNESS are every where clearly seen; in the air and in the water, in the heavens and on the earth; Thou providest for the various winged fowl, and the innumerable inhabitants of the water; Thou givest cold and heat, rain and sunshine in their season, and to the fruits of the earth increase.

Praised be Thy Name forever.

I believe Thou hast given life to Thy creatures that they might live, and art not delighted with violent death and bloody sacrifices.

Praised be Thy Name forever.

Thou abhorrest in Thy creatures treachery and deceit, malice, revenge, Intemperance and every other hurtful Vice; but Thou art a Lover of justice and sincerity, of friendship, benevolence and every virtue. Thou art my Friend, my Father, and my Benefactor.

Praised be Thy Name, O God, forever. Amen.[60]

That I may be preserved from atheism and infidelity, impiety and profaneness, and in my addresses to Thee carefully avoid irreverence and ostentation, formality and odious hypocrisy,

Help me, O Father.[61]

And forasmuch as ingratitude is one of the most odious of vices, let me not be unmindful gratefully to acknowledge the favours I receive from Heaven....For all Thy innumerable benefits; For life and reason, and the use of speech, for health and joy and every pleasant hour, my Good God, I thank Thee.[62]

Franklin wrote his own version of the Lord's Prayer:

Heavenly Father, May all revere Thee, And become Thy dutiful children and faithful subjects. May thy Laws be obeyed on earth as perfectly as they are in Heaven. Provide for us this day as Thou hast hitherto daily done. Forgive us our trespasses, and enable us likewise to forgive those that offend us. Keep us out of temptation and deliver us from Evil.[63]

Benjamin Franklin listed topics and doctrines, which he considered of vital importance, to be shared and preached:

That there is one God Father of the Universe.

That He [is] infinitely good, powerful and wise.

That He is omnipresent.

That He ought to be worshipped, by adoration, prayer and thanksgiving both in publick and private.

That He loves such of His creatures as love and do good to others: and will reward them either in this world or hereafter.

That men's minds do not die with their bodies, but are

made more happy or miserable after this life according to their actions.

That virtuous men ought to league together to strengthen the interest of virtue, in the world: and so strengthen themselves in virtue.

That knowledge and learning is to be cultivated, and ignorance dissipated. That none but the virtuous are wise.

That man's perfection is in virtue.[64]

Benjamin Franklin comments on his beliefs concerning God:

Next to the praise resulting from and due to His wisdom, I believe He is pleased and delights in the happiness of those He has created; and since without virtue man can have no happiness in this world, I firmly believe He delights to see me virtuous, because He is pleased when He sees me happy....

I love Him therefore for His Goodness, and I adore Him for His Wisdom.[65]

Benjamin Franklin

Benjamin Franklin wrote his own epitaph:

THE BODY
of
BENJAMIN FRANKLIN
Printer
Like the cover of an old book,
Its contents torn out,
And stripped of its lettering and gilding
Lies here, food for worms;
Yet the work itself shall not be lost,
For it will (as he believed) appear once more,
In a new,
And more beautiful edition,
Corrected and amended
By The AUTHOR[66]

On Franklin's family pew in Christ Church, a plaque reads:

Here worshipped Benjamin Franklin, philosopher and patriot.... Member of the Committee which erected the Spire of the Church. Interred according to the terms of his will in this churchyard.[67]

❦

Theodore Frelinghuysen (1787-1862), a U.S. Senator, was the chancellor of the University of New York, 1839-1850, and president of Rutgers College, 1850-1861. Theodore Frelinghuysen corresponded with Presidential candidate Henry Clay after Clay had narrowly failed to be elected:

> Let us look away to the brighter and better prospects and surer hopes in the promise and consolations of the Gospel of our Saviour. I pray, my honored sir, that your heart may seek this blessed refuge, stable as the everlasting hills, and let this be the occasion to prompt an earnest, prayerful, and, the Lord grant it may be, a joyful search after the truth as it is in Christ Jesus.[68]

While serving in the office of the President of the American Bible Society, 1846-1861, Theodore Frelinghuysen wrote in a letter:

> The Bible has done it sir! Seal up this one Volume and in a half century all these hopes would wither and these prospects perish forever. These sacred temples would crumble or become the receptacles of pollution and crime....
>
> The influence of this sacred Volume alone can achieve it. Let it find its way into every cottage until the whole mass of our population shall yield to its elevating power; and under the benignant smiles of Him who delights to bless the Word, our government, the last hope of liberty, will rest on foundations against which the winds and waves shall beat in vain.[69]

❦

James Anthony Froude (1818-1894), an English historian and professor at Oxford, published his famous work, *History of England from the Fall of Wolsey to the Defeat of the Spanish Armada*, in twelve volumes. James Anthony Froude professed:

> The Bible, thoroughly known, is literature in itself—the rarest and richest in all departments of thoughts and imagination which exists.[70]

❦

G

Galileo Galilei (1564-1642), was the famous Italian astronomer who conceived the idea for the isochronous pendulum, invented the sector-compass and made the first practical use of the telescope. He discovered the four bright satellites of Jupiter, discovered the famous *Law of Falling Bodies,* and was the first mathematician at the University of Pisa. Galileo stated:

> I am inclined to think that the authority of Holy Scripture is intended to convince men of those truths which are necessary for their salvation, which, being far above man's understanding, can not be made credible by any learning, or any other means than revelation by the Holy Spirit.[1]

In a letter, Galileo wrote:

> I send you a rose, which ought to please you extremely, seeing what a rarity it is at this season. And with the rose you must accept its thorns, which represent the bitter suffering of our Lord, while the green leaves represent the hope we may entertain, that through the same sacred passion we, having passed through the darkness of this short winter of our mortal life, may attain to the brightness and felicity of an eternal spring in Heaven.[2]

๛

Gallup Poll 1986, indicated that 81% of the American people identify themselves as Christian.[3]

In a more recent Gallup poll, reported by Ari Goldman in the *New York Times* on February 27, 1993, 96% of Americans believe in God. Among those polled, 82% identify themselves as Christians,

---

(being 56% Protestant, 25% Roman Catholic), and 2% of Americans identified themselves as Jewish.[4]

ૐ

James Abram Garfield (1831-1881 assassinated), was the 20th President of the United States of America, and after serving only four months he was shot, becoming the fourth President to die in office.

James Garfield had been a remarkable teacher at Hiram College in Ohio and, at the age of twenty-six, he was chosen as the College's president. It was there that he studied law and preached an occasional sermon at the Disciples of Christ church, of which he was a member. Garfield was strongly anti-slavery, and at the out-break of the Civil War was made a Lieutenant Colonel in the Union Army. After defeating a superior Confederate force, he was promoted to Brigadier General, then to Major General.

James Abram Garfield

While still in the military, he was elected to Congress, taking the position at the wishes of President Lincoln. On April 15, 1865, after overcoming the shock of Lincoln's assassination, James Garfield exhorted his countrymen in a speech given in New York:

> Fellow citizens! God reigns, and the Government at Washington still lives![5]

After serving in Congress 18 years, Garfield was elected as a Senator from Ohio. A truly unusual turn of circumstances occurred when James Garfield was asked to give the nomination speech for John Sherman at the opening of the Republican Convention in 1880. His speech received such a standing ovation, that the convention decided to nominate him instead of John Sherman. James Abram Garfield, who was elected President in 1881, proclaimed:

> Now more than ever before, the people are responsible for the

character of their Congress. If that body be ignorant, reckless, and corrupt, it is because the people tolerate ignorance, recklessness, and corruption. If it be intelligent, brave, and pure, it is because the people demand these high qualities to represent them in the national legislature....

If the next centennial does not find us a great nation...it will be because those who represent the enterprise, the culture, and the morality of the nation do not aid in controlling the political forces.[6]

In describing the Chancellor of the newly united German Empire, President James Garfield stated:

I am struck with the fact that Bismarck, the great statesman of Germany, probably the foremost man in Europe today, stated as an unquestioned principle, that the support, the defense, and propagation of the Christian Gospel is the central object of the German government.[7]

In concluding a letter to a friend, showing his submission to the death of his little son, Garfield wrote:

In the hope of the Gospel, which is so precious in this hour of affliction, I am affectionately your brother in Christ.[8]

James Garfield wrote:

The world's history is a Divine poem, of which the history of every nation is a canto, and every man a word. Its strains have been pealing along down the centuries, and though there have been mingled the discords of warring cannon and dying men, yet to the Christian philosopher and historian—the humble listener—there has been a Divine melody running through the song which speaks of hope and halcyon days to come.[9]

While a student at Williams College, James Garfield, along with other students, climbed one of the high peaks seven miles distant, on "Mountain Day." The surrounding scenery was enough to awaken religious awe. Just then young Garfield broke the silence:

Boys, it is a habit of mine to read a chapter in the Bible every evening with my absent mother. Shall I read aloud?

The little company assented; and, drawing from his pocket a well-worn Testament, he read in soft, rich tones the chapter which his mother in Ohio was reading at the same time, and then he called on a classmate, who was on the mountain top, to pray.[10]

&

Giuseppe Garibaldi (1807-1882), the famous Italian general and nationalist leader, freed Italy from foreign rule and saw Rome once again become its capital. Of the Bible, General Garibaldi said:

> This is the cannon that will make Italy free.[11]

In his *Autobiography*, General Giuseppe Garibaldi wrote:

> I am a Christian, and I speak to Christians—I am a true Christian, and I speak to true Christians. I love and venerate the religion of Christ, because Christ came into the world to deliver humanity from slavery, for which God had not created it....You who are here—you, the educated and cultivated portion of the citizenship—you have the duty to educate the people—educate the people—educate them to be Christians—educate them to be Italians....Viva Italia! Viva Christianity![12]

&

William Lloyd Garrison (1805-1879), was a famous abolitionist leader and the publisher of *The Liberator*, an anti-slavery paper in Boston. He founded the *American Anti-Slavery Society* in 1833 and suffered hundreds of threats upon his life for his politically incorrect stand that a human being was not property. In the face of pro-slavery government, laws, court decisions, public opinion, and even pseudo "scientific theories" that Negroes were "biologically inferior" and therefore denied the right to life and freedom, William Lloyd Garrison printed the first issue of *The Liberator* on January 1, 1831:

> It is pretended, that I am retarding the cause of emancipation by

the coarseness of my invective and the precipitancy of my measures. The charge is not true. On this question my influence,—humble as it is,—is felt at this moment to a considerable extent, and shall be felt in coming years—not perniciously, but beneficially—not as a curse, but as a blessing; and posterity will bear testimony that I was right. I desire to thank God, that he enables me to disregard "the fear of man which bringeth a snare," and to speak his truth in its simplicity and power. And here I close with this fresh dedication:

> "...I swear, while life-blood warms my throbbing veins,
> Still to oppose and thwart, with heart and hand,
> Thy brutalizing sway—till Afric's chains
> Are burst, and Freedom rules the rescued land,
> Trampling Oppression and his iron rod:
> Such is the vow I take—SO HELP ME GOD!"[13]

In his writings, *W.P. and F.J.T. Garrison*, published 1885-1889, William Lloyd Garrison explained:

> Wherever there is a human being, I see God-given rights inherent in that being, whatever may be the sex or complexion.[14]

❧

Colony of Georgia 1732, named in honor of King George II, was founded by James Edward Oglethorpe as a refuge for poor debtors from England and persecuted Protestants from Europe.[15] One hundred settlers moved into the area, quickly followed by the Moravians, who were enthusiastic Christian missionaries, and other Christian groups. As the settlers touched the shore, they kneeled and declared:

*James Edward
Oglethorpe*

> Our end in leaving our native country is not to gain riches and honor, but singly this: to live wholly to the glory of God.[16]

Their object was:

> To make Georgia a religious colony.[17]

John and Charles Wesley, who led the Methodist movement, served in Georgia as ministers and missionaries to the Indians. The famous George Whitefield built an orphanage there.[18]

John Wesley

Charles Wesley

&

Provincial Congress of Georgia July 4, 1775, stated:

The Congress being returned, a motion was made and seconded, that the thanks of this Congress be given to the Rev. Doctor Zubly, for the excellent Sermon he preached this day to the Members; which was unanimously agreed to.[19]

&

Provincial Congress of Georgia July 5, 1775, stated:

A motion was made and seconded, that this Congress apply to his Excellency the Governour, by message, requesting him to appoint a day of Fasting and Prayer throughout this Province, on account of the disputes subsisting between America and the Parent State; which being unanimously passed in the affirmative.[20]

&

GEORGIA.

Seal of Georgia

Provincial Congress of Georgia July 7, 1775, received from Savannah, his Excellency's Answer to the message sent from Congress:

Gentlemen: I have taken the opinion of His Majesty's Council relative to the request made by the gentlemen who have assembled together by the name of a Provincial Congress, and must premise, that I cannot consider that meeting as constitutional; but as the request is expressed in such loyal and dutiful terms, and the ends proposed being such as every good man must most ardently wish for, I will certainly appoint a day of Fasting and Prayer to be observed throughout this Province. Jas. Wright.[21]

ভ

Constitution of the State of Georgia 1777, stated:

We, the people of Georgia, relying upon protection and guidance of Almighty God, do ordain and establish this Constitution.[22]

ভ

Kahlil Gibran (1883-1931), was a Syrian-born American poet and painter, noted for his mystic perspective on life. In his 1923 work, *The Prophet*, Kahlil Gibran wrote *On Prayer:*

You pray in your distress and in your need; would that you might pray also in the fullness of your joy and in your days of abundance.[23]

ভ

John Bannister Gibson (1780-1853), Chief Justice of Pennsylvania and jurist, declared:

Give Christianity a common law trial; submit the evidence pro and con to an impartial jury under the direction of a competent court, and the verdict will assuredly be in its favor.[24]

John Bannister Gibson

ভ

William Ewart Gladstone (1809-1898), author and British Prime Minister four different times during Queen Victoria's reign, asserted:

I have known ninety-five of the world's great men in my time, and of these eighty-seven were followers of the Bible. The Bible is stamped with a Specialty of Origin, and an immeasurable distance separates it from all competitors.[25]

Most men at the head of great movements are Christian men. During the many years in the Cabinet I was brought in contact with some sixty master minds, and not more than perhaps three or four of whom were in sympathy with the skeptical movements of the day.[26]

In his book, *The Impregnable Rock of Holy Scripture*, the Right Honorable W.E. Gladstone writes:

They lead upward and onwards to the idea that the Scriptures are well called Holy Scriptures; and that, though assailed by camp, by battery, and by mine, they are, nevertheless, an house built upon a rock, and that rock impregnable; that the weapon of offense which shall impair their efficiency for aiding in the redemption of mankind has not yet been forged; that the Sacred Canon, which it took (perhaps) two thousand years from the accumulations of Moses down to the acceptance of the Apocalypse to construct, is like to wear out the storms and the sunshine of the world, and all the wayward aberrations of humanity, not merely for a term as long, but until time shall be no more.[27]

The Christian faith and the Holy Scriptures arm us with the means of neutralizing and repelling the assaults of evil in and from ourselves. Mist may rest upon the surrounding landscape, but our own path is visible from hour to hour, from day to day.

"I do not ask to see
The distant scene; one step enough for me."

Our Saviour astonished the people because, instead of being lost in the mazes of arbitrary and vicious excrescences that darkened the face of religion, He taught them "with authority," and "not as the scribes."

If God has given us a revelation of His will, whether in the laws of our nature, or in the kingdom of grace, that revelation not only illuminates, but binds. Like the credentials of an earthly ambassador, it is just and necessary that the credentials of that revelation should be tested.

But if it be found genuine, if we have proofs of its being genuine, equal to those of which, in ordinary concerns of life, reason acknowledges the obligatory character, then we find ourselves to be not independent beings, engaged in an optional inquiry, but the servants of a Master, the pupils of a Teacher, the children of a Father, and each of us already bound with the bonds which those relations imply.[28]

&

Johann Wolfgang von Goethe (1749-1832), was perhaps the most famous German author, poet and novelist of international acclaim. His most popular works include *The Sorrows of Werther*, 1774; *Iphigenie*, 1787; *Torquato Tasso*, 1790; and *Faust*, 1808-1832. Goethe contended:

> Let mental culture go on advancing, let the natural sciences progress in ever greater extent and depth, and the human mind widen itself as much as it desires; beyond the elevation and moral culture of Christianity, as it shines forth in the gospels, it will not go.[29]

> It is a belief in the Bible, the fruit of deep meditation, which has served me as the guide of my moral and literary life. I have found it a capital safely invested, and richly productive of interest.[30]

In his *Conversations with Eckermann*, 1828-1829, Johann Wolfgang von Goethe wrote:

> I esteem the Gospels to be thoroughly genuine, for there shines from them the reflected splendor of a sublimity proceeding from the person of Jesus Christ of so Divine a kind as only the Divine could ever have manifested on earth.[31]

In *Aus Makarieus Archiv W. Meister*, 1786-1830, Goethe wrote:

> I am persuaded that the Bible becomes evermore beautiful the more it is understood; that is, the more we consider that every word which we apply to ourselves has had at first a particular, peculiar, immediate reference to certain special circumstances.[32]

Johann Wolfgang von Goethe wrote in his *Autobiography:*

> Nothing, therefore, remained to me but to part from this society; and as my love for the Holy Scriptures, as well as the Founder of Christianity, and its early professors, could not be taken from me, I

formed a Christianity for my private use, and sought to build it up by an attentive study of history.[33]

❧

Sabine Baring-Gould (1834-1924), in 1864, during the critical period of the Civil War, wrote a famous song, entitled *Onward, Christian Soldiers,* underscoring the spiritual battle each individual is engaged in:

Onward, Christian soldiers,
Marching as to war,
With the Cross of Jesus
Going on before![34]

❧

William Franklin "Billy" Graham (1918-   ), an American evangelist, author and statesman, wrote in *The Chicago American,* April 16, 1967:

The most eloquent prayer is the prayer through hands that heal and bless. The highest form of worship is the worship of unselfish Christian service. The greatest form of praise is the sound of consecrated feet seeking out the lost and helpless.[35]

❧

Ulysses S. Grant (1822-1885), was the 18th President of the United States of America and Union General-in-Chief during the Civil War. He received General Robert E. Lee's surrender in 1865. On June 6, 1876, President Ulysses S. Grant wrote from Washington to the Editor of the *Sunday School Times* in Philadelphia:

Ulysses S. Grant

Your favor of yesterday asking a message from me to the children and the youth of the United States, to accompany your Centennial number, is this morning received.

My advice to Sunday schools, no matter what their denomination, is: Hold fast to the Bible as the sheet anchor of your liberties; write its precepts in your hearts, and practice them in your lives.

To the influence of this Book are we indebted for all the progress made in true civilization, and to this must we look as our guide in the future. "Righteousness exalteth a nation; but sin is a reproach to any people."

Yours respectfully,
U. S. Grant[36]

Mrs. Ulysses S. Grant (nee Julia Dent)

General Ulysses S. Grant stated:

I believe in the Holy Scriptures, and whoso lives by them will be benefitted thereby. Men may differ as to the interpretation, which is human, but the Scriptures are man's best guide....

I did not go riding yesterday, although invited and permitted by my physicians, because it was the Lord's day, and because I felt that if a relapse should set in, the people who are praying for me would feel that I was not helping their faith by riding out on Sunday....

Yes, I know, and I feel very grateful to the Christian people of the land for their prayers in my behalf. There is no sect or religion, as shown in the Old or New Testament, to which this does not apply.[37]

Ulysses S. Grant

ᶻ⃝

Horace Greeley

Horace Greeley (1811-1872), was a tremendously influential American journalist, newspaper editor and politician. He made famous the phrase, "Go West, Young Man!" Horace Greeley founded and edited the *New York Tribune* daily paper and *The New Yorker* magazine.

Called by the poet John Greenleaf Whittier, "our later Franklin," Greeley's strong anti-slavery editorials helped to stir the North to oppose slavery. He was one of the founders of the Republican Party and used his influence to secure the nomination of Abraham Lincoln for the Presidency. In his *Autobiography*, Greeley wrote:

It is impossible to mentally or socially enslave a Bible-reading people. The principles of the Bible are the groundwork of human freedom.[38]

Your reference to the "blameless Christian wife"—and what is "more pleasing in the sight of God"?—impels me to say that I must consider Jesus of Nazareth a better authority as to what is Christian and what pleases God than you are.

His testimony on the subject is expressed and unequivocal (Matt. xix. 9) that a marriage can be ruthfully dissolved because of adultery alone. You well know that was not the law either of the Jews or Romans in His day, so that He can not have been misled by custom or tradition, even were it possible for Him to have been mistaken. I believe He was wholly right.[39]

I am not, therefore, to be classed with those who claim to have been converted from one creed to another by studying the Bible alone.

Certainly, upon re-reading that Book in the light of my new convictions, I found therein abundant proofs to their correctness in the averments of patriarchs, Genesis iii. 15; xii. 3; Prophets, Isaiah xxv. 8; Apostles, Romans v. 12-21; viii. 19-21; I. Cor. xv. 42-54; Eph. i.8-10; Col. i. 19-21; I. Tim. 2, 3-6; and of the Messiah Himself, Matthew xv. 13; John xii. 32....

In the light of this faith the dark problem of evil is irradiated, and virtually solved. "Perfect through suffering" was the way traced out by the great Captain of our Salvation.[40]

&

Nathaniel Greene (1742-1786), a general in the Revolutionary War, also served in the Rhode Island Legislature from 1770 to 1772 and again in 1775. While at Camp Prospect Hill, January 4, 1776, General Nathaniel Greene wrote a letter to Samuel Ward, Rhode Island's representative to the Continental Congress:

Permit me, then, to recommend from the sincerity of my heart, ready at all times to bleed in my country's cause, a declaration of independence; and call upon the world, and the great God who governs it, to witness the necessity, propriety and rectitude thereof....

Let us, therefore, act like men inspired with a resolution that nothing but the frowns of Heaven shall conquer us.[41]

&

Simon Greenleaf (1783-1853), the famous Royall Professor of Law at Harvard, succeeded Justice Joseph Story as the Dane Professor of Law. To the efforts of Story and Greenleaf is to be ascribed the rise of the Harvard Law School to its eminent position among the legal schools of the United States.[42]

Simon Greenleaf

Greenleaf produced a work entitled:*A Treatise On the Law of Evidence*, still considered to be the greatest single authority on evidence of all the literature on legal procedure. Chief Justice Fuller of the United States Supreme Court described Greenleaf by saying, "He is the highest authority in our courts."[43]

In correspondence with the American Bible Society, Cambridge, November 6, 1852, Simon Greenleaf wrote:

> Of the Divine character of the Bible, I think no man who deals honestly with his own mind and heart can entertain a reasonable doubt. For myself, I must say, that having for many years made the evidences of Christianity the subject of close study, the result has been a firm and increasing conviction of the authenticity and plenary inspiration of the Bible. It is indeed the Word of God.[44]

In his *A Treatise on the Law of Evidence*, Simon Greenleaf propounded:

> If a close examination of the evidences of Christianity may be expected of one class of men more than another, it would seem incumbent upon lawyers who make the law of evidence one of our peculiar studies. Our profession leads us to explore the mazes of falsehood, to detect its artifices, to pierce its thickest veils, to follow and expose its sophistries, to compare the statements of different witnesses with severity, to discover truth and separate it from error.[45]

> The religion of Jesus Christ...not only solicits the grave attention of all, to whom its doctrines are presented, but it demands their cordial belief as a matter of vital concernment. These are no ordinary claims; and it seems hardly possible for a rational being to regard them with even a subdued interest; much less to treat them with mere indifference and contempt.

If not true, they are little else then the pretensions of a bold imposter....but if they are well founded and just they can be no less than the high requirements of heaven, addressed by the voice of God to the reason and understanding of man...such was the estimate taken of religion, even the religion of pagan Rome, by one of the greatest lawyers of antiquity, when he argued that it was either nothing at all or everything. *Aut undique religionem tolle, aut usquequa que conserva.*[46]

In reference to the apostles, Greenleaf said:

They had every possible motive to review carefully the grounds of their faith, and the evidences of the great facts and truths which they asserted....And their writings show them to have been men of vigorous understandings. If then, their testimony was not true, there was no possible motive for this fabrication.[47]

✓ In his work entitled *Examination of the Testimony of the Four Evangelists by the Rules of Evidence Administered in Courts of Justice, with an Account of the Trial of Jesus,* Simon Greenleaf stated:

The character they portrayed is perfect. It is the character of a sinless Being—One supremely wise and supremely good....

The doctrines and precepts of Jesus are in strict accordance with the attributes of God, agreeable to the most exalted ideas which we can form of them, from reason or revelation. They are strictly adapted to the capacities of mankind, and yet are delivered with a simplicity wholly Divine. "He spake as never man spake." He spake with authority, yet addressed Himself to the reason and understanding of men, and He spake with wisdom which men could neither gainsay nor resist.[48]

❧

Hugo Grotius (1583-1645), the renowned Dutch jurist, statesman and theologian, was the founder of the science of International Law. At the age of 24, he was appointed Advocate General for the provinces of Holland and Zealand; and at the age of 30, he became the Chief Magistrate of Rotterdam. In 1619, Grotius was sentenced to life imprisonment by Prince Maurice of Nassau for his support of the Arminian faith. However in 1621, with his wife's help, Grotius escaped to France, hidden in a linen chest. In 1625, Hugo

Grotius, or Huig de Groot in the Dutch language, published his famous work *De Jure Belli et Pacis (On the Law of War and Peace)*. He later served as the Swedish ambassador to France from 1635 till his death. President James Madison described him as:

The father of the modern code of nations.[49]

In *On the Law of War and Peace*, Hugo Grotius explained:

Among all good men one principle at any rate is established beyond controversy, that if the authorities issue any order that is contrary to the law of nature or to the commandments of God, the order should not be carried out. For when the Apostles said that obedience should be rendered to God rather than men, they appealed to an infallible rule of action, which is written in the hearts of all men.[50]

If it were not permitted to punish certain Criminals with Death, nor to defend the Subject by Arms against Highwaymen and Pyrates, there would of Necessity follow a terrible Inundation of Crimes, and a Deluge of Evils, since even now that Tribunals are erected, it is very difficult to restrain the Boldness of profligate Persons.
Wherefore if it had been the Design of CHRIST to have introduced a new Kind of Regulation, as was never heard of before, he would certainly have declared in most distinct and plain Words, that none should pronounce Sentence of Death against a Malefactor, or carry Arms in Defence of one's Country.[51]

Especially, however, Christian kings and states are bound to pursue this method of avoiding wars....Both for this and for other reasons it would be advantageous to hold certain conferences of Christian powers, where those who have no interest at stake may settle the disputes of others, and where, in fact, steps may be taken to compel parties to accept peace on fair terms.[52]

Hugo Grotius expounded:

He knows not how to rule a kingdome, that cannot manage a Province; nor can he wield a Province, that cannot order a City; nor he order a City, that knows not how to regulate a Village; nor he a Village, that cannot guide a Family; nor can that man Govern well a Family that knows not how to Govern himselfe; neither can any Govern himselfe unless reason be Lord, Will and Appetite her Vassals: nor can Reason rule unlesse herselfe be ruled by God, and (wholy) be obedient to Him.[53]

Whatever God has shown to be his will that is Law.[54]

In *The Truth of the Christian Religion,* Hugo Grotius wrote:

There is no reason for Christians to doubt the credibility of these Books (of the Bible), because there are testimonies in our books out of almost every one of them, the same as they are found in the Hebrew.

Nor did Christ, when He reproved many things in the teachings of the Law, and in the Pharisees of His time, ever accuse them of falsifying the Books of Moses and the Prophets, or of using supposititious or altered books.

And it can never be proved, or made credible, that after Christ's time the Scripture should be corrupted in anything of moment, if we consider how far and wide the Jewish nation, who everywhere kept these Books, was dispersed over the whole world.[55]

ء

Johannes Gutenberg (1400-1468), was the German inventor of the movable type printing press, which helped to revolutionize the western world. This invention prepared Europe for the rapid spread of ideas, making the Reformation possible. The first book of significance ever printed was the 42 line Gutenberg Bible, known as the *Mazarin Bible,* 1455. Johannes Gutenberg wrote:

God suffers in the multitude of souls whom His word can not reach. Religious truth is imprisoned in a small number of manuscript books which confine instead of spread the public treasure. Let us break the seal which seals up holy things and give wings to Truth in order that she may win every soul that comes into the world by her word no longer written at great expense by hands easily palsied, but multiplied like the wind by an untiring machine.[56]

Yes, it is a press, certainly, but a press from which shall flow in inexhaustible streams the most abundant and most marvelous liquor that has ever flowed to relieve the thirst of men. Through it, God will spread His word; a spring of pure truth shall flow from it; like a new star it shall scatter the darkness of ignorance, and cause a light hithertofore unknown to shine among men.[57]

ء

ℋ

Everett Hale (1822-1909), was a popular American author who wrote *The Man Without a Country*, 1863, and over fifty other books. He was the editor of the *Boston Daily Advertiser* and later became Chaplain of the United States Senate. Everett Hale was the nephew of Nathan Hale, the revolutionary patriot who was executed by the British after uttering his famous last words, "I only regret that I have but one life to lose for my country." Everett Hale proclaimed:

> I am only one, but I am one. I cannot do everything, but I can do something. What I can do, I should do and, with the help of God, I will do![1]

&

Sir Matthew Hale (1609-1676), an English jurist who held the highly influential position of Lord Chief-Justice of the King's Bench in England, testified:

> There is no book like the Bible for excellent wisdom and use.[2]

> Every morning read seriously and reverently a portion of the Holy Scriptures, and acquaint yourselves with the history and doctrine thereof; it is a Book full of light and wisdom, and will make you wise unto eternal life.
> Who was it that thus suffered? It was Christ Jesus, the eternal Son of God, clothed in our flesh; God and Man united in one person; His manhood giving Him capacity for suffering, and His Godhead giving a value to suffering; and each nature united in one person to make a complete Redeemer; the Heir of all things; the Prince of Life; the Light that lighteneth every man that cometh into the world. As touching His

Divine nature, God over all, blessed forever; and as touching His human nature, full of grace and truth; and in both, the beloved Son of the eternal God, in whom He proclaimed Himself well pleased.[3]

Mary Washington, the mother of George Washington, had in her possession Sir Matthew Hale's work, *Meditations Moral and Divine*, published in 1679 in London. The chapter that she had especially marked and studied was entitled, "The Great Audit With the Account of the Good Steward":

> The Great Lord of the World hath placed the Children of Men in this Earth as his Stewards; and according to the Parable in Matthew 25, He delivers to every person his Talents, a Stock of Advantages or opportunities: to some he commits more, to some less, to all some....
>
> That in that due and regular employment, each man might be in some measure serviceable and advantageous to another. That although the great Lord of this Family, can receive no Advantage by the Service of His Creature, because he is Perfect and All-sufficient in himself; yet he receives Glory and Praise by it, and a Complacency in the beholding a Conformity in the Creature, to his own most Perfect Will....
>
> Lord, before I enter into Account with thy Majesty, I must confess, that if thou shouldst enter into Judgement with me, and demand that Account which in Justice thou mayst require of me, I should be found thy Debtor: I confess I have not improved my Talents according to that measure of ability that thou has lent me: I therefore most humbly offer unto thee the redundant Merit of thy own Son to supply my defects, and to make good what is wanting in my account: yet according to thy command, I do humbly render my Discharge of the Trust thou has committed to me, as followeth.[4]

❧

Tony P. Hall (1942-   ), as a member of the 100th Congress, strongly supported President Ronald Reagan's signing of Public Law 100-307, on January 25, 1988, setting aside the first Thursday of each May to celebrate a National Day of Prayer. As a U.S. Representative from Ohio, Congressman Tony P. Hall proclaimed:

> The *National Day of Prayer* offers a tremendous opportunity for our entire nation to be humbly united in communication with God. Prayer

is a "toll-free-lifeline" to our most important Friend. I can't imagine facing the many challenges of service in Congress without prayer. Prayer truly is a two-way exchange with God. In some way, often unexpected, I discover that my concerns are answered through new insights to peaceful understanding that I could never have obtained without spiritual assistance. I urge everyone to discover the powerful potential of prayer.[5]

Alexander Hamilton (1757-1804), was not only a signer of the Constitution of the United States, but was known as the "Ratifier of the Constitution." It is probable that without his efforts the Constitution may not have been ratified by the states, particularly his own important state of New York.

Alexander Hamilton

Alexander Hamilton authored 51 of the 85 *Federalist Papers*, which were of immense consequence in influencing the ratification of the Constitution, (which needed to be passed in two-thirds of the states in order to go into effect).

During the Revolutionary War, he was captain of a New York artillery unit, then appointed by George Washington as his aide-de-camp and staff lawyer, and later promoted to Lieutenant Colonel. He was the first Secretary of the Treasury, founder of one of the first banks in New York, and the founder of the *New York Post*.

Shortly after the Constitutional Convention of 1787, Alexander Hamilton stated:

> For my own part, I sincerely esteem it a system which without the finger of God, never could have been suggested and agreed upon by such a diversity of interests.[6]

Alexander Hamilton, who led his household regularly in the observance of family prayers[7], wrote to his friend James Bayard

*Alexander
Hamilton*

in April of 1802, revealing the important connection between Christianity and Constitutional freedom:

> In my opinion, the present constitution is the standard to which we are to cling. Under its banner bona fide must we combat our political foes, rejecting all changes but through the channel itself provided for amendments. By these general views of the subject have my reflections been guided.
> I now offer you the outline of the plan they have suggested. Let an association be formed to be denominated "The Christian Constitutional Society," its object to be first: The support of the Christian religion. second: The support of the United States.[8]

Alexander Hamilton expounded:

> I have carefully examined the evidences of the Christian religion, and if I was sitting as a juror upon its authenticity I would unhesitatingly give my verdict in its favor. I can prove its truth as clearly as any proposition ever submitted to the mind of man.[9]

In refuting those who had a misunderstanding of the nature of liberty, Alexander Hamilton explained:

> The fundamental source of all your errors, sophisms, and false reasoning, is a total ignorance of the natural rights of mankind. Were you once to become acquainted with these, you could never entertain a thought, that all men are not, by nature, entitled to a parity of privileges.
> You would be convinced, that natural liberty is a gift of the beneficent Creator, to the whole human race; and that civil liberty is founded in that; and cannot be wrested from any people, without the most manifest violation of justice.[10]

On July 12, 1804, Alexander Hamilton was shot by Aaron Burr in a duel. A few hours later he received last rites from Benjamin Moore, the Episcopalian Bishop of New York.[11] His dying words were:

I have a tender reliance on the mercy of the Almighty, through the merits of the Lord Jesus Christ. I am a sinner. I look to Him for mercy; pray for me.[12]

Alexander Hamilton was quoted in the eulogy given for him as saying:

Mortals hastening to the tomb, and once the companions of my pilgrimage, take warning, and avoid my errors. Cultivate the virtues I have recommended. Choose the Saviour I have chosen. Live disinterestedly, and would you rescue anything from final dissolution, lay it up in God.[13]

Alexander Hamilton

&

John Hancock (1737-1793), an American merchant and Revolutionary leader, was the president of the Provincial Congress of Massachusetts. He became well-known for having been the first member of the Continental Congress to sign the Declaration of Independence.

John Hancock   On April 15, 1775, the Provincial Congress of Massachusetts declared *A Day of Public Humiliation, Fasting and Prayer*, signed by the President of the Provincial Congress, John Hancock:

In circumstances dark as these, it becomes us, as Men and Christians, to reflect that, whilst every prudent Measure should be taken to ward off the impending Judgements....All confidence must be withheld from the Means we use; and reposed only on that GOD who rules in the Armies of Heaven, and without whose Blessing the best human Counsels are but Foolishness—and all created Power Vanity;

It is the Happiness of his Church that, when the Powers of Earth and Hell combine against it...that the Throne of Grace is of the easiest access—and its Appeal thither is graciously invited by the Father of Mercies, who has assured it, that when his Children ask Bread he will not give them a Stone....

RESOLVED, That it be, and hereby is recommended to the good

The Boston Tea Party.

People of this Colony of all Denominations, that THURSDAY the Eleventh Day of May next be set apart as a Day of Public Humiliation, Fasting and Prayer...to confess the sins...to implore the Forgiveness of all our Transgression...and a blessing on the Husbandry, Manufactures, and other lawful Employments of this People; and especially that the union of the American Colonies in Defence of their Rights (for hitherto we desire to thank Almighty GOD) may be preserved and confirmed.... And that AMERICA may soon behold a gracious Interposition of Heaven.

> By Order of the [Massachusetts] Provincial Congress, John Hancock, President.[14]

(See also *Boston Tea Party.*)

On November 8, 1783, Governor John Hancock, from Boston, Massachusetts, issued *A Proclamation for a Day of Thanksgiving* to celebrate the victorious conclusion of the Revolutionary War:

John Hancock, Esquire
Governor of the Commonwealth of Massachusetts
A Proclamation for a Day of Thanksgiving:
    Whereas...these United States are not only happily rescued from the Danger and Calamities to which they have been so long exposed,

John Hancock

but their Freedom, Sovereignty and Independence ultimately acknowledged.

And whereas...the Interposition of Divine Providence in our Favor hath been most abundantly and most graciously manifested, and the Citizens of these United States have every Reason for Praise and Gratitude to the God of their salvation.

Impressed therefore with an exalted Sense of the Blessings by which we are surrounded, and of our entire Dependence on that Almighty Being from whose Goodness and Bounty they are derived;

I do by and with the Advice of the Council appoint Thursday the Eleventh Day of December next (the Day recommended by the Congress to all the States) to be religiously observed as a Day of Thanksgiving and Prayer, that all the People may then assemble to celebrate...that he hath been pleased to continue to us the Light of the Blessed Gospel;...That we also offer up fervent Supplications...to cause pure Religion and Virtue to flourish...and to fill the World with his glory.[15]

❧

George Frederick Handel (1685-1759), the German musical composer, is world renowned for having written the immortal oratorio, *Messiah*, 1742, which he completed in twenty-five days. Composed for the benefit program of the Dublin Foundling Hospital, this masterpiece was so stirring that when King George II heard the "Hallelujah Chorus," he rose to his feet, at which point the entire audience stood. In speaking of composing the "Hallelujah Chorus" in the *Messiah*, Handel confided:

I did think I did see all heaven before me, and the great God Himself.[16]

George Frederick Handel wrote operas, oratorios, orchestra concertos, organ concertos, as well as music for the wind instruments, drums and harpsichord. A tremendously talented composer, Handel also was known for having a temper in his youth. An interesting event was an argument he had with another young musician. Challenged to a sword duel, Handel would have been killed had not his opponent's sword struck a button on his coat.

As he was taken in his last illness, after having been blind for seven years, Handel expressed he was:

> In hopes of meeting his good God, his sweet (precious) Saviour, on the day of His resurrection.[17]

Within his famous masterpiece *Messiah*, George Frederick Handel wrote this line:

> I know that my Redeemer liveth.[18]

❧

Warren Gamaliel Harding (1865-1923), was the 29th President of the United States of America. He had been a prominent newspaper editor in Ohio, a state senator and a U.S. Senator. In his Inaugural Address, March 4, 1921, President Warren Gamaliel Harding recognized:

Warren Gamaliel Harding

> What doth the Lord require of thee but to do justly and to love mercy, and to walk humbly with thy God?[19]

> I have always believed in the inspiration of the Holy Scriptures, whereby they have become the expression to man of the Word and Will of God.[20]

❧

John Harris (1666-1719), was an English mathematician and the editor of *The Dictionary of Arts and Sciences*, published in 1704, which was the first real encyclopedia in the English language. He was vice-president of the Royal Society and participated in giving the *Boyle Lectures* which defended the Christian faith.

The lectures John Harris gave in 1698 were entitled:

Atheistical Objections Against the Being of God and His Attributes, Fairly Considered and Fully Refuted.[21]

Benjamin Harrison

Benjamin Harrison (1833-1901), the 23rd President of the United States, was the grandson of the 9th President, William Henry Harrison, and great-grandson of the signer of the Declaration of Independence, Benjamin Harrison. He fought in the Civil War with General Sherman, promoted to the rank of brigadier general, and became a U.S. Senator. In his Inaugural Address, March 4, 1889, President Benjamin Harrison stated:

> We may reverently invoke and confidently extend the favor and help of Almighty God-that He will give to me wisdom, strength, fidelity, and to our people a spirit of fraternity and a love of righteousness and peace.[22]

President Benjamin Harrison wrote to his son, Russell:

> It is a great comfort to trust God - even if His providence is unfavorable. Prayer steadies one, when he is walking in slippery places - even if things asked for are not given.[23]

William Henry Harrison (1773-1841), the 9th President of the United States, was the son of Benjamin Harrison, signer of the Declaration of Independence, and grandfather of Benjamin Harrison, the 23rd President. President William Henry Harrison served only one month in office before he died. In his Inaugural Address, March 4, 1841, he stated:

William Henry Harrison

I deem the present occasion sufficiently important and solemn to justify me in expressing to my fellow citizens a profound reverence for the Christian religion, and a thorough conviction that sound morals, religious liberty, and a just sense of religious responsibility are essentially connected with all true and lasting happiness.[24]

John Harvard (1607-1638), who came to America to be a clergyman in Charlestown, Massachusetts, contributed his library and property in 1636 for the founding of the first college in America, which was subsequently named in his honor. According to the *Old South Leaflets:*

After God had carried us safe to New-England, and wee had builded our houses, provided necessaries for our livelihood, rear'd convenient places for God's worship, and setled the Civill Government: One of the next things we longed for, and looked after was to advance Learning and to perpetuate it to Posterity; dreading to leave an illiterate Ministry to the Churches, when our present Ministers shall lie in the Dust. And as wee were thinking and consulting how to effect this great Work, it pleased God to stir up the heart of one Mr. Harvard, a godly gentleman and a lover of learning there living amongst us, to give the one half of his estate...towards the erecting of a college and all his Library...[25]

Harvard University 1636, was founded in Cambridge, Massachusetts, from the donation of property and the library of Rev. John Harvard. Originally called the College at Cambridge, Harvard was the first college in America, being established only sixteen years after the landing of the Pilgrims. The declared purpose of the college was:

To train a literate clergy.[26]

The *Rules and Precepts* that were observed at Harvard, September 26, 1642, stated:

1. When any Schollar...is able to make [write] and speak true Latine in Verse and Prose....And decline perfectly the paradigims of Nounes and Verbes in the Greek tongue...[he is capable] of admission into the college.

2. Let every Student be plainly instructed, and earnestly pressed to consider well, the maine end of his life and studies is, to know God and Jesus Christ which is eternall life, John 17:3 and therefore to lay Christ in the bottome, as the only foundation of all sound knowledge and Learning. And seeing the Lord only giveth wisedome, Let every one seriously set himself by prayer in secret to seeke it of him Prov. 2, 3.

3. Every one shall so exercise himselfe in reading the Scriptures twice a day, that he shall be ready to give such an account of his proficiency therein, both in Theoreticall observations of Language and Logick, and in practicall and spirituall truths, as his Tutor shall require, according to his ability; seeing the entrance of the word giveth light, it giveth understanding to the simple, Psalm, 119:130.

4. That they eshewing all profanation of God's name, Attributes, Word, Ordinances, and times of Worship, do studie with good conscience carefully to retaine God, and the love of his truth in their mindes, else let them know, that (notwithstanding their Learning) God may give them up to strong delusions, and in the end to a reprobate minde, 2 Thes. 2:11, 12. Rom. 1:28.

5. That they studiously redeeme the time; observe the generall houres...diligently attend the Lectures, without any disturbance by word or gesture....

6. None shall...frequent the company and society of such men as lead an unfit, and dissolute life. Nor shall any without his Tutors leave, or without the call of Parents or Guardians, goe abroad to other Townes.

7. Every Scholar shall be present in his Tutors chamber at the 7th houre in the morning, immediately after the sound of the Bell, at his opening the Scripture and prayer, so also at the 5th houre at night, and then give account of his owne private reading....But if any...shall absent himself from prayer or Lectures, he shall bee lyable to Admonition, if he offend above once a weeke.

8. If any Scholar shall be found to transgresse any of the Lawes of God, or the Schoole...he may bee admonished at the publick monethly Act.[27]

Prior to the Revolution, ten of the twelve presidents of Harvard were ministers,[28] and according to reliable calculations, over fifty percent of the seventeenth-century Harvard graduates became ministers.[29] It is worthy of note that 106 of the first 108 schools in

America were founded on the Christian faith.[30]

Harvard College was founded in "Christi Gloriam" and later dedicated "Christo et Ecclesiae." The founders of Harvard believed that:

> All knowledge without Christ was vain. [31]

The word *Veritas,* still on the college seal, means divine truth. [32] The motto of Harvard was officially:

> For Christ and the Church. [33]

At Harvard University, the following inscription remains on the wall by the old iron gate at the main entrance to the campus. Found also in the catalog of the Harvard Divinity School, the dedication reads:

> After God had carried us safe to New England and we had builded our houses, provided necessaries for our livelihood, reared convenient places for God's worship and settled the civil government, one of the next things we longed for and looked after was to advance learning and perpetuate it to posterity, dreading to leave an illiterate ministry to the churches when our present ministers lie in the dust. [34]

In May of 1775, the president of Harvard, Samuel Langdon, addressed the Provincial Congress of Massachusetts:

> We have rebelled against God. We have lost the true spirit of Christianity, though we retain the outward profession and form of it .... By many, the Gospel is corrupted into a superficial system of moral philosophy, little better than ancient Platonism....
>
> My brethren, let us repent and implore the divine mercy. Let us amend our ways and our doings, reform everything that has been provoking the Most High, and thus endeavor to obtain the gracious interpositions of providence for our deliverance....
>
> May the Lord hear us in this day of trouble .... We will rejoice in His salvation, and in the name of our God, we will set up our banners! [35]

Mark O. Hatfield (1922-   ), being a member of the 100th
Congress, strongly supported President Ronald Reagan's signing
of Public Law 100-307, on January 25, 1988, setting aside the first
Thursday of each May to celebrate a National Day of Prayer. As
a United States Senator from Oregon, Mark Hatfield asserted:

> For the Christian man to reason that God does not want him
> involved in politics because there are too many evil men in government
> is as insensitive as for a Christian doctor to turn his back on an
> epidemic because there are too many germs there.[36]

Nathaniel Hawthorne (1804-1864), an American
author and poet, became famous through his
novel, *The Scarlet Letter*, published in 1850. He
was a friend of Henry Wadsworth Longfellow
and Franklin Pierce, the 14th President of the
United States. Other well known works of his
include: *The House of Seven Gables, Twice-Told
Tales, Blithedale Romance* and *Mosses from an Old
Manse.* In his poem, *The Star of Calvary*, Nathaniel
Hawthorne wrote:

*Nathaniel
Hawthorne*

It is the same infrequent star,
   The all mysterious light,
That, like a watcher gazing on
   The changes of the night,
Toward the hill of Bethlehem, took
   Its solitary flight.

It is the same infrequent star;
   Its sameness startleth me;
Although the disk is red a-blood
   And downward silently
It looketh on another hill,
   The hill of Calvary.

Behold, O Israel! behold!
   It is no human One

> That ye have dared to crucify.
>   What evil hath he done?
> It is your King, O Israel,
>   The God-begotten Son![37]

In *Ethan Brand*, written in 1850, Nathaniel Hawthorne wrote:

> "What is the Unpardonable Sin?" asked the lime-burner....
> "It is a sin that grew within my own breast," replied Ethan Brand...."The sin of an intellect that triumphed over the sense of brotherhood with man and reverence for God."[38]

ta

John Milton Hay (1838-1905), an ambassador to Great Britain under President McKinley, was renowned for being the Secretary of State who helped negotiate over fifty treaties. From the Open-Door policy with China, to the Panama Canal, to the Alaskan boundary, to the Philippine policy, he exerted a lasting impact on American foreign policy. In addition to serving as private secretary to President Lincoln, he was a poet and editorial writer for the *New York Tribune*. John Hay composed the poem:

John Milton Hay

> *Sinai and Calvary*
>
> But Calvary stands to ransom
>   The earth from utter loss;
> In shade than light more glorious
>   The shadow of the Cross.
> To heal a sick world's trouble,
>   To soothe its woe and pain,
> On Calvary's sacred summit
>   The Pascal Lamb was slain.
> Almighty God! direct us
>   To keep Thy perfect Law!

O blessed Saviour, help us
Nearer to Thee to draw!
Let Sinai's thunder aid us
To guard our feet from sin,
And Calvary's light inspire us
The love of God to win.[39]

ॐ

Franz Joseph Haydn (1732-1809), a remarkable Austrian musical composer, was considered the first master of the symphony, setting an example which Mozart and Beethoven later followed. He developed the string choir which has become the backbone of the modern orchestra. His works include 104 symphonies, 83 quartets, 42 sonatas, 24 concertos, 14 operas, 8 oratorios as well as the Austrian national anthem. His musical scores were replete with such phrases as "In nomine Domini," "Soli Deo Gloria," or "Laus Deo." Franz Joseph Haydn declared:

When I think of my God, my heart dances within me for joy, and then my music has to dance, too.[40]

When asked by Emperor Franz which of his oratorios he preferred, he replied:

"The Creation!...because in *The Creation* angels speak, and their talk is of God....I was never so pious as during the time that I worked on *The Creation.* Daily I fell on my knees, and begged God to vouchsafe to me strength for the fortunate outcome of the work."[41]

Haydn's last public appearance was on March 27, 1808, when the Society of Amateurs in Vienna performed *The Creation* oratorio. When the performance produced a thunderous applause by the audience, Haydn pointed up and exclaimed:

It came from above![42]

ॐ

Rutherford Birchard Hayes (1822-1893), the 19th President of the United States, had served as a Major General in the Civil War, a U.S. Congressman and a three-term Governor of Ohio. In his Inaugural Address, March 5, 1877, President Rutherford Birchard Hayes acknowledged he was:

> Looking for the guidance of that Divine Hand by which the destinies of nations and individuals are shaped.[43]

Rutherford Birchard Hayes

President Rutherford B. Hayes declared:

> I am a firm believer in the Divine teachings, perfect example, and atoning sacrifice of Jesus Christ. I believe also in the Holy Scriptures as the revealed Word of God to the world for its enlightenment and salvation.[44]

❧

Reginald Heber (1783-1826), was an English missionary and hymn writer. He was the first Anglican bishop sent to India, where he baptized the first Christian convert in East India. In 1827, Reginald Heber wrote the immortal words to the hymn, *Holy, Holy, Holy:*

> Holy, Holy, Holy! Lord God Almighty!
> Early in the morning our song shall rise to Thee:
> Holy, Holy, Holy! Merciful and Mighty!
> God in Three Persons, Blessed Trinity.[45]

❧

Felicia Dorothea Browne Hemans (1793-1835), was an English poet noted for her naturalness and simplicity. Sir Walter Scott wrote the epilogue for her play, *The Vespers of Palermo*. Felicia Hemans is best known to American readers for her work, *The Landing of the Pilgrim Fathers*, in which she penned:

Ay, call it holy ground,
The soil where they first trod!
They have left unstained what there they found—
Freedom to worship God.[46]

❧

Patrick Henry (1736-1799), was an American Revolutionary leader and orator, who spoke the now famous phrase, "Give me Liberty or give me death!" He was Commander-in-Chief of the Virginia Militia, a member of the Continental Congress, a member of the Virginia General Assembly and House of Burgesses, and was instrumental in writing the Constitution of Virginia. He was the five-time Governor of the State of Virginia, (the only governor in United States history to be elected and reelected five times).

Patrick Henry

Patrick Henry was offered numerous positions by President George Washington and Congress, but he declined them all, including: Secretary of State, Chief Justice of the Supreme Court, U.S. Minister to Spain, U.S. Minister to France and U.S. Senator.

Prior to the Revolution, in 1768, Patrick Henry rode for miles on horseback to a trial in Spottsylvania County. He entered the rear of the courtroom where three Baptist ministers were being tried for having preached without the sanction of the Episcopalian Church. In the midst of the proceedings, he interrupted:

> May it please your lordships, what did I hear read? Did I hear an expression that these men, whom you worships are about to try for misdemeanor, are charged with preaching the gospel of the Son of God?[47]

On March 23, 1775, the Second Virginia Convention had been moved from the House of Burgesses to St. John's Church in Richmond, because of the mounting tension between the Colonies and the British Crown. It was here that Patrick Henry delivered his fiery patriotic oration:

Patrick Henry

For my own part I consider it as nothing less than a question of freedom or slavery....It is only in this way that we can hope to arrive at truth, and fulfill the great responsibility which we hold to God and our country...

Sir, we have done everything that could be done to avert the storm which is now coming on. We have petitioned; we have remonstrated; we have supplicated; we have prostrated ourselves before the throne, and have implored its interposition to arrest the tyrannical hands of the ministry and parliament. Our petitions have been slighted; our remonstrances have produced additional violence and insult; our supplications have been disregarded; and we have been spurned, with contempt....An appeal to arms and to the God of Hosts is all that is left us!

....Sir, we are not weak, if we make a proper use of the means which the God of nature hath placed in our power. Three millions of people, armed in the Holy cause of Liberty, and in such a country as that which we possess, are invincible by any force which our enemy can send against us.

Besides, sir, we shall not fight our battle alone. There is a just God who presides over the destinies of nations; and who will raise up friends to fight our battle for us. The battle, sir, is not to the strong alone; it is to the vigilant, the active, the brave....

Is life so dear, or peace so sweet, as to be purchased at the price of chains and slavery? Forbid it, Almighty God! I know not what course others may take; but as for me, give me liberty or give me death![48]

On June 12, 1776, as a member of the committee chosen to draft the first constitution of the commonwealth of Virginia, Patrick Henry helped champion article 16 of the Virginia Bill of Rights:

That religion, or the duty which we owe to our Creator, and the manner of discharging it, can be directed only by reason and conviction, not by force or violence; and therefore all men are equally entitled to the free exercise of religion, according to the dictates of conscience; and that it is the mutual duty of all to practice Christian forbearance, love, and charity towards each other.[49]

Patrick Henry wrote on the back of *The Stamp Act Resolves,* passed in the House of Burgesses in May of 1765, a summary of the pivotal events preceding the Revolution. Patrick Henry ended his writing with the following admonition:

Patrick Henry protests the Stamp Act in the House of Burgesses

This brought on the war which finally separated the two countries and gave independence to ours. Whether this will prove a blessing or a curse, will depend upon the use our people make of the blessings, which a gracious God hath bestowed on us.

If they are wise, they will be great and happy. If they are of a contrary character, they will be miserable.

Righteousness alone can exalt them as a nation. Reader! Whoever thou art, remember this, and in thy sphere practice virtue thyself, and encourage it in others.   - (signed) P. Henry [50]

Patrick Henry is attributed with the statement:

It cannot be emphasized too strongly or too often that this great nation was founded, not by religionists, but by Christians; not on religions, but on the Gospel of Jesus Christ. For this very reason peoples of other faiths have been afforded asylum, prosperity, and freedom of worship here. [51]

Patrick Henry, once interrupted while engaged in reading Scriptures, held up the Bible and said:

The Bible is worth all other books which have ever been printed. [52]

Patrick Henry wrote to his sister, Ann, in Kentucky, upon learning of the death of her husband, Colonel William Christian:

Would to God I could say something to give relief to the dearest of women and sisters....

My heart is full. Perhaps I may never see you in this world. O may we meet in heaven, to which the merits of Jesus will carry those who love and serve Him. Heaven will, I trust, give you its choicest comfort and preserve your family. Such is the prayer of him who thinks it his honor and pride to be, Your Affectionate Brother, Patrick Henry.[53]

On November 20, 1798, in his *Last Will and Testament*, Patrick Henry wrote:

This is all the inheritance I give to my dear family. The religion of Christ will give them one which will make them rich indeed.[54]

While Patrick Henry was dying, he spoke:

Doctor, I wish you to observe how real and beneficial the religion of Christ is to a man about to die....I am, however, much consoled by reflecting that the religion of Christ has, from its first appearance in the world, been attacked in vain by all the wits, philosophers, and wise ones, aided by every power of man, and its triumphs have been complete.[55]

Patrick Henry's grandson, William Wirt Henry, described Henry as one who:

Looked to the restraining and elevating principles of Christianity as the hope of his country's institutions.[56]

Patrick Henry Fontaine, also a grandson, said Patrick Henry had committed himself to the:

Earnest efforts to establish true Christianity in our country.[57]

❧

Sir John Frederick Herschel (1792-1871), an outstanding English astronomer and the son of the great astronomer Sir William Herschel, discovered and catalogued over 500 new stars and nebulae of both northern and southern hemispheres. Concerning the Bible, he asserted:

All human discoveries seem to be made only for the purpose of confirming more and more strongly the truths that come from on high and are contained in the Sacred Writings.[58]

ૐ

Sir William Herschel (1738-1822), the renowned English astronomer who discovered the planet "Uranus," in addition to noting the recognition of double stars, constructed the greatest reflecting telescopes of his time with which he cataloged and studied the nebulae and galaxies as had never been done before. It was Herschel who insisted:

The undevout astronomer must be mad.[59]

ૐ

Benjamin Harvey Hill (1823-1882), a noted statesman and orator from Georgia who opposed secession prior to the Civil War, later became a U.S. Senator. In a tribute to Robert E. Lee, Benjamin Hill expressed:

He was a foe without hate, a friend without treachery, a soldier without cruelty, and a victim without murmuring. He was a public officer without vices, a private citizen without wrong, a neighbor without reproach, a Christian without hypocrisy, and a man without guile. He was a Caesar without his ambition, a Frederick without his tyranny, a Napoleon without his selfishness, and a Washington without his reward.[60]

ૐ

Conrad Nicholson Hilton (1887-1979), founder of the American hotel chain, was known as "the biggest hotel man in the world." After having served in World War I, he was involved in the banking business, and his father's mercantile concerns. In 1919, he purchased his first hotel in Cisco, Texas, which began his world-impacting career. On May 7, 1952, Conrad Hilton gave an address, entitled, *A Battle for Peace:*

OUR FATHER IN HEAVEN:
WE PRAY that YOU save us from ourselves.
The world that YOU have made for us, to live in peace,
    we have made into an armed camp.
We live in fear of war to come.
We are afraid of "the terror that flies by night,
    and the arrow that flies by day,
    the pestilence that walks in darkness
    and the destruction that wastes at noon-day."
We have turned from YOU to go our selfish way.
We have broken YOUR commandments and denied YOUR
    truth.
We have left YOUR altars to serve the false gods of money
    and pleasure and power.
FORGIVE US AND HELP US
Now, darkness gathers around us and we are confused
    in all our counsels.
Losing faith in YOU,
    we lose faith in ourselves.
Inspire us with wisdom, all of us of every color, race and
    creed,
        to use our wealth, our strength to help our brother,
        instead of destroying him.
Help us to do YOUR will as it is done in heaven
    and to be worthy of YOUR promise of peace on earth.
Fill us with new faith, new strength and new courage,
    that we may win the Battle for Peace.
Be swift to save us, dear God,
    before the darkness falls.[61]

ᑤ

Archibald Alexander Hodge (1823-1886), was a prominent author, lecturer and theologian at Princeton College. In 1873, he explicated to America:

A Christian is just as much under the obligation to obey God's will in the most secular of his daily business as he is in his closet or at the communion table. He has no right to separate his life into two realms, and acknowledge different moral codes in each...

The kingdom of God includes all sides of human life, and it is a kingdom of absolute righteousness. You are either a loyal subject or a traitor. When the king comes, how will he find you doing?[62]

If professing Christians are unfaithful to the authority of their Lord in their capacity as citizens of the State, they cannot expect to be blessed by the indwelling of the Holy Ghost in their capacity as members of the Church. The kingdom of God is one, it cannot be divided...

If the Church languishes, the State cannot be in health; and if the State rebels against its Lord and King, the Church cannot enjoy his favour...

I charge you, citizens of the United States, afloat on your wide sea of politics, THERE IS ANOTHER KING, ONE JESUS: THE SAFETY OF THE STATE CAN BE SECURED ONLY IN THE WAY OF HUMBLE AND WHOLE-SOULED LOYALTY TO HIS PERSON AND OF OBEDIENCE TO HIS LAW.[63]

ða

Josiah Gilbert Holland (1819-1881), was one of the founders and the editor of the popular *Scribner's Monthly* (later renamed *Century Magazine*), and the *Springfield Republican*. He established the publishing policies of using contributors' names and receiving payment for everything published. A celebrated speaker on social topics and conduct of life, Josiah Gilbert Holland also wrote under the pen name "Timothy Titcomb." His well-read narrative works include the poems *Kathrina* and *Bitter-Sweet*. In 1872, Holland wrote in his *Gradatim:*

Heaven is not reached in a single bound.[64]

In his work, *Wanted*, also written in 1872, Josiah Gilbert Holland penned:

God give us men! A time like this demands
Strong minds, great hearts, true faith, and ready hands;
Men whom the lust of office does not kill;
Men whom the spoils of office cannot buy;
Men who possess opinions and a will;
Men who have honor; men who will not lie.[65]

ða

Oliver Wendell Holmes, Jr. (1841-1935), known as the "Great Dissenter," was one of the most influential associate justices of the United States Supreme Court. He was appointed in 1902 by President Theodore Roosevelt and served for 30 years.

The son of Oliver Wendell Holmes, the famous author and physician, Oliver Wendell Holmes, Jr. graduated from Harvard College, served in the Union Army during the Civil War, and later became the editor of the *American Law Review.* He was a professor at the Harvard Law School before becoming the Chief Justice of the Supreme Court of Massachusetts. Known for his remarkable brilliance and humor, Oliver Wendell Holmes, Jr. wrote to William James in 1907, saying:

> The great act of faith is when man decides that he is not God.[66]

In a letter to John C. H. Wu, dated 1924, Holmes wrote:

> Have faith and pursue the unknown end.[67]

On March 8, 1931, in reply to a reporter's question on his ninetieth birthday, Oliver Wendell Holmes, Jr. stated:

> Young man, the secret of my success is that at an early age I discovered I was not God.[68]

֍

Thomas Hooker (1586-1647), one of the founders of Hartford, Connecticut, in 1636, was a principal organizer of the New England colonies into the defensive confederation, known as the "United Colonies of New England," 1643. A Cambridge University graduate, Thomas Hooker was persecuted in England after becoming involved with the Christian movement known as the Puritans. He was forced to flee, first to Holland, and then, in 1633, to America.

A prominent and highly influential leader in the colonies, his sermon before the General Court of Connecticut propounded such unprecedented democratic principles, that it inspired the writing of Connecticut's Constitution, which was called the *Fundamental Constitutions of Connecticut, 1639.*This constitution was so significant, that it became a model for all other constitutions in the colonies, including the United States Constitution. Thomas Hooker explained:

> Mutual covenanting and confederating of the saints in the fellowship of the faith according to the order of the Gospel, is that which gives constitution and being to a visible church....Mutual subjection is the sinews of society, by which it is sustained and supported.[69]

Herbert Clark Hoover

Herbert Clark Hoover (1874-1964), the 31st President of the United States, was the first president elected out of a business career. He had made a fortune as a mining engineer, and then, at the outbreak of World War I, became the food administrator of the United States. From there he accepted a post on President Harding's cabinet, followed by the presidential nomination by the Republican party. In his Inaugural Address, March 4, 1929, President Herbert Clark Hoover entreated:

> This occasion is not alone the administration of the most sacred oath which can be assumed by an American citizen. It is a dedication and consecration under God to the highest office in service of our people.
>
> I assume this trust in the humility of knowledge that only through the guidance of Almighty Providence can I hope to discharge its ever-increasing burdens....
>
> I ask the help of Almighty God in this service.[70]

In an address at Valley Forge, May 30, 1931, President Hoover stated:

> If those few thousand men endured that long winter of privation and suffering, humiliated by the despair of their countrymen, and deprived of support save their own indomitable will, yet held their countrymen to the faith, and by that holding held fast the freedom of America, what right have we to be of little faith?[71]

In *The Challenge of Liberty*, 1934, Herbert Clark Hoover declared:

> While I can make no claim for having introduced the term, "rugged individualism," I should be proud to have invented it. It has been used by American leaders for over a half-century in eulogy of those God-fearing men and women of honesty whose stamina and character and fearless assertion of rights led them to make their own way in life.[72]

Herbert Hoover, in 1943, issued a joint statement along with Mrs. Calvin Coolidge, Mrs. Theodore Roosevelt, Mrs. William H. Taft, Mrs. Benjamin Harrison, Mrs. Grover Cleveland, Alfred Smith, Alfred Landon, James M. Cox, and John W. Davis:

> Menaced by collectivist trends, we must seek revival of our strength in the spiritual foundations which are the bedrock of our republic. Democracy is the outgrowth of the religious conviction of the sacredness of every human life. On the religious side, its highest embodiment is The Bible; on the political side, the Constitution.[73]

After his term in office, former President Herbert Clark Hoover sought a reorganization of the United Nations, excluding Communist countries. The speech, delivered to the American Newspaper Publishers Association, was broadcast across the nation on April 27, 1950:

> What the world needs today is a definite, spiritual mobilization of the nations who believe in God against this tide of Red agnosticism. It needs a moral mobilization against the hideous ideas of the police state and human slavery....
>
> I suggest that the United Nations should be reorganized without the Communist nations in it. If that is impractical, then a definite New United Front should be organized of those peoples who disavow communism, who stand for morals and religion, and who love freedom....
>
> It is a proposal based solely upon moral, spiritual and defense foundations. It is a proposal to redeem the concept of the United Nations to the high purpose for which it was created. It is a proposal for moral and spiritual cooperation of God-fearing free nations.
>
> And in rejecting an atheistic other world, I am confident that the Almighty God will be with us.[74]

President Herbert Hoover stated:

> The whole inspiration of our civilization springs from the teachings of Christ and the lessons of the prophets. To read the Bible for these fundamentals is a necessity of American life.[75]

J. (John) Edgar Hoover (1895-1972), the American director of the Federal Bureau of Investigation (FBI), became famous for his dramatic campaigns to stop organized crime. J. Edgar Hoover explained:

> The criminal is the product of spiritual starvation. Someone failed miserably to bring him to know God, love Him and serve Him.[76]

Gerard Manley Hopkins (1844-1889), an English poet and artist of significant impact, composed in his work, *No. 28, The Wreck of the Deutschland:*

> Thou mastering me
> God! giver of breath and bread;
> World's strand, sway of the sea;
> Lord of the living and dead;
> Thou hast bound bones and veins in me, fastened me flesh,
> And after it almost unmade, what with dread,
> Thy doing: and dost thou touch me afresh?
> Over again I feel thy finger and find thee.[77]

In *No. 31, God's Grandeur*, Gerard Manley Hopkins wrote:

> The world is charged with the grandeur of God.[78]

Hornbook, during the period 1442 to 1800, was the schoolbook used in early English and American schools to teach children to read. Invented in response to the expense and scarcity of paper, the hornbook consisted of one sheet of paper pasted to a flat board with a handle and covered over with a thin piece of transparent cow's horn, giving the appearance of a protective plastic cover. On the paper was printed the Criss-Cross Row (a Criss-Cross followed by the alphabet), the Benediction, the Lord's Prayer, and the Roman numerals.[79]

The Criss-Cross—originating in 1475 from the Middle English *Christ's-Cross*, and earlier, 1390, from *Cros-Kryst*—was the mark + or *X* written before the alphabet. (The Greek symbol ×, abbreviation of *Christos*, is of the same origin as *X-mas* for "Christmas.")[80] Learning the "Criss-Cross Row," therefore, was the expression used for learning the alphabet. The mark stood for the phrase *Christ-Cross me speed* ("May Christ's Cross give me success"), an invocation said before reciting the alphabet.[81] The Criss-Cross or Christ's-Cross (X) was also a form of written oath to God used before signing one's name on a document; and in the event a person could not write, it was used in place of his or her signature.[82]

The hornbook ceased being used in the early 1800s, when paper became less expensive and more easily available.

&

Oliver Otis Howard (1830-1909), was an illustrious Union General during the Civil War and the Superintendent of West Point Academy. He was appointed by President Lincoln to lead the Freedmen's Bureau, assisting former slaves after the war; he then went on to found Howard University for freed slaves in 1867. General Oliver Otis Howard, whose strong belief in the gospel created controversy when he integrated a church, also served as the Chairman of the American Tract Society.

Oliver Otis Howard

He was known by his soldiers as the "Old Prayer Book" because he never drank, smoke or swore. In 1869, as Superintendent of West Point, he personally presented each incoming cadet with a Bible, a practice which continues today.

In 1863, Major General Oliver Otis Howard addressed the officers and troops of the 127th Pennsylvania Volunteers:

I am glad to see so many of you out to hear preaching this Sabbath morning, and I would to God, that all the men of my command were true followers of Christ Jesus, the Lord. Soldiers, allow me to express, with your chaplain, the sincere desire of my heart, that we may meet at the right hand of the Great Judge in that day, which he has described to us.[83]

Major General Oliver Otis Howard declared:

I go to the Scriptures daily for spiritual food, and have done so for thirty-five years. God, as revealed to me in the crucified, the risen, and the ascended Christ, meets all my personal wants.[84]

At a Union camp chapel service, a missionary in the Christian Commission recorded General Howard's message:

The General spoke of the Saviour, his love for Him and his peace in His service, as freely and simply as he could have spoken in his own family circle.[85]

ૐ

Julia Ward Howe (1819-1910), was the author of the famous Civil War song, *The Battle Hymn of the Republic*, which was a favorite of President Abraham Lincoln. She was the daughter of a Wall Street banker, and wife of Doctor Samuel Gridley Howe.

Julia Ward Howe

Julia Ward Howe was very active in the abolition of the slavery movement, and later became a leader in the women's suffrage movement. In 1907, she became the first woman member of the American Academy of Arts and Letters. She and her husband worked hard against slavery and even entertained John Brown in their home.

In 1861 she traveled to Washington, D.C., and saw the city teeming with military, horses galloping all around and innumerable campfires burning. Sleeping unsoundly one night, she wrote the words to her poem. In February, 1862, the poem, *The Battle Hymn of the Republic*, was published in the *Atlantic Monthly*

Magazine (She received $5 for the poem.)

Mine eyes have seen the glory of the coming of the Lord: He is trampling out the vintage where the grapes of wrath are stored; He has loosed the fateful lighting of His terrible swift sword: His truth is marching on.

I have seen Him in the watch-fires of a hundred circling camps; They have builded Him an altar in the evening dews and damps; I can read His righteous sentence by the dim and flaring lamps: His day is marching on.

I have read a fiery gospel writ in burnished rows of steel; 'As ye deal with my contemners, so with you my grace shall deal; Let the Hero, born of woman, crush the serpent with his heel, Since God is marching on.

He has sounded forth the trumpet that shall never call retreat; He is sifting out the hearts of men before His judgement-seat: Oh, be swift, my soul, to answer Him! Be jubilant, my feet! Our God is marching on.

In the beauty of the lilies Christ was born across the sea; With a glory in his bosom that transfigures you and me: As he died to make men holy, let us die to make men free, While God is marching on.[86]

&

William Dean Howells (1837-1920), an editor, poet, novelist and literary critic, was one of America's first realistic fiction writers. He was the United States Consul in Venice, a writer for the *New York Tribune* and the *Nation,* assistant editor of the *Atlantic Monthly,* and in 1886 joined the staff of *Harper's Monthly.*

Elected the first president of the American Academy of Arts and Letters, William Dean Howells was a friend of Mark Twain, James Russell Lowell, Oliver Wendell Holmes, Henry Wadsworth Longfellow, Nathaniel Hawthorne and Walt Whitman. His works include: *A Boy's Town; Their Wedding Journey; A Modern Instance; A Foregone Conclusion; Hazard of New Fortunes;* and *The Rise of Silas Lapham,* 1885.

In his work *A Thanksgiving,* William Dean Howells wrote:

Lord, for the erring thought
Not for the evil wrought:
Lord, for the wicked will
Betrayed and baffled still:
For the heart from itself kept,
Our thanksgiving accept.[87]

&

Victor Marie Hugo (1802-1885), the famous French author who wrote *The Hunchback of Notre Dame*, 1831; *Les Contemplations*, 1856; *Les Miserables*, 1862; *Legend of the Centuries*, 1859-1883; and numerous other great works, was deeply involved in politics, and was exiled from France a number of times. Victor Marie Hugo avouched:

England has two books, the Bible and Shakespeare. England made Shakespeare, but the Bible made England.[88]

Victor Hugo remarked:

Courage for the great sorrows of life, and patience for the small ones, and when you have laboriously accomplished your daily task, go to sleep in peace. God is awake.[89]

&

John Hus (1370-1415), was a professor of philosophy and the rector of the University of Prague, in Bohemia. He insisted on teaching and expounding the Scriptures in the language of the people, and inspired a great following, similar to John Wycliffe in England. Amidst great controversy, he was betrayed and martyred. His last words were:

O holy simplicity![90]

&

Thomas Henry Huxley (1825-1895), was an English naturalist who strongly propounded the theory of evolution. In spite of his ardent support of that theory, Thomas Henry Huxley expressed:

> The Bible has been the Magna Charta of the poor and oppressed. The human race is not in a position to dispense with it.[91]

ᨺ

Henry J. Hyde (1924-   ), a U.S. Representative from Illinois, delivered a powerful speech after receiving the "Defender of Life" Award at the Constitutional Litigation Conference, July 16, 1993:

> "That all men are created equal and are endowed by their Creator." Human beings upon creation, not upon birth. That is where our human dignity comes from. It comes from the Creator. It is an endowment, not an achievement.
>
> By membership in the human family, we are endowed by our Creator with "inalienable rights." They can't be voted away by a jury or a court.
>
> "Among which are life"—the first inalienable right, the first endowment from the Creator. That is mainstream America, the predicate for our Constitution, our country's birth certificate. To respect the right to life as an endowment from the Creator....
>
> It is the unborn who are the least of God's creatures. We have been told that whatsoever we do for the least of these we do unto Jesus.[92]

ᨺ

I

Constitution of the State of Idaho 1889, states:

Preamble. We, the people of the State of Idaho, grateful to Almighty God for our freedom, to secure its blessings and promote our common welfare do establish this Constitution.[1]

ॐ

State of Idaho October 16, 1994, issued an Executive Proclamation declaring October 16-22, 1994, as "Christian Heritage Week." (A similar Proclamation was also signed March 23, 1992.):

WHEREAS, the Preamble to the Constitution of the State of Idaho declares that "We, the people of the State of Idaho, grateful to Almighty God for our freedom, to secure its blessings and promote our common welfare do establish this Constitution."; and

WHEREAS, Idaho has been richly blessed in natural beauty, reflecting God's miracle of creation; and the importance of our Christian Heritage to the traditions and values of Idaho is immeasurable; and

WHEREAS, the Christian Heritage of our nation is recognized in the writings and accomplishments of our citizens and in public documents and utterances made by many prominent Americans including Benjamin Franklin, George Washington, Thomas Jefferson, James Madison, and Patrick Henry; and

WHEREAS, the history of Christian faith and traditions of our people is reflected in practices in our public institutions and by our government officials; and

WHEREAS, the importance of our Christian Heritage to our institutions' values and vision is invaluable, and teaching future generations the all-important role of Christian Heritage is meaningful to peoples of all faiths, with our community churches serving a vital function in binding citizens together and providing crucial education and charitable services; and

WHEREAS, it is appropriate to set aside a specific time for celebrating our Christian Heritage;

NOW, THEREFORE, I, Cecil D. Andrus, Governor of the State of Idaho, do hereby proclaim October 16 through 22, 1994, to be

"CHRISTIAN HERITAGE WEEK"

in Idaho, and I encourage our citizens to acknowledge and appreciate the religious heritage of our great state and nation and to observe this week with appropriate ceremonies, activities and programs.

In Witness Whereof, I have hereunto set my hand and caused to be affixed the Great Seal of the State of Idaho at the Capitol of Boise.

> Cecil D. Andrus   Pete T. Cenarrusa
> Governor   Secretary of State[2]

ða

Constitution of the State of Illinois 1870, stated:

We, the people of the State of Illinois, grateful to Almighty God for the civil, political and religious liberty which He hath so long permitted us to enjoy, and looking to Him for a blessing upon our endeavors to secure and transmit the same unimpaired to succeeding generation...[3]

ða

State of Illinois June 24, 1993, proclaimed November 21-27, 1993 as Christian Heritage Week:

WHEREAS, religious holidays, festivals, and celebrations add to the cultural mosaic of our state; and

WHEREAS, churches are a functional part of the communities in our state, often providing charitable assistance to our citizens; and

WHEREAS, Thanksgiving week is an appropriate time to center attention on the religious heritage of our state and nation;

THEREFORE, I, Jim Edgar, Governor of the State of Illinois, proclaim November 21-27, 1993, as CHRISTIAN HERITAGE WEEK in Illinois.

In Witness Whereof, I hereunto set my hand and caused the Great Seal of the State of Illinois to be affixed. Done at the Capital, in the City of Springfield, this twenty-four day of June, in the Year of Our Lord one thousand nine hundred and ninety-three, and of the State of Illinois, the one hundred and seventy-fifth.

> George H. Ryan   Jim Edgar
> Secretary of State   Governor[4]

State of Indiana April 18,1994 issued an Executive Proclamation declaring November 20-26,1994, as "Christian Heritage Week," signed by Governor Evan Bayh and Secretary of State Joseph H. Hogsett. (A similar Proclamation was signed October 12, 1993):

> WHEREAS, Religious holidays, festivals and celebrations add to the cultural mosaic of our state; and
>
> WHEREAS, Churches are a functional part of the many communities in our state, often providing charitable assistance to those in need;
>
> WHEREAS, Thanksgiving week is a fitting time to center attention on the religious heritage of our state;
>
> THEREFORE, 1, Evan Bayh, Governor of the State of Indiana, do hereby proclaim November 20 - 26, 1994, as
>
> "CHRISTIAN HERITAGE WEEK"
>
> in the state of Indiana.
>
> In Testimony Whereof, I have hereunto set my hand and caused to be affixed the Great Seal of the State of Indiana at the Capitol in Indianapolis on this 18th day of April, 1994.
>
> Evan Bayh   Attest: Joseph H. Hogsett
> By The Governor: Evan Bayh   Secretary of State. [5]
> Governor of Indiana

State of Iowa May 23,1992, Governor Terry Edward Branstad joined the thousands in Des Moines and the estimated 600,000 worldwide in the first international *March For Jesus.* With over 142 U.S. cities participating and 50 nations, this yearly event has grown to include an estimated 25 million participants globally. At the end of the march, Governor Terry Branstad addressed the crowd, stating:

> It is exciting to see people from all over the world marching today in this very special March For Jesus. We all come together with a common belief in God, and we recognize that we are dependent on the Lord for guidance, that we can't do it by ourselves. [6]

Queen Isabella *(1451-1504),* was the Queen of Castile, who, along with her husband, King Ferdinand of Aragon, financed Christopher Columbus' expedition to the Indies, which resulted in the discovery of America. In her commission to Columbus, she recited that the purpose of the voyage was:

> For the Glory of God....it is hoped that by God's assistance some of the continents and islands in the oceans will be discovered.[7]

Isabel I (Isabella the Catholic)

Queen Isabella informed the Pope of Columbus' attempt:

> To bear the light of Christ west to the heathen undiscovered lands.[8]

On February 15, 1493, on his return trip from having discovered America, Columbus wrote to Queen Isabella and King Ferdinand from on board the ship *Caravel* anchored off the Canary Islands:

> Praise be to our eternal God, our Lord, who gives to all those who walk in His ways victory over all things which seem impossible; of which this is signally one, for, although others have spoken or written concerning these countries, it was all conjecture, as no one could say that he had seen them—it amounting only to this, that those who heard listened the more, and regarded the matter rather as a fable than anything else.

Christopher Columbus

> But our Redeemer has granted this victory to our illustrious King and Queen and their kingdoms, which have acquired great fame by an event of such high importance, in which all Christendom ought to rejoice, and which it ought to celebrate with great festivals and the offering of solemn thanks to the Holy Trinity with many sincere prayers, both for the great exaltation which may accrue to them in turning so many nations to our holy faith, and also for the temporal benefits which will bring great refreshment and gain, not only to Spain, but to all Christians.
>
> Done on board the Caravel, off the Canary Islands, on the fifteenth day of February, Fourteen hundred and ninety-three. At your orders,
>
> The Admiral.[9]

ɂ

J

Andrew Jackson (1767-1845), the 7th President
of the United States of America, was also a lawyer,
a Congressman, a U.S. Senator and a judge on
the Tennessee Supreme Court. Andrew Jackson
is credited with proposing the state's name,
"Tennessee," while being a member of the state's
first convention which adopted its constitution.
Known as "Old Hickory," he was a victorious
Major General in the army, winning the *Battle of*
New Orleans and capturing Florida. On January 8, 1815, Andrew
Jackson wrote to his friend Robert Hays regarding the victorious
Battle of New Orleans, during the War of 1812:

Andrew Jackson

> It appears that the unerring hand of Providence shielded my men
> from the shower of balls, bombs, and rockets, when every ball and
> bomb from our guns carried with them a mission of death.[1]

Concerning that same battle, Jackson wrote to Secretary of
War James Monroe:

> Heaven, to be sure, has interposed most wonderfully in our
> behalf, and I am filled with gratitude, when I look back to what we
> have escaped.[2]

In 1832, President Andrew Jackson vetoed the *Bank Renewal*
Bill, preventing the establishment of the Bank of the United
States, recognizing that a federal bank would be detrimental to
the freedoms of Americans:

It is easy to conceive that great evils to our country and its institutions might flow from such a concentration of power in the hands of a few men irresponsible to the people....

Their power would be great whenever they might choose to exert it...to influence elections or control the affairs of the nation. But if any private citizen or public functionary should interpose to curtail its powers or prevent a renewal of its privileges, it can not be doubted that he would be made to feel its influence....

Controlling our currency, receiving our public moneys, and holding thousands of our citizens in dependence, it would be more formidable and dangerous than the naval and military power of the enemy...

To this conclusion I can not assent. Mere precedent is a dangerous source of authority, and should not be regarded as deciding questions of constitutional power....

It is to be regretted that the rich and powerful too often bend the acts of government to their selfish purposes....

In the full enjoyment of the gifts of Heaven and the fruits of superior industry, economy, and virtue, every man is equally entitled to protection by law; but when the laws undertake to add to these natural and just advantages artificial distinctions, to grant titles, gratuities, and exclusive privileges, to make the rich richer and the potent more powerful, the humble members of society—the farmers, mechanics, and laborers—who have neither the time nor the means of securing like favors to themselves, have a right to complain of the injustice of their Government.

There are no necessary evils in government. Its evils exist only in its abuses. If it would confine itself to equal protection, and, as Heaven does its rains, shower its favors alike on the high and the low, the rich and the poor, it would be an unqualified blessing. In the act before me there seems to be a wide and unnecessary departure from these just principles.[3]

On March 4, 1833, in his Second Inaugural Address, President Andrew Jackson stated:

Finally, it is my fervent prayer to that Almighty Being...that He will so overrule all my intentions and actions and inspire the hearts of my fellow-citizens that we may be preserved from dangers of all kinds and continue forever a united happy people.[4]

Andrew Jackson wrote to Mary and Andrew Jackson

Hutchings on the death of their firstborn in 1834:

> My dear Hutchings...I am truly happy to find that you both have met this severe bereavement with that Christian meekness and submission as was your duty. This charming babe was only given you from your Creator and benefactor....He has a right to take away, and we ought humbly to submit to His will and be always ready to say, blessed be His name. We have one consolation under this severe bereavement, that this babe is now in the bosom of its Saviour.[5]

On September 11, 1834, Andrew Jackson wrote a letter to his son, Andrew, Jr.:

> I nightly offer up my prayers to the throne of grace for the health and safety of you all, and that we ought all to rely with confidence on the promises of our dear Redeemer, and give Him our hearts. This is all he requires and all that we can do, and if we sincerely do this, we are sure of salvation through his atonement.[6]

Andrew Jackson wrote a letter to comfort the family of General Coffee who had recently died:

> Rely on our dear Saviour. He will be father to the fatherless and husband to the widow. Trust in the mercy and goodness of Christ, and always be ready to say with heartfelt resignation, "may the Lord's will be done."[7]

In January of 1835, an assassination attempt was perpetrated on President Andrew Jackson. A bearded man, at point blank range, fired two pistols at him, but for some reason the guns failed to discharge. The King of England heard of the incident and expressed his concern. President Jackson wrote back, exclaiming:

> A kind of Providence had been pleased to shield me against the recent attempt upon my life, and irresistibly carried many minds to the belief in a superintending Providence.[8]

On March 25, 1835, Andrew Jackson wrote in a letter:

I was brought up a rigid Presbyterian, to which I have always adhered. Our excellent Constitution guarantees to every one freedom of religion, and charity tells us (and you know Charity is the real basis of all true religion)...judge the tree by its fruit.

All who profess Christianity believe in a Saviour, and that by and through Him we must be saved. We ought, therefore, to consider all good Christians whose walks correspond with their professions, be they Presbyterian, Episcopalian, Baptist, Methodist or Roman Catholic.[9]

On December 30, 1836, President Andrew Jackson wrote to Mr. Andrew Donelson after hearing that his wife, Emily, had died:

My dear Andrew, we cannot recall her, we are commanded by our dear Saviour, not to mourn for the dead, but for the living. I am sure from my dream that she is happy, she has changed a world of woe, for a world of eternal happiness, and we ought to prepare, as we too, must follow....

It becomes our duty to submit to this heavy bereavement with due submission, and control our passions, submit to the will of God who holds our lives in his hand and say with humble and contrite hearts, "The Lord's will be done on earth as it is in heaven."[10]

On March 4, 1837, President Jackson delivered his *Farewell Address:*

You have the highest of human trusts committed to your care. Providence has showered on this favored land blessings without number, and has chosen you as the guardians of freedom, to preserve it for the benefit of the human race. May He who holds in His hands the destinies of nations, make you worthy of the favors He has bestowed, and enable you, with pure hearts and hands and sleepless vigilance, to guard and defend to the end of time, the great charge He has committed to your keeping.[11]

Andrew Jackson

On September 20, 1838, Andrew Jackson wrote a letter upon receiving the news that his old friend, Ralph Earl, had suddenly died:

I must soon follow him, and hope to meet him and those friends who have gone before me in the realms of bliss through the mediation of a dear Redeemer, Jesus Christ.[12]

When Andrew Jackson was away in Washington, D.C., he wrote to his wife concerning his faith:

I trust that the God of Isaac and of Jacob will protect you, and give you health in my absence. In Him alone we ought to trust; He alone can preserve and guide us through this troublesome world, and I am sure He will hear your prayers. We are told that the prayers of the righteous prevaileth much, and I add mine for your health and preservation until we meet again.[13]

Andrew Jackson, on June 8, 1845, said in reference to the Bible:

That book, Sir, is the Rock upon which our republic rests.[14]

Peter Cartwright, the famous Methodist circuit-riding preacher was invited by Andrew Jackson to be a guest in his home for Sunday lunch. Another guest, a young lawyer from Nashville, attempted to draw Cartwright into an argument. He asked:

Peter Cartwright

"Mr. Cartwright, do you believe there is any such place as hell, a place of torment?"
Cartwright replied, "Yes I do."
Laughing, the young lawyer responded, "Well, I thank God I have too much sense to believe in such a thing!"
Andrew Jackson was unable to hold his composure longer, and sternly addressed the lawyer, "Well, sir, I thank God that there is such a place of torment as hell!"
The astonished young lawyer responded, "Why, General Jackson, what do you want with such a place as hell?"
Jackson confronted him saying, "To put such damned rascals as you are in, that oppose and vilify the Christian religion!"
And the young man, embarrassed, left the room.[15]

Andrew Jackson stated:

> We who are frequently visited by this chastening rod, have the consolation to read in the Scriptures that whomever He chasteneth He loveth, and does it for their good to make them mindful of their mortality and that this earth is not our abiding place; and afflicts us that we may prepare for a better world, a happy immortality.[16]

> Go to the Scriptures...the joyful promises it contains will be a balsam to all your troubles.[17]

On May 29, 1845, just a few weeks before he died, Andrew Jackson said:

> Sir, I am in the hands of a merciful God. I have full confidence in his goodness and mercy....The Bible is true. I have tried to conform to its spirit as near as possible. Upon that sacred volume I rest my hope for eternal salvation, through the merits and blood of our blessed Lord and Saviour, Jesus Christ.[18]

June 1, 1845, though in great pain, Jackson replied to those visiting him:

> When I have suffered sufficiently, the Lord will then take me to Himself—but what are all my sufferings compared to those of the Blessed Saviour, who died upon that cursed tree for me? Mine are nothing.[19]

On June 8, 1845, just moments before his death, Andrew Jackson called his family and servants to his bedside and told them:

> My dear children, do not grieve for me; it is true, I am going to leave you; I am well aware of my situation. I have suffered much bodily pain, but my sufferings are but as nothing compared with that which our blessed Redeemer endured upon the accursed Cross, that all might be saved who put their trust in Him...God will take care of you for me. I am my God's. I belong to Him. I go but a short time before you, and...I hope and trust to meet you all in Heaven, both white and black.[20]

As everyone began crying and weeping, Jackson exhorted with his last breath:

> Oh, do not cry. Be good children, and we will all meet in Heaven.[21]

The first clause of Andrew Jackson's *Will* states:

> The Bible is true. Upon that sacred Volume I rest my hope of eternal salvation through the merits of our blessed Lord and Saviour Jesus Christ.
> First, I bequeath my body to the dust whence it comes, and my soul to God who gave it, hoping for a happy immortality through the atoning merits of our Lord Jesus Christ, the Saviour of the world.[22]

Thomas Jonathan "Stonewall" Jackson (1824-1863), known as one of the country's greatest generals, served under General Robert E. Lee in the Confederate Army. General Jackson's tremendous success in combat against great odds was observed in numerous battles, including the *Battle of Bull Run, Shenandoah Valley, Cross Keys, Port Republic, Seven Day's Battle, Second Battle of Bull Run,* etc. When he died, General Lee exclaimed, "I have lost my right arm."

Thomas Jonathan "Stonewall" Jackson

As professor of philosophy and tactics at Virginia Military Institute, General Jackson once said:

> When we take our meals, there is the grace. When I take a draught of water, I always pause...to lift up my heart to God in thanks and prayer for the water of life. Whenever I [send] a letter...I send a petition along with it, for God's blessing upon its mission and upon the person to whom it is sent.
> When I [open] a letter...I stop to pray to God that He may prepare me for its contents...When I go to my class-room and await the arrangement of the cadets in their places, that is my time to intercede with God for them.[23]

In 1842, Jackson wrote to his uncle, Alfred Neale, concerning the sudden death of his brother, Warren:

> I have received no answer to my last communication conveying the sad news of my brother's premature death. He died in the hope of a bright immortality at the right hand of His Redeemer...
>
> As time is knowledge I must hasten my pen forward. We have received the smile of Bounteous Providence in a favorable Spring. There is a volunteer company being formed here to march to Texas, in order to assist in the noble cause of liberty.[24]

In 1852, Jackson wrote to his aunt, Mrs. Clementine (Alfred) Neale, from Lexington, Virginia:

> The subject of becoming herald of the cross has often seriously engaged my attention, and I regard it as the most noble of all professions. It is the profession of our divine Redeemer, and I should not be surprised were I to die upon a foreign field, clad in ministerial armor, fighting under the banner of Jesus. What could be more glorious?
>
> But my conviction is that I am doing good here; and that for the present I am where God would have me be. Within the last few days I have felt an unusual religious joy. I do rejoice to walk in the love of God. My heavenly Father condescended to use me as an instrument in getting up a large Sabbath school for the negroes here. He has greatly blessed it, and, I trust, all who are connected with it.[25]

On July 22, 1861, General Stonewall Jackson wrote to his wife, Mary Ann, from Manassas:

> My precious Pet,—Yesterday, we fought a great battle and gained a great victory for which all the glory is due to God alone...My preservation was entirely due, as was the glorious victory, to our God, to whom be all the honor, grace, and glory.[26]

On the battlefield in Manassas, General Stonewall Jackson prayed:

> Oh God, let this horrible war quickly come to an end that we may all return home and engage in the only work that is worthwhile—and that is the salvation of men.[27]

General Jackson's old servant said he:

> ...could always tell when a battle was near at hand, by seeing the general get up a great many times in the night to pray.[28]

After the *Battle of Cross Keys*, Chaplain Bennett recorded a soldier's remarks:

> I saw something today which affected me more than anything I ever saw or read on religion. While the battle was raging and the bullets were flying, Jackson rode by, calm as if he were at home, but his head was raised toward heaven, and his lips were moving, evidently in prayer.[29]

In a letter to his wife, General Stonewall Jackson wrote:

> Don't trouble yourself...these things are earthly and transitory. There are real and glorious blessings, I trust, in reserve for us, beyond this life. It is best for us to keep our eyes fixed upon the throne of God....It is gratifying to be beloved, and to have our conduct approved by our fellow men; but this is not worthy to be compared with the glory that is in reservation for us, in the presence of the glorified Redeemer...knowing that there awaits us "a far more exceeding and eternal weight of glory."[30]

General Stonewall Jackson had faithfully taught a colored Sunday school class in Lexington, Virginia. He wrote to his pastor, the Reverend Dr. White:

> My dear Pastor,
> In my tent last night, after a fatiguing day's service, I remembered that I had failed to send you my contribution for our colored Sunday School. Enclosed you will find my check for that object, which please acknowledge at your earliest convenience and oblige yours faithfully,
> T. Jackson.[31]

General Jackson was instrumental in organizing the Chaplains' Association within the southern ranks. When it was reported to him how his army responded by attending religious services,

---

Jackson replied:

> That is good—very good—we ought to thank God for that.[32]

In 1862, during the midst of the Civil War, Stonewall Jackson wrote to his wife, who was ill:

> I trust you and all I have in the hands of an ever kind Providence, knowing that all things work together for the good of His people. So live that your sufferings may be sanctified to you; remember that our light afflictions, which are but for a moment, work out for us a far more exceeding and eternal weight of glory.[33]

On May 2, 1863, the seemingly invincible Confederate Army won a tremendous victory at Chancellorville. This victory was offset by the setback of General Stonewall losing his left arm. The next day, when visited by Chaplain Lacy, Jackson remarked:

> You see me severely wounded but not depressed....I am sure that my Heavenly Father designs this affliction for my good. I am perfectly satisfied, that either in this life, or in that which is to come, I shall discover that what is now regarded as a calamity, is a blessing....If it were in my power to replace my arm, I would not dare to do it, unless I could know it was the will of my Heavenly Father.[34]

On May 10, 1863, while scouting ahead of his troops at twilight, General Jackson was accidently shot by his own troops. This tragedy so affected the Confederate troops, that they never fully recovered. His wife, who had been called to his side, comforted him, saying, "Do you not feel willing to acquiesce in God's allotment, if He wills you to go today....Well, before this day closes, you will be with the blessed Saviour in His glory." Jackson responded:

> I will be an infinite gainer to be translated.[35]

General Stonewall Jackson, in his restless sleep, uttered his final words:

Let us pass over the river, and rest under the shade of the trees.[36]

❧

William James (1842-1910), considered by some to be the father of modern psychology, was a psychologist and philosopher. He developed a theory of ethics called *pragmatism*, where the distinction between truth and falsity, even in the area of religion and morals, was not considered important as long as problems got solved.[37]

In examining the source of current nontraditional trends, today's prevailing psychological agenda can be seen reflected in his statement:

> There is nothing so absurd but if you repeat it often enough people will believe it.[38]

❧

John Jay

John Jay (1745-1829), was the first Chief Justice of the United States Supreme Court, having been appointed by President George Washington. He was a Founding Father, a member of the First and Second Continental Congresses and served as the President of the Continental Congress. He was very instrumental in causing the Constitution to be ratified, by writing the *Federalist Papers*, along with James Madison and Alexander Hamilton. In 1777, John Jay helped to write the Constitution of New York, and from 1795-1801 held the position of Governor of the State of New York.

John Jay negotiated the peace treaty to end the War with England (along with John Adams and Benjamin Franklin). He was Secretary of Foreign Affairs under the Articles of Confederation, U.S. Minister to Spain and, in 1794, he authored the *Jay Treaty*, which prevented the United States from getting involved in the war between France and England.

George Washington

On October 12, 1816, John Jay admonished:

> Providence has given to our people the choice of their rulers, and it is the duty, as well as the privilege and interest of our Christian nation to select and prefer Christians for their rulers.[39]

In addition to being appointed by President George Washington as the first Chief Justice of the United States Supreme Court, John Jay was also elected president of the Westchester Bible Society in 1818 and president of the American Bible Society in 1821.

On May 13, 1824, while serving as its president, John Jay gave an address to the American Bible Society:

> By conveying the Bible to people thus circumstanced, we certainly do them a most interesting kindness. We thereby enable them to learn that man was originally created and placed in a state of happiness, but, becoming disobedient, was subjected to the degradation and evils which he and his posterity have since experienced.
>
> The Bible will also inform them that our gracious Creator has provided for us a Redeemer, in whom all the nations of the earth shall be blessed; that this Redeemer has made atonement "for the sins of the whole world," and thereby reconciling the Divine justice with the Divine mercy has opened a way for our redemption and salvation; and that these inestimable benefits are of the free gift and grace of God, not of our deserving, nor in our power to deserve.[40]

John Jay stated:

> In forming and settling my belief relative to the doctrines of Christianity, I adopted no articles from creeds but such only as, on careful examination, I found to be confirmed by the Bible....At a party in Paris, once, the question fell on religious matters. In the course of it, one of them asked me if I believed in Christ? I answered that I did, and that I thanked God that I did.[41]

In 1826, John Jay was sent a letter from the corporation of the City of New York, asking him to join with them in the celebration of America's fiftieth anniversary. John Jay replied, expressing his:

> Earnest hope that the peace, happiness, and prosperity enjoyed by our beloved country may induce those who direct her national counsels to recommend a general and public return of praise to Him from whose goodness these blessings descend.[42]

Mrs. John Jay (nee Sarah Van Brugh Livingston)

In his *Last Will and Testament*, John Jay wrote:

> Unto Him who is the author and giver of all good, I render sincere and humble thanks for His merciful and unmerited blessings, and especially for our redemption and salvation by his beloved Son.[43]

On May 17, 1829, John Jay was drawing near death after a life of serving his country. As recorded by his son, Judge William Jay, John Jay was asked if he had any final words for his children, to which he responded:

> They have the Book.[44]

&

John Jay (1817-1894), a lawyer and diplomat, was the son of Judge William Jay and the grandson of John Jay, the Founding Father who was the first Chief Justice of the Supreme Court. He was the manager of the New York Young Men's Anti-Slavery Society in 1834; secretary of the Irish Relief Commission during the potato famine in 1847; U.S. Minister to Austria, 1869-75; and the vice-president of the Civil Service Reform Association of the State of New York. He served as the president of the American Historical Society, 1890, as well as being an active member of the Metropolitan Museum of Art and the National Academy of Design. John Jay authored many papers, including: "America Free or America Slave," 1856; "On the Passage of the Constitutional Amendment," 1864; and "Abolishing Slavery," 1864.

In 1887, as the president of the Westchester County Bible Society, John Jay delivered his message "National Perils and Opportunities":

"It is high time to wake out of sleep!" This gathering of citizens from distant parts, representing the millions who hold to the Bible, and cherish the institutions founded upon its inspired truths, shows that the nation is awakening to the perils, foreign and domestic, which threatens the purity of its Christian civilization.

Its intellectual and moral strength in our Revolutionary struggle were recognized by the world, and Burke rightly attributed that strength to the character of the emigrants from various lands exhibiting "the dissidence of dissent and the Protestantism of the Protestant religion." They brought with them the best and most heroic blood of the peoples of Europe—of the Hollanders, the Waloons of Flanders, the Huguenots of France, the English, Welsh, Scotch, and Irish, of the Norwegians and Swedes, the Germans and the Swiss, of the Bohemian followers of John Hus, of the Albigenses and Waldenses of the Italian Alps, of the Salzbury exiles, the Moravian brothers, with refugees from the Pallatinate, Alsace and southern Germany.

They all brought the Bible, for which they and their ancestors had been ready to suffer and to die; and their devotion to that Book descended to the Continental Congress, which, a week before it was driven from Philadelphia, ordered an importation of twenty thousand Bibles.

At the Centennial celebration, at Philadelphia, of the Declaration of Independence, the Acting Vice-President, Ferry, said that the American statesmen who had to choose between the royal authority or popular sovereignty had been inspired by the truth uttered on Mars Hill, and repeated in the opening prayer of the morning, that "God hath made of one blood all nations of men."[45]

ॐ

William Jay (1789-1858), was the son of John Jay, the first Chief Justice of the Supreme Court and the father of John Jay, the influential diplomat. He was a successful attorney, author and judge in Westchester County, New York. William Jay took the unpopular and politically incorrect stance of opposing slavery, and in 1833, helped found the New York City Anti-Slavery

Society. He was a founder of the American Bible Society, 1816, and served as the director of the American Tract Society.

William Jay

William Jay wrote several books against slavery, including: *American Anti-Slavery Societies*, 1835; *Miscellaneous Writings on Slavery*, 1853; *War and Peace: The Evils of the First and a Plan for Preserving the Last*, 1842; and, in 1849, wrote this testimony in the introduction to one of his works:

> The writer is a believer in the Divine authority of the Scriptures—he acknowledges no standard of right and wrong but the Will of God, and denies the expediency of any act which is forbidden by laws dictated by Infinite Wisdom and Goodness.
>
> This avowal will prepare the reader to find in the following pages many opinions not having the stamp of public approbation. Patriotism, honor, glory, and national prosperity, are terms to which the Christian and the mere politician attach different ideas, and estimate by different standards.
>
> He who admits the authority of the Bible will not readily acknowledge that whatever is "highly esteemed among men" must be right, nor that which is unpopular is, of course, wrong.[46]

Sir James Hopwood Jeans

Sir James Hopwood Jeans (1877-1946), an English physicist and astronomer, studied the nature of gases and sun radiations. Educated at Cambridge, he went on to become a professor at Princeton in the area of applied mathematics. In his work, *The Mysterious Universe*, 1930, Sir James Hopwood Jeans stated:

> All the pictures which science now draws of nature and which alone seem capable of according with observational fact are mathematical pictures....From the intrinsic evidence of his creation, the Great Architect of the Universe now begins to appear as a pure mathematician.[47]

Thomas Jefferson

Thomas Jefferson (1743-1826), author, architect, educator and scientist, was the 3rd President of the United States of America. In 1774, while serving in the Virginia Assembly, he personally introduced a resolution calling for a Day of Fasting and Prayer.[48]

Thomas Jefferson penned the words of the Declaration of Independence, on July 4th, 1776:

When in the Course of human events, it becomes necessary for one people to dissolve the political bands which have connected them with another, and to assume among the powers of the earth, the separate and equal station to which the Laws of Nature and of Nature's God entitles them...

We hold these truths to be self-evident, that all men are created equal. That they are endowed by their Creator with certain inalienable rights, that among these are life...

We, Therefore, the Representatives of the United States of America, in General Congress, Assembled, appealing to the Supreme Judge of the world for the rectitude of our intentions...

And for the support of this Declaration, with a firm reliance on the protection of Divine Providence, we mutually pledge to each other our Lives, our Fortunes, and our sacred Honor.[49]

Shortly after the signing of the Declaration of Independence, a committee was appointed to draft a seal for the newly united states which would express the spirit of the nation. Thomas Jefferson proposed:

The children of Israel in the wilderness, led by a cloud by day, and a pillar of fire by night.[50]

During the period between 1779-1781, Thomas Jefferson served as the Governor of Virginia, where he decreed a day of:

Thomas Jefferson designed and built Monticello, his home in Virginia.

Public and solemn thanksgiving and prayer to Almighty God.[51]

In 1781, Thomas Jefferson made this statement in *Query XVIII* of his *Notes on the State of Virginia.* Excerpts of these statements are engraved on the Jefferson Memorial in Washington, D.C.:

God who gave us life gave us liberty. And can the liberties of a nation be thought secure when we have removed their only firm basis, a conviction in the minds of the people that these liberties are of the Gift of God? That they are not to be violated but with His wrath? Indeed, I tremble for my country when I reflect that God is just; that His justice cannot sleep forever.[52]

In *Query XIX* of his *Notes on the State of Virginia,* Thomas Jefferson wrote:

Those who labor in the earth are the chosen people of God...whose breasts He has made His peculiar deposit for substantial and genuine virtue.[53]

On August 19, 1785, Jefferson wrote in a letter to Peter Carr:

He who permits himself to tell a lie once, finds it much easier to do it a second and third time, till at length it becomes habitual; he tells lies without attending to it, and truths without the world's believing him. This falsehood of the tongue leads to that of the heart, and in time depraves all its good dispositions.[54]

In 1798, Thomas Jefferson wrote at the occasion of the *Kentucky Resolution:*

No power over the freedom of religion...[is] delegated to the United States by the Constitution.[55]

In a letter to Dr. Benjamin Rush, September 23, 1800, Thomas Jefferson wrote:

I have sworn upon the altar of God eternal hostility against every form of tyranny over the mind of man.[56]

In 1801, President Thomas Jefferson stated in his First Inaugural Address:

And let us reflect that having banished from our land that religious intolerance under which mankind so long bled and suffered, we have yet gained little if we countenance a political intolerance as despotic, as wicked, and capable of as bitter and bloody persecutions....

Let us, then, with courage and confidence pursue our own federal and republican principles....enlightened by a benign religion, professed, indeed, and practiced in various forms, yet all of them including honesty, truth, temperance, gratitude, and the love of man; acknowledging and adoring an overruling Providence, which by all its dispensations proves that it delights in the happiness of man here and his greater happiness hereafter;

With all these blessings, what more is necessary to make us a happy and prosperous people? Still one thing more, fellow citizens— a wise and frugal government...which shall leave them otherwise free to regulate their own pursuits of industry and improvement, and shall not take from the mouth of labor the bread it has earned....

And may that Infinite Power which rules the destinies of the universe, lead our councils to what is best, and give them a favorable issue for your peace and prosperity.[57]

Thomas Jefferson, while U.S. President (1801-1809), chaired the school board for the District of Columbia, where he authored the first plan of education adopted by the city of Washington. This plan used the Bible and *Isaac Watts' Psalms, Hymns and Spiritual Songs*, 1707, as the principal books for teaching reading to students.[58]

On March 23, 1801, Thomas Jefferson wrote from Washington, D.C., to Moses Robinson:

The Christian Religion, when divested of the rags in which they [the clergy] have enveloped it, and brought to the original purity and simplicity of its benevolent institutor, is a religion of all others most friendly to liberty, science, and the freest expansion of the human mind.[59]

On January 1, 1802, Jefferson wrote a letter to the Danbury Baptist Association of Danbury, Connecticut, calming their fears that Congress was not in the process of choosing any one single Christian denomination to be the "state" denomination, as was the case with the Anglican Church in England and Virginia.

Thomas Jefferson

In his letter to the Danbury Baptists, who had experienced severe persecution for their faith, Jefferson borrowed phraseology from the famous Baptist minister Roger Williams who said, "...the hedge or wall of separation between the garden of the church and the wilderness of the world, God hath ever broke down the wall...."[60] Jefferson's letter included:

> Believing with you that religion is a matter which lies solely between man and his God, that he owes account to none other for faith or his worship, that the legislative powers of government reach actions only, and not opinions, I contemplate with solemn reverence that act of the whole American people which declared that their legislature should "make no law respecting an establishment of religion, or prohibiting the free exercise thereof," thus building a wall of separation between Church and State.[61]

This personal letter reassured the Baptists that the government's hands were tied from interfering with, or in any way controlling, the affairs or decisions of the churches in America.

Thomas Jefferson did not sign the Constitution, nor was he present at the Constitutional Convention of 1787. Neither was he present when the First Amendment and religious freedom were debated in the first session of Congress in 1789, as he was out of the country in France as a U.S. Minister.[62] Due to his not being present to hear all the comments of the Founding Fathers regarding the First Amendment, Thomas Jefferson had to rely on second-hand information to learn what had transpired in that first session of Congress. This rendered his letter to the Danbury Baptists (which was written 13 years *after* the First Amendment)[63] ineligible to be considered a "first-hand" reflection of the intent of the constitutional delegates.

Thomas Jefferson, April 30, 1802, signed the enabling act for Ohio to become a state. It stated that the government in this new state "not be repugnant to the [Northwest] Ordinance":[64]

> The Northwest Ordinance—*Article III* Religion, morality, and knowledge being necessary to good government and the happiness of

mankind, schools and the means of education shall be forever encouraged.[65]

Thomas Jefferson, on April 21, 1803, wrote to Dr. Benjamin Rush, (also a signer of the Declaration of Independence):

> My views...are the result of a life of inquiry and reflection, and very different from the anti-christian system imputed to me by those who know nothing of my opinions. To the corruptions of Christianity I am, indeed, opposed; but not to the genuine precepts of Jesus himself. I am a Christian in the only sense in which he wished any one to be; sincerely attached to his doctrines in preference to all others....[66]

On December 3, 1803, it was recommended by President Thomas Jefferson that the Congress of the United States pass a treaty with the Kaskaskia Indians. Included in this treaty was the annual support to a Catholic missionary priest of $100, to be paid out of the Federal treasury. Later in 1806 and 1807, two similar treaties were made with the Wyandotte and Cherokee tribes.[67]

President Thomas Jefferson also extended, three times, a 1787 act of Congress in which special lands were designated:

> For the sole use of Christian Indians and the Moravian Brethren missionaries for civilizing the Indians and promoting Christianity.[68]

On June 17, 1804, in a letter to Henry Fry, Thomas Jefferson writes:

> I consider the doctrines of Jesus as delivered by himself to contain the outlines of the sublimest system of morality that has ever been taught but I hold in the most profound detestation and execration the corruptions of it which have been invented...[69]

In a letter to Abigail Adams, September 11, 1804, Thomas Jefferson wrote:

> Nothing in the Constitution has given them [the federal judges] a right to decide for the Executive, more than to the Executive to decide

for them....But the opinion which gives to the judges the right to decide what laws are constitutional, and what not, not only for themselves in their own sphere of action, but for the legislature and executive also, in their spheres, would make the judiciary a despotic branch.[70]

On March 4, 1805, in his Second Inaugural Address, President Thomas Jefferson declared:

In matters of religion I have considered that its free exercise is placed by the Constitution independent of the powers of the General Government. I have therefore undertaken, on no occasion, to prescribe the religious exercise suited to it; but have left them, as the Constitution found them, under the direction and discipline of state and church authorities by the several religious societies.[71]

Thomas Jefferson

I shall now enter on the duties to which my fellow-citizens have again called me, and shall proceed in the spirit of those principles which they have approved....

I shall need, therefore, all the indulgence I have heretofore experienced...I shall need, too, the favor of that Being in whose hands we are, who led our forefathers, as Israel of old, from their native land and planted them in a country flowing with all the necessities and comforts of life, who has covered our infancy with His Providence and our riper years with His wisdom and power, and to whose goodness I ask you to join with me in supplications that He will so enlighten the minds of your servants, guide their councils and prosper their measures, that whatever they do shall result in your good, and shall secure to you the peace, friendship and approbation of all nations.[72]

President Thomas Jefferson, March 4, 1805, offered *A National Prayer for Peace:*

Almighty God, Who has given us this good land for our heritage; We humbly beseech Thee that we may always prove ourselves a people mindful of Thy favor and glad to do Thy will. Bless our land with honorable ministry, sound learning, and pure manners.

Save us from violence, discord, and confusion, from pride and arrogance, and from every evil way. Defend our liberties, and fashion into one united people the multitude brought hither out of many kindreds and tongues.

Endow with Thy spirit of wisdom those to whom in Thy Name we entrust the authority of government, that there may be justice and peace at home, and that through obedience to Thy law, we may show forth Thy praise among the nations of the earth.

In time of prosperity fill our hearts with thankfulness, and in the day of trouble, suffer not our trust in Thee to fail; all of which we ask through Jesus Christ our Lord, Amen.[73]

As President, Thomas Jefferson not only signed bills which appropriated financial support for chaplains in Congress and in the armed services, but he also signed the Articles of War, April 10, 1806, in which he:

Earnestly recommended to all officers and soldiers, diligently to attend divine services.[74]

On January 23, 1808, Thomas Jefferson wrote to Samuel Miller:

I consider the government of the U.S. as interdicted [prohibited] by the Constitution from intermeddling with religious institutions, their doctrines, discipline, or exercises. This results not only from the provision that no law shall be made respecting the establishment, or free exercise, of religion, but from that also which reserves to the states the powers not delegated to the U.S. [10th Amendment].

Certainly no power to prescribe any religious exercise, or to assume authority in religious discipline, has been delegated to the general government. It must then rest with the states as far as it can be in any human authority.[75]

In a letter to John Adams, dated 1813, Thomas Jefferson wrote:

In extracting the pure principles which Jesus taught, we should have to strip off the artificial vestments in which they have been muffled...there will be found remaining the most sublime and benevolent code of morals which has ever been offered to man.[76]

On September 18, 1813, in a letter to William Canby, Thomas Jefferson wrote:

An eloquent preacher of your religious society, Richard Mote, in a discourse of much emotion and pathos, is said to have exclaimed aloud to his congregation that he did not believe there was a Quaker, Presbyterian, Methodist, or Baptist in heaven, having paused to give his hearers time to stare and to wonder. He added, that in Heaven, God knew no distinctions....[77]

In a letter to Horatio G. Spafford, dated March 17, 1814, Thomas Jefferson wrote:

Merchants have no country. The mere spot they stand on does not constitute so strong an attachment as that from which they draw their gains.[78]

On September 26, 1814, Thomas Jefferson wrote to Miles King:

...Nay, we have heard it said that there is not a Quaker or a Baptist, a Presbyterian or an Episcopalian, a Catholic or a Protestant in heaven; that on entering that gate, we leave those badges of schism behind...Let us not be uneasy about the different roads we may pursue, as believing them the shortest, to that our last abode; but following the guidance of a good conscience, let us be happy in the hope that by these different paths we shall all meet in the end. And that you and I may meet and embrace, is my earnest prayer. And with this assurance I salute you with brotherly esteem and respect.[79]

In 1816, Thomas Jefferson wrote in his own handwriting "a wee book"[80] for his personal study, entitled:

The Life and Morals of Jesus of Nazareth, extracted textually from the Gospels in Greek, Latin, French and English with the table of contents reading "A Table of the Texts from the Evangelists employed in this Narrative and the order of their arrangement."[81]

In 1904, the fifty-seventh Congress, in an effort to restrain unethical behavior, voted:

That there be printed and bound, by photolithographic process, with an introduction of not to exceed twenty-five pages, to be prepared by Dr. Cyrus Adler, Librarian of the Smithsonian Institution, for the use of Congress, 9,000 copies of Thomas Jefferson's *Morals of Jesus of*

Nazareth, as the same appears in the National Museum; 3,000 copies for the use of the Senate and 6,000 copies for the use of the House.[82]

On September 6, 1819, Thomas Jefferson wrote:

The Constitution is a mere thing of wax in the hands of the judiciary, which they may twist and shape into any form they please.[83]

On September 28, 1820, Jefferson wrote to William Jarvis:

You seem...to consider the judges as the ultimate arbiters of all constitutional questions; a very dangerous doctrine indeed, and one which would place us under the despotism of an oligarchy. Our judges are as honest as other men, and not more so....and their power [is] the more dangerous, as they are in office for life and not responsible, as the other functionaries are, to the elective control. The Constitution has erected no such single tribunal, knowing that to whatever hands confided, with corruptions of time and party, its members would become despots.[84]

On November 4, 1820, Thomas Jefferson wrote to Jared Sparks:

I hold the precepts of Jesus as delivered by Himself, to be the most pure, benevolent and sublime which have ever been preached to man...[85]

In 1821, Jefferson wrote to Mr. Hammond:

The germ of dissolution of our federal government is in...the federal judiciary; an irresponsible body (for impeachment is scarcely a scare-crow) working like gravity by night and by day, gaining a little today and a little to-morrow, and advancing its noiseless step like a thief, over the field of jurisdiction, until all shall be usurped from the States.[86]

Seal of Thomas Jefferson, bearing the inscription: "Rebellion to tyrants is obedience to God."

On June 12, 1823, in a letter to Justice William Johnson regarding the meaning to the Constitution, Thomas Jefferson wrote:

On every question of construction, carry ourselves back to the time when the Constitution was adopted, recollect the spirit manifested in the debates, and instead of trying what meaning may be squeezed out of the text, or invented against it, conform to the probable one in which it was passed. [87]

On August 30, 1823, in a letter to James Madison, Thomas Jefferson commented on his authorship of the Declaration of Independence:

I know that I turned to neither book nor pamphlet while writing it. I did not consider it as any part of my charge to invent new ideas altogether, and to offer no sentiments which had never been expressed before... I pray God that these principles may be eternal, and close the prayer with my affectionate wishes for yourself of long life, health and happiness. [88]

In establishing the University of Virginia, Thomas Jefferson not only encouraged the teaching of religion, but set aside a place inside the Rotunda for chapel services. [89] Thomas Jefferson also spoke highly of the use, in his home town, of the local courthouse for religious services. [90]

While in Philadelphia, Thomas Jefferson attended Christ Church, along with George Washington, Benjamin Franklin, Robert Morris, Alexander Hamilton, Francis Hopkins and Betsy Ross. In Virginia, Jefferson attended Bruton Parish Church (Episcopalian) in Williamsburg, where George and Martha Washington were also members. [91] His own Bible, a well-worn, four-volume set, held preeminence in his personal library. In the catalog he had written, listing all the books in his library, Jefferson wrote this on the title page:

I am for freedom of Religion, and against all maneuvers to bring about a legal ascendancy of one sect over another. [92]

In a letter to Charles Thomson, January 9, 1816, Thomas Jefferson wrote regarding his book, *The Life and Morals of Jesus of Nazareth*:

A more beautiful or precious morsel of ethics I have never seen; it is a document in proof that I am a real Christian; that is to say, a disciple of the doctrines of Jesus. [93]

Of all the systems of morality, ancient or modern, which have come under my observation, none appear to me so pure as that of Jesus.[94]

The doctrines which flowed from the lips of Jesus himself are within the comprehension of a child; but thousands of volumes have not yet explained the Platonisms engrafted on them.[95]

Had the doctrines of Jesus been preached always as pure as they came from his lips, the whole civilized world would now have been Christians.[96]

I have always said, I always will say, that the studious perusal of the sacred volume will make better citizens, better fathers, and better husbands.[97]

1. The doctrines of Jesus are simple and tend to the happiness of man.
2. There is only one God, and He is all perfect.
3. There is a future state of rewards and punishment.
4. To love God with all the heart and thy neighbor as thyself is the sum of all. These are the great points on which to reform the religion of the Jews.[98]

No one sees with greater pleasure than myself the progress of reason in its advance toward rational Christianity, and my opinion is that if nothing had ever been added to what flowed from His lips, the whole world would at this day been Christian....Had there never been a commentator there never would have been an infidel. I have little doubt that the whole country will soon be rallied to the unity of our Creator, and, I hope, to the pure doctrines of Jesus also.[99]

Thomas Jefferson and John Adams were on the opposite sides of several major political issues, many times resulting in heated debates. John Adams, the 2nd President, was succeeded in office by Thomas Jefferson. So strong were John Adam's feelings against Jefferson at the time, that Adams even left Washington, D.C., to avoid being at Jefferson's Inauguration.
Later in life, however, the two became the

John Adams

best of friends. Their correspondence reveals not only their faith, but their friendship. In a providential coincidence, Thomas Jefferson and John Adams both died on the same day, July 4, 1826, exactly 50 years after they both had signed the Declaration of Independence. Once hardened political opponents, John Adams' last words were:

Thank God, Jefferson lives![100]

Thomas Jefferson's epitaph, which he wrote himself, is inscribed on his tombstone:

Here lies buried Thomas Jefferson, author of the Declaration of Independence, author of the Statutes for Religious Freedom in Virginia, and father of the University of Virginia.[101]

The Jefferson Memorial, on the south banks of Washington D.C.'s Tidal Basin, has inscribed in marble Thomas Jefferson's own words:

Almighty God hath created the mind free. All attempts to influence it by temporal punishments or burdens...are a departure from the plan of the Holy Author of our religion.[102]

No men shall...suffer on account of his religious opinions or belief, but all men shall be free to profess and by argument to maintain, their opinion in matters of religion. I know but one code of morality for men whether acting singly or collectively.[103]

Commerce between master and slave is despotism. Nothing is more certainly written in the Book of Life than that these people are to be free.[104]

The precepts of philosophy and of the Hebrew code, laid hold of actions only. [Jesus] pushed his scrutinies into the heart of man, erected his tribunal in the regions of his thoughts, and purified the waters at the fountain head.[105]

Jefferson declared that religion is:

Deemed in other countries incompatible with good government and yet proved by our experience to be its best support.[106]

❧

Andrew Johnson (1808-1875), the 17th President of the United States, had been President Abraham Lincoln's Vice-President. He assumed the office of the presidency when Lincoln was shot. Andrew Johnson continued Lincoln's plan of Reconstruction of the South and pardoned those who had seceded. Andrew Johnson had also been Governor of Tennessee and a U.S. Senator.

Andrew Johnson

I do believe in Almighty God! And I believe also in the Bible.[107]

Let us look forward to the time when we can take the flag of our country and nail it below the Cross, and there let it wave as it waved in the olden times, and let us gather around it and inscribe for our motto: "Liberty and Union, one and inseparable, now and forever," and exclaim, Christ first, our country next![108]

Is there a crusade to be commenced against the Church to satiate disappointed party vengeance? Are the persecutions of olden times to be revived? Are the ten thousand temples that have been erected, based upon the sufferings and atonement of our crucified Saviour, with their glittering spires wasting themselves in the very heavens, all to topple and to fall, crushed and buried beneath the ravings of party excitement? Is man to be set upon man, and in the name of God lift his hand against the throat of his fellow?...

Are the fires of heaven that have been lighted up by the Cross, and now burning upon so many altars consecrated to the true and living God, to be quenched in the blood of their innocent and defenseless worshipers, and the gutters of our streets made to flow with human gore? This is but a faint reality of what is shadowed forth in the gentleman's speech.[109]

❧

James Weldon Johnson (1871-1938), was a popular American

Negro poet who was best known for writing a series of verse entitled *God's Trombones.* James Weldon Johnson was a United States Consul in Venezuela and Nicaragua, a professor at Fisk University and served as the secretary of the National Association for the Advancement of Colored People. In *God's Trombones,* 1927, Johnson wrote *The Creation:*

> And God stepped out on space,
> And He looked around and said,
> "I'm lonely—
> I'll make me a world."....
>
> And God smiled again,
> And the rainbow appeared,
> And curled itself around his shoulder....
> With his head in his hands,
> God thought and thought,
> Till he thought: I'll make me a man![110]

✥

Lyndon Baines Johnson (1908-1973), the 36th President of the United States, assumed that position after President John F. Kennedy was assassinated. In his Inaugural Address, January 20, 1965, President Johnson said:

Lyndon Baines Johnson

> If we fail now...we will have forgotten that democracy rests on faith.[111]

> For myself, I ask only in the words of an ancient leader (Solomon): "Give me now wisdom and knowledge that I may go out and come in before this people.[112]

> Come now, let us reason together.[113]

✥

Samuel Johnson (1709-1784), a famous English lexicographer and writer, wrote one of the first dictionaries in the English language. A man of highly respected judgment coupled with a probing wit, Johnson organized the London Literary Club. He wrote the significant work, *The Lives of the Poets*, 1779-1781, wherein he gives profound critical examination of 52 famous English poets. Samuel Johnson attested:

> It appears evident that the writers of the Old Testament were the original and best writers, and that from them are borrowed numerous ideas attributed to the poets themselves.[114]

> Almighty God, the Giver of all good things, without whose help all labor is ineffectual, and without whose grace all wisdom is folly, grant, I beseech Thee, that in this undertaking Thy Holy Spirit may not be withheld from me, but that I may promote Thy glory and the salvation of myself and others; grant this, O Lord, for the sake of Thy Son, Jesus Christ.[115]

> I bless Thee for creation, preservation, and redemption; for the knowledge of Thy Son, Jesus Christ....Create in me a contrite heart that I may worthily lament my sins and acknowledge my wickedness, and obtain remission and forgiveness through the satisfaction of Jesus Christ....Grant this, Almighty God, for the merits and through the mediation of our most holy and blessed Saviour, Jesus Christ; to whom, with Thee and the Holy Spirit, three Persons in one God, be all honor and glory, world without end. Amen.[116]

In 1763, Samuel Johnson wrote:

> Sir, I think all Christians, whether Papists or Protestants, agree in the essential articles and that their differences are trivial, and rather political than religious.[117]

In 1772, Johnson commented:

> All denominations of Christians have really little difference in point of doctrine, though they may differ widely in external forms.[118]

Samuel Johnson's last words, December 13, 1784, were:

> God bless you, my dear![119]

William Samuel Johnson

William Samuel Johnson (1727-1819), one of the signers of the Constitution of the United States, was a distinguished lawyer, having received an honorary doctorate in civil law from Oxford in 1766. He was a delegate to the Stamp Act Convention, a Commissioner to England, a member of the Continental Congress, as well as a state representative, U.S. Senator and a Connecticut Supreme Court Justice. William Samuel Johnson, the son of the well-known Anglican minister, Samuel Johnson, also was the President of Columbia College from 1787 to 1800.

Johnson's great grandfather, Robert Johnson, came to America in 1638:

> To assist in founding a "Godly Commonwealth" at New Haven.[120]

As President of Columbia University (formerly King's College), William Samuel Johnson gave these profound remarks to the first graduating class after the Revolutionary War:

> You this day, gentlemen, assume new characters, enter into new relations, and consequently incur new duties. You have, by the favor of Providence and the attention of friends, received a public education, the purpose whereof hath been to qualify you the better to serve your Creator and your country....
>
> Your first great duties, you are sensible, are those you owe to Heaven, to your Creator and Redeemer. Let these be ever present to your minds, and exemplified in your lives and conduct.
>
> Imprint deep upon your minds the principles of piety towards God, and a reverence and fear of His holy name. The fear of God is the beginning of wisdom and its consummation is everlasting felicity. Possess yourselves of just and elevated notions of the Divine character, attributes, and administration, and of the end and dignity of your own immortal nature as it stands related to Him.
>
> Reflect deeply and often upon those relations. Remember that it is in God you live and move and have your being,—that in the language

---

of David He is about your bed and about your path and spieth out all your ways,—that there is not a thought in your hearts, nor a word upon your tongues, but lo! He knoweth them altogether, and that he will one day call you to a strict account for all your conduct in this mortal life.

Remember, too, that you are the redeemed of the Lord, that you are bought with a price, even the inestimable price of the precious blood of the Son of God. Adore Jehovah, therefore, as your God and your Judge. Love, fear, and serve Him as your Creator, Redeemer, and Sanctifier. Acquaint yourselves with Him in His word and holy ordinances.

Make Him your friend and protector and your felicity is secured both here and hereafter. And with respect to particular duties to Him, it is your happiness that you are well assured that he best serves his Maker, who does most good to his country and to mankind.[121]

ॐ

John Paul Jones (1747-1792), called the "Father of the American Navy," was known for his courage in fighting against larger and better equipped enemy fleets. In 1779 he took command of the *Bonhomme Richard (Poor Richard)*, which he named in honor of the American statesman Benjamin Franklin, author of *Poor Richard's Almanac.*

On September 23, 1779, the *Bonhomme Richard* attacked a large British convoy, led by the *Serapis.* The ships got so close that the masts were entangled and the muzzles of their guns touched. After an intense naval combat which nearly destroyed the *Bonhomme Richard,* the British commander yelled, asking if the American ship was ready to surrender, to which John Paul Jones responded:

I have not yet begun to fight.[122]

The British convoy finally surrendered after three hours of fighting.

ॐ

John William Jones (1836-1909), as a chaplain in Robert E. Lee's Army of Northern Virginia, played a major role in the numerous revivals that swept through General Lee's troops, resulting in over 100,000 conversions. Chaplain J. William Jones had been ordained a Baptist missionary and was preparing to leave for China when the war broke out. He enlisted as a private in the Confederate Army and within a year began serving as a chaplain. His reports of the ongoing revival that he had witnessed among the Confederate troops are recorded in his work *Christ in the Camp,* published in 1887:

> Any history of this army which omits an account of the wonderful influence of religion upon it—which fails to tell how the courage, discipline, and morale was influenced by the humble piety and evangelical zeal of many of its officers and men—would be incomplete and unsatisfactory.[123]

> It is believed that no army in the world's history ever had in it so much of genuine, devout piety, so much of active work for Christ, as the Army of Northern Virginia, under the command of our noble Christian leader.[124]

> On the bloody campaign from the Rapidan to Cold Harbor in 1864, when the army was constantly in the trenches or on the march, and fought almost daily, Bryan's Georgia Brigade had a season of comparative repose, while held in reserve, when they had from three to five [religious] meetings a day, which resulted in about fifty professions of conversions, most of whom...[were] baptized in a pond which was exposed to the enemy's fire, and where several men were wounded while the ordinance was being administered.[125]

Chaplain Jones writes of a Captain in the Georgia Brigade who was converted at one of the prayer meetings. The Captain professed publicly:

> Men, I have led you into many a battle....Alas! I have (also) led you into all manner of wickedness and vice....I have enlisted under the banner of the Cross, and mean, by God's help, to prove a faithful soldier of Jesus....I call upon you, my brave boys, to follow me, as I shall try to follow 'the Captain of our salvation.'[126]

Chaplain Jones records that one evening General Stonewall

Jackson had discussed strategies with his generals. As they left the meeting, A.P. Hill remarked to Richard Ewell, "Well, I suppose Jackson wants time to pray over it." Later Richard Ewell found General Jackson on his knees fervently praying for guidance, and exclaimed, "If that is religion, I must have it."[127]

August 21, 1863, had been declared a day of fasting, humiliation and prayer for the South. Chaplain J. William Jones took note of the response:

> I can never forget the effect produced by the reading of this order....A precious revival was already in progress in many of the commands....The work of grace among the troops widened and deepened and went gloriously on until over fifteen thousand of the soldiers of Lee's army professed repentance toward God and faith in Jesus Christ as a personal Saviour.[128]

Chaplain J. William Jones had visited General Robert E. Lee's tent, along with Chaplain B.T. Lacey, who was Stonewall Jackson's Chaplain. They told the General that he was being prayed for by all the chaplains. As Jones recorded, tears came to General Lee's eyes as he said:

> Please thank them for that, sir—I warmly appreciate it. And I can only say that I am nothing but a poor sinner, trusting in Christ alone for salvation, and need all of the prayers they can offer me.[129]

Robert E. Lee

After the war, Robert E. Lee accepted the invitation to serve as the President of Washington College. In 1869, he invited his former chaplain, John William Jones, to address the student body. Afterward he said:

> Our great want is a revival which shall bring these young men to Christ. We poor sinners need to come back from our wanderings to seek pardon through the all-sufficient merits of our Redeemer. And we need to pray earnestly for the power of the Holy Spirit to give us a precious revival in our hearts and among the unconverted.[130]

K

Queen Ka'ahumanu (d. 1832), the wife of King Kamehameha the Great of Hawaii, served as queen regent–prime minister *(kahina nui)* after her husband's death, from 1819 to 1832. Queen Ka'ahumanu, along with her son, King Kamehameha II *(Liholiho)*, commanded the cessation of the social taboos, idolatry and human sacrifice, known as *kapu*, that had controlled Hawaii for centuries. Their edict, issued in 1819, went out to all the islands, causing the destruction of numerous idols and temples *(heiaus)*.

The following year, Hiram Bingham and a group of Protestant missionaries came to Hawaii on the brig *Thaddeus*. Queen Ka'ahumanu received Christ and helped spread the Gospel throughout the islands, resulting in "The Great Awakening" of the 1830s and 1840s. Just prior to her death, Queen Ka'ahumanu was presented with the newly completed version of the New Testament in the Hawaiian language. She declared it good *(maika)*, and then spoke her last words to Rev. Bingham:

> I am going where the mansions are ready.[1]

The High Chiefess Kapiolani of Kealekekua Bay was baptized by the early Christian missionaries, and proceeded to introduce her village of Kaawaloa to Christ. In helping the Hilo missionaries win the people from ancient superstitions and human sacrifice to Pele (the volcano goddess), Kapiolani traveled a hundred miles to the rim of the volcano Kilauea, descended into the crater and defied Pele by eating some of the goddess' sacred *ohelo* berries. She then praised "the one true God" and proclaimed:

Jehovah is my God. He kindled these fires. I fear not Pele. All the gods of Hawaii are vain.[2]

This courageous act of the High Chiefess Kapiolani greatly advanced Christianity in Hawaii, leading many Hawaiians to become missionaries to other islands. One such missionary, Rev. Kauwealoha, stopped the ritual of cannibalism and planted numerous churches and schools.

ঞ

Immanuel Kant (1724-1804), was a famous German philosopher, whose major philosophical work, *Critique of Pure Reason,* published in 1781, is comparable to the works of Plato or Aristotle in importance. Immanuel Kant stated:

> The existence of the Bible, as a book for the people, is the greatest benefit which the human race has ever experienced. Every attempt to belittle it is a crime against humanity.[3]
>
> In the life and the Divine doctrine of Christ which are recorded in the Gospel, example and precept conspire to call men to the regular discharge of every moral duty for its own sake, and to the universal practice of pure virtue. "He can't be wrong whose life is in the right."
>
> The Sermon on the Mount, in particular, comprises so pure a doctrine of religion, which Jesus obviously had the intention of introducing among the Jews, that we can not avoid considering it the Word of God.
>
> Beyond doubt, Christ is the Founder of the first true Church; that is, that Church which, purified from the folly of superstition and the meanness of fanaticism, exhibits the moral kingdom of God upon the earth as far as can be done for man.[4]

ঞ

Helen Adams Keller (1880-1968), was a famous American author and lecturer who overcame the tremendous obstacles of being both blind and deaf. Having suffered a debilitating illness at the age of two, her parents took her to Dr. Alexander Graham Bell, who recommended her to the Perkins Institute for the Blind

Helen Adams Keller

in Boston. It was there, at the age of seven, that Anne Sullivan began tutoring her through the sense of touch, eventually teaching her to read Braille.

Helen Keller attended Radcliffe College, where Anne Sullivan interpreted the lectures to her, and she was able to type on a special Braille typewriter. Helen Keller became concerned about the conditions of the blind, especially those blinded in World War II. The recipient of innumerable national and international honors for her efforts to help the blind, Helen Keller wrote several books, including: *The Story of My Life*, 1903; *Optimism*, 1903; *The World I Live In*, 1908; *The Song of the Stone Wall*, 1910; *Out of the Dark*, 1913; *My Religion*, 1927; *Midstream*, 1930; *Let Us Have Faith*, 1941; and *The Open Door*, 1957. Helen Keller declared:

> Just as all things upon earth represent and image forth all the realities of another world, so the Bible is one mighty representative of the whole spiritual life of humanity.[5]

> I thank God for my handicaps, for, through them, I have found myself, my work, and my God.[6]

> Four things to learn in life:
>   To think clearly without hurry or confusion;
>   To love everybody sincerely;
>   To act in everything with the highest motives;
>   To trust God unhesitatingly.[7]

❧

Howard A. Kelly (1858-1943), was a renowned American surgeon and premier gynecologist in America in the early 20th century. For 22 years he was Professor of Gynecology and Obstetrics at Johns Hopkins University. Among his many authoritative medical works, was a book he wrote entitled:

Howard A. Kelly

A Scientific Man and His Bible.[8]

&

Sir William Thompson, Lord Kelvin (1824-1907), the famous scientist who developed degrees Kelvin to record temperatures on an absolute scale, held the chair of Natural Philosophy at the University of Glasgow for 54 years. He formulated the First and Second Laws of *Thermodynamics*, introduced the *Concept of Energy*, and made enormous advancements in the areas of mathematics and physics. Among his great contributions were the invention of a ship's compass which was largely freed from the magnetic influence of the iron in the ship, as well as helping to design and lay the first trans-atlantic telegraph cable.

In 1903, Lord Kelvin made the statement:

> With regard to the origin of life, science...positively affirms creative power.[9]

On May 23, 1889, in his address as the Chairman of the *Christian Evidence Society* in London, Lord Kelvin explained:

> My primary reason for accepting the invitation to preside was that I wished to show sympathy with this great Society which has been established for the purpose of defending Christianity as a Divine Revelation.
>
> I also thought something was due from Science. I have long felt that there was a general impression in the non-scientific world that the scientific world believes Science has discovered ways of explaining all the facts of nature without adopting any definite belief in a Creator. I have never doubted that impression was utterly groundless.
>
> It seems to me that when a scientific man says—as it has been said from time to time—that there is no God, he does not express his own ideas clearly. He is, perhaps, struggling with difficulties; but when he says that he does not believe in a creative power I am convinced he does not faithfully express what is in his mind. He is out of his depth....
>
> I may refer to that old but never uninteresting subject of the miracles of geology. Physical Science does something for us here.

Peter speaks of scoffers who said that "all things continue as they were from the beginning," but the Apostle affirms himself that "all these things shall be dissolved."

It seems to me that even physical science absolutely demonstrates the scientific truth of these words. We feel that there is no possibility of things going on forever as they have done for the last six thousand years. In science, as in morals and politics, there is absolutely no periodicity.[10]

🙚

Thomas a' Kempis (1380-1471), a writer during the Middle Ages, became well-known for writing the famous devotional, *Imitation of Christ*, in 1420. This work has greatly influenced western writers, including Martin Luther, Samuel Johnson, George Eliot and Lamartine. In it, Thomas a' Kempis wrote:

Be not angry that you cannot make others as you wish them to be, since you cannot make yourself as you wish to be.[11]

Man proposes, but God disposes.[12]

Love is swift, sincere, pious, pleasant, gentle, strong, patient, faithful, prudent, longsuffering, manly and never seeking her own; for wheresoever a man seeketh his own, there he falleth from love.[13]

🙚

Dr. D. James Kennedy (1930-), an authoritative author, lecturer and pastor of Coral Ridge Presbyterian Church in Florida, was quoted in 1987 in Dr. Tim LaHaye's book, *Faith of Our Founding Fathers*. In his message entitled "Church and State," Dr. D. James Kennedy articulated:

In reading over the Constitutions of all fifty of our states, I discovered something which some of you may not know: there is in all fifty, without exception, an appeal or a prayer to the Almighty God of the universe....Through all fifty state Constitutions, without exception, there runs this same appeal and reference to God who is the Creator of our liberties and the preserver of our freedoms.[14]

❧

John Fitzgerald Kennedy (1917-1963, assassinated) was the 35th President of the United States of America, the youngest man ever elected to that position. A graduate from Harvard, he served in World War II as a PT boat commander in the Pacific. He was elected as a U.S. Congressman, then as a U.S. Senator. Nominated as the Democratic candidate for president, John F. Kennedy was the first Roman Catholic ever to be elected to the highest executive office. In his Inaugural Address, January 20, 1961, President Kennedy proclaimed:

John Fitzgerald Kennedy

> The rights of man come not from the generosity of the state but from the hand of God.[15]

> The energy, the faith, the devotion which we bring to this endeavor will light our country and all who serve it—and the glow from that fire can truly light the world.
> And so, my fellow Americans—ask not what your country can do for you—ask what you can do for your country....Let us go forth to lead the land we love, asking His blessing and His help, but knowing that here on earth God's work must truly be our own.[16]

On November 22, 1963, President John F. Kennedy was killed in an assassination plot. The speech he was about to deliver concluded with these words:

> We in this country, in this generation, are—by destiny rather than choice—the watchmen on the walls of world freedom. We ask, therefore, that we may be worthy of our power and responsibility, that we may exercise our strength with wisdom and restraint, and that we may achieve in our time and for all time the ancient vision of peace on earth, goodwill toward men. That must always be our goal....For as was written long ago, "Except the Lord keep the city, the watchman waketh but in vain."[17]

President John F. Kennedy stated:

The question for our time is not whether all men are brothers. That question has been answered by God who placed us on this earth together. The question is whether we have the strength and the will to make the brotherhood of man the guiding principle of our daily lives.[18]

&

James Kent (1763-1847), was the Chief Justice of the Supreme Court of New York and the Head of the Court of Chancery for nine years. Considered the premier jurist in the development of the legal practice in the United States, James Kent authored the *Commentaries on American Law*. In the case of *The People v. Ruggles*, 1811, James Kent rendered the opinion of the Court:

James Kent

The defendant was indicted...in December, 1810, for that he did, on the 2nd day of September, 1810...wickedly, maliciously, and blasphemously, utter, and with a loud voice publish, in the presence and hearing of divers good and Christian people, of and concerning the Christian religion, and of and concerning Jesus Christ, the false, scandalous, malicious, wicked and blasphemous words following: "Jesus Christ was a bastard, and his mother must be a whore," in contempt of the Christian religion...the defendant was tried and found guilty, and was sentenced by the court to be imprisoned for three months, and to pay a fine of $500.[19]

Such words uttered with such a disposition were an offense at common law. In *Taylor's* case the defendant was convicted upon information of speaking similar words, and the Court...said that Christianity was parcel of the law, and to cast contumelious reproaches upon it, tended to weaken the foundation of moral obligation, and the efficacy of oaths.

And in the case of *Rex v. Woolston*, on a like conviction, the Court said...that whatever strikes at the root of Christianity tends manifestly to the dissolution of civil government....the authorities show that blasphemy against God and...profane ridicule of Christ or the Holy Scriptures (which are equally treated as blasphemy), are offenses punishable at common law, whether uttered by words or writings...because it tends to corrupt the morals of the people, and to destroy good order.

Such offenses have always been considered independent of any religious establishment or the rights of the Church. They are treated as affecting the essential interests of civil society....

We stand equally in need, now as formerly, of all the moral discipline, and of those principles of virtue, which help to bind society together.

The people of this State, in common with the people of this country, profess the general doctrines of Christianity, as the rule of their faith and practice; and to scandalize the author of these doctrines is not only...impious, but...is a gross violation of decency and good order.

Nothing could be more injurious to the tender morals of the young, than to declare such profanity lawful...

The free, equal, and undisturbed enjoyment of religious opinion, whatever it may be, and free and decent discussions on any religious subject, is granted and secured; but to revile...the religion professed by almost the whole community, is an abuse of that right....

We are a Christian people, and the morality of the country is deeply engrafted upon Christianity, and not upon the doctrines or worship of those impostors [other religions]....

[We are] people whose manners are refined and whose morals have been elevated and inspired with a more enlarged benevolence, by means of the Christian religion. Though the constitution has discarded religious establishments, it does not forbid judicial cognizance of those offenses against religion and morality which have no reference to any such establishment....

This [constitutional] declaration (noble and magnanimous as it is, when duly understood) never meant to withdraw religion in general, and with it the best sanctions of moral and social obligation from all consideration and notice of the law....

To construe it as breaking down the common law barriers against licentious, wanton, and impious attacks upon Christianity itself, would be an enormous perversion of its meaning....

Christianity in its enlarged sense, as a religion revealed and taught in the Bible, is part and parcel of the law of the land....

Nor are we bound by any expression of the Constitution, as some have strangely supposed, either not to punish at all, or to punish indiscriminately like attacks upon the religion of Mahomet and the Grand Lama; and for this plain reason, that we are a Christian people, and the morality of the country is deeply engrafted upon Christianity, and not upon the doctrines or worship of these impostors....

The Court is accordingly of the opinion that the judgement...must be affirmed.[20]

In an address before the American Bible Society, Chief Justice

Kent expressed:

The Bible is equally adapted to the wants and infirmities of every human being....

It brings life and immortality to light, which until the publication of the Gospel, were hidden from the scrutiny of the ages. The gracious Revelation of a future state is calculated to solve the mysteries of Providence in the dispensations of this life, to reconcile us to the inequalities of our present condition, and to inspire unconquerable fortitude and the most animating consolations when all other consolations fail....

The Bible also unfolds the origin and deep foundations of depravity and guilt, and the means and hopes of salvation through the mediation of our Redeemer. Its doctrines, its discoveries, its code of morals, and its means of grace are not only overwhelming evidence of its Divine origin, but they confound the pretensions of all other systems by showing the narrow range of and the feeble efforts of human reason, even when under the sway of the most exalted understanding, and enlightened by the accumulated treasures of science and learning.[21]

Kentucky Resolutions November 16, 1798, stated:

No power over the freedom of religion...[is] delegated to the United States by the Constitution.[22]

State of Kentucky 1992, passed the following bill in the Legislature, and Governor Brereton Jones signed it into law:

Local school boards may allow any teacher or administrator in a public school district of the Commonwealth to read or post in a public school building, classroom, or event any excerpts or portions of the National Motto, the National Anthem, the Pledge of Allegiance, the Preamble to the Kentucky Constitution, the Declaration of Independence, the Mayflower Pact, the writings, speeches, documents, and proclamations of the founding fathers and presidents of the United States, U.S. Supreme Court decisions, and acts of the U.S. Congress, including the published text of the Congressional Record. There shall be no content-based censorship of American history of heritage in the Commonwealth based on religious references in these writings, documents, and records.[23]

≥≥

Johann Kepler (1571-1630), the founder of physical astronomy, discovered the laws governing planetary motion and pioneered the discipline of celestial mechanics. He proved the heliocentric nature of the solar system, with all planets revolving around the sun. His publishing of the ephemeris tables, necessary for plotting star movement, contributed to the theory of calculus.

In regard to his invaluable scientific discoveries, Johann Kepler declared:

> O, Almighty God, I am thinking Thy thoughts after Thee! Nothing holds me! I will indulge in my sacred fury, I will triumph over mankind by the proud confession that I have stolen the golden vases to build up a tabernacle for my God, far away from the confines of Egypt. If you forgive me, I rejoice; if you be angry, I can bear it. The die is cast; the book is written, to be read either now or by posterity, I care not which. It may be well to wait a century for a reader, as God has waited six thousand years for an observer.[24]

In the conclusion of his treatise *Harmony of Worlds*, Kepler wrote:

> I thank Thee, my Creator and Lord, that Thou hast given me this joy in Thy creation, this delight in the works of Thy hands; I have shown the excellency of Thy works unto man, so far as my finite mind was able to comprehend Thine infinity; if I have said aught of Thy glory, graciously forgive it.[25]

In *Homage to the Book*, Johann Kepler stated:

> We astronomers say, with the common people, the planets stand still or go down; the sun rises or sets. How much less should we require than the Scriptures of Divine inspiration, setting aside the common mode of speech, should shape their words according to the model of the natural scientist, and, by employing a dark and inappropriate phraseology about things which surpass the comprehension of those whom it designs to instruct, perplex the

people of God, and thus obstruct its own way towards the attainment of the far more exalted object at which it aims.[26]

❧

Francis Scott Key

Francis Scott Key (1779-1843), an American lawyer and poet from Washington, D.C., was on a diplomatic mission to free a popular American doctor held captive aboard the British flagship in Chesapeake Bay. On that fateful night of September 14, 1814, Francis Scott Key's ship was commandeered by the British, and he was forced to watch as the British unmercifully bombarded the American Fort McHenry.

As the smoke of the night passed and the morning light began to dawn, Key saw "Old Glory" still waving. So inspired was he that he penned *The Star Spangled Banner*, later adding the music from the old hymn "To Anacreon in Heaven." Within weeks it was being sung all over the country, and on March 3, 1931, by official act of Congress (36 U.S.C. Sec.170),[27] it became the National Anthem of the United States. The fourth verse is as follows:

> O! thus be it ever when free men shall stand
> Between their loved home and the war's desolation;
> Blest with vict'ry and peace, may the Heav'n-rescued land
> Praise the Pow'r that hath made and preserved us a nation!
> Then conquer we must, when our cause it is just;
> And this be our motto, "In God is our trust!"
> And the star spangled banner in triumph shall wave
> O'er the land of the free and the home of the brave![28]

As a poet, Frances Scott Key also expressed an unusual depth:

Praise for Pardoning Grace

> Lord, with glowing heart I'd praise Thee
>   For the bliss Thy love bestows;
> For the pardoning grace that saves me,
>   And the peace that from it flows.

> Help, O God, my weak endeavor,
>   This dull soul to rapture raise;
> Thou must light the flame, or never
>   Can my love be warmed to praise.[29]

In an oration delivered before the Washington Society of Alexandria on February 22, 1812, Francis Scott Key declared:

> The patriot who feels himself in the service of God, who acknowledges Him in all his ways, has the promise of Almighty direction, and will find His Word in his greatest darkness, 'a lantern to his feet and a lamp unto his paths.' He will therefore seek to establish for his country in the eyes of the world, such a character as shall make her not unworthy of the name of a Christian nation....[30]

৵

Joyce Kilmer (1886-1918), an American poet and journalist, was educated at Rutgers College and Columbia University and worked for the *New York Times*. He was killed in World War I by a German machine-gun nest along the Ourcq River in France. His most famous poem was "Trees," 1913, in which he wrote:

> I think that I shall never see
> A poem lovely as a tree...
> Poems are made by fools like me,
> But only God can make a tree.[31]

৵

Cyrus King (1772-1817), a member of the United States Congress and on a Senate and House Joint Committee, was the brother of Rufus King, a signer of the Constitution of the United States. Cyrus King served as Major General of the 6th Division of the Massachusetts Militia, and founded Thorton Academy. In response to Thomas Jefferson's announcing his plans to donate his personal library of 6,487 books to the Library of Congress, Cyrus King, before the committee, moved:

To report a new section authorizing the Library Committee, as soon as said library shall be received at Washington, to select there from all books of an atheistical, irreligious, and immoral tendency, if any such there be, and send the same back to Mr. Jefferson without any expense to him.[32]

&

Martin Luther King, Jr. (1929-1968), was a prominent American civil rights leader. In his address at Montgomery, Alabama, December 31, 1955, Martin Luther King declared:

If you will protest courageously, and yet with dignity and Christian love, when the history books are written in future generations, the historians will have to pause and say, "There lived a great people—a black people—who injected new meaning and dignity into the veins of civilization."[33]

On August 28, 1963, on the occasion of the Civil Rights March on Washington, Martin Luther King declared:

I have a dream that one day on the red hills of Georgia the sons of former slaves and the sons of former slaveowners will be able to sit down together at the table of brotherhood....

I have a dream that my four little children will one day live in a nation where they will not be judged by the color of their skin, but by the content of their character.[34]

In accepting the Nobel Peace Prize on December 11, 1964, Martin Luther King admonished:

Nonviolence is the answer to the crucial political and moral questions of our time; the need for man to overcome oppression and violence without resorting to oppression and violence.

Man must evolve for all human conflict a method which rejects revenge, aggression and retaliation. The foundation of such a method is love.[35]

In *The Trumpet of Conscience*, Martin Luther King explains:

The limitation of riots...is that they cannot win...and their participants know it. Hence, rioting is not revolutionary but reactionary because it invites defeat. It involves an emotional catharsis, but it must be followed by a sense of futility.[36]

Martin Luther King, Jr. remarked:

> If a man is called to be a streetsweeper, he should sweep streets as Michelangelo painted, or Beethoven composed music, or Shakespeare wrote poetry. He should sweep streets so well that all the hosts of heaven and earth will pause to say, here lived a great streetsweeper who did his job well.[37]

On April 3, 1968, the evening before his assassination, Martin Luther King gave an address in Birmingham, Alabama:

> I just want to do God's will. And He's allowed me to go to the mountain. And I've looked over, and I've seen the promised land...[38]

ஐ

Rufus King (1755-1827), one of the signers of the Constitution of the United States, was a member of the Continental Congress, a diplomat, a lawyer, a minister to England, and a U.S. Senator from New York. He also served as an aide to General Sullivan during the Revolutionary War. Rufus King, a 32-year-old graduate of Harvard, was one of the youngest delegates at the Constitutional Convention.

Rufus King

In a speech made before the Senate at the time Missouri was petitioning for statehood, Rufus King stated:

> I hold that all laws or compacts imposing any such condition [as involuntary servitude] upon any human being are absolutely void because contrary to the law of nature, which is the law of God.[39]

ஐ

(Joseph) Rudyard Kipling (1865-1936), was a renowned British novelist, who wrote *Wee Willie Winkie and Other Children's Stories*, 1888; *Barrack Room Ballads*, 1892-93; *The Jungle Book*, 1894; *Kim*,

1901; and many other famous works. He was born in Bombay, educated in England, and in 1882 returned to India as a journalist. In 1889 Kipling arrived back in England, where his popularity as a writer grew tremendously. In 1907, he received the Nobel Prize for literature. In his work, *Gunga Din*, 1892, Rudyard Kipling penned:

> Though I've belted you and flayed you,
> By the livin' Gawd that made you,
> You're a better man than I am, Gunga Din.[40]

Kipling wrote his noblest poem, *Recessional-Jubilee Hymn for Queen Victoria's Reign*, in 1899, in honor of Queen Victoria's diamond jubilee. In it he admonished:

> Be careful lest thou forget the Lord thy God...and say in thine heart, my power and the might of mine hand hath gotten me this wealth. But thou shalt remember the Lord thy God; for it is He that giveth thee power to get wealth, that He may establish His covenant which He swear unto thy fathers, as it is this day—Deuteronomy 8:11, 17, 18.[41]

> God of our fathers, known of old—
>   Lord of our far-flung battle-line—
> Beneath whose awful hand we hold
>   Dominion over pal and pine—
> Lord God of Hosts, be with us yet,
> Lest we forget—lest we forget!

> The tumult and the shouting dies;
>   The captains and the kings depart;
> Still stands thine ancient Sacrifice,
>   An humble and a contrite heart.
> Lord God of Hosts, be with us yet,
> Lest we forget—lest we forget!

> Far called, our navies melt away—
>   On dune and headland sinks the fire—
> Lo, all our pomp of yesterday
>   Is one with Nineveh and Tyre!
> Judge of the Nations, spare us yet,
> Lest we forget—lest we forget!

If, drunk with sight of power, we loose
　　Wild tongues that have not Thee in awe
Such boasting as the Gentiles use,
　　Or lesser breeds without the Law-
Lord God of Hosts, be with us yet,
　　Lest we forget-lest we forget!

For heathen heart that puts her trust
　　In reeking tube and iron shard-
All valiant dust that builds on dust
　　And guarding calls not Thee to guard-
For frantic boast and foolish word,
Thy mercy on thy people. Lord!
　　　　　　　　Amen. [42]

In his *Ballad of East and West,* 1889, Rudyard Kipling penned:

Oh, East is East, and West is West,
And never the twain shall meet,
Till earth and sky stand presently
At God's great judgement seat. [43]

In The Glory of the Garden, 1911, Rudyard Kipling wrote:

Oh, Adam was a gardener, and God who made him sees
That half a proper gardener's work is done upon his knees. [44]

ða

William **Kirby** (1759-1850), a well-known English entomologist, wrote many significant scientific works, including one entitled:

On the Power and Wisdom of God and His Goodness as Manifested in the Creation of Animals. [45]

ða

John Knox (1505-1572), the leader of the Protestant Reformation in Scotland, stated:

A man with God is always in the majority. [46]

ða

L

Edwin Herbert Land (1909-1991), was the U.S. inventor and manufacturer of the Polaroid Land Camera, which developed pictures inside the camera through a process of light polarization. In 1977, when presented with a statement that the only thing that mattered was the bottom line on a balance sheet, Edwin Herbert Land replied:

> The bottom line is in heaven.[1]

ﻙ

Walter Savage Landor (1775-1864), an English author and poet, whose best-known work, *Imaginary Conversations,* was published between 1824-1829. Walter Savage Landor declared:

> To say nothing of its holiness or authority, the Bible contains more specimens of genius and taste than any other volume in existence.[2]

ﻙ

John Langdon (1741-1819), was a signer of the Constitution of the United States of America, a U.S. Senator, the President (Governor) of New Hampshire, and a merchant and soldier. John Langdon, a sixth generation American, was the first citizen of considerable wealth to put himself and his fortune in jeopardy during the Revolution. He not only supplied arms and money to the Continental Army, but fought as a

John Langdon

colonel in the militia as well.

Langdon considered slothfulness the same as infidelity, as he stated in a speech before Congress:

> There was evidence in New Hampshire of an "infidel age" in which the indolent, extravagant and wicked may divide the blessings of life with the industrious, the prudent and the virtuous. [3]

John Langdon, as President (Governor) of New Hampshire, made this official *Proclamation for a General Thanksgiving* to the State on October 21,1785:

A Proclamation For A General Thanksgiving
THE munificent Father of Mercies, and
Sovereign Disposer of Events, having been gra-

Seal of New Hampshire

ciously pleased to relieve the UNITED STATES of AMERICA from the Calamities of a long and dangerous war: through the whole course of which, he continued to smile on the Labours of our Husbandmen, thereby preventing Famine (the almost inseparable Companion of War) from entering our Borders;-eventually restored to us the blessings of Peace, on Terms advantageous and honourable:

And since the happy Period, when he silenced the Noise of contending Armies, has graciously smiled on the Labours of our Hands, caused the Earth to bring forth her increase in plentiful Harvests, and crowned the present Year with new and additional Marks of his unlimited Goodness:

It therefore becomes our indispensable Duty, not only to acknowledge, in general with the rest of Mankind, our dependence on the Supreme Ruler of the Universe, but as a People peculiarly favoured, to testify our Gratitude to the Author of all our Mercies, in the most solemn and public manner.

I DO therefore, agreeably to a Vote of the General Court, appointing Thursday the 24th Day of November next, to be observed and kept as a Day of GENERAL THANKSGIVING throughout this State, by and with the Advice of Council, issue this Proclamation, recommending to the religious Societies of every Denomination, to assemble on that Day, to celebrate the Praises of our divine Benefactor;

to acknowledge our own Unworthiness, confess our manifold Transgressions, implore his Forgiveness, and intreat the continuance of those Favours which he had been graciously pleased to bestow upon us;

that he would inspire our Rulers with Wisdom, prosper our Trade and Commerce, smile upon our Husbandry, bless our Seminaries of Learning, and spread the Gospel of his Grace over all the Earth.

And all servile Labour is forbidden on said Day.

GIVEN at the Council-Chamber in Concord, this Twenty-first Day of October, in the Year of our LORD, One Thousand Seven Hundred and Eighty-five, and in the Tenth Year of the Independence of the UNITED STATES of AMERICA. [4]

As President (Governor) of the State of New Hampshire, John Langdon issued *A Proclamation for a Day of Public Fasting and Prayer* on February 21, 1786:

A Proclamation For A Day of Public FASTING and PRAYER Throughout this State [1786]:

Vain is the acknowledgment of a Supreme Ruler of the Universe, unless such acknowledgments influence our practice, and call forth those expressions of homage and adoration that are due to his character and providential government, agreeably to the light of nature, enforced by revelation, and countenanced by the practice of civilized nations, in humble and fervent application to the throne for needed mercies, and gratitude for favors received.

It having been the laudable practice of this State, at the opening of the Spring, to set apart a day for such denomination, to assemble together on said day, in their respective places of public worship;

that the citizens of this State may with one heart and voice, penitently confess their manifold sins and transgressions, and fervently implore the divine benediction, that a true spirit of repentance and humiliation may be poured out upon all orders and degrees of men, and a compleat and universal reformation take place:

that he who gave wisdom and fortitude in the scenes of battle, would give prudence and direction to extricate us from succeeding embarrassments, build up, support and establish this rising Empire;

particularly, that he would be pleased to bless the great Council of the United States of America, and direct their deliberations to the wise and best determinations, succeed our embassies at foreign Courts, bless our Allies, and national Benefactors:

that he would always be pleased, to keep this State under his most holy protection: that all in the legislature, executive and judicial departments, may be guided and supported by wisdom, integrity and firmness, that all the people through this State, and through the land, may be animated by a true estimation of their privileges, and taught to secure, by their patriotism and virtue, what they have acquired by their valour:

that a spirit of emulation, industry, economy and frugality, may be diffused abroad, and that we may all be disposed to lead quiet and peaceable lives, in all godliness and honesty:

that he would be graciously pleased to bless us in the seasons of the year, and cause the earth to yield her increase, prosper our husbandry, merchandise, navigation and fishery, and all the labour of our hands, and give us to hear the voice of health in our habitations, and enjoy plenty of our borders:

that unanimity, peace and harmony, may be promoted and continue, and a spirit of universal philanthropy pervade the land: that he would be pleased to smile upon the means of education, and bless every institution of useful knowledge;

and above all, that he would rain down righteousness upon the earth, revive religion, and spread abroad the knowledge of the true GOD, the Saviour of man, throughout the world.

And all servile labour and recreations are forbidden on said day.

GIVEN at the Council-Chamber in Portsmouth, this twenty-first day of February, in the year of our LORD, one thousand seven hundred and eighty-six, and in the tenth year of the Sovereignty and Independence of the United States of America.[5]

John Langdon was one of the founders and the first President of the New Hampshire Bible Society, whose goal was to place a Bible into every home in New Hampshire.[6]

Governor John Langdon was visited by President Monroe in 1817, as the President was making a tour of the New England States. The local newspaper reported the following article:

James Monroe

While at Portsmouth, the President spent that part of the Sabbath which was not devoted to public divine service, with that eminent patriot and Christian, John Langdon. His tarry at the mansion of Gov. L. was probably longer than the time devoted to any individual in New England. It is thus that the President has evinced his partiality to our most distinguished and illustrious citizen.[7]

ॐ

Samuel Langdon (1723-1797), the president of Harvard University, was a member of the New Hampshire Convention to ratify the U.S. Constitution in 1788, and an original member of the American

Academy of Arts and Sciences. In May of 1775, Harvard President Samuel Langdon was invited to give an address to the Provincial Congress of Massachusetts. In it he stated:

> We have rebelled against God. We have lost the true spirit of Christianity, though we retain the outward profession and form of it....By many, the Gospel is corrupted into a superficial system of moral philosophy, little better than ancient Platonism....
>
> My brethren, let us repent and implore the divine mercy. Let us amend our ways and our doings, reform everything that has been provoking the Most High, and thus endeavor to obtain the gracious interpositions of providence for our deliverance....
>
> May the Lord hear us in this day of trouble....We will rejoice in His salvation, and in the name of our God, we will set up our banners![8]

ఎ

Bartolomé de Las Casas (1474-1566), called "the Apostle of the Indies," was one of the first Christian missionaries to America. As the first priest ordained in the New World, he became known for his devotion to the oppressed and enslaved natives. He provided a great literary service by copying Columbus' original *Journal of the First Voyage (El Libro de la Primera Navegacion)* into an abstract. He also wrote *Apologetic History of the Indies (Apologetica Historia de las Indias)*, in 1530, in which he stated (translated by George Sanderlin):

> It clearly appears that there are no races in the world, however rude, uncultivated, barbarous, gross, or almost brutal they may be, who cannot be persuaded and brought to a good order and way of life, and made domestic, mild and tractable, provided...the method that is proper and natural to men is used; that is, love and gentleness and kindness.[9]

In the prologue of his book, *Historia de las Indias*, written 1550-1563, Bartolomé de Las Casas stated (translated by Rachel Phillips):

> The main goal of divine Providence in [allowing] the discovery of these tribes and lands...is...the conversion and well-being of souls, and to this goal everything temporal must necessarily be subordinated and directed.[10]

ða

Hugh Latimer (1485-1555), was bishop of Worcester, England, during the reign of King Henry VIII. He refused to condemn Martin Luther's writings and strongly supported the Protestant Reformation. He was imprisoned for a total of seven years, after which Queen Mary condemned him to be burned at the stake. On October 16, 1555, while Hugh Latimer and Nicholas Ridley were being brought to their place of execution at Oxford, Latimer exhorted his companion:

> Play the man, Master Ridley. We shall this day light such a candle, by God's grace, in England, as I trust shall never be put out.[11]

ða

William Edward Hartpole Lecky (1838-1903), the famous Irish historian, said concerning Christ:

> Amid all the sins and failings, amid all the...persecution and fanaticism that have defaced the church, it has preserved in the character and example of its founder (Jesus), an enduring principle of regeneration.[12]

ða

Richard Henry Lee (1732-1794), a signer of the Declaration of Independence, was also a member of the Virginia House of Burgesses, a delegate to the First Continental Congress and a U.S. Senator. On November 1, 1777, as recorded in the *Journals of Congress*, Richard Henry Lee along with the committee of Samuel Adams and General Daniel Roberdeau, recommended a resolution setting apart:

Richard Henry Lee

> Thursday, the 18th of December next, for solemn thanksgiving and praise, that with one heart and one voice the good people may express the grateful feelings of their hearts, and consecrate themselves to the service of their Divine Benefactor; and that, together with their

sincere acknowledgments and offerings, they may join the penitent confession of their manifold sins, whereby they had forfeited every favor, and their humble and earnest supplication that it may please God, through the merits of Jesus Christ, mercifully to forgive and blot them out of remembrance.[13]

&

Robert Edward Lee (1807-1870), the General of the Confederate Army, was the son of the Revolutionary leader, "Light-Horse Harry" Lee, and the son-in-law of George Washington's adopted grandson, George Washington Parke Custis. Robert E. Lee and his wife, Mary Ann Randolph, inherited the 1,100 acre Washington estate directly across the Potomac from Washington, D.C. Tutored and home-schooled as a child, Robert E. Lee excelled at West Point, and distinguished himself in the Mexican-American War. From San Antonio, Texas, he engineered the American troops' passage across the difficult Mexican mountains so they could quickly take Mexico City.

Robert Edward Lee

Henry Lee ("Light-Horse Harry" Lee)

Lee was against slavery and a number of years before the war he freed his own slaves. He was so highly respected, that when war looked imminent, President Abraham Lincoln offered him the Field Command of the United States Army. He struggled all night with his decision, finally resolving to the obligation of loyalty to his home state and the South. He resigned from the U.S. Army and in a letter to his sister, explained:

> With all my devotion to the union and the feelings of loyalty and duty of an American citizen, I have not been able to make up my mind to raise my hand against my relatives, my children, my home.[14]

On December 27, 1856, Robert E. Lee wrote to his wife:

> Slavery as an institution is a moral and political evil in any

country....I think, however, a greater evil to the white than to the black race...

The doctrines and miracles of our Saviour have required nearly two thousand years to convert but a small part of the human race, and even among the Christian nations what gross errors still exist![15]

In 1859, Robert E. Lee's most reliable general, Stonewall Jackson, wrote to his wife, Mrs. Mary Ann Jackson:

Is there not comfort in prayer, which is not elsewhere to be found?[16]

General Robert E. Lee's military expertise was so formidable that, for the first two years of the Civil War, it looked as if the South had won. Stonewall Jackson's continued victories kept pushing the North back until Lee's troops were dangerously close to attacking Washington, D.C., itself.

On December 25, 1862, General Robert E. Lee wrote to his wife from Fredericksburg, Virginia:

My heart is filled with gratitude to Almighty God for his unspeakable mercies with which He has blessed us in this day. For those He granted us from the beginning of life, and particularly for those He has vouchsafed us during the past year. What should have become of us without His crowning help and protection?

Oh, if our people would only recognize it and cease from self-boasting and adulation, how strong would be my belief in the final success and happiness to our country! But what a cruel thing is war; to separate and destroy families and friends, and mar the purest joys and happiness God has granted us in this world; to fill our hearts with hatred instead of love for our neighbors, to devastate the fair face of this beautiful world!

I pray that on this day when only peace and good-will are preached to mankind, better thoughts may fill the hearts of our enemies and turn them to peace.[17]

On May 31, 1863, General Robert E. Lee wrote to his wife as he prepared the Confederate Army of Northern Virginia for its next major northern thrust:

I pray that our merciful Father in heaven may protect and direct us. In that case I fear no odds and no numbers.[18]

On April 8, 1864, General Robert E. Lee issued orders for his troops to observe the "day of fasting, humiliation, and prayer" that had been proclaimed:

> Soldiers! Let us humble ourselves before the Lord, our God, asking through Christ, the forgiveness of our sins, beseeching the aid of the God of our forefathers in the defense of our homes and our liberties, thanking Him for His past blessings, and imploring their continuance upon our cause and our people.[19]

General Robert E. Lee wrote:

> Knowing that intercessory prayer is our mightiest weapon and the supreme call for all Christians today, I pleadingly urge our people everywhere to pray. Believing that prayer is the greatest contribution that our people can make in this critical hour, I humbly urge that we take time to pray—to really pray.
>
> Let there be prayer at sunup, at noonday, at sundown, at midnight—all through the day. Let us pray for our children, our youth, our aged, our pastors, our homes. Let us pray for our churches.
>
> Let us pray for ourselves, that we may not lose the word "concern" out of our Christian vocabulary. Let us pray for our nation. Let us pray for those who have never known Jesus Christ and redeeming love, for moral forces everywhere, for our national leaders. Let prayer be our passion. Let prayer be our practice.[20]

General Lee once remarked to Chaplain John William Jones regarding the Bible:

> There are things in the old Book which I may not be able to explain, but I fully accept it as the infallible Word of God, and receive its teachings as inspired by the Holy Spirit.[21]

General Robert E. Lee was visited in his tent by Chaplain J. William Jones and General Stonewall Jackson's Chaplain, B.T. Lacey. They told the General that all the chaplains were praying for him. As Jones recorded, tears came to General Lee's eyes as he said:

> Please thank them for that, sir—I warmly appreciate it. And I can only say that I am nothing but a poor sinner, trusting in Christ alone for salvation, and need all of the prayers they can offer me.[22]

One night around the campfire, Chaplain Jones overheard some soldiers discussing the recent invention of the theory of evolution, when one soldier replied:

> Well, boys, the rest of us may have developed from monkeys; but I tell you, none the less than God could have made such a man as Marse Robert.[23]

Near the final end of the War, after such a tremendous loss of life, one of Lee's generals suggested rallying more recruits to the Confederate cause. General Lee responded:

> General, you and I as Christian men...must consider its effects on the country as a whole. Already it is demoralized by four years of war. If I took your advice, the men...would become mere bands of marauders, and the enemy's cavalry would pursue them and overrun many wide sections....We would bring on a state of affairs it would take the country years to recover from.[24]

General Robert E. Lee surrendered to General Ulysses S. Grant on April 9, 1865 at Appomattox, Virginia. Lee took off his sword and handed it to Grant, and Grant handed it back.

The next day, April 10, 1865, General Lee issued his final order to his army:

Ulysses S. Grant

> I have determined to avoid the useless sacrifice of those whose past services have endeared them to their countrymen. By the terms of the agreement, officers and men can return to their homes....I earnestly pray that a merciful God will extend to you His blessing and protection.[25]

Robert E. Lee confided:

> In all my perplexities and distresses, the Bible has never failed to give me light and strength.[26]

In a church service on June 4, 1865, as reported by Colonel T.L. Broun, there was a shock when a Negro advanced to the communion table. But then:

Robert Edward Lee

[General Lee] arose in his usual dignified and self-possessed manner...and reverently knelt down to partake of the communion, not far from the Negro.[27]

In June of 1865, Robert E. Lee was indicted for treason by the United States Grand Jury in Norfolk, Virginia. When some friends voiced their indignation, Lee calmly responded:

I have fought against the people of the North because I believed they were seeking to wrest from the South dearest rights. But I have never cherished toward them bitter or vindictive feelings, and have never seen the day when I did not pray for them.[28]

After the war, a southern clergyman spoke critically of the recent actions of the federal government. Following a pause, Robert E. Lee asked:

Doctor, there is a good old book which...says "Love your enemies." Do you think your remarks this evening were quite in the spirit of that teaching?[29]

In August of 1865, Robert E. Lee accepted the invitation to become the President of Washington College at Lexington, Virginia, (later changed to Washington and Lee University, in his honor). In 1869, Robert E. Lee invited his former chaplain, John William Jones to speak. In thanking him, Lee remarked:

Oh, doctor, if I could only know that all the young men in this College were good Christians I should have nothing more to desire.

I wish, sir, to thank you for your address. It was just what we needed. Our great want is a revival which shall bring these young men to Christ.

I should be disappointed, sir, and shall fail in the leading object that brought me here, unless these young men all become Christians; and I wish you and others of your sacred profession to do all you can to accomplish it.

We poor sinners need to come back from our wanderings to seek pardon through the all-sufficient merits of our Redeemer. And we need to pray earnestly for the power of the Holy Spirit to give us a precious revival in our hearts and among the unconverted.[30]

੨ਂ

Paul Lemoine (1878-1940), was the director of the Natural History Museum in Paris, President of the Geological Society of France, and a chief editor of the 1937 edition of the *Encyclopedia Francaise*. In writing an article on evolution, he stated:

> The theory of evolution is impossible. At base, in spite of appearances, no one any longer believes in it....Evolution is a kind of dogma which the priests no longer believe, but which they maintain for their people.[31]

੨ਂ

"C.S." Clive Staples Lewis (1898-1963), a professor at Oxford University, 1925-1954, and a professor at Cambridge University, 1954-1963, became a renowned English novelist, whose works include the famous *Chronicles of Narnia,* and *Out of the Silent Planet,* 1938; *The Problem of Pain,* 1940; *The Screwtape Letters,* 1942; and *Mere Christianity,* 1952. Having once been an agnostic, C.S. Lewis expressed:

> I am trying to prevent anyone from saying the really foolish thing that people often say about Him: "I am ready to accept Jesus as a great moral teacher, but I don't accept His claims to be God." That is one thing we must not say.
> A man who was merely a man and said the sort of things that Jesus said would not be a great moral teacher. He would either be a lunatic— on a level with the man who says he is a poached egg—or else he would be the devil of hell.
> You must make your choice. Either this man was, and is , the Son of God: or else a madman or something worse.[32]

In *The Screwtape Letters,* 1942, C.S. Lewis wrote:

> The safest road to Hell is the gradual one—the gentle slope, soft underfoot, without sudden turnings, without milestones, without signposts.[33]

In *Mere Christianity*, 1952, C.S. Lewis wrote:

> The Eternal Being, who knows everything and who created the whole universe, became not only a man but (before that) a baby, and before that a fetus in a woman's body.[34]

C.S. Lewis remarked:

> God cannot give us happiness and peace apart from Himself, because it is not there. There is no such thing.[35]

ॠ

The Liberty Bell

August 1752, was cast in England by an order of the Pennsylvania Assembly to commemorate the fiftieth anniversary of the colony's existence. Founded in 1701, when William Penn wrote the *Charter of Privileges*, the colony's Assembly, in 1751, declared a "Year of Jubilee," commissioning the bell to be put in the Philadelphia State House. Isaac Norris, the Speaker of the Assembly and a strong Quaker, chose the 10th verse of Leviticus chapter 25 for the occasion:

The inscription cast onto the Liberty Bell in August 1752 is an excerpt from Leviticus 25:10.

> And ye shall make hallow the fiftieth year, and proclaim liberty throughout all the land unto all the inhabitants thereof; it shall be a jubilee.[36]

The inscription cast onto the bell, August 1752, read:

> Proclaim liberty through all the land and to all the inhabitants thereof. (Leviticus XXV. 10)[37]

The Liberty Bell got its name from being rung July 8, 1776, at the first public reading of the Declaration of Independence.[38] It cracked as it rang at the funeral for Chief Justice Marshall in 1835.[39]

꙳

The Statue of Liberty Enlightening the World July 4, 1884, was given by the nation of France to the United States as a symbol of friendship between the two nations. The Statue of Liberty has since become a symbol of freedom throughout the world. The largest of its kind, the statue weighs 450,000 pounds and stands 305 feet above the base of the pedestal. Conceived by Edouard de Laboulaye and constructed over a steel structure built by Gustave Eiffel, the Statue was sculpted by the French sculptor Frederic Auguste Bartholdi.

Bartholdi wrote:

> The statue was born for this place which inspired its conception. May God be pleased to bless my efforts and my work, and to crown it with success, the duration and the moral influence which it ought to have.[40]

On October 28, 1886, the inauguration ceremony of the *Statue of Liberty Enlightening the World* was begun with a prayer by Reverend Richard S. Storrs, D.D.:

> Almighty God, our Heavenly Father, who art of infinite majesty and mercy, by whose counsel and might the courses of the worlds are wisely ordained and irresistibly established, yet who takest thought of the children of men, and to whom our homage in all our works is justly due: We bless and praise Thee....
> It is in Thy favor, and through the operation of the Gospel of Thy grace, that cities stand in quiet prosperity; that peaceful commerce covers the seas....

We pray that the Liberty which it represents may continue to enlighten with beneficent instruction, and to bless with majestic and wide benediction, the nations which have part in this work of renown ....

We pray for all the nations of the earth; that in equity and charity their sure foundations may be established; that in piety and wisdom they may find a true welfare, in obedience to Thee, glory and praise; and that, in all the enlargements of their power, they may be ever the joyful servants of Him to whose holy dominion and kingdom shall be no end. [41]

ૐ

Liberty Tree Flag 1776, was adopted by the Massachusetts Council and became the original flag that the *Sons of Liberty* met under just before the Boston Tea Party. It derived its name from the elm tree in Hanover Square, Boston, where the patriots first met to protest the Stamp Act. The flag is a green tree on a white background, inscribed with the words *Liberty Tree* and:

Appeal to God. [42]

ૐ

Library of Congress 1800, was set up primarily to assist Congressmen in preparing laws, although it is open to all scholars. Burned by the British during the War of 1812, it was subsequently rebuilt. In 1897, it was relocated into its present building, and an annex was added in 1938. Numerous quotations from Scripture can be found within the halls of the Library of Congress. President Eliot of Harvard selected the following verse to be inscribed on the walls:

He hath showed thee, O man, what is good; and what doth the Lord require of thee, but to do justly and love mercy and walk humbly with thy God. (Micah 6:8) [43]

The lawmakers' library has engraved the quote from the Psalmist:

The heavens declare the glory of God, and the firmament showeth His handiwork. (Psalm 19:1) [44]

Also inscribed is the verse:

> The light shineth in darkness, and the darkness comprehendeth it
> not. (John 1:5)[45]

&

Rush Limbaugh (1951-   ), hosts America's most popular radio
talk show, reaching over 20 million listeners a week. Additionally,
he airs a syndicated TV show which blankets nearly 99% of
America. Rush Limbaugh is the author of the best-selling books,
The Way Things Ought to Be, 1992; and *See, I Told You So*, 1993; and
the publisher of *The Limbaugh Letter*, which receives national
notoriety. Born in Cape Girardeau, Missouri, Rush went from
being a Top-40 deejay, to being a successful radio talk-show host
at KFBK in Sacramento, California, to being heard in over 616
markets across the country.

In the book *See, I Told You So*, Rush Limbaugh communicates
in his straightforward style:

> Well, folks, let's allow our real, undoctored-American-history
> lesson to unfold further. If our schools and the media have twisted the
> historical record when it comes to Columbus, they have obliterated
> the contributions of America's earliest permanent settlers—the
> Pilgrims. Why? Because they were a people inspired by profound
> religious beliefs to overcome incredible odds....
>   On August 1, 1620, the *Mayflower* set sail. It carried a total of 102
> passengers, including forty Pilgrims led by William Bradford. On the
> journey, Bradford set up an agreement, a contract, that established just
> and equal laws for all members of their new community, irrespective
> of their religious beliefs. Where did the revolutionary ideas expressed
> in the Mayflower Compact come from? From the Bible. The Pilgrims
> were a people completely steeped in the lessons of the Old and New
> Testaments. They looked to the ancient Israelites for their example.
> And, because of the biblical precedents set forth in Scripture, they
> never doubted that their experiment would work....
>   But guess what? There's even more that is being deliberately
> withheld from our modern textbooks. For example, one of those
> attracted to the New World by the success of Plymouth was Thomas
> Hooker, who established his own community in Connecticut the first

full-fledged constitutional community and perhaps the most free society the world had ever known. Hooker's community was governed by the Fundamental Orders of Connecticut, which established strict limits on the powers of government. So revolutionary and successful was this idea that Massachusetts was inspired to adopt its Body of Liberties, which included ninety-eight separate protections of individual rights, including: "no taxation without representation," "due process of law," "trial by a jury of peers," and prohibitions against "cruel and unusual punishment."

Does all that sound familiar? It should. These are ideas and concepts that led directly to the U.S. Constitution and Bill of Rights. Nevertheless, the Pilgrims and Puritans of early New England are often vilified today as witch-burners and portrayed as simpletons. To the contrary, it was their commitment to pluralism and free worship that led to these ideals being incorporated into American life. Our history books purposely conceal the fact that these notions were developed by communities of devout Christians who studied the Bible and found it prescribes limited, representative government and free enterprise as the best political and economic systems.

There's only one word for this, folks: censorship.[46]

With piercing humor, Rush Limbaugh offers the following definitions:

> ...I offer you this guide to the esoteric jargon of liberalism...
>
> **academic freedom:** freedom of student or teacher to hold or express views without fear of arbitrary interference, except when such ideas are deemed racist, bigoted, homophobic, insensitive, chauvinistic, jingoistic, imperialistic, religious, conservative, or politically incorrect...
>
> **Declaration of Independence:** a historical document that should not be read or displayed in public schools because of its overt religious nature...
>
> **prayer:** the only kind of speech the First Amendment doesn't protect...[47]

Commenting on the current popular movement, Rush Limbaugh profoundly states:

> What's new about the "New Age"? In spite of what Shirley MacLaine and *Algore* might tell you, it's nothing more than recycled paganism.[48]

❧

Abraham
Lincoln

Abraham Lincoln (1809-1865, assassinated) was the 16th President of the United States of America. Under his courageous leadership, America survived the Civil War and remained the "United States."

A man of highest moral character, who was nicknamed "Honest Abe," Abraham Lincoln never lost touch with the common people. From being raised in a log cabin and working at clearing land and splitting rails, Lincoln taught himself law, gained a respected reputation as a lawyer, and became the Eighth Circuit Judge in Illinois. Abraham Lincoln was elected to the Illinois State Legislature, to the United States Congress, and, after becoming a national figure through debating against Stephen A. Douglas' pro-slavery bill, he was nominated as the Republican candidate for President.

Only one week after he was inaugurated as President, the southern states formed the Confederacy, and within a month the Civil War had begun, with the Confederate Army firing on Fort Sumter, April 12, 1861. The Civil War ended four years later, April 9, 1865, with the surrender of General Robert E. Lee to General Ulysses S. Grant at Appomattox, Virginia. By the conclusion of the war, over a half million men had died, which is more than the combined casualties of all other wars America has been in to date. Five days later, on April 14, 1865, after he had freed millions of slaves, Abraham Lincoln was assassinated in Ford's Theater by John Wilkes Booth.

At age 28, Abraham Lincoln wrote to a friend, Joshua Speed, who was a slaveholder:

> I also acknowledge your rights and my obligations, under the Constitution, in regards to your slaves. I confess I hate to see the poor creatures hunted down and caught and carried back to their stripes and unrewarded toils; I bite my lip and keep quiet. In 1841, you and I had together a tedious low-water trip on a steamboat from Louisville to St. Louis. You may remember, as I well do, that from Louisville to the mouth of the Ohio, there were on board ten or a dozen slaves shackled together with irons.

That sight was a continual torment to me; I see something like it every time I touch the Ohio, or any other slave border. It is hardly fair for you to assume that I have no interest in a thing which has, and continually exercises, the power of making me miserable.[49]

In a speech on January 27, 1837, Abraham Lincoln forewarned:

At what point then is the approach of danger to be expected? I answer, if it ever reach us, it must spring up amongst us; it cannot come from abroad. If destruction be our lot we must ourselves be its author and finisher. As a nation of freemen we must live through all time, or die by suicide.[50]

In 1846, when Lincoln was running for Congress from the seventh district of Illinois, a rumor began to spread that he was not a Christian. In response to this, Lincoln made a public statement, published in the *Illinois Gazette*, August 15, 1846, which read:

That I am not a member of any Christian Church, is true; but I have never denied the truth of the Scriptures; and I have never spoken with intentional disrespect of religion in general, or of any denomination of Christians in particular....I do not think I could, myself, be brought to support a man for office whom I knew to be an open enemy of, and scoffer at religion.[51]

In 1851, during the last illness of his father, Abraham Lincoln wrote his step-brother, encouraging him:

I sincerely hope father may recover his health; but at all events tell him to remember to call upon and confide in our great and good and merciful Maker, who will not turn away from him in any extremity. He notes the fall of a sparrow and numbers the hairs of our head, and He will not forget the dying man who puts his trust in Him.[52]

On August 24, 1855, in a letter to Joshua F. Speed, Abraham Lincoln wrote:

How can anyone who abhors the oppression of Negroes be in favor of degrading classes of white people? Our progress in degeneracy appears to me to be pretty rapid. As a nation we began by declaring that "all men are created equal." We now practically read it "all men are created equal, except Negroes." When the Know-Nothings get control, it will read "all men are created equal, except Negroes and foreigners and Catholics." When it comes to this, I shall prefer emigrating to some country where they make no pretense of loving liberty—to Russia, for instance, where despotism can be taken pure, and without the base alloy of hypocrisy.[53]

Abraham Lincoln, in the closing remarks of a debate with Judge Douglas, asserted:

> That is the issue that will continue in this country when these poor tongues of Judge Douglas and myself shall be silent. It is the eternal struggle between these two principles—right and wrong—throughout the world. They are the two principles that have stood face to face from the beginning of time, and will ever continue to struggle.[54]

On July 10, 1858, Abraham Lincoln gave a speech in a debate with Stephen A. Douglas:

> It is said in one of the admonitions of our Lord, "As your Father in Heaven is perfect, be ye also perfect." The Saviour, I suppose, did not expect that any human being could be perfect as the Father in Heaven; but He said, "As your Father in Heaven is perfect, be ye also perfect." He set that up as a standard, and He who did most toward reaching that standard attained the highest degree of moral perfection.[55]

On September 11, 1858, Abraham Lincoln delivered a speech at Edwardsville, Illinois:

> Our reliance is in the love of liberty which God has planted in us. Our defense is in the spirit which prized liberty as the heritage of all men, in all lands everywhere. Destroy this spirit and you have planted the seeds of despotism at your own doors. Familiarize yourselves with the chains of bondage and you prepare your own limbs to wear them. Accustomed to trample on the rights of others, you have lost the genius of your own independence and become the fit subjects of the first cunning tyrant who rises among you.[56]

On April 6, 1859, Lincoln wrote a letter to H.L. Pierce and others, insisting:

This is a world of compensation; and he who would be no slave must consent to have no slave. Those who deny freedom to others deserve it not for themselves, and under a just God, cannot long retain it.[57]

On February 11, 1861, newly elected President Abraham Lincoln delivered a farewell speech to his home state in Springfield, Illinois, as he left for Washington, D.C.:

I now leave, not knowing when or whether ever I may return, with a task before me greater than that which rested upon Washington. Without the assistance of that Divine Being who ever attended him, I cannot succeed. With that assistance I cannot fail. Trusting in Him who can go with me, and remain with you, and be everywhere for good, let us confidently hope that all will yet be well.[58]

On February 22, 1861, in a Speech at Independence Hall, Philadelphia, President Lincoln declared:

The Declaration of Independence which gave liberty not alone to the people of this country, but hope to all the world, for all future time. It was that which gave promise that in due time the weights would be lifted from the shoulders of all men, and that all should have an equal chance. This is the sentiment embodied in the Declaration of Independence....I would rather be assassinated on this spot than surrender it.[59]

On February 23, 1861, Abraham Lincoln replied to William Dodge:

With the support of the people and the assistance of the Almighty, I shall undertake to perform it....

Freedom is the natural condition of the human race, in which the Almighty intended men to live. Those who fight the purpose of the Almighty will not succeed. They always have been, they always will be, beaten.[60]

In his Inaugural Address, March 4, 1861, President Abraham Lincoln commented on his disagreement with the 1857 Supreme Court case of *Dred Scott v. Sanford*, wherein Chief Justice Roger B. Taney decided that slaves were not persons or citizens, but were the property of the owner, the same as their body, horse, cattle, etc., and the owner had the freedom of choice to decide what they wanted to do with their own property:

> I do not forget the position assumed by some that constitutional questions are to be decided by the Supreme Court....At the same time, the candid citizen must confess that if the policy of the Government upon vital questions affecting the whole people is to be irrevocably fixed by decisions of the Supreme Court, the instant they are made...the people will have ceased to be their own rulers, having...resigned their Government into the hands of the eminent tribunal....
>
> Intelligence, patriotism, Christianity, and a firm reliance on Him who has never yet forsaken this favored land, are still competent to adjust in the best way all our present difficulty.[61]

In 1861, President Abraham Lincoln addressed the New Jersey State Senate:

> I am exceedingly anxious that this Union, the Constitution, and the liberties of the people shall be perpetuated in accordance with the original idea for which that struggle was made. And I shall be most happy, indeed, if I shall be an humble instrument in the hands of the Almighty...for perpetuating the object of that struggle.[62]

President Abraham Lincoln once told Noah Brooks, his intended secretary:

> I have been driven many times upon my knees by the overwhelming conviction that I had nowhere else to go. My own wisdom, and that of all about me, seemed insufficient for that day.[63]

In July of 1861, after the Union army was defeated at the *Battle of Bull Run*, President Abraham Lincoln declared the fourth Thursday in September, the 26th, as a *National Day of Prayer and Fasting:*

> It is fit and becoming in all people, at all times, to acknowledge and revere the Supreme Government of God; to bow in humble submission to his chastisement; to confess and deplore their sins and transgressions in the full conviction that the fear of the Lord is the beginning of wisdom; and to pray, with all fervency and contrition, for

the pardon of their past offenses, and for a blessing upon their present and prospective action.[64]

And whereas when our own beloved country, once, by the blessings of God, united, prosperous and happy, is now afflicted with faction and civil war, it is peculiarly fit for us to recognize the hand of God in this terrible visitation, and in sorrowful remembrance of our own faults and crimes as a nation and as individuals, to humble ourselves before Him and to pray for His mercy...that the inestimable boon of civil and religious liberty, earned under His guidance and blessing by the labors and sufferings of our fathers, may be restored.[65]

In 1862, President Lincoln restored the lands in California that had been taken from the missions after the *Mexican Secularization Act:*

Now know ye...pursuant to the provisions of the Act of Congress...I give and grant unto the said Joseph G. Alemony, Bishop of Monterrey..."in trust for the religious purposes and uses to which the same have been respectively appropriated" the tracts of land embraced and described in the foregoing survey....Given under my hand..this 23rd day of May, in the year of our Lord one thousand eight hundred and 62.[66]

In June of 1862, President Abraham Lincoln spoke to the chairman of the House Judiciary Committee, James Wilson, in regard to God's direction:

I trust that as He shall further open the way, I will be ready to walk therein, relying on His help and trusting in His goodness and wisdom.[67]

In delivering an address on colonization to a Negro deputation at Washington, August 14, 1862, President Abraham Lincoln pronounced:

It is difficult to make a man miserable while he feels he is worthy of himself and claims kindred to the great God who made him.[68]

In September of 1862, President Lincoln declared to a delegation from Chicago:

I am approached with the most opposite opinions and advice, and that by religious men, who are equally certain that they represent the divine will. I am sure that either the one or the other class is mistaken in that belief, and perhaps, in some respects, both.

I hope it will not be irreverent for me to say that if it is probable that God would reveal His will to others on a point so connected with my duty, it might be supposed He would reveal it directly to me; for, unless I am more deceived in myself than I often am, it is my earnest desire to know the will of Providence in this matter. And if I can learn what it is, I will do it.[69]

In September of 1862, in the darkest moment of the War, after losing the *Second Battle of Bull Run,* Lincoln wrote his *Meditation on the Divine Will:*

The will of God prevails. In great contests each party claims to act in accordance with the will of God. Both may be, and one must be wrong. God can not be for and against the same thing at the same time. In the present civil war it is quite possible that God's purpose is something different from the purpose of either party—and yet the human instrumentalities, working just as they do, are of the best adaptation to effect His purpose.

I am almost ready to say this is probably true—that God wills this contest, and wills that it shall not end yet. By his mere quiet power, on the minds of the now contestants, He could have either saved or destroyed the Union without a human contest. Yet the contest began. And having begun He could give the final victory to either side any day. Yet the contest proceeds.[70]

√ On September 22, 1862, after the massive Confederate Army lost to the Union troops at the *Battle at Antietam,* President Lincoln addressed his Cabinet:

I made a solemn vow before God, that if General Lee were driven back from Pennsylvania, I would crown the result by the declaration of freedom to the slaves.[71]

On September 22, 1862, President Abraham Lincoln, in direct disregard to the Supreme Court's 1857 *Dred Scott v. Sanford* decision, proceeded to issue the famous *Emancipation Proclamation,* to go into effect January 1, 1863, granting the right to life, freedom and citizenship to all persons irregardless of race, origin, circumstance, etc.:

On the first day of January, in the year of our Lord one thousand eight hundred and sixty-three, all persons held as slaves within any State, or designated part of a State, the people whereof shall then be in rebellion against the United States, shall be then, thenceforward, and forever free...

And by virtue of the power and for the purpose aforesaid, I do order and declare that all persons held as slaves within said designated States and parts of States are, and henceforward shall be, free; and that the Executive Government of the United States, including the military and naval authorities thereof, shall recognize and maintain the freedom of said persons.

And I hereby enjoin upon the people so declared to be free to abstain from all violence, unless in necessary self-defense; and I recommend to them that, in all cases where allowed, they labor faithfully for reasonable wages....

And upon this act, sincerely believed to be an act of justice, warranted by the Constitution upon military necessity, I invoke the considerate judgement of mankind and the gracious favor of Almighty God.

In witness whereof, I have hereunto set my hand and caused the seal of the United States to be affixed...

By the President: Abraham Lincoln
William H. Seward, Secretary of State.[72]

This courageous position of valuing all human life had been embraced by the Congress on June 9, 1862, when they prohibited legalized slavery in the free territories.

On October 6, 1862, President Lincoln confided with Eliza Gurney and three other Quakers:

If I had my way, this war would never have been commenced. If I had been allowed my way, this war would have ended before this. But we find it still continues; and we must believe that He permits it for some wise purpose of His own, mysterious and unknown to us; and though with our limited understandings we may not be able to comprehend it, yet we cannot but believe, that He who made the world still governs it.[73]

We are indeed going through a great trial—a fiery trial. In the very responsible position in which I happen to be placed, being a humble instrument in the hands of our Heavenly Father, as I am, and as we all are, to work out His great purposes, I have desired that all my works and acts may be according to His will, and that it might be so, I have sought His aid.[74]

On December 1, 1862, President Lincoln concluded his Second Annual Address to Congress:

In giving freedom to the slave, we assure freedom to the free—honorable alike in what we give and what we preserve. We shall nobly save—or meanly lose—the last, best hope of earth. Other means may succeed; this could not fail. The way is plain, peaceful, generous, just—a way which if followed the world will forever applaud and God must forever bless.[75]

In December of 1862, President Abraham Lincoln related to J.A. Reed:

I hold myself in my present position and with the authority vested in me as an instrument of Providence. I have my own views and purposes, I have my convictions of duty, and my notions of what is right to be done. But I am conscious every moment that all I am and all I have is subject to the control of a Higher Power, and that Power can use me or not use me in any manner, and at any time, as in His wisdom and might may be pleasing to Him.[76]

Near the end of December, 1862, President Lincoln spoke with Reverend Byron Sunderland, pastor of the First Presbyterian Church of Washington, D.C., where Lincoln had attended. He shared:

The ways of God are mysterious and profound beyond all comprehension—"Who by searching can find Him out?" God only knows the issue of this business. He has destroyed nations from the map of history for their sins. Nevertheless, my hopes prevail generally above my fears for our Republic. The times are dark, the spirits of ruin are abroad in all their power, and the mercy of God alone can save us.[77]

During 1862, tragedy struck the Lincolns as their son, Willie, died at the age of 12 years. "Many noticed that he was seen more frequently with a Bible in his hand and that he spent more time in prayer....From this time on, Lincoln regularly attended the New York Avenue Presbyterian Church on Sundays — often even going to the Wednesday evening prayer meeting — until his untimely death three years later."[78] Dr. Phineas Gurley, who was Lincoln's pastor at the New York Avenue Presbyterian Church, affirmed that "the death of Willie Lincoln in 1862 and the visit to the Gettysburg battlefield in 1863 finally led Lincoln to personal faith in Christ."[79]

On January 1, 1863, the *Emancipation Proclamation* went into effect in:

> Arkansas, Texas, Louisiana..., Mississippi, Alabama, Florida, Georgia, South Carolina, North Carolina, Virginia.[80]

Abraham Lincoln

On March 30, 1863, President Abraham Lincoln issued a historic *Proclamation Appointing a National Fast Day:*

Whereas, the Senate of the United States devoutly recognizing the Supreme Authority and just Government of Almighty God in all the affairs of men and of nations, has, by a resolution, requested the President to designate and set apart a day for national prayer and humiliation:

And whereas, it is the duty of nations as well as of men to own their dependence upon the overruling power of God, to confess their sins and transgressions in humble sorrow yet with assured hope that genuine repentance will lead to mercy and pardon, and to recognize the sublime truth, announced in the Holy Scriptures and proven by all history: that those nations only are blessed whose God is the Lord:

And, insomuch as we know that, by His divine law, nations like individuals are subjected to punishments and chastisement in this world, may we not justly fear that the awful calamity of civil war, which now desolates the land may be but a punishment inflicted upon us for our presumptuous sins to the needful end of our national reformation as a whole people?

We have been the recipients of the choicest bounties of Heaven. We have been preserved these many years in peace and prosperity. We have grown in numbers, wealth and power as no other nation has ever grown.

But we have forgotten God. We have forgotten the gracious Hand which preserved us in peace, and multiplied and enriched and strengthened us; and we have vainly imagined, in the deceitfulness of our hearts, that all these blessings were produced by some superior wisdom and virtue of our own.

Intoxicated with unbroken success, we have become too self-sufficient to feel the necessity of redeeming and preserving grace, too proud to pray to the God that made us!

It behooves us then to humble ourselves before the offended Power, to confess our national sins and to pray for clemency and forgiveness.

Now, therefore, in compliance with the request and fully concurring in the view of the Senate, I do, by this my proclamation, designate and set apart Thursday, the 30th day of April, 1863, as a day of national humiliation, fasting and prayer.

And I do hereby request all the people to abstain on that day from their ordinary secular pursuits, and to unite, at their several places of public worship and their respective homes, in keeping the day holy to the Lord and devoted to the humble discharge of the religious duties proper to that solemn occasion.

All this being done, in sincerity and truth, let us then rest humbly in the hope authorized by the Divine teachings, that the united cry of the nation will be heard on high and answered with blessing no less than the pardon of our national sins and the restoration of our now divided and suffering country to its former happy condition of unity and peace.

In witness whereof, I have hereunto set my hand and caused the seal of the United States to be affixed. By the President: Abraham Lincoln.[81]

In June of 1863, just weeks before the Battle of Gettysburg, a college president asked Lincoln if he thought the country would survive. President Lincoln replied:

Abraham Lincoln

I do not doubt that our country will finally come through safe and undivided. But do not misunderstand me....I do not rely on the patriotism of our people...the bravery and devotion of the boys in blue...(or) the loyalty and skill of our generals....

But the God of our fathers, Who raised up this country to be the refuge and asylum of the oppressed and downtrodden of all nations, will not let it perish now. I may not live to see it...I do not expect to see it, but God will bring us through safe.[82]

On October 3, 1863, President Abraham Lincoln issued a formal proclamation, passed by an Act of Congress, initiating the first annual *National Day of Thanksgiving:*

No human counsel hath devised, nor hath any mortal hand worked out these great things. They are the gracious gifts of the most high God, who, while dealing with us in anger for our sins, hath nevertheless remembered mercy...

I do, therefore, invite my fellow citizens in every part of the United States, and those who are sojourning in foreign lands, to set apart and observe the last Thursday of November next as a day of Thanksgiving and Praise to our beneficent Father who dwelleth in the heavens....[it is] announced in the Holy Scriptures and proven by all history, that those nations are blessed whose God is the Lord....It has seemed to me fit and proper that God should be solemnly, reverently and gratefully acknowledged, as with one heart and one voice, by the whole American people.[83]

On October 24, 1863, Abraham Lincoln said in a speech to the Presbyterians of Baltimore:

I have often wished that I was a more devout man than I am. Nevertheless, amid the greatest difficulties of my Administration, when I could not see any other resort, I would place my whole reliance in God, knowing that all would go well, and that He would decide for the right.[84]

As General Lee led his army of 76,000 men into Pennsylvania, panic took hold of Washington, D.C. In the midst, President Lincoln remained strangely confident. He later related to a general wounded at Gettysburg:

When everyone seemed panic-stricken...I went to my room...and got down on my knees before Almighty God and prayed....Soon a sweet comfort crept into my soul that God Almighty had taken the whole business into His own hands....[85]

On November 19, 1863, President Abraham Lincoln delivered his Gettysburg Address. The Battle of Gettysburg, consisting of three intense days of fighting with over 50,000 deaths, was the beginning of the end for the valiant Confederate Army. His ten-sentence speech of 267 words has become world renowned and is engraved in stone in the Lincoln Memorial in Washington, D.C.:

Fourscore and seven years ago our fathers brought forth upon this continent a new nation, conceived in liberty, and dedicated to the proposition that all men are created equal. Now we are engaged in a great civil war, testing whether that nation, or any nation so conceived and so dedicated, can long endure.

We are met on a great battlefield of that war. We have come to dedicate a portion of that field as a final resting place for those who here gave their lives that that nation might live. It is altogether fitting and proper that we should do this.

But in a larger sense we cannot dedicate, we cannot consecrate, we cannot hallow this ground. The brave men, living and dead, who struggled here, have consecrated it far above our poor power to add or detract.

The world will little note, nor long remember, what we say here, but it can never forget what they did here. It is for us, the living, rather to be dedicated here to the unfinished work which they who fought here have thus far so nobly advanced.

It is rather for us to be here dedicated to the great task remaining before us—that from these honored dead we take increased devotion to that cause for which they gave the last full measure of devotion—that we here highly resolve that these dead shall not have died in vain—that this nation, under God, shall have a new birth of freedom—and that government of the people, by the people, for the people, shall not perish from the earth.[86]

In his Gettysburgh Address, Lincoln proclaimed: "...That we here highly resolve that these dead shall not have died in vain—that this nation, under God, shall have a new birth of freedom...."

*The Battle of Gettysburgh was the beginning of the end
for the valiant Confederate Army.*

On December 23, 1863, President Lincoln related to John Hay:

Common-looking people are the best in the world; that is the reason the Lord makes so many of them.[87]

In speaking to a minister of the Christian Commission, an organization that ministered to the soldiers during the Civil War, President Lincoln said:

If it were not for my firm belief in an overruling Providence, it would be difficult for me, in the midst of such complications of affairs, to keep my reason on its seat. But I am confident that the Almighty has His plans, and will work them out; and, whether we see it or not, they will be the best for us.[88]

During the Civil War, President Lincoln overheard someone remark that he hoped "the Lord was on the Union's side." Lincoln gave a straightforward reply:

I am not at all concerned about that, for I know that the Lord is always on the side of the right. But it is my constant anxiety and prayer that I and this nation should be on the Lord's side.[89]

In the summer of 1864, an old friend of Lincoln's, Joshua Speed, observed the President reading a Bible, and remarked:

I am glad to see you so profitably engaged...if you have recovered from your skepticism; I am sorry to say that I have not.

Putting his hand on his friend's shoulder, Lincoln replied:

You are wrong, Speed. Take all that you can of this book upon reason, and the balance on faith, and you will live and die a happier man.[90]

As reported in the *Washington Chronicle*, September 5, 1864, President Abraham Lincoln addressed the Committee of Colored People from Baltimore, acknowledging the elegant Bible they had presented him:

In regard to this Great Book, I have but to say, I believe the Bible is the best gift God has given to man. All the good Saviour gave to the world was communicated through this Book. But for this

Abraham Lincoln

Book we could not know right from wrong. All things most desirable for man's welfare, here and hereafter, are to be found portrayed in it. To you I return my most sincere thanks for the elegant copy of the great Book of God which you present.[91]

On October 21, 1864, President Abraham Lincoln issued the second annual *Day of National Thanksgiving* on the last Thursday, in November:

And I do further recommend to my fellow-citizens aforesaid, that on that occasion they do reverently humble themselves in the dust, and from thence offer up penitent and fervent prayers and supplications to the great Disposer of events for a return of the inestimable blessings of peace, union, and harmony throughout the land which it has pleased Him to assign as a dwelling-place for ourselves and for our posterity throughout all generations.[92]

On November 21, 1864, President Lincoln sent a letter to Mrs. Lydia Bixby of Boston, who had lost five sons in the Civil War:

> Dear Madam, I have been shown in the files of the War Department a statement of the Adjutant-General of Massachusetts that you are the mother of five sons who have died gloriously on the field of battle.
>
> I feel how weak and fruitless must be any words of mine which should attempt to beguile you from the grief of a loss so overwhelming. But I cannot refrain from tendering to you the consolation that may be found in the thanks of the Republic they died to save.
>
> I pray that our Heavenly Father may assuage the anguish of your bereavement, and leave you only the cherished memory of the loved and lost, and the solemn pride that must be yours to have laid so costly a sacrifice upon the altar of freedom.[93]

In his Second Inaugural Address, March 4, 1865, just 45 days before his assassination, President Abraham Lincoln gave his historic speech reflecting on the War between the North and the South:

> Neither party expected for the war the magnitude or the duration which it has already attained....
>
> Both read the same Bible and pray to the same God, and each invokes His aid against the other. It may seem strange that any men should dare ask a just God's assistance in wringing their bread from the sweat of other men's faces, but let us judge not, that we be not judged.
>
> The prayers of both could not be answered. That of neither has been answered fully. The Almighty has His own purposes. "Woe unto the world because of offenses; for it must needs be that offenses come, but woe to that man by whom the offense cometh."
>
> If we shall suppose that American slavery is one of those offenses which, in the providence of God, must needs come, but which, having continued through His appointed time, He now wills to remove, and that He gives to both North and South this terrible war as the woe due to those by whom the offense came, shall we discern therein any departure from those divine attributes which the believers in a living God always ascribe to Him?
>
> Fondly do we hope, fervently do we pray, that this mighty scourge of war may speedily pass away. Yet, if God will that it continue until all the wealth piled by the bondsmen's two hundred and fifty years of unrequited toil shall be sunk, and until every drop of blood drawn with the lash shall be paid by another drawn with the

sword, as was said three thousand years ago, so still it must be said "the judgements of the Lord are true and righteous altogether."

With malice toward none, with charity for all, with firmness in the right, as God gives us to see the right, let us strive on to finish the work we are in, to bind up the nation's wounds, to care for him who shall have borne the battle, and for his widow, and his orphan—to do all which may achieve and cherish a just and lasting peace among ourselves and with all nations.[94]

On March 17, 1865, President Lincoln addressed the Indiana Regiment:

Whenever I hear anyone arguing for slavery, I feel a strong impulse to see it tried on him personally.[95]

In 1865, President Lincoln made his last speech to a crowd in front of the White House:

The evacuation of Petersburg and Richmond, and the surrender of the principal insurgent army, give hope of a righteous and speedy peace, whose joyous expression cannot be restrained. In the midst of this, however, He from whom all blessings flow must not be forgotten. A call for a national thanksgiving is being prepared and will be duly promulgated.[96]

In answering a question of L.E. Chittenden, Register of the Treasury, President Lincoln expounded:

That the Almighty does make use of human agencies, and directly intervenes in human affairs, is one of the plainest statements of the Bible. I have had so many evidences of his direction—so many instances when I have been controlled by some other power than my own will— that I cannot doubt that this power comes from above.

I frequently see my way clear to a decision when I have no sufficient facts upon which to found it. But I cannot recall one instance in which I have followed my own judgement, founded upon such a decision, where the results were unsatisfactory; whereas, in almost every instance where I have yielded to the views of others, I have had occasion to regret it.

I am satisfied that when the Almighty wants me to do or not to do a particular thing, He finds a way of letting me know it. I am confident that it is His design to restore the Union. He will do it in his own good time.[97]

In 1865, shortly before Lee's surrender, Abraham Lincoln began his second term. In visiting with State Senator James Scovel of New Jersey, he shared:

> Young man, if God gives me four years more to rule this country, I believe it will become what it ought to be-what its Divine Author intended it to be-no longer one vast plantation for breeding human beings for the purpose of lust and bondage. But it will become a new Valley of Jehoshaphat, where all the nations of the earth will assemble together under one flag, worshiping a common God, and they will celebrate the resurrection of human freedom. [98]

On April 14,1865, just five days after the Civil War had ended, Abraham Lincoln went to Ford's theater with his wife, Mary Todd Lincoln. She recalled his last words as they sat there:

> He said he wanted to visit the Holy Land and see those places hallowed by the footprints of the Saviour. He was saying there was no city he so much desired to see as Jerusalem. And with the words half spoken on his tongue, the bullet of the assassin entered the brain, and the soul of the great and good President was carried by the angels to the New Jerusalem above. [99]

Abraham Lincoln stated:

> Here without contemplating consequences, before High Heaven, and in the face of the world, I swear eternal fidelity to the just cause, as I deem it, of the land of my life, my liberty, and my love .... Let none falter, who thinks he is right, and we may succeed. [100]

> I have always taken Counsel of Him, and referred to Him my plans, and have never adopted a course of proceeding without being assured, as far as I could be, of His approbation. [101]

> Surely God would not have created such a being as man, with an ability to grasp the infinite, to exist only for a day. No, no, man was made for immortality. [102]

> Whenever any church will inscribe over its altar as a qualification for membership the Savior's statement of the substance of the law and gospel, "Thou shalt love the Lord Thy God with all thy heart, and with all thy soul, and with all thy mind, and thy neighbor as thyself," that church will I join with all my heart and soul. [103]

The character of the Bible is easily established, at least to my satisfaction. We have to believe many things which we do not comprehend. The Bible is the only history that claims to be God's Book-to comprise His laws, His history. It contains an immense amount of evidence as to its authenticity....

Now let us treat the Bible fairly. If we had a witness on the stand whose general story was true, we would believe him even when he asserted the facts of which we have no other evidence. We ought to treat the Bible with equal fairness. I decided long ago that it was less difficult to believe that the Bible was what it claimed to be than to disbelieve it. [104]

No man is poor who has had a godly mother. [105]

Abraham Lincoln is attributed with the observations:

The philosophy of the school room in one generation will be the philosophy of government in the next. [106]

The only assurance of our nation's safety is to lay our foundation in morality and religion. [107]

In describing President Abraham Lincoln, Count Leo Tolstoi, the famous Russian novelist and playwright, declared him:

A Christ in miniature. [108]

In 1896, President William McKinley gave his assessment of President Abraham Lincoln:

The purposes of God, working through the ages, were, perhaps, more clearly revealed to him than to any other.... He was the greatest man of his time, especially approved of God for the work He gave him to do. [109]

William McKinley

In a Memorial Address for President Lincoln, April 24, 1865, Schuyler Colfax, Speaker of the House of Representatives stated:

Nor should I forget to mention here that the last act of Congress ever signed by him was one requiring that the motto, in which he sincerely believed, "In God We Trust," should hereafter be inscribed upon all our national coin. [110]

Abraham Lincoln's own words are inscribed into the walls of the Lincoln Memorial in Washington D.C.:

> That this Nation, under God, shall have a new birth of freedom, and that government of the people, by the people, for the people, shall not perish from the earth.

At the opposite end, on the north wall, his Second Inaugural Address alludes to "God," the "Bible," "providence," "the Almighty," and "divine attributes." It then continues:

> As was said 3000 years ago, so it still must be said, "The judgements of the Lord are true and righteous altogether."[111]

ᐖ

(Nicholas) Vachel Lindsay (1879-1931), known as "the vagabond poet," was a popular American poet and lecturer whose rhythmical verse carried an impressive effect as he would read it aloud. Among his most admired volumes are: *General Booth Enters into Heaven and Other Poems*, 1913; *The Congo and Other Poems*, 1914; and *The Chinese Nightingale*. In his poem, *General Booth Enters into Heaven*, Vachel Lindsay wrote:

> Booth died blind and still by faith he trod,
> Eyes still dazzled by the ways of God.[112]

ᐖ

William Linn on May 1, 1789, was elected by the United States House of Representatives as its chaplain, and a salary of $500 was appropriated from the Federal treasury. Being a respected minister in New York City, and the father of the famous poet John Blair Linn (1777-1804), William Linn alleged:[113]

> Let my neighbor once persuade himself that there is no God, and he will soon pick my pocket, and break not only my leg but my neck. If there be no God, there is no law, no future account; government then is the ordinance of man only, and we cannot be subject for conscience sake.[114]

❧

Carolus Linnaeus (1707-1788), a Swedish botanist, was considered the father of modern botany because he was the first naturalist to classify plants. He introduced the use of two Latin names, identifying genus and species, to classify all plants and animals. His works include: *Bibliotheca Botanica, Systema Naturae,* 1735; *Genera Plantarum,* 1737; and *Species Plantarum,* 1753. Carolus Linnaeus had the following words inscribed over the door of his bedchamber:

> Live innocently; God is here.[115]

❧

Joseph Lister (1827-1912), the English surgeon who developed "antiseptic surgery" by the application of chemical disinfectants, was the founder of the *Lister Institute of Preventive Medicine in London.* He also served as the President of the British Association and the Royal Society. Lord Lister, who was of Quaker background, stated:

> I am a believer in the fundamental doctrines of Christianity.[116]

❧

William Livingston (1723-1790), who was 61 years old when he signed the Constitution of the United States of America, was also a member of the first and second Continental Congresses. He served as the first Governor of New Jersey, and was reelected for 14 years. William Livingston had previously held the rank of a Brigadier General in the militia.

William Livingston

Growing up on the frontier around Albany, William Livingston knew the missionaries who worked among the Mohawks. He graduated first in his class from Yale and went on to study law. While living in New York, he published articles defending the faith, many of which were published in *The*

Independent Reflector,[117] such as *No. 46:*

> I believe the Scriptures of the Old and New Testaments, without any foreign comments or human explanations...I believe that he who feareth God and worketh righteousness will be accepted of Him....I believe that the virulence of some...proceeds not from their affection to Christianity, which is founded on too firm a basis to be shaken by the freest inquiry, and the Divine authority of which I sincerely believe without receiving a farthing for saying so.[118]

In 1768, William Livingston said:

> The land we possess is the gift of heaven to our fathers, and Divine Providence seems to have decreed it to our latest posterity.[119]

Alexander Hamilton

In 1772, Livingston took in Alexander Hamilton, who was 16 years old at the time, and opened the doors for him to attend King's College (Columbia University) in New York. Hamilton went on to become the first Secretary of the Treasury.[120]

On March 16, 1776, as recorded in the *Journal of Congress,* General William Livingston presented this resolution in Congress, which passed without dissent:

> We earnestly recommend that Friday, the 17th day of May next, be observed by the colonies as a day of humiliation, fasting, and prayer, that we may with united hearts confess and bewail our manifold sins and transgressions, and by a sincere repentance and amendment of life appease God's righteous displeasure, and through the merits and mediation of Jesus Christ obtain His pardon and forgiveness.[121]

In a letter, William Livingston wrote:

> If the history (New Testament) be not true, then all the whole laws of nature were changed; all the motives and incentives to human actions that ever had obtained in this world have been entirely inverted; the wickedest men in the world have taken the greatest pains and endured the greatest hardship and misery to invent, practice, and propagate the most holy religion that ever was.[122]

ია

David Livingstone (1813-1873), was the famous Scottish missionary and African explorer who discovered Lake Ngami and the Zuga River in 1849, the Zambezi River in 1851, Victoria Falls in 1855, and Lake Nyasa and Lake Shirwa in 1858-62. In 1866-73 he ventured forth searching for the source of the Nile, and was met by Henry M. Stanley, a correspondent of the *New York Herald*, at Ujiji on Lake Tanganyika in late 1871. So loved was he by his African followers, that when he died on the shore of Lake Bangweulu in 1873, they buried his heart in Africa, and sent his body, packed in salt, back to England. David Livingstone once declared:

> All that I am I owe to Jesus Christ, revealed to me in His divine Book.[123]

In his work, *Missionary Travels and Researches in South Africa*, David Livingstone wrote:

> Great pains had been taken by my parents to instill the doctrines of Christianity into my mind, and I had no difficulty in understanding the theory of free salvation by the atonement of our Savior; but it was only about this time that I really began to feel the necessity and value of a personal application of the provisions of the atonement to my own case. The change was like that of "colorblindness."
>
> The perfect fullness with which the pardon of all our guilt is offered in God's Book drew forth feelings of affectionate love to Him who bought us with His blood, and a sense of deep obligation to Him for His mercy has influenced, in some small measure, my conduct ever since. This book will speak, not so much of what has been done, as of what remains to be performed before the Gospel can be said to be preached to all nations.
>
> In the glow of love which Christianity inspires I soon resolved to devote my life to the alleviation of human misery.[124]

In 1872, Henry Morton Stanley (1841-1904), the famous English correspondent for the *New York Herald*, found David Livingstone at Ujiji on Lake Tanganyika in the heart of Africa. He greeted him with the now-classic salutation, "Dr. Livingstone, I presume?" Henry M. Stanley described the famous old missionary:

Here is a man who is manifestly sustained as well as guided by influences from Heaven. The Holy Spirit dwells in him. God speaks through him. The heroism, the nobility, the pure and stainless enthusiasm as the root of his life come, beyond question, from Christ.

There must, therefore, be a Christ; and it is worth while to have such a Helper and Redeemer as this Christ undoubtedly is, and as He here reveals Himself to this wonderful disciple.[125]

John Locke (1632-1704), was an English philosopher whose writings had a profound influence on our Founding Fathers and, in turn, on the writing of the Constitution. Of nearly 15,000 items of the Founding Fathers which were reviewed, including books, newspaper articles, pamphlets, monographs, etc., John Locke was the third most frequently quoted author.[126] In his *Two Treatises of Government*, 1690, he cited 80 references to the Bible in the first treatise and 22 references to the Bible in the second.

Thomas Jefferson

John Locke elaborated on fundamental concepts, such as: unalienable rights, separation of powers, parental authority, private property, the right to resist unlawful authority, and government by consent (whereby governments "derive their just powers from the consent of the governed"). He built the understanding of the "social compact" (a constitution between the people and the government) upon:

That Paction which God made with Noah after the Deluge.[127]

His classification of the basic natural rights of man as the right to "life, liberty and property," not only influenced Thomas Jefferson in the writing of the Declaration of Independence, but also can be seen reflected in the Fifth and Fourteenth Amendments.

In 1689, John Locke published his treatise *Of Civil Government* in which he asserted:

[The] great and Chief End, therefore, of Mens uniting into Commonwealths, and putting themselves under Government, is the preservation of their property....

For Men being all the Workmanship of one Omnipotent, and

infinitely wise Maker: all the Servants of one Sovereign Master, sent into the World by his Order, and about his Business, they are his Property, whose Workmanship they are, made to last during his, not one another's Pleasure....

Those Grants God made of the World to Adam, and to Noah, and his Sons...has given the Earth to the Children of Men, given it to Mankind in common....

God, who hath given the World to Men in common, hath also given them reason to make use of it to the best Advantage of Life and Convenience.[128]

On August 23, 1689, in his work, *Two Treatises on Civil Government*, John Locke wrote on natural law and natural rights:

The obligations of the Law of Nature cease not in society, but only in many cases are drawn closer, and have, by human laws, known penalties annexed to them to enforce their observation.

Thus the Law of Nature stands as an eternal rule to all men, legislators as well as others. The rules that they make for other men's actions must...be conformable to the Law of Nature, i.e. to the will of God, of which that is a declaration, and the fundamental Law of Nature being the preservation of mankind, no human sanction can be good or valid against it.[129]

John Locke wrote in *The Second Treatise on Civil Government*, 1690:

Human Laws are measures in respect of Men whose Actions they must direct, albeit such measures they are as have also their higher Rules to be measured by, which Rules are two, the Law of God, and the Law of Nature; so that Laws Human must be made according to the general Laws of Nature, and without contradiction to any positive Law of Scripture, otherwise they are ill made.[130]

In addition to writing paraphrases of the books of Romans, First and Second Corinthians, Galatians and Ephesians, John Locke wrote, in 1695, a seldom mentioned book entitled *A Vindication of the Reasonableness of Christianity*.[131] In it he wrote:

He that shall collect all the moral rules of the philosophers and compare them with those contained in the New Testament will find them to come short of the morality delivered by our Saviour and taught by His disciples: a college made up of ignorant but inspired fishermen....

Such a law of morality Jesus Christ has given in the New Testament, but by the latter of these ways, by revelation, we have from Him a full and sufficient rule for our direction, and conformable to that of reason. But the word and obligation of its precepts have their force, and are past doubt to us, by the evidence of His mission.

He was sent by God: His miracles show it; and the authority of God in His precepts can not be questioned. His morality has a sure standard, that revelation vouches, and reason can not gainsay nor question; but both together witness to come from God, the great Lawgiver.

And such a one as this, out of the New Testament, I think, they would never find, nor can anyone say is anywhere else to be found....

To one who is persuaded that Jesus Christ was sent by God to be a King and a Saviour to those who believe in Him, all His commands become principles; there needs no other proof for the truth of what He says, but that He said it; and then there needs no more but to read the inspired books to be instructed.[132]

Our Saviour's great rule, that we should love our neighbors as ourselves, is such a fundamental truth for the regulating of human society, that, by that alone, one might without difficulty determine all the cases and doubts in social morality.[133]

John Locke stated:

The Bible is one of the greatest blessings bestowed by God on the children of men.—It has God for its author; salvation for its end, and truth without any mixture for its matter.—It is all pure, all sincere; nothing too much; nothing wanting.[134]

ع

James Logan (1674-1751), the private Secretary of William Penn and Chief Justice of the Supreme Court of Pennsylvania, stated:

Remember thou art by profession a Christian; that is, one who art called after the immaculate Lamb of God, who, by offering Himself a sacrifice for thee, atoned for thy sins....Rouse with the more simple servants of nature, and borrowing one hour from the sleep of sluggards, spend it in thy chamber in dressing thy soul with prayer and meditation, reading the Scriptures....

Remember that the same enemy that caused thy first parents to forfeit their blessed condition, notwithstanding the gate is now open for restoration, is perpetually using his whole endeavors to prevent thee from attaining this, and frustrate to thee the passion of thy Redeemer.[135]

꙼

John Alexander Logan (1826-1886), a Major General during the Civil War, served with General Grant at Vicksburg, Mississippi, and with General Sherman on his march through Georgia to the sea. He was elected a U.S. Congressman from Illinois, 1858, and a U.S. Senator, 1871. On *Decoration Day*, 1886, in an oration at Riverside Park in New York, John Logan said:

John Alexander Logan

But the beautiful ceremonies of love and remembrance, now so universally performed with flowers, came to the fullest expansion through the growth of the Christian religion. Branches of palms were thrown in the path of our Saviour as He entered Jerusalem. The crucified Christ received a crown of thorns from His executioners, but flowers strewn by unseen hands exhaled their fragrance around the cave where His body was laid.[136]

꙼

Henry Wadsworth Longfellow (1807-1882), a renowned poet, served for 20 years as Professor of Belles-Lettres at Harvard University, 1834-54. He wrote such famous poems as: *Evangeline*, 1847; *The Song of Hiawatha*, 1855; *The Courtship of Miles Standish*, 1858; and *Paul Revere's Ride*, 1861. In his brother's *Ordination Hymn*, Longfellow wrote:

Christ to the young man said:
"Yet one thing more:
If thou wouldst perfect be,
Sell all thou hast, and give it to the poor,
And come and follow me!"

Within this temple Christ again, unseen,
Those sacred words hath said,

And His invisible hands to-day have been
Laid upon a young man's head.

And evermore beside him on his way
The unseen Christ shall move,
That he may lean upon His arm and say,
"Dost Thou, dear Lord, approve?"

Beside him at the marriage feast shall be
To make the scene more fair:
Beside him in the dark Gethsemane
Of pain and midnight prayer.

O holy trust! O endless sense of rest!
Like the beloved John
To lay his head upon our Saviour's breast,
And thus to journey on.[137]

Henry Wadsworth Longfellow remarked:

Man is unjust, but God is just; and finally justice triumphs.[138]

Nothing with God can be accidental.[139]

&

James Longstreet (1821-1904), a Confederate Major General in the Civil War, went on to become a diplomat, serving as the U.S. Minister to Turkey, 1880-81, and the U.S. Railroad Commissioner, 1898-1904. He wrote in a letter:

Replying to your request, I am pleased to say: I believe in God, the Father, and in His only begotten Son, Jesus Christ, our Lord. It is my custom to read one or more chapters of my Bible daily for comfort, guidance, and instruction. Knowing myself a sinner, I am greatly relieved by the happy assurance that for such our Saviour died, and that under lowly penitence He will surely forgive, and make our acceptance certain through His holy pleasure.[140]

&

State of Louisiana June 30, 1993, issued the following Proclamation, signed by Governor Edwin W. Edwards:

WHEREAS, throughout the history of our country, prayer has been recognized by our leaders in times of war and peace as a vital part of maintaining a strong national character, and necessary to procure the blessings of a just and benevolent God upon our government and people; and

WHEREAS, the first national Thanksgiving Proclamation was put forth by Samuel Adams as a "National Day of Humiliation, Fasting and Prayer" and was observed by Washington's army in the snowy fields of Valley Forge; and

WHEREAS, the observance of prayer encourages Americans to affirm our nation's spiritual roots, to acknowledge dependence on God and to enlist prayer for local, state and national leaders; and

WHEREAS, it is certainly fitting and proper that we in Louisiana observe a time where all in our communities may acknowledge our many blessings and express gratitude to God for them while recognizing the need for strengthening religious and moral values in our land; and

WHEREAS, it is important that we remember the need to stand in the grace of God every day and we should acknowledge the need to pray for our leaders in government; and

WHEREAS, a time should be set aside to focus on the wisdom of God in the heritage of the United States and the intention of our founding fathers that the counsel of God be always deeply rooted in our makeup and progress as a nation; and

NOW THEREFORE, I, Edwin W. Edwards, Governor of the State of Louisiana, do hereby proclaim November 21-27, 1993 as

CHRISTIAN HERITAGE WEEK

in the State of Louisiana, and encourage all citizens to acknowledge and appreciate the religious heritage of our great state and nation.

In Witness Whereof, I have hereunto set my hand officially and caused to be affixed the Great Seal of the State of Louisiana at the Capital in the City of Baton Rouge, on this the 30th day of June A.D. 1993. Attest by the Governor.

Edwin W. Edwards
Governor of Louisiana[141]

છ

James Russell Lowell (1819-1891), an American editor, poet and diplomat, was the son of Charles Lowell, minister of the famous West Church in Boston. A graduate of Harvard Law School, James Russell Lowell wrote poetry and prose which received wide acclaim. His well-known works include *Fable For Critics*, 1848; and *Biglow Papers*, 1848-67. He edited the *Atlantic Monthly*,

1857-61; and the *North American Review*, 1862-72.

He received honorary degrees from both Oxford and Cambridge, and became a professor at Harvard. Lowell was appointed by President Rutherford B. Hayes as U.S. Minister to Spain, 1877-80, and England, 1880-85, where he was immensely popular. James Russell Lowell was once asked by Francois Guizot (1787-1874), the French historian and diplomat, "How long will the American Republic endure?" Lowell replied:

> As long as the ideas of the men who founded it continue dominant.[142]

On November 20, 1885, in his *International Copyright*, James Russell Lowell stated:

> In vain we call old notions fudge,
> And bend our conscience to our dealing;
> The Ten Commandments will not budge,
> And stealing will continue stealing.[143]

In volume II of his *Literary Essays*, 1810-1890, James Russell Lowell wrote *New England Two Centuries Ago:*

> Puritanism, believing itself quick with the seed of religious liberty, laid, without knowing it, the egg of democracy.[144]

ᵶ

Stephen Bleecker Luce (1827-1917), was promoted to Commodore, 1881, and to Rear Admiral, 1885, in the United States Navy. During the Civil War, he commanded the monitor *Nantucket*, the frigate *Wabash*, the double-ender *Sonoma*, the *Canadaiqua*, and the *Pontiac*. Stephen Bleecker Luce founded the United States Naval War College at Newport, Rhode Island, considered the highest educational institution in the United States Navy. As the first president of this college, Stephen Bleecker Luce attested in 1884:

Stephen Bleecker Luce

Surely seamen are worthy to appear in your "Cloud of Witnesses." Not only did our Saviour consort with the seamen of Galilee, but there are many examples in history of noted naval heroes who exhibited the highest Christian virtues. I wish to be counted among this great company of believers in the divinity of Christ, and in the inspiration of all Scripture.[145]

ᛈ

Sir Lionel Luckhoo (1914-   ), the ambassador of Barbados and Guyana, is the only person ever to have been an ambassador for two sovereign nations simultaneously. He was knighted twice by the Queen of England, served as Lord Mayor of Georgetown, Guyana, and presided as Judge of the Supreme Court in Guyana. Sir Lionel Luckhoo holds the distinction of being the world's most successful criminal attorney, with over 245 successive murder acquittals; this record is acknowledged in the Guinness Book of World Records.[146]

*Sir Lionel
Luckhoo*

Sir Lionel Luckhoo has spoken at the United Nations, to presidents, kings, parliaments, bar associations, cabinets, etc., all over the world. He has written several books that he gives away gratis. After having diligently studied Buddha, Confucius, Mohammed and numerous other religious leaders, Sir Lionel accepted Jesus as his personal Lord and Saviour on November 7, 1978. He elucidated:

The bones of Muhammad are in Medina, the bones of Confucius are in Shantung, the cremated bones of Buddha are in Nepal. Thousands pay pilgrimages to worship at their tombs which contain their bones. But in Jerusalem there is a cave cut into the rock. This is the tomb of Jesus. IT IS EMPTY! YES, EMPTY! BECAUSE HE IS RISEN! He died, physically and historically. He arose from the dead, and now sits at the right hand of God.[147]

ᛈ

Martin Luther (1483-1546), leader of the Protestant Reformation in Germany, was renowned for his enduring literary contribution of translating the Bible into the German language. He received his doctor of divinity and was appointed professor of philosophy at the University of Wittenberg, where he was promoted to the position of district vicar.

Martin Luther preached daily, and grew immensely popular through explaining the scriptures in the common language. After objecting to the methods Johann Tetzel was using to sell indulgences, Luther posted his famous 95 Theses to debate. This was the spark that lead to the Reformation, with Martin Luther being the most prominent leader.

Among Luther's many works, he wrote:

> I am much afraid that schools will prove to be the great gates of hell unless they diligently labor in explaining the Holy Scriptures, engraving them in the hearts of youth.
>
> I advise no one to place his child where the scriptures do not reign paramount. Every institution in which men are not increasingly occupied with the Word of God must become corrupt.[148]

> The Bible was written for men with a head upon their shoulders.[149]

> If I profess with the loudest voice and clearest exposition every portion of the truth of God except precisely that little point which the world and the devil are at that moment attacking, I am not confessing Christ, however boldly I may be professing Christ.
>
> Where the battle rages, there the loyalty of the soldier is proved and to be steady on all the battlefield besides is mere flight and disgrace if he flinches at that one point.[150]

> Where there are no Christians, or perverse and false Christians, it would be well for the authorities to allow them, like heathens, to put away their wives, and to take others, in order that they may not, with their discordant lives, have two hells, both here and there. But let them know that by their divorce they cease to be Christians, and become heathens, and are in the state of damnation.[151]

> In his life, Christ is an example, showing us how to live; in his death, he is a sacrifice, satisfying our sins; in his resurrection, a conqueror; in his ascension, a king; in his intercession, a high priest.[152]

On April 18, 1521, in his famous speech at the *Diet of Worms*,

Martin Luther declared:

> Here I stand; I can do no other. God help me. Amen.[153]

In 1529, Martin Luther wrote his famous hymn, *A Mighty Fortress (Ein 'Feste Burg):*

> A mighty fortress is our God,
> A bulwark never failing.
> Our helper He amid the flood
> Of mortal ills prevailing.[154]

Martin Luther wrote in *Table Talk*, 1569:

> Reason is the greatest enemy that faith has: it never comes to the aid of spiritual things, but—more frequently than not—struggles against the divine Word, treating with contempt all that emanates from God.[155]

Martin Luther remarked:

> Our Lord has written the promise of the resurrection not in books alone, but in every leaf in the springtime.[156]

&

M

Alexander MacAlister (1844-1919), professor of anatomy at Cambridge, was a distinguished author of textbooks on physiology and zoology. He related:

I think the widespread impression of the agnosticism of scientific men is largely due to the attitude taken up by a few of the great popularizers of science, like Tyndall and Huxley.

It has been my experience that the disbelief in the revelation that God has given, in the life and work, death and resurrection of our Savior, is more prevalent among what I may call the camp followers of science than amongst those to whom scientific work is the business of their lives.[1]

❧

Douglas MacArthur (1880-1964), the Supreme Commander of Allied Forces in the Pacific during World War II, was celebrated for having liberated the Philippine Islands from oppression and for having received the surrender of the Japanese forces in Tokyo Bay on the *U.S.S. Missouri*, September 3, 1945. A five star General and Commander of the U.N. forces during the Korean War, General MacArthur recounted:

History fails to record a single precedent in which nations subject to moral decay have not passed into political and economic decline. There has been either a spiritual awakening to overcome the moral lapse, or a progressive deterioration leading to ultimate national disaster.[2]

On October 22, 1944, upon landing on Leyte, General Douglas

MacArthur declared:

> I have returned. By the grace of Almighty God, our forces stand again on Philippine soil.[3]

Douglas MacArthur remarked:

> Build me a son, O Lord, who will be strong enough to know when he is weak, brave enough to face himself when he is afraid, one who will be proud and unbending in honest defeat, and humble and gentle in victory.[4]

ða

Thomas Babington, Lord Macaulay (1800-1859), was a renowned English statesman, essayist, historian and poet. He was a member of Parliament, 1830-56, an eloquent debater, and he served on the Supreme Council in India. His writings were highly popular, as he made historical figures come alive with a vivid style. His works include the *Lays of Ancient Rome* and *The History of England from the Accession of James II*, 5 vols., 1849-61.

In his piece entitled *On John Dryden*, 1828, Lord Macaulay stated:

> The English Bible—a book which if everything else in our language should perish, would alone suffice to show the whole extent of its beauty and power.[5]

In 1830, while commenting on Southey's edition of John Bunyan's classic book, *Pilgrim's Progress*, Lord Macaulay said:

> That wonderful book, while it obtains admiration from the most fastidious critics, is loved by those who are too simple to admire it.[6]

In *On Lord Bacon*, 1837, Lord Macaulay concluded:

> To sum up the whole, we should say that the aim of the Platonic philosophy was to exalt man into a god.[7]

æ

George MacDonald (1824-1905), was a Scottish novelist and writer of children's fairy tales. His best remembered stories include: *The Princess and the Goblins* and *The Fairy Fleet.* Beginning his career as a Congregational minister, he later took up writing and became close friends with the well-known writers, John Ruskin and Lewis Carroll. Carroll first recited his stories of *Alice in Wonderland* to George MacDonald's children, whose delighted response convinced Carroll to publish them.

In *David Elginbrod,* published in 1863, George MacDonald wrote:

> Here lie I, Martin Elginbrodde:
> Hae mercy o' my soul, Lord God;
> As I wad do, were I Lord God,
> And ye were Martin Elginbrodde.[8]

æ

James Madison (1751-1836), known as the "Chief Architect of the Constitution," was the 4th President of the United States, 1809-17. He was an instrumental member of the Constitutional Convention, speaking 161 times (more than any other founder except Gouverneur Morris). James Madison's records of the debates in the Constitutional Convention are the most accurate and detailed that exist. At the Convention, James Madison moved, seconded by Roger Sherman, that Benjamin Franklin's famous appeal for prayer be enacted in their assembly.[9]

James Madison

James Madison authored 29 of the 85 *Federalist Papers,* which argued successfully in favor of the ratification of the Constitution. He was also a member of the first United States Congress, where he introduced the Bill of Rights, which addressed religious freedom as the first item.

He was appointed by President Thomas Jefferson as U.S.

Secretary of State, and while in the office, he engineered the Louisiana Purchase of 1803. As acting President and Commander-in-Chief during the War of 1812, James Madison had to flee the White House before it was captured and burned by the British.

In addition to being a lawyer and planter, he was a member of the House of Delegates. As a Virginia Legislator, he helped write the Constitution of Virginia. Home-schooled as a child, Madison attended Princeton University under the direction of Reverend John Witherspoon, one of the nation's premier theologians and legal scholars. The University's first president, Jonathan Dickinson, had declared: "Cursed be all that learning that is contrary to the cross of Christ." [10]

On February 24, 1813, in a message to Congress, President James Madison stated:

> The Government of Great Britain had already introduced into her commerce during the war a system which, at once violating the rights of other nations and resting on a mass of forgery and perjury unknown to other times, was making an unfortunate progress in undermining those principles of morality and religion which are the best foundation of national happiness.... The general tendency of these demoralizing and disorganizing contrivances will be reprobated by the civilized and Christian world. [11]

In the 1785 session of the General Assembly of the State of Virginia, James Madison explained in his *Religious Freedom, A Memorial and Remonstrance* why he was against the Establishment of Religion by Law:

> It is the duty of every man to render to the Creator such homage.... Before any man can be considered as a member of Civil Society, he must be considered as a subject of the Governor of the Universe. [12]

> Because the policy of the bill is adverse to the diffusion of the light of Christianity. The first wish of those who ought to enjoy this precious gift, ought to be, that it may be imparted to the whole race of mankind. Compare the number of those who have as yet received it, with the number still remaining under the dominions of false religions, and how small is the former! Does the policy of the bill tend to lessen the disproportion? No; it at once discourages those who are strangers to the light of Truth, from coming into the regions of it. [13]

Whilst we assert for ourselves a freedom to embrace, to profess, and to observe the Religion which we believe to be of divine origin, we cannot deny an equal freedom to those whose minds have not yet yielded to the evidence which has convinced us. If this freedom be abused, it is an offence against God, not against man: To God, therefore, not to man, must an account of it be rendered. [14]

Earnestly praying, as we are in duty bound, that the Supreme Lawgiver of the Universe by illuminating those to whom it is addressed, may, on the one hand, turn their councils from every act which would affront His holy prerogative, or violate the trust committed to them; and, on the other, guide them into every measure which may be worthy of His blessing. [14]

In *Federalist Paper #39,* James Madison wrote:

That honourable determination which animates every votary of freedom, to rest all our political experiments on the capacity of mankind for self-government. [15]

James Madison, in a quotation attributed to him, 1778, stated:

We have staked the whole future of American civilization, not upon the power of government, far from it. We have staked the future of all of our political institutions upon the capacity of mankind for self- government; upon the capacity of each and all of us to govern ourselves, to control ourselves, to sustain ourselves according to the Ten Commandments of God. [16]

James Madison, known to regularly lead his household in the observance of family devotions, [17] was an adamant defender of religious liberty. His strong position of defending religious freedom began when, as a youth, he stood with his father outside a jail in the village of Orange and listened to several Baptists preach from their cell windows, having been imprisoned for their religious opinions. [18] James Madison, who had studied for the ministry before he took up the study of law, said:

James Madison

Religion, or the duty we owe to our Creator, and manner of discharging it, can be directed only by reason and conviction, not by force or violence; and, therefore, that all men should enjoy the fullest toleration in the exercise of religion according to the dictates of conscience, unpunished and unrestrained by the magistrate, unless under color of

James Madison

religion any man disturb the peace, the happiness, or safety of society, and that it is the mutual duty of all to practice Christian forbearance, love and charity toward each other.[19]

On November 20, 1825, James Madison wrote in a letter to Frederick Beasley:

The belief in a God All Powerful wise and good, is so essential to the moral order of the World and to the happiness of man, that arguments which enforce it cannot be drawn from too many sources nor adapted with too much solicitude to the different characters and capacities to be impressed with it.[20]

On October 15, 1788, James Madison wrote:

As the courts are generally the last in making the decision [on laws], it results to them, by refusing or not refusing to execute a law, to stamp it with its final character. This makes the Judiciary dept paramount in fact to the Legislature, which was never intended, and can never be proper.[21]

On March 4, 1809, President James Madison explained in his Inaugural Address:

We have all been encouraged to feel in the guardianship and guidance of that Almighty Being, whose power regulates the destiny of nations.[22]

James Madison, who made copious notes in his personal Bible, wrote in Acts chapter 19:

Believers who are in a State of Grace, have need of the word of God for their Edification and Building up therefore implies a possibility of falling. v. 32.
Grace, it is the free gift of God. Luke. 12. v. 32.
Giver more blessed than the Receiver. v. 35.
To neglect the means for our own preservation is to Tempt God: and to trust to them is to neglect him. v. 3 & Ch. 27. v. 31.

Humility, the better any man is, the lower thoughts he has of himself. v. 19.

Ministers to take heed to themselves & their flock. v. 28.

The apostles did greater Miracles than Christ, in the matter, not manner, of them. v. 11.[23]

Among his manuscripts on the Gospels and the Acts of the Apostles, Madison commends the Bereans as more noble than the Thessalonians, describing them:

Dolly Madison (Mrs. James Madison, nee Dorothea Payne)

As a noble example for all succeeding Christians to imitate.[24]

In another place he states:

It is not the talking but the walking and working person that is the true Christian.[25]

Again James Madison writes:

Christ's Divinity appears by St. John, chapter xx, 2: 'And Thomas answered and said unto Him, my Lord and my God!' Resurrection testified to and witnessed by the Apostles, Acts iv, 33: 'And with great power gave the apostles witness of the resurrection of the Lord Jesus, and great grace was upon them all.'[26]

James Madison, who outlived all of the other 54 founders of the American Republic, wrote on November 9, 1772, to his close college friend, William Bradford:

A watchful eye must be kept on ourselves lest while we are building ideal monuments of Renown and Bliss here we neglect to have our names enrolled in the Annals of Heaven.

[Bad health has] intimated to me not to expect a long or healthy life, yet it may be better with me after some time tho I hardly dare expect it and therefore have little spirit and alacrity to set about any thing that is difficult in acquiring and useless in possessing after one has exchanged Time for Eternity.[27]

ða

Magna Carta 1215, known as the "cornerstone of English liberty," was signed by King John of England in the meadow of Runymeade, under pressure from the English barons. This was the first time the absolute power of a king was limited, guaranteeing certain rights to his subjects. Included in the provisions were:

> Clause 39. No freeman shall be taken, or imprisoned, or outlawed, or exiled, or in any way harmed, nor will we go upon him nor will we send upon him, except by legal judgement of his peers or by the law of the land.

> Clause 40. To none will we sell, to none deny or delay, right or justice.[28]

ða

Charles Habib Malik (1906-1967), the Ambassador to the United Nations from Lebanon, was a member of the U.N. Security Council, 1953-54, and President of the 13th Session of the United Nations General Assembly in 1959. Charles Habib Malik, in 1958, recognized:

> The good (in the United States) would never have come into being without the blessing and power of Jesus Christ....Whoever tries to conceive the American word without taking full account of the suffering and love and salvation of Christ is only dreaming.
> I know how embarrassing this matter is to politicians, bureaucrats, businessmen and cynics; but, whatever these honored men think, the irrefutable truth is that the soul of America is at its best and highest, Christian.[29]

ða

André Malraux (1901-1976), a French essayist and novelist, was involved in the civil strife in China in the 1920s, the Republican forces during the Spanish Civil War and the French Resistance during World War II. He later served as minister of cultural affairs under French President de Gaulle.

His works include: *Man's Estate*, 1933; *Days of Hope*, 1938; *Voices of Silence*, 1953; and *Museum without Walls*, 1967. In his volume of memoirs, entitled *Anti-Memoirs*, 1967, André Malraux declared:

> The genius of Christianity is to have proclaimed that the path to the deepest mystery is the path of love.[30]

&

Clarence E. Manion (1896-1983), was dean of the Notre Dame College of Law, 1941-52, and Professor of Constitutional Law at the University of Notre Dame, 1925-1952. In 1946, Dean Manion was quoted regarding the Declaration of Independence in Verne Paul Kaub's book, *Collectivism Challenges Christianity*:

> Look closely at these self-evident truths, these imperishable articles of American Faith upon which all our government is firmly based. First and foremost is the existence of God. Next comes the truth that all men are equal in the sight of God. Third is the fact of God's great gift of unalienable rights to every person on earth. Then follows the true and single purpose of all American Government, namely, to preserve and protect these God-made rights of God-made man.[31]

&

Francis Marion (1732-1795), was a courageous Major General in the Revolutionary War. His daring tactics and exploits earned him the nickname "Old Swamp Fox" by the British General Banastre Tarleton, who spent much time and energy vainly pursuing, but never apprehending, Marion.

"Marion's Brigade" was a volunteer force that could assemble at a moment's notice and attack everywhere at once, or so it seemed to the British. Taking part in several important battles, and capturing many prisoners, General Francis Marion made communication impossible for the British troops in the Carolinas.

Marion's grandfather, a French Protestant Huguenot who fled to America in 1690 for religious freedom, settled on a farm in South Carolina. In 1775, Francis Marion was elected a member of the South Carolina Provincial Congress and, after the War, served in the State Senate of South Carolina for several terms. He stated:

> Who can doubt that God created us to be happy, and thereto made us to love one another? It is plainly written as the Gospel. The heart is sometimes so embittered that nothing but Divine love can sweeten it, so enraged that devotion can only becalm it, and so broken down that it takes all the forces of heavenly hope to raise it. In short, the religion of Jesus Christ is the only sure and controlling power over sin.[32]

John Marshall

John Marshall (1755-1835), the Chief Justice of the United States Supreme Court, was appointed by President John Adams and held that position for 34 years. He had been a captain in the Revolutionary War and had served with General George Washington during the freezing winter at Valley Forge in 1777-78.

John Marshall was a member of the Virginia House of Burgesses and strongly advocated the ratification of the Constitution. He turned down President George Washington's offer to be the United States Attorney General, though he later served as U.S. Minister to France, gaining recognition for his refusal to take French bribes during the "XYZ Affair."

After having been a U.S. Congressman, John Marshall was appointed Secretary of State, and finally Chief Justice of the Supreme Court in 1801. His influence helped form the judicial branch of the government. In the 1833 case of *Barron v. Baltimore*, Marshall emphasized that the Bill of Rights restricted only the national government.[33] The country mourned at his death, and it was at his funeral, in 1835, that the Liberty Bell cracked.[34]

At John Marshall's funeral in 1835, the Liberty Bell cracked.

The *Winchester Republican* newspaper published the following occurrence involving Chief Justice John Marshall at McGuire's Hotel in Winchester, after he had encountered trouble with his carriage along the road:

> The shafts of his ancient gig were broken and "held together by switches formed from the bark of a hickory sapling"; he was negligently dressed, his knee buckles loosened. In the tavern a discussion arose among some young men concerning "the merits of the Christian religion." The debate grew warm and lasted "from six o'clock until eleven." No one knew Marshall, who sat quietly listening.

> Finally one of the youthful combatants turned to him and said: Well, my old gentleman, what think you of these things?"
>
> Marshall responded with a "most eloquent and unanswerable appeal." He talked for an hour, answering "every argument urged against" the teachings of Jesus. "In the whole lecture, there was so much simplicity and energy, pathos and sublimity, that not another word was uttered."
>
> The listeners wondered who the old man could be. Some thought him a preacher; and great was their surprise when they learned afterwards that he was the Chief Justice of the United States.[35]

John Marshall

John Marshall, who had previously fought with Washington in the Revolutionary War and served with him at Valley Forge, described General Washington in these terms:

> Without making ostentatious professions of religion, he was a sincere believer in the Christian faith, and a truly devout man.[36]

John Marshall's daughter makes this statement regarding her father's religious views:

> He told me that he believed in the truth of the Christian Revelation...during the last months of his life he read *Keith on Prophecy*, where our Saviour's divinity is incidentally treated, and was convinced by this work, and the fuller investigation to which it led, of the supreme divinity of our Saviour. He determined to apply to the communion of our Church, objecting to communion in private, because he thought it his duty to make a public confession of the Saviour....[37]

In the case of *McCulloch v. Maryland*, 4 Wheaton 316, 431, 1819, John Marshall stated the profound truth:

> The power to tax involves the power to destroy.[38]

&

Peter Marshall (1902-1949), Chaplain of the United States Senate, emigrated from Scotland in 1927, and was ordained a Presbyterian minister in 1931. On January 13, 1947, as Chaplain of the U.S. Senate, Peter Marshall remonstrated Americans, saying:

> The choice before us is plain: Christ or chaos, conviction or compromise, discipline or disintegration. I am rather tired of hearing about our rights and privileges as American citizens. The time is come—it is now—when we ought to hear about the duties and responsibilities of our citizenship. America's future depends upon her accepting and demonstrating God's government.[39]

&

Luther Martin (1748-1826), was an American Revolutionary leader, who played an active role as a delegate to the Constitutional Convention. He gave 53 speeches, proposed the "electoral college" system for selecting the President, and strongly opposed a central government which would usurp the sovereignty of the states.

He was the Attorney General of Maryland for 28 years, the longest record in American history, and was one of the most eminent lawyers in the United States. Luther Martin described himself as being devoted to:

Luther Martin

> The sacred truths of the Christian religion.[40]

&

Charter of Maryland June 20, 1632, named in honor of Queen

George Calvert,
1st Baron
Baltimore

Henrietta Maria, was issued by King Charles I to First Lord Baltimore George Calvert, the Secretary of State for King James I, but he died before he could embark. It was then reissued to his son, Cecilius Calvert, Second Lord Baltimore. The Charter of Maryland proclaims:

> Our well beloved and right trusty Subject Caecilius Calvert, Baron of Baltimore...being animated with a laudable, and pious Zeal for extending the Christian Religion...hath humbly besought Leave of Us that he may transport...a numerous Colony of the English Nation, to a certain Region...in a Country hitherto uncultivated...and partly occupied by Savages, having no Knowledge of the Divine Being.[41]

Colony of Maryland March 25, 1634, began when Second Lord Baltimore Cecilius Calvert commissioned his brother, Leonard Calvert (1606-1647), to sail to the Chesapeake Bay area with 230 emigrants on the ships, the *Ark* and the *Dove*, and then to serve as the colony's governor. Initially founded as a refuge for persecuted Catholics, the colony granted Christians of all denominations religious freedom with the passage of the famous *Toleration Act of 1649*. The act declared:

Cecilius Calvert,
2nd Baron
Baltimore

> No person professing to believe in Jesus Christ shall from henceforth be troubled or molested on account of religion.[42]

The governors of Maryland annually took an oath not:

> By themselves, or indirectly, to trouble, molest, or discountenance any person professing to believe in Jesus Christ, for or in respect of religion; and if any such were so molested, to protect the person molested, and punish the offender.[43]

One of the colonists, Father White, described their initial arrival, on March 25, 1634, as they founded Saint Mary's City on Saint Clement's Island:

> We celebrated mass....This had never been done before in this part of the world. After we had completed, we took on our shoulders a great cross, which we had hewn out of a tree, and advancing in order to the appointed place, with the assistance of the Governor and his associates...we erected a trophy to Christ the Savior.[44]

ଈ

The Maryland Toleration Act April 21, 1649, stated:

> Be it therefore...enacted...that no person or persons whatsoever within this province...professing to believe in Jesus Christ shall...henceforth be any ways troubled, molested (or disapproved of)...in respect of his or her religion nor in the free exercise thereof...[45]

ଈ

MARYLAND

Seal of Maryland

Constitution of the State of Maryland August 14, 1776, stated:

> We, the people of the state of Maryland, grateful to Almighty God for our civil and religious liberty...[46]

> *Article XXXV* That no other test or qualification ought to be required, on admission to any office of trust or profit, than such oath of support and fidelity to this State and such oath of office, as shall be directed by this Convention, or the Legislature of this State, and a declaration of a belief in the Christian religion.[47]

Article XXXVI That the manner of administering an oath to any person, ought to be such, as those of the religious persuasion, profession, or denomination, of which such person is one, generally esteem to most effectual confirmation, by the attestation of the Divine Being.[48]

That, as it is the duty of every man to worship God in such a manner as he thinks most acceptable to him; all persons professing the Christian religion, are equally entitled to protection in their religious liberty;

wherefore no person ought by any law to be molested...on account of his religious practice; unless, under the color [pretense] of religion, any man shall disturb the good order, peace or safety of the State, or shall infringe the laws of morality...yet the Legislature may, in their discretion, lay a general and equal tax, for the support of the Christian religion.(until 1851)[49]

In 1851, the Constitution of the State of Maryland declared that no other test or qualification for admission to any office of trust or profit shall be required than the official oath and:

A declaration of belief in the Christian religion; and if the party shall profess to be a Jew the declaration shall be of his belief in a future state of rewards and punishments.[50]

In 1864, the Constitution of the State of Maryland required all State officers to make:

A declaration of belief in the Christian religion, or of the existence of God, and in a future state of rewards and punishments.[51]

༚

Supreme Court of Maryland 1799, decided the case of *M'Creery's Lessee v. Allender*, a dispute over whether an Irish emigrant, Thomas M'Creery, had become a naturalized American citizen and was thereby able to leave an estate to a relative who still lived in Ireland. The court decided in M'Creery's favor, based on a certificate executed before Justice Samuel Chase. The certificate reads:

Thomas M'Creery, in order to become...naturalized according to the Act of Assembly...on the 30th of September, 1795, took the oath...before the Honorable Samuel Chase, Esquire, then being the Chief Judge of the State of Maryland...and did then and there receive from the said Chief Judge, a certificate thereof...:

Maryland; I, Samuel Chase, Chief Judge of the State of Maryland, do hereby certify all whom it may concern, that...personally appeared before me Thomas M'Creery, and did repeat and subscribe a declaration of his belief in the Christian Religion, and take the oath required by the Act of Assembly of this State, entitled, "An Act for Naturalization."[52]

꙰

Supreme Court of Maryland 1799, in the case of *Runkel v. Winemiller*, rendered its opinion:

> Religion is of general and public concern, and on its support depend, in great measure, the peace and good order of government, the safety and happiness of the people. By our form of government, the Christian religion is the established religion; and all sects and denominations of Christians are placed upon the same equal footing, and are equally entitled to protection in their religious liberty.[53]

꙰

George Mason (1725-1792), was a famous American Revolutionary statesman and delegate from Virginia to the Constitutional Convention. He was a member of the Virginia House of Burgesses, a lawyer, judge, political philosopher and planter. The richest man in Virginia, he owned 15,000 acres in Virginia and 80,000 acres in the Ohio area. George Mason was the author of the Virginia Constitution and the Virginia Bill of Rights.

He was a delegate to the Constitutional Convention of the United States, but refused to sign the Constitution as it did not sufficiently limit the government's power from infringing on the rights of citizens. George Mason disapproved strongly of the slave trade and mortally hated paper money. He disliked the idea of a strong federal government as he feared it would usurp the sovereignty of the individual states.

He is called the "Father of the Bill of Rights," as he insisted that Congress add the Bill of Rights (the first ten amendments) to the Constitution. His influence is worldwide, as virtually all succeeding constitutions have incorporated the pattern he set forth.

George Mason practically wrote the first ten amendments to the United States Constitution, limiting the power of the government; these rights are expressed also in the Virginia Bill of Rights, which he wrote:

Virginia Bill of Rights June 12, 1776:
Article XVI That Religion, or the Duty which we owe our Creator, and the Manner of discharging it, can be directed only by Reason and Convictions, not by Force or Violence; and therefore all Men are equally entitled to the free exercise of Religion, according to the Dictates of Conscience; and that it is the mutual Duty of all to practice Christian Forbearance, Love, and Charity towards each other.[54]

George Mason stated before the General Court of Virginia:

The laws of nature are the laws of God, whose authority can be superseded by no power on earth.[55]

This phrase of George Mason's was later incorporated into the Declaration of Independence as, "the laws of nature and nature's God."[56]

On August 22, 1787, George Mason, one of the largest plantation owners in Virginia, stated his views on national accountability during the debates of the Constitutional Convention:

Every master of slaves is born a petty tyrant. They bring the judgement of heaven upon a country. As nations cannot be rewarded or punished in the next world, they must be in this. By an inevitable chain of causes and effects, Providence punishes national sins, by national calamities.[57]

On Tuesday, March 9, 1773, George Mason's wife died after a painful illness. In his own handwriting, he wrote inside their 1759 Family Bible:

...about three o'clock in the morning, died at Gunston-Hall...Mrs. Ann Mason, in the thirty-ninth year of her age; after a painful and tedious illness of more than nine months, which she bore with truly Christian Patience and resignation, in faithful hope of eternal Happiness in the world to come....

For many days before her death she had lost all hopes of recovery, and endeavour'd to wean herself from the affections of this life, saying that tho' it must cost her a hard struggle to reconcile herself to the hopes of parting with her husband and children, she hoped God would enable her to accomplish it...

An easy and agreeable companion, a kind neighbor, a steadfast friend, a humane mistress, a prudent and tender mother, a faithful, affectionate and most obliging wife; charitable to the poor and pious to her Maker, her virtue and religion were unmixed with hypocrisy or ostentation.[58]

In his *Last Will and Testament*, George Mason wrote:

I, George Mason, of "Gunston Hall", in the parish of Truro and county of Fairfax, being of perfect and sound mind and memory and in good health, but mindful of the uncertainty of human life and the imprudence of man's leaving his affairs to be settled upon a deathbed, do make and appoint this my last Will and Testament.

My soul, I resign into the hands of my Almighty Creator, whose tender mercies are over all His works, who hateth nothing that He hath made and to the Justice and Wisdom of whose dispensation I willingly and cheerfully submit, humbly hoping from His unbounded mercy and benevolence, through the merits of my blessed Savior, a remission of my sins.[59]

❧

First Charter of Massachusetts March 4, 1629, granted by King Charles I, stated:

For the directing, ruling, and disposeing of all other Matters and Things, whereby our said People...maie be soe religiously, peaceablie, and civilly governed, as their good life and orderlie Conversation, maie wynn and incite the Natives of the Country to the Knowledg and Obedience of the onlie true God and Savior of Mankinde, and the Christian Fayth, which, in our Royall Intention, and the Adventurers free profession, is the principall Ende of this Plantatiion....[60]

❧

Massachusetts Bay Colony June 1630, was founded by Governor John Winthrop, a successful lawyer and strong Puritan. He led over 700 Puritans, in eleven ships, from England for religious freedom. Governor John Winthrop landed in Massachusetts Bay ten years after the Pilgrims founded the Plymouth Colony, and there authored his famous work, *A Model of Christian Charity*, which became a guideline for the constitutional covenants of the colonies. In it he wrote:

> We are a Company professing our selues fellow members of Christ...knit together by this bond of loue....Wee are entered into Covenant with him for this worke....
>
> For wee must Consider that wee shall be as a City vpon a Hill, the eies of all people are vpon vs;
>
> soe that if wee shall deale falsely with our God in this worke wee have vndertaken and soe cause him to withdrawe his present help from vs, wee shall be made a story and a by-word through the world.[61]

ક

Massachusetts Body of Liberties 1641, stated:

> The free fruition of such liberties Immunities and priveledges as humanities, Civilitie and Christianitie call for as due every man in his place and proportion without impeachment and Infringement hath ever bene and ever will be the tranqualities and Stabilities of Churches and Commonwealths. And the deniall or deprivall thereof, the disturbance if not the ruine of both.[62]

ક

Colony of Massachusetts 1642, along with the Colony of Connecticut in 1647, passed the *Old Deluder Satan Law* to prevent illiteracy and the abuse of power over a population ignorant of Scriptures, as had been the case in Europe. The law instituted:

> It being one chiefe project of that old deluder, Sathan, to keepe men from the knowledge of the scriptures, as in former time....
>
> It is therefore ordered...[that] after the Lord hath increased [the settlement] to the number of fifty howshoulders, [they] shall forthwith appoint one within theire towne, to teach all such children as shall resorte to him, to write and read....
>
> and it is further ordered, That where any towne shall increase to the number of one hundred families or howshoulders, they shall sett

---

up a grammar schoole for the university.[63]

🐦

Boston, Massachusetts, 1765, was the place where the famous Congregational Minister, Jonathan Mayhew of West Church, gave a patriotic sermon which reflected the Colonists' feelings toward King George III's hated Stamp Act:

Jonathan Mayhew

The king is as much bound by his oath not to infringe the legal rights of the people, as the people are bound to yield subjection to him. From whence it follows that as soon as the prince sets himself above the law, he loses the king in the tyrant. He does, to all intents and purposes, un-king himself.[64]

🐦

Provincial Congress of Massachusetts October 22, 1774, concurred with the declaration of its President, John Hancock:

We think it is incumbent upon this people to humble themselves before God on account of their sins, for He hath been pleased in His righteous judgement to suffer a great calamity to befall us, as the present controversy between Great Britain and the Colonies. [And] also to implore the Divine Blessing upon us, that by the assistance of His grace, we may be enabled to reform whatever is amiss among us, that so God may be pleased to continue to us the blessings we enjoy, and remove the tokens of His displeasure, by causing harmony and union to be restored...[65]

John Hancock

🐦

Provincial Congress of Massachusetts 1774, resolved:

Resistance to tyranny becomes the Christian and social duty of each individual....Continue steadfast, and with a proper sense of your dependence on God, nobly defend those rights which heaven gave, and no man ought to take from us.[66]

&

Minuteman stands as a monument at Lexington, Massachusetts.

Provincial Congress of Massachusetts 1774, reorganized the Massachusetts militia, providing that over one-third of all new regiments be made up of "Minutemen." The minutemen, known as such because they would be ready to fight at a minute's notice, would drill as citizen soldiers on the parade ground, then go to the church to hear exhortation and prayer. Many times the deacon of the church, or even the pastor, would lead the drill. They proclaimed, "Our cause is just" and believed it was their Christian duty to defend it.[67] The Provincial Congress of Massachusetts charged the minutemen:

You...are placed by Providence in the post of honor, because it is the post of danger....The eyes not only of North America and the whole British Empire, but of all Europe, are upon you. Let us be, therefore, altogether solicitous that no disorderly behavior, nothing unbecoming our characters as Americans, as citizens and Christians, be justly chargeable to us.[68]

&

Provincial Congress of Massachusetts April 15, 1775, just four days before the famous *Battle of Lexington*, declared *A Day of Public Humiliation, Fasting and Prayer*, signed by President of the Provincial Congress, John Hancock:

In circumstances dark as these, it becomes us, as Men and Christians, to reflect that, whilst every prudent Measure should be taken to ward off the impending Judgements....All confidence must be withheld from the Means we use; and reposed only on that GOD who rules in the Armies of Heaven, and without whose Blessing the best human Counsels are but Foolishness—and all created Power Vanity;

It is the Happiness of his Church that, when the Powers of Earth and Hell combine against it...that the Throne of Grace is of the easiest access—and its Appeal thither is graciously invited by the Father of Mercies, who has assured it, that when his Children ask Bread he will not give them a Stone....

RESOLVED, That it be, and hereby is recommended to the good People of this Colony of all Denominations, that THURSDAY the Eleventh Day of May next be set apart as a Day of Public Humiliation, Fasting and Prayer...to confess the sins...to implore the Forgiveness of all our Transgression...and a blessing on the Husbandry, Manufactures, and other lawful Employments of this People; and especially that the union of the American Colonies in Defence of their Rights (for hitherto we desire to thank Almighty GOD) may be preserved and confirmed....And that AMERICA may soon behold a gracious Interposition of Heaven.

By Order of the [Massachusetts] Provincial Congress, John Hancock, President.[69]

(See also *Boston Tea Party*.)

ॐ

Provincial Congress of Massachusetts May 31, 1775, just three weeks after the victory of Fort Ticonderoga, invited Samuel Langdon, President of Harvard College, to address them. He declared:

We have rebelled against God. We have lost the true spirit of Christianity, though we retain the outward profession and form of it....By many, the Gospel is corrupted into a superficial system of moral philosophy, little better than ancient Platonism....

My brethren, let us repent and implore the divine mercy. Let us amend our ways and our doings, reform everything that has been provoking the Most High, and thus endeavor to obtain the gracious interpositions of providence for our deliverance....

If God be for us, who can be against us? The enemy has reproached us for calling on His name and professing our trust in Him. They have made a mock of our solemn fasts and every appearance of serious Christianity in the land...

May our land be purged from all its sins! Then the Lord will be our refuge and our strength, a very present help in trouble, and we will have no reason to be afraid, though thousands of enemies set themselves against us round about.

May the Lord hear us in this day of trouble....We will rejoice in His salvation, and in the name of our God, we will set up our banners![70]

❧

Constitution of the State of Massachusetts 1780, stated:

We, therefore, the people of Massachusetts, acknowledging, with grateful hearts, the goodness of the great Legislator of the universe, in affording us, in the course of His providence [an opportunity to form a compact];...and devoutly imploring His direction in so interesting a design,...[establish this Constitution].[71]

MASSACHUSETTS.

Seal of Massachusetts

The Governor shall be chosen annually; and no person shall be eligible to this office, unless, at the time of his election...he shall declare himself to be of the Christian religion.[72]

Chapter VI, Article I [All persons elected to State office or to the Legislature must] make and subscribe the following declaration, viz. "I, _____, do declare, that I believe the Christian religion, and have firm persuasion of its truth."[73]

Part I, Article II It is the right, as well as the duty, of all men in society, publicly, and at stated seasons, to worship the Supreme Being, the Great Creator and Preserver of the Universe. And no subject shall be hurt, molested, or restrained, in his person, liberty, or estate, for worshipping God in the manner and seasons, most agreeable to the dictates of his own conscience.[74]

Part I, Article III And every denomination of Christians, demeaning themselves peaceably, and as good subjects of the commonwealth, shall be equally under the protection of the law: and no subordination of any sect or denomination to another shall ever be established by law.[75]

The Constitution of the State of Massachusetts, through 1862, included:

The right of the people of this commonwealth to...invest their Legislature with power to authorize and require, the several towns, parishes, precincts, and other bodies-politic or religious societies to make suitable provision, at their own expense, for the institution of the public worship of God and for the support and maintenance of public Protestant teachers of piety, religion, and morality in all cases where such provision shall not be made voluntary.[76]

ža.

Commonwealth (State) of Massachusetts November 8, 1783, issued *A Proclamation for a Day of Thanksgiving,* signed by Governor John Hancock, to celebrate the victorious conclusion of the Revolutionary War:

John Hancock, Esquire
Governor of the Commonwealth of Massachusetts
A Proclamation for a Day of Thanksgiving:
Whereas...these United States are not only happily rescued from the Danger and Calamities to which they have been so long exposed, but their Freedom, Sovereignty and Independence ultimately acknowledged.
And whereas...the Interposition of Divine Providence in our Favor hath been most abundantly and most graciously manifested, and the Citizens of these United States have every Reason for Praise and Gratitude to the God of their salvation.
Impressed therefore with an exalted Sense of the Blessings by which we are surrounded, and of our entire Dependence on that Almighty Being from whose Goodness and Bounty they are derived;
I do by and with the Advice of the Council appoint Thursday the Eleventh Day of December next (the Day recommended by the Congress to all the States) to be religiously observed as a Day of Thanksgiving and Prayer, that all the People may then assemble to celebrate...that he hath been pleased to continue to us the Light of the Blessed Gospel;....That we also offer up fervent Supplications...to cause pure Religion and Virtue to flourish...and to fill the World with his glory.[77]

ža.

Massachusetts Grand Jury 1802, members were appointed by Judge Nathaniel Freeman, who defined:

The laws of the Christian system, as embraced by The Bible, must be respected as of high authority in all our courts and it cannot be thought improper for the officers of such government to acknowledge their obligation to be governed by its rule....

[Our government] originating in the voluntary compact of a people who in that very instrument profess the Christian religion, it may be considered, not as republic Rome was, a Pagan, but a Christian republic.[78]

[Of note is that the State of Massachusetts paid the salaries of the Congregational ministers in that state until 1833.][79]

❧

Supreme Court of Massachusetts 1838, heard the case of *Commonwealth v. Abner Kneeland,* 37 Mass. (20 Pick) 206, 216-217 1838, which involved a Universalist who claimed the right of "freedom of the press" as a defense for publishing libelous and defamatory remarks about Christianity and God. The Court delivered its decision, stating that "freedom of press" was not a license to print without restraint, otherwise:

According to the argument...every act, however injurious or criminal, which can be committed by the use of language may be committed...if such language is printed. Not only therefore would the article in question become a general license for scandal, calumny and falsehood against individuals, institutions and governments, in the form of publication...but all incitation to treason, assassination, and all other crimes however atrocious, if conveyed in printed language, would be dispunishable.[!].[80]

The statute, on which the question arises, is as follows:

"That if any person shall willfully blaspheme the holy name of God, by denying, cursing, or contumeliously reproaching God, his creation, government, or final judging of the world," &....

In general, blasphemy [libel against God] may be described, as consisting in speaking evil of the Deity...to alienate the minds of others from the love and reverence of God. It is purposely using words concerning God...to impair and destroy the reverence, respect, and confidence due him....

It is a wilful and malicious attempt to lessen men's reverence of God by denying his existence, of his attributes as an intelligent creator, governor and judge of men, and to prevent their having confidence in him....

But another ground for arresting the judgement, and one apparently most relied on and urged by the defendant, is, that this statute itself is repugnant to the constitution...and therefore wholly void....

[This law] was passed very soon after the adoption of the constitution, and no doubt, many members of the convention which framed the constitution, were members of the legislature which passed this law....

In New Hampshire, the constitution of which State has a similar declaration of [religious] rights, the open denial of the being and existence of God or of the Supreme Being is prohibited by statute, and declared to be blasphemy.

In Vermont, with a similar declaration of rights, a statute was passed in 1797, by which it was enacted, that if any person shall publicly deny the being and existence of God or the Supreme Being, or shall contumeliously reproach his providence and government, he shall be deemed a disturber of the peace and tranquility of the State, and an offender against the good morals and manners of society, and shall be punishable by fine....

√ The State of Maine also, having adopted the same constitutional provision with that of Massachusetts, in her declaration of rights, in respect to religious freedom, immediately after the adoption of the constitution reenacted, the Massachusetts statue against blasphemy....

In New York the universal toleration of all religious professions and sentiments, is secured in the most ample manner. It is declared in the constitution...that the free exercise and enjoyment of religious worship, without discrimination or preference, shall for ever be allowed in this State to all mankind....

Notwithstanding this constitutional declaration carrying the doctrine of unlimited toleration as far as the peace and safety of any community will allow, the courts have decided that blasphemy was a crime at common law and was not abrogated by the constitution [*People v. Ruggles*].[81]

[The First Amendment] embraces all who believe in the existence of God, as well...as Christians of every denomination....This provision does not extend to atheists, because they do not believe in God or religion; and therefore...their sentiments and professions, whatever they may be, cannot be called religious sentiments and professions.[82]

δ

Cotton Mather (1663-1728), an American colonial clergyman, received his degree from Harvard at the age of 18 and joined his father, Increase Mather, in the pastorate of Second Church in Boston. Author of 450 books and a Fellow of the Royal Society, Cotton Mather was regarded as the most brilliant man in New England in his time. Among his many accomplishments is the introduction of the smallpox inoculation in 1721, during an epidemic.

Cotton Mather

In 1702, Cotton Mather wrote *Magnalia Christi Americana, (The Great Achievement of Christ in America)*, the most detailed history written of the first 50 years of New England. In it he wrote:

> I write the wonders of the Christian religion, flying from the depravations of Europe, to the American strand: and, assisted by the Holy Author of that religion, I do, with all conscience of truth, required therein by Him, who is the Truth itself, report the wonderful displays of His infinite power, wisdom, goodness, and faithfulness, wherewith his Divine Providence hath irradiated an Indian wilderness....[83]

> The sum of the matter is that from the beginning of the Reformation in the English nation, there had always been a generation of godly men, desirous to pursue the reformation of religion, according to the Word of God....[though withstood by those with] power...in their hands...not only to stop the progress of the desired reformation but also, with innumerable vexation, to persecute those that heartily wish well unto it....[The Puritans were] driven to seek a place for the exercise of the Protestant religion, according to the light of conscience, in the deserts of America.[84]

In observing the trend in the Colonies, after their prayers for blessing were answered, Cotton Mather wrote:

> Religion begat prosperity, and the daughter devoured the mother.[85]

Cotton Mather proffered this advice to the young Benjamin Franklin as Franklin approached a low-hanging beam in Mather's parsonage:

You are young and have the world before you; stoop as you go through it, and you will miss many hard bumps.[86]

&

Increase Mather

Increase Mather (1639-1723), President of Harvard, was a primary leader in colonial America, and the key representative of the Colonists to England. He was the father of Cotton Mather, who became one of the most influential figures in Massachusetts. When King Charles II demanded the return of the charter of Massachusetts, Increase Mather prepared this response:

To submit and resign their charter would be inconsistent with the main end of their fathers' coming to New England....[Although resistance would provoke] great sufferings, [it was] better to suffer than sin. Let them trust in the God of their fathers, which is better than to put confidence in princes. And if they suffer, because they dare not comply with the wills of men against the will of God, they suffer in a good cause.[87]

&

Matthew Fontaine Maury

Matthew Fontaine Maury (1806-1873), scientist and pioneer hydrographer, was known as the "Pathfinder of the Seas" for having charted the sea and wind currents while serving in the U.S. Navy. Considered the founder of modern hydrography and oceanography, he was Professor of Meteorology at Virginia Military Institute. In his book *Physical Geography of the Sea*, 1855, Matthew Fontaine Maury wrote:

I have always found in my scientific studies, that, when I could get the Bible to say anything on the subject it afforded me a firm platform to stand upon, and a round in the ladder by which I could safely ascend.

As our knowledge of nature and her laws has increased, so has our knowledge of many passages of the Bible improved.

The Bible called the earth "the round world," yet for ages it was the most damnable heresy for Christian men to say that the world is round; and, finally, sailors circumnavigated the globe, and proved the Bible to be right, and saved Christian men of science from the stake.

And as for the general system of circulation which I have been so long endeavoring to describe, the Bible tells it all in a single sentence: "The wind goeth toward the South and returneth again to his circuits."[88]

Engraved on his tombstone at the U.S. Naval Academy is the verse from Psalm 8 which had inspired him all his life:

Whatsoever passeth through the paths of the seas.[89]

❧

Mayflower Compact November 11, 1620, America's first great governmental document, was signed by the Pilgrims before they disembarked their ship, the *Mayflower*. This covenant was so revolutionary that it has influenced all other constitutional instruments in America since. It reads:

A replica of the Mayflower anchors in Plymouth Bay.

In ye name of God, Amen. We whose names are underwritten, the loyall subjects of our dread soveraigne Lord, King James, by ye grace of God, of Great Britaine, France, & Ireland king, defender of ye faith, etc., having undertaken, for ye glorie of God, and advancemente of ye Christian faith, and honour of our king & countrie, a voyage to plant ye first colonie in ye Northerne parts of Virginia, doe by these presents solemnly & mutually in ye presence of God, and one of another, covenant & combine our selves togeather into a civill body politick, for our better ordering & preservation & furtherance of ye ends aforesaid;

and by vertue hearof to enacte, constitute, and frame such just & equall lawes, ordinances, acts, constitutions & offices, from time to time, as shall be thought most meete & convenient for ye generall good of ye Colonie, unto which we promise all due submission and obedience.

In witnes wherof we have hereunder subscribed our names at Cap-Codd ye 11. of November, in ye year of ye raigne of our soveraigne lord, King James, of England, France, & Ireland ye eighteenth, and by Scotland ye fiftie fourth. Ano:Dom. 1620.[90]

Jonathan Mayhew (1720-1766), was the famous Congregational minister of West Church in Boston. Having graduated with honors from Harvard in 1747, he was given the distinguished position of Dudlein Lecturer at Harvard in 1765. Reflecting the colonists' feelings toward King George III's hated Stamp Act, Jonathan Mayhew delivered a powerful patriotic sermon in 1765, stating:

Jonathan Mayhew

The king is as much bound by his oath not to infringe the legal rights of the people, as the people are bound to yield subjection to him. From whence it follows that as soon as the prince sets himself above the law, he loses the king in the tyrant. He does, to all intents and purposes, un-king himself.[91]

In response to the English Parliament's plan to impose the Episcopal Church as America's State Church, Jonathan Mayhew gave his sermon, *Concerning Unlimited Submission to the Higher Powers*, to the Council and House of Representatives in Colonial New England in 1749. He asserted:

It is hoped that but few will think the subject of it an improper one to be discoursed in the pulpit, under a notion that this is preaching politics instead of Christ. However, to remove all prejudices of this sort, I beg it may be remembered that "all Scripture is profitable for doctrine, for reproof, for correction, for instruction in righteousness."

Why, then, should not those parts of Scripture which relate to civil government be examined and explained from the desk, as well as others?...

It is evident that the affairs of civil government may properly fall under a moral and religious consideration...For, although there be a sense, and a very plain and important sense, in which Christ's Kingdom is not of this world, His inspired apostles have nevertheless, laid down some general principles concerning the office of civil rulers, and the duty of subjects, together with the reason and obligation of that duty.

And...it is proper for all who acknowledge the authority of Jesus Christ, and the inspiration of His apostles, to endeavor to understand what is in fact the doctrine which they have delivered concerning this matter....

Civil tyranny is usually small at the beginning, like "the drop of a bucket," till at length, like a mighty torrent, or the raging waves of the sea, it bears down all before it, and deluges whole countries and empires....[92]

&

James McGready (1758-1817), was a pastor in Orange County, North Carolina, in 1790; then in 1796, he pastored three small congregations in Logan County, Kentucky. He was responsible for the great revivals of 1797, 1798, and 1799, which were predecessors to the Great Revival of 1800. He also pioneered churches in South Indiana in 1811. He wrote *A Short Narrative of the Revival of Religion in Logan County in the State of Kentucky and the Adjacent Settlements in the State of Tennessee from May 1797 until 1800.*

As a young pastor, in 1797, James McGready entered into a covenant with his small congregations in Kentucky, vowing:

Therefore, we bind ourselves to observe the third Saturday of each month for one year as a day of fasting and prayer for the conversion of sinners in Logan County and throughout the world. We also engage to spend one half hour every Saturday evening, beginning at the setting of the sun, and one half hour every Sabbath morning at the rising of the sun in pleading with God to revive His work.[93]

In June of 1800, the five hundred members of McGready's three congregations gathered at Red River for a "camp meeting" which lasted several days. On the last day:

"A mighty effusion of [God's] Spirit" came on everyone "and the floor was soon covered with the slain; their screams for mercy pierced the heavens."[94]

In late July of 1800, they planned another camp meeting at Gaspar River. To their amazement 8,000 people arrived, some from distances over 100 miles away. Baptist, Methodist and Presbyterian ministers all worked together. On the third night:

The power of God seemed to shake the whole assembly. Towards the close of the sermon, the cries of the distressed arose almost as loud as his voice. After the congregation was dismissed the solemnity increased, till the greater part of the multitude seemed engaged in the most solemn manner. No person seemed to wish to go home—hunger and sleep seemed to affect nobody—eternal things were the vast concern. Here awakening and converting work was to be found in every part of the multitude; and even some things strangely and wonderfully new to me.[95]

In August of 1801, Barton W. Stone (1772-1844), with numerous Baptist, Methodist and Presbyterian ministers, planned a camp meeting at Cane Ridge, Kentucky. A multitude of 25,000 people came, from as far away as Ohio and Tennessee. (The immensity of this crowd is appreciated when one considers that Lexington, the largest town in Kentucky, only had 1,800 citizens.) Rev. Moses Hoge described the meeting:

The careless fall down, cry out, tremble, and not infrequently are affected with convulsive twitchings....

Nothing that imagination can paint, can make a stronger impression upon the mind, than one of those scenes. Sinners dropping down on every hand, shrieking, groaning, crying for mercy, convulsed; professors praying, agonizing, fainting, falling down in distress, for sinners or in raptures of joy!...

As to the work in general there can be no question but it is of God. The subjects of it, for the most part are deeply wounded for their sins, and can give a clear and rational account of their conversion....[96]

꣠

William Holmes McGuffey (1800-1873), an American educator, was the president of Ohio University, professor at the University of Virginia and the department chairman at the Miami University of Ohio. He was responsible for forming the first teachers' association in that part of the nation.

William Holmes McGuffey

Considered the "Schoolmaster of the Nation," McGuffey published the first edition of his *McGuffey's Reader* in 1836. This book was the mainstay in public education in America till 1920. As of 1963, 125 million copies had been sold, making it one of the most widely used and influential textbooks of all times.

Millions of American children learned to read and write from that reader. In its foreword, McGuffey wrote:

> The Christian religion is the religion of our country. From it are derived our prevalent notions of the character of God, the great moral governor of the universe. On its doctrines are founded the peculiarities of our free institutions.[97]

> The Ten Commandments and the teachings of Jesus are not only basic but plenary.[98]

Lesson 37 of McGuffey's *Eclectic First Reader* is entitled "Evening Prayer":

> At the close of the day, before you go to sleep, you should not fail to pray to God to keep you from sin and from harm. You ask your friends for food, and drink, and books, and clothes; and when they give you these things, you thank them, and love them for the good they do you. So you should ask your God for those things which he can give you, and which no one else can give you.
>
> You should ask him for life, and health, and strength; and you should pray to him to keep your feet from the ways of sin and shame. You should thank him for all his good gifts; and learn, while young, to put your trust in him; and the kind care of God will be with you, both in your youth and in your old age.[99]

Lesson 62 of McGuffey's *Eclectic First Reader* is entitled, "Don't Take Strong Drink":

No little boy or girl should ever drink rum or whiskey, unless they want to become drunkards. Men who drink are glad to have any excuse for doing it....and the man who uses it, becomes a sot. Then he is seen tottering through the streets, a shame to himself and to all his family. And oh, how dreadful to die a drunkard. The Bible says that no drunkard shall inherit the kingdom of heaven. Whiskey makes the happy miserable, and it causes the rich to become poor.[100]

In the preface to his 1837 *Eclectic Third Reader*, McGuffey states:

In making [my] selections, [I have] drawn from the purest fountains of English literature....For the copious extracts made from the Sacred Scripture, [I make] no apology.[101]

Indeed, upon a review of the work, [I am] not sure but an apology may be due for [my] not having still more liberally transferred to [my] pages the chaste simplicity, the thrilling pathos, the living descriptions, and the matchless sublimity of the sacred writings.[102]

From no source has the author drawn more copiously than from the Sacred Scriptures. For this [I] certainly apprehend no censure. In a Christian country, that man is to be pitied, who, at this day, can honestly object to imbuing the minds of youth with the language and spirit of the Word of God.[103]

In his 1837 *Eclectic Third Reader*, McGuffey instructs:

1. The design of the Bible is evidently to give us correct information concerning the creation of all things, by the omnipotent Word of God; to make known to us the state of holiness and happiness of our first parents in paradise, and their dreadful fall from that condition by transgression against God, which is the original cause of all our sin and misery....

3. The Scriptures are especially designed to make us wise unto salvation through faith in Christ Jesus; to reveal to us the mercy of the Lord in him; to form our minds after the likeness of God our Saviour; to build up our souls in wisdom and faith, in love and holiness; to make us thoroughly furnished unto good works, enabling us to glorify

God on earth; and, to lead us to an imperishable inheritance among the spirits of just men made perfect, and finally to be glorified with Christ in heaven.[104]

In Lesson 21 of McGuffey's *Eclectic Third Reader,* the character of Jesus Christ is taught:

1. The morality taught by Jesus Christ was purer, sounder, sublimer and more perfect than had ever before entered into the imagination, or proceeded from the lips of man...[105]

✓Lesson 31 in McGuffey's *Eclectic Third Reader* is entitled, "On Speaking Truth":

1. A little girl once came into the house, and told her mother a story about something which seemed very improbable.
2. The persons who were sitting in the room with her mother did not believe the little girl, for they did not know her character. But the mother replied at once, "I have no doubt that it is true, for I never knew my daughter to tell a lie." Is there not something noble in having such a character as this?
3. Must not that little girl have felt happy in the consciousness of thus possessing her mother's entire confidence? Oh, how different must have been her feelings from those of the child whose words cannot be believed, and who is regarded by every one with suspicion? Shame, shame on the child who has not magnanimity enough to tell the truth....
10. How awful must be the scene which will open before you, as you enter the eternal world! You will see the throne of God: how bright, how glorious, will it burst upon your sight! You will see God, the Savior, seated upon the majestic throne. Angels, in number more than can be counted, will fill the universe, with their glittering wings, and their rapturous songs. Oh, what a scene to behold! And then you will stand in the presence of this countless throng, to answer for every thing you have done while you lived.
11. Every action and every thought of your life will then be fresh in your mind. You know it is written in the Bible, "God will bring every work into judgement, with every secret thing, whether it be good or whether it be evil." How must the child then feel who has been guilty of falsehood and deception, and who sees it then all brought to light! No liar can enter the kingdom of heaven. Oh, how dreadful must be the confusion and shame, with which the deceitful child will then be overwhelmed! The angels will all see your sin and disgrace.

12. And do you think they will wish to have a liar enter heaven and be associated with them? No! They will turn from you with disgust. The Savior will look upon you in his displeasure. Conscience will read your soul. And you must hear the awful sentence, "Depart from me, into everlasting fire, prepared for the devil and his angels."

Questions: 1.What is the subject of this Lesson? 2.What did the little girl do? 3. What did the company think? 4. What did her mother say of her? 5. How must the little girl have felt when her mother said she could not doubt her word?...[106]

On August 7, 1873, in Elmira, New York, the National Education Association honored McGuffey at his death with this resolution:

> In the death of William H. McGuffey, late Professor of Moral Philosophy in the University of Virginia, the Association feels that they have lost one of the great lights of the profession....in offices as teacher of common schools, college professor and college president, and as author of text books; his almost unequalled industry; his power in the lecture room; his influence upon his pupils and community; his care for the public interests of education; his lofty devotion to duty; his conscientious Christian character—all these have made him one of the noblest ornaments of our profession in this age, and entitled to the grateful remembrance of this Association and of the teachers of America.
>
> Elmira, New York, August 7, 1873.[107]

ð

James McHenry (1753-1816), one of the signers of the Constitution of the United States, was a member of the Continental Congress, a state legislator, a soldier and the U.S. Secretary of War, who supervised the establishment of the United States Military Academy at West Point.

He was also a physician, having studied under the renowned Dr. Benjamin Rush, himself a signer of the Declaration of Independence. James McHenry served with distinction under General Washington on the medical staff during the Revolutionary War. Fort McHenry,

James McHenry

where, in 1812, the battle with Britain occasioned the writing of our national anthem, was named after him.

In 1813, he became the president of the first Bible society in Baltimore. He conveys the urgency of distributing Bibles to the public in an article to solicit funds for the society:

> Neither, in considering this subject, let it be overlooked, that public utility pleads most forcibly for the general distribution of the Holy Scriptures.
>
> The doctrine they preach, the obligations they impose, the punishment they threaten, the rewards they promise, the stamp and image of divinity they bear, which produces a conviction of their truths, can alone secure to society, order and peace, and to our courts of justice and constitutions of government, purity, stability and usefulness.
>
> In vain, without the Bible, we increase penal laws and draw intrenchments around our institutions. Bibles are strong intrenchments. Where they abound, men cannot pursue wicked courses, and at the same time enjoy quiet conscience.
>
> Consider also, the rich do not possess aught more precious than their Bible, and that the poor cannot be presented by the rich with anything of greater value. Withhold it not from the poor. It is a book of councils and directions, fitted to every situation in which man can be placed. It is an oracle which reveals to mortals the secrets of heavens and the hidden will of the Almighty....
>
> It is an estate, whose title is guaranteed by Christ, whose delicious fruits ripen every season, survive the worm, and keep through eternity. It is for the purpose of distributing this divine book more effectually and extensively among the multitudes, whose circumstances render such a donation necessary, that your cooperation is most earnestly requested.[108]

❧

William McKinley (1843-1901, assassinated) was the 25th President of the United States of America. His administration was responsible for America becoming a world power after the victory of the Spanish-American War, through the annexation of the Hawaiian Islands, Puerto Rico, Guam and the Philippine Islands. Under his administration, the United States was given the permanent lease of Guantanamo Bay in Cuba, the Panama Canal was planned, and the Boxer Rebellion was put down in China.

William McKinley

William McKinley had a reputation for honesty, great tact, personal charm and a marked religious attitude. He began his career as a Union major in the Civil War, became a lawyer, was elected to the U.S. Congress, and in 1891 became the governor of Ohio. The nation mourned when he was assassinated shortly after beginning his second term as president.

On July 4, 1892, in an address to the Baptist Young People's Union in Lakeside, Ohio, Governor William McKinley shared:

> Lincoln, like Washington, illustrated in his administration faith in God. On March 4, 1861, he said: "Intelligence, patriotism, Christianity, and a firm reliance upon Him who has never forgotten this favored land are still competent to adjust in the best way all our present difficulties."[109]

On June 29, 1893, before the First International Convention of the Epworth League in Cleveland, Governor William McKinley declared:

> We live to make our Church a power in the land while we love every other Church that exalts our Christ. That broad Christian liberality lies at the basis of your work....Every organization of this kind demonstrates that Christian character is helpful in every avenue or emergency of life....The demand of the time is the young man thoroughly grounded in Christianity and its Book.[110]

On July 14, 1894, in Cleveland, Ohio, Governor McKinley stated in a speech to the Christian Endeavor's International Convention:

> There is no currency in this world that passes at such a premium anywhere as good Christian character....The time has gone by when the young man or the young woman in the United States has to apologize for being a follower of Christ....No cause but one could have brought together so many people, and that is the cause of our Master.[111]

In 1896, while speaking of the attributes of Abraham Lincoln, William McKinley declared:

Abraham Lincoln

> The purposes of God, working through the ages, were, perhaps, more clearly revealed to him than to any other....He was the greatest man of his time, especially approved of God for the work He gave him to do.[112]

On March 4, 1897, in his Inaugural Address, President William McKinley proclaimed:

> Let me repeat the oath administered by the Chief Justice: "I will faithfully administer the office of the President of the United States...." This is the obligation I have reverently taken before the Lord this day. To keep it will be my single purpose and my prayer.[113]

> Our faith teaches that there is no safer reliance than upon the God of our fathers...who will not forsake us so long as we obey His commandments and walk humbly in His footsteps.[114]

President William McKinley stated:

> The Christian religion is no longer the badge of weaklings and enthusiasts, but of distinction, enforcing respect.[115]

In respect to the Bible, President McKinley announced:

> The more profoundly we study this wonderful Book, and the more closely we observe its divine precepts, the better citizens we will become and the higher will be our destiny as a nation.[116]

੨੦

John McLean (1785-1861), Justice of the United States Supreme Court from 1829 until 1861, had previously served as a U.S. Congressman from Ohio, an Ohio Supreme Court Judge, and the U.S. Postmaster General.

On November 4, 1852, in a letter from Chapel Wood, John McLean wrote to the American Bible Society:

No one can estimate or describe the salutary influence of the Bible. What would the world be without it? Compare the dark places of the earth, where the light of the Gospel has not penetrated, with those where it has been proclaimed and embraced in all its purity. Life and immortality are brought to light by the Scriptures.

Aside from Revelation, darkness rests upon the world and upon the future. There is no ray of light to shine upon our pathway; there is no star of hope. We begin our speculations as to our destiny in conjecture, and they end in uncertainty. We know not that there is a God, a heaven, or a hell, or any day of general account, when the wicked and the righteous shall be judged.

The Bible has shed a glorious light upon the world. It shows us that in the coming day we must answer for the deeds done in the body. It has opened us to a new and living way, so plainly marked out that no one can mistake it. The price paid for our redemption shows the value of our immortal souls.[117]

ᐱ

George Gordon Meade (1815-1872), was the Major General of the United States Army who led the Union troops to victory at the *Battle of Gettysburg*, thus turning the tide of the Civil War. Colonel George Meade, the son of General Meade, reported the facts surrounding his father's last days in 1872:

George Gordon Meade

Death came suddenly, with the sound of a foot-fall. There were a few days when friends waited on medical skill, but his heart was on the country whither he was going. He looked to the Saviour, who was the only one in Heaven or earth who could help him. He asked for the Holy Communion, and by the Lord's table gathered manna for the last journey. The words of penitence and the look of faith were blended with his dying prayers.

General Meade's religious principles were exhibited in his daily life, in his intercourse with his fellow men, and the Christian example he set. As far as his outward profession of belief was concerned, he was an active and attentive communicant in our Church from an early day, and died in the triumphs of faith in the great Captain of his salvation.[118]

ᐱ

Wesley Merritt (1834-1910), a Major General in the Union Army during the Civil War, was the Superintendent of the United States Military Academy at West Point, 1882-87, and commanded the first Philippine expedition to occupy Manila in August of 1898. He expressed:

> The principles of life as taught in the Bible, the inspired Word, and exemplified in the matchless Life of Him "who spake as never man spake," are the rules of moral action which have resulted in civilizing the world.
>
> The testimony of great men, like Gladstone and his fellow statesmen; like Havelock and his fellow soldiers, who have made the teachings of the Scriptures their rule of conduct in life, are wonderful helps to men of lesser note and smaller intellectual and moral powers. One example, even of the smallest of these, more than offsets the efforts of an hundred unbelievers in active opposition.
>
> They are the worthy followers of the religion of the Bible, and in their daily lives interpret the inimitable example and Divine precepts of the Son of God, our Saviour.[119]

٢٨

Michelangelo Buonarroti (1475-1564), one of the greatest artists in history, lived during the Italian Renaissance. His paintings, sculptures and architectural designs portrayed a living strength and energy. Among his most celebrated works are the painting of the ceiling of the Sistine Chapel, and the sculptures: David; Moses; Bound Captives; and the Pietá, a touching depiction of Christ in His mother's arms after He was taken down from the cross. In his *Sonnet*, Michelangelo wrote:

> If it be true that any beautiful thing raises the pure and just desire of man from earth to God, the eternal fount of all, such I believe my love.[120]

> I live and love in God's peculiar light.[121]

٢٨

Michigan Federal Court 1965, in the case of *Reed v. van Hoven*, 237

F. Supp. 48, 51 (W. D. Mich. 1965), rendered this opinion:

> The child is not the mere creature of the state.[122]

ʂ●

John Milton (1608-1674), was the famous English poet and political writer who wrote the epics, *Paradise Lost,* 1667; and *Paradise Regained,* 1671. Tremendously gifted, Milton aggressively defended the Puritan cause, by writing, among others, *Pro Populo Anglicano,* 1651; *The Tenure of Kings and Magistrates,* 1649; *The Tetrachordon,* 1645; and *The Reason of Church Government,* 1642; which declares that governments are to have no control over the local churches.

John Milton faced his greatest difficulty when he went blind in his middle forties, followed by his wife dying in childbirth. He continued creating his most renowned works by dictating them to his daughters, including *Paradise Lost* and *Paradise Regained.* John Milton expressed:

> There are no songs comparable to the songs of Zion; no orations equal to those of the prophets; and no politics like those which the Scriptures teach.[123]

In 1629, in the composition *On the Morning of Christ's Nativity,* John Milton wrote:

> This is the month, and this the happy morn,
> Wherein the Son of Heav'n's eternal King,
> Of wedded maid and virgin mother born,
> Our great redemption from above did bring;
> For so the holy sages once did sing,
> That He our deadly forfeit should release,
> And with His Father work us a perpetual peace.[124]

John Milton, in 1631, penned *Il Penseroso,* in which he said:

> And storied windows richly dight,
> Casting a dim religious light,

There let the pealing organ blow,
To the full-voiced choir below,
In service high, and anthems clear
As may, with sweetness, through mine ear
Dissolve me into ecstasies,
And bring all Heaven before mine eyes.[125]

In 1634, John Milton wrote in *Comus:*

That power
Which erring men call chance.[126]

In *Lycidas,* 1637, Milton composed:

Last came, and last did go,
The Pilot of the Galilean lake;
Two massy keys he bore of metals twain,
(The golden opes, the iron shuts amain).[127]

In his work, *Animadversions upon the Reply of Smectymnuus,* 1642, John Milton wrote:

Let us all go, every true protested Briton, throughout the three kingdoms, and render thanks, to God, the Father of light, and fountain of heavenly grace, and to His Son, Christ the Lord.[128]

In *Tractate of Education,* 1644, Milton wrote:

Inflamed with the study of learning and the admiration of virtue; stirred up with high hopes of living to be brave men and worthy patriots, dear to God, and famous to all ages.[129]

In *Areopagitica,* 1644, considered the best of his prose works, John Milton wrote:

As good almost kill a man as kill a good book: who kills a man kills a reasonable creature, God's image; but he who destroys a good book kills reason itself.[130]

In *On the Late Massacre in Piedmont,* 1655, Milton wrote:

Avenge, O Lord, thy slaughtered saints, whose bones
Lie scattered on the Alpine mountains cold;
Ev'n them who kept thy truth so pure of old
When all our fathers worshipped stocks and stones
Forget not.[131]

John Milton declared in his *True Religion, Heresy, Schism, Toleration*, 1673:

No man or angel can know how God would be worshiped and served unless God reveal it: He hath revealed and taught it us in the Holy Scriptures by inspired ministers, and in the Gospel by His own Son, and His apostles, with strictest command to reject all other traditions or additions whatever.[132]

In *Paradise Lost*, written in 1667, John Milton coined the lines:

A heaven on earth.[133]

All hell broke loose.[134]

So vivid were his depictions in *Paradise Lost*, that it has become a classic which has endured the ages:

Of Man's first disobedience, and the fruit
Of that forbidden tree whose mortal taste
Brought death into the world, and all our woe,
With loss of Eden....

What in men is dark
Illumine, what is low raise and support;
That to the height of this great argument
I may assert eternal Providence,
And justify the ways of God to men....

The infernal serpent; he it was, whose guile,
Stirred up with envy and revenge, deceived
The mother of mankind....

Him the Almighty Power
Hurled headlong flaming from th' ethereal sky
With hideous ruin and combustion down

To bottomless perdition, there to dwell
In adamantine chains and penal fire,
Who durst defy th' Omnipotent to arms....

Thus Belial with words clothed in reason's garb
Counseled ignoble ease, and peaceful sloth,
Not peace.[135]

&

Constitution of the State of Mississippi 1817, stated:

No person who denies the being of God or a future state of rewards and punishments shall hold any office in the civil department of the State.[136]

Article IX, Section 16 Religion, morality, and knowledge, being necessary to good government, the preservation of liberty and the happiness of mankind, schools and the means of education shall be forever encouraged in this state.[137]

&

Ormsby Macknight Mitchell (1810-1862), a Major General in the Civil War, and a renowned astronomer, was famous for having led the raid which captured Huntsville, Alabama, in April of 1862.

As director of the Dudley Observatory in Albany, New York, Ormsby Mitchell wrote *Planetary and Stellar Worlds,* 1848; and *Popular Astronomy,* 1860; and a book entitled, *The Astronomy of the Bible,* in which he stated:

Let us turn to the language of the Bible; it furnishes the only vehicle to express the thoughts which overwhelm us, and we break out involuntarily in the language of God's own inspiration:

"Have ye not known, hath it not been told to you from the beginning, have ye not understood from the foundation of the earth? It is He who sitteth upon the circle of the earth, that stretcheth out the heavens like a curtain, and spreadeth them out as a tent to dwell in.

"Lift up your eyes on high, and behold. Who hath created all these things, that bringeth out their host by number? It is He who meted out the heavens with a span, and comprehended the dust of the earth in a measure, and weighed the mountains in scales and the hills in balances.

"It is He who stretcheth out the north over the empty place, and hangeth the earth upon nothing. He telleth the number of the stars. He calleth them all by their names."[138]

☙

James Monroe (1758-1831), who served in public office for fifty years, was elected the 5th President of the United States in 1817. Home schooled as a child by the Reverend William Douglas, he was a fellow student with John Marshall, who became the Chief Justice of the Supreme Court.

James Monroe

Beginning as a lieutenant colonel in the Revolutionary Army, James Monroe served in the Virginia Assembly, the Constitutional

Mrs. James Monroe (nee Eliza Kortright)

Convention, the U.S. Senate, as governor of Virginia, and Minister to France, Great Britain, and Spain. He was appointed as Secretary of State, and also served as the U.S. Secretary of War. He helped negotiate the *Louisiana Purchase* from Napoleon, which doubled the size of the United States. He also negotiated the acquiring of Florida from Spain; the addition of Maine, Illinois, Missouri, Alabama and Mississippi as states in the Union; and was responsible for the *Monroe Doctrine*, which forbade European powers from interfering with the independent nations of the Western Hemisphere.

On March 5, 1821, in his Second Inaugural Address, President James Monroe stated:

> The liberty, prosperity, and happiness of our country will always be the object of my most fervent prayers to the Supreme Author of All Good.[139]

☙

Baron Charles Louis Joseph de Secondat Montesquieu (1689-

1755), was an authoritative French professor, author and legal philosopher, who, in 1748, wrote the highly influential book, *The Spirit of the Laws.* This book greatly impacted the formation of the American government, as it was read and studied intently in America. In reviewing nearly 15,000 items written by the Founding Fathers, (including newspaper articles, monographs, books, pamphlets, etc.), Baron Charles Montesquieu was the most frequently quoted source next to the Bible. [140]

Montesquieu's philosophy was based on the premise that humanity is basically selfish, and, opportunity provided, individuals would accumulate more and more power unto themselves, eventually becoming despots. This reflected the concept of the fallen nature of man expressed Jeremiah 17:9:

The heart is deceitful above all things and desperately wicked: who can know it? [142]

In order to prevent the accumulation of power, Montesquieu proposed separating the powers of government into three branches and pitting them against each other, allowing the greed and ambition of one to check the greed and ambition of the others. This idea of dividing a monarch's power into Judicial, Legislative and Executive branches reflected Isaiah 33:22:

For the Lord is our Judge, the Lord is our Lawgiver, the Lord is our King. [141]

In 1748, Montesquieu wrote in The Spirit of the Laws:

Nor is there liberty if the power of judging is not separated from legislative power and from executive power. If it [the power of judging] were joined to legislative power, the power over life and liberty of the citizens would be arbitrary, for the judge would be the legislator. If it were joined to executive power, the judge could have the force of an oppressor. All would be lost if the same... body of principal men... exercised these three powers. [144]

The Christian religion, which orders men to love one another, no doubt wants the best political laws and the best civil laws for each people, because those laws are, after [the Christian religion], the greatest good that men can give and receive. [143]

In Book XXIV of *The Spirit of the Laws,* Montesquieu wrote:

I have always respected religion; the morality of the Gospel is the noblest gift ever bestowed by God on man. We shall see that we owe to Christianity, in government, a certain political law, and in war a certain law of nations—benefits which human nature can never sufficiently acknowledge.

The principles of Christianity, deeply engraved on the heart, would be infinitely more powerful than the false honor of monarchies, than the humane virtues of republics, or the servile fear of despotic states.

It is the Christian religion that, in spite of the extent of empire and the influence of climate, has hindered despotic power from being established in Ethiopia, and has carried into the heart of Africa the manners and laws of Europe.

The Christian religion is a stranger to mere despotic power. The mildness so frequently recommended in the Gospel is incompatible with the despotic rage with which a prince punishes his subjects, and exercises himself in cruelty.[145]

Society...must repose on principles that do not change.[146]

ᎧᎧ

James Montgomery (1771-1854), was a well-known Scottish newspaperman and poet. He edited the Sheffield *Iris,* and wrote many hymns, including *What Is Prayer?,* in which he penned:

Prayer is the soul's sincere desire
Uttered or unexpressed;
The motion of a hidden fire
That trembles in the breast.[147]

ᎧᎧ

Benjamin Franklin Morris (1810-1867), a notable American historian, wrote his insightful work, *The Christian Life and Character of the Civil Institutions of the United States,* 1864. Benjamin Franklin Morris expounded:

These fundamental objects of the Constitution are in perfect harmony with the revealed objects of the Christian religion. Union, justice, peace, the general welfare, and the blessings of civil and religious liberty, are the objects of Christianity, and always secured under its practical and beneficent reign.[148]

The state must rest upon the basis of religion, and it must preserve this basis, or itself must fall. But the support which religion gives to the state will obviously cease the moment religion loses its hold upon the popular mind.[149]

This is a Christian nation, first in name, and secondly because of the many and mighty elements of a pure Christianity which have given it character and shaped its destiny from the beginning. It is pre-eminently the land of the Bible, of the Christian Church, and of the Christian Sabbath....The chief security and glory of the United States of America has been, is now, and will be forever, the prevalence and domination of the Christian Faith.[150]

Gouverneur Morris (1752-1816), writer of the final draft of the Constitution of the United States, and head of the Committee on Style, was the originator of the phrase "We the people of the United States." He was 35 years old when he served as one of the members of the Continental Congress, and he spoke 173 times during the Constitutional debates (more than any other delegate).

Gouverneur Morris

He was the first U.S. Minister to France, a U.S. Senator and helped to write the New York Constitution. A graduate of King's College (Columbia University), he was a merchant, lawyer, planter, financier and pioneer promoter of the Erie Canal.

When France was in the process of establishing a new form of government, Gouverneur Morris offered to them his expertise in government formation by writing *Observation on Government, Applicable to the Political State of France* and *Notes on the Form of a Constitution for France:*

Religion is the only solid basis of good morals; therefore education should teach the precepts of religion, and the duties of man toward God.[151]

Gouverneur Morris wrote to his Tory mother:

There is one Comforter who weighs our Minutes and Numbers

out our Days.[152]

Near the end of his life, Gouverneur Morris stated that he would soon:

Descend towards the grave full of gratitude to the Giver of all good.[153]

🙚

Jedediah Morse (1761-1826), was a pioneer American educator and geographer, and was called the "Father of American Geography." He was also the father of Samuel F.B. Morse, inventor of the telegraph and the Morse Code.

Having taught in the New Haven schools for several years, Jedediah Morse compiled his notes and published them in his highly successful work, in 1784, entitled *Geography Made Easy.*

Jedediah Morse

Setting a standard for American Geography, he authored other books, including: *The American Geography,* 1789; *Elements of Geography,* 1795; *The American Gazetteer,* 1797; *A New Gazetteer of the Eastern Continent,* 1802; *A Compendious History of New England,* 1804; and *Annals of the American Revolution.* Jedediah was also a founder of the *New England Tract Society,* 1814; *The American Bible Society,* 1816; and was a member of the *American Board of Commissioners for Foreign Missions,* 1811-1819.

In 1799, Jedediah Morse stated:

To the kindly influence of Christianity we owe that degree of civil freedom, and political and social happiness which mankind now enjoys. In proportion as the genuine effects of Christianity are diminished in any nation, either through unbelief, or the corruption of its doctrines, or the neglect of its institutions; in the same proportion will the people of that nation recede from the blessings of genuine freedom, and approximate the miseries of complete despotism.

All efforts to destroy the foundations of our holy religion, ultimately tend to the subversion also of our political freedom and happiness.

Whenever the pillars of Christianity shall be overthrown, our present republican forms of government, and all the blessings which flow from them, must fall with them.[154]

❧

Samuel Finley Breese Morse (1791-1872), was not only the inventor of the Morse Code, but he developed the telegraph and built the first camera in America. He was the son of Jedediah Morse, the famous educator and textbook writer known as "The Father of American Geography."

Samuel Finley Breese Morse

Samuel F.B. Morse was also one of the greatest portrait artists of all time. He was the founder and president for 20 years of the National Academy of Design, and in 1831, received the distinction of being appointed to the first chair of fine arts in America, the Professor of Sculpture and Painting at New York University.

In 1844, Samuel F.B. Morse erected the first telegraph lines between Baltimore and the chamber of the United States Supreme Court in Washington, D.C. The first message, only four words, ever sent over this new communication system which would revolutionize the world, was a verse from the Bible, found in Numbers 23:23:

> "What hath God Wrought!"[155]

Samuel F.B. Morse wrote to his wife during those anxious days between failure and success:

> The only gleam of hope, and I can not underrate it, is from confidence in God. When I look upward it calms my apprehensions for the future, and I seem to hear a voice saying: 'If I clothe the lilies of the field, shall I not also clothe you?' Here is my strong confidence, and I will wait patiently for the direction of Providence.[156]

Later in life, when informed of his wife's death, Samuel F.B. Morse wrote to his father:

> Oh, is it possible? Is it possible? Shall I never see my wife again?

But I can not trust myself to write on this subject. I need your prayers and those of Christian friends.[157]

Samuel F.B. Morse graduated in 1810 from Yale College, having studied under the godly influence of its famous President, Timothy Dwight. Four years before his death, Samuel F.B. Morse gave this strong testimony of his faith:

> The nearer I approach to the end of my pilgrimage, the clearer is the evidence of the divine origin of the Bible, the grandeur and sublimity of God's remedy for fallen man are more appreciated, and the future is illumined with hope and joy.[158]

ও

Wolfgang Amadeus Mozart (1756-1791), was a master German musical composer and pianist. Living only till the age of 35, Mozart has forever earned a place as one the most renowned geniuses in the history of music. He composed symphonies, operas, concertos, sonatas, and choral and chamber pieces—more than 600 works—for royalty all across Europe. Mozart also met the famous composer, Franz Josef Haydn.

On July 3, 1778, Wolfgang Amadeus Mozart wrote from Paris to a friend:

> Mourn with me! This has been the most melancholy day of my life; I am now writing at two o'clock in the morning. I must tell you that my mother, my darling mother, is no more. God has called her to Himself; I clearly see that it was His will to take her from us, and I must learn to submit to the will of God. The Lord giveth and the Lord taketh away....I am fully convinced that God has so ordained it.
>
> All I would ask of you at present is, to act the part of a true friend, by preparing father by degrees for this sad intelligence....May God give him strength and courage! My dear friend, I am consoled not only now, but I have been for some time past.
>
> By the mercy of God, I have borne it with all firmness and composure. When the danger became imminent, I prayed my heavenly Father for only two things—a happy death for my mother, and strength and courage for myself, and our gracious God heard my prayer, and conferred those two boons fully upon me.[159]

In a letter, Mozart wrote:

> It is a great consolation for me to remember that the Lord, to whom I had drawn near in humble and child-like faith, has suffered and died for me, and that He will look on me in love and compassion.[160]

Wolfgang Amadeus Mozart insisted:

> Neither a lofty degree of intelligence nor imagination nor both together go to the making of genius. Love, love, love, that is the soul of genius.[161]

ð

Malcolm Thomas Muggeridge (1903-1990), was a well-known British author, columnist, philosopher and lecturer. In his 1975 work, entitled *Jesus*, Malcolm Muggeridge wrote:

> As Man alone, Jesus could not have saved us; as God alone, he would not; Incarnate, he could and did.[162]

ð

Henry Melchior Muhlenberg (1711-1787), one of the founders of the Lutheran Church in America, was the father of John Peter Gabriel Muhlenberg, the Lutheran clergyman who became a major general in the Continental Army and U.S. Senator. During the Revolutionary War, Henry Melchior Muhlenberg pastored the Lutheran Church near Valley Forge. He commented regarding George Washington:

Henry Melchior Muhlenberg

> I heard a fine example today, namely that His Excellency General Washington rode around among his army yesterday and admonished each and every one to fear God, to put away wickedness that has set in and become so general, and to practice Christian virtues.
>
> From all appearances General Washington does not belong to the so-called world of society, for he respects God's Word, believes in the atonement through Christ, and bears himself in humility and gentleness.

Therefore, the Lord God has also singularly, yea, marvelously preserved him from harm in the midst of countless perils, ambuscades, fatigues, etc., and has hitherto graciously held him in his hand as a chosen vessel.[163]

꙳

John Peter Gabriel Muhlenberg (1746-1807), a member of the Virginia House of Burgesses in 1774, was a 30-year-old pastor who preached on the Christian's responsibility to be involved in securing freedom for America. He was the son of Henry Melchior Muhlenberg, one of the founders of the Lutheran Church in America.

John Peter Muhlenberg

In 1775, after preaching a message on Ecclesiastes 3:1, "For everything there is a season, and a time for every matter under heaven," John Peter Muhlenberg closed his message by saying:

In the language of the Holy Writ, there is a time for all things. There is a time to preach and a time to fight. And now is the time to fight.[164]

He then threw off his clerical robes to reveal the uniform of an officer in the Revolutionary Army. That afternoon, at the head of 300 men, John Peter Muhlenberg marched off to join General Washington's troops and became Colonel of the 8th Virginia Regiment. He served until the end of the war, during which he was promoted to the rank of Major General.

In 1785 he became the Vice-President of Pennsylvania, and in 1790 was a member of the Pennsylvania Constitutional Convention. He then served as a U.S. Congressman from Pennsylvania, and in 1801 he was elected to the United States Senate. In 1889, the State of Pennsylvania placed his statue in the Statuary Hall at Washington.

꙳

N

Napoleon Bonaparte I (1769-1821), was the Emperor of France from 1804 to 1815. He was first given command of the French army in Italy in 1796, where he turned near defeat by the Austrians into victory over Milan, Mantua, Sardinia and Naples. This victory was followed by the papacy suing for peace. Napoleon then obtained the Directory's support for conquering Egypt and India. In 1799, he became the first consul in the French government, formed after the Roman model. In 1802, he became consul for life; and in 1804, he proclaimed himself Emperor.

He defeated the Austrians in 1802, and in 1805 renewed the war with Italy, Germany and Switzerland. Needing money for his military campaigns, he gave up his idea of a colony in America and, in 1803, sold the Louisiana Territory to the United States for $15,000,000. This single purchase of over a million square miles, at about 2½ cents an acre, more than doubled the size of the United States of America.

Napoleon was defeated on the sea by British Lord Horatio Nelson at Trafalgar, but commenced tremendous victories on land at Austerlitz, Jena and Friedland. In 1812, Napoleon invaded Russia with over a half a million men, but nearly 400,000 of them died in the brutal Russian winter. In 1813, he was defeated at Leipzig, forced to abdicate and exiled to Elba. Napoleon escaped Elba in 1815, and returned to a hero's welcome in Paris, where he led France for the famous Hundred Days in an attempt to regain his former power. In one of the most decisive battles in history, Napoleon was defeated at Waterloo by the British Duke of Wellington, June 18, 1815. He was then captured and banished to the island of St. Helena, off the west coast of Africa, where he lived for the remainder of his life.

At Paris, January 23, 1814, Napoleon remarked:

> France is invaded; I am leaving to take command of my troops, and, with God's help and their valor, I hope soon to drive the enemy beyond the frontier.[1]

In communicating with General Bertrand on the island of St. Helena, Napoleon wrote in *On St. Helena*, 1816:

> The Gospel possesses a secret virtue, a mysterious efficacy, a warmth which penetrates and soothes the heart. One finds in meditating upon it that which one experiences in contemplating the heavens.
>
> The Gospel is not a book; it is a living being, with an action, a power, which invades everything that opposes its extension.
>
> Behold it upon this table, this book surpassing all others (here the Emperor solemnly placed his hand upon it): I never omit to read it, and every day with new pleasure.
>
> Nowhere is to be found such a series of beautiful ideas, and admirable moral maxims, which pass before us like the battalions of a celestial army....The soul can never go astray with this book for its guide....
>
> Everything in Christ astonishes me. His spirit overawes me, and His will confounds me. Between Him and whoever else in the world there is no possible term of comparison; He is truly a Being by Himself. His ideas and His sentiments, the truth which He announces, His manner of convincing, are not explained either by human organization or by the nature of things.
>
> Truth should embrace the universe. Such is Christianity, the only religion which destroys sectional prejudices, the only one which proclaims the unity and the absolute brotherhood of the whole human family, the only one which is purely spiritual; in fine, the only one which assigns to all, without distinction, for a true country, the bosom of the Creator, God.
>
> Christ proved that He was the Son of the Eternal by His disregard of time. All His doctrines signify one only and the same thing— eternity. What a proof of the divinity of Christ! With an empire so absolute, he has but one single end—the spiritual melioration of individuals, the purity of the conscience, the union to that which is true, the holiness of the soul....
>
> Not only is our mind absorbed, it is controlled; and the soul can never go astray with this book for its guide. Once master of our spirit, the faithful Gospel loves us. God even is our friend, our father, and

truly our God. The mother has no greater care for the infant whom she nurses....

If you [General Bertrand] do not perceive that Jesus Christ is God, very well: then I did wrong to make you a general.[2]

Napoleon's famous statement, in another rendering from the French language, declares:

The Bible is no mere book, but a Living Creature, with a power that conquers all that oppose it.[3]

Napoleon I, in a discussion with Count de Motholon, stated:

I know men; and I tell you that Jesus Christ is not a man. Superficial minds see a resemblance between Christ and the founders of empires, and the gods of other religions. That resemblance does not exist.

There is between Christianity and whatever other religions the distance of infinity....His religion is a revelation from an intelligence which certainly is not that of man.

The religion of Christ is a mystery which subsists by its own force, and proceeds from a mind which is not a human mind. We find in it a marked individuality, which originated a train of words and actions unknown before.

Jesus is not a philosopher, for His proofs are miracles, and from the first His disciples adored Him.

Alexander, Caesar, Charlemagne, and myself founded empires; but upon what foundation did we rest the creations of our genius? Upon force! But Jesus Christ founded His upon love; and at this hour millions of men would die for Him.[4]

Emperor Napoleon Bonaparte I stated:

All systems of morality are fine. The Gospel alone has exhibited a complete assemblage of the principles of morality, divested of all absurdity. It is not composed, like your creed, of a few commonplace sentences put into bad verse. Do you wish to see that which is really sublime? Repeat the Lord's Prayer.[5]

The nature of Christ's existence is mysterious, I admit;...Reject it and the world is an inexplicable riddle; believe it and the history of our race is satisfactorily explained.[6]

The loftiest intellects since the advent of Christianity have had faith, a practical faith, in the doctrines of the Gospel:...Descrates and Newton, Liebnitz and Pascal, Racine and Corneille, Charlemagne and Louis XIV.[7]

Upon receiving a copy of Pierre Simon de Laplace's book, *Mecanique Celeste*, Napoleon Bonaparte remarked:

You have written this huge book on the system of the world without once mentioning the author of the universe.[8]

Napoleon remarked:

All things proclaim the existence of God.[9]

&

National Day of Prayer January 25, 1988, which was ratified by a Joint Resolution of the 100th Congress, declared the first Thursday of each May to be recognized as *National Day of Prayer*.

PUBLIC LAW 100-307—MAY 5, 1988
One Hundredth Congress of the United States of America
AT THE SECOND SESSION
Begun and held at the City of Washington on Monday, the twenty-fifth day of January, one thousand nine hundred and eighty-eight
AN ACT
To provide for setting aside the first Thursday in May as the date on which the National Day of Prayer is celebrated.

Be it enacted by the Senate and House of Representatives of the United States of America in Congress assembled, That the joint resolution entitled "Joint Resolution to provide for setting aside an appropriate day as a National Day of Prayer," approved April 17, 1952 (Public Law 82-324; 66 Stat. 64), is amended by striking "a suitable day each year, other than a Sunday," and inserting in lieu thereof "the first Thursday in May in each year."

Speaker of the House of Representatives
President of the Senate Pro Tempore
APPROVED
May 5, 1988
Ronald Reagan[10]

ка

John Mason Neale (1818-1866), an English poet and language scholar, knew over 20 languages. In 1842, he was ordained a clergyman and translated many hymns from their original Greek and Latin tongues. Many famous Christmas hymns were written or translated by him, including *Jerusalem the Golden; The Day is Past and Over; Come, Ye Faithful;* and the favorite *Good King Wenceslas:*

> Good King Wenceslas looked out
> On the feast of Stephen,
> When the snow lay round about,
> Deep and crisp and even. [11]

In 1861, he translated the twelfth century Latin hymn *Veni, Veni, Emmanuel* into English:

> O come, O come, Emmanuel,
> And ransom captive Israel. [12]

ка

Constitution of the State of Nebraska June 12,1875, stated:

> *Article 1, Section IV* Religion, morality, and knowledge, however, being essential to good government, it shall be the duty of the legislature to pass suitable laws...to encourage schools and the means of instruction. [13]

ка

Horatio Nelson (1758-1805), the famous British Admiral and naval hero, defeated the French fleet of Napoleon at the Battle of the Nile, August 1, 1798, and won one of the most decisive battles in naval history, the Battle of Trafalgar, October 21, 1805. Although he soundly defeated the combined French and Spanish fleets, Lord Nelson was wounded at the height of the battle. Carried below deck, he spoke these dying words:

Thank God I have done my duty.[14]

ᐧᐁ

New England, (Synod of) Churches September 30, 1648, defined the duties of citizens, functions of civil magistrates and the nature of civil government:

> *I.* God, Supreme Lord and King of all the world, hath ordained civil magistrates to be under him, over the people, and for his own glory and the public good; and to this end hath armed them with the power of the sword for the defense and encouragement of them that do well, and for the punishment of evil-doers.
>
> *II.* It is lawful for Christians to accept and execute the office of magistrate when called thereunto. In the management whereof, as they ought especially to maintain piety, justice, and peace, according to the wholesome laws of the Commonwealth, so for that end they may lawfully now, under the New Testament, wage war upon just and necessary occasions....
>
> *IV.* It is the duty of the people to pray for magistrates, to honor their persons, to pay them tribute and other dues, to obey their lawful commands, and to be subject to their authority for conscience's sake.[15]

ᐧᐁ

Constitution of the New England Confederation May 19, 1643, as covenanted together by the colonists of New Plymouth, New Haven, Massachusetts & Connecticut, stated:

> The Articles of Confederation between the plantations under the government of Massachusetts, the plantations under the government of New Plymouth, the plantations under the government of Connecticut, and the government of New Haven with the plantations in combination therewith:
> Whereas we all came to these parts of America with the same end and aim, namely, to advance the Kingdome of our Lord Jesus Christ, and to injoy the liberties of the Gospell thereof with purities and peace, and for preserving and propagating the truth and liberties of the gospell.[16]

ᐧᐁ

New England Primer 1691, was entering its second edition, as advertised by Benjamin Harris of Boston. The oldest extant copy available is dated 1737. This famous little book was used to teach colonial era children the alphabet, using rhyme and illustrations:

A In ADAM's Fall
We sinned all.

B Heaven to find,
The Bible Mind.

C Christ crucify'd
For sinners dy'd.

D The Deluge drown'd
The Earth around.

E ELIJAH hid
By Ravens fed.

F The judgment made
FELIX afraid.

G As runs the Glass,
Our Life doth pass.

H My Book and Heart
Must never part.

J JOB feels the Rod,
Yet blesses GOD.

K Proud Korah's troop
Was swallowed up.

L LOT fled to *Zoar*,
Saw fiery Shower
On *Sodom* pour.

M MOSES was he
Who *Israel's* Host
Led thro' the Sea.

N NOAH did view
The old world & new.

O Young OBADIAS,
DAVID, JOSIAS
All were pious.

P PETER deny'd
His Lord and cry'd.

Q Queen ESTHER sues
And saves the *Jews*.

R Young pious RUTH,
Left all for Truth.

S Young SAM'L dear
The Lord did fear.

T Young TIMOTHY
Learnt sin to fly.

V VASTHI for Pride,
Was set aside.

W Whales in the Sea,
GOD's Voice obey.

X XERXES did die,
And so must I.

Y While youth do chear
Death may be near.

Z ZACCHEUS he
Did climb the Tree
Our Lord to see.[17]

Originally recorded in the *Enchiridion Leonis*, dated 1160 A.D., the *New England Primer* contained this cherished prayer:

> Now I lay me down to sleep,
> I pray the Lord my soul to keep;
> If I should die before I wake,
> I pray the Lord my soul to take.[18]

❧

New Guide to the English Tongue 1740, published first in England by Thomas Dilworth, gained universal adoption in the New England schools by 1765. This book contained spelling, reading and grammar lessons, "adorned with proper Scriptures." Its first lesson, having words only three letters long or less, stated:

> No Man may put off the Law of God.
> The Way of God is no ill Way.
> My Joy is in God all the Day.
> A bad Man is a Foe to God.[19]

Noah Webster, known as the "Schoolmaster to America," used only the Bible and Thomas Dilworth's book in his earliest school. Thomas Dilworth said he wanted to rescue:

> Poor creatures from the Slavery of Sin and Satan by setting the word of God for a Lantern to our feet and a Light to our Paths.[20]

❧

Exeter, New Hampshire August 4, 1639, the colonists defined the purpose for government, stating:

> Considering with ourselves the holy will of God and our own necessity, that we should not live without wholesome laws and civil government among us, of which we are altogether destitute, do, in the name of Christ and in the sight of God, combine ourselves together to erect and set up among us such governments as shall be, to our best discerning, agreeable to the will of God....[21]

NEW HAMPSHIRE

Seal of
New Hampshire

Constitution of the State of New Hampshire
1784, 1792, required senators and representatives to be of the:

Protestant religion.(in force until 1877)[22]

The Constitution stipulated:

Part One, Article I, Section V. Every individual has a natural and unalienable right to worship God according to the dictates of his own conscience, and reason...[23]

Article I, Section VI. And every denomination of Christians demeaning themselves quietly, and as good citizens of the state, shall be equally under the protection of the laws. And no subordination of any one sect or denomination to another, shall ever be established by law.[24]

ᨀ

State of New Hampshire October 21, 1785, issued this official proclamation of the State, signed by President (Governor) John Langdon of New Hampshire:

John Langdon

A Proclamation For A General Thanksgiving
THE munificent Father of Mercies, and Sovereign Disposer of Events, having been graciously pleased to relieve the UNITED STATES of AMERICA from the Calamities of a long and dangerous war:
through the whole course of which, he continued to smile on the Labours of our Husbandmen, thereby preventing Famine (the almost inseparable Companion of War) from entering our Borders;—eventually restored to us the blessings of Peace, on Terms advantageous and honourable:
And since the happy Period, when he silenced the Noise of contending Armies, has graciously smiled on the Labours of our Hands, caused the Earth to bring forth her increase in plentiful

Harvests, and crowned the present Year with new and additional Marks of his unlimited Goodness:

It therefore becomes our indispensable Duty, not only to acknowledge, in general with the rest of Mankind, our dependence on the Supreme Ruler of the Universe, but as a People peculiarly favoured, to testify our Gratitude to the Author of all our Mercies, in the most solemn and public manner.

I DO therefore, agreeably to a Vote of the General Court, appointing Thursday the 24th Day of November next, to be observed and kept as a Day of GENERAL THANKSGIVING throughout this State, by and with the Advice of Council, issue this Proclamation, recommending to the religious Societies of every Denomination, to assemble on that Day, to celebrate the Praises of our divine Benefactor;

to acknowledge our own Unworthiness, confess our manifold Transgressions, implore his Forgiveness, and intreat the continuance of those Favours which he had been graciously pleased to bestow upon us;

that he would inspire our Rulers with Wisdom, prosper our Trade and Commerce, smile upon our Husbandry, bless our Seminaries of Learning, and spread the Gospel of his Grace over all the Earth.

And all servile Labour is forbidden on said Day.

GIVEN at the Council-Chamber in Concord, this Twenty-first Day of October, in the Year of our LORD, One Thousand Seven Hundred and Eighty-five, and in the Tenth Year of the Independence of the UNITED STATES of AMERICA. [25]

&

State of New Hampshire, February 21, 1786, under President (Governor) John Langdon of New Hampshire, made this official proclamation to the State:

A Proclamation For A Day of Public FASTING and PRAYER Throughout this State [1786]:

Vain is the acknowledgment of a Supreme Ruler of the Universe, unless such acknowledgments influence our practice, and call forth those expressions of homage and adoration that are due to his character and providential government, agreeably to the light of nature, enforced by revelation, and countenanced by the practice of civilized nations, in humble and fervent application to the throne for needed mercies, and gratitude for favors received.

It having been the laudable practice of this State, at the opening of the Spring, to set apart a day for such denomination, to assemble together on said together on said day, in their respective places of public worship;

that the citizens of this State may with one heart and voice, penitently confess their manifold sins and transgressions, and fervently implore the divine benediction, that a true spirit of repentance and humiliation may be poured out upon all orders and degrees of men, and a compleat and universal reformation take place:

that he who gave wisdom and fortitude in the scenes of battle, would give prudence and direction to extricate us from succeeding embarrassments, build up, support and establish this rising Empire;

particularly, that he would be pleased to bless the great Council of the United States of America, and direct their deliberations to the wise and best determinations, succeed our embassies at foreign Courts, bless our Allies, and national Benefactors:

that he would always be pleased, to keep this State under his most holy protection: that all in the legislature, executive and judicial departments, may be guided and supported by wisdom, integrity and firmness, that all the people through this State, and through the land, may be animated by a true estimation of their privileges, and taught to secure, by their patriotism and virtue, what they have acquired by their valour:

that a spirit of emulation, industry, economy and frugality, may be diffused abroad, and that we may all be disposed to lead quiet and peaceable lives, in all godliness and honesty:

that he would be graciously pleased to bless us in the seasons of the year, and cause the earth to yield her increase, prosper our husbandry, merchandise, navigation and fishery, and all the labour of our hands, and give us to hear the voice of health in our habitations, and enjoy plenty of our borders:

that unanimity, peace and harmony, may be promoted and continue, and a spirit of universal philanthropy pervade the land: that he would be pleased to smile upon the means of education, and bless every institution of useful knowledge;

and above all, that he would rain down righteousness upon the earth, revive religion, and spread abroad the knowledge of the true GOD, the Saviour of man, throughout the world.

And all servile labour and recreations are forbidden on said day.

GIVEN at the Council-Chamber in Portsmouth, this twenty-first day of February, in the year of our LORD, one thousand seven hundred and eighty-six, and in the tenth year of the Sovereignty and Independence of the United States of America. [26]

੨

New Haven Colony Charter April 3, 1644, adopted the rules for governing the courts of the New Haven Colony, stating:

> The judicial laws of God, as they were delivered by Moses...[are to] be a rule to all the courts in this jurisdiction...[27]

ða

New Jersey Colony 1697, Governor Basse proclaimed:

> It being very necessary for the good and prosperity of this province that our principal care be, in obedience to the laws of God, to endeavor as much as in us lyeth the extirpation of all sorts of looseness and profanity, and to unite in the fear and love of God and one another,..
>
> Take due care that all laws made and provided for the suppression of vice and encouraging of religion and virtue, particularly the observance of the Lord's day, be duly put into execution.[28]

Inscribed on the Provincial Seal of New Jersey was Proverbs 14:34:

> Righteousness exalteth a nation.[29]

ða

NEW JERSEY.

Seal of New Jersey

Constitution of the State of New Jersey 1844, reads:

> We, the people of the State of New Jersey, grateful to Almighty God for the civil and religious liberty which He hath so long permitted us to enjoy, and looking to Him for a blessing upon our endeavors to secure and transmit the same unimpaired to succeeding generations, do ordain and establish this Constitution.[30]

ða

Board of Education of Netcong, New Jersey prior to 1970, endorsed this public school policy:

> On each school day before class instruction begins, a period of not
> more that five minutes shall be available to those teachers and students
> who may wish to participate voluntarily in the free exercise of religion
> as guaranteed by the United States Constitution...[31]

ॐ

Sir Isaac Newton (1642-1727), the famous discoverer of the laws
of universal gravitation, also formulated the three laws of motion,
which aided in advancing the discipline of dynamics, and helped
develop calculus into a comprehensive branch of mathematics.

Sir Isaac Newton was a mathematician, scientist, and
philosopher. He constructed the first reflecting telescope, laid the
foundation for the great law of energy conservation and developed
the *particle theory* of light propagation. In 1704, Sir Isaac Newton
wrote his work entitled *Optics*, in which he stated:

> God in the beginning formed matter in solid, massy, hard,
> impenetrable, movable particles, of such sizes and figures, and with
> such other properties, and in such proportion to space, as most
> conduced to the end for which he formed them.[32]

Sir Isaac Newton asserted:

> We account the Scriptures of God to be the most sublime
> philosophy. I find more sure marks of authenticity in the Bible than in
> any profane history whatsoever....Worshipping God and the Lamb in
> the temple: God, for his benefaction in creating all things, and the
> Lamb, for his benefaction in redeeming us with his blood.[33]

> There is one God, the Father, ever-living, omnipresent, omniscient,
> almighty, the Maker of heaven and earth, and one Mediator between
> God and man, the man Christ Jesus....
> To us there is but one God, the Father, of whom are all things, and
> one Lord Jesus Christ, by whom are all things, and we by Him. That is,
> we are to worship the Father alone as God Almighty, and Jesus alone
> as the Lord, the Messiah, the Great King, the Lamb of God who was
> slain, and hath redeemed us with His blood, and made us kings and
> priests.[34]

> The Book of Revelation exhibits to us the same peculiarities as that

of Nature....The history of the Fall of Man—of the introduction of moral and physical evil, the prediction of the Messiah, the actual advent of our Saviour, His instructions, His miracles, His death, His resurrection, and the subsequent propagation of His religion by the unlettered fishermen of Galilee, are each a stumbling-block to the wisdom of this world....

But through the system of revealed truth which this Book contains is, like that of the universe, concealed from common observation, yet the labors of the centuries have established its Divine origin, and developed in all its order and beauty the great plan of human restoration.[35]

John Newton (1725-1807), was the captain of a slave trading ship who became converted and wrote the famous spiritual song *Amazing Grace*. He was so depraved in his former profession that even his crew became disgusted. Once in a drunken stupor he fell overboard, and to save him his crew threw a harpoon through his leg and yanked him back aboard. His constant limp thereafter was a reminder to him of how God could save such a wretch. He wrote:

> Amazing Grace, How sweet the sound,
> That saved a wretch like me.
> I once was lost, but now am found,
> Was blind, but now I see.[36]

Colonial Legislature of New York Colony 1665, passed this act:

> Whereas, The public worship of God is much discredited for want of painful [laborious] and able ministers to instruct the people in the true religion, it is ordered that a church shall be built in each parish, capable of holding two hundred persons; that ministers of every church shall preach every Sunday, and pray for the king, queen, the Duke of York, and the royal family; and to marry persons after legal publication of license...
>
> Sunday is not to be profaned by traveling, by laborers, or vicious persons...

Church wardens to report twice a year all misdemeanors, such as swearing, profaneness, Sabbath-breaking, drunkenness, fornication, adultery, and all such abominable sins.[37]

୬

NEW YORK.

Seal of New York

Constitution of the State of New York 1777, stated:

The free exercise and enjoyment of religious profession and worship, without discrimination or preference, shall forever hereafter be allowed, within this State, to all mankind: Provided, that the liberty of conscience, hereby granted, shall not be so construed as to excuse acts of licentiousness.[38]

୬

Preamble of the Constitution of the State of New York 1846, reads:

We, the people of the State of New York, grateful to Almighty God for our freedom: in order to secure its blessings, do establish this Constitution.[39]

୬

Chester County, New York August 23, 1831, as related in *The New York Spectator*, reported that a judge refused to admit the evidence of a man who declared he did not believe in God, on the grounds that the witness had destroyed beforehand all confidence of the court in his testimony. The newspaper explained:

The court of commons pleas of Chester county (New York), a few days since rejected a witness who declared his disbelief in the existence of God. The presiding judge remarked, that he had not before been aware that there was a man living who did not believe in the existence of God; that this belief constituted the sanction of all testimony in a court of justice: and that he knew of no cause in a Christian country, where a witness had been permitted to testify without such belief.[40]

ટ્ર

Supreme Court of New York 1811, in the case of the *People v. Ruggles*, 8 Johns 545-547, Chief Justice Chancellor Kent stated:

> The defendant was indicted...in December, 1810, for that he did, on the 2nd day of September, 1810...wickedly, maliciously, and blasphemously, utter, and with a loud voice publish, in the presence and hearing of divers good and Christian people, of and concerning the Christian religion, and of and concerning Jesus Christ, the false, scandalous, malicious, wicked and blasphemous words following: "Jesus Christ was a bastard, and his mother must be a whore," in contempt of the Christian religion...the defendant was tried and found guilty, and was sentenced by the court to be imprisoned for three months, and to pay a fine of $500.[41]

The argument which the prosecuting attorney had presented to the court, explained:

> While the constitution of the State has saved the rights of conscience, and allowed a free and fair discussion of all points of controversy among religious sects, it has left the principal engrafted on the body of our common law, that Christianity is part of the laws of the State, untouched and unimpaired.[42]

Chief Justice Kent delivered the courts decision in this case:

> Such words uttered with such a disposition were an offense at common law. In *Taylor's* case the defendant was convicted upon information of speaking similar words, and the Court...said that Christianity was parcel of the law, and to cast contumelious reproaches upon it, tended to weaken the foundation of moral obligation, and the efficacy of oaths.
> And in the case of *Rex v. Woolston,* on a like conviction, the Court said...that whatever strikes at the root of Christianity tends manifestly to the dissolution of civil government....the authorities show that blasphemy against God and...profane ridicule of Christ or the Holy Scriptures (which are equally treated as blasphemy), are offenses punishable at common law, whether uttered by words or writings...because it tends to corrupt the morals of the people, and to destroy good order.
> Such offenses have always been considered independent of any

religious establishment or the rights of the Church. They are treated as affecting the essential interests of civil society....

We stand equally in need, now as formerly, of all the moral discipline, and of those principles of virtue, which help to bind society together.

The people of this State, in common with the people of this country, profess the general doctrines of Christianity, as the rule of their faith and practice; and to scandalize the author of these doctrines is not only, in a religious point of view, extremely impious, but, even in respect to the obligations due to society, is a gross violation of decency and good order.

Nothing could be more injurious to the tender morals of the young, than to declare such profanity lawful....

The free, equal, and undisturbed enjoyment of religious opinion, whatever it may be, and free and decent discussions on any religious subject, is granted and secured; but to revile....the religion professed by almost the whole community, is an abuse of that right....

We are a Christian people, and the morality of the country is deeply engrafted upon Christianity, and not upon the doctrines or worship of those impostors [other religions]....

[We are] people whose manners are refined and whose morals have been elevated and inspired with a more enlarged benevolence, by means of the Christian religion. Though the constitution has discarded religious establishments, it does not forbid judicial cognizance of those offenses against religion and morality which have no reference to any such establishment....[offenses which] strike at the root of moral obligation, and weaken the security of the social ties....

This [constitutional] declaration (noble and magnanimous as it is, when duly understood) never meant to withdraw religion in general, and with it the best sanctions of moral and social obligation from all consideration and notice of the law....

To construe it as breaking down the common law barriers against licentious, wanton, and impious attacks upon Christianity itself, would be an enormous perversion of its meaning....

Christianity, in its enlarged sense, as a religion revealed and taught in the Bible, is not unknown to our law....

The Court are accordingly of opinion that the judgement....must be affirmed.[43]

ଌ

Supreme Court of New York stated in the case of *Lindenmuller v. The People*, 33 Barbour, 561:

Christianity...is in fact, and ever has been, the religion of the people. This fact is everywhere prominent in all our civil and political history, and has been, from the first, recognized and acted upon by the people, as well as by constitutional conventions, by legislatures and by courts of justice.[44]

&

Supreme Court of New York 1958, stated in the case of *Baer v. Kolmorgen*, 181 N. Y. S. 2d. 230, 237 (Sup. Ct. N. Y. 1958):

Much has been written in recent years concerning Thomas Jefferson's reference in 1802 to "a wall of separation between church and State." ...Jefferson's figure of speech has received so much attention that one would almost think at times that it is to be found somewhere in our Constitution.[45] *IT IS NOT found IN THE CONSTITUTION*

&

Supreme Court of New York December 30, 1993, in the Appellate Division, stated in the case of *Alfonso v. Fernandez*, that the public schools in New York City are:

Prohibited from dispensing condoms to unemancipated minor students without the prior consent of their parents or guardians, or without an opt-out provision....

[The condom distribution plan] is tantamount to condoning promiscuity and sexual permissiveness, and that the exposure to condoms and their ready availability may encourage sexual relations among adolescents at an earlier age and/or with more frequency, thereby weakening their moral and religious values....

[The court agrees that] supplying condoms to students upon request has absolutely nothing to do with education, [but is a] health service....

[Parents should not be] compelled by state authority to send their children into an environment where they will be permitted, even encouraged, to obtain a contraceptive device, which the parents disfavor as a matter of private belief....

The amici miss the point. The primary purpose of the Board of Education is not to serve as a health provider. Its reason for being is education. No judicial or legislative authority directs or permits teachers and other public school educators to dispense condoms to minor, unemancipated students without the knowledge or consent of their parents. Nor do we believe that they have any inherent authority to do so....

[Parents] enjoy a well-recognized liberty interest in rearing and educating their children to accord with their own views, [citing U.S. Supreme Court cases from the 1920's, *Pierce v. Society of Sisters* and *Meyer v. Nebraska*] The Constitution gives parents the right to regulate their children's sexual behavior as best they can, [a contraceptive decision] is clearly within the purview of the petitioners' constitutionally protected right to rear their children....

[The AIDS problem cannot force parents] to surrender a parenting right—specifically, to influence and guide the sexual activity of their children without state interference....

The threat of AIDS cannot summarily obliterate this Nation's fundamental values....We conclude that the condom availability component of the program violates the petitioners' constitutional due process rights to direct the upbringing of their children.[46]

ə.

Robert Carter Nicholas (1715-1780) served in the Virginia House of Burgesses as a representative of James City and was appointed Judge of the High Court of Chancery and Court of Appeals. He was a member of the Committees of Correspondence, attended all major conventions, and served as President Pro-tem of the Continental Convention in 1775.

After the British navy closed the port of Boston, in retaliation for the tea dumped into the harbor to protest taxes, the colonies surrounding Massachusets responded with sympathy and action.

On May 24, 1773, Robert Carter Nicholas, Treasurer of the House of Burgesses in Virginia, proposed a *Day of Fasting, Humiliation and Prayer*. It was approved with virtually no argument:

> This House, being deeply impressed with apprehension of the great dangers to be derived to British America from the hostile invasion of the city of Boston in our Sister Colony of Massachusetts Bay, whose commerce and harbor are, on the first day of June next, to be stopped by an armed force, deem it highly necessary that the said first day of June be set apart, by the members of this House, as a Day of Fasting, Humiliation and Prayer, devoutly to implore the Divine interposition, for averting the heavy calamity which threatens

destruction to our civil rights and the evils of civil war;

to give us one heart and mind firmly opposed, by all just and proper means, every injury to American rights;

and that the minds of His Majesty and his Parliament, may be inspired from above with wisdom, moderation and justice, to remove from the loyal people of America all cause of danger from a continued pursuit of measures pregnant with their ruin.[47]

❧

Reinhold Niebur (1892-1971), was an internationally known writer, teacher, lecturer. Graduating from Yale Divinity School, he became a minister known for being concerned with the needs of the poor. He later became the dean of the Union Theological Seminary in New York City. Reinhold Niebur wrote *The Serenity Prayer* in 1934:

God, give us grace to accept with serenity the things that cannot be changed, courage to change the things which should be changed, and the wisdom to distinguish the one from the other.[48]

In *Discerning the Signs of the Times*, 1949, Reinhold Niebur wrote:

Humor is a prelude to faith and
Laughter is the beginning of prayer.[49]

❧

Martin Niemoeller (1892-1984), a German citizen during the Nazi regime, stated:

In Germany they came first for the Communists, and I didn't speak up because I wasn't a Communist. Then they came for the Jews, and I didn't speak up because I wasn't a Jew. Then they came for the trade unionists, and I didn't speak up because I wasn't a trade unionist. Then they came for the Catholics, and I didn't speak up because I was a Protestant. Then they came for me, and by that time no one was left to speak up.[50]

❧

Richard Milhous Nixon (1913-1994), the 37th President of the United States, declared in his Inaugural Address, January 20, 1969:

> Let us go forward firm in our faith....sustained by our confidence in the will of God.[51]

❧

North American Review 1867, reported:

> The American government and the Constitution is the most precious possession which the world holds, or which the future can inherit. This is true—true because the American system is the political expression of Christian ideas.[52]

❧

Colony of Carolina 1650, was originally named "Carolana" or "Charles' land," after King Charles I of England who granted it to Sir Robert Heath in 1629. Carolina was originally part of Virginia, named after the "Virgin Queen" Elizabeth by Sir Walter Raleigh, who explored the area and attempted to found a settlement on Roanoke Island beginning April 9, 1585.

Elizabeth I (Elizabeth Tudor; the "Virgin Queen")

On August 13, 1587, the members of the colony converted the Indian Manteo and he was baptized into the Christian faith. That same month the first child was born in America, and she was baptized Virginia Dare. The Roanoke Colony was unsuccessful and later became known as the "Lost Colony."[53]

It wasn't until the 1650's that English colonists began settling the area permanently. The first governor, William Sayle, was a Nonconformist and allowed religious toleration to all denominations: Calvinists and Baptists from England and parts of New England, Huguenots (French Protestants), Episcopalians, Scotch-Irish Presbyterians, Lutherans, German Reformed, Moravians, etc.[54]

Of the many Christians that began to settle in North Carolina, beginning in 1653, the Quaker missionaries were among the most notable, with even George Fox, the founder of Quakerism, preaching there. At a later date, the Quaker family of Daniel Boone, along with other Quaker families, pioneered the Yadkin River Valley along the North Carolina frontier. In 1727 the first Baptist congregation was formed, followed by the Methodists, who preached strongly against slavery and recognized Negro ministers.[55]

ᴥ

Charter of Carolina 1663, was granted by King Charles II to Sir William Berkeley and the seven other lord proprietors. (This area initially had been granted by King Charles I to Sir Robert Heath in 1629.) The Charter stated:

> Being excited with a laudable and pious zeal for the propagation of the Christian faith....[they] have humbly besought leave of us...to transport and make an ample colony...unto a certain country...in the parts of America not yet cultivated or planted, and only inhabited by some barbarous people, who have no knowledge of Almighty God.[56]

ᴥ

Fundamental Constitutions of the Carolinas 1663, drawn up by the famous philosopher, John Locke, at the request of Sir William Berkeley and the seven other lord proprietors of the colony,[57] stated:

> No man shall be permitted to be a freeman of Carolina, or to have any estate of habitation within it that doth not acknowledge a God, and that God is publicly and solemnly to be worshiped.[58]

ᴥ

North Carolina, Mecklenburg County Resolutions May 20, 1775, written in Charlotte by a convention of Scotch-Irish Presbyterians, prepared by the elder Ephraim Brevard and sent by special courier to the Continental Congress. It reads:

> We do hereby dissolve the political bands which have connected us with the mother-country, and hereby absolve ourselves from all allegiance to the British crown....
>
> Resolved, That we hereby declare ourselves a free and independent people; are, and of a right ought to be, a sovereign and self-governing association, under control of no power other than that of our God and the general government of Congress; to the maintenance of which we solemnly pledge to each other our mutual cooperation and our lives, our fortunes and our most sacred honor.[59]

Constitution of the State of North Carolina
1776, stated:

NORTH CAROLINA

> There shall be no establishment of any one religious church or denomination in this State in preference to any other.[60]

Seal of North Carolina

> *Article XXXII* That no person who shall deny the being of God, or the truth of the Protestant religion, or the divine authority of the Old or New Testaments, or who shall hold religious principles incompatible with the freedom and safety of the State, shall be capable of holding any office or place of trust or profit in the civil department within this State. (until 1876)[61]

In 1835, the word "Protestant" was changed to "Christian."[62]

In 1868, among the persons disqualified for office were:

> All persons who shall deny the being of Almighty God.[63]

Preamble of the Constitution of the State of North Carolina
1868, reads:

> We the people of the State of North Carolina, grateful to Almighty

God, the sovereign ruler of nations, for the preservation of the American Union and the existence of our civil, political, and religious liberties, and acknowledging our dependence upon Him for the continuance of those blessings to us and our posterity, do, for the more certain security thereof and for the better government of this State, ordain and establish this constitution.[64]

꽈

Northwest Ordinance July 13, 1787, passed as "An Ordinance for the Government of the Territory of the United States, North-West of the River Ohio." Its name was later shortened to the Northwest Ordinance. This Ordinance, recognized in *The United States Code Annotated* as one of America's four most significant governmental documents, was later passed by the United States Congress, July 21, 1789, and signed into law by President Washington, August 4, 1789, during the same time the First Amendment was being formulated. It stated:

SECTION 13. And, for extending the fundamental principles of civil and religious liberty, which form the basis whereon these republics, their laws and constitutions are erected:

to fix and establish those principles as the basis of all laws, constitutions and governments, which forever hereafter shall be formed in the said territory:

to provide also for the establishment of states, and permanent government therein, and for their admission to a share in the federal councils in an equal footing with the original states, at as early period as may be consistent with the general interest:

SECTION 14. It is hereby ordained and declared by the authority aforesaid, That the following articles shall be considered as articles of compact, between the original states and the people and states of the said territory, and forever remain unalienable, unless by common consent, to wit:

ARTICLE I. No person, demeaning himself in a peaceable and orderly manner, shall ever be molested on account of his mode of worship or religious sentiments in the said territory....

ARTICLE III. Religion, morality, and knowledge being necessary to good government and the happiness of mankind, schools and the means of education shall forever be encouraged.[65]

꽈

O

Daniel O'Connell (1775-1847), was an Irish patriotic leader and member of the English Parliament, 1829-1847. A famous orator, O'Connell was known as "The Liberator" because he was responsible for the Catholic Emancipation Act in England:

Nothing is politically right which is morally wrong.[1]

ð

Flannery O'Connor (1925-1964), born in Savannah, Georgia, was a famous American author, whose published works include *Wise Blood*, 1952; *A Good Man is Hard to Find*, 1955; *The Violent Bear It Away*, 1960; *Everything That Rises Must Converge*; and *Mystery and Manners*. Flannery O'Connor stated in a talk at Notre Dame University in the spring of 1957:

Southern culture has fostered a type of imagination that has been influenced by Christianity of a not too unorthodox kind and by a strong devotion to the Bible, which has kept our minds attached to the concrete and the living symbol.[2]

ð

James Edward Oglethorpe (1696-1785), was the founder of the Colony of Georgia, named for King George II, in 1732. The colony was conceived as a place of refuge for poor debtors from England and persecuted Protestants from Europe.[3] One hundred settlers moved into the area, quickly followed by the Moravians, who were enthusiastic Christian missionaries, and other Christian groups. As the settlers touched the shore, they knelt and declared:

Our end in leaving our native country is not to gain riches and honor, but singly this: to live wholly to the glory of God.[4]

Their object was:

To make Georgia a religious colony.[5]

James Edward Oglethorpe

Constitution of the State of Ohio November 1, 1802, stated:

Article VIII, Section 3. Religion, morality, and knowledge, being essentially necessary to the good government and the happiness of mankind, schools and the means of instruction shall forever be encouraged by legislative provision.[6]

Motto of the State of Ohio 1959, stated:

With God All Things are Possible[7]

State of Ohio February 18, 1992, declared:

STATE OF OHIO
Executive Department
Office of the Governor
COLUMBUS
PROCLAMATION

WHEREAS, the National Day of Prayer is a tradition first proclaimed by the Continental Congress in 1775; and

WHEREAS, In 1988, legislation was unanimously ratified by both Houses of Congress and signed by President Ronald Reagan stating that the National Day of Prayer was to be observed on the first Thursday of every May; and

WHEREAS, President George Bush has set aside May 7, 1992, as the 41st consecutive observance of the National Day of Prayer; and

WHEREAS, it is fitting and proper to give thanks to the Lord by observing this day in Ohio when all may acknowledge our blessing and express gratitude for them, while recognizing the need for strengthening religious and moral values in our state and nation;

NOW, THEREFORE, I, GEORGE V. VOINOVICH, Governor of the State of Ohio, do hereby proclaim May 7, 1992, as

A DAY OF PRAYER IN OHIO

throughout the state of Ohio. I urge all citizens to observe this day in ways appropriate to its importance and significance.

In Testimony Whereof, I have hereunto subscribed my name and caused the Great Seal of the State of Ohio to be affixed at Columbus, this eighteenth day of February in the year of our Lord, one thousand nine hundred and ninety two.

George V. Voinovich	Bob Taft
Governor of the State of Ohio	Secretary of State[8]

❧

State of Oklahoma District Court—Tulsa County July 15, 1993, in the case of *Crowley, Gaines and Ries v. Tilton*, District Judge Robert J. Scott granted the defendants summary judgement, stating:

> Initially Christianity was taught by Christ. He then taught disciples who went out over the world to teach others. This process has spread to a major world body of believers. Religion should be permitted to use contemporary means to communicate religious messages in the form of TV appeal to mass audiences, follow-up communication by computerized mailing designed to convert and symbolic tokens to cause response to the messages.
>
> The context of the message is belief, and the freedom for belief is absolute. When a minister or a church urges one to take certain actions based upon a representation that God will act toward that person in positive and rewarding ways, they are entitled to absolute protection as a belief.[9]

❧

Old Deluder Satan Law 1647, was passed by the Colonies of Massachusetts and Connecticut to prevent illiteracy and to preclude the abuse of power over a population ignorant of Scriptures, as had been the case in Europe. It stated:

> It being one chiefe project of that old deluder, Sathan, to keepe

men from the knowledge of the scriptures, as in former time...

It is therefore ordered....[that] after the Lord hath increased [the settlement] to the number of fifty howshoulders, [they] shall forthwith appoint one within theire towne, to teach all such children as shall resorte to him, to write and read...

and it is further ordered, That where any towne shall increase to the number of one hundred families or howshoulders, they shall sett up a grammar schoole for the university.[10]

ﾞﾞ

Henry Opukahai'a (d.1818), was the first Hawaiian convert to Christianity. Orphaned at age 10, he was raised by his uncle to be a pagan priest (kahuna) of the Hawaiian religion. He grew disillusioned with the rituals and chants, and left on an American ship bound for New England with his Hawaiian friend, Thomas Hopu. There he was befriended by students and professors of Yale College and soon became a Christian. He studied Greek and Hebrew and translated sections of the Bible into the Hawaiian language. In his memoirs, which sold 500,000 copies after his death, Henry Opukahai'a wrote:

My poor countrymen, without knowledge of the true God, and ignorant of the future world, have no Bible to read, no Sabbath....[11]

Henry Opukahai'a's zeal for Christ and love for the Hawaiian people inspired the first American Board of Missions to Hawaii in 1820. It was led by his friend, Thomas Hopu, Hiram Bingham, and a small group of New Englanders. They reduced the Hawaiian language to writing, set up schools and churches, and convinced the Hawaiian women to wear dresses. Amid much solemnity and rejoicing the remains of Henry Opukahai'a were returned to Hawaii in 1993, 175 years after his death in Connecticut, and were reinterred at Napo'opo'o, Kona, Hawaii.[12]

ﾞﾞ

℗

Robert Morris Page (1903-1970), was the physicist who invented pulsation radar used for the detection of aircraft. He served with the Naval Research Laboratory in Washington, D.C., received the U.S. Navy Distinguished Civilian Service Award, the Presidential Certificate of Merit, the IRE Fellowship Harry Diamond Memorial Award, and the Stuart Ballantyne Medal of the Franklin Institute. Robert Morris Page held thirty-seven patents, mostly in radar. He wrote:

> The authenticity of the writings of the prophets, though the men themselves are human, is established by such things as the prediction of highly significant events far in the future that could be accomplished only through a knowledge obtained from a realm which is not subject to the laws of time as we know them.
>
> One of the great evidences is the long series of prophecies concerning Jesus the Messiah. These prophecies extend hundreds of years prior to the birth of Christ. They include a vast amount of detail concerning Christ himself, His nature and the things He would do when He came—things which to the natural world, or the scientific world, remain to this day completely inexplicable.[1]

Thomas Paine (1737-1809), was the American Revolutionary author who wrote a famous 16-pamphlet series entitled, *The American Crisis*, which he signed "Common Sense." Greatly fanning the flames of colonial independence, his first essay, issued December 23, 1776, was read aloud to the Colonial Army at Valley Forge by order of General Washington. In it, Paine wrote:

Thomas Paine

Tyranny, like hell, is not easily conquered; yet we have this consolation with us, that the harder the conflict, the more glorious the triumph. What we obtain too cheaply, we esteem too lightly; 'tis dearness only that gives everything its value. Heaven knows how to put a price upon its goods; and it would be strange indeed if so celestial an article as freedom should not be highly rated.[2]

George Washington

The cause of America is in a great measure the cause of all mankind. Where, say some, is the king of America? I'll tell you, friend, He reigns above.[3]

Yet that we may not appear to be defective even in earthly honors, let a day be solemnly set apart for proclaiming the charter; let it be placed on the divine law, the Word of God; let a crown be placed thereon.[4]

The Almighty implanted in us these inextinguishable feelings for good and wise purposes. They are the guardians of His image in our heart. They distinguish us from the herd of common animals.[5]

Thomas Paine lost his popularity when he wrote *The Age of Reason,* a work embracing French Rationalism. In his later years, though, he had a profound change and wrote:

I would give worlds, if I had them, if *The Age of Reason* had never been published. O Lord, help! Stay with me! It is hell to be left alone.[6]

Thomas Paine, a man who was an "Englishman by birth, French citizen by decree, and American by adoption," gave his last words:

I die in perfect composure and resignation to the will of my Creator, God.[7]

❧

Ambroise Paré (1517-1590), was a pioneer French surgeon, who greatly raised the standards for surgery. He rose to fame as a field surgeon in the French army; he discarded the common practice of using boiling oils and hot irons in favor of cleansing wounds with ointments and surgically tying off major arteries. Ambroise Paré was so successful that he was appointed to the court and served four different kings. The favorite saying of Ambroise Paré was:

> I treated him, God cured him.[8]

ہ

Theodore Parker (1810-1860), was an American abolitionist, clergyman, and graduate of Harvard. He spoke strongly against slavery, declaring:

> The Bible goes equally to the cottage of the peasant, and the palace of the king. It is woven into literature, and colors the talk of the street. The bark of the merchant cannot sail without it; and no ship of war goes to the conflict but it is there. It enters men's closets; directs their conduct, and mingles in all the grief and cheerfulness of life.[9]

Theodore Parker

On May 29, 1850, Theodore Parker wrote *The American Idea*, in which he stated:

> A democracy—that is a government of all the people, by all the people, for all the people; of course, a government of the principles of eternal justice, the unchanging law of God; for shortness' sake I will call it the idea of Freedom.[10]

ہ

Blaise Pascal (1623-1662), was renowned as the "Father of the Science of Hydrostatics." He helped establish the principles of hydrodynamics and made invaluable contributions in the areas of mathematical treatment of conic sections, the theory of probability, and differential calculus, with the invention of Pascal's triangle for calculating the coefficients of a binomial expansion. He also helped develop the barometer through his discoveries in fluid mechanics, known as "Pascal's Principle." He wrote his

Lettres provinciales in 1656-57; and in 1670 published his highly influential religious work, entitled *Pensees sur la religion.* In it, Blaise Pascal wrote:

> Men blaspheme what they don't know.[11]

Blaise Pascal was well-known for his famous "Wager of Pascal":

> How can anyone lose who chooses to become a Christian? If, when he dies, there turns out to be no God and his faith was in vain, he has lost nothing—in fact, he has been happier in life than his nonbelieving friends. If, however, there is a God and a heaven and hell, then he has gained heaven and his skeptical friends will have lost everything in hell![12]

In his work, *Thoughts, Letters, and Opuscules,* Blaise Pascal declared:

> We know God only through Jesus Christ. Without this Mediator, is taken away all communication with God; through Jesus Christ we know God. All those who have pretended to know God, and prove Him without Jesus Christ, have only had impotent proofs.
>
> But, to prove Jesus Christ we have the prophecies which are good and valid proofs. And those prophecies, being fulfilled, and truly proved by the event, indicate the certainty of these truths, and therefore the truth of the divinity of Jesus Christ. In Him, and by Him, then, we know God. Otherwise, and without Scripture, without original sin, without a necessary Mediator, we can not absolutely prove God, nor teach a good doctrine and sound morals.
>
> But by Jesus Christ and in Jesus Christ, we prove God and teach doctrine and morals. Jesus Christ, then, is the true God of men. Not only do we know God only through Jesus Christ, but we know ourselves only through Jesus Christ.
>
> We know life, death, only through Jesus Christ. Except by Jesus Christ we know not what life is, what our death is, what God is, what we ourselves are. Thus, without Scripture, which has only Jesus Christ for its object, we know nothing, and we see not only obscurity and confusion in the nature of God, but in nature herself. Without Jesus Christ, man must be in sin and misery; with Jesus Christ, man is exempt from sin and misery. In Him is all our virtue, and all our felicity. Out of Him, there is nothing but sin, misery, error, darkness,

death, and despair.[13]

After his death, this writing was found in Pascal's effects:

"The God of Abraham, the God of Isaac, the God of Jacob," not of philosophers and scholars.[14]

ð›

Louis Pasteur(1822-1895), was the French scientist who developed the process of "pasteurization" for milk, the vaccines for anthrax and chicken cholera in 1881, and the rabies vaccine in 1885. As a physicist and chemist, he revolutionized the medical field by establishing the germ theory of disease, organic basis and regulation of fermentation, and bacteriology. His research laid the foundation for the control of tuberculosis, cholera, diphtheria, tetanus, and many other diseases. In 1854 he was appointed dean of the faculty of sciences at Lille University, and in 1888 the Pasteur Institute was founded to treat rabies and for advanced biological research.

In describing anaerobic bacteria, Louis Pasteur commented:

The more I study nature, the more I stand amazed at the work of the Creator. Into his tiniest creatures, God has placed extraordinary properties that turn them into agents of destruction of dead matter.[15]

Louis Pasteur was questioned in his older years concerning faith. He replied:

The more I know, the more does my faith approach that of the Breton peasant. Could I but know all, I would have the faith of a Breton peasant woman.[16]

Being one of the first European scientists to reject the theory of spontaneous generation and evolution, Louis Pasteur insisted that life only arises from life. He explained:

Microscopic beings must come into the world from parents similar to themselves....There is something in the depths of our souls which tells us that the world may be more than a mere combination of events.[17]

✳Louis Pasteur declared in one of his lectures:

> Science brings man nearer to God.[18]

૪

William Paterson (1745-1806), one of the signers of the Constitution, was a member of the Continental Congress, a lawyer, a state attorney general and a U.S. senator. He also served as Governor of New Jersey (after Governor Livingston died), and in 1793 he was appointed by President George Washington to be a justice on the United States Supreme Court. The people of his state esteemed him so much that they named the city of Paterson, New Jersey, after him.

William Paterson

William Paterson moved from Ireland with his strong Presbyterian family when he was two years old. He attended Princeton College during a time when there was a strong evangelical movement (of the 18 students in his class, 12 became ministers). The official motto of Princeton was:

> Under God's Power She Flourishes.[19]

The first president of Princeton, Jonathan Dickinson, declared:

> Cursed be all that learning that is contrary to the cross of Christ.[20]

Jonathan Dickinson

An entry in Paterson's personal journal, during a visit in 1776 to the West Indies, gives insight into his character:

> On my arrival in the West Indies in the year 1776, a new scene was

opened to me for which I was little prepared, for I had previously lived with religious people, and my new acquaintances, and those with whom I was to transact business, were the reverse of this.

No one went there to settle for life; all were in quest of fortune, to retire and spend it elsewhere; character was little thought of. Of course it required the utmost circumspection and caution to steer clear of difficulties.

A kind superintending Providence, in this, as in many other concerns of my life, enabled me, however, to surmount every difficulty, young and inexperienced as I then was.[21]

William Penn (1644-1718), the founder of Pennsylvania, was the son of the famous British Navy Admiral William Penn, who discovered Bermuda and helped strengthen Charles II's throne in England. William studied at Oxford University, and later studied law. At the age of 22, William Penn was touched through a sermon delivered by Thomas Loe, entitled, "The Sandy Foundation Shaken." To the heartbreak of his father, he gave up his brilliant future to convert to the Christian truths of the Society of Friends, or Quakers, who at that time were greatly scorned and ridiculed.[22]

William Penn

In his *Treatise on the Religion of the Quakers*, William Penn proclaimed:

> I do declare to the whole world that we believe the Scriptures to contain a declaration of the mind and will of God in and to those ages in which they were written; being given forth by the Holy Ghost moving in the hearts of holy men of God; that they ought also to be read, believed, and fulfilled in our day; being used for reproof and instruction, that the man of God may be perfect. They are a declaration and testimony of heavenly things themselves, and, as such, we carry a high respect for them. We accept them as the words of God Himself.[23]

Young Penn became a Quaker preacher and writer, suffering imprisonment over three times for his faith. Once he was imprisoned in the Tower of London for eight months, during which time he wrote the classic book, *No Cross, No Crown:*[24]

> No pain, no palm; no thorns, no throne; no gall, no glory; no cross, no crown....[25]

✓ Christ's cross is Christ's way to Christ's crown. This is the subject of the following discourse, first written during my confinement in the Tower of London in the year of 1668, now reprinted with great enlargement of matter and testimonies, that thou mayest be won to Christ, or if won already, brought nearer to Him. It is a path which God in his everlasting kindness guided my feet into, in the flower of my youth, when about two and twenty years of age.

He took me by the hand and led me out of the pleasures, vanities and hopes of the world. I have tasted of Christ's judgements, and of his mercies, and of the world's frowns and reproaches. I rejoice in my experience, and dedicate it to thy service in Christ....

The unmortified Christian and the heathen are of the same religion, and the deity they truly worship is the god of this world. What shall we eat? What shall we drink? What shall we wear? And how shall we pass away our time? Which way may we gather and perpetuate our names and families in the earth? It is a mournful reflection, but a truth which will not be denied, that these worldly lusts fill up a great part of the study, care and conversation of Christendom.

The false notion that they may be children of God while in a state of disobedience to his holy commandments, and disciples of Jesus though they revolt from his cross, and members of his true church, which is without spot or wrinkle, notwithstanding their lives are full of spots and wrinkles, is of all other deceptions upon themselves the most pernicious to their eternal condition for they are at peace in sin and under a security in their transgression.[26]

William Penn admonished:

Read my "No Cross, No Crown." There is instruction. Make your conversation with the most eminent for wisdom and piety, and shun all wicked men as you hope for the blessing of God and the comfort of your father's living and dying prayers. Be sure you speak evil of none, not of the meanest, much less of your superiors as magistrates, guardians, teachers, and elders in Christ.[27]

William Penn traveled and preached with George Fox, the founder of Quakerism, throughout Holland and Germany. There he met many persecuted Quakers, as well as Christians of other denominations who desired to worship God in their own way, without fear.[28] In his work, *Travels in Holland and Germany,* William Penn recorded:

> As I have been traveling, the great work of Christ in the earth has often been presented to my view, and the day of the Lord hath been deeply impressed upon me, and my soul and spirit hath frequently been possessed with an holy and weighty concern for the glory and name of the Lord and the spreading of his everlasting truth.[29]

It was at this time that his father, who had been a courageous Admiral in the King's Navy, died. King Charles owed him a tremendous amount of money, but being short on funds, he decided to repay him with a land grant in America.[30]

In 1681, William Penn received the grant, as heir of his father's estate, from King Charles II. The grant consisted of all the land between Maryland and New York. The following year, the Duke of York gave Penn the area that is now Delaware. William Penn had named the area, "Sylvania," meaning "woodland," but King Charles changed it to "Pennsylvania." The state has also become known as "The Quaker State," as the Society of Friends (Quakers) helped found it.[31]

On January 1, 1681, William Penn wrote to a friend concerning the land given to him, declaring he would:

> Make and establish such laws as shall best preserve true Christian and civil liberty, in all opposition to all unchristian...practices.[32]

> I eyed the Lord in obtaining it and more was I drawn inward to look to Him, and to owe it to His hand and power than to any other way. I have so obtained it, and desire to keep it that I may not be unworthy of His love. God that has given it to me through many difficulties, will, I believe, bless and make it the seed of a nation.[33]

One of Penn's first acts was to make friends with the Indians. He insisted on buying the land from the Indians, rather than just taking it. As a result of his fair dealings with them, his colony was never attacked by the Indians, according to historical records.[34] On August 18, 1681, in a letter sent ahead to the Indians in Pennsylvania, William Penn wrote:

My Friends:

There is one great God and Power that hath made the world and all things therein, to whom you and I and all people owe their being and well-being, and to whom you and I must one day give an account, for all that we doe in the world; This great God hath written His law in our hearts by which we are taught and commanded to love and help and doe good to one another and not to doe harm and mischief one unto another....

Now this great God hath pleased to make me concerned in my parts of the world, and the king of the country where I live, hath given unto me a great province therein, but I desire to enjoy it with your love and consent, that we may always live together as neighbors and friends, else what would the great God say to us, who hath made us not to devour and destroy one another, but to live soberly and kindly together in the world....

I have great love and regard towards you, and I desire to gain your love and friendship by a kind, just and peaceable life, and the people I send are of the same mind, and shall in all things behave themselves accordingly....

I shall shortly come to you myself at which time we may more freely and largely confer and discourse of these matters. Receive those presents and tokens which I have sent to you as a testimony to my goodwill to you and my resolution to live justly, peaceably and friendly with you.

I am your loving friend, William Penn.[35]

On April 25, 1682, William Penn wrote the famous *Frame of Government* for his new colony. This writing demonstrated such wisdom that it strongly influenced the charters of the other colonies. In it Penn stated:

The origination and descent of all human power [is] from God..first, to terrify evil doers; secondly, to cherish those who do well;...

Government seems to me to be a part of religion itself—a thing sacred in its institutions and ends....

Government, like clocks, go from the motion men give them; and as governments are made and moved by men, so by them they are ruined too. Wherefore governments rather depend upon men, than men upon governments. Let men be good, and the government cannot be bad....

That, therefore, which makes a good constitution must keep it,— namely men of wisdom and virtue,—qualities that, because they descend not with worldly inheritance, must be carefully propagated

by a virtuous education of youth....
[It is therefore enacted] that all persons...having children...shall cause such to be instructed in reading and writing, so that they may be able to read the Scriptures and to write by the time they attain to 12 years of age.[36]

William Penn, who had experienced so much religious persecution for his faith in England, saw the colony as a land of religious freedom, granting religious toleration to Christians of every denomination. He printed advertisements for his colony in six different languages and sent them across Europe.

Soon the Quakers, Mennonites, Lutherans, Dunkards (Church of the Brethren), Moravians, Schwenkfelders, etc., from England, Sweden, Wales, Germany, Scotland and Ireland all began arriving in his colony.

His emphasis on Christians working together in love was demonstrated in his founding of the city Philadelphia, "The City of Brotherly Love." To the Quaker, religion consisted not of a Sunday ceremonial ritual, but as the daily basis and inspiration for life.[37]

In 1684, William Penn delivered his *Prayer for Philadelphia*, which now appears on a plaque in the Philadelphia City Hall:

And thou, Philadelphia, the Virgin settlement of this province named before thou wert born, what love, what care, what service and what travail have there been to bring thee forth and preserve thee from such as would abuse and defile thee.

O that thou mayest be kept from the evil that would overwhelm thee. That faithful to the God of thy mercies, in the Life of Righteousness, thou mayest be preserved to the end. My soul prays to God for thee, that thou mayest stand in the day of trial, that thy children may be blest of the Lord and thy people saved by His Power.[38]

In 1701, William Penn, in his *Charter of Privileges* granted to the province of Pennsylvania, stated:

Almighty God being the only Lord of Conscience...and Author as well as object of all Divine Knowledge, faith and worship, who only doth enlighten the minds and persuade and convince the understandings of people, I do hereby grant and declare:

All persons living in this province, who confess and acknowledge the One Almighty and Eternal God to be the Creator, Upholder, and Ruler of the world, and that hold themselves obliged in conscience to live peaceably and justly in civil society, shall in no wise be molested or prejudiced for their religious persuasion or practice.

And that all persons who also profess to believe in Jesus Christ, the Savior of the World, shall be capable to serve this government in any capacity, both legislatively or executively.[39]

No people can be truly happy, though under the greatest enjoyment of civil liberties, if abridged of...their religious profession and worship....[40]

William Penn wrote to Peter the Great, Czar of Russia:

If thou wouldst rule well, thou must rule for God, and to do that, thou must be ruled by him....Those who will not be governed by God will be ruled by tyrants.[41]

William Penn stated:

True Godliness doesn't turn men out of the World, but enables them to live better in it, and excites their endeavors to mend it.[42]

William Penn had written on the title page of his *Book of Psalms:*

Set forth and allowed to be sung in all churches, of all the people together, before and after morning and evening prayer, and moreover in private houses for their godly solace and comfort, laying apart all ungodly songs and ballads: which tend only to the nourishing of vice and corruption of youth.[43]

William Penn, in his profound sermon, entitled, *A Summons or call to Christendom—In an earnest expostulation with her to prepare for the Great and Notable Day of the Lord that is at the Door,* wrote:

For in Jesus Christ, the light of the world, are hid all the treasures of wisdom and knowledge; redemption and glory; they are hid from the worldly Christian, from all that are captivated by the spirit and lusts of the world: and whoever would see them (for therein consists the things that belong to their eternal peace) must come to Christ Jesus the true light in their consciences, bring their deeds to Him, love Him and obey Him; whom God hath ordained a light to lighten the Gentiles, and for His salvation to the ends of the earth....[44]

William Penn wrote to his wife and children, not knowing if he would ever see them again:

My dear Wife and Children:

My love, which neither sea nor land nor death itself can extinguish or lessen toward you, most endearly visits you with eternal embraces, and will abide with you forever; and may the God of my life watch over you and bless you, and do good in this world and forever!

Some things are upon my spirit to leave with you in your respective capacities, as I am to the one a husband and to the rest a father, if I should never see you more in this world.

My dear wife, remember thou wast the love of my youth and much the joy of my life; the most beloved as well as the most worthy of all my earthly comforts; and the reason of that love was more thy inward than thy outward excellencies, which yet were many.

God knows, and thou knowest it, I can say it was a match of Providence's making and God's image in us both was the first thing, and the most amiable and engaging ornament in our eyes. Now I am to leave thee, and that without knowing whether I shall ever see thee more in this world; take my counsel into thy bosom and let it dwell with thee in my stead while thou livest.

First: Let the fear of the Lord and a zeal and love to his glory dwell richly in thy heart; and thou wilt watch for good over thyself and thy dear children and family, that no rude, light, or bad thing be committed; else God will be offended, and He will repent Himself of the good He intends thee and thine....

And now, my dearest, let me recommend to thy care my dear children; abundantly beloved of me as the Lord's blessings, and the sweet pledges of our mutual and endeared affection. Above all things endeavor to breed them up in the love and virtue, and that holy plain way of it which we have lived in, that the world in no part of it get into my family.

I had rather they were homely than finely bred as to outward behavior; yet I love sweetness mixed with gravity and cheerfulness tempered with sobriety. Religion in the heart leads into this true civility, teaching men and women to be mild and courteous in their behavior, an accomplishment worthy indeed of praise....[45]

In 1819, the *Biographical Review* in London described William

Penn as one who:

> Established an absolute toleration; it was his wish that every man who believed in God should partake of the rights of a citizen; and that every man who adored Him as a Christian, of whatever sect he might be, should be a partaker in authority.[46]

ะ

Charter of Pennsylvania 1681, granted to William Penn by King Charles II of England, consisted of all the land between Maryland and New York. Added to this the following year was the area of Delaware, which was given him by the Duke of York. William Penn had named the area, "Sylvania," meaning "woodland," but King Charles changed it to "Pennsylvania." The goal of the plantation, as stated in the Charter, was:

> To reduce the savage natives by gentle and just manners to the Love of Civil Societe and Christian religion.[47]

ะ

Fundamental Constitutions of Pennsylvania 1682, written by William Penn, formulated the government of the colony, stating:

> I Constitution.
> Considering that it is impossible that any People or Government should ever prosper, where men render not unto God, that which is God's, as well as to Caesar, that which is Caesar's;
> and also perceiving that disorders and Mischiefs that attend those places where force is used in matters of faith and worship, and seriously reflecting upon the tenure of the new and Spiritual Government, and that both Christ did not use force and that he did expressly forbid it in his holy Religion, as also that the Testimony of his blessed Messengers was, that the weapons of the Christian warfare were not Carnall but Spiritual....
> Therefore, in reverence to God the Father of lights and spirits, the Author as well as object of all divine knowledge, faith and worship, I do hereby declare for me and myn and establish it for the first fundamental of the Government of my Country;
> that every Person that does or shall reside therein shall have and

enjoy the Free Possession of his or her faith and exercise of worship towards God, in such way and manner as every Person shall in Conscience believe is most acceptable to God and so long as every such Person useth not this Christian liberty to Licentiousness, that is to say to speak loosely and prophainly of God, Christ or Religion, or to Committ any evil in their Conversation [lifestyle], he or she shall be protected in the enjoyment of the aforesaid Christian liberty by the civill Magistrate....[48]

&

Great Law of Pennsylvania April 25, 1682, was the first legislative act of Pennsylvania. It proclaimed:

Whereas the glory of Almighty God and the good of mankind is the reason and the end of government, and, therefore government itself is a venerable ordinance of God....[there shall be established] laws as shall best preserve true Christian and civil liberty, in opposition to all unchristian, licentious, and unjust practices, whereby God may have his due, and Caesar his due, and the people their due, from tyranny and oppression.[49]

&

Charter of Privileges of Pennsylvania 1701, granted by William Penn to the province of Pennsylvania, stated:

Almighty God being the only Lord of Conscience...and Author as well as object of all Divine Knowledge, faith and worship, who only doth enlighten the minds and persuade and convince the understandings of people, I do hereby grant and declare: that no person or persons, inhabiting in this province or territory who shall confess and acknowledge our Almighty God and Creator, Upholder and Ruler of the world; and profess him or themselves obliged to live quietly under civil government, shall be in any case molested or prejudiced in his or her person or estate....

And that all persons who also profess to believe in Jesus Christ, the Savior of the World, shall be capable to serve this government in any capacity, both legislatively or executively.[50]

No people can be truly happy, though under the greatest enjoyment of civil liberties, if abridged of...their religious profession and worship....[51]

ᴈ

PENNSYLVANIA.

*Seal of
Pennsylvania*

Constitution of the State of Pennsylvania 1776, stated:

We, the people of Pennsylvania, grateful to Almighty God for the blessings of civil and religious liberty, and humbly invoking His guidance, do ordain and establish this Constitution....[52]

Frame of Government, Section 10. And each member [of the legislature], before he takes his seat, shall make and subscribe the following declaration, viz: "I do believe in one God, the Creator and Governour of the universe, the rewarder of the good and punisher of the wicked, and I do acknowledge the Scriptures of the Old and New Testament to be given by Divine Inspiration."[53]

ᴈ

*√***Supreme Court of Pennsylvania** 1815, in the case of *The Commonwealth v. Jesse Sharpless and others,* 2 Serg.& R. 91-92, 97, 101-104 (1815), rendered the grand jury indictment as follows:

Jesse Sharpless...John Haines...George Haines...John Steel...Ephriam Martin...and Mayo...designing, contriving, and intending the morals, as well of youth as of divers other citizens of this commonwealth, to debauch and corrupt, and to raise and create in their minds inordinate and lustful desires...in a certain house there...scandalously did exhibit and show for money...a certain lewd...obscene painting, representing a man in an obscene...and indecent posture with a woman, to the manifest corruption and subversion of youth, and other citizens of this commonwealth... offending...[the] dignity of the Commonwealth of Pennsylvania.[54]

Judge Duncan delivered the court's verdict:

The defendants have been convicted, upon their own confession, of conduct indicative of great moral depravity....This court is...invested with power to punish not only open violations of decency and morality, but also whatever secretly tends to undermine the principles of society....

Whatever tends to the destruction of morality, in general, may be punishable criminally. Crimes are public offenses, not because they are perpetrated publicly, but because their effect is to injure the public. Burglary, though done in secret, is a public offense; and secretly destroying fences is indictable.

Hence, it follows, that an offence may be punishable, if in its nature and by its example, it tends to the corruption of morals; although it be not committed in public.

The defendants are charged with exhibiting and showing...for money, a lewd...and obscene painting. A picture tends to excite lust, as strongly as writing; and the showing of a picture is as much a publication as the selling of a book....

If the privacy of the room was a protection, all the youth of the city might be corrupted, by taking them, one by one, into a chamber, and there inflaming their passions by the exhibition of lascivious pictures. In the eye of the law, this would be a publication, and a most pernicious one.[55]

In a demonstration of the strong feelings of the court on this issue, a second Justice, by the name of Judge Yeates, added to the pronouncement of the court's decision:

Although every immoral act, such as lying, etc., is not indictable, yet where the offence charged is destructive of morality in general....it is punishable at common law.

The destruction of morality renders the power of the government invalid....

The corruption of the public mind, in general, and debauching the manners of youth, in particular, by lewd and obscene pictures exhibited to view, must necessarily be attended with the most injurious consequences....

No man is permitted to corrupt the morals of the people; secret poison cannot be thus disseminated.[56]

ॐ

Supreme Court of Pennsylvania 1817, in the case of *The Commonwealth v. Wolf,* 3 Serg. & R. 48, 50 (1817), stated the court's opinion as follows:

Laws cannot be administered in any civilized government unless the people are taught to revere the sanctity of an oath, and look to a future state of rewards and punishments for the deeds of this life. It is of the utmost moment, therefore, that they should be reminded of their religious duties at stated periods....A wise policy would naturally lead to the formation of laws calculated to subserve those salutary purposes.

The invaluable privilege of the rights of conscience secured to us by the constitution of the commonwealth, was never intended to shelter those persons, who, out of mere caprice, would directly oppose those laws for the pleasure of showing their contempt and abhorrence of the religious opinions of the great mass of the citizens.[57]

Supreme Court of Pennsylvania 1824, in the case of *Updegraph v. The Commonwealth*, 11 Serg. & R. 393-394, 398-399, 402-407 (1824), recorded the court's declaration that:

Abner Updegraph...on the 12th day of December [1821]...not having the fear of God before his eyes...contriving and intending to scandalize, and bring into disrepute, and vilify the Christian religion and the scriptures of truth, in the presence and hearing of several persons...did unlawfully, wickedly and premeditatively, despitefully and blasphemously say..."The Holy Scriptures were a mere fable: that they were a contradiction, and that although they contained a number of good things, yet they contained a great many lies." To the great dishonor of Almighty God, to the great scandal of the profession of the Christian religion....

The jury...finds a malicious intention in the speaker to vilify the Christian religion and the scriptures, and this court cannot look beyond the record, nor take any notice of the allegation, that the words were uttered by the defendant, a member of a debating association, which convened weekly for discussion and mutual information....

That there is an association in which so serious a subject is treated with so much levity, indecency and scurrility...I am sorry to hear, for it would prove a nursery of vice, a school of preparation to qualify young men for the gallows, and young women for the brothel, and there is not a skeptic of decent manners and good morals, who would not consider such debating clubs as a common nuisance and disgrace to the city....

It was the out-pouring of an invective, so vulgarly shocking and insulting, that the lowest grade of civil authority ought not to be subject to it, but when spoken in a Christian land, and to a Christian audience, the highest offence *contra bonos mores;* and even if Christianity was not part of the law of the land, it is the popular religion of the country, an insult on which would be indictable....

[Their] assertion is once more made, that Christianity never was received as part of the common law of this Christian land; and...[they] added, that if it was, it was virtually repealed by the constitution of the United States, and of this state....If the argument be worth anything, all the laws which have Christianity for their object—all would be carried away at one fell swoop—the act against cursing and swearing, and breach of the Lord's day; the act forbidding incestuous marriages, perjury by taking a false oath upon the book, fornication and adultery...for all these are founded on Christianity—for all these are restraints upon civil liberty....

We will first dispose of what is considered the grand objection— the constitutionality of Christianity—for, in effect, that is the question. Christianity, general Christianity, is and always has been a part of the common law...not Christianity founded on any particular religious tenets; not Christianity with an established church...but Christianity with liberty of conscience to all men....

I would have it taken notice of, that we do not meddle with the difference of opinion, and that we interfere only where the root of Christianity is struck as....The true principles of natural religion are part of the common law; the essential principles of revealed religion are part of the common law; so that a person vilifying, subverting or ridiculing them may be prosecuted at common law; but temporal punishments ought not to be inflicted for mere opinions;

Thus this wise legislature framed this great body of laws, for a Christian country and Christian people. This is the Christianity of the common law...and thus, it is irrefragably proved, that the laws and institutions of this state are built on the foundation of reverence for Christianity....In this the Constitution of the United States has made no alteration, nor in the great body of the laws which was an incorporation of the common-law doctrine of Christianity...without which no free government can long exist.

To prohibit the open, public and explicit denial of the popular religion of a country is a necessary measure to preserve the tranquillity of a government. Of this, no person in a Christian country can complain....In the Supreme Court of New York it was solemnly determined, that Christianity was part of the law of the land, and that to revile the Holy Scriptures was an indictable offence. The case assumes, says Chief Justice Kent, that we are a Christian people, and the morality of the country is deeply engrafted on Christianity. *The People v. Ruggles.*

No society can tolerate a wilful and despiteful attempt to subvert its religion, no more than it would to break down its laws—a general, malicious and deliberate intent to overthrow Christianity, general Christianity.

Religion and morality...are the foundations of all governments. Without these restraints no free government could long exist.

It is liberty run mad to declaim against the punishment of these offenses, or to assert that the punishment is hostile to the spirit and genius of our government. They are far from being true friends to liberty who support this doctrine, and the promulgation of such opinions, and general receipt of them among the people, would be the sure forerunners of anarchy, and finally, of despotism.

No free government now exists in the world unless where Christianity is acknowledged, and is the religion of the country....Its foundations are broad and strong, and deep....it is the purest system of morality, the firmest auxiliary, and only stable support of all human laws....

Christianity is part of the common law; the act against blasphemy is neither obsolete nor virtually repealed; nor is Christianity inconsistent with our free governments of the genius of the people.

While our own free constitution secures liberty of conscience and freedom of religious worship to all, it is not necessary to maintain that any man should have the right publicly to vilify the religion of his neighbors and of the country; these two privileges are directly opposed.[58]

❧

Samuel Pepys (1633-1703), a clerk in the British Navy, was later promoted to secretary of the Admiralty, where he instituted many of the administrative methods of the British Navy. He was also elected the president of the Royal Society. His famous *Diary*, which he kept from the years of 1660-1669, has become a vivid and popular picture of life in England during this period, including descriptions of the Restoration, the Plague, and the Fire of London. His *Diary*, which was written in code and translated in the 19th century, was made into the 1928 play, *And So To Bed*.

In his *Diary*, Samuel Pepys wrote on March 22, 1660:

I pray God to keep me from being proud.[59]

On February 23, 1667, he wrote:

This day I am, by the blessing of God, 34 years old, in very good health and mind's content, and in condition of estate much beyond whatever my friends could expect of a child of theirs, this day 34 years. The Lord's name be praised! and may I be thankful for it.[60]

In the final entry of his diary, made before the most active period of his life with the British government, Samuel Pepys wrote on May 31, 1669:

> And so I betake myself to that course, which is almost as much as to see myself go into my grave; for which, and all the discomforts that will accompany my being blind, the good God prepares me![61]

ಶಿ

Matthew Calbraith Perry (1794-1858), was the U.S. Navy Commodore who opened Japan to world trade through a dramatic show of force on July 8, 1853, and again in February of 1854. He was also the brother of Captain Oliver Hazard Perry who won fame in the War of 1812. Commodore Matthew Calbraith Perry declared:

Matthew Calbraith Perry

> I have just finished the Bible; I make it a point to read it through every cruise. It is certainly a wonderful Book—a most wonderful Book.... From boyhood I have taken a deep interest in Christianizing the heathen, and in imparting a knowledge of God's revealed truth everywhere.[62]

On a Sunday in 1853, on his way to Japan to protect American seamen, Commodore Perry set his Bible on the capstan, read Psalm 100, then sang:

> Before Jehovah's awful throne
> Ye nations bow with sacred joy.[63]

ಶಿ

Oliver Hazard Perry (1785-1819), the brother of Commodore Matthew C. Perry, was a U.S. Navy Captain who, in the War of

1812, was responsible for the spectacular victory over the British fleet on Lake Erie, September 10, 1813. The sailors on deck with him heard him say:

> The prayers of my wife are answered.[64]

He then dispatched a message to the Secretary of the Navy, saying:

> It has pleased the Almighty to give the arms of the United States a signal victory over their enemies on this lake. The British squadron, consisting of two ships, two brigs, one schooner, and one sloop have this moment surrendered to the force of my command after a sharp conflict.[65]

ଈ

Sir William Phipps (1651-1695), the Governor of Massachusetts and American colonial administrator, professed:

> I have divers times been in danger of my life; and I have been brought to see that I owe my life to Him who has given His precious life for me. I thank God He has led me to see myself altogether unhappy without an interest in the Lord Jesus Christ, and to close heartily with Him, desiring Him to execute all His offices on my behalf. I have now, for some time, been under serious resolution, that I should avoid whatever I knew to be displeasing to God, that I should serve Him all the days of my life....
>
> I knew that if God had a people anywhere, it was here, and I resolved to rise or fall with them; neglecting very great advantages for my worldly interests, that I might come and enjoy the ordinances of the Lord Jesus here.[66]

ଈ

Franklin Pierce (1804-1869), the 14th President of the United States, asserted in his Inaugural Address, March 4, 1853:

> It must be felt that there is no national security but in the nation's humble, acknowledged dependence upon God and His overruling providence.[67]

On December 5, 1853, in his first annual address to Congress,

President Franklin Pierce stated:

> Recognizing the wisdom of the broad principles of absolute religious toleration proclaimed in our fundamental law, and rejoicing in the benign influence which it has exerted upon our social and political condition, I should shrink from a clear duty if I failed to express my deepest conviction that we can place no secure reliance upon any apparent progress if it be not sustained by national integrity, resting upon the great truths affirmed and illustrated by Divine Revelation.[68]

Franklin Pierce

಍

Charles Cotesworth Pinckney (1746-1825), one of the signers of the Constitution of the United States, was a delegate to the Constitutional Convention and helped to write the Constitution of the State of South Carolina. He was a Presidential and Vice-Presidential candidate, a lawyer, planter, statesman, soldier, an aide-de-camp to General Washington, and a Brigadier General.

Charles Cotesworth Pinckney

Pinckney turned down many offers from President Washington for positions within government, including several cabinet appointments and a place on the U.S. Supreme Court, though finally he accepted the position of U.S. Minister to France. He helped found the Charleston Bible Society and served as its first president.

He studied for his military career at the Royal Military Academy of France, after having studied law at the Westminster School at Oxford under Sir William Blackstone. Sir William Blackstone, the second most quoted legal authority by our Founding Fathers, gave evidence of the views he taught, stating:

> Blasphemy against the Almighty is denying his being or providence, or uttering contumelious reproaches on our Savior Christ. It is punished, at common law by fine and imprisonment, for Christianity is part of the laws of the land.[69]

And consequently, as man depends absolutely upon his Maker for every thing, it is necessary that he should, in all points, conform to his Maker's will. This will of his Maker, is called the law of nature.[70]

Charles Cotesworth Pinckney was very involved in forming the Constitution of the State of South Carolina. The South Carolina Constitution contains the following article:

SOUTH CAROLINA, 1778. *Article XXXVIII.* That all persons and religious societies who acknowledge that there is one God, and a future state of rewards and punishments, and that God is publicly to be worshipped, shall be freely tolerated....That all denominations of Christian[s]...in this State, demeaning themselves peaceably and faithfully, shall enjoy equal religious and civil privileges.[71]

In a personal letter to a military friend, Pinckney wrote:

The great art of government is not to govern too much.[72]

Charles Cotesworth Pinckney, since a child, had learned "to love Christ and the Church."[73] As the first president of the Charleston Bible Society, he distributed Bibles to Negroes, putting aside finances to evangelize the slaves and teach them to read the Holy Scriptures.[74]

The elder Charles Pinckney, who was the Chief Justice of South Carolina, wrote in his will concerning his young son, Charles Cotesworth Pinckney:

To the end that my beloved son Charles Cotesworth may the better be enabled to become the head of his family and prove not only of service and advantage to his country, but also an Honour to his Stock and kindred, my order and direction is that my said son be virtuously, religiously and liberally brought up and Educated in the Study and practice of the Laws of England;

and from said son I hope, as he would have the blessings of Almighty God, and deserve the Countenance and favour of all good men, and answer my expectations of him, that he will employ all his future abilities in the service of God, and his Country, in the Cause of virtuous liberty as well religious as Civil; and in support of private right and Justice between Man and Man;

and that he do by no means debase the dignity of his human nature, nor the honour of his profession, by giving countenance to, or ever appearing in favour of irreligion, injustice or wrong, oppression or tyranny of any sort, public or private;

but that he make the glory of God and the good of Mankind, the relief of the poor and distressed, the widow and the fatherless, and such as have none else to help them, his principal aim and study.[75]

At his death in 1825, the following resolutions were read:

The Board of Managers of the Charleston Bible Society, entertaining a high sense of the benefits conferred on his country and on society, by their late revered President General CHARLES COTESWORTH PINCKNEY, in the course of a long life, steadily and honorably devoted to the service of both;

and of the fidelity, zeal and ability, with which he fulfilled the duties of the important and responsible public functions, to which he was called; as well as of the virtues, which adorned his private life and character, and by which he justly earned and secured the permanent respect, veneration and affection of all his fellow citizens....

That they give devout thanks to Almighty God for the invaluable services which the life, influence and example of their late revered President, have rendered to the cause of religion, virtue and good order, to his country and to mankind;

and that they submit themselves to this painful dispensation of Providence, with a sorrow mitigated by the grateful remembrance of his virtue, and by a pious trust in Divine mercy....

For fifteen years past he presided over our Society, and at our Board. Our meetings were held at his house. We will long remember his kindness and hospitality to us all, while the patience, industry, perseverance and zeal, which he exercised to promote the interests of our Society, merit the approbation of the cause in which we were engaged.

The last time he met our Society he was so feeble that it was necessary to support him to the chair. It was evident to all of us, that his long and useful life was drawing to a close. He seemed to come among us to show that in his last hours the cause of the Bible was nearest his heart, to give us his blessing and to bid us farewell;

for from that day [I am informed] he was confined to his chamber; and after having lived nearly fourscore years, an age seldom attained, he soon after fell to the ground, like as a shuck of corn cometh forth in his season.[76]

Charles Cotesworth Pinckney's parents were also very loved and respected for their godly and patriotic influence. President Washington himself, at his own request, served as a pallbearer at his mother, Elizabeth Pinckney's, funeral.[77]

ૐ

Charter of the Plymouth Council November 3, 1620, granted by King James I (1566-1625), declared the purpose of the colony was:

> In the hope thereby to advance the enlargement of the Christian religion, to the glory of God Almighty.[78]

ૐ

Edgar Allen Poe (1809-1849), was a famous American poet, literary critic and story writer. His best known works include: *The Fall of the House of Usher*, 1840; *The Raven*, 1845; and the short stories: *The Cask of Amontillado, The Purloined Letter, The Masque of the Red Death*, and *The Pit and the Pendulum*. In *Tamerlane*, 1827, Edgar Allen Poe wrote:

> O, human love! thou spirit given,
> On Earth, of all we hope in Heaven.[79]

ૐ

James Knox Polk (1795-1849), was the 11th President of the United States of America. In his Inaugural Address, March 4, 1845, President James Knox Polk expressed:

> I fervently invoke the aid of that Almighty Ruler of the Universe in whose hands are the destinies of nations.[80]

James Knox Polk

> I enter upon the discharge of the high duties which have been assigned to me by the people, again humbly supplicating that Divine Being, who has watched over and protected our beloved country from its infancy to the present hour, to continue

His gracious benedictions upon us, that we may continue to be prosperous and happy people....[81]

ও

Pope John Paul I (1912-1978), Albino Luciani, in the homily of the mass celebrating his installation, September 3, 1978, stated:

If all the sons and daughters of the Church would know how to be tireless missionaries of the Gospel, a new and flowering of holiness and renewal would spring up, in this world that thirsts for love and for truth.[82]

ও

Pope John Paul II (1920-), whose given name is Karol Wojtyla, has held the position of Pope since 1978. Arriving at Stapleton International Airport in Denver, Colorado, on August 12, 1993, Pope John Paul stated:

The best tradition of your love presumes respect for those who cannot defend themselves.[83]

Later that day, at Regis University, in the presence of President Bill Clinton, Pope John Paul II addressed the crowd:

The inalienable dignity of every human being and the rights which flow from that dignity—in the first place the right to life and the defense of life—as well as the well-being and full human development of individuals and peoples, are at the heart of the church's message and action in the world....No country, not even the most powerful, can endure if it deprives its own children of this essential good.[84]

It is he, Jesus Christ, the true life who gives hope and purpose to our earthly existence, opens our minds and hearts to the goodness and beauty of the world around us.[85]

I greet each one with sincere friendship, in spite of divisions among Christians, 'all those justified by faith through baptism are incorporated into Christ...brothers and sisters in the Lord.'[86]

Following his address on the "moral crisis," the Pontiff gave

President Clinton a Gutenberg Bible.

On Thursday night, August 12, 1993, in an address to 90,000 young people in Denver's Mile High Stadium, Pope John Paul II declared:

> Jesus has called each of you to Denver for a purpose. You must live these days in such a way that, when the time comes to return home, each of you will have a clearer idea of what Christ expects of you.[87]

During the Saturday night prayer vigil, August 14, 1993, at Cherry Creek State Park, the Pope spoke to nearly a quarter of a million people, warning:

> There is spreading an anti-life mentality—an attitude of hostility to life in the womb and life in its last stages. Precisely when science and medicine are achieving a greater capacity to safeguard health and life, the threats against life are becoming more insidious. Abortion and euthanasia—the actual killing of another human being—are hailed as 'rights' and solutions to 'problems'—an individual's or society's.[88]

On Sunday, August 15, 1993, Pope John Paul II addressed a crowd of over 375,000 people from 70 different countries in a Mass celebrated at Cherry Creek State Park, Colorado, as a part of "World Youth Day." With Vice-President Al Gore in attendance, the Pope exclaimed:

> A 'culture of death' seeks to impose itself on our desire to live, and live to the full....In our own century, as at no other time in history, the 'culture of death' has assumed a social and institutional form of legality to justify the most horrible crimes against humanity: genocide, 'final solutions,' 'ethnic cleansings' and massive taking of lives of human beings even before they are born, or before they reach the natural point of death....
>
> In much of contemporary thinking, any reference to a 'law' guaranteed by the Creator is absent. There remains only each individual's choice of this or that objective as convenient or useful in a given set of circumstances. No longer is anything considered intrinsically 'good' and 'universally binding.'
>
> ...Vast sectors of society are confused about what is right and what is wrong and are at the mercy of those with the power to 'create' opinion and impose it on others....

The family especially is under attack. And the sacred character of Human Life is denied. Naturally, the weakest members of society are the most at risk. The unborn, children, the sick, the handicapped, the old, the poor and unemployed, the immigrant and refugee....

Do not be afraid to go out on the streets and into public places....This is no time to be ashamed of the Gospel. It is a time to preach it from the rooftops....

You must feel the full urgency of the task. Woe to you if you do not succeed in defending life. The church needs your energies, your enthusiasm, your youthful ideas, in order to make the Gospel of Life penetrate the fabric of society, transforming people's hearts and the structures of society in order to create a civilization of true justice and love.[89]

On August 15, 1993, in his farewell address from Stapleton International Airport, Denver, Colorado, Pope John Paul II reiterated:

The 'culture of life' means respect for nature and protection of God's work of creation....In a special way, it means respect for Human Life from the first moment of conception until its natural end.[90]

࡝

Pope Leo XIII (1810-1903), whose given name was Gioacchino Pecci, in his encyclical on the condition of labor, *Rerum Novarum*, May 15, 1891, stated:

Every man has by nature the right to possess property as his own.[91]

࡝

Pope Pius XI (1857-1939), who held the position of Pontiff from 1922-1939, exclaimed:

Christian teaching alone, in its majestic integrity, can give full meaning and compelling motive to the demand for human rights and liberties, because it alone gives worth and dignity to human personality.[92]

In light of current trends, Pope Pius XI spoke:

Woman apparently is doing everything possible to destroy in herself those very qualifications which render her beautiful, namely, modesty, purity, and chastity. It is a blindness which can only be explained by the fascination of that vanity of which Scriptures speak with such severity.[93]

&

Pope Pius XII (1876-1958), whose given name was Eugenio Pacelli, in a radio broadcast on September 1, 1944, stated:

Private property is a natural fruit of labor, a product of intense activity of man, acquired through his energetic determination to ensure and develop with his own strength his own existence and that of his family, and to create for himself and his own an existence of just freedom, not only economic, but also political, cultural and religious.[94]

&

David Dixon Porter (1813-1891), was the second man to hold the position of Admiral in the United States Navy (the first was his adopted brother, David Farragut). In the Civil War, David Dixon Porter helped Ulysses S. Grant at the siege of Vicksburg, Mississippi, in 1863, and at the attack of Fort Fisher in North Carolina. He eventually became the superintendent of the United States Naval Academy at Annapolis. Admiral David Dixon Porter explained:

David Dixon Porter

David Glasgow Farragut

When one sees how much has been done for the world by the disciples of Christ and those professing the Christian religion, he must be astonished to find anyone who hesitates to believe in the Divine origin of Jesus and the wonderful works He performed, all of which are so beautifully portrayed by the author of the work under consideration; and no man or woman of real intelligence would hesitate to believe that it is only through Christ that sinners can be saved, unless their vanity is so great that they are capable of saving themselves without an intermediary. [95]

❧

John Pory (1572-1635), was an Englishman who traveled to Jamestown, where he became Secretary to Virginia's Council at Jamestown in 1619. He was also an author and geographer. On July 30, 1619 the House of Burgesses opened with prayer, then chose John Pory as speaker. The assembly sought to plan the method of government which would be used in the future:

> But, forasmuch as men's affairs do little prosper when God's service is neglected, all the burgesses took their place ... till prayer was said by Mr. Bucke, the minister, that it would please God to guide and sanctify all our proceedings to His own glory, and the good of this plantation. Prayer being ended, to the intent that as we had begun at God Almighty so we might proceed w[ith] awful and due respect toward his lieutenant, [the King of England]....
>
> *Be it enacted* by this present Assembly that for laying a surer foundation for the conversion of the Indians to Christian religion, each town, city, borough, and particular plantation do obtain unto themselves, by just means, a certain number of the natives' children to be educated by them in true religion and a civil course of life;
>
> of which children the mostly toward boys in wit and graces of nature to be brought up by them in the first elements of literature, so as to be fitted for the college intended for them; that from thence they may be sent to that work of conversion...
>
> All ministers shall duly read divine service and exercise their ministerial function according to the ecclesiastical laws and orders of the Church of England, and every Sunday in the afternoon shall catechize such as are not yet ripe to come to the communion.
>
> And whosoever of them shall be found negligent or faulty in this kind shall be subjected to the censure of the governor and Council of Estate. [96]

❧

William Prescott (1726-1795), was an American Colonel during the Revolutionary War. He built the fortifications at Breed's Hill and commanded the Colonial Militia at the Battle of Bunker Hill. William Prescott wrote in support of the citizens of Boston when the British blockaded the port in 1774:

We heartily sympathize with you, and are always ready to do all in our power for your support, comfort and relief, knowing that Providence has placed you where you must stand the first shock.

We consider that we are all embarked in (the same boat) and must sink or swim together....Let us all be of one heart, and stand fast in the liberty wherewith Christ has made us free.

And may He, of His infinite mercy, grant us deliverance of all our troubles.[97]

Princeton University 1746, originally called "The College of New Jersey," was founded in Princeton, New Jersey by the Presbyterian Church. Until 1902, every president of Princeton was a minister.[98] The University's official motto was:

Under God's Power She Flourishes.[99]

The Rev. Jonathan Dickinson, who was its first president, declared:

Jonathan Dickinson

Cursed be all that learning that is contrary to the cross of Christ.[100]

Samuel de Pufendorf (1632-1694), Professor of the Law of Nature at the University of Heidelberg in Germany and the University of Lund in Sweden, was famous for writing *The Law of Nature and Nations,* which greatly influenced our Founding Fathers. The son of a Lutheran minister, Pufendorf studied at the University of Leipzig. He became the royal historian for Elector Frederick II of Brandenburg, after serving in that position for Sweden. His works were standard in colonial colleges and highly recommended by the writers of our Constitution. Pufendorf stated:

Atheists are not, strictly speaking, God's Enemies...but His Rebellious Subjects, and consequently guilty of Treason against the Divine Majesty....It is no such obscure matter, therefore to assign the particular Species of Sin, to which Atheism belongs....[101]

Q

Queen Elizabeth I (1533-1603), the Queen of England from 1558 to 1603, answered the question at her Coronation in 1558 as to the presence of Christ in the Sacrament, by saying:

> Christ was the Word that spake it,
> He took the bread and brake it,
> And what that Word did make it,
> I do believe and take it.[1]

Elizabeth I (Elizabeth Tudor; The "Virgin Queen")

Queen Elizabeth I asserted:

> I am your Queen. I will never be by violence constrained to do anything. I thank God I am endued with such qualities that if I were turned out of the Realm in my petticoat I were able to live in any place in Christendom.[2]

In 1601, Queen Elizabeth gave *The Golden Speech*, saying:

> Though God hath raised me high, yet this I count the glory of my crown: that I have reigned with your loves.[3]

Queen Elizabeth I spoke to her ladies regarding her epitaph, saying:

> I am no lover of pompous title, but only desire that my name may be recorded in a line or two, which shall briefly express my name, my virginity, the years of my reign, the reformation of religion under it, and my preservation of peace.[4]

&

Queen Isabella (1451-1504), was the Queen of Castile, who, along with her husband, King Ferdinand of Aragon, financed Christopher Columbus' expedition to the Indies which resulted in the discovery of America. In her commission to Columbus, she recited that the purpose of the voyage was:

> For the Glory of God....it is hoped that by God's assistance some of the continents and islands in the oceans will be discovered.[5]

Isabel I
(Isabella the Catholic)

Queen Isabella informed the Pope of Columbus' attempt:

> To bear the light of Christ west to the heathen undiscovered lands.[6]

On February 15, 1493, on his return trip from having discovered America, Christopher Columbus wrote to Queen Isabella and King Ferdinand from on board the ship, *Caravel*, anchored off the Canary Islands:

> Praise be to our eternal God, our Lord, who gives to all those who walk in His ways victory over all things which seem impossible; of which this is signally one, for, although others have spoken or written concerning these countries, it was all conjecture, as no one could say that he had seen them—it amounting only to this, that those who heard listened the more, and regarded the matter rather as a fable than anything else.
>
> But our Redeemer has granted this victory to our illustrious King and Queen and their kingdoms, which have acquired great fame by an event of such high importance, in which all Christendom ought to rejoice, and which it ought to celebrate with great festivals and the offering of solemn thanks to the Holy Trinity with many sincere prayers, both for the great exaltation which may accrue to them in turning so many nations to our holy faith, and also for the temporal benefits which will bring great refreshment and gain, not only to Spain, but to all Christians.
>
> Done on board the Caravel, off the Canary Islands, on the fifteenth day of February, Fourteen hundred and ninety-three. At your orders, The Admiral.[7]

❧

Queen Ka'ahumanu (d. 1832), the wife of King Kamehameha, served as queen regent of Hawaii from 1819 to 1832. Along with her son, King Kamehameha II, she ended the social taboos, idolatry and human sacrifice that had controlled Hawaii for centuries. Their edict caused the destruction of numerous idols and temples.

The following year, Hiram Bingham and a group of missionaries came to Hawaii. Queen Ka'ahumanu received Christ and helped spread the Gospel, resulting in "The Great Awakening" (1830s and 1840s). Just prior to her death, Queen Ka'ahumanu was presented with the newly completed Hawaiian translation of the New Testament. She declared it good, then spoke her last words:

> I am going where the mansions are ready.[8]

The High Chiefess Kapiolani was baptized by the early Christian missionaries. She helped to win the people from superstitions and human sacrifice to Pele, the volcano goddess. Kapiolani descended into the crater of the volcano Kilauea and defied Pele by eating the goddess' sacred berries. She then proclaimed:

> Jehovah is my God. He kindled these fires. I fear not Pele. All the gods of Hawaii are vain.[9]

This courageous act greatly advanced Christianity in Hawaii, leading many to become missionaries to other islands. One such missionary, Rev. Kauwealoha, stopped the ritual of cannibalism. [See *Ka'ahumanu, Queen.*]

❧

Queen Victoria (1819-1901), was Queen of England, 1837 to 1901, and Empress of India, 1876 to 1901. Upon her coronation, June 28, 1837, three gifts were given to her: the Sword of State, the Imperial Robe, and the Bible. These words accompanied the Bible:

> Our gracious Queen, we present you this Book, the most valuable thing the world affords. Here is wisdom; this is the royal law; these are the timely oracles of God. Blessed is he that readeth and they that hear the words of this Book; that keep and do the things contained in it. For

these are the words of eternal life, able to make you wise unto salvation, and so happy forever more, through faith in Christ Jesus, to whom be the glory forever and ever. Amen.[10]

In commenting on the Bible, the Queen stated:

That book accounts for the supremacy of England.[11]

In 1849, the Queen instructed the Earl of Chichester to write the African Chieftain, Sagbua, a letter which contained the words:

Commerce alone will not make a nation great and happy like England. England has become great and happy by the knowledge of the true God through Jesus Christ. In order to show how much the queen values God's Word, she sends with this as a present a copy of the Word.[12]

ಶಿ

Josiah Quincy (1744-1775), was an American Revolutionary patriot, lawyer, and orator of freedom. He wrote many patriotic articles and signed them, "An Independent" or, "An Old Man." His most notable work was *Observations of the Act of Parliament Commonly called the Boston Port Bill with Thoughts on Civil Society and Standing Arms*, 1774. He was sent on a mission to England to argue the cause of the Colonists in 1774, and died at sea on April 26, 1775, during his return trip. His son, Josiah Quincy (1772-1864), was a U.S. Congressman, 1805-1818, and president of Harvard, 1829-1845.

Josiah Quincy
(1744-1775)

In response to the 1774 closing of the Boston harbor by the British, Josiah Quincy declared:

Blandishments will not fascinate us, nor will threats of a "halter" intimidate. For, under God, we are determined that wheresoever, whensoever, or howsoever we shall be called to make our exit, we will die free men.[13]

Josiah Quincy
(1772-1864)

ಶಿ

R

Sir Walter Raleigh (1552-1618), was an English navigator, writer, courtier and colonizer. He explored the eastern seaboard of America and named it "Virginia" after the "Virgin Queen," Elizabeth. Sir Walter Raleigh received the first colonial grant to America in 1584, authorizing him to enact statutes for the government of the proposed colony, provided that:

Sir Walter Raleigh

They be not against the true Christian Faith....[1]

In his Bible, found in the Gatehouse at Westminster after his death, Sir Walter Raleigh left this version of his earlier poem:

> Even such is time, that takes in trust
> Our youth, our joys, our all we have,
> And pays us but with age and dust;
> Who in the dark and silent grave,
> When we have wandered all our ways,
> Shuts up the story of our days.
> And from which earth, and grave, and dust,
> The Lord shall raise me up, I trust.[2]

≈

Samuel Jackson Randall (1828-1890), who was a U.S. Congressman and twice Speaker of the House, stated in the *Washington Papers:*

> Gentlemen, Christianity is true. The man who doubts it discredits his own intelligence. I have examined this matter for myself.
> I know that God has given me influence among my fellow men, and as I have a prospect of recovery I want henceforth to use the

influence of my example on the side of Christianity.[3]

ॐ

Edmund Jennings Randolph (1753-1813), was an American Revolutionary leader, member of the Continental Congress and delegate to the Constitutional Convention. He was the Governor of Virginia, U.S. Attorney General and U.S. Secretary of State.

Edmund Jennings Randolph

On June 28, 1787, at the Constitutional Convention in Philadelphia, following the historical address and appeal for prayer by Dr. Benjamin Franklin (which ended the heated debates over state representation), Edmund Jennings Randolph of Virginia further moved:

> That a sermon be preached at the request of the convention on the 4th of July, the anniversary of Independence; & thenceforward prayers be used in ye Convention every morning.[4]

[Of note is the fact that prayers have opened both houses of Congress ever since.][5]

On July 4th, according to the proposal by Edmund Jennings Randolph of Virginia, the entire Constitutional Convention assembled in the Reformed Calvinistic Church to hear a sermon by Rev. William Rogers. His prayer was a reflection of the hearts of all the delegates, following the convicting admonition of Dr. Franklin:

> We fervently recommend to the fatherly notice...our federal convention....Favor them, from day to day, with thy inspiring presence; be their wisdom and strength; enable them to devise such measures as may prove happy instruments in healing all divisions and prove the good of the great whole...that the United States of America may form one example of a free and virtuous government....
>
> May we...continue, under the influence of republican virtue, to partake of all the blessings of cultivated and Christian society.[6]

ॐ

John Ray (1627-1705), a scientist and a founder of the Royal Society, was considered the father of English natural history. A respected expert in the fields of botany and zoology, he compiled an extensive catalogue of English flora. One of the books he authored was entitled:

> The Wisdom of God Manifested in the Works of Creation.[7]

In it, John Ray stated that God's works of creation were:

> The works created by God at first, and by Him conserved to this day in the same state and condition in which they were first made.[8]

George Read (1733-1798), was a signer of the Declaration of Independence, a signer of the Constitution of the United States, a delegate from Delaware to the Constitutional Convention, U.S. Senator, and Chief Justice of the Supreme Court of Delaware. As a youth, George Read studied at the seminary of Rev. Dr. Allison at New London. At the age of 17 he began reading law with John Moland Esq., and two years later was admitted to the bar.[9] In 1769, he married the daughter of Reverend George Ross, who was the pastor of Immanuel Church in Newcastle for 50 years. George Read's wife was described as:

George Read

> Beautiful, her manners elegant and her piety exemplary.[10]

Known as "the Father of Delaware," George Read wrote "the first edition of her laws"[11] and the Constitution of the State of Delaware. The requirements, stated in the state's Constitution, necessary for holding office include:

DELAWARE

Seal of Delaware

> DELAWARE 1776. *Article XXII.* Every person who shall be chosen a member of either house, or appointed to any office or place of trust...shall... make and subscribe the following declaration, to

wit: "I, _____, do profess faith in God the Father, and in Jesus Christ His only Son, and in the Holy Ghost, one God, blessed for evermore; and I do acknowledge the holy scriptures of the Old and New Testament to be given by divine inspiration."[12]

Ronald Wilson Reagan (1911-2004), the 40th President of the United States of America, in 1980, said:

> The time has come to turn to God and reassert our trust in Him for the healing of America...our country is in need of and ready for a spiritual renewal....[13]

President Ronald Reagan, October 4, 1982, as authorized and requested by a Joint Resolution of the 97th Congress of the United States of America, held at the City of Washington, designated 1983 as the national "Year of the Bible." The Resolution, *Public Law 97-280*, declared:

> WHEREAS the Bible, the Word of God, has made a unique contribution in shaping the United States as a distinctive and blessed nation and people;
>
> WHEREAS deeply held religious convictions springing from the Holy Scriptures led to the early settlement of our Nation;
>
> WHEREAS Biblical teachings inspired concepts of civil government that are contained in our Declaration of Independence and Constitution of the United States;
>
> WHEREAS many of our great national leaders—among them Presidents Washington, Jackson, Lincoln, and Wilson—paid tribute to the surpassing influence of the Bible in our country's development, as in the words of President Jackson that the Bible is "the Rock on which our Republic rests";
>
> WHEREAS the history of our Nation clearly illustrates the value of voluntarily applying the teachings of the Scriptures in the lives of individuals, families, and societies;
>
> WHEREAS this Nation now faces great challenges that will test this Nation as it has never been tested before; and
>
> WHEREAS that renewing our knowledge of and faith in God through Holy Scripture can strengthen us as a nation and a people: NOW, THEREFORE, be it
>
> Resolved by the Senate and House of Representatives of the United States of America in Congress assembled, That the President is

authorized and requested to designate 1983 as a national "Year of the Bible" in recognition of both the formative influence the Bible has been for our Nation, and our national need to study and apply the teachings of the Holy Scriptures.

Thomas P. O'Neill   Strom Thurmond
Speaker of the House   President of the Senate - Pro Tempore

Approved
October 4, 1982
Ronald Reagan[14]

In his profound work, entitled "Abortion and the Conscience of the Nation," first published in *The Human Life Review*, 1983, President Ronald Reagan stated:

> Abraham Lincoln recognized that we could not survive as a free land when some men could decide that others were not fit to be free and should therefore be slaves. Likewise, we cannot survive as a free nation when some men decide that others are not fit to live and should be abandoned to abortion or infanticide. My administration is dedicated to the preservation of America as a free land, and there is no cause more important for preserving that freedom than affirming the transcendent right to life of all human beings, the right without which no other rights have any meaning.[15]

On January 25, 1984, President Ronald Reagan explained:

> America was founded by people who believed that God was their rock of safety. I recognize we must be cautious in claiming that God is on our side, but I think it's all right to keep asking if we're on His side.[16]

On August 23, 1984, following the enactment of the "Equal Access Bill of 1984," President Ronald Reagan spoke at the Ecumenical Prayer Breakfast at Reunion Arena in Dallas, Texas:

> In 1962, the Supreme Court in the New York prayer case banned the...saying of prayers. In 1963, the Court banned the reading of the Bible in our public schools. From that point on, the courts pushed the meaning of the ruling ever outward, so that now our children are not allowed voluntary prayer.
> We even had to pass a law—pass a special law in the Congress just a few weeks ago—to allow student prayer groups the same access to school rooms after classes that a Young Marxist Society, for example,

would already enjoy with no opposition....

The 1962 decision opened the way to a flood of similar suits. Once religion had been made vulnerable, a series of assaults were made in one court after another, on one issue after another.

Cases were started to argue against tax-exempt status for churches. Suits were brought to abolish the words "Under God" from the Pledge of Allegiance, and to remove "In God We Trust" from public documents and from our currency.

Without God there is no virtue because there is no prompting of the conscience....without God there is a coarsening of the society; without God democracy will not and cannot long endure....If we ever forget that we are One Nation Under God, then we will be a Nation gone under.[17]

On January 25, 1988, the 100th Congress of the United States of America, by a Joint Resolution, declared the first Thursday of each May to be recognized as a *National Day of Prayer*. Wholly concurring with Congress, President Ronald Reagan signed the bill into law:

PUBLIC LAW 100-307—MAY 5, 1988
One Hundredth Congress of the United States of America
AT THE SECOND SESSION
Begun and held at the City of Washington on Monday, the twenty-fifth day of January, one thousand nine hundred and eighty-eight
AN ACT
To provide for setting aside the first Thursday in May as the date on which the National Day of Prayer is celebrated.

Be it enacted by the Senate and House of Representatives of the United States of America in Congress assembled, That the joint resolution entitled "Joint Resolution to provide for setting aside an appropriate day as a National Day of Prayer," approved April 17, 1952 (Public Law 82-324; 66 Stat. 64), is amended by striking "a suitable day each year, other than a Sunday," and inserting in lieu thereof "the first Thursday in May in each year."

Speaker of the House of Representatives
President of the Senate Pro Tempore
APPROVED May 5, 1988
Ronald Reagan[18]

President Ronald Reagan in his 1988 *National Day of Prayer Proclamation*, expressed:

Let us, young and old, join together, as did the First Continental Congress, in the first step—humble, heartfelt prayer. Let us do so for the Love of God and His great goodness, in search of His guidance, and the grace of repentance, in seeking His blessings, His peace, and the resting of His kind and holy hands on ourselves, our Nation, our friends in the defense of freedom, and all mankind, now and always.[19]

President Ronald Reagan declared:

There are times when I'm in church, I think God might recognize the magnitude of my responsibility and give me an extra portion of His grace...and I don't feel guilty for feeling that way.[20]

President Ronald Reagan wrote:

The family has always been the cornerstone of American society. Our families nurture, preserve, and pass on to each succeeding generation the values we share and cherish, values that are the foundation for our freedoms. In the family we learn our first lessons of God and man, love and discipline, rights and responsibilities, human dignity and human frailty.

Our families give us daily examples of these lessons being put into practice. In raising and instructing our children, in providing personal and compassionate care for the elderly, in maintaining the spiritual strength of religious commitment among our people—in these and other ways, America's families make immeasurable contributions to America's well-being.

Today more than ever, it is essential that these contributions not be taken for granted and that each of us remember that the strength of our families is vital to the strength of our nation.[21]

We cannot diminish the value of one category of human life—the unborn—without diminishing the value of all human life....There is no cause more important.[22]

ﻌ

William Hubbs Rehnquist (1924-   ), an Associate Justice of the United States Supreme Court, stated in the 1985 case of *Wallace v. Jafree*, 472 U.S. 38, 99:

It is impossible to build sound constitutional doctrine upon a mistaken understanding of Constitutional history....The establishment clause had been expressly freighted with Jefferson's misleading metaphor for nearly forty years....

There is simply no historical foundation for the proposition that the framers intended to build a wall of separation [between church and state]....The recent court decisions are in no way based on either the language or intent of the framers.[23]

&

Joseph Ernest Renan (1823-1890), a French historian and philosopher, was elected to the French Academy in 1878. He was famous for his *Life of Jesus; History of the People of Israel;* and *Philosophical Dramas*. In *La Vie de Jesus*, 1863, Renan stated in his introduction concerning Jesus:

The whole of history is incomprehensible without him.[24]

In *Les Apotres*, 1866, Renan wrote:

Religion is not a popular error; it is a great instinctive truth, sensed by the people, expressed by the people.[25]

&

Charter of Rhode Island and Providence Plantations July 8, 1663, was granted by King Charles II to Roger Williams. In 1636, Williams left Massachusetts with his followers, for the purpose of religious freedom, and founded Providence Plantation. There they established the First Baptist Church in America in 1639. The colonial patent of 1644 was confirmed by the Royal Charter of 1663, which read:

We submit our persons, lives, and estates unto our Lord Jesus Christ, the King of kings and Lord of lords and to all those perfect and most absolute laws of His given us in His Holy Word.[26]

That they, pursueing, with peaceable and loyall mindes, sober, serious and religious intentions, of godlie edifieing themselves, and one another, in the holie Christian ffaith and worshipp...together with the gaineing over and conversione of the poore ignorant Indian natives...to sincere professions and obedienc of the same faith and worship....a most flourishing civill state may stand and best bee maintained....grounded upon gospell principles.[27]

୨⊷

RHODE ISLAND

Seal of Rhode Island

Seal of the State of Rhode Island 1797, reflected the sentiments of the state's 69,122 population. On the seal, over the picture of an anchor, is inscribed the motto:

IN GOD WE HOPE.[28]

୨⊷

Constitution of the State of Rhode Island 1842, stated:

We, the people of the State of Rhode Island and Providence Plantations, grateful to Almighty God for the civil and religious liberty which He hath so long permitted us to enjoy, and looking to Him for a blessing upon our endeavors to secure and to transmit the same unimpaired to succeeding generations, do ordain and establish this constitution of Government.[29]

୨⊷

Richard Rich (fl.1610), in his narrative poem *Newes from Virginia: The Flock Triumphant,* recounted his voyage to Virginia with Captain Christopher Newport. In it he gives the account of a shipwreck on the Bermudas, which is the likely source of Shakespeare's play, *The Tempest.* Richard Rich wrote:

God will not let us fall...
For...our work is good,
We hope to plant a nation,
Where none before hath stood.[30]

୨⊷

Edward Vernon "Eddie" Rickenbacker (1892-1973), was the most celebrated American aviator in France during World War I. Having begun his career as an auto racer, he grew to international fame before the war. In 1917 he was sent to France as the personal chauffeur of General John J. Pershing.

Requesting transfer to the air service, Eddie Rickenbacker soon became the commanding officer of the 94th Aero Pursuit Squadron, which was responsible for destroying sixty-nine enemy aircraft. This was the highest number shot down by any American Squadron, with Eddie himself earning the Congressional Medal of Honor for shooting down twenty-six. He wrote of his World War I experiences in the book *Fighting the Flying Circus* (1919).

After the war, he successfully worked in the auto and aircraft industries. In 1938, he became the president of Eastern Airlines. He also was the president of the Indianapolis Motor Speedway Corporation, which holds the annual 500 mile auto race.

During World War II, he was asked to go on a special mission to inspect the Pacific air bases for Secretary of War Henry L. Stimson. It was during one of these tours that his plane was shot, and he had to make a forced landing in the Pacific. For twenty-four days, in almost hopeless conditions, Eddie Rickenbacker and seven others drifted aimlessly on the open sea.

Succumbing to exposure and dehydration, the crew would have died had not Eddie Rickenbacker, the oldest person on the raft, continued to encourage them that they would make it. The exciting story of their survival is written in his book *Seven Came Through* (1943). Eddie Rickenbacker said:

> I pray to God every night of my life to be given the strength and power to continue my efforts to inspire in others the interest, the obligation and the responsibilities that we owe to this land for the sake of future generations—for my boys and girls—so that we can always look back when the candle of life burns low and say "Thank God I have contributed my best to the land that contributed so much to me."[31]

æ

M.G. "Pat" Robertson (1930-   ), is an internationally renowned broadcaster; founder of: The Christian Broadcasting Network, Inc., airing in over 70 countries; *The 700 Club*, reaching an average of one million households daily; International Family Entertainment, Inc., a publicly held company on the New York Stock Exchange; The Family Channel, a commercial television

Pat Robertson

network reaching 95% of all cable households and 62% of all households in the U.S.; Regent University, offering master's and doctoral degrees, accredited by the Commission on Colleges of the Southern Association of Colleges and Schools; Operation Blessing International Relief and Development Corporation, a nonprofit humanitarian organization, providing over $440 million in relief to nearly 114 million people in 50 states and 71 foreign countries since 1978. A graduate of Yale University Law School, 1955, and a candidate for the U.S. Presidency, 1988, Pat Robertson has authored nine books, including: *Turning the Tide; The New Millennium; The New World Order; The Secret Kingdom,* on the *New York Times* best-seller list, 1983; and *America's Dates with Destiny,* in which he wrote:

On September 17, 1787, the day our Constitution was signed, the absolute monarch Ch'ien Lung, emperor of the Manchu (or Ch'ing) Dynasty, reigned supreme over the people of China. To guard against revolt, Chinese officials could not hold office in their home provinces, and...revolts were put down by ruthless military force.

In Japan the shogun (warriors) of the corrupt Tokugawa chamberlain Tanuma Okitsugu exercised corrupt and totalitarian authority over the Japanese.

In India, Warren Hastings, the British Governor of Bengal, had successfully defeated the influence of the fragmented Mogul dynasties that ruled India since 1600.

Catherine II was the enlightened despot of all the Russias.

Joseph II was the emperor of Austria, Bohemia and Hungary.

For almost half a century, Frederick the Great had ruled Prussia.

Louis XVI sat uneasily on his throne in France just years away from revolution, a bloody experiment in democracy, and the new tyranny of Napoleon Bonaparte.

A kind of a constitutional government had been created in the Netherlands in 1579 by the Protestant Union of Utrecht, but that constitution was really a loose federation of the northern provinces for a defense against Catholic Spain....

What was happening in America had no real precedent, even as far back as the city-states of Greece. The only real precedent was established thousands of years before by the tribes of Israel in the covenant with God and with each other....[32]

ஃ

John Robinson (1576-1625), was a leader of the Pilgrim Church in England and Holland, before their departure to America. On July 22, 1620, while on board the *Speedwell,* Pastor John Robinson gave this admonition to the Pilgrims just before they set sail from Delft Haven, Holland, for England, and then for the New World:

> Lastly, whereas you are become a body politic, using amongst yourselves civil government, let your wisdom and godliness appear not only in choosing such persons as do entirely love and will promote the common good, but also in yielding unto them all due honor and obedience in their lawful administrations; not beholding in them the ordinariness of their persons, but God's ordinance for your good....[33]

> Someone or few must needs be appointed over the assembly [for]...discussing and determining of all matters, so in this royal assembly, the church of Christ, though all be Kings, yet some most faithful and most able, are to be set over the rest...wherein...they are...charged to minister according to the Testament of Christ.[34]

In his famous Leyden letter, Pastor John Robinson declared:

> Thus this holy army of saints is marshalled here on earth by these officers, under the conduct of their glorious Emperor, Christ. Thus it marches in this most heavenly order and gracious array, against all enemies, both bodily and ghostly: peaceable in itself, as Jerusalem, terrible to the enemy as an army with banners, triumphing over their tyranny with patience, their cruelty with meekness, and over death itself with dying.
>
> Thus, through the Blood of that spotless Lamb, and that Word of their testimony, they are more than conquerors, bruising the head of the Serpent; yea, through the power of His Word, they have power to cast down Satan like lightning; to tread upon serpents and scorpions; to cast down strongholds, and everything that exalteth itself against God.
>
> The gates of hell, and all the principalities and powers on earth shall not prevail against it. Romans 12; I Corinthians 12; Revelation 14:1, 2; Song 6:3; Revelation 12:11; Luke 10:18, 19; 2 Corinthians 10:15; Matthew 16:18, Romans 8:38, 39....[35]

ஃ

Carlos Peña Romulo (1899-1985), a famous Philippine general, diplomat and journalist, was renowned for his heroic activities during World War II. He was an aide-de-camp to U.S. General Douglas MacArthur on Corregidor Island and in Australia. He won the Pulitzer Prize in 1941, and in 1948 he served as president of the United Nations Conference on Freedom of Information in Geneva. He was president of the U.N. General Assembly, 1949-1950; Philippine ambassador to the United States, 1952; chairman of the U.N. Security Council, 1957; and was the president of the University of the Philippines. General Carlos P. Romulo stated:

> Never forget, Americans, that yours is a spiritual country. Yes, I know you're a practical people. Like others, I've marvelled at your factories, your skyscrapers, and your arsenals. But underlying everything else is the fact that America began as a God-loving, God-fearing, God-worshipping people.[36]

Franklin Delano Roosevelt (1882-1945), the 32nd President of the United States, addressed the nation, which had just entered the Great Depression, in his First Inaugural Address, March 4, 1933:

Franklin Delano Roosevelt

> The only thing we have to fear is fear itself....We face arduous days that lie before us in the warm courage of national unity; with the clear consciousness of seeking old and precious moral values....

In this dedication of a nation we humbly ask the blessing of God. May He protect each and every one of us! May He guide me in the days to come![37]

On December 6, 1933, in his address to the Federal Council of Churches of Christ, President Franklin D. Roosevelt stated:

> If I were asked to state the great objective which Church and State are both demanding for the sake of every man and woman and child in this country, I would say that that great objective is "a more abundant life."[38]

In a 1935 radio broadcast, Franklin D. Roosevelt declared:

We cannot read the history of our rise and development as a nation, without reckoning with the place the Bible has occupied in shaping the advances of the Republic....[W]here we have been the truest and most consistent in obeying its precepts, we have attained the greatest measure of contentment and prosperity.[39]

In his Second Inaugural Address on January 20, 1937, he said:

Franklin Delano Roosevelt

I shall do my utmost....seeking Divine guidance.[40]

On January 6, 1941, President Franklin D. Roosevelt gave his *Four Freedoms Speech* to Congress:

Today, thank God, one hundred and thirty million Americans, in forty-eight States, have forgotten points of the compass in our national unity....

We look forward to a world founded upon four essential human freedoms. The first in freedom of speech and expression....

The second is freedom of every person to worship God in his own way....

This nation has placed its destiny in the hands and heads and hearts of its millions of free men and women; and its faith in freedom under the guidance of God.[41]

In his Third Inaugural Address on January 20, 1941, he said:

We go forward in the service of our country by the will of God.[42]

On January 25, 1941, President Roosevelt inscribed a moving prologue to a special edition New Testament published by The Gideons. This New Testament (& Psalms), printed by the National Bible Press, Philadelphia, was distributed to the soldiers as they left for service during World War II. The prologue stated:

THE WHITE HOUSE
WASHINGTON
January 25, 1941

To the Armed Forces:

As Commander-in-Chief, I take pleasure in commending the reading of the Bible to all who serve in the armed forces of the United States. Throughout the centuries men of many faiths and diverse origins have found in the Sacred Book words of wisdom, counsel and inspiration. It is a fountain of strength and now, as always, an aid in attaining the highest aspirations of the human soul.

Very sincerely yours,
(signed) Franklin D. Roosevelt.[43]

On January 20, 1945, in his Fourth Inaugural Address, President Franklin D. Roosevelt said:

So we pray to Him now for the vision to see our way clearly...to the achievement of His will, to peace on earth.[44]

In a mid-Atlantic summit with British Prime Minister Winston Churchill, in the darkest hours of World War II, President Franklin Delano Roosevelt asked the crew of an American warship to join him in a rousing chorus of the hymn, "Onward, Christian Soldiers," after having described the United States as:

The lasting concord between men and nations, founded on the principles of Christianity. [45]

છ

Theodore Roosevelt (1858-1919), the 26th President of the United States, was a soldier, author and Nobel Prize Winner (1906). Upon assuming office September 14, 1901, he stated:

Theodore Roosevelt

I earnestly recommend all the people to assemble on that day in their respective places of divine worship, there to bow down in submission to the will of Almighty God.[46]

President Theodore Roosevelt stated:

The true Christian is the true citizen, lofty of purpose, resolute in endeavor, ready for a hero's deeds, but never looking down on his task because it is cast in the day of small things; scornful of baseness, awake to his own duties as well as to his rights, following the higher law with reverence, and in this world doing all that in his power lies, so that when death comes he may feel that mankind is in some degree better because he lived. [47]

A thorough knowledge of the Bible is worth more than a college education. [48]

On March 4, 1905, President Theodore Roosevelt proclaimed in his Second Inaugural Address:

No people on earth have more cause to be thankful than ours, and this is said reverently, in no spirit of boastfulness in our own strength, but with the gratitude to the Giver of good who has blessed us.[49]

President Theodore Roosevelt, in 1909, said:

After a week on perplexing problems...it does so rest my soul to come into the house of The Lord and to sing and mean it, "Holy, Holy, Holy, Lord God Almighty"....(my) great joy and glory that, in occupying an exalted position in the nation, I am enabled, to preach the practical moralities of The Bible to my fellow-countrymen and to hold up Christ as the hope and Savior of the world. [50]

In 1909, with grave intuition, President Roosevelt gave this ominous warning:

Progress has brought us both unbounded opportunities and unbridled difficulties. Thus, the measure of our civilization will not be that we have done much, but what we have done with that much. I believe that the next half century will determine if we will advance the cause of Christian civilization or revert to the horrors of brutal paganism. The thought of modern industry in the hands of Christian charity is a dream worth dreaming. The thought of industry in the hands of paganism is a nightmare beyond imagining. The choice between the two is upon us.[51]

In 1910, President Theodore Roosevelt gave his message on *The New Nationalism:*

The material progress and prosperity of a nation are desirable chiefly so far as they lead to the moral and material welfare of all citizens. Just in proportion as the average man and woman are honest, capable of sound judgement and high ideals, active in public affairs—but, first of all, sound in their home life, and the father and mother of healthy children whom they bring up well—just so far, and no further, we may count our civilization a success.

We must have—I believe we have already—a genuine and permanent moral awakening, without which no wisdom of legislation or administration really means anything.[52]

President Theodore Roosevelt explained:

Every thinking man, when he thinks, realizes that the teachings of the Bible are so interwoven and entwined with our whole civic and social life that it would be literally impossible for us to figure ourselves what that life would be if these standards were removed. We would lose almost all the standards by which we now judge both public and private morals; all the standards towards which we, with more or less resolution, strive to raise ourselves. [53]

President Theodore Roosevelt said concerning President Abraham Lincoln:

If ever there lived a President who, during his term of service, needed all the consolation and strength that he could draw from the Unseen Power above him, it was President Lincoln—sad, patient, mighty Lincoln, who worked and suffered for the people and, when he had lived for them at good end, gave up his life. If there ever was a man who practically applied what was taught in our churches, it was Abraham Lincoln.[54]

On June 17, 1912, in a speech at the Progressive Party Convention in Chicago, Theodore Roosevelt said:

We stand at Armageddon and we battle for the Lord.[55]

In a letter to Sir Edward Grey, written November 15, 1913, Theodore Roosevelt declared:

There is absolutely nothing to be said for government by a plutocracy, for government by men very powerful in certain lines and gifted with "the money touch," but with ideals which in their essence are merely those of so many glorified pawnbrokers.[56]

ра

William Rosecrans (1819-1898), was a General in the Union Army during the Civil War. He was noted for having increased the number of chaplains in his company, insisting that his troops not fight on the Sabbath, and conversing often with his staff in religious discussions, once till 4 a.m. for ten nights in a row. Having been a significant part of many major battles, General Rosecrans' motto was:

God never fails those who truly trust.[57]

ક

Jean Jacques Rousseau (1712-1778), a famous French author and philosopher, in *Emilius and Sophia*, Vol.III, Book IV, wrote:

I will confess to you, that the majesty of the Scriptures strikes me with admiration, as the purity of the Gospel has its influence upon my heart. Peruse the works of our philosophers; with all their pomp of diction, how mean, how contemptible, are they, compared with the Scriptures! Is it possible that a Book at once so simple and sublime should be merely the work of man?

It is possible that the Person whose history it relates be Himself a mere man? Does it contain the language of an enthusiast or an ambitious sectary? What sweetness, what purity in His manners! What affecting goodness in His instructions! What sublimity in His maxims! What profound wisdom in His discourses! What presence of mind! What sagacity and propriety in His answers! How great the command over His passions! Where is the man, where the philosopher, who could so live, suffer, and die, without weakness and without ostentation!...

The Jewish authors were incapable of the diction, and strangers to the morality contained in the Gospel, the marks of whose truths are so striking and inimitable that the inventor would be a more astonishing character than the hero....

Yes, if the life and death of Socrates are those of a philosopher, the life and death of Jesus Christ are those of a God.

Should we suppose the Gospel was a story, invented to please? It is not in this manner that we forge tales; for the actions of Socrates, of which no person has the least doubt, are less satisfactorily attested than those of Jesus Christ. Such a supposition, in fact, only shifts the difficulty without removing it; it is more conceivable that a number of persons should agree to write such a history, than that one should furnish the subject of it.[58]

In 1762, in his work *Emile; ou, De l'Education,* Jean Jacques Rousseau verbalized:

> Everything is good when it leaves the hands of the Creator; everything degenerates in the hands of man.[59]

> I shall always maintain that whoso says in his heart, "There is no God," while he takes the name of God upon his lips, is either a liar or a madman.[60]

> Where is the man who owes nothing to the land in which he lives? Whatever that land may be, he owes to it the most precious thing possessed by man, the morality of his actions and the love of virtue.[61]

Benjamin Rush

Benjamin Rush (1745-1813), was a physician, signer of the Declaration of Independence, "father of public schools" and a principal promoter of the American Sunday School Union. He also served as the Surgeon General of the Continental Army, helped to write the Pennsylvania Constitution, and was the treasurer of the U.S. Mint. In 1786, Dr. Benjamin Rush established the first free medical clinic and later helped found the first American anti-slavery society. In 1798, after the adoption of the Constitution, Benjamin Rush declared:

> The only foundation for...a republic is to be laid in Religion. Without this there can be no virtue, and without virtue there can be no liberty, and liberty is the object and life of all republican governments.[62]

In his work, *Essays, Literary, Moral, and Philosophical,* published in 1798, Dr. Benjamin Rush stated:

> I know there is an objection among many people to teaching children doctrines of any kind, because they are liable to be controverted. But let us not be wiser than our Maker. If moral precepts alone could have reformed mankind, the mission of the Son of God into all the world would have been unnecessary. The perfect morality of the Gospel rests upon the doctrine which, though often controverted

has never been refuted: I mean the vicarious life and death of the Son of God.[63]

Benjamin Rush described himself:

I have alternately been called an Aristocrat and a Democrat. I am neither. I am a Christocrat.[64]

During his final illness, Benjamin Rush wrote to his wife:

My excellent wife, I must leave you, but God will take care of you. By the mystery of Thy holy incarnation; by Thy holy nativity; by Thy baptism, fasting, and temptation; by Thine agony and bloody sweat; by Thy cross and passion; by Thy precious death and burial; by Thy glorious resurrection and ascension, and by the coming of the Holy Ghost, blessed Jesus, wash away all my impurities, and receive me into Thy everlasting kingdom.[65]

 è‌

John Ruskin (1819-1900), an English author, critic and philanthropist, pronounced:

Whatever merit there is in anything that I have written is simply due to the fact that when I was a child my mother daily read me a part of the Bible and daily made me learn a part of it by heart. [66]

To my early knowledge of the Bible I owe the best part of my taste in literature, and the most precious, and on the whole, the one essential part of my education. [67]

In Volume II of *Ruskin's Praeterita*, he wrote:

A firm word concerning Christianity itself...what was the total meaning of it?...The total meaning was, and is, that the God who made earth and its creatures took at a certain time upon the earth the flesh and form of man; in that flesh sustained pain, and died the death of the creature He had made; rose again after the dead into a glorious human life, and when the date of the human race is ended will return in visible form and render to every man according to his work. Christianity is the belief in, and the love of, God thus manifested.[68]

In the Preface to *The Crown of Olives*, John Ruskin exclaimed:

The English people are in possession of a Book which tells them, straight from the lips of God, all they ought to do and need to know. I have read that Book with as much care as the most of them for some forty years; and am thankful that on those who trust it I can press its pleadings.

My endeavor has uniformly been to make them trust it more deeply than they do; trust it, not in their own favorite verses only, but in the sum of all; trust it, not as a fetich or talisman which they are to be saved by daily repetition of, but as a Captain's order, to be obeyed at their peril.[69]

To *The Pall Mall Gazette*, John Ruskin expounded:

I see in your columns, as in other literary journals, more and more buzzing and fussing about what M. Renan has found the Bible to be; or Mr. Huxley, not to be; or the school-board, that it must not be; etc., etc., etc. Let me tell your readers who care to know, in the fastest possible words, what it is.

It is the grandest group of writings existent in the rational world, translated in the first strength of the Christian faith; translated with beauty and felicity into every language of the Christian world; and the guide, so translated, of all the arts and acts of that world which has been noble, fortunate, and happy.[70]

ॐ

Rutgers University 1766, originally founded in New Jersey as "Queen's College," was greatly influenced by Rev. Theodore Jacobus Frelinghuysen, 1692-1747, a Dutch minister. Formerly a Pietist minister in Germany, he was schooled in Holland, and later emigrated to New Jersey. Rev. Frelinghuysen concluded:

> The largest portion of the faithful have been poor and of little account in the world.[71]

Henry Rutgers

Queen's College was changed to Rutgers University in 1825, in honor of Henry Rutgers. He had served as a captain in the 1st Regiment of the New York Militia, was a member of the New York Assembly, and gave land for the 2nd Free School for the city's poor. He was a regent for the U. State of N.Y., and a trustee of Princeton and Queens College. Henry Rutgers was the president of the board of the Dutch Reformed Church, and gave the land for the Rutgers Street Presbyterian Church.

Rutgers University had as its official motto:

> Son of Righteousness, Shine upon the West also. [72]

&

Samuel Rutherford (1600-1661), was an English leader, who, in 1644, wrote the tremendously influential book *Lex, Rex or The Law and the Prince.* This book challenged the "divine right of kings," which said the king was God's appointed regent. Rutherford stated instead that all men, even the king, were under the law and not above it. He agreed that rulers derived their authority from God, as written in Romans 13:1-4, but he stressed that God gives this authority through the people. He cited the following biblical passages in support:

> II Samuel 16:18, "Hushai said to Absalom, Nay, but whom the Lord and the people, and all the men of Israel choose, his will I be, and with him will I abide'; Judges 8:22, 'The men of Israel said to Gideon, Rule thou over us'; Judges 9:6, 'The men of Shechem made Abimelech king'; II Kings 14:21, 'The people made Azariah king'; I Samuel 12:1, II Chronicles 23:3. [73]

This book, which created an immediate controversy, was banned in Scotland and publicly burned in England. Rutherford, who was one of the Scottish commissioners at Westminster Abbey in London and Rector of St. Andrew's Church in Scotland, was placed under house arrest and summoned to trial before the Parliament in Edinburgh. He died shortly thereafter, before the orders could be carried out. In his book *Lex, Rex,* Samuel Rutherford introduced the political concept:

> All men are created equal. [14]

&

S

Carl Sandburg (1878-1967), a famous American poet and biographer, received the Pulitzer Prizes for History and Poetry, in 1940 and 1951, respectively. He also was honored with Gold Medals from the American Academy of Arts & Letters and the Poetry Society of America. His noted works include: *Chicago Poems*, 1915; *American Songbag*, 1927; and the famous *Abraham Lincoln, The Prairie Years and The War Years*, 1954. The acclaim resulted in his being asked to address a joint session of Congress on the 150th anniversary of Lincoln's birthday.

Carl Sandburg acknowledged:

> A baby is God's opinion that the world should go on.[1]

❧

George Santayana (1863-1952), was an American philosopher, essayist and poet. He taught philosophy at Harvard University for 23 years. His works include *The Sense of Beauty*, 1896; *Character and Opinion in the United States*, 1920; *The Realm of Truth*, 1920-40; *The Last Puritan*, 1935; *Persons and Places*, 1945; and *The Idea of Christ in the Gospels*, 1946. George Santayana taught:

> Those who cannot remember the past are condemned to repeat it.[2]

In his *Dialogues in Limbo*, 1926, George Santayana wrote:

> Religion in its humility restores man to his only dignity, the courage to live by grace.[3]

In *The Genteel Tradition at Bay*, 1931, George Santayana wrote:

There is nothing impossible in the existence of the supernatural: its existence seems to me decidedly probable.[4]

❧

Francis August Schaeffer (1912-1983), a renowned philosopher, author and commentator, wrote in his book, *A Christian Manifesto:*

It follows from [Samuel] Rutherford's thesis that citizens have a moral obligation to resist unjust and tyrannical government. While we must always be subject to the office of the magistrate, we are not to be subject to the man in that office who commands that which is contrary to the Bible.

Rutherford suggested that there are three appropriate levels of resistance: First, he must defend himself by protest (in contemporary society this would most often be by legal action); second, he must flee if at all possible; and third, he may use force, if necessary, to defend himself.

One should not employ force if he may save himself by flight; nor should one employ flight if he can save himself and defend himself by protest and the employment of constitutional means of redress. Rutherford illustrated this pattern of resistance from the life of David [fleeing from King Saul] as it is recorded in the Old Testament.[5]

The civil government, as all life, stands under the Law of God....when any office commands that which is contrary to the Word of God, those who hold that office abrogate their authority and they are not to be obeyed.[6]

[Justice is] based on God's written Law, back through the New Testament to Moses' written Law; and the content and authority of that written Law is rooted back to Him who is the final reality. Thus, neither church nor state were equal to, let alone above, that Law. The base for law is not divided, and no one has the right to place anything, including king, state or church, above the contents of God's Law.[7]

In *Escape from Reason*, Francis A. Schaeffer wrote:

Modern man has not only thrown away Christian theology, he has thrown away the possibility of what our forefathers had as a basis for morality and law.[8]

&

H. Norman Schwarzkopf (1934-   ), was commander-in-chief of the Coalition Forces in Operation Desert Storm. Having acknowledged during an interview, in 1991, that he kept a Bible by his bed, General Schwarzkopf was asked if he had a favorite verse. He replied:

> Actually, it's a prayer of St. Francis: "Lord, make me an instrument of Thy peace."[9]

One of the key decisions of General Schwarzkopf's was an extreme flanking maneuver of the 101st Airborne, nicknamed *Hail Mary*, which cut off the retreat of the Iraqi Republican Guard. He commented:

> I began to believe that, when my forward commander radioed that they had reached the Euphrates River ahead of schedule. I waited for the other shoe to fall. "General," he said, "I've got to tell you about the casualties." I braced myself. "One man was slightly wounded." That's when I knew God was with us.[10]

&

Robert Falcon Scott (1868-1912), the English explorer of the Antarctic, reached the south pole on January 18, 1912. Caught in a snowstorm on their return trip, both he and the four other men in his expedition died. He kept a journal up to the day of his death; his final entry on Thursday, March 29, 1912, stated:

> For God's sake look after our people.[11]

&

Sir Walter Scott (1771-1832), was a famous Scottish novelist and poet, whose works include: *The Lay of the Last Minstrel*, 1805; *Lady of the Lake*, 1810; *Ivanhoe*, 1819; and *The Talisman*, 1825. In chapter XII of *The Monastery*, 1920, Sir Walter Scott wrote:

> Oh, on that day, that wrathful day,

> When man to judgment wakes from clay,
> Be Thou, O Christ, the sinner's stay
> Though heaven and earth shall pass away.
> Within this awful Volume lies
> The mystery of mysteries.
> Happiest they, of human race,
> To whom our God has granted grace
> To read, to fear, to hope, to pray,
> To lift the latch, and force the way;
> And better had they ne'er been born
> Who read to doubt, or read to scorn.[12]

In commenting on the Scriptures, Sir Walter Scott expounded:

> The most learned, acute, and diligent student cannot, in the longest life, obtain an entire knowledge of this one Volume. The most deeply he works the mine, the richer and more abundant he finds the ore; new light continually beams from this source of heavenly knowledge to direct the conduct, and illustrate the work of God and the ways of men; and he will at last leave the world confessing that the more he studied the Scriptures the fuller conviction he had of his own ignorance, and of their inestimable value.[13]

During his final illness he expressed a desire that someone should read to him. When asked what book, he replied:

> Need you ask? There is but one!—St. John's Gospel.[14]

&

Edmund Hamilton Sears (1810-1876), an American clergyman who ministered in Wayland, Massachusetts, 1848-66; and in Weston, Massachusetts, 1866-76. In 1850, Edmund Hamilton Sears wrote *The Angel's Song:*

> It came upon the midnight clear,
> That glorious song of old,
> From Angels bending near the earth
> To touch their harps of gold:
> "Peace on earth, good will to men
> From heav'n's all gracious King."
> The world in solemn stillness lay
> To hear the angels sing.[15]

ॐ

William Henry Seward (1801-1872), was Governor of New York, 1839-1843; a U.S. Senator 1849-1861, and Secretary of State under President Lincoln during the Civil War, 1861-1865. Lincoln's assassins also attempted to kill him as one of John Wilkes Booth's accomplices broke into Seward's home and wounded him. He was Secretary of State under President Andrew Johnson, 1865-1869, working to implement "reconstruction" of the South.

William Henry Seward

Among his accomplishments was the negotiation of the purchase of Alaska from Russia, 1867, at the time mockingly called "Seward's Folly," as the land was thought of no use, though later it proved to be of tremendous benefit. William H. Seward stated:

> I do not believe human society, including not merely a few persons in any state, but whole masses of men, ever have attained, or ever can attain, a high state of intelligence, virtue, security, liberty, or happiness without the Holy Scriptures;
> Even the whole hope of human progress is suspended on the ever growing influence of the Bible.[16]

William Henry Seward gave an oration entitled *The Destiny of America,* in which he stated:

> Shall we look to the sacred desk? Yes, indeed; for it is of Divine institution, and is approved by human experience. The ministers of Christ, inculcating Divine morals, under Divine authority, with Divine sanction, and sustained and aided by special cooperating influences of the Divine Spirit, are now carrying further and broadly onward the great work of the renewal of the civilization of the world, and its emancipation from superstition and despotism.[17]

In 1836, as vice-president of the American Bible Society, William Henry Seward expressed:

I know not how long a republican government can flourish among a great people who have not the Bible; the experiment has never been tried; but this I do know: that the existing government of this country never could have had existence but for the Bible.

And, further, I do, in my conscience, believe that if at every decade of years a copy of the Bible could be found in every family in the land its republican institutions would be perpetuated.[18]

⋆

Horatio Seymour (1810-1886), was the Governor of New York, 1853-55, and the War Governor of New York during the Civil War, 1863-65. Horatio Seymour, who was instrumental in gaining government sanction for the building of Erie Canal, was also the Democratic Presidential candidate in 1868.

Horatio Seymour

On July 4, 1876, Horatio Seymour gave an oration entitled *The Future of the Human Race*, delivered at Rome, New York. In it, he declared:

He who studies with care the jurisprudence of the Old Testament will see that this feeling of reverence for forefathers and devotion to country is made the substance of positive law in the command that men should honor their fathers and mothers. But sacred poetry is filled with appeals to these sentiments, and the narratives of the Bible abound with proofs of the great truth that the days of those who fear them shall be long upon the land which God hath given them.

Men cross the ocean and encounter the fatigues, dangers of a journey to the other side of the earth, that they may walk through the streets of Jerusalem where our Saviour trod, or look out from the hill of Zion, or wander amid sacred places. These scenes bring to their minds the story of the past in a way that thrills their nerves....

You will find that all history, all jurisprudence, all just reasonings, force us to the conclusion that not only does a Divine command, but that reason and justice call upon us all to honor our ancestors, and that there is a great practical truth which concerns the welfare and the power of all communities in the words of the inspired penman: "Honor thy father and thy mother that thy days may be long in the land which the Lord thy God giveth thee."[19]

⋆

William Shakespeare (1564-1616), was the most famous English playwright and poet, whose works have had an enduring world-wide impact. In 1591, Shakespeare introduced his play, *King Henry the Sixth,* in which he wrote in Part II, act II, scene i, line 34:

> Blessed are the peacemakers on earth.[20]

In line 66, he wrote:

> Now, God be praised, that to the believing souls
> Gives light in darkness, comfort in despair![21]

In scene iii, line 55, he exclaimed:

> God defend the right![22]

In Part III, act V, scene v, line 7, he penned:

> So part we sadly in this troublous world
> To meet with joy in sweet Jerusalem.[23]

William Shakespeare wrote in *King Richard the Third,* 1592-1593, act I, scene iv:

> O, I have passed a miserable night,
> So full of ugly sights, of ghastly dreams,
> That, as I am a Christian faithful man,
> I would not spend another such a night,
> Though 'twere to but a world of happy days.[24]

> Before I be convict by course of law,
> To threaten me with death is most unlawful.
> I charge you, as you hope for any goodness,
> By Christ's dear blood shed for our grievous sins
> That you depart and lay no hands on me.[25]

In *King Richard the Second,* 1595-1596, act IV, scene i, line 97, Shakespeare wrote:

> Many a time hath banished Norfolk fought
> For Jesus Christ in glorious Christian field,
> Streaming the ensign of the Christian Cross,

> And there at Venice, gave
> His body to that pleasant country's earth,
> And his pure soul unto his captain Christ,
> Under whose colors he had fought so long.[26]

In line 170, Shakespeare wrote:

> So Judas did to Christ: but he, in twelve,
> Found truth in all but one; I, in twelve thousand, none.
> God save the king! Will no man say, amen?[27]

In line 239, he wrote:

> Some of you with Pilate wash your hands,
> Showing an outward pity.[28]

In the play, *The Merchant of Venice,* act I, scene ii, line 59, Shakespeare penned:

> God made him, and therefore let him pass for a man.[29]

In scene iii, line 99, he wrote:

> Mark you this, Bassanio:
> The devil can cite Scripture for his own purpose.
> An evil soul, producing holy witness,
> Is like a villain with a smiling cheek,
> A goodly apple rotten at the heart.[30]

In act IV, scene i, line 184, he wrote:

> The quality of mercy is not strained,
> It droppeth as the gentle rain from heaven
> Upon the place beneath: it is twice blessed;
> It blessed him that gives and him that takes:
> Tis mightiest in the mightiest; it becomes
> The throned monarch better than his crown;
> His scepter shows the force of temporal power,
> The attribute to awe and majesty,
> Wherein doth sit the dread and fear of kings,
> But mercy is above this sceptered sway,
> It is enthroned in the hearts of kings,
> It is an attribute to God himself,

And earthly power doth then show likest God's
When mercy seasons justice. Therefore...
Though justice be thy plea, consider this,
That in the course of justice, none of us
Should see salvation: we do pray for mercy,
And that same prayer doth teach us all to render
The deeds of mercy.[31]

In his play, *King Henry the Fourth*, Part I, act i, scene 1, line 18, published in 1598, Shakespeare wrote:

Therefore friends,
As far as to the sepulchre of Christ,
Whose soldier now, under whose blessed cross
We are impressed and engaged to fight....
To chase these pagans in those holy fields.
Over whose acres walk'd those blessed feet,
Which fourteen hundred years ago were nail'd
For our advantage on the bitter cross.[32]

In *King Henry the Fifth*, 1598-1600, act III, scene vi, line 181, William Shakespeare wrote:

We are in God's hand.[33]

In act IV, scene i, line 309, he wrote:

O God of battles! steel my soldiers' hearts;
Possess them not with fear; take from them now
The sense of reckoning, if the opposed numbers
Pluck their hearts from them.[34]

In *Hamlet*, 1600-1601, act I, scene I, Shakespeare wrote:

Some say—that ever 'gainst that season comes
Wherein our Saviour's birth is celebrated
The bird of dawning singeth all night long.[35]

In act III, scene i, line 150, he wrote:

I have heard of your paintings too, well enough;
God has given you one face, and you make yourselves
another.[36]

In scene iv, line 149, he wrote:

> Confess yourself to heaven;
> Repent what's past; avoid what is to come.[37]

In act V, scene i, line 84, he wrote:

> A politician...one that would circumvent God.[38]

William Shakespeare wrote in *Othello*, 1604-1605, act I, scene i, line 108:

> You are one of those that will not serve God if the devil bid you.[39]

In act II, scene iii, line 106, he wrote:

> Well, God's above all; and there be souls must be saved, and there be souls must not be saved.[40]

In line 293, he wrote:

> O God! that men should put an enemy in their mouths to steal away their brains; that we should, with joy, pleasance, revel, and applause, transform ourselves into beasts.[41]

William Shakespeare wrote in *King Henry the Eighth*, 1613, act III, scene ii, line 456:

> Had I but served my God with half the zeal
> I served my king, he would not in mine age
> Have left me naked to mine enemies.[42]

In act V, scene v, line 51, he wrote:

> Whenever the bright sun of heaven shall shine,
> His honor and the greatness of his name
> Shall be, and make new nations.[43]

William Shakespeare remarked:

> God's goodness hath been great to thee;
> Let never day nor night unhallowed pass,

But still remember what the Lord hath done.[44]

In his last *Will*, dated the year of his death, 1616, the first clause reads:

In the name of God, Amen! I, William Shakespeare, of Stratford-upon-Avon, in the county of Warr., gent., in perfect health and memory, God be praised, do make and ordain this my last will and testament in manner and form following, that is to say, first, I commend my soul into the hands of God, my Creator, hoping and assuredly believing, through the only merits of Jesus Christ, my Saviour, to be made partaker of life everlasting, and my body to the earth whereof it is made.[45]

Carved on William Shakespeare's Tombstone are the lines:

Good Friend For Jesus Sake Forbeare,
To Digg The Dust Enclosed Heare.
Blese Be Ye Man [who] Spares Thes Stones,
And Curst Be He [who] Moves My Bones.[46]

之

John Sherman (1823-1900), was a U.S. Congressman, 1855-61; a U.S. Senator, 1861-77, and again in 1881-97; Secretary of the Treasury under President Hayes, 1877-81; and Secretary of State under President McKinley, 1897-98. John Sherman was the younger brother of Union General William Tecumseh Sherman of Civil War fame. John Sherman is noted for having introduced the *Sherman Anti-Trust Act*, 1879, in an effort to curb the monopolies of big businesses. He stated:

John Sherman

I appreciate the Holy Bible as the highest gift of God to man, unless it be the "unspeakable Gift" of Jesus Christ as the Saviour of the world. It is the Divine assurance that our life does not end with death, and it is the strongest incentive to honorable, charitable Christian deeds.[47]

≈

Roger Sherman (1721-1793), was an American Revolutionary patriot, politician and jurist, who was the only one of the Founding Fathers to sign all four of the major founding documents: The Articles of Association, 1774; The Declaration of Independence, 1776; The Articles of Confederation, 1777; and The Constitution of the United States, 1787.

Roger Sherman

He served on the committee that drafted the Declaration of Independence, was a member of the Continental Congress and made 138 speeches at the Constitutional Convention. Roger Sherman was also a U.S. Congressman, 1789-91; a U.S. Senator, 1791-93 (elected at the age of 70); a state senator; a self-taught lawyer; superior court judge; and a judge in Connecticut for fourteen years. Prior to his political career, he was a surveyor, merchant and shoe cobbler.

Benjamin Franklin

During the almost fatal crisis at the Constitutional Convention, Thursday, June 28, 1787, Roger Sherman seconded the motion to have Dr. Benjamin Franklin's famous request, that Congress be opened with prayer every day, enacted.[48](A practice which continues to this day.)

The extremely heated dispute which arose at the Constitutional Convention was over how Congress would insure that the smaller states would be equally represented in comparison with the larger states. This debate grew so serious that it began to threaten the convention itself, as some delegates had already left.

Shortly after Franklin's call for prayer, Roger Sherman made the suggestion that state representation in the Senate be equal and that state representation in the House be based on population. This historic proposal, which came to be called the "Connecticut Compromise," was adopted and is the system in use today.[49]

Roger Sherman was also on the committee which decided the

George Wythe

John Adams

wording of the First Amendment. (Roger Sherman was originally opposed to the First Amendment, considering it unnecessary, since Congress had no authority delegated from the Constitution in such areas.)[50]

In February 1776, Roger Sherman, along with John Adams and George Wythe of Virginia, were on the committee responsible for creating instructions for the embassy headed for Canada. The instructions directed:

> You are further to declare that we hold sacred the rights of conscience, and may promise to the whole people, solemnly in our name, the free and undisturbed exercise of their religion. And...that all civil rights and the right to hold office were to be extended to persons of any Christian denomination.[51]

Roger Sherman also successfully worked to have President Washington officially declare a national Thanksgiving Day holiday. His remarks were recorded in the *Journals of Congress:*

> Mr. Sherman justified the practice of thanksgiving, on any signal event, not only as a laudable one in itself, but as warranted by a number of precedents in Holy Writ: for instance, the solemn thanksgivings and rejoicings which took place in the time of Solomon, after the building of the temple, was a case in point. This example, he thought, worthy of Christian imitation on the present occasion.[52]

While he was in Congress, Roger Sherman objected to a report from the War Committee which would have allowed the army to give five hundred lashes to a delinquent soldier at a court-martial. He successfully opposed the proposal, basing his arguments on the scripture Deuteronomy XXV:3:

> Forty stripes he may give him, and not exceed: lest, if he should exceed, and beat him above these with many stripes, then thy brother should seem vile unto thee.[53]

In one of his speeches, Roger Sherman pointed out the necessity of:

> Admiring and thankfully acknowledging the riches of redeeming love, and earnestly imploring that divine assistance which may enable us to live no more to ourselves, but to him who loved us and gave himself to die for us.[54]

Roger Sherman joined the Congregational Church in 1742 and faithfully served as deacon, clerk and treasurer. He spoke very highly of his pastor, the Reverend Jonathan Edwards, the younger:

> I esteem him one of the best of preachers that I am acquainted with, sound in faith, and pious and diligent in his studies and attention to the duties of his office.[55]

In 1788, as a member of the White Haven Congregational Church, Roger Sherman was asked to use his expertise in revising the wording of their creed. In his own handwriting, he wrote the following:

> I believe that there is one only living and true God, existing in three persons, the Father, the Son, and the Holy Ghost, the same in substance equal in power and glory.
>
> That the scriptures of the old and new testaments are a revelation from God, and a complete rule to direct us how we may glorify and enjoy him.
>
> That God has foreordained whatsoever comes to pass, so as thereby he is not the author or approver of sin.
>
> That he creates all things, and preserves and govern all creatures and all their actions, in a manner perfectly consistent with the freedom of will in moral agents, and the usefulness of means.
>
> That he made man at first perfectly holy, that the first man sinned, and as he was the public head of his posterity, they all became sinners in consequence of his first transgression, are wholly indisposed to that which is good and inclined to evil, and on account of sin are liable to all the miseries of this life, to death, and to the pains of hell forever.
>
> I believe that God having elected some of mankind to eternal life, did send his own Son to

Roger Sherman

become man, die in the room and stead of sinners and thus to lay a foundation for the offer of pardon and salvation to all mankind, so as all may be saved who are willing to accept the gospel offer:

also by his special grace and spirit, to regenerate, sanctify and enable to persevere in holiness, all who shall be saved; and to procure in consequence of their repentance and faith in himself their justification by virtue of his atonement as the only meritorious cause.

I believe a visible church to be a congregation of those who make a credible profession of their faith in Christ, and obedience to him, joined by the bond of the covenant....

I believe that the souls of believers are at their death made perfectly holy, and immediately taken to glory: that at the end of this world there will be a resurrection of the dead, and a final judgement of all mankind, when the righteous shall be publicly acquitted by Christ the Judge and admitted to everlasting life and glory, and the wicked be sentenced to everlasting punishment.[56]

President John Adams described Roger Sherman as:

John Adams

...an old Puritan, as honest as an angel and as firm in the cause of American Independence as Mount Atlas.[57]

Engraved on Roger Sherman's tomb is the Epitaph:

IN MEMORY OF
THE HON. ROGER SHERMAN, ESQ.
MAYOR OF THE CITY OF NEW HAVEN,
AND SENATOR OF THE UNITED STATES.
HE WAS BORN AT NEWTOWN, IN MASSACHUSETTS,
APRIL 19th,1721
AND DIED IN NEW HAVEN, JULY 23rd, A.D. 1793,
AGED LXXII.
...He ever adorned
the profession of Christianity
which he made in youth;
and, distinguished through life
for public usefulness,
died in the prospect
of a blessed immortality.[58]

❧

Jonathan Shipley 1774, bishop of St. Asaph Anglican Church in London, appealed in the House of Lords:

> At present we force every North American to be our enemy....It is a strange idea we have taken up, to cure their resentments by increasing provocation....That just God, whom we have all so deeply offended, can hardly inflict a severer national punishment than by committing us to the natural consequences of our own conduct.[59]

Edward Rowland Sill (1841-1887), in writing *The Fool's Prayer*, stated:

> But Lord,
> Be merciful to me, a fool![60]

Benjamin Silliman (1779-1864), an honored physicist, chemist and geologist, was the Yale College professor, who, in 1818, founded and edited the *American Journal of Science and Arts*. He also was an original member of the National Academy of Sciences in 1863. Benjamin Silliman published his research on the potential uses of crude oil in his respected *Silliman Report*, 1855, which was of significant importance in establishing the American oil industry. The mineral sillimanite (a form of aluminum silicate, Al_2SiO_5) is named for him.

Benjamin Silliman

Having been profoundly influenced by the faith of Yale President Timothy Dwight, Professor Benjamin Silliman wrote concerning the atmosphere on the Yale campus during Dwight's tenure:

> It would delight your heart to see how the trophies of the cross are multiplied in this institution. Yale College is a little temple: prayer and praise seem to be the delight of the greater part of the students.[61]

Benjamin Silliman stated:

> The relation of geology, as well as astronomy, to the Bible, when both are well understood, is that of perfect harmony. The Bible nowhere limits the age of the globe, while its chronology assigns a recent origin to the human race; and geology not only confirms that the Genesis presents a true statement of the progress of the terrestrial arrangements, and of the introduction of living beings in the order in which their fossil remains are found entombed in the strata.
>
> The Word and the works of God cannot conflict, and the more they are studied the more perfect will their harmony appear.[62]

On June 13, 1855, he concluded his course of college lectures with the prayer:

> Thus, O Almighty God, hast Thou led me on in mercy almost to the close of a long life....For myself, in the evening of my life, may I be every day ready to die, trusting in Thy mercy through the Redeemer of men; and if power and opportunity to be useful are still continued to me, may I have a disposition, as well as ability, to honor Thee, and to benefit my fellow men.
>
> For my salvation I depend entirely upon the Redeemer. In the sight of God I have no merits of my own, and feel deeply that if I am saved it will be of grace and not of works. I have none to offer that are worthy of Thine acceptance. And now, my Heavenly Father, I implore Thy blessing upon my dear children and their children, and upon the faithful and devoted companion whom Thou hast in mercy given me.
>
> I implore it, also, for the precious youth who are about to go into the world. Bless them all in time and eternity through Christ our Lord and Redeemer.[63]

અ

Sir James Young Simpson (1811-1870), pioneered modern anesthesiology through his discovery of "Chloroform" in 1847. He stated that his research was inspired by the "deep sleep" that Adam was put into.

Sir James Young Simpson, considered a chief founder of the medical field of gynecology, served as Professor of Obstetric Medicine at Edinburgh University. He invented the Simpson forceps, introduced iron wire sutures, and acupressure. His writings on medical history, fetal pathology and hermaphroditism are highly regarded.

James Simpson declared his greatest discovery was:

> That I have a Saviour![64]

A gospel tract he wrote concludes:

> But again I looked and saw Jesus, my substitute, scourged in my stead and dying on the cross for me. I looked and cried and was forgiven. And it seems to be my duty to tell you of that Saviour, to see if you will not also look and live. "He was wounded for our transgressions....and with His stripes we are healed"(Isaiah 53:5, 6).[65]

Sir James Young Simpson stated:

> The unregenerate, unbelieving soul is compared to a corpse; it is "dead in sins." Of all of you who are now living by faith in Christ it may be truthfully said to-day, as it was said eighteen centuries ago of the Ephesian converts to whom the Apostle Paul wrote, "You hath He quickened, who were dead."
>
> As many of you as are unbelievers are, in the strong language of Scripture, "dead." You are dead in the eye of Divine justice; for as the condemned criminal is as a "dead man," when his crimes have brought on him the legal doom of death, you are likewise "dead," because "he that believeth not is condemned already."
>
> Further, you are also spiritually dead on account of being cut off by your sins from communion with the living God. For as a corpse moves not, stirs not, feels not, and can not be aroused, so are you dead to all love of God, and to everything pertaining to the wondrous Gospel of Jesus Christ. Of the dread and crushing burden of their own sins your souls are not all conscious; for the dead feel not.
>
> But in the infinitude of His love to our fallen race, God offers to each of us individually a free and full pardon, and life now and forever, if we only believe on Jesus Christ, His Son, whom He sent to suffer in our stead—to die that we might live—if we rely and rest entirely on Him as the all-sufficient sacrifice for our sins—as our substitute and security.[66]

&

Jedediah Strong Smith (1798-1831), was an American trader and explorer, whose expeditions were exceeded in importance only by those of Lewis and Clark. He led expeditions across the Rocky

Mountains, 1822-26; from California to the Oregon coast; across the Mojave desert and the Sierra Nevadas; and along the famous Sante Fe Trail, 1826-29. With two other partners, he operated a successful fur-trading company in Salt Lake City.

Renowned for having escaped being killed by Indians numerous times, Jedediah was once mauled by a grizzly. While he was recovering apart from the camp, an Indian raid killed all the rest in his group. Arriving back at the camp, he found only a rifle, knife, flint, and his Bible. He let it fall open, and his eyes fell on a verse that would change his life:

> He is chastened also with pain upon his bed, and the multitude of his bones with strong pain....Yes, his soul draweth near to the grave, and his life to the destroyers. His flesh shall be fresher than a child's; he shall return to the days of his youth. He shall pray unto God, and He will be favorable unto him.[67]

&

Samuel Francis Smith (1808-1895), was an American poet and clergyman, who, in 1832, wrote the famous patriotic hymn, *My Country 'Tis Of Thee*. He graduated from Harvard University in the same class as the poet Oliver Wendell Holmes. Smith continued his studies through seminary, becoming a Baptist minister and professor of modern languages at Waterville College. He edited *The Christian Review* and devoted much time to helping the American Baptist Missionary Union. As a 23-year-old seminary student, Samuel was inspired after hearing the national anthems for England, Sweden and Russia, and within a half hour wrote:

Samuel Francis Smith

> My Country 'tis of thee,
> Sweet land of liberty,
> Of thee I sing;
> Land where my fathers died,
> Land of the Pilgrim's pride,
> From every mountainside,
> Let freedom ring.[68]

The fourth verse proclaims:

> Our fathers' God, to thee,
> Author of liberty,
> To Thee we sing;
> Long may our land be bright
> With freedom's holy light:
> Protect us by Thy might,
> Great God, our King.[69]

ॐ

Sydney Smith (1771-1845), was a famous English humorist, known for his wit and satirical humor. He is best known for his *Peter Plymley Letters*, which were highly instrumental in forwarding the cause of granting Catholics in England the right to vote. In his 1855 work, entitled *Lady Holland's Memoir*, Sydney Smith wrote:

> Take short views, hope for the best, and trust in God.[70]

ॐ

Alexander Solzhenitsyn (1918-   ), a famous Russian author, was imprisoned by Joseph Stalin from 1945-1953. He received the Nobel Prize for Literature in 1970 and was expelled from the country in 1974. Alexander Solzhenitsyn proceeded to publish his telling book *The Gulag Archipelago*, 1974-79, which won international acclaim. In May of 1983, as he received the Templeton Prize for Progress in Religion, Solzhenitsyn expressed:

> Instead of the ill-advised hopes of the last two centuries, which have reduced us to insignificance and brought us to the brink of nuclear and non-nuclear death, we can only reach with determination for the warm hand of God, which we have so rashly and self-confidently pushed away.[71]

Alexander Solzhenitsyn, in commenting on the forces precipitating our culture's decay, stated laconically:

> Man has forgotten God, that is why this has happened.[72]

ॐ

Walter Raleigh

South Carolina 1650, was originally named "Carolana" or "Charles' land," after King Charles I of England, who granted it to Sir Robert Heath in 1629. The Colony of Carolina was originally part of Virginia, named after the "Virgin Queen" Elizabeth by Sir Walter Raleigh, who explored the area and attempted to found a settlement on Roanoke Island beginning April 9, 1585.

On August 13, 1587, the members of the colony converted the Indian Manteo and he was baptized into the Christian faith. That same month the first child was born in America, and she was baptized Virginia Dare. The Roanoke Colony was unsuccessful and later became known as the "Lost Colony."[73]

It wasn't until the 1650s that English colonists began settling the area permanently. The first governor, William Sayle, was a Nonconformist and allowed religious toleration of all denominations: Calvinists and Baptists from England and parts of New England, Huguenots (French Protestants), Episcopalians, Scotch-Irish Presbyterians, Lutherans, German Reformed, Moravians, etc.[74]

Of the many Christians that began to settle in North Carolina, beginning in 1653, the Quaker missionaries were among the most notable, with even George Fox, the founder of Quakerism, preaching there. At a later date, the Quaker family of Daniel Boone, with other Quaker families, pioneered the Yadkin River Valley along the North Carolina frontier. In 1727 the first Baptist congregation was formed, followed by the Methodists, who preached strongly against slavery and recognized Negro ministers.[75]

ॐ

Charter of Carolina 1663, was granted by King Charles II to Sir William Berkeley and seven other lord proprietors. (Initially, this area was granted by King Charles I to Sir Robert Heath in 1629.) The Charter stated:

Being excited with a laudable and pious zeal for the propagation of the Christian faith...[they] have humbly besought leave of us...to transport and make an ample colony...unto a certain country...in the parts of America not yet cultivated or planted, and only inhabited by some barbarous people, who have no knowledge of Almighty God.[76]

ぃ

Fundamental Constitutions of the Carolinas 1663, was drawn up by the famous philosopher, John Locke, at the request of Sir William Berkeley and the seven other lord proprietors of the colony.[77] It stated:

No man shall be permitted to be a freeman of Carolina, or to have any estate of habitation within it that doth not acknowledge a God, and that God is publicly and solemnly to be worshiped.[78]

ぃ

SOUTH CAROLINA

Seal of South Carolina

Constitution of the State of South Carolina
1778, stated:

We, the people of the State of South Carolina,...grateful to God for our liberties, do ordain and establish this Constitution.[79]

Article XXXVIII. That all persons and religious societies who acknowledge that there is one God, and a future state of rewards and punishments, and that God is publicly to be worshipped, shall be freely tolerated....That all denominations of Christian[s]...in this State, demeaning themselves peaceably and faithfully, shall enjoy equal religious and civil privileges.[80]

ぃ

Supreme Court of South Carolina 1846, in the case of *City of Charleston v. S.A. Benjamin*, cites an individual who wilfully broke an Ordinance which stated:

No person or persons whatsoever shall publicly expose to sale, or sell...any goods, wares or merchandise whatsoever upon the Lord's day.[81]

The prosecuting attorney astutely explained the premise, stating:

Christianity is a part of the common law of the land, with liberty of conscience to all. It has always been so recognized .... If Christianity is a part of the common law, its disturbance is punishable at common law. The U.S. Constitution allows it as a part of the common law.

The President is allowed ten days [to sign a bill], with the exception of Sunday. The Legislature does not sit, public offices are closed, and the Government recognizes the day in all things .... The observance of Sunday is one of the usages of the common law, recognized by our U.S. and State Governments .... The Sabbath is still to be supported;

Christianity is part and parcel of the common law .... Christianity has reference to the principles of right and wrong .... it is the foundation of those morals and manners upon which our society is formed; it is their basis. Remove this and they would fall .... [Morality] has grown upon the basis of Christianity.
[82]

The Supreme Court of South Carolina delivered its decision, declaring:

The Lord's day, the day of the Resurrection, is to us, who are called Christians, the day of rest after finishing a new creation. It is the day of the first visible triumph over death, hell and the grave! It was the birth day of the believer in Christ, to whom and through whom it opened up the way which, by repentance and faith, leads unto everlasting life and eternal happiness! On that day we rest, and to us it is the Sabbath of the Lord-its decent observance, in a Christian community, is that which ought to be expected....

What gave to us this noble safeguard of religious toleration? It was Christianity .... But this toleration, thus granted, is a religious toleration; it is the free exercise and enjoyment of religious profession and worship, with two provisos, one of which, that which guards against acts of licentiousness, testifies to the Christian construction, which this section should receive!

What are acts "of licentiousness" within the meaning of this section? Must they not be such public acts, as are calculated to shock the moral sense of the community where they take place? The orgies of Bacchus, among the ancients, were not offensive! At a later day, the Carnivals of Venice went off without note or observation. Such could not be allowed now! Why? Public opinion, based on Christian morality, would not suffer it!

What constitutes the standard of good morals? Is it not Christianity?

There certainly is none other. Say that cannot be appealed to, and I don't know what would be good morals. The day of moral virtue in which we live would, in an instant, if that standard were abolished, lapse into the dark and murky night of Pagan immorality.

In the Courts over which we preside, we daily acknowledge Christianity as the most solemn part of our administration. A Christian witness, having no religious scruple about placing his hand upon the book, is sworn upon the holy Evangelists—the books of the New Testament, which testify of our Savior's birth, life, death, and resurrection; this is so common a matter, that it is little thought of as an evidence of the part which Christianity has in the common law.

I agree fully to what is beautifully and appropriately said in *Updegraph v. The Commonwealth*...Christianity, general Christianity, is, and always has been, a part of the common law: "not Christianity with an established church...but Christianity with liberty of conscience to all men."[83]

ða

State of South Carolina November 20, 1994, issued an Executive Proclamation, signed by Governor Carroll A. Campbell, Jr. (A similar Proclamation was signed November 21, 1993.):

WHEREAS, We each have been richly blessed by The Almighty whose divine providence our founding fathers sought as they established these United States of America as a free and independent nation; and WHEREAS, the contributions of faith and traditions of our people are often reflected in the prayers offered preceding each day's opening of Congress and the General Assembly of this state; and WHEREAS, The importance of our Christian Heritage to the institutions, values and vision of our nation is immeasurable; and WHEREAS, Our Christian Heritage is further reflected by our people and our leaders, past and present, in our individual and collective efforts as a nation of peacekeepers and peacemakers to provide for other people, both in America and abroad, by providing humanitarian assistance to our fellow men, women and children; and WHEREAS, It is appropriate to recognize the Pilgrims' first Thanksgiving for God's providence as a special time and reason for celebrating our nation's Christian heritage. NOW, THEREFORE, I, Carroll A. Campbell, Jr., Governor of the State of South Carolina, do hereby proclaim November 20-26, 1994, as "CHRISTIAN HERITAGE WEEK" in South Carolina.[84]

ða

Motto of the State of South Dakota 1889, states:

> Under God The People Rule[85]

ๆ

Robert Louis Stevenson (1850-1894), was the famous British novelist who wrote *New Arabian Nights,* 1882; *Treasure Island,* 1883; *Dr. Jekyll and Mr. Hyde,* 1886; and *Kidnapped,* 1886.

In *Songs of Travel—If This Were Faith,* Stevenson wrote:

> God, if this were enough,
> That I see things bare to the buff.[86]

In 1889, in his work *The Master of Ballantrae—Mr. Mackellar's Journey,* Stevenson wrote:

> Not every man is so great a coward as he thinks he is—nor yet so good a Christian.[87]

Shortly before he died, Stevenson wrote:

> Written in the East, these characters live forever in the West; written in one province, they pervade the world; penned in rude times, they are prized more and more as civilization advances; product of antiquity, they come home to the bosoms of men, women, and children in modern days. Then is it any exaggeration to say that the "characters of the Scripture are a marvel of the mind?"[88]

On the bronze memorial to him in St. Giles Cathedral, Edinburgh, Scotland, Robert Louis Stevenson's prayer is engraved:

> Give us grace and strength to forbear and to persevere. Give us courage and gaiety and the quiet mind, spare to us our friends, soften to us our enemies.[89]

ๆ

Ezra Stiles (1727-1795), was a founder of Rhode Island College (now Brown University) in 1763, the president of Yale College, and was the president of the first society for the abolition of slavery formed in Connecticut, in 1790.

On May 8, 1783, as the president of Yale College, Ezra Stiles gave a major Election Address, entitled "The United States Elevated to Glory and Honor," before the Governor and the General Assembly of Connecticut, declaring:

> All forms of civil polity have been tried by mankind, except one, and that seems to have been reserved in Providence to be realized in America.[90]

> Our system of dominion and civil polity would be imperfect without the true religion; or that from the diffusion of virtue among the people of any community would arise their greatest secular happiness: which will terminate in this conclusion, that holiness ought to be the end of all civil government. "That thou mayest be a holy people unto the Lord thy God."[91]

> In our lowest and most dangerous state, in 1776 and 1777, we sustained ourselves against the British Army of sixty thousand troops, commanded by...the ablest generals Britain could procure throughout Europe, with a naval force of twenty-two thousand seamen in above eighty men-of-war.
> Who but a Washington, inspired by Heaven, could have conceived the surprise move upon the enemy at Princeton—that Christmas eve when Washington and his army crossed the Delaware?
> Who but the Ruler of the winds could have delayed the British reinforcements by three months of contrary ocean winds at a critical point of the war?
> Or what but "a providential miracle" at the last minute detected the treacherous scheme of traitor Benedict Arnold, which would have delivered the American army, including George Washington himself, into the hands of the enemy?
> On the French role in the Revolution, it is God who so ordered the balancing interests of nations as to produce an irresistible motive in the European maritime powers to take our part....
> The United States are under peculiar obligations to become a holy people unto the Lord our God.[92]

ช

Charles Milton Stine (1882-1954), was the director of Research for the E.I. Dupont Company. He was an organic chemist and leader in the development of significant new products and patents, most of which were connected with propellant powder, high explosives, dyes, artificial leather, and paints. In the book he authored, entitled, *A Chemist and His Bible,* Charles Stine stated:

> The world about us, far more intricate than any watch, filled with checks and balances of a hundred varieties, marvelous beyond even the imagination of the most skilled scientific investigator, this beautiful and intricate creation, bears the signature of its Creator, graven in its works.[93]

Richard Stockton

Richard Stockton (1730-1781), a signer of the Declaration of Independence, was a member of the Continental Congress, 1776; an associate justice of the New Jersey Supreme Court, 1774-76; and a member of the Executive Council of New Jersey, 1768-76.

His son, Richard, was a U.S. Senator, 1796-99; and a U.S. Congressman, 1813-15. Another son, Robert, served with prominence as a U.S. Naval officer in the War of 1812; helped freed slaves to found the country of Liberia, West Africa in 1821; and conquered California, proclaiming it a U.S. Territory, on August 17, 1846. Robert also served as a U.S. Senator, 1851-53; and was honored when Stockton, California, was named after him.

In his *Will,* Richard Stockton wrote:

> As my children will have frequent occasion of perusing this instrument, and may probably be peculiarly impressed with the last words of their father, I think proper here, not only to subscribe to the entire belief of the great leading doctrine of the Christian religion...but also in the heart of a father's affection, to charge and exhort them to remember "that the fear of the Lord is the beginning of wisdom."[94]

Joseph Story (1779-1845), a U.S. Congressman, 1808-9, was appointed in 1811 as a Justice to the United States Supreme Court by President James Madison ("The Chief Architect of the Constitution"). Being the youngest person ever to serve in that position, Joseph Story continued on the bench for 34 years, until

Joseph Story

his death in 1845. He was instrumental in establishing federal supremacy in *Martin v. Hunter's Lessee*, 1816; and in establishing the illegality of the slave trade in the *Amistad case*. A professor at the Harvard Law School, 1821- 45, Joseph Story wrote tremendously influential works, including: *Bailments, 1832; Commentaries on the Constitution of the United States, 1833; Equity Jurisprudence*, 1836; and *A Familiar Exposition of the Constitution of the United States, 1840*. In 1829, Justice Joseph Story explained in a speech at Harvard:

> There never has been a period of history, in which the Common Law did not recognize Christianity as lying at its foundation. [95]

In his work, *A Familiar Exposition of the Constitution of the United States,* 1840, Justice Joseph Story, stated:

> We are not to attribute this prohibition of a national religious establishment [in the First Amendment] to an indifference to religion in general, and especially to Christianity (which none could hold in more reverence than the framers of the Constitution)....
>
> Probably, at the time of the adoption of the Constitution, and of the Amendment to it now under consideration, the general, if not the universal, sentiment in America was, that Christianity ought to receive encouragement from the State so far as was not incompatible with the private rights of conscience and the freedom of religious worship.
>
> Any attempt to level all religions, and to make it a matter of state policy to hold all in utter indifference, would have created universal disapprobation, if not universal indignation. [96]

In Commentaries on the Constitution of the United States, 1833, Vol. 111, Justice Joseph Story stated:

> It yet remains a problem to be solved in human affairs, whether any free government can be permanent, where the public worship of God, and the support of religion, constitute no part of the policy or duty of the state in any assignable shape. [97]

In the 1844 case of *Vidal v. Girard's Executors,* Justice Story delivered the United States Supreme Court's unanimous opinion:

Christianity...is not to be maliciously and openly reviled and blasphemed against, to the annoyance of believers or the injury of the public....

It is unnecessary for us, however, to consider the establishment of a school or college, for the propagation of...Deism, or any other form of infidelity. Such a case is not to be presumed to exist in a Christian country....

Why may not laymen instruct in the general principles of Christianity as well as ecclesiastics....And we cannot overlook the blessings, which such [lay]men by their conduct, as well as their instructions, may, nay must, impart to their youthful pupils.

Why may not the Bible, and especially the New Testament, without note or comment, be read and taught as a Divine Revelation in the [school]—its general precepts expounded, its evidences explained and its glorious principles of morality inculcated?

What is there to prevent a work, not sectarian, upon the general evidences of Christianity, from being read and taught in the college by lay teachers? It may well be asked, what is there in all this, which is positively enjoined, inconsistent with the spirit or truths of the religion of Christ? Are not these truths all taught by Christianity, although it teaches much more?

Where can the purest principles of morality be learned so clearly or so perfectly as from the New Testament?[98]

In his commentary of the First Amendment's original meaning, Justice Joseph Story clarified:

The real object of the First Amendment was not to countenance, much less to advance Mohammedanism, or Judaism, or infidelity, by prostrating Christianity, but to exclude all rivalry among Christian sects [denominations] and to prevent any national ecclesiastical patronage of the national government.[99]

Justice Joseph Story insured:

There is not a truth to be gathered from history more certain, or more momentous, than this: that civil liberty cannot long be separated from religious liberty without danger, and ultimately without destruction to both.

Wherever religious liberty exists, it will, first or last, bring in and establish political liberty.[100]

&

Harriet Beecher Stowe

Harriet Beecher Stowe (1811-1896), was a teacher who became famous for authoring the book *Uncle Tom's Cabin*. She was the daughter of the famous New England minister Lyman Beecher, and the sister of Henry Ward Beecher, one of the most renowned preachers of the day.

Her book, *Uncle Tom's Cabin*, published first in serial form between 1851-1852, gained international fame and greatly stirred up the abolitionist movement. When President Lincoln met her, he greeted her by saying:

So you're the little lady who started the big war.[101]

Her book ends by saying:

A day of grace is yet held out to us. Both North and South have been guilty before God; and the Christian church has a heavy account to answer. Not by combining together, to protect injustice and cruelty, and making a common capital of sin, is this Union to be saved, but by repentance, justice and mercy.[102]

ख

William Strong (1808-1880), an Associate Justice of United States Supreme Court, 1870-1880, had previously served his country as a U.S. Congressman, 1847-51, and as a justice on the Pennsylvania Supreme Court, 1857-68. Justice William Strong stated:

William Strong

You ask me what I think of Christ? He is the Chiefest among ten thousand, and altogether lovely—my Lord, my Saviour, and my God.

What do I think of the Bible? It is the infallible Word of God, a light erected all along the shores of time to warn against the rocks and breakers, and to show the only way to the harbor of eternal rest.[103]

ख

Lord Rayleigh John Strutt (1842-1919), was a leading scientist at

Cambridge, 1879-84; a member of the Royal Institution, 1887- 1905; and the chancellor of Cambridge, 1908-1919. He was the co-discoverer of argon, 1895, and other rare gases. He pioneered the studies of electromagnetic wave motion, optics, sonics, gas dynamics, as well as perfecting similitude and dimensional analysis as scientific tools. A pioneer in developing molecular acoustics, Lord Rayleigh John Strutt was awarded the Nobel Prize for Physics in 1904.

In the introduction to his published papers, he stated:

> The works of the Lord are great, sought out of all them that have pleasure therein. [104]

ࢫ

George Hay Stuart, 1861-65, was a philanthropist who served as the president of the Christian Commission during the Civil War. Under his direction, that organization was responsible for distributing over 30 million gospel tracts and New Testaments to the soldiers. One of the workers was D.L. Moody, who later became a world renowned minister. George Hay Stuart said:

> I have prayed for this union; and I have labored for it, simply because I believed that it would bring glory to my blessed Lord and Master, Jesus Christ....
> I have labored and prayed for it, because it would bring brethren together, now unhappily divided, to see eye to eye, that the nations that have so long bowed down to idols might learn of Jesus and Him crucified ... Since these twenty-four hours have passed away eighty-six thousand four hundred immortal souls have gone to the judgment seat of Christ....
> I never hear the funeral bell toll without asking myself the question, "What have I done to point that departed soul to the Lamb of God that died to save a perishing world?"
> Brethren, buckle on your armor for a great conflict; buckle it on for giving the glorious Gospel of the Son of God to the millions of the earth who are perishing for lack of knowledge. [105]

ࢫ

Charles Sumner (1811-1874), was a United States Senator from Massachusetts for 23 years, 1851-74. He was strongly opposed to slavery and was persecuted for taking that unpopular stand. So firm was his conviction against slavery, that he was once physically assaulted on the floor of the House by Congressman Preston S. Brooks of South Carolina. He never fully recovered from the injuries incurred. As one of the founders of the Republican Party, Charles Sumner declared:

Charles Sumner

Familiarity with that great story of redemption, when God raised up the slave-born Moses to deliver His chosen people from bondage, and with that sublimer story where our Saviour died a cruel death that all men, without distinction of race, might be saved, makes slavery impossible.

Because Christians are in the minority there is no reason for renouncing Christianity, or for surrendering to the false religions; nor do I doubt that Christianity will yet prevail over the earth as the waters cover the sea.[106]

*William Ashley
"Billy" Sunday*

William Ashley "Billy" Sunday (1862-1935), was a famous American baseball player, 1883-91, who, after working with the Y.M.C.A. from 1891-1895, became a nationally renowned evangelist, 1896-1935. He declared:

Going to church doesn't make you a Christian any more than going to a garage makes you an automobile.[107]

T

William Howard Taft (1857-1930), became the 27th President of the United States, 1909-1913; and served nine years as the Chief Justice of the Supreme Court, 1921-1930. He was also the first Governor of the Philippines, 1901-1904; and served as the Secretary of War under President Theodore Roosevelt, 1904-1908. In his Inaugural Address, March 4, 1909, William Howard Taft proclaimed:

William Howard Taft

> I invoke the considerate sympathy and support of my fellow-citizens and the aid of the Almighty God in the discharge of my responsible duties.[1]

ᘓ

Nahum Tate (1652-1715), honored by England's royalty by being appointed poet-laureate in 1692, was renowned for his version of Shakespeare's *King Lear,* and for being coauthor of Dryden's *Absalom and Achitopel.* In 1700, Nahum Tate composed his *Christmas Hymn,* in which he wrote:

> While shepherds watched their flocks by night,
> All seated on the ground,
> The angel of the Lord came down,
> And glory shone around.[2]

ᘓ

Zachary Taylor (1784-1850), the 12th President of the United States, was a military hero of both the Mexican War and the War of 1812. On February 14, 1849, a delegation of ladies from Frankfurt, Kentucky, presented President Taylor with a beautifully bound

Bible and a copy of the Constitution of the United
States. He sent a message acknowledging their
kindness, which was printed in the *Frankfort
Commonwealth*, February 21, 1849:

Zachary Taylor

> I accept with gratitude and pleasure your
> gift of this inestimable Volume. It was for the love
> of the truths of this great Book that our fathers
> abandoned their native shores for the wilderness.
> Animated by its lofty principles they toiled and
> suffered till the desert blossomed as a rose.
>
> The same truths sustained them in their resolutions to become a
> free nation; and guided by the wisdom of this Book they founded a
> government under which we have grown from three millions to more
> than twenty millions of people, and from being but a stock on the
> borders of this Continent we have spread from the Atlantic to the
> Pacific.
>
> I trust that their principles of liberty may extend, if without
> bloodshed, from the northern to the southern extremities of the
> Continent. If there were in that Book nothing but its great precept, "All
> things whatsoever ye would that men should do unto you, do ye even
> so to them," and if that precept were obeyed, our government might
> extend over the whole Continent.
>
> Accept...my sincere thanks for the kind manner in which you have
> discharged this duty; and expressing again my hearty gratitude to the
> ladies for their beautiful gift, I pray that health, peace, and prosperity
> may long be continued to them.[3]

❧

William Temple (1881-1944), was the Archbishop of York, 1929-
42, and of Canterbury, 1942-44. Active in economic and social
matters, William Temple wrote in *The Malvern Manifesto:*

> There is no structural organization of society which can bring
> about the coming of the Kingdom of God on earth, since all systems
> can be perverted by the selfishness of man.[4]

❧

Constitution of the State of Tennessee 1796, stated:

Article VIII, Section II. No person who denies the being of God, or a future state of rewards and punishments, shall hold any office in the civil department of this State.[5]

&

Supreme Court of Tennessee 1975, in the case of *Swann v. Pack,* 527 S.W. 2d 99, 101 (Sup. Ct. Tn. 1975), asserted:

> The scales are always weighed in favor of free exercise of religion, and the State's interest must be compelling, it must be substantial, and the danger must be clear and present and so grave as to endanger paramount public interests before the state can interfere with the free exercise of religion.[6]

&

Alfred, Lord Tennyson (1809-1892), 1st Baron Tennyson, was accorded the royal honor of being named an English poet-laureate. He authored the famous poem, *Idylls of the King,* 1859-1885, which described the legends of King Arthur's Court, the Knights of the Round Table, Queen Guinevere, Lancelot, and the search for the Holy Grail. Alfred, Lord Tennyson acknowledged that:

> Bible reading is an education in itself.[7]

> The life after death is the cardinal point of Christianity. I believe that God reveals Himself in every individual soul; and my idea of heaven is the perpetual ministry of one soul to another. There are two things which I believe to be beyond the intelligence of man: the one the intellectual genius of Shakespeare, and the other the religious genius of Christ.[8]

In 1850, Alfred, Lord Tennyson wrote his famous work *In Memoriam.* Queen Victoria once said, "Next to the Bible, *'In Memoriam'* is my comfort."[9] In it Tennyson wrote:

> And so the Word had breath, and wrought
> With human hands the creed of creeds
> In loveliness of perfect deeds,
> More strong than all poetic thought.[10]

Ring in the valiant man and free,
The larger heart, the kindlier hand;
Ring out the darkness of the land,
Ring in the Christ that is to be.[11]

In *Ode on the Death of the Duke of Wellington*, 1852, st. 9, Tennyson wrote:

Speak no more of his renown.
Lay your earthly fancies down,
And in the vast cathedral leave him.
God accept him, Christ receive him.[12]

In *Maud*, 1855, Part II, sec. iv, st. 3, Tennyson wrote:

Oh, Christ, that it were possible
For one short hour to see
The souls we loved, that they might tell us
What and where they be.[13]

In *Enoch Arden*, 1864, line 222, Tennyson wrote:

Cast all your cares on God; that anchor holds.[14]

In *The Higher Pantheism*, 1869, st. 6, Tennyson wrote:

Speak to Him thou for He hears, and Spirit with Spirit can meet—
Closer is He than breathing, and nearer than hands and feet.[15]

In other works, Alfred, Lord Tennyson wrote:

In Grief

Strong Son of God! Immortal Love,
Whom we, that have not seen Thy face,
By faith, and faith alone, embrace,
Believing where we can not prove!

Thine are these orbs of light and shade;
Thou madest life in man and brute;
Thou madest Death; and lo, Thy foot
Is on the skull which Thou hast made!

Thou wilt not leave us in the dust;
Thou madest man, he knows not why;
He thinks he was not made to die;
And Thou hast made Him: Thou art just.

Thou seemest human and Divine,
The highest, holiest manhood, Thou;
Our wills are ours, we know not how;
Our wills are ours to make them Thine.[16]

Lazarus

When Lazarus left his charnel-cave,
And home to Mary's house returned,
Was this demanded—if he yearned
To hear her weeping by his grave?

"Where wert thou, brother, those four days?"
There lives no record of reply,
Which, telling what it is to die,
Had surely added praise to praise.

From every house the neighbors met,
The streets were filled with joyful sound;
A solemn gladness even crowned
The purple brows of Olivet.

Behold a man raised up by Christ;
The rest remained unrevealed;
He told it not, or something sealed
The lips of that Evangelist.[17]

In *Flower in the Crannied Wall*, 1869, Tennyson wrote:

Flower in the crannied wall,
I pluck you out of the crannies,
I hold you here, root and all, in my hand,
Little flower—but if I could understand
What you are, root and all, and all in all,
I should know what God and man is.[18]

In *Idylls of the King*, 1859-1885, Tennyson wrote *The Passing of*

Arthur, line 9:

> I found Him in the shining of the stars,
> I marked Him in the flowering of His fields,
> But in His ways with men I find Him not.[19]

In line 407:

> And slowly answered Arthur from the barge:
> The old order changeth, yielding place to new;
> And God fulfills himself in many ways,
> Lest one good custom should corrupt the world.[20]

In *Crossing the Bar*, 1889, st. 3, Tennyson wrote:

> I hope to see my Pilot face to face
> When I have crossed the bar.[21]

ે.

Mother Teresa of Calcutta (1910-   ), an internationally renowned Catholic nun, was awarded the Nobel Prize in 1979 for her work among the poor and outcast. She confessed:

> Many people mistake our work for our vocation. Our vocation is the love of Jesus.[22]

> God hasn't called me to be successful. He's called me to be faithful.[23]

> We can do no great things, only small things with great love.[24]

> If you want to pray better, you must pray more.[25]

> I see Jesus in every human being. I say to myself, this is hungry Jesus, I must feed him. This is sick Jesus. This one has leprosy or gangrene; I must wash him and tend to him. I serve because I love Jesus.[26]

On February 3, 1994, Mother Teresa spoke at the National Prayer Breakfast in Washington, D.C., before an audience of 3,000, including President and Mrs. Bill Clinton and Vice-President Al Gore. The frail 83-year-old Mother Teresa spoke simply, yet with a powerful directness to America, saying:

> Jesus died on the Cross because that is what it took for Him to do good to us—to save us from our selfishness in sin....to show us that we too must be willing to give up everything to do God's will....
>
> But I feel that the greatest destroyer of peace today is abortion, because it is a war against the child, a direct killing of the innocent child, murder by the mother herself and if we accept that a mother can kill even her own child, how can we tell other people not to kill one another?
>
> How do we persuade a woman not to have an abortion? As always, we must persuade her with love and we remind ourselves that love means to be willing to give until it hurts. Jesus gave even His life to love us. So the mother who is thinking of abortion, should be helped to love, that is, to give until it hurts her plans or her free time, to respect the life of her child.
>
> The father of that child, whoever he is, must also give until it hurts. By abortion, the mother does not learn to love, but kills even her own child to solve her problems. And, by abortion, the father is told that he does not have to take any responsibility for the child he has brought into the world. The father is likely to put other women into the same trouble. So abortion just leads to more abortion.
>
> Any country that accepts abortion is not teaching its people to love, but to use violence to get what they want. That is why the greatest destroyer of love and peace is abortion.
>
> Many people are very, very concerned with the children of India, with the children of Africa where quite a few die of hunger, and so on. Many people are also concerned about all the violence in this great country of the United States. These concerns are very good. But often these same people are not concerned with the millions who are being killed by the deliberate decision of their own mothers....
>
> We have sent word to the clinics, to the hospitals and police stations: "Please don't destroy the child; we will take the child." So we always have someone tell the mothers in trouble: "Come, we will take care of you, we will get a home for your child." And we have a tremendous demand from couples who cannot have a child....
>
> Jesus said, "Anyone who receives a child in my name, receives me." By adopting a child, these couples receive Jesus but by aborting a child, a couple refuses to receive Jesus.
>
> Please don't kill the child. I want the child. Please give me the child. I am willing to accept any child who would be aborted and to give that child to a married couple who will love the child and be loved by the child. From our children's home in Calcutta alone, we have saved over 3,000 children from abortion....

If we remember that God loves us, and that we can love others as He loves us, then America can become a sign of peace for the world. From here, a sign of care for the weakest of the weak—the unborn child—must go out to the world. If you become a burning light of justice and peace in the world, then really you will be true to what the founders of this country stood for. God bless you![27]

&

Texas Declaration of Independence March 2, 1836:

UNANIMOUS DECLARATION OF INDEPENDENCE
BY THE DELEGATES OF THE PEOPLE OF TEXAS IN GENERAL CONVENTION AT THE TOWN OF WASHINGTON. ON THE SECOND DAY OF MARCH, 1836.

When a government has ceased to protect the lives, liberty, and property of the people...and...becomes an instrument in the hands of evil rulers for their oppression....in such a crisis...the inherent and inalienable right of the people to...take their political affairs into their own hands in extreme cases, enjoins it as a right towards themselves and a sacred obligation to their posterity to abolish such government, and create another in its stead, calculated to rescue them from impending dangers, and to secure their welfare and happiness....

The late changes made in the government by General Antonio Lopez Santa Ana, who having overturned the constitution of his country, now offers, as the cruel alternative, either abandon our homes acquired by so many privations, or submit to the most intolerable of all tyranny....

It denies us the right of worshipping the Almighty according to the dictates of our own conscience, by the support of a National Religion, calculated to promote the temporal interest of its human functionaries, rather than the glory of the true and living God.

It has demanded us to deliver up our arms, which are essential to our defence—the rightful property of freemen—and formidable only to tyrannical governments....

It has, through its emissaries, incited the merciless savage, with the tomahawk and scalping knife, to massacre the inhabitants of our defenceless frontiers....

We, therefore...DECLARE, that our political connection with the Mexican nation has forever ended, and that the people of Texas, do now constitute a FREE, SOVEREIGN, and INDEPENDENT REPUBLIC...

Conscious of the rectitude of our intentions, we fearlessly and confidently commit the issue to the decision of the Supreme Arbiter of the destinies of nations.[28]

ð

Supreme Court of Texas June 30, 1993, in the case of *Ex Parte: Reverend Keith Tucci*, declared that a proposed 100-foot "speech free zone" around abortion facilities violated the Constitution of the State of Texas. The Texas Supreme Court Opinion stated:

> Today our court continues to favor the growth and enhancement of freedom, not its constraint. The fact that vigorous debate of public issues in our society may produce speech considered obnoxious or offensive by some is a necessary cost of that freedom. Our Constitution calls on this court to maintain a commitment to expression that is strong and uncompromising for friend and foe alike.[29]

ð

Cal Thomas 1983, in his published work entitled *Book Burning*, exposed the bias embedded in current media trends. A graduate of American University in Washington, D.C., Cal Thomas' background with NBC and numerous other broadcast companies has given him over 32 years of journalism experience in radio and T.V. Nationally acclaimed as a reporter, news commentator, author and syndicated columnist, Cal Thomas remonstrated:

> All we are asking for is balance. I would like to think that I could walk into a public library and find not only works by Gloria Steinem but also those of Phyllis Schlafly. I would like to think that a teenager could be taught in sex education that a serious alternative to abortion is teenage abstinence, or should pregnancy occur, that adoption might be preferable. I am not trying, as the ad says, to shove religion down anyone's throat. But I do think everyone has a right, and that the Christian voice is being choked off.[30]

ð

Norman Mattoon Thomas (1884-1968), was a U.S. socialist leader, reformer and author. He stated in a speech before an anti-war protest in Washington, D.C., November 27, 1965:

> I'd rather see America save her soul than her face.[31]

ð

Leo Nikolaevich Tolstoi (1828-1910), was a renowned Russian writer and playwright. In *War and Peace*, 1865-1869, book XIV, chapter 18, he wrote:

> For us, with the rule of right and wrong given us by Christ, there is nothing for which we have no standard. And there is no greatness where there is not simplicity, goodness and truth.[32]

In describing President Abraham Lincoln after his death, Count Leo Tolstoi, declared him:

> A Christ in miniature.[33]

🙋

Augustus Montague Toplady (1740-1778), composed the world-famous hymn *Rock of Ages*, which first appeared in the *Gospel Magazine* in October of 1775. Toplady wrote:

> Rock of Ages, cleft for me,
> Let me hide myself in Thee.[34]

🙋

Harry S. Truman (1884-1972), was the 33rd President of the United States of America, after having served as Vice-President under President Roosevelt. On April 12, 1945, the day after Franklin D. Roosevelt's funeral, President Harry S. Truman concluded his first address before a joint session of Congress:

Harry S. Truman

> At this moment I have in my heart a prayer. As I have assumed my heavy duties, I humbly pray to Almighty God in the words of King Solomon, "Give therefore Thy servant an understanding heart to judge Thy people that I may discern between good and bad; for who is able to judge this Thy so great a people?" I ask only to be a good and faithful servant of my Lord and my people.[35]

To Pope Pius XII, in 1947, President Truman wrote of America:

> This is a Christian nation.[36]

On November 29, 1948, in a personal letter to Dr. Chaim Weizmann, President of the State of Israel, President Harry S. Truman wrote:

> I want to tell you how happy and impressed I have been at the remarkable progress made by the new State of Israel.[37]

In his Inaugural Address, January 20, 1949:

> We believe that all men are created equal because they are created in the image of God....With God's help the future of mankind will be assured in a world of justice, harmony and peace.[38]

President Harry S. Truman, in 1950, stated:

> But all of us—at home, at war, wherever we may be—are within the reach of God's love and power. We all can pray. We all should pray. We should ask the fulfillment of God's will. We should ask for courage, wisdom, for the quietness of soul which comes alone to them who place their lives in His hands.[39]

President Truman commented on peace:

> Peace is the goal of my life. I'd rather have lasting peace in the world than be President. I wish for peace, I work for peace and I pray for peace continually.[40]

President Truman recorded his favorite prayer:

> O Almighty and Everlasting God, Creator of Heaven, Earth and the Universe:
> Help me to be, to think, to act what is right, because it is right; make me truthful, honest and honorable in all things; make me intellectually honest for the sake of right and honor and without thought of reward to me. Give me the ability to be charitable, forgiving and patient with my fellow men—help me to understand their motives and their shortcomings—even as thou understandest mine! Amen, Amen, Amen.[41]

President Harry S. Truman gave this admonition:

> The fundamental basis of this nation's laws was given to Moses on the Mount. The fundamental basis of our Bill of Rights comes from the teachings we get from Exodus and St. Matthew, from Isaiah and St. Paul. I don't think we emphasize that enough these days. If we don't have a proper fundamental moral background, we will finally end up

with a totalitarian government which does not believe in rights for anybody except the State![42]

&

Jonathan Trumbull (1710-1785), was the British Governor of Connecticut who had been appointed by King George III. He was also the father of the famous Revolutionary artist of the same name (1756-1843). Jonathan Trumbull became sympathetic to the American cause and, in 1773, he openly shared:

Jonathan Trumbull

> It is hard to break connections with our mother country, but when she strives to enslave us, the strictest union must be dissolved...."The Lord reigneth; let the earth rejoice; let the multitudes of isles be glad thereof"—the accomplishment of such noble prophecies is at hand.[43]

In the early 1770s, as the tension was mounting in the Colonies prior to the Revolution, another governor who had been appointed by King George III, wrote to the Board of Trade in England:

> If you ask an American, who is his master? He will tell you he has none, nor any governor but Jesus Christ.[44]

On April 19, 1775, Governor Trumbull of the Connecticut Colony proclaimed a day of Fasting and Prayer, asking that:

> God would graciously pour out His Holy Spirit on us to bring us to a thorough Repentance and effectual Reformation that our iniquities may not be our ruin; that He would restore, preserve and secure the Liberties of this and all the other British American colonies, and make the Land a mountain of Holiness, and Habitation of Righteousness forever.[45]

On July 13, 1775, Governor Jonathan Trumbull wrote from Lebanon, Connecticut, to George Washington, informing him of the Continental Fast Day and exhorting him as the General of the Continental Army:

The Honorable Congress have proclaimed a Fast to be observed by the inhabitants of all the English Colonies on this continent, to stand before the Lord in one day, with public humiliation, fasting, and prayer, to deplore our many sins, to offer up our joint supplications to God, for forgiveness, and for his merciful interposition for us in this day of unnatural darkness and distress.

They have, with one united voice, appointed you to the high station you possess. The Supreme Director of all events hath caused a wonderful union of hearts and counsels to subsist among us. Now therefore, be strong and very courageous.

May the God of the armies of Israel shower down the blessings of his Divine Providence on you, give you wisdom and fortitude, cover your head in the day of battle and danger, add success, convince our enemies of their mistaken measures, and that all their attempts to deprive these Colonies of their inestimable constitutional rights and liberties are injurious and vain.[46]

In August of 1776, in response to General Washington's desperate plea for reinforcements, Governor Trumbull called for nine more regiments of volunteers. He sent out this appeal:

In this day of calamity, to trust altogether to the justice of our cause, without our utmost exertion, would be tempting Providence....March on!—This shall be your warrant: Play the man for God, and for the cities of our God. May the Lord of Hosts, the God of the armies of Israel, be your Captain, your Leader, your Conductor, and Saviour.[47]

ใ๏

Sojourner Truth (1797-1883), was a freed slave who moved with her family to New York. She then heard "a voice from Heaven," and began to travel the country preaching truth. She became a strong part of the abolitionist movement:

When I left the house of bondage I left everything behind. I wanted to keep nothing of Egypt on me, and so I went to the Lord and asked him to give me a new name....

I set up my banner, and then I sing, and then folks always comes up 'round me, and then...I tells them about Jesus.[48]

ใ๏

Harriet Tubman (1821-1913), was a former slave who repeatedly risked her life to free over 300 slaves, through what came to be known as the *Underground Railroad*. After the Civil War she helped set up schools for freed slaves. She said:

> I always told God: I'm gwine to hole stiddy on to you, and you got to see me trou...Jes so long as He wants to use me, He'll tak ker of me, and when He don't want me any longer, I'm ready to go.[49]

To her biographer, Sarah H. Bradford, Harriet Tubman related in 1868:

> 'Twant me, 'twas the Lord. I always told him, "I trust to you. I don't know where to go or what to do, but I expect you to lead me," and he always did.[50]

Mark Twain (1835-1910), whose given name was Samuel Langhorne Clemens, took the pen name "Mark Twain" from a Mississippi river pilot. He wrote many famous novels, including: *The Adventures of Huckleberry Finn*, 1884; *The Adventures of Tom Sawyer*, 1876; *Life on the Mississippi*, 1883; *The Prince and the Pauper*, 1882; *A Connecticut Yankee at King Arthur's Court*, 1889; *Joan of Arc*, 1896; and many more. In the midst of cynics who doubted the authenticity of the Bible, he remarked:

Mark Twain

> If the Ten Commandments were not written by Moses, then they were written by another fellow of the same name.[51]

In *Innocents Abroad*, 1869, which solidly established his reputation, Mark Twain wrote:

> It is hard to make a choice of the most beautiful passage in a book which is so gemmed with beautiful passages as the Bible....
> Who taught these ancient writers the simplicity of language, their felicity of expression, their pathos, and, above all, their faculty of sinking themselves entirely out of sight of the reader and making the narrative stand out alone and seem to tell itself? Shakespeare is always

present when one reads his book; Macaulay is present when we follow the march of his stately sentences; but the Old Testament writers are hidden from view.[52]

We dismounted on those shores which the feet of the Saviour had made holy ground....We left Capernaum behind us. It was only a shapeless ruin. It bore no semblance to a town. But, all desolate and unpeopled as it was, it was illustrious ground. From it sprang that tree of Christianity whose broad arms overshadow so many distant lands today. Christ visited his old home at Nazareth, and saw His brothers Joses, Judas, James, and Simon....

Who wonders what passed in their minds when they saw this brother (who was only a brother to them, however He might be to others a mysterious stranger; who was a God, and had stood face to face with God above the clouds) doing miracles, with crowds of astonished people for witnesses?[53]

One of the most astonishing things that has yet fallen under our observation is the exceedingly small portion of the earth from which sprang the new flourishing plant of Christianity. The longest journey our Saviour ever performed was from here to Jerusalem—about one hundred to one hundred and twenty miles....Leaving out two or three short journeys, He spent His life, preaching His Gospel, and performing His miracles, within a compass no larger than an ordinary county of the United States....

In the starlight, Galilee has no boundaries but the broad compass of the heavens, and is a theatre meet for great events; meet for the birth of a religion able to save the world; and meet for the stately figure appointed to stand upon its stage and proclaim high decrees.[54]

In *The Adventures of Tom Sawyer*, 1876, Mark Twain wrote:

There was no getting around the stubborn fact that taking sweetmeats was only "hooking," while taking bacon and hams and such valuables was plain simple stealing—and there was a command against that in the Bible. So they inwardly resolved that so long as they remained in the business, their piracies should not again be sullied with the crime of stealing.[55]

In *The Tragedy of Pudd'nhead Wilson*, 1894, Mark Twain penned:

Adam and Eve had many advantages, but the principal one was that they escaped teething.[56]

Adam was but human—this explains it all. He did not want the apple for the apple's sake, he wanted it because it was forbidden.[57]

Whoever has lived long enough to find out what life is, knows how deep a debt of gratitude we owe to Adam, the first great benefactor of our race. He brought death into the world.[58]

It is by the goodness of God that in our country we have those three unspeakably precious things: freedom of speech, freedom of conscience, and the prudence never to practice either of them.[59]

Mark Twain quipped:

The calm confidence of a Christian with four aces.[60]

From Albert Bigelow Paine's *Mark Twain*, 1912, Mark Twain is quoted as saying:

As out of place as a Presbyterian in Hell.[61]

From Bernard De Voto's *Mark Twain in Eruption*, 1940, Mark Twain is quoted as saying:

I believe that our Heavenly Father invented man because he was disappointed with the monkey.[62]

ᴥ

John Tyndall (1820-1893), was a British physicist and philosopher who became the director of the Royal Institute. His scientific studies included: glacier flow, transmission and radiation of heat, and the Tyndall effect, which demonstrates how light is scattered by microscopic particles such as dust and colloids in suspension. In *Fragments of Science*, vol. II, "Professor Virchow and Evolution," Tyndall stated:

Religious feeling is as much a verity as any other part of human consciousness; and against it, on the subjective side, the waves of science beat in vain.[63]

ᴥ

U

United States Supreme Court 1789, was "ordained and established" by the Judiciary Act of Congress. Originally consisting of 6 justices, it has since been increased to 9. The Supreme Court Building in Washington, D.C., designed by Cass Gilbert, was completed in 1935. Engraved in stone above the head of the Chief Justice are the Ten Commandments with the great American eagle protecting them. Moses is included among the great lawgivers in Herman A. MacNeil's marble-sculpture relief on the East Portico. At the beginning of each session of the court, as the Justices stand before their desks, the crier opens with the invocation:

> God save the United States and this Honorable Court.[1]

&.

United States Supreme Court 1844, in the case of *Vidal v. Girard's Executors*, 43 U.S. 126, 132, Justice Joseph Story delivered the court's opinion. The case concerned one Stephen Girard, a deist from France, who had moved to Philadelphia and later died. In his will he left his entire estate, valued at over $7 million, to establish an orphanage and school, with the stipulation that no religious influence be allowed. The city rejected the proposal, as their lawyers declared:

> The plan of education proposed is anti-christian, and therefore repugnant to the law....The purest principles of morality are to be taught. Where are they found? Whoever searches for them must go to the source from which a Christian man derives his faith—the Bible....There is an obligation to teach what the Bible alone can teach,

viz. a pure system of morality....

Both in the Old and New Testaments [religious instruction's] importance is recognized. In the Old it is said, "Thou shalt diligently teach them to thy children," and the New, "Suffer the little children to come unto me and forbid them not...." No fault can be found with Girard for wishing a marble college to bear his name for ever, but it is not valuable unless is has a fragrance of Christianity about it.[2]

The United States Supreme Court rendered its unanimous opinion, stating:

Christianity...is not to be maliciously and openly reviled and blasphemed against, to the annoyance of believers or the injury of the public....It is unnecessary for us, however, to consider the establishment of a school or college, for the propagation of...Deism, or any other form of infidelity.

Such a case is not to be presumed to exist in a Christian country....Why may not laymen instruct in the general principles of Christianity as well as ecclesiastics....

And we cannot overlook the blessings, which such [lay]men by their conduct, as well as their instructions, may, nay must impart to their youthful pupils. Why may not the Bible, and especially the New Testament, without note or comment, be read and taught as a divine revelation in the [school]—its general precepts expounded, its evidences explained and its glorious principles of morality inculcated?...

Where can the purest principles of morality be learned so clearly or so perfectly as from the New Testament?[3]

It is also said, and truly, that the Christian religion is a part of the common law of Pennsylvania....[4]

&

United States Supreme Court 1878, rendered its opinion on the case of *Reynolds v. United States*, 98 U.S. 145, 165 (1878). The same men that successfully passed the act creating religious freedom in Virginia, also passed very strict laws against polygamy and sexual immorality, as documented in the Supreme Court's decision of 1878:

It is a significant fact that on the 8th of December, 1788, after the passage of the act establishing religious freedom, and after the convention of Virginia had recommended as an amendment to the Constitution of the United States the declaration in a bill of rights that "all men have an equal, natural, and unalienable right to the free exercise of religion, according to the dictates of conscience,"[that] the legislature of that State substantially enacted the...death penalty...[for polygamy].[5]

United States Supreme Court 1884, in reference to the individual's God-given rights, stated:

> These inherent rights have never been more happily expressed than in the Declaration of Independence, "we hold these truths to be self-evident"—that is so plain that their truth is recognized upon their mere statement—"that all men are endowed"—not by edicts of emperors or decrees of parliament, or acts of Congress, but "by their Creator with certain inalienable rights and that among these are life, liberty and the pursuit of happiness, and to secure these"—not grant them but secure them—"governments are instituted among men."[6]

United States Supreme Court 1885, in the case of *Murphy v. Ramsey & Others*, 144 U.S. 15, 45 (1885), gave its opinion:

> Every person who has a husband or wife living...and marries another...is guilty of polygamy, and shall be punished....Certainly no legislation can be supposed more wholesome and necessary in the founding of a free, self-governing commonwealth...than that which seeks to establish it on the basis of the idea of the family, as consisting in and springing from the union for life of one man and one woman in the holy estate of matrimony; [the family is] the sure foundation of all that is stable and noble in our civilization; the best guarantee of that reverent morality which is the source of all beneficent progress in social and political improvement.[7]

United States Supreme Court 1889, stated in the case of *Davis v. Beason*, 133 U.S. 333, 341-343, 348 (1890), that the United States considers bigamy and polygamy as crimes. The State of Idaho also declared bigamy and polygamy illegal, and declared that anyone who commits it, teaches it or even encourages it, is forbidden from voting or holding office in that Territory.

A man named Samuel Davis was caught in the crime, fined and jailed. He argued that he was being imprisoned for his religious belief and that he should have the freedom to commit bigamy and polygamy under the First Amendment. The decision of the Court was delivered by Justice Stephen Field, who had been appointed by President Abraham Lincoln in 1863. It stated:

> Bigamy and polygamy are crimes by the laws of all civilized and Christian countries. They are crimes by the laws of the United States, and they are crimes by the laws of Idaho. They tend to destroy the purity of the marriage relation, to disturb the peace of families, to degrade woman and debase man....
>
> To extend exemption from punishment for such crimes would be to shock the moral judgement of the community. To call their advocacy a tenet of religion is to offend the commons sense of mankind.
>
> There have been sects which denied as a part of their religious tenets that there should be any marriage tie, and advocated promiscuous intercourse of the sexes as prompted by the passions of its members....
>
> Should a sect of either of these kinds ever find its way into this country, swift punishment would follow the carrying into effect of its doctrines, and no heed would be given to the pretence that...their supporters could be protected in their exercise by the Constitution of the United States.
>
> Probably never before in the history of this country has it been seriously contended that the whole punitive power of the government for acts, recognized by the general consent of the Christian world...must be suspended in order that the tenets of a religious sect...may be carried out without hindrance.
>
> The constitutions of several States, in providing for religious freedom, have declared expressly that such freedom shall not be construed to excuse acts of licentiousness....
>
> The constitution of New York of 1777 provided: The free exercise and enjoyment of religious profession and worship, without discrimination or preference, shall forever hereafter be allowed, within this State, to all mankind: Provided, That the liberty of conscience, hereby granted, shall not be so construed as to excuse acts of licentiousness....The constitutions of California, Colorado, Connecticut,

Florida, Georgia, Illinois, Maryland, Minnesota, Mississippi, Missouri, Nevada and South Carolina contain a similar declaration. [8]

৯৯

United States Supreme Court 1890, in the case of *The Church of Jesus Christ of Latter Day Saints v. United States,* 136 U.S. 1 (1890), forbade the practice of polygamy in the United States, stating:

> It is contrary to the spirit of Christianity and the civilization which Christianity has produced in the Western world. [9]

৯৯

United States Supreme Court February 29, 1892, in the case of *Church of the Holy Trinity v. United States,* 143 US 457-458,465-471, 36 L ed 226, Justice Josiah Brewer rendered the high court's decision:

> No purpose of action against religion can be imputed to any legislation, state or national, because this is a religious people. This is historically true. From the discovery of this continent to the present hour, there is a single voice making this affirmation.
>
> The commission to Christopher Columbus ... [recited] that "it is hoped that by God's assistance some of the continents and islands in the ocean will be discovered..."
>
> The first colonial grant made to Sir Walter Raleigh in 1584 ... and the grant authorizing him to enact statutes for the government of the proposed colony provided that they "be not against the true Christian faith...."
>
> The first charter of Virginia, granted by King James I in 1606 ... commenced the grant in these words: "...in propagating of Christian Religion to such People as yet live in Darkness...."
>
> Language of similar import may be found in the subsequent charters of that colony ... in 1609 and 1611; and the same is true of the various charters granted to the other colonies. In language more or less emphatic is the establishment of the Christian religion declared to be one of the purposes of the grant. The celebrated compact made by the Pilgrims in the Mayflower, 1620, recites: "Having undertaken for the Glory of God, and advancement of the Christian faith... a voyage to plant the first colony in the northern parts of Virginia..."
>
> The fundamental orders of Connecticut, under which a provisional

government was instituted in 1638-1639, commence with this declaration: "...And well knowing where a people are gathered together the word of God requires that to maintain the peace and union... there should be an orderly and decent government established according to God ... to maintain and preserve the liberty and purity of the gospel of our Lord Jesus which we now profess ... of the said gospel [which] is now practiced amongst us."

In the charter of privileges granted by William Penn to the province of Pennsylvania, in 1701, it is recited: "...no people can be truly happy, though under the greatest enjoyment of civil liberties, if abridged of ... their religious profession and worship...."

Coming nearer to the present time, the Declaration of Independence recognizes the presence of the Divine in human affairs in these words:

"We hold these truths to be self-evident, that all men are created equal, that they are endowed by their Creator with certain unalienable Rights ... appealing to the Supreme Judge of the world for the rectitude of our intentions .... And for the support of this Declaration, with firm reliance on the Protection of Divine Providence, we mutually pledge to each other our Lives, our Fortunes, and our sacred Honor."...

We find everywhere a clear recognition of the same truth... because of a general recognition of this truth, the question has seldom been presented to the courts....

There is no dissonance in these declarations. There is a universal language pervading them all, having one meaning; they affirm and reaffirm that this is a religious nation. These are not individual sayings, declarations of private persons: they are organic utterances; they speak the voice of the entire people.

While because of a general recognition of this truth the question has seldom been presented to the courts, yet we find that in *Updegraph v. The Commonwealth,* it was decided that, Christianity, general Christianity, is, and always has been, a part of the common law.... not Christianity with an established church ... but Christianity with liberty of conscience to all men.

And in *The People v. Ruggles,* Chancellor Kent, the great commentator on American law, speaking as Chief Justice of the Supreme Court of New York, said:

"The people of this State, in common with the people of this country, profess the general doctrines of Christianity, as the rule of their faith and practice.... We are a Christian people, and the morality of the country is deeply engrafted upon Christianity, and not upon the doctrines or worship of those impostors."

And in the famous case of *Vidal v. Girard's Executors,* this Court... observed: "It is also said, and truly, that the Christian religion is a part of the common law..."

If we pass beyond these matters to a view of American life as expressed by its laws, its business, its customs and its society, we find everywhere a clear recognition of the same truth. Among other matters note the following: The form of oath universally prevailing, concluding with an appeal to the Almighty; the custom of opening sessions of all deliberative bodies and most conventions with prayer; the prefatory words of all wills, "In the name of God, amen"; the laws respecting the observance of the Sabbath, with the general cessation of all secular business, and the closing of courts, legislatures, and other similar public assemblies on that day; the churches and church organizations which abound in every city, town and hamlet; the multitude of charitable organizations existing everywhere under Christian auspices; the gigantic missionary associations, with general support, and aiming to establish Christian missions in every quarter of the globe.

These, and many other matters which might be noticed, add a volume of unofficial declarations to the mass of organic utterances that this is a Christian nation .... we find everywhere a clear recognition of the same truth. [10]

The happiness of a people and the good order and preservation of civil government essentially depend upon piety, religion and morality. [11]

Religion, morality, and knowledge [are] necessary to good government, the preservation of liberty, and the happiness of mankind. [11]

A commentary on *Church of the Holy Trinity v. US* summarized:

Our laws and our institutions must necessarily be based upon and embody the teachings of the Redeemer of mankind. It is impossible that it should be otherwise; and in this sense and to this extent our civilization and our institutions are emphatically Christian. [12]

ã€€

United States Supreme Court 1895, in the case of *Pollock v. Farmers' Loan and Trust Co.,* 157, U.S. 429,574,596 (1895), declared income tax unconstitutional. The court's membership consisted of Chief Justice Melville W. Fuller, Ill.; Justice David Josiah Brewer, Kan.; Justice Horace Gray, Mass.; Justice John M. Harlan, Ky.; Justice Henry B. Brown, Mich.; Justice Stephen J. Field, Ca.; Justice George Shiras, Jr., Pa.; Justice Howell E. Jackson, Tenn.; and Justice Edward D. White, La. [13]

Chief Justice Melville W. Fuller stated:

The original expectation was that the power of direct taxation would be exercised only in extraordinary exigencies, and down to August 15, 1894, this expectation has been realized.[14]

Justice Stephen J. Field stated:

The income tax law under consideration is marked by discriminating features which affect the whole law. It discriminates between those who receive an income of four thousand dollars and those who do not....

The legislation, in the discrimination it makes, is class legislation. Whenever a distinction is made in the burdens a law imposes or in the benefits it confers on any citizens by reason of their birth, or wealth, or religion, it is class legislation, and leads inevitably to oppression and abuses, and to general unrest and disturbance in society. It was hoped and believed that the great amendments to the Constitution which followed the late civil war had rendered such legislation impossible for all future time. But the objectional legislation reappears in the act under consideration. It is the same in essential character as that of the English income statute of 1691, which taxed Protestants at a certain rate, Catholics, as a class, at double the rate of Protestants, and Jews at another and separate rate.[15]

૨**

United States Supreme Court 1925, in the case of *Pierce v. Society of Sisters*, 268 U.S. 510 (1925), stated:

The fundamental theory upon which all governments in this Union repose excludes any general power of the state to standardize its children.[16]

The child is not the mere creature of the state.[17]

૨**

United States Supreme Court 1931, in the case of *United States v. Macintosh*, 283 U.S. 605, 625 (1931), Justice George Sutherland delivered the court's decision regarding a Canadian seeking naturalization by reiterating the Court's decision of 1892:

We are a Christian people...according to one another the equal right of religious freedom, and acknowledge with reverence the duty of obedience to the will of God.[18]

ϧ

United States Supreme Court 1939, in the case of *Hague v. C.I.O.*, 307 U.S. 496, 515 (1939), stated:

Wherever the title of streets and parks may rest, they have immemorially been held in trust for the use of the public, and time out of mind, have been used for the purposes of assembly, communicating thoughts between citizens, and discussing public questions.[19]

ϧ

United States Supreme Court 1948, in the case of *McCollum v. Board of Education*, 333 U.S. 203, Justice Felix Frankfurter rendered the court's opinion:

Traditionally, organized education in the Western world was Church education. It could hardly be otherwise when the education of children was primarily study of the Word and the ways of God. Even in the Protestant countries, where there was a less close identification of Church and State, the basis of education was largely the Bible, and its chief purpose inculcation of piety....[20]

ϧ

United States Supreme Court 1952, in the case of *Zorach v. Clauson*, 343 US 306 307 313, Justice William O. Douglas delivered the court's decision, stating:

The First Amendment, however, does not say that in every respect there shall be a separation of Church and State. Rather, it studiously defines the manner, the specific ways, in which there shall be no concert or union or dependency one on the other.

That is the common sense of the matter. Otherwise the state and religion would be aliens to each other—hostile, suspicious, and even unfriendly....

Municipalities would not be permitted to render police or fire protection to religious groups. Policemen who helped parishioners into their places of worship would violate the Constitution. Prayers in our legislative halls; the appeals to the Almighty in the messages of the Chief Executive; the proclamation making Thanksgiving Day a holiday; "so help me God" in our courtroom oaths—these and all other references to the Almighty that run through our laws, our public rituals, our ceremonies, would be flouting the First Amendment. A fastidious atheist or agnostic could even object to the supplication with which the Court opens each session: God save the United States and this Honorable Court.

We are a religious people and our institutions presuppose a Supreme Being....When the state encourages religious instruction or cooperates with religious authorities by adjusting the schedule of public events to sectarian needs, it follows the best of our traditions.

For it then respects the religious nature of our people and accommodates the public service to their spiritual needs. To hold that it may not would be to find in the Constitution a requirement that the government show a callous indifference to religious groups. That would be preferring those who believe in no religion over those who do believe....

We find no constitutional requirement makes it necessary for government to be hostile to religion and to throw its weight against the efforts to widen the scope of religious influence. The government must remain neutral when it comes to competition between sects....

We cannot read into the Bill of Rights such a philosophy of hostility to religion.[21]

ða

United States Supreme Court 1962, in the case of *Engle v. Vitale;* as quoted in *Stone v. Graham*, 449 U.S. 39, 46 (1980) and *Abington v. Schempp*, 374 U.S. 203, 212 (1963), stated:

The history of man is inseparable from the history of religion.[22]

ða

United States Supreme Court 1963, in the case of *School District of Abington Township v. Schempp*, 374 U.S. 203, 212, 225 (1963), pp. 21, 71, records Associate Justice Tom Clark, writing the Court's opinion:

It is true that religion has been closely identified with our history and government. As we said in *Engle v. Vitale*, "The history of man is inseparable from the history of religion."[23]

Secularism is unconstitutional....preferring those who do not believe over those who do believe....It is the duty of government to deter no-belief religions....Facilities of government cannot offend religious principles....[24]

[T]he State may not establish a 'religion of secularism' in the sense of affirmatively opposing or showing hostility to religion, thus preferring those who believe in no religion over those who do believe.[25]

It might well be said that one's education is not complete without a study of comparative religion or the history of religion and its relationship to the advancement of civilization. It certainly may be said that the Bible is worthy of study for its literary and historic qualities. Nothing we have said here indicates that such study of the Bible or of religion, when presented objectively as part of a secular program of education, may not be effected consistently with the First Amendment.[26]

⁊⋆

United States Supreme Court 1969, in the case of *Tinker v. Des Moines Independent School District*, 393 U.S. 503, 506, 512, 513 (1969), stated:

It can hardly be argued that either students or teachers shed their constitutional rights to freedom of speech or expression at the schoolhouse gate. [Student's rights apply] in the cafeteria, or on the playing field, or on campus during authorized hours....[27]

School officials do not possess absolute authority over their students.[28]

⁊⋆

United States Supreme Court 1973, in the case of *Anderson v. Salt Lake City Corp*, 475 F. 2d 29, 33, 34 (10th Cir. 1973), cert. denied, 414 U.S. 879, stated:

But this creed does not include any element of coercion concerning these beliefs unless one considers it coercive to look upon the Ten

Commandments. Although they are in plain view, no one is required to read or recite them.

It does not seem reasonable to require removal of a passive monument, involving no compulsion, because its accepted precepts, as a foundation for law, reflect the religious nature of an ancient era. [29]

ॐ

United States Supreme Court 1980, in the case of *Stone v. Graham,* 449 U.S. 39, 42, 46 (1980), stated:

Religion has been closely identified with our history and government, *Abington School District,* 1963, and that the history of man is inseparable from the history of religion. *Engle v. Vitale,* 1962. [30]

The Bible may constitutionally be used in an appropriate study of history, civilization, ethics, comparative religion, or the like. [31]

ॐ

United States Supreme Court 1981, in the case of *Widmar v. Vincent,* 454 U.S. 263, 269 (1981), stated:

Religious worship and discussion ... are forms of speech and association protected by the First Amendment. [32]

ॐ

United States Supreme Court 1982, in the case of *Chambers v. Marsh,* 675 F. 2d 228,233 (8th Cir. 1982); review allowed, 463 U.S. 783 (1982), recorded Chief Justice Warren E. Burger's delivery of the court's opinion:

The legislature by majority vote invites a clergyman to give a prayer, neither the inviting nor the giving nor the hearing of the prayer is making a law. On this basis alone... the saying of prayers, per se, in the legislative halls at the opening session is not prohibited by the First and Fourteenth Amendments. [33]

The case of *Bogen v. Doty...* involved a county board's practice of opening each of its public meetings with a prayer offered by a local member of the clergy....This Court upheld that practice, finding that it advanced a clearly secular purpose of establishing a solemn atmosphere and serious tone for the board meetings....establishing solemnity is the primary effect of all invocations at gatherings of persons with differing views on religion.[34]

The men who wrote the First Amendment religion clause did not view paid legislative chaplains and opening prayers as a violation of that amendment....the practice of opening sessions with prayer has continued without interruption ever since that early session of Congress.[35]

It can hardly be thought that in the same week the members of the first Congress voted to appoint and pay a chaplain for each House and also voted to approve the draft of the First Amendment...(that) they intended to forbid what they had just declared acceptable.[36]

[Chaplains and prayer] are deeply embedded in the history and tradition of this country.[37]

ôa

United States Supreme Court 1983, in the case of *United States v. Grace*, 461 U.S. 171, 177 (1983), stated:

Streets, sidewalks, and parks, are considered, without more, to be public forums.[38]

ôa

*United States Supreme Court*1985, in the case of*Lynch v. Donnelly,* 465 U.S. 668, 669-670 (1985), Chief Justice Warren Burger rendered the court's opinion upholding that the city of Pawtucket, R.I., did not violate the Constitution by displaying a Nativity scene. The decision noted that presidential orders and proclamations from Congress have designated Christmas as a national holiday in religious terms since 1789:

The city of Pawtucket, R.I., annually erects a Christmas display in a park....The creche [nativity] display is sponsored by the city to celebrate the Holiday recognized by Congress and national tradition and to depict the origins of that Holiday; these are legitimate secular purposes....The creche...is no more an advancement or endorsement of religion than the congressional and executive recognition of the origins of Christmas....

It would be ironic if...the creche in the display, as part of a celebration of an event acknowledged in the Western World for 20 centuries, and in this country by the people, the Executive Branch, Congress, and the courts for 2 centuries, would so 'taint' the exhibition as to render it violative of the Establishment Clause. To forbid the use of this one passive symbol...would be an overreaction contrary to this Nation's history.[39]

There is an unbroken history of official acknowledgement by all three branches of government of the role of religion in American life....

The Constitution does not require a complete separation of church and state. It affirmatively mandates accommodation, not merely tolerance, of all religions and forbids hostility towards any.[40]

ૐ

United States Supreme Court 1985, in the case of *Wallace v. Jafree*, 472 U.S., 38, 99, Associate Justice William Rehnquist rendered the court's decision:

It is impossible to build sound constitutional doctrine upon a mistaken understanding of Constitutional history....The establishment clause had been expressly freighted with Jefferson's misleading metaphor for nearly forty years....

There is simply no historical foundation for the proposition that the framers intended to build a wall of separation [between church and state]....The recent court decisions are in no way based on either the language or intent of the framers.[41]

ૐ

United States Supreme Court 1986, in the case of *Bowers v. Hardwick*, 478 U.S. 186, 92 L Ed 2d 140, 106 S. Ct. 2841, p. 149, Chief Justice Warren E. Burger delivered the court's decision censuring the act of sodomy:

Condemnation of those practices is firmly rooted in Judeo-Christian moral and ethical standards.[42]

Sodomy was a criminal offense at common law and was forbidden by the laws of the original 13 States when they ratified the Bill of Rights. In 1868, when the Fourteenth Amendment was ratified, all but five of the 37 States in the Union had criminal sodomy laws. In fact, until 1961, all 50 states outlawed sodomy...provid[ing] criminal penalties for sodomy performed in private and between consenting adults.[43]

ᨠ

United States Supreme Court June 4, 1990, in the case of *Westside Community Schools v. Mergens*, 496, U.S. 226, 250, (1990), No. 88-1597 Part III was delivered by Justice O'Connor and No. 88-1597-CONCUR Part II was delivered by Justice Kennedy and Justice Scalia. By this 8 to 1 decision, the Supreme Court ruled to allow the formation of Christian clubs on the campuses of public schools, provided they were student initiated. Students were to be granted identical rights which other non-curricular groups were enjoying:[44]

There is a crucial difference between government speech endorsing religion, which the Establishment Clause forbids, and private speech endorsing religion, which the Free speech and Free Exercise Clauses protect.[45]

If a State refused to let religious groups use facilities open to others, then it would demonstrate not neutrality but hostility toward religion. The Establishment Clause does not license government to treat religion and those who teach or practice it, simply by virtue of their status as such, as subversive of American ideals and therefore subject to unique disabilities.[46]

Indeed, as the Court noted in *Widmar*, a denial of equal access to religious speech might well create greater entanglement problems in the form of invasive monitoring to prevent religious speech at meetings at which such speech might occur. See *Widmar*, 454 U.S., at 272, n.11.[47]

I should think it inevitable that a public high school "endorses" a religious club, in a common-sense use of the term, if the club happens to be one of many activities that the school permits students to choose in order to further the development of their intellect and character in an extracurricular setting.

But no constitutional violation occurs if the school's action is based upon a recognition of the fact that membership in a religious club is one of many permissible ways for a student to further his or her own personal enrichment. [48]

৵

United States Supreme Court 1992, in the case of *Lee v. Weisman,* 112 S. Ct. 2649 (1992), by only a one-vote majority, the court ruled that a commencement prayer is not to be given by clergy. Justice Kennedy delivered the decision. In a strong dissenting opinion, Justice Antonin Scalia, joined by Chief Justice William Rehnquist, Justice Byron White and Justice Clarence Thomas, stated that invocations and benedictions may continue to be offered, provided a notice is included in the commencement program that participation is voluntary:

> The Court lays waste a longstanding American tradition of nonsectarian prayer to God at public celebrations .... There is simply no support for the proposition that the officially sponsored nondenominational invocation and benediction read by Rabbi Gutterman - with no one legally coerced to recite them - violated the Constitution of the United States.
>
> To the contrary, they are so characteristically American they could have come from the pen of George Washington or Abraham Lincoln himself....
>
> That obvious fact recited the graduates and their parents may proceed to thank God, as Americans have always done, for the blessings He has generously bestowed on them and their country. [49]

In pointing out the incongruity of the decision, Justice Scalia observed:

> If students were psychologically coerced to remain standing during the invocation, they must also have been psychologically coerced moments before, to stand for the Pledge. [50]

৵

United States Supreme Court 1993, in the case of *Jayne Bray v. Alexandria Women's Health Clinic,* Justice Scalia delivered the majority decision, which held that:

> A value judgement favoring childbirth over abortion is proper and reasonable enough to be implemented by the allocation of public funds.[51]

ᴥ

United States Supreme Court June 7, 1993, in the case of *Lamb's Chapel v. Center Moriches Union Free School District,* rendered a 9-0 unanimous decision, overturning a ruling by the Second U.S. Circuit Court of Appeals. The case involved a New York school district that had rejected the request for facilities, which are made available for other noncurricular uses, to be used for the showing of Dr. James Dobson's film, *Turn Your Heart Toward Home.*

The Supreme Court allowed the film to be shown, thereby upholding the right of freedom of speech, including *religious* free speech, within the public arena.[52] Free speech, even involving religious content, cannot be restricted by the New York education law, which permits public school facilities to be rented for the purpose of:

> Holding social, civic, and recreational meetings and entertainments, and other uses pertaining to the welfare of the community.[53]

During the proceedings, Supreme Court Justice Scalia questioned the school board's attorney:

> *Justice Scalia:* You are here representing both respondents [the school board and the State of New York]...in this argument, and the Attorney General of New York, in his brief defending...the New York rule says that 'Religious advocacy serves the community only in the eyes of its adherents and yields a benefit only to those who already believe.'
>
> Does New York State—I grew up in New York State, and in those days they—they used to have a tax exemption for religious property. Is that still there?
>
> *Counsel:* Yes, Your Honor, it still is.
>
> *Justice Scalia:* But they've changed their view, apparently, that—

Counsel: Well, Your Honor—
Justice Scalia: You see—it used to be thought that—that religion—
it didn't matter what religion, but it—some code of morality always
went with it and was thought, you know, what was called a God-
fearing person might be less likely to mug me and rape my sister. That
apparently is not the view of New York anymore.
Counsel: Well I'm not sure that that's—that—
Justice Scalia: Has this new regime worked very well?
(Laughter)[54]

Justice White, writing the opinion, stated:

The government violates the First Amendment when it denies
access to a speaker solely to suppress the point of view he espouses on
an otherwise inculpable subject....[the] First Amendment forbids the
government to regulate speech in ways that favor some viewpoints or
ideas at the expense of others.[55]

Justice Scalia, in his concurring opinion, wrote:

That was not the view of those who adopted our Constitution,
who believed that the public virtues inculcated by religion are a public
good. It suffices to point out that during the summer of 1789, when it
was in the process of drafting the First Amendment, Congress enacted
the famous Northwest Territory Ordinance of 1789, Article III of
which provides, "Religion, morality, and knowledge, being necessary
to good government and the happiness of mankind, schools and the
means of education shall forever be encouraged.[56]

❧

United States Supreme Court June 7, 1993, in the case of *Jones v.
Clear Creek Independent School District*, 977 F.2d 963, 972 (5th Cir.
1992), upheld the Fifth Circuit Court of Appeals decision
permitting student-initiated prayer at high school graduation
ceremonies, providing a majority of the class votes to do so:[57]

A majority of students can do what the State acting on its own
cannot do to incorporate prayer in public high school graduation
ceremonies.[58]

There is a crucial difference between government speech endorsing religion, which the Establishment Clause forbids, and private speech endorsing religion, which the Free speech and Free Exercise Clauses protect.[59]

ð

United States Court of Appeals—6th Circuit 1992, in the case of *Americans United for Separation of Church and State v. City of Grand Rapids*, 980 F.2d 1538, 1555, stated:

What the members of Chabad House seek in this court is fully consistent with, and does not violate, our traditional division between church and state....They merely ask that they not be spurned because they choose to praise God. Instead of forcing them to remain on our sidelines, our Constitution offers them platform from which to proclaim their message. In a traditional public forum, as at the ballot box, all citizens are insiders as they seek to influence our civic life.[60]

ð

United States Court of Appeals—7th Circuit 1992, in the case of *Doe v. Small*, 964 F.2d 611, 618 (7th Cir. 1992), stated:

The Supreme Court has refused to find the Establishment Clause to be a sufficiently compelling interest to exclude private religious speech even from a limited public forum created by the government.[61]

ð

United States Court of Appeals—7th Circuit May 17, 1993, rendered its opinion in the case of *Walsh v. Boy Scouts of America*. In 1989, Elliott Walsh of Hinsdale, an agnostic, had sued the Boy Scouts on behalf of his 10-year-old son, Mark, claiming religious discrimination against the West Suburban Council Tiger Cub Scout chapter. The court ruled that the Boy Scouts could keep the phrase "duty to God" in their oath, and as a private organization they had the right to exclude anyone who refused to take the oath.[62]

Judge John Coffey, in delivering the 2-1 majority opinion, stated the Boy Scouts did not violate the 1964 Civil Rights Act, as scouting was an activity and not a facility, a membership organization, rather than a "place of public accommodation":[63]

> The leadership of many in our government is a testimonial to the success of Boy Scout activities....In recent years, single-parent families, gang activity, the availability of drugs and other factors have increased the dire need for support structures like the Scouts.
>
> When the government, in this instance, through the courts, seeks to regulate the membership of an organization like the Boy Scouts in a way that scuttles its founding principles, we run the risk of undermining one of the seedbeds of virtue that cultivate the sorts of citizens our nation so desperately needs.[64]

ₓ₳

United States Court of Appeals—8th Circuit 1980, in the case of *Florey v. Sioux Falls School District*, 619 F. 2d 1311, 1314 (8th Cir. 1980), stated that the performance and study of religious songs, inclusive of Christmas carols, is constitutional, provided the purpose is the:

> Advancement of the students' knowledge of society's cultural and religious heritage, as well as the provision of an opportunity for students to perform a full range of music, poetry, and drama that is likely to be of interest to the students and their audience.[65]

ₓ₳

United States Court of Appeals—9th Circuit 1993, in the case of *Kreisner v. City of San Diego*, 1 F.3d 775, 785, held:

> The Committee [seeking to erect the display], like other citizens of diverse views, has a right to express its views publicly in areas traditionally held open for all manner of speech.[66]

ₓ₳

United States Court of Appeals—10th Circuit July 12, 1993, in the case of *Cannon v. City and County of Denver*, rendered a unanimous decision in favor of two women who picketed near an abortion clinic, stating:

We are convinced that here the message on the signs did not amount to fighting words under the Supreme Court's standards ....Furthermore they played an important role in the exposition of ideas. We hold therefore that the rights of the protestors to picket on the public sidewalks in front of the clinic with signs was a clearly established constitutional right at the time of the 1988 arrests in question.[67]

ૹ

United States Court of Appeals—11th Circuit October 18, 1993, in the case of *Chabad—Lubavitch of Georgia v. Miller*, No. 92-8008 stated:

Because the religious speech is communicated in a true public forum...the state, by definition, neither endorses nor disapproves of the speech. By permitting religious speech in a public forum—whether in the heart of a core government building, in the Georgia Governor's mansion, or in the outer reaches of some state-owned pasture—the state simply does not endorse, but rather acts in a strictly neutral manner toward, private speech.[68]

ૹ

United States District Court March 18, 1992, Western District of Texas—Austin Division, *Word of Faith v. Attorney General*, Civil No. A-92-CA-089, U.S. District Judge Sam Sparks renders the decision:

On January 13, 1992...the Attorney General of Texas sent to the Plaintiffs, by facsimile transmission, a demand for documents....Both the nature and extent of the documents demanded were not reasonable and included documents clearly the Attorney General was not entitled to obtain from any religious organization and/or church.

The church...clearly had First Amendment rights to assert....Now, after the filing of this lawsuit, the Attorney General admits its demand for documents...and its petition in quo warranto were inappropriate....

The Court finds from the evidence that the conduct of the Attorney General and his personnel...was neither professional nor responsible, bordering on the unethical and constitutes "bad faith." This conduct is not what is expected of attorneys charged with the responsibility of being the legal representatives of the State of Texas.

It is beyond dispute freedoms of religious worship and of association are foundation pillars of our country....For generations Americans have died and been persecuted defending these specific rights.

In this particular case, the Attorney General of the State of Texas has utilized its own interpretation of a statute...to publicly accuse a church of fraud and demand documents clearly constitutionally protected.

The accusation and demand for documents and records are enforced by pleading in quo warranto requesting dissolution of the corporate church, appointment of a receiver to manage its affairs, and an Injunction against its ministers from conducting the business of the church which is admitted (by stipulation) to be a bona fide religious organization.

These circumstances satisfy, in this Court's judgment,...the conduct of the Attorney General as "bad faith, harassment or any other unusual circumstance that would require equitable relief."

...the Court finds from the evidence that the Plaintiffs have established that their declining to deliver the records and documents demanded by the Attorney General was an exercise of legitimate and valid First Amendment rights, i.e. constitutionally protected.

Contributors to the church do not seek to purchase goods or services. Plaintiffs do not advertise goods or services for sale. Contributors to the church are not required to give donations in order to receive pamphlets, books or other goods. Nor is a donation required before [someone] will pray over a prayer request or perform other acts.

There is nothing to make contributors to the church believe their contributions are in return for requested materials or acts by the church... In fact, not only do members sometimes make "vows" or contributions without requesting any materials or acts to be performed...but the church makes it a practice to inform persons who seek to "purchase" items that the church no longer sells any-thing....Contributors to the church are not "consumers," and the Attorney General may not bring a DTPA action to protect their interests....

The Attorney General demanded, amongst other things...[the] list of all persons who have sent contributions to the Church...including name, address, telephone number, amount and date of contribution ....The scope and substance of these requests are clearly uncon-stitutional.

The State has no constitutional authority to know a person's membership in or support of any church. The State has no constitutional authority to know what a person believes, how he or she practices religion, or how he or she supports religious activities. Nor does the State have constitutional authority to probe into the internal operations of a church....The First Amendment right to freedom of religious belief and freedom of association protects this kind of information.

Implicit in these First Amendments freedoms is privacy of belief and association....Disclosure of who belongs to a group or who contributes to a group, and how much, has been vigorously safeguarded by the United States Supreme Court....The Court has recognized that disclosure to the public, or to the State, of a group's members or contributors can harm the group by subjecting them to harassment or causing new members to not join for fear of disclosure or harassment or other reprisal.

In order to withstand attack under the Establishment Clause, three requirements must be met:

First, the statute must have a secular legislative purpose; second its principal or primary effect must be one that neither advances nor inhibits religion; finally, the statute must not foster an excessive government entanglement with religion....

Plaintiffs' pamphlets, advertisements, television broadcasts, sermons, etc., would be subject to inspection and approval by the Attorney General. Certainly this continual monitoring of the Plaintiffs' activities by the Attorney General would constitute an excessive entanglement....

This would also require the Attorney General to make determinations as to which representations are purely religious and which are secular. The Assistant Attorney Generals assure this Court they can distinguish purely religious assertions from secular assertions....Despite the Assistant Attorney Generals' confidence, this Court does not believe they or any other state officials are authorized to make those kind of determinations.

See e.g. *Cantwell v. Connecticut,* 310 U.S. 296, 305-06, 60 S.CT. 900, 904 (1940) (state could not give a state official the power to determine if a solicitation was for a religious cause or not;) Lemon, 403 U.S. at 618-19,91 S.Ct. at 2114 ("With the best of intentions such a teacher would find it hard to make a total separation between secular teaching and religious doctrine.")

It is simply not the business of courts or the State to "approve, classify, regulate, or in any manner control sermons delivered at religious meetings" or other forms of religious expression. See *Fowler v. Rhode Island,* 345 U.S. 526, 527, 73 S.Ct. 526, 527 (1953)....

The Attorney General sought forfeiture of [the church's] charter and dissolution of the corporation and appointment of a Receiver to take possession of the affairs of the [church], to rehabilitate, reorganize, conserve or liquidate the affairs of the corporation and sought a permanent Injunction against the [church], its officers, directors, stockholder, agents, employees, and representatives whomsoever from conducting any business of the [church]....

Application of these remedies to the Plaintiffs is clearly unconstitutional.

It is absurd for the Attorney General to think that it can deprive the Plaintiffs of their rights to freely worship as a group altogether as punishment for the Plaintiffs initial assertion of their First Amendment rights to not produce constitutionally protected documents....

A fine for exercising one's First Amendment rights would clearly be unconstitutional....Imprisonment would also clearly be unconstitutional, both as a punishment for exercising one's constitutional rights and because it would wholly prevent...exercising an important part of their religious beliefs, which is to spread their religious faith to others.

The Attorney General argues that because Section 501(c)(3) of the Internal Revenue Code includes a corporation operated for religious purposes the Church is a charitable entity. This Court disagrees. A church is not organized for a "civic or public purpose." If the Legislature had intended to incorporate any entity described in the Internal Revenue Code...it could have easily done so.

The church is not a charitable trust, and because jurisdiction in the Travis County Probate Court is based on the church being a charitable trust, that jurisdiction is improper....

The Attorney General cannot, in turn, use allegations of fraud as a sword to violate the Plaintiffs' First Amendment rights....

Article 1396-2.23A specifically exempts a religious institution from having to maintain, and make available to the public financial records "with respect to all financial transaction of the corporation"....

The Attorney General of Texas, is permanently enjoined from pursuing further its...demand for documents and investigation.[69]

かわ

United States District Court July 1993, in the case of *Black v. City of Atlanta*, ordered the City of Atlanta, Georgia, to adopt procedures respecting the rights of pro-life protestors. The ruling encompassed:

1. The fundamental rights of speech, press and religion includes the freedom to engage in prayer, conversation, oratory, display and/or distribution of literature, display of picket signs, reading of scriptures, singing and chanting.

2. City authorities will not interfere with, restrict, or deny the rights of speech, press, or religion, unless an actual obstruction or impediment occurs. Circumstances where physical passage is possible, but discomfort with the messages of a speaker causes a person to avoid the abortion location, are not considered an obstruction or impediment.

3. Public streets and public sidewalks located adjacent to abortion facilities in Atlanta are public forums. The City of Atlanta and its law enforcement personnel shall respect the exercise of free speech rights on these public forums.

Atlanta's law enforcement personnel must allow the greatest tolerance for political and religious expression by its citizens. The Atlanta Police Department's Field Manual will be revised to include the guidelines set forth in the court order. Copies of the court order will be distributed to all police zone and watch commanders.[70]

ð

Constitution of the United Soviet Socialist Republic (1922-1991), stated:

> *Article 124:* In order to ensure to citizens freedom of conscience, the church in the U.S.S.R. is separated from the State, and the school from the church.[71]

ð

Tomb of the Unknown Soldier November 11, 1921, was originated three years after the end of World War I. The records disclose how six soldiers were sent back to France for a special assignment. Outside the chapel at Chalons-sur-Marne, an officer met them with the instructions, "Men, it is my task to choose one of you to perform a great and sacred duty." Handing a rose to Sgt. Edward Younger, the officer continued, "In this church are four caskets. In them lie the bodies of four nameless American soldiers. Go into the chapel and place a rose on one of the caskets."

After the casket was chosen, it was brought back to America

and placed in the Tomb of the Unknown Soldier in Arlington Cemetery, Virginia, to represent all of those brave men who died so our country could remain free. The inscription reads:

> Here rests in honored glory an American soldier known only to God.[72]

On Memorial Day, 1958, two more unknown soldiers, from World War II and the Korean War, were buried there as well. During his administration, President Ronald Reagan, along with citizens of the United States, laid the fourth soldier to rest in the tomb.

❧

V

Cesar Vallejo (1892-1938), in *Poemas Humanos*, 1939, *Whatever May Be the Cause*, wrote:

Whatever may be the cause I have to defend before God, beyond death I have a defender: God.[1]

❧

Martin Van Buren (1782-1862), was the 8th President of the United States, 1837-41; a New York state senator, 1813-20; the Attorney General of New York, 1816-21; a U.S. Senator, 1821-28; Governor of New York, 1828-29; and Vice-President under President Andrew Jackson, 1832-36. President Martin Van Buren declared:

Martin Van Buren

I only look to the gracious protection of that Divine Being whose strengthening support I humbly solicit, and whom I fervently pray to look down upon us all. May it be among the dispensations of His Providence to bless our beloved country with honors and length of days; may her ways be pleasantness, and all her paths peace.[2]

During his last illness he made this confession:

The atonement of Jesus Christ is the only remedy and rest for my soul.[3]

❧

Sir Henry Vane (1612-1662), was an English colonial administrator, statesman and the Governor of Massachusetts in 1636. He was knighted by King Charles I in 1640 and elected to Long and Short Parliaments. He also served as joint treasurer of the English Navy. Sir Henry Vane is noted for having helped Roger Williams secure the Rhode Island Charter in 1644, which bore Vane's signature as one of the commissioners for the plantation.

After Oliver Cromwell's "Protectorate" government, 1653-59, Charles II took the throne and executed Cromwell's loyal followers, one of whom was Sir Henry Vane, who wrote:

> They that press so earnestly to carry on my trial do little know what the presence of God may be afforded me in it, and issue out of it to the magnifying of Christ in my body, by life or by death. Nor can they, I am sure, imagine how much I desire to be dissolved and be with Christ, which of all things which can befall me I account the best.[4]

> As the present storm we now lie under, the dark clouds that yet hang over the Reformed Churches of Christ, which are coming thicker and faster, so the coming of Jesus Christ in these clouds in order to a speedy and sudden revival of His cause, and spread of His kingdom over the face of the whole earth, is most clear to the eye of faith, even the faith in which I die, whereby the kingdoms of this world shall become the kingdoms of our Lord and of His Christ, Amen! Even so come, Lord Jesus![5]

Henry Vaughan (1622-1695), was an English poet and physician. Born in Wales, he was educated at Jesus College, Oxford, and practiced medicine in Brecon. In 1655, he composed his collection of poetry, entitled *Silex Scintillans*, in which he wrote the poem, *The Night:*

> Dear Night! This world's defeat;
> The stop to busy fool; care's check and curb;
> The day of spirits; my soul's calm retreat
> Which none disturb!
> Christ's progress, and His prayer-time;
> The hours to which high Heaven doth chime.[6]

In *Peace*, he wrote:

My soul, there is a country
Far beyond the stars
Where stands a winged sentry
All skillful in the wars:
There, above noise and danger,
Sweet Peace is crowned with smiles,
And One born in a manger
Commands the beauteous files.[7]

ðə

William Henry Venable (1836-1920), in *Johnny Appleseed*, st. 25, wrote:

Remember Johnny Appleseed,
All ye who love the apple;
He served his kind by word and deed,
In God's grand greenwood chapel.[8]

ðə

Constitution of the State of Vermont 1786, stated:

Frame of Government, *Section 9*. And each member [of the Legislature], before he takes his seat, shall make and subscribe the following declaration, viz: "I do believe in one God, the Creator and Governor of the universe, the rewarder of the good and punisher of the wicked. And I do acknowledge the Scripture of the Old and New Testament to be given by divine inspiration, and own and profess the [Christian] religion. And no further or other religious test shall ever, hereafter, be required of any civil officer or magistrate in this State."[9]

ðə

Queen Victoria (1819-1901), was the Queen of England, 1837-1901, and the Empress of India, 1876-1901. When she was crowned at Westminster Abbey, June 28, 1837, three presents were given to her: the Sword of State, the Imperial Robe, and the Holy Bible. These words accompanied the Bible:

Our gracious Queen, we present you this Book, the most valuable thing the world affords. Here is wisdom; this is the royal law; these are the timely oracles of God. Blessed is he that readeth and they that hear the words of this Book; that keep and do the things contained in it. For these are the words of eternal life, able to make you wise unto salvation, and so happy forever more, through faith in Christ Jesus, to whom be the glory forever and ever. Amen.[10]

In commenting on the Bible, the Queen stated:

That book accounts for the supremacy of England.[11]

In 1849, the Queen instructed the Earl of Chichester to write the African Chieftain, Sagbua, a letter which contained the words:

Commerce alone will not make a nation great and happy like England. England has become great and happy by the knowledge of the true God through Jesus Christ. In order to show how much the Queen values God's Word, she sends with this as a present a copy of the Word.[12]

&

First Charter of Virginia April 10, 1606, was granted by King James I to those who would endeavor to settle "Jamestown Colony" in Virginia:

We, greatly commending and graciously accepting of their Desires for the Furtherance of so noble a Work, which may, by the Providence of Almighty God, hereafter tend to the Glory of His Divine Majesty, in propagating of Christian Religion to such People, as yet live in Darkness and miserable Ignorance of the true Knowledge and Worship of God, and may in time bring the Infidels and Savages, living in those Parts, to human Civility, and to a settled and quiet Government....[13]

&

Colony of Virginia May 14, 1607, was planted with settlers who had left England in December of 1606. Their settlement at Jamestown was the first permanent settlement in North America. (Sir Walter Raleigh, who was responsible for naming Virginia after the "Virgin Queen" Elizabeth I, had attempted a previous settlement in 1585, but it proved unsuccessful.)

Sir Walter
Raleigh

Queen
Elizabeth I
(Elizabeth
Tudor;
the "Virgin
Queen")

The Colonists' first act, after landing at Cape Henry, April 27, 1607, was to erect a large wooden cross and hold a prayer meeting.[14] Their minister, the Reverend Robert Hunt, conducted this premier service honoring the Lord for the first time in this new land. Later that year, at Reverend Robert Hunt's death, the settlers gave this tribute to him:

1607. To the glory of God and in memory of the Reverend Robert Hunt, Presbyter, appointed by the Church of England. Minister of the Colony which established the English Church and English Civilization at Jamestown, Virginia, in 1607.

His people, members of the Colony, left this testimony concerning him. He was an honest, religious and courageous Divine.

He preferred the Service of God in so good a voyage to every thought of ease at home. He endured every privation, yet none ever heard him repine. During his life our factions were ofte healed, and our greatest extremities so comforted that they seemed easy in comparison with what we endured after his memorable death.

We all received from him the Holy Communion together, as a pledge of reconciliation, for we all loved him for his exceeding goodness. He planted the First Protestant Church in America and laid down his life in the foundation of America.[15]

❧

Second Charter of Virginia May 23, 1609, granted by King James I, stated:

Because the principal Effect which we can expect or desire of this Action is the Conversion and reduction of the people in those parts unto the true worship of God and the Christian Religion.[16]

❧

Colony of Virginia 1613, in the Jamestown Settlement, baptized

Pocahontas, the Indian princess, into the Christian faith. She received the Christian name of Rebekah as the Reverend Richard Bucke, second chaplain to the Virginia Colony, performed the ceremony. In 1614 she married John Rolfe, a council member of the Jamestown Colony, and later they had a son named Thomas, (whose descendants included the statesman John Randolph of Roanoke, and Edith Galt, who married President Woodrow Wilson in 1915).[17]

The original painting of Pocahontas, by the artist Brooke, is in the National Portrait Gallery of the Smithsonian Institution. The inscription painted on the portrait states:

> Matoaks ats Rebecka, daughter of the mighty Prince Powhatan Emperour of Attanoughknomouck ats Virginia converted and baptized in the Christian faith, and wife to the wor. Mr. Tho:Rolff.[18]

ها

Colony of Virginia July 30, 1619, was ordered by the Virginia Company to hold the first Representative Assembly in the New World at Jamestown. The secretary of the Virginia Colony, John Pory recorded the meeting:

VIRGINIA.

Seal of Virginia

> But foreasmuch as men's affaires doe little prosper, where God's service is neglected, all the Burgesses tooke their places in the Quire till prayer was said by Mr. Bucke the Minister, that it would please God to guide and sanctifie all our proceedings, to His own glory and the good of this plantation.[19]

ها

Colony of Virginia December 4, 1619, records how 38 colonists landed in a place they called Berkeley Hundred. In their charter, they instructed:

> We ordain that the day of our ship's arrival...in the land of Virginia shall be yearly and perpetually kept holy as a day of

Thanksgiving to Almighty God.[20]

❧

Colony of Virginia March 22, 1622, saw the Jamestown Settlement saved from a massacre by the warning of a young Indian, named Chanco. A marker within the reconstructed interior of the original church at Jamestown Island, Virginia, commemorates the event:

> In memory of Chanco, an Indian youth converted to Christianity, who resided in the household of Richard Pace across the river from Jamestown and who, on the eve of the Indian massacre of March 22, 1622, warned Pace of the murderous plot thus enabling Pace to cross the river in a canoe to alert and save the Jamestown settlement from impending disaster.[21]

❧

Colony of Virginia 1623, enacted legislation requiring civil magistrates:

> To see that the Sabbath was not profaned by working or any employments, or journeying from place to place.[22]

❧

Virginia Bill of Rights June 12, 1776, states:

> *Article XVI* That Religion, or the Duty which we owe our Creator, and the Manner of discharging it, can be directed only by Reason and Convictions, not by Force or Violence; and therefore all Men are equally entitled to the free exercise of Religion, according to the Dictates of Conscience; and that it is the mutual Duty of all to practice Christian Forbearance, Love, and Charity towards each other.[23]

❧

Virginia Statute of Religious Liberty January 16, 1786, states:

> Well aware that Almighty God hath created the mind free; that all attempts to influence it by temporal punishments or burdens, or by

civil incapacitations...are a departure from the plan of the Holy Author of our religion.[24]

ka

State of Virginia March 13, 1994, issued an Executive Proclamation declaring March 13-19, 1994, as "Christian Heritage Week":

> WHEREAS, The Constitution of the Commonwealth of Virginia states "That religion or the duty which we owe to our creator, and the manner of discharging it, can be directed only by reason and conviction; not by force or violence; and, therefore, all men are equally entitled to the free exercise of religion, according to the dictates of conscience; and that it is the mutual duty of all to practice Christian forbearance, love, and charity towards each other;" and WHEREAS, Benjamin Franklin, at the Constitutional Convention in 1787 stated: "It is impossible to build an empire without our Father's aid. I believe the sacred writings which say that 'Except the Lord build the house, they labor in vain that build it,'" (Psalm 127:1); and WHEREAS, George Washington enunciated "animated alone by the pure spirit of Christianity, and conducting ourselves as the faithful subjects of our free government, we may enjoy every temporal and spiritual felicity;" and WHEREAS, Thomas Jefferson, author of the Declaration of Independence, wrote: "Can the liberties of a nation be secure when we have removed the conviction that these liberties are the gift of God?" and WHEREAS, James Madison, father of the U.S. Constitution, advocated "the diffusion of the light of Christianity in our nation" in his Memorial and Remonstrance; and WHEREAS, Patrick Henry quoted Proverbs 14:34 for our nation: "Righteousness alone can exalt a nation, but sin is a disgrace to any people;" and WHEREAS, George Mason, in his Virginia Declaration of Rights, forerunner to our U.S. Bill of Rights, affirmed: "That it is the mutual duty of all to practice Christian forbearance, love and charity towards each other;" and WHEREAS, these, and many other truly great men and women of America, giants in the structuring of American history, were Christian statesmen of calibre and integrity who did not hesitate to express their faith;
>
> NOW, THEREFORE, I, George Allen, Governor, do hereby recognize March 13-19, 1994 as CHRISTIAN HERITAGE WEEK, in the Commonwealth of Virginia, and I call this observance to the attention of all our citizens.

George Allen   Betsy Davis Beamer
Governor   Secretary of the Commonwealth.[25]

ka

W

William Walker 1833, of the Wyandot Indian tribe, wrote a letter in 1833 to the *Christian Advocate & Journal*. He described how he had encountered four Indians, one of the Flathead tribe and three of the Nez Perces tribe, who had traveled 3,000 miles to St. Louis, Missouri, because they heard that:

> The white people away toward the rising sun had been put in possession of the true mode of worshipping the Great Spirit; they had a Book containing directions.[1]

Lew Wallace (1827-1905), was a Major General in the Civil War, a diplomat and the author of the famous novel, *Ben-Hur*, 1880. He became the Governor of New Mexico, 1878-81, and served as the U.S. minister to Turkey, 1881-85.

On February 2, 1893, he wrote in the *Youth Companion*:

Lew Wallace

At that time (1875), speaking candidly, I was not in the least influenced by religious sentiment. I had no conviction about God and Christ. I neither believed nor disbelieved them....

I had been listening to a discussion which involved such elemental points as God, Heaven, life hereafter, Jesus Christ, and His Divinity. Trudging on in the dark, alone, except as one's thoughts may be company, good or bad, a sense of the importance of the theme struck me for the first time with a force both singular and persistent. I was ashamed of myself, and make haste now to declare that mortification of pride I then endured, or, if it be preferred, the punishment of spirit, ended in a resolution to study the whole matter, if only for the gratification there might be in having convictions of one kind or another.

Forthwith a number of practical suggestions assailed me. How could I conduct the study? Delve into theology? I shuddered....There were the sermons and commentaries. The very thought of them overwhelmed me with an idea of the shortness of life. No, I would read the Bible and the four Gospels. A lawyer of fifteen or twenty years of practice attains a confidence peculiar in his mental muscularity, so to speak....

The manuscript in my desk ended with the birth of Christ; why not make it the first book of a volume, and go on to His death? I halted—there was light!...I had my opening; it was the birth of Christ. Could anything be more beautiful? As a mere story, the imagination of man has conceived nothing more crowded with poetry, mystery, and incidents, pathetic and sublime, nothing sweeter with human interest, nothing so nearly a revelation of God in person.

So, too, I saw a fitting conclusion. Viewed purely and professionally as a climax or catastrophe to be written up to, the final scene of the last act of the tragedy, what could be more stupendous than the Crucifixion?...Wanting a connecting thread for the whole story—that given to Christ the Child and that given to Christ the Saviour, I kept Belthasar alive to the end....

I determined to withhold the reappearance of the Saviour until the very last hours. Meanwhile, He should always be coming—today I would have Him, as it were, just over the hill yonder—tomorrow He will be here, and then tomorrow....Finally when He was come, I would be religiously careful that every word He uttered should be a literal quotation from one of His sainted biographers....

The name "Ben-Hur" was chosen because it was biblical, and easily spelled, printed and pronounced.

As this article is in the nature of confessions, here is one which the readers of the *Youth's Companion* may excuse, and accept at the same time as a fitting conclusion: Long before I was through with my book I became a believer in God and Christ.[2]

ও

William Ross Wallace (1819-1881), in *The Hand That Rules the World*, stated:

The hand that rocks the cradle is the hand that rules the world.[3]

ੈ

John Wanamaker (1838-1922), was the U.S. Postmaster General, 1889-93; a financier; a pioneer business tycoon; and founder of John Wanamaker and Company, a men's clothing business, which grew into one of the largest department stores in the United States. He made numerous advancements in the field of advertising within the retail industry, having run the first full-page mercantile advertisement in an American paper. In addition, the two magazines he founded to carry advertising copy became precursors to today's mail-order catalogues. His store in Philadelphia boasted of displaying priceless paintings of Christ, and a 33,000-pipe organ which was played every day of business.

John Wanamaker

John Wanamaker founded and was senior elder of the Bethany Presbyterian Church in Philadelphia. He led a *John Wesley Class Meeting* and for 65 years was the active Sunday school superintendent, with attendance growing from 27 to over 5,000 people.

Of the prayer meetings, John Wanamaker said:

> I like to be present at the meeting, in the middle of the week, feeling, as I sit among the people gathered, some of them deaf, hearing hardly a spoken word and others with failing sight, that as the Lord passed around amongst them He might give me a blessing too.[4]

At one of the prayer meetings, John Wanamaker prayed:

> Ever-living God, our Father, we have come into Thy house again through Thy mercy which has kept us alive. We would worship Thee with reverence. We hallow Thy name, O God, our Father, the name which is above every other name. We worship Thee, O Christ, God manifest in the flesh.
>
> We hear Thee speak, O Christ, who walked the pathways of this very earth and talked and did things like a man, and left the earth richer for the charity of thy words and the work of Thy dear, kindly hands. Thou hast written Thy name on so much of daily life that we

cannot walk or talk or open the doors of our homes without thinking of Thee and Thy ways in Galilee.

Oh Lord, Thou hast told us how to pray. Help us to shut the door, shutting out the world, and the enemy and any fear or doubt which spoils prayer. May there be no distance between our souls and Thee.

Our Father, we have come to sit down together to rest, after a busy week, and to think. We are not satisfied with ourselves for we all, like sheep, have gone astray. What we have done is what we ought not to have done. We are stung to the quick with disappointment, sorrow and desolation. It seems as though there were a cankerworm eating at the core of our hearts, and there is no rest for our souls day or night. Have pity on us, Lord, and cut us not down in Thy displeasure. We confess our sin and bring it to Thee. Let our prayers prevail in Heaven, and do Thou heal and help us to a new life in Christ Jesus. Amen.[5]

John Wanamaker declared:

> I cannot too greatly emphasize the importance and value of Bible study—more important than ever before in these days of uncertainties, when men and women are apt to decide questions from the standpoint of expediency rather than of the eternal principles laid down by God, Himself.[6]

On July 9-11, 1889, in Philadelphia, during the Eighth Annual Conference of the Young People's Society of Christian Endeavor, John Wanamaker exhorted:

> I came only to salute you, as one working with you, and as one in sympathy with you. Whatever skepticism of the day may say, there is a power in the Gospel of the Lord Jesus Christ. Keep uppermost the profound conviction that it is the Gospel that is to win the heart and convert the world. The things that were sweet dreams in our childhood are now being worked out. The procession is being made longer and longer; the letters of Christ's name are becoming larger and larger.[7]

&

Anna Bartlett Warner (1827-1915), in 1858, wrote *The Love of Jesus:*

> Jesus loves me—this I know,
> For the Bible tells me so.[8]

ᨠ

James Warren (1726-1808), was the president of the Massachusetts Provincial Congress; a Major General in the Provincial Militia; a member of the Navy board for the Eastern Department; a member of the Governor's Council, 1792-94; and a presidential elector from Massachusetts, 1804. He was married to Mercy Warren, 1724-1814, a remarkable author of the Revolutionary period, whose correspondence with numerous founding fathers has granted invaluable insight into our nation's history. In 1805, she wrote the *History of the Rise, Progress and Termination of the American Revolution,* in 3 volumes.

It was James Warren who first proposed the famous Committees of Correspondence to Samuel Adams. These committees were of inestimable influence in inspiring the spirit of freedom among the Colonies.

On June 16, 1775, President James Warren and the Provincial Congress of Massachusetts resolved:

In *Provincial Congress, Watertown,* June 16th, 1775.

As it has pleased Almighty GOD in his Providence to suffer the Calamities of an unnatural War to take Place among us, in Consequence of our sinful Declensions from Him, and our great Abuse of those inestimable Blessings bestowed upon us. And as we have Reason to fear, that unless we become a penitent and reformed People, we shall feel still severer Tokens of his Displeasure.

And as the most effectual Way to escape those desolating Judgements, which so evidently hang over us, and if it may be obtain the Restoration of our former Tranquility, will be—That we repent and return every one from his Iniquities, unto him that correcteth us, which if we do in Sincerity and Truth, we have no Reason to doubt but he will remove his Judgements—cause our Enemies to be at Peace with us—and prosper the Work of our Hands.

And as among the prevailing Sins of this Day, which threaten the Destruction of this Land, we have Reason to lament the frequent Prophanation of the Lord's-Day, or Christian Sabbath; many spending their Time in Idleness and Sloth, others in Diversion, and others in Journeying of Business, which is not necessary on said Day:

And as we earnestly desire that a Stop might be put to this great and prevailling Evil:

It is therefore RESOLVED, That it be recommended by this Congress, to the People of all Ranks and Denominations throughout this Colony, that they not only pay a religious Regard to that Day, and to the public Worship of God thereon; but that they also use their Influence to discountenance and suppress any Prophanations thereof in others.

And it is further RESOLVED, That it be recommended to the Ministers of the Gospel to read this Resolve to their several Congregations, accompanied with such Exhortations as they shall think proper.

And whereas there is great Danger that the Prophanation of the Lord's-Day will prevail in the Camp:

We earnestly recommend to all the Officers, not only to set good Examples; but that they strictly require of their Soldiers to keep up a religious Regard to that Day, and attend upon the public Worship of God thereon, so far as may be consistent with other Duties.

> A true Copy from the Minutes,
> Attest. Samuel Freeman, Secry.
> By Order of the Congress,
> James Warren, Prefident.[9]

Booker Taliaferro Washington (1856-1915), once a slave, became one of America's greatest reformers, educators and writers. After having taught at Malden, West Virginia, and at the Hampton Institute, Booker T. Washington founded the famous Tuskegee Institute. He wrote *Up From Slavery*, 1901; and *The Future of the American Negro*, 1899. Booker T. Washington declared:

Booker T. Washington

I shall allow no man to belittle my soul by making me hate him.[10]

George Washington (1732-1799), the 1st President of the United States, was the Commander-in-Chief of the Continental Army during the Revolutionary War. He was also a surveyor, a planter,

a soldier, and a statesman. In addition to being politically involved as the chairman of the Constitutional Convention, George Washington was also an active Episcopalian. Considered the most popular man in the Colonies, George Washington was described by Henry "Light Horse Harry" Lee in his now famous tribute, as "First in war, first in peace, first in the hearts of his countrymen."

George Washington

Henry Lee ("Light-Horse Harry" Lee)

The son of Augustine Washington and his second wife, Mary Ball, George Washington was also a descendant of King John of England and nine of the twenty-five Baron Sureties of the Magna Carta. His father died, in 1743, when he was eleven years old, and from then until the age of sixteen, George lived with his elder half-brother, Augustine, in Westmoreland County, Virginia, just 40 miles outside of Fredericksburg. Most of George's education was through home schooling and tutoring. He received his surveyor's license in 1749 from William and Mary College, and later, from 1788 until his death, he was the college's chancellor.

At age 15, George Washington copied, in his own handwriting, *110 Rules of Civility and Decent Behavior in Company and Conversation.* Among them were:

108) When you speak of God, or His attributes, let it be seriously and with reverence. Honor and obey your natural parents although they be poor.

109) Let your recreations be manful not sinful.

110) Labour to keep alive in your breast that little spark of celestial fire called conscience.[11]

When George Washington was leaving home to begin what would become a lifelong service for his country, he recorded the parting words of his mother, Mrs. Mary Washington:

> Remember that God is our only sure trust. To Him, I commend you .... My
> son, neglect not the duty of secret prayer. [12]

The account of George Washington at the *Battle at the Monongahela*
was included in student textbooks in America until 1934. During the
French & Indian War, George Washington fought alongside British
General Edward Braddock. On July 9,1755, the British were on the way to
Fort Duquesne, when the French surprised them in an ambush attack.

The British, who were not accustomed to fighting unless in an open
field, were being annihilated. Washington rode back and forth across the
battle delivering General Braddock's orders. As the battle raged, every
other officer on horseback, except Washington, was shot down. Even
General Braddock was killed, at which point the troops fled in confusion.
After the battle, on July 18, 1755, Washington wrote to his brother, John
A. Washington:

> But by the all-powerful dispensations of Providence, I have been protected
> beyond all human probability or expectation; for I had four bullets through my
> coat, and two horses shot under me, yet escaped unhurt, although death was
> leveling my companions on every side of me! [13]

Fifteen years later, Washington and Dr. Craik, a close friend of his from
his youth, were traveling through those same woods near the Ohio River
and Great Kanawha River. They were met by an old Indian chief, who
addressed Washington through an interpreter:

> I am a chief and ruler over my tribes. My influence extends to the
> waters of the great lakes and to the far blue mountains.
> I have traveled a long and weary path that I might see the young
> warrior of the great battle. It was on the day when the white man's blood
> mixed with the streams of our forests that I first beheld this chief
> [Washington].
> I called to my young men and said, mark yon tall and daring warrior?
> He is not of the red-coat tribe - he hath an Indian's wisdom, and his
> warriors fight as we do - himself alone exposed.
> Quick, let your aim be certain, and he dies. Our rifles were leveled,
> rifles which, but for you, knew not how to miss - 'twas all in

vain, a power mightier far than we, shielded you.

Seeing you were under the special guardianship of the Great Spirit, we immediately ceased to fire at you. I am old and soon shall be gathered to the great council fire of my fathers in the land of shades, but ere I go, there is something bids me speak in the voice of prophecy:

Listen! The Great Spirit protects that man [pointing at Washington], and guides his destinies—he will become the chief of nations, and a people yet unborn will hail him as

George Washington addresses his troops.

the founder of a mighty empire. I am come to pay homage to the man who is the particular favorite of Heaven, and who can never die in battle.[14]

The famous Indian warrior, who was in that battle, said:

Washington was never born to be killed by a bullet! I had seventeen fair fires at him with my rifle, and after all could not bring him to the ground![15]

On June 1, 1774, as the Colonies were seeking God's will as to whether they should break ties with England, George Washington made this entry in his diary:

Went to church and fasted all day.[16]

On July 4, 1775, in his General Orders from the Headquarters at Cambridge, General George Washington gave the order:

Newly appointed as Commander-in-Chief, George Washington took command of the army at Cambridge, Massachusetts, after his arrival on July 2, 1775.

The General most earnestly requires and expects a due observance of those articles of war established for the government of the Army which forbid profane cursing, swearing and drunkenness. And in like manner he requires and expects of all officers and soldiers not engaged in actual duty, a punctual attendance of Divine services, to implore the blessing of Heaven upon the means used for our safety and defense.[17]

On July 20, 1775, General Washington issued the order:

The General orders this day to be religiously observed by the forces under his Command, exactly in manner directed by the Continental Congress. It is therefore strictly enjoined on all officers and soldiers to attend Divine service. And it is expected that all those who go to worship do take their arms, ammunition and accoutrements, and are prepared for immediate action, if called upon.[18]

The Navy cruisers commissioned by General Washington during the Revolutionary War flew as their ensign a white flag with a green pine tree, and above it the inscription:

An Appeal to Heaven.[19]

On July 2, 1776, from his headquarters in New York, General Washington issued this order:

> The time is now near at hand which must probably determine whether Americans are to be freemen or slaves; whether they are to have any property they can call their own; whether their houses and farms are to be pillaged and destroyed, and themselves consigned to a state of wretchedness from which no human efforts will deliver them.
>
> The fate of unborn millions will now depend, under God, on the courage of this army. Our cruel and unrelenting enemy leaves us only the choice of brave resistance, or the most abject submission. We have, therefore to resolve to conquer or die.[20]

On July 9, 1776, the Continental Congress authorized the Continental Army to provide chaplains for their troops. General George Washington then issued the order and appointed chaplains to every regiment.[21] On that same day, he issued the general order to his troops, stating:

> The General hopes and trusts that every officer and man, will endeavor so to live, and act, as becomes a Christian Soldier defending the dearest Rights and Liberties of his country.[22]

On August 27, 1776, British General Howe had trapped General Washington and his 8,000 troops on Brooklyn Heights, Long Island, intending to advance the next morning to crush them. In a desperate move, Washington gathered every vessel, from fishing boats to row boats, and spent all night ferrying his army across the East River. When the morning came, there was still a large number of his troops dangerously exposed to the British, but in a most unusual change in weather, the fog did not lift from the river. It stayed thick, covering Washington's retreat until the entire army had evacuated and escaped! Never again did the British have such a rare chance of winning the war.[23] Major Ben Tallmadge, who was Washington's Chief of Intelligence, wrote of that morning:

> As the dawn of the next day approached, those of us who remained

in the trenches became very anxious for our own safety, and when the dawn appeared there were several regiments still on duty. At this time a very dense fog began to rise [out of the ground and off the river], and it seemed to settle in a peculiar manner over both encampments. I recollect this peculiar providential occurrence perfectly well, and so very dense was the atmosphere that I could scarcely discern a man at six yards distance....we tarried until the sun had risen, but the fog remained as dense as ever.[24]

In the freezing winter of 1777, General George Washington was burdened with the lack of supplies for his troops camped at Valley Forge, and with the overwhelming superiority of the British forces. Soldiers died at the rate of twelve per day, with many not even having blankets or shoes. The Commander-in-Chief himself, records the desperate state:

> No history now extant can furnish an instance of an army's suffering such uncommon hardships as ours has done and bearing them with the same patience and fortitude. To see men without clothes to cover their nakedness, without blankets to lie on, without shoes (for the want of which their marches might be traced by the blood from their feet)...and submitting without a murmur, is a proof of patience and obedience which in my opinion can scarce be paralleled.[25]

A Committee from Congress reported "feet and legs froze till they became black, and it was often necessary to amputate them." Sights of bloody footprints in the snow and lack of food and shelter caused the Commander-in-Chief to seek divine assistance. The famous account of his resolution was given by Isaac Potts, who was General Washington's temporary landlord at Valley Forge:

> In 1777 while the American army lay at Valley Forge, a good old Quaker by the name of Potts had occasion to pass through a thick woods near headquarters. As he traversed the dark brown forest, he heard, at a distance before him, a voice which as he advanced became more fervid and interested.
> Approaching with slowness and circumspection, whom should he behold in a dark bower, apparently formed for the purpose, but the Commander-in-Chief of the armies of the United Colonies on his knees in the act of devotion to the Ruler of the Universe!
> At the moment when Friend Potts, concealed by the trees, came

up, Washington was interceding for his beloved country. With tones of gratitude that labored for adequate expression he adored that exuberant goodness which, from the depth of obscurity, had exalted him to the head of a great nation, and that nation fighting at fearful odds for all the world holds dear....

Soon as the General had finished his devotions and had retired, Friend Potts returned to his house, and threw himself into a chair by the side of his wife. "Heigh! Isaac!" said she with tenderness, "thee seems agitated; what's the matter?"

"Indeed, my dear" quoth he, "if I appear agitated 'tis no more than what I am. I have seen this day what I shall never forget. Till now I have thought that a Christian and a soldier were characters incompatible; but if George Washington be not a man of God, I am mistaken, and still more shall I be disappointed if God does not through him perform some great thing for this country."[26]

Henry Muhlenberg, pastor of the Lutheran church near Valley Forge and one of the founders of the Lutheran Church in America, noted concerning General Washington:

Henry Muhlenberg

I heard a fine example today, namely, that His Excellency General Washington rode around among his army yesterday and admonished each and every one to fear God, to put away the wickedness that has set in and become so general, and to practice the Christian virtues. From all appearances, this gentleman does not belong to the so-called world of society, for he respects God's Word, believes in the atonement through Christ, and bears himself in humility and gentleness. Therefore, the Lord God has also singularly, yea, marvelously, preserved him from harm in the midst of countless perils, ambuscades, fatigues, etc., and has hitherto graciously held him in His hand as a chosen vessel.[27]

In 1775, John Peter Muhlenberg, who was a pastor like his father Henry, preached a message on Ecclesiastes 3:1, "For everything there is a season, and a time for every matter under heaven." He closed his message by saying:

John Peter Muhlenberg

In the language of the Holy Writ, there is a time for all things. There is a time to preach and a time to fight.[28]

He then threw off his robes to reveal the uniform of an officer in the Revolutionary Army. That afternoon, at the head of 300 men, he marched off to join General Washington's troops. He became Colonel of the 8th Virginia Regiment and served until the end of the war; during this time, he was promoted to Major General. In 1785, he became the Vice-President of Pennsylvania, and in 1790 was a member of the Pennsylvania Constitutional Convention. He then served as a U.S. Congressman from Pennsylvania, and in 1801 John Peter Muhlenberg was elected to the United States Senate.

Prussian General Friedrich Wilhelm Augustus Baron von Steuben (1730-1794) worked with the Continental army at Valley Forge, continually drilling them until they could, with precision, deliver a volley of gunfire every 15 seconds. An article appeared in the *Pennsylvania Packet,* a Philadelphia newspaper, during that fateful winter:

> Our attention is now drawn to one point: the enemy grows weaker every day, and we are growing stronger. Our work is almost done, and with the blessing of heaven, and the valor of our worthy General, we shall soon drive these plunderers out of our country![29]

On March 10, 1778, as recorded in *The Writings of George Washington* (March 1 to May 31, 1778, 11:83-84, published by the U.S. Government Printing Office, 1934), is the following incident:

> At a General Court Marshall whereof Colo. Tupper was President (10th March 1778) Lieutt. Enslin of Colo. Malcom's Regiment tried for attempting to commit sodomy, with John Monhort a soldier; Secondly, For Perjury in swearing to false Accounts, found guilty of the charges exhibited against him, being breaches of 5th. Article 18th. Section of the Articles of War and do sentence him to be dismiss'd the service with Infamy. His Excellency the Commander in Chief [George Washington] approves the sentence and with Abhorrence and Detestation of such Infamous Crimes orders Liett. Enslin to be drummed out of Camp tomorrow morning by all the Drummers and Fifers in the Army never to return; The Drummers and Fifers to attend on the Grand parade at Guard mounting for that Purpose.[30]

On May 2, 1778, General George Washington issued these orders to his troops at Valley Forge:

George Washington

While we are zealously performing the duties of good citizens and soldiers, we certainly ought not to be inattentive to the higher duties of religion.

To the distinguished character of Patriot, it should be our highest Glory to laud the more distinguished Character of Christian.

The signal instances of Providential goodness which we have experienced and which have now almost crowned our labors with complete success demand from us in a peculiar manner the warmest returns of gratitude and piety to the Supreme Author of all good.[31]

On May 5, 1778, upon receiving news that France had joined the War on the side of the Colonies, General Washington issued this order from his headquarters at Valley Forge:

It having pleased the Almighty Ruler of the universe to defend the cause of the United American States, and finally to raise up a powerful friend among the princes of the earth, to establish our liberty and independence upon a lasting foundation, it becomes us to set apart a day for gratefully acknowledging the divine goodness, and celebrating the important event, which we owe to His divine interposition.[32]

On August 20, 1778, General George Washington wrote to his friend, Brigadier General Thomas Nelson in Virginia:

The hand of Providence has been so conspicuous in all this (the course of the war) that he must be worse than an infidel that lacks faith, and more wicked that has not gratitude to acknowledge his obligations; but it will be time enough for me to turn Preacher when my present appointment ceases.[33]

[Profuse instances of "Providential" intervention are documented in *The Light and the Glory* by Peter Marshall and David Manuel, (Old Tappan, New Jersey: Fleming H. Revell Company, 1977), and in *The American Covenant* by Marshall Foster, (Thousand Oaks, California: The Mayflower Institute, 1992).]

On May 12, 1779, General George Washington was visited at his Middle Brook military encampment by the Chiefs of the Delaware Indian tribe. They had brought three youths to be trained in the American schools. Washington assured them, commenting:

> Congress will look upon them as their own Children....You do well to wish to learn our arts and ways of life, and above all, the religion of Jesus Christ. These will make you a greater and happier people than you are. Congress will do everything they can to assist you in this wise intention.[34]

In June of 1779, near his headquarters on the Hudson River, General George Washington's private prayer was recorded:

> And now, Almighty Father, if it is Thy holy will that we shall obtain a place and name among the nations of the earth, grant that we may be enabled to show our gratitude for Thy goodness by our endeavors to fear and obey Thee. Bless us with Thy wisdom in our counsels, success in battle, and let all our victories be tempered with humanity. Endow, also, our enemies with enlightened minds, that they become sensible of their injustice, and willing to restore our liberty and peace. Grant the petition of Thy servant, for the sake of Him whom Thou hast called Thy beloved Son; nevertheless, not my will, but Thine be done.[35]

In June of 1780, Hessian General Wilhelm von Knyphausen, with 5,000 troops, crossed over to New Jersey from Staten Island. Encountering unexpected resistance at the little village of Springfield, they were driven back, but not before they shot the wife of Reverend James Caldwell, a mother of nine, and burned their home to the ground.

George Washington

Two weeks later they repeated their attempt to advance, aided by British General Clinton's troops, and they again met resistance. The patriots in General Nathaniel Greene's regiment were courageously firing from behind the church fence when they suddenly ran out of the paper wadding used to hold the gunpowder in place in their muskets.

Chaplain James Caldwell quickly ran past the British fire, entered the Presbyterian church and collected all the copies he could carry of *Isaac Watts' Psalms, Hymns and Spiritual Songs,* 1707. Distributing them to the thankful troops, he exclaimed, "Now put Watts into'em, boys! Give 'em Watts!" The Americans held their ground, and by the next day the enemy had withdrawn.[36]

On Monday, September 25, 1780, almost by accident, the plot of Benedict Arnold, Commander of West Point, to betray the Continental Army into the hands of the British was discovered. In response to the miraculous deliverance thereof, General George Washington issued the following circular to his troops:

> General Orders—Head Quarters, Orangetown, September 26, 1780, Tuesday.
> Treason of the blackest dye was yesterday discovered! General Arnold who commanded at Westpoint, lost to every sentiment of honor, of public and private obligation, was about to deliver up that important Post into the hands of the enemy. Such an event must have given the American cause a deadly wound if not fatal stab. Happily the treason had been timely discovered to prevent the fatal misfortune. The providential train of circumstances which led to it affords the most convincing proof that the Liberties of America are the object of divine Protection.[37]

On January 1, 1781, circumstances were desperate for the Continental Army. The Pennsylvania line troops, being paid with worthless paper currency, revolted. Short enlistments threatened the discipline of the ranks.

In a bold move, on January 17, 1781, George Washington's southern army, led by General George Morgan, defeated the entire detachment of British Colonel Tarleton's troops at Cowpens. Lord Cornwallis was infuriated and immediately began pursuing the American troops. He decided to wait the night at the Catawba River, which the American troops had crossed just two hours earlier, but to his distress, a storm began during the night, causing the river to be uncrossable for days.

On February 3, Lord Cornwallis nearly overtook the American troops again at the Yadkin River. He watched the American troops getting out of the river on the other side, but before his troops could cross, a sudden flood ran the river over its banks, preventing the British from crossing.

On February 13, only a few hours ahead of the British, the American troops crossed the Dan River into Virginia. When the British arrived, again, the river had risen, stopping the British from pursuing. British Commander-in-Chief Henry Clinton wrote, explaining the incident:

> Here the royal army was again stopped by a sudden rise of the waters, which had only just fallen (almost miraculously) to let the enemy over, who could not else have eluded Lord Cornwallis' grasp, so close was he upon their rear.[38]

On October 19, 1781, the British troops under Lord Cornwallis surrendered at Yorktown. The following day, General George Washington called for a service to render thanksgiving to God:

> The commander-in-chief earnestly recommends that the troops not on duty should universally attend with that seriousness of deportment and gratitude of heart which the recognition of such reiterated and astonishing interposition of Providence demands of us.[39]

On November 15, 1781, General George Washington wrote to the President of the Continental Congress, Thomas McKean:

> I take a particular pleasure in acknowledging that the interposing Hand of Heaven, in the various instances of our extensive Preparation for this Operation [Yorktown], has been most conspicuous and remarkable.[40]

On June 14, 1783, at the conclusion of the Revolutionary War, General George Washington sent a farewell circular letter from his headquarters in Newburgh, New York, to all thirteen Governors of the newly freed states. He stated:

> I now make it my earnest prayer that God would have you, and the State over which you preside, in his holy protection...that he would most graciously be pleased to dispose us all to do justice, to love mercy, and to demean ourselves with that charity, humility, and pacific temper of mind, which were the characteristics of the Divine Author of our blessed religion, and without an humble imitation of whose example in these things, we can never hope to be a happy nation.[41]

Washington's Prayer for the United States of America appears on a plaque in St. Paul's Chapel in New York City and at Pohick Church, Fairfax County, Virginia, where Washington was a vestryman from 1762 to 1784:

> Almighty God; We make our earnest prayer that Thou wilt keep the United States in Thy Holy protection; and Thou wilt incline the hearts of the Citizens to cultivate a spirit of subordination and obedience to Government; and entertain a brotherly affection and love for one another and for their fellow Citizens of the United States at large, and particularly for their brethren who have served in the Field.
>
> And finally that Thou wilt most graciously be pleased to dispose us all to do justice, to love mercy, and to demean ourselves with that Charity, humility, and pacific temper of mind which were the Characteristics of the Divine Author of our blessed Religion, and without a humble imitation of whose example in these things we can never hope to be a happy nation.
>
> Grant our supplication, we beseech Thee, through Jesus Christ our Lord. Amen.[42]

On December 23, 1783, from the Maryland Capitol at Annapolis, General George Washington addressed Congress regarding the official resignation of his military commission:

> I resign with satisfaction the appointment...my abilities to accomplish so arduous a task, were superceded by...the patronage of Heaven....My gratitude for the interposition of Providence...increases with every review of the momentous contest....
>
> I consider it an indispensable duty to close this last solemn act of my Official life by commending the Interest of our dearest Country to the protection of Almighty God, and those who have the superintendence of them, to his holy keeping.[43]

On May 14, 1787, the Constitutional Convention met at the State House (Independence Hall) for the purpose of revising the Articles of Confederation and formulating the Constitution. George Washington, who had been unanimously elected as president of the Convention, rose during the Convention and admonished the delegates:

> If to please the people, we offer what we ourselves disapprove, how can we afterward defend our work? Let us raise a standard to

which the wise and the honest can repair; the event is in the Hand of God![44]

On July 30, 1787, George Washington wrote to Joseph Rakestraw of Philadelphia, concerning his desire to place a "Dove of Peace" (Genesis 8:11-12) atop the weathervane of his home in Mount Vernon:

> I should like to have a bird (in place of the Vane) with an olive branch in its mouth....[45]

On June 29, 1788, George Washington sent a letter to General Benjamin Lincoln, his deputy in the War, who had accepted British General Cornwallis' sword at the surrender at Yorktown:

> No Country upon Earth ever had it more in its power to attain these blessings....Much to be regretted indeed would it be, were we to neglect the means and depart from the road which Providence has pointed us to, so plainly; I cannot believe it will ever come to pass. The Great Governor of the Universe has led us too long and too far...to forsake us in the midst of it....We may, now and then, get bewildered; but I hope and trust that there is good sense and virtue enough left to recover the right path.[46]

On July 20, 1788, George Washington wrote to Jonathan Trumbull, the British Governor of Connecticut, who had become loyal to the cause of American Independence:

> We may, with a kind of grateful and pious exultation, trace the finger of Providence through those dark and mysterious events, which first induced the States to appoint a general Convention and then led them one after another into an adoption of the system recommended by that general Convention; thereby in all human probability, laying a lasting foundation for tranquillity and happiness.[47]

Jonathan Trumbull

At the start of the Revolutionary War, George Washington had moved his mother into the village of Fredericksburg for

This illustration depicts Washington's triumphant reception in Trenton, scene of one of his greatest victories, while en route to his inauguration in New York in 1789.

safety. She remained there for the entire duration of the War. In October of 1781, when informed of British General Cornwallis' surrender, Mary Washington lifted her hands toward heaven in gratitude and exclaimed:

> Thank God! War will now be ended, and peace, independence and happiness bless our country![48]

On Tuesday, April 14, 1789, George Washington received the official notification that he had been elected as the first President of the United States. Before leaving for New York, he insisted on visiting his ailing mother. George Washington's adopted grandson, George Washington Parke Custis, records what would be the last visit between the first President and his mother:

An affected scene ensued. The son feelingly remarked the ravages which a torturing disease (cancer) had made upon the aged frame of the mother, and addressed her with these words:

"The people, madam, have been pleased, with the most flattering unanimity, to elect me to the Chief magistracy of these United States, but before I can assume the functions of my office, I have come to bid you an affectionate farewell. So soon as the weight of public business, which must necessarily attend the outset of a new government, can be disposed of, I shall hasten to Virginia, and,"(here the matron interrupted with—)

"and you will see me no more; my great age, and the disease which is fast approaching my vitals, warn me that I shall not be long in this world; I trust in God that I may be somewhat prepared for the better. But go, George, fulfill the high destinies which Heaven appears to have intended for you; go, my son, and may that Heaven's and a mother's blessing be with you always."[49]

On August 5, 1789, less than 4 months later, Mrs. Mary Washington died at 82 years of age.

A week prior to Washington's Inauguration, April 23, 1789, the schedule of events for that special day was published in the newspaper, *Daily Advertiser:*

On the morning of the day on which our illustrious President will be invested with his office, the bells will ring at nine o'clock, when the people may go up and in a solemn manner commit the new Government, with its important train of consequences, to the holy protection and blessings of the Most High. An early hour is prudently fixed for this peculiar act of devotion, and it is designed wholly for prayer.[50]

On April 27, 1789, the Senate, and two days later the House, passed a resolution in Congress giving instructions with regard to the Inauguration of George Washington as the first President of the United States:

Resolved, That after the oath shall have been administered to the President, he, attended by the Vice President, and the members of the Senate, and House of Representatives, proceed to St. Paul's Chapel, to hear divine service, to be performed by the Chaplain of Congress already appointed.[51]

George Washington took the oath of office, April 30, 1789,
on the balcony of Federal Hall, in New York City,
with his hand upon an open Bible.

The *Annals of Congress* give a record of the events on April 30, 1789, following President George Washington's Inauguration:

> The President, the Vice President, the Senate, and House of Representatives, &c., then proceeded to St. Paul's Chapel, where divine service was preformed by the Chaplains of Congress.[52]

George Washington took the oath of office, April 30, 1789, on the balcony of Federal Hall, in New York City, with his hand upon an open Bible. Then, embarrassed at the thunderous ovation which followed, the pealing church bells and the roaring of artillery, he went inside to deliver his inaugural address to Congress.[53]

In his Inaugural Address to Both Houses of Congress, April 30, 1789, George Washington proclaimed:

> Such being the impressions under which I have, in obedience to the public summons, repaired to the present station, it would be peculiarly improper to omit, in this first official act, my fervent

supplications to that Almighty Being who rules over the universe, who presides in the councils of nations and whose providential aids can supply every human defect,

that His benediction may consecrate to the liberties and happiness of the people of the United States a Government instituted by themselves for these essential purposes; and may enable every instrument employed in its administration to execute with success, the functions allotted to his charge.

In tendering this homage to the Great Author of every public and private good, I assure myself that it expresses your sentiments not less than my own; nor those of my fellow-citizens at large, less than either.

No people can be bound to acknowledge and adore the Invisible Hand which conducts the affairs of men more than the people of the United States.

Every step by which they have advanced to the character of an independent nation seems to have been distinguished by some token of providential agency;

and in the important revolution just accomplished in the system of their United government, the tranquil deliberations and voluntary consent of so many distinct communities, from which the event has resulted can not be compared with the means by which most governments have been established, without some return of pious gratitude, along with an humble anticipation of the future blessings which the past seem to presage.

These reflections, arising out of the present crisis, have forced themselves too strongly on my mind to be suppressed. You will join with me I trust in thinking, that there are none under the influence of which the proceedings of a new and free Government can more auspiciously commence.

We ought to be no less persuaded that the propitious smiles of Heaven can never be expected on a nation that disregards the eternal rules of order and right which Heaven itself has ordained; and since the preservation of the sacred fire of liberty and the destiny of the republican model of government are justly considered as deeply, perhaps finally, staked of the experiment....

I shall take my present leave; but not without resorting once more to the Benign Parent of the Human Race, in humble supplication that, since He has been pleased to favor the American people with opportunities for deliberating in perfect tranquillity, and dispositions for deciding with unparalleled unanimity on a form of government for the security of their union and the advancement of their happiness, so His divine blessings may be equally conspicuous in the enlarged views, the temperate consultations and the wise measures on which the success of this Government must depend.[54]

To a gathering of Episcopalians, Washington declared:

> That Government alone can be approved by Heaven, which promotes peace and secures protection to its Citizens in every thing that is dear and interesting to them....[55]

In addressing the General Committee representing the United Baptist Churches of Virginia, on May 10, 1789, Washington stated:

> If I could have entertained the slightest apprehension that the Constitution framed by the Convention, where I had the honor to preside, might possibly endanger the religious rights of any ecclesiastical Society, certainly I would never have placed my signature to it;
> ...I beg you will be persuaded that no one would be more zealous than myself to establish effectual barriers against...every species of religious persecution.[56]

On May 29, 1789, in a letter to the Methodist Episcopal Bishop of New York, George Washington wrote:

> It shall still be my endeavor to manifest, by overt acts, the purity of my inclination for promoting the happiness of mankind, as well as the sincerity of my desires to contribute whatever may be in my power towards the preservation of the civil and religious liberties of the American People.[57]

In July of 1789, in a letter to the Directors of the Society of the United Brethren for Propagating the Gospel among the Heathen, President Washington committed that government should:

George Washington

> Co-operate, as far as the circumstances may conveniently admit, with the disinterested endeavors of your Society to civilize and Christianize the Savages of the Wilderness.[58]

In October of 1789, President Washington addressed the Quakers at their yearly meeting for Pennsylvania, New Jersey, Delaware, and the western part of Virginia and Maryland, stating:

> The liberty enjoyed by the People of these States of worshipping Almighty God agreeable to their consciences is not only among the

choicest of their blessings, but also of their rights.

While men perform their social duties faithfully, they do all that society or the state can with propriety demand or expect; and remain responsible only to their Maker for the religion, or modes of faith, which they may prefer or profess.[59]

George Washington issued from New York a *National Day of Thanksgiving Proclamation* on October 3, 1789:

Whereas it is the duty of all nations to acknowledge the providence of Almighty God, to obey His will, to be grateful for his benefits, and humbly to implore His protection and favor....

George Washington

Now, therefore, I do recommend and assign Thursday, the twenty-sixth day of November next, to be devoted by the people of these United States to the service of that great and glorious Being, who is the beneficent Author of all the good that was, that is, or that will be. That we then may all unite unto Him our sincere and humble thanks for His kind care and protection of the people of this country previous to their becoming a nation; for the signal and manifold mercies and the favorable interpositions of His providence in the course and conclusion of the late war;

for the great degree of tranquility, union, and plenty which we have since enjoyed; for the peaceable and rational manner in which we have been enabled to establish constitutions of government for our safety and happiness, and particularly the national one now lately instituted; for the civil and religious liberty with which we are blessed....

And also that we may then unite in most humbly offering our prayers and supplications to the great Lord and Ruler of Nations, and beseech Him to pardon our national and other transgressions, to enable us all, whether in public or private stations, to perform our several and relative duties properly and punctually, to render our national government a blessing to all the People, by constantly being a government of wise, just and constitutional laws, discreetly and faithfully executed and obeyed, to protect and guide all Sovereigns and Nations (especially such as have shown kindness unto us) and to bless them with good government, peace, and concord, to promote the knowledge and practice of the true religion and virtue, and the increase of science among them and Us, and generally to grant unto all Mankind such a degree of temporal prosperity as He alone knows to be best.

Given under my hand, at the city of New York, the 3rd of October, A.D. 1789.—G̲o̲ Washington.[60]

On October 9, 1789, President George Washington wrote to the Synod of the Dutch Reformed Churches in North America:

George Washington

> While just government protects all in their religious rights, true religion affords to government its surest support.[61]

On March 15, 1790, to the Roman Catholics of the nation, President Washington spoke of:

> The pure spirit of Christianity.[62]

On March 11, 1792, from Philadelphia, President George Washington wrote a letter to John Armstrong:

> I am sure that never was a people, who had more reason to acknowledge a Divine interposition in their affairs, than those of the United States; and I should be pained to believe that they have forgotten that agency, which was so often manifested during our Revolution, or that they failed to consider the omnipotence of that God who is alone able to protect them.[63]

On January 27, 1793, to the congregation of the New Church in Baltimore, President George Washington exclaimed:

> We have abundant reason to rejoice that in this Land the light of truth and reason has triumphed over the power of bigotry and super-stition, and that every person may here worship God according to the dictates of his own heart. In this enlightened Age and in this Land of equal liberty it is our boast, that a man's religious tenets will not forfeit the protection of the Laws, nor deprive him of the right of attaining and holding the highest offices that are known in the United States.[64]

In writing to the Hebrew Congregations of the City of Savanah, Georgia, President George Washington petitioned:

> May the same wonder-working Deity, who long since delivering the Hebrews from their Egyptian Oppressors planted them in the promised land—whose providential agency has lately been conspicuous in establishing these United States as an independent Nation—still continue to water them with the dews of Heaven and to

make the inhabitants of every denomination participate in the temporal and spiritual blessings of that people whose God is Jehovah.[65]

On November 19, 1794, following the Whiskey Rebellion, President Washington stated in his sixth Annual Address:

> Let us unite, therefore, in imploring the Supreme Ruler of nations, to spread his holy protection over these United States; to turn the machinations of the wicked to the confirming of our constitutions; to enable us at all times to root out internal sedition, and put invasion to flight; to perpetuate to our country that prosperity, which his goodness has already conferred, and to verify the anticipation of this government being a safeguard to human rights.[66]

On January 1, 1795, President George Washington issued another _National Thanksgiving Proclamation:_

> It is in an especial manner our duty as a people, with devout reverence and affectionate gratitude, to acknowledge our many and great obligations to Almighty God, and to implore Him to continue and confirm the blessings we experienced.
>
> Deeply penetrated with this sentiment, I, George Washington, President of the United States, do recommend to all religious societies and denominations, and to all persons whomsoever within the United States, to set apart and observe Thursday, the 19th day of February next, as a day of public thanksgiving and prayer,
>
> and on that day to meet together and render sincere and hearty thanks to the great Ruler of nations for the manifold and signal mercies which distinguish our lot as a nation;
>
> particularly for the possession of constitutions of government which unite and, by their union, establish liberty with order; for the preservation of our peace, foreign and domestic; for the reasonable control which has been given to a spirit of disorder in the suppression of the late insurrection, and generally for the prosperous condition of our affairs, public and private,
>
> and at the same time humbly and fervently beseech the kind Author of these blessings graciously to prolong them to us;
>
> to imprint on our hearts a deep and solemn sense of our obligations to Him for them; to teach us rightly to estimate their immense value;
>
> to preserve us from the arrogance of prosperity, and from hazarding the advantages we enjoy by delusive pursuits,
>
> to dispose us to merit the continuance of His favors by not abusing them, by our gratitude for them, and by a corresponding conduct as citizens and as men to render this country more and more a safe and

propitious asylum for the unfortunate of other countries; to extend among us true and useful knowledge;

to diffuse and establish habits of sobriety, order, and morality and piety, and finally to impart all the blessings we possess or ask for ourselves to the whole family of mankind.

In testimony whereof, I have caused the seal of the United States of America to be affixed to these presents, and signed the same with my hand. Done at the city of Philadelphia the first day of January, 1795.   (signed) George Washington.[67]

In 1752, George Washington created a personal prayer book, consisting of 24 pages in his field notebook, in his own handwriting:

SUNDAY MORNING....Almighty God, and most merciful Father, who didst command the children of Israel to offer a daily sacrifice to Thee, that thereby they might glorify and praise Thee for Thy protection both night and day, receive O Lord, my morning sacrifice which I now offer up to Thee;

I yield Thee humble and hearty thanks, that Thou hast preserved me from the dangers of the night past and brought me to the light of this day, and the comfort thereof, a day which is consecrated to Thine own service and for Thine own honour.

Let my heart therefore gracious God be so affected with the glory and majesty of it, that I may not do mine own works but wait on Thee, and discharge those weighty duties Thou required of me:

and since Thou art a God of pure eyes, and will be sanctified in all who draw nearer to Thee, who dost not regard the sacrifice of fools, nor hear sinners who tread in Thy courts, pardon I beseech Thee, my sins, remove them from Thy presence, as far as the east is from the west, and accept of me for the merits of Thy

George Washington

son Jesus Christ,

that when I come into Thy temple and compass Thine altar, my prayer may come before Thee as incense, and as I desire Thou wouldst hear me calling upon Thee in my prayers, so give me peace to hear Thee calling on me in Thy word, that it may be wisdom, righteousness, reconciliation and peace to the saving of my soul in the day of the Lord Jesus.

Grant that I may hear it with reverence, receive it with meekness, mingle it with faith, and that it may accomplish in me gracious God, the good work for which Thou hast sent it.

Bless my family, kindred, friends and country, be our God and guide this day and forever for His sake, who lay down in the grave and arose again for us, Jesus Christ our Lord. Amen.[68]

SUNDAY EVENING....O most Glorious God, in Jesus Christ my merciful and loving Father, I acknowledge and confess my guilt, in the weak and imperfect performance of the duties of this day. I have called on Thee for pardon and forgiveness of sins....Let me live according to those holy rules which Thou hast this day prescribed in Thy holy word;

make me to know what is acceptable in Thy sight, and therein to delight, open the eyes of my understanding, and help me thoroughly to examine myself concerning my knowledge, faith and repentance, increase my faith, and direct me to the true object, Jesus Christ the Way, the Truth and the Life, bless, O Lord, all the people of this land, from the highest to the lowest, particularly those whom Thou hast appointed to rule us in church & state.

Continue Thy goodness to me this night. These weak petitions, I humbly implore Thee to hear, accept and answer for the sake of Thy Dear Son, Jesus Christ our Lord, Amen.[69]

MONDAY MORNING....O eternal and everlasting God, I presume to present myself this morning before Thy Divine Majesty, beseeching Thee to accept of my humble and hearty thanks....Direct my thoughts, words and work, wash away my sins in the immaculate Blood of the Lamb, and purge my heart by Thy Holy Spirit....Daily frame me more and more into the likeness of Thy Son, Jesus Christ, that living in Thy fear, and dying in Thy favor, I may in Thy appointed time attain the resurrection of the just unto eternal life. Bless my family, friends and kindred, and unite us all in praising and glorifying Thee in all our works.[70]

MONDAY EVENING....Most Gracious Lord God, from whom proceedeth every good and perfect gift, I offer to Thy Divine Majesty my unfeigned praise and thanksgiving for all Thy mercies towards me....I have sinned and done very wickedly, be merciful to me, O God, and pardon me for Jesus Christ sake....Thou gavest Thy Son to die for me; and hast given me assurance of salvation, upon my repentance and sincerely endeavoring to conform my life to His holy precepts and example....

Bless O Lord the whole race of mankind, and let the world be filled with the knowledge of Thee and Thy Son, Jesus Christ....I beseech Thee to defend me this night from all evil, and do more for me than I can think or ask, for Jesus Christ sake, in whose most holy Name and Words, I continue to pray, Our Father, who art in heaven, hallowed be Thy Name....[71]

TUESDAY MORNING....O Lord our God, most mighty and merciful Father, I, thine unworthy creature and servant, do once more approach Thy presence. Though not worthy to appear before Thee, because of my natural corruptions, and the many sins and transgressions which I have committed against Thy Divine Majesty; yet I beseech Thee, for the sake of Him in whom Thou are well pleased, the Lord Jesus Christ, to admit me to render Thee deserved thanks and praises for Thy manifold mercies extended toward me....

Bless the people of this land, be a Father to the fatherless, a Comforter to the comfortless, a Deliverer to the captives, and a Physician to the sick. Let Thy blessing be upon our friends, kindred and families. Be our Guide this day and forever through Jesus Christ in whose blessed form of prayer I conclude my weak petitions—Our Father, who art in heaven, hallowed be Thy Name....[72]

TUESDAY EVENING....Most gracious God and heavenly Father, we cannot cease, but must cry unto Thee for mercy, because my sins cry against me for justice....That I may know my sins are forgiven by His death and passion. Embrace me in the arms of Thy mercy; vouchsafe to receive me unto the bosom of Thy love, shadow me with Thy wings, that I may safely rest under Thy protection this night;

and so into Thy hands I commend myself, both soul and body, in the name of Thy son, Jesus Christ, beseeching Thee, when this life shall end, I may take my everlasting rest with Thee in Thy heavenly kingdom. Bless all in authority over us, be merciful to all those afflicted with Thy cross or calamity, bless all my friends, forgive my enemies and accept my thanksgiving this evening for all the mercies and favors afforded me;

hear and graciously answer these my requests, and whatever else Thou see'st needful grant us, for the sake of Jesus Christ in whose blessed Name and Words I continue to pray, Our Father, who art in heaven, hallowed be Thy Name....[73]

WEDNESDAY MORNING .... Almighty and eternal Lord God, the great Creator of heaven and earth, and the God and Father of our Lord Jesus Christ; look down from heaven, in pity and compassion upon me Thy servant, who humbly prostrate myself before Thee, sensible of Thy mercy and my own misery.... Help all in affliction or adversity - give them patience and a sanctified use of their affliction, and in Thy good time, deliverance from them; forgive my enemies, take me unto Thy protection this day, keep me in perfect peace, which I ask in the name and for the sake of Jesus. Amen. [74]

George Washington is attributed with the statement:

It is impossible to rightly govern the world without God and the Bible. [75]

In James K. Paulding's *A Life of Washington*, published in New York, 1835 by Harper & Brothers, George Washington is recorded as saying:

It is impossible to account for the creation of the universe, without the agency of a Supreme Being. It is impossible to govern the universe without the aid of a Supreme Being. It is impossible to reason without arriving at a Supreme Being.

Religion is as necessary to reason, as reason is to religion. The one cannot exist without the other. A reasoning being would lose his reason, in attempting to account for the great phenomena of nature, had he not a Supreme Being to refer to.[76]

George Washington stated, as recorded in the *Maxims of Washington*:

The sentiments we have mutually expressed of profound gratitude to the Source of those numerous blessings - the Author of all good obligations to unite our sincere and zealous endeavours, as the instruments of Divine Providence, to preserve and perpetuate them. [77]

Providence has heretofore taken us up when all other means and hope seemed to be departing from us, in this I will confide. [78]

On September 9,1786, from Mt. Vernon, George Washington wrote to John F. Mercer:

It being among my first wishes to see some plan adopted by which slavery in this country may be abolished by law. [79]

George Washington stated in his Farewell Address, September 19, 1796:

Profoundly penetrated with this idea, I shall carry it with me to the grave, as a strong incitement to unceasing vows that Heaven may continue to you the choicest tokens of its beneficence - that your union and brotherly affection may be perpetual - that the free constitution, which is the work of your hands, may be sacredly maintained - that its administration in every department may be stamped with wisdom and virtue....

The name of AMERICAN, which belongs to you, in your national capacity, must always exalt the just pride of Patriotism, more than any appellation derived from local discriminations. With slight shades of difference, you have the same Religion, Manners, Habits, and political Principles....

Of all the dispositions and habits which lead to political prosperity, Religion and morality are indispensable supports.

In vain would that man claim the tribute of Patriotism, who should labor to subvert these great Pillars of human happiness, these firmest props of the duties of Men and Citizens.

The mere Politician, equally with the pious man, ought to respect and to cherish them. A volume could not trace all their connections with private and public felicity.

Let it simply be asked where is the security for prosperity, for reputation, for life, if the sense of religious obligation desert the oaths, which are the instruments of investigation in the Courts of Justice?

And let us with caution indulge the supposition, that morality can be maintained without religion.

Whatever may be conceded to the influence of refined education on minds of peculiar structure, reason and experience both forbid us to expect that national morality can prevail in exclusion of religious principle.

Tis substantially true, that virtue or morality is a necessary spring of popular government.

The rule indeed extends with more or less force to every species of Free Government. Who that is a sincere friend to it, can look with indifference upon attempts to shake the foundation of the fabric?

Observe good faith and justice towards all Nations. Cultivate peace and harmony with all. Religion and Morality enjoin this conduct; and can it be that good policy does not equally enjoin it?...Can it be that Providence has not connected the permanent felicity of a Nation with its virtue?

Though, in reviewing the incidents of my Administration, I am unconscious of intentional error, I am nevertheless too sensible of my defects not to think it probable that I may have committed many errors. Whatever they may be I fervently beseech the Almighty to avert or mitigate the evils to which they may tend.

I shall also carry with me the hope that my country will never cease to view them with indulgence; and that after forty-five years of my life dedicated to its service, with an upright zeal, the faults of incompetent abilities will be consigned to oblivion, as myself must soon be to the mansions of rest.[80]

Of note are other passages from Washington's Farewell Speech, September 19, 1796:

And of fatal tendency…to put, in the place of the delegated will of the Nation, the will of a party;—often a small but artful and enterprising minority.…they are likely, in the course of time and things, to become potent engines, by which cunning, ambitious, and unprincipled men will be enabled to subvert the Power of the People and to usurp for the themselves the reins of Government; destroying afterwards the very engines which have lifted them to unjust dominion.…

But this leads at length to a more formal and permanent despotism—The disorders and miseries, which result, gradually incline the minds of men to seek security and repose in the absolute power of an Individual…:[who] turns this disposition to the purposes of his own elevation, on the ruins of Public Liberty.…

The spirit of encroachment tends to consolidate the powers of all the departments in one, and thus to create, whatever the form of government, a real despotism.…

by unnecessarily parting with what ought to have been retained, and by exciting jealousy, ill-will, and a disposition to retaliate.…it gives to ambitious, corrupted, or deluded citizens…facility to betray, or sacrifice the interests of their own country, without odium, sometimes even with popularity:—gilding with the appearances of a virtuous sense of obligation, a commendable deference for public opinion, or a laudable zeal for public good, the base or foolish compliances of ambition, corruption or infatuation.

…ill founded jealousies and false alarms, kindles the animosity of one part against another, foments occasionally riot and insurrection.— It opens the doors to foreign influence and corruption, which find a facilitated access to the Government itself through the channels of party passions. Thus the policy and the will of one country, are subjected to the policy and will of another.[81]

On December 7, 1796, in his eighth Annual Address to Congress, President George Washington stated:

The situation in which I now stand, for the last time, in the midst of the Representatives of the People of the United States, naturally recalls the period when the Administration of the present form of Government commenced; and I cannot omit the occasion, to congratulate you and my Country, on the success of the experiment; nor to repeat my fervent supplications to the Supreme Ruler of the Universe, and Sovereign Arbiter of Nations, that his Providential care may still be extended to the United States; that the virtue and happiness of the People, may be preserved; and that the Government, which they have instituted, for the protection of their liberties, may be perpetual.[82]

On May 30, 1799, only six months before his death, George Washington corresponded with his intimate friend and pastor, Reverend William White of Christ Church, Philadelphia:

Rev. Dear Sir, The Sermon on the duty of civil obedience as required in Scripture, which you had the goodness to send me, came safe a Post or two ago; and for which I pray you to accept my grateful acknowledgements. The hurry in which it found me engaged, in a matter that pressed, has not allowed me time to give it a perusal yet; but I anticipate the pleasure of the edification I shall find when it is in my power to do it. With every respectful wish, in which Mrs. Washington unites, for yourself and the young ladies of your family, I am with great esteem and regard, Dear Sir, your most obedient and humble servant, George Washington.[83]

The Reverend Mason L. Weems, pastor of the Pohick Church, where George Washington and his family attended, wrote a book in 1796, entitled, *The Immortal Mentor: or Man's Unerring Guide to a Healthy, Wealthy, and Happy Life*. George Washington wrote this recommendation in the inside page of his copy:

RECOMMENDATION BY GEORGE WASHINGTON
Mount Vernon, July 3, 1799
Rev. Sir,

For your kind compliment, "The Immortal Mentor," I beg you to accept my best thanks. I have perused it with singular satisfaction; and hesitate not to say that it is, in my opinion at least, an invaluable compilation. I cannot but hope that a book whose contents do such credit to its title, will meet a very generous patronage. Should that patronage equal my wishes, you will have no reason to regret that you ever printed the Immortal Mentor. With respect I am, Rev. Sir, Your most obedient, humble servant, George Washington.[84]

In his *Last Will and Testament*, George Washington wrote:

In the name of God, Amen....All my debts, of which there are but few, and none of magnitude, are to be punctually and speedily paid....To my dearly beloved wife, Martha Washington, I give and bequeath the use, profit, and benefit of my whole estate, real and

Martha Washington

personal, for the term of her natural life....Upon the decease of my wife it is my will and desire that all slaves whom I hold in my own right shall receive their freedom...And to my mulatto man, William, (calling himself William Lee), I give immediate freedom, or, if he should prefer it (on account of the accidents which have befallen him, and which have rendered him incapable of walking, or of any active employment), to remain in the situation he now is, it shall be optional in him to do so: In either case, however, I allow him an annuity of thirty dollars during his natural life, which shall be independent of the victuals and clothes he has been accustomed to receive, if he choose the last alternative; but in full with his freedom if he prefers the first: — and this I give him, as a testimony of my sense of his attachment to me, and for his faithful services during the Revolutionary War.[85]

Rev. J.T. Kirkland said, after Washington's death, December 14, 1799:

> The virtues of our departed friend were crowned by piety. He is known to have been habitually devout. To Christian institutions he gave the countenance of his example; and no one could express, more fully, his sense of the Providence of God, and the dependence of man.[86]

John Marshall

John Marshall, Chief Justice of the Supreme Court, who had previously fought with Washington in the Revolutionary War and served with him at Valley Forge, said of Washington:

> Without making ostentatious professions of religion, he was a sincere believer in the Christian faith, and a truly devout man.[87]

William White gives evidence of Washington's personal life in his *Washington's Writing*:

> It seems proper to subjoin to this letter what was told to me by Mr. Robert Lewis, at Fredricksburg, in the year 1827. Being a nephew of Washington, and his private secretary during the first part of his presidency, Mr. Lewis lived with him on terms of intimacy, and had

the best opportunity for observing his habits.

Mr. Lewis said that he had accidentally witnessed his private devotions in his library both morning and evening; that on those occasions he had seen him in a kneeling posture with a Bible open before him, and that he believed such to have been his daily practice. [88]

George Washington's Bible was donated by his adopted grandson, George Washington Parke Custis, to the Pohick Church in Truro Parish, where Washington served as a vestryman from October 25, 1762 to February 23, 1784. The inscription reads:

Presented to Truro Parish for the use of Pohick Church, July 11, 1802. With the request that should said church cease to be appropriated to Divine worship which God forbid, and for the honor of Christianity, it is hoped will never take place. In such case I desire that the vestry will preserve this Bible as a testimony of regard from the subscriber after a residence of 19 years in the Parish.

George Washington Parke Custis. [89]

Being in communion with the Anglican Church, serving for over twenty years as a vestryman (trustee), and on at least three different occasions serving as churchwarden, Washington would have regularly repeated the Apostle's Creed, which begins:

I believe in God, the Father Almighty, Maker of heaven and earth, and in Jesus Christ, His only Son, our Lord. [90]

On the rear wall of Washington's tomb is engraved the verse from the Book of John, chapter 11:

I am the Resurrection and the Life; sayeth the Lord. He that believeth in Me, though he were dead yet shall he live. And whosoever liveth and believeth in Me shall never die. [91]

The Washington Monument, in Washington, D.C., stands over 555 feet high. Engraved on the metal cap are the words:

Praise be to God.

Along the stairway on the inside of the monument the following verses are carved on the tribute blocks:

SUFFER THE LITTLE CHILDREN TO COME UNTO ME AND FORBID THEM NOT; FOR SUCH IS THE KINGDOM OF GOD. (Luke 18:16)

TRAIN UP A CHILD IN THE WAY HE SHOULD GO AND WHEN HE IS OLD, HE WILL NOT DEPART FROM IT. (Proverbs 22:6)

SEARCH THE SCRIPTURES. (John 5:39; Acts 17:11)

HOLINESS UNTO THE LORD. (Exodus 28:36; 39:30; Zechariah 14:20)

IN GOD WE TRUST

GOD AND OUR NATIVE LAND

MAY HEAVEN TO THIS UNION CONTINUE ITS BENEFICENCE[92]

&

Isaac Watts (1674-1748), a poet, a theologian, and hymn writer, composed over 600 hymns. His most famous work, *Isaac Watts' Psalms, Hymns and Spiritual Songs,* 1707, was chosen, along with the Bible, by President Thomas Jefferson as the principal textbooks to teach reading in the schools of the District of Columbia. (Jefferson, being the third President, chaired the school board for the District of Columbia, where he authored the first plan of education adopted by the city of Washington.)[93] Isaac Watts' works include:

Thomas Jefferson

The Excellency of the Bible

The stars, that in their courses roll,
Have much instruction given;
But thy good Word informs my soul
How I may climb to heaven.[94]

Praise for the Gospel

How glad the heathens would have been,
That worship idols, wood and stone,
If they the book of God had seen,
'Or Jesus and his gospel known![95]

Praise to God for Learning to Read

Dear Lord, this Book of thine
Informs me where to go,
For grace to pardon all my sin,
And make me holy too.[96]

In 1707, Isaac Watts published his *Psalms, Hymns and Spiritual Songs,* which included the Christmas carol, "Joy to the World":

Joy to the World, the Lord is come,
Let earth receive her King;
Let every heart, prepare Him room,
And Heaven and nature sing,
And Heaven and nature sing,
And Heaven, and Heaven, and nature sing!

Joy to the World, the Savior reigns,
Let men their songs employ;
While fields and floods, rocks, hills and plains
Repeat the sounding joy,
Repeat the sounding joy,
Repeat, Repeat, the sounding joy!

He rules the world with truth and grace,
And makes the nations prove,
The glories of His righteousness
And wonders of His love,
And wonders of His love,
And wonders, and wonders, of His love![97]

In *Psalm 90,* 1719, st. I, Isaac Watts wrote:

O God, our help in ages past,
Our hope for years to come,
Our shelter from the stormy blast,
And our eternal home.[98]

≈

Francis Wayland (1796-1865), was the president of Brown University, 1827-55, and the first president of the American Institute of Instruction, 1830. He was instrumental in devising the

Francis Wayland

school system for Providence, R.I. A graduate of Union College and Harvard University, Francis Wayland wrote: *Elements of Moral Science*, 1835; *Elements of Political Economy*, 1837; *Thoughts on the Present Collegiate System in the United States*, 1842; and *A Memoir of the Life of the Rev. Adoniram Judson, D.D.*, 1842. As a well-recognized American clergyman, Francis Wayland stated:

That the truths of the Bible have the power of awakening an intense moral feeling in every human being; that they make bad men good, and send a pulse of healthful feeling through all the domestic, civil, and social relations;

that they teach men to love right, and hate wrong, and seek each other's welfare as children of a common parent; that they control the baleful passions of the heart, and thus make men proficient in self government;

and finally that they teach man to aspire after conformity to a Being of infinite holiness, and fill him with hopes more purifying, exalted, and suited to his nature than any other book the world has ever known—these are facts as incontrovertible as the laws of philosophy, or the demonstrations of mathematics.[99]

ॐ

Daniel Webster

Daniel Webster (1782-1852), was a famous American politician and diplomat. He is considered one of the greatest orators in American history. He served as a U.S. Congressman, a U.S. Senator and as the Secretary of State for three different Presidents: William Henry Harrison, John Tyler and Millard Fillmore. His political career spanned almost four decades.

Daniel Webster stated:

If there is anything in my thoughts or style to commend, the credit is due to my parents for instilling in me an early love of the Scriptures. If we abide by the principles taught in the Bible, our country will go on prospering and to prosper; but if we and our posterity neglect its instructions and authority, no man can tell how sudden a catastrophe may overwhelm us and bury all our glory in profound obscurity.[100]

Daniel Webster, in speaking at the bicentennial celebration of the landing of the Pilgrims at Plymouth Rock, December 22, 1820, declared:

Lastly, our ancestors established their system of government on morality and religious sentiment. Moral habits, they believed, cannot safely be trusted on any other foundation than religious principle, nor any government be secure which is not supported by moral habits....Whatever makes men good Christians, makes them good citizens.[101]

Cultivated mind was to act on uncultivated nature; and more than all, a government and a country were to commence, with the very first foundations laid under the divine light of the Christian religion. Happy auspices of a happy futurity! Who would wish that his country's existence had otherwise begun?[102]

Finally, let us not forget the religious character of our origin. Our fathers were brought hither by their high veneration for the Christian religion. They journeyed by its light, and labored in its hope. They sought to incorporate its principles with the elements of their society, and to diffuse its influence through all their institutions, civil, political, or literary.
Let us cherish these sentiments, and extend this influence still more widely; in full conviction that that is the happiest society which partakes in the highest degree of the mild and peaceful spirit of Christianity.[103]

On June 17, 1825, fifty years after the battle, the cornerstone for the Bunker Hill Monument was laid. As the guest speaker, Daniel Webster spoke to a crowd of twenty thousand people, including General Marquis de Lafayette:

We wish that this column, rising towards heaven among the pointed spires of so many temples dedicated to God, may contribute also to produce in all minds a pious feeling of dependence and gratitude.[104]

Let our object be—our country, our whole country, and nothing but our country. And by the blessing of God, may that country itself become a vast and splendid monument—not of oppression and terror, but of Wisdom, of Peace, and of Liberty, upon which the world may gaze with admiration forever.[105]

On August 2, 1826, in a discourse commemorating Adams and Jefferson at Faneuil Hall, Boston, Daniel Webster declared:

> It is my living sentiment, and by the blessing of God it shall be my dying sentiment—Independence now and Independence forever.[106]

Daniel Webster delivered these words in his second speech on Foote's Resolution, January 26, 1830:

> When my eyes shall be turned to behold for the last time the sun in heaven, may I not see him shining on the broken and dishonored fragments of a once glorious Union; on States disevered, discordant, belligerent; on a land rent with civil feuds, or drenched, it may be, in fraternal blood.[107]

> Behold the gorgeous ensign of the Republic, now known and honored throughout the earth, still full high advanced, its arms and trophies streaming in their original luster, not a stripe erased or polluted, nor a single star obscured....[It does not bear the motto] "Liberty first and Union afterwards," but everywhere, spread all over in characters of living light, blazing on all its ample folds, as they float over the sea and over the land, and in every wind under the whole heavens, that other sentiment, dear to every true American heart— Liberty and Union, now and forever, one and inseparable![108]

On April 6, 1830, in presenting an argument on the murder of Captain White, Daniel Webster spoke:

> A sense of duty pursues us ever. It is omnipresent, like the Deity. If we take to ourselves the wings of the morning, and dwell in the uttermost parts of the sea, duty performed or duty violated is still with us, for our happiness or our misery. If we say the darkness shall cover us, in the darkness as in the light our obligations are yet with us.[109]

In a speech on June 3, 1834, Daniel Webster exclaimed:

> God grants liberty only to those who love it, and are always ready to guard and defend it.[110]

In 1837, speaking on the Constitution, Daniel Webster gave a famous appeal for the Union:

> I regard it as the work of the purest patriots and wisest statesmen that ever existed, aided by the smiles of a benignant Providence; for when we regard it as a system of government growing out of the discordant opinions and conflicting interests of thirteen independent States, it almost appears a Divine interposition in our behalf....The hand that destroys the Constitution rends our Union asunder forever.[111]

In a speech at the Bunker Hill Monument, Charleston, Massachusetts, on June 17, 1843, Daniel Webster spoke of the Founding Fathers' regard for the Bible:

> The Bible came with them. And it is not to be doubted, that to free and universal reading of the Bible, in that age, men were much indebted for right views of civil liberty.
>
> The Bible is a book of faith, and a book of doctrine, and a book of morals, and a book of religion, of special revelation from God; but it is also a book which teaches man his own individual responsibility, his own dignity, and his equality with his fellow-man.[112]
>
> Thank God! I—I also—am an American![113]

Daniel Webster stated:

> If religious books are not widely circulated among the masses in this country, I do not know what is going to become of us as a nation. If truth be not diffused, error will be;
>
> If God and His Word are not known and received, the devil and his works will gain the ascendancy; If the evangelical volume does not reach every hamlet, the pages of a corrupt and licentious literature will;
>
> If the power of the Gospel is not felt throughout the length and breadth of the land, anarchy and misrule, degradation and misery, corruption and darkness will reign without mitigation or end.[114]
>
> If we work on marble, it will perish; if on brass, time will efface it; if we rear up temples, they will crumble into dust; but if we work upon immortal minds and imbue them with principles, with the just fear of God and the love of our fellow men, we engrave on those tablets something that will brighten to all eternity.[115]

The Lord's Day is the day on which the Gospel is preached...and although we live in a reading age and in a reading community, yet the preaching of the Gospel is the human agency which has been and still is most efficaciously employed for the spiritual good of men. That the poor had the Gospel preached to them was an evidence of His mission which the Author of Christianity Himself proclaimed.[116]

I believe that the Bible is to be understood and received in the plain and obvious meaning of its passages; for I cannot persuade myself that a book intended for the instruction and conversion of the whole world should cover its true meaning in any such mystery and doubt that none but critics and philosophers can discover it.[117]

I shall stand by the Union, and by all who stand by it. I shall do justice to the whole country...in all I say, and act for the good of the whole country in all I do. I mean to stand upon the Constitution. I need no other platform. I shall know but one country. The ends I aim at shall be my country's, my God's, and Truth's. I was born an American; I will live an American; I shall die an American; and I intend to perform the duties incumbent upon me in that character to the end of my career.[118]

In a discussion as he sat in a drawing room, Daniel Webster laid his hand on a copy of the Holy Scriptures and proclaimed:

This is the Book. I have read the Bible through many times, and now make it a practice to read it through once every year.—It is a book of all others for lawyers, as well as divines; and I pity the man who cannot find in it a rich supply of thought and of rules for conduct. It fits man for life—it prepares him for death.

My brother knew the importance of Bible truths. The Bible led him to prayer, and prayer was his communion with God. On the day he died he was engaged in an important cause in the courts then in session. But this cause, important as it was, did not keep him from his duty to God. He found time for prayer; for on his desk which he had just left was found a prayer written by him on that day, which for fervent piety, a devotedness to his heavenly Master, and for expressions of humility I think was never excelled.[119]

In stating his convictions, Daniel Webster declared:

The Gospel is either true history, or it is a consummate fraud; it is either a reality or an imposition. Christ was what He professed to be, or He was an imposter. There is no other alternative. His spotless life in His earnest enforcement of the truth—His suffering in its defense, forbid us to suppose that He was suffering an illusion of a heated brain. Every act of His pure and holy life shows that He was the author of truth, the advocate of truth, the earnest defender of truth, and the uncompromising sufferer for truth.

Now, considering the purity of His doctrines, the simplicity of His life, and the sublimity of His death, is it possible that he would have died for an illusion? In all His preaching the Saviour made no popular appeals; His discourses were always directed to the individual. Christ and His apostles sought to impress upon every man the conviction that he must stand or fall alone—he must live for himself, and die for himself, and give up his account to the omniscient God as though he were the only dependent creature in the universe.

The Gospel leaves the individual sinner alone with himself and his God. To his own Master he stands or falls. He has nothing to hope from the aid and sympathy of associates. The deluded advocates of new doctrines do not so preach. Christ and His apostles, had they been deceivers, would not so have preached. If clergymen in our days would return to the simplicity of the Gospel, and preach more to individuals and less to the crowd, there would not be so much complaint of the decline of true religion.

Many of the ministers of the present day take their text from St. Paul, and preach from the newspapers. When they do so, I prefer to enjoy my own thoughts rather than to listen. I want my Pastor to come to me in the spirit of the Gospel, saying: "You are mortal! Your probation is brief; your work must be done speedily; you are immortal, too. You are hastening to the bar of God; the Judge standeth at the door." When I am thus admonished, I have no disposition to muse or to sleep.[120]

In a speech, July 4, 1851, Daniel Webster expounded:

Let the religious element in man's nature be neglected, let him be influenced by no higher motives than low self-interest, and subjected to no stronger restraint than the limits of civil authority, and he becomes the creature of selfish passion or blind fanaticism.

On the other hand, the cultivation of the religious sentiment represses licentiousness...inspires respect for law and order, and gives strength to the whole social fabric, at the same time that it conducts the human soul upward to the Author of its being.[121]

When asked the question, "What is the greatest thought that ever passed through your mind?" Daniel Webster responded:

My accountability to God.[122]

On October 10, 1852, just two weeks before he died, Mr. Webster dictated what he desired to be engraved as an epitaph upon his tomb:

"LORD, I BELIEVE; HELP THOU MINE UNBELIEF."

Philosophical
argument, especially
that drawn from the vastness of the
Universe in comparison with the apparent insignificance of this globe, has sometimes
shaken my reason for the faith which is in me;
but my heart has always assured and reassured me that
the Gospel of Jesus Christ must be a Divine Reality. The Sermon on the Mount can not be a
merely human production. This belief
enters into the very depths of my
conscience. The whole history
of man proves it.
Daniel Webster[123]

After executing his *Will*, Daniel Webster remarked:

I thank God for strength to perform a sensible act....And now unto God, the Father, the Son, and the Holy Ghost, be praise for evermore. Peace on earth, and good will toward men. That is happiness—the essence—good will toward men.[124]

On October 24, 1852, only a few hours before his death, Daniel Webster said slowly:

The great mystery is Jesus Christ—the Gospel. What would the condition of any of us be if we had not the hope of immortality?...Thank God, the Gospel of Jesus Christ brought life and immortality to light, rescued it—brought it to light.[125]

Having begun to recite the Lord's Prayer, he said:

Hold me up; I do not wish to pray with a fainting voice....[126]

Daniel Webster's last coherent words were:

> I still live.[127]

In the Eulogy for Daniel Webster given in the United States Senate, Senator Lewis Cass stated:

> And beyond all this he died in the faith of the Christian—humble, but hopeful—adding another to the long list of eminent men who have searched the Gospel of Jesus Christ, and have found it to be the word and the will of God.[128]

๖

Noah Webster (1758-1843), was a statesman, educator, lexicographer and the author of *Webster's Dictionary*. Known as "the Schoolmaster of the Nation," Noah Webster published the first edition of his *American Dictionary of the English Language* in November, 1828. It contained the greatest number of biblical definitions given in any secular volume.

Noah Webster

Noah Webster, who had served as a soldier in the Revolutionary War, was also elected to the Connecticut General Assembly for nine terms, the Legislature of Massachusetts for three terms, and served as a judge. He was also largely responsible for Article I, Section 8, of the United States Constitution. During his tenure in the Massachusetts Legislature, Noah Webster labored to have funds appropriated for education. He declared government was responsible to:

> Discipline our youth in early life in sound maxims of moral, political, and religious duties.[129]

Webster's *American Spelling Book*, first written in the 1780s while he taught in New York, became the most popular book in American education. The famous "blue-backed speller" set a publishing record of a million copies a year for one hundred years. Americans from north to south and from east to west learned their letters, morality and patriotism from Webster's dictionaries, spellers, catechisms, history books, etc. His early "blue-backed speller" even contained a "Moral Catechism" with rules from the Scriptures upon which to base moral conduct.

In 1790, in his *American Spelling Book—Containing an easy Standard of Pronunciation* (which was the first part of a *Grammatical Institute of the English Language),* Noah Webster wrote on the second page a dedication to Ezra Stiles, President of Yale College:

> This first part of a Grammatical Institute of the English Language, is, with permission, most humbly inscribed, as a testimony of my veneration, for the superior talents, piety and patriotism, which enable him to preside over that seat of literature, with distinguished reputation, which render him an ornament to the Christian Profession, and give him an eminent rank among the illustrious characters that adorn the revolution.[130]

Noah Webster stated concerning education:

> Education is useless without the Bible.[131]

> The Bible was America's basic text book in all fields.[132]

> God's Word, contained in the Bible, has furnished all necessary rules to direct our conduct.[133]

In 1823, Noah Webster wrote in his textbook:

> It is alleged by men of loose principles, or defective views of the subject, that religion and morality are not necessary or important qualifications for political stations. But the Scriptures teach a different doctrine. They direct that rulers should be men who rule in the fear of God, able men, such as fear God, men of truth, hating covetousness.
> But if we had no divine instruction on the subject, our own interest would demand of us a strict observance of the principle of these injunctions. And it is to the neglect of this rule of conduct in our citizens, that we must ascribe the multiplied frauds, breeches of trust, peculations and embezzlements of public property which astonish even ourselves; which tarnish the character of our country; which disgrace a republican government; and which will tend to reconcile men to monarchs in other countries and even our own.[134]

In 1828, Noah Webster completed his 26-year project of writing *An American Dictionary of the English Language—with pronouncing vocabularies of Scripture, classical and geographical names.* It contained 70,000 entries and 12,000 new definitions. For the first time in English-speaking history, English vocabulary words had a standardized spelling. In the preface to this great work, Noah Webster wrote:

> In my view, the Christian religion is the most important and one of the first things in which all children, under a free government ought to be instructed....No truth is more evident to my mind than that the Christian religion must be the basis of any government intended to secure the rights and privileges of a free people.[135]

> To that great and benevolent Being, who, during the preparation of this work, has sustained a feeble constitution amidst obstacles and toils, disappointments, infirmities and depression; who has borne me and my manuscripts in safety across the Atlantic, and given me strength and resolution to bring the work to a close, I would present the tribute of my most grateful acknowledgements.
> And if the talent which He entrusted to my care, has not been put to the most profitable use in his service, I hope it has not been "kept laid up in a napkin" and that any misapplication of it may be graciously forgiven.
>
> New Haven
> Noah Webster.[136]

Noah Webster's 1828 edition of the *American Dictionary* contained a profuse amount of Holy Scripture, as he would use verses from the Old and New Testaments to clarify the context in which a word was to be used. For example, the definition of the word *Faith* includes the following sentences:

> Being justified by faith. Rom.v.
> Without faith it is impossible to please God. Heb.xi.
> For we walk by faith, not by sight. 2Cor.v.
> With the heart man believeth to righteousness. Rom.x.
> Your faith is spoken of throughout the whole world. Rom.i.
> Hast thou faith? Have it to thyself before God. Rom.xiv.
> Children in whom is no faith. Deut.xxxii.[137]

In *Webster's Dictionary*, the definition of the word *Property* is given as:

> The exclusive right of possessing, enjoying and disposing of a thing; ownership. In the beginning of the world, the Creator gave to man dominion over the earth, over the fish of the sea and the fowls of the air, and over every living thing. This is the foundation of man's property in the earth and all its productions....The labor of inventing, making or producing any thing constitutes one of the highest titles to property...It is one of the greatest blessings of civil society that the property of citizens is well secured.[138]

In *Webster's Dictionary*, the definition of the word *Providence* is given as:

> The care and superintendence which God exercises over his creatures....Some persons admit a general providence, but deny a particular providence, not considering that a general providence consists of particulars. A belief in divine providence is a source of great consolation to good men. By divine providence is understood God himself.[139]

In 1832, Noah Webster published his *History of the United States*, in which he wrote:

> The brief exposition of the constitution of the United States, will unfold to young persons the principles of republican government; and it is the sincere desire of the writer that our citizens should early understand that the genuine source of correct republican principles is the Bible, particularly the New Testament or the Christian religion.[140]

> The religion which has introduced civil liberty is the religion of Christ and His apostles, which enjoins humility, piety, and benevolence; which acknowledges in every person a brother, or a sister, and a citizen with equal rights. This is genuine Christianity, and to this we owe our free Constitutions of Government.[141]

> The moral principles and precepts contained in the Scriptures ought to form the basis of all of our civil constitutions and laws....All the miseries and evils which men suffer from vice, crime, ambition, injustice, oppression, slavery and war, proceed from their despising or neglecting the precepts contained in the Bible.[142]

> When you become entitled to exercise the right of voting for

public officers, let it be impressed on your mind that God commands you to choose for rulers just men who will rule in the fear of God. The preservation of a republican government depends on the faithful discharge of this duty;

If the citizens neglect their duty and place unprincipled men in office, the government will soon be corrupted; laws will be made not for the public good so much as for selfish or local purposes;

Corrupt or incompetent men will be appointed to execute the laws; the public revenues will be squandered on unworthy men; and the rights of the citizens will be violated or disregarded.

If a republican government fails to secure public prosperity and happiness, it must be because the citizens neglect the divine commands, and elect bad men to make and administer the laws. [143]

In *Advice to the Young,* published 1832, Noah Webster wrote:

> The 'Advice to the Young,'...will be useful in enlightening the minds of youth in religious and moral principles, and serve... to restrain some of the common vices of our country.... To exterminate our popular vices is a work of far more importance to the character and happiness of our citizens than any other improvements in our system of education. [144]

In 1833, Noah Webster translated the *Common Version of the Holy Bible, containing the Old and New Testament, with Amendments of the Language.* The preface reads:

> The Bible is the Chief moral cause of all that is good, and the best corrector of all that is evil, in human society; the best book for regulating the temporal concerns of men, and the only book that can serve as an infallible guide to future felicity .... It is extremely important to our nation, in a political as well as religious view, that all possible authority and influence should be given to the scriptures, for these furnish the best principles of civil liberty, and the most effectual support of republican government.
>
> The principles of genuine liberty, and of wise laws and administrations, are to be drawn from the Bible and sustained by its authority. The man, therefore, who weakens or destroys the divine authority of that Book may be accessory to all the public disorders which society is doomed to suffer....
>
> There are two powers only, sufficient to control men and secure the rights of individuals and a peaceable administration; these are the

combined force of religion and law, and the force or fear of the bayonet.

> Noah Webster
> New Haven 1833.[145]

In his *Dictionary*, published 1848, Noah Webster wrote in the preface:

> If the language can be improved in regularity, so as to be more easily acquired by our own citizens and by foreigners, and thus be rendered a more useful instrument for the propagation of science, arts, civilization and Christianity....[146]

Noah Webster stated:

> For this reason society requires that the education of youth should be watched with the most scrupulous attention. Education, in a great measure, forms the moral characters of men, and morals are the basis of government.
>
> Education should therefore be the first care of a legislature; not merely the institution of schools, but the furnishing of them with the best men for teachers. A good system of education should be the first article in the code of political regulations; for it is much easier to introduce and establish an effectual system for preserving morals, than to correct by penal statutes the ill effects of a bad system.
>
> The goodness of a heart is of infinitely more consequence to society than an elegance of manners; nor will any superficial accomplishments repair the want of principle in the mind. It is always better to be vulgarly right than politely wrong....
>
> The education of youth [is] an employment of more consequence than making laws and preaching the gospel, because it lays the foundation on which both law and gospel rest for success.[147]

> Republican government loses half of its value, where the moral and social duties are....negligently practised. To exterminate our popular vices is a work of far more importance to the character and happiness of our citizens, than any other improvements in our system of education.[148]

> By taking revenge, a man is even with his enemy, but by passing it over, he is superior.[149]

In 1843, just before his death, Noah Webster publicly professed:

I know whom I have believed, and that He is able to keep that which I have committed to Him against that day.[150]

&

Charles Wesley (1707-1788), the famous hymn writer, was the brother of John Wesley who founded Methodism. In 1739, Charles Wesley published his *Hymns and Sacred Poems*, which contained the famous song, "Christ, the Lord, Is Risen Today":

Charles Wesley

"Christ, the Lord, is risen today,"
Sons of men and angels say,
Raise your joys and triumphs high,
Sing, ye heavens, and earth reply.[151]

In his hymn, "Jesus, Lover of My Soul," 1740, Charles Wesley wrote:

Jesus, lover of my soul,
Let me to Thy bosom fly,
While the nearer waters roll,
While the tempest still is high!
Hide me, O my Savior, hide,
Till the storm of life is past;
Safe into the haven glide,
O receive my soul at last.[152]

In 1742, Charles Wesley wrote "Gentle Jesus, Meek and Mild":

Gentle Jesus, meek and mild,
Look upon a little child;
Pity my simplicity,
Suffer me to come to Thee.[153]

In 1749, Charles Wesley composed "Soldiers of Christ, Arise":

Soldiers of Christ, arise,
And put your armor on.[154]

In the famous Christmas hymn, 1753, Charles Wesley wrote:

Hark the herald angels sing,
Glory to the new-born king;
Peace on earth, and mercy mild,
God and sinners reconciled.
Joyful all ye nations rise,
Join the triumph of the skies;
With th' angelic host proclaim
Christ is born in Bethlehem.
Hark the herald angels sing,
Glory to the new-born king.[155]

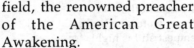

John Wesley (1703-1791), was the founder of the Methodist denomination and one of the greatest evangelists in the 1700s. An Oxford graduate, he became a missionary to Georgia, along with his brother, Charles Wesley. The Wesleys were close

John Wesley

friends with George Whitefield, the renowned preacher of the American Great Awakening.

John and Charles Wesley sailed from England to America to serve as missionaries in Georgia. Their experiences with the Moravians awakened within John Wesley a knowledge that something was missing in his experience.[156] John Wesley wrote in his journal recounting his conversion:

George Whitefield

On shipboard...I was again active in outward works: where it pleased God, of his free mercy, to give me twenty-six of the Moravian brethren for companions, who endeavored to shew me a more excellent way. But I understood it not at first. I was too learned and too wise; so that it seemed foolishness unto me. And I continued...trusting in that righteousness whereby no flesh can be justified.

All the time I was at Savannah I was thus *beating the air*. Being ignorant of the righteousness of Christ, which, by a living faith in him bringeth salvation *to every one that believeth,* I sought to establish my own righteousness, and so laboured in the fire all my days.

In my return to England, January 1738, being in imminent danger of death, and very uneasy on that account, I was strongly convinced that the cause of uneasiness was unbelief, and that the gaining a true, living faith was the one thing needful for me....So that when Peter Boehler, whom God prepared for me as soon as I came to London, affirmed of true faith in Christ...that it has those two fruits inseparably attending it, "Dominion over sin, and constant peace, from a sense of forgiveness," I was quite amazed, and looked upon it as a new Gospel....

In the evening, I went very unwillingly to a Society in Aldersgate-Street, where one was reading Luther's preface to the Epistle to the Romans. About a quarter before nine, while he was describing the change which God works in the heart through faith in Christ, I felt my heart strangely warmed. I felt I did trust in Christ; Christ alone, for salvation; and an assurance was given me, that he had taken away my sins, even mine, and saved me from the law of sin and death.[157]

In his *Journal*, June 11, 1739, John Wesley wrote:

I look upon the world as my parish.[158]

In his *Journal*, February 12, 1772, John Wesley wrote:

That execrable sum of all villainies, commonly called the Slave Trade.[159]

John Wesley's *Rule*, stated:

Do all the good you can,
By all the means you can,
In all the ways you can,
In all the places you can,
At all the times you can,
To all the people you can,
As long as ever you can.[160]

≈

Samuel West (1731-1807), was a Chaplain in the Continental Army during the Revolutionary War. He was noted for greatly assisting General George Washington by deciphering a letter of treason from Dr. Benjamin Church intended for the British Admiral at Newport, R.I.

A graduate of Harvard in 1754, Samuel West was a member of the committee to frame the Constitution of Massachusetts, and a member of the Massachusetts Convention to adopt the U.S. Constitution. In July of 1776, as Dartmouth's minister, Samuel West spoke in Boston concerning the War for Independence:

> Our cause is so just and good that nothing can prevent our success but only our sins. Could I see a spirit of repentance and reformation prevail throughout the land, I should not have the least apprehension or fear of being brought under the iron rod combined against us. And though I confess that the irreligion and profaneness which are so common among us gives something of a damp to my spirits yet I cannot help hoping and even believing, that Providence has designed this continent for to be the asylum of liberty and true religion.[161]

George Whitefield

George Whitefield (1714-1770), was the famous evangelist of the Great Awakening in the American colonies prior to the Revolutionary War. His preaching up and down the Eastern seaboard of America did more than anything else to turn the thirteen isolated, individual colonies into one country.

George Whitefield had gone to Oxford with John and Charles Wesley, who began the Methodist movement. As George Whitefield's preaching confronted the established churches, doors were closed, forcing him to preach out-of-doors. Crowds grew until he was preaching to over thirty thousand people at once, with no amplification. Benjamin Franklin wrote in his autobiography that he was able to hear his voice nearly a mile away!

Benjamin Franklin was so impressed by his preaching that he built an auditorium in Philadelphia for Whitefield to preach in. That auditorium became the first building of the University of Pennsylvania, and has a bronze statue of George Whitefield in front. Franklin also printed Whitefield's *Journal*, which grew to be tremendously popular.

When he was converted in 1733, George Whitefield exclaimed:

Ben Franklin

> Joy—joy unspeakable—joy that's full of, big with glory![162]

In a sermon, George Whitefield proclaimed:

> Never rest until you can say, "the Lord our righteousness." Who knows but the Lord may have mercy, nay, abundantly pardon you? Beg of God to give you faith; and if the Lord give you that, you will by it receive Christ, with his righteousness, and his all....
>
> None, none can tell, but those happy souls who have experienced it with what demonstration of the Spirit this conviction comes....Oh, how amiable, as well as all sufficient, does the blessed Jesus now appear! With what new eyes does the soul now see the Lord its righteousness! Brethren, it is unutterable....
>
> Those who live godly in Christ, may not so much be said to live, as Christ to live in them....They are led by the Spirit as a child is led by the hand of its father....
>
> They hear, know, and obey his voice....Being born again in God they habitually live to, and daily walk with God.[163]

George Whitefield declared:

> Would you have peace with God? Away, then, to God through Jesus Christ, who has purchased peace; the Lord Jesus has shed his heart's blood for this. He died for this; he rose again for this; he ascended into the highest heaven, and is now interceding at the right hand of God.[164]

Jonathan Edwards

Sarah Edwards, the wife of Jonathan Edwards, wrote to her brother in New Haven concerning the effects of George Whitefield's ministry:

> It is wonderful to see what a spell he casts over an audience by proclaiming the simplest truths of the Bible....Our mechanics shut up their shops, and the day laborers throw down their

tools to go and hear him preach, and few return unaffected. [165]

Benjamin Franklin wrote in his autobiography of the effect George Whitefield's preaching was having on the colonies:

> It was wonderful to see the change soon made in the manners of our inhabitants. From being thoughtless or indifferent about religion, it seemed as if all the world were growing religious, so that one could not walk thro' the town in an evening without hearing psalms sung in different families of every street. [166]

In 1752, George Whitefield wrote to his friend Benjamin Franklin:

> My Dear Doctor .... I find that you grow more and more famous in the learned world. [167]

In 1764, George Whitefield received a letter from Benjamin Franklin, in which Franklin closed:

> Your frequently repeated Wishes and Prayers for my Eternal as well as temporal Happiness are very obliging. I can only thank you for them, and offer you mine in return. [168]

In 1769, George Whitefield wrote Benjamin Franklin on the night before his last trip to America. In this last surviving letter, Whitefield shared his desire that both he and Franklin would:

> Be in that happy number of those who in the midst of the tremendous final blaze shall cry Amen. [169]

The last letter George Whitefield received from Benjamin Franklin revealed Franklin's heart:

> Life, like a dramatic piece, should ... finish handsomely. Being now in the last act, I began to cast about for something fit to end with .... I sometimes wish, that you and I were jointly employ'd by the Crown to settle a colony on the Ohio... to settle in that fine country a strong body of religious and industrious people!... Might it not greatly facilitate the introduction of pure religion among the heathen, if we could, by such a colony, show them a better sample of Christians than they commonly see in our Indian traders? [170]

In 1770, as he was dying, Whitefield declared:

> How willing I would ever live to preach Christ! But I die to be with Him![171]

ॐ

Alfred North Whitehead (1861-1947), was a renowned British philosopher and mathematician. His works include: *Principia Mathematica* (1910-1913); *Principles of Natural Knowledge* (1919); and *The Concept of Nature*. In *Science and the Modern World* (1925), chapter 12, Alfred North Whitehead wrote:

> The religious vision, and its history of persistent expansion, is our one ground for optimism. Apart from it, human life is a flash of occasional enjoyments lighting up a mass of pain and misery, a bagatelle of transient experience.[172]

ॐ

William Whiting (1825-1878), wrote *The Hymn of the U.S. Navy* in 1860, entitled *Eternal Father, Strong to Save*, st. I:

> Eternal Father, strong to save,
> Whose arm doth bind the restless wave,
> Who bidd'st the mighty ocean deep
> Its own appointed limits keep,
> O, hear us when we cry to Thee
> For those in peril on the sea![173]

ॐ

Marcus Whitman (1802-1847), was an American pioneer, doctor and missionary to the Indians in the Pacific Northwest. Dr. Marcus Whitman had practiced medicine for eight years in Rushville, N.Y., and in Canada before being appointed, in 1836, as a missionary-physician to Oregon, with his wife Narcissa, by the American Board of Foreign Missions. They set up missions at Waiilatpu near Walla Walla, Washington, and at Laowai.

In 1842-43, responding to a potential threat of closure, Marcus Whitman made a famous 3,000-mile trek east to persuade the Mission Board not to disband the mission. He also endeavored to interest the Government in settling the Oregon country, and, in 1843, saw the first large wagon train head west on the *Oregon Trail*. In 1923, President Warren G. Harding praised Dr. Marcus Whitman in a speech celebrating the *Oregon Trail*, at Meacham, Oregon:

> It was that of a religious enthusiast, tenaciously earnest yet revealing no suggestion of fanaticism, bronzed from exposure to pitiless elements and seamed with deep lines of physical suffering, a rare combination of determination and gentleness—obviously a man of God, but no less a man among men. Such was Marcus Whitman, the missionary hero of the vast, unsettled, unexplored Oregon country, who had come out of the West to plead that the State should acquire for civilization the Empire that the churches were gaining for Christianity....
>
> Then turning to President [Tyler], he added quietly but beseechingly:
>
> "All I ask is that you will not barter away Oregon or allow English interference until I can lead a band of stalwart American settlers across the plains. For this I shall try to do!"
>
> "Dr. Whitman," he rejoined sympathetically, "your long ride and frozen limbs testify to your courage and your patriotism. Your credentials establish your character. Your request is granted!"
>
> Never in the history of the world has there been a finer example of civilization following Christianity....
>
> I rejoice particularly in the opportunity afforded me of voicing my appreciation both as President of the United States and as one who honestly tries to be a Christian soldier, of the signal service of the martyred Whitman.[174]

≈

Walt Whitman (1819-1892), was an American poet. As a young man he worked as a teacher, journalist and printer. He gained renown through his poems *Leaves of Grass*, 1855-1892. During the Civil War, he nursed wounded soldiers, eventually becoming ill himself. His free-verse poems expressed a democratic idealism, as seen in his "Democratic Vistas." In "Starting from Paumanok," from his *Leaves of Grass,* Walt Whitman wrote:

> I say the whole earth and all the stars in the sky are for religion's sake....
> I say that the real and permanent grandeur of these States must be their religion.[175]

ፊ

John Greenleaf Whittier (1807-1892), was one of the best-known American poets. He was known as the "Quaker Poet," as his faith was exhibited in his life and poetry. He wrote *Panorama,* in 1856, which included the favorites "Barefoot Boy," and "Maud Muller." His other renowned works include: *Song of the Vermonteers,* 1779; *Lays of My Home and other poems,* 1843; *Voices of Freedom,* 1846; *Snowbound,* 1866; *Justice and Expediency, Dear Lord* and *Father of Mankind.*

John Greenleaf Whittier

He was the editor of the *American Manufacturer,* the *Essex Gazette, The Pennsylvania Freeman,* and the *National Era.* He bitterly opposed slavery, to the extent that once he was mobbed and severely beaten during a speaking tour. Later, his office in Philadelphia was burned. John Greenleaf Whittier, one of the first to suggest the creation of a Republican Party, wrote:

> I believe in the Scriptures because they repeat the warnings and promises of the indwelling Light and Truth; I find in them the eternal precepts of the Divine Spirit declared and repeated. They testify of Christ within....My ground of hope for myself and for humanity is in that Divine fullness which was manifested in the life, teachings, and self-sacrifice of Christ. In the infinite mercy of God so revealed, and not in any work or merit of my own nature, I humbly, yet very hopefully, trust.[176]

In 1876, one hundred years after the signing of the Declaration of Independence and shortly after the Civil War had ended, John Greenleaf Whittier wrote his famous *Centennial Hymn:*

We meet today, united free,
And loyal to our land and Thee,
To thank Thee for the era done,
And trust Thee for the opening one.

O make Thou us, through centuries long,
In peace secure, in justice strong;
Around our gift of freedom draw
The safeguards of Thy righteous law:
And, cast in some diviner mould,
Let the new cycle shame the old![177]

In poetic verse, John Greenleaf Whittier expressed:

The Word of God

Voice of the Holy Spirit, making known
Man to himself, a witness swift and sure,
Warning, approving, true and wise and pure,
Counsel and guidance that misleadeth none!
By Thee the mystery of Life is read;
The picture writing of the world's gray seers,
The myths and parables of the primal years,
Whose letter kills, by thee interpreted
Take healthful meanings fitted to our needs,
And in the soul's vernacular express
The common law of simple righteousness.
Hatred of cant and doubt of human creeds
May well be felt the unpardonable sin
Is to deny the Word of God within![178]

Our Master

We may not climb the heavenly steeps
To bring the Lord Christ down;
In vain we search the lowest deeps,
For Him no depths can drown.

O Lord and Master of us all!
Whate'er our name or sign,
We own Thy sway, we hear Thy call,
We test our lives by Thine.

Deep strike Thy roots, O heavenly Vine,
Within our earthly sod,
Most human and yet most Divine,
The flower of Man and God![179]

૨&

Oscar Fingal O'Flahertie Wills Wilde (1854-1900), in the *Ballad of Reading Gaol*, 1898, Pt. V, st. 14, stated:

How else but through a broken heart
May the Lord Christ enter in?[180]

૨&

Emma Willard

Emma Willard (1787-1870), an American educator and historian, was a leader in the movement to provide higher education among women. Emma was born in Berlin, Connecticut, and began teaching at the age of sixteen. She was married to John Willard in 1809, and with his help she established a girl's boarding school and later a girl's seminary at Middleton, Vermont. The seminary was moved to New York and became the famous *Emma Willard School*. She wrote many successful books and later built a school for women in Athens, Greece.[181]

In 1843, American historian Emma Willard wrote:

The government of the United States is acknowledged by the wise and good of other nations, to be the most free, impartial, and righteous government of the world; but all agree, that for such a government to be sustained for many years, the principles of truth and righteousness, taught in the Holy Scriptures, must be practised. The rulers must govern in the fear of God, and the people obey the laws.[182]

In 1857, Emma Willard published a book for children entitled, *Morals for the Young: or, Good Principles Instilling Wisdom*. In it she stated:

My Dear Children and Youth:—

Since, then, wisdom teaches us to rate everything at its just value, it is wise to seek the favor and fear the frown of God, rather than to seek the favor, and fear the frown of men....

Look upon a Savior's cross...ask pardon...and the Holy Spirit's guidance...receive the Christian's armor.[183]

૨**

William I (1533-1584), Prince of Orange (known as William the Silent), served Charles V, King of Spain, as commander of the troops in France. When Charles died, Philip II became King. Philip not only hated William, but proceeded to stamp out the Protestants in Holland. William turned on the King, eventually gaining freedom from Spain and forming the Dutch Republic. In 1581, Philip offered a bounty for William's death, and three years later William was assassinated. His last words were:

My God, have mercy on my soul and on my poor people.[184]

૨**

College of William and Mary 1693, was founded in Williamsburg, Virginia, through the efforts of Rev. James Blair. The College of William and Mary is the oldest college in America. (Harvard is the oldest University.) George Washington received his surveyor's commission there in 1749, and later became the college's Chancellor. Benjamin Franklin received an honorary degree of Master of Arts from the College in 1756. In 1782, Thomas Jefferson received the degree of Doctor of Civil Law under George Wythe. President James Monroe; President John Tyler; Chief Justice John Marshall; and Peyton Randolph, first President of the Continental Congress; as well as sixteen members of the Continental Congress also studied there.[185]

Its charter, 1693, stated:

William and Mary, by the grace of God, of England, Scotland, France and Ireland, King and Queen, Defenders of the Faith, to all whom these our present Letters shall come, greeting.

Forasmuch as our well-beloved and trusty Subjects, constituting the General Assembly of our Colony of Virginia, have had it in their minds, and have proposed to themselves, to the end that the Church of Virginia may be furnished with a Seminary of Ministers of the Gospel, and that the Youth may be piously educated in Good Letters and Manners, and that the Christian Faith may be propagated amongst the Western Indians, to the glory of God .... [186]

&

George Williams (1821-1905), was the founder of the Young Men's Christian Association (YMCA) in 1844. He declared:

My life-long experience as a business man, and as a Christian worker among young men, has taught me that the only power in this world that can effectually keep one from evil and sin, in all the varied and often attractive forms which they assume, is that which comes from an intimate knowledge of the Lord Jesus Christ as a present Saviour. And I can also heartily testify that the safe Guide-Book by which one may be led to Christ is the Bible, the Word of God, which is inspired by the Holy Ghost. [187]

&

Roger Williams (1603-1683), known as the "Father of Rhode Island," was the founder of the Providence and Rhode Island Plantations. [188] He was ordained a Puritan minister in the Church of England, but his sermons in favor of religious liberty caused him to be persecuted, eventually forcing him to flee to America. Williams criticized the state church in Massachusetts and was sentenced to be sent back to England. He escaped and lived among the Indians, befriending them and learning their language.

In 1636 he founded the town of Providence on the land which the Narragansett Indians gave him. This was the first place ever where the freedom to worship God was separated from the control of the state. There he organized the first Baptist Church in the New World, with one of the principal foundations being that the state could not interfere or restrict the free and open worship of God according to the Bible.

The *Charter of Rhode Island,* which was granted by King Charles II to Roger Williams in July, 1663, stated:

> That they, pursueing, with peaceable and loyall mindes, sober, serious and religious intentions...in the holie Christian faith...a most flourishing civil state may stand and best bee maintained...grounded upon gospell principles.[189]

In one of his messages, Roger Williams wrote:[190]

> When they have opened a gap in the hedge or wall of separation between the garden of the church and the wilderness of the world, God hath ever broken down the wall itself....And that there fore if He will eer please to restore His garden and paradise again, it must of necessity be walled in peculiarly unto Himself from the world....[191]

On January 9, 1872, Senator Henry Bowen Anthony delivered a Eulogy of Roger Williams in Congress:

Henry Bowen Anthony

> He knew, for God, whose prophet he was, revealed it to him, that the great principles for which he contended, and for which he suffered, founded in the eternal fitness of things, would endure forever. He did not inquire if his name would survive a generation. In his vision of the future he saw mankind emancipated from...the blindness of bigotry, from the cruelties of intolerance. He saw the nations walking forth into the liberty wherewith Christ had made them free.[192]

❧

Hugh Williamson (1735-1819), a signer of the Constitution of the United States of America, was also a member of the Continental Congress, a member of the U.S. House of Representatives, a land speculator and a scientist (having joined with Dr. Franklin in many of his electrical experiments).

As a young man, Hugh Williamson studied for the ministry, visiting and praying for the sick in his neighborhood. After his father died, he pursued the study of divinity and went on to become a preacher:

Hugh Williamson

In 1759 he went to Connecticut, where he pursued his theological studies and was licensed to preach. After returning from Connecticut, he was admitted to membership in the Presbytery of Philadelphia...[and] preached nearly two years.[193]

Unfortunately, it became apparent that a chronic weakness in his chest would not permit him to continue in a career of public speaking.[194] Hugh Williamson then entered medical school, working as a professor in mathematics to finance his education. After graduation, he practiced in Philadelphia, and following travels in Europe became surgeon general, distinguishing himself in medical service during the Revolutionary War.

After his service in Congress, Williamson became wealthy through investments and land speculations. He then wrote extensively for medical and literary societies, winning much acclaim.

In 1811, Hugh Williamson wrote a powerful book refuting the "higher criticism" of Scripture. His book, entitled *Observations of the Climate in Different Parts of America*, provided a scientific explanation for the credibility of the Holy Scriptures in regard to Noah's flood and the events of Moses' exodus.[195]

&

Henry Wilson

Henry Wilson (1812-1875), was a U.S. Senator, 1855-72, and Vice-President under Ulysses S. Grant, 1873-75. He took a strong stand against slavery, and in 1848 he helped found the Free Soil Party. Henry Wilson declared:

Men who see not God in our history have surely lost sight of the fact that, from the landing of the Mayflower to this hour, the great men whose names are indissolubly associated with the colonization, rise, and progress of the Republic have borne testimony to the vital truths of Christianity.[196]

On December 23, 1866, in speaking at Natick, Massachusetts,

to the Young Men's Christian Association, Henry Wilson said:

> God has given us an existence in this Christian republic, founded
> by men who proclaim as their living faith, amid persecution and exile:
> "We give ourselves to the Lord Jesus Christ and the Word of His Grace,
> for the teaching, ruling and sanctifying of us in matters of worship and
> conversation."
>
> Privileged to live in an age when the selectest influences of the
> religion of our fathers seem to be visibly descending upon our land,
> we too often hear the Providence of God, the religion of our Lord and
> Saviour Jesus Christ, the inspiration of the Holy Bible doubted,
> questioned, denied with an air of gracious condescension.
>
> Remember ever, and always, that your country was founded, not
> by the "most superficial, the lightest, the most irreflective of all
> European races," but by the stern old Puritans who made the deck of
> the Mayflower an altar of the living God, and whose first act on
> touching the soil of the new world was to offer on bended knees
> thanksgiving to Almighty God.[197]

James Wilson

James Wilson (1742-1798), appointed as a
Supreme Court Justice by President George
Washington in 1789, held the distinction of being
one of six Founding Fathers to sign both the
Declaration of Independence and the Consti-
tution. James Wilson was very active in the
Constitutional Convention, having spoken 168
times. He also, in 1790, became the first Law
Professor of the University of Pennsylvania.

In the Pennsylvania Supreme Court records of *Updegraph v.
Commonwealth*, 1824, Judge James Wilson is mentioned:

> The late Judge Wilson, of the Supreme Court of the United States,
> Professor of Law in the College in Philadelphia, was appointed in
> 1791, unanimously, by the House of Representatives of this state....He
> had just risen from his seat in the convention which formed the
> constitution of the United States, and of this state; and it is well known,
> that for our present form of government we are greatly indebted to his
> exertions and influence. With his fresh recollections of both
> constitutions, in his Course of Lectures (3d vol. of his Works, 122), he
> states that....Christianity is part of the common-law.[198]

Woodrow Wilson (1856-1924), became the 28th President of the United States, after having served as the Governor of New Jersey. He was an educator, author and the President of Princeton University. In his Inaugural Address, March 4, 1913, President Woodrow Wilson stated:

Woodrow Wilson

> God's own presence, where justice and mercy are reconciled and the Judge and the Brother are one....God helping me, I will not fail....[199]

Woodrow Wilson remarked:

> A man had deprived himself of the best there is in the world who has deprived himself of this, a knowledge of the Bible. When you have read the Bible, you will know it is the Word of God, because you will have found it the key to your own heart, your own happiness and your own duty.[200]

> I am sorry for the men who do not read the Bible every day. I wonder why they deprive themselves of the strength and of the pleasure.[201]

On July 4, 1913, in a message delivered at Gettysburg, Pennsylvania, President Woodrow Wilson declared:

> Here is the nation God has builded by our hands. What shall we do with it?[202]

In 1911, at a Denver rally, Woodrow Wilson remarked:

> A nation which does not remember what it was yesterday, does not know what it is today, nor what it is trying to do. We are trying to do a futile thing if we do not know where we came from or what we have been about....
>
> The Bible...is the one supreme source of revelation of the meaning of life, the nature of God and spiritual nature and needs of men. It is the only guide of life which really leads the spirit in the way of peace and salvation.
>
> America was born a Christian nation. America was born to

exemplify that devotion to the elements of righteousness which are derived from the revelations of Holy Scripture.[203]

President Woodrow Wilson stated:

The history of Liberty is a history of limitations of governmental power, not the increase of it. When we resist, therefore, the concentration of power, we are resisting the powers of death, because concentration of power is what always precedes the destruction of human liberties.[204]

There are a good many problems before the American people today, and before me as President, but I expect to find the solution to those problems just in the proportion that I am faithful in the study of the Word of God.[205]

On March 5, 1917, President Woodrow Wilson said in his Second Inaugural Address:

I pray God that I may be given the wisdom and prudence to do my duties in the true spirit of this great people.[206]

In 1917, President Woodrow Wilson gave his *War Message* to Congress. He concluded it by saying:

To such a task we can dedicate our lives and our fortunes, everything that we are and everything that we have, with the pride of those who know that the day has come when America is privileged to spend her blood and her might for the principles that gave her birth and happiness and the peace which she has treasured. God helping her, she can do no other.[207]

President Woodrow Wilson commented on business:

Business underlies everything in our national life, including our spiritual life. Witness the fact that in the Lord's Prayer the first petition is for daily bread. No one can worship God or love his neighbor on an empty stomach.[208]

☙

Edward Winslow (1595-1655), one of the Pilgrim administrators of the Plymouth Colony, 1621, was the colony's English agent, 1629-32. He served as the Governor of the colony, 1633-34, 1636-37, and 1644-45. In 1646, he stayed in England to serve Oliver Cromwell. Edward Winslow, who kept detailed records of the Pilgrims' experiences, recounted:

> [The prolonged] drought and the like considerations moved not only every good man privately to enter into examination with his own estate between God and his conscience, and so to humiliation before Him, but also to humble ourselves together before the Lord by fasting and prayer.[209]

John Winthrop

John Winthrop, (1588-1649), was the founder, 1630, and first Governor of the Massachusetts Bay Colony, being elected 12 consecutive times. He was a successful lawyer and a strong Puritan leader. Oliver Cromwell pleaded with him to join the revolution in England, but John Winthrop declined the offer, deciding rather to leave England for religious freedom.

On May 15, 1629, in a letter to his wife, John Winthrop wrote:

> Be of good comfort; the hardest that can come shall be a means to mortify this body of corruption, which is a thousand times more dangerous to us than any outward tribulation, and to bring us into nearer communion with our Lord Jesus Christ, and more assurance of His kingdom.[210]

In June of 1630, ten years after the Pilgrims founded the Plymouth Colony, Governor John Winthrop landed in Massachusetts Bay with 700 people in 11 ships (thus beginning the Great Migration, which lasted 16 years and saw more than 20,000 Puritans embark for New England).[211]

On June 11, 1630, aboard *Arbella,* John Winthrop authored his famous work, *A Model of Christian Charity,* which became a guideline for future constitutional covenants of the Colonies:

> This love among Christians is a real thing, not imaginary...as absolutely necessary to the [well] being of the Body of Christ, as the sinews and other ligaments of a natural body are to the [well] being of that body....
>
> We are a Company, professing ourselves fellow members of Christ, [and thus] we ought to account ourselves knit together by this bond of love....For the work we have in hand, it is by a mutual consent through a special overruling providence, and a more than an ordinary approbation of the Churches of Christ to seek out a place of Cohabitation and Consortship under a due form of Government both civil and ecclesiastical....
>
> Thus stands the cause between God and us: we are entered into covenant with Him for this work. We have taken out a Commission; the Lord hath given us leave to draw our own articles....
>
> If the Lord shall please to hear us, and bring us in peace to the place we desire, then hath He ratified this Covenant and sealed our Commission, [and] will expect a strict performance of the Articles...the Lord will surely break out in wrath against us.
>
> Now the only way to avoid this shipwreck and to provide for our posterity, is to follow the counsel of Micah, to do justly, to love mercy, to walk humbly with our God. For this end, we must be knit together in this work as one man....
>
> We must hold a familiar commerce together in each other in all meekness, gentleness, patience, and liberality. We must delight in each other, make one another's condition our own, rejoice together, mourn together, labor and suffer together, always having before our eyes our Commission and Community in this work, as members of the same body. So shall we keep the unity of the Spirit in the bond of peace....
>
> We shall find that the God of Israel is among us, when ten of us shall be able to resist a thousand of our enemies, when He shall make us a praise and glory, that men of succeeding plantations shall say, "The Lord make it like that of New England."
>
> For we must Consider that we shall be as a City upon a Hill, the eyes of all people are upon us;
>
> so that if we shall deal falsely with our God in this work we have undertaken and so cause him to withdraw his present help from us, we shall be made a story and a by-word through the world.[212]

John Winthrop stated:

I will ever walk humbly before my God, and meekly, mildly, and gently towards all men...to give myself—my life, my wits, my health, my wealth—to the service of my God and Saviour.[213]

Teach me, O Lord, to put my trust in Thee, then shall I be like Mount Sion that cannot be moved....Before the week was gone...I waxed exceeding discontent and impatient...then I acknowledged my unfaithfulness and pride of heart, and turned again to my God, and humbled my soul before Him, and He returned and accepted me, and so I renewed my Covenant of walking with my God.[214]

The Covenant between you and us is the oath you have taken of us, which is to this purpose, that we shall govern you and judge your causes by the rules of God's law.[215]

On May 19, 1643, he organized the New England Confederation among the colonists of New Plymouth, New Haven, Massachusetts and Connecticut. They covenanted together under the *Constitution of the New England Confederation:*

Whereas we all came to these parts of America with the same end and aim, namely, to advance the kingdome of our Lord Jesus Christ, and to injoy the liberties of the Gospell thereof with purities and peace, and for preserving and propagating the truth and liberties of the gospell.[216]

ße

Robert Charles Winthrop (1809-1894), an American legislator, author and orator, was a descendant of Governor John Winthrop. On May 28, 1849, Robert Charles Winthrop spoke at the Annual Meeting of the Massachusetts Bible Society in Boston, stating:

The voice of experience and the voice of our own reason speak but one language....Both united in teaching us, that men may as well build their houses upon the sand and expect to see them stand, when the rains fall, and the winds blow, and the floods come, as to found free institutions upon any other basis than that of morality and virtue, of which the Word of God is the only authoritative rule, and the only adequate sanction.

All societies of men must be governed in some way or other. The less they have of stringent State Government, the more they must have of individual self-government. The less they rely on public law or physical force, the more they must rely on private moral restraint.

Men, in a word, must necessarily be controlled either by a power within them, or a power without them; either by the word of God, or by the strong arm of man; either by the Bible or by the bayonet.

It may do for other countries, and other governments to talk about the State supporting religion. Here, under our own free institutions, it is Religion which must support the State.[217]

Winthrop stated:

The Bible itself is its own best witness. No evolution produced that Volume, and no revolution of thought, or action, or human will can ever prevail against it. Revisions and new versions may improve or may impair the letter, but they can never change its essential character. The Gospel of Jesus Christ, through which He brought life and immortality to light, like its Divine Author, is the same "yesterday, today, and forever."[218]

In 1866, Robert Winthrop addressed the American Bible Society in New York on its jubilee, saying:

Beyond all doubt, my friends, we are dealing here today with the great enginery of the world's progress, with the greatest of all instrumentalities for social advancement as well as for individual salvation.[219]

કે

John Witherspoon (1723-1794), a signer of the Declaration of Independence, was a member of the Continental Congress who served on over 100 Congressional committees. An American Revolutionary patriot of Scottish birth, John Witherspoon became a famous educator, clergyman and the President of Princeton College.

John Witherspoon

Reverend John Witherspoon's emphasis of biblical principles impacting government was tremendously felt in the Colonies during the foundation of America. His influence continued through his students, who included:

A President, Vice-President, three Supreme Court Justices, ten Cabinet members, twelve Governors, twenty-one Senators, thirty-nine Representatives, as well as numerous delegates to the Constitutional Convention and state leaders. His numerous students included leaders, such as, Gunning Bedford of Delaware, David Brearly of New Jersey and James Madison, who served eight years as Secretary of State and eight years as President.[220]

Princeton College, originally called "The College of New Jersey," was founded in 1746 in Princeton, New Jersey, by the Presbyterian Church. Its official motto was:

Under God's Power She Flourishes.[221]

Every president of Princeton was a minister until 1902.[222] Its first president, the predecessor of John Witherspoon, was the Rev. Jonathan Dickinson, who declared:

Jonathan Dickinson

Cursed be all that learning that is contrary to the cross of Christ.[223]

John Witherspoon stated:

It is in the man of piety and inward principle, that we may expect to find the uncorrupted patriot, the useful citizen, and the invincible soldier.—God grant that in America true religion and civil liberty may be inseparable and that the unjust attempts to destroy the one, may in the issue tend to the support and establishment of both.[224]

On May 17, 1776, the Continental Congress declared a *National Day of Fasting, Humiliation and Prayer*. John Witherspoon concurred, and in a speech at the College of New Jersey (Princeton), he declared:

While we give praise to God, the supreme disposer of all events, for His interposition on our behalf, let us guard against the dangerous error of trusting in, or boasting of, an arm of flesh....
If your cause is just, if your principles are pure, and if your conduct is prudent, you need not fear the multitude of opposing hosts.
What follows from this? That he is the best friend to American

liberty, who is most sincere and active in promoting true and undefiled religion, and who sets himself with the greatest firmness to bear down profanity and immorality of every kind.

Whoever is an avowed enemy of God, I scruple not [do not hesitate] to call him an enemy of his country.[225]

As a convention delegate from the colony of New Jersey, Rev. Witherspoon debated the separation from England, declaring:

Gentlemen, New Jersey is ready to vote for independence. In our judgement, the country is not only ripe for independence, but we are in danger of becoming rotten for the want of it, if we delay any longer![226]

Reverend John Witherspoon, who had lost two sons in the Revolutionary War, was the epitome of a patriot.[227] After his wife died in October of 1789, he re-entered politics, heading up a committee in the New Jersey legislature to abolish slavery.[228] Following Witherspoon's death, John Adams admired him as:

A true son of liberty. So he was. But first, he was a son of the Cross.[229]

ઢ

William Wordsworth (1770-1850), one of the first English Romantic poets, published his *Lyrical Ballads* in 1798 and *Poems in Two Volumes* in 1807. Other works include *The Excursion, The White Doe of Rylstone, Memorials of a Tour of the Continent* and *Ecclesiastical Sketches.* Greatly criticized at first, his works gradually became recognized, and in 1843, Queen Victoria appointed him Poet-Laureate of England:

Trust in the Saviour

But Thou art true, Incarnate Lord!
Who didst vouchsafe for man to die;
Thy smile is sure, Thy plighted Word
No charge can falsify.[230]

Hymn for the Boatman

Jesus, bless our slender boat,
By the current swept along!
Loud its threatenings—let them not
Drown the music of a song
Breathed Thy mercy to implore,
Where the troubled waters roar.
Saviour, for our warning, seen
Bleeding on that precious rood;
If, while through the meadows green
Gently wound the peaceful flood,
We forget Thee, do not Thou
Disregard Thy suppliants now.[231]

Translation of the Bible

But to outweigh all harm, the sacred Book,
In dusty sequestration wrapt too long,
Assumes the accents of our native tongue;
And he who guides the plow or wields the crook
With understanding spirit now may look
Upon her records, listen to her song,
And sift her laws—much wondering that the wrong
Which Faith hath suffered, Heaven could calmly brook.
Transcendent boon! Noblest that earthly king
Ever bestowed to equalize and bless
Under the weight of mortal wretchedness.[232]

ঝ

Rev. Heinrich Richard Wurmbrand (1909-   ), was released in 1964, after having spent 14 years in prison in Romania for his faith. A Lutheran minister, he has since become an internationally known speaker. He wrote *Tortured for Christ; Christ in the Communist Prison*, 1968; and *My Answer to the Moscow Atheists*, 1975. Rev. Wurmbrand gave the world's view of America in 1967:

Every freedom-loving man has two fatherlands; his own and America. Today, America is the hope of every enslaved man, because it is the last bastion of freedom in the world. Only America has the power and spiritual resources to stand as a barrier between militant Communism and the people of the world.

It is the last "dike" holding back the rampaging floodwaters of militant Communism. If it crumples, there is no other dike, no other dam; no other line of defense to fall back upon.

America is the last hope of millions of enslaved peoples. They look to it as their second fatherland. In it lies their hopes and prayers.

I have seen fellow-prisoners in Communist prisons beaten, tortured, with 50 pounds of chains on their legs—praying for America....that the dike will not crumple; that it will remain free.[233]

John Wycliffe (1320-1384), a professor at Oxford University, became one of the greatest English religious reformers. His most outstanding achievement was being the first to translate the Bible into English. Known as the "Morning Star of the Reformation," John Wycliffe wrote in the General Prologue of his 1384 Bible:

The Bible is for the Government of the People, by the People, and for the People.[234]

George Wythe (1726-1806), one of the signers of the Declaration of Independence, was a member of the Continental Congress, a member of the House of Burgesses and the Mayor of Williamsburg. He served as Attorney General of the Virginia Colony and established the first law professorship in the United States at William and Mary College.[235]

George Wythe

In February of 1776, George Wythe, Roger Sherman and John Adams, comprised a committee responsible for establishing guidelines for an embassy bound for Canada. Their instructions stated:

You are further to declare that we hold sacred the rights of conscience, and may promise to the whole people, solemnly in our name, the free and undisturbed exercise of their religion. And....that all civil rights and the right to hold office were to be extended to persons of any Christian denomination.[236]

Y

Elihu Yale

Yale College 1701, was founded as the Collegiate School at Saybrook, Connecticut, by ten Congregational ministers. It was moved to New Haven, Connecticut, and renamed for Elihu Yale (1649-1721), an American-born English merchant and governor of the East India Company. Elihu Yale donated books and goods from his fortune to the college in the amount of $2,800. The General Court which passed the act authorizing the new college, declared it to be an institution where:

> Youth may be instructed in the Arts and Sciences who through the blessing of Almighty God may be fitted for Publick employment both in Church and Civil State.[1]

Its purpose, as stated by the trustees on November 11, 1701, was:

> To plant, and under ye Divine blessing to propagate in this Wilderness, the blessed Reformed, Protestant Religion, in ye purity of its Order, and Worship.[2]

The founders set down specific rules for Yale College:

> Whereunto the Liberal, and Religious Education of Suitable youth is under ye blessing of God, a chief, & most probable expedient...we agree to...these Rules:
>
> 1. The said rector shall take Especial Care as of the moral Behaviour of the Students at all Times so with industry to Instruct and Ground

Them well in Theoretical devinity...and [not to] allow them to be Instructed and Grounded in any other Systems or Synopses....To recite the Assemblies Catechism in Latin...[with] such Explanations as may be (through the Blessing of God) most Conducive to their Establishment in the Principles of the Christian protestant Religion.

2. That the said Rector shall Cause the Scriptures Daily...morning and evening to be read by the Students at the times of prayer in the School...Expound practical Theology...Repeat Sermons...studiously Indeavor[ing] in the Education of said students to promote the power and the Purity of Religion and Best Edification and peace of these New England Churches.[3]

The requirements for the students included:

All scholars shall live religious, godly, and blameless lives according to the rules of God's Word, diligently reading the Holy Scriptures, the fountain of light and truth; and constantly attend upon all the duties of religion, both in public and secret.[4]

Seeing God is the giver of all wisdom, every scholar, besides private or secret prayer, where all we are bound to ask wisdom, shall be present morning and evening at public prayer in the hall at the accustomed hour.[5]

The primary goal, as outlined by the founders, stated:

Every student shall consider the main end of his study to wit to know God in Jesus Christ and answerably to lead a Godly, sober life.[6]

The Yale Charter of 1745 clarified the intention of the college:

Which has received the favourable bene-factions of many liberal [generous] and piously disposed persons, and under the blessing of Almighty God has trained up many worthy persons for the service of God in the state as well as in the church.[7]

Timothy Dwight

Benjamin Silliman, a well-known American science educator and editor, was a Yale faculty member during the era of Yale President Timothy Dwight, 1795-1817. He wrote concerning the

Benjamin
Silliman

atmosphere that existed on the Yale campus:

> It would delight your heart to see how the trophies of the cross are multiplied in this institution. Yale College is a little temple: prayer and praise seem to be the delight of the greater part of the students.[8]

&

Year of the Bible 1983, was declared on October 4, 1982, by a Joint Resolution of both the Senate and House of Representatives in the second session of the 97th Congress of the United States of America, held at the City of Washington:

Public Law 97-280.

WHEREAS the Bible, the Word of God, has made a unique contribution in shaping the United States as a distinctive and blessed nation and people;

WHEREAS deeply held religious convictions springing from the Holy Scriptures led to the early settlement of our Nation;

WHEREAS Biblical teachings inspired concepts of civil government that are contained in our Declaration of Independence and Constitution of the United States;

WHEREAS many of our great national leaders—among them Presidents Washington, Jackson, Lincoln, and Wilson—paid tribute to the surpassing influence of the Bible in our country's development, as in the words of President Jackson that the Bible is "the Rock on which our Republic rests";

WHEREAS the history of our Nation clearly illustrates the value of voluntarily applying the teachings of the Scriptures in the lives of individuals, families, and societies;

WHEREAS this Nation now faces great challenges that will test this Nation as it has never been tested before; and

WHEREAS that renewing our knowledge of and faith in God through Holy Scripture can strengthen us as a nation and a people: NOW, THEREFORE, be it

Resolved by the Senate and House of Representatives of the United States of America in Congress assembled, That the President is authorized and requested to designate 1983 as a national "Year of the Bible" in recognition of both the formative influence the Bible has been for our Nation, and our national need to study and apply the teachings of the Holy Scriptures.

Thomas P. O'Neill
Speaker of the House

Strom Thurmond
President of the Senate - Pro Tempore

Approved
October 4, 1982
Ronald Reagan[9]

◈

William Butler Yeats (1865-1939), was an Irish author, theatrical producer and politician. In 1923 he received the Nobel Prize for literature. He wrote in *The Wind Among the Reeds*, 1899, *Into the Twilight:*

And God stands winding His lonely horn,
And time and the world are ever in flight.[10]

In *The Tower*, 1928, *Two Songs from a Play*, II, st. I, Yeats wrote:

Odor of blood when Christ was slain
Made all Platonic tolerance vain
And vain all Doric discipline.[11]

In *The Winding Stair and Other Poems*, 1933, *For Anne Gregory*, st. 3, Yeats wrote:

Only God, my dear,
Could love you for yourself alone
And not your yellow hair.[12]

◈

Notes

A

¹ **School District of Abington Township, Pennsylvania.** Prior to 1963 school policy. *Abington v. Schempp,* 374 U.S. 211 (1963). David Barton, *The Myth of Separation* (Aledo, TX: WallBuilder Press, 1991), p. 149.

² **Lord John Emerich Edward Dalberg Acton.** 1877. Keith Fournier, *In Defense of Liberty* (Virginia Beach, VA: Law & Justice, 1993), Vol. 2, No. 2, p. 7.

³ **Lord John Emerich Edward Dalberg Acton.** April 5, 1881, in a letter to Bishop Mandell Creighton. John Bartlett, *Bartlett's Familiar Quotations* (Boston: Little, Brown and Company, 1855, 1980), p. 615. *The World Book Encyclopedia,* 22 vols. (Chicago, IL: World Book, Inc., 1989; W.F. Quarrie and Company, 8 vols., 1917), Vol. 1, p. 31. Marshall Foster and Mary-Elaine Swanson, *The American Covenant - The Untold Story* (Roseburg, OR: Foundation for Christian Self-Government, 1981; Thousand Oaks, CA: The Mayflower Institute, 1983, 1992), p. 135.

⁴ **Abigail Adams.** October 16, 1774, writing to her husband John Adams from their home in Braintree, Massachusetts, just prior to the outbreak of war. *Letters of Abigail Adams to Her Husband* (Old South Leaflets, No. 6, Fourth Series, 1886), pp. 1-3. Catherine Millard, *The Rewriting of America's History* (Camp Hill, PA: Horizon House Publishers, 1991), p. 85.

⁵ **Abigail Adams.** June 18, 1775, in writing to her husband John Adams, in the midst of the conflict with Britain. Charles Francis Adams (son of John Quincy Adams and grandson of John Adams), *Familiar Letters of John Adams with his wife Abigail Adams - during the Revolution* (NY: Hurd and Houghton, 1876), Vol. XXVI, pp. 3-4. Catherine Millard, *The Rewriting of America's History* (Camp Hill, PA: Horizon House Publishers, 1991), p. 88.

⁶ **Abigail Adams.** September 16, 1775, Sunday, in writing to her husband, John Adams. *Letters of Abigail Adams to her Husband* (Old South Leaflets, No. 6, Fourth Series, 1886), pp. 4-6. Catherine Millard, *The Rewriting of America's History* (Camp Hill, PA: Horizon House Publishers, 1991), pp. 85-86.

⁷ **Abigail Adams.** November 5, 1775(circa), in a letter to her friend, Mercy Warren. *Warren-Adams Letters, 1743-1777* (Massachusetts Historical Society Collections), Vol. I, p. 72. L.H. Butterfield, ed., *Adams Family Correspondence* (Cambridge, MA: The Belknap Press of Harvard University Press, 1963), Vol. I, p. 323. Edmund Fuller and David E. Green, *God in the White House - The Faiths of American Presidents* (NY: Crown Publishers, Inc., 1968), p. 22. Jan Payne Pierce, *The Patriot Primer III* (Fletcher, NC: New Puritan Library, Inc., 1987), p. 44. David Barton, *The Myth of Separation,* (Aledo, TX: WallBuilder Press, 1991), pp. 95, 249. Peter Marshall and David Manuel, *The Glory of America* (Bloomington, MN: Garborg's Heart'N Home, Inc., 1991), 3.11. D.P. Diffine, Ph.D., *One Nation Under God - How Close a Separation?* (Searcy, Arkansas: Harding University, Belden Center for Private Enterprise Education, 6th edition, 1992), p. 7. Stephen McDowell and Mark Beliles, "The Providential Perspective" (Charlottesville, VA: The Providence Foundation, P.O. Box 6759, Charlottesville, Va. 22906, January 1994), Vol. 9, No. 1, p. 7.

⁸ **Abigail Adams.** June 20, 1776, in a letter to her husband, John Adams, in Philadelphia. L.H. Butterfield, ed., *Adams Family Correspondence* (Cambridge, MA: The Belknap Press of Harvard University Press, 1963), Vol. II, p. 16. Peter Marshall and David Manuel, *The Light and the Glory* (Old Tappan, New Jersey: Fleming H. Revell Co., 1977), p. 303. Peter Marshall and David Manuel, *The Glory of America* (Bloomington, MN: Garborg's Heart'N Home, Inc., 1991), 6.20.

⁹ **Abigail Adams.** March 20, 1780, in writing to her son, John Quincy Adams. David Barton, *The WallBuilder Report* (Aledo, TX: WallBuilder Press, Summer 1993), p. 2.

¹⁰ **Abigail Adams.** February 8, 1797, in writing to her husband, John Adams, at the occasion of his election as the 2nd President of the United States. Charles Francis Adams (son of John Quincy Adams and grandson of John Adams), *Familiar Letters of John Adams with his wife Abigail Adams - during the Revolution* (NY: Hurd and Houghton, 1876), p. XXVI. Catherine Millard, *The Rewriting of America's History* (Camp Hill, PA: Horizon House Publishers, 1991), p. 86.

¹¹ **John Adams.** February 22, 1756, in a diary entry. L.H. Butterfield, ed., *Diary and Autobiography of John Adams* (Cambridge, MA: Belknap Press of Harvard University Press, 1961), Vol. III, p. 9. L.H. Butterfield, *The Earliest Diary of John Adams* (Cambridge, MA: The Belknap Press of Harvard University Press, 1966), Vol. 1, p. 9. *Life and Works of John Adams,* Vol. XI, pp. 6-7. Stephen Abbott Northrop, D.D., *A Cloud of Witnesses* (Portland, OR: American Heritage Ministries, 1987; Mantle Ministries, 228 Still Ridge, Bulverde, Texas, 78163), p. 2. David Barton, *The Myth of Separation* (Aledo, TX: WallBuilder Press, 1991), pp. 123, 150. D.P. Diffine, Ph.D., *One Nation Under God - How Close a Separation?* (Searcy, Arkansas: Harding University, Belden Center for Private Enterprise Education, 6th edition, 1992), p. 6.

¹² **John Adams.** February 1765, in his notes for *A Dissertation on the Canon and Feudal Law.* Benjamin Franklin Morris, *The Christian Life and Character of the Civil Institutions of the United States* (Philadelphia: George W. Childs, 1864), p. 109. John Bartlett, *Bartlett's Familiar Quotations* (Boston: Little, Brown and Company, 1855, 1980), p. 380. Norman Cousins, *In God We Trust - The Religious Beliefs and Ideas of the American Founding Fathers* (NY: Harper & Brothers, 1958), p. 84. Earnest Lee Tuveson, *Redeemer Nation,* (Chicago & London: University of Chicago Press, 1974), p. 25. Gary DeMar, *God and Government - A Biblical and Historical Study* (Atlanta, GA: American Vision Press, 1982), p. 117. John Eidsmoe, *Christianity and the Constitution - The Faith of Our Founding Fathers* (Grand Rapids, MI: Baker Book House, A Mott Media Book, 1987; 6th printing, 1993), p. 266. Peter Marshall and David Manuel, *The Glory of America* (Bloomington, MN: Garborg's Heart'N Home, Inc., 1991), 2.1.

¹³ **John Adams.** February 9, 1772, Sunday, in a diary entry. David Barton, "The WallBuilder Report" (Aledo, TX: WallBuilder Press, Fall 1993), pp. 3-4.

¹⁴ **John Adams.** July 4, 1774, in a letter to his wife, Abigail Adams, from Patten's at Arundel. Charles Francis Adams (son of John Quincy Adams and grandson of John Adams), *Familiar Letters of John Adams with his wife Abigail Adams - during the Revolution* (NY: Hurd and Houghton, 1876), p. 10. Catherine Millard, *The Rewriting of America's History* (Camp Hill, PA: Horizon House Publishers, 1991), p. 83.

¹⁵ **John Adams.** September 7, 1774, in a letter to his wife Abigail, relating the events of the first day of the Continental Congress. *First Prayer in Congress - Beautiful Reminiscence* (Washington, D.C.: Library of Congress). John S.C. Abbot, *George Washington*

(NY: Dodd, Mead & Co., 1875, 1917), p. 187. Gary DeMar, *God and Government - A Biblical and Historical Study* (Atlanta, GA: American Vision Press, 1982), Vol. I, p. 108. David Barton, *The Myth of Separation* (Aledo, TX: WallBuilder Press, 1991), pp. 101-102.
[16] **John Adams.** September 7, 1774, in a letter to his wife Abigail relating the events of the First Continental Congress. *John and Abigail Adams*, Vol. I, pp. 23-24. Charles Francis Adams (son of John Quincy Adams and grandson of John Adams), ed., *Letters of John Adams - Addressed To His Wife* (Boston: Charles C. Little and James Brown, 1841), Vol. I, pp. 23-24. Edmund Fuller and David E. Green, *God in the White House - The Faiths of American Presidents* (NY: Crown Publishers, Inc., 1968), pp. 21-22. L.H. Butterfield, Marc Frielander, and Mary-Jo King, eds., *The Book of Abigail and John - Selected Letters of The Adams Family 1762-1784* (Cambridge, Massachusetts and London, England: Harvard University Press, 1975), p. 76. Phyllis Lee Levin, *Abigail Adams* (NY: St. Martin's Press, 1987), p. 55. David Barton, *The Myth of Separation* (Aledo, TX: WallBuilder Press, 1991), p. 101.
[17] **John Adams.** October 9, 1774, in a letter to his wife, Abigail Adams, sent from Philadelphia during the First Continental Congress. Charles Francis Adams (son of John Quincy Adams and grandson of John Adams), ed., *Letters of John Adams with his wife Abigail Adams - during the Revolution* (NY: Hurd and Houghton, 1876), p. 46. Catherine Millard, *The Rewriting of America's History* (Camp Hill, PA: Horizon House Publishers, 1991), pp. 84-85.
[18] **John Adams.** 1774, in his commentary entitled, *Novanglus: A History of the Dispute with America, from its Origin, in 1754, to the Present Time*. Norman Cousins, ed., *'In God We Trust': The Religious Beliefs and Ideas of the American Founding Fathers* (New York: Harper & Brothers, 1958), pp. 89-90. John Eidsmoe, *Christianity and the Constitution - The Faith of Our Founding Fathers* (Grand Rapids, MI: Baker House, A Mott Media Book, 1987; 6th printing, 1993), p. 296. Gary DeMar, "Why the Religious Right is Always Right - Almost" (Atlanta, GA: *The Biblical Worldview*, An American Vision Publication - American Vision, Inc., November 1992), p. 5. Gary DeMar, *America's Christian History: The Untold Story* (Atlanta, GA: American Vision Publishers, Inc., 1993), pp. 96-97.
[19] **John Adams.** June 21, 1776. Charles Francis Adams (son of John Quincy Adams and grandson of John Adams), ed., *The Works of John Adams - Second President of the United States* (Boston: Little, Brown, & Co., 1854), Vol. IX, p. 401. "Our Christian Heritage," *Letter from Plymouth Rock* (Marlborough, NH: The Plymouth Rock Foundation), p. 3. Russ Walton, *One Nation Under God* (NH: Plymouth Rock Foundation, 1993), p. 115. David Barton, *The Myth of Separation* (Aledo, TX: WallBuilder Press, 1991), p. 123. David Barton, *The WallBuilder Report* (Aledo, TX: WallBuilder Press, Winter 1993), p. 2.
[20] **John Adams.** In contemplating the personal effect that separation from England would produce. Henry Steele Commager and Richard B. Morris, eds., *Spirit of Seventy-Six* (New York: The Bobbs-Merrill Co., Inc., 1958), p. 26. Peter Marshall and David Manuel, *The Glory of America* (Bloomington, MN: Garborg's Heart'N Home, Inc., 1991), 6.5.
[21] **John Adams.** July 1, 1776, in speaking to the delegates of the Continental Congress. William H. McGuffey, *McGuffey's Eclectic Fifth Reader* (NY: American Book Company, 1907; revised 1920), p. 199. Charles Fadiman, ed., *The American Treasury* (NY: Harper & Brothers, Publishers, 1955), p. 369. Dan Smoot, *America's Promise* (Dallas, TX: The Dan Smoot Report, 1960), p. 6. Peter Marshall and David Manuel, *The Light and the Glory* (Old Tappan, NJ: Fleming H. Revell Company, 1977), pp. 307-308. Lucille Johnston, *Celebrations of a Nation* (Arlington, VA: The Year of Thanksgiving Foundation, 1987), p. 83. Peter Marshall and David Manuel, *The Glory of America* (Bloomington, MN: Garborg's Heart 'N Home, 1991), 7.1. William Safire, ed., *Lend Me Your Ears - Great Speeches in History* (NY: W.W. Norton & Company, 1992), p. 163. D.P. Diffine, Ph.D., *One Nation Under God - How Close a Separation?* (Searcy, Arkansas: Harding University, Belden Center for Private Enterprise Education, 6th edition, 1992), p. 7.
[22] **John Adams.** July 3, 1776, in a letter to his wife, Abigail Adams, following Congress' approval of the Declaration of Independence. L.H. Butterfield, ed., *Adams Family Correspondence* (Cambridge: Harvard University Press, 1963), Vol. II, p. 28-31. Peter Marshall and David Manuel, *The Light and the Glory* (Old Tappan, NJ: Fleming H. Revell, 1977), pp. 310-311.
[23] **John Adams.** July 3, 1776, in a letter to his wife Abigail Adams, in relation to the state of the Cause of Independence. Charles Francis Adams (son of John Quincy Adams and grandson of John Adams), ed., *Letters of John Adams - Addressed To His Wife* (Boston: Charles C. Little and James Brown, 1841), Vol. I, p. 128. *Old South Leaflets* (Boston: Directors of the Old South Meeting House, 1902). John Bartlett, *Bartlett's Familiar Quotations* (Boston: Little, Brown and Company, 1855, 1980), p. 381. *The World Book Encyclopedia*, 18 vols. (Chicago, IL: Field Enterprises, Inc., 1957; W.F. Quarrie and Company, 8 vols., 1917; World Book, Inc., 22 vols., 1989), Vol. 9, p. 3683. Charles E. Kistler, *This Nation Under God* (Boston: Richard T. Badger, 1924), p. 71. Henry Steele Commager and Richard B. Morris, eds., *The Spirit of 'Seventy-Six* (NY: Bobbs-Merrill Co., Inc., 1958; NY: Harper & Row, Publishers, 1967), p. 321. L.H. Butterfield, ed., *Adams Family Correspondence* (Cambridge: Harvard University Press, 1963), Vol. II, p. 28-31. L.H. Butterfield, Marc Frielander, and Mary-Jo King, eds., *The Book of Abigail and John - Selected Letters of The Adams Family 1762-1784* (Cambridge, Massachusetts and London, England: Harvard University Press, 1975), p. 142. Peter Marshall and David Manuel, *The Light and the Glory* (Old Tappan, NJ: Fleming H. Revell, 1977), pp. 310-311. Lucille Johnston, *Celebrations of a Nation* (Arlington, VA: The Year of Thanksgiving Foundation, 1987), p. 87. David Barton, *The Myth of Separation* (Aledo, TX: WallBuilder Press, 1991), p. 98. Catherine Millard, *The Rewriting of America's History* (Camp Hill, PA: Horizon House Publishers, 1991), p. 77. D.P. Diffine, Ph.D., *One Nation Under God - How Close a Separation?* (Searcy, Arkansas: Harding University, Belden Center for Private Enterprise Education, 6th edition, 1992), p. 6. Catherine Millard, *A Children's Companion Guide to America's History* (Camp Hill, PA: Horizon House Publishers, 1993), p. 43.
[24] **John Adams.** June 2, 1778, in a diary entry made while in Paris, France. L.H. Butterfield, ed., *Diary and Autobiography of John Adams* (Cambridge, MA: Belknap Press of Harvard University Press, 1961), Vol. IV, p. 123. David Barton, *The Myth of Separation* (Aledo, TX: WallBuilder Press, 1991), p. 248.
[25] **John Adams.** In writing to his wife Abigail Adams, regarding their sons. Philip Greven, *The Protestant Temperament: Patterns of Child-Rearing, Religious Experience, and Self in Early America* (New York: Alfred A. Knopf, 1977), p. 346. Gary DeMar, *America's Christian History: The Untold Story* (Atlanta, GA: American Vision Publishers, Inc., 1993), p. 96.
[26] **John Adams.** July 12, 1782, in a letter regarding politics, written from Holland. W. Cleon Skousen, *The Making of America* (Washington: The National Center for Constitutional Studies, 1985), p. 195. Tim LaHaye, *Faith of Our Founding Fathers* (Brentwood, TN: Wolgemuth & Hyatt, Publishers, Inc., 1987), pp. 89-90.
[27] **John Adams.** July 26, 1796, writing in his diary a disapproval of Thomas Paine's assertions. Norman Cousins, *In God We Trust - The Religious Beliefs and Ideas of the American Founding Fathers* (NY: Harper & Brothers, 1958), p. 99. L.H. Butterfield, ed., *The Diary and Autobiography of John Adams* (Cambridge, MA: The Belknap Press of Harvard University Press, 1962), Vol. 3, pp. 233-234. Edmund Fuller and David E. Green, *God in the White House - The Faiths of American Presidents* (NY: Crown Publishers, Inc., 1968), p. 25. Christopher Collier, *Roger Sherman's Connecticut* (Middleton, CT: Wesleyan University Press, 1971), p. 185. John Eidsmoe, *Christianity and the Constitution - The Faith of Our Founding Fathers* (Grand Rapids, MI: Baker Book House, A Mott

Media Book, 1987; 6th printing, 1993), p. 277. David Barton, *The Myth of Separation* (Aledo, TX: WallBuilder Press, 1991), p. 123. Gary DeMar, "Why the Religious Right is Always Right - Almost" (Atlanta, GA: *The Biblical Worldview*, An American Vision Publication - American Vision, Inc., November 1992), p. 12. Gary DeMar, *America's Christian History: The Untold Story* (Atlanta, GA: American Vision Publishers, Inc., 1993), p. 95.

[28] **John Adams.** March 4, 1797, Saturday, in his Inaugural Address, given in Philadelphia, Pennsylvania. James D. Richardson (U.S. Representative from Tennessee), ed., *A Compilation of the Messages and Papers of the Presidents 1789-1897*, 10 vols. (Washington, D.C.: U.S. Government Printing Office, published by Authority of Congress, 1897, 1899; Washington, D.C.: Bureau of National Literature and Art, 1789-1902, 11 vols., 1907, 1910), Vol. I, pp. 228-232. *Inaugural Addresses of the Presidents of the United States - From George Washington 1789 to Richard Milhous Nixon 1969* (Washington, D.C.: United States Government Printing Office; 91st Congress, 1st Session, House Document 91-142, 1969), pp. 7-11. Charles E. Rice, *The Supreme Court and Public Prayer* (New York: Fordham University Press, 1964), pp. 178-179. *Proclaim Liberty* (Dallas, TX: Word of Faith), p. 1. J. Michael Sharman, J.D., *Faith of the Fathers* (Culpepper, Virginia: Victory Publishing, 1995), p. 22.

[29] **John Adams.** October 11, 1798, in a letter to the officers of the First Brigade of the Third Division of the Militia of Massachusetts. Charles Francis Adams (son of John Quincy Adams and grandson of John Adams), ed., *The Works of John Adams - Second President of the United States: with a Life of the Author, Notes, and Illustration* (Boston: Little, Brown, & Co., 1854), Vol. IX, pp. 228-229. Richard John Neuhaus, *The Naked Public Square* (Grand Rapids, MI: William B. Eerdman Publishing Company, 1984), p. 95. *War on Religious Freedom* (Virginia Beach, Virginia: Freedom Council, 1984), p. 1. A. James Reichley, *Religion in American Public Life* (Washington, D.C.: The Brookings Institute, 1985), p. 105. Pat Robertson, *America's Dates With Destiny* (Nashville, TN: 1986), pp. 93-95. Charles Colson, *Kingdoms in Conflict* (Grand Rapids, MI: Zondervan Publishing House, 1987), pp. 47, 120. Tim LaHaye, *Faith of Our Founding Fathers* (Brentwood, TN: Wolgemuth & Hyatt, Publishers, Inc., 1987), p. 194. John Eidsmoe, *Christianity and the Constitution - The Faith of Our Founding Fathers* (Grand Rapids, MI: Baker Book House, A Mott Media Book, 1987; 6th printing, 1993), pp. 273, 292, 381. Gary DeMar, "Is the Constitution Christian?" (Atlanta, GA: *The Biblical Worldview*, An American Vision Publication - American Vision, Inc., December 1989), p. 2. Peter Marshall and David Manuel, *The Glory of America* (Bloomington, MN: Garborg's Heart 'N Home, 1991), 8.11. David Barton, *The Myth of Separation* (Aledo, TX: WallBuilder Press, 1991), p. 123. David Barton, *America - To Pray or Not to Pray* (Aledo, Texas: Wallbuilder Press, 1991), p. 89. Kerby Anderson, "Christian Roots of the Declaration" (Dallas, TX: *Freedom Club Report*, July 1993), p. 6. Rush H. Limbaugh III, *See, I Told You So* (New York, NY: reprinted by permission of Pocket Books, a division of Simon & Schuster Inc., 1993), pp. 73-76. Stephen McDowell and Mark Beliles, "The Providential Perspective" (Charlottesville, VA: The Providence Foundation, P.O. Box 6759, Charlottesville, Va. 22906, January 1994), Vol. 9, No. 1, p. 4.

[30] **John Adams.** March 6, 1799, in a Proclamation of a National Day of Humiliation, Fasting, and Prayer. James D. Richardson (U.S. Representative from Tennessee), ed., *A Compilation of the Messages and Papers of the Presidents 1789-1897*, 10 vols. (Washington, D.C.: U.S. Government Printing Office, published by Authority of Congress, 1897, 1899; Washington, D.C.: Bureau of National Literature and Art, 1789-1902, 11 vols., 1907, 1910), Vol. I, pp. 284-286. Benjamin Franklin Morris, *The Christian Life and Character of the Civil Institutions of the United States* (Philadelphia: George W. Childs, 1864), pp. 547-548. Gary DeMar, *The Biblical Worldview* (Atlanta, GA: An American Vision Publication - American Vision, Inc., 1992), Vol. 8, No. 12, p. 9. Gary DeMar, *America's Christian History: The Untold Story* (Atlanta, GA: American Vision Publishers, Inc., 1993), p. 78. Stephen McDowell and Mark Beliles, "The Providential Perspective" (Charlottesville, VA: The Providence Foundation, P.O. Box 6759, Charlottesville, Va. 22906, January 1994), Vol. 9, No. 1, pp. 4, 6.

[31] **John Adams.** November 1800, in a letter to his wife, Abigail Adams, in which he composed a prayer, which was later engraved upon the mantel in the State Dining Room of the White House. John Adams, *John Adam's Prayer* (Washington, D.C.: White House Collection, engraved upon the mantel, State Dining Room). John Bartlett, *Bartlett's Familiar Quotations* (Boston: Little, Brown and Company, 1855, 1980), p. 382. Charles Fadiman, ed., *The American Treasury* (NY: Harper & Brothers, Publishers, 1955), p. 317. Catherine Millard, *The Rewriting of America's History* (Camp Hill, PA: Horizon House Publishers, 1991), p. 78.

[32] **John Adams.** February 16, 1809, in a letter to Judge F.A. Van der Kemp. Norman Cousins, ed., *'In God We Trust': The Religious Beliefs and Ideas of the American Founding Fathers* (New York: Harper & Brothers, 1958), pp. 102-103. Russell Kirk, *Roots of American Order* (LaSalle, IL.: Open Court, 1974), p. 17. Charles Colson, *Kingdoms in Conflict* (Grand Rapids, MI: Zondervan Publishing House, 1987), p. 228. Gary DeMar, *America's Christian History: The Untold Story* (Atlanta, GA: American Vision Publishers, Inc., 1993), p. 96.

[33] **John Adams.** August 28, 1811, to Dr. Benjamin Rush. Charles Francis Adams (son of John Quincy Adams and grandson of John Adams), ed., *The Works of John Adams - Second President of the United States* (Boston: Little, Brown, & Co., 1854), Vol. IX, p. 636. Norman Cousins, *In God We Trust - The Religious Beliefs and Ideas of the American Founding Fathers* (NY: Harper & Brothers, 1958), p. 101. David Barton, *The Myth of Separation*, (Aledo, TX: WallBuilder Press, 1991), p. 123.

[34] **John Adams.** In a letter to Mr. Warren. *Warren-Adams Letters* (Boston, MA: Massachusetts Historical Society, 1917), Vol. I, p. 222. Verna M. Hall, *The Christian History of the American Revolution - Consider and Ponder* (San Francisco: Foundation for American Christian Education, 1976), p. 615. Philip Greven, *The Protestant Temperament - Patterns of Childrearing, Religious Experience, and Self in Early America* (NY: Alfred A. Knopf, 1977), p. 346. David Barton, *The Myth of Separation* (Aledo, TX: WallBuilder Press, 1991), p. 247. Gary DeMar, *America's Christian History: The Untold Story* (Atlanta, GA: American Vision Publishers, Inc., 1993), p. 96. Stephen McDowell and Mark Beliles, "The Providential Perspective" (Charlottesville, VA: The Providence Foundation, P.O. Box 6759, Charlottesville, Va. 22906, January 1994), Vol. 9, No. 1, p. 5.

[35] **John Adams.** June 28, 1813, in a letter to Thomas Jefferson. Norman Cousins, *In God We Trust - The Religious Beliefs and Ideas of the American Founding Fathers* (NY: Harper & Brothers, 1958), p. 230. Lester J. Capon, ed., *The Adams-Jefferson Letters*, 2 vols. (Chapel Hill, NC: University of North Carolina Press, 1959), Vol. 2, pp. 339-340. Gary DeMar, *The Biblical Worldview* (Atlanta, GA: An American Vision Publication - American Vision, Inc., 1992), Vol. 8, No. 12, p. 9. Gary DeMar, *America's Christian History: The Untold Story* (Atlanta, GA: American Vision Publishers, Inc., 1993), pp. 78, 121.

[36] **John Adams.** In a letter to Thomas Jefferson. Richard K. Arnold, ed., *Adams to Jefferson/Jefferson to Adams - A Dialogue from their Correspondence* (San Francisco: Jerico Press, 1975), pp. 330-31. Catherine Millard, *The Rewriting of America's History* (Camp Hill, PA: Horizon House Publishers, 1991), p. 80.

[37] **John Adams.** December 25, 1813, in a letter to Thomas Jefferson. Norman Cousins, *In God We Trust - The Religious Beliefs and Ideas of the American Founding Fathers* (NY: Harper & Brothers, 1958), p. 256. L.J. Capon, ed., *The Adams-Jefferson Letters* (Chapel Hill, NC: University of North Carolina Press, 1959), 2:412. Stephen Abbott Northrop, D.D., *A Cloud of Witnesses* (Portland, OR: American Heritage Ministries, 1987; Mantle Ministries, 228 Still Ridge, Bulverde, Texas), p. 2. Peter Marshall and David Manuel,

The *Glory of America* (Bloomington, MN: Garborg's Heart 'N Home, 1991), 7.10. D.P. Diffine, Ph.D., *One Nation Under God - How Close a Separation?* (Searcy, Arkansas: Harding University, Belden Center for Private Enterprise Education, 6th edition, 1992), p. 6. Gary DeMar, *America's Christian History: The Untold Story* (Atlanta, GA: American Vision Publishers, Inc., 1993), p. 58.

[38] **John Adams.** June 20, 1815, in a letter to Thomas Jefferson. Paul Wilstach, ed., *The Correspondence of John Adams and Thomas Jefferson, 1812-1826* (Indianapolis: The Bobbs-Merrill Publishers, 1925), p. 112. Catherine Millard, *The Rewriting of America's History* (Camp Hill, PA: Horizon House Publishers, 1991), pp. 82-83.

[39] **John Adams.** November 4, 1816, in a letter to Thomas Jefferson. Paul Wilstach, ed., *The Correspondence of John Adams and Thomas Jefferson, 1812-1826* (Indianapolis: The Bobbs-Merrill Publishers, 1925), p. 112. Norman Cousins, *In God We Trust - The Religious Beliefs and Ideas of the American Founding Fathers* (NY: Harper & Brothers, 1958), p. 280. Catherine Millard, *The Rewriting of America's History* (Camp Hill, PA: Horizon House Publishers, 1991) p. 83.

[40] **John Adams.** December 27, 1816, in a letter to Judge F.A. Van de Kemp. Norman Cousins, *In God We Trust - The Religious Beliefs and Ideas of the American Founding Fathers* (NY: Harper & Brothers, 1958), pp. 104-105. John Eidsmoe, *Christianity and the Constitution - The Faith of Our Founding Fathers* (Grand Rapids, MI: Baker Book House, A Mott Media Book, 1987; 6th printing, 1993), p. 286. Gary DeMar, "Why the Religious Right is Always Right - Almost" (Atlanta, GA: *The Biblical Worldview*, An American Vision Publication - American Vision, Inc., November 1992), p. 6. Gary DeMar, *America's Christian History: The Untold Story* (Atlanta, GA: American Vision Publishers, Inc., 1993), p. 95.

[41] **John Adams.** April 19, 1817, in a letter to Thomas Jefferson. Norman Cousins, *In God We Trust - The Religious Beliefs and Ideas of the American Founding Fathers* (NY: Harper & Brothers, 1958), p. 282. Edmund Fuller and David E. Green, *God in the White House - The Faiths of American Presidents* (NY: Crown Publishers, Inc., 1968), p. 26. Richard K. Arnold, ed., *Adams to Jefferson/Jefferson to Adams - A Dialogue from their Correspondence* (San Francisco: Jerico Press, 1975), p. 25. Catherine Millard, *The Rewriting of America's History* (Camp Hill, PA: Horizon House Publishers, 1991), p. 80.

[42] **John Adams.** October 7, 1818, in a letter to Thomas Jefferson, regarding the impending death of his wife, Abigail Adams. Richard K. Arnold, ed., *Adams to Jefferson/Jefferson to Adams - A Dialogue from their Correspondence* (San Francisco: Jerico Press, 1975), p. 27. Catherine Millard, *The Rewriting of America's History* (Camp Hill, PA: Horizon House Publishers, 1991), p. 80.

[43] **John Adams.** *Life and Works of John Adams,* Vol. X, p. 390. Stephen Abbott Northrop, D.D., *A Cloud of Witnesses* (Portland, Oregon: American Heritage Ministries, 1987; Mantle Ministries, 228 Still Ridge, Bulverde, Texas), pp. 2-3.

[44] **John Adams.** July 4, 1826, his last words. James H. Huston, "John Adams," *The World Book Encyclopedia,* 22 vols. (Chicago, IL: World Book, Inc., 1989; W.F. Quarrie and Company, 8 vols., 1917), Vol. 1, p. 39. Peter Marshall and David Manuel, *The Glory of America* (Bloomington, MN: Garborg's Heart'N Home, Inc., 1991), 7.12.

[45] **John Quincy Adams.** In reply to an inquiry as to his unpopular stance against slavery. David Barton, *The WallBuilder Report* (Aledo, TX: WallBuilder Press, Summer 1993), p. 3.

[46] **John Quincy Adams.** September 1811, in a letter to his son written while serving as U.S. Minister in St. Petersburg, Russia. James L. Alden, *Letters of John Quincy Adams to His Son on the Bible and Its Teachings* (1850), pp. 6-21. Henry H. Halley, *Halley's Bible Handbook* (Grand Rapids, MI: Zondervan Publishing House, 1927, 1965), p. 19. Verna M. Hall, *The Christian History of the American Revolution - Consider and Ponder* (San Francisco: Foundation for American Christian Education, 1976), pp. 615-616. Verna M. Hall and Rosalie J. Slater, *The Bible and the Constitution of the United States of America* (San Francisco: Foundation for American Christian Education, 1983), p. 17. Tim LaHaye, *Faith of Our Founding Fathers* (Brentwood, TN: Wolgemuth & Hyatt, Publishers, Inc., 1987), pp. 90-91. David Barton, *The Myth of Separation* (Aledo, TX: WallBuilder Press, 1991), p. 124. D.P. Diffine, Ph.D., *One Nation Under God - How Close a Separation?* (Searcy, Arkansas: Harding University, Belden Center for Private Enterprise Education, 6th edition, 1992), p. 6.

[47] **John Quincy Adams.** December 31, 1812, in a diary entry. Allan Nevins, ed., *The Diary of John Quincy Adams* (NY: Longmans, Green & Co., 1928), p. 103. Peter Marshall and David Manuel, *From Sea to Shining Sea* (Old Tappan, N.J.: Fleming H. Revell Company, 1986), p. 181. Peter Marshall and David Manuel, *The Glory of America* (Bloomington, MN: Garborg's Heart 'N Home, Inc., 1991), 12.31. D.P. Diffine, Ph.D., *One Nation Under God - How Close a Separation?* (Searcy, Arkansas: Harding University, Belden Center for Private Enterprise Education, 6th edition, 1992), p. 10.

[48] **John Quincy Adams.** December 24, 1814, in writing from London to Boston, after negotiating the Treaty of Ghent. Worthington Chauncey Ford, ed., *Writings of John Quincy Adams* (New York: Macmillan, 1915), Vol. 5, p. 362. Peter Marshall and David Manuel, *From Sea to Shining Sea* (Old Tappan, NJ: Fleming H. Revell Company, 1986), p. 185.

[49] **John Quincy Adams.** December 24, 1814, in writing from London to Boston, after negotiating the Treaty of Ghent. Adams, *Writings,* Vol. VI, p. 329. Worthington Chauncey Ford, ed., *Writings of John Quincy Adams* (New York: Macmillan, 1915), Vol. 5, pp. 431-433. Peter Marshall and David Manuel, *From Sea to Shining Sea* (Old Tappan, NJ: Fleming H. Revell Company, 1986), pp. 185-186. Peter Marshall and David Manuel, *The Glory of America* (Bloomington, MN: Garborg's Heart'N Home, Inc., 1991), 5.5.

[50] **John Quincy Adams.** December 24, 1814, in writing from London to Boston, after negotiating the Treaty of Ghent. Worthington Chauncey Ford, *Writing of John Quincy Adams* (New York: Macmillan, 1916), Vol. 6, pp. 135-136. Peter Marshall and David Manuel, *From Sea to Shining Sea* (Old Tappan, NJ: Fleming H. Revell Company, 1986), p. 186.

[51] **John Quincy Adams.** July 4, 1821. John Wingate Thornton, *The Pulpit of the American Revolution 1860* (reprinted NY: Burt Franklin, 1860; 1970), p. XXIX. Verna M. Hall, comp., *Christian History of the Constitution of the United States of America* (San Francisco: Foundation for American Christian Education, 1976), p. 372. Marshall Foster and Mary-Elaine Swanson, *The American Covenant - The Untold Story* (Roseburg, OR: Foundation for Christian Self-Government, 1981; Thousand Oaks, CA: The Mayflower Institute, 1983, 1992), p. 18. David Barton, *The Myth of Separation* (Aledo, TX: WallBuilder Press, 1991), p. 151.

[52] **John Quincy Adams.** Statement. John Wingate Thornton, *The Pulpit of the American Revolution 1860* (NY: Burt Franklin, 1860; 1970), p. XXIX. David Barton, *The Myth of Separation* (Aledo, TX: WallBuilder Press, 1991), p. 151. D.P. Diffine, Ph.D., *One Nation Under God - How Close a Separation?* (Searcy, Arkansas: Harding University, Belden Center for Private Enterprise Education, 6th edition, 1992), p. 11.

[53] **John Quincy Adams.** July 4, 1837, in his work entitled, *An Oration Delivered Before the Inhabitants of the Town of Newburyport at their Request on the Sixty-First Anniversary of the Declaration of Independence* (Newburyport: Charles Whipple, 1837), pp. 5-6. Marshall Foster and Mary-Elaine Swanson, *The American Covenant - The Untold Story* (Roseburg, OR: Foundation for Christian Self-Government, 1981; Thousand Oaks, CA: The Mayflower Institute, 1983, 1992), pp. 18-19. Peter Marshall and David Manuel, *The Glory of America* (Bloomington, MN: Garborg's Heart'N Home, Inc., 1991), 12.25. David Barton, *The Myth of Separation* (Aledo, TX: WallBuilder Press, 1992), pp. 125, 151. D.P. Diffine, Ph.D., *One Nation Under God - How Close a Separation?* (Searcy,

Arkansas: Harding University, Belden Center for Private Enterprise Education, 6th edition, 1992), p. 12. David Barton, *America's Godly Heritage* (Aledo, TX: WallBuilder Press, 1993), pp. 6-7. Russ Walton, *One Nation Under God* (NH: Plymouth Rock Foundation, 1993), p. 20. Stephen McDowell and Mark Beliles, "The Providential Perspective" (Charlottesville, VA: The Providence Foundation, P.O. Box 6759, Charlottesville, Va. 22906, January 1994), Vol. 9, No. 1, p. 6.

[54] **John Quincy Adams.** June 16; July 7, 1838, in speaking before Congress. Stephen Abbott Northrop, D.D., *A Cloud of Witnesses* (Portland, OR: American Heritage Ministries, 1987; Mantle Ministries, 228 Still Ridge, Bulverde, Texas), p. 3.

[55] **John Quincy Adams.** In a diary entry. Charles Francis Adams (son of John Quincy Adams and grandson of John Adams), ed., *Memoirs of John Quincy Adams*, 2 vols. (Philadelphia: J.B. Lippincott & Co., 1874-77), IX:289. Peter Marshall and David Manuel, *The Glory of America* (Bloomington, MN: Garborg's Heart 'N Home, 1991), 11.7.

[56] **John Quincy Adams.** Statement. Robert Flood, *The Rebirth of America* (Philadelphia: Arthur S. DeMoss Foundation, 1986), p. 37. Gary DeMar, *America's Christian History: The Untold Story* (Atlanta, GA: American Vision Publishers, Inc., 1993), p. 59.

[57] **John Quincy Adams.** Statement. Tryon Edwards, D.D., *The New Dictionary of Thoughts - A Cyclopedia of Quotations* (Garden City, NY: Hanover House, 1852; revised and enlarged by C.H. Catrevas, Ralph Emerson Browns and Jonathan Edwards [descendent, along with Tryon, of Jonathan Edwards (1703-1758), president of Princeton], 1891; The Standard Book Company, 1955, 1963), p. 48. Gary DeMar, "Censoring America's Christian History" (Atlanta, GA: *The Biblical Worldview*, An American Vision Publication - American Vision, Inc., July 1990), p. 6. D.P. Diffine, Ph.D., *One Nation Under God - How Close a Separation?* (Searcy, Arkansas: Harding University, Belden Center for Private Enterprise Education, 6th edition, 1992), p. 10. Gary DeMar, *America's Christian History: The Untold Story* (Atlanta, GA: American Vision Publishers, Inc., 1993), p. 59.

[58] **John Quincy Adams.** Statement. Tryon Edwards, D.D., *The New Dictionary of Thoughts - A Cyclopedia of Quotations* (Garden City, NY: Hanover House, 1852; revised and enlarged by C.H. Catrevas, Ralph Emerson Browns and Jonathan Edwards [descendent, along with Tryon, of Jonathan Edwards (1703-1758), president of Princeton], 1891; The Standard Book Company, 1955, 1963), p. 45.

[59] **John Quincy Adams.** Statement. Stephen Abbott Northrop, D.D., *A Cloud of Witnesses* (Portland, Oregon: American Heritage Ministries, 1987; Mantle Ministries, 228 Still Ridge, Bulverde, Texas), p. introduction.

[60] **John Quincy Adams.** Statement. Robert Flood, *The Rebirth of America* (Philadelphia: Arthur S. DeMoss Foundation, 1986), p. 16.

[61] **John Quincy Adams.** February 27, 1844, as a U.S. Congressman, addressing the American Bible Society, of which he was the chairman. Stephen Abbott Northrop, D.D., *A Cloud of Witnesses* (Portland, Oregon: American Heritage Ministries, 1987; Mantle Ministries, 228 Still Ridge, Bulverde, Texas), p. 4. Peter Marshall and David Manuel, *The Glory of America* (Bloomington, MN: Garborg's Heart 'N Home, Inc., 1991), 2.27.

[62] **John Quincy Adams.** December 3, 1844, in a diary entry, after hearing that his efforts to rescind the infamous *Gag Rule* had finally succeeded. Champ Bennett Clark, *John Quincy Adams: "Old Man Eloquent"* (Boston: Little, Brown, & Co., 1932), p. 407. Peter Marshall and David Manuel, *The Glory of America* (Bloomington, MN: Garborg's Heart 'N Home, Inc., 1991), 12.3.

[63] **John Quincy Adams.** July 11, 1846, in a diary entry made on his 80th birthday. Charles Francis Adams (son of John Quincy Adams and grandson of John Adams), ed., *Memoirs of John Quincy Adams*, 2 vols. (Philadelphia: J.B. Lippincott & Co., 1874-77), Vol. XII, p. 268. Peter Marshall and David Manuel, *The Glory of America* (Bloomington, MN: Garborg's Heart 'N Home, Inc., 1991), 7.11.

[64] **John Quincy Adams.** June 14, 1890, statement published in *The Churchman.* Stephen Abbott Northrop, D.D., *A Cloud of Witnesses* (Portland, OR: American Heritage Ministries, 1987; Mantle Ministries, 228 Still Ridge, Bulverde, Texas), p. 4.

[65] **John Quincy Adams.** In a diary entry near the end of his life. Charles Francis Adams (son of John Quincy Adams and grandson of John Adams), ed., *Memoirs of John Quincy Adams*, 2 vols. (Philadelphia: J.B. Lippincott & Co., 1874-77), XII:277. Peter Marshall and David Manuel, *The Glory of America* (Bloomington, MN: Garborg's Heart 'N Home, 1991), 10.31.

[66] **John Quincy Adams.** February 21, 1848, statement. Charles Francis Adams (son of John Quincy Adams and grandson of John Adams), ed., *Memoirs of John Quincy Adams*, 2 vols. (Philadelphia: J.B. Lippincott & Co., 1874-77), p. 14. Peter Marshall and David Manuel, *The Glory of America* (Bloomington, MN: Garborg's Heart 'N Home, 1991), 2.21. D.P. Diffine, Ph.D., *One Nation Under God - How Close a Separation?* (Searcy, Arkansas: Harding University, Belden Center for Private Enterprise Education, 1992), p. 13.

[67] **Samuel Adams.** November 20, 1772, in his pamphlet entitled, *The Rights of the Colonists*, in section: "The Rights of the Colonist as Christians." *The Rights of the Colonists* (Boston: *Old South Leaflets*), Vol. VII, 1772. Adams, *Writings*. Selim H. Peabody, ed., *American Patriotism - Speeches, Letters, and Other Papers Which Illustrate the Foundation, the Development, the Preservation of the United States of America* (NY: American Book Exchange, 1880), p. 34. Charles E. Kistler, *This Nation Under God* (Boston: Richard T. Badger, 1924), p. 73. *The Annals of America*, 20 vols. (Chicago, IL: Encyclopedia Britannica, 1968), Vol. 2, pp. 218-219. Verna M. Hall, *The Christian History of the Constitution of the United States of America - Christian Self-Government* (San Francisco: Foundation for American Christian Education, 1976), p. xiii. Marshall Foster and Mary-Elaine Swanson, *The American Covenant - The Untold Story* (Roseburg, OR: Foundation for Christian Self-Government, 1981; Thousand Oaks, CA: The Mayflower Institute, 1983, 1992), p. 112. Pat Robertson, *America's Dates with Destiny* (Nashville: Thomas Nelson Publishers, 1986), p. 91. John Eidsmoe, *Christianity and the Constitution - The Faith of Our Founding Fathers* (Grand Rapids, MI: Baker Book House, A Mott Media Book, 1987; 6th printing, 1993), p. 254. "Our Christian Heritage," *Letter from Plymouth Rock* (Marlborough, NH: The Plymouth Rock Foundation), pp. 2, 4. Peter Marshall and David Manuel, *The Glory of America* (Bloomington, MN: Garborg's Heart 'N Home, 1991), 1.19. David Barton, *The Myth of Separation* (Aledo, TX: WallBuilder Press, 1992), p. 93-94. D.P. Diffine, Ph.D., *One Nation Under God - How Close a Separation?* (Searcy, Arkansas: Harding University, Belden Center for Private Enterprise Education, 6th edition, 1992), p. 5.

[68] **Samuel Adams.** September 6, 1774, in a proposition for prayer given the second day of the Continental Congress. Key Paton, "Notable Chaplains," *Eternity* (November 1986), p. 28. Gary DeMar, *America's Christian History: The Untold Story* (Atlanta, GA: American Vision Publishers, Inc., 1993), p. 51.

[69] **Samuel Adams.** 1776, statement made while the Declaration of Independence was being signed. Charles E. Kistler, *This Nation Under God* (Boston: Richard G. Badger, The Gorham Press, 1924), p. 71. Peter Marshall and David Manuel, *The Light and the Glory* (NJ: Fleming H. Revell Co., 1977), p. 309. "Our Christian Heritage," *Letter from Plymouth Rock* (Marlborough, NH: The Plymouth Rock Foundation), p. 8. David Barton, *The Myth of Separation* (Aledo, TX: WallBuilder Press, 1991), p. 98. D.P. Diffine, Ph.D., *One Nation Under God - How Close a Separation?* (Searcy, Arkansas: Harding University, Belden Center for Private Enterprise Education, 6th edition, 1992), p. 6.

[70] **Samuel Adams**. February 12, 1779, in a letter to James Warren. Harry Alonzo Cushing, ed., *The Writings of Samuel Adams* (New York: G.P. Putnam's Sons, 1905), Vol. 4, p. 124. Rosalie Slater, *Teaching and Learning America's Christian Heritage (San* Francisco: Foundation for American Christian Education, American Revolution Bicentennial edition, 1975), p. 251. Verna M. Hall, *The Christian History of the Constitution of the United States of America - Christian Self-Government with Union* (San Francisco: Foundation for American Christian Education, 1976), p. 4. Stephen K. McDowell and Mark A. Beliles, *America's Providential History* (Charlottesville, VA: Providence Press, 1988), pp. 148, 179. Peter Marshall and David Manuel, *The Glory of America* (Bloomington, MN: Garborg's Heart'N Home, Inc., 1991), 9.27. Stephen McDowell and Mark Beliles, "The Providential Perspective" (Charlottesville, VA: The Providence Foundation, P.O. Box 6759, Charlottesville, Va. 22906, January 1994), Vol. 9, No. 1, p. 4.

[71] **Samuel Adams**. Statement made in a political essay, printed in *The Public Advisor*, p. 1749. William V. Wells, *The Life and Public Service of Samuel Adams* (Boston: Little, Brown, & Co., 1865), Vol. 1, p. 22. Tim LaHaye, *Faith of Our Founding Fathers* (Brentwood, TN: Wolgemuth & Hyatt, Publishers, Inc., 1987), p. 196. David Barton, *The Myth of Separation* (Aledo, TX: WallBuilder Press, 1991), p. 246. Stephen McDowell and Mark Beliles, "The Providential Perspective" (Charlottesville, VA: The Providence Foundation, P.O. Box 6759, Charlottesville, Va. 22906, January 1994), Vol. 9, No. 1, p. 4.

[72] **Samuel Adams**. 1750, statement. William V. Wells, *The Life and Public Services of Samuel Adams* (Boston: Little, Brown & Co., 1865). Rosalie J. Slater, *Teaching and Learning America's Christian History* (San Francisco: Foundation for American Christian Education, 1975). Peter Marshall, David Manuel, *The Glory of America* (Bloomington, MN: Garborg's Heart'N Home, Inc., 1991), 11.3.

[73] **Samuel Adams**. October 4, 1790, in a letter to his cousin, Vice-President John Adams. *Four Letters, Being an Interesting Correspondence Between John Adams and Samuel Adams* (Boston: Adams & Rhoades, 1802). Charles Francis Adams (son of John Quincy Adams and grandson of John Adams), ed., *The Works of John Adams-Second President of the United States* (Boston: Little, Brown & Co., 1854) Vol. VI, p. 414. William V. Wells, *The Life and Public Services of Samuel Adams* (Boston: Little, Brown & Co., 1865), Vol. III, p. 301. Verna M. Hall, comp., *Christian History of the Constitution of the United States of America* (San Francisco: Foundation for American Christian Education, 1976), p. XIV. Marshall Foster and Mary-Elaine Swanson, *The American Covenant - The Untold Story* (Roseberg, OR: Foundation for Christian Self-Government, 1981; Thousand Oaks, CA: The Mayflower Institute, 1983, 1992), p. xvi.

[74] **Samuel Adams**. October 18, 1790, Vice-President John Adams wrote his reply to his cousin, Samuel Adams. *Four Letters, Being an Interesting Correspondence Between John Adams and Samuel Adams* (Boston: Adams & Rhoades, 1802). Charles Francis Adams (son of John Quincy Adams and grandson of John Adams), ed., *The Works of John Adams-Second President of the United States* (Boston: Little, Brown & Co., 1854), Vol. VI, p. 414. William V. Wells, *The Life and Public Services of Samuel Adams* (Boston: Little, Brown & Co., 1865), Vol. III, p. 304. David Barton, *The Myth of Separation* (Aledo, TX: WallBuilder Press, 1991), p. 117.

[75] **Samuel Adams**. 1794, in an address to the State Legislature of Massachusetts, having recently risen from Lieutenant Governor to Governor, following the death of Governor John Hancock. "Our Christian Heritage," *Letter from Plymouth Rock* (Marlborough, NH: The Plymouth Rock Foundation), p. 4.

[76] **Samuel Adams**. March 20, 1797, as Governor of Massachusetts, in a *Proclamation of a Day of Fast*. Harry Alonzo Cushing, ed., *The Writings of Samuel Adams* (New York: G.P. Putman's Sons, 1905), Vol. II, pp. 355-356. John Eidsmoe, *Christianity and the Constitution - The Faith of Our Founding Fathers* (Grand Rapids, MI: Baker Book House, A Mott Media Book, 1987, 6th printing, 1993), p. 254.

[77] **Samuel Adams**. November 22, 1780, to T. Wells, his daughter's fiancee. Norman Cousins, *In God We Trust - The Religious Beliefs and Ideas of the American Founding Fathers* (NY: Harper & Brothers, 1958), p. 354. Verna M. Hall, *The Christian History of the Constitution of the United States of America - Christian Self-Government* (San Francisco: Foundation for American Christian Education, 1976), p. 71. Peter Marshall and David Manuel, *The Glory of America* (Bloomington, MN: Garborg's Heart'N Home, Inc., 1991), 11.15. D.P. Diffine, Ph.D., *One Nation Under God - How Close a Separation?* (Searcy, Arkansas: Harding University, Belden Center for Private Enterprise Education, 6th edition, 1992), p. 5.

[78] **Samuel Adams**. Statement in his *Last Will and Testament*. Stephen Abbott Northrop, D.D., *A Cloud of Witnesses* (Portland, Oregon: American Heritage Ministries, 1987; Mantle Ministries, 228 Still Ridge, Bulverde, Texas), p. 5. Peter Marshall and David Manuel, *The Glory of America* (Bloomington, MN: Garborg's Heart'N Home, Inc., 1991),10.2

[79] **Robert Aitken**. January 21, 1781, statement presented in Congress. *Memorial of Robert Aitken to Congress* (Washington, D.C.: National Archives, January 21, 1781). David Barton, *The Myth of Separation* (Aledo, TX: WallBuilder Press, 1991), p. 106. "Our Christian Heritage," *Letter form Plymouth Rock* (Marlborough, NH: The Plymouth Rock Foundation), p. 4. Robert Flood, *The Rebirth of America* (Philadelphia: Arthur S. DeMoss Foundation, 1986), p. 39.

[80] **Robert Aitken**. September 10, 1782, the Continental Congress granted approval to print an edition of the Bible. *Bible for the Revolution* (NY: Arno Press, 1782, reprinted 1968), cover page. *Journals of Continental Congress 1774-1789* (Washington, D.C.: Government Printing Office, 1905), Vol. XXIII, 1782, p. 574. Robert Flood, *The Rebirth of America* (Philadelphia: Arthur S. DeMoss Foundation, 1986), p. 39. "Our Christian Heritage," *Letter from Plymouth Rock* (Marlborough, NH: The Plymouth Rock Foundation), p. 4. David Barton, *The Myth of Separation* (Aledo, TX: WallBuilder Press, 1991), p. 106.

[81] **Alabama Courts**. 1983, in the case of *Jaffree v. Board of School Commissioners of Mobile County*, 544 F. Supp, 1104 (S.D. Ala. 1983), Judge Brevard Hand, quoting from the 19th-century United States Supreme Court Justice Joseph Story. Russell Kirk, ed., *The Assault on Religion: Commentaries on the Decline of Religious Liberty* (Lanham, NY: University Press of America, 1986), p. 84. Gary DeMar, *America's Christian History - The Untold Story* (Atlanta, GA: American Vision Publishers, Inc., 1993), p. 113.

[82] **Ethan Allen**. May 10, 1775, statement made in demanding that Captain de la Place surrender Fort Ticonderoga on Lake Champlain to the Green Mountain Boys of the Continental Army. Ethan Allen, *A Narrative of Colonel Ethan Allen's Captivity* (Burlington: 1779, 4th ed., 1846). Washington Irving, *Life of Washington* (1855-1859), Vol. 1, ch. 38. John Bartlett, *Bartlett's Familiar Quotations* (Boston: Little, Brown and Company, 1855, 1980), p. 385. Charles Fadiman, ed., *The American Treasury* (NY: Harper & Brothers, Publishers, 1955), p. 371. Henry Steele Commager and Richard B. Morris, eds., *The Spirit O'Seventy-Six* (NY: Bobbs-Merrill Co., Inc., 1958; reprinted, NY: Harper & Row, Publishers, 1967), p. 103. Burton Stevenson, *The Home Book of Quotations - Classical & Modern* (New York: Dodd, Mead and Company, 1967), p. 61. Peter Beilenson, ed., *Spirit of '76* (NY: Peter Pauper Press, 1974), p. 35. *Boston Globe*, June 8, 1975, p. 15. Peter Marshall and David Manuel, *The Light and the Glory* (Old Tappan, NJ: Fleming H. Revell Co., 1977), p. 276.

[83] **Fisher Ames.** August 20, 1789, wording for the First Amendment to the Constitution, suggested in and adopted by the U.S. House during the First Session of the U.S. Congress. *Annals of the Congress of the United States - First Congress* (Washington, D.C.: Gales & Seaton, 1834), Vol. I, p. 766. David Barton, *The Myth of Separation* (Aledo, TX: WallBuilder Press, 1991), p. 27.

[84] **Fisher Ames.** Statement concerning education. Stephen Abbott Northrop, D.D., *A Cloud of Witnesses* (Portland, Oregon: American Heritage Ministries, 1987; Mantle Ministries, 228 Still Ridge, Bulverde, Texas), p. 12. Peter Marshall and David Manuel, *The Glory of America* (Bloomington, MN: Garborg's Heart'N Home, Inc., 1991), 12.27. David Barton, "The Truth About Thomas Jefferson And The First Amendment" (Aledo, TX: WallBuilder Press, 1992), p. 8. D.P. Diffine, Ph.D., *One Nation Under God - How Close a Separation?* (Searcy, Arkansas: Harding University, Belden Center for Private Enterprise Education, 6th edition, 1992), p. 13.

[85] **Fisher Ames.** September 20, 1789, in an article published in the *Palladium* magazine. D. James Kennedy, "The Great Deception" (Fort Lauderdale, Florida: Coral Ridge Ministries, 1989; 1993), p. 3.

[86] **Proclamation of Amnesty.** December 8, 1863; March 26, 1864, in Proclamations of Amnesty and Pardon to the participants of the Confederate insurrection, issued by President Abraham Lincoln; also in Proclamations of Amnesty and Pardon issued by President Andrew Johnson, May 29, 1865; September 7, 1867. James D. Richardson (U.S. Representative from Tennessee), ed., *A Compilation of the Messages and Papers of the Presidents 1789-1897*, 10 vols. (Washington, D.C.: U.S. Government Printing Office, published by Authority of Congress, 1897, 1899; Washington, D.C.: Bureau of National Literature and Art, 1789-1902, 11 vols., 1907, 1910), Vol. VI, pp. 213-215, 310-311, 548-549. Charles W. Eliot, LL.D., ed., *American Historical Documents 1000-1904* (New York: P.F. Collier & Son Company, *The Harvard Classics*, 1910), Vol. 43, p. 443.

[87] **Andre Marie Ampere.** In a note written on a piece of paper before his death. Philip Gilbert Hamerton, *Modern Frenchmen*, p. 334. Stephen Abbott Northrop, D.D., *A Cloud of Witnesses* (Portland, Oregon: American Heritage Ministries, 1987; Mantle Ministries, 228 Still Ridge, Bulverde, Texas), p. 13.

[88] **Hans Christian Andersen.** 1855, in his work entitled, *The Fairy Tale of My Life*. Stephen Abbott Northrop, D.D., *A Cloud of Witnesses* (Portland, Oregon: American Heritage Ministries, 1987; Mantle Ministries, 228 Still Ridge, Bulverde, Texas), p. 13.

[89] **Hans Christian Andersen.** Verses of "Barn (Child) Jesus," one of Denmark's best-known carols. Walter Ehret and George K. Evans, comps., *The International Book of Christmas Carols* (Englewood Cliffs, N.J.: Prentice-Hall, 1963), p. 193. Elizabeth Silverthorne, *Christmas in Texas* (College Station, TX: Texas A & M University Press, 1990), pp. 110-111.

[90] **Henry Bowen Anthony.** January 9, 1872, as U.S. Senator, delivering the eulogy for Roger Williams in Congress. Stephen Abbott Northrop, D.D., *A Cloud of Witnesses* (Portland, Oregon: American Heritage Ministries, 1987; Mantle Ministries, 228 Still Ridge, Bulverde, Texas), p. 16.

[91] **Motto of The State of Arizona** 1912 (originally adopted in 1863). John Wilson Taylor, M.A., Ph.D., et al., *The Lincoln Library of Essential Information* (Buffalo, New York: The Frontier Press Company, 1935), p. 2067. *The World Book Encyclopedia*, 18 vols. (Chicago, IL: Field Enterprises, Inc., 1957; W.F. Quarrie and Company, 8 vols., 1917; World Book, Inc., 22 vols., 1989), Vol. 1, p. 410.

[92] **Constitution of the State of Arkansas.** 1874, Preamble; Article II, Section 24; Article XIX, Section 1. Frances Newton Thorpe, ed., *Federal and State Constitutions, Colonial Charters, and Other Organic Laws of the States, Territories, and Colonies now or heretofore forming the United States*, 7 vols. (Washington: Government Printing Office, 1905; 1909; St. Clair Shores, MI: Scholarly Press, 1968). Charles E. Rice, *The Supreme Court and Public Prayer* (New York: Fordham University Press, 1964), pp. 167-168; "Hearings, Prayers in Public Schools and Other Matters," Committee on the Judiciary, U.S. Senate (87th Cong., 2nd Sess.), 1962, pp. 268 et seq. Miller, *The First Liberty - Religion and the American Republic*, p. 109. Gary DeMar, "God and the Constitution" (Atlanta, GA: *Biblical Worldview*, An American Vision Publication - American Vision, Inc., December 1993), p. 11.

[93] **Supreme Court of Arkansas.** *Shover v. The State*, 10 English, 263. David Josiah Brewer, U.S. Supreme Court Justice, *The United States - A Christian Nation* (Philadelphia: The John C. Winston Company, 1905, Supreme Court Collection). Catherine Millard, *The Rewriting of America's History* (Camp Hill, PA: Horizon House Publishers, 1991), pp. 387-393.

[94] **John Armstrong.** Statement. Alfred Nevin, *Centennial Biography, Men of Mark of the Cumberland Valley*, p. 78. Stephen Abbott Northrop, D.D., *A Cloud of Witnesses* (Portland, Oregon: American Heritage Ministries, 1987; Mantle Ministries, 228 Still Ridge, Bulverde, Texas), p. 17.

[95] **Chester Alan Arthur.** Statement. Joan Bumann and John Patterson, *Our American Presidents* (St. Petersburg, FL: Willowisp Press, 1993), p. 78.

[96] **Articles of Confederation.** November 15, 1777, proposed by the Continental Congress; signed July 9, 1778; ratified March 1, 1781. Charles W. Eliot, LL.D., ed., *American Historical Documents 1000-1904* (New York: P.F. Collier & Son Company, *The Harvard Classics*, 1910), Vol. 43, pp. 168-179. John Wilson Taylor, M.A., Ph.D., et al., *The Lincoln Library of Essential Information* (Buffalo, New York: The Frontier Press Company, 1935), pp. 1392-1394. "Our Christian Heritage," *Letter from Plymouth Rock* (Marlborough, NH: The Plymouth Rock Foundation), p. 3.

[97] **Articles of Confederation.** November 15, 1777, proposed by the Continental Congress; signed July 9, 1778; ratified March 1, 1781. Charles W. Eliot, LL.D., ed., *American Historical Documents 1000-1904* (New York: P.F. Collier & Son Company, *The Harvard Classics*, 1910), Vol. 43, pp. 168-179. John Wilson Taylor, M.A., Ph.D., et al., *The Lincoln Library of Essential Information* (Buffalo, New York: The Frontier Press Company, 1935), pp. 1392-1394. "Our Christian Heritage," *Letter from Plymouth Rock* (Marlborough, NH: The Plymouth Rock Foundation), p. 3. Michael R. Farris, Esq., *Constitutional Law* (Paeonian Springs, VA: Home School Legal Defense Association, 1991), pp. 20-29.

B

[1] **Johann Sebastian Bach.** In a cantata he composed entitled, *Jesus, Meine Freude*. Philip Spitta, *His Work and Influence in the Music of Germany*, Vol. III, pp. 601, 267. Stephen Abbott Northrop, D.D., *A Cloud of Witnesses* (Portland, OR: American Heritage Ministries, 1987; Mantle Ministries, 228 Still Ridge, Bulverde, Texas), p. 21.

[2] **Johann Sebastian Bach.** Statement regarding music. G. Schirmer Music Publishing Catalogue.

[3] **Sir Francis Bacon.** Statement. Henry M. Morris, *Men of Science-Men of God* (El Cajon, CA: Masters Books, A Division of Creation Life Publishers, Inc., 1990), pp. 13-15.

[4] **Sir Francis Bacon.** In his work entitled, *Essays: Of Goodness*. Tryon Edwards, D.D., *The New Dictionary of Thoughts - A Cyclopedia of Quotations* (Garden City, NY: Hanover House, 1852; revised and enlarged by C.H. Catrevas, Ralph Emerson Browns and Jonathan Edwards [descendent, along with Tryon, of Jonathan Edwards (1703-1758), president of Princeton], 1891; The

Notes

Standard Book Company, 1955, 1963), p. 91. Burton Stevenson, *The Home Book of Quotations - Classical & Modern* (New York: Dodd, Mead and Company, 1967), p. 265

[5] **Sir Francis Bacon.** 1605, in his work entitled, *The Advancement of Learning*, book II, chapter xx, p. 8. John Bartlett, *Bartlett's Familiar Quotations* (Boston: Little, Brown and Company, 1855, 1980), p. 179.

[6] **Sir Francis Bacon.** 1605, in his work entitled, *The Advancement of Learning*, book II, chapter. xxii, p. 14. John Bartlett, *Bartlett's Familiar Quotations* (Boston: Little, Brown and Company, 1855, 1980), p. 179.

[7] **Sir Francis Bacon.** In his work entitled, *Of Atheism*. John Bartlett, *Bartlett's Familiar Quotations* (Boston: Little, Brown and Company, 1855, 1980), p. 180.

[8] **Sir Francis Bacon.** *Literary and Religious Works of Francis Bacon*, Vol. II, pp. 152-154. Stephen Abbott Northrop, D.D., *A Cloud of Witnesses* (Portland, Oregon: American Heritage Ministries, 1987; Mantle Ministries, 228 Still Ridge, Bulverde, Texas), p. 22.

[9] **Sir Francis Bacon.** 1626, statement in his *Last Will and Testament*. John Bartlett, *Bartlett's Familiar Quotations* (Boston: Little, Brown and Company, 1855, 1980), p. 181.

[10] **Abraham Baldwin.** 1785, Charter of the College of Georgia. Charles C. Jones, *Biographical Sketches of the Delegates from Georgia* (Tustin, CA: American Biography Service), pp. 6-7. Tim LaHaye, *Faith of Our Founding Fathers* (Brentwood, TN: Wolgemuth & Hyatt, Publishers, Inc., 1987), pp. 146-147.

[11] **Stanley Baldwin.** Statement made during the period he served as British Prime Minister, 1923-1937. Tryon Edwards, D.D., *The New Dictionary of Thoughts - A Cyclopedia of Quotations* (Garden City, NY: Hanover House, 1852; revised and enlarged by C.H. Catrevas, Ralph Emerson Browns and Jonathan Edwards [descendent, along with Tryon, of Jonathan Edwards (1703-1758), president of Princeton], 1891; The Standard Book Company, 1955, 1963), p. 47.

[12] **Second Lord Baltimore Cecilius Calvert.** 1632. *Charter of Maryland*, issued by King Charles I. William McDonald, ed., *Documentary Source Book of American History 1606-1889* (NY: The Macmillan Company, 1909), p. 32. Henry Steele Commager, ed., *Documents of American History*, 2 vols. (NY: F.S. Crofts and Company, 1934; Appleton-Century-Crofts, Inc., 1948, 6th edition, 1958; Englewood Cliffs, NJ: Prentice Hall, Inc., 9th edition, 1973), p. 21. David Barton, *The Myth of Separation* (Aledo, TX: WallBuilder Press, 1991), p. 86.

[13] **Second Lord Baltimore Cecilius Calvert.** March 25, 1634, in Father White's account of founding the Colony of Maryland. Joseph Banvard, *Tragic Scenes in the History of Maryland and the Old French War* (Boston: Gould and Lincoln, 1856), p. 32. J. Moss Ives, *The Ark and the Dove* (NY: Cooper Square Publishers, Inc., 1936, 1969), p. 119. David Barton, *The Myth of Separation* (Aledo, TX: WallBuilder Press, 1991), p. 86.

[14] **Second Lord Baltimore Cecilius Calvert.** 1649, an oath prescribed in the Colony of Maryland, during Governor Stone's period. Stephen Abbott Northrop, D.D., *A Cloud of Witnesses* (Portland, OR: American Heritage Ministries, 1987; Mantle Ministries, 228 Still Ridge, Bulverde, Texas), p. 69.

[15] **Second Lord Baltimore Cecilius Calvert.** 1650, in a vote passed by the Maryland Assembly in eulogy of Leonard Calvert. Spark's *Library of American Biography*, Vol. XIX, pp. 178, 227. Stephen Abbott Northrop, D.D., *A Cloud of Witnesses* (Portland, Oregon: American Heritage Ministries, 1987; Mantle Ministries, 228 Still Ridge, Bulverde, Texas), p. 69.

[16] **George Bancroft.** 1834, in his work entitled, *History of the United States of America*, Vol. I, p. 318. Stephen Abbot Northrop, D.D., *A Cloud of Witnesses* (Portland, Oregon: American Heritage Ministries, 1987; Mantle Ministries, 228 Still Ridge, Bulverde, Texas), p. 24.

[17] **George Bancroft.** In an address entitled, "The Progress of Mankind." George Bancroft, *Literary and Historical Miscellanies*, pp. 502, 504. Stephen Abbott Northrop, D.D., *A Cloud of Witnesses* (Portland, Oregon: American Heritage Ministries, 1987; Mantle Ministries, 228 Still Ridge, Bulverde, Texas), pp. 24-25.

[18] **Phineas Taylor Barnum.** Statement. Stephen Abbott Northrop, D.D., *A Cloud of Witnesses* (Portland, Oregon: American Heritage Ministries, 1987; Mantle Ministries, 228 Still Ridge, Bulverde, Texas), p. 25.

[19] **Frederic Auguste Bartholdi.** Statement as sculptor of the Statue of Liberty. Frederic Auguste Bartholdi, *The Statue of Liberty Enlightening the World*. (New York: North American Review, Published for the benefit of the Pedestal Fund, 1885). Catherine Millard, *The Rewriting of America's History* (Camp Hill, PA: Horizon House Publishers, 1991), p. 329.

[20] **Bruce Barton.** Statement. Tryon Edwards, D.D., *The New Dictionary of Thoughts - A Cyclopedia of Quotations* (Garden City, NY: Hanover House, 1852; revised and enlarged by C.H. Catrevas, Ralph Emerson Browns and Jonathan Edwards [descendent, along with Tryon, of Jonathan Edwards (1703-1758), president of Princeton], 1891; The Standard Book Company, 1955, 1963), pp. 46-47.

[21] **Bruce Barton.** Statement. Tryon Edwards, D.D., *The New Dictionary of Thoughts - A Cyclopedia of Quotations* (Garden City, NY: Hanover House, 1852; revised and enlarged by C.H. Catrevas, Ralph Emerson Browns and Jonathan Edwards [descendent, along with Tryon, of Jonathan Edwards (1703-1758), president of Princeton], 1891; The Standard Book Company, 1955, 1963), p. 47.

[22] **Richard Bassett.** Tim LaHaye, *Faith of Our Founding Fathers* (Brentwood, TN: Wolgemuth & Hyatt, Publishers, Inc., 1987), p. 148.

[23] **Richard Bassett.** M.E. Bradford, *A Worthy Company* (Marlborough, NH: Plymouth Rock Foundation, 1982), p. 110-111. Tim LaHaye, *Faith of Our Founding Fathers* (Brentwood, TN: Wolgemuth & Hyatt, Publishers, Inc., 1987), p. 148. M.E. Bradford, *Religion & The Framers: The Biographical Evidence* (Marlborough, NH: The Plymouth Rock Foundation, 1991), p. 6.

[24] **Richard Bassett.** 1787, Major William Pierce of Georgia in his description of Richard Bassett at the Constitutional Convention. W. Cleon Skousen, *The Making of America* (Washington: The National Center for Constitutional Studies, 1985), p. xv. Tim LaHaye, *Faith of Our Founding Fathers* (Brentwood, TN: Wolgemuth & Hyatt, Publishers, Inc., 1987), p. 148.

[25] **Richard Bassett.** 1776, Constitution of the State of Delaware, Article XXII. *The Constitutions of the Several Independent States of America - Published by Order of Congress* (Boston: Norman & Bowen, 1785), pp. 99-100. *Church of the Holy Trinity v. U.S.* 143 US 457, 469-470 (1892). Frances Newton Thorpe, ed., *Federal and State Constitutions, Colonial Charters and Other Organic Laws of the States, Territories, and Colonies now or heretofore forming the United States*, 7 vols. (Washington: Government Printing Office, 1905; 1909; St. Clair Shores, MI: Scholarly Press, 1968), Vol. I, p. 142. M.E. Bradford, *A Worthy Company* (NH: Plymouth Rock Foundation, 1982), p. x. Tim LaHaye, *Faith of Our Founding Fathers* (Brentwood, TN: Wolgemuth & Hyatt, Publishers, Inc., 1987), pp. 180-181. Gary DeMar, "Censoring America's Christian History" (Atlanta, GA: *The Biblical Worldview*, An American Vision Publication - American Vision, Inc., July 1990), p. 7. "Our Christian Heritage," *Letter from Plymouth Rock* (Marlborough, NH: The Plymouth Rock Foundation), p. 3. David Barton, *The Myth of Separation* (Aledo, TX: WallBuilder Press, 1991), pp. 23, 33. Gary DeMar, *America's Christian History: The Untold Story* (Atlanta, GA: American Vision Publishers, Inc., 1993), pp. 67-68. David

Barton, *Keys to Good Government* (Aledo, TX: WallBuilder Press, 1994), p. 3.
[26] **Katherine Lee Bates.** 1892, verses in the song she composed entitled, *America the Beautiful.* Michael Drury, *Why She Wrote America's Favorite Song* (NY: *Woman's Day,* January 1978, reprinted: Pleasantville, NY: *Reader's Digest,* The Reader's Digest Association, Inc., July 1993). Robert Flood, *The Rebirth of America* (Philadelphia: Arthur S. DeMoss Foundation, 1986), p. 13. Tim LaHaye, *Faith of Our Founding Fathers* (Brentwood, TN: Wolgemuth & Hyatt, Publishers, Inc., 1987), p. 96.
[27] **Richard Baxter.** 1681, in his work entitled, *Poetical Fragments-Love Breathing Thanks and Praise.* John Bartlett, *Bartlett's Familiar Quotations* (Boston: Little, Brown and Company, 1855, 1980), p. 294.
[28] **Gunning Bedford.** Allen Johnson, ed., *Dictionary of American Biography* (New York: Charles Scribner's Sons, 1964), I:123. Tim LaHaye, *Faith of Our Founding Fathers* (Brentwood, TN: Wolgemuth & Hyatt, Publishers, Inc., 1987), p. 149.
[29] **Gunning Bedford.** Tim LaHaye, *Faith of Our Founding Fathers* (Brentwood, TN: Wolgemuth & Hyatt, Publishers, Inc., 1987), pp. 148-149.
[30] **Gunning Bedford.** 1776, Constitution of the State of Delaware, Article XXII. *The Constitutions of the Several Independent States of America - Published by Order of Congress* (Boston: Norman & Bowen, 1785), pp. 99-100. *Church of the Holy Trinity v. U.S.* 143 US 457, 469-470 (1892). Frances Newton Thorpe, ed., *Federal and State Constitutions, Colonial Charters, and Other Organic Laws of the States, Territories, and Colonies now or heretofore forming the United States* 7 vols. (Washington: Government Printing Office, 1905; 1909; St. Clair Shores, MI: Scholarly Press, 1968), Vol. I, p. 142. M.E. Bradford, *A Worthy Company* (NH: Plymouth Rock Foundation, 1982), p. x. Tim LaHaye, *Faith of Our Founding Fathers* (Brentwood, TN: Wolgemuth & Hyatt, Publishers, Inc., 1987), pp. 180-181. Gary DeMar, "Censoring America's Christian History" (Atlanta, GA: *The Biblical Worldview,* An American Vision Publication - American Vision, Inc., July 1990), p. 7. "Our Christian Heritage," *Letter from Plymouth Rock* (Marlborough, NH: The Plymouth Rock Foundation), p. 3. David Barton, *The Myth of Separation* (Aledo, TX: WallBuilder Press, 1991), pp. 23, 33. Gary DeMar, *America's Christian History: The Untold Story* (Atlanta, GA: American Vision Publishers, Inc., 1993), pp. 67-68. David Barton, *Keys to Good Government* (Aledo, TX: WallBuilder Press, 1994), p. 3.
[31] **Henry Ward Beecher.** Mark Galli, "The Gallery: Firebrands and Visionaries - Leading people in religion and politics during the Civil War era" (Carol Stream, IL: *Christian History,* Christianity Today, Inc., 1992), Issue 33, Vol. XI, No. 1, p. 18.
[32] **Henry Ward Beecher.** Tryon Edwards, D.D., *The New Dictionary of Thoughts - A Cyclopedia of Quotations* (Garden City, NY: Hanover House, 1852; revised and enlarged by C.H. Catrevas, Ralph Emerson Browns and Jonathan Edwards [descendent, along with Tryon, of Jonathan Edwards (1703-1758), president of Princeton], 1891; The Standard Book Company, 1955, 1963), p. 47.
[33] **Henry Ward Beecher.** Life Thoughts. Burton Stevenson, *The Home Book of Quotations* (New York: Dodd, Mead & Company, 1967), p. 264. Carroll E. Simcox, *3000 Quotations on Christian Themes* (Grand Rapids, Michigan: Baker Book House 1989), p. 164. Bob Cutshall, *More Light for the Day* (Minneapolis, MN: Northwest Products, Inc., 1991), 9.11.
[34] **Henry Ward Beecher.** Tryon Edwards, D.D., *The New Dictionary of Thoughts - A Cyclopedia of Quotations* (Garden City, NY: Hanover House, 1852; revised and enlarged by C.H. Catrevas, Ralph Emerson Browns and Jonathan Edwards [descendent, along with Tryon, of Jonathan Edwards (1703-1758), president of Princeton], 1891; The Standard Book Company, 1955, 1963), p. 89.
[35] **Henry Ward Beecher.** Tryon Edwards, D.D., *The New Dictionary of Thoughts - A Cyclopedia of Quotations* (Garden City, NY: Hanover House, 1852; revised and enlarged by C.H. Catrevas, Ralph Emerson Browns and Jonathan Edwards [descendent, along with Tryon, of Jonathan Edwards (1703-1758), president of Princeton], 1891; The Standard Book Company, 1955, 1963), p. 91.
[36] **Henry Ward Beecher.** Tryon Edwards, D.D., *The New Dictionary of Thoughts - A Cyclopedia of Quotations* (Garden City, NY: Hanover House, 1852; revised and enlarged by C.H. Catrevas, Ralph Emerson Browns and Jonathan Edwards [descendent, along with Tryon, of Jonathan Edwards (1703-1758), president of Princeton], 1891; The Standard Book Company, 1955, 1963), p. 91.
[37] **Henry Ward Beecher.** Bob Cutshall, *More Light for the Day* (Minneapolis, MN: Northwestern Products, Inc., 1991), 3.24.
[38] **Henry Ward Beecher.** Alfred Armand Montapert, *Distilled Wisdom* (Englewood Cliffs, NJ: Prentice Hall, 1965), p. 36.
[39] **Lyman Beecher.** 1831, in a newspaper article he wrote entitled, "The Spirit of the Pilgrims." Perry Miller, *The Life of the Mind in America from the Revolution to the Civil War-Books 1-3* (New York: Harcourt, Brace & World, 1966), p. 36. Peter Marshall and David Manuel, *The Glory of America* (Bloomington, MN: Garborg's Heart'N Home, Inc., 1991), 12.5.
[40] **Lyman Beecher.** In his Autobiography. Barbara M. Cross, ed., *The Autobiography of Lyman Beecher,* 2 vols. (Cambridge: Harvard University Press, Belknap Press, 1961), pp. 125-126. Peter Marshall and David Manuel, *From Sea to Shining Sea* (Old Tappan, NJ: Fleming H. Revell Company, 1986), pp. 10, 95, 102, 112-116, 119, 312-316, 371-372, 396. Peter Marshall and David Manuel, *The Glory of America* (Bloomington, MN: Garborg's Heart 'N Home, Inc., 1991), 1.3.
[41] **Lyman Beecher.** Statement reflecting on his life. Barbara M. Cross, *The Autobiography of Lyman Beecher,* 2 vols. (Cambridge: Harvard University Press, Belknap Press, 1961), Vol. I, p. 105. Peter Marshall and David Manuel, *From Sea to Shining Sea* (Old Tappan, NJ: Fleming H. Revell Company, 1986). Peter Marshall and David Manuel, *The Glory of America* (Bloomington, MN: Garborg's Heart 'N Home, Inc., 1991), 1.10.
[42] **Ludwig van Beethoven.** Statement recorded in the work *Franklin Square Song Collection.* Stephen Abbott Northrop, D.D., *A Cloud of Witnesses* (Portland, OR: American Heritage Ministries, 1987; Mantle Ministries, 228 Still Ridge, Bulverde, Texas), p. 29.
[43] **Ludwig van Beethoven.** Statement recorded by Nathan Haskell Dole, *A Score of Musical Composers.* Stephen Abbott Northrop, D.D., *A Cloud of Witnesses* (Portland, Oregon: American Heritage Ministries, 1987; Mantle Ministries, 228 Still Ridge, Bulverde, Texas), p. 29.
[44] **George Eugene Belknap.** Statement. Stephen Abbott Northrop, D.D., *A Cloud of Witnesses* (Portland, Oregon: American Heritage Ministries, 1987; Mantle Ministries, 228 Still Ridge, Bulverde, Texas), p. 59.
[45] **George Eugene Belknap.** Statement. Stephen Abbott Northrop, D.D., *A Cloud of Witnesses* (Portland, Oregon: American Heritage Ministries, 1987; Mantle Ministries, 228 Still Ridge, Bulverde, Texas), p. 59.
[46] **Charles Bell.** In his work entitled, *Bridgewater Treatise.* Henry M. Morris, *Men of Science - Men of God* (El Cajon, CA: Master Books, Creation Life Publishers, Inc., 1990), p. 40.
[47] **Francis Bellamy.** September 8, 1892, *Pledge of Allegiance.* John Bartlett, *Bartlett's Familiar Quotations* (Boston: Little, Brown and Company, 1855, 1980), p. 677. *The World Book Encyclopedia,* 18 vols. (Chicago, IL: Field Enterprises, Inc., 1957; W.F. Quarrie and Company, 8 vols., 1917; World Book, Inc., 22 vols., 1989), Vol. 13, p. 6419. Catherine Millard, *The Rewriting of America's History*

Notes

(Camp Hill, PA: Horizon House Publishers, 1991), pp. 273-274.

[48] **Francis Bellamy.** June 14, 1954, President Eisenhower signed House Joint Resolution 243 into law as Public Law 83-396, which added Abraham Lincoln's phrase from the *Gettysburg Address*, "under God," to the *Pledge of Allegiance* (Public Law 287); the *Pledge* was originally adopted by the 79th Congress on December 28, 1945, as Public Law 287. *The World Book Encyclopedia* 20 vols. (Chicago, IL: Field Enterprises Educational Corporation, 1970; W.F. Quarrie and Company, 8 vols., 1917), Vol. 15, p. 508. "Our Christian Heritage," *Letter from Plymouth Rock* (Marlborough, NH: The Plymouth Rock Foundation), p. 7. D.P. Diffine, Ph.D., *One Nation Under God - How Close a Separation?* (Searcy, Arkansas: Harding University, Belden Center for Private Enterprise Education, 6th edition, 1992), p. 17. Gary DeMar, *America's Christian History: The Untold Story* (Atlanta, GA: American Vision Publishers, Inc., 1993), p. 104.

[49] **Francis Bellamy.** June 14, 1954, in a speech by President Dwight David Eisenhower confirming the Act of Congress which added the phrase "Under God" to the *Pledge of Allegiance*. U.S. Marine Corps, *How to Respect and Display Our Flag* (Washington: U.S. Government Printing Office, 1977), p. 31.

[50] **Francis Bellamy.** June 14, 1954, President Eisenhower on the steps of the Capitol Building. *The Capitol* (Washington D.C.: United States Government Printing Office, 7th edition, 1979), pp. 24-25. Gary DeMar, *America's Christian History: The Untold Story* (Atlanta, GA: American Vision Publishers, Inc., 1993), p. 53.

[51] **George Bennard.** 1913, in the hymn he composed entitled, *The Old Rugged Cross*. John Bartlett, *Bartlett's Familiar Quotations* (Boston: Little, Brown and Company, 1855, 1980), p. 738.

[52] **Sir Risdon Bennett.** 1890, recorded in the *Report of the Christian Evidence Society*, pp. 41-42. Stephen Abbott Northrop, D.D., *A Cloud of Witnesses* (Portland, Oregon: American Heritage Ministries, 1987; Mantle Ministries, 228 Still Ridge, Bulverde, Texas), p. 30.

[53] **William W. Bennett.** 1877, in his work entitled, *A Narrative of the Great Revival Which Prevailed in the Southern Armies*. John Williams Jones, D.D., *Christ in the Camp* (Richmond, VA: B.F. Johnson & Co., 1887, 1897; The Martin & Hoyt Co., 1904; Harrisonburg, VA: Sprinkle Publications, 1986), p. 390. Gardiner H. Shattuck, Jr., "Revivals in the Camp - Reports of the Revival" (Carol Stream, IL: *Christian History*, Christianity Today, Inc., 1992), Vol. XI, No. 1, Issue 33, p. 29. Peter Marshall and David Manuel, *The Glory of America* (Bloomington, MN: Garborg's Heart'N Home, Inc., 1991), 1.15.

[54] **William W. Bennett.** 1877, in his work entitled, *A Narrative of the Great Revival Which Prevailed in the Southern Armies*. Gardiner H. Shattuck, Jr., "Revivals in the Camp - Reports of the Revival" (Carol Stream, IL: *Christian History*, Christianity Today, Inc., 1992), Vol. XI, No. 1, Issue 33, p. 29.

[55] **William W. Bennett.** 1877, in his work entitled, *A Narrative of the Great Revival Which Prevailed in the Southern Armies*. Gardiner H. Shattuck, Jr., "Revivals in the Camp - Reports of the Revival" (Carol Stream, IL: *Christian History*, Christianity Today, Inc., 1992), Vol. XI, No. 1, Issue 33, p. 29.

[56] **William W. Bennett.** 1862, report of a soldier to Chaplain William W. Bennett after the *Battle of Cross Keys*, regarding General Stonewall Jackson. William W. Bennett, *A Narrative of the Great Revival Which Prevailed in the Southern Armies*, p. 67. Peter Marshall and David Manuel, *The Glory of America* (Bloomington, MN: Garborg's Heart'N Home, Inc., 1991), 8.13.

[57] **William W. Bennett.** The last words of soldier T.S. Chandler of the 6th South Carolina Regiment. Chaplain William W. Bennett, *A Narrative of the Great Revival Which Prevailed in the Southern Armies*, p. 243. Peter Marshall and David Manuel, *The Glory of America* (Bloomington, MN: Garborg's Heart'N Home, Inc., 1991), 9.29.

[58] **William W. Bennett.** Spring 1865, in a Resolution of five Georgia Brigades of the Confederate Army. William W. Bennett, *A Narrative of the Great Revival Which Prevailed in the Southern Armies*, p. 420. Peter Marshall and David Manuel, *The Glory of America* (Bloomington, MN: Garborg's Heart'N Home, Inc., 1991), 3.21.

[59] **Arthur Christopher Benson.** 1902, in his work entitled, *Land of Hope and Glory*. John Bartlett, *Bartlett's Familiar Quotations* (Boston: Little, Brown and Company, 1855, 1980), p. 699.

[60] **Irving Berlin.** 1938, in the patriotic hymn he composed entitled, *God Bless America*. John Bartlett, *Bartlett's Familiar Quotations* (Boston: Little, Brown and Company, 1855, 1980), p. 802. Tim LaHaye, *Faith of Our Founding Fathers* (Brentwood, TN: Wolgemuth & Hyatt, Inc., 1987), p. 96. (ed. note: The song may actually have been written about 20 years earlier, but Berlin felt it was not the right time for it's release. - from Larry King Live, taped 12-27-94).

[61] *Holy Bible.* 1760-1805. Donald S. Lutz and Charles S. Hyneman, "The Relative Influence of European Writers on Late Eighteenth-Century American Political Thought," *American Political Science Review* 189 (1984): 189-197. (Courtesy of Dr. Wayne House of Dallas Theological Seminary.) John Eidsmoe, *Christianity and the Constitution - The Faith of Our Founding Fathers* (Grand Rapids, MI: Baker Book House, A Mott Media Book, 1987; 6th printing, 1993), pp. 51-53. *Origins of American Constitutionalism*, (1987). Stephen K. McDowell and Mark A. Beliles, *America's Providential History* (Charlottesville, VA: Providence Press, 1988), p. 156. David Barton, *The Myth of Separation* (Aledo, TX: WallBuilder Press, 1991), pp. 195, 201.

[62] **Jean Baptiste LeMoyne Sieur de Bienville.** 1768, statement in his *Last Will and Testament*. Grace King, *Makers of America Series-Jean Baptiste Le Moyne, Sieur de Bienville*, p. 325. Stephen Abbott Northrop, D.D., *A Cloud of Witnesses* (Portland, Oregon: American Heritage Ministries, 1987; Mantle Ministries, 228 Still Ridge, Bulverde, Texas), p. 32.

[63] **John Armor Bingham.** Statement. Stephen Abbott Northrop, D.D., *A Cloud of Witnesses* (Portland, Oregon: American Heritage Ministries, 1987; Mantle Ministries, 228 Still Ridge, Bulverde, Texas), p. 20. Peter Marshall and David Manuel, *The Glory of America* (Bloomington, MN: Garborg's Heart 'N Home, Inc., 1991), 1.7.

[64] **Otto Eduard Leopold von Bismarck.** Statement. Charles Lowe, *Prince Bismarck: An Historical Biography*, Vol. II, pp. 351, 353. Stephen Abbott Northrop, D.D., *A Cloud of Witnesses* (Portland, Oregon: American Heritage Ministries, 1987; Mantle Ministries, 228 Still Ridge, Bulverde, Texas), p. 32.

[65] **Otto Eduard Leopold von Bismarck.** February 6, 1888, in a speech to the Reichstag. John Bartlett, *Bartlett's Familiar Quotations* (Boston: Little, Brown and Company, 1855, 1980), p. 553.

[66] **Otto Eduard Leopold von Bismarck.** 1871, James A. Garfield's description of the Chancellor of the newly united German Empire. S.P. Linn, *Golden Gleams of Thought*, p. 154. Stephen Abbott Northrop, D.D., *A Cloud of Witnesses* (Portland, Oregon: American Heritage Ministries, 1987; Mantle Ministries, 228 Still Ridge, Bulverde, Texas), p. 164.

[67] **Hugo La Fayette Black.** 1962, in court a decision. Tim LaHaye, *Faith of Our Founding Fathers* (Brentwood, TN: Wolgemuth & Hyatt, Publishers, Inc., 1987), p. 73.

[68] **Jeremiah Sullivan Black.** August 1881, in an article he authored entitled, "The Claims of the Christian Religion," *North American Review* (August, 1881). Stephen Abbott Northrop, D.D., *A Cloud of Witnesses* (Portland, Oregon: American Heritage Ministries, 1987; Mantle Ministries, 228 Still Ridge, Bulverde, Texas), p. 31.

[69] **Sir William Blackstone.** 1826-1830, as cited in a work written by Chancellor James Kent of New York entitled, *Commentaries on American Law*, (1826-1830). Robert K. Dorman and Csaba Vedlik, Jr., *Judicial Supremacy: The Supreme Court of Trial* (Massachusetts: Plymouth Rock Foundation, 1986), p. 10. David Barton, *The Myth of Separation* (Aledo, TX: WallBuilder Press, 1991), p. 197.

[70] **Sir William Blackstone.** 1760-1805, being the second most frequently quoted author by the framers of the Constitution; cited by Donald S. Lutz and Charles S. Hyneman, "The Relative Influence of European Writers on Late Eighteenth-Century American Political Thought," *American Political Science Review* 189 (1984): 189-197. (Courtesy of Dr. Wayne House of Dallas Theological Seminary.) John Eidsmoe, *Christianity and the Constitution - The Faith of Our Founding Fathers* (Grand Rapids, MI: Baker Book House, A Mott Media Book, 1987; 6th printing, 1993), pp. 51-53. *Origins of American Constitutionalism*, (1987). Stephen K. McDowell and Mark A. Beliles, *America's Providential History* (Charlottesville, VA: Providence Press, 1988), p. 156. David Barton, *The Myth of Separation* (Aledo, TX: WallBuilder Press, 1991), pp. 195, 201.

[71] **Sir William Blackstone.** 1821, Thomas Jefferson approval of Sir William Blackstone's work entitled, *Commentaries on the Laws of England*, (1765-1770). Verna M. Hall, *The Christian History of the Constitution of the United States of America* (San Francisco: Foundation for American Christian Education, 1962, 1979), pp. 140-146. John Eidsmoe, *Christianity and the Constitution - The Faith of Our Founding Fathers* (Grand Rapids, MI: Baker Book House, A Mott Media Book, 1987; 6th printing, 1993), pp. 57-58. David Barton, *The Myth of Separation* (Aledo, TX: WallBuilder Press, 1991), p. 197.

[72] **Sir William Blackstone.** 1765-1770, in his work entitled, *Commentaries on the Laws of England*, Robert Bell, ed., (Philadelphia: Union Library, 1771), p. 39. William Blackstone, *Commentaries on the Laws of England*, Tucker, ed., (1803), p. 39. Sir William Blackstone, *Commentaries on the Laws of England* (Philadelphia: J.B. Lippincott and Co., 1879), Vol. I, p. 39. Verna M. Hall, *Christian History of the Constitution of the United States of America* (San Francisco: Foundation for American Christian Education, 1962, 1979), pp. 140-146. John Whitehead, *The Second American Revolution* (Elgin, IL: David C. Cook; Wheaton, Illinois: Crossway Books, 1982), pp. 30-32. Pat Robertson, *America's Dates with Destiny* (Nashville: Thomas Nelson Publishers, 1986), p. 66. Tim LaHaye, *Faith of Our Founding Fathers* (Brentwood, TN: Wolgemuth & Hyatt, Publishers, Inc., 1987) pp. 86-87. John Eidsmoe, *Christianity and the Constitution - The Faith of Our Founding Fathers* (Grand Rapids, MI: Baker Book House, A Mott Media Book, 1987; 6th printing, 1993), pp. 57-58. David Barton, *The Myth of Separation* (Aledo, TX: WallBuilder Press, 1991, 1992), p. 197.

[73] **Sir William Blackstone.** 1765-1770, in his work entitled, *Commentaries on the Law of England* (Oxford: Clarendon Press, 1769). Sir William Blackstone, *Commentaries on the Laws of England* (Philadelphia: J.B. Lippincott and Co., 1879), Vol. I, pp. 39, 41, 42. Verna M. Hall, *The Christian History of the Constitution of the United States of America - Christian Self-Government with Union* (San Francisco: Foundation for American Christian Education, 1962, 1976, 1979), pp. 140-146. John Eidsmoe, *Christianity and the Constitution - The Faith of Our Founding Fathers* (Grand Rapids, MI: Baker Book House, A Mott Media Book, 1987; 6th printing, 1993), pp. 57-58. David Barton, *The Myth of Separation* (Aledo, TX: WallBuilder Press, 1991), p. 197. David Barton, *The WallBuilder Report* (Aledo, TX: WallBuilder Press, Winter 1993), p. 2.

[74] **Sir William Blackstone.** 1765-1770, in his work entitled, *Commentaries on the Laws of England* (Oxford: Clarendon Press, 1769). Sir William Blackstone, *Commentaries on the Laws of England* (Philadelphia: J.B. Lippincott and Co., 1879), Vol. I, pp. 39, 41, 42. Verna M. Hall, *The Christian History of the Constitution of the United States of America - Christian Self-Government with Union* (San Francisco: Foundation for American Christian Education, 1962, 1976, 1979), pp. 140-146. John Whitehead, *The Second American Revolution* (Elgin, IL: David C. Cook, 1982), pp. 30-32. Tim LaHaye, *Faith of Our Founding Fathers* (Brentwood, TN: Wolgemuth & Hyatt, Publishers, Inc., 1987) pp. 86-87. John Eidsmoe, *Christianity and the Constitution - The Faith of Our Founding Fathers* (Grand Rapids, MI: Baker Book House, A Mott Media Book, 1987; 6th printing, 1993), pp. 57-58. David Barton, *The Myth of Separation* (Aledo, TX: WallBuilder Press, 1991), p. 197. David Barton, *The WallBuilder Report* (Aledo, TX: WallBuilder Press, Winter 1993), p. 2.

[75] **Sir William Blackstone.** 1765-1770, in his work entitled, *Commentaries on the Laws of England* (Philadelphia: J.B. Lippincott and Co., 1879), Vol. II, p. 59; as cited in the case *Updegraph v. The Commonwealth*, 11 Ser. & R. 396 (1824). David Barton, *The Myth of Separation* (Aledo, TX: WallBuilder Press, 1991), p. 52.

[76] **Sir William Blackstone.** 1765-1770, in his work entitled *Commentaries on the Laws of England*. Robert K. Dorman and Csaba Vedlik, Jr., *Judicial Supremacy: The Supreme Court of Trial* (MA: Plymouth Rock Foundation, 1986), p. 10. David Barton, *The Myth of Separation* (Aledo, TX: WallBuilder Press, 1991), p. 223.

[77] **Sir William Blackstone.** 1765-1770, in his work entitled *Commentaries on the Laws of England*. Wendell's *Blackstone's Commentaries*, Vol. IV, p. 59. Stephen Abbott Northrop, D.D., *A Cloud of Witnesses* (Portland, Oregon: American Heritage Ministries, 1987; Mantle Ministries, 228 Still Ridge, Bulverde, Texas), p. 33.

[78] **Sir William Blackstone.** 1765-1770, in his work entitled, *Commentaries on the Laws of England*. Wendell's *Blackstone's Commentaries*, Vol. IV, p. 43. Stephen Abbott Northrop, D.D., *A Cloud of Witnesses* (Portland, Oregon: American Heritage Ministries, 1987; Mantle Ministries, 228 Still Ridge, Bulverde, Texas), p. 33.

[79] **James Gillespie Blaine.** In the work by Hon. James G. Blaine, J.W. Buel, Prof. John Ridpath, and Hon. Benjamin Butterworth, *Columbus and Columbia: a Pictorial History of the Man and the Nation*. Stephen Abbott Northrop, D.D., *A Cloud of Witnesses* (Portland, Oregon: American Heritage Ministries, 1987; Mantle Ministries, 228 Still Ridge, Bulverde, Texas), p. 34.

[80] **John Blair.** In a letter to his sister at the time of her husband's death. Frederick Horner, *History of the Blair, Banister and Braxton Families* (Philadelphia: J.B. Lippincott Co., 1898), pp. 68-69. Tim LaHaye, *Faith of Our Founding Fathers* (Brentwood, TN: Wolgemuth & Hyatt, Publishers, Inc., 1987), pp. 149-151.

[81] **Edward William Bok.** September 1894, as editor, in an article he wrote for *The Ladies' Home Journal*. Stephen Abbott Northrop, D.D., *A Cloud of Witnesses* (Portland, Oregon: American Heritage Ministries, 1987; Mantle Ministries, 228 Still Ridge, Bulverde, Texas), p. 20.

[82] **Frank Borman.** December 24, 1968, in a television up-linked message broadcast from the Apollo VIII spacecraft, as it circled the moon. Peter Marshall and David Manuel, *The Glory of America* (Bloomington, MN: Garborg's Heart'N Home, Inc., 1991), 12.24. D.P. Diffine, Ph.D., *One Nation Under God - How Close a Separation?* (Searcy, Arkansas: Harding University, Belden Center for Private Enterprise Education, 6th edition, 1992), p. 17.

[83] **Boston, Massachusetts.** 1765, in a sermon by Congregational Minister Jonathan Mayhew at West Church, Boston, following the issuance of King George III's Stamp Act. Clinton Rossiter, *Seedtime of the Republic* (New York: Harcourt, Brace & World, Inc., 1953), p. 241. Peter Marshall and David Manuel, *The Glory of America* (Bloomington, MN: Garborg's Heart'N Home, Inc., 1991), 2.18.

[84] **Boston Gazette.** September 1768, in an article. George Bancroft, *Bancroft's History of the United States*, 10 vols. (Boston: Charles

Notes

C. Little & James Brown, Third Edition, 1838), Vol. VI, p. 195. Peter Marshall and David Manuel, *The Glory of America* (Bloomington, MN: Garborg's Heart'N Home, Inc., 1991), 9.12.

[85] **Boston Tea Party.** 1773, in a unanimous declaration by the men of Marlborough, Massachusetts. Charles E. Kistler, *This Nation Under God* (Boston: Richard G. Badger, The Gorham Press, 1924), p. 56. Peter Marshall and David Manuel, *The Glory of America* (Bloomington, MN: Garborg's Heart 'N Home, Inc., 1991), 1.2.

[86] **Boston Tea Party.** June 1, 1774, in a Day of Fasting and Prayer issued by the Colonies, following the Committee of Correspondence report of the passage of the Boston Port Bill. Verna M. Hall and Rosalie J. Slater, *The Bible and the Constitution of the United States of America* (San Francisco: Foundation for American Christian Education, 1983), p. 31. David Barton, *The Myth of Separation* (Aledo, TX: WallBuilder Press, 1991), pp. 95-96.

[87] **Boston Tea Party.** August 1774, William Prescott's statement to the inhabitants of Boston while delivering supplies from Pepperell, Massachusetts. George Bancroft, *History of the United States of America*, 6 vols. (Boston: Charles C. Little and James Brown, 1838; 1859, Third Edition), Vol. VII, p. 99. Lucille Johnston, *Celebrations of a Nation* (Arlington, VA: The Year of Thanksgiving Foundation, 1987), p. 76. Peter Marshall, & David Manuel, *The Glory of America* (Bloomington, MN: Garborg's Heart 'N Home, 1991), 7.27. David Barton, *The Myth of Separation* (Aledo, TX: WallBuilder Press, 1992), p. 96.

[88] **Boston Tea Party.** 1774, the respondence of the inhabitants of Boston, Massachusetts, to the support given by the other Colonies. Verna M. Hall and Rosalie J. Slater, *The Bible and the Constitution of the United States of America* (San Francisco: Foundation for American Christian Education, 1983), p. 31. David Barton, *The Myth of Separation* (Aledo, TX: WallBuilder Press, 1991), p. 96.

[89] **Boston Tea Party.** 1774, Josiah Quincy speaking in response to the *Boston Port Bill*, in which the British closed the Boston harbor. John Bartlett, *Bartlett's Familiar Quotations* (Boston: Little, Brown and Company, 1855, 1980), p. 393. Peter Marshall and David Manuel, *The Glory of America* (Bloomington, MN: Garborg's Heart'N Home, 1991), 2.10.

[90] **Boston Tea Party.** 1774, report of the Crown-appointed Governor of Boston, Massachusetts, sent to the Board of Trade in England. Hezekiah Niles, *Principles and Acts of the Revolution in America* (Baltimore: William Ogden Niles, 1822), p. 418. David Barton, *The Myth of Separation* (Aledo, TX: WallBuilder Press, 1991), p. 96.

[91] **Boston Tea Party.** 1774, colonial motto issued through the Committees of Correspondence from Boston, Massachusetts. Peter Powers' Election Sermon entitled *Jesus Christ the King* (Newburyport, 1778). Clifford K. Shipton, *Sibley's Harvard Graduates* (Boston: Massachusetts Historical Society, 1965), Vol. XIII, pp. 475-476. Cushing Strout, *The New Heavens and the New Earth* (NY: Harper & Row, 1974), p. 59. David Barton, *The Myth of Separation* (Aledo, TX: WallBuilder Press, 1991), p. 97.

[92] **Boston Tea Party.** September 5, 1774, *Day of Fasting and Prayer.* Verna M. Hall and Rosalie J. Slater, *The Bible and the Constitution of the United States of America* (San Francisco: Foundation for American Christian Education, 1983), p. 31. David Barton, *The Myth of Separation* (Aledo, TX: WallBuilder Press, 1991), pp. 95-96.

[93] **Boston Tea Party.** October 22, 1774, a Proclamation of the Provincial Congress of Massachusetts, signed by President John Hancock. George Bancroft, *Bancroft's History of the United States*, 10 vols. (Boston: Charles C. Little & James Brown, 1838), Vol. VII, p. 229. Peter Marshall and David Manuel, *The Light and the Glory* (Old Tappan, NJ: Fleming H. Revell, 1977), p. 269. D.P. Diffine, Ph.D., *One Nation Under God - How Close a Separation?* (Searcy, Arkansas: Harding University, Belden Center for Private Enterprise Education, 6th edition, 1992), pp. 5-6.

[94] **Boston Tea Party.** 1774, in a Resolution issued by the Provincial Congress of Massachusetts to the inhabitants of Massachusetts Bay. George Bancroft, *Bancroft's History of the United States*, 10 vols. (Boston: Charles C. Little & James Brown, 1838), Vol. VII, p. 229. Peter Marshall and David Manuel, *The Light and the Glory* (Old Tappan, NJ: Fleming H. Revell, 1977), p. 269. Peter Marshall and David Manuel, *The Glory of America* (Bloomington, MN: Garborg's Heart'N Home, Inc., 1991), 8.31.

[95] **Boston Tea Party.** 1774, Minutemen of the Massachusetts Militia, organized by order of the Provincial Congress of Massachusetts. Richard Frothingham, *Rise of the Republic of the United States* (Boston: Little Brown & Co., 1872), pp. 393, 458. David Barton, *The Myth of Separation* (Aledo, TX: WallBuilder Press, 1991), p. 94.

[96] **Boston Tea Party.** The Provincial Congress of Massachusetts 1774, Charge to the Minutemen of the Massachusetts Militia by the Provincial Congress of Massachusetts. Richard Frothingham, *Rise of the Republic of the United States* (Boston: Little, Brown & Co., 1872), p. 393. David Barton, *The Myth of Separation* (Aledo, TX: WallBuilder Press, 1991), pp. 94-95.

[97] **Elias Boudinot.** Statement made as President of Continental Congress and President of the American Bible Society. George Adam Boyd, *Elias Boudinot: Patriot and Statesman 1740-1821* (Princeton: Princeton University Press, 1952). Verna M. Hall, *The Christian History of the American Revolution* (San Francisco: Foundation for American Christian Education, 1976), p. xxv. M.E. Bradford, *Religion & The Framers: The Biographical Evidence* (Marlborough, NH: Plymouth Rock Foundation, 1991), p. 6. Peter Marshall and David Manuel, *The Glory of America* (Bloomington, MN: Garborg's Heart'N Home, Inc., 1991), 5.2. In *An Oration, Delivered at Elizabeth-town, New Jersey...on the Fourth of July*, pp. 14-15, (David Barton, *Keys to Good Government* (Aledo, TX: WallBuilder Press, 1994), p. 16), July 4, 1793, Elias Boudinot spoke at a Fourth of July celebration in Elizabethtown, New Jersey:
"If the moral character of a people once degenerate, their political character must soon follow....These considerations should lead to an attractive solicitude...to be religiously careful in our choice of all public officers...and judge of the tree by its fruits."

[98] **Professor Louis Bounoure.** March 8, Thursday, 1984, as quoted in *The Advocate. The Revised Quotebook* (Sunnybank, Brisbane, Australia: Creation Science Foundation Ltd., 1990), p. 5.

[99] **Robert Boyle.** Statement. *Allibone's Quotations*, p. 104. Stephen Abbott Northrop, D.D., *A Cloud of Witnesses* (Portland, OR: American Heritage Ministries, 1987; Mantle Ministries, 228 Still Ridge, Bulverde, Texas), p. 43.

[100] **Robert Boyle.** In his work entitled, *Some Considerations Touching the Style of the Holy Scriptures.* Stephen Abbott Northrop, D.D., *A Cloud of Witnesses* (Portland, Oregon: American Heritage Ministries, 1987; Mantle Ministries, 228 Still Ridge, Bulverde, Texas), p. 43-44.

[101] **William Bradford.** 1650, in his famous work entitled, *The History of Plymouth Plantation 1608-1650* (Boston, Massachusetts: Massachusetts Historical Society, 1856; Boston, Massachusetts: Wright and Potter Printing Company, 1898, 1901, from the Original Manuscript, Library of Congress Rare Book Collection, Washington, D.C.; rendered in Modern English, Harold Paget, 1909; NY: Russell and Russell, 1968; NY: Random House, Inc., Modern Library College edition, 1981; San Antonio, TX: American Heritage Classics, Mantle Ministries, 228 Still Ridge, Bulverde, Texas, 1988). Catherine Millard, *The Rewriting of America's History* (Camp Hill, PA: Horizon House Publishers, 1991), p. 14.

[102] **William Bradford.** 1607, in his work entitled, *The History of Plymouth Plantation 1608-1650* (Boston, Massachusetts: Massachusetts Historical Society, 1856; Boston, Massachusetts: Wright and Potter Printing Company, 1898, 1901, from the

Original Manuscript, Library of Congress Rare Book Collection, Washington, D.C.; rendered in Modern English, Harold Paget, 1909; NY: Russell and Russell, 1968; NY: Random House, Inc., Modern Library College edition, 1981; San Antonio, TX: American Heritage Classics, Mantle Ministries, 228 Still Ridge, Bulverde, Texas, 1988). Verna M. Hall, comp., *Christian History of the Constitution of the United States of America* (San Francisco: Foundation for American Christian Education, 1976), p. 186. Marshall Foster and Mary-Elaine Swanson, *The American Covenant - The Untold Story* (Roseburg, OR: Foundation for Christian Self-Government, 1981; Thousand Oaks, CA: The Mayflower Institute, 1983, 1992), p. 32. Catherine Millard, *The Rewriting of America's History* (Camp Hill, PA: Horizon House Publishers, 1991), p. 16. Catherine Millard, *A Children's Companion Guide to America's History* (Camp Hill, PA: Horizon House Publishers, 1993), p. 21.

[103] **William Bradford.** 1650, in his work entitled, *The History of Plymouth Plantation 1608-1650* (Boston, Massachusetts: Massachusetts Historical Society, 1856; Boston, Massachusetts: Wright and Potter Printing Company, 1898, 1901, from the Original Manuscript, Library of Congress Rare Book Collection, Washington, D.C.; rendered in Modern English, Harold Paget, 1909; NY: Russell and Russell, 1968; NY: Random House, Inc., Modern Library College edition, 1981; San Antonio, TX: American Heritage Classics, Mantle Ministries, 228 Still Ridge, Bulverde, Texas, 1988). Verna M. Hall, comp., *Christian History of the Constitution of the United States of America* (San Francisco: Foundation for American Christian Education, 1976), p. 185. Marshall Foster and Mary-Elaine Swanson, *The American Covenant - The Untold Story* (Roseburg, OR: Foundation for Christian Self-Government, 1981; Thousand Oaks, CA: The Mayflower Institute, 1983, 1992), p. 62.

[104] **William Bradford.** 1618, Church of Leyden Articles sent to the Counsel of England. Henry Steele Commager, ed., *Documents of American History*, 2 vols. (NY: F.S. Crofts and Company, 1934; Appleton-Century-Crofts, Inc., 1948, 6th edition, 1958; Englewood Cliffs, NJ: Prentice Hall, Inc., 9th edition, 1973), pp. 14-15. Catherine Millard, *The Rewriting of America's History* (Camp Hill, PA: Horizon House Publishers, 1991), pp. 17-18. Catherine Millard, *A Children's Companion Guide to America's History* (Camp Hill, PA: Horizon House Publishers, 1993), p. 17.

[105] **William Bradford.** December 15, 1617, in a letter from John Robinson and William Brewster in Leyden, Holland, to Sir Edwin Sandys in London, England. William Bradford (Governor of Plymouth Colony), *The History of Plymouth Plantation 1608-1650* (Boston, Massachusetts: Massachusetts Historical Society, 1856; Boston, Massachusetts: Wright and Potter Printing Company, 1898, from the original manuscript; rendered in Modern English, Harold Paget, 1909; NY: Russell and Russell, 1968; San Antonio, TX: American Heritage Classics, Mantle Ministries, 228 Still Ridge, Bulverde, Texas, 1988), p.28. Sacvan Bercovitch, ed., *Typology and Early American Literature* (Cambridge: University of Massachusetts Press, 1972), p. 104. Peter Marshall and David Manuel, *The Glory of America* (Bloomington, MN: Garborg's Heart'N Home, Inc., 1991), 11.16.

[106] **William Bradford.** July 1620, in a day of solemn humiliation prior to the Pilgrims' departure from Leyden, Holland. William Bradford (Governor of Plymouth Colony), *The History of Plymouth Plantation 1608-1650* (Boston, Massachusetts: Massachusetts Historical Society, 1856; Boston, Massachusetts: Wright and Potter Printing Company, 1898, from the original manuscript; rendered in Modern English, Harold Paget, 1909; NY: Russell and Russell, 1968; San Antonio, TX: American Heritage Classics, Mantle Ministries, 228 Still Ridge, Bulverde, Texas, 1988), pp. 49-50.

[107] **William Bradford.** November 12, 1620, in recounting the Pilgrims' first full day in Cape Cod, Massachusetts, in his work entitled, *The History of Plymouth Plantation 1608-1650* (Boston, Massachusetts: Massachusetts Historical Society, 1856; Boston, Massachusetts: Wright and Potter Printing Company, 1898, 1901, from the Original Manuscript, Library of Congress Rare Book Collection, Washington, D.C.; rendered in Modern English, Harold Paget, 1909; NY: Russell and Russell, 1968; NY: Random House, Inc., Modern Library College edition, 1981; San Antonio, TX: American Heritage Classics, Mantle Ministries, 228 Still Ridge, Bulverde, Texas, 1988), ch. 9, p. 64. John Bartlett, *Bartlett's Familiar Quotations* (Boston: Little, Brown and Company, 1855, 1980), p. 265.

[108] **William Bradford.** November 11, 1620, in the *Mayflower Compact*. William Bradford (Governor of Plymouth Colony), *The History of Plymouth Plantation 1608-1650* (Boston, Massachusetts: Massachusetts Historical Society, 1856; Boston, Massachusetts: Wright and Potter Printing Company, 1898, 1901, from the Original Manuscript, Library of Congress Rare Book Collection, Washington, D.C.; rendered in Modern English, Harold Paget, 1909; NY: Russell and Russell, 1968; NY: Random House, Inc., Modern Library College edition, 1981; San Antonio, TX: American Heritage Classics, Mantle Ministries, 228 Still Ridge, Bulverde, Texas, 1988), pp. 75-76. Marshall Foster and Mary-Elaine Swanson, *The American Covenant - The Untold Story* (Roseburg, OR: Foundation for Christian Self-Government, 1981; Thousand Oaks, CA: The Mayflower Institute, 1983, 1992), p. vii. D.P. Diffine, Ph.D., *One Nation Under God - How Close a Separation?* (Searcy, Arkansas: Harding University, Belden Center for Private Enterprise Education, 6th edition, 1992), p. 3.

[109] **William Bradford.** March 16, 1621. William Bradford (Governor of Plymouth Colony), *The History of Plymouth Plantation 1608-1650* (Boston, Massachusetts: Massachusetts Historical Society, 1856; Boston, Massachusetts: Wright and Potter Printing Company, 1898, 1901, from the Original Manuscript, Library of Congress Rare Book Collection, Washington, D.C.; rendered in Modern English, Harold Paget, 1909; NY: Russell and Russell, 1968; NY: Random House, Inc., Modern Library College edition, 1981; San Antonio, TX: American Heritage Classics, Mantle Ministries, 228 Still Ridge, Bulverde, Texas, 1988), pp. 79-80. *The Annals of America*, 20 vols. (Chicago, IL: Encyclopedia Britannica, 1968), Vol. 1, p. 66. Marshall Foster and Mary-Elaine Swanson, *The American Covenant - The Untold Story* (Roseburg, OR: Foundation for Christian Self-Government, 1981; Thousand Oaks, CA: The Mayflower Institute, 1983, 1992), p. 28.

[110] **William Bradford.** November 29, 1623, in an official Thanksgiving Proclamation. William Bradford (Governor of Plymouth Colony), *The History of Plymouth Plantation 1608-1650* (Boston, Massachusetts: Massachusetts Historical Society, 1856; Boston, Massachusetts: Wright and Potter Printing Company, 1898, 1901, from the Original Manuscript, Library of Congress Rare Book Collection, Washington, D.C.; rendered in Modern English, Harold Paget, 1909; NY: Russell and Russell, 1968; NY: Random House, Inc., Modern Library College edition, 1981; San Antonio, TX: American Heritage Classics, Mantle Ministries, 228 Still Ridge, Bulverde, Texas, 1988). Herbert V. Prochnow, *5100 Quotations for Speakers and Writers* (Grand Rapids, MI: Baker Book House, 1992), p. 529.

[111] **William Bradford.** 1650, in his work entitled, *The History of Plymouth Plantation 1608-1650* (Boston, Massachusetts: Massachusetts Historical Society, 1856; Boston, Massachusetts: Wright and Potter Printing Company, 1898, 1901, from the Original Manuscript, Library of Congress Rare Book Collection, Washington, D.C.; rendered in Modern English, Harold Paget, 1909; NY: Russell and Russell, 1968; NY: Random House, Inc., Modern Library College edition, 1981; San Antonio, TX: American Heritage Classics, Mantle Ministries, 228 Still Ridge, Bulverde, Texas, 1988), p. 21. David Barton, *The Myth of Separation* (Aledo, TX: WallBuilder Press, 1991), p. 86.

[112] **William Bradford.** 1650, in his work entitled, *The History of Plymouth Plantation 1608-1650* (Boston, Massachusetts:

Massachusetts Historical Society, 1856; Boston, Massachusetts: Wright and Potter Printing Company, 1898, 1901, from the Original Manuscript, Library of Congress Rare Book Collection, Washington, D.C.; rendered in Modern English, Harold Paget, 1909; NY: Russell and Russell, 1968; NY: Random House, Inc., Modem Library College edition, 1981; San Antonio, TX: American Heritage Classics, Mantle Ministries, 228 Still Ridge, Bulverde, Texas, 1988), p. 21. Jordan D. Fiore, ed., *Mourt's Relation: A Journal of the Pilgrims of Plymouth* (Plymouth, MA: Plymouth Rock Foundation, 1841, 1865, 1985), pp. 10-11. William T. Davis, ed., *History of Plymouth Plantation* (NY: Charles Scribner's Sons, 1908), p. 46. *The Annals of America*, 20 vols. (Chicago, IL: Encyclopedia Britannica, 1968), Vol. 1, p. 66. Verna M. Hall, comp., *Christian History of the Constitution of the United States of America* (San Francisco: Foundation for American Christian Education, 1976), p. 193.

[113] **William Bradford**. 1650, in his work entitled, The *History of Plymouth Plantation 1608-1650* (Boston, Massachusetts: Massachusetts Historical Society, 1856; Boston, Massachusetts: Wright and Potter Printing Company, 1898, 1901, from the Original Manuscript, Library of Congress Rare Book Collection, Washington, D.C.; rendered in Modern English, Harold Paget, 1909; NY: Russell and Russell, 1968; NY: Random House, Inc., Modern Library College edition, 1981; San Antonio, TX: American Heritage Classics, Mantle Ministries, 228 Still Ridge, Bulverde, Texas, 1988), p. 236. John Bartlett, *Bartlett's Familiar Quotations* (Boston: Little, Brown and Company, 1855, 1980), p. 265. Fleming, *One Small Candle. The Pilgrim's First Year in America*, p. 218. Peter Marshall and David Manuel, *The Glory of America* (Bloomington, MN: Garborg's Heart'N Home, Inc., 1991), 11.25. D.P. Diffine, Ph.D., *One Nation Under God - How Close a Separation?* (Searcy, Arkansas: Harding University, Belden Center for Private Enterprise Education 6th edition, 1992), p. 4.

[114] **William Bradford**. 1650, in his work entitled, The *History of Plymouth Plantation 1608-1650* (Boston, Massachusetts: Massachusetts Historical Society, 1856; Boston, Massachusetts: Wright and Potter Printing Company, 1898, 1901, from the Original Manuscript, Library of Congress Rare Book Collection, Washington, D.C.; rendered in Modern English, Harold Paget, 1909; NY: Russell and Russell, 1968; NY: Random House, Inc., Modern Library College edition, 1981; San Antonio, TX: American Heritage Classics, Mantle Ministries, 228 Still Ridge, Bulverde, Texas, 1988).

[115] **William Bradford**. 1657, engraved on grave at Burial Hill in Plymouth, Massachusetts.

[116] **Omar Bradley**. November 11, 1948, in an address delivered on Armistice Day, or Veteran's Day. John Bartlett, *Bartlett's Familiar Quotations* (Boston: Little, Brown and Company, 1855, 1980), p. 825.

[117] **Wernher Magnus Maximilian von Braun**. Statement. Charles E. Jones, *The Books You Read* (Harrisburg, PA: Executive Books, 1985), p. 120.

[118] **Wernher Magnus Maximilian von Braun**. Statement from the foreword to his anthology concerning creation and design exhibited in nature. Henry M. Morris, *Men of Science - Men of God* (El Cajon, CA: Master Books, Creation Life Publishers, Inc., 1990), p. 85.

[119] **Wernher Magnus Maximilian von Braun**. May 1974, in an article he authored entitled, *Applied Christianity*, published in the *Bible Science Newsletter*, May 1974, p. 8. Dennis R. Petersen, B.S., M.A., *Unlocking the Mysteries of Creation* (El Cajon, CA: Master Books, 1988), p. 63.

[120] **David Brearly**. Biographical description. Dorothy McGee, *Framers of the Constitution* (New York: Dodd, Mead, 1968), p. 133. Tim LaHaye, *Faith of Our Founding Fathers* (Brentwood, TN: Wolgemuth & Hyatt, Publishers, Inc., 1987), pp. 151-152.

[121] **David Josiah Brewer**. February 29,1892, delivering the court's opinion in the case *Church of the Holy Trinity v. United States*, 143 US 457-458,465471, 36 L ed 226, (submitted and argued January 7,1892). "Our Christian Heritage," *Letter from Plymouth Rock* (Marlborough, NH: The Plymouth Rock Foundation), p. 6. David Barton, *The Myth of Separation* (Aledo, TX: WallBuilder Press, 1991), pp. 47-51. D.P. Diffine, Ph.D., *One Nation Under God - How Close a Separation?* (Searcy, Arkansas: Harding University, Belden Center for Private Enterprise Education, 6th edition, 1992), p. 3. Gary DeMar, *America's Christian History: The Untold Story* (Atlanta, GA: American Vision Publishers, Inc., 1993), p. 21.

[122] **David Josiah Brewer**. 1892, in rendering the United States Supreme Court's opinion in the case *Church of the Holy Trinity v. U.S.*, 143 U.S. 457,469 (1892).

[123] **David Josiah Brewer**. A commentary on the United States Supreme Court's decision on the case *Church of the Holy Trinity v. U.S.*, 143 U.S. (1892). Robert Flood, *The Rebirth of America* (Philadelphia: Arthur S. DeMoss Foundation, 1986), p. 21. "Our Christian Heritage" *Letter from Plymouth Rock* (Marlborough, NH: The Plymouth Rock Foundation), p. 6. D. James Kennedy, *What if Jesus Had Never Been Born?* (Nashville, TN: Thomas Nelson, Inc., 1994), p. 73. Tal Brooke, *America's Waning Light* (Chicago: Moody Press, 1994), pp. 20-21.

[124] **David Josiah Brewer**. Statement. Stephen Abbott Northrop, D.D., *A Cloud of Witnesses* (Portland, Oregon: American Heritage Ministries, 1987; Mantle Ministries, 228 Still Ridge, Bulverde, Texas), p. 46.

[125] **Sir David Brewster**. Statement. John Macaulay, *Short Biographies for the People*, Vol. 11. Stephen Abbott Northrop, D.D., *A Cloud of Witnesses* (Portland, OR. American Heritage Ministries, 1987; Mantle Ministries, 228 Still Ridge, Bulverde, Texas), pp. 46-47.

[126] **George Nixon Briggs**. May 1850, in Buffalo, addressing the missionaries of the American Baptist Missionary Union. Stephen Abbott Northrop, D.D., *A Cloud of Witnesses* (Portland, Oregon: American Heritage Ministries, 1987; Mantle Ministries, 228 Still Ridge, Bulverde, Texas), p. 48.

[127] **Rupert Brooke**. *Peace*. John Bartlett, *Bartlett's Familiar Quotations* (Boston: Little, Brown and Company, 1855, 1980), p. 797.

[128] **John Brooks**. *Dixwell's Memoirs*. Stephen Abbott Northrop, D.D., *A Cloud of Witnesses* (Portland, Oregon: American Heritage Ministries, 1987; Mantle Ministries, 228 Still Ridge, Bulverde, Texas), p. 50.

[129] **Phillips Brooks**. 1867, wrote his famous song, O *Little Town of Bethlehem*. John Bartlett, *Bartlett's Familiar Quotations (Boston: Little, Brown and Company, 1855, 1980)*, p. 619.

[130] **Phillips Brooks**. In his sermon, *Going Up to Jerusalem*. John Bartlett, *Bartlett's Familiar Quotations* (Boston: Little, Brown and Company, 1855, 1980), p. 619.

[131] **Jacob Broom**. Rev. William Campbell, *Papers of the Historical Society of Delaware* (Wilmington, Del.: Historical Society of Delaware, 1909), pp. 27, 35. Tim LaHaye, *Faith of Our Founding Fathers* (Brentwood, TN: Wolgemuth & Hyatt, Publishers, Inc., 1987), p. 153.

[132] **Jacob Broom**. 1776, Constitution of the State of Delaware, Article XXII. Thomas McKean and George Read wrote the Oath of Office in use until 1792. *The Constitutions of the Several Independent States of America - Published by Order of Congress* (Boston: Norman & Bowen, 1785), pp. 99-100. *Church of the Holy Trinity v. U.S.* 143 US 457, 469-470 (1892). Frances Newton Thorpe, ed., *Federal and State Constitutions, Colonial Charters, and Other Organic Laws of the States, Territories, and Colonies now or heretofore*

forming the United States, 7 vols. (Washington: Government Printing Office, 1905; 1909; St. Clair Shores, MI: Scholarly Press, 1968), Vol. I, p. 142. M.E. Bradford, *A Worthy Company* (NH: Plymouth Rock Foundation, 1982), p. x. Tim LaHaye, *Faith of Our Founding Fathers* (Brentwood, TN: Wolgemuth & Hyatt, Publishers, Inc., 1987), pp. 180-181. Gary DeMar, "Censoring America's Christian History" (Atlanta, GA: *The Biblical Worldview*, An American Vision Publication - American Vision, Inc., July 1990), p. 7. "Our Christian Heritage," *Letter from Plymouth Rock* (Marlborough, NH: The Plymouth Rock Foundation), p. 3. David Barton, *The Myth of Separation* (Aledo, TX: WallBuilder Press, 1991), pp. 23, 33. Gary DeMar, *America's Christian History: The Untold Story* (Atlanta, GA: American Vision Publishers, Inc., 1993), pp. 67-68. David Barton, *Keys to Good Government* (Aledo, TX: WallBuilder Press, 1994), p. 3.

[133] **Jacob Broom.** 1794, in a letter to his son who was a senior at Princeton. Rev. William Campbell, *Papers of the Historical Society of Delaware* (Wilmington: Historical Society of Delaware, 1909), p. 27. Tim LaHaye, *Faith of Our Founding Fathers* (Brentwood, TN: Wolgemuth & Hyatt, Publishers, Inc., 1987), p. 153.

[134] **William Bross.** Wilbur F. Crafts, *Successful Business Men of Today*, p. 232. Stephen Abbott Northrop, D.D., *A Cloud of Witnesses* (Portland, Oregon: American Heritage Ministries, 1987; Mantle Ministries, 228 Still Ridge, Bulverde, Texas), p. 49.

[135] **John Brown.** Statement by John Brown. Richard O. Boyer, *The Legend of John Brown* (NY: Alfred A. Knopf, 1973), p. 314. Peter Marshall and David Manuel, *From Sea to Shining Sea* (Old Tappan, N.J.: Fleming H. Revell Company, 1986), p. 401.

[136] **John Brown.** In a letter. Frank B. Sanborn, *Life and Letters of John Brown*, p. 580. Stephen Abbott Northrop, D.D., *A Cloud of Witnesses* (Portland, Oregon: American Heritage Ministries, 1987; Mantle Ministries, 228 Still Ridge, Bulverde, Texas), p. 55.

[137] **Joseph Emerson Brown.** Stephen Abbott Northrop, D.D., *A Cloud of Witnesses* (Portland, Oregon: American Heritage Ministries, 1987; Mantle Ministries, 228 Still Ridge, Bulverde, Texas), p. 54.

[138] **Robert Browning.** Herbert V. Prochnow, *5100 Quotations for Speakers and Writers* (Grand Rapids, MI: Baker Book House, 1992), p. 354.

[139] **Robert Browning.** 1842, in *The Guardian Angel*, l. 33. John Bartlett, *Bartlett's Familiar Quotations* (Boston: Little, Brown and Company, 1855, 1980), p. 540.

[140] **Robert Browning.** 1845, in *Instans Tyrannus*, st. 7. John Bartlett, *Bartlett's Familiar Quotations* (Boston: Little, Brown and Company, 1855, 1980), p. 540.

[141] **William Cullen Bryant.** Park Goodwin, *Life of William Cullen Bryant.* Stephen Abbott Northrop, D.D., *A Cloud of Witnesses* (Portland, OR: American Heritage Ministries, 1987; Mantle Ministries, 228 Still Ridge, Bulverde, Texas), p. 57.

[142] **William Cullen Bryant.** John Bigelow, *Life of William Cullen Bryant*, p. 275. Stephen Abbott Northrop, D.D., *A Cloud of Witnesses* (Portland, OR: American Heritage Ministries, 1987; Mantle Ministries, 228 Still Ridge, Bulverde, Texas), pp. 57-58.

[143] **James Buchanan.** 1832-1833, in a letter to his brother, a Presbyterian minister, while serving in Russia as the U.S. Minister. Edmund Fuller and David E. Green, *God in the White House - The Faiths of American Presidents* (NY: Crown Publishers, Inc., 1968), p. 98.

[144] **James Buchanan.** February 29, 1844, in a letter to his brother, written from Washington, D.C. Stephen Abbott Northrop, D.D., *A Cloud of Witnesses* (Portland, Oregon: American Heritage Ministries, 1987; Mantle Ministries, 228 Still Ridge, Bulverde, Texas), p. 56.

[145] **James Buchanan.** In a letter written near the end of his life. George Tichnor Curtis, *Life of James Buchanan.* Stephen Abbott Northrop, D.D., *A Cloud of Witnesses* (Portland, OR: American Heritage Ministries, 1987; Mantle Ministries, 228 Still Ridge, Bulverde, Texas), p. 56.

[146] **Peter Bulkeley.** 1651. *The Gospel Covenant; or the Covenant of Grace Opened* (London: 2nd edition, 1651), pp. 431-32. *The Annals of America*, 20 vols. (Chicago, IL: Encyclopedia Britannica, 1968), Vol. I, pp. 221-212. Peter Marshall and David Manuel, *The Glory of America* (Bloomington, MN: Garborg's Heart'N Home, Inc., 1991), 11.23.

[147] **John Bunyan.** 1678, *Pilgrim's Progress*, pt. II, *Shepherd Boy's Song*. John Bartlett, *Bartlett's Familiar Quotations* (Boston: Little, Brown and Company, 1855, 1980), p. 302.

[148] **Warren Earl Burger.** 1982, United States Supreme Court case of *Marsh v. Chambers*, 675 F. 2d 228, 233 (8th Cir. 1982); review allowed, 463 U.S. 783 (1982). "Our Christian Heritage," *Letter from Plymouth Rock* (Marlborough, NH: The Plymouth Rock Foundation), p. 7.

[149] **Warren Earl Burger.** 1982, United States Supreme Court case of *Marsh v. Chambers*, 675 F. 2d 228, 233 (8th Cir. 1982); review allowed, 463 U.S. 783 (1982). Tracy Everback, *Dallas Morning News*, March 16, 1993, pp. 1A, 8A.

[150] **Warren Earl Burger.** 1982, United States Supreme Court case of *Marsh v. Chambers*, 675 F. 2d 228, 233 (8th Cir. 1982); review allowed, 463 U.S. 783 (1982). Tracy Everback, *Dallas Morning News*, March 16, 1993, pp. 1A, 8A. David Barton, *The Myth of Separation* (Aledo, TX: WallBuilder Press, 1991), p. 187.

[151] **Warren Earl Burger.** 1985, United States Supreme Court case of *Lynch v. Donnelly*, 465 U.S. 668, 669-670, 673 (1985). John Whitehead, *The Rights of Religious Persons in Public Education* (Wheaton, IL: Crossway Books, Good News Publishers, 1991), pp. 49, 52. Tracy Everback, *Dallas Morning News*, March 16, 1993, pp. 1A, 8A. David Barton, *The Myth of Separation* (Aledo, TX: WallBuilder Press, 1991), p. 189.

[152] **Edmund Burke.** March 22, 1775, in an address to Parliament, entitled *Second Speech on the Conciliation with America-The Thirteen Resolutions*. Sidney Carelton Newsom, ed., *Burke's Speech on Conciliation with America* (New York: The Macmillan Company, 1899; 1913), pp. 28-29. John Bartlett, *Bartlett's Familiar Quotations* (Boston: Little, Brown and Company, 1855, 1980), p. 372. Ernest R. Clark, ed., *Burke's Speech on the Conciliation with the American Colonies* (New York, American Book Company, 1895; 1911) p. 34. Tim LaHaye, *Faith of Our Founding Fathers* (Brentwood, TN: Wolgemuth & Hyatt, Publishers, Inc., 1987), p. 67.

[153] **Edmund Burke.** March 22, 1775, in an address to Parliament, entitled *Second Speech on the Conciliation with America-The Thirteen Resolutions*. Sidney Carelton Newsom, ed., *Burke's Speech on Conciliation with America* (New York: Macmillan Company, 1899; 1913). John Bartlett, *Bartlett's Familiar Quotations* (Boston: Little, Brown and Company, 1855, 1980), p. 373.

[154] **Edmund Burke.** March 22, 1775, in an address to Parliament entitled *Second Speech on the Conciliation with America-The Thirteen Resolutions*. Sidney Carelton Newsom, ed., *Burke's Speech on Conciliation with America* (New York: The Macmillan Company, 1899; 1913), p. 32. Ernest R. Clark, ed., *Burke's Speech on the Conciliation with the American Colonies* (New York, American Book Company, 1895; 1911) p. 36.

[155] **Edmund Burke.** *The Works and Correspondence of the Right Honorable Edmund Burke.* Vol. VI, p. 90. Stephen Abbott Northrop, D.D., *A Cloud of Witnesses* (Portland, Oregon: American Heritage Ministries, 1987; Mantle Ministries, 228 Still Ridge, Bulverde, Texas), p. 64.

[156] **Edmund Burke.** 1790, in his *Reflections on the Revolution in France.* John Bartlett, *Bartlett's Familiar Quotations* (Boston: Little, Brown and Company, 1855, 1980), p. 373.
[157] **Edmund Burke.** May 28, 1794, in the *Impeachment of Warren Hastings.* John Bartlett, *Bartlett's Familiar Quotations* (Boston: Little, Brown and Company, 1855, 1980), p. 373.
[158] **Edmund Burke.** January 9, 1795, in a letter to William Smith. John Bartlett, *Bartlett's Familiar Quotations* (Boston: Little, Brown & Co., 1863, 1980), p. 374. Edward L.R. Elson, D.D., Lit.D., LL.D., *America's Spiritual Recovery* (Westwood, N.J.: Fleming H. Revell Company, 1954), p. 174. David Barton, *The Myth of Separation* (Aledo, TX: WallBuilder Press, 1991), p. 262. Carroll E. Simcox, comp., *4400 Quotations for Christian Communicators* (Grand Rapids, MI: Baker Book House, 1991), p. 124. D.P. Diffine, Ph.D., *One Nation Under God - How Close a Separation?* (Searcy, Arkansas: Harding University Belden Center for Private Enterprise Education, 6th edition, 1992), p. 20.
[159] **Edmund Burke.** 1797, *Letters on a Regicide Peace.* Carroll E. Simcox, comp., *4400 Quotations for Christian Communicators* (Grand Rapids, MI: Baker Book House, 1991), p. 52.
[160] **Edmund Burke.** 1791, in "A Letter to a Member of the National Assembly." Theodore Roosevelt, "Fifth Annual Message to Congress," December 5, 1905. *A Compilation of the Messages and Papers of the Presidents* 20 vols. (New York: Bureau of National Literature, Inc., prepared under the direction of the Joint Committee on Printing, of the House and Senate, pursuant to an Act of the Fifty-Second Congress of the United States, 1893, 1923), Vol. XIV, p. 6986. Keith Fournier, *In Defense of Liberty* (Virginia Beach, VA: Law & Justice, 1993), Vol. 2, No. 2, p. 5. Rush H. Limbaugh III, *See, I Told You So* (New York, NY: reprinted by permission of Pocket Books, a division of Simon & Schuster Inc., 1993), pp. 73-76.
[161] **Edmund Burke.** Robert Bissel, *Life of Edmund Burke,* Vol. II, p. 441. Stephen Abbott Northrop, D.D., *A Cloud of Witnesses* (Portland, OR: American Heritage Ministries, 1987; Mantle Ministries, 228 Still Ridge, Bulverde, Texas), p. 64.
[162] **George Herbert Walker Bush.** May 3, 1990, in a *Proclamation of a National Day of Prayer.* "Our Christian Heritage," *Letter from Plymouth Rock* (Marlborough, NH: The Plymouth Rock Foundation), p. 8.
[163] **George Herbert Walker Bush.** 1992, in a *Proclamation of a National Day of Prayer.* Mrs. James Dobson (Shirley), chairman, *The Annual National Day of Prayer* (Colorado Springs, CO: National Day of Prayer, 1993).
[164] **Benjamin Franklin Butler.** 1834, from an address delivered as the U.S. attorney general at Alexandria, D.C. (Benjamin Franklin Butler is distinguished from the army officer, governor and congressman by the same name, 1818-1893.) Stephen Abbott Northrop, D.D., *A Cloud of Witnesses* (Portland, OR: American Heritage Ministries, 1987; Mantle Ministries, 228 Still Ridge, Bulverde, Texas), pp. 64-65.
[165] **Robert Byrd.** July 27, 1962, in a message delivered in Congress by United States Senator from West Virginia two days after the Supreme Court declared prayer in schools unconstitutional. Robert Flood, *The Rebirth of America* (Philadelphia: Arthur S. DeMoss Foundation, 1986), pp. 66-69.
[166] **Robert Byrd.** July 27, 1962, in a message delivered in Congress by United States Senator from West Virginia two days after the Supreme Court declared prayer in schools unconstitutional. Robert Flood, *The Rebirth of America* (Philadelphia: Arthur S. DeMoss Foundation, 1986), pp. 66-69.

C

[1] **John Caldwell Calhoun.** 1850, in his last speech to the Senate before he died, warning of the impending civil war. Richard D. Heffner, *A Documentary History of the United States* (New York: The New American Library of World Literature, Inc., 1961), pp. 120-121.
[2] **Supreme Court of California.** 1980, *Devin Walker v. First Presbyterian Church,* 760-028.9. "Our Christian Heritage," *Letter from Plymouth Rock* (Marlborough, NH: The Plymouth Rock Foundation), p. 7.
[3] **Thomas Carlyle.** Henry H. Halley, *Halley's Bible Handbook* (Grand Rapids, MI: Zondervan Publishing House, 1927, 1965), p. 18.
[4] **Thomas Carlyle.** Lewis C. Henry, *Best Quotations For All Occasions* (Greenwich, CONN: Fawcett Publications, Inc., 1961), p. 21.
[5] **Thomas Carlyle.** *Miscellaneous Papers,* p. 388. Stephen Abbott Northrop, D.D., *A Cloud of Witnesses* (Portland, Oregon: American Heritage Ministries, 1987; Mantle Ministries, 228 Still Ridge, Bulverde, Texas), p. 73.
[6] **Thomas Carlyle.** *Essays: Corn-Law Rhymes.* Stephen Abbott Northrop, D.D., *A Cloud of Witnesses* (Portland, Oregon: American Heritage Ministries, 1987; Mantle Ministries, 228 Still Ridge, Bulverde, Texas), p. 73.
[7] **Thomas Carlyle.** *Critical and Miscellaneous Essays.* Stephen Abbott Northrop, D.D., *A Cloud of Witnesses* (Portland, Oregon: American Heritage Ministries, 1987; Mantle Ministries, 228 Still Ridge, Bulverde, Texas), p. 73.
[8] **Thomas Carlyle.** 1827, in *The State of German Literature, Critical and Miscellaneous.* John Bartlett, *Bartlett's Familiar Quotations* (Boston: Little, Brown and Company, 1855, 1980), p. 472.
[9] **Thomas Carlyle.** *Sartor Resartus,* Book III, Chapter III. Stephen Abbott Northrop, D.D., *A Cloud of Witnesses* (Portland, Oregon: American Heritage Ministries, 1987; Mantle Ministries, 228 Still Ridge, Bulverde, Texas), p. 73.
[10] **Thomas Carlyle.** 1833-1834, in *Sartor Resartus.* John Bartlett, *Bartlett's Familiar Quotations* (Boston: Little, Brown and Company, 1855, 1980), p. 473.
[11] **William Bliss Carman.** *Vestigia,* st. I. John Bartlett, *Bartlett's Familiar Quotations* (Boston: Little, Brown and Company, 1855, 1980), p. 696.
[12] **Colony of Carolina.** 1650, first permanent settlement; April 9, 1585, the Roanoke Settlement was begun, later to be called The Lost Colony; August 13, 1587, members of the colony converted an Indian named Manteo; August 18, 1587, the first child, Virginia Dare was born in America. *The World Book Encyclopedia,* 18 vols. (Chicago, IL: Field Enterprises, Inc., 1957; W.F. Quarrie and Company, 8 vols., 1917; World Book, Inc., 22 vols., 1989), Vol. 12, p. 5732; Vol. 10, p. 4596.
[13] **Colony of Carolina.** 1653. *The World Book Encyclopedia,* 18 vols. (Chicago, IL: Field Enterprises, Inc., 1957; W.F. Quarrie and Company, 8 vols., 1917; World Book, Inc., 22 vols., 1989), Vol. 15, p. 7587; Vol. 12, p. 5732.
[14] **Colony of Carolina.** August 13, 1587. Roanoke Settlement-The Lost Colony. *The World Book Encyclopedia,* 18 vols. (Chicago, IL: Field Enterprises, Inc., 1957; W.F. Quarrie and Company, 8 vols., 1917; World Book, Inc., 22 vols., 1989), Vol. 12, p. 5732.
[15] **Charter of Carolina.** 1663. Frances Newton Thorpe, ed., *Federal and State Constitutions, Colonial Charters, and Other Organic Laws of the States, Territories, and Colonies now or heretofore forming the United States,* 7 vols. (Washington: Government Printing Office, 1905; 1909; St. Clair Shores, MI: Scholarly Press, 1968), Vol. 5, p. 2743. Hugh Talmage Lefler, ed., *North Carolina History* (Chapel

Hill: Univ. of North Carolina Press, 1934, 1956), p. 16. Pat Robertson, *America's Dates With Destiny* (Nashville, TN: Thomas Nelson Publishers, 1986), p. 32. David Barton, *The Myth of Separation* (Aledo, TX: WallBuilder Press, 1991), p. 86.

[16] **Fundamental Constitutions of the Carolinas.** 1663, John Locke.*The World Book Encyclopedia*, 18 vols. (Chicago, IL: Field Enterprises, Inc., 1957; W.F. Quarrie and Company, 8 vols., 1917; World Book, Inc., 22 vols., 1989), Vol. 12, p. 5736, Vol. 15, p. 7591.

[17] **Fundamental Constitutions of the Carolinas.** 1663. Supreme Court Justice David Josiah Brewer, who served 1890-1910, in his work, *The United States - A Christian Nation* (Philadelphia: The John C. Winston Company, 1905, Supreme Court Collection). Catherine Millard, *The Rewriting of America's History* (Camp Hill, PA: Horizon House Publishers, 1991), p. 389.

[18] **James Earl "Jimmy" Carter, Jr.** January 20, 1977, Thursday, in his Inaugural Address. "Our Christian Heritage," *Letter from Plymouth Rock* (Marlborough, NH: The Plymouth Rock Foundation), p. 7. J. Michael Sharman, J.D., *Faith of the Fathers* (Culpepper, Virginia: Victory Publishing, 1995), p. 121.

[19] **James Earl "Jimmy" Carter, Jr.** March 16, 1976, in an interview with Robert L. Turner. John Bartlett, *Bartlett's Familiar Quotations* (Boston: Little, Brown and Company, 1855, 1980), p. 903.

[20] **Robert "King" Carter.** July 22, 1720, in a letter to Mr. Perry in England. Louis B. Wright, ed., *Letters of Robert Carter, 1720-1727* (San Marino: The Hunting Library, 1940), p. 34. Catherine Millard, *The Rewriting of America's History* (Camp Hill, PA: Horizon House Publishers, 1991), pp. 281-282.

[21] **Robert "King" Carter.** July 23, 1720, in a letter to his son John in England. Louis B. Wright, ed., *Letters of Robert Carter, 1720-1727* (San Marino: The Hunting Library, 1940), p. 37. Catherine Millard, *The Rewriting of America's History* (Camp Hill, PA: Horizon House Publishers, 1991), p. 282.

[22] **Robert "King" Carter.** August 4, 1732, on his epitaph in Christ Church, Lancaster County, Virginia. Louis Morton, *Robert Carter of Nomini Hall*, pp. 23-24. Catherine Millard, *The Rewriting of America's History* (Camp Hill, PA: Horizon House Publishers, 1991), p. 283.

[23] **Peter Cartwright.** "The Return of the Spirit" (Carol Stream, IL: Christian History), Vol. VIII, No. 3, Issue 23, p. 26.

[24] **Peter Cartwright.** Peter Cartwright, *The Autobiography of Peter Cartwright* (New York: Carlton & Porter, 1856), p. 38. Peter Marshall and David Manuel, *The Glory of America* (Bloomington, MN: Garborg's Heart'N Home, Inc., 1991), 9.1.

[25] **George Washington Carver.** 1920, in speaking at Blue Ridge, North Carolina to the Young Mens Christian Association. Ethel Edwards, *Carver of Tuskegee* (Cincinnati, Ohio: Ethel Edwards & James T. Hardwick, a limited edition work compiled in part from over 300 personal letters written by Dr. Carver to James T. Hardwick between 1922-1937, available from the Carver Memorial in Locust Grove, Diamond, Mo., 1971), pp. 114-117.

[26] **George Washington Carver.** 1920, in speaking at Blue Ridge, North Carolina to the Young Mens Christian Association. Ethel Edwards, *Carver of Tuskegee* (Cincinnati, Ohio: Ethel Edwards & James T. Hardwick, a limited edition work compiled in part from over 300 personal letters written by Dr. Carver to James T. Hardwick between 1922-1937, available from the Carver Memorial in Locust Grove, Diamond, Mo., 1971), pp. 114-117.

[27] **George Washington Carver.** 1921, in an address before the Senate Ways and Means Committee. Charles E. Jones, *The Books You Read* (Harrisburg, PA: Executive Books, 1985), p. 132.

[28] **George Washington Carver.** November 19, 1924, in a speech before 500 people of the Women's Board of Domestic Missions in New York City's Marble Collegiate Church. Ethel Edwards, *Carver of Tuskegee* (Cincinnati, Ohio: Ethel Edwards & James T. Hardwick, a limited edition work compiled in part from over 300 personal letters written by Dr. Carver to James T. Hardwick between 1922-1937, available from the Carver Memorial in Locust Grove, Diamond, Mo., 1971), pp. 141-142.

[29] **George Washington Carver.** Ethel Edwards, *Carver of Tuskegee* (Cincinnati, Ohio: Ethel Edwards & James T. Hardwick, a limited edition work compiled in part from over 300 personal letters written by Dr. Carver to James T. Hardwick between 1922-1937, available from the Carver Memorial in Locust Grove, Diamond, Mo., 1971), pp. 183,199.

[30] **George Washington Carver.** 1928, Tuskegee Institute. Ethel Edwards, *Carver of Tuskegee* (Cincinnati, Ohio: Ethel Edwards & James T. Hardwick, a limited edition work compiled in part from over 300 personal letters written by Dr. Carver to James T. Hardwick between 1922-1937, available from the Carver Memorial in Locust Grove, Diamond, Mo., 1971), pp. 157-160.

[31] **George Washington Carver.** 1939, in the citation made at the presentation of the Roosevelt Medal. Henry M. Morris, *Men of Science - Men of God* (El Cajon, CA: Master Books, Creation Life Publishers, Inc., 1990), pp. 81-83.

[32] **George Washington Carver.** *Bless Your Heart* (series II) (Eden Prairie, MN: Heartland Samplers, Inc., 1990), 7.12.

[33] **Lewis Cass.** Tryon Edwards, D.D., *The New Dictionary of Thoughts - A Cyclopedia of Quotations* (Garden City, NY: Hanover House, 1852; revised and enlarged by C.H. Catrevas, Ralph Emerson Browns and Jonathan Edwards [descendent, along with Tryon, of Jonathan Edwards (1703-1758), president of Princeton], 1891; The Standard Book Company, 1955, 1963), p. 90.

[34] **Lewis Cass.** 1846, in a letter dated from Washington. Stephen Abbott Northrop, D.D., *A Cloud of Witnesses* (Portland, Oregon: American Heritage Ministries, 1987; Mantle Ministries, 228 Still Ridge, Bulverde, Texas), p. 76. Peter Marshall & David Manuel, *The Glory of America* (Bloomington, MN: Garborg's Heart 'N Home, 1991), 10.9. D.P. Diffine, Ph.D., *One Nation Under God - How Close a Separation?* (Searcy, Arkansas: Harding University, Belden Center for Private Enterprise Education, 6th edition, 1992), p. 12.

[35] **Lewis Cass.** December 14, 1852, in the Obituary Address for Daniel Webster. Stephen Abbott Northrop, D.D., *A Cloud of Witnesses* (Portland, Oregon: American Heritage Ministries, 1987; Mantle Ministries, 228 Still Ridge, Bulverde, Texas), p. introduction.

[36] **Lewis Cass.** December 14, 1852, in the Obituary Address for Daniel Webster. Stephen Abbott Northrop, D.D., *A Cloud of Witnesses* (Portland, Oregon: American Heritage Ministries, 1987; Mantle Ministries, 228 Still Ridge, Bulverde, Texas), p. 76.

[37] **(Jay David) Whittaker Chambers.** (1901-1961), American journalist and recanted Communist agent. Whittaker Chambers, *Witness* (New York: Random House, 1952), p. 16. John Eidsmoe, *God & Caesar-Christian Faith & Political Action* (Westchester, IL: Crossway Books, a Division of Good News Publishers, 1984), p. 85.

[38] **(Jay David) Whittaker Chambers.** Robert Flood, *The Rebirth of America* (Philadelphia: Arthur S. DeMoss Foundation, 1986), p. 90.

[39] **Salmon Portland Chase.** November 20, 1861, in correspondence to the Director of the Mint, Philadelphia. Catherine Millard, *The Rewriting of America's History* (Camp Hill, PA: Horizon House Publishers, 1991), pp. 380-381.

[40] **Salmon Portland Chase.** December 9, 1863, in correspondence to the James Pollock, Director of the Mint, Philadelphia. Catherine Millard, *The Rewriting of America's History* (Camp Hill, PA: Horizon House Publishers, 1991), pp. 380-381.

[41] **Salmon Portland Chase.** "Our Christian Heritage," *Letter from Plymouth Rock* (Marlborough, NH: The Plymouth Rock

Foundation), p. 6. Keith J. Hardman, *Christianity & The Civil War-The Christian History Timeline* (Carol Stream, IL: Christian History, 1992), Vol. XI, No. 1, p. 33.

[42] **Salmon Portland Chase.** J.W. Schnuckers, *Life and Public Services of Salmon P. Chase.* Stephen Abbott Northrop, D.D., *A Cloud of Witnesses* (Portland, OR: American Heritage Ministries, 1987; Mantle Ministries, 228 Still Ridge, Bulverde, Texas), p. 79.

[43] **Salmon Portland Chase.** Robert B. Warden, *Private Life and Public Services of Salmon P. Chase.* Stephen Abbott Northrop, D.D., *A Cloud of Witnesses* (Portland, Oregon: American Heritage Ministries, 1987; Mantle Ministries, 228 Still Ridge, Bulverde, Texas), p. 79-80.

[44] **Samuel Chase.** *Runkel v. Winemiller,* 4 Harris & McHenry 276, 288 (Sup. Ct. Md. 1799). *Runkel v. Winemiller,* 4 Harris & McHenry (MD) 429 1 AD 411, 417 (Justice Chase). David Barton, *The Myth of Separation* (Aledo, TX: WallBuilder Press, 1991), pp. 64, 151. David Barton, *America's Godly Heritage,* Video Transcript (Aledo, TX: WallBuilder, 1993), p. 13. "Our Christian Heritage," *Letter from Plymouth Rock* (Marlborough, NH: The Plymouth Rock Foundation), p. 4.

[45] **Samuel Chase.** *M'Creery's Lessee v. Allender,* 4 H. & Mett. 259 (1799). David Barton, *The Myth of Separation* (Aledo, TX: WallBuilder Press, 1991) p. 63.

[46] **Francois Rene' de Chateaubriand.** 1802, in writing on his conversion in *Le Genie du Christianisme.* John Bartlett, *Bartlett's Familiar Quotations* (Boston: Little, Brown and Company, 1855, 1980), p. 419.

[47] **Geoffrey Chaucer.** *Canterbury Tales.* Stephen Abbott Northrop, D.D., *A Cloud of Witnesses* (Portland, Oregon: American Heritage Ministries, 1987; Mantle Ministries, 228 Still Ridge, Bulverde, Texas), p. 82.

[48] **Geoffrey Chaucer.** *Canterbury Tales.* Stephen Abbott Northrop, D.D., *A Cloud of Witnesses* (Portland, Oregon: American Heritage Ministries, 1987; Mantle Ministries, 228 Still Ridge, Bulverde, Texas), p. 82.

[49] **Geoffrey Chaucer.** 1387, *Canterbury Tales, Prologue,* l. 527. John Bartlett, *Bartlett's Familiar Quotations* (Boston: Little, Brown and Company, 1855, 1980), p. 146.

[50] **Geoffrey Chaucer.** *Canterbury Tales, The Man of Law's Tale,* l. 194, 582. John Bartlett, *Bartlett's Familiar Quotations* (Boston: Little, Brown and Company, 1855, 1980), p. 147.

[51] **John Cheever.** 1957, in *The Wapshot Chronicle,* ch. 36, end. John Bartlett, *Bartlett's Familiar Quotations* (Boston: Little, Brown and Company, 1855, 1980), p. 879.

[52] **Gilbert Keith Chesterton.** 1910, in his work, *What's Wrong with the World,* pt. 1, ch. 5. John Bartlett, *Bartlett's Familiar Quotations* (Boston: Little, Brown and Company, 1855, 1980), p. 742. Perry Tanksley, *To Love is to Give* (Jackson, Mississippi: Allgood Books, Box 1329; Parthenon Press, 201 8th Ave., South, Nashville, Tennessee, 1972), p. 31.

[53] **Charles Chiniquy.** *The Finished Wonder* (Seattle, WA: Life Messengers, 1984), pp. 20-22.

[54] **Rufus Choate.** *Appleton's Cyclopedia of American Biography,* Volume I. Stephen Abbott Northrop, D.D., *A Cloud of Witnesses* (Portland, Oregon: American Heritage Ministries, 1987; Mantle Ministries, 228 Still Ridge, Bulverde, Texas), p. 83.

[55] **Rufus Choate.** Tryon Edwards, D.D., *The New Dictionary of Thoughts - A Cyclopedia of Quotations* (Garden City, NY: Hanover House, 1852; revised and enlarged by C.H. Catrevas, Ralph Emerson Browns and Jonathan Edwards [descendent, along with Tryon, of Jonathan Edwards (1703-1758), president of Princeton], 1891; The Standard Book Company, 1955, 1963), p. 47.

[56] **Dame Agatha Christie.** 1977, *An Autobiography,* Pt. III, *Growing Up.* John Bartlett, *Bartlett's Familiar Quotations* (Boston: Little, Brown and Company, 1855, 1980), p. 817.

[57] **Sir Winston Leonard Spencer Churchill.** June 16, 1941, in a radio broadcast to America on receiving the honorary degree of Doctor of Laws from the University of Rochester, New York. John Bartlett, *Bartlett's Familiar Quotations* (Boston: Little, Brown and Company, 1855, 1980), p. 745.

[58] **Sir Winston Leonard Spencer Churchill.** October 29, 1941, in an address at Harrow School. John Bartlett, *Bartlett's Familiar Quotations* (Boston: Little, Brown and Company, 1855, 1980), p. 745.

[59] **Sir Winston Leonard Spencer Churchill.** December 30, 1941, in a speech to the Canadian Senate and House of Commons in Ottawa. John Bartlett, *Bartlett's Familiar Quotations* (Boston: Little, Brown and Company, 1855, 1980), p. 745.

[60] **Tom Campbell Clark.** Supreme Court Justice. Herbert V. Prochnow, *5100 Quotations for Speakers and Writers* (Grand Rapids, MI: Baker Book House, 1992), p. 343.

[61] **Cassius Marcellus Clay.** Stephen Abbott Northrop, D.D., *A Cloud of Witnesses* (Portland, OR: American Heritage Ministries, 1987; Mantle Ministries, 228 Still Ridge, Bulverde, Texas), p. 86.

[62] **Henry Clay.** *The World Book Encyclopedia,* 18 vols. (Chicago, IL: Field Enterprises, Inc., 1957; W.F. Quarrie and Company, 8 vols., 1917; World Book, Inc., 22 vols., 1989), Vol. 3, p. 1472.

[63] **Henry Clay.** 1829, in a speech at Frankfort to the Kentucky Colonization Society. Stephen Abbott Northrop, D.D., *A Cloud of Witnesses* (Portland, Oregon: American Heritage Ministries, 1987; Mantle Ministries, 228 Still Ridge, Bulverde, Texas), p. 87.

[64] **Henry Clay.** June 30, 1852, in the obituary address given by Congressman John C. Breckinridge in the House and Senate at the occasion of Henry Clay's death. Stephen Abbott Northrop, D.D., *A Cloud of Witnesses* (Portland, OR: American Heritage Ministries, 1987; Mantle Ministries, 228 Still Ridge, Bulverde, Texas), p. 87.

[65] **Henry Clay.** June 30, 1852, quoted by Congressman Venable in the obituary address of Henry Clay, delivered in the House and Senate. Stephen Abbott Northrop, D.D., *A Cloud of Witnesses* (Portland, OR: American Heritage Ministries, 1987; Mantle Ministries, 228 Still Ridge, Bulverde, Texas), p. 87. Peter Marshall, & David Manuel, *The Glory of America* (Bloomington, MN: Garborg's Heart 'N Home, 1991), 6.29.

[66] **Stephen Grover Cleveland.** March 4, 1885, Wednesday, in his First Inaugural Address. James D. Richardson (U.S. Representative from Tennessee), ed., *A Compilation of the Messages and Papers of the Presidents 1789-1897,* 10 vols. (Washington, D.C.: U.S. Government Printing Office, published by Authority of Congress, 1897, 1899; Washington, D.C.: Bureau of National Literature and Art, 1789-1902, 11 vols., 1907, 1910), Vol. 8, pp. 300, 303. *Inaugural Addresses of the Presidents of the United States - From George Washington 1789 to Richard Milhous Nixon 1969* (Washington, D.C.: United States Government Printing Office; 91st Congress, 1st Session, House Document 91-142, 1969), pp. 149-152. Davis Newton Lott, *The Inaugural Addresses of the American Presidents* (NY: Holt, Rinehart and Winston, 1961), p. 142. Charles E. Rice, *The Supreme Court and Public Prayer* (New York: Fordham University Press, 1964), pp. 186-187. Benjamin Weiss, *God in American History - A Documentation of America's Religious Heritage* (Grand Rapids, MI: Zondervan, 1966), p. 109. Willard Cantelon, *Money Master of the World* (Plainfield, NJ: Logos International, 1976), p. 120. Peter Marshall and David Manuel, *The Glory of America* (Bloomington, MN: Garborg's Heart 'N Home, Inc., 1991), 3.18. *Proclaim Liberty* (Dallas, TX: Word of Faith), p. 2. J. Michael Sharman, J.D., *Faith of the Fathers* (Culpepper, Virginia: Victory Publishing, 1995), p. 73.

[67] **Stephen Grover Cleveland.** Charles W. Skelton, reporting a meeting with President Grover Cleveland regarding the Indians.

Stephen Abbott Northrop, D.D., *A Cloud of Witnesses* (Portland, OR: American Heritage Ministries, 1987; Mantle Ministries, 228 Still Ridge, Bulverde, Texas), p. 90.

[68] **Stephen Grover Cleveland.** George F. Parker, ed., *The Writings and Speeches of Grover Cleveland,* pp. 182-183. Stephen Abbott Northrop, D.D., *A Cloud of Witnesses* (Portland, Oregon: American Heritage Ministries, 1987; Mantle Ministries, 228 Still Ridge, Bulverde, Texas), p. 90. Peter Marshall and David Manuel, *The Glory of America* (Bloomington, MN: Garborg's Heart'N Home, Inc., 1991), 3.19. D.P. Diffine, Ph.D., *One Nation Under God - How Close a Separation?* (Searcy, Arkansas: Harding University, Belden Center for Private Enterprise Education, 6th edition, 1992), p. 16.

[69] **Francis Marion Cockrell.** 1875. Stephen Abbott Northrop, D.D., *A Cloud of Witnesses* (Portland, Oregon: American Heritage Ministries, 1987; Mantle Ministries, 228 Still Ridge, Bulverde, Texas), p. 102.

[70] **Samuel Taylor Coleridge.** Tryon Edwards, D.D., *The New Dictionary of Thoughts - A Cyclopedia of Quotations* (Garden City, NY: Hanover House, 1852; revised and enlarged by C.H. Catrevas, Ralph Emerson Browns and Jonathan Edwards [descendent, along with Tryon, of Jonathan Edwards (1703-1758), president of Princeton], 1891; The Standard Book Company, 1955, 1963), p. 47.

[71] **Samuel Taylor Coleridge.** *Specimen of Table-Talk of Samuel Taylor Coleridge.* Stephen Abbott Northrop, D.D., *A Cloud of Witnesses* (Portland, OR: American Heritage Ministries, 1987; Mantle Ministries, 228 Still Ridge, Bulverde, Texas), p. 92.

[72] **Samuel Taylor Coleridge.** 1798, in *The Rime of the Ancient Mariner,* pt. VII, st. 23. John Bartlett, *Bartlett's Familiar Quotations* (Boston: Little, Brown and Company, 1855, 1980), p. 435.

[73] **Samuel Taylor Coleridge.** In an autographed letter in the Wellesley College Library. Stephen Abbott Northrop, D.D., *A Cloud of Witnesses* (Portland, OR: American Heritage Ministries, 1987; Mantle Ministries, 228 Still Ridge, Bulverde, Texas), p. 92.

[74] **Samuel Taylor Coleridge.** J.C. Shairp, Principal of the United States College of the St. Salvador and St. Leonard, *Studies in Poetry and Philosophy.* Stephen Abbott Northrop, D.D., *A Cloud of Witnesses* (Portland, OR: American Heritage Ministries, 1987; Mantle Ministries, 228 Still Ridge, Bulverde, Texas), p. 92.

[75] **Schuyler Colfax.** O.J. Hollister, *Life of Schuyler Colfax,* p. 453. Stephen Abbott Northrop, D.D., *A Cloud of Witnesses* (Portland, OR: American Heritage Ministries, 1987; Mantle Ministries, 228 Still Ridge, Bulverde, Texas), p. 93.

[76] **Schuyler Colfax.** O.J. Hollister, *Life of Schuyler Colfax,* p. 20. Stephen Abbott Northrop, D.D., *A Cloud of Witnesses* (Portland, OR: American Heritage Ministries, 1987; Mantle Ministries, 228 Still Ridge, Bulverde, Texas), pp. 93-94.

[77] **Samuel Colgate.** 1890, Colgate University named after the Colgate soap manufacturing family. *The World Book Encyclopedia,* 18 vols. (Chicago, IL: Field Enterprises, Inc., 1957; W.F. Quarrie and Company, 8 vols., 1917; World Book, Inc., 22 vols., 1989), Vol. 3, pp. 1550-1551. Stephen Abbott Northrop, D.D., *A Cloud of Witnesses* (Portland, Oregon: American Heritage Ministries, 1987; Mantle Ministries, 228 Still Ridge, Bulverde, Texas), p. 93.

[78] **Alfred Holt Colquitt.** December 7, 1887, in an address at the Evangelical Alliance in Washington. Stephen Abbott Northrop, D.D., *A Cloud of Witnesses* (Portland, Oregon: American Heritage Ministries, 1987; Mantle Ministries, 228 Still Ridge, Bulverde, Texas), p. 91.

[79] **Chuck W. Colson.** 1981, Chuck W. Colson, *Is There a Better Way? A Perspective on American Prisons* (Washington, D.C.: Prison Fellowship, 1981). David Rotham, *The Invention of the Penitentiary,* Criminal Law Bulletin, September 1972 (vol.8), pp. 585, 586. Thorsten Sellin, "The Origin of the Pennsylvania System of Prison Disciple," in George Killinger and Paul Cromwell, Jr., editors, *Penology: the Evolution of Corrections in America* (St. Paul, Minn: West Publishing, 1973), pp. 13ff. John Eidsmoe, *God & Caesar-Christian Faith & Political Action* (Westchester, IL: Crossway Books, a Division of Good News Publishers, 1984), p. 203.

[80] **Columbia University.** 1754, Seal of Columbia University. Gabriel Sivan, *The Bible and Civilization* (New York: Quandrangle/The New York Times Book Co., 1973), p. 237. Gary Demar, *God and Government* (Atlanta: American Vision Press, 1984), p. 23.

[81] **Christopher Columbus.** *Book of Prophecies.* Washington Irving, *Life and Voyages of Christopher Columbus* (NY: The Cooperative Publication Society, Inc., 1892), p. 41. August J. Kling, "Columbus-A Layman Christ-bearer to Uncharted Isles." (*The Presbyterian Layman,* October 1971). Peter Marshall and David Manuel, *The Light and the Glory* (NJ: Fleming H. Revell Co., 1977), pp. 31-33. Gary DeMar, *God and Government* (Atlanta: American Vision Press, 1982), p. 126. Stephen K. McDowell and Mark A. Beliles, *America's Providential History* (Charlottesville, VA: Providence Press, 1988), p. 39. Steve Wilkins, *America: The First 350 Years, Tape Album and Study Guide* (224 Auburn Avenue, Monroe, LA. 71201, 1988), pp. 3-4. Catherine Millard, *The Rewriting of America's History* (Camp Hill, PA: Horizon House Publishers, 1991), pp. 3-5. John Eidsmoe, *Columbus & Cortez, Conquerors for Christ* (Green Forest, AR: New Leaf Press, 1992), pp. 90-91. Rick Wood, *Christopher Columbus* (Pasadena, CA: Mission Frontiers-U.S.Center for World Missions, 1992), Vol. 14, No. 9-12, September-December. Kay Brigham, *Christopher Columbus - His life and discovery in the light of his prophecies* (Terrassa, Barcelona: CLIE Publishers, 1990; rendered from the original Spanish Language *a compilation of passages from the Bible which the Admiral believed were pertinent to his mission of discovery, selected by Columbus himself with the help of his friend, Fray Gaspar de Gorricio, from Columbus' Libro de las profecias;* also in Transcription of Interview, broadcast on the 700 Club, Virginia Beach: Christian Broadcasting Network, October 12, 1992), pp. 53, 61, 82, 85, 86, 115, 124, 125, 127, 129, 131, 167:

"At this time I have seen and put in study to look into all the Scriptures, cosmography, histories, chronicles and philosophy and other arts, which our Lord opened to my understanding (I could sense His hand upon me), so that it became clear to me that it was feasible to navigate from here to the Indies; and He unlocked within me the determination to execute the idea. And I came to your Highnesses with this ardor.

"All those who heard about my enterprise rejected it with laughter, scoffing at me. Neither the sciences which I mentioned above, nor the authoritative citations from them, were of any avail. In only your Highnesses remained faith and constancy. Who doubts that this illumination was from the Holy Spirit? I attest that He (the Spirit), with marvelous rays of light, consoled me through the holy and sacred Scriptures...encouraging me to proceed, and, continually, without ceasing for a moment, they inflame me with a sense of great urgency....

"I am the worst of sinners. The pity and mercy of our Lord have completely covered me whenever I have called(on Him) for them. I have found the sweetest consolation in casting away all my anxiety, so as to contemplate His marvelous presence.

"I have already said that for the execution of the enterprise of the Indies, neither reason, nor mathematics, nor world maps were profitable to me; rather the prophecy of Isaiah was completely fulfilled....

"Your Highnesses, remember the Gospel texts and the many promises which our Savior made to us, and how all this has been put to a test: (for example) St. Peter, when he leapt into the sea, walked upon(the water) as long as his faith remained firm. The mountains will obey anyone who has faith the size of a kernel of Indian corn. All that is requested by anyone who has faith will be granted. Knock and it will be opened to you.

"No one should be afraid to take on any enterprise in the name of our Savior, if it is right and if the purpose is purely for His holy service....The working out of all things was entrusted by our Lord to each person (but it happens) in conformity with His sovereign will, even though he gives advice to many. He lacks nothing that it may be in the power of men to give him.

"O, how good is the Lord who wishes people to perform that for which he holds himself responsible! Day and night, and at every moment, everyone should give Him their most devoted thanks."

[82] **Christopher Columbus.** *Church of the Holy Trinity v. U.S.*, 143 U.S. 465-468 (1892). David Barton, *The Myth of Separation* (Aledo, TX: WallBuilder Press, 1991), p. 48.

[83] **Christopher Columbus.** Queen Isabella's Commission to Christopher Columbus circa 1490-1492. *Letter from Plymouth Rock* (Marlborough, NH: The Plymouth Rock Foundation), p. 1.

[84] **Christopher Columbus.** August 3, 1492, as recounted by Bartolome' de Las Casas. Samuel Eliot Morison, *Admiral of the Ocean Sea* (Boston: Little, Brown & Co., 1942), p. 149. John Eidsmoe, *Columbus & Cortez, Conquerors for Christ* (Green Forest, AR: New Leaf Press, 1992), p. 106.

[85] **Christopher Columbus.** John Eidsmoe, *Columbus & Cortez, Conquerors for Christ* (Green Forest, AR: New Leaf Press, 1992), p. 107.

[86] **Christopher Columbus.** John Eidsmoe, *Columbus & Cortez, Conquerors for Christ* (Green Forest, AR: New Leaf Press, 1992), p. 107.

[87] **Christopher Columbus.** John Eidsmoe, *Columbus & Cortez, Conquerors for Christ* (Green Forest, AR: New Leaf Press, 1992), p. 107.

[88] **Christopher Columbus.** 1492, in the opening of the journal of his first voyage. Samuel Eliot Morison, *Journals & Other Documents on the Life & Voyage of Christopher Columbus* (New York: Heritage Press, 1963), pp. 47-48. John Eidsmoe, *Columbus & Cortez, Conquerors for Christ* (Green Forest, AR: New Leaf Press, 1992), p. 84.

[89] **Christopher Columbus.** October 8, 10, 12, 16, 28, November 6, 27, December 12, 16, 22, 24, 1492, in his *Journal of the First Voyage* (*El Libro de la Primera Navegacion*), as recounted in Bartolome' de Las Casas' abstract, translated into English by Samuel Eliot Morison, *Journals & Other Documents on the Life & Voyage of Christopher Columbus* (New York: Heritage Press, 1963), pp. 65, 72. John Bartlett, *Bartlett's Familiar Quotations* (Boston: Little, Brown and Company, 1855, 1980), pp. 150-151. John Eidsmoe, *Columbus & Cortez, Conquerors for Christ* (Green Forest, AR: New Leaf Press, 1992), pp. 85-86. Bjorn Landstrom, *Columbus* (New York: The Macmillan Co., 1966), pp. 66-75. Peter Marshall and David Manual, *The Light and the Glory* (Old Tappan, NJ: Fleming H. Revell Company, 1977), p. 42.

[90] **Christopher Columbus.** Bjorn Landstrom, *Columbus* (New York: The Macmillan Co., 1966), pp. 66-75. Peter Marshall and David Manuel, *The Light and the Glory* (Old Tappan, NJ: Fleming H. Revell Company, 1977), p. 41.

[91] **Christopher Columbus.** Bjorn Landstrom, *Columbus* (New York: The Macmillan Co., 1966), pp. 66-75. Peter Marshall and David Manuel, *The Light and the Glory* (Old Tappan, NJ: Fleming H. Revell Company, 1977), p. 43. Zvi Dor-Ner, *Columbus and the Age of Discovery* (New York: Morrow & Co., 1991), p. 150. John Eidsmoe, *Columbus & Cortez, Conquerors for Christ* (Green Forest, AR: New Leaf Press, 1992), p. 108.

[92] **Christopher Columbus.** Personal log. "Our Christian Heritage," *Letter from Plymouth Rock* (Marlborough, NH: The Plymouth Rock Foundation), p. 1.

[93] **Christopher Columbus.** *Book of Prophecies.* Facsimile manuscript pages with English translation by Kay Brigham. Catherine Millard, *A Children's Companion Guide to America's History* (Camp Hill, PA: Horizon House Publishers, 1993), p. 5.

[94] **Christopher Columbus.** January 13, 1493, in his journal, as recounted by Bartolome' de Las Casas. Samuel Eliot Morison, *Journals & Other Documents on the Life & Voyages of Christopher Columbus* (New York: Heritage Press, 1963), p. 152. John Eidsmoe, *Columbus & Cortez, Conquerors for Christ* (Green Forest, AR: New Leaf Press, 1992), p. 110.

[95] **Christopher Columbus.** February 15, 1493, in a letter to Luis de Sant Angel, Treasurer of Aragon and Chancellor of the Exchequer, sent with correspondence to their Highnesses, King Ferdinand and Queen Isabella of Spain, from on board the ship *Caravel* anchored off the Canary Islands. Samuel Eliot Morison, *Journals & Other Documents on the Life & Voyages of Christopher Columbus* (New York: Heritage Press, 1963), pp. 182-186. John Eidsmoe, *Columbus & Cortez, Conquerors for Christ* (Green Forest, AR: New Leaf Press, 1992), pp. 86-88, 108. J.M. Dickey, compiler, *Christopher Columbus and his Monument*, p. 321. Stephen Abbott Northrop, D.D., *A Cloud of Witnesses* (Portland, Oregon: American Heritage Ministries, 1987; Mantle Ministries, 228 Still Ridge, Bulverde, Texas), p. 95. Also in another translation taken from the *American History Leaflets*, Professors Hart and Channing, editors. Charles W. Eliot, LL.D., ed., *American Historical Documents 1000-1904* (New York: P.F. Collier & Son Company, *The Harvard Classics*, 1910), Vol. 43, pp. 22-28.

[96] **Christopher Columbus.** March 15, 1493, in his *Journal of the First Voyage* (*El Libro de la Primera Navegacion*), as recounted in Bartolome' de Las Casas' abstract, translated into English by Samuel Eliot Morison, *Journals & Other Documents on the Life & Voyages of Christopher Columbus* (New York: Heritage Press, 1963), pp. 65, 72. John Bartlett, *Bartlett's Familiar Quotations* (Boston: Little, Brown and Company, 1855, 1980), pp. 150-151. John Eidsmoe, *Columbus & Cortez, Conquerors for Christ* (Green Forest, AR: New Leaf Press, 1992), pp. 85-86. Bjorn Landstrom, *Columbus* (New York: The Macmillan Co., 1966), pp. 66-75. Peter Marshall and David Manual, *The Light and the Glory* (Old Tappan, NJ: Fleming H. Revell Company, 1977), p. 42.

[97] **Christopher Columbus.** In his letter to Gabriel Sanchez, Spain's General Treasurer 1493. *Letter from Plymouth Rock* (Marlborough, NH: The Plymouth Rock Foundation), p. 1.

[98] **Christopher Columbus.** Samuel Eliot Morrison, "Christopher Columbus-Mariner" (*American Heritage*, December 1955), p. 93. Paul G. Humber, *Columbus and His Creator* (El Cajon, CA: Impact, Institute for Creation Research, October 1991), No. 220, p. ii.

[99] **Christopher Columbus.** In a letter from Queen Isabella to the Pope. Cecil Jane, trans. & ed., *The Voyages of Christopher Columbus* (London: Argonaut Press, 1930), p. 146. Peter Marshall and David Manuel, *The Glory of America* (Bloomington, MN: Garborg's Heart'N Home, Inc., 1991), 10.11.

[100] **Christopher Columbus.** April 9, 1493, in a letter to King Ferdinand and Queen Isabella requesting permission for his second voyage. Samuel Eliot Morison, *Journals & Other Documents on the Life & Voyages of Christopher Columbus* (New York: Heritage Press, 1963), p. 200. John Eidsmoe, *Columbus & Cortez, Conquerors for Christ* (Green Forest, AR: New Leaf Press, 1992), p. 112.

[101] **Christopher Columbus.** May 29, 1493, permission granted Columbus for a second voyage by the Sovereigns, King Ferdinand and Queen Isabella. Samuel Eliot Morison, *Journals & Other Documents on the Life & Voyages of Christopher Columbus* (New York: Heritage Press, 1963), pp. 204-204. John Eidsmoe, *Columbus & Cortez, Conquerors for Christ* (Green Forest, AR: New Leaf Press, 1992), pp. 112-113.

¹⁰² **Christopher Columbus.** November 1495. Michele de Cuneo in a letter to a friend. Samuel Eliot Morison, *Journals & Other Documents on the Life & Voyages of Christopher Columbus* (New York: Heritage Press, 1963), pp. 211-220. John Eidsmoe, *Columbus & Cortez, Conquerors for Christ* (Green Forest, AR: New Leaf Press, 1992), pp. 113, 137-138.

¹⁰³ **Christopher Columbus.** Letter of Dr. Diego Alvarez Chanca. Felipe Fernandez-Arnesto, *Columbus and the Conquest of the Impossible* (New York: Saturday Review Press, 1974), p. 118. John Eidsmoe, *Columbus & Cortez, Conquerors for Christ* (Green Forest, AR: New Leaf Press, 1992), pp. 136-137.

¹⁰⁴ **Christopher Columbus.** *Letter from Don Cristobal Colon to his son, Don Diego*, published by the Duchess of Berwick y Alba. Maurice David, *Who was Christopher Columbus?* (New York: The Research Publishing Company, 1933), p. 92. Catherine Millard, *The Rewriting of America's History* (Camp Hill, PA: Horizon House Publishers, 1991), p. 3. Catherine Millard, *A Children's Companion Guide to America's History* (Camp Hill, PA: Horizon House Publishers, 1993), p. 5.

¹⁰⁵ **Christopher Columbus.** October 18, 1498, in a letter to the Sovereigns of Spain while on his third voyage. John Bartlett, *Bartlett's Familiar Quotations* (Boston: Little, Brown and Company, 1855, 1980), p. 151.

¹⁰⁶ **Christopher Columbus.** Letter from Don Cristobal Colon to his son, Don Diego, published by the Duchess of Berwick y Alba. Maurice David, *Who was Christopher Columbus?* (New York: The Research Publishing Company, 1933), pp. 68-69. Catherine Millard, *A Children's Companion Guide to America's History* (Camp Hill, PA: Horizon House Publishers, 1993), p. 5.

¹⁰⁷ **Christopher Columbus.** December 26, 1499, Christopher Columbus, as quoted by Ferdinand Columbus, *The Life of the Admiral Christopher Columbus*, trans. by Benjamin Keen (New Brunswick, NJ: Rutgers University Press, 1959), p. 219. John Eidsmoe, *Columbus & Cortez, Conquerors for Christ* (Green Forest, AR: New Leaf Press, 1992), p. 117.

¹⁰⁸ **Christopher Columbus.** October 1500, in letter to Dona Juana de Torres, as Columbus was being taken as a prisoner from the Indies to Cadiz. Samuel Eliot Morison, *Journals & Other Documents on the Life & Voyages of Christopher Columbus* (New York: Heritage Press, 1963), pp. 290-296. John Eidsmoe, *Columbus & Cortez, Conquerors for Christ* (Green Forest, AR: New Leaf Press, 1992), pp. 118-119. John Bartlett, *Bartlett's Familiar Quotations* (Boston: Little, Brown and Company, 1855, 1980), p. 151.

¹⁰⁹ **Christopher Columbus.** Samuel Eliot Morrison, *Admiral of the Ocean Sea* (Boston: Little, Brown and Co., 1942), pp. 6, 206, 476, 494. Paul G. Humber, *Columbus and His Creator* (El Cajon, CA: Impact, Institute for Creation Research, 1991), No. 220, p. iv, October 1991.

¹¹⁰ **Christopher Columbus.** Simon Wiesenthal, *Sails of Hope* (New York: Macmillan Publishing Co., Inc., 1973), p. 122. Paul G. Humber, *Columbus and His Creator* (El Cajon, CA: Impact, Institute for Creation Research, 1991), No. 220, pp. iii-iv, October 1991.

¹¹¹ **Christopher Columbus.** 1501, Christopher Columbus in his *Book of Prophecies*. Salvador de Madariaga, *Christopher Columbus, Being the Life of the Very Magnificent Lord Don Cristobal* (New York: Frederick Ungar, 1940, 1967), p. 361. Kay Brigham, *Christopher Columbus - His life and discovery in the light of his prophecies* (Terrassa, Barcelona: CLIE Publishers, 1990; rendered from the original Spanish Language as *a compilation of passages from the Bible which the Admiral believed were pertinent to his mission of discovery, selected by Columbus himself with the help of his friend, Fray Gaspar de Gorricio*), pp. 53, 61, 82, 85, 86, 115, 124, 125, 127, 129, 167. Paul G. Humber, *Columbus and His Creator* (El Cajon, CA: Impact, Institute for Creation Research, 1991), No. 220, pp. iii-iv, October 1991. John Eidsmoe, *Columbus & Cortez, Conquerors for Christ* (Green Forest, AR: New Leaf Press, 1992), p. 88.

¹¹² **Christopher Columbus.** July 7, 1503, in his *Lettera Rarissima* to Sovereigns, written while shipwrecked on the coast of Jamaica. Samuel Eliot Morison, *Journals & Other Documents on the Life & Voyages of Christopher Columbus* (New York: Heritage Press, 1963), p. 378. John Eidsmoe, *Columbus & Cortez, Conquerors for Christ* (Green Forest, AR: New Leaf Press, 1992), pp. 122-124.

¹¹³ **Christopher Columbus.** July 7, 1503, in his *Lettera Rarissiam to the Sovereigns*, while on his fourth and final voyage, as translated by Milton Anastos. Notarized English translation. Library of Congress Rare Manuscript Collection, Washington, D.C. Catherine Millard, *A Children's Companion Guide to America's History* (Camp Hill, PA: Horizon House Publishers, 1993), p. 5. John Bartlett, *Bartlett's Familiar Quotations* (Boston: Little, Brown and Company, 1855, 1980), pp. 151-152.

¹¹⁴ **Christopher Columbus.** Columbus, *Libro de las profecias (Book of Prophecies)*. Kay Brigham, *Christopher Columbus - His life and discovery in the light of his prophecies* (Terrassa, Barcelona: CLIE Publishers, 1990), p. 97. Peter Marshall and David Manuel, *The Glory of America* (Bloomington, MN: Garborg's Heart'N Home, Inc., 1991), 10.13.

¹¹⁵ **Christopher Columbus.** Signature. Catherine Millard, *The Rewriting of America's History* (Camp Hill, PA: Horizon House Publishers, 1991), p. 2. Catherine Millard, *A Children's Companion Guide to America's History* (Camp Hill, PA: Horizon House Publishers, 1993), p. 3.

¹¹⁶ **Christopher Columbus.** Ferdinand Columbus, *The Life of the Admiral Christopher Columbus*, trans. by Benjamin Keen (New Brunswick, NJ: Rutgers University Press, 1959), pp. 4-5, 9. John Eidsmoe, *Columbus & Cortez, Conquerors for Christ* (Green Forest, AR: New Leaf Press, 1992), pp. 79-80, 95-96.

¹¹⁷ **Christopher Columbus.** Bartolome' de Las Casas, *Historie de las Indias*. Samuel Eliot Morison, *Admiral of the Ocean Sea* (Boston: Little, Brown & Co., 1942), pp. 45-46. John Eidsmoe, *Columbus & Cortez, Conquerors for Christ* (Green Forest, AR: New Leaf Press, 1992), pp. 96-97.

¹¹⁸ **Christopher Columbus.** Ferdinand Columbus, *The Life of the Admiral Christopher Columbus*, trans. Benjamin Keen (New Brunswick, NJ: Rutgers University Press, 1959), pp. 284-285. Wilbur E. Garrett, *Columbus and the New World* (National Geographic, November 1986), p. 564. John Eidsmoe, *Columbus & Cortez, Conquerors for Christ* (Green Forest, AR: New Leaf Press, 1992), p. 125.

¹¹⁹ **Congress of Massachusetts, Provincial.** October 22, 1774, in a Declaration by President John Hancock. George Bancroft, *Bancroft's History of the United States* (Boston: Charles C. Little & James Brown, 1838), Vol. VII, p. 229. Peter Marshall and David Manuel, *The Light and the Glory* (Old Tappan, NJ: Fleming H. Revell Company, 1977), p. 269.

¹²⁰ **Congress of Massachusetts, Provincial.** 1774. George Bancroft, *Bancroft's History of the United States* (Boston: Charles C. Little & James Brown, 1838), Vol. VII, p. 229. Peter Marshall and David Manuel, *The Glory of America* (Bloomington, MN: Garborg's Heart'N Home, Inc., 1991), 8.31.

¹²¹ **Congress of Massachusetts, Provincial.** 1774, Minutemen. Richard Frothingham, *Rise of the Republic of the United States* (Boston: Little Brown & Co., 1872), pp. 393, 458. David Barton, *The Myth of Separation* (Aledo, TX: WallBuilder Press, 1991), p. 94.

¹²² **Congress of Massachusetts, Provincial.** 1774, Charge to the Minutemen. Richard Frothingham, *Rise of the Republic of the United States* (Boston: Little, Brown & Co., 1872), p. 393. David Barton, *The Myth of Separation* (Aledo, TX: WallBuilder Press, 1991), pp. 94-95.

¹²³ **Continental Congress.** September 6, 1774. *The Journals of the Continental Congress 1774-1789* (Washington, D.C.: Government Printing Office, 1905), Vol. I, p. 26. David Barton, *The Myth of Separation* (Aledo, TX: WallBuilder Press, 1991), p. 100.

Notes

[124] **Continental Congress.** September 7, 1774. *The Journals of the Continental Congress 1774-1789* (Washington, D.C.: Government Printing Office, 1905), Vol. I, p. 27. David Barton, *The Myth of Separation* (Aledo, TX: WallBuilder Press, 1991), p. 101.

[125] **Continental Congress.** September 7, 1774. *First Prayer in Congress - Beautiful Reminiscence* (Washington, D.C.: Library of Congress). John S.C. Abbot, *George Washington* (NY: Dodd, Mead & Co., 1875, 1917), p. 187. Gary DeMar, *God and Government - A Biblical and Historical Study* (Atlanta, GA: American Vision Press, 1982), Vol. I, p. 108. David Barton, *The Myth of Separation* (Aledo, TX: WallBuilder Press, 1991), pp. 101-102.

[126] **Continental Congress.** September 7, 1774. Charles Francis Adams (son of John Quincy Adams and grandson of John Adams), ed., *Letters of John Adams Addressed To His Wife* (Boston: Charles C. Little and James Brown, 1841), Vol. I, pp. 23-24. Edmund Fuller and David E. Green, *God in the White House - The Faiths of American Presidents* (NY: Crown Publishers, Inc., 1968), pp. 21-22. L.H. Butterfield, Marc Frielander, and Mary-Jo King, eds., *The Book of Abigail and John - Selected Letters of The Adams Family 1762-1784* (Cambridge, Massachusetts and London, England: Harvard University Press, 1975), p. 76. David Barton, *The Myth of Separation* (Aledo, TX: WallBuilder Press, 1991), p. 101.

[127] **Continental Congress.** September 7, 1774, Rev. Mr. Duche' reading Psalm 35. "Our Christian Heritage," *Letter from Plymouth Rock* (Marlborough, NH: The Plymouth Rock Foundation), pp. 2-3. Catherine Millard, *The Rewriting of America's History* (Camp Hill, PA: Horizon House Publishers, 1991), p. 249.

[128] **Continental Congress.** September 7, 1774. *First Prayer in Congress - Beautiful Reminiscence* (Washington, D.C.: Library of Congress) Gary DeMar, *God and Government - A Biblical and Historical Study* (Atlanta, GA: American Vision Press, 1982), Vol. I, p. 108. John S.C. Abbot, *George Washington* (NY: Dodd, Mead & Co., 1875, 1917), p. 187. David Barton, *The Myth of Separation* (Aledo, TX: WallBuilder Press, 1991), pp. 101-102. Reynolds, *The Maine Scholars Manual* (Portland, ME: Dresser, McLellan & Co., 1880).

[129] **Continental Congress.** September 7, 1774. *First Prayer in Congress - Beautiful Reminiscence* (Washington, D.C.: Library of Congress). Gary DeMar, *God and Government - A Biblical and Historical Study* (Atlanta, GA: American Vision Press, 1982), Vol. I, p. 108. John S.C. Abbot, *George Washington* (NY: Dodd, Mead & Co., 1875, 1917), p. 187. David Barton, *The Myth of Separation* (Aledo, TX: WallBuilder Press, 1991), pp. 101-102.

[130] **Continental Congress.** September 1774, Article X of the Articles of Association. Catherine Millard, *The Rewriting of America's History* (Camp Hill, PA: Horizon House Publishers, 1991), pp. 77-78.

[131] **Continental Congress.** June 12, 1775. *The Journals of the Continental Congress 1774-1789* (Washington, D.C.: Government Printing Office, 1905), Vol. II, p. 87. "Our Christian Heritage," *Letter from Plymouth Rock* (Marlborough, NH: The Plymouth Rock Foundation), p. 3. David Barton, *The Myth of Separation* (Aledo, TX: WallBuilder Press, 1991), p. 98. Verna M. Hall, *Christian History of the American Revolution - Consider and Ponder* (San Francisco: Foundation for American Christian Education, 1976), p. 506. Lucille Johnston, *Celebrations of a Nation* (Arlington, VA: The Year of Thanksgiving Foundation, 1987), pp. 75-76.

[132] **Continental Congress** July 6, 1775, passed *The Declaration of the Causes and Necessity for Taking Up Arms*, composed by Thomas Jefferson. *Journals of the American Congress - from 1774 to 1788*, Vol. I, Thursday, July 6, 1775. Henry Steele Commager, ed., *Documents of American History*, 2 vols. (NY: F.S. Crofts and Company, 1934; Appleton-Century-Crofts, Inc., 1948, 6th edition, 1958; Englewood Cliffs, NJ: Prentice Hall, Inc., 9th edition, 1973), Vol. I, p. 95. *The Annals of America*, 20 vols. (Chicago, IL: Encyclopedia Britannica, 1968, 1977), Vol. 2, pp. 337-341. Richard Maxfield, K. De Lynn Cook, and W. Cleon Skousen, *The Real Thomas Jefferson* (Washington, D.C.: National Center for Constitutional Studies, 2nd edition, 1981, 1983), p. 403. Marshall Foster and Mary-Elaine Swanson, *The American Covenant - The Untold Story* (Roseburg, OR: Foundation for Christian Self-Government, 1981; Thousand Oaks, CA: The Mayflower Institute, 1983, 1992), p. 33. John Eidsmoe, *Christianity and the Constitution - The Faith of Our Founding Fathers* (Grand Rapids, MI: Baker Book House, A Mott Media Book, 1987; 6th printing, 1993), p. 227. Peter Marshall, & David Manuel, *The Glory of America* (Bloomington, MN: Garborg's Heart 'N Home, 1991), 7.6.

[133] **Continental Congress.** April 15, 1775. *The Journals of the Continental Congress 1774-1789* (Washington, D.C.: Government Printing Office, 1905), Vol. II, p. 192. David Barton, *The Myth of Separation* (Aledo, TX: WallBuilder Press, 1991), p. 103.

[134] **Continental Congress.** March 16, 1776, passed a resolution declaring May 17, 1776, as a *National Day of Humiliation, Fasting and Prayer*, presented by General William Livingston. *Journals of Congress*, Vol. II, p. 93. *The Journals of the Continental Congress 1774-1789* (Washington, D.C.: Government Printing Office, 1905), Vol. IV, pp. 208-209. Carl E. Prince, ed., *The Papers of William Livingston*, 5 vols. (Trenton: New Jersey Historical Commission, 1979), Vol. I, pp. 43-44. Stephen Abbott Northrop, D.D., *A Cloud of Witnesses* (Portland, Oregon: American Heritage Ministries, 1987; Mantle Ministries, 228 Still Ridge, Bulverde, Texas), pp. 287-288. "Our Christian Heritage," *Letter from Plymouth Rock* (Marlborough, NH: The Plymouth Rock Foundation), p. 3. M.E. Bradford, *Religion & The Framers - The Biographical Evidence* (Marlborough, NH: Plymouth Rock Foundation, 1991), p. 5. David Barton, *The Myth of Separation* (Aledo, TX: WallBuilder Press, 1991), p. 103.

[135] **Continental Congress.** July 1, 1776, in a speech by John Adams. Dan Smoot, *America's Promise* (Dallas, TX: The Dan Smoot Report, 1960), p. 6. Peter Marshall and David Manuel, *The Glory of America* (Bloomington, MN: Garborg's Heart 'N Home, Inc., 1991), 7.1. D.P. Diffine, Ph.D., *One Nation Under God - How Close a Separation?* (Searcy, Arkansas: Harding University, Belden Center for Private Enterprise Education, 1992), p. 7.

[136] **Continental Congress.** July 2, 1776, The Declaration of Independence, Philadelphia, PA. Charles W. Eliot, LL.D., ed., *American Historical Documents 1000-1904* (New York: P.F. Collier & Son Company, The Harvard Classics, 1910), Vol. 43, pp. 160-165. United States Supreme Court, *Church of the Holy Trinity v. United States*, 143 US 457, 458, 465-471, 36 L ed 226, (1892), Justice David Josiah Brewer. "Our Christian Heritage," *Letter from Plymouth Rock* (Marlborough, NH: The Plymouth Rock Foundation), p. 6. David Barton, *The Myth of Separation* (Aledo, TX: WallBuilder Press, 1991), pp. 47-51, 269-272. D.P. Diffine, Ph.D., *One Nation Under God - How Close a Separation?* (Searcy, Arkansas: Harding University, Belden Center for Private Enterprise Education, 6th edition, 1992), p. 6. Stephen McDowell and Mark Beliles, "The Providential Perspective" (Charlottesville, VA: The Providence Foundation, P.O. Box 6759, Charlottesville, Va. 22906, January 1994), Vol. 9, No. 1, p. 2.

[137] **Continental Congress.** July 2, 1776. Charles E. Kistler, *This Nation Under God* (Boston: Richard G. Badger, The Gorham Press, 1924), p. 71. Peter Marshall and David Manuel, *The Light and the Glory* (NJ: Fleming H. Revell Co., 1977), p. 309. David Barton, *The Myth of Separation* (Aledo, TX: WallBuilder Press, 1991), p. 98. "Our Christian Heritage," *Letter from Plymouth Rock* (Marlborough, NH: The Plymouth Rock Foundation), p. 8. D.P. Diffine, Ph.D., *One Nation Under God - How Close a Separation?* (Searcy, Arkansas: Harding University, Belden Center for Private Enterprise Education, 6th edition, 1992), p. 6.

[138] **Continental Congress.** July 3, 1776, in a message given by John Adams given to Congress. Catherine Millard, *The Rewriting of America's History* (Camp Hill, PA: Horizon House Publishers, 1991) p. 77.

[139] **Continental Congress.** July 3, 1776, John Adams, in a letter to his wife Abigail. Charles Francis Adams (son of John Quincy

Adams and grandson of John Adams), ed.,*Letters of John Adams-Addressed to His Wife* (Boston: Charles C. Little and James Brown, 1841), Vol. I, p. 1 28. *The World Book Encyclopedia*, 18 vols. (Chicago, IL: Field Enterprises, Inc., 1957; W.F. Quarrie and Company, 8 vols., 1917; World Book, Inc., 22 vols., 1989), Vol. 9, p. 3683. L.H. Butterfield, ed., *Adams Family Correspondence* (Cambridge: Harvard University Press, 1963), Vol. II, p. 28-31. Peter Marshall and David Manuel, *The Light and the Glory* (Old Tappan, NJ: Fleming H. Revell, 1977), pp. 310-311. Catherine Millard, *The Rewriting of America's History* (Camp Hill, PA: Horizon House Publishers, 1991) p. 77. David Barton, *The Myth of Separation* (Aledo, TX: WallBuilder Press, 1991), p. 98. D.P. Diffine, Ph.D.,*One Nation Under God - How Close a Separation?* (Searcy, Arkansas: Harding University, Belden Center for Private Enterprise Education, 6th edition, 1992), p. 6.

[140] **Continental Congress.** July 4, 1776, Declaration of Independence. Dan Valentine,*Spirit of America - American Essays* (Salt Lake City, UT: Geo. Mc Co., 1972), No. 9, p. 37.

[141] **Continental Congress.** July 8, 1776. Charles Francis Adams (son of John Quincy Adams and grandson of John Adams), ed., *Letters of John Adams Addressed to His Wife* (Boston: Charles C. Little and James Brown, 1841), Vol. I, p. 152. David Barton, *The Myth of Separation* (Aledo, TX: WallBuilder Press, 1991), p. 104. John Adams and Abigail Adams, *The Book of Abigail and John - Selected Letters from The Adams Family 1762-1784*, L.H. Butterfield, Marc Frielander and Mary-Jo Kings, eds. (Cambridge, MA: Harvard University Press, 1975), August 14, 1776, p. 154. David Barton, *The Myth of Separation* (Aledo, TX: WallBuilder Press, 1991), p. 104. "Our Christian Heritage," *Letter from Plymouth Rock* (Marlborough, NH: The Plymouth Rock Foundation), p. 3.

[142] **Continental Congress.** July 8, 1776. Charles Francis Adams (son of John Quincy Adams and grandson of John Adams), ed., *Letters of John Adams Addressed to His Wife* (Boston: Charles C. Little and James Brown, 1841), Vol. I, p. 152. David Barton, *The Myth of Separation* (Aledo, TX: WallBuilder Press, 1991), p. 104. "Our Christian Heritage," *Letter from Plymouth Rock* (Marlborough, NH: The Plymouth Rock Foundation), p. 3.

[143] **Continental Congress.** July 9, 1776. *The Journals of the Continental Congress 1774-1789* (Washington, D.C.: Government Printing Office, 1905), Vol. V, 1776, p. 530. Charles Francis Adams (son of John Quincy Adams and grandson of John Adams), *Familiar Letters of John Adams with his wife Abigail Adams - during the Revolution* (NY: Hurd and Houghton, 1876), p. 320. Anson Phelps Stokes and Leo Pfeffer,*Church and State in the United States* (NY: Harper and Row, Publishers, 1950, revised one-volume edition, 1964), p. 83. David Barton, *The Myth of Separation* (Aledo, TX: WallBuilder Press, 1991), pp. 103-104.

[144] **Continental Congress.** July 9, 1776. John Clement Fitzpatrick, ed., *The Writings of George Washington, from the Original Manuscript Sources 1749-1799*, 39 vols. (Washington, D.C.: United States Government Printing Office, 1931-1944), Vol. V, pp. 244-245. *American Army Chaplaincy - A Brief History* (prepared in the Office of the Chief of Chaplains: 1946), p. 6. Anson Phelps Stokes and Leo Pfeffer,*Church and State in the United States* (NY: Harper and Row, Publishers, 1950, revised one-volume edition, 1964), p. 35. "Our Christian Heritage," *Letter from Plymouth Rock* (Marlborough, NH: The Plymouth Rock Foundation), p. 3. David Barton, *The Myth of Separation* (Aledo, TX: WallBuilder Press, 1991), p. 104. Pay for chaplains was previously $20.00 a month, approved July 1775. *American Army Chaplaincy - A Brief History* (prepared in the Office of the Chief of Chaplains: 1946), p. 6. Anson Phelps Stokes and Leo Pfeffer, *Church and State in the United States* (NY: Harper and Row, Publishers, 1950, revised one-volume edition, 1964), p. 35.

[145] **Continental Congress.** July 9, 1776, authorized the Continental Army to provide chaplains for their troops to be paid the rate of pay for captains; Commander in Chief, General George Washington, following the reading of the Declaration of Independence, issued the order from his headquarters in New York to appoint chaplains to every regiment. *Writings of George Washington*, (Sparks ed.), XII, 401, citing *Orderly Book*; also orders of August 3, 1776, in ibid., IV, 28 n. Abraham Lincoln quoted this order of Washington's on November 15, 1862, to have his troops maintain regular sabbath observances. Abraham Lincoln, *Letters and Addresses and Abraham Lincoln* (NY: Unit Book Publishing Co., 1907), p. 261. John Clement Fitzpatrick, ed., *The Writings of George Washington, from the Original Manuscript Sources 1749-1799*, 39 vols. (Washington, D.C.: United States Government Printing Office, 1931-1944), Vol. V, p. 245. William Barclay Allen, ed.,*George Washington - A Collection* (Indianapolis: Liberty Classics, Liberty Fund, Inc., 7440 N. Shadeland, Indianapolis, Indiana 46250, 1988; based almost entirely on materials reproduced from *The Writings of George Washington, from the original manuscript sources, 1745-1799*/John Clement Fitzpatrick, editor), p. 73. John F. Schroeder, ed., *Maxims of Washington* (Mt. Vernon: Mt. Vernon Ladies' Association, 1942), p. 299. Saxe Commins, ed., *The Basic Writings of George Washington* (NY: Random House, 1948), p. 236. Anson Phelps Stokes and Leo Pfeffer, *Church and State in the United States* (NY: Harper and Row, Publishers, 1950, revised one-volume edition, 1964), p. 35. Norman Cousins,*In God We Trust - The Religious Beliefs and Ideas of the Founding Fathers* (NY: Harper & Brothers, 1958), p. 50. Paul F. Boller, Jr., *George Washington and Religion* (Dallas: Southern Methodist University Press, 1963), p. 69. Frank Donovan, *Mr. Jefferson's Declaration* (New York: Dodd Mead & Co., 1968), p. 192. A. James Reichley, *Religion in American Public Life* (Washington, D.C.: The Brookings Institute, 1985), p. 99. Tim LaHaye, *Faith of Our Founding Fathers* (Brentwood, TN: Wolgemuth & Hyatt, Publishers, Inc., 1987), p. 108. John Eidsmoe, *Christianity and The Constitution - The Faith of Our Founding Fathers* (Grand Rapids, MI: Baker Book House, A Mott Media Book, 1987, 6th printing 1993), pp. 120-121. David Barton, *The Myth of Separation* (Aledo, TX: WallBuilder Press, 1991), p. 98. During the Civil War, a complaint was made concerning the lack of chaplains to serve Jewish soldiers. New wording was written on July 12, 1862, to include ministers of the Hebrew faith. The previous law had read: "The chaplain so appointed must be a regular ordained minister of a Christian denomination." Anson Phelps Stokes and Leo Pfeffer, *Church and State in the United States* (NY: Harper and Row, Publishers, 1950, revised one-volume edition, 1964), p. 473.

[146] **Continental Congress.** September 11, 1777. Robert Flood,*The Rebirth of America* (Philadelphia: Arthur S. DeMoss Foundation, 1986), p. 39.*Journals of the Continental Congress 1774-1789* (Washington, D.C.: Government Printing Office, 1905), book 146, Vol. VIII, pp. 731-735. *Journal of the American Congress, 1774-1788* (Washington: 1823), Vol. II, pp. 261-262. David Barton, *The Myth of Separation* (Aledo, TX: WallBuilder Press, 1991), p. 104. Tim LaHaye, *Faith of Our Founding Fathers* (Brentwood, TN: Wolgemuth & Hyatt, Publishers, Inc., 1987), p. 96. Benjamin Franklin Morris, *The Christian Life and Character of the Civil Institutions of the United States* (Philadelphia, PA: G.W. Childs, 1864), pp. 215-216. Gary DeMar, *America's Christian History: The Untold Story* (Atlanta, GA: American Vision Publishers, Inc., 1993), pp. 47-48. D.P. Diffine, Ph.D., *One Nation Under God - How Close a Separation?* (Searcy, Arkansas: Harding University, Belden Center for Private Enterprise Education, 6th edition, 1992), p. 2.

[147] **Continental Congress.** November 1, 1777, Congress ordered a National Day of Thanksgiving to Almighty God, signed by Henry Laurens, President of the Continental Congress. Papers of the Continental Congress,*National Thanksgiving Proclamation*, November 1, 1777, National Archives Collection, Washington, D.C.*Journals of the Continental Congress 1774-1789* (Washington, D.C.: Government Printing Office, 1905), Vol. IX, pp. 854-855. National Archives Collection, Washington, D.C. David Barton, *The Myth of Separation* (Aledo, TX: WallBuilder Press, 1991), p. 105. "Our Christian Heritage," *Letter from Plymouth Rock*

Notes

(Marlborough, NH: The Plymouth Rock Foundation), pp. 3-4. Catherine Millard, *The Rewriting of America's History* (Camp Hill, PA: Horizon House Publishers, 1991), pp. 303-304. Catherine Millard, *A Children's Companion Guide to America's History* (Camp Hill, PA: Horizon House Publishers, 1993), p. 23.

148 Continental Congress. November 15, 1777, proposed the Articles of Confederation; signed in Congress, July 9, 1778, and ratified by the States, March 1, 1781. Charles W. Eliot, LL.D., ed., *American Historical Documents 1000-1904* (New York: P.F. Collier & Son Company, *The Harvard Classics,* 1910), Vol. 43, pp. 168-179. John Wilson Taylor, M.A., Ph.D., et al., *The Lincoln Library of Essential Information* (Buffalo, New York: The Frontier Press Company, 1935), pp. 1392-1394. "Our Christian Heritage," *Letter from Plymouth Rock* (Marlborough, NH: The Plymouth Rock Foundation), p. 3.

149 Continental Congress. November 15, 1777, proposed the Articles of Confederation; signed in Congress, July 9, 1778, and ratified by the States, March 1, 1781. Charles W. Eliot, LL.D., ed., *American Historical Documents 1000-1904* (New York: P.F. Collier & Son Company, *The Harvard Classics,* 1910), Vol. 43, pp. 168-179. John Wilson Taylor, M.A., Ph.D., et al., *The Lincoln Library of Essential Information* (Buffalo, New York: The Frontier Press Company, 1935), pp. 1392-1394. "Our Christian Heritage," *Letter from Plymouth Rock* (Marlborough, NH: The Plymouth Rock Foundation), p. 3. Michael R. Farris, Esq., *Constitutional Law* (Paeonian Springs, VA: Home School Legal Defense Association, 1991), pp. 20-29.

150 Continental Congress. October 18, 1780. *The Journals of the Continental Congress 1774-1789* (Washington, D.C.: Government Printing Office, 1905), Vol. XVIII, pp. 950-951. David Barton, *The Myth of Separation* (Aledo, TX: WallBuilder Press, 1991), pp. 105-106.

151 Congress of the Confederation. September 10, 1782, under the Articles of Confederation, granted approval to a request, January 21, 1781, for Robert Aitken of Philadelphia, to print an edition of the Bible, known as *Bible of the Revolution. Journals of the Continental Congress 1774-1798* (Washington: Government Printing Office, 1907), Vol. VIII pp. 731-735. Tim LaHaye, *Faith of Our Founding Fathers* (Brentwood, TN: Wolgemuth & Hyatt, Publishers, Inc., 1987), p. 96. *Memorial of Robert Aitken to Congress,* 21 January, 1781, obtained from National Archives, Washington D.C. David Barton, *The Myth of Separation* (Aledo, TX: WallBuilder Press, 1991), p. 106. "Our Christian Heritage," *Letter from Plymouth Rock* (Marlborough, NH: The Plymouth Rock Foundation), p. 4.

152 Congress of the Confederation. September 10, 1782, under the Articles of Confederation, granted approval to a request, January 21, 1781, for Robert Aitken of Philadelphia, to print an edition of the Bible, known as *Bible of the Revolution. Journals of Continental Congress 1774-1789* (Washington, D.C.: Government Printing Office, 1905), Vol. XXIII, p. 574. *Bible for the Revolution* (NY: Arno Press, 1782, reprinted 1968), cover page. David Barton, *The Myth of Separation* (Aledo, TX: WallBuilder Press, 1991), p. 106. "Our Christian Heritage," *Letter from Plymouth Rock* (Marlborough, NH: The Plymouth Rock Foundation), p. 4.

153 Congress of the Confederation. January 14, 1784, under the Articles of Confederation, ratified the peace treaty with Great Britain, which had been signed in Paris on September 3, 1783, by D. Hartley, John Adams, B. Franklin, and John Jay, thereby officially ending the Revolutionary War. William M. Malloy, compiler, *Treaties, Conventions, International Acts, Protocols and Agreements between the United States of America and Other Powers, 1776-1909,* 4 vols. (New York: Greenwood Press, 1910, 1968), 2:1786. Charles W. Eliot, LL.D., ed., *American Historical Documents 1000-1904* (New York: P.F. Collier & Son Company, *The Harvard Classics,* 1910), Vol. 43, pp. 185-191. Gary DeMar, *America's Christian History: The Untold Story* (Atlanta, GA: American Vision Publishers, Inc., 1993), p. 84.

154 Congress of the Confederation. 1787, under the Articles of Confederation, approved a *Treaty with the Kaskaskia Indians,* extended under President Thomas Jefferson, December 3, 1803; also in the *Treaty with the Wyandotte Indians,* 1806; and the *Treaty with the Cherokee Indians,* 1807. Daniel L. Driesbach, *Real Threat and Mere Shadow: Religious Liberty and the First Amendment* (Westchester, IL: Crossway Books, 1987), p. 127. Richard Peters, ed., *The Public Statutes at Large of the United States of America* (Boston: Charles C. Little and James Brown, 1846), *A Treaty Between the United States and the Kaskaskia Tribe of Indians,* 23 December 1803, Art. III, Vol. VII, pp. 78-79., *Treaty with the Wyandots, etc.,* 1805, Vol. VII, Art. IV, p. 88, *Treaty with the Cherokees,* 1806, Vol. VII, Art. II, p. 102. Robert L. Cord, *Separation of Church and State* (NY: Lambeta Press, 1982), p. 39. David Barton, *The Myth of Separation* (Aledo, TX: WallBuilder Press, 1991), p. 176.

155 Constitutional Convention. May 14, 1787, admonition by President George Washington to the delegates. John Fiske, *The Critical Period of American History: 1783-1789* (Boston and New York: Houghton, Mifflin & Co., 1898), pp. 231-232. Marshall Foster and Mary-Elaine Swanson, *The American Covenant - The Untold Story* (Roseburg, OR: Foundation for Christian Self-Government, 1981; Thousand Oaks, CA: The Mayflower Institute, 1983, 1992), p. 42.

156 Constitutional Convention. June 28, 1787, in an address by Benjamin Franklin. James Madison, *Notes of Debates in the Federal Convention of 1787* (1787; Athens, OH: Ohio University Press, 1966, 1985; NY: W.W. Norton & Co., 1987), pp. 209-210. Albert Henry Smyth, ed., *The Writings of Benjamin Franklin* (New York: The Macmillan Company, 1905-7), IX:600-1. Gaillard Hunt and James B. Scott, ed., *The Debates in the Federal Convention of 1787 Which Framed the Constitution of the United States of America* (New York: Oxford University Press, 1920), pp. 181-182. Andrew M. Allison, W. Cleon Skousen, and M. Richard Maxfield, *The Real Benjamin Franklin* (Salt Lake City, Utah: The Freeman Institute, 1982, pp. 258-259. John Eidsmoe, *Christianity and the Constitution - The Faith of Our Founding Fathers* (Grand Rapids, MI: Baker Book House, A Mott Media Book, 1987; 6th printing, 1993), pp. 12-13, 208. Tim LaHaye, *Faith of Our Founding Fathers* (Brentwood, TN: Wolgemuth & Hyatt, Publishers, Inc., 1987), pp. 122-124. David Barton, *The Myth of Separation* (Aledo, TX: WallBuilder Press, 1991), p. 108-109. D.P. Diffine, Ph.D., *One Nation Under God - How Close a Separation?* (Searcy, Arkansas: Harding University, Belden Center for Private Enterprise Education, 6th edition, 1992), p. 8.

157 Constitutional Convention. June 28, 1787, Jonathan Dayton recorded the response to Benjamin Franklin's address. E.C. M'Guire, *The Religious Opinions and Character of Washington* (NY: Harper & Brothers, 1836), p. 151. David Barton, *The Myth of Separation* (Aledo, TX: WallBuilder Press, 1991), p. 109.

158 Constitutional Convention. June 28, 1787, in a motion by James Madison. Irving Brant, *James Madison, Father of the Constitution 1787-1800* (New York: Bobbs-Merrill, 1950), Vol. III, p. 84. Tim LaHaye, *Faith of Our Founding Fathers* (Brentwood, TN: Wolgemuth & Hyatt, Publishers, Inc., 1987), p. 126.

159 Constitutional Convention. June 28, 1787, Roger Sherman seconding a motion following Benjamin Franklin's address. James Madison, *Notes of Debates in the Federal Convention of 1787* (1787; reprinted NY: W. W. Norton & Co., 1987), p. 210. David Barton, *The Myth of Separation* (Aledo, TX: WallBuilder Press, 1991), p. 109.

160 Constitutional Convention. June 28, 1787, motion by Edmund Jennings Randolph of Virginia following Benjamin Franklin's address. James Madison, *Notes of Debates in the Federal Convention of 1787* (1787; reprinted NY: W.W.Norton & Co., 1987), pp. 210-211. David Barton, *The Myth of Separation* (Aledo, TX: WallBuilder Press, 1991), p. 109.

[161] **Constitutional Convention.** June 28, 1787, following Benjamin Franklin's address. Tim LaHaye, *Faith of Our Founding Fathers* (Brentwood, TN: Wolgemuth & Hyatt, Publishers, Inc., 1987), p. 57.

[162] **Constitutional Convention.** July 2, 1787, as recorded in Jonathan Dayton. E.C. M'Guire, *The Religious Opinions and Character of Washington* (NY: Harper & Brothers, 1836), p. 152. David Barton, *The Myth of Separation* (Aledo, TX: WallBuilder Press, 1991), p. 110.

[163] **Constitutional Convention.** July 4, 1787, in a sermon by Rev. William Rogers to the delegates. Benjamin Franklin Morris, *The Christian Life and Character of the Civil Institutions of the United States* (Philadelphia: George W. Childs, 1864), pp. 253-254. David Barton, *The Myth of Separation* (Aledo, TX: WallBuilder Press, 1991), p. 110.

[164] **Congress of the Confederation.** July 13, 1787, under the Articles of Confederation, approved THE NORTHWEST ORDINANCE OF 1787, Section 13, 14; Article I, III. Journal of Congress (ed. 1800) (early proposals of the bill) Vol. IX, pp. 109-110. *The Constitutions of the United States of America with the Latest Amendments* (Trenton: Moore & Lake, 1813), p. 364. *Revised Statutes of the United States relating to the District of Columbia and Post Roads...together with the Public Treaties in force on the first day of December 1873* (ed. 1878). *Life, Journal and Correspondence of Manasseh Cutler*, Vol. I, chap. 8. William MacDonald, *Select Documents Illustrative of the History of the United States, 1776-1861* (NY: Macmillan Company, 1897, 1898), p. 26. Frances Newton Thorpe, ed., *Federal and State Constitutions, Colonial Charters, and Other Organic Laws of the States, Territories, and Colonies now or heretofore forming the United States*, 7 vols. (Washington: Government Printing Office, 1905; 1909; St. Clair Shores, MI: Scholarly Press, 1968), Vol. I, pp. 957-962. Henry Steele Commager, ed., *Documents of American History*, 2 vols. (NY: F.S. Crofts and Company, 1934; Appleton-Century-Crofts, Inc., 1948, 6th edition, 1958; Englewood Cliffs, NJ: Prentice Hall, Inc., 9th edition, 1973), p. 131. Paul M. Angle, ed., *By These Words* (NY: Rand McNally & Company, 1954), pp. 91-93. Lillian W. Kay, ed., *The Ground on Which We Stand - Basic Documents of American History* (NY: Franklin Watts, Inc, 1969), p. 38-39. Daniel L. Driesbach, *Real Threat and Mere Shadow - Religious Liberty and the First Amendment* (Westchester, IL: Crossway Books, 1987), Vol. I, pp. 427-428. Edwin S. Gaustad, *Neither King nor Prelate - Religion and the New Nation, 1776-1826* (Grand Rapids, MI: William B. Eerdmans Publishing Company, 1993), (complete text including drafts and proposals), pp. 153-158. Poole, *North American Rev.*, (includes history of the act) CXXII: 229-65. *Article III of An Ordinance for the Government of the Territory of the United States, North-West of the River Ohio (Northwest Ordinance)*. David Barton, *The Myth of Separation* (Aledo, TX: WallBuilder Press, 1991), pp. 37-39. William Benton, *The Annals of America*, 20 vols. (Chicago, IL: Encyclopedia Britannica, 1968, 1977), Vol, III, pp. 194-195. Tim LaHaye, *Faith of Our Founding Fathers* (Brentwood, TN: Wolgemuth & Hyatt, Publishers, Inc., 1987), p. 91. D.P. Diffine, Ph.D., *One Nation Under God - How Close a Separation?* (Searcy, Arkansas: Harding University, Belden Center for Private Enterprise Education, 6th edition, 1992), p. 3.

[165] **Constitutional Convention.** September 17, 1787. *Foundations of Freedom - The Constitution & Bill Of Rights* (Chesapeake, VA: The National Legal Foundation, 1985), pp. 18-20.

[166] **Constitutional Convention.** September 17, 1787. M.E. Bradford, *A Worthy Company: Brief Lives of the Framers of the United States Constitution* (Marlborough, NH: Plymouth Rock Foundation, 1982), pp. iv-v, viii-ix. John Eidsmoe, *Christianity and the Constitution - The Faith of Our Founding Fathers* (Grand Rapids, MI: Baker Book House, A Mott Media Book, 1987; 6th printing, 1993), pp. 41-43. Tim LaHaye, *Faith of Our Founding Fathers* (Brentwood, TN: Wolgemuth & Hyatt, Publishers, Inc., 1987), p. 30. David Barton, *The Myth of Separation* (Aledo, TX: WallBuilder Press, 1991), pp. 24-25.

[167] **Constitutional Convention.** September 17, 1787, in the Preamble to the Constitution of the United States. Charles W. Eliot, LL.D., ed., *American Historical Documents 1000-1904* (New York: P.F. Collier & Son Company, *The Harvard Classics*, 1910), Vol. 43, p. 192. "Our Christian Heritage," *Letter from Plymouth Rock* (Marlborough, NH: The Plymouth Rock Foundation), p. 4.

[168] **Constitutional Convention.** September 17, 1787, Constitution of the United States, Article I, Section 7, Paragraph 2. Charles W. Eliot, LL.D., ed., *American Historical Documents 1000-1904* (New York: P.F. Collier & Son Company, *The Harvard Classics*, 1910), Vol. 43, p. 196. David Barton, *The Myth of Separation* (Aledo, TX: WallBuilder Press, 1991), p. 111. "Our Christian Heritage," *Letter form Plymouth Rock* (Marlborough, NH: The Plymouth Rock Foundation), p. 4.

[169] **Constitutional Convention.** September 17, 1787, Constitution of the United States. Charles W. Eliot, LL.D., ed., *American Historical Documents 1000-1904* (New York: P.F. Collier & Son Company, *The Harvard Classics*, 1910), Vol. 43, p. 205. Gary DeMar, *God and Government - A Biblical and Historical Study* (Atlanta, GA: American Vision Press, 1982), pp. 163, 172. "Our Christian Heritage," *Letter from Plymouth Rock* (Marlborough, NH: The Plymouth Rock Foundation), p. 4.

[170] **Congress of the United States of America.** April 27, 1789, prior to the Inauguration of President George Washington. *Annals of Congress 1789-1791* (Washington, D.C: Gales & Seaton, 1843), Vol. I, p. 25. *Journal of the First Session of th Senate of the United States of America* (Washington: Gales & Seton, 1820), book no. 50; *Senate Journal*, under April 27 and April 30, 1789. David Barton, *The Myth of Separation* (Aledo, TX: WallBuilder Press, 1991), p. 112.

[171] **Congress of the United States of America.** April 23, 1789, article in the newspaper, *Daily Advertiser*. Benjamin Franklin Morris, *The Christian Life and Character of the Civil Institutions of the United States* (Philadelphia: George W. Childs, 1864), p. 272. David Barton, *The Myth of Separation* (Aledo, TX: WallBuilder Press, 1991), p. 112.

[172] **Congress of the United States of America.** April 30, 1789, following President George Washington's Inauguration. *Annals of Congress 1789-1791* (Washington, D.C.: Gales & Seaton, 1843), Vol. I, p. 29. David Barton, *The Myth of Separation* (Aledo, TX: WallBuilder Press, 1991), p. 113.

[173] **Congress of the United States of America.** April 30, 1789, George Washington being inaugurated as president. Charles W. Eliot, LL.D., ed., *American Historical Documents 1000-1904* (New York: P.F. Collier & Son Company, *The Harvard Classics*, 1910), Vol. 43, pp. 241-245. Charles E. Kistler, *This Nation under God* (Boston: Richard G. Badger, The Gorham Press, 1924), p. 97. William J. Johnson, *George Washington, the Christian* (Nashville, TN: Abingdon Press, 1919), pp. 161-162. *Inaugural Addresses of the Presidents of the United States - From George Washington 1789 to Richard Milhous Nixon 1969* (Washington, D.C.: United States Government Printing Office; 91st Congress, 1st Session, House Document 91-142, 1969), pp. 1-4. Charles E. Rice, *The Supreme Court and Public Prayer* (New York: Fordham University Press, 1964), pp. 177-178. Peter Marshall and David Manuel, *The Light and the Glory* (Old Tappan, NJ: Fleming H. Revell Company, 1977), p. 349. John W. Whitehead, *The Separation Illusion* (Milford, MI: Mott Media, 1977), p. 123. Gary DeMar, *God and Government* (Atlanta, GA: American Vision Press, 1984), p. 170. Tim LaHaye, *Faith of Our Founding Fathers* (Brentwood, TN: Wolgemuth & Hyatt, Publishers, Inc., 1987), pp. 63-64. J. Michael Sharman, J.D., *Faith of the Fathers* (Culpepper, Virginia: Victory Publishing, 1995), pp. 18-19.

[174] **Congress of the United States of America.** April 30, 1789, Thursday, in President George Washington's First Inaugural Address. National Archives, Original work and facsimile, (complete text), No. 22 (Washington: 1952). Jared Sparks, ed., *The Writings of George Washington* 12 vols. (Boston: American Stationer's Company, 1837, NY: F. Andrew's, 1834-1847), Vol. XII, pp.

Notes

2-5. James D. Richardson (U.S. Representative from Tennessee), ed., *A Compilation of the Messages and Papers of the Presidents 1789-1897*, 10 vols. (Washington, D.C.: U.S. Government Printing Office, published by Authority of Congress, 1897, 1899; Washington, D.C.: Bureau of National Literature and Art, 1789-1902, 11 vols., 1907, 1910), Vol. 1, pp. 52-53. Charles W. Eliot, LL.D., ed., *American Historical Documents 1000-1904* (New York: P.F. Collier & Son Company, *The Harvard Classics*, 1910), Vol. 43, pp. 241-245. William J. Johnson, *George Washington - The Christian* (St. Paul, MN: William J. Johnson, Merriam Park, February 23, 1919; Nashville, TN: Abingdon Press, 1919; reprinted Milford, MI: Mott Media, 1976; reprinted Arlington Heights, IL: Christian Liberty Press, 502 West Euclid Avenue, Arlington Heights, Illinois, 60004, 1992), pp. 161-162. John Clement Fitzpatrick, ed., *The Writings of George Washington, from the Original Manuscript Sources 1749-1799*, 39 vols. (Washington, D.C.: United States Government Printing Office, 1931-1944), Vol. XXX, pp. 291-296. William Barclay Allen, ed., *George Washington - A Collection* (Indianapolis: Liberty Classics, Liberty Fund, Inc., 7440 N. Shadeland, Indianapolis, Indiana 46250, 1988; based almost entirely on materials reproduced from *The Writings of George Washington from the original manuscript sources, 1745-1799 / John Clement Fitzpatrick, editor*), pp. 460-463. Henry Steele Commager, ed., *Documents of American History*, 2 vols. (New York: F.S. Crofts and Company, 1934; Appleton-Century-Crofts, Inc., 1948, 6th edition, 1958; Englewood Cliffs, NJ: Prentice Hall, Inc., 9th edition, 1973), Vol. I, pp. 152-154. John F. Schroeder, ed., *Maxims of Washington* (Mt. Vernon: Mt. Vernon Ladies' Association, 1942), pp. 287-288. Saxe Commins, ed., *The Basic Writings of George Washington* (NY: Random House, 1948), complete work, pp. 599-602. Frederick C. Packard, Jr., ed., *Are You an American? - Great Americans Speak* (NY: Charles Scribner's Sons, 1951), pp. 14-18. Paul M. Angle, ed., *By These Words* (NY: Rand McNally & Company, 1954), pp. 128-131. Davis Newton Lott, *The Inaugural Addresses of the American Presidents* (NY: Holt, Rinehart and Winston, 1961), p. 3-5. Daniel Boorstin, Jr., ed., *An American Primer* (Chicago: The University of Chicago Press, 1966), complete work, pp. 172-174. Gary DeMar, *God and Government, A Biblical and Historical Study* (Atlanta, GA: American Vision Press, 1984), p. 127-28. Pat Robertson, *America's Dates With Destiny* (Nashville, TN: Thomas Nelson Publishers, 1986), p. 104. Tim LaHaye, *Faith of Our Founding Fathers* (Brentwood, TN: Wolgemuth & Hyatt, Publishers, Inc., 1987), pp. 63-64, 107. John Eidsmoe, *Christianity and the Constitution - The Faith of Our Founding Fathers* (Grand Rapids, MI: Baker Book House, A Mott Media Book, 1987; 6th printing, 1993), pp. 117, 123. David Barton, *The Myth of Separation* (Aledo, TX: WallBuilder Press, 1991), p. 113. "Our Christian Heritage," *Letter from Plymouth Rock* (Marlborough, NH: The Plymouth Rock Foundation), p. 4. D.P. Diffine, Ph.D., *One Nation Under God - How Close a Separation?* (Searcy, Arkansas: Harding University, Belden Center for Private Enterprise Education, 6th edition, 1992), p. 2. Charles E. Kistler, *This Nation under God* (Boston: Richard G. Badger, The Gorham Press, 1924), p. 97. *Inaugural Addresses of the Presidents of the United States - From George Washington 1789 to Richard Milhous Nixon 1969* (Washington, D.C.: United States Government Printing Office; 91st Congress, 1st Session, House Document 91-142, 1969), pp. 1-4. Charles E. Rice, *The Supreme Court and Public Prayer* (New York: Fordham University Press, 1964), pp. 177-178. Peter Marshall and David Manuel, *The Light and the Glory* (Old Tappan, NJ: Fleming H. Revell Company, 1977), p. 349. John W. Whitehead, *The Separation Illusion* (Milford, MI: Mott Media, 1977), p. 123. Gary DeMar, *God and Government* (Atlanta, GA: American Vision Press, 1984), p. 170. J. Michael Sharman, J.D., *Faith of the Fathers* (Culpepper, Virginia: Victory Publishing, 1995), pp. 18-19.

[175] **Congress of the United States of America.** May 1, 1789, in the United States House of Representatives. "Our Christian Heritage," *Letter from Plymouth Rock* (Marlborough, NH: The Plymouth Rock Foundation), p. 4. Gary DeMar, *America's Christian History: The Untold Story* (Atlanta, GA: American Vision Publishers, Inc., 1993), p. 51.

[176] **Congress of the United States of America.** August 4, 1789, Congress repassed the *Northwest Ordinance. Article III of An Ordinance for the Government of the Territory of the United States, North-West of the River Ohio.* Henry Steele Commager, ed., *Documents of American History*, 2 vols. (NY: F.S. Crofts and Company, 1934; Appleton-Century-Crofts, Inc., 1948, 6th edition, 1958; Englewood Cliffs, NJ: Prentice Hall, Inc., 9th edition, 1973), p. 131. David Barton, *The Myth of Separation* (Aledo, TX: WallBuilder Press, 1991), pp. 37-38. D.P. Diffine, Ph.D., *One Nation Under God - How Close a Separation?* (Searcy, Arkansas: Harding University, Belden Center for Private Enterprise Education, 6th edition, 1992), p. 3.

[177] **Congress of the United States of America.** September 25, 1789, the First Amendment. Michael J. Malbin, *Religion and Politics - The Intentions of the Authors of the First Amendment* (Washington: 1978). William Miller, *The First Liberty - Religion and the American Republic* (NY: 1986). Linda DePauw, et al., eds., *Documentary History of the First Federal Congress...* (Baltimore: 1972 and following) (work in progress). David Barton, *The Myth of Separation* (Aledo, TX: WallBuilder Press, 1991), p. 28. M.E. Bradford, *Religion & The Framers: The Biographical Evidence* (Marlborough, NH: The Plymouth Rock Foundation, 1991), p. 12. Wells Bradley, "Religion and Government: The Early Days" (Tulsa, Ok: *Tulsa Christian Times*, October 1992), p. 7. Edwin S. Gaustad, *Neither King nor Prelate - Religion and the New Nation, 1776-1826* (Grand Rapids, MI: William B. Eerdmans Publishing Company, 1993), pp. 157-158.

[178] **Congress of the United States of America.** June 8, 1789, James Madison introducing the initial version of the First Amendment. *Annals of the Congress of the United States - First Congress, The Debates and Proceedings in the Congress of the United States with an Appendix Containing Important State Papers and Public Documents and All the Laws of a Public Nature - with a Copious Index* 42 vols. (Washington, D.C.: Gales & Seaton, 1834-56), Vol. I, p. 434. Gaillard Hunt, ed., *Writings of James Madison, comprising his public papers and his private correspondence, for the first time printed*, 9 vols. (NY: G.P. Putnam's Sons, 1900-1910). Norman Cousins, *In God We Trust - The Religious Beliefs and Ideas of the American Founding Fathers* (NY: Harper & Brothers, 1958), pp. 316-317. *Foundations of Freedom-The Constitution & Bill of Rights* (Chesapeake, VA: The National Legal Foundation, 1985), p. 22. John Eidsmoe, *Christianity and the Constitution - The Faith of Our Founding Fathers* (Grand Rapids, MI: Baker Book House, A Mott Media Book, 1987; 6th printing, 1993), p. 109. David Barton, *The Myth of Separation* (Aledo, TX: WallBuilder Press, 1991), p. 27. Wells Bradley, "Religion and Government: The Early Days" (Tulsa, OK: *Tulsa Christian Times*, October 1992), p. 7. Edwin S. Gaustad, *Neither King nor Prelate - Religion and the New Nation, 1776-1826* (Grand Rapids, MI: William B. Eerdmans Publishing Company, 1993), p. 157.

[179] **Congress of the United States of America.** August 15, 1789, the House Select version of the First Amendment. *Annals of the Congress of the United States - First Congress* (Washington, D.C.: Gales & Seaton, 1834), Vol. I, p. 434. David Barton, *The Myth of Separation* (Aledo, TX: WallBuilder Press, 1991), p. 27. Wells Bradley, "Religion and Government: The Early Days" (Tulsa, OK: *Tulsa Christian Times*, October 1992), p. 7. Edwin S. Gaustad, *Neither King nor Prelate - Religion and the New Nation, 1776-1826* (Grand Rapids, MI: William B. Eerdmans Publishing Company, 1993), p. 157.

[180] **Congress of the United States of America.** August 15, 1789, Peter Sylvester of New York debating the First Amendment. M.E. Bradford, *Religion & The Framers: The Biographical Evidence* (Marlborough, NH: The Plymouth Rock Foundation, 1991), p. 11. Wells Bradley, "Religion and Government: The Early Days" (Tulsa, OK: *Tulsa Christian Times*, October 1992), p. 7.

[181] **Congress of the United States of America.** August 1789, James Madison in the debates on the First Amendment. Wells

Bradley, "Religion and Government: The Early Days" (Tulsa, OK: *Tulsa Christian Times*, October 1992), p. 7.

[182] **Congress of the United States of America.** August 1789, Benjamin Huntington, in the debates on the First Amendment. M.E. Bradford, *Religion & The Framers: The Biographical Evidence* (Marlborough, NH: The Plymouth Rock Foundation, 1991), p. 11. Wells Bradley, "Religion and Government: The Early Days" (Tulsa, OK: *Tulsa Christian Times*, October 1992), p. 7.

[183] **Congress of the United States of America.** August 1789, Benjamin Huntington proposing adjustment to the wording of the First Amendment. M.E. Bradford, *Religion & The Framers: The Biographical Evidence* (Marlborough, NH: The Plymouth Rock Foundation, 1991), p. 11. Wells Bradley, "Religion and Government: The Early Days" (Tulsa, OK: *Tulsa Christian Times*, October 1992), p. 7.

[184] **Congress of the United States of America.** August 1789, James Madison notes on the debates of the First Amendment. Philip B. Kurland and Ralph Lerner, eds., *The Founders' Constitution*, 5 vols. (Chicago: University of Chicago Press, 1987), Vol. V, p. 93. M.E. Bradford, *Religion & The Framers-The Biographical Evidence* (Marlborough, NH: The Plymouth Rock Foundation, Inc., 1991), p. 12.

[185] **Congress of the United States of America.** August 1789, James Madison's response to Benjamin Huntington and Peter Sylvester regarding the First Amendment. Philip B. Kurland and Ralph Lerner, eds., *The Founders' Constitution*, 5 vols. (Chicago: University of Chicago Press, 1987), Vol. V, p. 93. M.E. Bradford, *Religion & The Framers-The Biographical Evidence* (Marlborough, NH: The Plymouth Rock Foundation, Inc., 1991), p. 12.

[186] **Congress of the United States of America.** August 15, 1789, Samuel Livermore of New Hampshire proposed wording of the First Amendment. Wells Bradley, "Religion and Government: The Early Days" (Tulsa, OK: *Tulsa Christian Times*, October 1992), p. 7. *Annals of the Congress of the United States - First Congress* (Washington, D.C.: Gales & Seaton, 1834), Vol. I, pp. 729, 731. David Barton, *The Myth of Separation* (Aledo, TX: WallBuilder Press, 1991), p. 27. Edwin S. Gaustad, *Neither King nor Prelate - Religion and the New Nation*, 1776-1826 (Grand Rapids, MI: William B. Eerdmans Publishing Company, 1993), p. 157.

[187] **Congress of the United States of America.** August 20, 1789, Fisher Ames of Massachusetts introduced language for the First Amendment. Wells Bradley, "Religion and Government: The Early Days" (Tulsa, OK: *Tulsa Christian Times*, October 1992), p. 7. *Annals of the Congress of the United States - First Congress* (Washington, D.C.: Gales & Seaton, 1834), Vol. I, pp. 729, 731. David Barton, *The Myth of Separation* (Aledo, TX: WallBuilder Press, 1991), p. 27. Edwin S. Gaustad, *Neither King nor Prelate - Religion and the New Nation*, 1776-1826 (Grand Rapids, MI: William B. Eerdmans Publishing Company, 1993), p. 157.

[188] **Congress of the United States of America.** September 3, 1789, the Senate proposed several versions of the First Amendment. *Annals of the Congress of the United States - First Congress* (Washington, D.C.: Gales & Seaton, 1834), Vol. I, pp. 729, 731. David Barton, *The Myth of Separation* (Aledo, TX: WallBuilder Press, 1991), p. 27.

[189] **Congress of the United States of America.** September 3, 1789, the Senate proposed several versions of the First Amendment. *Annals of the Congress of the United States - First Congress* (Washington, D.C.: Gales & Seaton, 1834), Vol. I, pp. 729, 731. David Barton, *The Myth of Separation* (Aledo, TX: WallBuilder Press, 1991), p. 27. S.E. Morrison, ed., *Sources and Documents Illustrating the American Revolution, 1754-1788, and the Formation of the Federal Constitution* (New York: Oxford University Press, 1923), p. 158. Edwin S. Gaustad, *Neither King nor Prelate - Religion and the New Nation*, 1776-1826 (Grand Rapids, MI: William B. Eerdmans Publishing Company, 1993), p. 158.

[190] **Congress of the United States of America.** September 3, 1789, the Senate proposed several versions of the First Amendment. *Annals of the Congress of the United States - First Congress* (Washington, D.C.: Gales & Seaton, 1834), Vol. I, pp. 729, 731. David Barton, *The Myth of Separation* (Aledo, TX: WallBuilder Press, 1991), p. 27. S.E. Morrison, ed., *Sources and Documents Illustrating the American Revolution, 1754-1788, and the Formation of the Federal Constitution* (New York: Oxford University Press, 1923), p. 158. Edwin S. Gaustad, *Neither King nor Prelate - Religion and the New Nation*, 1776-1826 (Grand Rapids, MI: William B. Eerdmans Publishing Company, 1993), p. 158.

[191] **Congress of the United States of America.** September 3, 1789, the Senate accepted this version of the First Amendment. *Annals of the Congress of the United States - First Congress* (Washington, D.C.: Gales & Seaton, 1834), Vol. I, pp. 729, 731. David Barton, *The Myth of Separation* (Aledo, TX: WallBuilder Press, 1991), p. 27. Edwin S. Gaustad, *Neither King nor Prelate - Religion and the New Nation*, 1776-1826 (Grand Rapids, MI: William B. Eerdman Publishing Company, 1993), p. 158. S.E. Morrison, ed., *Sources and Documents Illustrating the American Revolution, 1754-1788, and the Formation of the Federal Constitution* (New York: Oxford University Press, 1923), p. 158.

[192] **Congress of the United States of America.** September 9, 1789, the Senate agreed of this version of the First Amendment. Wells Bradley, "Religion and Government: The Early Days" (Tulsa, OK: *Tulsa Christian Times*, October 1992), p. 7. *Annals of the Congress of the United States - First Congress* (Washington, D.C.: Gales & Seaton, 1834), Vol. I, pp. 729, 731. David Barton, *The Myth of Separation* (Aledo, TX: WallBuilder Press, 1991), p. 27. Edwin S. Gaustad, *Neither King nor Prelate - Religion and the New Nation*, 1776-1826 (Grand Rapids, MI: William B. Eerdmans Publishing Company, 1993), p. 158. S.E. Morrison, ed., *Sources and Documents Illustrating the American Revolution, 1754-1788, and the Formation of the Federal Constitution* (New York: Oxford University Press, 1923), p. 158.

[193] **Congress of the United States of America.** September 25, 1789, wording agreed upon by a joint committee of the House and Senate. Wells Bradley, "Religion and Government: The Early Days" (Tulsa, OK: *Tulsa Christian Times*, October 1992), p. 7. *Annals of the Congress of the United States - First Congress* (Washington, D.C.: Gales & Seaton, 1834), Vol. I, pp. 729, 731. David Barton, *The Myth of Separation* (Aledo, TX: WallBuilder Press, 1991), pp. 27-28. S.E. Morrison, ed., *Sources and Documents Illustrating the American Revolution, 1754-1788, and the Formation of the Federal Constitution* (New York: Oxford University Press, 1923), p. 158. Edwin S. Gaustad, *Neither King nor Prelate - Religion and the New Nation*, 1776-1826 (Grand Rapids, MI: William B. Eerdmans Publishing Company, 1993), p. 158.

[194] **Congress of the United States of America.** September 25, 1789, the *Bill of Rights* were passed by Congress, December 15, 1791, they were ratified by the states. Charles W. Eliot, LL.D., ed., *American Historical Documents 1000-1904* (New York: P.F. Collier & Son Company, *The Harvard Classics*, 1910), Vol. 43, pp. 206-208. David Barton, *The Myth of Separation* (Aledo, TX: WallBuilder Press, 1991), p. 284. *Foundations of Freedom-The Constitution & Bill of Rights* (Chesapeake, VA: The National Legal Foundation, 1985), p. 23.

[195] **Congress of the United States of America.** September 25, 1789, recommending a *National Day of Public Thanksgiving and Prayer. Annals of the Congress of the United States - First Congress, The Debates and Proceedings in the Congress of the United States with an Appendix Containing Important State Papers and Public Documents and All the Laws of a Public Nature - with a Copious Index* 42 vols. (Washington, D.C.: Gales & Seaton, 1834-56), Vol. I:914. David Barton, *The Myth of Separation* (Aledo, TX: WallBuilder Press, 1991), p. 114. Gary DeMar, *America's Christian History: The Untold Story* (Atlanta, GA: American Vision Publishers, Inc.,

1993), pp. 53, 113. *The Annals of America*, 20 vols. (Chicago, IL: Encyclopedia Britannica, 1968, 1977), Vol. I, p. 914. Gary DeMar, *Ruler of the Nations* (Ft. Worth, TX: Dominion Press, 1987), p. 231. Gary DeMar, "Censoring America's Christian History" (Atlanta: *The Biblical Worldview*, An American Vision Publication - American Vision, Inc., July 1990), p. 5. Gary DeMar, "Does Anyone Have a Prayer?" (Atlanta: *The Biblical Worldview*, An American Vision Publication - American Vision, Inc.), p. 2.

[196] **Congress of the United States of America.** September 1789, Roger Sherman's comments justifying the National Day of Thanksgiving. *Annals of the Congress of the United States - First Congress, The Debates and Proceedings in the Congress of the United States with an Appendix Containing Important State Papers and Public Documents and All the Laws of a Public Nature - with a Copious Index* 42 vols. (Washington, D.C.: Gales & Seaton, 1834-56), 1789-1791, Vol. I, p. 914. David Barton, *The Myth of Separation* (Aledo, TX: WallBuilder Press, 1991), p. 114.

[197] **Congress of the United States of America.** October 3, 1789, *National Day of Thanksgiving Proclamation* issued by President George Washington from the city of New York. Jared Sparks, ed., *The Writings of George Washington* 12 vols. (Boston: American Stationer's Company, 1837, NY: F. Andrew's, 1834-1847), Vol. XII, p. 119. William Barclay Allen, ed., *George Washington - A Collection* (Indianapolis: Liberty Classics, Liberty Fund, Inc., 7440 N. Shadeland, Indianapolis, Indiana 46250, 1988; based almost entirely on materials reproduced from *The Writings of George Washington from the original manuscript sources, 1745-1799/* John Clement Fitzpatrick, editor), pp. 513-514. John Clement Fitzpatrick, ed., *The Writings of George Washington, from the Original Manuscript Sources 1749-1799*, 39 vols. (Washington, D.C.: United States Government Printing Office, 1931-1944). James D. Richardson (U.S. Representative from Tennessee), ed., *A Compilation of the Messages and Papers of the Presidents 1789-1897*, 10 vols. (Washington, D.C.: U.S. Government Printing Office, published by Authority of Congress, 1897, 1899; Washington, D.C.: Bureau of National Literature and Art, 1789-1902, 11 vols., 1907, 1910), Vol. 1, p. 64. William J. Johnson, *George Washington - The Christian* (St. Paul, MN: William J. Johnson, Merriam Park, February 23, 1919; Nashville, TN: Abingdon Press, 1919; reprinted Milford, MI: Mott Media, 1976; reprinted Arlington Heights, IL: Christian Liberty Press, 502 West Euclid Avenue, Arlington Heights, Illinois, 60004, 1992), pp. 173-174. John F. Schroeder, ed., *Maxims of Washington* (Mt. Vernon: Mt. Vernon Ladies' Association, 1942), p. 287. Anson Phelps Stokes and Leo Pfeffer, *Church and State in the United States*, 3 vols. (NY: Harper & Brothers, 1950), p. 87. Pat Robertson, *America's Dates with Destiny* (Nashville: Thomas Nelson Publishers, 1986), p. 112. John Eidsmoe, *Christianity and the Constitution - The Faith of Our Founding Fathers* (Grand Rapids, MI: Baker Book House, A Mott Media Book, 1987, 6th printing 1993), p. 118. Tim LaHaye, *Faith of Our Founding Fathers* (Brentwood, TN: Wolgemuth & Hyatt, Publishers, Inc., 1987), pp. 105-106. David Barton, *The Myth of Separation* (Aledo, TX: WallBuilder Press, 1991), p. 115. D.P. Diffine, Ph.D., *One Nation Under God - How Close a Separation?* (Searcy, Arkansas: Harding University, Belden Center for Private Enterprise Education, 6th edition, 1992), p. 9. Gary DeMar, *The Biblical Worldview* (Atlanta, GA: An American Vision Publication - American Vision, Inc., 1992), Vol. 8, No. 12, p. 8. Gary DeMar, *America's Christian History: The Untold Story* (Atlanta, GA: American Vision Publishers, Inc., 1993), pp. 76-77.

[198] **Congress of the United States of America.** January 1, 1795, *National Thanksgiving Proclamation*, issued from Philadelphia, by President George Washington. Library of Congress Rare Book Collection, Washington, D.C. Jared Sparks, ed., *The Writings of George Washington* 12 vols. (Boston: American Stationer's Company, 1837; NY: F. Andrew's, 1834-1847), Vol. XII, pp. 132-134. James D. Richardson (U.S. Representative from Tennessee), ed., *A Compilation of the Messages and Papers of the Presidents 1789-1897*, 10 vols. (Washington, D.C.: U.S. Government Printing Office, published by Authority of Congress, 1897, 1899; Washington, D.C.: Bureau of National Literature and Art, 1789-1902, 11 vols., 1907, 1910), Vol. I, pp. 179-180. William J. Johnson, *George Washington - The Christian* (St. Paul, MN: William J. Johnson, Merriam Park, February 23, 1919; Nashville, TN: Abingdon Press, 1919; reprinted Milford, MI: Mott Media, 1976; reprinted Arlington Heights, IL: Christian Liberty Press, 502 West Euclid Avenue, Arlington Heights, Illinois, 60004, 1992), pp. 215-217. Catherine Millard, *The Rewriting of America's History* (Camp Hill, PA: Horizon House Publishers, 1991), pp. 61-62. Catherine Millard, *A Children's Companion Guide to America's History* (Camp Hill, PA: Horizon House Publishers, 1993), p. 23.

[199] **Congress of the United States of America.** April 30, 1802, Congress passed the enabling act for Ohio. *C. 40, 2 Stat. 173 at 174.* David Barton, *The Myth of Separation* (Aledo, TX: WallBuilder Press, 1991), p. 38.

[200] **Congress of the United States of America.** April 30, 1802. *Article III of An Ordinance for the Government of the Territory of the United States, North-West of the River Ohio.* Henry Steele Commager, ed., *Documents of American History*, 2 vols. (NY: F.S. Crofts and Company, 1934; Appleton-Century-Crofts, Inc., 1948, 6th edition, 1958; Englewood Cliffs, NJ: Prentice Hall, Inc., 9th edition, 1973), p. 131. David Barton, *The Myth of Separation* (Aledo, TX: WallBuilder Press, 1991), pp. 37-38. D.P. Diffine, Ph.D., *One Nation Under God - How Close a Separation?* (Searcy, Arkansas: Harding University, Belden Center for Private Enterprise Education, 6th edition, 1992), p. 3.

[201] **Congress of the United States of America.** December 3, 1803, President Thomas Jefferson signs the *Treaty with the Kaskaskia Indians, 1806 with the Wyandotte Indians, and 1807 Cherokee Indians.* Daniel L. Driesbach, *Real Threat and Mere Shadow: Religious Liberty and the First Amendment* (Westchester, IL: Crossway Books, 1987), p. 127. Richard Peters, ed., *The Public Statutes at Large of the United States of America* (Boston: Charles C. Little and James Brown, 1846), *A Treaty Between the United States and the Kaskaskia Tribe of Indians*, 23 December 1803, Art. III, Vol. VII, pp. 78-79., *Treaty with the Wyandots, etc.*, 1805, Vol. VII, Art. IV, p. 88, *Treaty with the Cherokees*, 1806, vol.VII, Art. II, p. 102. Robert L. Cord, *Separation of Church and State* (NY: Lambeta Press, 1982), p. 39. David Barton, *The Myth of Separation* (Aledo, TX: WallBuilder Press, 1991), p. 176. "A Treaty Between the United States of America and the Kaskaskian Tribe of Indians." 7 Stat. 78-9 (1846). Daniel L. Driesbach, *Real Threat and Mere Shadow - Religious Liberty and the First Amendment* (Westchester, IL: Crossway Books, 1987), p. 127.

[202] **Congress of the United States of America.** June 4, 1805, United States Senate drafted a *Treaty of Peace and Amity with Tripoli*, ratified April 12, 1806, Article XIV. Gary DeMar, "The Treaty of Tripoli" (Atlanta, GA: *The Biblical Worldview*, An American Vision Publication - American Vision, Inc., December 1992), Vol. 8, No. 12, pp. 7-12. "Our Christian Heritage," *Letter from Plymouth Rock* (Marlborough, NH: The Plymouth Rock Foundation), p. 5.

[203] **Congress of the United States of America.** June 7, 1797, *Treaty with Tripoli.* Charles Bevans, *Treaties and Other International Agreements of the United States of America 1776-1959* (Washington, D.C.: Department of State, 1974), 11:1070. Gary DeMar, "The Treaty of Tripoli" (Atlanta, GA: *The Biblical Worldview*, An American Vision Publication - American Vision, Inc., December 1992), Vol. 8, No. 12, pp. 7-12.

[204] **Congress of the United States of America.** June 7, 1797, *Treaty with Tripoli.* Dr. C. Snouck Hurgronje of Leyden, Netherlands in his 1930 retranslation of the original treaty from Arabic into English. Gary DeMar, "The Treaty of Tripoli" (Atlanta, GA: *The Biblical Worldview*, An American Vision Publication - American Vision, Inc., December 1992), Vol. 8, No. 12, pp. 7-12. Gary DeMar, *America's Christian History: The Untold Story* (Atlanta, GA: American Vision Publishers, Inc., 1993), p. 80.

[205] **Congress of the United States of America.** April 13, 1816, Congress passed *The Enabling Act for Indiana. C. 56, 3 Stat. 289.* Frances Newton Thorpe, ed., *Federal and State Constitutions, Colonial Charters, and Other Organic Laws of the States, Territories, and Colonies now or heretofore forming the United States,* 7 vols. (Washington: Government Printing Office, 1905; 1909; St. Clair Shores, MI: Scholarly Press, 1968). David Barton, *The Myth of Separation* (Aledo, TX: WallBuilder Press, 1991), p. 38.

[206] **Congress of the United States of America.** April 13, 1816, in passing the *Enabling Act of Indiana. Article III of An Ordinance for the Government of the Territory of the United States, North-West of the River Ohio.* Henry Steele Commager, ed., *Documents of American History,* 2 vols. (NY: F.S. Crofts and Company, 1934; Appleton-Century-Crofts, Inc., 1948, 6th edition, 1958; Englewood Cliffs, NJ: Prentice Hall, Inc., 9th edition, 1973), p. 131. David Barton, *The Myth of Separation* (Aledo, TX: WallBuilder Press, 1991), pp. 37-38. D.P. Diffine, Ph.D., *One Nation Under God - How Close a Separation?* (Searcy, Arkansas: Harding University, Belden Center for Private Enterprise Education, 6th edition, 1992), p. 3.

[207] **Congress of the United States of America.** March 1, 1817, Congress passed the *Enabling Act for Mississippi. C.23, 3 Stat. 348* at 349. Frances Newton, ed., *Federal and State Constitutions, Colonial Charters and Other Organic Laws of the States, Territories, and Colonies now or heretofore forming the United States,* 7 vols. (Washington: Government Printing Office, 1909). David Barton, *The Myth of Separation* (Aledo, TX: WallBuilder Press, 1991), pp. 38-39.

[208] **Congress of the United States of America.** March 1, 1817, Congress passes the *Enabling Act of Mississippi. Article III of An Ordinance for the Government of the Territory of the United States, North-West of the River Ohio.* Henry Steele Commager, ed., *Documents of American History,* 2 vols. (NY: F.S. Crofts and Company, 1934; Appleton-Century-Crofts, Inc., 1948, 6th edition, 1958; Englewood Cliffs, NJ: Prentice Hall, Inc., 9th edition, 1973), pp. 37-38. D.P. Diffine, Ph.D., *One Nation Under God - How Close a Separation?* (Searcy, Arkansas: Harding University, Belden Center for Private Enterprise Education, 6th edition, 1992), p. 3.

[209] **Congress of the United States of America.** 1822, both the House and Senate of the United States, along with Great Britain and Ireland, ratified the *Convention for Indemnity under Award of Emperor of Russia as to the True Construction of the First Article of the Treaty of December 24, 1814.* William M. Malloy, compiler, *Treaties, Conventions, International Acts, Protocols and Agreements between the United States of America and Other Powers 1776-1909,* 4 vols. (New York: Greenwood Press, 1910, 1968), 1:634. Gary DeMar, *The Biblical Worldview* (Atlanta, GA: An American Vision Publication - American Vision, Inc., 1992), Vol. 8, No. 12, p. 12. Congress of the United States of America, February 2, 1848, ratified the peace treaty with Mexico which ended the Mexican War and brought the territories of California, Nevada, Utah, and parts of Arizona, New Mexico, Colorado and Wyoming, into the Union, concluded at Guadalupe Hidalgo; ratified with amendments by U.S. Senate, March 10, 1848; ratified by President, March 16, 1848; ratifications exchanged at Queretaro, May 30, 1848; proclaimed July 4, 1848. Charles W. Eliot, LL.D., ed., *American Historical Documents 1000-1904* (New York: P.F. Collier & Son Company, *The Harvard Classics,* 1910), Vol. 43, pp. 309-326. The treaty began:
    "In the Name of Almighty God:
    "The United States and the United Mexican States animated by a sincere desire to put an end to the calamities of the war....who, after a reciprocal communication of their respective full powers, have, under the protection of Almighty God, the Author of Peace, arranged, agreed upon, and signed the following: Treaty of Peace, Friendship, Limits, and Settlement between the United States of America and the Mexican Republic....
    "If (which is not to be expected, and which God forbid) war should unhappily break out between the two republics, they do now, with a view to such calamity, solemnly pledge themselves to each other and to the world to observe the following rules....
    "All churches, hospitals, schools, colleges, libraries, and other establishments for charitable and beneficent purposes, shall be respected, and all persons connected with the same protected in the discharge of their duties, and the pursuit of their vocations....
    "Done in quintuplicate, at the city of Guadalupe Hidalgo, on the second day of February, in the year of the Lord one thousand eight hundred and forty-eight."

[210] **Congress of the United States of America.** 1838. Benjamin Franklin Morris, *The Christian Life and Character of the Civil Institutions of the United States* (Philadelphia: George W. Childs, 1864), p. 318. David Barton, *The Myth of Separation* (Aledo, TX: WallBuilder Press, 1991), p. 130.

[211] **Congress of the United States of America.** January 19, 1853, Mr. Badger giving report of Congressional investigations. Benjamin Franklin Morris, *The Christian Life and Character of the Civil Institutions of the United States* (Philadelphia: George W. Childs, 1864), pp. 324-327. David Barton, *The Myth of Separation* (Aledo, TX: WallBuilder Press, 1991), pp. 31, 132.

[212] **Congress of the United States of America.** January 19, 1853, Mr. Badger, as part of a Congressional investigation, delivers the report of the Senate Judiciary Committee. Benjamin Franklin Morris, *The Christian Life and Character of the Civil Institutions of the United States* (Philadelphia: George W. Childs, 1864), p. 326. David Barton, *The Myth of Separation* (Aledo, TX: WallBuilder Press, 1991), p. 183.

[213] **Congress of the United States of America.** January 19, 1853, in a Senate Judiciary Report. Benjamin Franklin Morris, *The Christian Life and Character of the Civil Institutions of the United States* (Philadelphia: George W. Childs, 1864), p. 326. David Barton, *The Myth of Separation* (Aledo, TX: WallBuilder Press, 1991), pp. 111, 132.

[214] **Congress of the United States of America.** January 19, 1853, in the Senate Judiciary Committee report. Benjamin Franklin Morris, *The Christian Life and Character of the Civil Institutions of the United States* (Philadelphia: George W. Childs, 1864), p. 326. David Barton, *The Myth of Separation* (Aledo, TX: WallBuilder Press, 1991), pp. 130-132.

[215] **Congress of the United States of America.** March 27, 1854, Mr. Meacham giving report of the House Committee on the Judiciary. Benjamin Franklin Morris, *The Christian Life and Character of the Civil Institutions of the United States* (Philadelphia: George W. Childs, 1864), pp. 317, 320-327. David Barton, *The Myth of Separation* (Aledo, TX: WallBuilder Press, 1991), pp. 31, 133, 144. "Our Christian Heritage," *Letter from Plymouth Rock* (Marlborough, NH: The Plymouth Rock Foundation), pp. 5-6.

[216] **Congress of the United States of America.** May 1854. A Resolution passed in the House. Benjamin Franklin Morris, *The Christian Life and Character of the Civil Institutions of the United States* (Philadelphia: George W. Childs, 1864), p. 328. David Barton, *The Myth of Separation* (Aledo, TX: WallBuilder Press, 1991), p. 133. Stephen McDowell and Mark Beliles, "The Providential Perspective" (Charlottesville, VA: The Providence Foundation, P.O. Box 6759, Charlottesville, Va. 22906, January 1994), Vol. 9, No. 1, p. 7.

[217] **Congress of the United States of America.** March 3, 1863, resolution passed in the third session Thirty-Seventh Congress. *Congressional Globe,* pp. 1148-1501. Stephen Abbott Northrop, D.D., *A Cloud of Witnesses* (Portland, OR: American Heritage Ministries, 1987; Mantle Ministries, 228 Still Ridge, Bulverde, Texas), p. 453.

Notes

[218] **Congress of the United States of America** March 30, 1863, received President Abraham Lincoln's *Proclamation Appointing a National Fast Day*. James D. Richardson (U.S. Representative from Tennessee), ed., *A Compilation of the Messages and Papers of the Presidents 1789-1897*, 10 vols. (Washington, D.C.: U.S. Government Printing Office, published by Authority of Congress, 1897, 1899; Washington, D.C.: Bureau of National Literature and Art, *1789-1902*, 11 vols., 1907, 1910), Vol. VI, p. 164. Benjamin Weiss, *God in American History: A Documentation of America's Religious Heritage* (Grand Rapids, MI: Zondervan, 1966), p. 92. Willard Cantelon, *Money Master of the World* (Plainfield, NJ: Logos International, 1976), p. 120. Gary DeMar, *God and Government - A Biblical and Historical Study* (Atlanta, GA: American Vision Press, 1984), p. 128-29. David Barton, *The Myth of Separation* (Aledo, TX: WallBuilder Press, 1991), p. 259. "Our Christian Heritage," *Letter from Plymouth Rock* (Marlborough, NH: The Plymouth Rock Foundation), p. 6. Gary DeMar, *America's Christian History: The Untold Story* (Atlanta, GA: American Vision Publishers, Inc., 1993), p. 5.

[219] **Congress of the United States of America** October 3, 1863, passed an Act of Congress designating an annual *National Day of Thanksgiving and Praise*, signed by President Abraham Lincoln. Library of Congress Rare Book Collection, Washington, D.C. James D. Richardson (U.S. Representative from Tennessee), ed., *A Compilation of the Messages and Papers of the Presidents 1789-1897*, 10 vols. (Washington, D.C.: U.S. Government Printing Office, published by Authority of Congress, 1897, 1899; Washington, D.C.: Bureau of National Literature and Art, *1789-1902*, 11 vols., 1907, 1910), Vol. VI, pp. 172-173. William J. Johnson, *Abraham Lincoln, The Christian* (NY: The Abington Press, 1913), pp. 124-125. David Manuel, *The Glory of America* (Bloomington, MN: Garborg's Heart'N Home, Inc., 1991), 10.4. Gary DeMar, *America's Christian History: The Untold Story* (Atlanta, GA: American Vision Publishers, Inc., 1993), pp. 16-17. Catherine Millard, *A Children's Companion Guide to America's History* (Camp Hill, PA: Horizon House Publishers, 1993), p. 23.

[220] **Congress of the United States of America.** March 3, 1865, Congress approves instructions to the Secretary of the Treasury. "Our Christian Heritage," *Letter from Plymouth Rock* (Marlborough, NH: The Plymouth Rock Foundation), p. 6. Keith J. Hardman, *Christianity & The Civil War-The Christian History Timeline* (Carol Stream, IL: Christian History, 1992), Vol. XI, No. 1, p. 33.

[221] **Congress of the United States of America.** March 3, 1931, adopted *The Star Spangled Banner* as our National Anthem, 36 U.S.C. Sec.170, (H.R. 14; Public, No. 823; Session III; 1508 Seventy-First Congress. Sess. III. Chs. 436, 437. 1931. Chap. 436. - An Act To make The Star-Spangled Banner the national anthem of the United States of America. Courtesy of Bruce Barilla, Christian Heritage Week Ministry (P.O. Box 58, W.V. 24712; 304-384-7707, 304-384-9044 fax). Francis Scott Key's *The Star Spangled Banner*. (36 U.S.C. Sec.170). Hearings before Subcommittee No. 4 of the Committee Judiciary, 85th Congress, 2nd Session. May 21, 22 & 28, 1958, p. 6. Catherine Millard, *The Rewriting of America's History* (Camp Hill, PA: Horizon House Publishers, 1991), pp. 272-273. Tim LaHaye, *Faith of Our Founding Fathers* (Brentwood, TN: Wolgemuth & Hyatt, Publishers, Inc., 1987), p. 95. United States Congress. "Our Christian Heritage," *Letter from Plymouth Rock* (Marlborough, NH: The Plymouth Rock Foundation), p. 6. D.P. Diffine, Ph.D., *One Nation Under God - How Close a Separation?* (Searcy, Arkansas: Harding University, Belden Center for Private Enterprise Education, 6th edition, 1992), p. 17.

[222] **Congress of the Unites States of America.** June 14, 1954, approved the Joint Resolution 243, signed by President Eisenhower. (Public Law 83-396; Chapter 297; Sec. 7), June 22, 1942, 36 U.S.C. sec. 172); December 28, 1945, as Public Law 287.) Courtesy of Bruce Barilla, Christian Heritage Week Ministry (P.O. Box 58, W.V. 24712; 304-384-7707, 304-384-9044 fax). D.P. Diffine, Ph.D., *One Nation Under God - How Close a Separation?* (Searcy, Arkansas: Harding University, Belden Center for Private Enterprise Education, 6th edition, 1992), p. 17.

[223] **Congress of the United States of America.** September 8, 1892, *Pledge of Allegiance*. *The World Book Encyclopedia*, 18 vols. (Chicago, IL: Field Enterprises, Inc., 1957; W.F. Quarrie and Company, 8 vols., 1917; World Book, 22 vols., 1989), Vol. 13, p. 6419. Catherine Millard, *The Rewriting of America's History* (Camp Hill, PA: Horizon House Publishers, 1991), pp. 273-274.

[224] **Congress of the United States of America.** June 14, 1954, in a speech confirming the Act of Congress which added the phrase *Under God* to the *Pledge of Allegiance*. U.S. Marine Corps, *How to Respect and Display Our Flag* (Washington: U.S. Government Printing Office, 1977), p. 31.

[225] **Congress of the United States of America.** June 14, 1954, President Eisenhower signed House Joint Resolution 243 into law as Public Law 83-396, which added the phrase, "under God," to the *Pledge of Allegiance* (Public Law 287). "Our Christian Heritage," *Letter from Plymouth Rock* (Marlborough, NH: The Plymouth Rock Foundation), p. 7. Gary DeMar, *America's Christian History: The Untold Story* (Atlanta, GA: American Vision Publishers, Inc., 1993), pp. 53, 104. D.P. Diffine, Ph.D., *One Nation Under God - How Close a Separation?* (Searcy, Arkansas: Harding University, Belden Center for Private Enterprise Education, 6th edition, 1992), p. 17. *The Capitol* (Washington D.C.: United States Government Printing Office, 7th edition, 1979), pp. 24-25.

[226] **Congress of the United States of America.** 1954, Willard Cantelon, *Money Master of the World* (Plainfield, NJ: Logos International, 1976), p. 135. Robert Byrd, United States Senator from West Virginia, July 27, 1962. In a message delivered in Congress two days after the Supreme Court declared prayer in schools unconstitutional. Robert Flood, *The Rebirth of America* (Philadelphia: Arthur S. DeMoss Foundation, 1986), pp. 66-69.

[227] **Congress of the United States of America.** July 27, 1962, in an address by U.S. Senator Robert Byrd from West Virginia delivered in Congress two days after the Supreme Court declared prayer in schools unconstitutional. Robert Flood, *The Rebirth of America* (Philadelphia: Arthur S. DeMoss Foundation, 1986), pp. 66-69. Gary DeMar, *America's Christian History: The Untold Story* (Atlanta, GA: American Vision Publishers, Inc., 1993), pp. 54-56.

[228] **Congress of the United States of America.** July 20, 1956, bill for national motto, in the 84th Congress, 2nd session, adopted House Joint Resolution 396, introduced by Rep. Charles E. Bennett's (FL); April 18 (legislative day, April 9,) 1956; read twice and referred to the Committee on the Judiciary. Passed the House of Representatives April 16, 1956. Attest: Ralph R. Roberts, Clerk. "Our Christian Heritage," *Letter from Plymouth Rock* (Marlborough, NH: The Plymouth Rock Foundation), p. 7. Christine F. Hart, *One Nation Under God* (NJ: American Tract Society, reprinted by Gospel Tract Society, Inc.), p. 5. Gary DeMar, *America's Christian History: The Untold Story* (Atlanta, GA: American Vision Publishers, Inc., 1993), pp. 52, 104. Courtesy of Bruce Barilla, Christian Heritage Week Ministry (P.O. Box 58, W.V. 24712; 304-384-7707, 304-384-9044 fax).

[229] **Congress of the United States of America.** 1977, in Public Law 77-379. Gary DeMar, *America's Christian History: The Untold Story* (Atlanta, GA: American Vision Publishers, Inc., 1993), p. 53.

[230] **Congress of the United States of America.** October 4, 1982, by a Joint Resolution of the Senate and House in the second session of the 97th Congress, held at the City of Washington, passed Public Law 97-280, 96 Stat. 1211, declaring 1983 the "Year of the Bible." John Eidsmoe, *Christianity and the Constitution - The Faith of Our Founding Fathers* (Grand Rapids, MI: Baker Book House, A Mott Media Book, 1987; 6th printing, 1993), p. 355. "Our Christian Heritage," *Letter from Plymouth Rock* (Marlborough, NH:

The Plymouth Rock Foundation), p. 7. Gary DeMar, *America's Christian History: The Untold Story* (Atlanta, GA: American Vision Publishers, Inc., 1993), p. 53. Congress of the United States of America February 22, 1990, in Senate Joint Resolution 164, authorized and requested President George Bush to issue a Presidential Proclamation declaring 1990 the *International Year of Bible Reading*. In his Proclamation, President Bush stated:

"Among the great books produced throughout the history of mankind, the Bible has been prized above all others by generations of men and women around the world - by people of every age, every race, and every walk of life.

"The Bible has had a critical impact upon the development of Western civilization. Western literature, art, and music are filled with images and ideas that can be traced to its pages. More important, our moral tradition has been shaped by the laws and teachings it contains. It was a biblical view of man - one affirming the dignity and worth of the human person, made in the Image of our Creator - that inspired the principles upon which the United States is founded. President Jackson called the Bible "the Rock on which our Republic rests" because he knew that it shaped the Founding Fathers' concept of individual liberty and their vision of a free and just society.

"The Bible has not only influenced the development of our Nation's values and institutions but also enriched the daily lives of millions of men and women who have looked to it for comfort, hope, and guidance. On the American frontier, the Bible was often the only book a family owned. For those pioneers living far from any church or school, it served both as a source of religious instruction and as the primary text from which children learned to read. The historic speeches of Abraham Lincoln and Dr. Martin Luther King, Jr., provide compelling evidence of the role Scripture played in shaping the struggle against slavery and discrimination. Today the Bible continues to give courage and direction to those who seek truth and righteousness. In recognizing its enduring value, we recall the words of the prophet Isaiah, who declared, 'The grass withereth, the flower fadeth; but the word of our God shall stand forever.'

"Containing revelations of God's intervention in human history, the Bible offers moving testimony to His love for mankind. Treasuring the Bible as a source of knowledge and inspiration. President Abraham Lincoln call this Great Book 'the best gift God has given to man.' President Lincoln believed that the Bible not only reveals the infinite goodness of our Creator, but also reminds us of our worth as individuals and our responsibilities toward one another.

"President Woodrow Wilson likewise recognized the importance of the Bible to its readers. 'The Bible is the word of life,' he once said. Describing its contents, he added:

"'You will find it full of real men and women not only but also of the things you have wondered about and been troubled about all your life, as men have been always; and the more you will read it the more it will become plain to you what things are worth while and what are not, what things make men happy - loyalty, right dealing, speaking the truth...and the things that are guaranteed to make men unhappy - selfishness, cowardice, greed, and everything that is low and mean. When you have read the Bible you will know that it is the Word of God, because you will have found it the key to your own heart, your own happiness, and your own duty.'"

"President Wilson believed that the Bible helps its readers find answers to the mysteries and sorrows that often trouble the souls of men.

"Cherished for centuries by men and women around the world, the Bible's value is timeless. Its significance transcends the boundaries between nations and languages because it carries a universal message to every human heart. This year numerous individuals and associations around the world will join in a campaign to encourage voluntary study of the Bible. Their efforts are worthy of recognition and support.

"In acknowledgement of the inestimable value and timeless appeal of the Bible, the Congress, by Senate Joint Resolution 164, has designated the year 1990 as the 'International Year of Bible Reading' and has authorized and requested the President to issue a proclamation in observance of this year.

"NOW, THEREFORE, I, GEORGE BUSH, President of the United States of America, do hereby proclaim the year 1990 as the International Year of Bible Reading. I invite all Americans to discover the great inspiration and knowledge that can be obtained through thoughtful reading of the Bible.

"IN WITNESS WHEREOF, I have hereunto set my hand this twenty-second day of February, in the year of our Lord nineteen hundred and ninety, and of the Independence of the United States of America the two hundred and fourteenth. George Bush.

[231] **Congress of the United States of America.** August 11, 1984, the Equal Access Act became law. (20 U.S.C. §§ 4071-74). *The Equal Access Act and the Public Schools-Questions and Answers* (available from the Christian Legal Society, P.O. Box 1492, Merrifield, Va. 22116.), pp. 1, 3.

[232] **Congress of the United States of America.** January 25, 1988 in the Second Session of the One Hundredth Congress. *Public Law 100-307 - May 5, 1988* [Legislative History - S. 1378]; May 5, 1988. 36 USC 169th, Congressional Record, Vol. 134 (1988), Apr.22, considered and passed Senate, May 2, considered and passed House. 102 STAT. 456. Mrs. James Dobson (Shirley), chairman, *The National Day of Prayer Information Packet* (Colorado Springs, CO: National Day of Prayer Task Force, May 6, 1993). Gary DeMar, *America's Christian History: The Untold Story* (Atlanta, GA: American Vision Publishers, Inc., 1993), p. 53. April 17, 1952, by a Joint Resolution of the House and Senate, passed Public Law 82-324; 66 Stat. 64, to provide for setting aside an appropriate day as a National Day of Prayer. Courtesy of Bruce Barilla, Christian Heritage Week Ministry (P.O. Box 58, W.V. 24712; 304-384-7707, 304-384-9044 fax).

[233] **Fundamental Orders (Constitution) of Connecticut.** January 14, 1639. *Old South Leaflets*, No. 8. John Fiske, *The Beginning of New England* (Boston: Houghton, Mifflin & Co., 1889, 1898), p. 127-128. David Barton, *The Myth of Separation* (Aledo, TX: WallBuilder Press, 1991), p. 87.

[234] **Fundamentals Orders (Constitution) of Connecticut.** January 14, 1639. *Old South Leaflets*, No. 8.*The World Book Encyclopedia*, 18 vols. (Chicago, IL: Field Enterprises, Inc., 1957; W.F. Quarrie and Company, 8 vols., 1917; World Book, Inc., 22 vols., 1989), Vol. 3, p. 1675.

[235] **Fundamental Orders (Constitution) of Connecticut.** January 14, 1639. John Wingate Thornton, *The Pulpit of the American Revolution, 1860* (reprinted NY: Burt Franklin, 1970), p. XIX. David Barton, *The Myth of Separation* (Aledo, TX: WallBuilder Press, 1991), p. 87.

[236] **Fundamental Orders (Constitution) of Connecticut.** January 14, 1639, Connecticut Towns of Hartford, Wethersfield, and Windsor. *Old South Leaflets*, No. 8. *Connecticut Colonial Records*, Vol. 1, pp. 20-25. *Old South Leaflets*, Published by the Directors of the Old South Work, Old South Meeting House, Boston, n.d. *The Code of 1650, Being a Compilation of the Earliest Laws and Orders of the General Court of Connecticut* (Hartford: Silus Andrus, 1822), p. 2. Perley Poore, ed.,*The Federal and State Constitutions, Colonial*

Notes

Charters, and Other Organic Laws of the United States (Washington, 1877), Part I:249-251. *Church of the Holy Trinity v. U.S.*, 143 U.S. 457, 458, 465-471, 36 L ed 226, (1892), Justice David Josiah Brewer. Henry Steele Commager, ed., *Documents of American History*, 2 vols. (NY: F.S. Crofts and Company, 1934; Appleton-Century-Crofts, Inc., 1948, 6th edition, 1958; Englewood Cliffs, NJ: Prentice Hall, Inc., 9th edition, 1973), Vol. I, pp. 22-23. Paul M. Angle, ed., *By These Words* (NY: Rand McNally & Company, 1954), pp. 6-7. Verna M. Hall, *The Christian History of the Constitution of the United States of America* (San Francisco, CA: Foundation for American Christian Education, 1960, 1980), pp. 253-257. *The Annals of America*, 20 vols. (Chicago, IL: Encyclopedia Britannica, 1968, 1977), Vol. I. p. 157. "Our Christian Heritage," *Letter from Plymouth Rock* (Marlborough, NH: The Plymouth Rock Foundation), pp. 2, 6. Michael P. Farris, *Constitutional Law for Christian Students* (Paeonian Springs, VA: Home School Legal Defense Association, 1991), p. 8. David Barton, *The Myth of Separation* (Aledo, TX: WallBuilder Press, 1991), pp. 47-51, 88. Gary DeMar, *America's Christian History: The Untold Story* (Atlanta, GA: American Vision Publishers, Inc., 1993), p. 37. Stephen McDowell and Mark Beliles, "The Providential Perspective" (Charlottesville, VA: The Providence Foundation, P.O. Box 6759, Charlottesville, Va. 22906, January 1994), Vol. 9, No. 1, p. 1.

236 Fundamental Orders (Constitution) of Connecticut. 1639, in the articles of the constitution of Connecticut drawn up in Quinipiack (New Haven), Connecticut. Benjamin Franklin Morris, *The Christian Life and Character of the Civil Institutions of the United States* (Philadelphia: George W. Childs, 1864), pp. 67-68. Gary DeMar, *God and Government - A Biblical and Historical Study* (Atlanta, GA: American Vision Press, 1982), pp. 113-114.

238 Fundamental Orders (Constitution) of Connecticut. 1639, charge to the governor by Rev. Mr. Davenport. Benjamin Franklin Morris, *The Christian Life and Character of the Civil Institutions of the United States* (Philadelphia: George W. Childs, 1864), p. 114. Gary DeMar, *God and Government - A Biblical and Historical Study* (Atlanta, GA: American Vision Press, 1982), p. 114.

239 General Court of Connecticut. 1639, established under the Constitution of Connecticut. Benjamin Franklin Morris, *The Christian Life and Character of the Civil Institutions of the United States* (Philadelphia: George W. Childs, 1864), p. 68. Gary DeMar, *God and Government - A Biblical and Historical Study* (Atlanta, GA: American Vision Press, 1982), p. 114. Peter Marshall and David Manuel, *The Glory of America* (Bloomington, MN: Garborg's Heart'N Home, Inc., 1991), 1.9. D.P. Diffine, Ph.D., *One Nation Under God - How Close a Separation?* (Searcy, Arkansas: Harding University, Belden Center for Private Enterprise Education, 6th edition, 1992), p. 4. *The Code of 1650 - Being a Compilation of the Earliest Laws and Orders of the General Court of Connecticut, etc., etc.,* (Hartford: Silus Andrus, 1822), complete work pages, pp. 20-94. *The Annals of America*, 20 vols. (Chicago, IL: Encyclopedia Britannica, 1968, 1977), Vol. I, p. 200.

240 Colony of Connecticut. 1647. *Old Deluder Satan Law. The Code of 1650 - Being a Compilation of the Earliest Laws and Orders of the General Court of Connecticut* (Hartford: Silus Andrus, 1822), pp. 20-91, 92-94. *The Laws and Liberties of Massachusetts, 1648* (reprinted Cambridge: 1929), cited in *McCollum v. Board of Education*, 68 S.Ct. 461, 333 U.S. 203 (1948). *Records of the Governor of the Massachusetts Bay in New England*, II:203. Henry Steele Commager, ed., *Documents of American History*, 2 vols. (NY: F.S. Crofts and Company, 1934; Appleton-Century-Crofts, Inc., 1948, 6th edition, 1958; Englewood Cliffs, NJ: Prentice Hall, Inc., 9th edition, 1973), Vol. I, p. 29. John Wilson Taylor, M.A., Ph.D., et al., *The Lincoln Library of Essential Information* (Buffalo, New York: The Frontier Press Company, 1935), p. 1623. *The Annals of America*, 20 vols. (Chicago, IL: Encyclopedia Britannica, 1968, 1977), Vol. I, p. 203. John Eidsmoe, *Christianity and the Constitution - The Faith of Our Founding Fathers* (Grand Rapids, MI: Baker Book House, A Mott Media Book, 1987, 6th printing 1993), p. 28. David Barton, *The Myth of Separation* (Aledo, TX: WallBuilder Press, 1991), p. 90. D.P. Diffine, Ph.D., *One Nation Under God - How Close a Separation?* (Searcy, Arkansas: Harding University, Belden Center for Private Enterprise Education, 6th edition, 1992), p. 2.

241 Constitution of the State of Connecticut. 1776. Benjamin Franklin Morris, *The Christian Life and Character of the Civil Institutions of the United States* (Philadelphia: George W. Childs, 1864). Benjamin Weiss, *God in American History: A Documentation of America's Religious Heritage* (Grand Rapids, MI: Zondervan, 1966), p. 155. Frances Newton Thorpe, ed., *Federal and State Constitutions, Colonial Charters, and Other Organic Laws of the States, Territories, and Colonies now or heretofore forming the United States*, 7 vols. (Washington: Government Printing Office, 1905; 1909; St. Clair Shores, MI: Scholarly Press, 1968). Gary DeMar, *God and Government* (Atlanta, GA: American Vision Press, 1984), p. 164. Gary DeMar, "Censoring America's Christian History" (Atlanta, GA: *The Biblical Worldview*, An American Vision Publication - American Vision, Inc., July 1990), p. 7. Gary DeMar, *America's Christian History: The Untold Story* (Atlanta, GA: American Vision Publishers, Inc., 1993), p. 65. William Miller, *The First Liberty - Religion and the American Republic* (NY: 1986), p. 109.

242 State of Connecticut. 1785-1786. Allen Nevins, *The American States During and After the Revolution: 1770-1789* (New York: MacMillan, 1924), p. 426. Tim LaHaye, *Faith of Our Founding Fathers* (Brentwood, TN: Wolgemuth & Hyatt, Publishers, Inc., 1987), p. 254.

243 Constitution of the United States of America. September 17, 1787, Preamble. "Our Christian Heritage," *Letter from Plymouth Rock* (Marlborough, NH: The Plymouth Rock Foundation), p. 4.

244 Constitution of the United States of America. September 17, 1787, Article I, Section 7, Paragraph 2. David Barton, *The Myth of Separation* (Aledo, TX: WallBuilder Press, 1991), p. 111. "Our Christian Heritage," *Letter form Plymouth Rock* (Marlborough, NH: The Plymouth Rock Foundation), p. 4.

245 Constitution of the United States of America. September 17, 1787. "Our Christian Heritage," *Letter from Plymouth Rock* (Marlborough, NH: The Plymouth Rock Foundation), p. 4.

246 Continental Congress. September 17, 1787. M.E. Bradford, *A Worthy Company: Brief Lives of the Framers of the United States Constitution* (Marlborough, NH: Plymouth Rock Foundation, 1982), p. viii-ix. John Eidsmoe, *Christianity and the Constitution - The Faith of Our Founding Fathers* (Grand Rapids, MI: Baker Book House, A Mott Media Book, 1987, 6th printing 1993), p. 43. Tim LaHaye, *Faith of Our Founding Fathers* (Brentwood, TN: Wolgemuth & Hyatt, Publishers, Inc., 1987), p. 30. David Barton, *The Myth of Separation* (Aledo, TX: WallBuilder Press, 1991), pp. 24-25.

247 (John) Calvin Coolidge. May 31, 1923, Memorial Day, as Vice-President under President Harding, speaking on the motives of the Puritan forefathers in his message entitled "The Destiny of America." *The Price of Freedom - Speeches and Addresses* (NY: 1924), pp. 1331-1353. *The Annals of America*, 20 vols. (Chicago, IL: Encyclopedia Britannica, 1968, 1977), Vol. XIV, pp. 410-414. Peter Marshall and David Manuel, *From Sea to Shining Sea* (Old Tappan, NJ: Fleming H. Revell Company, 1986). Peter Marshall and David Manuel, *The Glory of America* (Bloomington, MN: Garborg's Heart'N Home, Inc., 1991), 1.5, 5.30. D.P. Diffine, Ph.D., *One Nation Under God - How Close a Separation?* (Searcy, Arkansas: Harding University, Belden Center for Private Enterprise Education, 6th edition, 1992), p. 17.

248 (John) Calvin Coolidge. August 4, 1923, in a Proclamation of a National Day of Mourning and Prayer issued from the White House. *A Compilation of the Messages and Papers of the Presidents* 20 vols. (New York: Bureau of National Literature, Inc., prepared under the direction of the Joint Committee on Printing, of the House and Senate, pursuant to an Act of the Fifty-Second Congress of the United States, 1893, 1923), Vol. XVIII, pp. 9321-9322.

²⁴⁹ **(John) Calvin Coolidge.** March 4, 1925, in his Inaugural Address. *Inaugural Addresses of the Presidents of the United States - From George Washington 1789 to Richard Milhous Nixon 1969* (Washington, D.C.: United States Government Printing Office; 91st Congress, 1st Session, House Document 91-142, 1969), pp. 215-223. Calvin Coolidge, *Foundations of the Republic - Speeches and Addresses* (New York: Charles Scribner's Sons, 1926), p. 205. McCollister, *So Help Me God*, p. 137. Charles E. Rice, *The Supreme Court and Public Prayer* (New York: Fordham University Press, 1964), p. 190. Benjamin Weiss, *God in American History: A Documentation of America's Religious Heritage* (Grand Rapids, MI: Zondervan, 1966), p. 131. Lott, ed., *The Inaugural Addresses of the American Presidents*, p. 221. Reid, ed., *Three Centuries of American Rhetorical Discourse*, p. 667. Willard Cantelon, *Money Master of the World* (Plainfield, NJ: Logos International, 1976), p. 121. Peter Marshall and David Manuel, *The Glory of America* (Bloomington, MN: Garborg's Heart 'N Home, Inc., 1991), 1.4. *Proclaim Liberty* (Dallas, Tx: Word of Faith), p. 2. J. Michael Sharman, J.D., *Faith of the Fathers* (Culpepper, Virginia: Victory Publishing, 1995), pp. 92-93.

²⁵⁰ **(John) Calvin Coolidge.** September of 1923, in a letter to Rev. James E. Freeman, Bishop of Washington; Rev. James E. Freeman quoted from the letter in his Memorial Address for Coolidge before the House of Representatives on January 16, 1933. Hon. Arthur Prentice Rugg, "Calvin Coolidge - Memorial Address - Delivered Before the Joint Meeting of the Two Houses of Congress as a Tribute of Respect to the Late President of the United States," February 6, 1933. 72d Congress, Senate Document No. 186, *In Memoriam - Calvin Coolidge - Late President of the United States* (Washington, D.C.: United States Government Printing Office, 1933), pp. 66- 67.

²⁵¹ **(John) Calvin Coolidge.** 1923, statement. Charles Fadiman, ed., *The American Treasury* (NY: Harper & Brothers, Publishers, 1955), p. 127. Robert Flood, *The Rebirth of America* (Philadelphia: Arthur S. DeMoss Foundation, 1986), p. 37. Gary DeMar, "Censoring America's Christian History" (Atlanta, GA: *The Biblical Worldview*, An American Vision Publication - American Vision, Inc., July 1990), p. 6. David Barton, *The Myth of Separation* (Aledo, TX: WallBuilder Press, 1991), p. 249. Peter Marshall and David Manuel, *The Glory of America* (Bloomington, MN: Garborg's Heart'N Home, Inc., 1991), 8.3. D.P. Diffine, Ph.D., *One Nation Under God - How Close a Separation?* (Searcy, Arkansas: Harding University, Belden Center for Private Enterprise Education, 6th edition, 1992), p. 17. Gary DeMar, *America's Christian History: The Untold Story* (Atlanta, GA: American Vision Publishers, Inc., 1993), p. 60.

²⁵² **Resolution of the City of Coppell, Texas.** April 27, 1993. *Resolution No. 042793.1*, duly passed and approved by the City Council of Coppell, Texas, Mark Wolfe, Mayor, Linda Grau, Assistant City Secretary, b:\Pub Sch Pra.Res.

²⁵³ **Hernando Cortez.** February 10, 1519, in an address to his men as they embark for Mexico. Henry Morton Robinson, *Stout Cortez: A Biography of the Spanish Conquest* (New York: Century Co., 1931), pp. 47-48. John Eidsmoe, *Columbus & Cortez, Conquerors for Christ* (Green Forest, AR: New Leaf Press, 1992), p. 165-166.

²⁵⁴ **Hernando Cortez.** July 10, 1519, Hernando Cortez sent his *First Dispatch* to Queen Juana and her son, Charles V, from the city of Vera Cruz. John Bartlett, *Bartlett's Familiar Quotations* (Boston: Little, Brown and Company, 1855, 1980), p. 156.

²⁵⁵ **Hernando Cortez.** 1519. Francisco Lopez de Gomara, *Cortez: The Life of the Conqueror by His Secretary* (Berkeley: University of California Press, 1552, 1964). Bernal Diaz del Castillo, *The True History of the Conquest of New Spain by Bernal Diaz del Castillo, One of Its Conquerors* (London: Hakluyt Society, 1568, 1908). John Eidsmoe, *Columbus & Cortez, Conquerors for Christ* (Green Forest, AR: New Leaf Press, 1992), pp. 147-170.

²⁵⁶ **Hernando Cortez.** 1519, in Cozumel, Mexico. Francisco Lopez de Gomara, *Cortez: The Life of the Conqueror by His Secretary* (Berkeley: University of California Press, 1552, 1964), chap. 13, p. 33. John Eidsmoe, *Columbus & Cortez, Conquerors for Christ* (Green Forest, AR: New Leaf Press, 1992), p. 170.

²⁵⁷ **Hernando Cortez.** 1519, to the Tabascan tribe in Mexico. Francisco Lopez de Gomara, *Cortez: The Life of the Conqueror by His Secretary* (Berkeley: University of California Press, 1552, 1964), chap. 23, p. 51. John Eidsmoe, *Columbus & Cortez, Conquerors for Christ* (Green Forest, AR: New Leaf Press, 1992), p. 173.

²⁵⁸ **Hernando Cortez.** 1519, in referring to the Cempoallan tribe. Bernal Diaz del Castillo, *The True History of the Conquest of New Spain by Bernal Diaz del Castillo, One of Its Conquerors* (London: Hakluyt Society, 1568, 1908), Vol. I, chap. 51, p. 186. John Eidsmoe, *Columbus & Cortez, Conquerors for Christ* (Green Forest, AR: New Leaf Press, 1992), p. 190.

²⁵⁹ **Hernando Cortez.** 1519, in fighting the Tlaxcalan tribe. Bernal Diaz del Castillo, *The True History of the Conquest of New Spain by Bernal Diaz del Castillo, One of Its Conquerors* (London: Hakluyt Society, 1568, 1908), Vol. I, chap. 62, p. 228. John Eidsmoe, *Columbus & Cortez, Conquerors for Christ* (Green Forest, AR: New Leaf Press, 1992), p. 192.

²⁶⁰ **Hernando Cortez.** 1519, in talking with Montezuma's ambassadors. Bernal Diaz del Castillo, *The True History of the Conquest of New Spain by Bernal Diaz del Castillo, One of Its Conquerors* (London: Hakluyt Society, 1568, 1908), Vol. I, chap. 40, pp. 148-149. John Eidsmoe, *Columbus & Cortez, Conquerors for Christ* (Green Forest, AR: New Leaf Press, 1992), p. 187.

²⁶¹ **Hernando Cortez.** In discoursing with Montezuma. Diaz, Bernal Diaz del Castillo, *The True History of the Conquest of New Spain by Bernal Diaz del Castillo, One of Its Conquerors* (London: Hakluyt Society, 1568, 1908), Vol. II, chap. 89, p. 54. John Eidsmoe, *Columbus & Cortez, Conquerors for Christ* (Green Forest, AR: New Leaf Press, 1992), p. 200.

²⁶² **Hernando Cortez.** 1519. Maurice Collis, *Cortez and Montezuma* (London: Faber & Faber, 1954), pp. 56-57. John Eidsmoe, *Columbus & Cortez, Conquerors for Christ* (Green Forest, AR: New Leaf Press, 1992), p. 184.

²⁶³ **Hernando Cortez.** 1519 in a discourse with Montezuma. Bernal Diaz del Castillo, *The True History of the Conquest of New Spain by Bernal Diaz del Castillo, One of Its Conquerors* (London: Hakluyt Society, 1568, 1908), Vol. II, chap. 90, pp. 56-57. John Eidsmoe, *Columbus & Cortez, Conquerors for Christ* (Green Forest, AR: New Leaf Press, 1992), pp. 200-201.

²⁶⁴ **Hernando Cortez.** 1519, in discoursing with Montezuma. Bernal Diaz del Castillo, *The True History of the Conquest of New Spain by Bernal Diaz del Castillo, One of Its Conquerors* (London: Hakluyt Society, 1568, 1908), Vol. II, chap. 92, p. 78. John Eidsmoe, *Columbus & Cortez, Conquerors for Christ* (Green Forest, AR: New Leaf Press, 1992), p. 205.

²⁶⁵ **Hernando Cortez.** 1519, at the death of Montezuma. Bernal Diaz del Castillo, *The True History of the Conquest of New Spain by Bernal Diaz del Castillo, One of Its Conquerors* (London: Hakluyt Society, 1568, 1908), Vol. II, chap. 126, p. 238. John Eidsmoe, *Columbus & Cortez, Conquerors for Christ* (Green Forest, AR: New Leaf Press, 1992), p. 225.

²⁶⁶ **Hernando Cortez.** December 26, 1520, in addressing his troop prior to marching to Mexico city the second time. Francisco Lopez de Gomara, *Cortez: The Life of the Conqueror by His Secretary* (Berkeley: University of California, 1552, 1964), chap. 120, pp. 241-242. John Eidsmoe, *Columbus & Cortez, Conquerors for Christ* (Green Forest, AR: New Leaf Press, 1992), pp. 236-237.

²⁶⁷ **Hernando Cortez.** Inscription on his coat of arms. John Eidsmoe, *Columbus & Cortez, Conquerors for Christ* (Green Forest, AR: New Leaf Press, 1992), p. 265.

²⁶⁸ **John Cotton.** 1636. Benjamin Fletcher Wright, Jr., *American Interpretations of Natural Law* (New York: Russell & Russell, 1962), pp. 17-18. John Eidsmoe, *Christianity and the Constitution - The Faith of Our Founding Fathers* (Grand Rapids, MI: Baker Book House, A Mott Media Book, 1987; 6th printing, 1993), p. 32.

²⁶⁹ **John Cotton.** 1636. Benjamin Fletcher Wright, Jr., *American Interpretations of Natural Law* (New York: Russell & Russell, 1962), pp. 17-18. John Eidsmoe, *Christianity and the Constitution - The Faith of Our Founding Fathers* (Grand Rapids, MI: Baker Book House, A Mott Media Book, 1987, 6th printing 1993), p. 32.

²⁷⁰ **John Cotton.** Perry Miller and Thomas H. Johnson, *The Puritans: A Sourcebook of Their Writings* Vol. I (New York: Harper & Row, 1938, 1963), pp. 212-214. John Eidsmoe, *Christianity and the Constitution - The Faith of Our Founding Fathers* (Grand Rapids, MI: Baker Book House, A Mott Media Book, 1987; 6th printing, 1993), pp. 34-35.

²⁷¹ **John Cotton.** Samuel Eliot Morison, "John Winthrop and the Founding of New England," Davis R. B. Ross, Alden T. Vaughan, and John B. Duff, eds., *Colonial America: 1607-1763* (New York: Thomas Y. Crowell Co., 1970), p. 25. Peter Marshall and David Manuel, *The Light and the Glory* (Old Tappan, NJ: Fleming H. Revell, 1977), p. 157. Peter Marshall and David Manuel, *The Glory of America* (Bloomington, MN: Garborg's Heart'N Home, Inc., 1991), 12.4.

²⁷² **John Cotton.** Stephen Foster, *Their Solitary Way* (New Haven: Yale University Press, 1971), p. 58. Peter Marshall and David Manuel, *The Glory of America* (Bloomington, MN: Garborg's Heart'N Home, Inc., 1991), 12.11.

²⁷³ **William Cowper.** 1785, in *The Task*, Vol. VI, "Winter Walk at Noon," l. 223. John Bartlett, *Bartlett's Familiar Quotations* (Boston: Little, Brown and Company, 1855, 1980), p. 377.

²⁷⁴ **Samuel Sullivan Cox.** Samuel Sullivan Cox addressing Congress. *Memorial Addresses* (United States Congress, 1890). Stephen Abbott Northrop, D.D., *A Cloud of Witnesses* (Portland, OR: American Heritage Ministries, 1987; Mantle Ministries, 228 Still Ridge, Bulverde, Texas), pp. 101-102.

²⁷⁵ **Richard Crashaw.** 1652, in the *Hymn of the Nativity, st. 6.* John Bartlett, *Bartlett's Familiar Quotations* (Boston: Little, Brown and Company, 1855, 1980), p. 292.

²⁷⁶ **Oliver Cromwell.** August 3, 1650, spoken before his defeat of the Royalist Scots at the Battle of Dunbar, September 3, 1650. John Bartlett, *Bartlett's Familiar Quotations* (Boston: Little, Brown and Company, 1855, 1980), p. 272.

²⁷⁷ **Oliver Cromwell.** September 12, 1654, in a message to Parliament. John Bartlett, *Bartlett's Familiar Quotations* (Boston: Little, Brown and Company, 1855, 1980), p. 272.

²⁷⁸ **Oliver Cromwell.** *Hood's Cromwell*, Chap. 17, p. 223. *Knight's England*, Vol. IV, p. 215. Stephen Abbott Northrop, D.D., *A Cloud of Witnesses* (Portland, OR: American Heritage Ministries, 1987; Mantle Ministries, 228 Still Ridge, Bulverde, Texas), p. 104.

²⁷⁹ **William Thomas Cummings.** 1942, in a field sermon at Bataan. Carlos P. Romulo, *I Saw the Fall of the Philippines* (1942). John Bartlett, *Bartlett's Familiar Quotations* (Boston: Little, Brown and Company, 1855, 1980), p. 857.

¹ **Dallas High Schools.** September 1946, E.B. Comstock, Assistant Superintendent in Charge of High Schools, "Foreword," *Bible Study Course - New Testament Bulletin No.170* (Dallas, TX: Dallas Public Schools Printshop, Authorized by Board of Education, April 23, 1946; reprinted Aledo, TX: WallBuilder Press, 1993), p. iii.

² **Dallas High Schools.** September 1946, *Bible Study Course - New Testament Bulletin No.170* (Dallas, TX: Dallas Public Schools Printshop, Authorized by Board of Education, April 23, 1946; reprinted Aledo, TX: WallBuilder Press, 1993), p. ix.

³ **Dallas High Schools.** September 1946, *Bible Study Course - New Testament Bulletin No.170* (Dallas, TX: Dallas Public Schools Printshop, Authorized by Board of Education, April 23, 1946; reprinted Aledo, TX: WallBuilder Press, 1993), p. x.

⁴ **Dallas High Schools.** September 1946, *Bible Study Course - New Testament Bulletin No.170* (Dallas, TX: Dallas Public Schools Printshop, Authorized by Board of Education, April 23, 1946; reprinted Aledo, TX: WallBuilder Press, 1993), appendix, pp. 99-105.

⁵ **Charles Anderson Dana.** Stephen Abbott Northrop, D.D., *A Cloud of Witnesses* (Portland, Oregon: American Heritage Ministries, 1987; Mantle Ministries, 228 Still Ridge, Bulverde, Texas), p. 112-113.

⁶ **James Dwight Dana.** Henry M. Morris, *Men of Science - Men of God* (El Cajon, CA: Master Books, Creation Life Publishers, Inc., 1990), pp. 56-57.

⁷ **Charles Robert Darwin.** 1859, in his *Origin of Species by Means of Natural Selection*. Charles Darwin, *Origin of Species* (London: J.M. Dent & Sons Ltd., 1971), p. 167. Dr. Andrew Snelling, *The Revised Quotebook* (Brisbane, Queensland, Australia: Creation Science Foundation, 1990), p. 18.

⁸ **Charles Robert Darwin.** 1859, in his *Origin of Species by Means of Natural Selection*. Charles Darwin, *Origin of Species-'On the imperfection of the geological record'* (London: J.M. Dent & Sons Ltd., 1971), Ch. X, pp. 292-293. Dr. Andrew Snelling, *The Revised Quotebook* (Brisbane, Queensland, Australia: Creation Science Foundation, 1990), p. 7.

⁹ **Charles Robert Darwin.** 1859, in his *Origin of Species by Means of Natural Selection*. Charles Darwin, *Introduction to Origin of Species*, p. 2. "John Lofton's Journal" (*The Washington Times*, February 8, 1984). Dr. Andrew Snelling, *The Revised Quotebook* (Brisbane, Queensland, Australia: Creation Science Foundation, 1990), p. 3.

¹⁰ **Charles Robert Darwin.** 1859, in his work, *The Origin of Species*, Chapter 15. John Bartlett, *Bartlett's Familiar Quotations* (Boston: Little, Brown and Company, 1855, 1980), p. 515.

¹¹ **Charles Robert Darwin.** "Darwin on His Deathbed" (*Christian Reader's Digest*, December 1941; reprinted from *Christian Witness*, 147 Commonwealth St., Sydney, Australia), p. 24.

¹² **Charles Robert Darwin.** "Darwin on His Deathbed" (*Christian Reader's Digest*, December 1941; reprinted from *Christian Witness*, 147 Commonwealth St., Sydney, Australia), p. 24.

¹³ **Charles Robert Darwin.** "Darwin on His Deathbed" (*Christian Reader's Digest*, December 1941; reprinted from *Christian Witness*, 147 Commonwealth St., Sydney, Australia), p. 24.

¹⁴ **Charles Robert Darwin.** "Darwin on His Deathbed" (*Christian Reader's Digest*, December 1941; reprinted from *Christian Witness*, 147 Commonwealth St., Sydney, Australia), p. 24.

¹⁵ **Jonathan Dayton.** June 28, 1787, in the Constitutional Convention. E.C. M'Guire, *The Religious Opinions and Character of Washington* (NY: Harper & Brothers, 1836), p. 151. David Barton, *The Myth of Separation* (Aledo, TX: WallBuilder Press, 1991), p. 109.

¹⁶ **Declaration of Independence.** July 4, 1776, in Philadelphia, PA. Charles W. Eliot, LL.D., ed., *American Historical Documents 1000-1904* (New York: P.F. Collier & Son Company, *The Harvard Classics*, 1910), Vol. 43, pp. 160-165. *Church of the Holy Trinity*

v. United States, 143 US 457, 458, 465-471, 36 L ed 226, (1892), Justice David Josiah Brewer. David Barton, *The Myth of Separation* (Aledo, TX: WallBuilder Press, 1991), pp. 47-51, 269-272. "Our Christian Heritage," *Letter from Plymouth Rock* (Marlborough, NH: The Plymouth Rock Foundation), p. 6. Stephen McDowell and Mark Beliles, "The Providential Perspective" (Charlottesville, VA: The Providence Foundation, P.O. Box 6759, Charlottesville, Va. 22906, January 1994), Vol. 9, No. 1, p. 2. D.P. Diffine, Ph.D., *One Nation Under God - How Close a Separation?* (Searcy, Arkansas: Harding University, Belden Center for Private Enterprise Education, 6th edition, 1992), p. 6.

[17] **Declaration of Independence.** July 3, 1776, John Adams in a letter to his wife Abigail. Charles Francis Adams (son of John Quincy Adams and grandson of John Adams), ed., *Letters of John Adams Addressed to His Wife* (Boston: Charles C. Little and James Brown, 1841), Vol. I, p. 128. *The World Book Encyclopedia*, 18 vols. (Chicago, IL: Field Enterprises, Inc., 1957; W.F. Quarrie and Company, 8 vols., 1917; World Book, Inc., 22 vols., 1989), Vol. 9, p. 3683. David Barton, *The Myth of Separation* (Aledo, TX: Wallbuilder Press, 1991), p. 98.

[18] **Declaration of Independence.** August 2, 1776, Samuel Adams addressing the members of Congress after they had finished signing the parchment copy of the *Declaration of Independence*. Charles E. Kistler, *This Nation Under God* (Boston: Richard G. Badger, The Gorham Press, 1924), p. 71. Peter Marshall and David Manuel, *The Light and the Glory* (NJ: Fleming H. Revell Co., 1977), p. 309. David Barton, *The Myth of Separation* (Aledo, TX: WallBuilder Press, 1991), p. 98. "Our Christian Heritage," *Letter from Plymouth Rock* (Marlborough, NH: The Plymouth Rock Foundation), p. 8.

[19] **Daniel Defoe.** *A Selection from the Works of Daniel Defoe*, Vol. III, p. 187. Stephen Abbott Northrop, D.D., *A Cloud of Witnesses* (Portland, Oregon: American Heritage Ministries, 1987; Mantle Ministries, 228 Still Ridge, Bulverde, Texas), p. 116.

[20] **Daniel Defoe.** *A Selection from the Works of Daniel Defoe*, Vol. III, p. 102. Stephen Abbott Northrop, D.D., *A Cloud of Witnesses* (Portland, Oregon: American Heritage Ministries, 1987; Mantle Ministries, 228 Still Ridge, Bulverde, Texas), pp. 116-117.

[21] **Daniel Defoe.** 1701, in his satirical poem, *The True Born Englishman, Part I, Line 1*. Lewis C. Henry, *Best Quotations For All Occasions* (Greenwich, CONN: Fawcett Publications, Inc., 1961), p. 38. John Bartlett, *Bartlett's Familiar Quotations* (Boston: Little, Brown and Company, 1855, 1980), p. 318.

[22] **DeKalb County Community School District.** prior to 1967, kindergarten poem. *DeSpain v. DeKalb County Comm. School Dist.*, 384 F. 2d 655, 835 (N. D. Ill. 1966), cert. denied, 390 U.S. 906 (1967). David Barton, *The Myth of Separation* (Aledo, TX: WallBuilder Press, 1991), p. 159.

[23] **Constitution of the State of Delaware.** 1776, Constitution of the State of Delaware, Article XXII, oath of office authored by George Read and Thomas McKean; until 1792. *The Constitutions of the Several Independent States of America, Published by Order of Congress* (Boston: Norman & Bowen, 1785), pp. 99-100. *Church of the Holy Trinity v. U.S.* 143 US 457, 469-470 (1892). Benjamin Franklin Morris, *The Christian Life and Character of the Civil Institutions of the United States* (Philadelphia, PA: L. Johnson & Co., 1863; George W. Childs, 1864), pp. 233-234. Frances Newton Thorpe, ed., *Federal and State Constitutions, Colonial Charters, and Other Organic Laws of the States, Territories, and Colonies now or heretofore forming the United States*, 7 vols. (Washington: Government Printing Office, 1905; 1909; St. Clair Shores, MI: Scholarly Press, 1968), Vol. I, p. 142. M.E. Bradford, *A Worthy Company* (NH: Plymouth Rock Foundation, 1982), p. x. Tim LaHaye, *Faith of Our Founding Fathers* (Brentwood, TN: Wolgemuth & Hyatt, Publishers, Inc., 1987), pp. 180-181. "Our Christian Heritage," *Letter from Plymouth Rock* (Marlborough, NH: The Plymouth Rock Foundation), p. 3. Gary DeMar, "Censoring America's Christian History" (Atlanta, GA: *The Biblical Worldview*, An American Vision Publication - American Vision, Inc., July 1990), p. 7. David Barton, *The Myth of Separation* (Aledo, TX: WallBuilder Press, 1991), pp. 23, 33, 143. Gary DeMar, *America's Christian History: The Untold Story* (Atlanta, GA: American Vision Publishers, Inc., 1993), pp. 67-68. David Barton, *Keys to Good Government* (Aledo, TX: WallBuilder Press, 1994), p. 3.

[24] **Constitution of the State of Delaware.** 1831, Article I. Frances Newton Thorpe, ed., *Federal and State Constitutions, Colonial Charters, and Other Organic Laws of the States, Territories, and Colonies now or heretofore forming the United States*, 7 vols. (Washington: Government Printing Office, 1905; 1909; St. Clair Shores, MI: Scholarly Press, 1968). Edwin S. Gaustad, *Neither King nor Prelate - Religion and the New Nation, 1776-1826* (Grand Rapids, MI: William B. Eerdmans Publishing Company, 1993), pp. 161-162. Charles E. Rice, *The Supreme Court and Public Prayer* (New York: Fordham University Press, 1964), p. 168; "Hearings, Prayers in Public Schools and Other Matters," Committee on the Judiciary, U.S. Senate (87th Cong., 2nd Sess.), 1962, pp. 268 et seq. Gary DeMar, *God and Government, A Biblical and Historical Study* (Atlanta, Georgia: American Vision Press), Vol. 1, pp. 164-165. *Church of the Holy Trinity v. U.S.*, 143 U.S. 457, 469-470. David Barton, *The Myth of Separation* (Aledo, TX: WallBuilder Press, 1991), p. 143. as recorded in The State of Delaware Executive Proclamation of November 14 - 20, 1993, as "Christian Heritage Week," signed by Governor Thomas R. Caper, and Lieutenant Governor Ruth Ann Minner. Courtesy of Bruce Barilla, Christian Heritage Week Ministry (P.O. Box 58, W.V. 24712; 304-384-7707, 304-384-9044 fax).

[25] ***Denver Post.*** January 20, 1905. Robert Flood, *The Rebirth of America* (Philadelphia: Arthur S. DeMoss Foundation, 1986), p. 65.

[26] **Alexis de Tocqueville.** Robert N. Bellah, et. al., *Habits of the Heart*, p. viii. Gary DeMar, *The Biblical Worldview* (Atlanta, GA: An American Vision Publication - American Vision Inc., 1993), Vol. 9, No. 2, p. 14.

[27] **Alexis de Tocqueville.** Statement. Alexis de Tocqueville, *Democracy in America* (New York: Vintage Books, 1945), Vol. I, p. 319. Tim LaHaye, *Faith of Our Founding Fathers* (Brentwood, TN: Wolgemuth & Hyatt, Publishers, Inc., 1987), p. 97. Alexis de Tocqueville, *The Republic of the United States of America and Its Political Institutions, Reviewed and Examined*, Henry Reeves, trans., (Garden City, NY: A.S. Barnes & Co., 1851), Vol. I, p. 337. David Barton, *The Myth of Separation* (Aledo, TX: WallBuilder Press, 1991), p. 135. Francis J. Grund, a publicist, wrote his work *The Americans in Their Moral, Social and Political Relations* in 1837, in which he observed the trends of religious influence in America: "The religious habits of the Americans form not only the basis of their private and public morals, but have become so thoroughly interwoven with their whole course of legislation, that it would be impossible to change them, without affecting the very essence of their government." Francis J. Grund, *The Americans in Their Moral, Social and Political Relations*, (1837), Vol. I, pp. 281, 292, 294. Anson Phelps Stokes and Leo Pfeffer, *Church and State in the United States* (NY: Harper and Row, Publishers, 1950, revised one-volume edition, 1964), p. 210.

[28] **Alexis de Tocqueville.** Alexis de Tocqueville, *Democracy in America* (New York: Vintage Books, 1945), Vol. I, p. 316. Tim LaHaye, *Faith of Our Founding Fathers* (Brentwood, TN: Wolgemuth & Hyatt, Publishers, Inc., 1987), p. 97. Alexis de Tocqueville, *The Republic of the United States of America and Its Political Institutions, Reviewed and Examined*, Henry Reeves, trans., (Garden City, NY: A.S. Barnes & Co., 1851), Vol. I, p. 334. David Barton, *The Myth of Separation* (Aledo, TX: WallBuilder Press, 1991), p. 135. Verna M. Hall, *Christian History* (San Francisco: Foundation for Christian Education), Vol. I, p. 372. Francis J. Grund, a publicist, wrote his work *The Americans in Their Moral, Social and Political Relations* in 1837, in which he observed the trends of religious influence in America: "The Americans look upon religion as a promoter of civil and political liberty; and have, therefore, transferred to it a large portion of the affection which they cherish for the institutions of their country." Francis J. Grund, *The*

Notes

Americans in Their Moral, Social and Political Relations, (1837),Vol. I, pp. 281, 292, 294. Anson Phelps Stokes and Leo Pfeffer, Church and State in the United States (MY: Harper and Row, Publishers, 1950, revised one-volume edition, 1964), p. 210.

[29] **Alexis de Tocqueville.** Democracy in America, 2 vols. (New York: Alfred A. Knopf, 1945), Vol. I p 303. Gary DeMar, The Biblical Worldview (Atlanta, GA: An American Vision Publication - American Vision, Inc., 1993), Vol. 9, No. 2, p. 14. "Our Christian Heritage," Letter from Plymouth Rock (Marlborough, NH: The Plymouth Rock Foundation), p. 5. Alexis de Tocqueville, Democracy in America (New York: Vintage Books, 1945), Vol. I, pp. 314-315. Tim LaHaye, Faith of Our Founding Fathers (Brentwood, TN: Wolgemuth & Hyatt, Publishers, Inc., 1987), p. 97.

[30] **Alexis de Tocqueville.** 1835, 1840. Alexis de Tocqueville, The Republic of the United States and Its Political Institutions, Revised and Examined, Henry Reeves, translator (Garden City, NY: A.S. Barnes & Co., 1851), Vol. 1, p. 331-332. Alexis de Tocqueville, Democracy in America, 2 vols. (NY: Alfred A. Knopf, 1945), Vol. I, p. 303. Alexis de Tocqueville, Democracy in America (New York: Vintage Books, 1945), Vol. I, pp. 314-315. Gary DeMar, "The Christian America Debate" (Atlanta, GA: The Biblical Worldview, An American Vision Publication- American Vision, Inc., February 1993), Vol. 9, No. 2, p. 14.

[31] **Alexis de Tocqueville.** Alexis de Tocqueville, The Republic of the United States of America and Its Political Institutions, Revised and Examined, Henry Reeves, trans., (Garden City, NY: A.S. Barnes & Co., 1851), Vol. 1, p. 334. David Barton, The Myth of Separation (Aledo, TX: WallBuilder Press, 1991), p. 32. Francis J. Grund, a publicist, wrote his work The Americans in Their Moral, Social and Political Relations, 1837, in which he observed the trends of religious influence in America: "Although the most perfect tolerance exists with regard to particular creeds, yet it is absolutely necessary that a man should belong to some persuasion of other, lest his Fellow-citizens should consider him an outcast from society. The Jews are tolerated in America with the same liberality as any denomination of Christians; but if a person were to call himself a Deist or an Atheist, it would excite universal execration. Yet there are religious denominations in the United States whose creeds are very nearly verging on Deism; but taking their arguments from the Bible, and calling themselves followers of Christ, they and their doctrines are tolerated, together with their form of worship." Francis J. Grund, The Americans in Their Moral, Social and Political Relations, (1837), Vol. 1, pp. 281, 292, 294. Anson Phelps Stokes and Leo Pfeffer, Church and State in the United States (MY: Harper and Row, Publishers, 1950, revised one-volume edition, 1964), p. 210.

[32] **Alexis de Tocqueville.** Alexis De Tocqueville, Democracy in America (New York: Vintage Books, 1945), Vol. 1, p. 314-315. Tim LaHaye, Faith of Our Founding Fathers (Brentwood, TN: Wolgemuth & Hyatt, Publishers, Inc., 1987), p. 98.

[33] **Alexis de Tocqueville.** Alexis De Tocqueville, Democracy in America (New York: Vintage Books, 1945), Vol. 1, p. 314-315. Tim LaHaye, Faith of Our Founding Fathers (Brentwood, TN: Wolgemuth & Hyatt, Publishers, Inc., 1987), p. 98. Alexis de Tocqueville, The Republic of the United States of America and Its Political Institutions, Revised and Examined, Henry Reeves, trans., (Garden City, NY: A.S. Barnes & Co., 1851), Vol. I, p. 333. David Barton, The Myth of Separation (Aledo, TX: WallBuilder Press, 1991), p. 135.

[34] **Alexis de Tocqueville.** Alexis de Tocqueville, The Republic of the United States of America and its Political Institutions, Reviewed and Examined, Henry Reeves, trans., (Garden City, NY: A.S. Barnes & Co., 1851), Vol. I, p. 44. David Barton, The Myth of Separation (Aledo, TX: WallBuilder Press, 1991), p. 246.

[35] **Alexis de Tocqueville.** The Republic of the United States of America and Its Political Institutions, Reviewed and Examined, Henry Reeves, trans., (Garden City, NY: A.S. Barnes & Co., 1851), Vol. 1, p. 335. David Barton, The Myth of Separation (Aledo, TX: WallBuilder Press, 1991), pp. 32,135.

[36] **Alexis de Tocqueville.** Tryon Edwards, D.D., The New Dictionary of Thoughts - A Cyclopedia of Quotations (Garden City, NY: Hanover House, 1852; revised and enlarged by C.H. Catrevas, Ralph Emerson Browns and Jonathan Edwards [descendent, along with Tryon, of Jonathan Edwards (1703-1758), president of Princeton 1891; The Standard Book Company, 1955,1963), p. 90.

[37] **Alexis de Tocqueville.** The Republic of the United States of America and Its Political Institutions, Reviewed and Examined, Henry Reeves, trans., (Garden City, NY: A.S. Barnes & Co., 1851), Vol. 1, p. 328. David Barton, The Myth of Separation (Aledo, TX: WallBuilder Press, 1991), p. 135.

[38] **Alexis de Tocqueville.** Alexis de Tocqueville, The Republic of the United States of America and Its Political Institutions, Reviewed and Examined, Henry Reeves, trans., (Garden City, NY: A.S. Barnes & Co., 1851), Vol. I, p. 5. David Barton, The Myth Separation (Aledo, TX: WallBuilder Press, 1991), p. 263.

[39] **Alexis de Tocqueville.** Democracy in America, 2 vols. (New York: Alfred A. Knopf, 1945), Vol. I, p. 305. Gary DeMar, The Biblical Worldview (Atlanta, GA: An American Vision Publication - American Vision, Inc., 1993), Vol. 9, No. 2, p. 15.

[40] **Alexis de Tocqueville.** The Republic of the United States of America and Its Political Institutions, Reviewed and Examined, Henry Reeves, trans., (Garden City, NY: A.S. Barnes & Co., 1851), Vol. 1, p. 337. David Barton, The Myth of Separation (Aledo, TX: WallBuilder Press, 1991), p. 130.

[41] **Alexis de Tocqueville.** Attributed. Robert Flood, The Rebirth of America (The Arthur S. DeMoss Foundation, 1986), p. 32. The New American, December 12, 1986, p. 10. Russell P. McRory, "Faith of Our Founding Fathers" (Wall Street Journal, Letter to the Editor, June 1993). D.P. Diffine, Ph.D.,One Nation Under God - How Close a Separation? (Searcy, Arkansas: Harding University, Belden Center for Private Enterprise Education, 6th edition, 1992), p. 1.

[42] **Alexis de Tocqueville.** August 1831. Alexis de Tocqueville, The Republic of the United States of America and Its Political Institutions - Reviewed and Examined, Henry Reeves, trans., (Garden City, NY: A.S. Barnes & Co., 1851), Vol. 1, p. 334. Alexis de Tocqueville, Democracy in America, 2 vols. (NY: Alfred A. Knopf, 1945), Vol. 1, pp. 311, 319-320. Alexis de Tocqueville, Democracy in America, George Lawrence, translator, (NY: Harper & Row, 1998) p. 47. Tryon Edwards, D.D., The New Dictionary of Thoughts - A Cyclopedia of Quotations (Garden City, NY: Hanover House, 1852; revised and enlarged by C.H. Catrevas, Ralph Emerson Browns and Jonathan Edwards [descendent, along with Tryon, of Jonathan Edwards (1703-1758), president of Princeton], 1891; The Standard Book Company, 1955, 1963), p. 337. The Annals of America, 20 vols. (Chicago, IL: Encyclopedia Britannica, 1968, 1977), Vol. 5, pp. 486-487, 497. Sidney E. Ahlstrom, A Religious History of the American People (New Haven, CT: Yale University Press, 1972), p. 386. Frederick Kershner, Jr., ed., Tocqueville's America - The Great Quotations (Athens, Ohio: Ohio University Press, Cooper Industries, 1993), p. 62. Charles Colson, Kingdoms in Conflict (Grand Rapids, MI: Zondervan Publishing House, 1987), pp. 228-229, 273. John Eidsmoe, Christianity and the Constitution - The Faith of Our Founding Fathers (Grand Rapids, MI: Baker Book House, A Mott Media Book, 1987; 6th printing, 1993), p. 408. Pat Robertson, The

Turning Tide (Dallas: Word Publishing, 1993), p. 270.

⁴³ **Charles Dickens.** Henry H. Halley, *Halley's Bible Handbook* (Grand Rapids, MI: Zondervan Publishing House, 1927, 1965), p. 19.

⁴⁴ **Charles Dickens.** 1843. Tiny Tim's line in the famous novel,*A Christmas Carol*. Lewis C. Henry,*Best Quotations For All Occasions* (Greenwich, CONN: Fawcett Publications, Inc., 1961), p. 24.

⁴⁵ **Charles Dickens.** *Bless Your Heart (series II)* (Eden Prairie, MN: Heartland Sampler, Inc., 1990), 7.15.

⁴⁶ **Charles Dickens.** 1849, in a literary work for his children. Marie Dickens, *The Life of Our Lord* (London, E.C.4, Great Britain: Associated Newspapers Ltd., 1934). *Life of Our Lord* (Nashville, TN: Oliver-Nelson Books, division of Thomas Nelson, Inc., Publishers, 1991), pp. 1-2.

⁴⁷ **Charles Dickens.** 1849, in a literary work for his children not intended for publication, Charles Dickens wrote *The Life of Our Lord*. Kept in the possession of Charles Dickens' sister-in-law, Miss Georgia Hogarth, till her death in 1917, when it came into the possession of Charles Dickens' son, Sir Henry Fielding Dickens. Sir Henry Fielding Dickens provided in his *Last Will and Testament*, that if the majority of his family were in favor, it may be published. Marie Dickens first published it in 1934 in newspaper serial form. Charles Dickens,*The Life of Our Lord* (London, E. C. 4, Great Britain: Associated Newspapers Ltd., 1934). *Life of Our Lord* (Nashville, TN: Oliver-Nelson Books, division of Thomas Nelson, Inc., Publishers, 1991), pp. 3,7-8, 11-13, 17-18, 21, 41, 52, 56-57, 59-61, 63-65.

⁴⁸ **Charles Dickens.** In a letter to his youngest son, Edward. Mamie Dickens, eldest daughter of Charles Dickens, "What My Father Taught Us" (*The Ladies' Home Journal*, February 1892). Stephen Abbott Northrop, D.D., *A Cloud of Witnesses* (Portland, OR: American Heritage Ministries, 1987; Mantle Ministries, 228 Still Ridge, Bulverde, Texas), p. 125.

⁴⁹ **Charles Dickens.** Mamie Dickens, eldest daughter of Charles Dickens, "What My Father Taught Us" (*The Ladies' Home Journal*, February 1892). Stephen Abbott Northrop, D.D., *A Cloud of Witnesses* (Portland, Oregon: American Heritage Ministries, 1987; Mantle Ministries, 228 Still Ridge, Bulverde, Texas), pp. 125-126.

⁵⁰ **Charles Dickens.** In his *Last Will and Testament*. Mamie Dickens, eldest daughter of Charles Dickens, "What My Father Taught Us" (*The Ladies' Home Journal*, February 1892). Stephen Abbott Northrop, D.D., *A Cloud of Witnesses* (Portland, OR: American Heritage Ministries, 1987; Mantle Ministries, 228 Still Ridge, Bulverde, Texas), p. 125.

⁵¹ **John Dickinson.** Milton E. Fowler, *John Dickinson: Conservative Revolutionary* (Charlottesville: University Press of Virginia, 1983), p. 287. M.E. Bradford, *Religion & The Framers: The Biographical Evidence* (Marlborough, NH: Plymouth Rock Foundation, 1991), p. 8.

⁵² **John Dickinson.** Forrest McDonald, ed., *Empire and Nation* (Englewood Cliffs, NJ: Prentice-Hall, 1962), pp. 15, 17, 20, 28, 83. Tim LaHaye, *Faith of Our Founding Fathers* (Brentwood, TN: Wolgemuth & Hyatt, Publishers, Inc., 1987), pp. 156-157.

⁵³ **John Dickinson.** 1776. Charles Stille, *The Life and Times of John Dickinson* (New York: Burt Franklin, 1968), pp. 187-188. Tim LaHaye, *Faith of Our Founding Fathers* (Brentwood, TN: Wolgemuth & Hyatt, Publishers, Inc., 1987), pp. 157-158.

⁵⁴ **John Dickinson.** Charles Stille,*The Life and Times of John Dickinson* (New York: Burt Franklin, 1968), p. 185. Tim LaHaye, *Faith of Our Founding Fathers* (Brentwood, TN: Wolgemuth & Hyatt, Publishers, Inc., 1987), p. 157.

⁵⁵ **John Dickinson.** 1768, in *The Liberty Song*. John Bartlett, *Bartlett's Familiar Quotations* (Boston: Little, Brown and Company, 1863, 1980), p. 378.

⁵⁶ **Thomas Dilworth.** 1740, *New Guide to the English Tongue*, London, 1740. H.R. Warfel, *Noah Webster, Schoolmaster to America* (New York: Octagon Press, 1966), pp. 11-13. Tim LaHaye, *Faith of Our Founding Fathers* (Brentwood, TN: Wolgemuth & Hyatt, Publishers, Inc., 1987), pp. 75-76. D.P. Diffine, Ph.D., *One Nation Under God - How Close a Separation?* (Searcy, Arkansas: Harding University, Belden Center for Private Enterprise Education, 6th edition, 1992), p. 5.

⁵⁷ **Thomas Dilworth.** 1740, *New Guide to the English Tongue*, London, 1740. H.R. Warfel, *Noah Webster, Schoolmaster to America* (New York: Octagon Press, 1966), pp. 11-13. Tim LaHaye, *Faith of Our Founding Fathers* (Brentwood, TN: Wolgemuth & Hyatt, Publishers, Inc., 1987), pp. 75-76.

⁵⁸ **Benjamin Disraeli.** *Are All Great Men Infidels?* (Winnipeg, Canada: Hull Publishing Co.), p. 7. Willard Cantelon, *New Money or None?* (Plainfield, NH: Logos International, 1979), p. 229.

⁵⁹ **Dr. James C. Dobson.** January 1994, in the "Focus on the Family" newsletter, (Colorado Springs, CO.), pp. 6-7.

⁶⁰ **John Donne.** 1624, *Devotions upon Emergent Occasions, No. 17*. John Donne, *Poems* (1633). John Bartlett, *Bartlett's Familiar Quotations* (Boston: Little, Brown and Company, 1855, 1980), p. 254.

⁶¹ **John Donne.** 1609-1617, in his*Holy Sonnets*, No. 14, Line 1. John Donne,*Poems* (1633). John Bartlett,*Bartlett's Familiar Quotations* (Boston: Little, Brown and Company, 1855, 1980), p. 254.

⁶² **John Donne.** Autumn 1622, in a message delivered to the Earl of Carlisle. John Donne, *LXXX Sermons*, (1640), No. 76. John Bartlett, *Bartlett's Familiar Quotations* (Boston: Little, Brown and Company, 1855, 1980), p. 254-255.

⁶³ **John Donne.** 1625, in a message delivered Christmas Day. John Donne, *LXXX Sermons*, (1640), No. 3. John Bartlett, *Bartlett's Familiar Quotations* (Boston: Little, Brown and Company, 1855, 1980), p. 255.

⁶⁴ **John Donne.** December 12, 1626, in a message delivered at the funeral of Sir William Cokayne. *LXXX Sermons* (1640), No. 80. John Bartlett, *Bartlett's Familiar Quotations* (Boston: Little, Brown and Company, 1855, 1980), p. 255.

⁶⁵ **Fedor Mikhailovich Dostoevski.** 1879-1880, in*Brothers Karamazov*, Book II, Chapter 6, (translated by Constance Garnett). John Bartlett, *Bartlett's Familiar Quotations* (Boston: Little, Brown and Company, 1855, 1980), p. 581.

⁶⁶ **William Orville Douglas.** 1952,*United States Supreme Court. Zorach v. Clauson*, 343 US 306 307 313, Justice William O. Douglas. Dr. Ed Rowe, *The ACLU and America's Freedom* (Washington: Church League of America, 1984), pp. 20-21. Tim LaHaye, *Faith of Our Founding Fathers* (Brentwood, TN: Wolgemuth & Hyatt, Publishers, Inc., 1987), pp. 9-10. Martin Shapiro and Roco Tresolini, eds., *American Constitutional Law* (NY: Macmillan Publishing, 5th edition, 1979), p. 445. David Barton, *The Myth of Separation* (Aledo, TX: WallBuilder Press, 1992), p. 77. John Whitehead, *The Rights of Religious Persons in Public Education* (Wheaton IL: Crossway Books, Good News Publishers, 1991), p. 284. "Our Christian Heritage," *Letter from Plymouth Rock* (Marlborough, NH: The Plymouth Rock Foundation), p. 7.

⁶⁷ **Frederick Douglass.** Page Smith, *The Nation Comes of Age* (NY: McGraw-Hill Book Co., 1981), Vol. 4, p. 584. Peter Marshall and David Manuel, *The Glory of America* (Bloomington, MN: Garborg's Heart'N Home, Inc., 1991), 2.20.

⁶⁸ **Frederick Douglass.** 1845, in *Narrative of the Life of Frederick Douglass*, Chapter 2. John Bartlett, *Bartlett's Familiar Quotations* (Boston: Little, Brown and Company, 1855, 1980), p. 556.

⁶⁹ **Jacob Duche'.** September 6, 1774. *The Journals of the Continental Congress 1774-1789* (Washington, D.C.: Government Printing Office, 1905), Vol. I, p. 26. David Barton, *The Myth of Separation* (Aledo, TX: WallBuilder Press, 1991), p. 100.

Notes

[70] **Jacob Duche'.** September 7, 1774, Rev. Mr. Duche' reading Psalm 35. "Our Christian Heritage," *Letter from Plymouth Rock* (Marlborough, NH: The Plymouth Rock Foundation), pp. 2-3. Catherine Millard, *The Rewriting of America's History* (Camp Hill, PA: Horizon House Publishers, 1991), p. 249.

[71] **Jacob Duche'.** September 7, 1774. *First Prayer in Congress - Beautiful Reminiscence* (Washington, D.C.: Library of Congress). John Adams and Abigail Adams, *The Book of Abigail and John - Selected Letters of The Adams Family 1762-1784*, L.H. Butterfield, Marc Frielander, and Mary-Jo King, eds. (Cambridge, MA: Harvard University Press, 1975), p. 76. Reynolds, *The Maine Scholars Manual* (Portland, ME: Dresser, McLellan & Co., 1880). Edmund Fuller and David E. Green, *God in the White House - The Faiths of American Presidents* (NY: Crown Publishers, Inc., 1968), pp. 21-22. Gary DeMar, *God and Government-A Biblical and Historical Study* (Atlanta, GA: American Vision Press, 1982), Vol. I, p. 108. John S.C. Abbot, *George Washington* (NY: Dodd, Mead & Co., 1875, 1917), p. 187. David Barton, *The Myth of Separation* (Aledo, TX: WallBuilder Press, 1991), pp. 101-102.

[72] **Jacob Duche'.** September 7, 1774. *The Journals of the Continental Congress 1774-1789* (Washington, D.C.: Government Printing Office, 1905), Vol. I, p. 27. David Barton, *The Myth of Separation* (Aledo, TX: WallBuilder Press, 1991), p. 101. On May 17, 1776, in the *Journals of Congress*, Vol. IV, p. 530, it was recorded: "*Resolved*, That the Rev. Mr. Duche' be appointed chaplain to Congress, and that he be desired to attend every morning at 9 O'Clock." Charles Francis Adams (son of John Quincy Adams and grandson of John Adams), ed., *Familiar Letters of John Adams and his Wife, Abigail Adams, during the Revolution*, p. 320. Anson Phelps Stokes and Leo Pfeffer, *Church and State in the United States* (NY: Harper and Row, Publishers, 1950, revised one-volume edition, 1964), p. 83. David Barton, *The Myth of Separation* (Aledo, TX: WallBuilder Press, 1991), p. 104.

[73] **Pierre Samuel du Pont de Nemours.** 1802, in a report to President Thomas Jefferson. DuPont de Nemours, *National Education in the United States of America* (Newark, DE: The University of Delaware Press, 1923), pp. 3-5. R.J. Rushdoony, *The Messianic Character of American Education*, (Nutley, N.J.: Prague Press, 1963), pp. 329-330. John Eidsmoe, *God & Caesar-Christian Faith & Political Action* (Westchester, IL: Crossway Books, a Division of Good News Publishers, 1984), p. 144. John Eidsmoe, *Christianity and the Constitution - The Faith of Our Founding Fathers* (Grand Rapids, MI: Baker Book House, A Mott Media Book, 1987, 6th printing 1993), pp. 22-23. Benjamin Hart, *Faith & Freedom - The Christian Roots of American Liberty* (Dallas, TX: Lewis and Stanley, 1988), pp. 360-361.

[74] **Timothy Dwight.** July 4th, 1798, as president of Yale College delivered an address entitled, *The Duty of Americans, at the Present Crisis, Illustrated in a Discourse, Preached on the Fourth of July, 1798*. (#Ital original). *The Annals of America*, 20 vols. (Chicago, IL: Encyclopedia Britannica, 1968, 1977), Vol. I, pp. 33-36. Peter Marshall and David Manuel, *The Glory of America* (Bloomington, MN: Garborg's Heart 'N Home, Inc., 1991), 1.11. Peter Marshall and David Manuel, *From Sea to Shining Sea* (Old Tappan, NJ: Fleming H. Revell Company, 1986).

[75] **Timothy Dwight.** Timothy Dwight, *Travels; in New England and New York* (New Haven, 1821-1822), Vol. IV, pp. 403-404. Charles Roy Keller, *The Second Great Awakening in Connecticut* (New Haven: Yale University Press, 1942), p. 36. David Barton, *The Myth of Separation* (Aledo, TX: WallBuilder Press, 1991), p. 246. Peter Marshall and David Manuel, *The Light and the Glory* (Old Tappan, New Jersey: Fleming H. Revell Co., 1977), p. 350.

[76] **Timothy Dwight.** Tryon Edwards, D.D., *The New Dictionary of Thoughts - A Cyclopedia of Quotations* (Garden City, NY: Hanover House, 1852; revised and enlarged by C.H. Catrevas, Ralph Emerson Browns and Jonathan Edwards [descendent, along with Tryon, of Jonathan Edwards (1703-1758), president of Princeton], 1891; The Standard Book Company, 1955, 1963), p. 44.

[77] **Timothy Dwight.** Stephen E. Berk, *Calvinism Versus Democracy* (Hamden, Conn.: Archon Books, 1974), p. 94. Peter Marshall and David Manuel, *The Glory of America* (Bloomington, MN: Garborg's Heart'N Home, Inc., 1991), 5.14.

E

[1] **Jonathan Edwards.** Marshall Foster, *Winning the Battle for the 21st Century* (Thousand Oaks, CA: Mayflower Institute, 1993), p. 39.

[2] **Jonathan Edwards.** *The Works of President Edwards* (Isaiah Thomas, editor), Vol. III, pp. 14-19. Peter Marshall and David Manuel, *The Light and The Glory* (Old Tappan, NJ: Fleming H. Revell Company), pp. 241-243.

[3] **Jonathan Edwards.** Tryon Edwards, D.D., *The New Dictionary of Thoughts - A Cyclopedia of Quotations* (Garden City, NY: Hanover House, 1852; revised and enlarged by C.H. Catrevas, Ralph Emerson Browns and Jonathan Edwards [descendent, along with Tryon, of Jonathan Edwards (1703-1758), president of Princeton], 1891; The Standard Book Company, 1955, 1963), p. 91.

[4] **Albert Einstein.** Philip Frank, *Einstein, His Life and Times* (1947). ("I shall never believe that God plays dice with the world.") John Bartlett, *Bartlett's Familiar Quotations* (Boston: Little, Brown and Company, 1855, 1980), p. 763. *Unlocking the Mysteries of Creation*, Dennis R. Petersen, B.S., M.A. (El Cajon, CA: Master Books, 1988), p. 79. Willard Cantelon, *New Money or None?* (Plainfield, NJ: Logos International, 1979), p. 239.

[5] **Albert Einstein.** Engraved over the fireplace in Fine Hall, Princeton, N.J. Burton Stevenson, *The Home Book of Quotations - Classical & Modern* (New York: Dodd, Mead and Company, 1967). ("Raffiniert ist der Herr Gott, aber Boshaft ist er nicht,"-"The Lord God is subtle, but malicious he is not.") John Bartlett, *Bartlett's Familiar Quotations* (Boston: Little, Brown and Company, 1855, 1980), p. 764.

[6] **Dwight David Eisenhower.** July 10, 1943 quoted from Charles L. Allen. Herbert V. Prochnow, *5100 Quotations for Speakers and Writers* (Grand Rapids, MI: Baker Book House, 1992), p. 347.

[7] **Dwight David Eisenhower.** June 14, 1954, in a speech confirming the Act of Congress which added the phrase *Under God* to the *Pledge of Allegiance*. U.S. Marine Corps, *How to Respect and Display Our Flag* (Washington: U.S. Government Printing Office, 1977), p. 31.

[8] **Dwight David Eisenhower.** June 14, 1954, President Eisenhower on the steps of the Capitol Building. *The Capitol* (Washington D.C.: United States Government Printing Office, 7th edition, 1979), pp. 24-25. Gary DeMar, *America's Christian History: The Untold Story* (Atlanta, GA: American Vision Publishers, Inc., 1993), p. 53.

[9] **Dwight David Eisenhower.** June 14, 1954, President Eisenhower signs House Joint Resolution 243 into law as Public Law 287, the *Pledge of Allegiance*. "Our Christian Heritage," *Letter from Plymouth Rock* (Marlborough, NH: The Plymouth Rock Foundation), p. 7. D.P. Diffine, Ph.D., *One Nation Under God - How Close a Separation?* (Searcy, Arkansas: Harding University, Belden Center for Private Enterprise Education, 6th edition, 1992), p. 17.

[10] **Dwight David Eisenhower.** September 8, 1892. *Pledge of Allegiance. The World Book Encyclopedia*, 18 vols. (Chicago, IL: Field Enterprises, Inc., 1957; W.F. Quarrie and Company, 8 vols., 1917; World Book, Inc., 22 vols., 1989), Vol. 13, p. 6419. Catherine

Millard, *The Rewriting of America's History* (Camp Hill, PA: Horizon House Publishers, 1991), pp. 273-274.

[11] **Dwight David Eisenhower.** 1954. "Our Christian Heritage," *Letter from Plymouth Rock* (Marlborough, NH: The Plymouth Rock Foundation), p. 7.

[12] **Dwight David Eisenhower.** January 21, 1957, Monday, in his Second Inaugural Address. *Inaugural Addresses of the Presidents of the United States - From George Washington 1789 to Richard Milhous Nixon 1969* (Washington, D.C.: United States Government Printing Office; 91st Congress, 1st Session, House Document 91-142, 1969), pp. 263-266. Benjamin Weiss, *God in American History: A Documentation of America's Religious Heritage* (Grand Rapids, MI: Zondervan, 1966), p. 145. Davis Newton Lott, *The Inaugural Addresses of the American Presidents* (NY: Holt, Rinehart and Winston, 1961), p. 263. Charles E. Rice, *The Supreme Court and Public Prayer* (New York: Fordham University Press, 1964), p. 193. Charles Wallis, ed., *Our American Heritage* (NY: Harper & Row, Publishers, Inc., 1970), p. 54. Willard Cantelon, *Money Master of the World* (Plainfield, NJ: Logos International, 1976), p. 121. *Proclaim Liberty* (Dallas, TX: Word of Faith), p. 3. J. Michael Sharman, J.D., *Faith of the Fathers* (Culpepper, Virginia: Victory Publishing, 1995), p. 109.

[13] **Dwight David Eisenhower.** Robert Flood, *The Rebirth of America* (Philadelphia: Arthur S. DeMoss Foundation, 1986), p. 190.

[14] **Dwight David Eisenhower.** *The Bible—The Book that Shaped a Nation.* Gary DeMar, *America's Christian History: The Untold Story* (Atlanta, GA: American Vision Publishers, Inc., 1993), p. 60.

[15] **John Eliot.** 1633, in a letter to Sir Simonds D'Ewes; Manuscript in the British Museum. *The Annals of America,* 20 vols. (Chicago, IL: Encyclopedia Britannica, 1968, 1977), Vol. I, p. 130.

[16] **John Eliot.** 1640, The *Bay Psalm Book.* Sydney E. Ahlstrom, *A Religious History of the American People* (New Haven, CT: Yale University Press, 1972), pp. 149-150. Gary DeMar, *America's Christian History: The Untold Story* (Atlanta, GA: American Vision Publishers, Inc., 1993), pp. 45-46.

[17] **Queen Elizabeth I.** Her response to the question as to Christ's presence in the Sacrament of Eucharist. S. Clarke, *Marrow of Ecclesiastical History* [ed. 1675], pt. II, *Life of Queen Elizabeth.* John Bartlett, *Bartlett's Familiar Quotations* (Boston: Little, Brown and Company, 1855, 1980), p. 164. Burton Stevenson, *The Home Book of Quotations - Classical & Modern* (New York: Dodd, Mead & Company, 1967).

[18] **Queen Elizabeth I.** Chamberlin, *Sayings of Queen Elizabeth.* John Bartlett, *Bartlett's Familiar Quotations* (Boston: Little, Brown and Company, 1855, 1980), p. 163.

[19] **Queen Elizabeth I.** 1601, in *The Golden Speech.* John Bartlett, *Bartlett's Familiar Quotations* (Boston: Little, Brown and Company, 1855, 1980), p. 164.

[20] **Queen Elizabeth I.** Speaking to her ladies regarding her epitaph. John Bartlett, *Bartlett's Familiar Quotations* (Boston: Little, Brown and Company, 1855, 1980), p. 164.

[21] **(Henry) Havelock Ellis.** 1923, in *The Dance of Life,* chapter 5. John Bartlett, *Bartlett's Familiar Quotations* (Boston: Little, Brown and Company, 1855, 1980), p. 690.

[22] **Ralph Waldo Emerson.** Henry Steele Commager and Richard B. Morris, eds., *Spirit of Seventy-Six* (New York: The Bobbs-Merrill Co., Inc., 1958), p. 156. Peter Marshall and David Manuel, *The Glory of America* (Bloomington, MN: Garborg's Heart'N Home, Inc., 1991), 5.25. *Bless Your Heart (series II)* (Eden Prairie, MN: Heartland Sampler, Inc., 1990), 7.14.

[23] **Magnus Eriksson II.** 1354, in a commission to Paul Knudsen authorizing an expedition to Greenland. Hjalmar R. Holand, *A Pre-Columbian Crusade to America* (New York: Twayne Publishers, 1962), p. 24; cf. Ingstad, *Pole Star,* p. 167. John Eidsmoe, *Columbus & Cortez, Conquerors for Christ* (Green Forest, AR: New Leaf Press, 1992), p. 37.

[24] **Edward Everett.** Tryon Edwards, D.D., *The New Dictionary of Thoughts - A Cyclopedia of Quotations* (Garden City, NY: Hanover House, 1852; revised and enlarged by C.H. Catrevas, Ralph Emerson Browns and Jonathan Edwards [descendent, along with Tryon, of Jonathan Edwards (1703-1758), president of Princeton], 1891; The Standard Book Company, 1955, 1963), p. 46.

[25] **Edward Everett.** In a speech at the opening of the Dudley Observatory in Albany, New York entitled "Uses of Astronomy," William H. McGuffey, *McGuffey's Eclectic Sixth Reader* (NY: American Book Company, 1907, revised 1920), p. 69.

[26] **Johannes Ewald.** Tryon Edwards, D.D., *The New Dictionary of Thoughts - A Cyclopedia of Quotations* (Garden City, NY: Hanover House, 1852; revised and enlarged by C.H. Catrevas, Ralph Emerson Browns and Jonathan Edwards [descendent, along with Tryon, of Jonathan Edwards (1703-1758), president of Princeton], 1891; The Standard Book Company, 1955, 1963), p. 46.

F

[1] **Henri Fabre.** Henry M. Morris, *Men of Science - Men of God* (El Cajon, CA: Master Books, Creation Life Publishers, Inc., 1990), pp. 62-63.

[2] **Michael Faraday.** Walter Jerrold, *Michael Faraday, Man of Science,* p. 120. Stephen Abbott Northrop, D.D., *A Cloud of Witnesses* (Portland, OR: American Heritage Ministries, 1987; Mantle Ministries, 228 Still Ridge, Bulverde, Texas), p. 147.

[3] **Michael Faraday.** George Wilson, *Short Biographies for the People,* Vol. IV. Stephen Abbott Northrop, D.D., *A Cloud of Witnesses* (Portland, Oregon: American Heritage Ministries, 1987; Mantle Ministries, 228 Still Ridge, Bulverde, Texas), p. 147-8. Ken Curtis, Ph.D., et. al., "Michael Faraday: At Play in the Fields of the Lord" Stories Behind Great Scientists - Fifth in a Series (Worcester, PA: *Glimpses,* published by the Christian History Institute, 1995), p. 2. Charles Ludwig, *Michael Faraday - Father of Electronics* (Herald Press, 1978).

[4] **David Glasgow Farragut.** Loyall Farragut, son of Admiral D.C. Farragut, *Life and Letters of Admiral D.C. Farragut,* p. 548. Stephen Abbott Northrop, D.D., *A Cloud of Witnesses* (Portland, Oregon: American Heritage Ministries, 1987; Mantle Ministries, 228 Still Ridge, Bulverde, Texas), p. 148.

[5] **David Glasgow Farragut.** Loyall Farragut, the son of Admiral D.G. Farragut, *Life and Letters of Admiral D.C. Farragut,* p. 548. Stephen Abbott Northrop, D.D., *A Cloud of Witnesses* (Portland, Oregon: American Heritage Ministries, 1987; Mantle Ministries, 228 Still Ridge, Bulverde, Texas), p. 148.

[6] **Federalist Paper No. 47.** (1787-1788). Gary DeMar, *God and Government-A Biblical and Historical Study* (Atlanta, GA: American Vision Press, 1982), p. 132.

[7] **Federalist Papers No. 51.** James Madison, *The Federalist No. 51, The Federalist Papers,* Clinton Rossiter, ed., (New York: Mentor Books, 1961), p. 322. John Eidsmoe, *Christianity and the Constitution - The Faith of Our Founding Fathers* (Grand Rapids, MI: Baker Book House, A Mott Media Book, 1987, 6th printing 1993), p. 102. David A. Noebel, *Understanding The Times - The Story of the Biblical Christian, Marxist/Leninist and Secular Humanist Worldviews* (Manitou Springs, CO: Summit Press, a branch of Summit Ministries, P.O. Box 207, Manitou Springs, Co., 80829, 1993), pp. 623-624.

[8] **Federalist Paper No. 81.** (1787-1788), written by Alexander Hamilton. David Barton, *The Myth of Separation* (Aledo, TX: WallBuilder Press, 1991), p. 224.

[9] **Henry Fielding.** 1742, in *Joseph Andrews*, book III, chapter 5. John Bartlett, *Bartlett's Familiar Quotations* (Boston: Little, Brown and Company, 1855, 1980), p. 349.

[10] **James Thomas Fields.** 1858, in *The Captain's Daughter; or, The Ballad of the Tempest*, st. 5. John Bartlett, *Bartlett's Familiar Quotations* (Boston: Little, Brown and Company, 1855, 1980), p. 557.

[11] **Charles Grandison Finney.** "In the Wake of the Second Great Awakening" (Carol Stream, IL: Christian History), Vol. VIII, No. 3, Issue 23, p. 31.

[12] **Charles Grandison Finney.** Charles G. Finney, *Memoirs* (NY: A.S. Barnes, 1876). *Revival Lectures* (reprinted Old Tappan, NJ: Fleming Revell Co., 1970), *Lecture XV*, pp. 336-337. David Barton, *The Myth of Separation* (Aledo, TX: WallBuilder Press, 1991), p. 265. Pat Robertson, *America's Dates with Destiny* (Nashville: Thomas Nelson Publishers, 1986), (some differences in language), p. 144. Peter Marshall & David Manuel, *The Glory of America* (Bloomington, MN: Garborg's Heart 'N Home, 1991), 11.2.

[13] **First Amendment to the Constitution of the United States.** December 15, 1791. Henry B. Watson, *The Key to the Constitution of the United States* (Alexandria, VA: Patriotic Education Incorporated, 1988), p. 34.

[14] **St. Johns River Settlement, Florida.** June 30, 1564, as recorded by French Huguenot leader, Rene de Laudonniere. Diana Karter Appelbaum, *Thanksgiving: An American Holiday, An American History* (New York: Facts on File Publications, 1984), pp. 14-15. Gary DeMar, *America's Christian History: The Untold Story* (Atlanta, GA: American Vision Publishers, Inc., 1993), p. 22.

[15] **Gerald Rudolph Ford.** August 9, 1974, after swearing in as the 38th President of the United States, in an address to Chief Justice Warren E. Burger, members of Congress and the citizens of America. *Weekly Compilation of Presidential Documents*, August 12, 1974. *The Annals of America*, 20 vols. (Chicago, IL: Encyclopedia Britannica, 1968, 1977), Vol. 20, pp. 30-32. Benjamin Weiss, *God in American History: A Documentation of America's Religious Heritage* (Grand Rapids, MI: Zondervan, 1966), p. 158. Willard Cantelon, *Money Master of the World* (Plainfield, NJ: Logos International, 1976), p. 122.

[16] **Gerald Rudolph Ford.** December 5, 1974. Mrs. James Dobson (Shirley), chairman, *The National Day of Prayer Information Packet* (Colorado Springs, CO: National Day of Prayer Tack Force, May 6, 1993).

[17] **Kirk Fordice.** "U.S.New & World Report" (November 30, 1992), p. 21. Gary DeMar, *The Biblical Worldview* (Atlanta, GA: An American Vision Publication - American Vision, Inc., 1993), Vol. 9, No. 2, p. 12.

[18] **Kirk Fordice.** Richard L. Berke, "Religion Issue Stirs Noise in G.O.P. Governors' 'Tent,'" *The New York Times* (November 18, 1992), p. A13. Gary DeMar, *America's Christian History: The Untold Story* (Atlanta, GA: American Vision Publishers, Inc., 1993), p. 33.

[19] **Howell M. Forgy.** December 7, 1941, to the men on the navy cruiser where he serving as chaplain. These words became the basis for Frank Loesser's song, *Praise the Lord and Pass the Ammunition*, 1942. John Bartlett, *Bartlett's Familiar Quotations* (Boston: Little, Brown and Company, 1855, 1980), p. 871.

[20] **Henry Emerson Fosdick.** 1920, in *The Meaning of Service*. John Bartlett, *Bartlett's Familiar Quotations* (Boston: Little, Brown and Company, 1855, 1980), p. 759.

[21] **George Fox.** 1694, in his journal. John Bartlett, *Bartlett's Familiar Quotations* (Boston: Little, Brown and Company, 1855, 1980), p. 300.

[22] **Anne Frank.** March 7, 1944, in *Anne Frank: The Diary of a Young Girl*, (translated by B.M. Mooyart, published 1952). John Bartlett, *Bartlett's Familiar Quotations* (Boston: Little, Brown and Company, 1855, 1980), p. 909.

[23] **Benjamin Franklin.** *Poor Richard's Almanac*. Carroll E. Simcox, comp., *4400 Quotations for Christian Communicators* (Grand Rapids, MI: Baker Book House, 1991), p. 185.

[24] **Benjamin Franklin.** 1733, in *Poor Richard's Almanac*. Raymond A. St. John, *American Literature for Christian Schools* (Greenville, SC: Bob Jones University Press, Inc., 1979), p. 126. John Bartlett, *Bartlett's Familiar Quotations* (Boston: Little, Brown and Company, 1855, 1980), p. 347.

[25] **Benjamin Franklin.** May 1757, in *Poor Richard's Almanac*. Carroll E. Simcox, comp., *4400 Quotations for Christian Communicators* (Grand Rapids, MI: Baker Book House, 1991), p. 297. John Bartlett, *Bartlett's Familiar Quotations* (Boston: Little, Brown and Company, 1855, 1980), p. 347.

[26] **Benjamin Franklin.** September 3, 1783, signed the Treaty of Paris, officially ending the Revolutionary War with Great Britain; ratified by Congress January 14, 1784, under the Articles of Confederation. William M. Malloy, compiler, *Treaties, Conventions, International Acts, Protocols and Agreements between the United States of America and Other Powers, 1776-1909*, 4 vols. (New York: Greenwood Press, 1910, 1968), 2:1786. Charles W. Eliot, LL.D., ed., *American Historical Documents 1000-1904* (New York: P.F. Collier & Son Company, *The Harvard Classics*, 1910), Vol. 43, pp. 185-191. W. Cleon Skousen, *The Making of America* (Washington: The National Center for Constitutional Studies, 1985), 139. Tim LaHaye, *Faith of Our Founding Fathers* (Brentwood, TN: Wolgemuth & Hyatt, Publishers, Inc., 1987), p. 115. Gary DeMar, *America's Christian History: The Untold Story* (Atlanta, GA: American Vision Publishers, Inc., 1993), p. 84.

[27] **Benjamin Franklin.** Carl Van Doren, *Benjamin Franklin* (NY: Viking Press, 1938), p. 188. John Eidsmoe, *Christianity and The Constitution* (Grand Rapids, MI: Baker Book House, 1987), p. 209. Peter Marshall and David Manuel, *The Glory of America* (Bloomington, MN: Garborg's Heart'N Home, Inc., 1991), 1.17.

[28] **Benjamin Franklin.** August 23, 1750, in a letter to Dr. Samuel Johnson, President of King's College (now Columbia University). Verna M. Hall, *The Christian History of the American Revolution* (San Francisco: Foundation for Christian Education, 1976), p. 221.

[29] **Benjamin Franklin.** June 6, 1753, in a letter from Philadelphia to Joseph Huey. Jared Sparks, *Works of Benjamin Franklin* (Boston: 1840), Vol. VII. Albert Henry Smyth, ed., *The Writings of Benjamin Franklin*, 10 vols. (NY: The Macmillan Co., 1905-07), Vol. II, p. 144. Verna M. Hall, *The Christian History of the American Revolution* (San Francisco: Foundation for Christian Education, 1976), pp. 189-190. Perry Tanksley, *To Love is to Give* (Jackson, Mississippi: Allgood Books, Box 1329; Parthenon Press, 201 8th Ave., South, Nashville, Tennessee, 1972), p. 27. John Eidsmoe, *Christianity and the Constitution - The Faith of Our Founding Fathers* (Grand Rapids, MI: Baker Book House, A Mott Media Book, 1987; 6th printing, 1993), p. 200.

[30] **Benjamin Franklin.** 1751. Benjamin Franklin, *Some Account of the Pennsylvania Hospital from its first rise, to the beginning of the fifth month, called May 1754* (Philadelphia: B. Franklin and D. Hall, Rare Book Collection, Library of Congress). Catherine Millard, *The Rewriting of America's History* (Camp Hill, PA: Horizon House Publishers, 1991), pp. 117-119.

[31] **Benjamin Franklin.** 1755, inscription he composed for the cornerstone of Pennsylvania Hospital. Catherine Millard, *The Rewriting of America's History* (Camp Hill, PA: Horizon House Publishers, 1991), p. 117.

[32] **Benjamin Franklin.** 1757, in *The Way to Wealth*. Raymond A. St. John, *American Literature for Christian Schools* (Greenville, SC: Bob Jones University Press, Inc., 1979), p. 128.

[33] **Benjamin Franklin.** List of Virtues. The Autobiography of Benjamin Franklin.

[34] **Benjamin Franklin.** Personal Prayer. *The Autobiography of Benjamin Franklin*. Norman Cousins, *In God We Trust - The Religious Beliefs and Ideas of the American Founding Fathers* (NY: Harper & Brothers, Publishers, 1955), p. 30.

[35] **Benjamin Franklin.** 1781, in his second Autobiography. Benjamin Franklin, *Autobiography, 11* (1784). Carl Van Dorn, ed.,*Franklin's Autobiographical Writings*, Carl Van Dorn, ed., (NY: Viking Press, 1945), p. 624. Norman Cousins, In *God We Trust - The Religious Beliefs and Ideas of the American Founding Fathers* (NY: Harper & Brothers, Publishers, 1955), pp. 25-26. Raymond A. St. John, *American Literature for Christian Schools* (Greenville, SC: Bob Jones University Press, Inc., 1979), pp. 121-17'). John Eidsmoe, *Christianity and the Constitution - The Faith of our Founding Fathers* (Grand Rapids, MI: Baker Book House, A Mott Media Book, 1987, 6th printing, 1993), pp. 195-193.

[36] **Benjamin Franklin.** William S. Pfaff, ed., *Maxims and Morals of Benjamin Franklin* (New Orleans: Searcy and Pfaff, Ltd., 1927).

[37] **Benjamin Franklin.** 1739. Benjamin Franklin, *The Autobiography of Benjamin Franklin* (New York Books, Inc., 1791), p. 146. Benjamin Franklin, *Autobiography, 1771-75* (Reprinted Garden City, NY: Garden City Publishing Co., Inc., 1916), Vol. 1, pp. 191- 192. John Pollack, *George Whitefield and the Great Awakening* (Garden City New Jersey: Doubleday and Co., 1972), p. 117. John Eidsmoe, *Christianity and The Constitution - The Faith of the Founding Fathers* (Grand Rapids, MI: Baker Book House, 1987), p. 204. Tim LaHaye, *Faith of Our Founding Fathers* (Brentwood, TN: Wolgemuth & Hyatt, Publishers, Inc., 1987), p. 116. Peter Marshall & David Manuel, *The Glory of America* (Bloomington, MN: Garborg's Heart'N Home, 1991), 12.18.

[38] **Benjamin Franklin.** 1752, in a letter from George Whitefield. Frank Lambert, *The Religious Odd Couple* (Carol Stream, IL: Christian History), Vol. XII, No. 2, Issue 38, p. 31.

[38] **Benjamin Franklin.** 1764, in ending a letter written to George Whitefield. Frank Lambert, *The Religious Odd Couple* (Carol Stream, IL: Christian History), Vol. XII, No. 2, Issue 38, p. 31.

[39] **Benjamin Franklin.** 1769, in the last surviving letter from George Whitefield to Benjamin Franklin. Frank Lambert, The *Religious Odd Couple* (Carol Stream, IL: Christian History), Vol. XII, No. 2, Issue 38, pp. 31-32.

[40] **Benjamin Franklin.** In his last letter to George Whitefield. Frank Lambert, *The Religious Odd Couple* (Carol Stream, IL: Christian History), Vol. XII, No. 2, issue 38, p. 31.

[41] **Benjamin Franklin.** August 14,1776. Charles Francis Adams (son of John Quincy Adams and grandson of John Adams), ed., *Letters of John Adams, Addressed to His Wife*, (Boston: Charles C. Little and James Brown, 1841), Vol. 1, p. 152. L.H. Butterfield, Marc Frielander and Mary-Jo Kings, eds., The *Book of Abigail and John - Selected Letters from The Adams Family 1^62-1^84* (Cambridge, MA: Harvard University Press, 1975), p. 154.

[43] **Benjamin Franklin.** Attributed, March 1778, in a letter to the French ministry. Charles E. Kistler, *This Nation Under God* (Boston: Richard G. Badger, The Gorham Press, 1924), p. 83, Peter Marshall and David Manuel, *The Light and the Glory* (NJ: Fleming H. Revell Co., 1977), p. 370, n. 10. Burton Stevenson, *The Home Book of Quotations-Classical & Modern* (New York: Dodd, Mead and Company, 1967), p. 265. D.P. Diffine, Ph.D., *One Nation Under God - How Close a Separation?* (Searcy, Arkansas: Harding University, Belden Center for Private Enterprise Education, 6th edition, 1992), p. 9.

[44] **Benjamin Franklin.** Tryon Edwards, D.D., *The New Dictionary of Thoughts - A Cyclopedia of Quotations* (Garden City, NY: Hanover House, 1852; revised and enlarged by C.H. Catrevas, Ralph Emerson Browns and Jonathan Edwards [descendent, along with Tryon, of Jonathan Edwards (1703-1758), president of Princeton], 1891; The Standard Book Company, 1955, 1963), pp. 49, 338.

[45] **Benjamin Franklin.** 1754. Benjamin Franklin, *Information on Those Who Would Remove to America* (London: M. Gurney, 1754), pp. 22, 23. "Advice on Coming to America," George D. Youstra, ed., *America in Person* (Greenville, SC: Bob Jones University Press, 1975), p. 109. Tim LaHaye, *Faith of Our Founding Fathers* (Brentwood, TN: Wolgemuth & Hyatt, Publishers, Inc. 1987), p. 31. Benjamin Franklin, *Works of the Late Doctor Benjamin Franklin Consisting of his Life, Written by Himself, Together with Essays, Humorous, Moral & Literary, Chiefly in the Manner of the Spectator*, Richard Price, ed., (Dublin: P. Wogan, P. Byrne, J. Moore, and W. Jones, 1793), p. 289. David Barton, *The Myth of Separation* (Aledo, TX: WallBuilder Press, 1991), p. 100.

[46] **Benjamin Franklin.** 1784, in a letter to Robert Livingston. William S. Pfaff, ed, *The Pith of Franklin's Letter* (New Orleans: Searcy and Pfaff, Ltd., 1927).

[47] **Benjamin Franklin.** April 17, 1787, in a letter. Albert Henry Smyth, ed., *The Writings of Benjamin Franklin*, 10 vols. (New York-. Macmillan Co., 1905-7), 9:569, reprinted (NY: Haskell House Publishers, 1970), Vol. IX, p. 569. Albert Henry Smyth, ed., *The Writings of Benjamin Franklin 10* vols. (NY: The Macmillan Co., 1905-07), Vol. X, p. 50. Norman Cousins, *In God We Trust - The Religious Beliefs and Ideas of the American Founding Fathers* (NY: Harper & Brothers, Publishers, 1955), p. 393. Andrew W. Allison, Cleon Skousen and M. Richard Maxfield, *The Real Benjamin Franklin* (Salt Lake City, Utah; The Freeman Institute, 1982), p. 313. John Eidsmoe, *Christianity and The Constitution - The Faith of our Founding Fathers* (Grand Rapids, MI: Baker Book House, 1987), p. 211. Tim LaHaye, *Faith of Our Founding Fathers* (Brentwood, TN: Wolgemuth & Hyatt, Publishers, Inc., 1987), p. 196. Stephen McDowell and Mark Beliles, "The Providential Perspective" (Charlottesville, VA: The Providence Foundation, P.O. Box 6759, Charlottesville, Va. 22906, January 1994), Vol. 9, No. 1, p. 4.

[48] **Benjamin Franklin.** June 28,1787. James Madison, *Notes of Debates in the Federal Convention of 1^8^* (NY: W.W. Morton & Co., Original 1787 reprinted 1987), Vol. I, p. 504, 451-21. James Madison, *Notes of Debates in the Federal Convention of 1^8^* (Athens, Ohio: Ohio University Press, 1966, 1985), pp. 209-10. George Bancroft, *Bancroft's History of the Constitution of the United States* vols. I-X (Boston: Charles C. Little & James Brown, 1838), Vol. II. Albert Henry Smyth, ed. ,*The Writings of Benjamin Franklin* (New York: The Macmillan Company, 1905-7), Vol. IX, pp. 600-601. Gaillard Hunt and James B. Scott, ed., *The Debates in the Federal Convention of 1^8^ Which Framed the Constitution of the United States of America*, reported by James Madison (New York: Oxford University Press, 1920), pp. 181-182. Andrew M. Allison, W. Cleon Skousen, and M. Richard Maxfield, *The Real Benjamin Franklin* (Salt Lake City, Utah: The Freeman Institute, 1982, pp. 258-259. John *Eidsmoe, Christianity and the Constitution - The Faith of Our Founding Fathers* (Grand Rapids, MI: Baker Book House, A Mott Media Book, 1987, 6th printing 1993), pp. 12-13, 208. Tim

Notes

LaHaye, *Faith of Our Founding Fathers* (Brentwood, TN: Wolgemuth & Hyatt, Publishers, Inc., 1987), pp. 122-124. Stephen Abbott Northrop, D.D., *A Cloud of Witnesses* (Portland, Oregon: American Heritage Ministries, 1987; Mantle Ministries, 228 Still Ridge, Bulverde, Texas), p. 159-160. David Barton, *The Myth of Separation* (Aledo, TX: WallBuilder Press, 1991), p. 108-109. D.P. Diffine, Ph.D., *One Nation Under God - How Close a Separation?* (Searcy, Arkansas: Harding University, Belden Center for Private Enterprise Education, 6th edition, 1992), p. 8. Stephen McDowell and Mark Beliles, "The Providential Perspective" (Charlottesville, VA: The Providence Foundation, P.O. Box 6759, Charlottesville, Va. 22906, January 1994), Vol. 9, No. 1, pp. 5-6.

[49] **Benjamin Franklin.** June 28, 1787, records of Jonathan Dayton. E.C. M'Guire, *The Religious Opinions and Character of Washington* (NY: Harper & Brothers, 1836), p. 151. David Barton, *The Myth of Separation* (Aledo, TX: WallBuilder Press, 1991), p. 109.

[50] **Benjamin Franklin.** Irving Brant, *James Madison, Father of the Constitution, 1787-1800* (New York: Bobbs-Merrill, 1950), Vol. III, p. 84. Tim LaHaye, *Faith of Our Founding Fathers* (Brentwood, TN: Wolgemuth & Hyatt, Publishers, Inc., 1987), p. 126.

[51] **Benjamin Franklin.** James Madison, *Notes of Debates in the Federal Convention of 1787* (1787; reprinted NY: W. W. Norton & Co., 1987), p. 210. David Barton, *The Myth of Separation* (Aledo, TX: WallBuilder Press, 1991), p. 109.

[52] **Benjamin Franklin.** June 28, 1787. James Madison, *Notes of Debates in the Federal Convention of 1787* (1787; reprinted NY: W.W. Norton & Co., 1987), pp. 210-211. David Barton, *The Myth of Separation* (Aledo, TX: WallBuilder Press, 1991), p. 109.

[53] **Benjamin Franklin.** Tim LaHaye, *Faith of Our Founding Fathers* (Brentwood, TN: Wolgemuth & Hyatt, Publishers, Inc., 1987), p. 57.

[54] **Benjamin Franklin.** E.C. M'Guire, *The Religious Opinions and Character of Washington* (NY: Harper & Brothers, 1836), p. 152. David Barton, *The Myth of Separation* (Aledo, TX: WallBuilder Press, 1991), p. 110.

[55] **Benjamin Franklin.** Benjamin Franklin Morris, *The Christian Life and Character of the Civil Institutions of the United States* (Philadelphia: George W. Childs, 1864), pp. 253-254. David Barton, *The Myth of Separation* (Aledo, TX: WallBuilder Press, 1991), p. 110.

[56] **Benjamin Franklin.** In a toast at a dinner of foreign ambassadors in Versailles, France. John Bartlett, *Bartlett's Familiar Quotations* (Boston: Little, Brown and Company, 1855, 1980), p. 348.

[57] **Benjamin Franklin.** March 9, 1790, in a letter to Ezra Stiles, President of Yale University. Tryon Edwards, D.D., *The New Dictionary of Thoughts - A Cyclopedia of Quotations* (Garden City, NY: Hanover House, 1852; revised and enlarged by C.H. Catrevas, Ralph Emerson Browns and Jonathan Edwards [descendent, along with Tryon, of Jonathan Edwards (1703-1758), president of Princeton], 1891; The Standard Book Company, 1955, 1963), p. 91. Albert Henry Smyth, ed., *The Writings of Benjamin Franklin* (New York: MacMillan, 1905-7), Vol. 10, p. 84. John Bigelow, *Complete Words of Benjamin Franklin*. Stephen Abbott Northrop, D.D., *A Cloud of Witnesses* (Portland, OR: American Heritage Ministries, 1987; Mantle Ministries, 228 Still Ridge, Bulverde, Texas), p. 159. Carl Van Dorn, ed., *The Autobiography of Benjamin Franklin* (NY: Viking Press, 1945), p. 783. Norman Cousins, *In God We Trust - The Religious Beliefs and Ideas of the American Founding Fathers* (NY: Harper & Brothers, Publishers, 1955), p. 42. Frank B. Carlson, *Our Presbyterian Heritage,* (1973), p. 25. Raymond A. St. John, *American Literature for Christian Schools* (Greenville, SC: Bob Jones University Press, Inc., 1979), p. 131. Tim LaHaye, *Faith of Our Founding Fathers* (Brentwood, TN: Wolgemuth & Hyatt, Publishers, Inc., 1987), p. 116. John Eidsmoe, *Christianity and The Constitution - The Faith of Our Founding Fathers* (Grand Rapids, MI: Baker Book House, 1987), p. 210. D.P. Diffine, Ph.D., *One Nation Under God - How Close a Separation?* (Searcy, Arkansas: Harding University, Belden Center for Private Enterprise Education, 6th edition, 1992), p. 8.

[58] **Benjamin Franklin.** 1728, in his "Articles of Belief and Acts of Religion." Jared Sparks, ed., *The Writings of Benjamin Franklin* (Boston: Tappan, Whittemore and Mason, 1840), Vol. II, pp. 1-3. Carl Van Dorn, *Benjamin Franklin* (NY: Viking Press, 1938), p. 188. Carl Becker, *Benjamin Franklin* (New York: Cornell University, 1946), p. 81. Leonard Labaree, ed., *The Papers of Benjamin Franklin* (New Haven: Yale University Press, 1959), Vol. I, p. 103. *The Annals of America,* 20 vols. (Chicago, IL: Encyclopedia Britannica, 1968), Vol. 1, pp. 373-74. John Eidsmoe, *Christianity and The Constitution - The Faith of Our Founding Fathers* (Grand Rapids, MI: Baker Book House, 1987), p. 209. Tim LaHaye, *Faith of Our Founding Fathers* (Brentwood, TN: Wolgemuth & Hyatt, Publishers, Inc., 1987), pp. 118-122.

[59] **Benjamin Franklin.** Carl Becker, *Benjamin Franklin* (New York: Cornell University, 1946), p. 81. Tim LaHaye, *Faith of Our Founding Fathers* (Brentwood, TN: Wolgemuth & Hyatt, Publishers, Inc., 1987), p. 122.

[60] **Benjamin Franklin.** Leonard Labaree, ed., *The Papers of Benjamin Franklin* (New Haven: Yale University Press, 1959), Vol. I, pp. 104-105. Carl Becker, *Benjamin Franklin* (New York: Cornell University, 1946), p. 81. Tim LaHaye, *Faith of Our Founding Fathers* (Brentwood, TN: Wolgemuth & Hyatt, Publishers, Inc., 1987), p. 119, 122.

[61] **Benjamin Franklin.** Leonard Labaree, ed., *The Papers of Benjamin Franklin* (New Haven: Yale University Press, 1959), Vol. I, p. 108. Tim LaHaye, *Faith of Our Founding Fathers* (Brentwood, TN: Wolgemuth & Hyatt, Publishers, Inc., 1987), p. 120.

[62] **Benjamin Franklin.** Leonard Labaree, ed., *The Papers of Benjamin Franklin* (New Haven: Yale University Press, 1959), Vol. I, p. 109. Tim LaHaye, *Faith of Our Founding Fathers* (Brentwood, TN: Wolgemuth & Hyatt, Publishers, Inc., 1987), p. 120.

[62] **Benjamin Franklin.** William B. Wilcox, ed., *The Papers of Benjamin Franklin* (New Haven: Yale University Press, 1972), Vol. 15, p. 301. Tim LaHaye, *Faith of Our Founding Fathers* (Brentwood, TN: Wolgemuth & Hyatt, Publishers, Inc., 1987), p. 124. Norman Cousins, *In God We Trust - The Religious Beliefs and Ideas of the American Founding Fathers* (NY: Harper & Brothers, Publishers, 1955), p. 20.

[64] **Benjamin Franklin.** Leonard Labaree, ed., *The Papers of Benjamin Franklin* (New Haven: Yale University Press, 1959), Vol. I, p. 213. Tim LaHaye, *Faith of Our Founding Fathers* (Brentwood, TN: Wolgemuth & Hyatt, Publishers, Inc., 1987), p. 120.

[65] **Benjamin Franklin.** 1728, in his "Articles of Belief and Acts of Religion." Jared Sparks, ed., *The Writings of Benjamin Franklin* (Boston: Tappan, Whittemore and Mason, 1840), Vol. II, pp. 1-3. *The Annals of America,* 20 vols. (Chicago, IL: Encyclopedia Britannica, 1968), Vol. 1 pp. 373-74.

[66] **Benjamin Franklin.** *Autobiography of Benjamin Franklin* (Note: Franklin's Epitaph, written by himself in 1728, is engraved on his gravestone), p. 401. Tim LaHaye, *Faith of Our Founding Fathers* (Brentwood, TN: Wolgemuth & Hyatt, Publishers, Inc., 1987), p. 121. *The Annals of America,* 20 vols. (Chicago, IL: Encyclopedia Britannica, 1968), Vol. I, p. 374.

[67] **Benjamin Franklin.** Christ Church, plaque on Franklin's family pew. Catherine Millard, *The Rewriting of America's History* (Camp Hill, PA: Horizon House Publishers, 1991), p. 129.

[68] **Theodore Frelinghuysen.** In a letter he wrote to Presidential Candidate Henry Clay after receiving news of his defeat. Stephen Abbott Northrop, D.D., *A Cloud of Witnesses* (Portland, Oregon: American Heritage Ministries, 1987; Mantle Ministries, 228 Still Ridge, Bulverde, Texas), p. 158.

[69] **Theodore Frelinghuysen.** In a letter he wrote while President of the American Bible Society, 1846-1861. Stephen Abbott

Northrop, D.D., *A Cloud of Witnesses* (Portland, Oregon: American Heritage Ministries, 1987; Mantle Ministries, 228 Still Ridge, Bulverde, Texas), p. 158.
[70] **James Anthony Froude.** Tryon Edwards, D.D., *The New Dictionary of Thoughts - A Cyclopedia of Quotations* (Garden City, NY: Hanover House, 1852; revised and enlarged by C.H. Catrevas, Ralph Emerson Browns and Jonathan Edwards [descendent, along with Tryon, of Jonathan Edwards (1703-1758), president of Princeton], 1891; The Standard Book Company, 1955, 1963), p. 47.

G

[1] **Galileo Galilei.** Sarah K. Bolton, *Famous Men of Science*, p. 16. Stephen Abbott Northrop, D.D., *A Cloud of Witnesses* (Portland, OR: American Heritage Ministries, 1987; Mantle Ministries, 228 Still Ridge, Bulverde, Texas), p. 165. Ken Curtis, Ph.D., et. al., "More Than Man Can Understand By Himself" (Worcester, PA: *Glimpses*, published by the Christian History Institute, 1995), p. 1.
[2] **Galileo Galilei.** Sarah K. Bolton, *Famous Men of Science*, p. 18. Stephen Abbott Northrop, D.D., *A Cloud of Witnesses* (Portland, Oregon: American Heritage Ministries, 1987; Mantle Ministries, 228 Still Ridge, Bulverde, Texas), p. 165.
[3] **Gallup Poll.** Tim LaHaye, *Faith of Our Founding Fathers* (Brentwood, TN: Wolgemuth & Hyatt, Publishers, Inc., 1987), p. 70. Paul Vitz, *Censorship - Evidence of Bias in Our Children's Textbooks* (Ann Arbor, MI: Servant Books, 1986), p. 87. David Barton, *The Myth of Separation* (Aledo, TX: WallBuilder Press, 1992), p. 231.
[4] **Gallup Poll.** February 27, 1993, as reported by Ari Goldman in the *New York Times*. Keith A. Fournier, Esq., "To Whom Will We Give Thanks?" Law & Justice (Virginia Beach, VA: The American Center For Law And Justice, November 1993), p. 2.
[5] **James Abram Garfield.** April 15, 1865, at a speech in New York at Lincoln's assassination. John Bartlett, *Bartlett's Familiar Quotations* (Boston: Little, Brown and Company, 1855, 1980), p. 609. Edmund Fuller and David E. Green, *God in the White House - The Faiths of American Presidents* (NY: Crown Publishers, Inc., 1968), p. 144.
[6] **James Abram Garfield.** 1876, in a speech commemorating the centennial of the Declaration of Independence. "A Century of Congress," by James A. Garfield, published in *Atlantic*, July 1877. John M. Taylor, *Garfield of Ohio - The Available Man* (NY: W.W. Norton and Company, Inc.), p. 180. David Barton, *The Myth of Separation*, (Aledo, TX: WallBuilder Press, 1991), p. 266. David Barton, *Keys to Good Government*, audio tape (Aledo, TX: WallBuilder Press, 1994).
[7] **James Abram Garfield.** 1871, in describing the Chancellor of the new united German Empire, Otto Eduard Leopold von Bismarck (1815-1898). S. P. Linn, *Golden Gleams of Thought*, p. 154. Stephen Abbott Northrop, D.D., *A Cloud of Witnesses* (Portland, Oregon: American Heritage Ministries, 1987; Mantle Ministries, 228 Still Ridge, Bulverde, Texas), p. 164.
[8] **James Abram Garfield.** 1876, in a letter to a friend, regarding the death of his son, Edward Garfield, (1874-1876). S. P. Linn, *Golden Gleams of Thought*, p. 154. Stephen Abbott Northrop, D.D., *A Cloud of Witnesses* (Portland, OR: American Heritage Ministries, 1987; Mantle Ministries, 228 Still Ridge, Bulverde, Texas), p. 164.
[9] **James Abram Garfield.** John C. Ridpath, *Life of Garfield*. Stephen Abbott Northrop, D.D., *A Cloud of Witnesses* (Portland, OR: American Heritage Ministries, 1987; Mantle Ministries, 228 Still Ridge, Bulverde, Texas), p. 164.
[10] **James Abram Garfield.** Stephen Abbott Northrop, D.D., *A Cloud of Witnesses* (Portland, Oregon: American Heritage Ministries, 1987; Mantle Ministries, 228 Still Ridge, Bulverde, Texas), p. 164.
[11] **Giuseppe Garibaldi.** Tryon Edwards, D.D., *The New Dictionary of Thoughts - A Cyclopedia of Quotations* (Garden City, NY: Hanover House, 1852; revised and enlarged by C.H. Catrevas, Ralph Emerson Browns and Jonathan Edwards [descendent, along with Tryon, of Jonathan Edwards (1703-1758), president of Princeton], 1891; The Standard Book Company, 1955, 1963), p. 47.
[12] **Giuseppe Garibaldi.** Theodore Dwight, *General Garibaldi's Autobiography*, translated from his private papers, p. 444. Stephen Abbott Northrop, D.D., *A Cloud of Witnesses* (Portland, Oregon: American Heritage Ministries, 1987; Mantle Ministries, 228 Still Ridge, Bulverde, Texas), p. 165-166.
[13] **William Lloyd Garrison.** January 1, 1831, *The Liberator*. Richard D. Heffner, *A Documentary History of the United States* (New York: The New American Library of World Literature, Inc., 1961), pp. 110-111.
[14] **William Lloyd Garrison.** 1885-1889, in his writings *W.P. and F.T.J. Garrison*, Vol. III, p. 390. John Bartlett, *Bartlett's Familiar Quotations* (Boston: Little, Brown and Company, 1855, 1980), p. 505.
[15] **Colony of Georgia.** 1732. *The World Book Encyclopedia*, 18 vols. (Chicago, IL: Field Enterprises, Inc., 1957; W.F. Quarrie and Company, 8 vols., 1917; World Book, Inc., 22 vols., 1989), Vol. 7, p. 2950, Vol. 12, p. 5857.
[16] **Colony of Georgia.** Stephen K. McDowell and Mark A. Beliles, *America's Providential History* (Charlottesville, VA: Providence Press, 1988), p. 55. David Barton, *The Myth of Separation* (Aledo, TX: WallBuilder Press, 1991), p. 87.
[17] **Colony of Georgia.** Stephen K. McDowell and Mark A. Beliles, *America's Providential History* (Charlottesville, VA: Providence Press, 1988), p. 55. David Barton, *The Myth of Separation* (Aledo, TX: WallBuilder Press, 1991), p. 87.
[18] **Colony of Georgia.** Stephen K. McDowell and Mark A. Beliles, *America's Providential History* (Charlottesville, VA: Providence Press, 1988), p. 55. David Barton, *The Myth of Separation* (Aledo, TX: WallBuilder Press, 1991), p. 87.
[19] **Provincial Congress of Georgia.** July 4, 1775. Verna M. Hall and Rosalie J. Slater, *The Christian History of the American Revolution* (San Francisco: Foundation for American Christian Education, 1976), p. 523.
[20] **Provincial Congress of Georgia.** July 5, 1775. Verna M. Hall and Rosalie J. Slater, *The Christian History of the American Revolution* (San Francisco: Foundation for American Christian Education, 1976), p. 523.
[21] **Provincial Congress of Georgia.** July 7, 1775. Verna M. Hall and Rosalie J. Slater, *The Christian History of the American Revolution* (San Francisco: Foundation for American Christian Education, 1976), p. 525-526.
[22] **Constitution of the State of Georgia.** 1777, Preamble; Article VI; Article LVI. Benjamin Franklin Morris, *The Christian Life and Character of the Civil Institutions of the United States* (Philadelphia, PA: L. Johnson & Co., 1863; George W. Childs, 1864), p. 235. Frances Newton Thorpe, ed., *Federal and State Constitutions, Colonial Charters, and Other Organic Laws of the States, Territories, and Colonies now or heretofore forming the United States*, 7 vols. (Washington: Government Printing Office, 1905; 1909; St. Clair Shores, MI: Scholarly Press, 1968). Edwin S. Gaustad, *Neither King nor Prelate - Religion and the New Nation*, 1776-1826 (Grand Rapids, MI: William B. Eerdmans Publishing Company, 1993), p. 162. Gary DeMar, "Censoring America's Christian History" (Atlanta, GA: *The Biblical Worldview*, An American Vision Publication - American Vision, Inc., July 1990), p. 7. Charles E. Rice, *The Supreme Court and Public Prayer* (New York: Fordham University Press, 1964), p. 169; "Hearings, Prayers in Public Schools and Other Matters," Committee on the Judiciary, U.S. Senate (87th Cong., 2nd Sess.), 1962, pp. 268 et seq. Benjamin Weiss, *God in American*

Notes

History: A Documentation of America's Religious Heritage (Grand Rapids, MI: Zondervan, 1966), p. 155. Gary DeMar, *America's Christian History: The Untold Story* (Atlanta, GA: American Vision Publishers, Inc., 1993), p. 65.

[23] **Kahlil Gibran.** 1923, in *The Prophet; On Prayer*. John Bartlett, *Bartlett's Familiar Quotations* (Boston: Little, Brown and Company, 1855, 1980), p. 782.

[24] **John Bannister Gibson.** Chief Justice of Pennsylvania. Tryon Edwards, D.D., *The New Dictionary of Thoughts - A Cyclopedia of Quotations* (Garden City, NY: Hanover House, 1852; revised and enlarged by C.H. Catrevas, Ralph Emerson Browns and Jonathan Edwards [descendent, along with Tryon, of Jonathan Edwards (1703-1758), president of Princeton], 1891; The Standard Book Company, 1955, 1963), p. 90.

[25] **William Ewart Gladstone.** Henry H. Halley, *Halley's Bible Handbook* (Grand Rapids, MI: Zondervan Publishing House, 1927, 1965), p. 18.

[26] **William Ewart Gladstone.** Right Hon. W.E. Gladstone, *The Impregnable Rock of Holy Scripture*, p. 7. Stephen Abbott Northrop, D.D., *A Cloud of Witnesses* (Portland, Oregon: American Heritage Ministries, 1987; Mantle Ministries, 228 Still Ridge, Bulverde, Texas), pp. intro, 171.

[27] **William Ewart Gladstone.** Right Hon. W.E. Gladstone, *The Impregnable Rock of Holy Scripture*, p. 353. Stephen Abbott Northrop, D.D., *A Cloud of Witnesses* (Portland, Oregon: American Heritage Ministries, 1987; Mantle Ministries, 228 Still Ridge, Bulverde, Texas), pp. intro, 171.

[28] **William Ewart Gladstone.** Right Hon. W.E. Gladstone, *The Impregnable Rock of Holy Scripture*, p. 355. Stephen Abbott Northrop, D.D., *A Cloud of Witnesses* (Portland, Oregon: American Heritage Ministries, 1987; Mantle Ministries, 228 Still Ridge, Bulverde, Texas), pp. intro, 172.

[29] **Johann Wolfgang von Goethe.** Henry H. Halley, *Halley's Bible Handbook* (Grand Rapids, MI: Zondervan Publishing House, 1927, 1965), p. 19.

[30] **Johann Wolfgang von Goethe.** Tryon Edwards, D.D., *The New Dictionary of Thoughts - A Cyclopedia of Quotations* (Garden City, NY: Hanover House, 1852; revised and enlarged by C.H. Catrevas, Ralph Emerson Browns and Jonathan Edwards [descendent, along with Tryon, of Jonathan Edwards (1703-1758), president of Princeton], 1891; The Standard Book Company, 1955, 1963), p. 46. Alfred Armand Montapert, *Distilled Wisdom* (Englewood Cliffs, NJ: Prentice I, 1965), p. 36.

[31] **Johann Wolfgang von Goethe.** *Conversations with Eckermann*, Vol. III, p. 371. Stephen Abbott Northrop, D.D., *A Cloud of Witnesses* (Portland, OR: American Heritage Ministries, 1987; Mantle Ministries, 228 Still Ridge, Bulverde, Texas), p. 174.

[32] **Johann Wolfgang von Goethe.** *Aus Makarieus Archiv W. Meister.* Stephen Abbott Northrop, D.D., *A Cloud of Witnesses* (Portland, OR: American Heritage Ministries, 1987; Mantle Ministries, 228 Still Ridge, Bulverde, Texas), p. 174.

[33] **Johann Wolfgang von Goethe.** *Autobiography*, p. 208. Stephen Abbott Northrop, D.D., *A Cloud of Witnesses* (Portland, Oregon: American Heritage Ministries, 1987; Mantle Ministries, 228 Still Ridge, Bulverde, Texas), p. 174.

[34] **Sabine Baring-Gould.** 1864, first stanza of *Onward, Christian Soldiers.* John Bartlett, *Bartlett's Familiar Quotations* (Boston: Little, Brown and Company, 1855, 1980), p. 616.

[35] **William Franklin "Billy" Graham.** April 16, 1967, *The Chicago American.* Carroll E. Simcox, comp., *4400 Quotations for Christian Communicators* (Grand Rapids, MI: Baker Book House, 1991), p. 296.

[36] **Ulysses Simpson Grant.** June 6, 1876, in a letter from Washington during his term as President, to the Editor of the *Sunday School Times* in Philadelphia. Stephen Abbott Northrop, D.D., *A Cloud of Witnesses* (Portland, OR: American Heritage Ministries, 1987; Mantle Ministries, 228 Still Ridge, Bulverde, Texas), p. 195. Peter Marshall and David Manuel, *The Glory of America* (Bloomington, MN: Garborg's Heart 'N Home, Inc., 1991), 4.27. Tryon Edwards, D.D., *The New Dictionary of Thoughts - A Cyclopedia of Quotations* (Garden City, NY: Hanover House, 1852; revised and enlarged by C.H. Catrevas, Ralph Emerson Browns and Jonathan Edwards [descendent, along with Tryon, of Jonathan Edwards (1703-1758), president of Princeton], 1891; The Standard Book Company, 1955, 1963), p. 48. Henry Halley, *Halley's Bible Handbook* (Grand Rapids, MI: Zondervan, 1927, 1965), p. 18. W. David Stedman and LaVaughn G. Lewis, *Our Ageless Constitution* (Asheboro, NC: W. Stedman Associates, 1987), p. 162. Gary DeMar, *America's Christian History: The Untold Story* (Atlanta, GA: American Vision Publishers, Inc., 1993), pp. 59-60. Edmund Fuller and David E. Green, *God in the White House - The Faiths of American Presidents* (NY: Crown Publishers, Inc., 1968), p. 130. D.P. Diffine, Ph.D., *One Nation Under God - How Close a Separation?* (Searcy, Arkansas: Harding University, Belden Center for Private Enterprise Education, 6th edition, 1992), p. 16.

[37] **Ulysses Simpson Grant.** 1884, during his final illness. James P. Boyd, *Military and Civil Life of General Ulysses S. Grant*, pp. 709-710. Stephen Abbott Northrop, D.D., *A Cloud of Witnesses* (Portland, OR: American Heritage Ministries, 1987; Mantle Ministries, 228 Still Ridge, Bulverde, Texas), p. 195.

[38] **Horace Greeley.** *Autobiography of Horace Greeley*, p. 70. Stephen Abbott Northrop, D.D., *A Cloud of Witnesses* (Portland, OR: American Heritage Ministries, 1987; Mantle Ministries, 228 Still Ridge, Bulverde, Texas), p. 197. Tryon Edwards, D.D., *The New Dictionary of Thoughts - A Cyclopedia of Quotations* (Garden City, NY: Hanover House, 1852; revised and enlarged by C.H. Catrevas, Ralph Emerson Browns and Jonathan Edwards [descendent, along with Tryon, of Jonathan Edwards (1703-1758), president of Princeton], 1891; The Standard Book Company, 1955, 1963), p. 48. Henry H. Halley, *Halley's Bible Handbook* (Grand Rapids, MI: Zondervan Publishing House, 1927, 1965), p. 19. David Barton, *The Myth of Separation* (Aledo, TX: WallBuilder Press, 1991), p. 260.

[39] **Horace Greeley.** *Autobiography of Horace Greeley*, p. 71. Stephen Abbott Northrop, D.D., *A Cloud of Witnesses* (Portland, OR: American Heritage Ministries, 1987; Mantle Ministries, 228 Still Ridge, Bulverde, Texas), p. 197.

[40] **Horace Greeley.** *Autobiography of Horace Greeley*, p. 559. Stephen Abbott Northrop, D.D., *A Cloud of Witnesses* (Portland, OR: American Heritage Ministries, 1987; Mantle Ministries, 228 Still Ridge, Bulverde, Texas), p. 197.

[41] **Nathaniel Greene.** January 4, 1776, in a letter to Samuel Ward while serving as a general in the Revolutionary Army. Henry Steele Commager, ed., *The Great Declaration - A Book for Young Americans* (Indianapolis: The Bobbs-Merrill Co., Inc., 1958), p. 43.

[42] **Simon Greenleaf.** Wilbur Smith, *Therefore Stand: Christian Apologetics* (Grand Rapids, MI: Baker Book House). Willard Cantelon, *New Money or None?* (Plainfield, NJ: Logos International, 1979), pp. 243-245.

[43] **Simon Greenleaf.** Irwin H. Linton, *A Lawyer Examines the Bible: A Defense of the Faith* (Grand Rapids, MI: Baker Book House, 1977), p. 36. Willard Cantelon, *New Money or None?* (Plainfield, NH: Logos International, 1979), p. 244.

[44] **Simon Greenleaf.** November 6, 1852, in correspondence with the American Bible Society, Cambridge. Stephen Abbott Northrop, D.D., *A Cloud of Witnesses* (Portland, OR: American Heritage Ministries, 1987; Mantle Ministries, 228 Still Ridge, Bulverde, Texas), p. 198.

[45] **Simon Greenleaf**. Simon Greenleaf, *A Treatise on the Law of Evidence* (New York: Arno Press), p. 13. Willard Cantelon, *New Money or None?* (Plainfield, NH: Logos International, 1979). p. 244.

[46] **Simon Greenleaf**. Simon Greenleaf, *A Treatise on the Law of Evidence* (New York: Arno Press), p. 13. Willard Cantelon, *New Money or None?* (Plainfield, NH: Logos International, 1979). pp. 244-245.

[47] **Simon Greenleaf**. Simon Greenleaf, *A Treatise on the Law of Evidence* (New York: Arno Press), p. 41. Willard Cantelon, *New Money or None?* (Plainfield, NH: Logos International, 1979). pp. 244-245.

[48] **Simon Greenleaf**. *Examination of the Testimony of the Four Evangelists by the Rules of Evidence Administered in Courts of Justice, with an Account of the Trial of Jesus*. Stephen Abbott Northrop, D.D., *A Cloud of Witnesses* (Portland, Oregon: American Heritage Ministries, 1987; Mantle Ministries, 228 Still Ridge, Bulverde, Texas), pp. 198-199.

[49] **Hugo Grotius**. James Madison, *Examination of the British Doctrine*, 1806. Verna M. Hall, *Christian History of the Constitution of the United States of America: Christian Self-Government* (San Francisco: Foundation for American Christian Education, 1966, 1980), p. 250. John Eidsmoe, *Christianity and the Constitution - The Faith of Our Founding Fathers* (Grand Rapids, MI: Baker Book House, A Mott Media Book, 1987; 6th printing, 1993), p. 62.

[50] **Hugo Grotius**. 1625. Hugo Grotius, *The Rights of War and Peace*, (Amsterdam, 1933), 1:4.1.3. William Vasilio Sotirovich, *Grotius' Universe: Divine Law and a Quest for Harmony* (New York: Vantage Press, 1978), p. 51. John Eidsmoe, *Christianity and the Constitution - The Faith of Our Founding Fathers* (Grand Rapids, MI: Baker Book House, A Mott Media Book, 1987; 6th printing, 1993), p. 63.

[51] **Hugo Grotius**. 1625. Hugo Grotius, *The Rights of War and Peace*. Verna M. Hall, *Christian History of the Constitution of the United States of America - Christian Self-Government with Union* (San Francisco: Foundation for American Christian Education, 1979), p. 251. John Eidsmoe, *Christianity and the Constitution - The Faith of Our Founding Fathers* (Grand Rapids, MI: Baker Book House, A Mott Media Book, 1987; 6th printing, 1993), p. 64.

[52] **Hugo Grotius**. 1625. Hugo Grotius, *The Rights of War and Peace*, II:23:3.4. William Vasilio Sotirovich, *Grotius' Universe: Divine Law and a Quest for Harmony* (New York: Vantage Press, 1978), p. 58. John Eidsmoe, *Christianity and the Constitution - The Faith of Our Founding Fathers* (Grand Rapids, MI: Baker Book House, A Mott Media Book, 1987; 6th printing, 1993), p. 64.

[53] **Hugo Grotius**. Verna M. Hall and Rosalie J. Slater, *Teaching and Learning America's Christian History* (San Francisco, CA: Foundation for American Christian Education, 1975), p. 69. Gary DeMar, *God and Government-A Biblical and Historical Study* (Atlanta, GA: American Vision Press, 1984), p. 12.

[54] **Hugo Grotius**. Hugo Grotius, *Commentary on the Law of Prize and Booty*, (Oxford: Clarendon Press, 1950), p. 8. William Vasilio Sotirovich, *Grotius' Universe - Divine Law and a Quest for Harmony* (New York: Vantage Press, 1978), p. 46. John Eidsmoe, *Christianity and the Constitution - The Faith of Our Founding Fathers* (Grand Rapids, MI: Baker Book House, A Mott Media Book, 1987, 6th printing 1993), p. 63. David Barton, *The Myth of Separation* (Aledo, TX: WallBuilder Press, 1991), p. 199.

[55] **Hugo Grotius**. *The Truth of the Christian Religion*. Stephen Abbott Northrop, D.D., *A Cloud of Witnesses* (Portland, OR: American Heritage Ministries, 1987; Mantle Ministries, 228 Still Ridge, Bulverde, Texas), p. 200.

[56] **Johannes Gutenberg**. Alphonse De Lamartine, *Memories of Celebrated Characters*, p. 277. Stephen Abbott Northrop, D.D., *A Cloud of Witnesses* (Portland, Oregon: American Heritage Ministries, 1987; Mantle Ministries, 228 Still Ridge, Bulverde, Texas), p. 202. Gary DeMar, *God and Government* (Atlanta, GA: American Vision Press, 1984), Vol. 2, p. vi. Also rendered from the German tongue as, "Religious truth is captive in a small number of little manuscripts, which guard the common treasures instead of expanding them. Let us break the seal which binds these holy things; let us give wings to truth that it may fly with the Word, no longer prepared at vast expense, but multiplied everlasting by a machine which never wearies - to every soul which enters life." Gary DeMar, *America's Christian History: The Untold Story* (Atlanta, GA: American Vision Publishers, Inc., 1993), p. 44.

[57] **Johannes Gutenberg**. Alphonse De Lamartine, *Memories of Celebrated Characters*, p. 287. Stephen Abbott Northrop, D.D., *A Cloud of Witnesses* (Portland, Oregon: American Heritage Ministries, 1987; Mantle Ministries, 228 Still Ridge, Bulverde, Texas), p. 202.

H

[1] **Everett Hale**. Robert Flood, *The Rebirth of America* (Philadelphia: Arthur S. DeMoss Foundation, 1986), p. 223.

[2] **Sir Matthew Hale**. Tryon Edwards, D.D., *The New Dictionary of Thoughts - A Cyclopedia of Quotations* (Garden City, NY: Hanover House, 1852; revised and enlarged by C.H. Catrevas, Ralph Emerson Browns and Jonathan Edwards [descendent, along with Tryon, of Jonathan Edwards (1703-1758), president of Princeton], 1891; The Standard Book Company, 1955, 1963), p. 45.

[3] **Sir Matthew Hale**. *British Plutarch*, Vol. IV, pp. 56, 70. Stephen Abbott Northrop, D.D., *A Cloud of Witnesses* (Portland, Oregon: American Heritage Ministries, 1987; Mantle Ministries, 228 Still Ridge, Bulverde, Texas), p. 205.

[4] **Sir Matthew Hale**. 1679. *Meditations Moral and Divine*, published in London. The chapter entitled "The Great Audit With the Account of the Good Steward" was marked and studied by Mary Washington, mother of George Washington. Rosalie J. Slater, "Reflective Education: The Principle Approach" (San Francisco, CA: *Principally Speaking*, The Foundation for American Christian Education, November 1992), Vol. 2, No. 3, p. 1.

[5] **Tony P. Hall**. Member of the Congress of the United States of America, speaking on the "National Day of Prayer." Mrs. James Dobson (Shirley), chairman, *The Annual National Day of Prayer* (Colorado Springs, CO: National Day of Prayer, 1993).

[6] **Alexander Hamilton**. 1787. Christine F. Hart, *One Nation Under God* (NJ: American Tract Society, reprinted by Gospel Tract Society, Inc.), p. 2. D.P. Diffine, Ph.D., *One Nation Under God - How Close a Separation?* (Searcy, Arkansas: Harding University, Belden Center for Private Enterprise Education, 6th edition, 1992), p. 9.

[7] **Alexander Hamilton**. M.E. Bradford, *Religion & The Framers: The Biographical Evidence* (Marlborough, NH: The Plymouth Rock Foundation, 1991), p. 8.

[8] **Alexander Hamilton**. April 16-21, 1802, in writing to James Bayard. Claude G. Bowers, *Jefferson and Hamilton: The Struggle for Democracy in America* (Boston: Houghton Mifflin Co., 1925, 1937), p. 40. Broadus Mitchell, *Alexander Hamilton: The National Adventure 1788-1804* (NY: MacMillan, 1962), pp. 513-514. Allan M. Hamilton, *The Intimate Life of Alexander Hamilton* (Philadelphia: Richard West, 1979), p. 335. Morton J. Frisch, ed., *Selected Writings and Speeches of Alexander Hamilton*, (Washington, D.C.: American Enterprise Institute for Public Policy Research, 1985), p. 511, April 16-21, 1802. Henry Cabot Lodge, *American Statesmen Series*. Stephen Abbott Northrop, D.D., *A Cloud of Witnesses* (Portland, OR: American Heritage Ministries, 1987; Mantle Ministries, 228 Still Ridge, Bulverde, Texas), p. 208. Tim LaHaye, *Faith of Our Founding Fathers* (Brentwood, TN:

Notes

Wolgemuth & Hyatt, Publishers, Inc., 1987), p. 140. David Barton, *The Myth of Separation* (Aledo, TX: WallBuilder Press, 1991), p. 124. John Eidsmoe, *Christianity and the Constitution - The Faith of Our Founding Fathers* (Grand Rapids, MI: Baker Book House, A Mott Media Book, 1987; 6th printing, 1993), p. 146.

[9] **Alexander Hamilton.** Sarah K. Bolton, *Famous American Statesmen*, p. 126. Stephen Abbott Northrop, D.D., *A Cloud of Witnesses* (Portland, OR: American Heritage Ministries, 1987; Mantle Ministries, 228 Still Ridge, Bulverde, Texas), p. 208.

[10] **Alexander Hamilton.** Keith Fournier, *In Defense of Liberty* (Virginia Beach, VA: Law & Justice, Spring 1993), Vol. 2, No. 2, p. 7.

[11] **Alexander Hamilton.** M.E. Bradford, *A Worthy Company* (Marlborough, NH: Plymouth Rock Foundation, 1982), p. 49. Tim LaHaye, *Faith of Our Founding Fathers* (Brentwood, TN: Wolgemuth & Hyatt, Publishers, Inc., 1987), p. 141.

[12] **Alexander Hamilton.** July 11, 1804, on his deathbed. William Coleman, ed., *A Collection of Facts and Documents, relating to the Death of...Alexander Hamilton* (NY: Hopkins and Seymour, 1804), pp. 50-55. Broadus Mitchell, *Alexander Hamilton: The National Adventure 1788-1804* (NY: MacMillan, 1962), pp. 536-357. Edward J. Giddings, *American Christian Rulers*. Stephen Abbott Northrop, D.D., *A Cloud of Witnesses* (Portland, OR: American Heritage Ministries, 1987; Mantle Ministries, 228 Still Ridge, Bulverde, Texas), p. 208. John Eidsmoe, *Christianity and the Constitution - The Faith of Our Founding Fathers* (Grand Rapids, MI: Baker Book House, A Mott Media Book, 1987; 6th printing, 1993), p. 161. M.E. Bradford, *Religion and the Framers: The Biographical Evidence* (Marlborough, NH: Plymouth Rock Foundation, 1991), p. 8.

[13] **Alexander Hamilton.** President Nott's Eulogy of Alexander Hamilton. Stephen Abbott Northrop, D.D., *A Cloud of Witnesses* (Portland, Oregon: American Heritage Ministries, 1987; Mantle Ministries, 228 Still Ridge, Bulverde, Texas), p. 208.

[14] **John Hancock.** April 15, 1775, Massachusetts Provincial Congress declaring a *Day of Public Humiliation, Fasting and Prayer. Proclamation of John Hancock from Concord* (from an original in the Evans collection, #14220, by the American Antiquarian Society. David Barton, *The Myth of Separation* (Aledo, TX: WallBuilder Press, 1991), pp. 102-103. William Lincoln, ed., *The Journals of Each Provincial Congress of Massachusetts, 1774-1775* (Boston: Dutton & Wentworth, 1838), pp. 114-145.

[15] **John Hancock.** November 8, 1783, *A Proclamation for a Day of Thanksgiving* - signed by Governor John Hancock from Boston, Massachusetts. From an original in the Evans collection, #18025, by the American Antiquarian Society. David Barton, *The Myth of Separation* (Aledo, TX: WallBuilder Press, 1991), pp. 106-107.

[16] **George Frederick Handel.** Eliza Clark, *The World's Worker*. Stephen Abbott Northrop, D.D., *A Cloud of Witnesses* (Portland, OR: American Heritage Ministries, 1987; Mantle Ministries, 228 Still Ridge, Bulverde, Texas), p. 212.

[17] **George Frederick Handel.** *Messiah*. Eliza Clark, *The World's Workers*. Stephen Abbott Northrop, D.D., *A Cloud of Witnesses* (Portland, Oregon: American Heritage Ministries, 1987; Mantle Ministries, 228 Still Ridge, Bulverde, Texas), p. 212.

[18] **George Frederick Handel.** *Messiah*. Eliza Clark, *The World's Workers*. Stephen Abbott Northrop, D.D., *A Cloud of Witnesses* (Portland, Oregon: American Heritage Ministries, 1987; Mantle Ministries, 228 Still Ridge, Bulverde, Texas), p. 213.

[19] **Warren Gamaliel Harding.** March 4, 1921, Friday, in his Inaugural Address. *A Compilation of the Messages and Papers of the Presidents* 20 vols. (New York: Bureau of National Literature, Inc., prepared under the direction of the Joint Committee on Printing, of the House and Senate, pursuant to an Act of the Fifty-Second Congress of the United States, 1893, 1923), Vol. XVIII, pp. 8923-8930. *Inaugural Addresses of the Presidents of the United States - From George Washington 1789 to Richard Milhous Nixon 1969* (Washington, D.C.: United States Government Printing Office; 91st Congress, 1st Session, House Document 91-142, 1969), pp. 207-214. Charles E. Rice, *The Supreme Court and Public Prayer* (New York: Fordham University Press, 1964), pp. 189-190. Benjamin Weiss, *God in American History: A Documentation of America's Religious Heritage* (Grand Rapids, MI: Zondervan, 1966), p. 126. Willard Cantelon, *Money, Master of the World* (Plainfield, NJ: Logos International, 1976), p. 126. Davis Newton Lott, *The Inaugural Addresses of the American Presidents* (NY: Holt, Rinehart and Winston, 1961), p. 207. Arthur Schlesinger Jr., ed., *The Chief Executive* (NY: Chelsea House Publishers, 1965), pp. 232, 238. J. Michael Sharman, J.D., *Faith of the Fathers* (Culpepper, Virginia: Victory Publishing, 1995), pp. 89-90.

[20] **Warren Gamaliel Harding.** Tryon Edwards, D.D., *The New Dictionary of Thoughts - A Cyclopedia of Quotations* (Garden City, NY: Hanover House, 1852; revised and enlarged by C.H. Catrevas, Ralph Emerson Browns and Jonathan Edwards [descendent, along with Tryon, of Jonathan Edwards (1703-1758), president of Princeton], 1891; The Standard Book Company, 1955, 1963), p. 47.

[21] **John Harris.** 1698, title of lectures. Henry M. Morris, *Men of Science - Men of God* (El Cajon, CA: Master Books, Creation Life Publishers, Inc., 1990), p. 30.

[22] **Benjamin Harrison.** March 4, 1889, in his Inaugural Address. James D. Richardson (U.S. Representative from Tennessee), ed., *A Compilation of the Messages and Papers of the Presidents 1789-1897*, 10 vols. (Washington, D.C.: U.S. Government Printing Office, published by Authority of Congress, 1897, 1899; Washington, D.C.: Bureau of National Literature and Art, *1789-1902*, 11 vols., 1907, 1910), Vol. IX, pp. 6-13. *Inaugural Addresses of the Presidents of the United States - From George Washington 1789 to Richard Milhous Nixon 1969* (Washington, D.C.: United States Government Printing Office; 91st Congress, 1st Session, House Document 91-142, 1969), pp. 153-162. Davis Newton Lott, *The Inaugural Addresses of the American Presidents* (NY: Holt, Rinehart and Winston, 1961), pp. 155-162. Charles E. Rice, *The Supreme Court and Public Prayer* (New York: Fordham University Press, 1964), p. 187. Arthur Schlesinger Jr., ed., *The Chief Executive* (NY: Chelsea House Publishers, 1965), pp. 171-179. Benjamin Weiss, *God in American History: A Documentation of America's Religious Heritage* (Grand Rapids, MI: Zondervan, 1966), p. 110. Willard Cantelon, *Money, Master of the World* (Plainfield, NJ: Logos International, 1976), p. 120. J. Michael Sharman, J.D., *Faith of the Fathers* (Culpepper, Virginia: Victory Publishing, 1995), p. 75.

[23] **Benjamin Harrison.** In a letter to his son Russell Benjamin Harrison (1854-1936). McCollister, *Help*, p. 107. Edmund Fuller and David E. Green, *God in the White House - The Faiths of American Presidents* (NY: Crown Publishers, Inc., 1968), p. 155. Peter Marshall and David Manuel, *The Glory of America* (Bloomington, MN: Garborg's Heart'N Home, Inc., 1991), 3.13.

[24] **William Henry Harrison.** March 4, 1841, Thursday, in his Inaugural Address. James D. Richardson (U.S. Representative from Tennessee), ed., *A Compilation of the Messages and Papers of the Presidents 1789-1897*, 10 vols. (Washington, D.C.: U.S. Government Printing Office, published by Authority of Congress, 1897, 1899; Washington, D.C.: Bureau of National Literature and Art, *1789-1902*, 11 vols., 1907, 1910), Vol. 4, pp. 6-20. Benjamin Franklin Morris, *The Christian Life and Character of the Civil Institutions of the United States* (Philadelphia: George W. Childs, 1864), p. 605. *Inaugural Addresses of the Presidents of the United States - From George Washington 1789 to Richard Milhous Nixon 1969* (Washington, D.C.: United States Government Printing Office; 91st Congress, 1st Session, House Document 91-142, 1969), pp. 71-87. Davis Newton Lott, *The Inaugural Addresses of the American Presidents* (NY: Holt, Rinehart and Winston, 1961), p. 86. Charles E. Rice, *The Supreme Court and Public Prayer* (New York: Fordham University Press, 1964), p. 182. Arthur Schlesinger Jr., ed., *The Chief Executive* (NY: Chelsea House Publishers, 1965),

pp. 93-94. Stephen Abbott Northrop, D.D., *A Cloud of Witnesses* (Portland, Oregon: American Heritage Ministries, 1987; Mantle Ministries, 228 Still Ridge, Bulverde, Texas), p. 215. Peter Marshall and David Manuel, *The Glory of America* (Bloomington, MN: Garborg's Heart 'N Home, Inc., 1991), 4.4. J. Michael Sharman, J.D., *Faith of the Fathers* (Culpepper, Virginia: Victory Publishing, 1995), pp. 43-44.

25 **John Harvard.** 1642. *Old South Leaflets.* Peter Marshall and David Manuel, *The Glory of America* (Bloomington, MN: Garborg's Heart'N Home, Inc., 1991), 9.28. "New England's First Fruits in Respect to the Progress of Learning in the College at Cambridge in Massachusetts Bay," in Verna M. Hall, comp., and Rosalie J. Slater, developer, *Teaching and Learning America's Christian History* (San Francisco: Foundation for American Christian Education, 1975), frontpiece. Peter G. Mode, ed., *Sourcebook and Bibliography Guide for American Church History* (Menasha, WI: George Banta Publishing Company, 1920), pp. 73-74. Pat Robertson, *America's Dates With Destiny* (Nashville, TN: Thomas Nelson Publishers, 1986), pp. 43-44.

26 **John Harvard.** 1636. Tim LaHaye, *Faith of Our Founding Fathers* (Brentwood, TN: Wolgemuth & Hyatt, Publishers, Inc., 1987), p. 32.

27 **Harvard University.** 1636. *Old South Leaflets.* Peter G. Mode, ed., *Sourcebook and Biographical Guide for American Church History* (Menasha, WI: George Banta Publishing Co., 1921), pp. 74-75. David Barton *The Myth of Separation* (Aledo, TX: WallBuilder Press, 1991), p. 91. Robert Flood, *The Rebirth of America* (Philadelphia: Arthur S. DeMoss Foundation, 1986), p. 41. "Our Christian Heritage," *Letter from Plymouth Rock* (Marlborough, NH: The Plymouth Rock Foundation), p. 2. Pat Robertson, *America's Dates With Destiny* (Nashville, TN: Thomas Nelson Publishers, 1986), pp. 44-45. Gary DeMar, *America's Christian History: The Untold Story* (Atlanta, GA: American Vision Publishers, Inc., 1993), p. 40. Rosalie J. Slater, "New England's First Fruits, 1643," *Teaching and Learning America's Christian History* (San Francisco: Foundation for Christian Education, 1980), p. vii. Stephen McDowell and Mark Beliles, "The Providential Perspective" (Charlottesville, VA: The Providence Foundation, P.O. Box 6759, Charlottesville, Va. 22906, January 1994), Vol. 9, No. 1, p. 3. D.P. Diffine, Ph.D., *One Nation Under God - How Close a Separation?* (Searcy, Arkansas: Harding University, Belden Center for Private Enterprise Education, 6th edition, 1992), p. 4.

28 **Harvard University.** 1636. Stephen K. McDowell and Mark A. Beliles, *America's Providential History* (Charlottesville, VA: Providence Press, 1988), p. 91. David Barton, *The Myth of Separation* (Aledo, TX: WallBuilder Press, 1991), p. 91.

29 **Harvard University.** 1636. Quoted in Nancy Leigh DeMoss, ed., "How Christians Started the Ivy League," *The Rebirth of America* (Philadelphia, PA: Arthur S. DeMoss Foundation, 1986), p. 41. Peter Gay, *A Loss of Mastery: Puritan Historians in Colonial America* (Berkeley, CA: University of California Press, 1966), p. 23. Gary DeMar, *America's Christian History: The Untold Story* (Atlanta, GA: American Vision Publishers, Inc., 1993), p. 41.

30 **Harvard University.** 1636. "Our Christian Heritage," *Letter from Plymouth Rock* (Marlborough, NH: The Plymouth Rock Foundation), p. 2.

31 **Harvard University.** 1636. "Our Christian Heritage," *Letter from Plymouth Rock* (Marlborough, NH: The Plymouth Rock Foundation), p. 2.

32 **Harvard University.** 1636. "Our Christian Heritage," *Letter from Plymouth Rock* (Marlborough, NH: The Plymouth Rock Foundation), p. 2.

33 **Harvard University.** 1636. Stephen K. McDowell and Mark A. Beliles, *America's Providential History* (Charlottesville, VA: Providence Press, 1988), p. 91. David Barton, *The Myth of Separation* (Aledo, TX: WallBuilder Press, 1991), p. 91.

34 **Harvard University.** 1636. Tim LaHaye, *Faith of Our Founding Fathers* (Brentwood, TN: Wolgemuth & Hyatt, Publishers, Inc., 1987), p. 75. Robert Flood, *The Rebirth of America* (Philadelphia: Arthur S. DeMoss Foundation, 1986), p. 41. Also found in the catalog for the Harvard Divinity School. Gary DeMar, *America's Christian History: The Untold Story* (Atlanta, GA: American Vision Publishers, Inc., 1993), p. 41.

35 **Harvard University.** May 31, 1775, in the Election Day sermon, entitled "The Wall," delivered to the Provincial Congress of Massachusetts by Harvard President Samuel Langdon. A.W. Plumstead, ed., *The Wall and the Garden, Selected Massachusetts Election Sermons, 1670-1775* (Minneapolis: University of Minnesota Press, 1968), pp. 364-373. Verna M. Hall, *Christian History of the American Revolution - Consider and Ponder* (San Francisco: Foundation for American Christian Education, 1976), p. 506. Peter Marshall and David Manuel, *The Light and the Glory* (Old Tappan, New Jersey: Fleming H. Revell Co., 1977), p. 278. Lucille Johnston, *Celebrations of a Nation* (Arlington, VA: The Year of Thanksgiving Foundation, 1987), p. 77. Peter Marshall and David Manuel, *The Light and the Glory* (Old Tappan, NJ: Fleming H. Revell, 1977), pp. 277-278. Peter Marshall and David Manuel, *The Glory of America* (Bloomington, MN: Garborg's Heart'N Home, Inc., 1991), 6.3.

36 **Mark Hatfield.** U.S. Senator Mark Hatfield, "How Can a Christian Be in Politics?", Robert G. Clouse, Robert Linder and Richard V. Pierard, eds., *Protest and Politics: Christianity and Contemporary Affairs* (Greenwood, SC: Attic Press, 1968), pp. 13-14. John Eidsmoe, *God & Caesar-Christian Faith & Political Action* (Westchester, IL: Crossway Books, a Division of Good News Publishers, 1984), p. 57.

37 **Nathaniel Hawthorne.** *The Star of Calvary.* Stephen Abbott Northrop, D.D., *A Cloud of Witnesses* (Portland, Oregon: American Heritage Ministries, 1987; Mantle Ministries, 228 Still Ridge, Bulverde, Texas), p. 221-2.

38 **Nathaniel Hawthorne.** 1850, in *Ethan Brand.* John Bartlett, *Bartlett's Familiar Quotations* (Boston: Little, Brown and Company, 1855, 1980), p. 503.

39 **John Milton Hay.** Stephen Abbott Northrop, D.D., *A Cloud of Witnesses* (Portland, Oregon: American Heritage Ministries, 1987; Mantle Ministries, 228 Still Ridge, Bulverde, Texas), p. 245.

40 **Franz Joseph Haydn.** Nathan Haskell Dole, *A Score of Famous Composers.* Stephen Abbott Northrop, D.D., *A Cloud of Witnesses* (Portland, Oregon: American Heritage Ministries, 1987; Mantle Ministries, 228 Still Ridge, Bulverde, Texas), p. 220-1.

41 **Franz Joseph Haydn.** Nathan Haskell Dole, *A Score of Famous Composers.* Stephen Abbott Northrop, D.D., *A Cloud of Witnesses* (Portland, Oregon: American Heritage Ministries, 1987; Mantle Ministries, 228 Still Ridge, Bulverde, Texas), pp. 220-221.

42 **Franz Joseph Haydn.** March 27, 1808, as the Society of Amateurs in Vienna, Austria, performed his oratorio, *The Creation.* Nathan Haskell Dole, *A Score of Famous Composers.* Stephen Abbott Northrop, D.D., *A Cloud of Witnesses* (Portland, Oregon: American Heritage Ministries, 1987; Mantle Ministries, 228 Still Ridge, Bulverde, Texas), pp. 220-221.

43 **Rutherford Birchard Hayes.** March 5, 1877, Monday, in his Inaugural Address. James D. Richardson (U.S. Representative from Tennessee), ed., *A Compilation of the Messages and Papers of the Presidents 1789-1897*, 10 vols. (Washington, D.C.: U.S. Government Printing Office, published by Authority of Congress, 1897, 1899; Washington, D.C.: Bureau of National Literature and Art, 1789-1902, 11 vols., 1907, 1910), Vol. 7, pp. 446-447. *Inaugural Addresses of the Presidents of the United States - From George Washington 1789 to Richard Milhous Nixon 1969* (Washington, D.C.: United States Government Printing Office; 91st Congress, 1st Session, House Document 91-142, 1969), pp. 135-140. Davis Newton Lott, *The Inaugural Addresses of the American Presidents*

Notes

(NY: Holt, Rinehart and Winston, 1961), p. 141. Charles E. Rice, *The Supreme Court and Public Prayer* (New York: Fordham University Press, 1964), p. 186. Arthur Schlesinger Jr., ed., *The Chief Executive* (NY: Chelsea House Publishers, 1965), p. 155. Benjamin Weiss, *God in American History. A Documentation of America's Religious Heritage* (Grand Rapids, MI: Zondervan, 1966), p. 103. Willard Cantelon, *Money Master of the World* (Plainfield, NJ: Logos International, 1976), p. 170. 1. Michael Sharman, J.D., *Faith of the Fathers* (Culpepper, Virginia: Victory Publishing, 1995), pp. 66-67.

[44] **Rutherford Birchard Hayes**. Stephen Abbott Northrop, D.D., *A Cloud of Witnesses* (Portland, Oregon: American Heritage Ministries, 1987, Mantle Ministries, 228 Still Ridge, Bulverde, Texas), p. 223.

[45] **Reginald Heber**. 1827, in the hymn, *Holy, Holy, Holy*. John Bartlett, *Bartlett's Familiar Quotations* (Boston: Little, Brown and Company, 1855, 1980), p. 452.

[46] **Felicia Dorothea Browne Hemans**. *The Landing of the Pilgrim Fathers, st*, 10. John Bartlett, *Bartlett's Familiar Quotations (Boston:* Little, Brown and Company, 1855,1980), p. 470.

[47] **Patrick Henry**. Allen Nevins, *The American States During and After the Revolution: 1770-1789* (New York: MacMillan, 1924), pp. 431-432, Tim LaHaye, *Faith of Our Founding Fathers* (Brentwood, TN: Wolgemuth & Hyatt, Publishers, Inc., 1987), p. 257.

[48] **Patrick Henry.** March 23, 1775, in The Second Virginia Convention given at St. John's Church in Richmond Virginia. *The Annals of America*, 20 vols. (Chicago, IL: Encyclopedia Britannica, 1968), Vol. 2, pp. 322-333. William Wirt, *Sketches of the Life and Character of Patrick Henry* (Philadelphia: Claxton, 1818; Revised edition, NY: M'Elrath & Sons, 1835), pp. 137-142. George Bancroft, *History of the United States of America*, 6 vols. (Boston: Charles C. Little and James Brown, Third Edition, 1&38), p. 29. Frederick C. Packard, Jr., ed.,*Are You an American? - Great Americans Speak* (NY: Charles Scribner's Sons, 1951), pp. 1-4. A. Craig Baird, *American Public Addresses* (NY: McGraw Hill, 1956), complete speech, pp. 29-36. Ronald Reid, ed., *Three Centuries of American Rhetorical Discourse - An Anthology and a Review* (Prospect Heights, IU: Waveland Press, Inc., 1988), pp. 115-116. Peter Marshall and David Manual, *The Light and the Glory* (Old Tappan, NJ: Fleming Revell Co., 1977), p. 269. William Satire, ed., *Lend Me Your Ears - Great Speeches in History* (NY: W.W. Norton & Company 1992), pp. 86-89.

[49] **Patrick Henry**. June 12, 1776, Article XVI of the Virginia Bill of Rights. John Bartlett, *Bartlett's Familiar Quotations* (Boston: Little, Brown and Company, 1855,1980), p. 383. D.P. Diffine, Ph.D., *One Nation Under God - How Close a Separation?* (Searcy, Arkansas; Harding University, Belden Center for Private Enterprise Education, 6th edition, 1992), p. 9.

[50] **Patrick Henry**. May 1765, written on the back of the Stamp Act resolves passed in the House of Burgesses in Virginia. William Wirt Henry, *Patrick Henry - Life, Correspondence and Speeches* (NY: Burt Franklin, 1969), Vol. 1, pp. 91-93. E.L. Magoon, *Orators of the American Revolution* (New York: Charles Scribner, 1857, reprinted by Sightext Publications, El Segundo, CA: 1969), p. 253. Magoon, ed., *Orators of the American Revolution*, p. 253. Norine Dickson Campbell, *Patrick Henry: Patriot and Statesman (Old* Greenwich, CT: Devin Adair, 1969,1975), p. 57. John Eidsmoe, *Christianity and the Constitution - The Faith of Our Founding Fathers* (Grand Rapids, M: Baker Book House, A Mott Media Book, 1987; 6th printing, 1993), p. 302. Peter Marshall and David Manuel, *The Glory of America* (Bloomington, MN: Garborg's Heart'N Home, Inc., 1991), 6.6. Stephen McDowell and Mark Beliles, "The Providential Perspective' (Charlottesville, VA: The Providence Foundation, P.O. Box 6759, Charlottesville, Va. 2.2906, January 1994), Vol. 9, No. 1, p. 4.

[51] **Patrick Henry**. Attributed. Steve C. Dawson, *God's Providence in America's History* (Rancho Cordova, CA: Steve C. Dawson, 1988), Vol. I, p. 5. David Barton, *The Myth of Separation* (Aledo, TX: WallBuilder Press, 1991), pp. 25,158. M.E. Bradford, *The Trumpet Voice of Freedom: Patrick Henry of Virginia* (Marlborough, NH: Plymouth Rock Foundation, 1991), p. iii. "The Voice of America's Past," *Torch* (Dallas, TX: Texas Eagle Forum, February 1994), Vol. 1, No. 7, p. 5.

[52] **Patrick Henry**. William Wirt, *The Life and Character of Patrick Henry* (Philadelphia: James Webster, 1818), p. 402. Henry H. Halley, *Halley's Bible Handbook* (Grand Rapids, MI: Zondervan Publishing House, 1927,1965), p. 18. John Eidsmoe, *Christianity and the Constitution - The Faith of Our Founding Fathers* (Grand Rapids, MI: Baker Book House, A Mott Media Book, 1987; 6th printing 1993), p. 150. David Barton, *The Myth of Separation* (Aledo, TX: WallBuilder Press, 1991), pp. 119,150.

[53] **Patrick Henry**. 1786, in a letter to his sister, Ann Christian, at the time of her husband's death. Anson Phelps Stokes and Leo Pfeffer, *Church and State in the United States*, 3 vols. (NY: Harper & Brothers, Publishers, 1955), p. 415. Norine Dickson Campbell, *Patrick Henry: Patriot and Statesman* (Greenwich, Connecticut: Devin-Adair Co., 1969), p. 271. John Eidsmoe, *Christianity and the Constitution - The Faith of Our Founding Fathers* (Grand Rapids, W: Baker Book House, A Mott Media Book, 1987; 6th printing, 1993), p. 314. Peter Marshall & David Manuel, *The Glory of America* (Bloomington, MN: Garborg's Heart'N Home, 1991),9.18. M.E. Bradford, *Religion & The Framers: The Biographical Evidence* (Marlborough NH: Plymouth Rock Foundation, 1991), pp. 4- 5.

[54] **Patrick Henry**. November 20,1798, in a Certified Copy of Last Will and Testament of Patrick Henry. William Wirt Henry, *Patrick Henry: Life, Correspondence and Speeches* (NY: Charles Scribner's Sons, 1891), Vol. H, p. 631. Moses Coit Tyler, *Patrick Henry* (NY: Frederick Ungar Publishing Company), p. 395. Tryon Edwards, D.D., *The New Dictionary of Thoughts - A Cyclopedia of Quotations* (Garden City, NY: Hanover House, 1852; revised and enlarged by C.H. Catrevas, Ralph Emerson Browns and Jonathan Edwards [descendent, along with Tryon, of Jonathan Edwards (1703-1758), president of Princeton], 1891; The Standard Book Company, 1955,1963), p. 542. Norine Dickson Campbell, *Patrick Henry: Patriot and Statesman* (Greenwich, Connecticut: Devin-Adair Co., 1969), p. 428. John Eidsmoe, *Christianity and The Constitution - The Faith of our Founding Fathers* (Grand Rapids, MI: Baker Book House, 1987), p. 315. M.E. Bradford, *Religion & The Framers: The Biographical Evidence* (Marlborough, NH: Plymouth Rock Foundation, 1991), pp. 4-5. Peter Marshall and David Manuel, *The Glory of America* (Bloomington, MN: Garborg's Heart'N Home, Inc., 1991), 11.20. D.P. Diffine, Ph.D., *One Nation Under God - How Close a Separation?* (Searcy, Arkansas: Harding University, Belden Center for Private Enterprise Education, 6th edition, 1992), p. 9.

[55] **Patrick Henry**. Prof. Tyler, biography. Stephen Abbott Northrop, D.D., *A Cloud of Witnesses* (Portland, Oregon: American Heritage Ministries, 1987; Mantle Ministries, 228 Still Ridge, Bulverde, Texas), p. 227.

[56] **Patrick Henry**. William Wirt Henry, Patrick's grandson comments concerning his grandfather. William Wirt Henry, *Patrick Henry.-Life, Correspondence and Speeches* (NY: Burt Franklin, 1969), Vol. H, p. 621. Norine Dickson Campbell, *Patrick Henry* (Old Greenwich, CT: Devin-Adair Co., 1969), p. 415. David Barton, *The Myth of Separation* (Aledo, TX: WallBuilder Press, 1991), p. 118.

[57] **Patrick Henry**. Patrick Henry Fontaine, grandson, writing concerning his grandfather John Eidsmoe, *Christianity and the Constitution - The Faith of Our Founding Fathers* (Grand Rapids, NH: Baker Book House, A Mott Media Book, 1987; 6th printing 1993), p. 314. David Barton, *The Myth of Separation* (Aledo, TX: WallBuilder Press, 1991), p. 118.

[58] **Sir John Frederick Herschel.** Tryon Edwards, D.D., *The New Dictionary of Thoughts - A Cyclopedia of Quotations* (Garden City, NY: Hanover House, 1852; revised and enlarged by C.H. Catrevas, Ralph Emerson Browns and Jonathan Edwards [descendent, along with Tryon, of Jonathan Edwards (1703-1758), president of Princeton], 1891; The Standard Book Company, 1955, 1963), p. 49. Henry H. Halley, *Halley's Bible Handbook* (Grand Rapids, MI: Zondervan Publishing House, 1927, 1965), p. 19. *Allibone's Prose Quotations*, p. 72 and from his *Discourse on Natural Philosophy*. Stephen Abbott Northrop, D.D., *A Cloud of Witnesses* (Portland, Oregon: American Heritage Ministries, 1987; Mantle Ministries, 228 Still Ridge, Bulverde, Texas), p. 227.

[59] **Sir William Herschel.** Henry M. Morris, *Men of Science-Men of God* (El Cajon, CA: Masters Books, A Division of Creation Life Publishers, Inc., 1990), pp. 29-30.

[60] **Benjamin Harvey Hill.** In a *Tribute to Robert E. Lee*. Thomas Nelson Page, *Robert E. Lee*, (1911). John Bartlett, *Bartlett's Familiar Quotations* (Boston: Little, Brown and Company, 1855, 1980), p. 592.

[61] **Conrad Nicholson Hilton.** May 7, 1952, in an address entitled "The Battle for Peace." Mrs. James Dobson (Shirley), chairman, *The National Day of Prayer Information Packet* (Colorado Springs, CO: National Day of Prayer Task Force, May 6, 1993).

[62] **Archibald A. Hodge.** Princeton College theologian. A.A. Hodge, *Evangelical Theology* (Carlisle, PA: The Banner of Truth Trust, 1873, 1977), pp. 280-281. Gary DeMar, *God and Government-A Biblical and Historical Study* (Atlanta, GA: American Vision Press, 1982), pp. 70-71.

[63] **Archibald A. Hodge.** Princeton College theologian. A.A. Hodge, *Evangelical Theology* (Carlisle, PA: The Banner of Truth Trust, 1873, 1977), pp. 246-248. Gary DeMar, *God and Government-A Biblical and Historical Study* (Atlanta, GA: American Vision Press, 1982), p. ix.

[64] **Josiah Gilbert Holland.** 1872, in his *Gradatim*, st. I. John Bartlett, *Bartlett's Familiar Quotations* (Boston: Little, Brown and Company, 1855, 1980), p. 566.

[65] **Josiah Gilbert Holland.** 1872, in his work, *Wanted*, l. I. John Bartlett, *Bartlett's Familiar Quotations* (Boston: Little, Brown and Company, 1855, 1980), p. 566. Carl Van Dorn, ed., *Patriotic Anthology* (NY: Literary Guild of America, Inc, 1941), p. 390. Charles Wallis, ed., *Our American Heritage* (NY: Harper & Row, Publishers, Inc., 1970), p. 163. Peter Marshall & David Manuel, *The Glory of America* (Bloomington, MN: Garborg's Heart 'N Home, 1991), 7.24.

[66] **Oliver Wendell Holmes, Jr.** 1907, in a letter to William James. John Bartlett, *Bartlett's Familiar Quotations* (Boston: Little, Brown and Company, 1855, 1980), p. 644. Carroll E. Simcox, *3000 Quotations on Christian Themes* (Grand Rapids, Michigan: Baker Book House 1989), p. 168.

[67] **Oliver Wendell Holmes, Jr.** 1924, in a letter to John C.H. Wu. John Bartlett, *Bartlett's Familiar Quotations* (Boston: Little, Brown and Company, 1855, 1980), p. 645.

[68] **Oliver Wendell Holmes, Jr.** March 8, 1931, in reply to a reporter's question on his ninetieth birthday. John Bartlett, *Bartlett's Familiar Quotations* (Boston: Little, Brown and Company, 1855, 1980), p. 645.

[69] **Thomas Hooker.** Clinton Rossiter, "Thomas Hooker," *New England Quarterly*, Vol. XXV, pp. 479-481. Peter Marshall and David Manuel, *The Light and the Glory* (Old Tappan, NJ: Fleming H. Revell, 1977), pp. 207-208. Peter Marshall and David Manuel, *The Glory of America* (Bloomington, MN: Garborg's Heart'N Home, Inc., 1991), 7.7.

[70] **Herbert Clark Hoover.** March 4, 1929, Monday, in his Inaugural Address. *Inaugural Addresses of the Presidents of the United States - From George Washington 1789 to Richard Milhous Nixon 1969* (Washington, D.C.: United States Government Printing Office; 91st Congress, 1st Session, House Document 91-142, 1969), pp. 225-233. Davis Newton Lott, *The Inaugural Addresses of the American Presidents* (NY: Holt, Rinehart and Winston, 1961), pp. 223, 229. Charles E. Rice, *The Supreme Court and Public Prayer* (New York: Fordham University Press, 1964), pp. 190-191. Arthur Schlesinger Jr., ed., *The Chief Executive* (NY: Chelsea House Publishers, 1965), pp. 250, 259. Benjamin Weiss, *God in American History: A Documentation of America's Religious Heritage* (Grand Rapids, MI: Zondervan, 1966), p. 132. Willard Cantelon, *Money Master of the World* (Plainfield, NJ: Logos International, 1976), p. 121. J. Michael Sharman, J.D., *Faith of the Fathers* (Culpepper, Virginia: Victory Publishing, 1995), p. 95.

[71] **Herbert Clark Hoover.** May 30, 1931, in an address at Valley Forge. Herbert Hoover, *The Memoirs of Herbert Hoover - The Great Depression 1929-1941* (New York: The MacMillan Company, 1952), p. 35.

[72] **Herbert Clark Hoover.** 1934, Herbert Clark Hoover, *The Challenge of Liberty* (New York: Charles Scribner's Sons, 1934), p. 54. John Bartlett, *Bartlett's Familiar Quotations* (Boston: Little, Brown and Company, 1855, 1980), p. 750.

[73] **Herbert Clark Hoover.** "Our Christian Heritage," *Letter from Plymouth Rock* (Marlborough, NH: The Plymouth Rock Foundation), p. 7.

[74] **Herbert Clark Hoover.** April 27, 1950, in a speech to the American Newspaper Publishers Association. Charles Hurd, ed., *A Treasury of Great American Speeches* (NY: Hawthorne Books, 1959), pp. 289-291.

[75] **Herbert Clark Hoover.** Charles E. Jones, *The Books You Read* (Harrisburg, PA: Executive Books, 1985), p. 116.

[76] **J. (John) Edgar Hoover.** Herbert V. Prochnow, *5100 Quotations for Speakers and Writers* (Grand Rapids, MI: Baker Book House, 1992), p. 489.

[77] **Gerard Manley Hopkins.** *No. 28, The Wreck of the Deutschland*, st. I. John Bartlett, *Bartlett's Familiar Quotations* (Boston: Little, Brown and Company, 1855, 1980), p. 655.

[78] **Gerard Manley Hopkins.** *No. 31, God's Grandeur*, l. I. John Bartlett, *Bartlett's Familiar Quotations* (Boston: Little, Brown and Company, 1855, 1980), p. 655.

[79] **Hornbook.** 1442-1800. *The World Book Encyclopedia*, 18 vols. (Chicago, IL: Field Enterprises, Inc., 1957; W.F. Quarrie and Company, 8 vols., 1917; World Book, Inc., 22 vols., 1989), Vol. 8, p. 3526. Gary DeMar, *God and Government - A Biblical And Historical Study* (Atlanta, GA: American Vision Press, 1982), Vol. 1, p. 18.

[80] **Hornbook.** 1442-1800. Victoria Neufeldt, editor, *Webster's New World Dictionary of American English* (New York, NY: Simon & Schuster, Third College Edition, 1988), p. 328. Gary DeMar, *God and Government - A Biblical And Historical Study* (Atlanta, GA: American Vision Press, 1982), Vol. 1, p. 18.

[81] **Hornbook.** 1442-1800. John Keats, *Life and Letters*, I.112, 1818. Robert K. Barnhart, editor, *The Barnhart Dictionary of Etymology* (Bronx, NY: H.W. Wilson Company, 1988), p. 235. J.A. Simpson and E.S.C. Weiner, editors, *The Oxford English Dictionary* (Oxford, England: Oxford University Press, Second Edition, 1989), Vol. 2, p. 29.

[82] **Hornbook.** 1442-1800. David B. Guralnik, General editor, *Webster's New World Dictionary of the American Language - Concise Edition* (New York: Rand McNally & Company, The World Publishing Company, 1966) p. 180. J.A. Simpson and E.S.C. Weiner, editors, *The Oxford English Dictionary* (Oxford, England: Oxford University Press, Second Edition, 1989), Vol. 2, p. 29. Victoria Neufeldt, editor, *Webster's New World Dictionary of American English* (New York, NY: Simon & Schuster, Third College Edition, 1988), p. 328.

[83] **Oliver Otis Howard.** 1863, in an address to the 127th Pennsylvania Volunteers. Greg, *Life*, p. 87. Peter Marshall and David Manuel, *The Glory of America* (Bloomington, MN: Garborg's Heart'N Home, Inc., 1991), 2.19. D.P. Diffine, Ph.D., *One Nation Under God - How Close a Separation?* (Searcy, Arkansas: Harding University, Belden Center for Private Enterprise Education, 6th edition, 1992), p. 14.

[84] **Oliver Otis Howard.** Stephen Abbott Northrop, D.D., *A Cloud of Witnesses* (Portland, Oregon: American Heritage Ministries, 1987; Mantle Ministries, 228 Still Ridge, Bulverde, Texas), p. 239. Peter Marshall and David Manuel, *The Glory of America* (Bloomington, MN: Garborg's Heart'N Home, Inc., 1991), 11.8.

[85] **Oliver Otis Howard.** Jeffery Warren Scott, *Fighters of Faith* (Carol Stream, IL: Christian History), Vol. XI, No. 1, Issue 33, pp. 36-37.

[86] **Julia Ward Howe.** *The Battle Hymn of the Republic* (Massachusetts: The Atlantic Monthly, February 1862), Vol. IX, No. LII, p. 10, Entered according to Act of Congress by Ticknor and Fields, in the Clerk's Office of the District Court of the District of Massachusetts. Mark Galli, *Christian History* (Carol Stream, IL: Christian History, 1992, Issue 33), Vol. XI, No. 1, p. 19. D.P. Diffine, Ph.D., *One Nation Under God - How Close a Separation?* (Searcy, Arkansas: Harding University, Belden Center for Private Enterprise Education, 6th edition, 1992), p. 14.

[87] **William Dean Howells.** *A Thanksgiving*. John Bartlett, *Bartlett's Familiar Quotations* (Boston: Little, Brown and Company, 1855, 1980), p. 631.

[88] **Victor Marie Hugo.** William Neil, Ph.D., D.D., *Concise Dictionary of Religious Quotations* (Grand Rapids, MI: William B. Eerdmans Publishing Company, 1974), p. 9.

[89] **Victor Marie Hugo.** *Bless Your Heart (series II)* (Eden Prairie, MN: Heartland Samplers, Inc., 1990), 4.3.

[90] **John Hus.** 1415, his last words. John Bartlett, *Bartlett's Familiar Quotations* (Boston: Little, Brown and Company, 1855, 1980), p. 148.

[91] **Thomas Henry Huxley.** Henry H. Halley, *Halley's Bible Handbook* (Grand Rapids, MI: Zondervan Publishing House, 1927, 1965), p. 18.

[92] **Henry J. Hyde.** July 16, 1993, in a speech delivered after receiving the "Defender of Life" Award at the Constitutional Litigation Conference, Virginia Beach, Virginia. *Law & Justice* (Virginia Beach, VA: The American Center for Law and Justice, October 1993), Vol. 2, No. 5, p. 6.

I

[1] **Constitution of the State of Idaho.** 1889, in the Preamble. Charles E. Rice, *The Supreme Court and Public Prayer* (New York: Fordham University Press, 1964), p. 169; "Hearings, Prayers in Public Schools and Other Matters," Committee on the Judiciary, U.S. Senate (87th Cong., 2nd Sess.), 1962, pp. 268 et seq. Recorded in the Executive Proclamation declaring October 16 - 22, 1994, as "Christian Heritage Week," signed in the Capitol City of Boise by Governor Cecil D. Andrus and Secretary of State Pete T. Cenarrusa. Courtesy of Bruce Barilla, Christian Heritage Week Ministry (P.O. Box 58, W.V. 24712; 304-384-7707, 304-384-9044 fax).

[2] **State of Idaho.** October 16, 1994, the State of Idaho issued an Executive Proclamation declaring October 16 - 22, 1994, as "Christian Heritage Week," signed by Governor Cecil D. Andrus and Secretary of State Pete T. Cenarrusa, in the Capitol City of Boise. A similar Proclamation was signed March 23, 1992. Courtesy of Bruce Barilla, Christian Heritage Week Ministry (P.O. Box 58, W.V. 24712; 304-384-7707, 304-384-9044 fax).

[3] **Constitution of the State of Illinois.** 1870, in the Preamble. Charles E. Rice, *The Supreme Court and Public Prayer* (New York: Fordham University Press, 1964), p. 169; "Hearings, Prayers in Public Schools and Other Matters," Committee on the Judiciary, U.S. Senate (87th Cong., 2nd Sess.), 1962, pp. 268 et seq. *Church of the Holy Trinity v. United States* 143 U.S. 457, (1892). Gary DeMar, *God and Government-A Biblical and Historical Study* (Atlanta: GA: American Vision Press, 1984), p. 143.

[4] **State of Illinois.** April 5, 1994, the State of Illinois issued an Executive Proclamation declaring August 28 - September 3, 1994, as "Christian Heritage Week," signed in the City of Springfield by Governor Jim Edgar and Secretary of State George H. Ryan. A similar Proclamation was also signed June 24, 1993. Courtesy of Bruce Barilla, Christian Heritage Week Ministry (P.O. Box 58, W.V. 24712; 304-384-7707, 304-384-9044 fax).

[5] **State of Indiana.** April 18, 1994, in an Executive Proclamation declaring November 20 - 26, 1993, as "Christian Heritage Week," signed by Governor Evan Bayh and Secretary of State Joseph H. Hogsett, in the Capitol City of Indianapolis. A similar Proclamation was also signed on October 12, 1993. Courtesy of Bruce Barilla, Christian Heritage Week Ministry (P.O. Box 58, W.V. 24712; 304-384-7707, 304-384-9044 fax).

[6] **State of Iowa.** May 23, 1992. Governor Terry Edward Branstad (1946-) addressed the participants in the *March For Jesus* event in Des Moines, Iowa. Tom Pelton, *March For Jesus* (Austin, TX: March For Jesus, P.O. Box 3216, 1993), p. 4.

[7] **Queen Isabella.** 1490-1492, in her commission to Christopher Columbus. *Letter from Plymouth Rock* (Marlborough, NH: The Plymouth Rock Foundation), p. 1. *Church of the Holy Trinity v. U.S.*, 143 U.S. 465-468 (1892). David Barton, *The Myth of Separation* (Aledo, TX: WallBuilder Press, 1991), p. 48.

[8] **Queen Isabella.** In a letter to the Pope. Cecil Jane, trans. & ed., *The Voyages of Christopher Columbus* (London: Argonaut Press, 1930), p. 146. Peter Marshall and David Manuel, *The Glory of America* (Bloomington, MN: Garborg's Heart'N Home, Inc., 1991), 10.11.

[9] **Queen Isabella.** February 15, 1493, included in correspondence from Columbus on his return trip from having discovered America, to their Highnesses, King Ferdinand and Queen Isabella of Spain, from on board the ship *Caravel* anchored off the Canary Islands, in a letter addressed to Luis de Sant Angel, Treasurer of Aragon and Chancellor of the Exchequer. J.M. Dickey, compiler, *Christopher Columbus and his Monument*, p. 321. Stephen Abbott Northrop, D.D., *A Cloud of Witnesses* (Portland, Oregon: American Heritage Ministries, 1987; Mantle Ministries, 228 Still Ridge, Bulverde, Texas), p. 95. Also in another translation by Professors Hart and Channing, *American History Leaflets*. Charles W. Eliot, LL.D., ed., *American Historical Documents 1000-1904* (New York: P.F. Collier & Son Company, *The Harvard Classics*, 1910), Vol. 43, pp. 22-28.

J

[1] **Andrew Jackson.** January 8, 1815, in a letter to his friend Robert Hays at the occasion of the *Battle of New Orleans*, during the War of 1812. Burke Davis, *Old Hickory: A Life of Andrew Jackson* (NY: Dial Press, 1977), p. 150. Peter Marshall and David Manuel, *From Sea to Shining Sea* (Old Tappan, NJ: Fleming H. Revell Company, 1986), p. 169. Peter Marshall and David Manuel, *The Glory*

of America (Bloomington, MN: Garborg's Heart 'N Home, Inc., 1991), 1.8.

² **Andrew Jackson.** 1815, in a letter to Secretary of War James Monroe at the occasion of the *Battle of New Orleans*, during the War of 1812. Burke Davis, *Old Hickory: A Life of Andrew Jackson* (NY: Dial Press, 1977), p. 150. Peter Marshall and David Manuel, *From Sea to Shining Sea* (Old Tappan, NJ: Fleming H. Revell Company, 1986), p. 169.

³ **Andrew Jackson.** 1832, *Veto of the Bank Renewal Bill.* James D. Richardson (U.S. Representative from Tennessee), ed., *A Compilation of the Messages and Papers of the Presidents 1789-1897*, 10 vols. (Washington, D.C.: U.S. Government Printing Office, published by Authority of Congress, 1897, 1899; Washington, D.C.: Bureau of National Literature and Art, *1789-1902*, 11 vols., 1907, 1910), Vol. II, pp. 576-591. Richard D. Heffner, *A Documentary History of the United States* (New York: The New American Library of World Literature, Inc., 1961), pp. 93-96.

⁴ **Andrew Jackson.** March 4, 1833, in his Inaugural Address. James D. Richardson (U.S. Representative from Tennessee), ed., *A Compilation of the Messages and Papers of the Presidents 1789-1897*, 10 vols. (Washington, D.C.: U.S. Government Printing Office, published by Authority of Congress, 1897, 1899; Washington, D.C.: Bureau of National Literature and Art, *1789-1902*, 11 vols., 1907, 1910), Vol. III, p. 5. *Inaugural Addresses of the Presidents of the United States - From George Washington 1789 to Richard Milhous Nixon 1969* (Washington, D.C.: United States Government Printing Office; 91st Congress, 1st Session, House Document 91-142, 1969), pp. 58-60. Davis Newton Lott, *The Inaugural Addresses of the American Presidents* (NY: Holt, Rinehart and Winston, 1961), p. 63. Charles E. Rice, *The Supreme Court and Public Prayer* (New York: Fordham University Press, 1964), p. 181. Arthur Schlesinger Jr., ed., *The Chief Executive* (NY: Chelsea House Publishers, 1965) p. 67. Benjamin Weiss, *God in American History: A Documentation of America's Religious Heritage* (Grand Rapids, MI: Zondervan, 1966), p. 73. Willard Cantelon, *Money Master of the World* (Plainfield, NJ: Logos International, 1976), p. 120. *Proclaim Liberty* (Dallas, TX: Word of Faith), p. 1. J. Michael Sharman, J.D., *Faith of the Fathers* (Culpepper, Virginia: Victory Publishing, 1995), p. 39.

⁵ **Andrew Jackson.** 1834, in writing to Mary and Andrew Jackson Hutchings on the death of their firstborn. Robert V. Remini, *Andrew Jackson and the Course of American Freedom, 1822-1832* (New York: Harper & Row, 1981), Vol. 2, p. 226. Peter Marshall and David Manuel, *The Glory of America* (Bloomington, MN: Garborg's Heart'N Home, Inc., 1991), 1.25.

⁶ **Andrew Jackson.** September 11, 1834, in a letter to his son, Andrew, Jr. Robert V. Remini, *Andrew Jackson and the Course of American Freedom, 1822-1832* (New York: Harper & Row, 1981), p. 184. Peter Marshall and David Manuel, *The Glory of America* (Bloomington, MN: Garborg's Heart'N Home, Inc., 1991), 9.11.

⁷ **Andrew Jackson.** In a letter to comfort the family of General Coffee who had recently died. Robert V. Remini, *Andrew Jackson and the Course of American Freedom, 1822-1832* (New York: Harper & Row, 1981), p. 91. Peter Marshall and David Manuel, *The Glory of America* (Bloomington, MN: Garborg's Heart'N Home, Inc., 1991), 11.6.

⁸ **Andrew Jackson.** January 1835, in a correspondence to the King of England, following the failed assassination attempt. Benton, *Thirty Years' View*, Vol. I, p. 524. Peter Marshall and David Manuel, *The Glory of America* (Bloomington, MN: Garborg's Heart 'N Home, Inc., 1991), 1.30.

⁹ **Andrew Jackson.** March 25, 1835, in a letter. Robert V. Remini, *Andrew Jackson and the Course of American Freedom, 1822-1832* (NY: Harper & Row, 1981), Vol. 2, p. 251. Peter Marshall and David Manuel, *The Glory of America* (Bloomington, MN: Garborg's Heart 'N Home, Inc., 1991), 3.25.

¹⁰ **Andrew Jackson.** December 30, 1836, in a letter to Mr. Andrew Donelson after hearing that his wife, Emily, had died. Robert V. Remini, *Andrew Jackson and the Course of American Freedom, 1822-1832* (NY: Harper & Row, 1981), Vol. 2, p. 350. Peter Marshall and David Manuel, *From Sea to Shining Sea* (Old Tappan, NJ: Fleming H. Revell Company, 1986). Peter Marshall and David Manuel, *The Glory of America* (Bloomington, MN: Garborg's Heart'N Home, Inc., 1991), 12.30.

¹¹ **Andrew Jackson.** March 4, 1837, in his Farewell Address. James D. Richardson (U.S. Representative from Tennessee), ed., *A Compilation of the Messages and Papers of the Presidents 1789-1897*, 10 vols. (Washington, D.C.: U.S. Government Printing Office, published by Authority of Congress, 1897, 1899; Washington, D.C.: Bureau of National Literature and Art, *1789-1902*, 11 vols., 1907, 1910), Vol. II, pp. 292-308. *The Annals of America*, 20 vols. (Chicago, IL: Encyclopedia Britannica, 1968), Vol. VI, p. 310. Peter Marshall and David Manuel, *The Glory of America* (Bloomington, MN: Garborg's Heart 'N Home, Inc., 1991), 3.3. D.P. Diffine, Ph.D., *One Nation Under God - How Close a Separation?* (Searcy, Arkansas: Harding University, Belden Center for Private Enterprise Education, 6th edition, 1992), p. 11.

¹² **Andrew Jackson.** September 20, 1838, in a letter written upon receiving the news that his old friend, Ralph Earl, had suddenly died. Robert V. Remini, *Andrew Jackson and the Course of American Freedom, 1822-1832* (New York: Harper & Row, 1981), p. 448. Peter Marshall and David Manuel, *The Glory of America* (Bloomington, MN: Garborg's Heart'N Home, Inc., 1991), 9.20.

¹³ **Andrew Jackson.** In a letter to his wife Rachel, written while away in Washington, D.C. Andrew Jackson, *Correspondence of Andrew Jackson*, John Spencer Bassett, ed., (Washington, D.C.: Carnegie Institution of Washington, 1927), 3:218. Peter Marshall and David Manuel, *From Sea to Shining Sea* (Old Tappan, NJ: Fleming H. Revell Company, 1986), p. 279.

¹⁴ **Andrew Jackson.** June 8, 1845. Henry Halley, *Halley's Bible Handbook* (Grand Rapids, MI: Zondervan, 1927, 1965), p. 18. Alfred Armand Montapert, *Distilled Wisdom* (Englewood Cliffs, NJ: Prentice Hall,Inc., 1965), p. 36. George Sivan, *The Bible and Civilization* (New York: Quadrangle/The New York Times Book Co., 1973), p. 178. George Herbert Walker Bush, February 22, 1990, at the request of Congress, Senate Joint Resolution 164, in a Presidential Proclamation declaring 1990 the *International Year of Bible Reading*. Courtesy of Bruce Barilla, Christian Heritage Week Ministry (P.O. Box 58, W.V. 24712; 304-384-7707, 304-384-9044 fax). "Our Christian Heritage," *Letter from Plymouth Rock* (Marlborough, NH: The Plymouth Rock Foundation), p. 5. Gary DeMar, *America's Christian History: The Untold Story* (Atlanta, GA: American Vision Publishers, Inc., 1993), p. 59. Stephen McDowell and Mark Beliles, "The Providential Perspective" (Charlottesville, VA: The Providence Foundation, P.O. Box 6759, Charlottesville, Va. 22906, January 1994), Vol. 9, No. 1, p. 6.

¹⁵ **Andrew Jackson.** In conversation with a young lawyer from Nashville, regarding Peter Cartwright, the famous Methodist circuit-riding preacher, who had been invited as a guest into Jackson's home for Sunday lunch. Robert V. Remini, *The Revolutionary Age of Andrew Jackson* (NY: Harper & Row, 1976), pp. 10-11. Peter Marshall and David Manuel, *From Sea to Shining Sea* (Old Tappan, NJ: Fleming H. Revell Company, 1986), pp. 279-280.

¹⁶ **Andrew Jackson.** Statement. Robert V. Remini, *Andrew Jackson and the Course of American Freedom, 1822-1832* (New York: Harper & Row, 1981), Vol. II, p. 443. Peter Marshall and David Manuel, *The Glory of America* (Bloomington, MN: Garborg's Heart'N Home, Inc., 1991), 8.15.

¹⁷ **Andrew Jackson.** Statement. Gabriel Sivan, *The Bible and Civilization* (New York: Quadrangle/The New York Times Book Co., 1973), p. 178. Robert Flood, *The Rebirth of America* (Philadelphia: Arthur S. DeMoss Foundation, 1986), p. 37. Gary DeMar, *America's Christian History: The Untold Story* (Atlanta, GA: American Vision Publishers, Inc., 1993), p. 59.

[18] **Andrew Jackson.** May 29, 1845, a few weeks before his death. Robert V. Remini, *Andrew Jackson and the Course of American Freedom, 1822-1832* (New York: Harper & Row, 1981), p. 519. Peter Marshall and David Manuel, *The Glory of America* (Bloomington, MN: Garborg's Heart'N Home, Inc., 1991), 5.29.

[19] **Andrew Jackson.** June 1, 1845, in speaking to those visiting him in his last illness. Robert V. Remini, *Andrew Jackson and the Course of American Freedom, 1822-1832* (New York: Harper & Row, 1981), p. 521. Peter Marshall and David Manuel, *The Glory of America* (Bloomington, MN: Garborg's Heart'N Home, Inc., 1991), 6.1.

[20] **Andrew Jackson.** June 8, 1845, in speaking from his bed to his family and servants just moments before his death. Sarah K. Bolton, *Famous American Statesmen*, p. 174. Robert V. Remini, *Andrew Jackson and the Course of American Freedom, 1822-1832* (New York: Harper & Row, 1981), p. 523. Stephen Abbott Northrop, D.D., *A Cloud of Witnesses* (Portland, Oregon: American Heritage Ministries, 1987; Mantle Ministries, 228 Still Ridge, Bulverde, Texas), p. 247. Peter Marshall and David Manuel, *The Glory of America* (Bloomington, MN: Garborg's Heart'N Home, Inc., 1991), 6.8.

[21] **Andrew Jackson.** June 8, 1845, in his last words to his family and servants. Kenneth W. Leish, et als., *The American Heritage Pictorial History of the Presidents of the United States* (United States of America: American Heritage Publishing Co., Inc., Simon and Schuster, 1968), p. 235. Robert V. Remini, *Andrew Jackson and the Course of American Freedom, 1822-1832* (New York: Harper & Row, 1981), p. 523. Peter Marshall and David Manuel, *The Glory of America* (Bloomington, MN: Garborg's Heart'N Home, Inc., 1991), 6.8.

[22] **Andrew Jackson.** First clause in his *Last Will and Testament*. B.M. Dusenberry, *Compilation of Speeches in Memory of General Jackson*. Stephen Abbott Northrop, D.D., *A Cloud of Witnesses* (Portland, OR: American Heritage Ministries, 1987; Mantle Ministries, 228 Still Ridge, Bulverde, Texas), p. 247.

[23] **Thomas Jonathan "Stonewall" Jackson.** Statement from General Robert E. Lee, upon receiving information of the death of General Thomas Jonathan "Stonewall" Jackson. Prof. R.L. Dabney, D.D., *Life and Campaigns of Lieut.-General Thomas J. (Stonewall) Jackson* (Harrisonburg, VA: Sprinkle Publications, 1983), pp. 106-107. Peter Marshall and David Manuel, *The Glory of America* (Bloomington, MN: Garborg's Heart'N Home, Inc., 1991), 1.23.

[24] **Thomas Jonathan "Stonewall" Jackson.** 1842, in a letter to his uncle, Alfred Neale, concerning the death of his brother, Warren. John G. Gittings, *Personal Recollections of Stonewall Jackson* (Cincinnati: The Editor Publishing Company, 1899), p. 32. Catherine Millard, *The Rewriting of America's History* (Camp Hill, PA: Horizon House Publishers, 1991), p. 192.

[25] **Thomas Jonathan "Stonewall" Jackson.** 1852, in a letter to his Aunt, Mrs. Clementine (Alfred) Neale, from Lexington, Virginia. Mary Ann Jackson, *Life and Letters by his Wife*. John G. Gittings, *Personal Recollections of Stonewall Jackson* (Cincinnati: The Editor Publishing Company, 1899), p. 32. Stephen Abbott Northrop, D.D., *A Cloud of Witnesses* (Portland, OR: American Heritage Ministries, 1987; Mantle Ministries, 228 Still Ridge, Bulverde, Texas), p. 248. Catherine Millard, *The Rewriting of America's History* (Camp Hill, PA: Horizon House Publishers, 1991), p. 191.

[26] **Thomas Jonathan "Stonewall" Jackson.** July 22, 1861, in writing to his wife, Mary Ann, from Manassas. *Memoirs of Stonewall Jackson* (Dayton: Morningside Bookshop, 1976), p. 131. John Eidsmoe, *God & Caesar-Christian Faith & Political Action* (Westchester, IL: Crossway Books, A Division of Good News Publishers, 1984), p. 137.

[27] **Thomas Jonathan "Stonewall" Jackson.** A prayer given on the battlefield in Manassas. Roy Bird Cook, *The Family and Early Life of Stonewall Jackson*, p. 92. Catherine Millard, *The Rewriting of America's History* (Camp Hill, PA: Horizon House Publishers, 1991), p. 192.

[28] **Thomas Jonathan "Stonewall" Jackson.** Statement of General Jackson's servant. John Williams Jones, D.D., *Christ in the Camp* (Richmond, VA: B.F. Johnson & Co., 1887, 1897; The Martin & Hoyt Co., 1904; Harrisonburg, VA: Sprinkle Publications, 1986), p. 88. Peter Marshall and David Manuel, *The Glory of America* (Bloomington, MN: Garborg's Heart'N Home, Inc., 1991), 4.2.

[29] **Thomas Jonathan "Stonewall" Jackson.** Confederate soldier's remark after the *Battle of Cross Keys*. William W. Bennett, *A Narrative of the Great Revival Which Prevailed in the Southern Armies* (1877), p. 67. Peter Marshall and David Manuel, *The Glory of America* (Bloomington, MN: Garborg's Heart'N Home, Inc., 1991), 8.13.

[30] **Thomas Jonathan "Stonewall" Jackson.** In a letter to his wife. Prof. R.L. Dabney, D.D., *Life and Campaigns of Lieut.-General Thomas J. (Stonewall) Jackson* (Harrisonburg, VA: Sprinkle Publications, 1983), p. 588. Peter Marshall and David Manuel, *The Glory of America* (Bloomington, MN: Garborg's Heart'N Home, Inc., 1991), 8.22.

[31] **Thomas Jonathan "Stonewall" Jackson.** In a letter to his pastor, Reverend Dr. White, concerning the Sunday School class General Jackson taught in Lexington. John G. Gittings, *Personal Recollections of Stonewall Jackson* (Cincinnati: The Editor Publishing Company, 1899), p. 65. Catherine Millard, *The Rewriting of America's History* (Camp Hill, PA: Horizon House Publishers, 1991), p. 192.

[32] **Thomas Jonathan "Stonewall" Jackson.** Statement made after hearing of soldiers attending religious services. John Williams Jones, D.D., *Christ in the Camp* (Richmond, VA: B.F. Johnson & Co., 1887, 1897; The Martin & Hoyt Co., 1904; Harrisonburg, VA: Sprinkle Publications, 1986), p. 93. Peter Marshall and David Manuel, *The Glory of America* (Bloomington, MN: Garborg's Heart'N Home, Inc., 1991), 9.4.

[33] **Thomas Jonathan "Stonewall" Jackson.** 1862, in a letter to his ill wife. Prof. R.L. Dabney, D.D., *Life and Campaigns of Lieut.-General Thomas J. (Stonewall) Jackson* (Harrisonburg, VA: Sprinkle Publications, 1983), p. 329. Peter Marshall and David Manuel, *The Glory of America* (Bloomington, MN: Garborg's Heart 'N Home, Inc., 1991), 4.7.

[34] **Thomas Jonathan "Stonewall" Jackson.** May 2, 1863, in a comment to Chaplain Lacy, following the loss his left arm in the *Battle of Chancellorville*. Prof. R.L. Dabney, D.D., *Life and Campaigns of Lieut.-General Thomas J. (Stonewall) Jackson* (Harrisonburg, VA: Sprinkle Publications, 1983), p. 707. Peter Marshall and David Manuel, *The Glory of America* (Bloomington, MN: Garborg's Heart'N Home, Inc., 1991), 5.3.

[35] **Thomas Jonathan "Stonewall" Jackson.** May 10, 1863, in response to his wife. Prof. R.L. Dabney, D.D., *Life and Campaigns of Lieut.-General Thomas J. (Stonewall) Jackson* (Harrisonburg, VA: Sprinkle Publications, 1983), pp. 722-723. Peter Marshall and David Manuel, *The Glory of America* (Bloomington, MN: Garborg's Heart'N Home, Inc., 1991), 5.10.

[36] **Thomas Jonathan "Stonewall" Jackson.** May 10, 1863, his last words. Prof. R.L. Dabney, D.D., *Life and Campaigns of Lieut.-General Thomas J. (Stonewall) Jackson* (Harrisonburg, VA: Sprinkle Publications, 1983), pp. 724-726. Peter Marshall and David Manuel, *The Glory of America* (Bloomington, MN: Garborg's Heart'N Home, Inc., 1991), 5.11.

[37] **William James.** *Webster's Family Encyclopedia* (NY: Ottenheimer Publishers, Inc., 1987), Vol. 6, p. 1347.

[38] **William James.** Statement. David Barton, *The Myth of Separation* (Aledo, TX: WallBuilder Press, 1991), p. 46.

[39] **John Jay.** October 12, 1816, in a statement. *The Correspondence and Public Papers of John Jay*, Henry P. Johnston, ed., (NY: Burt Franklin, 1970), Vol. IV, p. 393. Benjamin Franklin Morris, *Christian Life and Character of the Civil Institutions of the United States*

(Philadelphia: George W. Childs, 1864), p. 154. Peter Marshall and David Manuel, *The Glory of America* (Bloomington, MN: Garborg's Heart'N Home, Inc., 1991), 11.5. David Barton, *The Myth of Separation* (Aledo, TX: WallBuilder Press, 1991), pp. 35, 78, 119, 152. David Barton, *America - To Pray or Not to Pray* (Aledo, Texas: WallBuilder Press, 1991), p. 7. David Barton, *The Founding Fathers*, audio tape (Aledo, TX: WallBuilder Press, 1992), audio tape. D.P. Diffine, Ph.D., *One Nation Under God - How Close a Separation?* (Searcy, Arkansas: Harding University, Belden Center for Private Enterprise Education, 6th edition, 1992), p. 8. David Barton, *Keys to Good Government* (Aledo, TX: WallBuilder Press, 1994), p. 21.

[40] **John Jay.** May 13, 1824, in an address to the American Bible Society. Norman Cousins, *In God We Trust - The Religious Beliefs and Ideas of the American Founding Fathers* (NY: Harper & Brothers, 1958), p. 379. Stephen Abbott Northrop, D.D., *A Cloud of Witnesses* (Portland, Oregon: American Heritage Ministries, 1987; Mantle Ministries, 228 Still Ridge, Bulverde, Texas), p. 251. John Eidsmoe, *Christianity and the Constitution* (MI: Baker Book House, 1987), p. 170. Peter Marshall and David Manuel, *The Glory of America* (Bloomington, MN: Garborg's Heart'N Home, Inc., 1991), 5.13.

[41] **John Jay.** Statement. George Pellew, *American Statesman Series*, p. 360. Stephen Abbott Northrop, D.D., *A Cloud of Witnesses* (Portland, OR: American Heritage Ministries, 1987; Mantle Ministries, 228 Still Ridge, Bulverde, Texas), p. 251. In a letter to John Bristed, April 23, 1811, John Jay recounted a conversation he had with several atheists: "I was at a large party, of which were several of that description. They spoke freely and contemptuously of religion. I took no part in the conversation. In the course of it, one of them asked me if I believed in Christ. I answered that I did, and that I thanked God that I did. He [an atheist] was a sedate, decent man. I frequently observed him drawing the conversation towards religion, and I constantly gave it another direction. He, nevertheless, during one of his visits, very abruptly remarked that there was no God, and he hoped the time would come when there would be no religion in the world. I very concisely remarked that if there was no God there could be no moral obligations, and I did not see how society could subsist without them." Norman Cousins, *In God We Trust - The Religious Beliefs and Ideas of the American Founding Fathers* (NY: Harper & Brothers, 1958), pp. 364-365.

[42] **John Jay.** 1826, in a reply to the corporation of the City of New York, regarding the 50th Anniversary of the United States. Stephen Abbott Northrop, D.D., *A Cloud of Witnesses* (Portland, Oregon: American Heritage Ministries, 1987; Mantle Ministries, 228 Still Ridge, Bulverde, Texas), p. 249.

[43] **John Jay.** In his *Last Will and Testament*. William Jay, *The Life of John Jay with Selections from His Correspondence*, 3 vols. (New York: Harper, 1833), Vol. I, pp. 519-520. John Eidsmoe, *Christianity and The Constitution - The Faith of Our Founding Fathers* (Grand Rapids, MI: Baker Book House, 1987), p. 168. M.E. Bradford, *Religion & The Framers: The Biographical Evidence* (Marlborough, NH: Plymouth Rock Foundation, 1991), p. 5.

[44] **John Jay.** May 17, 1829, in his final words to his children. William Jay, *Life of John Jay, with Selections from His Correspondence*, 2 vols. (NY: Harper, 1833), Vol. I, p. 548. Benjamin Franklin Morris, *The Christian Life and Character of the Civil Institutions of the United States* (Philadelphia: George W. Childs, 1864), pp. 154-155. Frank Monaghan, *John Jay: Defender of Liberty* (Indianapolis: Bobbs-Merrill Co., 1935, 1972), p. 435. John Eidsmoe, *Christianity and The Constitution - The Faith of Our Founding Fathers* (Grand Rapids, MI: Baker Book House, 1987), p. 170. Stephen Abbott Northrop, D.D., *A Cloud of Witnesses* (Portland, Oregon: American Heritage Ministries, 1987; Mantle Ministries, 228 Still Ridge, Bulverde, Texas), p. 249. David Barton, *The Myth of Separation* (Aledo, TX: WallBuilder Press, 1991), p. 119. Peter Marshall and David Manuel, *The Glory of America* (Bloomington, MN: Garborg's Heart'N Home, Inc., 1991), 5.19.

[45] **John Jay.** 1887, in a message, delivered while president of the Westchester County Bible Society, entitled "National Perils and Opportunities," pp. 8-9. Stephen Abbott Northrop, D.D., *A Cloud of Witnesses* (Portland, Oregon: American Heritage Ministries, 1987; Mantle Ministries, 228 Still Ridge, Bulverde, Texas), p. 250.

[46] **William Jay.** 1849, in the introduction of one of his works. David Barton, *The WallBuilder Report* (Aledo, TX: WallBuilder, Inc., Winter, 1993), p. 3.

[47] **Sir James Hopwood Jeans.** 1930, in his work, *The Mysterious Universe*. John Bartlett, *Bartlett's Familiar Quotations* (Boston: Little, Brown and Company, 1855, 1980), p. 758.

[48] **Thomas Jefferson.** 1774, in a Resolution he introduced in the Virginia Assembly calling for a *Day of Fasting and Prayer. Resolution for a Day of Fasting and Prayer made in the Virginia General Assembly.* Stephen K. McDowell and Mark A. Beliles, *America's Providential History* (Charlottesville, VA: Providence Press, 1988, 1994), p. 131. David Barton, *The Myth of Separation* (Aledo, TX: WallBuilder Press, 1991), p. 175.

[49] **Thomas Jefferson.** United States Supreme Court. 1892. *Church of the Holy Trinity v. U.S.*, 143 U.S. 457, 469 (1892). "Our Christian Heritage," *Letter from Plymouth Rock* (Marlborough, NH: The Plymouth Rock Foundation), p. 6. David Barton, *The Myth of Separation* (Aledo, TX: WallBuilder Press, 1991), pp. 247, 269-272. D.P. Diffine, Ph.D., *One Nation Under God - How Close a Separation?* (Searcy, Arkansas: Harding University, Belden Center for Private Enterprise Education, 6th edition, 1992), p. 6. Stephen McDowell and Mark Beliles, "The Providential Perspective" (Charlottesville, VA: The Providence Foundation, P.O. Box 6759, Charlottesville, Va. 22906, January 1994), Vol. 9, No. 1, p. 2.

[50] **Thomas Jefferson.** July 3, 1776, in a proposition for a national seal. *Journals of the Continental Congress, 1776*, Vol. V, p. 530. Charles Francis Adams (son of John Quincy Adams and grandson of John Adams), ed., *Letters of John Adams, Addressed to His Wife* (Boston: Charles C. Little and James Brown, 1841), Vol. I, p. 152. David Barton, *The Myth of Separation* (Aledo, TX: WallBuilder Press, 1992) p. 104.

[51] **Thomas Jefferson.** November 11, 1779, as Governor of the State of Virginia, in a *Proclamation Appointing a Day of Thanksgiving and Prayer.* Charles E. Rice, *The Supreme Court and Public Prayer: The Need for Restraint* (New York: Fordham University Press, 1964), p. 63. Gary DeMar, *America's Christian History: The Untold Story* (Atlanta, GA: American Vision Publishers, Inc., 1993), p. 116. Stephen McDowell and Mark Beliles, "The Providential Perspective" (Charlottesville, VA: The Providence Foundation, P.O. Box 6759, Charlottesville, Va. 22906, January 1994), Vol. 9, No. 1, p. 6.

[52] **Thomas Jefferson.** 1781, in his *Notes on the State of Virginia*, Query XVIII, 1781, 1782, p. 237. Paul Leicester Ford, *The Writings of Thomas Jefferson* (New York: G.P. Putnam's Sons, the Knickerbocker Press, 1894), 3:267. A.A. Lipscomb and Albert Bergh, eds., *The Writings of Thomas Jefferson* 20 vols. (Washington, D.C.: The Thomas Jefferson Memorial Association, 1903-1904). Vol. IX, Vol. II, p. 227. Robert Byrd, United States Senator from West Virginia, July 27, 1962, in a message delivered in Congress two days after the Supreme Court declared prayer in schools unconstitutional. Merrill D. Peterson, ed., *Jefferson Writings* (NY: Literary Classics of the United States, Inc., 1984) p. 289. Robert Flood, *The Rebirth of America* (Philadelphia: Arthur S. DeMoss Foundation, 1986), pp. 66-69. Tim LaHaye, *Faith of Our Founding Fathers* (Brentwood, TN: Wolgemuth & Hyatt, Publishers, Inc., 1987), pp. 192-193. George Grant, *Third Time Around* (Brentwood, TN: Wolgemuth & Hyatt, Inc., 1991), p. 103. David Barton, *The Myth of Separation* (Aledo, TX: WallBuilder Press, 1992), pp. 176, 246. D.P. Diffine, Ph.D., *One Nation Under God - How Close*

Notes

a Separation? (Searcy, Arkansas: Harding University, Belden Center for Private Enterprise Education, 6th edition, 1992), p. 10. Gary DeMar, *America's Christian History: The Untold Story* (Atlanta, GA: American Vision Publishers, Inc., 1993), p. 56. Stephen McDowell and Mark Beliles, "The Providential Perspective" (Charlottesville, VA: The Providence Foundation, P.O. Box 6759, Charlottesville, Va. 22906, January 1994), Vol. 9, No. 1, p. 5.

[53] **Thomas Jefferson.** 1781-1785, in *Query XIX* of his *Notes on the State of Virginia.* John Bartlett, *Bartlett's Familiar Quotations* (Boston: Little, Brown and Company, 1855, 1980), p. 388. United States Department of the Interior pamphlet, Thomas Jefferson Memorial, Washington, D.C., U.S. Government Printing Office, document number 0—407791, 2d Reprinting, 1956.

[54] **Thomas Jefferson.** August 19, 1785, in a letter to Peter Carr. John Bartlett, *Bartlett's Familiar Quotations* (Boston: Little, Brown and Company, 1855, 1980), p. 388.

[55] **Thomas Jefferson.** November 16, 1798, in the *Kentucky Resolutions* of 1798, *Article III.* Jonathan Elliot, ed., *The Debates in the Several State Conventions on the Adoption of the Federal Constitution,* 5 vols. (Washington, D.C.: Jonathan Elliot, 1836, and reprinted Philadelphia, 1861), Vol. IV, p. 540-44. Henry Steele Commager, ed., *Documents of American History,* 2 vols. (NY: F.S. Crofts and Company, 1934; Appleton-Century-Crofts, Inc., 1948, 6th edition, 1958; Englewood Cliffs, NJ: Prentice Hall, Inc., 9th edition, 1973), Vol. I, p. 179. *The Annals of America,* 20 vols. (Chicago, IL: Encyclopedia Britannica, 1968), Vol. 4, p. 63. N.S. Shaler, *Kentucky,* Vol. IV, p. 409 ff. David Barton, *The Myth of Separation* (Aledo, TX: WallBuilder Press, 1992), pp. 42, 174.

[56] **Thomas Jefferson.** September 23, 1800, in a letter to Dr. Benjamin Rush. *Jefferson's Extracts from the Gospels,* p. 320. John Bartlett, *Bartlett's Familiar Quotations* (Boston: Little, Brown and Company, 1855, 1980), p. 388. Jefferson Memorial, Washington, D.C. Tim LaHaye, *Faith of Our Founding Fathers* (Brentwood, TN: Wolgemuth & Hyatt, Publishers, Inc., 1987), p. 28. John Eidsmoe, *Christianity and the Constitution - The Faith of Our Founding Fathers* (Grand Rapids, MI: Baker Book House, A Mott Media Book, 1987; 6th printing, 1993), pp. 235, 238.

[57] **Thomas Jefferson.** March 4, 1801, Wednesday, in his First Inaugural Address. James D. Richardson (U.S. Representative from Tennessee), ed., *A Compilation of the Messages and Papers of the Presidents 1789-1897,* 10 vols. (Washington, D.C.: U.S. Government Printing Office, published by Authority of Congress, 1897, 1899; Washington, D.C.: Bureau of National Literature and Art, *1789-1902,* 11 vols., 1907, 1910), Vol. I, p. 322-324. *Inaugural Addresses of the Presidents of the United States - From George Washington 1789 to Richard Milhous Nixon 1969* (Washington, D.C.: United States Government Printing Office; 91st Congress, 1st Session, House Document 91-142, 1969), pp. 13-16. H.A. Washington, ed., *The Writings of Thomas Jefferson - Being His Autobiography, Correspondence, Reports, Messages, Addresses, and Other Writings, Official and Private,* 9 vols. (NY: Derby & Jackson, 1859; Washington, 1853-54; Philadelphia, 1871), Vol. VIII, p. 6. Henry Steele Commager, ed., *Documents of American History,* 2 vols. (NY: F.S. Crofts and Company, 1934; Appleton-Century-Crofts, Inc., 1948, 6th edition, 1958; Englewood Cliffs, NJ: Prentice Hall, Inc., 9th edition, 1973), Vol. I, pp. 187-189. Frederick C. Packard, Jr., ed., *Are You an American? - Great Americans Speak* (NY: Charles Scribner's Sons, 1951), p. 21-24. Paul M. Angle, ed., *By These Words* (NY: Rand McNally & Company, 1954), pp. 157-159. Charles Hurd, ed., *A Treasury of Great American Speeches* (NY: Hawthorne Books, 1959), p. 50. Richard D. Heffner, *A Documentary History of the United States* (New York: The New American Library of World Literature, Inc., 1961), pp. 71-74. Davis Newton Lott, *The Inaugural Addresses of the American Presidents* (NY: Holt, Rinehart and Winston, 1961), p. 16-17. Charles E. Rice, *The Supreme Court and Public Prayer* (New York: Fordham University Press, 1964), p. 179. William Safire, ed., *Lend Me Your Ears - Great Speeches in History* (NY: W.W. Norton & Company 1992), pp. 727-729. J. Michael Sharman, J.D., *Faith of the Fathers* (Culpepper, Virginia: Victory Publishing, 1995), p. 24.

[58] **Thomas Jefferson.** 1801-1809, as chairman of the school board for the District of Columbia during his Presidential term, authored a plan of education for the city of Washington which used the Bible and *Isaac Watts' Psalms, Hymns and Spiritual Songs,* 1707, as the principle textbooks to teach reading to students. John W. Whitehead, *The Second American Revolution* (Elgin, IL: David C. Cook Publishing Co., 1982), p. 100. Quoting from J.O. Wilson, *Public School of Washington* (Washington, D.C.: Columbia Historical Society, 1897), Vol. 1, p. 5. David Barton, *The Myth of Separation* (Aledo, TX: WallBuilder Press, 1991), pp. 130, 175.

[59] **Thomas Jefferson.** March 23, 1801, in a letter from Washington, D.C. to Moses Robinson. Barnes Mayo, ed., *Jefferson Himself - The Personal Narrative of a many-sided American* (Boston: Houghton Mifflin Company, 1942), p. 231. Catherine Millard, *The Rewriting of America's History* (Camp Hill, PA: Horizon House Publishers, 1991), p. 92.

[60] **Thomas Jefferson.** January 1, 1802, in using phraseology of famous Baptist minister Roger Williams. Lynn R. Buzzard and Samuel Ericsson, *The Battle for Religious Liberty* (Elgin, IL: David C. Cook, 1982), p. 51. John Eidsmoe, *Christianity and the Constitution - The Faith of Our Founding Fathers* (Grand Rapids, MI: Baker Book House, A Mott Media Book, 1987, 6th printing 1993), pp. 215, 243. David Barton, *The Myth of Separation* (Aledo, TX: WallBuilder Press, 1991), p. 42.

[61] **Thomas Jefferson.** January 1, 1802, in a personal letter to Nehemiah Dodge, Ephraim Robbins, and Stephen Nelson of the Danbury Baptist Association, Danbury, Connecticut. *Reynolds v. U.S.,* 98 U.S. 164 (1878). A.A. Lipscomb and Albert Bergh, eds., *The Writings of Thomas Jefferson* 20 vols. (Washington, D.C.: The Thomas Jefferson Memorial Association, 1903-1904). Norman Cousins, *In God We Trust - The Religious Beliefs and Ideas of the American Founding Fathers* (NY: Harper & Brothers, 1958), p. 135. Arthur Frommer, *The Bible in the Public Schools* (New York, NY: Liberal Press, 1963), p. 19. Charles E. Rice, *The Supreme Court and Public Prayer: The Need for Restraint* (New York: Fordham University Press, 1964), p. 63. Merrill D. Peterson, *Jefferson Writings,* Merrill D. Peterson, ed., (NY: Literary Classics of the United States, Inc., 1984), p. 510. Henry Steele Commager, ed., *Freedom of Religion & Separation of Church and State* (Mount Vernon, New York: A. Colish, Inc., 1985), pp. 28-29. John Eidsmoe, *Christianity and the Constitution - The Faith of Our Founding Fathers* (Grand Rapids, MI: Baker Book House, A Mott Media Book, 1987, 6th printing 1993), pp. 215, 242. Gary Wills, *Under God* (NY: Simon & Schuster, 1990), p. 350. David Barton, *The Myth of Separation* (Aledo, TX: WallBuilder Press, 1991), p. 41. David Barton, "The Truth About Thomas Jefferson and the First Amendment" (Aledo, TX: WallBuilder Press, 1992), pp. 4-5. Gary DeMar, *America's Christian History: The Untold Story* (Atlanta, GA: American Vision Publishers, Inc., 1993), pp. 115-116. Letter transcribed in its entirety from the courthouse in Danbury, Connecticut, by William Vigue, 18 Clapboard Ridge Rd., Danbury, CT, 06811:

"The affectionate sentiments of esteem and approbation which you are so good as to express towards me, on behalf of the Danbury Baptists Association, give me the highest satisfaction. My duties dictate a faithful and zealous pursuit of my constituents, and in proportion as they are persuaded of my fidelity to those duties, the discharge of them becomes more and more pleasing. Believing with you that religion is a matter which lies solely between man and his God, that he owes account to none other for faith or his worship, that the legislative powers of government reach actions only, and not opinions, I contemplate with solemn reverence that act of the whole American people which declared that their legislature should 'make no law respecting an establishment of religion, or prohibiting the free exercise thereof,' thus building a wall of separation between Church and State. Adhering to this expression of the supreme will of the nation in behalf of the rights of conscience,

I shall see with sincere satisfaction the progress of those sentiments which tend to restore man to all his natural rights, convinced he has no natural right in opposition to his social duties. I reciprocate your kind prayers for the protection and blessing of the common Father and Creator of man, and tender you for yourselves and your religious association, assurances of my high respect and esteem. Thomas Jefferson."

⁶² **Thomas Jefferson.** John Eidsmoe, *Christianity and the Constitution* (MI: Baker Book House, 1987), pp. 242-243. David Barton, *The Myth of Separation* (Aledo, TX: WallBuilder Press, 1991), p. 44. Dr. Joseph Priestly wrote an article giving much credit for the Constitution to Jefferson. On June 19, 1802, President Thomas Jefferson wrote to him in reply, correcting:

"One passage in the paper you enclosed me must be corrected. It is the following, 'And all say it was yourself more than any other individual, that planned and established it,' i.e., the Constitution. I was in Europe when the Constitution was planned, and never saw it till after it was established."

David Barton, "The Truth About Thomas Jefferson And The First Amendment" (Aledo, TX: WallBuilder Press, 1992), pp. 2-3.

⁶³ **Thomas Jefferson.** John Eidsmoe, *Christianity and the Constitution* (MI: Baker Book House, 1987), pp. 242-243. David Barton, *The Myth of Separation* (Aledo, TX: WallBuilder Press, 1991), p. 44.

⁶⁴ **Thomas Jefferson.** April 30, 1802, c.40, 2 Stat. 173 at 174. David Barton, *The Myth of Separation* (Aledo, TX: WallBuilder Press, 1991), p. 38. "Our Christian Heritage," *Letter from Plymouth Rock* (Marlborough, NH: The Plymouth Rock Foundation), p. 4.

⁶⁵ **Thomas Jefferson.** Northwest Ordinance. Henry Steele Commager, ed., *Documents of American History*, 2 vols. (NY: F.S. Crofts and Company, 1934; Appleton-Century-Crofts, Inc., 1948, 6th edition, 1958; Englewood Cliffs, NJ: Prentice Hall, Inc., 9th edition, 1973), p. 131. William Benton, *The Annals of America*, 20 vols. (Chicago, IL: Encyclopedia Britannica, 1968), Vol.III, pp. 194-195. Tim LaHaye, *Faith of Our Founding Fathers* (Brentwood, TN: Wolgemuth & Hyatt, Publishers, Inc., 1987), p. 91. David Barton, *The Myth of Separation* (Aledo, TX: WallBuilder Press, 1991), pp. 37-39. D.P. Diffine, Ph.D., *One Nation Under God - How Close a Separation?* (Searcy, Arkansas: Harding University, Belden Center for Private Enterprise Education, 6th edition, 1992), p. 3.

⁶⁶ **Thomas Jefferson.** April 21, 1803, in a letter to Dr. Benjamin Rush. *The Writings of Thomas Jefferson*, Vol. X, p. 379. Barnes Mayo, ed., *Jefferson Himself - The Personal Narrative of a many-sided American* (Boston: Houghton Mifflin Company, 1942), pp. 231, 235. Thomas Jefferson, *The Life and Selected Writings of Thomas Jefferson*, Adrienne Koch and William Paden, eds. (NY: Random House, 1944), p. 567. Norman Cousins, *In God We Trust - The Religious Beliefs and Ideas of the American Founding Fathers* (NY: Harper & Brothers, 1958), p. 119. Burton Stevenson, *The Home Book of Quotations-Classical & Modern* (New York: Dodd, Mead and Company, 1967), pp. 265-266. *Library of American Literature*, Vol. III, p. 277. Stephen Abbott Northrop, D.D., *A Cloud of Witnesses* (Portland, OR: American Heritage Ministries, 1987; Mantle Ministries, 228 Still Ridge, Bulverde, Texas), p. 252. Catherine Millard, *The Rewriting of America's History* (Camp Hill, PA: Horizon House Publishers, 1991), p. 92.

⁶⁷ **Thomas Jefferson.** December 3, 1803, treaty with the Kaskaskia Indians, 1806 with the Wyandotte Indians, and 1807 Cherokee Indians. Daniel L. Driesbach, *Real Threat and Mere Shadow: Religious Liberty and the First Amendment* (Westchester, IL: Crossway Books, 1987), p. 127. Richard Peters, ed., *The Public Statutes at Large of the United States of America* (Boston: Charles C. Little and James Brown, 1846), *A Treaty Between the United States and the Kaskaskia Tribe of Indians*, 23 December 1803, Art. II, Vol. II, pp. 78-79., *Treaty with the Wyandots, etc.*, 1805, Vol. II, Art. V, p. 88, *Treaty with the Cherokees*, 1806, Vol. VII, Art. II, p. 102. Robert L. Cord, *Separation of Church and State* (NY: Lambeta Press, 1982), p. 39. David Barton, *The Myth of Separation* (Aledo, TX: WallBuilder Press, 1991), p. 176.

⁶⁸ **Thomas Jefferson.** December 3, 1803, treaty with the Kaskaskia Indians, 1806 with the Wyandotte Indians, and 1807 Cherokee Indians. Daniel L. Driesbach, *Real Threat and Mere Shadow: Religious Liberty and the First Amendment* (Westchester, IL: Crossway Books, 1987), p. 127. Richard Peters, ed., *The Public Statutes at Large of the United States of America* (Boston: Charles C. Little and James Brown, 1846), *A Treaty Between the United States and the Kaskaskia Tribe of Indians*, 23 December 1803, Art. III, Vol. VII, pp. 78-79., *Treaty with the Wyandots, etc.*, 1805, Vol. VII, Art. IV, p. 88, *Treaty with the Cherokees*, 1806, Vol.VII, Art,II, p. 102. Robert L. Cord, *Separation of Church and State* (NY: Lambeta Press, 1982), p. 39. David Barton, *The Myth of Separation* (Aledo, TX: WallBuilder Press, 1991), p. 176.

⁶⁹ **Thomas Jefferson.** June 17, 1804, in a letter to Henry Fry. Thomas Jefferson, *Jefferson's Writings*, Monticello, ed., 1905, Vol. IX, pp. 428-430. Catalogue of the Library of Thomas Jefferson, Vol. II. Rare Book Collection (Washington, D.C.: Library of Congress, 1953). Catherine Millard, *The Rewriting of America's History* (Camp Hill, PA: Horizon House Publishers, 1991), p. 99. John Eidsmoe, *Christianity and The Constitution - The Faith of Our Founding Fathers* (Grand Rapids, MI: Baker Book House, 1987), p. 244.

⁷⁰ **Thomas Jefferson.** September 11, 1804, in a letter to Abigail Adams. Thomas Jefferson, *Writings of Thomas Jefferson*, Albert Ellery Bergh, ed., (Washington, D.C.: Thomas Jefferson Memorial Association, 1904), Vol. X, pp. 50-51. David Barton, *The Myth of Separation* (Aledo, TX: WallBuilder Press, 1991), p. 177.

⁷¹ **Thomas Jefferson.** March 4, 1805, Monday, in his Second Inaugural Address. James D. Richardson (U.S. Representative from Tennessee), ed., *A Compilation of the Messages and Papers of the Presidents 1789-1897*, 10 vols. (Washington, D.C.: U.S. Government Printing Office, published by Authority of Congress, 1897, 1899; Washington, D.C.: Bureau of National Literature and Art, 1789-1902, 11 vols., 1907, 1910), Vol. I, p. 378-382. *Inaugural Addresses of the Presidents of the United States - From George Washington 1789 to Richard Milhous Nixon 1969* (Washington, D.C.: United States Government Printing Office; 91st Congress, 1st Session, House Document 91-142, 1969), pp. 17-21. Saul K. Padover, ed., *The Complete Jefferson, Containing His Major Writings, Published and Unpublished, Except His Letters* (NY: Duell, Sloan & Pearce, 1943), p. 412. Adrienne Koch and William Paden, eds., *The Life and Selected Writings of Thomas Jefferson* (NY: Random House, 1944), p. 341. Davis Newton Lott, *The Inaugural Addresses of the American Presidents* (NY: Holt, Rinehart and Winston, 1961), p. 22. Charles E. Rice, *The Supreme Court and Public Prayer* (New York: Fordham University Press, 1964), p. 179. Arthur Schlesinger Jr., ed., *The Chief Executive* (NY: Chelsea House Publishers, 1965), p. 20. Richard Maxfield, K. De Lynn Cook, and W. Cleon Skousen, *The Real Thomas Jefferson* (Washington, D.C.: National Center for Constitutional Studies, 2nd edition, 1981, 1983), pp. 403-440. Gary DeMar, *God and Government - A Biblical and Historical Study* (Atlanta, GA: American Vision Press, 1982), p. 166. John Eidsmoe, *Christianity and The Constitution - The Faith of Our Founding Fathers* (Grand Rapids, MI: Baker Book House, 1987), pp. 227-228, 243. David Barton, *The Myth of Separation* (Aledo, TX: WallBuilder Press, 1991), pp. 42, 174. John Whitehead, *The Rights of Religious Persons in Public Education* (Wheaton, IL: Crossway Books, Good News Publishers, 1991), p. 45. Catherine Millard, *The Rewriting of America's History* (Camp Hill, PA: Horizon House Publishers, 1991), pp. 91-92. Gary DeMar, *America's Christian History: The Untold Story* (Atlanta, GA: American Vision Publishers, Inc., 1993), p. 116. J. Michael Sharman, J.D., *Faith of the Fathers* (Culpepper, Virginia: Victory Publishing, 1995), pp. 25-26.

Notes

[72] **Thomas Jefferson.** March 4, 1805, Monday, in his Second Inaugural Address. James D. Richardson (U.S. Representative from Tennessee), ed., *A Compilation of the Messages and Papers of the Presidents 1789-1897*, 10 vols. (Washington, D.C.: U.S. Government Printing Office, published by Authority of Congress, 1897, 1899; Washington, D.C.: Bureau of National Literature and Art, 1789-1902, 11 vols., 1907, 1910), Vol. I, p. 378-382. *Inaugural Addresses of the Presidents of the United States - From George Washington 1789 to Richard Milhous Nixon 1969* (Washington, D.C.: United States Government Printing Office; 91st Congress, 1st Session, House Document 91-142, 1969), pp. 17-21. Saul K. Padover, ed., *The Complete Jefferson, Containing His Major Writings, Published and Unpublished, Except His Letters* (NY: Duell, Sloan & Pearce, 1943), p. 412. Adrienne Koch and William Paden, eds., *The Life and Selected Writings of Thomas Jefferson* (NY: Random House, 1944), p. 341. Davis Newton Lott, *The Inaugural Addresses of the American Presidents* (NY: Holt, Rinehart and Winston, 1961), p. 22. Charles E. Rice, *The Supreme Court and Public Prayer* (New York: Fordham University Press, 1964), p. 179. Arthur Schlesinger Jr., ed., *The Chief Executive* (NY: Chelsea House Publishers, 1965), p. 20. Richard Maxfield, K. De Lynn Cook, and W. Cleon Skousen, *The Real Thomas Jefferson* (Washington, D.C.: National Center for Constitutional Studies, 2nd edition, 1981, 1983), pp. 403-440. Gary DeMar, *God and Government - A Biblical and Historical Study* (Atlanta, GA: American Vision Press, 1982), p. 166. Gary DeMar, *Christianity and The Constitution - The Faith of Our Founding Fathers* (Grand Rapids, MI: Baker Book House, 1987), pp. 227-228, 243. David Barton, *The Myth of Separation* (Aledo, TX: WallBuilder Press, 1991), pp. 42, 174. John Whitehead, *The Rights of Religious Persons in Public Education* (Wheaton, IL: Crossway Books, Good News Publishers, 1991), p. 45. Catherine Millard, *The Rewriting of America's History* (Camp Hill, PA: Horizon House Publishers, 1991), pp. 91-92. Gary DeMar, *America's Christian History: The Untold Story* (Atlanta, GA: American Vision Publishers, Inc., 1993), p. 116. J. Michael Sharman, J.D., *Faith of the Fathers* (Culpepper, Virginia: Victory Publishing, 1995), pp. 25-26.

[73] **Thomas Jefferson.** March 4, 1805, offered a National Prayer for Peace. Adrienne Koch and William Paden, eds. *The Life and Selected Writings of Thomas Jefferson* (NY: Random House, 1944), p. 341. "Our Christian Heritage," *Letter from Plymouth Rock* (Marlborough, NH: The Plymouth Rock Foundation), p. 5.

[74] **Thomas Jefferson.** April 10, 1806, Articles of War, cited as Act of April 10, 1806, C. 20, 2 Stat. 359, 360. Charles E. Rice, *The Supreme Court and Public Prayer: The Need for Restraint* (New York: Fordham University Press, 1964), pp. 63-64. Gary DeMar, *America's Christian History: The Untold Story* (Atlanta, GA: American Vision Publishers, Inc., 1993), p. 116.

[75] **Thomas Jefferson.** January 23, 1808, in a letter to Samuel Miller. Thomas Jefferson, *Jefferson Writings*, Merrill D. Peterson, ed., (NY: Literary Classics of the United States, Inc., 1984), p. 1186-1187. Thomas Jefferson Randolph, ed., *Memoirs, Correspondence, and Private Papers of Thomas Jefferson*, 4 vols. (London and Charlottesville, VA: 1829), Vol. IV, p. 106. Paul Leicester Ford, ed., *The Writings of Thomas Jefferson*, 10 vols. (NY: G.P. Putnam's Sons, 1892-1899), Vol. IX, pp. 174-175. A.A. Lipscomb and Albert Bergh, eds., *The Writings of Thomas Jefferson* 20 vols. (Washington, D.C.: The Thomas Jefferson Memorial Association, 1903-1904), Vol. XI, p. 428. Thomas Jefferson, *Jefferson's Writings*, Monticello, ed., (1905), Vol. IX, p. 428-30. *The Annals of America*, 20 vols. (Chicago, IL: Encyclopedia Britannica, 1968), Vol. 4, p. 234. Henry Steele Commager, ed., *Freedom of Religion & Separation of Church and State* (Mount Vernon, New York: A. Colish, Inc., 1985), p. 29. Norman Cousins, *In God We Trust - The Religious Beliefs and Ideas of the American Founding Fathers* (NY: Harper & Brothers, 1958), pp. 136-1 37. John Eidsmoe, *Christianity and The Constitution - The Faith of Our Founding Fathers* (Grand Rapids, MI: Baker Book House, 1987), p. 244. David Barton, *The Myth of Separation* (Aledo, TX: WallBuilder Press, 1991), p. 42. Gary DeMar, *God and Government-A Biblical and Historical Study* (Atlanta, GA: American Vision Press, 1982), p. 173.

[76] **Thomas Jefferson.** 1813, in a letter to John Adams. Thomas Jefferson, *Writings*, Vol. XIII, p. 389. Douglas Lurton, "Foreword," *The Jefferson Bible* (Cleveland, OH: The Word Publishing Company, 1942), p. ix. Burton Stevenson, *The Home Book of Quotations-Classical & Modern* (New York: Dodd, Mead and Company, 1967), p. 266. Gary DeMar, *America's Christian History: The Untold Story* (Atlanta, GA: American Vision Publishers, Inc., 1993), p. 91. A. Douglas Lurton, *The Jefferson Bible* (Cleveland, OH:, The Word Publishing, Co., 1942), (Forward).

[77] **Thomas Jefferson.** September 18, 1813, in a letter to William Canby. Compiled for Senator A. Willis Robertson, *Letters of Thomas Jefferson on Religion* (Williamsburg, VA: The Williamsburg Foundation, April 27, 1960). Catherine Millard, *The Rewriting of America's History* (Camp Hill, PA: Horizon House Publishers, 1991), p. 107.

[78] **Thomas Jefferson.** March 17, 1814, in a letter to Horatio G. Spafford. John Bartlett, *Bartlett's Familiar Quotations* (Boston: Little, Brown and Company, 1855, 1980), p. 389.

[79] **Thomas Jefferson.** September 26, 1814, in a letter to Miles King. Compiled for Senator A. Willis Robertson, *Letters of Thomas Jefferson on Religion* (Williamsburg, VA: The Williamsburg Foundation, April 27, 1960). Catherine Millard, *The Rewriting of America's History* (Camp Hill, PA: Horizon House Publishers, 1991), pp. 107-108.

[80] **Thomas Jefferson.** *The Life and Morals of Jesus of Nazareth*, extracted textually from the Gospels in Greek, Latin, French and English. Library of the Smithsonian Institute National Museum. Catherine Millard, *The Rewriting of America's History* (Camp Hill, PA: Horizon House Publishers, 1991), p. 109.

[81] **Thomas Jefferson.** *The Life and Morals of Jesus of Nazareth*, extracted textually from the Gospels in Greek, Latin, French and English. Library of the Smithsonian Institute National Museum. Catherine Millard, *The Rewriting of America's History* (Camp Hill, PA: Horizon House Publishers, 1991), p. 97.

[82] **Thomas Jefferson.** 1816. *The Life and Morals of Jesus of Nazareth, extracted textually from the Gospels.* David Barton, *The WallBuilder Report* (Aledo, TX: WallBuilder, Summer 1993), p. 2. Catherine Millard, *The Rewriting of America's History* (Camp Hill, PA: Horizon House Publishers, 1991), pp. 97-99.

[83] **Thomas Jefferson.** September 6, 1819. Thomas Jefferson, *Jefferson Writings*, Merrill D. Peterson, ed., (NY: Literary Classics of the United States, Inc., 1984), p. 1426. David Barton, *The Myth of Separation* (Aledo, TX: WallBuilder Press, 1991), p. 236.

[84] **Thomas Jefferson.** September 28, 1820, in a letter to William Jarvis. Thomas Jefferson, *Jefferson's Letters*, Wilson Whitman, ed., (Eau Claire, WI: E.M. Hale & Co., 1900), p. 338. David Barton, *The Myth of Separation* (Aledo, TX: WallBuilder Press, 1991), p. 177. Gary DeMar, *God and Government-A Biblical and Historical* Study (Atlanta, GA: American Vision Press, 1982), p. 166.

[85] **Thomas Jefferson.** November 4, 1820, in a letter to Jared Sparks. Compiled for Senator A. Willis Robertson, *Letters of Thomas Jefferson* (Williamsburg, VA: The Williamsburg Foundation, April 27, 1960). Norman Cousins, *In God We Trust - The Religious Beliefs and Ideas of the American Founding Fathers* (NY: Harper & Brothers, 1958), p. 156. Catherine Millard, *The Rewriting of America's History* (Camp Hill, PA: Horizon House Publishers, 1991), p. 96.

[86] **Thomas Jefferson.** 1821, in a letter to Mr. Hammond. Thomas Jefferson, *Thomas Jefferson on Democracy*, Saul K. Padover, ed., (NY: D. Appleton-Century Co., 1939), p. 64. David Barton, *The Myth of Separation* (Aledo, TX: WallBuilder Press, 1991), pp. 177-178.

[87] **Thomas Jefferson**. June 12, 1823, in a letter to Justice William Johnson. Thomas Jefferson, *Jefferson Writings*, Merrill D. Peterson, ed., (NY: Literary Classics of the United States, Inc., 1984), p. 1475. David Barton, *The Myth of Separation* (Aledo, TX: WallBuilder Press, 1991), p. 170.

[88] **Thomas Jefferson**. August 30,1823, in a letter to James Madison regarding his authorship of the Declaration of Independence. *Old South Leaflets* (Boston: Directors of the Old South Meeting House, 1902).

[89] **Thomas Jefferson**. 1813, in his regulations for the University of Virginia. Saul K. Padover, ed., *The Complete Jefferson, Containing His Major Writings, Published and Unpublished, Except His letters* (KY: Duell, Sloan & Pearce, 1943), p. 111. John Whitehead, *The Rights of Religious Persons in Public Education* (Wheaton, IL: Crossway Books, Good News Publishers, 1991), p. 47. Philip Alexander Bruce, *The History of the University of Virginia 1819-1919* (NY: The Macmillan Co., 1920), Vol. II, p.367-69. Anson Phelps Stokes and Leo Pfeffer, *Church and State in the United States* (NY: Harper and Row, Publishers, 1950, revised one- volume edition, 1964), p. 54. Stephen K McDowell and Mark A. Beliles, *America's Providential History* (Charlottesville, VA: Providence Press, 1988), p. 152. David Barton, *The Myth of Separation* (Aledo, TX: WallBuilder Press, 1991), p. 175.

[90] **Thomas Jefferson**. University of Virginia, being established by Thomas Jefferson. Stephen K. McDowell and Mark A. Beliles, *America's Providential History* (Charlottesville, VA: Providence Press, 1988), p. 152. David Barton, *The Myth of Separation (Aledo, TX:* WallBuilder Press, 1991), p. 175.

[91] **Thomas Jefferson**. Bruton Parish Church (Episcopalian), Williamsburg, VA.

[92] **Thomas Jefferson**. Catalog of the Library of Thomas Jefferson, (Washington, D.C.: Rare Book Collection, Library of Congress, 1953), Vol. II.

[93] **Thomas Jefferson**. January 9,1816, in a letter to Charles Thomson. Henry S. Randall, *The Life of Thomas Jefferson* (NY: Derby and Jackson, 1958),Vol. 3, p. 451. Norman Cousins, *In God We Trust - The Religious Beliefs and Ideas of the American Founding Fathers* (NY: Harper & Brothers, 1958), p. 146. Edmund Fuller and David E. Green, *God in the White House - The Faiths of American Presidents* (NY: Crown Publishers, Inc., 1968), p. 35. Dickenson Adams, ed., *Jefferson's Extracts from the Gospels* (Princeton: Princeton University Press, 1983), p. 395. Pat Robertson, *America's Dates with Destiny* (Nashville: Thomas Nelson Publishers, 1986), p. 65.

[94] **Thomas Jefferson**. Thomas Jefferson, *Writings,* Vol. XIII, p. 377. Burton Stevenson, *The Home Book of Quotations-Classical and Modern* (New York: Dodd, Mead and Company, 1967), p. 266.

[95] **Thomas Jefferson**. *Writings,* Vol. XIV, p. 149. Burton Stevenson, *The Home Book of Quotations* (New York: Dodd, Mead and Company, 1967), p. 266.

[96] **Thomas Jefferson**. Tryon Edwards, D.D., *The New Dictionary of Thoughts - A Cyclopedia of Quotations* (Garden City, NY: Hanover House, 1852; revised and enlarged by C.H. Catrevas, Ralph Emerson Browns and Jonathan Edwards [descendent, along with Tryon, of Jonathan Edwards (1703-1758), president of Princeton] 1991; The Standard Book Company, 1955, 1963), p. 91.

[97] **Thomas Jefferson**. Tryon Edwards, D.D., *The New Dictionary of Thoughts - A Cyclopedia of Quotations* (Garden City, NY: Hanover House, 1852; revised and enlarged by C.H. Catrevas, Ralph Emerson Browns and Jonathan Edwards [descendent, along with Tryon, of Jonathan Edwards (1703-1758), president of Princeton], 1891; The Standard Book Company, 1955, 1963), p. 46. Herbert Lockyer, *Last Words of Saints and Sinners* (Grand Rapids, W: Kregel, 1969), p. 98. David Barton, *The Myth of Separation* (Aledo, TX: WallBuilder Press, 1991), pp. 130, 150, 176. D.P. Diffine, Ph.D., *One Nation Under God - How Close a Separation?* (Searcy, Arkansas: Harding University, Belden Center for Private Enterprise Education, 6th edition, 1992), p. 10.

[98] **Thomas Jefferson**. Shmucher, *Life of Jefferson.* Stephen Abbott Northrop, D.D., *A Cloud of Witnesses* (Portland, OR: American Heritage Ministries, 1987; Mantle Ministries, 228 Still Ridge, Bulverde, Texas), pp. 252-253.

[99] **Thomas Jefferson**. Library of American Literature, Vol. III, pp. 283-284. Stephen Abbott Northrop, D.D., *A Cloud of Witnesses* (Portland, Oregon: American Heritage Ministries, 1987; Mantle Ministries, 228 Still Ridge, Bulverde, Texas), p. 253.

[100] **Thomas Jefferson**. July 4,1826, his last words. James H. Huston, "John Adams," *The World Book Encyclopedia* 22 vols. (Chicago, IL: World Book, Inc., 1989; W.F. Quarrie and Company, 8 vols., 1917), Vol. 1, p. 39. Peter Marshall and David Manuel, *The Glory of America* (Bloomington, MN: Garborg's Heart'N Home, Inc., 1991), 7.12.

[101] **Thomas Jefferson**. July 4,1826, epitaph inscribed on his tombstone, which he authored himself.

[102] **Thomas Jefferson**. Jefferson Memorial, Washington D.C. January 16,1786, in a bill written by the Committee on Religion, Virginia Assembly. H.A. Washington, ed., *The Writings of Thomas Jefferson - Being His Autobiography, Correspondence, Reports, Messages, Addresses, and Other Writings, Official and Private,* 9 vols. (Jackson: 1859); (Washington: 1853-54); (Philadelphia: 1871), Vol. 8; (NY: Derby), Vol. VIII, p. 454-56. William Taylor Thom, *The Struggle for Religious Freedom in Virginia: The Baptists,* Johns Hopkins Studies in Historical and Political Science, Herbert B. Adams, ed., (Baltimore: Johns Hopkins, 1900), p. 79. *The Annals of America,* 20 vols. (Chicago, IL: Encyclopedia Britannica, 1968), Vol. 3, p. 53. Norman Cousins, *In God We Trust - The Religious Beliefs and Ideas of the American Founding Fathers* (NY: Harper & Brothers, 1958), p. 124. Tim LaHaye, *Faith of Our Founding Fathers* (Brentwood, TN: Wolgemuth & Hyatt, Publishers, Inc., 1987), pp. 192-193.

[103] **Thomas Jefferson**. Jefferson Memorial, Washington D.C. Tim LaHaye, *Faith of Our Founding Fathers* (Brentwood, TN: Wolgemuth & Hyatt, Publishers, Inc., 1987), pp. 192-193.

[104] **Thomas Jefferson**. Robert Byrd, United States Senator from West Virginia, July 27, 1962, in a message delivered in Congress two days after the Supreme Court declared prayer in schools unconstitutional. Robert Flood, *The Rebirth of America* (Philadelphia: Arthur S. DeMoss Foundation, 1986), pp. 66-69. Tim LaHaye, *Faith of Our Founding Fathers* (Brentwood, TN: Wolgemuth & Hyatt, Publishers, Inc., 1987), pp. 192-193.

[105] **Thomas Jefferson**. April 21, 1803, in a letter to Benjamin Rush. William Linn, *The Life of Thomas Jefferson* (Ithaca, NY: Mack & Andrus, 1834), p. 265. Norman Cousins, *In God We Trust - The Religious Beliefs and Ideas of the American Founding Fathers* (NY: Harper & Brothers, 1958), p. 170-171. Richard Maxfield, K. De Lynn Cook, and W. Cleon Skousen, *The Real Thomas Jefferson* (Washington, D.C.: National Center for Constitutional Studies, 2nd edition, 1981, 1983), pp. 495-496. John Eidsmoe, *Christianity and The Constitution - The Faith of Our Founding Fathers* (Grand Rapids, MI: Baker Book House, 1987), p. 230.

Notes

[106] **Thomas Jefferson.** Stephen K. McDowell and Mark A. Beliles, *America's Providential History* (Charlottesville, VA: Providence Press, 1988), p. 148. David Barton, *The Myth of Separation* (Aledo, TX: WallBuilder Press, 1991), p. 176. Stephen McDowell and Mark Beliles, "The Providential Perspective" (Charlottesville, VA: The Providence Foundation, P.O. Box 6759, Charlottesville, Va. 22906, January 1994), Vol. 9, No. 1, p. 7.

[107] **Andrew Johnson.** John Savage, *The Life and Public Services of Andrew Johnson*, p. 274. Stephen Abbott Northrop, D.D., *A Cloud of Witnesses* (Portland, Oregon: American Heritage Ministries, 1987; Mantle Ministries, 228 Still Ridge, Bulverde, Texas), p. 255.

[108] **Andrew Johnson.** John Savage, *The Life and Public Services of Andrew Johnson*, p. 247. Stephen Abbott Northrop, D.D., *A Cloud of Witnesses* (Portland, Oregon: American Heritage Ministries, 1987; Mantle Ministries, 228 Still Ridge, Bulverde, Texas), p. 255.

[109] **Andrew Johnson.** John Savage, *The Life and Public Services of Andrew Johnson*, p. 34. Stephen Abbott Northrop, D.D., *A Cloud of Witnesses* (Portland, Oregon: American Heritage Ministries, 1987; Mantle Ministries, 228 Still Ridge, Bulverde, Texas), p. 255.

[110] **James Weldon Johnson.** 1927, in *God's Trombones - The Creation*, (The Viking Press: 1927), st. I, 7, 10. John Bartlett, *Bartlett's Familiar Quotations* (Boston: Little, Brown and Company, 1855, 1980), p. 733. James Weldon Johnson, *God's Trombones* (NY: Penguin Books: 1985), pp. 17, 20.

[111] **Lyndon Baines Johnson.** January 20, 1965, Wednesday, in his Inaugural Address. *Inaugural Addresses of the Presidents of the United States - From George Washington 1789 to Richard Milhous Nixon 1969* (Washington, D.C.: United States Government Printing Office; 91st Congress, 1st Session, House Document 91-142, 1969), pp. 271-274. Benjamin Weiss, *God in American History: A Documentation of America's Religious Heritage* (Grand Rapids, MI: Zondervan, 1966), p. 151. Willard Cantelon, *Money Master of the World* (Plainfield, NJ: Logos International, 1976), p. 122. *Proclaim Liberty* (Dallas, TX: Word of Faith), p. 3. J. Michael Sharman, J.D., *Faith of the Fathers* (Culpepper, Virginia: Victory Publishing, 1995), p. 114.

[112] **Lyndon Baines Johnson.** January 20, 1965, Wednesday, in his Inaugural Address. *Inaugural Addresses of the Presidents of the United States - From George Washington 1789 to Richard Milhous Nixon 1969* (Washington, D.C.: United States Government Printing Office; 91st Congress, 1st Session, House Document 91-142, 1969), pp. 271-274. Benjamin Weiss, *God in American History: A Documentation of America's Religious Heritage* (Grand Rapids, MI: Zondervan, 1966), p. 151. Willard Cantelon, *Money Master of the World* (Plainfield, NJ: Logos International, 1976), p. 122. *Proclaim Liberty* (Dallas, TX: Word of Faith), p. 3. J. Michael Sharman, J.D., *Faith of the Fathers* (Culpepper, Virginia: Victory Publishing, 1995), p. 114.

[113] **Lyndon Baines Johnson.** Saying taken from Isaiah 1:18, 28:30. John Bartlett, *Bartlett's Familiar Quotations* (Boston: Little, Brown and Company, 1855, 1980), p. 872.

[114] **Samuel Johnson.** Dr. Johnson, *Oriental Eloquence of Collins*. Stephen Abbott Northrop, D.D., *A Cloud of Witnesses* (Portland, OR: American Heritage Ministries, 1987; Mantle Ministries, 228 Still Ridge, Bulverde, Texas), p. 256.

[115] **Samuel Johnson.** Prayer before writing *The Rambler*. Stephen Abbott Northrop, D.D., *A Cloud of Witnesses* (Portland, OR: American Heritage Ministries, 1987; Mantle Ministries, 228 Still Ridge, Bulverde, Texas), p. 256.

[116] **Samuel Johnson.** Extracts from a birthday prayer, transcribed June 26, 1768. Arthur Murphy, *Prayers and Meditations; The Works of Samuel Johnson, with an Essay on His Life and Genius* Vol. II. Stephen Abbott Northrop, D.D., *A Cloud of Witnesses* (Portland, Oregon: American Heritage Ministries, 1987; Mantle Ministries, 228 Still Ridge, Bulverde, Texas), p. 256.

[117] **Samuel Johnson.** 1763. James Boswell, *Life of Johnson* (1791, edited by G.B. Hill, revised by L.F. Powell, 1934). John Bartlett, *Bartlett's Familiar Quotations* (Boston: Little, Brown and Company, 1855, 1980), p. 354.

[118] **Samuel Johnson.** 1772. James Boswell, *Life of Johnson* (1791, edited by G.B. Hill, revised by L.F. Powell, 1934). John Bartlett, *Bartlett's Familiar Quotations* (Boston: Little, Brown and Company, 1855, 1980), p. 354.

[119] **Samuel Johnson.** December 13, 1784. James Boswell, *Life of Johnson* (1791, edited by G.B. Hill, revised by L.F. Powell, 1934). John Bartlett, *Bartlett's Familiar Quotations* (Boston: Little, Brown and Company, 1855, 1980), p. 357.

[120] **William Samuel Johnson.** M.E. Bradford, *A Worthy Company* (Marlborough, NH: Plymouth Rock Foundation, 1982), p. 30. Tim LaHaye, *Faith of Our Founding Fathers* (Brentwood,TN: Wolgemuth & Hyatt, Publishers, Inc., 1987), p. 158.

[121] **William Samuel Johnson.** John Irving, *A Discourse of the Advantages of Classical Learning* (New York: G. & C. & H. Carvill, 1830), pp. 141-143. Tim LaHaye, *Faith of Our Founding Fathers* (Brentwood, TN: Wolgemuth & Hyatt, Publishers, Inc., 1987), pp. 159-160.

[122] **John Paul Jones.** September 23, 1779, as commander of the American ship, *Bonhomme Richard*, in answering a call to surrender from the commander of the British ship, *Serapis*. John Bartlett, *Bartlett's Familiar Quotations* (Boston: Little, Brown & Company, 1855, 1980), p. 394. *The World Book Encyclopedia*, 18 vols. (Chicago, IL: Field Enterprises, Inc., 1957; W.F. Quarrie and Company, 8 vols., 1917; World Book, Inc., 22 vols., 1989), Vol. 9, pp. 4054-4055. *Oxford Dictionary of Quotations* (London: Oxford University Press, Second Edition, 1941, 1955), p. 279.

[123] **John William Jones.** 1887. John Williams Jones, D.D., *Christ in the Camp* (Richmond, VA: B.F. Johnson & Co., 1887, 1897; The Martin & Hoyt Co., 1904; Harrisonburg, VA: Sprinkle Publications, 1986). Mark Galli, "Firebrands and Visionaries" (Carol Stream, IL: Christian History), Vol. XI, No. 1, Issue 33, p. 20.

[124] **John William Jones.** John William Jones. Bradford, *Lee*, p. 242. Peter Marshall and David Manuel, *The Glory of America* (Bloomington, MN: Garborg's Heart'N Home, Inc., 1991), 2.4.

[125] **John William Jones.** 1887. John Williams Jones, D.D., *Christ in the Camp* (Richmond, VA: B.F. Johnson & Co., 1887, 1897; The Martin & Hoyt Co., 1904; Harrisonburg, VA: Sprinkle Publications, 1986). Gardiner H. Shattuck, Jr., *Revivals in the Camp* (Carol Stream, IL: Christian History), Vol. XI, No. 1, Issue 33, p. 29.

[126] **John William Jones.** In quoting a Captain of the Confederate Georgia Brigade. John Williams Jones, D.D., *Christ in the Camp* (Richmond, VA: B.F. Johnson & Co., 1887, 1897; The Martin & Hoyt Co., 1904; Harrisonburg, VA: Sprinkle Publications, 1986), p. 397. Peter Marshall and David Manuel, *The Glory of America* (Bloomington, MN: Garborg's Heart'N Home, Inc., 1991), 3.17.

[127] **John William Jones.** John Williams Jones, D.D., *Christ in the Camp* (Richmond, VA: B.F. Johnson & Co., 1887, 1897; The Martin & Hoyt Co., 1904; Harrisonburg, VA: Sprinkle Publications, 1986), p. 97. Peter Marshall and David Manuel, *The Glory of America* (Bloomington, MN: Garborg's Heart'N Home, Inc., 1991), 8.14.

[128] **John William Jones.** John Williams Jones, D.D., *Christ in the Camp* (Richmond, VA: B.F. Johnson & Co., 1887, 1897; The Martin & Hoyt Co., 1904; Harrisonburg, VA: Sprinkle Publications, 1986), p. 56. Peter Marshall and David Manuel, *The Glory of America* (Bloomington, MN: Garborg's Heart'N Home, Inc., 1991), 8.21.

[129] **John William Jones.** In a meeting with General Robert E. Lee and Chaplain Lacey. John Williams Jones, D.D., *Christ in the Camp* (Richmond, VA: B.F. Johnson & Co., 1887, 1897; The Martin & Hoyt Co., 1904; Harrisonburg, VA: Sprinkle Publications, 1986), p. 50. Peter Marshall and David Manuel, *The Glory of America* (Bloomington, MN: Garborg's Heart'N Home, Inc., 1991), 3.7.

¹³⁰ **John William Jones.** 1869, John William Jones speaking at Washington College at the request of its president Robert E. Lee. John William Jones, *Lee*. Peter Marshall and David Manuel, *The Glory of America* (Bloomington, MN: Garborg's Heart'N Home, Inc., 1991), 10.29.

𝒦

¹ **Queen Ka'ahumanu.** 1832, in her last words to Rev. Hiram Bingham. "Hawaii's heroes of the faith," (Hawaii: University of the Nations Newsletter, Youth With a Mission, 1993), p. 8.

² **Queen Ka'ahumanu.** High Chiefess Kapiolani's testimony. "Hawaii's heroes of the faith," (Hawaii: University of the Nations Newsletter, Youth With a Mission, 1993), p. 8.

³ **Immanuel Kant.** Henry H. Halley, *Halley's Bible Handbook* (Grand Rapids, MI: Zondervan Publishing House, 1927, 1965), p. 19.

⁴ **Immanuel Kant.** *An Inquiry into the Existence of God*, Stephen Abbott Northrop, D.D., *A Cloud of Witnesses* (Portland, Oregon: American Heritage Ministries, 1987; Mantle Ministries, 228 Still Ridge, Bulverde, Texas), p. 263.

⁵ **Helen Adams Keller.** Tryon Edwards, D.D., *The New Dictionary of Thoughts - A Cyclopedia of Quotations* (Garden City, NY: Hanover House, 1852; revised and enlarged by C.H. Catrevas, Ralph Emerson Browns and Jonathan Edwards [descendent, along with Tryon, of Jonathan Edwards (1703-1758), president of Princeton], 1891; The Standard Book Company, 1955, 1963), p. 46.

⁶ **Helen Adams Keller.** *Bless Your Heart (series II)* (Eden Prairie, MN: Heartland Samplers, Inc., 1990), 3.2.

⁷ **Helen Adams Keller.** *Bless Your Heart (series II)* (Eden Prairie, MN: Heartland Samplers, Inc., 1990), 4.7.

⁸ **Howard A. Kelly.** *A Scientific Man and His Bible.* Henry M. Morris, *Men of Science - Men of God* (El Cajon, CA: Master Books, Creation Life Publishers, Inc., 1990), pp. 80-81.

⁹ **Sir William Thompson, Lord Kelvin.** 1903. Henry M. Morris,*Men of Science - Men of God* (El Cajon, CA: Master Books, Creation Life Publishers, Inc., 1990), pp. 63-66.

¹⁰ **Sir William Thomson, Lord Kelvin.** May 23, 1889, in his address as the Chairman of the*Christian Evidence Society*, in London, at its nineteenth anniversary. Stephen Abbott Northrop, D.D., *A Cloud of Witnesses* (Portland, OR: American Heritage Ministries, 1987; Mantle Ministries, 228 Still Ridge, Bulverde, Texas), pp. 460-461.

¹¹ **Thomas a' Kempis.** 1420, in his work, *Imitation of Christ*, book. I, ch. 16. John Bartlett, *Bartlett's Familiar Quotations* (Boston: Little, Brown and Company, 1855, 1980), p. 149.

¹² **Thomas a' Kempis.** 1420, in his work, *Imitation of Christ*, book. I, ch. 19. John Bartlett, *Bartlett's Familiar Quotations* (Boston: Little, Brown and Company, 1855, 1980), p. 149.

¹³ **Thomas a' Kempis.** 1420, in his work, *Imitation of Christ*, book. III, ch. 5. John Bartlett, *Bartlett's Familiar Quotations* (Boston: Little, Brown and Company, 1855, 1980), p. 149.

¹⁴ **Dr. D. James Kennedy.** From the unabridged, printed sermon by D. James Kennedy, Ph.D., "Church and State." Tim LaHaye, *Faith of Our Founding Fathers* (Brentwood, TN: Wolgemuth & Hyatt, Publishers, Inc., 1987), p. 93.

¹⁵ **John Fitzgerald Kennedy.** January 20, 1961, Friday, in his Inaugural Address. *Inaugural Addresses of the Presidents of the United States - From George Washington 1789 to Richard Milhous Nixon 1969* (Washington, D.C.: United States Government Printing Office; 91st Congress, 1st Session, House Document 91-142, 1969), pp. 267-270. Davis Newton Lott, *The Inaugural Addresses of the American Presidents* (NY: Holt, Rinehart and Winston, 1961), p. 269. Charles E. Rice,*The Supreme Court and Public Prayer* (New York: Fordham University Press, 1964), p. 193. Benjamin Weiss,*God in American History: A Documentation of America's Religious Heritage* (Grand Rapids, MI: Zondervan, 1966), p. 146. *The Annals of America*, 20 vols. (Chicago, IL: Encyclopedia Britannica, 1968), Vol. XVIII, p. 7. Lillian W. Kay, ed., *The Ground on Which We Stand - Basic Documents of American History* (NY: Franklin Watts., Inc, 1969), p. 296. Willard Cantelon,*Money Master of the World* (Plainfield, NJ: Logos International, 1976), p. 121-122. Bob Arnebeck, "FDR Invoked God Too," *Washington Post*, September 21, 1986. Vincent J. Wilson, ed., *The Book of Great American Documents* (Brookfield, MD: American History Research Associates, 1987), p. 84. Halford Ross Ryan, *American Rhetoric from Roosevelt to Reagan* (Prospect Heights, IL: Waveland Press, 1987), p. 156. Jeffrey K. Hadden and Anson Shupe, *Televangelism - Power & Politics on God's Frontier* (NY: Henry Holt and Company, 1988), p. 272. Ronald Reid, ed., *Three Centuries of American Rhetorical Discourse: An Anthology and a Review* (Prospect Heights, Il: Waveland Press, Inc., 1988), p. 711. William Safire, ed.,*Lend Me Your Ears - Great Speeches in History* (NY: W.W. Norton & Company 1992), p. 812. Peter Marshall and David Manuel,*The Glory of America* (Bloomington, MN: Garborg's Heart 'N Home, Inc., 1991), 1.20. *Proclaim Liberty* (Dallas, TX: Word of Faith), p. 3. J. Michael Sharman, J.D., *Faith of the Fathers* (Culpepper, Virginia: Victory Publishing, 1995), pp. 111-112.

¹⁶ **John Fitzgerald Kennedy.** January 20, 1961, Friday, in his Inaugural Address. *Inaugural Addresses of the Presidents of the United States - From George Washington 1789 to Richard Milhous Nixon 1969* (Washington, D.C.: United States Government Printing Office; 91st Congress, 1st Session, House Document 91-142, 1969), p. 267-270. Davis Newton Lott, *The Inaugural Addresses of the American Presidents* (NY: Holt, Rinehart and Winston, 1961), p. 269. Charles E. Rice,*The Supreme Court and Public Prayer* (New York: Fordham University Press, 1964), p. 193. Benjamin Weiss,*God in American History: A Documentation of America's Religious Heritage* (Grand Rapids, MI: Zondervan, 1966), p. 146. *The Annals of America*, 20 vols. (Chicago, IL: Encyclopedia Britannica, 1968), Vol. XVIII, p. 7. Lillian W. Kay, ed., *The Ground on Which We Stand - Basic Documents of American History* (NY: Franklin Watts., Inc, 1969), p. 296. Willard Cantelon,*Money Master of the World* (Plainfield, NJ: Logos International, 1976), p. 121-122. Bob Arnebeck, "FDR Invoked God Too," *Washington Post*, September 21, 1986. Vincent J. Wilson, ed., *The Book of Great American Documents* (Brookfield, MD: American History Research Associates, 1987), p. 84. Halford Ross Ryan, *American Rhetoric from Roosevelt to Reagan* (Prospect Heights, IL: Waveland Press, 1987), p. 156. Jeffrey K. Hadden and Anson Shupe, *Televangelism - Power & Politics on God's Frontier* (NY: Henry Holt and Company, 1988), p. 272. Ronald Reid, ed., *Three Centuries of American Rhetorical Discourse: An Anthology and a Review* (Prospect Heights, Il: Waveland Press, Inc., 1988), p. 711. William Safire, ed.,*Lend Me Your Ears - Great Speeches in History* (NY: W.W. Norton & Company 1992), p. 812. Peter Marshall and David Manuel,*The Glory of America* (Bloomington, MN: Garborg's Heart 'N Home, Inc., 1991), 1.20. *Proclaim Liberty* (Dallas, TX: Word of Faith), p. 3. J. Michael Sharman, J.D., *Faith of the Fathers* (Culpepper, Virginia: Victory Publishing, 1995), pp. 111-112.

¹⁷ **John Fitzgerald Kennedy.** November 22, 1963, the conclusion to the speech he had prepared to give before he was shot. *The Annals of America*, 20 vols. (Chicago, IL: Encyclopedia Britannica, 1968), Vol. XVIII, p. 201. Peter Marshall and David Manuel, *The Glory of America* (Bloomington, MN: Garborg's Heart'N Home, Inc., 1991), 11.22.

¹⁸ **John Fitzgerald Kennedy.** Herbert V. Prochnow, *5100 Quotations for Speakers and Writers* (Grand Rapids, MI: Baker Book House, 1992), p. 479.

[19] **James Kent.** 1811, in the decision of Supreme Court of New York in the case, *The People v. Ruggles*, 8 Johns 545 (1811). James Kent, *Commentaries on American Law* (Boston: Little, Brown, 1826-1830, 1858), Vol. 2, pp. 35-36. (Emphasis original). Perry Miller, *The Life of the Mind in America* (London: Victor Gallanz, 1966), p. 66. David Barton, *The Myth of Separation* (Aledo, TX: WallBuilder Press, 1991), p. 55. John Whitehead, *The Second American Revolution* (Wheaton, Illinois: Crossway Books, 1982), p. 197. Gary DeMar, "The Treaty of Tripoli" (Atlanta, GA: *The Biblical Worldview*, An American Vision Publication - American Vision, Inc., December 1992), p. 12.

[20] **James Kent.** 1811, issuing his opinion as Chief Justice of the Supreme Court of New York in the case *The People v. Ruggles*, 8 Johns 545-547 (1811); cited by the United States Supreme Court in the case *Church of the Holy Trinity v. United States*, 143 US 457, 458, 465-471, 36 L ed 226, (1892), Justice David Josiah Brewer. James Kent, *Commentaries on American Law* (Boston: Little, Brown, 1826-1830, 1858), Vol. 2, pp. 35-36. Charles B. Galloway, *Christianity and the American Commonwealth* (Nashville, TN: Methodist Episcopal Church Publishing House, 1898), p. 169-70. *Johnson's Reports*, p. 290. Perry Miller, *The Life of the Mind in America* (London: Victor Gallanz, 1966), p. 66. John Whitehead, *The Second American Revolution* (Wheaton, Illinois: Crossway Books, 1982), p. 197. Stephen Abbott Northrop, D.D., *A Cloud of Witnesses* (Portland, OR: American Heritage Ministries, 1987; Mantle Ministries, 228 Still Ridge, Bulverde, Texas), p. 265. "Our Christian Heritage," *Letter from Plymouth Rock* (Marlborough, NH: The Plymouth Rock Foundation), p. 6. David Barton, *The Myth of Separation* (Aledo, TX: WallBuilder Press, 1991), pp. 47-51, 55-61. Gary DeMar, "The Treaty of Tripoli" (Atlanta, GA: *The Biblical Worldview*, An American Vision Publication - American Vision, Inc., December 1992), Vol. 8, No. 12, p. 12. Gary DeMar, *America's Christian History: The Untold Story* (Atlanta, GA: American Vision Publishers, Inc., 1993), p. 85.

[21] **James Kent.** Extracts from an Address before the American Bible Society. Stephen Abbott Northrop, D.D., *A Cloud of Witnesses* (Portland, Oregon: American Heritage Ministries, 1987; Mantle Ministries, 228 Still Ridge, Bulverde, Texas), pp. 265-266.

[22] **Kentucky Resolutions.** November 16, 1798. Jefferson, *Works*, (ed. 1856), IX:464-71. William McDonald, *Select Documents Illustrative of the History of United States, 1776-1861* (NY: Macmillan Company, 1897; 1898), p. 150. James Madison, *Writings of James Madison, comprising his public papers and his private correspondence, for the first time printed* (Madison's report on the debate and resolution, ed. 1865) IV: 515-55. Shaler, *Kentucky* (complete work), pp. 409-16. Warfield, *Kentucky Resolutions of 1789*. Henry Steele Commager, ed., *Documents of American History*, 2 vols. (NY: F.S. Crofts and Company, 1934; Appleton-Century-Crofts, Inc., 1948, 6th edition, 1958; Englewood Cliffs, NJ: Prentice Hall, Inc., 9th edition, 1973), p. 179. David Barton, *The Myth of Separation* (Aledo, TX: WallBuilder Press, 1991), p. 174.

[23] **State of Kentucky.** Henry S. Morris, *Acts & Facts* (El Cajon, CA: Institute For Creation Research, February 1993), Vol. 22, No. 2, p. 4.

[24] **Johann Kepler.** Sir David Brewster, biography. Stephen Abbott Northrop, D.D., *A Cloud of Witnesses* (Portland, OR: American Heritage Ministries, 1987; Mantle Ministries, 228 Still Ridge, Bulverde, Texas), p. 266. Henry M. Morris, *Men of Science - Men of God* (El Cajon, CA: Master Books, Creation Life Publishers, Inc., 1990), pp. 11-13.

[25] **Johann Kepler.** *Harmony of Worlds.* Stephen Abbott Northrop, D.D., *A Cloud of Witnesses* (Portland, OR: American Heritage Ministries, 1987; Mantle Ministries, 228 Still Ridge, Bulverde, Texas), p. 266.

[26] **Johann Kepler.** *Homage to the Book*, p. 84. Stephen Abbott Northrop, D.D., *A Cloud of Witnesses* (Portland, Oregon: American Heritage Ministries, 1987; Mantle Ministries, 228 Still Ridge, Bulverde, Texas), p. 266.

[27] **Francis Scott Key.** May 21, 22, 28, 1958, Hearings before the Subcommittee No. 4 of the Committee of the Judiciary, 85th Congress, 2nd Session, p. 6. Catherine Millard, *A Children's Companion Guide to America's History* (Camp Hill, PA: Horizon House Publishers, 1993), p. 1.

[28] **Francis Scott Key.** Tim LaHaye, *Faith of Our Founding Fathers* (Brentwood, TN: Wolgemuth & Hyatt, Publishers, Inc., 1987), p. 95. Charles Wallis, ed., *Our American Heritage* (NY: Harper & Row, Publishers, Inc., 1970), p. 144. Catherine Millard, *The Rewriting of America's History* (Camp Hill, PA: Horizon House Publishers, 1991), p. 272. D.P. Diffine, Ph.D., *One Nation Under God - How Close a Separation?* (Searcy, Arkansas: Harding University, Belden Center for Private Enterprise Education, 6th edition, 1992), p. 17.

[29] **Francis Scott Key.** *Praise for Pardoning Grace.* Stephen Abbott Northrop, D.D., *A Cloud of Witnesses* (Portland, Oregon: American Heritage Ministries, 1987; Mantle Ministries, 228 Still Ridge, Bulverde, Texas), p. 267.

[30] **Francis Scott Key.** February 22, 1812, in *An Oration before the Washington Society of Alexandria*, p. 9. Library of Congress Rare Book Collection. Catherine Millard, *A Children's Companion Guide to America's History* (Camp Hill, PA: Horizon House Publishers, 1993), p. 1.

[31] **Joyce Kilmer.** 1913, in his poem "Trees." John Bartlett, *Bartlett's Familiar Quotations* (Boston: Little, Brown and Company, 1855, 1980), p. 795.

[32] **Cyrus King.** David C. Mearns, *The Story Up to Now* (Washington: The Library of Congress, 1947), p. 19. Tim LaHaye, *Faith of Our Founding Fathers* (Brentwood, TN: Wolgemuth & Hyatt, Publishers, Inc., 1987), p. 162.

[33] **Martin Luther King, Jr.** December 31, 1955, in an address at Montgomery, Alabama. Carroll E. Simcox, comp., *4400 Quotations for Christian Communicators* (Grand Rapids, MI: Baker Book House, 1991), p. 49.

[34] **Martin Luther King, Jr.** August 28, 1963, on the occasion of the Civil Rights March on Washington. *The SCLC Story in Words and Pictures*, 1964, pp. 50-51. *The Annals of America*, 20 vols. (Chicago, IL: Encyclopedia Britannica, Inc., 1976), Vol. 18, pp. 156-159. John Bartlett, *Bartlett's Familiar Quotations* (Boston: Little, Brown and Company, 1855, 1980), p. 909.

[35] **Martin Luther King, Jr.** December 11, 1964, in accepting the Nobel Peace Prize. John Bartlett, *Bartlett's Familiar Quotations* (Boston: Little, Brown and Company, 1855, 1980), p. 909.

[36] **Martin Luther King, Jr.** *The Trumpet of Conscience.* Carroll E. Simcox, comp., *4400 Quotations for Christian Communicators* (Grand Rapids, MI: Baker Book House, 1991), p. 370.

[37] **Martin Luther King, Jr.** *Bless Your Heart (series II)* (Eden Prairie, MN: Heartland Samplers, Inc., 1990), 1.16.

[38] **Martin Luther King, Jr.** April 3, 1968, in an address at Birmingham, Alabama, the night before his death. Carroll E. Simcox, comp., *4400 Quotations for Christian Communicators* (Grand Rapids, MI: Baker Book House, 1991), p. 168.

[39] **Rufus King.** M.E. Bradford, *A Worthy Company* (Marlborough, NH: Plymouth Rock Foundation, 1982), p. 15. Tim LaHaye, *Faith of Our Founding Fathers* (Brentwood, TN: Wolgemuth & Hyatt, Publishers, Inc., 1987), p. 161.

[40] **(Joseph) Rudyard Kipling.** In *Gunga Din*. Lewis C. Henry, *Best Quotations For All Occasions* (Greenwich, CONN: Fawcett Publications, Inc., 1961), p. 143.

[41] **(Joseph) Rudyard Kipling.** Recessional, *Jubilee Hymn on the Queen Victoria's Reign*. Stephen Abbott Northrop, D.D., *A Cloud of Witnesses* (Portland, OR: American Heritage Ministries, 1987; Mantle Ministries, 228 Still Ridge, Bulverde, Texas), p. 266.

⁴² **(Joseph) Rudyard Kipling.** 1899, *Recessional - Jubilee Hymn on the Queen Victoria's Reign.* Stephen Abbott Northrop, D.D., *A Cloud of Witnesses* (Portland, OR: American Heritage Ministries, 1987; Mantle Ministries, 228 Still Ridge, Bulverde, Texas), p. 266. John Bartlett, *Bartlett's Familiar Quotations* (Boston: Little, Brown and Company, 1855, 1980), p. 709.

⁴³ **(Joseph) Rudyard Kipling.** In his *Ballad of East and West.* Lewis C. Henry, *Best Quotations For All Occasions* (Greenwich, CONN: Fawcett Publications, Inc., 1961), p. 33.

⁴⁴ **(Joseph) Rudyard Kipling.** *The Glory of the Garden,* st. 8. John Bartlett, *Bartlett's Familiar Quotations* (Boston: Little, Brown and Company, 1855, 1980), p. 710.

⁴⁵ **William Kirby.** Title of a scientific treatises he had written. Henry M. Morris, *Men of Science - Men of God* (El Cajon, CA: Master Books, Creation Life Publishers, Inc., 1990), pp. 43-44.

⁴⁶ **John Knox.** Inscription on the Reformation Monument in Geneva, Switzerland. John Bartlett, *Bartlett's Familiar Quotations* (Boston: Little, Brown and Company, 1855, 1980), p. 162.

L

¹ **Edwin Herbert Land.** 1977, in a reply when shown a balance sheet of a product. John Bartlett, *Bartlett's Familiar Quotations* (Boston: Little, Brown and Company, 1855, 1980), p. 876.

² **Walter Savage Landor.** Tryon Edwards, D.D., *The New Dictionary of Thoughts - A Cyclopedia of Quotations* (Garden City, NY: Hanover House, 1852; revised and enlarged by C.H. Catrevas, Ralph Emerson Browns and Jonathan Edwards [descendent, along with Tryon, of Jonathan Edwards (1703-1758), president of Princeton], 1891; The Standard Book Company, 1955, 1963), p. 46.

³ **John Langdon.** M.E. Bradford, *A Worthy Company* (Marlborough, NH: Plymouth Rock Foundation, 1982), p. 2. Tim LaHaye, *Faith of Our Founding Fathers* (Brentwood, TN: Wolgemuth & Hyatt, Publishers, Inc., 1987), p. 163.

⁴ **John Langdon.** October 21, 1785, John Langdon, as President (Governor) of New Hampshire, made an official *Proclamation for a General Thanksgiving.* Tim LaHaye, *Faith of Our Founding Fathers* (Brentwood, TN: Wolgemuth & Hyatt, Publishers, Inc., 1987), pp. 165-166.

⁵ **John Langdon.** February 21, 1786, John Langdon, as President (Governor) of the State of New Hampshire, issued *A Proclamation for a Day of Public Fasting and Prayer.* Tim LaHaye, *Faith of Our Founding Fathers* (Brentwood, TN: Wolgemuth & Hyatt, Publishers, Inc., 1987), pp. 163-165.

⁶ **John Langdon.** *John Langdon of New Hampshire,* p. 285. Tim LaHaye, *Faith of Our Founding Fathers* (Brentwood, TN: Wolgemuth & Hyatt, Publishers, Inc., 1987), p. 167.

⁷ **John Langdon.** *John Langdon of New Hampshire,* p. 286. Tim LaHaye, *Faith of Our Founding Fathers* (Brentwood, TN: Wolgemuth & Hyatt, Publishers, Inc., 1987), p. 167.

⁸ **Samuel Langdon.** May 31, 1775, address as Harvard President to the Provincial Congress of Massachusetts. May 31, 1775, in "The Wall," Election Day sermon, A.W. Plumstead, *The Wall and the Garden, Selected Massachusetts Election Sermons, 1670-1775* (Minneapolis: University of Minnesota Press, 1968), pp. 364-373. Verna M. Hall, *Christian History of the American Revolution - Consider and Ponder* (San Francisco: Foundation for American Christian Education, 1976), p. 506. Lucille Johnston, *Celebrations of a Nation* (Arlington, VA: The Year of Thanksgiving Foundation, 1987), p. 77. Peter Marshall and David Manuel, *The Light and the Glory* (Old Tappan, NJ: Fleming H. Revell, 1977), pp. 277-278. Peter Marshall and David Manuel, *The Glory of America* (Bloomington, MN: Garborg's Heart 'N Home, Inc., 1991), 6.3.

⁹ **Bartolome' de Las Casas.** 1530, in his *Apologetic History of the Indies (Apologetica Historia de las Indias),* ch. 48, translated by George Sanderlin. John Bartlett, *Bartlett's Familiar Quotations* (Boston: Little, Brown and Company, 1855, 1980), p. 154.

¹⁰ **Bartolome' de Las Casas.** 1550-1563, in the prologue of his book, *Historia de las Indias,* translated by Rachel Phillips. John Bartlett, *Bartlett's Familiar Quotations* (Boston: Little, Brown and Company, 1855, 1980), p. 154.

¹¹ **Hugh Latimer.** October 16, 1555, spoke his last words to Nicholas Ridley as they were being brought to their execution in Oxford, England. J.R Green, *A Short History of the English People* (1874), ch. 7. John Bartlett, *Bartlett's Familiar Quotations* (Boston: Little, Brown and Company, 1855, 1980), p. 158.

¹² **William Edward Hartpole Lecky.** William E. Lecky, *History of European Morals from Augustus to Charlemagne* (New York: Arno, 1975). William Cantelon, *New Money or None?* (Plainfield, NJ: Logos International, 1979), pp. 245-246.

¹³ **Richard Henry Lee.** *Journals of Congress,* Volume III, pp. 467-468. Stephen Abbott Northrop, D.D., *A Cloud of Witnesses* (Portland, Oregon: American Heritage Ministries, 1987; Mantle Ministries, 228 Still Ridge, Bulverde, Texas), pp. 279-280.

¹⁴ **Robert Edward Lee.** In a letter to his sister after resigning from the U.S. Army. *American Peoples Encyclopedia,* (Chicago: Spencer Press, 1954), Vol. 12, p. 120317. Catherine Millard, *The Rewriting of America's History* (Camp Hill, PA: Horizon House Publishers, 1991), p. 184.

¹⁵ **Robert Edward Lee.** December 27, 1956, in a letter to his wife. Ralston B. Lattimore, *The Story of Robert E. Lee, as told in his own words and those of his contemporaries* (Washington, D.C.: Colortone Press, 1964), pp. 22-23. Catherine Millard, *The Rewriting of America's History* (Camp Hill, PA: Horizon House Publishers, 1991), p. 184.

¹⁶ **Robert Edward Lee.** April 13, 1859, General Thomas Jonathan "Stonewall" Jackson, writing in a letter to his wife, Mary Ann Jackson. Prof. R.L. Dabney, D.D., *Life and Campaigns of Lieut.-General Thomas J. (Stonewall) Jackson* (Harrisonburg, VA: Sprinkle Publications, 1983), p. 329. Peter Marshall & David Manuel, *The Glory of America* (Bloomington, MN: Garborg's Heart 'N Home, 1991), 4.13.

¹⁷ **Robert Edward Lee.** December 25, 1862, in a letter to his wife from Fredericksburg, Virginia. Captain Robert E. Lee, *Recollections and Letters of General Robert E. Lee by his son* (New York: Doubleday, Page and Company, 1924), pp. 88-89. Catherine Millard, *The Rewriting of America's History* (Camp Hill, PA: Horizon House Publishers, 1991), pp. 186-187.

¹⁸ **Robert Edward Lee.** Captain Robert E. Lee, *Recollections and Letters of General Robert E. Lee by his son* (New York: Doubleday, Page and Company, 1924), p. 95. Peter Marshall and David Manuel, *The Glory of America* (Bloomington, MN: Garborg's Heart'N Home, Inc., 1991), 5.31.

¹⁹ **Robert Edward Lee.** April 8, 1864, issuing orders concurring with Confederate President Davis' proclamation of a day of fasting, humiliation, and prayer. John Williams Jones, D.D., *Christ in the Camp* (Richmond, VA: B.F. Johnson & Co., 1887, 1897; The Martin & Hoyt Co., 1904; Harrisonburg, VA: Sprinkle Publications, 1986), p. 58. Peter Marshall and David Manuel, *The Glory of America* (Bloomington, MN: Garborg's Heart'N Home, Inc., 1991), 4.8.

²⁰ **Robert Edward Lee.** Robert Flood, comp., *The Rebirth of America* (Philadelphia: Arthur S. DeMoss Foundation, 1986), p. 183.

Notes

Peter Marshall and David Manuel, *The Glory of America* (Bloomington, MN: Garborg's Heart'N Home, Inc., 1991), 7.28. D.P. Diffine, Ph.D., *One Nation Under God - How Close a Separation?* (Searcy, Arkansas: Harding University, Belden Center for Private Enterprise Education, 6th edition, 1992), p. 15.

[21] **Robert Edward Lee.** Young, *Marse Robert*, p. 344. Peter Marshall and David Manuel, *The Glory of America* (Bloomington, MN: Garborg's Heart'N Home, Inc., 1991), 8.9.

[22] **Robert Edward Lee.** In a meeting with Chaplains Jones and Lacey. John Williams Jones, D.D., *Christ in the Camp* (Richmond, VA: B.F. Johnson & Co., 1887, 1897; The Martin & Hoyt Co., 1904; Harrisonburg, VA: Sprinkle Publications, 1986), p. 50. Peter Marshall and David Manuel, *The Glory of America* (Bloomington, MN: Garborg's Heart'N Home, Inc., 1991), 3.7. D.P. Diffine, Ph.D., *One Nation Under God - How Close a Separation?* (Searcy, Arkansas: Harding University, Belden Center for Private Enterprise Education, 6th edition, 1992), p. 15.

[23] **Robert Edward Lee.** John William Jones, *Reminiscences*, p. 319. Peter Marshall and David Manuel, *The Glory of America* (Bloomington, MN: Garborg's Heart'N Home, Inc., 1991), 4.3.

[24] **Robert Edward Lee.** William J. Johnson, *Robert E. Lee, The Christian* (NY: Abington Press), p. 151. Peter Marshall and David Manuel, *The Glory of America* (Bloomington, MN: Garborg's Heart 'N Home, Inc., 1991), 4.10.

[25] **Robert Edward Lee.** April 10, 1865, in his final order to the Army of Northern Virginia. Charles W. Eliot, LL.D., ed., *American Historical Documents 1000-1904* (New York: P.F. Collier & Son Company, *The Harvard Classics*, 1910), Vol. 43, p. 449. Raymond A. St. John, *American Literature for Christian Schools* (Greenville, SC: Bob Jones University Press, Inc., 1979), p. 388. Lillian W. Kay, ed., *The Ground on Which We Stand - Basic Documents of American History* (NY: Franklin Watts., Inc, 1969), p. 207.

[26] **Robert Edward Lee.** Henry H. Halley, *Halley's Bible Handbook* (Grand Rapids, MI: Zondervan Publishing House, 1927, 1965), p. 19.

[27] **Robert Edward Lee.** June 4, 1865. Flood, *Lee*, pp. 65-66. Peter Marshall and David Manuel, *The Glory of America* (Bloomington, MN: Garborg's Heart'N Home, Inc., 1991), 6.4.

[28] **Robert Edward Lee.** William J. Johnson, *Robert E. Lee, The Christian* (NY: The Abington Press), p. 156. Peter Marshall and David Manuel, *The Glory of America* (Bloomington, MN: Garborg's Heart'N Home, Inc., 1991), 6.22.

[29] **Robert Edward Lee.** Pitts, *Chaplains*, p. 120. Peter Marshall and David Manuel, *The Glory of America* (Bloomington, MN: Garborg's Heart'N Home, Inc., 1991), 5.21.

[30] **Robert Edward Lee.** John William Jones, *Lee*. Peter Marshall and David Manuel, *The Glory of America* (Bloomington, MN: Garborg's Heart'N Home, Inc., 1991), 10.29. John Esten Cooke, *A Life of General Lee*, pp. 492-494. Stephen Abbott Northrop, D.D., *A Cloud of Witnesses* (Portland, Oregon: American Heritage Ministries, 1987; Mantle Ministries, 228 Still Ridge, Bulverde, Texas), p. 279.

[31] **Paul Lemoine.** Writing in an article. Henry M. Morris, *Men of Science - Men of God* (El Cajon, CA: Master Books, Creation Life Publishers, Inc., 1990), p. 84.

[32] **"C.S." Clive Staples Lewis.** Statement. Philip Schaff, *The Person of Jesus* (New York: American Tract Society), p. 40. Willard Cantelon, *New Money or None?* (Plainfield, NJ: Logos International, 1979), p. 243.

[33] **"C.S." Clive Staples Lewis.** 1942, in his work, *The Screwtape Letters*. Carroll E. Simcox, comp., *4400 Quotations for Christian Communicators* (Grand Rapids, MI: Baker Book House, 1991), p. 190. John Bartlett, *Bartlett's Familiar Quotations* (Boston: Little, Brown and Company, 1855, 1980), p. 842.

[34] **"C.S." Clive Staples Lewis.** 1952, in his work entitled, *Mere Christianity*. Carroll E. Simcox, comp., *4400 Quotations for Christian Communicators* (Grand Rapids, MI: Baker Book House, 1991), p. 207.

[35] **"C.S." Clive Staples Lewis.** Statement. *Bless Your Heart (series II)* (Eden Prairie, MN: Heartland Samplers, Inc., 1990), 1.18.

[36] **Liberty Bell.** Committee on the Restoration of Independence Hall, Mayor's Office. *Report.* Philadelphia, June 12, 1873. Library of Congress Rare Book Collection, Washington, D.C., pp. 2-3. Catherine Millard, *A Children's Companion Guide to America's History* (Camp Hill, PA: Horizon House Publishers, 1993), p. 31.

[37] **Liberty Bell.** "Our Christian Heritage," *Letter from Plymouth Rock* (Marlborough, NH: The Plymouth Rock Foundation), p. 2. D.P. Diffine, Ph.D., *One Nation Under God - How Close a Separation?* (Searcy, Arkansas: Harding University, Belden Center for Private Enterprise Education, 6th edition, 1992), p. 5.

[38] **Liberty Bell.** July 8, 1776. David Barton, *The Myth of Separation* (Aledo, TX: WallBuilder Press, 1991), p. 100.

[39] **Liberty Bell.** 1835. Catherine Millard, *The Rewriting of America's History* (Camp Hill, PA: Horizon House Publishers, 1991), p. 265.

[40] **Statue of Liberty Enlightening the World.** Frederic Auguste Bartholdi, sculptor, *The Statue of Liberty Enlightening the World* (New York: North American Review, Published for the benefit of the Pedestal Fund, 1885). Catherine Millard, *The Rewriting of America's History* (Camp Hill, PA: Horizon House Publishers, 1991), p. 329.

[41] **Statue of Liberty Enlightening the World.** October 28, 1886, prayer by Reverend Richard S. Storrs, D.D. opening the inauguration ceremony. *Inauguration of the Statue of Liberty Enlightening the World, by the President of the United States* (New York: D. Appleton and Company, 1887), pp. 18-21. Catherine Millard, *The Rewriting of America's History* (Camp Hill, PA: Horizon House Publishers, 1991), pp. 330-331.

[42] **Liberty Tree Flag.** 1776, adopted by the Massachusetts Council. *The World Book Encyclopedia*, 18 vols. (Chicago, IL: Field Enterprises, Inc., 1957; W.F. Quarrie and Company, 8 vols., 1917; World Book, Inc., 22 vols., 1989), Vol. 2, p. 917; Vol. 6, p. 2590b-c.

[43] **Library of Congress.** July 27, 1962, Senator Robert Byrd of West Virginia, in a message delivered in Congress two days after the Supreme Court declared prayer in schools unconstitutional. Robert Flood, *The Rebirth of America* (Philadelphia: Arthur S. DeMoss Foundation, 1986), pp. 66-69. Gary DeMar, *America's Christian History: The Untold Story* (Atlanta, GA: American Vision Publishers, Inc., 1993), p. 55.

[44] **Library of Congress.** July 27, 1962, Senator Robert Byrd of West Virginia, in a message delivered in Congress two days after the Supreme Court declared prayer in schools unconstitutional. Robert Flood, *The Rebirth of America* (Philadelphia: Arthur S. DeMoss Foundation, 1986), pp. 66-69. Gary DeMar, *America's Christian History: The Untold Story* (Atlanta, GA: American Vision Publishers, Inc., 1993), p. 55.

[45] **Library of Congress.** July 27, 1962, Senator Robert Byrd of West Virginia, in a message delivered in Congress two days after the Supreme Court declared prayer in schools unconstitutional. Robert Flood, *The Rebirth of America* (Philadelphia: Arthur S. DeMoss Foundation, 1986), pp. 66-69.

[46] **Rush Limbaugh.** COPYRIGHT© 1993 by Rush H. Limbaugh III, in his book, *See, I Told You So* (New York, NY: reprinted by

permission of Pocket Books, a division of Simon & Schuster Inc., 1993), pp. 69-73.
⁴⁷ Rush Limbaugh. COPYRIGHT© 1993 by Rush H. Limbaugh III, in his book, *See, I Told You So* (New York, NY: reprinted by permission of Pocket Books, a division of Simon & Schuster Inc., 1993), pp. 309-322.
⁴⁸ Rush Limbaugh. COPYRIGHT© 1993 by Rush H. Limbaugh III, in his book, *See, I Told You So* (New York, NY: reprinted by permission of Pocket Books, a division of Simon & Schuster Inc., 1993), p. 34.
⁴⁹ Abraham Lincoln. 1837, at age 28, in a letter to a pro-slavery friend, Joshua Speed. Roy P. Basler, ed., *The Collected Works of Abraham Lincoln* (New Brunswick, N.J.: Rutgers University Press, 1953), Vol. 2, p. 320. Peter Marshall and David Manuel, *From Sea to Shining Sea* (Old Tappan, N.J.: Fleming H. Revell Company, 1986), p. 403.
⁵⁰ Abraham Lincoln. January 27, 1837, in an address. *Letters and Addresses of Abraham Lincoln* (NY: Unit Book Publishing Co., 1907), p. 8. David Barton, *The Myth of Separation*, (Aledo, TX: WallBuilder Press, 1991), pp. 71, 247.
⁵¹ Abraham Lincoln. August 15, 1846, in a public statement published in the *Illinois Gazette*, August 15, 1846, during his race for the Congressional seat of the Seventh District of Illinois. P. Thomas Benjamin, *Abraham Lincoln* (New York: Knopf, 1953), pp. 108-109. Carl Sandberg, *Lincoln's Devotional* (NY: Channel Press, Inc., 1957), introduction. Edmund Fuller and David E. Green, *God in the White House - The Faiths of American Presidents* (NY: Crown Publishers, Inc., 1968), p. 170-108. Mark A. Knoll, *The Puzzling Faith of Abraham Lincoln* (Carol Stream, IL: Christian History), Vol. XI, No. 1, Issue 33, p. 14. Gary DeMar, "Why the Religious Right is Right...Almost" (Atlanta, GA: *The Biblical Worldview*, An American Vision Publication - American Vision, Inc., November 1992), pp. 8-9. Gary DeMar, *America's Christian History: The Untold Story* (Atlanta, GA: American Vision Publishers, Inc., 1993), p. 101.
⁵² Abraham Lincoln. 1851, in a letter to his step-brother on the occasion of his father's final illness. John G. Nicolay and John Hay, eds., *The Complete Works of Abraham Lincoln: Speeches, Letters and State Papers* (1905), 2:574. Clarence Edward Macartney, *Lincoln and the Bible* (Nashville, TN: Abingdon-Cokesbury Press, 1949), pp. 35-36. Mark A. Knoll, *The Puzzling Faith of Abraham Lincoln* (Carol Stream, IL: Christian History), Vol. XI, No. 1, Issue 33, p. 13. Gary DeMar, *America's Christian History: The Untold Story* (Atlanta, GA: American Vision Publishers, Inc., 1993), p. 98.
⁵³ Abraham Lincoln. August 24, 1855, in a letter to Joshua F. Speed. John Bartlett, *Bartlett's Familiar Quotations* (Boston: Little, Brown and Company, 1863, 1980), p. 520. Pat Robertson, *America's Dates With Destiny* (Nashville, TN: Thomas Nelson Publishers, 1986), pp. 155-156.
⁵⁴ Abraham Lincoln. 1858, in the closing remarks of a debate with Judge Douglas. Carroll E. Simcox, *3000 Quotations on Christian Themes* (Grand Rapids, MI: Baker Book House, 1989), p. 202, No. 2455.
⁵⁵ Abraham Lincoln. July 10, 1858, Chicago, Illinois, in a debate with Stephen A. Douglas. Osborn H. Oldroyd, ed., *The Lincoln Memorial Album of Immortelles*. Stephen Abbott Northrop, D.D., *A Cloud of Witnesses* (Portland, OR: American Heritage Ministries, 1987; Mantle Ministries, 228 Still Ridge, Bulverde, Texas), p. 258.
⁵⁶ Abraham Lincoln. September 11, 1858, in a speech at Edwardsville, Illinois. John Bartlett, *Bartlett's Familiar Quotations* (Boston: Little, Brown and Company, 1863, 1980), p. 520. Pat Robertson, *America's Dates With Destiny* (Nashville, TN: Thomas Nelson Publishers, 1986), p. 156.
⁵⁷ Abraham Lincoln. April 6, 1859, in a letter to H.L. Pierce and others. John Bartlett, *Bartlett's Familiar Quotations* (Boston: Little, Brown and Company, 1863, 1980), p. 521. Pat Robertson, *America's Dates With Destiny* (Nashville, TN: Thomas Nelson Publishers, 1986), p. 156.
⁵⁸ Abraham Lincoln. February 11, 1861, Springfield, Illinois, in a *Farewell Address* to his home as he left for Washington, D.C. John Bartlett, *Bartlett's Familiar Quotations* (Boston: Little, Brown and Company, 1855, 1980), p. 521. Christine F. Hart, *One Nation Under God* (NJ: American Tract Society, reprinted by Gospel Tract Society, Inc., Independence, Mo.), p. 3. "Unless the great God who assisted him [Washington] shall be with me and aid me, I must fail: but if the same omniscient mind and mighty arm that directed and protected him shall guide and support me, I shall not fail - I shall succeed. Let us all pray that the God of our fathers may not forsake us now." Carroll E. Simcox, *3000 Quotations on Christian Themes* (Grand Rapids, MI: Baker Book House, 1989), p. 12, No. 115.
⁵⁹ Abraham Lincoln. February 22, 1861, in a speech at Independence Hall, Philadelphia. John Bartlett, *Bartlett's Familiar Quotations* (Boston: Little, Brown and Company, 1863, 1980), pp. 520-524. Pat Robertson, *America's Dates With Destiny* (Nashville, TN: Thomas Nelson Publishers, 1986), p. 156.
⁶⁰ Abraham Lincoln. February 23, 1861, in a reply to William Dodge. L.E. Chittenden (Register of the Treasury under President Lincoln), *Recollections of President Lincoln, and his Administration*, p. 76. Peter Marshall and David Manuel, *The Glory of America* (Bloomington, MN: Garborg's Heart'N Home, Inc., 1991), 2.23. D.P. Diffine, Ph.D., *One Nation Under God - How Close a Separation?* (Searcy, Arkansas: Harding University, Belden Center for Private Enterprise Education, 6th edition, 1992), p. 13.
⁶¹ Abraham Lincoln. March 4, 1861, Monday, in his First Inaugural Address. James D. Richardson (U.S. Representative from Tennessee), ed., *A Compilation of the Messages and Papers of the Presidents 1789-1897*, 10 vols. (Washington, D.C.: U.S. Government Printing Office, published by Authority of Congress, 1897, 1899; Washington, D.C.: Bureau of National Literature and Art, 1789-1902, 11 vols., 1907, 1910), Vol. VI, pp. 9-11. *Inaugural Addresses of the Presidents of the United States - From George Washington 1789 to Richard Milhous Nixon 1969* (Washington, D.C.: United States Government Printing Office; 91st Congress, 1st Session, House Document 91-142, 1969), pp. 119-126. Benjamin Franklin Morris, *The Christian Life and Character of the Civil Institutions of the United States* (Philadelphia: George W. Childs, 1864), p. 611. Charles W. Eliot, LL.D., ed., *American Historical Documents 1000-1904* (New York: P.F. Collier & Son Company, *The Harvard Classics*, 1910), Vol. 43, pp. 334-343. Albert J. Beveridge, *The Life of John Marshall* (Boston: Houghton Mifflin, 1919), Vol. VI, p. 9. Roy Basler, ed., *Collected Works of Abraham Lincoln* (Rutgers University Press, 1953), Vol. IV, p. 271. Paul M. Angle, ed., *By These Words* (NY: Rand McNally & Company, 1954), p. 228. Davis Newton Lott, *The Inaugural Addresses of the American Presidents* (NY: Holt, Rinehart and Winston, 1961), p. 122. Richard D. Heffner, *A Documentary History of the United States* (New York: The New American Library of World Literature, Inc., 1961), pp. 144-146. Charles E. Rice, *The Supreme Court and Public Prayer* (New York: Fordham University Press, 1964), p. 184. David Barton, *The Myth of Separation* (Aledo, TX: WallBuilder Press, 1991), p. 242. Mark A. Knoll, *The Puzzling Faith of Abraham Lincoln* (Carol Stream, IL: Christian History), Vol. XI, No. 1, Issue 33, p. 11. William McKinley, July 4, 1892, while serving as Governor of Ohio, quoted Lincoln in an address to the Baptist Young People's Union in Lakeside, Ohio. Stephen Abbott Northrop, D.D., *A Cloud of Witnesses* (Portland, OR: American Heritage Ministries, 1987; Mantle Ministries, 228 Still Ridge, Bulverde, Texas), p. 313. William Safire, ed., *Lend Me Your Ears - Great Speeches in History* (NY: W.W. Norton & Company 1992), p. 746. J. Michael Sharman, J.D., *Faith of the Fathers* (Culpepper, Virginia: Victory Publishing, 1995), p. 58.
⁶² Abraham Lincoln. 1861, in an address to the New Jersey State Senate. Trueblood, *Abraham Lincoln: Theologian of American*

Anguish, p. 9. Peter Marshall and David Manuel, *The Glory of America* (Bloomington, MN: Garborg's Heart'N Home, Inc., 1991), 5.12.
63 Abraham Lincoln. In statement to Noah Brooks. Tryon Edwards, D.D., *The New Dictionary of Thoughts - A Cyclopedia of Quotations* (Garden City, NY: Hanover House, 1852; revised and enlarged by C.H. Catrevas, Ralph Emerson Browns and Jonathan Edwards [descendent, along with Tryon, of Jonathan Edwards (1703-1758), president of Princeton], 1891; The Standard Book Company, 1955, 1963), p. 486. Trueblood, *Abraham Lincoln: Theologian of American Anguish,* p. 76. Robert Flood, *The Rebirth of America* (Philadelphia: Arthur S. DeMoss Foundation, 1986), p. 182. *Bless Your Heart (series II)* (Eden Prairie, MN: Heartland Sampler, Inc., 1990), 12.18. *Christianity Today,* February 11, 1991. Peter Marshall and David Manuel, *The Glory of America* (Bloomington, MN: Garborg's Heart'N Home, Inc., 1991), 5.24.
64 Abraham Lincoln. August 12, 1861, in a Proclamation of a *National Day of Humiliation, Prayer, and Fasting,* issued after the Union army was defeated at the *Battle of Bull Run.* James D. Richardson (U.S. Representative from Tennessee), ed., *A Compilation of the Messages and Papers of the Presidents 1789-1897,* 10 vols. (Washington, D.C.: U.S. Government Printing Office, published by Authority of Congress, 1897, 1899; Washington, D.C.: Bureau of National Literature and Art, 1789-1902, 11 vols., 1907, 1910), Vol. VI, pp. 36-37. Benjamin Franklin Morris, *The Christian Life and Character of the Civil Institutions of the United States* (Philadelphia: George W. Childs, 1864), p. 557. William J. Johnson, *Abraham Lincoln, The Christian* (NY: The Abington Press, 1913), p. 76. Trueblood, *Abraham Lincoln: Theologian of American Anguish,* pp. 76-86. Peter Marshall and David Manuel, *The Glory of America* (Bloomington, MN: Garborg's Heart'N Home, Inc., 1991), 9.26, 8:12.
65 Abraham Lincoln. August 12, 1861, in a Proclamation of a *National Day of Humiliation, Prayer, and Fasting,* issued after the Union army was defeated at the *Battle of Bull Run.* James D. Richardson (U.S. Representative from Tennessee), ed., *A Compilation of the Messages and Papers of the Presidents 1789-1897,* 10 vols. (Washington, D.C.: U.S. Government Printing Office, published by Authority of Congress, 1897, 1899; Washington, D.C.: Bureau of National Literature and Art, 1789-1902, 11 vols., 1907, 1910), Vol. VI, pp. 36-37. Benjamin Franklin Morris, *The Christian Life and Character of the Civil Institutions of the United States* (Philadelphia: George W. Childs, 1864), p. 557. William J. Johnson, *Abraham Lincoln, The Christian* (NY: The Abington Press, 1913), p. 76. Trueblood, *Abraham Lincoln: Theologian of American Anguish,* pp. 76-86. Peter Marshall and David Manuel, *The Glory of America* (Bloomington, MN: Garborg's Heart'N Home, Inc., 1991), 9.26, 8:12.
66 Abraham Lincoln. May 23, 1862, restoring land back to the Missions in California after the 1833 *Mexican Secularization Act. Act of Congress* (San Diego, CA: Museum of San Diego de Alcala). Catherine Millard, *The Rewriting of America's History* (Camp Hill, PA: Horizon House Publishers, 1991), p. 223.
67 Abraham Lincoln. June of 1862, in speaking to James Wilson, chairman of the House Judiciary Committee. Trueblood, *Abraham Lincoln: Theologian of American Anguish,* p. 126. Peter Marshall and David Manuel, *The Glory of America* (Bloomington, MN: Garborg's Heart'N Home, Inc., 1991), 6.23.
68 Abraham Lincoln. August 14, 1862, in delivering an address on colonization to a Negro deputation at Washington, D.C. John Bartlett, *Bartlett's Familiar Quotations* (Boston: Little, Brown and Company, 1855, 1980), p. 522. Carroll E. Simcox, *3000 Quotations on Christian Themes* (Grand Rapids, MI: Baker Book House, 1989), p. 210, No. 2561.
69 Abraham Lincoln. September of 1862, in addressing a delegation from Chicago. William J. Johnson, *Abraham Lincoln, The Christian* (NY: The Abington Press, 1913), p. 94. Carroll E. Simcox, *3000 Quotations on Christian Themes* (Grand Rapids, MI: Baker Book House, 1989), p. 14, No. 130. Peter Marshall and David Manuel, *The Glory of America* (Bloomington, MN: Garborg's Heart'N Home, Inc., 1991), 9.17.
70 Abraham Lincoln. September 1862, in his *Meditations on the Divine Will,* written after the Union lost the *Second Battle of Bull Run,* August 29-30, 1862. John G. Nicolay and John Hay, eds., *The Complete Works of Abraham Lincoln: Speeches, Letters and State Papers* (1905). William J. Johnson, *Abraham Lincoln: The Christian* (NY: The Abington Press, 1913), pp. 94, 98. Charles Fadiman, ed., *The American Treasury* (NY: Harper & Brothers, Publishers, 1955), pp. 381, 391. Edmund Fuller and David E. Green, *God in the White House - The Faiths of American Presidents* (NY: Crown Publishers, Inc., 1968), p. 113. Mark A. Knoll, *The Puzzling Faith of Abraham Lincoln* (Carol Stream, IL: Christian History), Vol. XI, No. 1, Issue 33, p. 11. D.P. Diffine, Ph.D., *One Nation Under God - How Close a Separation?* (Searcy, Arkansas: Harding University, Belden Center for Private Enterprise Education, 6th edition, 1992), p. 14.
71 Abraham Lincoln. September 22, 1862, in addressing his Cabinet after the massive Confederate Army lost to the Union troops at the *Battle at Antietam.* Frank B. Carpenter, *Six Months at the White House* (1866), p. 89. Peter Marshall and David Manuel, *The Glory of America* (Bloomington, MN: Garborg's Heart'N Home, Inc., 1991), 9.22.
72 Abraham Lincoln. September 22, 1862, in the *Emancipation Proclamation,* to go into effect January 1, 1863. John Bartlett, *Bartlett's Familiar Quotations* (Boston: Little, Brown and Company, 1855, 1980), p. 522. James D. Richardson (U.S. Representative from Tennessee), ed., *A Compilation of the Messages and Papers of the Presidents 1789-1897,* 10 vols. (Washington, D.C.: U.S. Government Printing Office, published by Authority of Congress, 1897, 1899; Washington, D.C.: Bureau of National Literature and Art, 1789-1902, 11 vols., 1907, 1910), Vol. VI, pp. 157-159. Charles W. Eliot, LL.D., ed., *American Historical Documents 1000-1904* (New York: P.F. Collier & Son Company, *The Harvard Classics,* 1910), Vol. 43, pp. 344-346. Henry Steele Commager, ed., *Documents of American History,* 2 vols. (NY: F.S. Crofts and Company, 1934; Appleton-Century-Crofts, Inc., 1948, 6th edition, 1958; Englewood Cliffs, NJ: Prentice Hall, Inc., 9th edition, 1973), Vol. I, p. 421. Richard D. Heffner, *A Documentary History of the United States* (New York: The New American Library of World Literature, Inc., 1952), p. 151. Vincent J. Wilson, ed., *The Book of Great American Documents* (Brookfield, MD: American History Research Associates, 1987), p. 69.
73 Abraham Lincoln. October 6, 1862, in conversation with Eliza Gurney and three other Quakers. William J. Johnson, *Abraham Lincoln, The Christian* (NY: The Abington Press, 1913), p. 97. Peter Marshall and David Manuel, *The Glory of America* (Bloomington, MN: Garborg's Heart'N Home, Inc., 1991), 9.25.
74 Abraham Lincoln. October 6, 1862, in a meeting with Eliza Gurney and three other Quakers. William J. Johnson, *Abraham Lincoln, The Christian* (NY: The Abington Press, 1913), p. 97. Peter Marshall and David Manuel, *The Glory of America* (Bloomington, MN: Garborg's Heart'N Home, Inc., 1991), 10.6.
75 Abraham Lincoln. December 1, 1862, in concluding his Second Annual Message to Congress. John Bartlett, *Bartlett's Familiar Quotations* (Boston: Little, Brown and Company, 1863, 1980), pp. 520-524. John G. Nicolay and John Hay, eds., *The Complete Works of Abraham Lincoln: Speeches, Letters and State Papers* (1905), Vol. V, p. 537. James D. Richardson (U.S. Representative from Tennessee), ed., *A Compilation of the Messages and Papers of the Presidents 1789-1897,* 10 vols. (Washington, D.C.: U.S. Government Printing Office, published by Authority of Congress, 1897, 1899; Washington, D.C.: Bureau of National Literature and Art, 1789-1902, 11 vols., 1907, 1910), Vol. VI, p. 142. Pat Robertson, *America's Dates With Destiny* (Nashville, TN: Thomas Nelson Publishers,

1986), p. 157. Peter Marshall and David Manuel, *The Glory of America* (Bloomington, MN: Garborg's Heart'N Home, Inc., 1991), 12.1.
⁷⁶ Abraham Lincoln. December 1862, in relating to J.A. Reed. William J. Johnson, *Abraham Lincoln, The Christian* (NY: The Abington Press, 1913), p. 102. Peter Marshall and David Manuel, *The Glory of America* (Bloomington, MN: Garborg's Heart'N Home, Inc., 1991), 11.14.
⁷⁷ Abraham Lincoln. December 1862, in speaking with Reverend Byron Sunderland, pastor of the First Presbyterian Church of Washington, D.C.. William J. Johnson, *Abraham Lincoln, The Christian* (NY: The Abington Press, 1913), p. 101. Peter Marshall and David Manuel, *The Glory of America* (Bloomington, MN: Garborg's Heart'N Home, Inc., 1991), 12.26.
⁷⁸ Abraham Lincoln. 1862, after the death of their twelve-year-old son, William Wallace "Willie" Lincoln, February 20, 1862. Richard V. Pierard and Robert D. Linder, *Civil Religion and the Presidency* (Grand Rapids, MI: Zondervan/ Academie, 1988), pp. 96-97. Gary DeMar, *America's Christian History: The Untold Story* (Atlanta, GA: American Vision Publishers, Inc., 1993), pp. 101-102.
⁷⁹ Abraham Lincoln. 1863, as reported by Dr. Phineas Gurley, pastor of the New York Avenue Presbyterian Church, where Lincoln regularly attended after the death of their twelve-year-old son, William Wallace "Willie" Lincoln, February 20, 1862, and after the *Battle of Gettysburg*, July 1-3, 1863. Richard V. Pierard and Robert D. Linder, *Civil Religion and the Presidency* (Grand Rapids, MI: Zondervan/ Academie, 1988), p. 316, note 24. Gary DeMar, *America's Christian History: The Untold Story* (Atlanta, GA: American Vision Publishers, Inc., 1993), p. 102. [Other books evidencing Lincoln's faith are: William J. Wolf, *The Almost Chosen People: A Study in the Religion of Abraham Lincoln* (Garden City, NY: Doubleday, 1959), chap. 7, "The Best Gift God Has Given to Man," pp. 117-118. Mark A. Knoll, *One Nation Under God: Christian Faith and Political Action in America* (San Francisco, CA: Harper & Row, 1988), chap. 6, "The Transcendent Faith of Abraham Lincoln," pp. 90-104. Clarence Edward Macartney, *Lincoln and the Bible* (Nashville, TN: Abingdon-Cokesbury Press, 1949).]
⁸⁰ Abraham Lincoln. January 1, 1863, *Emancipation Proclamation*. John Bartlett, *Bartlett's Familiar Quotations* (Boston: Little, Brown and Company, 1855, 1980), p. 522. James D. Richardson (U.S. Representative from Tennessee), ed., *A Compilation of the Messages and Papers of the Presidents 1789-1897*, 10 vols. (Washington, D.C.: U.S. Government Printing Office, published by Authority of Congress, 1897, 1899; Washington, D.C.: Bureau of National Literature and Art, 1789-1902, 11 vols., 1907, 1910), Vol. VI, pp. 157-159. Charles W. Eliot, LL.D., ed., *American Historical Documents 1000-1904* (New York: P.F. Collier & Son Company, *The Harvard Classics*, 1910), Vol. 43, pp. 344-346. Henry Steele Commager, ed., *Documents of American History*, 2 vols. (NY: F.S. Crofts and Company, 1934; Appleton-Century-Crofts, Inc., 1948, 6th edition, 1958; Englewood Cliffs, NJ: Prentice Hall, Inc., 9th edition, 1973), Vol. I, p. 421. Richard D. Heffner, *A Documentary History of the United States* (New York: The New American Library of World Literature, Inc., 1952), pp. 150-151. Vincent J. Wilson, ed., *The Book of Great American Documents* (Brookfield, MD: American History Research Associates, 1987), p. 69.
⁸¹ Abraham Lincoln. March 30, 1863, in a Proclamation of a National Day of Humiliation, Fasting and Prayer. James D. Richardson (U.S. Representative from Tennessee), ed., *A Compilation of the Messages and Papers of the Presidents 1789-1897*, 10 vols. (Washington, D.C.: U.S. Government Printing Office, published by Authority of Congress, 1897, 1899; Washington, D.C.: Bureau of National Literature and Art, 1789-1902, 11 vols., 1907, 1910), Vol. VI, pp. 164-165. Benjamin Franklin Morris, *The Christian Life and Character of the Civil Institutions of the United States* (Philadelphia: George W. Childs, 1864), pp. 558-559. Roy Basler, ed., *Collected Works of Abraham Lincoln* (Rutgers University Press, 1953), Vol. 6, p. 179. Benjamin Weiss, *God in American History: A Documentation of America's Religious Heritage* (Grand Rapids, MI: Zondervan, 1966), p. 92. Willard Cantelon, *Money Master of the World* (Plainfield, NJ: Logos International, 1976), p. 120. Gary DeMar, *God and Government, A Biblical and Historical Study* (Atlanta, GA: American Vision Press, 1984), p. 128-29. David Barton, *The Myth of Separation* (Aledo, TX: WallBuilder Press, 1991), p. 259. "Our Christian Heritage," *Letter from Plymouth Rock* (Marlborough, NH: The Plymouth Rock Foundation), p. 6. D.P. Diffine, Ph.D., *One Nation Under God - How Close a Separation?* (Searcy, Arkansas: Harding University, Belden Center for Private Enterprise Education, 6th edition, 1992), pp. 14-15. Gary DeMar, *America's Christian History: The Untold Story* (Atlanta, GA: American Vision Publishers, Inc., 1993), pp. 53, 99.
⁸² Abraham Lincoln. June 1863, in a discourse with a college President, just weeks before the *Battle of Gettysburg*, July 1-3, 1863. William J. Johnson, *Abraham Lincoln, The Christian* (NY: The Abington Press, 1913), pp. 109-110. Peter Marshall and David Manuel, *The Glory of America* (Bloomington, MN: Garborg's Heart 'N Home, Inc., 1991), 4.26.
⁸³ Abraham Lincoln. October 3, 1863, in Proclamation of an annual *National Day of Thanksgiving*, concurring with an Act of Congress. Library of Congress Rare Book Collection, Washington, D.C. James D. Richardson (U.S. Representative from Tennessee), ed., *A Compilation of the Messages and Papers of the Presidents 1789-1897*, 10 vols. (Washington, D.C.: U.S. Government Printing Office, published by Authority of Congress, 1897, 1899; Washington, D.C.: Bureau of National Literature and Art, 1789-1902, 11 vols., 1907, 1910), Vol. VI, pp. 172-173. William J. Johnson, *Abraham Lincoln, The Christian* (NY: The Abington Press, 1913), pp. 124-125. Peter Marshall and David Manuel, *The Glory of America* (Bloomington, MN: Garborg's Heart'N Home, Inc., 1991), 10.4. Catherine Millard, *A Children's Companion Guide to America's History* (Camp Hill, PA: Horizon House Publishers, 1993), p. 23. Gary DeMar, *America's Christian History: The Untold Story* (Atlanta, GA: American Vision Publishers, Inc., 1993), pp. 16-17.
⁸⁴ Abraham Lincoln. October 24, 1863, in an address to the Presbyterians of Baltimore. Mark A. Knoll, "The Puzzling Faith of Abraham Lincoln" (Carol Stream, IL: Christian History), Vol. XI, No. 1, Issue 33, p. 13.
⁸⁵ Abraham Lincoln. 1863, in conversation with a General who was wounded at the *Battle of Gettysburg*, July 1-3, 1863, relating the panic in Washington, D.C., as General Robert E. Lee was leading his army of 76,000 men into Pennsylvania. Thomas Fleming, "Lincoln's Journey in Faith" (Carmel, NY: *Guideposts*, February 1994), p. 36.
⁸⁶ Abraham Lincoln. November 19, 1863, in his *Gettysburg Address*, commemorating the field where 50,000 men died in the *Battle of Gettysburg*, July 1-3, 1863. Engraved in stone in the Lincoln Memorial in Washington, D.C. John Bartlett, *Bartlett's Familiar Quotations* (Boston: Little, Brown and Company, 1855, 1980), p. 523. Charles W. Eliot, LL.D., ed., *American Historical Documents 1000-1904* (New York: P.F. Collier & Son Company, *The Harvard Classics*, 1910), Vol. 43, p. 441. *The World Book Encyclopedia*, 18 vols. (Chicago, IL: Field Enterprises, Inc., 1957; W.F. Quarrie and Company, 8 vols., 1917; World Book, Inc., 22 vols., 1989), Vol. 7, p. 2982. Henry Steele Commager, ed., *Documents of American History*, 2 vols. (NY: F.S. Crofts and Company, 1934; Appleton-Century-Crofts, Inc., 1948, 6th edition, 1958; Englewood Cliffs, NJ: Prentice Hall, Inc., 9th edition, 1973), p. 228. Frederick C. Packard, Jr., ed., *Are You an American? - Great Americans Speak* (NY: Charles Scribner's Sons, 1951), pp. 32-33. Roy Basler, ed., *Collected Works of Abraham Lincoln* (Rutgers University Press, 1953). Daniel Boorstin, Jr., ed., *An American Primer* (Chicago: The University of Chicago Press, 1966), p. 418. Lillian W. Kay, ed., *The Ground on Which We Stand - Basic Documents of American History*

(NY: Franklin Watts., Inc, 1969), pp. 197-198. Robert Flood, *The Rebirth of America* (The Arthur S. DeMoss Foundation, 1986), back cover. Catherine Millard, *The Rewriting of America's History* (Camp Hill, PA: Horizon House Publishers, 1991), pp. 166-167. William Safire, ed., *Lend Me Your Ears - Great Speeches in History* (NY: W.W. Norton & Company 1992), p. 50. D.P. Diffine, Ph.D., *One Nation Under God - How Close a Separation?* (Searcy, Arkansas: Harding University, Belden Center for Private Enterprise Education, 6th edition, 1992), p. 15.

[87] **Abraham Lincoln.** December 23, 1863, as he related to John Hay. John Bartlett, *Bartlett's Familiar Quotations* (Boston: Little, Brown and Company, 1855, 1980), p. 523.

[88] **Abraham Lincoln.** In speaking to a minister of the Christian Commission during the Civil War. Holland, *Lincoln*, p. 440. Peter Marshall and David Manuel, *The Glory of America* (Bloomington, MN: Garborg's Heart'N Home, Inc., 1991), 12.9. D.P. Diffine, Ph.D., *One Nation Under God - How Close a Separation?* (Searcy, Arkansas: Harding University, Belden Center for Private Enterprise Education, 6th edition, 1992), p. 13.

[89] **Abraham Lincoln.** 1863, in reply to a remark that "the Lord was on the Union's side." Frank B. Carpenter, *Six Months at the White House* (1866), p. 125. J.B. McClure, ed., *Abraham Lincoln's Stories and Speeches* (Chicago: Rhodes & McClure Pub. Co., 1896), pp. 185-186. John Wesley Hill, *Abraham Lincoln - Man of God* (NY: G.P. Putnam's Son's, 1920), p. 330. David Barton, *The Myth of Separation* (Aledo, TX: WallBuilder Press, 1991), p. 259. Peter Marshall & David Manuel, *The Glory of America* (Bloomington, MN: Garborg's Heart 'N Home, 1991), 2.12. D.P. Diffine, Ph.D., *One Nation Under God - How Close a Separation?* (Searcy, Arkansas: Harding University, Belden Center for Private Enterprise Education, 6th edition, 1992), p. 14. David Barton, *America's Godly Heritage*, Video Transcript (Aledo, TX: WallBuilder Press, 1993), p. 27.

[90] **Abraham Lincoln.** Summer of 1864, in a conversation with an old friend named Joshua Speed. William J. Johnson, *Abraham Lincoln, The Christian* (NY: The Abington Press, 1913), p. 148. Peter Marshall and David Manuel, *The Glory of America* (Bloomington, MN: Garborg's Heart'N Home, Inc., 1991), 8.26.

[91] **Abraham Lincoln.** September 5, 1864, in an address to the Committee of Colored People from Baltimore. *Washington Chronicle*. William J. Johnson, *Abraham Lincoln, The Christian* (NY: The Abington Press, 1913), p. 157. Clarence Edward McCartney, *Lincoln and the Bible* (Nashville, TN: Abington-Cokesbury Press, 1949), p. 35. Roy P. Basler, ed., *The Collected Works of Abraham Lincoln*, 9 vols. (New Brunswick, NJ: Rutgers University Press, 1953), Vol. 1, p. 382. Carl Sandberg, *Lincoln's Devotional* (NY: Channel Press, Inc., 1957), introduction, p. viii. Henry H. Halley, *Halley's Bible Handbook* (Grand Rapids, MI: Zondervan Publishing House, 1927, 1965), p. 18. George L. Hunt, *Calvinism and the Political Order* (Westminster Press, 1965), p. 33. Stephen Abbott Northrop, D.D., *A Cloud of Witnesses* (Portland, OR: American Heritage Ministries, 1987; Mantle Ministries, 228 Still Ridge, Bulverde, Texas), p. 285. George Herbert Walker Bush, February 22, 1990, at the request of Congress, Senate Joint Resolution 164, in a Presidential Proclamation declaring 1990 the *International Year of Bible Reading*. Courtesy of Bruce Barilla, Christian Heritage Week Ministry (P.O. Box 58, W.V. 24712; 304-384-7707, 304-384-9044 fax). "Our Christian Heritage," *Letter from Plymouth Rock* (Marlborough, NH: The Plymouth Rock Foundation), p. 6. Peter Marshall and David Manuel, *The Glory of America* (Bloomington, MN: Garborg's Heart'N Home, Inc., 1991), 9.7. Mark A. Noll, *A History of Christianity in the United States and Canada* (Grand Rapids, MI: William B. Eerdmans Publishing Company, 1992), *Christian History* (Carol Stream, IL: Christianity Today, Inc.), Issue 33, Vol. IX, No. 1, p. 3. D.P. Diffine, Ph.D., *One Nation Under God - How Close a Separation?* (Searcy, Arkansas: Harding University, Belden Center for Private Enterprise Education, 6th edition, 1992), p. 15. Gary DeMar, *America's Christian History: The Untold Story* (Atlanta, GA: American Vision Publishers, Inc., 1993), p. 59.

[92] **Abraham Lincoln.** October 20, 1864, in a Proclamation of a Second Annual National Day of Thanksgiving and Praise, on the last Thursday in November. William J. Johnson, *Abraham Lincoln, The Christian* (NY: The Abington Press, 1913), p. 159. James D. Richardson (U.S. Representative from Tennessee), ed., *A Compilation of the Messages and Papers of the Presidents 1789-1897*, 10 vols. (Washington, D.C.: U.S. Government Printing Office, published by Authority of Congress, 1897, 1899; Washington, D.C.: Bureau of National Literature and Art, 1789-1902, 11 vols., 1907, 1910), Vol. VI, pp. 228-229. Peter Marshall and David Manuel, *The Glory of America* (Bloomington, MN: Garborg's Heart'N Home, Inc., 1991), 10.21.

[93] **Abraham Lincoln.** November 21, 1864, in a letter to Mrs. Lydia Bixby of Boston, who had lost five sons in the Civil War. John Bartlett, *Bartlett's Familiar Quotations* (Boston: Little, Brown and Company, 1855, 1980), p. 524. *Boston Globe*, April 12, 1908. Charles W. Eliot, LL.D., ed., *American Historical Documents 1000-1904* (New York: P.F. Collier & Son Company, *The Harvard Classics*, 1910), Vol. 43, p. 446. Peter Marshall and David Manuel, *The Glory of America* (Bloomington, MN: Garborg's Heart'N Home, Inc., 1991), 11.21.

[94] **Abraham Lincoln.** March 4, 1865, Saturday, in his Second Inaugural Address. Abraham Lincoln, *Second Inaugural Address - 1865* (Washington, D.C.: Lincoln Memorial, inscribed on the North Wall). James D. Richardson (U.S. Representative from Tennessee), ed., *A Compilation of the Messages and Papers of the Presidents 1789-1897*, 10 vols. (Washington, D.C.: U.S. Government Printing Office, published by Authority of Congress, 1897, 1899; Washington, D.C.: Bureau of National Literature and Art, 1789-1902, 11 vols., 1907, 1910), Vol. VI, pp. 276-277. *Inaugural Addresses of the Presidents of the United States - From George Washington 1789 to Richard Milhous Nixon 1969* (Washington, D.C.: United States Government Printing Office; 91st Congress, 1st Session, House Document 91-142, 1969), pp. 127-128. John G. Nicolay and John Hay, eds., *The Complete Works of Abraham Lincoln: Speeches, Letters and State Papers* (1905), Vol. VIII, p. 333. Charles W. Eliot, LL.D., ed., *American Historical Documents 1000-1904* (New York: P.F. Collier & Son Company, *The Harvard Classics*, 1910), Vol. 43, pp. 450-452. Henry Steele Commager, ed., *Documents of American History*, 2 vols. (NY: F.S. Crofts and Company, 1934; Appleton-Century-Crofts, Inc., 1948, 6th edition, 1958; Englewood Cliffs, NJ: Prentice Hall, Inc., 9th edition, 1973), p. 443. Frederick C. Packard, Jr., ed., *Are You an American? - Great Americans Speak* (NY: Charles Scribner's Sons, 1951), p. 36. Roy Basler, ed., *Collected Works of Abraham Lincoln* (Rutgers University Press, 1953), Vol. VIII p. 33. Richard D. Heffner, *A Documentary History of the United States* (New York: The New American Library of World Literature, Inc., 1961), pp. 156-157. Charles E. Rice, *The Supreme Court and Public Prayer* (New York: Fordham University Press, 1964), pp. 184-185. Davis Newton Lott, *The Inaugural Addresses of the American Presidents* (NY: Holt, Rinehart and Winston, 1961), p. 126. Edmund Fuller and David E. Green, *God in the White House - The Faiths of American Presidents* (NY: Crown Publishers, Inc., 1968), p. 114. *The Annals of America*, 20 vols. (Chicago, IL: Encyclopedia Britannica, 1968), Vol. 9, p. 556. Lillian W. Kay, ed., *The Ground on Which We Stand - Basic Documents of American History* (NY: Franklin Watts., Inc, 1969), p. 201. Vincent J. Wilson, ed., *The Book of Great American Documents* (Brookfield, MD: American History Research Associates, 1987), p. 80. Ronald Reid, ed., *Three Centuries of American Rhetorical Discourse - An Anthology and a Review* (Prospect Heights, Ill: Waveland Press, Inc., 1988), p. 466. Mark A. Knoll, *The Puzzling Faith of Abraham Lincoln* (Carol Stream, IL: Christian History), Vol. XI, No. 1, Issue 33, p. 12. Peter Marshall and David Manuel, *The Glory of America* (Bloomington, MN: Garborg's Heart'N Home, Inc., 1991), 3.4. Catherine Millard, *The Rewriting of America's History* (Camp Hill, PA: Horizon House Publishers, 1991), pp. 168-169.

Michael Barone, "Who Was Lincoln?" *U.S. News & World Report* (October 5, 1992), p. 71. William Safire, ed., *Lend Me Your Ears - Great Speeches in History* (NY: W.W. Norton & Company 1992), p. 441. J. Michael Sharman, J.D., *Faith of the Fathers* (Culpepper, Virginia: Victory Publishing, 1995), p. 59-60.

[95] **Abraham Lincoln.** March 17, 1865, in an address to the Indiana Regiment. John Bartlett, *Bartlett's Familiar Quotations* (Boston: Little, Brown and Company, 1863, 1980), p. 524, Pat Robertson, *America's Dates With Destiny* (Nashville, TN: Thomas Nelson Publishers, 1986), p. 158.

[96] **Abraham Lincoln.** 1865, in his last address in front of the White House. John G. Nicolay and John Hay, eds., *The Complete Works of Abraham Lincoln: Speeches, Letters and State Papers* (1905), Vol. VIII, p. 395. Peter Marshall and David Manuel, *The Glory of America* (Bloomington, MN: Garborg's Heart'N Home, Inc., 1991), 4.11.

[97] **Abraham Lincoln.** In answering a question of L.E. Chittenden (Register of the Treasury under President Lincoln), Recollections *of President Lincoln, and his Administration.* Trueblood, *Abraham Lincoln: Theologian of American Anguish,* pp. 127-128. Peter Marshall and David Manuel, *The Glory of America* (Bloomington, MN: Garborg's Heart'N Home, Inc., 1991), 7.15, 16.

[98] **Abraham Lincoln.** 1865, in a conversation with state Senator James Scovel of New Jersey. William J. Johnson, *Abraham Lincoln, The Christian* (NY: The Abington Press, 1913),p. 179. Peter Marshall and David *Manuel The Glory of America* (Bloomington, MN: Garborg's Heart 'N Home, Inc., 1991), 4.12.

[99] **Abraham Lincoln** April 14,1865, Ford's Theater, his last words. Miner, *Lincoln,* p. 52. Peter Marshall and David Manuel, *The Glory of America* (Bloomington, MN: Garborg's Heart'N Home, Inc., 1991), 4.14.

[100] **Abraham Lincoln.** Roy Basler, ed., *Collected Works of Abraham Lincoln* (Rutgers University Press, 1953), Vol. 1, p. 178. Peter Marshall and David Manuel, *The Glory of America* (Bloomington, MN: Garborg's Heart'N Home, Inc., 1991),10.25.

[101] **Abraham Lincoln** Peter Marshall and David Manuel, *The Glory of America* (Bloomington, MN: Garborg's Heart'N Home, Inc., 1991), 11.29.

[102] **Abraham Lincoln.** Carroll E. Simcox, *3000 Quotations on Christian Themes* (Grand Rapids, MI: Baker Book House, 1989), p. 231, No. 2792.

[103] **Abraham Lincoln.** Carl Sandberg, *Lincoln's Devotional* (NY: Channel Press, Inc., 1957), introduction, p. xiii. Herbert V. Prochnow, *5100 Quotations for Speakers and Writers* (Grand Rapids, MI: Baker Book House, 1992), p. 352.

[104] **Abraham Lincoln.** L.E. Chittenden (Register of the Treasury under President Lincoln), *Recollections of President Lincoln, and his Administration,* pp. 450-451. Stephen Abbott Northrop, E).D., *A Cloud of Witnesses* (Portland, Oregon: American Heritage Ministries, 1987; Mantle Ministries, 228 Still Ridge, Bulverde, Texas), p. 286.

[105] **Abraham Lincoln.** *Bless Your Heart (series 11)* (Eden Prairie, MN: Heartland Prairie, Inc., 1990),8.17.

[106] **Abraham Lincoln.** Attributed. *Herald Star,* Steubenville, Ohio, 1984. Stephen K. McDowell and Mark A. Beliles, *America's Providential History* (Charlottesville, VA: Providence Press, 1988), p. 79. David Barton, *The Myth of Separation* (Aledo, TX: WallBuilder Press, 1991), p. 16. Karen Morgan, People of the Past, 517-A Greenville, N.E., Bristolville, Ohio, 44402, (216) 889-9746.

[107] **Abraham Lincoln.** Attributed. Stephen K. McDowell and Mark A. Beliles, America's Providential History (Charlottesville, VA: Providence Press, 1988), pp. 148, 179. Stephen McDowell and Mark Beliles, "The Providential Perspective" (Charlottesville, VA: The Providence Foundation, P.O. Box 6759, Charlottesville, Va. 22906, January 1994), Vol. 9, No. 1, p. 5.

[108] **Abraham Lincoln.** Count Leo Tolstoy eulogizing the President. William J. Johnson, *Abraham Lincoln, The Christian* (NY: The Abington Press, 1913), p. 187. Peter Marshall and David Manuel, *The Glory of America* (Bloomington MN: Garborg's Heart'N Home, Inc., 1991), 4.16.

[109] **Abraham Lincoln.** 1896. William McKinley, the 25th President, describing Lincoln. William J. Johnson, *Abraham Lincoln, The Christian* (NY: The Abington Press, 1913), p. 187. Peter Marshall and David Manuel, The *Glory of America* (Bloomington, MN: Garborg's Heart'N Home, Inc., 1991), 4.16.

[110] **Abraham Lincoln.** April 24, 1865, a Memorial Address delivered by Schuyler Colfax, Speaker of the House of Representatives. Colfax, *Lincoln,* p. 180. D.P. Diffine, Ph.D., *One Nation Under God - How Close a Separation?* (Searcy, Arkansas: Harding University, Belden Center for Private Enterprise Education, 6th edition, 1992), p. 15.

[111] **Abraham Lincoln.** Inscription of President Abraham Lincoln's words on the walls of the Lincoln Memorial in Washington D.C. Robert Byrd, US Senator from West Virginia, July 27, 1962. in a message to Congress two days after the Supreme Court declared prayer in schools unconstitutional. Robert Flood, *The Rebirth of America* (Philadelphia: Arthur S. DeMoss Foundation, 1986), pp. 66-69.

[112] **Vachel Lindsay.** 1913, in his poem *General Booth Enters into Heaven.* John Bartlett, *Bartlett's Familiar Quotations* (Boston: Little, Brown and Company, 1855, 1980), p. 765.

[113] **William Linn.** May 1, 1789. The United States House of Representatives. *"Our Christian Heritage," Letter from Plymouth Rock* (Marlborough, NH: The Plymouth Rock Foundation), p. 4.

[114] **William Linn.** Dickinson W. Adams, ed., *Jefferson's Extracts from the Gospels* (Princeton: Princeton University Press, 1983), p. II. Quoting from William Linn, *Serious Considerations on the Election Of a President: Addressed to the Citizens of the United States* (NY, 1800), p. 19.

[115] **Carolus Linnaeus.** Inscribed over the door of his bedchamber. Benjamin Daydon Jones, *Biography of Linnaeus,* ch. 15. John Bartlett, *Bartlett's Familiar Quotations* (Boston: Little, Brown and Company, 1855, 1980), p. 350.

[116] **Joseph Lister.** Henry M. Morris, *Men of Science - Men of God* (El Cajon, CA: Master Books, Creation Life Publishers, Inc., 1990), pp. 66-67.

[117] **William Livingston.** Vincent Wilson, Jr., *The Book of the Founding Fathers* (Brookeville, MD: American History Research Associates, 1974), p. 44. Tim LaHaye, *Faith of Our Founding Fathers* (Brentwood, TN: Wolgemuth & Hyatt, Publishers, Inc., 1987), p. 169.

[118] **William Livingston.** William Livingston, *The Independent Reflector-No. 46. Life and Letters of William Livingston,* reprinted by Theodore Sedgwick, Jr.. Stephen Abbott Northrop, D.D., *A Cloud of Witnesses* (Portland, OR.- American Heritage Ministries, 1987; Mantle Ministries, 228 Still Ridge, Bulverde, Texas), p. 298.

[119] **William Livingston.** 1768. *The World Book Encyclopedia* (Chicago, IL: Field Enterprises, Inc., 18 vols., 1957; W.F. Quarrie and Company, 8 vols., 1917; World Book, Inc., 22 vols., 1989). Peter Marshall and David Manuel, *The Glory of America* (Bloomington, MN: Garborg's Heart'N Home, Inc., 1991), 11.30.

[120] **William Livingston.** Vincent Wilson,Jr., *The Book of the Founding Fathers* (Brookeville, MD: American History Research Associates, 1974), p. 44. Tim LaHaye, *Faith of Our Founding Fathers* (Brentwood, TN: Wolgemuth & Hyatt, Publishers, Inc., 1987), p. 170.

[121] **William Livingston.** March 16, 1776, in a resolution passed in the Continental Congress declaring May 17, 1776, as a *National Day of Humiliation, Fasting and Prayer*, presented by General William Livingston. *Journal of Congress*, Vol. II, p. 93. Carl E. Prince, ed., *The Papers of William Livingston*, 5 vols. (Trenton: New Jersey Historical Commission, 1979), Vol. I, pp. 43-44. Stephen Abbott Northrop, D.D., *A Cloud of Witnesses* (Portland, Oregon: American Heritage Ministries, 1987; Mantle Ministries, 228 Still Ridge, Bulverde, Texas), p. 287-288. M.E. Bradford, *Religion & The Framers - The Biographical Evidence* (Marlborough, NH: Plymouth Rock Foundation, 1991), p. 5.

[122] **William Livingston.** *Livingston's Familiar Letters to a Gentleman, upon a variety of seasonable and important Subjects in Religion.* Stephen Abbott Northrop, D.D., *A Cloud of Witnesses* (Portland, OR: American Heritage Ministries, 1987; Mantle Ministries, 228 Still Ridge, Bulverde, Texas), pp. 287-288.

[123] **David Livingstone.** Tryon Edwards, D.D., *The New Dictionary of Thoughts - A Cyclopedia of Quotations* (Garden City, NY: Hanover House, 1852; revised and enlarged by C.H. Catrevas, Ralph Emerson Browns and Jonathan Edwards [descendent, along with Tryon, of Jonathan Edwards (1703-1758), president of Princeton], 1891; The Standard Book Company, 1955, 1963), p. 47.

[124] **David Livingstone.** David Livingstone, *Missionary Travels and Researches in South Africa.* Stephen Abbott Northrop, D.D., *A Cloud of Witnesses* (Portland, Oregon: American Heritage Ministries, 1987; Mantle Ministries, 228 Still Ridge, Bulverde, Texas), p. 287.

[125] **David Livingstone.** As described by Henry Morton Stanley. Stephen Abbott Northrop, D.D., *A Cloud of Witnesses* (Portland, OR: American Heritage Ministries, 1987; Mantle Ministries, 228 Still Ridge, Bulverde, Texas), p. 287.

[126] **John Locke.** Donald S. Lutz and Charles S. Hyneman, "The Relative Influence of European Writers on Late Eighteenth-Century American Political Thought," *American Political Review* 189 (1984): 189-197. (Courtesy of Dr. Wayne House of Dallas Theological Seminary.) John Eidsmoe, *Christianity and the Constitution - The Faith of Our Founding Fathers* (Grand Rapids, MI: Baker Book House, A Mott Media Book, 1987, 6th printing 1993), pp. 51-53. Stephen K. McDowell and Mark A. Beliles, *America's Providential History* (Charlottesville, VA: Providence Press, 1988), p. 156. [1760-1805], *Origins of American Constitutionalism*, (1987). David Barton, *The Myth of Separation* (Aledo, TX: WallBuilder Press, 1991), pp. 195, 201.

[127] **John Locke.** John Locke, *Of Civil Government, Book Two*, II:11, III:56; V:25, 55; XVIII:200. John Eidsmoe, *Christianity and the Constitution - The Faith of Our Founding Fathers* (Grand Rapids, MI: Baker Book House, A Mott Media Book, 1987, 6th printing 1993), p. 61.

[128] **John Locke.** 1689, in his work *Of Civil Government.* John Locke, *Two Treatises on Civil Government* (London: George Routledge and Sons, 1903) Book 2, p. 262. John Locke, *The Second Treatise Of Civil Government 1690* (Reprinted Buffalo, NY: Prometheus Books, 1986) p. 77. Frank Donovan, *Mr. Jefferson's Declaration* (New York: Dodd Mead & Co., 1968), p. 137. Pat Robertson, *America's Dates with Destiny* (Nashville: Thomas Nelson Publishers, 1986), p. 66. Verna M. Hall, *Christian History of the Constitution of the United States of America* (San Francisco: Foundation for American Christian Education, 1975), pp. 58, 63-64, 91. Marshall Foster and Mary-Elaine Swanson, *The American Covenant - The Untold Story* (Roseburg, OR: Foundation for Christian Self-Government, 1981; Thousand Oaks, CA: The Mayflower Institute, 1983, 1992), pp. 111-112.

[129] **John Locke.** August 23, 1689, in his work *Of Civil Government.* John Locke, *The Second Treatise on Civil Government*, 1690 (reprinted Buffalo, NY: Prometheus Books, 1986), p. 75. John Locke, *Two Treatises on Civil Government* (London: George Routledge and Sons, 1903), Book 2, p. 262. Verna M.Hall, *The Christian History of the Constitution of the United States of America - Christian Self-Government with Union* (San Francisco: Foundation for American Christian Education, 1976), p. 58. Marshall Foster and Mary-Elaine Swanson, *The American Covenant - The Untold Story* (Roseburg, OR: Foundation for Christian Self-Government, 1981; Thousand Oaks, CA: The Mayflower Institute, 1983, 1992), p. 108. David Barton, *The Myth of Separation* (Aledo, TX: WallBuilder Press, 1991), p. 199.

[130] **John Locke.** 1690, John Locke, *Of Civil Government, Book Two*, XI:136n. John Locke, *The Second Treatise on Civil Government*, 1690 (reprinted Buffalo, NY: Prometheus Books, 1986), p. 76, n. 1. Richard Hooker, *Of the Laws of Ecclesiastical Polity*, Book 1, section 10. John Eidsmoe, *Christianity and the Constitution - The Faith of Our Founding Fathers* (Grand Rapids, MI: Baker Book House, A Mott Media Book, 1987, 6th printing 1993), p. 62. David Barton, *The Myth of Separation* (Aledo, TX: WallBuilder Press, 1991), p. 199.

[131] **John Locke.** 1695, John Locke, *A Vindication of the Reasonableness of Christianity*, a paraphrase of the books of Romans, First and Second Corinthians, Galatians and Ephesians. Tim LaHaye, *Faith of Our Founding Fathers* (Brentwood, TN: Wolgemuth & Hyatt, Inc., 1987), pp. 51, 85-86.

[132] **John Locke.** 1695, John Locke, *A Vindication of the Reasonableness of Christianity*, a paraphrase of the books of Romans, First and Second Corinthians, Galatians and Ephesians. Stephen Abbott Northrop, D.D., *A Cloud of Witnesses* (Portland, OR: American Heritage Ministries, 1987; Mantle Ministries, 228 Still Ridge, Bulverde, Texas), pp. 289-290.

[133] **John Locke.** 1695, John Locke, *A Vindication of the Reasonableness of Christianity*, a paraphrase of the books of Romans, First and Second Corinthians, Galatians and Ephesians. John Churchill, *The Works of John Locke, Esq.*, 3 Vol. (1714). Verna M. Hall, *The Christian History of the Constitution of the United States of America - Christian Self-Government with Union* (San Francisco: Foundation for American Christian Education, 1976), Vol. I, op cit, 56. Russ Walton, *One Nation Under God* (NH: Plymouth Rock Foundation, 1993), p. 22.

[134] **John Locke.** Statement. Tryon Edwards, D.D., *The New Dictionary of Thoughts - A Cyclopedia of Quotations* (Garden City, NY: Hanover House, 1852; revised and enlarged by C.H. Catrevas, Ralph Emerson Browns and Jonathan Edwards [descendent, along with Tryon, of Jonathan Edwards (1703-1758), president of Princeton], 1891; The Standard Book Company, 1955, 1963), p. 46.

[135] **James Logan.** Wilson Armstead, *Memoirs of James Logan.* Stephen Abbott Northrop, D.D., *A Cloud of Witnesses* (Portland, Oregon: American Heritage Ministries, 1987; Mantle Ministries, 228 Still Ridge, Bulverde, Texas),

[136] **John Alexander Logan.** *Decoration Day*, 1886, in an oration at Riverside Park in New York. Stephen Abbott Northrop, D.D., *A Cloud of Witnesses* (Portland, OR: American Heritage Ministries, 1987; Mantle Ministries, 228 Still Ridge, Bulverde, Texas),

P. 290.

[137] **Henry Wadsworth Longfellow.** Henry Wadsworth Longfellow, *His Brother's Ordination Hymn.* Stephen Abbott Northrop, D.D., *A Cloud of Witnesses* (Portland, OR: American Heritage Ministries, 1987; Mantle Ministries, 228 Still Ridge, Bulverde, Texas), p. 292.

[138] **Henry Wadsworth Longfellow.** *Bless Your Heart (series 11)* (Eden Prairie, MN: Heartland Sampler, Inc., 1990), 6.12.

[139] **Henry Wadsworth Longfellow.** *Bless Your Heart (series 11)* (Eden Prairie, MN: Heartland Sampler, Inc., 1990), 12.17.

[140] **James Longstreet.** In a letter. Stephen Abbott Northrop, D.D., *A Cloud of Witnesses* (Portland, OR: American Heritage Ministries, 1987; Mantle Ministries, 228 Still Ridge, Bulverde, Texas), p. 291.

[141] **State of Louisiana.** March 23,1994, the state of Louisiana issued an Executive Proclamation declaring November 20 - November 26,1994, as "Christian Heritage Week," signed by Governor Edwin W. Edwards and Secretary of State, J.K, in the Capitol City of Baton Rouge. A similar Proclamation was also signed June 30, 1993. Courtesy of Bruce Barilla, Christian Heritage Week Ministry (P.O. Box 58, W.V. 24712; 304-384-7707, 304-384-9044 fax).

[142] **James Russell Lowell.** Daniel Marsh, *Unto The Generations* (Buena Park, CA: ARC, 1970), p. 51. David Barton, *The Myth of Separation,* (Aledo, TX: WallBuilder Press, 1991), p. 268. Tim LaHaye, Faith *of our Founding Fathers* (Brentwood, TN: Wolgemuth & Hyatt, Publishers, 1987), p. 48. Edward L.R. Elson, D.D., Lit.D., LL.D., *America's Spiritual Recovery* (Westwood, NJ.: Fleming H. Revell Company, 1954), p. 73.

[143] **James Russell Lowell.** November 20, 1885, in his *International Copyright.* John Bartlett, *Bartlett's Familiar Quotations* (Boston: Little, Brown and Company, 1855, 1980), p. 569.

[144] **James Russell Lowell.** 1810-1890, in his *Literary Essays, Vol. 11, New England Two Centuries Ago.* Charles Fadiman, ed., *The American Treasury* (NY: Harper & Brothers, Publishers, 1955), p. 119. James Russell Lowell, *Among My Books, New England Two Centuries Ago.* John Bartlett, *Bartlett's Familiar Quotations* (Boston: Little, Brown and Company, 1855, 1980), p. 569.

[145] **Stephen Bleecker Luce.** 1834. Stephen Abbott Northrop, D.D., *A Cloud of Witnesses* (Portland, OR: American Heritage Ministries, 1987; Mantle Ministries, 228 Still Ridge, Bulverde, Texas), p. 298.

[146] **Sir Lionel Alfred Luckhoo.** Norris McWhirter, *Guinness Book of World Records* (NY: Sterling Publishing Co., Inc., 1986), p. 271.

[147] **Sir Lionel Alfred Luckhoo.** Lionel Luckhoo, *The Quran is Not the Word of God* (Dallas, TX: Luckhoo Ministries, Box 815881, Dallas, Texas 75381), pp. 20-21.

[148] **Martin Luther.** Statement. Robert Flood, *The Rebirth of America* (Philadelphia: Arthur S. DeMoss Foundation, 1986), p. 127. David Barton, *The Myth of Separation* (Aledo, TX WallBuilder Press, 1991), p. 264.

[149] **Martin Luther.** Statement. William Neil, Ph.D., D.D., *Concise Dictionary of Religious Quotations* (Grand Rapids, MI: William B. Eerdmans Publishing Company, 1974). p. 9, No. 14.

[150] **Martin Luther.** Statement. Gary DeMar, *God and Government-A Biblical and Historical Study,* (Atlanta, GA: American Vision Press, 1984), Vol. 1, p. viii.

[151] **Martin Luther.** Statement. Ed Erlangen, *Luther's Werke,* Vol. 51, p. 37. Larry Christenson, *The Christian Family* (Minneapolis, MN: Bethany Fellowship, Inc., 1970), p. 25.

[152] **Martin Luther.** Statement. Tryon Edwards, D.D., *The New Dictionary of Thoughts - A Cyclopedia of Quotations* (Garden City, NY: Hanover House, 1852, revised by C.H. Catrevas, Ralph E. Browns and Jonathan Edwards, 1891; Standard Book Co., 1955, 1963), p. 88.

[153] **Martin Luther.** April 18, 1521, in his famous speech at the *Diet of Worms.* John Bartlett, *Bartlett's Familiar Quotations (Boston:* Little, Brown and Company, 1855, 1980), p. 155.

[154] **Martin Luther.** 1529, in his famous hymn, *A Mighty Fortress (Ein 'Feste Burg).* John Bartlett, *Bartlett's Familiar Quotations* (Boston: Little, Brown and Company, 1855, 1980), p. 156.

[155] **Martin Luther.** 1569, *Table Talk,* 353. *Bartlett's Familiar Quotations* (Boston: Little, Brown and Company, 1855, 1980), p. 156.

[156] **Martin Luther.** Statement. *Bless Your Heart (series 11)* (Eden Prairie, MN: Heartland Samplers, Inc., 1990),4.8.

M

[1] **Alexander MacAlister.** Henry M. Morris, *Men of Science - Men of God* (El Cajon, CA: Master Books, Creation Life Publishers, Inc., 1990), p. 79.

[2] **Douglas MacArthur.** John Stormer, *The Death of a Nation* (Florissant, MO: Liberty Bell Press, 1968), p. 128. John Eidsmoe, *God & Caesar-Christian Faith & Political Action* (Westchester, IL: Crossway Books, a Division of Good News Publishers, 1984), p. 68. 1

[3] **Douglas MacArthur.** October 20,1944, upon landing on Leyte, Philippines. John Bartlett, *Bartlett's Familiar Quotations* (Boston: Little, Brown and Company, 1855,1980), p. 771.

[4] **Douglas MacArthur.** Bob Cutshall, *More Light for the Day* (Minneapolis, MN: Northwestern Products, Inc., 1991), 6.21.

[5] **Thomas Babington, Lord Macaulay.** 1828, in his work *On John Dryden.* John Bartlett, *Bartlett's Familiar Quotations (Boston:* Little, Brown and Company, 1855, 1980), p. 487.

[6] **Thomas Babington, Lord Macaulay.** 1830, in commenting on Southey's edition of John Bunyan's classic book, *Pilgrim's Progress.* John Bartlett, *Bartlett's Familiar Quotations* (Boston: Little, Brown and Company, 1855, 1980), p. 487.

[7] **Thomas Babington, Lord Macaulay.** 1837, in writing *On Lord Bacon.* John Bartlett, *Bartlett's Familiar Quotations* (Boston: Little, Brown and Company, 1855, 1980), p. 488.

[8] **George MacDonald.** 1863, in *David Elginbrod,* Bk. 1, ch. 13. John Bartlett, *Bartlett's Familiar Quotations* (Boston, Little, Brown & Company, 1855, 1980), p. 595.

[9] **James Madison.** Irving Brant, *James Madison - Father of the Constitution, 1787-1800* (New York: Bobbs-Merrill, 1950), Vol. III, p. 84. Tim LaHaye, *Faith of Our Founding Fathers* (Brentwood, TN: Wolgemuth & Hyatt, Publishers; Inc., 1987), p. 126.

[10] **James Madison.** Princeton University. Stephen K. McDowell and Mark A. Beliles, *America's Providential History* (Charlottesville, VA: Providence Press 1988), p. 93. David Barton, *The Myth of Separation* (Aledo, TX: WallBuilder Press, 1991), pp. 92, 93, 119.

[11] **James Madison.** Feb. 24, 1813, message to Congress. James D. Richardson, ed., *A Compilation of the Messages and Papers of the Presidents, 1789-189*, 10 vols (Washington, D.C.: U.S. Government Printing Office, by authority of Congress, 1899), Vol. I, p. 522-523.

[12] **James Madison.** June 20, 1785. James Madison, *A Memorial and Remonstrance* (Washington, D.C.: Library of Congress, Rare

Book Collection, delivered to the General Assembly of the State of Virginia, 1785). Robert Rutland, ed., *The Papers of James Madison* (Chicago: University of Chicago Press, 1973), Vol. VIII, pp. 299, 304. David Barton, *The Myth of Separation* (Aledo, TX: WallBuilder Press, 1991), P. 120. Stephen McDowell and Mark Beliles, "The Providential Perspective" (Charlottesville, VA: The Providence Foundation, P.O. Box 6759, Charlottesville, Va. 22906, January 1994), Vol. 9, No. 1, p. 5.

[13] **James Madison**. 1785. James Madison, *A Memorial and Remonstrance* (Washington, D.C.: Library of Congress, Rare Book Collection, delivered to the General Assembly of the State of Virginia, 1785). Norman Cousins, *"In God We Trust"* (New York: Harper and Brothers, 1958), p. 309. John Eidsmoe, *Christianity and the Constitution - The Faith of Our Founding Fathers* (Grand Rapids, MI: Baker Book House, A Mott Media Book, 1987, 6th printing 1993), p. 108. Stephen McDowell and Mark Beliles, "The Providential Perspective" (Charlottesville, VA: The Providence Foundation, P.O. Box 6759, Charlottesville, Va. 22906, January 1994), Vol. 9, No. 1, p. 5.

[14] **James Madison**. 1785, James Madison, *A Memorial and Remonstrance* (Washington, D.C.: Library of Congress, Rare Book Collection, delivered to the General Assembly of the State of Virginia, 1785). James Madison, *Religious Freedom, A Memorial & Remonstrance to the General Assembly of Virginia, Session of 1785* (Boston: Lincoln and Edmands, 1819), p. 7. Tim LaHaye, *Faith of Our Founding Fathers* (Brentwood, TN: Wolgemuth & Hyatt, Publishers, Inc., 1987), p. 131. Norman Cousins, *"In God We Trust"* (New York: Harper and Brothers, 1958), p. 309. John Eidsmoe, *Christianity and the Constitution - The Faith of Our Founding Fathers* (Grand Rapids, MI: Baker Book House, A Mott Media Book, 1987, 6th printing 1993), p. 107.

[15] **James Madison**. James Madison, *Federalist Paper # 39*. James Madison, Alexander Hamilton, John Jay, *The Federalist on the New Constitution Written 1788* (Philadelphia: Benjamin Warner, 1818), pp. 203-204.

[16] **James Madison**. 1778, attributed. Frederick Nymeyer, *Progressive Calvinism*, (January 1958), Vol. 4, p. 31. Spiritual Mobilization Calendar (Los Angeles, CA: Spiritual Mobilization, First Congregational Church, 1958), inscription. Rousas J. Rushdoony, *Institutes of Biblical Law* (1973). Gary DeMar, *God and Government-A Biblical and Historical Study* (Atlanta, GA: American Vision Press, 1982), pp. 137-138. Stephen K. McDowell and Mark A. Beliles, *America's Providential History* (Charlottesville, VA: Providence Press, 1988), p. 221. Benjamin Hart, *Faith & Freedom - The Christian Roots of American Liberty* (Dallas, TX: Lewis and Stanley, 1988), p. 18. David Barton, *The Myth of Separation* (Aledo, TX: WallBuilder Press, 1991), p. 120. D.P. Diffine, Ph.D., *One Nation Under God - How Close a Separation?* (Searcy, Arkansas: Harding University, Belden Center for Private Enterprise Education, 6th edition, 1992), p. 7. Rush H. Limbaugh, III, *See, I Told You So* (New York, NY: reprinted by permission of Pocket Books, a division of Simon & Schuster Inc., 1993), pp. 73-76. Kirk Fordice, Governor of the State of Mississippi, along with the Secretary of State, D.M., in *An Executive Proclamation By The Governor of the State of Mississippi*, declaring November 20 - November 26, 1994, as "Christian Heritage Week," signed in the Capitol City of Jackson, August 24, 1994. A similar Proclamation was also signed August 23, 1993. Courtesy of Bruce Barilla, Christian Heritage Week Ministry (P.O. Box 58, W.V. 24712; 304-384-7707, 304-384-9044 fax).

[17] **James Madison**. M.E. Bradford, *Religion & The Framers: The Biographical Evidence* (Marlborough, NH: The Plymouth Rock Foundation, 1991), p. 8.

[18] **James Madison**. January 24, 1774, in a letter to William Bradford. James Madison, *The Papers of James Madison*, William T. Hutchinson and William M. Rachal, eds., (Chicago: University of Chicago Press), 1:104-6. Gaillard Hunt, *James Madison and Religious Liberty* (Washington: American Historical Association, Government Printing Office, 1902), p. 167. Gaillard Hunt, *The Life of James Madison* (New York: Russell & Russell, 1902, 1968), p. 12. John Eidsmoe, *Christianity and the Constitution - The Faith of Our Founding Fathers* (Grand Rapids, MI: Baker Book House, A Mott Media Book, 1987, 6th printing 1993), p. 105. Tim LaHaye, *Faith of Our Founding Fathers* (Brentwood, TN: Wolgemuth & Hyatt, Publishers, Inc., 1997), p. 128.

[19] **James Madison**. Gaillard Hunt, *James Madison and Religious Liberty* (Washington: American Historical Association, Government Printing Office, 1902), p. 166. Tim LaHaye, *Faith of Our Founding Fathers* (Brentwood, TN: Wolgemuth & Hyatt, Publishers, Inc., 1987), pp. 78, 127.

[20] **James Madison**. November 20, 1825, in a letter to Frederick Beasley. Norman Cousins, *In God We Trust - The Religious Beliefs and Ideas of the American Founding Fathers* (NY: Harper & Brothers, 1958), p. 321. A.D. Wainwright, ed., *Madison and Witherspoon: Theological Roots of American Political Thought* (The Princeton University Library Chronicle, Spring 1961), p. 125. Charles E. Rice, *The Supreme Court and Public Prayer* (New York- Fordham University Press, 1964), p. 45. Tim LaHaye, *Faith of Our Founding Fathers* (Brentwood, TN: Wolgemuth & Hyatt, Publishers, Inc., 1987), p. 131. "Our Christian Heritage," *Letter from Plymouth Rock* (Marlborough, NH: The Plymouth Rock Foundation), p. 4. John Eidsmoe, *Christianity and the Constitution - The Faith of Our Founding Fathers* (Grand Rapids, MI: Baker Book House, A Mott Media Book, 1987, 6th printing 1993), p. 110. Stephen McDowell and Mark Beliles, "The Providential Perspective" (Charlottesville, VA: The Providence Foundation, P.O. Box 6759, Charlottesville, Va. 27906, January 1994), Vol. 9, No. 1, p. 8.

[21] **James Madison**. October 15,1788. Robert Rutland, ed., *The Papers of James Madison* (Chicago: University of Chicago Press, 1973), Vol. VIII, p. 293. David Barton, *The Myth of Separation* (Aledo, TX: WallBuilder Press, 1991), p. 178.

[22] **James Madison**. March 4, 1809, Saturday, in his Inaugural Address. James D. Richardson (U.S. Representative from Tennessee), ed., *A Compilation of the Messages and Papers of the Presidents 1789-1897*, 10 vols. (Washington, D.C.: U.S. Government Printing Office, published by Authority of Congress, 1897, 1899; Washington, D.C.: Bureau of National Literature and Art, 1789-1902, 11 vols., 1907, 1910), Vol. 1, pp. 466-468. Irving Brant, *James Madison* (Indianapolis: Bobbs-Merrill, 1941), Vol. V, p. 19. *Inaugural Addresses of the Presidents of the United States - From George Washington 1789 to Richard Milhous Nixon 1969* (Washington, D.C.: United States Government Printing Office; 91st Congress, 1st Session, House Document 91-142, 1969), pp. 23-25. Davis Newton Lott, *The Inaugural Addresses of the American Presidents* (NY: Holt, Rinehart and Winston, 1961), p. 27. Charles E. Rice, *The Supreme Court and Public Prayer* (New York: Fordham University Press, 1964), pp. 179-180. Arthur M. Schlesinger, *The State of the Union Messages of the Presidents, 1790 -1966* (New York: Chelsea House,-Robert Hector, 1966); Adrienne Koch, *Madison's "Advice to My Country"* (Princeton: Princeton University Press, 1966), p. 43. Tim LaHaye, *Faith of Our Founding Fathers* (Brentwood, TN: Wolgemuth & Hyatt, Publishers, Inc., 1987), p. 131. John Eidsmoe, *Christianity and the Constitution - The Faith of Our Founding Fathers* (Grand Rapids, NU: Baker Book House, A Mott Media Book, 1987, 6th printing 1993), p. 110. J. Michael Sharman, J.D., *Faith of the Fathers* (Culpepper, Virginia: Victory Publishing, 1995), p. 28.

[23] **James Madison.** James Madison, *The Papers of James Madison*, William T. Hutchinson and William M. Rachal, eds., (Chicago: University of Chicago, 1912), Vol. I, pp. 7, 51-60. Tim LaHaye, *Faith of Our Founding Fathers* (Brentwood, TN: Wolgemuth & Hyatt, Publishers, Inc., 1987), p. 130. John Eidsmoe, *Christianity and the Constitution - The Faith of Our Founding Fathers* (Grand Rapids, MI: Baker Book House, A Mott Media Book, 1987, 6th printing 1993), p. 97.

[24] **James Madison.** William C. Rives, *Biography of James Madison*, Vol. I, pp. 33-34. Stephen Abbott Northrop, D.D., *A Cloud of Witnesses* (Portland, OR: American Heritage Ministries, 1987; Mantle Ministries, 228 Still Ridge, Bulverde, Texas), p. 307.

[25] **James Madison.** William C. Rives, *Biography of James Madison*, Vol. I, pp. 33-34. Stephen Abbott Northrop, D.D., *A Cloud of Witnesses* (Portland, OR: American Heritage Ministries, 1987; Mantle Ministries, 228 Still Ridge, Bulverde, Texas), p. 307.

[26] **James Madison.** William C. Rives, *Biography of James Madison*, Vol. I, pp. 33-34. Stephen Abbott Northrop, D.D., *A Cloud of Witnesses* (Portland, OR: American Heritage Ministries, 1987; Mantle Ministries, 228 Still Ridge, Bulverde, Texas), p. 307.

[27] **James Madison.** November 9, 1772, in writing to William Bradford. William T. Hutchinson and William M. Rachal, eds., *The Papers of James Madison* (Chicago: University of Chicago Press, 1962), Vol. I, p. 51-60, 75. Tim LaHaye, *Faith of Our Founding Fathers* (Brentwood, TN: Wolgemuth & Hyatt, Publishers, Inc., 1987), pp. 130-131. John Eidsmoe, *Christianity and the Constitution - The Faith of Our Founding Fathers* (Grand Rapids, MI: Baker Book House, A Mott Media Book, 1987, 6th printing 1993), p. 98.

[28] **Magna Carta.** 1215, signed by King John of England on the meadow of Runnymeade. John Bartlett, *Bartlett's Familiar Quotations* (Boston: Little, Brown and Company, 1855, 1980), p. 138. *The World Book Encyclopedia*, 18 vols. (Chicago, IL: Field Enterprises, Inc., 1957; W.F. Quarrie and Company, 8 vols., 1917; World Book, Inc., 22 vols., 1989), Vol. 11, p. 4709. Richard L. Perry, ed., *Sources of Our Liberties: Documentary Origins of Individual Liberties in the United States Constitution and Bill of Rights* (Chicago: American Bar Foundation, 1978; New York: 1952). Charles E. Rice, *The Supreme Court and Public Prayer* (New York: Fordham University Press, 1964), p. 159. Benjamin Hart, *Faith & Freedom - The Christian Roots of American Liberty* (Dallas, TX: Lewis and Stanley, 1988), p. 17.

[29] **Charles Habib Malik.** 1958. The Honorable Charles Malik, Ambassador to the United Nations from Lebanon, in his Farewell speech upon his retirement. "Our Christian Heritage," *Letter from Plymouth Rock* (Marlborough, NH: The Plymouth Rock Foundation), p. 7. Russ Walton, *Biblical Principles of Importance to Godly Christians* (Marlborough, NH: The Plymouth Rock Foundation, 1984), pp. 21, 23.

[30] **André Malraux.** 1967, *Anti-Memoirs*, sec. 6. John Bartlett, *Bartlett's Familiar Quotations* (Boston: Little, Brown and Company, 1855, 1980), p. 853.

[31] **Clarence E. Manion.** Verne Paul Kaub, *Collectivism Challenges Christianity* (Winona Lake, IN: Light and Life Press, 1946), p. 58. Tim LaHaye, *Faith of Our Founding Fathers* (Brentwood, TN: Wolgemuth & Hyatt, Publishers, Inc., 1987), p. 65.

[32] **Francis Marion.** General Henry and Mason Locke Weems, *Life of General Francis Marion*. Stephen Abbott Northrop, D.D., *A Cloud of Witnesses* (Portland, OR: American Heritage Ministries, 1987; Mantle Ministries, 228 Still Ridge, Bulverde, Texas), pp. 317-318.

[33] **John Marshall.** 1833, as Chief Justice of the United States Supreme Court. Robert K. Doman and Csaba Vedlik, Jr., *Judicial Supremacy: The Supreme Court on Trial* (MA: Plymouth Rock Foundation, 1986), p. 85. David Barton, *The Myth of Separation* (Aledo, TX: WallBuilder Press, 1991), p. 169.

[34] **John Marshall.** 1835, as Chief Justice of the United States Supreme Court. Catherine Millard, *The Rewriting of America's History* (Camp Hill, PA: Horizon House Publishers, 1991), p. 265.

[35] **John Marshall.** Chief Justice of the United States Supreme Court. Albert J. Beveridge, *The Life of John Marshall* (Boston: Houghton Mifflin, 1919, 1947), Vol. IV, pp. 70-71. David Barton, *The Myth of Separation* (Aledo, TX: WallBuilder Press, 1991), pp. 80-81.

[36] **John Marshall.** John F. Schroeder, ed., *Maxims of Washington* (Mt. Vernon: Mt. Vernon Ladies' Association, 1942), p. 274. Tim LaHaye, *Faith of Our Founding Fathers* (Brentwood, TN: Wolgemuth & Hyatt, Publishers, Inc., 1987), p. 102.

[37] **John Marshall.** Allen B. Magruder, *American Statesmen Series-"John Marshall,"* p. 265. Stephen Abbott Northrop, D.D., *A Cloud of Witnesses* (Portland, OR: American Heritage Ministries, 1987; Mantle Ministries, 228 Still Ridge, Bulverde, Texas), pp. 308-309.

[38] **John Marshall.** 1819, in the case of *McCulloch v. Maryland*, 4 Wheaton 316, 431. John Bartlett, *Bartlett's Familiar Quotations* (Boston: Little, Brown and Company, 1855, 1980), p. 402.

[39] **Peter Marshall.** 1947, in a message as Chaplain of the United States Senate. Robert Flood, *The Rebirth of America* (Philadelphia: Arthur S. DeMoss Foundation, 1986), p. 205. Peter Marshall and David Manuel, *The Glory of America* (Bloomington, MN: Garborg's Heart 'N Home, Inc., 1991), 1.13.

[40] **Luther Martin.** M.E. Bradford, *Religion & The Framers: The Biographical Evidence* (Marlborough, NH: The Plymouth Rock Foundation, 1991), p. 8. M.E. Bradford, *A Worthy Company* (Marlborough, NH: Plymouth Rock Foundation, 1982), p. 114. Tim LaHaye, *Faith of Our Founding Fathers* (Brentwood, TN: Wolgemuth & Hyatt, Publishers, Inc., 1987), p. 242.

[41] **Charter of Maryland.** June 20, 1632, issued by King Charles I to Cecilius Calvert, Second Lord Baltimore. Henry Steele Commager, ed., *Documents of American History*, 2 vols. (NY: F.S. Crofts and Company, 1934; Appleton-Century-Crofts, Inc., 1948, 6th edition, 1958; Englewood Cliffs, NJ: Prentice Hall, Inc., 9th edition, 1973), Vol. I, p. 21. William McDonald, ed., *Documentary Source Book of American History, 1606-1889* (NY: The Macmillan Company, 1909), p. 32. Charles E. Rice, *The Supreme Court and Public Prayer* (New York: Fordham University Press, 1964), pp. 160-161. Richard L. Perry, ed., *Sources of Our Liberties: Documentary Origins of Individual Liberties in the United States Constitution and Bill of Rights* (Chicago: American Bar Foundation, 1978; New York: 1952), p. 105. David Barton, *The Myth of Separation* (Aledo, TX: WallBuilder Press, 1991), p. 86. Pat Robertson, *America's Dates With Destiny* (Nashville, TN: Thomas Nelson Publishers, 1986), pp. 31-32. Frances Newton Thorpe, ed., *Federal and State Constitutions, Colonial Charters, and Other Organic Laws of the States, Territories, and Colonies now or heretofore forming the United States*, 7 vols. (Washington: Government Printing Office, 1905; 1909; St. Clair Shores, MI: Scholarly Press, 1968), Vol. III, pp. 1677 ff.

[42] **Colony of Maryland.** 1649, *Act Concerning Religion*. *The World Book Encyclopedia*, 18 vols. (Chicago, IL: Field Enterprises, Inc., 1957; W.F. Quarrie and Company, 8 vols., 1917; World Book, Inc., 22 vols., 1989), Vol. 11, p. 4833.

[43] **Colony of Maryland.** 1649, *Act of Toleration*. Samuel Wilberforce, *A History of the Protestant Episcopal Church in America* (Oxford, London: 1853). Verna M. Hall, *The Christian History of the American Revolution* (San Francisco: Foundation for Christian Education, 1976), p. 159.

[44] **Colony of Maryland.** March 25, 1634, as recorded by Father White. J. Moss Ives, *The Ark and the Dove* (NY: Cooper Square Publishers, Inc., 1936, 1969), p. 119. Joseph Banvard, *Tragic Scenes in the History of Maryland and the Old French War* (Boston: Gould

Notes

and Lincoln, 1856), p. 32. David Barton, *The Myth of Separation* (Aledo, TX: WallBuilder Press, 1991), p. 86.

⁴⁵ **Maryland Toleration Act.** April 21, 1649. *Act of Toleration.* W.H. Browne, ed., The Archives of Maryland, I:244ff. Henry Steele Commager, ed., *Documents of American History*, 2 vols. (NY: F.S. Crofts and Company, 1934; Appleton-Century-Crofts, Inc., 1948, 6th edition, 1958; Englewood Cliffs, NJ: Prentice Hall, Inc., 9th edition, 1973), Vol. I, p. 31. Lillian W. Kay, ed., *The Ground on Which We Stand - Basic Documents of American History* (NY: Franklin Watts., Inc, 1969), (portions), pp. 4-5. Samuel Wilberforce, *A History of the Protestant Episcopal Church in America* (Oxford, London: 1853). Verna M. Hall, *The Christian History of the American Revolution* (San Francisco: Foundation for Christian Education, 1976), p. 159. "Our Christian Heritage," *Letter from Plymouth Rock* (Marlborough, NH: The Plymouth Rock Foundation), p. 2. "An Act concerning Religion" issued by the Maryland Colonial Assembly. Anson Phelps Stokes and Leo Pfeffer, *Church and State in the United States* (NY: Harper and Row, Publishers, 1950, revised one-volume edition, 1964), p. 12.

⁴⁶ **Constitution of the State of Maryland.** 1776. Benjamin Weiss, *God in American History: A Documentation of America's Religious Heritage* (Grand Rapids, MI: Zondervan, 1966), p. 155. Gary DeMar, *America's Christian History: The Untold Story* (Atlanta, GA: American Vision Publishers, Inc., 1993), p. 65.

⁴⁷ **Constitution of the State of Maryland.** August 14, 1776, in Article XXXV. *The Constitutions of All the United States According to the Latest Amendments* (Lexington, KY: Thomas T. Skillman, 1817), p. 188. Benjamin Franklin Morris, *The Christian Life and Character of the Civil Institutions of the United States* (Philadelphia, PA: L. Johnson & Co., 1863; George W. Childs, 1864), p. 233. Frances Newton Thorpe, ed., *Federal and State Constitutions, Colonial Charters, and Other Organic Laws of the States, Territories, and Colonies now or heretofore forming the United States*, 7 vols. (Washington: Government Printing Office, 1905; 1909; St. Clair Shores, MI: Scholarly Press, 1968), Vol. III. *Federal and State Constitutions, Colonial Charters, and Other Organic Laws of the States, Territories, and Colonies now or heretofore forming the United States*, 7 vols. (Washington: Government Printing Office, 1909). Tim LaHaye, *Faith of Our Founding Fathers* (Brentwood, TN: Wolgemuth & Hyatt, Publishers, Inc., 1987), p. 74. Gary DeMar, "Censoring America's Christian History" (Atlanta, GA: *The Biblical Worldview*, An American Vision Publication - American Vision, Inc., July 1990), p. 7. David Barton, *The Myth of Separation* (Aledo, TX: WallBuilder Press, 1991), p. 24.

⁴⁸ **Constitution of the State of Maryland.** August 14, 1776, Article XXXVI. Frances Newton Thorpe, ed., *Federal and State Constitutions, Colonial Charters, and Other Organic Laws of the States, Territories, and Colonies now or heretofore forming the United States*, 7 vols. (Washington: Government Printing Office, 1905; 1909; St. Clair Shores, MI: Scholarly Press, 1968), Vol. III. Tim LaHaye, *Faith of Our Founding Fathers* (Brentwood, TN: Wolgemuth & Hyatt, Publishers, Inc., 1987), p. 74.

⁴⁹ **Constitution of the State of Maryland.** 1776, Article XIX, XXXIII. Benjamin Franklin Morris, *The Christian Life and Character of the Civil Institutions of the United States* (Philadelphia, PA: L. Johnson & Co., 1863; George W. Childs, 1864), p. 234. Frances Newton Thorpe, ed., *Federal and State Constitutions, Colonial Charters, and Other Organic Laws of the States, Territories, and Colonies now or heretofore forming the United States*, 7 vols. (Washington: Government Printing Office, 1905; 1909; St. Clair Shores, MI: Scholarly Press, 1968). Gary DeMar, *God And Government, A Biblical and Historical Study* (Atlanta, GA: American Vision Press, 1982), p. 164. Edwin S. Gaustad, *Neither King nor Prelate - Religion and the New Nation, 1776-1826* (Grand Rapids, MI: William B. Eerdmans Publishing Company, 1993), p. 164.

⁵⁰ **Constitution of the State of Maryland.** 1851. Supreme Court Justice David Josiah Brewer, who served 1890-1910, in his work, *The United States - A Christian Nation* (Philadelphia: The John C. Winston Company, 1905, Supreme Court Collection). Catherine Millard, *The Rewriting of America's History*, (Camp Hill, PA: Horizon House Publishers, 1991), p. 389. "Our Christian Heritage," *Letter from Plymouth Rock* (Marlborough, NH: The Plymouth Rock Foundation), p. 6.

⁵¹ **Constitution of the State of Maryland.** 1864. Benjamin Franklin Morris, *The Christian Life and Character of the Civil Institutions of the United States* (Philadelphia: George W. Childs, 1864). Supreme Court Justice David Josiah Brewer, who served 1890-1910, in his work, *The United States - Christian Nation* (Philadelphia: The John C. Winston Company, 1905, Supreme Court Collection). "Our Christian Heritage," *Letter from Plymouth Rock* (Marlborough, NH: The Plymouth Rock Foundation), p. 6. Catherine Millard, *The Rewriting of America's History* (Camp Hill, PA: Horizon House Publishers, 1991), p. 389.

⁵² **Supreme Court of Maryland.** 1799. *M'Creery's Lessee v. Allender*, 4 H. & Mett. 259 (1799). David Barton, *The Myth of Separation* (Aledo, TX: WallBuilder Press, 1991), p. 63.

⁵³ **Supreme Court of Maryland.** 1799, *Runkel v. Winemiller*, 4 Harris & McHenry 276, 288 (Sup. Ct. Md. 1799). David Barton, *The Myth of Separation* (Aledo, TX: WallBuilder Press, 1991), p. 64. *Runkel v. Winemiller*, 4 Harris & McHenry (MD) 429 1 AD 411, 417 (Justice Chase). "Our Christian Heritage," *Letter from Plymouth Rock* (Marlborough, NH: The Plymouth Rock Foundation), p. 4.

⁵⁴ **George Mason.** June 12, 1776, *Virginia Bill of Rights*, Article XVI. Frances Newton Thorpe, ed., *Federal and State Constitutions, Colonial Charters, and Other Organic Laws of the States, Territories, and Colonies now or heretofore forming the United States*, 7 vols. (Washington: Government Printing Office, 1905; 1909; St. Clair Shores, MI: Scholarly Press, 1968), Vol. VII, p. 3814. Henry Steele Commager, ed., *Documents of American History*, 2 vols. (NY: F.S. Crofts and Company, 1934; Appleton-Century-Crofts, Inc., 1948, 6th edition, 1958; Englewood Cliffs, NJ: Prentice Hall, Inc., 9th edition, 1973), pp. 103-104. Anson Phelps Stokes and Leo Pfeffer, *Church and State in the United States* (NY: Harper and Row, Publishers, 1950, revised one-volume edition, 1964), p. 42. *The Annals of America*, 20 vols. (Chicago, IL: Encyclopedia Britannica, 1968), Vol. 2, p. 433. Charles Fadiman, ed., *The American Treasury* (NY: Harper & Brothers, Publishers, 1955), p. 121. Pat Robertson, *America's Dates with Destiny* (Nashville: Thomas Nelson Publishers, 1986), pp. 80-81. "Our Christian Heritage," *Letter from Plymouth Rock* (Marlborough, NH: The Plymouth Rock Foundation), p. 3. Kate Mason Rowland, *The Life of George Mason*, Vol. I. p. 435. Catherine Millard, *The Rewriting of America's History* (Camp Hill, PA: Horizon House Publishers, 1991), p. 145.

⁵⁵ **George Mason.** In an address before the General Court of Virginia. Russ Walton, *Biblical Principles of Importance to Godly Christians* (Marlborough, NH: The Plymouth Rock Foundation, 1984), p. 358. David Barton, *The Myth of Separation* (Aledo, TX: WallBuilder Press, 1991), p. 200.

⁵⁶ **George Mason.** Russ Walton, *Biblical Principles of Importance to Godly Christians* (Marlborough, NH: The Plymouth Rock Foundation, 1984), p. 358. David Barton, *The Myth of Separation* (Aledo, TX: WallBuilder Press, 1991), p. 200.

⁵⁷ **George Mason.** August 22, 1787, in addressing the Continental Congress. James Madison, *Notes of Debates in the Federal Convention of 1787* (1787, reprinted NY: W.W. Norton Co., 1987), p. 504. David Barton, *The Myth of Separation* (Aledo, TX: WallBuilder Press, 1991), p. 217, 258. Robert A. Rutland, ed., *The Papers of George Mason*, 3 vols. (Chapel Hill, NC: The University of North Carolina Press, 1970), 3:1787. Marshall Foster and Mary-Elaine Swanson, *The American Covenant - The Untold Story* (Roseburg, OR: Foundation for Christian Self-Government, 1981; Thousand Oaks, CA: The Mayflower Institute, 1983, 1992), p. 142. Peter Marshall and David Manuel, *The Glory of America* (Bloomington, MN: Garborg's Heart'N Home, Inc., 1991), 1.31.

58 George Mason. March 9, 1773, writing in their Family Bible of his wife's death. George Mason, *Eulogy on Ann Mason* (Lorton, VA: Gunston Hall Plantation, inscribed in original 1759 Family Bible). Catherine Millard, *The Rewriting of America's History* (Camp Hill, PA: Horizon House Publishers, 1991), pp. 147-149.

59 George Mason. In his last *Will and Testament.* Robert C. Mason, *George Mason of Virginia - Citizen, Statesman and Philosopher* (New York: Oscar Aurelius Morgnor, An address Commemorative of the launching of the S.S. *Gunston Hall* at Alexandria, Virginia, January 1919), p. 10. Catherine Millard, *The Rewriting of America's History* (Camp Hill, PA: Horizon House Publishers, 1991), pp. 151-152.

60 First Charter of Massachusetts. March 4, 1629. Ebenezer Hazard, *Historical Collection - Consisting of State Papers and other Authentic Documents - Intended as Materials for an History of the United States of America* (Philadelphia: T. Dobson, 1792), Vol. I, p. 252. Benjamin Franklin Morris, *The Christian Life and Character of the Civil Institutions of the United States* (Philadelphia: George W. Childs, 1864), p. 56. William McDonald, ed., *Documentary Source Book of American History, 1606-1889* (NY: The Macmillan Company, 1909), p. 26. Frances Newton Thorpe, ed., *Federal and State Constitutions, Colonial Charters, and Other Organic Laws of the States, Territories, and Colonies now or heretofore forming the United States,* 7 vols. (Washington: Government Printing Office, 1905; 1909; St. Clair Shores, MI: Scholarly Press, 1968). Henry Steele Commager, ed., *Documents of American History,* 2 vols. (NY: F.S. Crofts and Company, 1934; Appleton-Century-Crofts, Inc., 1948, 6th edition, 1958; Englewood Cliffs, NJ: Prentice Hall, Inc., 9th edition, 1973), p. 16, 18. *The Annals of America,* 20 vols. (Chicago, IL: Encyclopedia Britannica, 1968), Vol. II, pp. 101, 103. Gary DeMar, *God and Government-A Biblical and Historical Study* (Atlanta, GA: American Vision Press, 1982), p. 112. "Our Christian Heritage," *Letter from Plymouth Rock* (Marlborough, NH: The Plymouth Rock Foundation), p. 2. David Barton, *The Myth of Separation* (Aledo, TX: WallBuilder Press, 1991), p. 85.

61 Massachusetts Bay Colony. June 1630. *A Model of Christian Charity.* Francis W. Coker, ed., *Democracy, Liberty, and Property: Readings in the American Political Tradition* (NY: The Macmillan Co., 1942), pp. 18-20. David Barton, *The Myth of Separation* (Aledo, TX: WallBuilder Press, 1991), pp. 85-86. John Bartlett, *Bartlett's Familiar Quotations* (Boston: Little, Brown and Company, 1855, 1980), p. 264.

62 Massachusetts Body of Liberties. 1641. *Massachusetts Colonial Records,* 1:174. Benjamin Fletcher Wright, Jr., *American Interpretations of Natural Law* (New York: Russell & Russell, 1962), p. 33. John Eidsmoe, *Christianity and the Constitution - The Faith of Our Founding Fathers* (Grand Rapids, MI: Baker Book House, A Mott Media Book, 1987, 6th printing 1993), p. 33. "Our Christian Heritage," *Letter from Plymouth Rock* (Marlborough, NH: The Plymouth Rock Foundation), p. 2.

63 Massachusetts Bay Colony. 1647. *Old Deluder Satan Law. The Code of 1650 - Being a Compilation of the Earliest Laws and Orders of the General Court of Connecticut* (Hartford: Silus Andrus, 1822), pp. 20-91, 92-94. *The Laws and Liberties of Massachusetts,* 1648 (reprinted Cambridge: 1929), cited in *McCollum v. Board of Education,* 68 S.Ct. 461, 333 U.S. 203 (1948). *Records of the Governor of the Massachusetts Bay in New England,* II:203. Henry Steele Commager, ed., *Documents of American History,* 2 vols. (NY: F.S. Crofts and Company, 1934; Appleton-Century-Crofts, Inc., 1948, 6th edition, 1958; Englewood Cliffs, NJ: Prentice Hall, Inc., 9th edition, 1973), Vol. I, p. 29. John Eidsmoe, *Christianity and the Constitution - The Faith of Our Founding Fathers* (Grand Rapids, MI: Baker Book House, A Mott Media Book, 1987, 6th printing 1993), p. 28. David Barton, *The Myth of Separation* (Aledo, TX: WallBuilder Press, 1991), p. 90. *The Annals of America,* 20 vols. (Chicago, IL: Encyclopedia Britannica, 1968), Vol. I, p. 203. John Wilson Taylor, M.A., Ph.D., et al., *The Lincoln Library of Essential Information* (Buffalo, New York: The Frontier Press Company, 1935), p. 1623. D.P. Diffine, Ph.D., *One Nation Under God - How Close a Separation?* (Searcy, Arkansas: Harding University, Belden Center for Private Enterprise Education, 6th edition, 1992), p. 2.

64 Boston, Massachusetts. 1765. In an address by Jonathan Mayhew. Clinton Rossiter, *Seedtime of the Republic* (New York: Harcourt, Brace & World, Inc., 1953), p. 241. Peter Marshall and David Manuel, *The Glory of America* (Bloomington, MN: Garborg's Heart'N Home, Inc., 1991), 2.18.

65 Provincial Congress of Massachusetts. October 1774. President John Hancock. George Bancroft, *Bancroft's History of the United States,* Vol. 1-X (Boston: Charles C. Little & James Brown, 3rd Edition, 1838) Vol. VII, p. 229. Peter Marshall and David Manuel, *The Light and the Glory* (Old Tappan, N.J.: Fleming H. Revell Company, 1977), pp. 268-269.

66 Provincial Congress of Massachusetts. 1774. George Bancroft, *Bancroft's History of the United States,* Vol. 1-X (Boston: Charles C. Little & James Brown, 3rd Edition, 1838) Vol. VII, p. 229. Peter Marshall and David Manuel, *The Glory of America* (Bloomington, MN: Garborg's Heart'N Home, Inc., 1991), 8.31.

67 Provincial Congress of Massachusetts. Minutemen. Richard Frothingham, *Rise of the Republic of the United States* (Boston: Little Brown & Co., 1872), pp. 393, 458. David Barton, *The Myth of Separation* (Aledo, TX: WallBuilder Press, 1991), p. 94.

68 Provincial Congress of Massachusetts. Charge to the Minutemen. Richard Frothingham, *Rise of the Republic of the United States* (Boston: Little, Brown & Co., 1872), p. 393. David Barton, *The Myth of Separation* (Aledo, TX: WallBuilder Press, 1991), pp. 94-95.

69 Provincial Congress of Massachusetts. April 15, 1775, in declaring a Day of Public Humiliation, Fasting and Prayer. Proclamation of John Hancock from Concord (from an original in the Evans Collection, #14220, by the American Antiquarian Society.) David Barton, *The Myth of Separation* (Aledo, TX: WallBuilder Press, 1991), pp. 102-103. William Lincoln, ed., *The Journals of Each Provincial Congress of Massachusetts, 1774-1775* (Boston: Dutton & Wentworth, 1838), pp. 114-145.

70 Provincial Congress of Massachusetts. May 31, 1775, address by Harvard President Samuel Langdon, reprinted by Plumstead, *The Wall,* pp. 364-373. Peter Marshall and David Manuel, *The Light and the Glory* (Old Tappan, NJ: Fleming H. Revell Company, 1977), pp. 277-278.

71 Constitution of the State of Massachusetts. 1780, in the Preamble. Henry Steele Commager, ed., *Documents of American History,* 2 vols. (NY: F.S. Crofts and Company, 1934; Appleton-Century-Crofts, Inc., 1948, 6th edition, 1958; Englewood Cliffs, NJ: Prentice Hall, Inc., 9th edition, 1973), Vol. I, pp. 107-108. *The Annals of America,* 20 vols. (Chicago, IL: Encyclopedia Britannica, 1968), Vol. I, pp. 322-333. Jacob C. Meyer, *Church and State in Massachusetts from 1740-1833* (Cleveland: Western Reserve Press, 1930), pp. 234-235. Anson Phelps Stokes and Leo Pfeffer, *Church and State in the United States* (NY: Harper and Row, Publishers, 1950, revised one-volume edition, 1964), p. 77. *The Constitutions of All the United States According to the Latest Amendments* (Lexington, KY: Thomas T. Skillman, 1817), p. 89. David Barton, *The Myth of Separation* (Aledo, TX: WallBuilder Press, 1991), p. 24. *The Constitutions of the Several Independent States of America* (Philadelphia: Bailey, published by order of the U.S. Continental Congress, 1781, in the Evans Collection, #17390), p. 138. Gary DeMar, "Censoring America's Christian History" (Atlanta, GA: *The Biblical Worldview,* An American Vision Publication - American Vision, Inc., July 1990), p. 7. Benjamin Weiss, *God in American History: A Documentation of America's Religious Heritage* (Grand Rapids, MI: Zondervan, 1966), p. 155. Gary DeMar, *America's Christian History: The Untold Story* (Atlanta, GA: American Vision Publishers, Inc., 1993), p. 65. Frances Newton Thorpe, ed.,

Federal and State Constitutions, Colonial Charters, and Other Organic Laws of the States, Territories, and Colonies now or heretofore forming the United States, 7 vols. (Washington: Government Printing Office, 1905; 1909; St. Clair Shores, MI: Scholarly Press, 1968), Vol. V, p. 38.

[72] **Constitution of the State of Massachusetts.** 1780, qualifications for the office of governor. Frances Newton Thorpe, ed., *Federal and State Constitutions, Colonial Charters, and Other Organic Laws of the States, Territories, and Colonies now or heretofore forming the United States*, 7 vols. (Washington: Government Printing Office, 1905; 1909; St. Clair Shores, MI: Scholarly Press, 1968), Vol. III, pp. 1900, 1908. Tim LaHaye, *Faith of Our Founding Fathers* (Brentwood, TN: Wolgemuth & Hyatt, Publishers, Inc., 1987), p. 266.

[73] **Constitution of the State of Massachusetts.** 1780, Chapter VI, Article I. *The Constitutions of All the United States According to the Latest Amendments* (Lexington, KY: Thomas T. Skillman, 1817), p. 89. David Barton, *The Myth of Separation*, (Aledo, TX: WallBuilder Press, 1991), p. 24.

[74] **Constitution of the State of Massachusetts.** 1780, Part I, Article II. *The Constitutions of All the United States According to the Latest Amendments* (Lexington, KY: Thomas T. Skillman, 1817), pp. 60, 62. Frances Newton Thorpe, ed., *Federal and State Constitutions, Colonial Charters, and Other Organic Laws of the States, Territories, and Colonies now or heretofore forming the United States*, 7 vols. (Washington: Government Printing Office, 1905; 1909; St. Clair Shores, MI: Scholarly Press, 1968), Vol. V, p. 38. Henry Steele Commager, ed., *Documents of American History*, 2 vols. (NY: F.S. Crofts and Company, 1934; Appleton-Century-Crofts, Inc., 1948, 6th edition, 1958; Englewood Cliffs, NJ: Prentice Hall, Inc., 9th edition, 1973), Vol. I, pp. 107-108. *The Annals of America*, 20 vols. (Chicago, IL: Encyclopedia Britannica, 1968), Vol. I, pp. 322-333. Jacob C. Meyer, *Church and State in Massachusetts from 1740-1833* (Cleveland: Western Reserve Press, 1930) pp. 234-235. Anson Phelps Stokes and Leo Pfeffer, *Church and State in the United States* (NY: Harper and Row, Publishers, 1950, revised one-volume edition, 1964), p. 77. *The Constitutions of the Several Independent States of America* (Philadelphia: Bailey, published by order of the U.S. Continental Congress, 1781, in the Evans Collection, #17390), p. 138. Gary DeMar, "Censoring America's Christian History" (Atlanta, GA: *The Biblical Worldview*, An American Vision Publication - American Vision, Inc., July 1990), p. 7. David Barton, *The Myth of Separation* (Aledo, TX: WallBuilder Press, 1991), p. 28.

[75] **Constitution of the State of Massachusetts.** 1780, Part I, Article III. *The Constitutions of the Several Independent States of America* (Philadelphia: Bailey, published by order of the U.S. Continental Congress, 1781, in the Evans Collection, #17390), p. 138. *The Constitutions of All the United States According to the Latest Amendments* (Lexington, KY: Thomas T. Skillman, 1817), pp. 60-62. Benjamin Franklin Morris, *The Christian Life and Character of the Civil Institutions of the United States* (Philadelphia, PA: L. Johnson & Co., 1863; George W. Childs, 1864), p. 229. Frances Newton Thorpe, ed., *Federal and State Constitutions, Colonial Charters, and Other Organic Laws of the States, Territories, and Colonies now or heretofore forming the United States*, 7 vols. (Washington: Government Printing Office, 1905; 1909; St. Clair Shores, MI: Scholarly Press, 1968), Vol. V, p. 38. Henry Steele Commager, ed., *Documents of American History*, 2 vols. (NY: F.S. Crofts and Company, 1934; Appleton-Century-Crofts, Inc., 1948, 6th edition, 1958; Englewood Cliffs, NJ: Prentice Hall, Inc., 9th edition, 1973), Vol. I, pp. 107-108. Jacob C. Meyer, *Church and State in Massachusetts from 1740-1833* (Cleveland: Western Reserve Press, 1930) pp. 234-235. Anson Phelps Stokes and Leo Pfeffer, *Church and State in the United States* (NY: Harper and Row, Publishers, 1950, revised one-volume edition, 1964), p. 77. *The Annals of America*, 20 vols. (Chicago, IL: Encyclopedia Britannica, 1968), Vol. I, pp. 322-333. Gary DeMar, *God and Government-A Biblical and Historical Study* (Atlanta, GA: American Vision Press, 1982), pp. 164-165. Gary DeMar, "Censoring America's Christian History" (Atlanta, GA: *The Biblical Worldview*, An American Vision Publication - American Vision, Inc., July 1990), p. 7. David Barton, *The Myth of Separation* (Aledo, TX: WallBuilder Press, 1991), pp. 24-28. Stephen McDowell and Mark Beliles, "The Providential Perspective" (Charlottesville, VA: The Providence Foundation, P.O. Box 6759, Charlottesville, Va. 22906, January 1994), Vol. 9, No. 1, p. 5.

[76] **Constitution of the State of Massachusetts.** 1780, Part I, Article III. *The Constitutions of the Several Independent States of America* (Philadelphia: Bailey, published by order of the U.S. Continental Congress, 1781, in the Evans Collection, #17390), p. 138. *The Constitutions of All the United States According to the Latest Amendments* (Lexington, KY: Thomas T. Skillman, 1817), pp. 60-62. Benjamin Franklin Morris, *The Christian Life and Character of the Civil Institutions of the United States* (Philadelphia, PA: L. Johnson & Co., 1863; George W. Childs, 1864), p. 229. Frances Newton Thorpe, ed., *Federal and State Constitutions, Colonial Charters, and Other Organic Laws of the States, Territories, and Colonies now or heretofore forming the United States*, 7 vols. (Washington: Government Printing Office, 1905; 1909; St. Clair Shores, MI: Scholarly Press, 1968), Vol. V, p. 38. Henry Steele Commager, ed., *Documents of American History*, 2 vols. (NY: F.S. Crofts and Company, 1934; Appleton-Century-Crofts, Inc., 1948, 6th edition, 1958; Englewood Cliffs, NJ: Prentice Hall, Inc., 9th edition, 1973), Vol. I, pp. 107-108. Jacob C. Meyer, *Church and State in Massachusetts from 1740-1833* (Cleveland: Western Reserve Press, 1930) pp. 234-235. Anson Phelps Stokes and Leo Pfeffer, *Church and State in the United States* (NY: Harper and Row, Publishers, 1950, revised one-volume edition, 1964), p. 77. *The Annals of America*, 20 vols. (Chicago, IL: Encyclopedia Britannica, 1968), Vol. I, pp. 322-333. Gary DeMar, *God and Government-A Biblical and Historical Study* (Atlanta, GA: American Vision Press, 1982), pp. 164-165. Gary DeMar, "Censoring America's Christian History" (Atlanta, GA: *The Biblical Worldview*, An American Vision Publication - American Vision, Inc., July 1990), p. 7. David Barton, *The Myth of Separation* (Aledo, TX: WallBuilder Press, 1991), pp. 24-28. Stephen McDowell and Mark Beliles, "The Providential Perspective" (Charlottesville, VA: The Providence Foundation, P.O. Box 6759, Charlottesville, Va. 22906, January 1994), Vol. 9, No. 1, p. 5.

[77] **Commonwealth (State) of Massachusetts.** November 8, 1783, A Proclamation for a Day of Thanksgiving - signed by Governor John Hancock from Boston (from an original in the Evans collection, #18025, by the American Antiquarian Society.) David Barton, *The Myth of Separation* (Aledo, TX: WallBuilder Press, 1991), pp. 106-107.

[78] **Massachusetts Grand Jury.** "Our Christian Heritage," *Letter from Plymouth Rock* (Marlborough, NH: The Plymouth Rock Foundation), pp. 4-5.

[79] **Massachusetts.** Tim LaHaye, *Faith of Our Founding Fathers* (Brentwood, TN: Wolgemuth & Hyatt, Publishers, Inc., 1987), p. 74.

[80] **Supreme Court of Massachusetts.** 1838. *Commonwealth v. Abner Kneeland*, 37 Mass. (20 Pick) 206, 216-217 (1838). David Barton, *The Myth of Separation* (Aledo, TX: WallBuilder Press, 1991), p. 58-61.

[81] **Supreme Court of Massachusetts.** 1838. *Commonwealth v. Abner Kneeland*, 37 Mass. (20 Pick) 206, 216-217 (1838). David Barton, *The Myth of Separation* (Aledo, TX: WallBuilder Press, 1991), p. 58-61.

[82] **Supreme Court of Massachusetts.** 1838. *Commonwealth v. Abner Kneeland*, 37 Mass. (20 Pick) 206, 233, 234 (Sup.Ct.Mass.1838). David Barton, *The Myth of Separation* (Aledo, TX: WallBuilder Press, 1991), p. 182.

[83] **Cotton Mather.** 1702, in the *Magnalia Christi Americana*, (*The Great Achievement of Christ in America*), introduction. John Bartlett,

Bartlett's Familiar Quotations (Boston: Little, Brown and Company, 1855, 1980), pp. 319-320.

[84] **Cotton Mather.** 1702. Cotton Mather, *Magnalia Christi Americana, (The Great Achievement of Christ in America),* 2 vols. (Edinburgh: The Banner of Truth Trust, 1702, 1979), 1:26. Gary DeMar, *America's Christian History: The Untold Story* (Atlanta, GA: American Vision Publishers, Inc., 1993), p. 47.

[85] **Cotton Mather.** Cotton Mather, *Magnalia Christi Americana.* Stephen Foster, *Their Solitary Way* (New Haven: Yale University Press, 1971) p. 121. Peter Marshall and David Manuel, *The Glory of America* (Bloomington, MN: Garborg's Heart'N Home, Inc., 1991), 2.14.

[86] **Cotton Mather.** Advice given to the young Benjamin Franklin who was visiting in his parsonage. Emily Morison Beck, *Sailor Historian: The Best of Samuel Eliot Morison* (1977). John Bartlett, *Bartlett's Familiar Quotations* (Boston: Little, Brown and Company, 1855, 1980), p. 320.

[87] **Increase Mather.** Lovejoy, *Revolution,* p. 154. Peter Marshall and David Manuel, *The Glory of America* (Bloomington, MN: Garborg's Heart'N Home, Inc., 1991), 6.21.

[88] **Matthew Fontaine Maury.** *Physical Geography of the Sea.* Stephen Abbott Northrop, D.D., *A Cloud of Witnesses* (Portland, OR: American Heritage Ministries, 1987; Mantle Ministries, 228 Still Ridge, Bulverde, Texas), p. 310.

[89] **Matthew Fontaine Maury.** Henry M. Morris, *Men of Science - Men of God* (El Cajon, CA: Master Books, Creation Life Publishers, Inc., 1990), p. 49.

[90] *Mayflower Compact.* November 11, 1620. William Bradford (Governor of Plymouth Colony), *The History of Plymouth Plantation 1608-1650* (Boston, Massachusetts: Massachusetts Historical Society, 1856; Boston, Massachusetts: Wright and Potter Printing Company, 1898, 1901, from the Original Manuscript, Library of Congress Rare Book Collection, Washington, D.C.; rendered in Modern English, Harold Paget, 1909; NY: Russell and Russell, 1968; NY: Random House, Inc., Modern Library College edition, 1981; San Antonio, TX: American Heritage Classics, Mantle Ministries, 228 Still Ridge, Bulverde, Texas, 1988), pp. 75-76. *Church of the Holy Trinity v. United States* 143 US 457, 458, 465-471, 36 L ed 226, (1892), Justice David Josiah Brewer. Marshall Foster and Mary-Elaine Swanson, *The American Covenant - The Untold Story* (Roseburg, OR: Foundation for Christian Self-Government, 1981; Thousand Oaks, CA: The Mayflower Institute, 1983, 1992), p. vii. John Eidsmoe, *Christianity and the Constitution - The Faith of Our Founding Fathers* (Grand Rapids, MI: Baker Book House, 1987, 6th printing 1993), p. 29. "Our Christian Heritage," *Letter from Plymouth Rock* (Marlborough, NH: The Plymouth Rock Foundation), p. 6. David Barton, *The Myth of Separation* (Aledo, TX: WallBuilder Press, 1991), pp. 47-51. D.P. Diffine, Ph.D., *One Nation Under God - How Close a Separation?* (Searcy, Arkansas: Harding University, Belden Center for Private Enterprise Education, 6th edition, 1992), p. 3. Stephen McDowell and Mark Beliles, "The Providential Perspective" (Charlottesville, VA: The Providence Foundation, P.O. Box 6759, Charlottesville, Va. 22906, January 1994), Vol. 9, No. 1, p. 1.

[91] **Jonathan Mayhew.** 1775. Clinton Rossiter, *Seedtime of the Republic* (New York: Harcourt, Brace & World, Inc., 1953), p. 241. Peter Marshall and David Manuel, *The Glory of America* (Bloomington, MN: Garborg's Heart'N Home, Inc., 1991), 2.18.

[92] **Jonathan Mayhew.** 1749, to the Council and House of Representatives in Colonial New England. Dorothy Dimmick, *Why Study the Election Sermons of Our Founding Generation?* (San Francisco, CA: The American Christian Prompter, Winter 1993), Vol. 4, No. 2, p. 3. Verna M. Hall, *The Christian History of the Constitution of the United States of America* (San Francisco: Foundation for American Christian Education, 1975), pp. 374-375. Marshall Foster and Mary-Elaine Swanson, *The American Covenant - The Untold Story* (Roseburg, OR: Foundation for Christian Self-Government, 1981; Thousand Oaks, CA: The Mayflower Institute, 1983, 1992), pp. 14-15.

[93] **James McGready.** 1797. Clarence Edward Noble MacCartney, *The Gospel of the Oregon Trail* (An Address, First Presbyterian Church, Pittsburgh, Pennsylvania, June 1, 1936). Catherine Millard, *The Rewriting of America's History* (Camp Hill, PA: Horizon House Publishers, 1991), p. 205.

[94] **James McGready.** June 1800. *The Return of the Spirit* (Carol Stream, IL: Christian History), Vol. VIII, No. 3, Issue 23, p. 25-26.

[95] **James McGready.** June 1800. *The Return of the Spirit* (Carol Stream, IL: Christian History), Vol. VIII, No. 3, Issue 23, p. 25-26.

[96] **James McGready.** June 1800, as accounted by Rev. Moses Hodge. "The Return of the Spirit" (Carol Stream, IL: Christian History), Vol. VIII, No. 3, Issue 23, p. 25-26.

[97] **William Holmes McGuffey.** 1836. in the Forward to his McGuffey's Reader. "Our Christian Heritage," *Letter from Plymouth Rock* (Marlborough, NH: The Plymouth Rock Foundation), p. 5. Stephen McDowell and Mark Beliles, "The Providential Perspective" (Charlottesville, VA: The Providence Foundation, P.O. Box 6759, Charlottesville, Va. 22906, January 1994), Vol. 9, No. 1, p. 8.

[98] **William Holmes McGuffey.** *Eclectic Reader.* D. James Kennedy, *What's Happened to American Education.* Robert Flood, *The Rebirth of America* (Philadelphia: Arthur S. DeMoss Foundation, 1986), p. 122.

[99] **William Holmes McGuffey.** *Eclectic First Reader-Lesson 37.* Catherine Millard, *The Rewriting of America's History* (Camp Hill, PA: Horizon House Publishers, 1991), p. 202.

[100] **William Holmes McGuffey.** *McGuffey's Eclectic First Reader-Lesson 62.* Catherine Millard, *The Rewriting of America's History* (Camp Hill, PA: Horizon House Publishers, 1991), pp. 202-203.

[101] **William Holmes McGuffey.** William Holmes McGuffey, *McGuffey's Eclectic Third Reader* (Cincinnati: Withrop B. Smith & Co., 1848), p. 5, preface. David Barton, *The Myth of Separation* (Aledo, TX: WallBuilder Press, 1991), p. 129.

[102] **William Holmes McGuffey.** William Holmes McGuffey, *McGuffey's Eclectic Third Reader* (Cincinnati: Withrop B. Smith & Co., 1848), p. 5, preface. David Barton, *The Myth of Separation* (Aledo, TX: WallBuilder Press, 1991), p. 129.

[103] **William Holmes McGuffey.** William Holmes McGuffey, *McGuffey's Eclectic Fourth Reader* (Cincinnati: Withrop B. Smith & Co., 1853), p. 3, preface. David Barton, *The Myth of Separation* (Aledo, TX: WallBuilder Press, 1991), p. 129.

[104] **William Holmes McGuffey.** 1837. William H. McGuffey, *Eclectic Third Reader* (Cincinnati: Van Antwerp, Bragg and Company, 1879). Catherine Millard, *The Rewriting of America's History* (Camp Hill, PA: Horizon House Publishers, 1991), p. 197.

[105] **William Holmes McGuffey.** 1837. William H. McGuffey, *Eclectic Third Reader* (Cincinnati: Van Antwerp, Bragg and Company, 1879). Catherine Millard, *The Rewriting of America's History* (Camp Hill, PA: Horizon House Publishers, 1991), p. 200.

[106] **William Holmes McGuffey.** *Eclectic Third Reader-Lesson 31.* Catherine Millard, *The Rewriting of America's History* (Camp Hill, PA: Horizon House Publishers, 1991), pp. 199-200.

[107] **William Holmes McGuffey.** August 7, 1873, in Elmira, New York, the National Education Association honored him with this resolution. John H. Westerhoff, III., *McGuffey and his Readers Piety, Morality and Education in 19th Century America* (Nashville: Abington Press), p. 13. Catherine Millard, *The Rewriting of America's History* (Camp Hill, PA: Horizon House Publishers, 1991), p. 196.

Notes

[108] **James McHenry.** Bernard Steiner, *One Hundred and Ten Years of Bible Society in Maryland* (Maryland: Maryland Bible Society, 1921), p. 14. Tim LaHaye, *Faith of Our Founding Fathers* (Brentwood, TN: Wolgemuth & Hyatt, Publishers, Inc., 1987), pp. 171-172. Peter Marshall & David Manuel, *The Glory of America* (Bloomington, MN: Garborg's Heart 'N Home, 1991), 8.17.

[109] **William McKinley.** July 4, 1892, as Governor of Ohio, in an address to the Baptist Young People's Union in Lakeside, Ohio. Stephen Abbott Northrop, D.D., *A Cloud of Witnesses* (Portland, OR: American Heritage Ministries, 1987; Mantle Ministries, 228 Still Ridge, Bulverde, Texas), p. 313. [quoting Abraham Lincoln. March 4, 1861, in his First Inaugural Address. Albert J. Beveridge, *The Life of John Marshall* (Boston: Houghton Mifflin, 1919), Vol. VI, p. 9. James D. Richardson (U.S. Representative from Tennessee), ed., *A Compilation of the Messages and Papers of the Presidents 1789-1897*, 10 vols. (Washington, D.C.: U.S. Government Printing Office, published by Authority of Congress, 1897, 1899; Washington, D.C.: Bureau of National Literature and Art, 1789-1902, 11 vols., 1907, 1910), Vol. VI, pp. 9-11. Roy Basler, ed., *Collected Works of Abraham Lincoln* (Rutgers University Press, 1953), Vol. IV, p. 271. Paul M. Angle, ed., *By These Words* (NY: Rand McNally & Company, 1954), p. 224. Davis Newton Lott, *The Inaugural Addresses of the American Presidents* (NY: Holt, Rinehart and Winston, 1961), p. 122. Richard D. Heffner, *A Documentary History of the United States* (New York: The New American Library of World Literature, Inc., 1961), pp. 144-146. David Barton, *The Myth of Separation* (Aledo, TX: WallBuilder Press, 1991), p. 242. Mark A. Knoll, *The Pu~zling Faith of Abraham Lincoln* (Carol Stream, IL: Christian History), Vol. XI, No. 1, Issue 33, p. 11. William Safire, ed., *Lend Me Your Ears - Great Speeches in History* (NY: W.W. Norton & Company 1992), p. 746.]

[110] **William McKinley.** June 29, 1893, before the First International Convention of the Epworth League in Cleveland. Stephen Abbott Northrop, D.D., *A Cloud of Witnesses* (Portland, OR: American Heritage Ministries, 1987; Mantle Ministries, 228 Still Ridge, Bulverde, Texas), p. 313.

[111] **William McKinley.** July 14, 1894, in a speech to the Christian Endeavor's International Convention in Cleveland, Ohio. Stephen Abbott Northrop, D.D., *A Cloud of Witnesses* (Portland, OR: American Heritage Ministries, 1987; Mantle Ministries, 228 Still Ridge, Bulverde, Texas), p. 313. Peter Marshall and David Manuel, *The Glory of America* (Bloomington, MN: Garborg's Heart'N Home, Inc., 1991), 7.14. D.P. Diffine, Ph.D., *One Nation Under God - How Close a Separation?* (Searcy, Arkansas: Harding University, Belden Center for Private Enterprise Education, 6th edition, 1992), p. 16.

[112] **William McKinley.** 1896, the 25th President describing Lincoln. William J. Johnson, *Abraham Lincoln, The Christian* (NY: The Abington Press, 1913), p. 187. Peter Marshall and David Manuel, *The Glory of America* (Bloomington, MN: Garborg's Heart 'N Home, Inc., 1991), 4.16.

[113] **William McKinley.** March 4, 1897, in his First Inaugural Address. *A Compilation of the Messages and Papers of the Presidents* 20 vols. (New York: Bureau of National Literature, Inc., prepared under the direction of the Joint Committee on Printing, of the House and Senate, pursuant to an Act of the Fifty-Second Congress of the United States, 1893, 1923), Vol. XIII, pp. 6236-6244. *Inaugural Addresses of the Presidents of the United States - From George Washington 1789 to Richard Milhous Nixon 1969* (Washington, D.C.: United States Government Printing Office; 91st Congress, 1st Session, House Document 91-142, 1969), pp. 169-177. Davis Newton Lott, *The Inaugural Addresses of the American Presidents* (NY: Holt, Rinehart and Winston, 1961), p. 171. Charles E. Rice, *The Supreme Court and Public Prayer* (New York: Fordham University Press, 1964), pp. 187-188. Arthur Schlesinger Jr., ed., *The Chief Executive* (NY: Chelsea House Publishers, 1965), p. 189. Benjamin Weiss, *God in American History: A Documentation of America's Religious Heritage* (Grand Rapids, MI: Zondervan, 1966) p. 115. Willard Cantelon, *Money Master of the World* (Plainfield, NJ: Logos International, 1976), p. 120. *Proclaim Liberty* (Dallas, TX: Word of Faith), p. 2. Stephen Abbott Northrop, D.D., *A Cloud of Witnesses* (Portland, OR: American Heritage Ministries, 1987; Mantle Ministries, 228 Still Ridge, Bulverde, Texas), p. 313. J. Michael Sharman, J.D., *Faith of the Fathers* (Culpepper, Virginia: Victory Publishing, 1995), p. 79.

[114] **William McKinley.** March 4, 1897, in his First Inaugural Address. *A Compilation of the Messages and Papers of the Presidents* 20 vols. (New York: Bureau of National Literature, Inc., prepared under the direction of the Joint Committee on Printing, of the House and Senate, pursuant to an Act of the Fifty-Second Congress of the United States, 1893, 1923), Vol. XIII, pp. 6236-6244. *Inaugural Addresses of the Presidents of the United States - From George Washington 1789 to Richard Milhous Nixon 1969* (Washington, D.C.: United States Government Printing Office; 91st Congress, 1st Session, House Document 91-142, 1969), pp. 169-177. Davis Newton Lott, *The Inaugural Addresses of the American Presidents* (NY: Holt, Rinehart and Winston, 1961), p. 171. Charles E. Rice, *The Supreme Court and Public Prayer* (New York: Fordham University Press, 1964), pp. 187-188. Arthur Schlesinger Jr., ed., *The Chief Executive* (NY: Chelsea House Publishers, 1965), p. 189. Benjamin Weiss, *God in American History: A Documentation of America's Religious Heritage* (Grand Rapids, MI: Zondervan, 1966) p. 115. Willard Cantelon, *Money Master of the World* (Plainfield, NJ: Logos International, 1976), p. 120. *Proclaim Liberty* (Dallas, TX: Word of Faith), p. 2. Stephen Abbott Northrop, D.D., *A Cloud of Witnesses* (Portland, OR: American Heritage Ministries, 1987; Mantle Ministries, 228 Still Ridge, Bulverde, Texas), p. 313. J. Michael Sharman, J.D., *Faith of the Fathers* (Culpepper, Virginia: Victory Publishing, 1995), p. 79.

[115] **William McKinley.** Stephen Abbott Northrop, D.D., *A Cloud of Witnesses* (Portland, Oregon: American Heritage Ministries, 1987; Mantle Ministries, 228 Still Ridge, Bulverde, Texas), p. introduction.

[116] **William McKinley.** Gary DeMar, *America's Christian History: The Untold Story* (Atlanta, GA: American Vision Publishers, Inc., 1993), p. 60.

[117] **John McLean.** November 4, 1852, in a letter to the American Bible Society from Chapel Wood. Stephen Abbott Northrop, D.D., *A Cloud of Witnesses* (Portland, OR: American Heritage Ministries, 1987; Mantle Ministries, 228 Still Ridge, Bulverde, Texas), p. 314. D.P. Diffine, Ph.D., *One Nation Under God - How Close a Separation?* (Searcy, Arkansas: Harding University, Belden Center for Private Enterprise Education, 6th edition, 1992), p. 13.

[118] **George Gordon Meade.** 1872, as reported by his son, Colonel George Meade. Stephen Abbott Northrop, D.D., *A Cloud of Witnesses* (Portland, OR: American Heritage Ministries, 1987; Mantle Ministries, 228 Still Ridge, Bulverde, Texas), p. 315.

[119] **Wesley Merritt.** Stephen Abbott Northrop, D.D., *A Cloud of Witnesses* (Portland, OR: American Heritage Ministries, 1987; Mantle Ministries, 228 Still Ridge, Bulverde, Texas), p. 316.

[120] **Michelangelo Buonarroti.** In his *Sonnet*. John Bartlett, *Bartlett's Familiar Quotations* (Boston: Little, Brown and Company, 1855, 1980), pp. 154-155.

[121] **Michelangelo Buonarroti.** In his *Sonnet*. John Bartlett, *Bartlett's Familiar Quotations* (Boston: Little, Brown and Company, 1855, 1980), p. 155.

[122] **Michigan Federal Court.** 1965. *Reed v. Van Hoven*, 237 F. Supp. 48, 51 (W. D. Mich. 1965). David Barton, *The Myth of Separation* (Aledo, TX: WallBuilder Press, 1991), p. 192.

[123] **John Milton.** Tryon Edwards, D.D., *The New Dictionary of Thoughts - A Cyclopedia of Quotations* (Garden City, NY: Hanover House, 1852; revised and enlarged by C.H. Catrevas, Ralph Emerson Browns and Jonathan Edwards [descendent, along with

Tryon, of Jonathan Edwards (1703-1758), president of Princeton], 1891; The Standard Book Company, 1955, 1963), p. 46.

[124] **John Milton.** 1629, in *On the Morning of Christ's Nativity,* st. I, l. I. I. John Bartlett, *Bartlett's Familiar Quotations* (Boston: Little, Brown and Company, 1855, 1980), p. 277.

[125] **John Milton.** 1631, in *Il Penseroso,* l. 159. John Bartlett, *Bartlett's Familiar Quotations* (Boston: Little, Brown and Company, 1855, 1980), pp. 278-279.

[126] **John Milton.** 1634, in *Comus,* l. 587. John Bartlett, *Bartlett's Familiar Quotation* (Boston: Little, Brown and Company, 1855, 1980), p. 279.

[127] **John Milton.** 1637, in *Lycidas,* l. 108. John Bartlett, *Bartlett's Familiar Quotations* (Boston: Little, Brown and Company, 1855, 1980), p. 280.

[128] **John Milton.** 1642 in *Animadversions upon the Reply of Smectymnuus.* Stephen Abbott Northrop, D.D., *A Cloud of Witnesses* (Portland, OR: American Heritage Ministries, 1987; Mantle Ministries, 228 Still Ridge, Bulverde, Texas), p. 320.

[129] **John Milton.** 1644, in *Tractate of Education.* John Bartlett, *Bartlett's Familiar Quotations* (Boston: Little, Brown and Company, 1855, 1980), p. 281.

[130] **John Milton.** 1644, in *Areopagitica.* John Bartlett, *Bartlett's Familiar Quotations* (Boston: Little, Brown and Company, 1855, 1980), p. 281.

[131] **John Milton.** 1655, in *On the Late Massacre in Piedmont.* John Bartlett, *Bartlett's Familiar Quotations* (Boston: Little, Brown and Company, 1855, 1980), p. 282.

[132] **John Milton.** *True Religion, Heresy, Schism, Toleration.* Stephen Abbott Northrop, D.D., *A Cloud of Witnesses* (Portland, OR: American Heritage Ministries, 1987; Mantle Ministries, 228 Still Ridge, Bulverde, Texas), p. 320.

[133] **John Milton.** 1667, in *Paradise Lost,* bk. IV, l. 208. John Bartlett, *Bartlett's Familiar Quotations* (Boston: Little, Brown and Company, 1855, 1980), p. 285. Lewis C. Henry, *Best Quotations For All Occasions* (Greenwich, CONN: Fawcett Publications, Inc., 1961), p. 104.

[134] **John Milton.** 1667 in *Paradise Lost,* bk. IV, l. 918. John Bartlett, *Bartlett's Familiar Quotations* (Boston: Little, Brown and Company, 1855, 1980), p. 286. Lewis C. Henry, *Best Quotations For All Occasions* (Greenwich, CONN: Fawcett Publications, Inc., 1961), p. 105.

[135] **John Milton.** 1667, in *Paradise Lost,* bk. I, l. 1, 22, 34, 44, bk. II, l. 226. John Bartlett, *Bartlett's Familiar Quotations* (Boston: Little, Brown and Company, 1855, 1980), pp. 282-289.

[136] **Constitution of the State of Mississippi.** 1817. Supreme Court Justice David Josiah Brewer, who served 1890-1910, in his work, *The United States - Christian Nation* (Philadelphia: The John C. Winston Company, 1905, Supreme Court Collection). Catherine Millard, *The Rewriting of America's History,* (Camp Hill, PA: Horizon House Publishers, 1991), p. 390. In 1890, the Constitution of the State of Mississippi stated: "*Preamble.* We, the people of Mississippi in convention assembled, grateful to Almighty God, and invoking His blessing on our work, do ordain and establish this Constitution....*Article XIV, Section 265.* No person who denies the existence of a Supreme Being shall hold any office in this state...." Charles E. Rice, *The Supreme Court and Public Prayer* (New York: Fordham University Press, 1964), pp. 171-172; "Hearings, Prayers in Public Schools and Other Matters," Committee on the Judiciary, U.S. Senate (87th Cong., 2nd Sess.), 1962, pp. 268 et seq.

[137] **Constitution of the State of Mississippi.** 1817, Article IX, Section 16. *The Constitutions of All the United States According to the Latest Amendments* (Lexington, KY: Thomas T. Skillman, 1817), p. 389. David Barton, *The Myth of Separation,* (Aledo, TX: WallBuilder Press, 1991), p. 39. Congressional Records, March 1, 1817, c. 23,3 Stat. 348 at 349. Frances Newton Thorpe, ed., *Federal and State Constitutions, Colonial Charters, and Other Organic Laws of the States, Territories, and Colonies now or heretofore forming the United States,* 7 vols. (Washington: Government Printing Office, 1905; 1909; St. Clair Shores, MI: Scholarly Press, 1968).

[138] **Ormsby Macknight Mitchell.** *Astronomy and the Bible.* Stephen Abbott Northrop, D.D., *A Cloud of Witnesses* (Portland, OR: American Heritage Ministries, 1987; Mantle Ministries, 228 Still Ridge, Bulverde, Texas), pp. 320-321.

[139] **James Monroe.** March 5, 1821, Monday, in his Second Inaugural Address. James D. Richardson (U.S. Representative from Tennessee), ed., *A Compilation of the Messages and Papers of the Presidents 1789-1897,* 10 vols. (Washington, D.C.: U.S. Government Printing Office, published by Authority of Congress, 1897, 1899; Washington, D.C.: Bureau of National Literature and Art, 1789-1902, 11 vols.), 1907, 1910), Vol. II, pp. 86-94. *Inaugural Addresses of the Presidents of the United States - From George Washington 1789 to Richard Milhous Nixon 1969* (Washington, D.C.: United States Government Printing Office; 91st Congress, 1st Session, House Document 91-142, 1969), pp. 37-45. Davis Newton Lott, *The Inaugural Addresses of the American Presidents* (NY: Holt, Rinehart and Winston, 1961), p. 48. Charles E. Rice, *The Supreme Court and Public Prayer* (New York: Fordham University Press, 1964), pp. 180-181. J. Michael Sharman, J.D., *Faith of the Fathers* (Culpepper, Virginia: Victory Publishing, 1995), p. 33.

[140] **Baron Charles Louis Joseph de Secondat Montesquieu.** Donald S. Lutz and Charles S. Hyneman, "The Relative Influence of European Writers on Late Eighteenth-Century American Political Thought," *American Political Review* 189 (1984): 189-197. (Courtesy of Dr. Wayne House of Dallas Theological Seminary.) John Eidsmoe, *Christianity and the Constitution - The Faith of Our Founding Fathers* (Grand Rapids, MI: Baker Book House, A Mott Media Book, 1987, 6th printing 1993), pp. 51-53. Stephen K. McDowell and Mark A. Beliles, *America's Providential History* (Charlottesville, VA: Providence Press, 1988), p. 156. [1760-1805], *Origins of American Constitutionalism,* (1987). David Barton, *The Myth of Separation* (Aledo, TX: WallBuilder Press, 1991), pp. 195, 201.

[141] **Baron Charles Louis Joseph de Secondat Montesquieu.** 1748. Baron Charles Montesquieu, *The Spirit of the Laws,* 1748, Anne Cohler, trans. (reprinted Cambridge: Cambridge University Press, 1989), p. 457. David Barton, *The Myth of Separation* (Aledo, TX: WallBuilder Press, 1991), pp. 195-196.

[142] **Baron Charles Louis Joseph de Secondat Montesquieu.** 1748. Baron Charles Montesquieu, *The Spirit of the Laws,* 1748, Anne Cohler, trans. (reprinted Cambridge: Cambridge University Press, 1989), p. 457. David Barton, *The Myth of Separation* (Aledo, TX: WallBuilder Press, 1991), pp. 195-196.

[143] **Baron Charles Louis Joseph de Secondat Montesquieu.** 1748. *The Spirit of the Laws* (New York: Hafner, 1949, 1962), 1:1-3. 1748. Anne Cohler, trans., *The Spirit of the Laws* (reprinted Cambridge: Cambridge University Press, 1989), p. 457. John Eidsmoe, *Christianity and the Constitution - The Faith of Our Founding Fathers* (Grand Rapids, MI: Baker Book House, A Mott Media Book, 1987, 6th printing 1993), pp. 54-55. David Barton, *The Myth of Separation* (Aledo, TX: WallBuilder Press, 1991), pp. 195-196.

[144] **Baron Charles Louis Joseph de Secondat Montesquieu.** 1748. Baron Charles Montesquieu, *The Spirit of the Laws,* 1748, Anne Cohler, trans. (reprinted Cambridge: Cambridge University Press, 1989), p. 157. David Barton, *The Myth of Separation* (Aledo, TX: WallBuilder Press, 1991), p. 227.

[145] **Baron Charles Louis Joseph de Secondat Montesquieu.** 1748. *The Spirit of the Laws* (New York: Hafner, 1949, 1962), 24:27-

29. John Eidsmoe, *Christianity and the Constitution - The Faith of Our Founding Fathers* (Grand Rapids, MI: Baker Book House, A Mott Media Book, 1987, 6th printing 1993), pp. 55-56. Stephen Abbott Northrop, D.D., *A Cloud of Witnesses* (Portland, OR: American Heritage Ministries, 1987; Mantle Ministries, 228 Still Ridge, Bulverde, Texas), p. 322.

[146] **Baron Charles Louis Joseph de Secondat Montesquieu.** George Bancroft,*Bancroft's History of the United States* (Boston: Little, Brown & Co., 1859), Vol. V, p. 24. David Barton, *The Myth of Separation* (Aledo, TX: WallBuilder Press, 1991), p. 196.

[147] **James Montgomery.** *What is Prayer?*, st. I. John Bartlett, *Bartlett's Familiar Quotations* (Boston: Little, Brown and Company, 1855, 1980), p. 429.

[148] **Benjamin Franklin Morris.** 1864, Benjamin Franklin Morris,*The Christian Life and Character of the Civil Institutions of the United States - developed in the Official and Historical Annals of the Republic* (Philadelphia, PA: George W. Childs; Cincinnati: Rickey & Carroll, 1864; located in the libraries of Case Western Reserve and the University of Cincinnati, Miami), p. 262. Gary DeMar, *God and Government-A Biblical and Historical Study* (Atlanta, GA: American Vision Press, 1984), p. 137.

[149] **Benjamin Franklin Morris.** 1864, Benjamin Franklin Morris,*The Christian Life and Character of the Civil Institutions of the United States - developed in the Official and Historical Annals of the Republic* (Philadelphia, PA: George W. Childs; Cincinnati: Rickey & Carroll, 1864; located in the libraries of Case Western Reserve and the University of Cincinnati, Miami). Stephen K. McDowell and Mark A. Beliles, *America's Providential History* (Charlottesville, VA: Providence Press, 1988), p. 94. David Barton, *The Myth of Separation*, (Aledo, TX: WallBuilder Press, 1991), p. 246.

[150] **Benjamin Franklin Morris.** 1864, Benjamin Franklin Morris,*The Christian Life and Character of the Civil Institutions of the United States - developed in the Official and Historical Annals of the Republic* (Philadelphia, PA: George W. Childs; Cincinnati: Rickey & Carroll, 1864; located in the libraries of Case Western Reserve and the University of Cincinnati, Miami), p. 11. David Barton, *The Myth of Separation* (Aledo, TX: WallBuilder Press, 1991), p. 135.

[151] **Gouverneur Morris.** circa 1792, in "Notes of the Form for the King of France." Jared Sparks, ed.,*The Life of Gouverneur Morris, with Selections from His Correspondence and Miscellaneous Papers,* 3 vols. (Boston: Gray and Bowen, 1832), Vol. III, p. 483. John Eidsmoe, *Christianity and The Constitution - The Faith of Our Founding Fathers* (Baker Book House, 1987), p. 188. David Barton, *The Myth of Separation* (Aledo, TX: WallBuilder Press, 1991), pp. 121, 130. Stephen McDowell and Mark Beliles, "The Providential Perspective" (Charlottesville, VA: The Providence Foundation, P.O. Box 6759, Charlottesville, Va. 22906, January 1994), Vol. 9, No. 1, p. 3.

[152] **Gouverneur Morris.** Max M. Mintz,*Gouverneur Morris and the American Revolution* (Norman: University of Oklahoma Press, 1970), p. 127. M.E. Bradford, *Religion & The Framers: The Biographical Evidence* (Marlborough, NH: The Plymouth Rock Foundation, 1991), p. 8.

[153] **Gouverneur Morris.** M.E. Bradford, *A Worthy Company* (Marlborough, NH: The Plymouth Rock Foundation, 1982), p. 91. Tim LaHaye, *Faith of Our Founding Fathers* (Brentwood, TN: Wolgemuth & Hyatt, Publishers, Inc., 1987), p. 133.

[154] **Jedediah Morse.** April 25, 1799, in Jedediah Morse's Election Sermon given at Charleston, Mass., taken from an original in the Evans collection compiled by the American Antiquarian Society. David Barton, *The Myth of Separation* (Aledo, TX: WallBuilder Press, 1991), p. 128. Verna M. Hall,*Christian History of the Constitution of the United States of America* (San Francisco: Foundation for America Christian Education, 1975), pp. v, 145. Peter Marshall and David Manuel, *The Glory of America* (Bloomington, MN: Garborg's Heart'N Home, Inc., 1991), 4.25, 8.5. Stephen McDowell and Mark Beliles, "The Providential Perspective" (Charlottesville, VA: The Providence Foundation, P.O. Box 6759, Charlottesville, Va. 22906, January 1994), Vol. 9, No. 1, p. 7.

[155] **Samuel Finley Breese Morse.** 1844. *Webster's Family Encyclopedia,* 13 vols. (NY: Ottenheimer Publishers, Inc., 1988), Vol. 8, p. 1763. Sarah K. Bolton, *Famous Men of Science.* Stephen Abbott Northrop, D.D., *A Cloud of Witnesses* (Portland, OR: American Heritage Ministries, 1987; Mantle Ministries, 228 Still Ridge, Bulverde, Texas), p. 327-328.

[156] **Samuel Finley Breese Morse.** Sarah K. Bolton, *Famous Men of Science.* Stephen Abbott Northrop, D.D., *A Cloud of Witnesses* (Portland, OR: American Heritage Ministries, 1987; Mantle Ministries, 228 Still Ridge, Bulverde, Texas), p. 327.

[157] **Samuel Finley Breese Morse.** Sarah K. Bolton, *Famous Men of Science.* Stephen Abbott Northrop, D.D., *A Cloud of Witnesses* (Portland, OR: American Heritage Ministries, 1987; Mantle Ministries, 228 Still Ridge, Bulverde, Texas), p. 327.

[158] **Samuel Finley Breese Morse.** 1868. Henry M. Morris,*Men of Science - Men of God* (El Cajon, CA: Master Books, Creation Life Publishers, Inc., 1990), p. 47.

[159] **Wolfgang Amadeus Mozart.** July 3, 1778, in a letter from Paris to a friend. Lady Wallace, *The Letters of Wolfgang Amadeus Mozart*, Vol. II, pp. 275-276. Stephen Abbott Northrop, D.D.,*A Cloud of Witnesses* (Portland, OR: American Heritage Ministries, 1987; Mantle Ministries, 228 Still Ridge, Bulverde, Texas), pp. 332-333.

[160] **Wolfgang Amadeus Mozart.** Lady Wallace, *The Letters of Wolfgang Amadeus Mozart*, Vol. I, pp. 210-211. Stephen Abbott Northrop, D.D., *A Cloud of Witnesses* (Portland, OR: American Heritage Ministries, 1987; Mantle Ministries, 228 Still Ridge, Bulverde, Texas), pp. 332-333.

[161] **Wolfgang Amadeus Mozart.** Attributed. John Bartlett, *Bartlett's Familiar Quotations* (Boston: Little, Brown and Company, 1855, 1980), p. 402.

[162] **Malcolm Muggeridge.** 1975 in *Jesus,* pt. I. John Bartlett, *Bartlett's Familiar Quotations* (Boston: Little, Brown and Company, 1855, 1980), p. 858.

[163] **Henry Melchior Muhlenberg.** Henry Melchior Muhlenberg, *The Notebook of a Colonial Clergyman,* translated and ed., by Theodore G. Tappert and John W. Doberstern (Philadelphia: Fortress Press, 1975), p. 195. Lucille Johnston, *Celebrations of a Nation* (Arlington, VA: The Year of Thanksgiving Foundation, 1987), p. 87. Peter Marshall and David Manuel, *The Light and the Glory* (Old Tappan, NJ: Fleming H. Revell Company, 1977), p. 323.

[164] **John Peter Muhlenberg.** 1775, in a sermon on Ecclesiastes 3:1. *The World Book Encyclopedia,* 18 vols. (Chicago, IL: Field Enterprises, Inc., 1957; W.F. Quarrie and Company, 8 vols., 1917; World Book, Inc., 22 vols., 1989), Vol. 11, p. 5324. Peter Marshall and David Manuel, *The Glory of America* (Bloomington, MN: Garborg's Heart'N Home, Inc., 1991), 6.25.

N

[1] **Napoleon Bonaparte.** January 23, 1814, at Paris. John Bartlett, *Bartlett's Familiar Quotations* (Boston: Little, Brown and Company, 1855, 1980), p. 420.

[2] **Napoleon Bonaparte.** At St. Helena, to General Bertrand. Tryon Edwards, D.D.,*The New Dictionary of Thoughts - A Cyclopedia of Quotations* (Garden City, NY: Hanover House, 1852; revised and enlarged by C.H. Catrevas, Ralph Emerson Browns and

Jonathan Edwards [descendent, along with Tryon, of Jonathan Edwards (1703-1758), president of Princeton], 1891; The Standard Book Company, 1955, 1963), p. 46. Charles E. Jones, *The Books You Read* (Harrisburg, PA: Executive Books, 1985), p. 134. John S.C. Abbott, *The History of Napoleon Bonaparte*, Vol. II, Chapter XXXIII. Canon Liddon, in his *Bampoton Lectures*, p. 148, names these authorities: Luthardt, *Apologetische Vortrage*, pp. 234, 293; M. Auguste Nicholas, *Etudes Philosophique sur le Christianisme*, Bruxelles, 1849, tom II., pp. 352, 256; Chevalier de Beauterne, *Sentiment de Napoleon sur le Christianisme*, edit. par M. Bathild Bouniol, Paris, 1864, pp. 87, 118. Stephen Abbott Northrop, D.D., *A Cloud of Witnesses* (Portland, Oregon: American Heritage Ministries, 1987; Mantle Ministries, 228 Still Ridge, Bulverde, Texas), p. 38.

[3] **Napoleon Bonaparte.** Henry H. Halley, *Halley's Bible Handbook* (Grand Rapids, MI: Zondervan Publishing House, 1927, 1965), p. 18.

[4] **Napoleon Bonaparte.** At St. Helena, to Count de Motholon. Major General Alfred Pleasonton. Stephen Abbott Northrop, D.D., *A Cloud of Witnesses* (Portland, OR: American Heritage Ministries, 1987; Mantle Ministries, 228 Still Ridge, Bulverde, Texas), pp. 361-362. Vernon C. Grounds, *The Reason for Our Hope* (Chicago: Moody Press), p. 37. Willard Cantelon, *New Money or None?* (Plainfield, NJ: Logos International, 1979), p. 246.

[5] **Napoleon Bonaparte.** Charles E. Jones, *The Books You Read* (Harrisburg, PA: Executive Books, 1985), p. 114.

[6] **Napoleon Bonaparte.** Tryon Edwards, D.D., *The New Dictionary of Thoughts - A Cyclopedia of Quotations* (Garden City, NY: Hanover House, 1852; revised and enlarged by C.H. Catrevas, Ralph Emerson Browns and Jonathan Edwards [descendent, along with Tryon, of Jonathan Edwards (1703-1758), president of Princeton], 1891; The Standard Book Company, 1955, 1963), p. 88. Frank S. Mead, *The Encyclopedia of Religious Quotations* (Old Tappan: Revell, 1976), p. 56. Willard Cantelon, *New Money or None?* (Plainfield, NJ: Logos International, 1979), p. 246.

[7] **Napoleon Bonaparte.** Stephen Abbott Northrop, D.D., *A Cloud of Witnesses* (Portland, Oregon: American Heritage Ministries, 1987; Mantle Ministries, 228 Still Ridge, Bulverde, Texas), p. introduction.

[8] **Napoleon Bonaparte.** His remark upon receiving a copy of *Mecanique Celeste* by Pierre Simon de Laplace. John Bartlett, *Bartlett's Familiar Quotations* (Boston: Little, Brown and Company, 1855, 1980), p. 397.

[9] **Napoleon Bonaparte.** *Bless Your Heart (series II)* (Eden Prairie, MN: Heartland Samplers, Inc., 1990), 5.31.

[10] **National Day of Prayer.** January 25, 1988 in the Second Session of the One Hundredth Congress. *Public Law 100-307 - May 5, 1988;* originally passed April 17, 1952, through a Joint Resolution the Congress of the United States of America as Public Law 82-324; 66 Stat. 64. Mrs. James Dobson (Shirley), chairman, *The National Day of Prayer Information Packet* (Colorado Springs, CO: National Day of Prayer Task Force, May 6, 1993). Gary DeMar, *America's Christian History: The Untold Story* (Atlanta, GA: American Vision Publishers, Inc., 1993), p. 53. Courtesy of Bruce Barilla, Christian Heritage Week Ministry (P.O. Box 58, W.V. 24712; 304-384-7707, 304-384-9044 fax).

[11] **John Mason Neale.** In *Good King Wenceslas*. John Bartlett, *Bartlett's Familiar Quotations* (Boston: Little, Brown and Company, 1855, 1980), p. 563.

[12] **John Mason Neale.** 1861, the twelfth century Latin hymn *Veni, Veni, Emmanuel*, which he translated into English. John Bartlett, *Bartlett's Familiar Quotations* (Boston: Little, Brown and Company, 1855, 1980), p. 563.

[13] **Constitution of the State of Nebraska.** June 12, 1875, Preamble; Article I, Section IV; Bill of Rights, Article I, Section 4. M.B.C. True, *A Manual of the History and Civil Government of the State of Nebraska* (Omaha: Gibson, Miller, & Richardson, 1885), p. 34. Frances Newton Thorpe, ed., *Federal and State Constitutions, Colonial Charters, and Other Organic Laws of the States, Territories, and Colonies now or heretofore forming the United States*, 7 vols. (Washington: Government Printing Office, 1905; 1909; St. Clair Shores, MI: Scholarly Press, 1968). Charles E. Rice, *The Supreme Court and Public Prayer* (New York: Fordham University Press, 1964), p. 172; "Hearings, Prayers in Public Schools and Other Matters," Committee on the Judiciary, U.S. Senate (87th Cong., 2nd Sess.), 1962, pp. 268 et seq. David Barton, *The Myth of Separation*, (Aledo, TX: WallBuilder Press, 1991), p. 39.

[14] **Horatio Nelson.** October 21, 1805, his dying words. *The World Book Encyclopedia*, 18 vols. (Chicago, IL: Field Enterprises, Inc., 1957; W.F. Quarrie and Company, 8 vols., 1917; World Book, Inc., 22 vols., 1989), Vol. 12, p. 5495.

[15] **New England, Synod of Churches.** September 30, 1648. Benjamin Franklin Morris, *The Christian Life and Character of the Civil Institutions of the United States* (Philadelphia: George W. Childs, 1864), pp. 53-54. Gary DeMar, *God and Government-A Biblical and Historical Study* (Atlanta, GA: American Vision Press, 1982), pp. 111-112.

[16] **Constitution of the New England Confederation.** May 19, 1643. Benjamin Franklin Morris, *The Christian Life and Character of the Civil Institutions of the United States* (Philadelphia: George W. Childs, 1864), p. 56. Henry Steele Commager, ed., *Documents of American History*, 2 vols. (NY: F.S. Crofts and Company, 1934; Appleton-Century-Crofts, Inc., 1948, 6th edition, 1958; Englewood Cliffs, NJ: Prentice Hall, Inc., 9th edition, 1973), Vol. I, pp. 26-27. William McDonald, ed., *Documentary Source Book of American History, 1606-1889* (NY: The Macmillan Company, 1909), p. 46. William Bradford (Governor of Plymouth Colony), *The History of Plymouth Plantation 1608-1650* (Boston, Massachusetts: Massachusetts Historical Society, 1856; Boston, Massachusetts: Wright and Potter Printing Company, 1898, 1901, from the Original Manuscript, Library of Congress Rare Book Collection, Washington, D.C.; rendered in Modern English, Harold Paget, 1909; NY: Russell and Russell, 1968; NY: Random House, Inc., Modern Library College edition, 1981; San Antonio, TX: American Heritage Classics, Mantle Ministries, 228 Still Ridge, Bulverde, Texas, 1988), pp. 321-324. *The Annals of America*, 20 vols. (Chicago, IL: Encyclopedia Britannica, 1968), Vol. 1, pp. 72-73. Gary DeMar, *God and Government* (Atlanta, GA: American Vision Press, 1984), p. 112. Lucille Johnston, *Celebrations of a Nation* (Arlington, VA: The Year of Thanksgiving Foundation, 1987), (part 1), p. 46. "Our Christian Heritage," *Letter from Plymouth Rock* (Marlborough, NH: The Plymouth Rock Foundation), p. 2. David Barton, *The Myth of Separation* (Aledo, TX: WallBuilder Press, 1991), p. 88. D.P. Diffine, Ph.D., *One Nation Under God - How Close a Separation?* (Searcy, Arkansas: Harding University, Belden Center for Private Enterprise Education, 6th edition, 1992), p. 4. Gary DeMar, *America's Christian History: The Untold Story* (Atlanta, GA: American Vision Publishers, Inc., 1993), pp. 37-38.

[17] *New England Primer.* 1737. *Alphabet of Religious Jingles*, Dover Publication, Inc., New York, N.Y., Gary DeMar, *God and Government, A Biblical and Historical Study* (Atlanta, GA: American Vision Press, 1984), p. 19. Tim LaHaye, *Faith of Our Founding Fathers* (Brentwood, TN: Wolgemuth & Hyatt, Publishers, Inc., 1987), p. 75. D.P. Diffine, Ph.D., *One Nation Under God - How Close a Separation?* (Searcy, Arkansas: Harding University, Belden Center for Private Enterprise Education, 6th edition, 1992), p. 4.

[18] *New England Primer.* 1691, second edition advertised, 1737, oldest extant copy, 1784, date of primer which contained the referenced version of the prayer, *Enchiridion Leonis*, dated 1160 A.D. John Bartlett, *Bartlett's Familiar Quotations* (Boston: Little, Brown and Company, 1855, 1980), p. 320.

[19] *New Guide to the English Tongue.* 1740, Thomas Dilworth, London. H.R. Warfel, *Noah Webster-Schoolmaster to America* (New York: Octagon Press, 1966), pp. 11-13. Tim LaHaye, *Faith of Our Founding Fathers* (Brentwood, TN: Wolgemuth & Hyatt,

Publishers, Inc., 1987), pp. 75-76. D.P. Diffine, Ph.D., *One Nation Under God - How Close a Separation?* (Searcy, Arkansas: Harding University, Belden Center for Private Enterprise Education, 6th edition, 1992), p. 5.

[20] *New Guide to the English Tongue.* 1740, Thomas Dilworth, (London). H.R. Warfel, *Noah Webster-Schoolmaster to America* (New York: Octagon Press, 1966), pp. 11-13. Tim LaHaye, *Faith of Our Founding Fathers* (Brentwood, TN: Wolgemuth & Hyatt, Publishers, Inc., 1987), pp. 75-76.

[21] **New Hampshire, City of Exeter.** August 4, 1639. Stephen K. McDowell and Mark A. Beliles, *America's Providential History* (Charlottesville, VA: Providence Press, 1988), p. 59. David Barton, *The Myth of Separation* (Aledo, TX: WallBuilder Press, 1991), p. 88. *Our Christian Heritage, Letter from Plymouth Rock* (Marlborough, NH: The Plymouth Rock Foundation), p. 2. Stephen McDowell and Mark Beliles, "The Providential Perspective" (Charlottesville, VA: The Providence Foundation, P.O. Box 6759, Charlottesville, Va. 22906, January 1994), Vol. 9, No. 1, p. 2.

[22] **Constitution of the State of New Hampshire.** 1784, 1792, (in force till 1877). Supreme Court Justice David Josiah Brewer, who served 1890-1910, in his work, *The United States - Christian Nation* (Philadelphia: The John C. Winston Company, 1905, Supreme Court Collection). Catherine Millard, *The Rewriting of America's History* (Camp Hill, PA: Horizon House Publishers, 1991), p. 389. *The Constitutions of the Several Independent States of America, Published by Order of Congress* (Boston: Norman & Bowen, 1785) p. 136. Frances Newton Thorpe, ed., *Federal and State Constitutions, Colonial Charters, and Other Organic Laws of the States, Territories, and Colonies now or heretofore forming the United States,* 7 vols. (Washington: Government Printing Office, 1905; 1909; St. Clair Shores, MI: Scholarly Press, 1968). Edwin S. Gaustad, *Neither King nor Prelate - Religion and the New Nation, 1776-1826* (Grand Rapids, MI: William B. Eerdmans Publishing Company, 1993), p. 166.

[23] **Constitution of the State of New Hampshire.** 1784, 1792, Part One, Article I, Section V. *The Constitutions of All the United States According to the Latest Amendments* (Lexington, KY: Thomas T. Skillman, 1817), pp. 27, 29. *The Constitutions of the Several Independent States of America, Published by Order of Congress* (Boston: Norman & Bowen, 1785) p. 3-4. Frances Newton Thorpe, ed., *Federal and State Constitutions, Colonial Charters, and Other Organic Laws of the States, Territories, and Colonies now or heretofore forming the United States,* 7 vols. (Washington: Government Printing Office, 1905; 1909; St. Clair Shores, MI: Scholarly Press, 1968). Charles E. Rice, *The Supreme Court and Public Prayer* (New York: Fordham University Press, 1964), p. 172; "Hearings, Prayers in Public Schools and Other Matters," Committee on the Judiciary, U.S. Senate (87th Cong., 2nd Sess.), 1962, pp. 268 et seq. *New Hampshire Manual* (1937), pp. 9-10.5. David Barton, *The Myth of Separation* (Aledo, TX: WallBuilder Press, 1991), p. 29. Edwin S. Gaustad, *Neither King nor Prelate - Religion and the New Nation, 1776-1826* (Grand Rapids, MI: William B. Eerdmans Publishing Company, 1993), p. 166.

[24] **Constitution of the State of New Hampshire.** June 2, 1784; 1792, Article I, Section VI. *The Constitutions of All the United States According to the Latest Amendments* (Lexington, KY: Thomas T. Skillman, 1817), pp. 27, 29, 37, 38. *The Constitutions of the Several Independent States of America, Published by Order of Congress* (Boston: Norman & Bowen, 1785), p. 3-4. *The Constitutions of the United States of America with the Latest Amendments* (Trenton: Moore & Lake, 1813), p. 37-38. Frances Newton Thorpe, ed., *Federal and State Constitutions, Colonial Charters, and Other Organic Laws of the States, Territories, and Colonies now or heretofore forming the United States,* 7 vols. (Washington: Government Printing Office, 1905; 1909; St. Clair Shores, MI: Scholarly Press, 1968). Richard L. Perry, ed., *Sources of Our Liberties - Documentary Origins of Individual Liberties in the United States Constitution and Bill of Rights* (Chicago: American Bar Foundation, 1978; New York: 1952), p. 382. Edwin S. Gaustad, *Neither King nor Prelate - Religion and the New Nation, 1776-1826* (Grand Rapids, MI: William B. Eerdmans Publishing Company, 1993), p. 166-167. David Barton, *The Myth of Separation* (Aledo, TX: WallBuilder Press, 1991), p. 29. Stephen McDowell and Mark Beliles, "The Providential Perspective" (Charlottesville, VA: The Providence Foundation, P.O. Box 6759, Charlottesville, Va. 22906, January 1994), Vol. 9, No. 1, p. 4.

[25] **State of New Hampshire.** October 21, 1785, proclamation signed by President (Governor) John Langdon of New Hampshire. Tim LaHaye, *Faith of Our Founding Fathers* (Brentwood, TN: Wolgemuth & Hyatt, Publishers, Inc., 1987), pp. 165-166.

[26] **State of New Hampshire.** February 21, 1786, proclamation signed by President (Governor) John Langdon of New Hampshire. Tim LaHaye, *Faith of Our Founding Fathers* (Brentwood, TN: Wolgemuth & Hyatt, Publishers, Inc., 1987), pp. 163-165.

[27] **New Haven Colony Charter.** April 3, 1644. John Fiske, *The Beginnings of New England* (Boston: Houghton, Mifflin & Co., 1898), p. 136. Russ Walton, *Biblical Principles of Importance to Godly Christians* (NH: Plymouth Rock Foundation, 1984), p. 356. David Barton, *The Myth of Separation* (Aledo, TX: WallBuilder Press, 1991), p. 88. "Our Christian Heritage," *Letter from Plymouth Rock* (Marlborough, NH: The Plymouth Rock Foundation), p. 2.

[28] **New Jersey Colony.** 1697. Benjamin Franklin Morris, *The Christian Life and Character of the Civil Institutions of the United States* (Philadelphia: George W. Childs, 1864), p. 91. Gary DeMar, *God and Government-A Biblical and Historical Study* (Atlanta, GA: American Vision Press, 1982), p. 116. Stephen K. McDowell and Mark A. Beliles, *America's Providential History* (Charlottesville, VA: Providence Press, 1988), p. 61. David Barton, *The Myth of Separation* (Aledo, TX: WallBuilder Press, 1991), p. 89.

[29] **Seal of the Province of New Jersey.** 1697. Stephen K. McDowell and Mark A. Beliles, *America's Providential History* (Charlottesville, VA: Providence Press, 1989, 1994), p. 90. David Barton, *The Myth of Separation* (Aledo, TX: WallBuilder Press, 1991), p. 89.

[30] **Constitution of the State of New Jersey.** 1844, 1947, Preamble; Article I, Section 3. Charles E. Rice, *The Supreme Court and Public Prayer* (New York: Fordham University Press, 1964), pp. 172-173; "Hearings, Prayers in Public Schools and Other Matters," Committee on the Judiciary, U.S. Senate (87th Cong., 2nd Sess.), 1962, pp. 268 et seq. Tim LaHaye, *Faith of Our Founding Fathers* (Brentwood, TN: Wolgemuth & Hyatt, Publishers, Inc., 1987), p. 92.

[31] **Board of Education of Netcong, New Jersey.** 1970, prior; public school policy. *State Board of Education v. Board of Education of Netcong,* 262 A.2d 21,23 (Sup. Ct. N.J. 1970), cert. denied, 401 U.S. 1013. David Barton, *The Myth of Separation* (Aledo, TX: WallBuilder Press, 1991), p. 155.

[32] **Sir Isaac Newton.** 1704, in *Optics.* John Bartlett, *Bartlett's Familiar Quotations* (Boston: Little, Brown and Company, 1855, 1980), p. 313.

[33] **Sir Isaac Newton.** Henry H. Morris, *Men of Science-Men of God* (El Cajon, CA: Master Books, A Division of Creation Life Publishers, Inc., 1988), pp. 23-26. Tryon Edwards, D.D., *The New Dictionary of Thoughts - A Cyclopedia of Quotations* (Garden City, NY: Hanover House, 1852; revised and enlarged by C.H. Catrevas, Ralph Emerson Browns and Jonathan Edwards [descendent, along with Tryon, of Jonathan Edwards (1703-1758), president of Princeton], 1891; The Standard Book Company, 1955, 1963), p. 47. Henry H. Halley, *Halley's Bible Handbook* (Grand Rapids, MI: Zondervan Publishing House, 1927, 1965), p. 19. Charles E. Jones, *The Books You Read* (Harrisburg, PA: Executive Books, 1985), p. 118.

[34] **Sir Isaac Newton.** Sir David Brewster, *Memoirs of the Life, Writings, and Discoveries of Sir Isaac Newton.* Stephen Abbott Northrop, D.D., *A Cloud of Witnesses* (Portland, OR: American Heritage Ministries, 1987; Mantle Ministries, 228 Still Ridge,

Bulverde, Texas), p. 338.
35 Sir Isaac Newton. T.H.L. Leary, *Short Biographies of the People - Life of Sir Isaac Newton*, Vol. VI. Stephen Abbott Northrop, D.D., *A Cloud of Witnesses* (Portland, OR: American Heritage Ministries, 1987; Mantle Ministries, 228 Still Ridge, Bulverde, Texas), p. 338.
36 John Newton. Robert Flood, *The Rebirth of America* (Philadelphia: Arthur S. DeMoss Foundation, 1986), pp. 178-179.
37 Colonial Legislature of New York Colony. 1665, in an act passed by the Legislature. Benjamin Franklin Morris, *The Christian Life and Character of the Civil Institutions of the United States* (Philadelphia: George W. Childs, 1864), p. 88. Gary DeMar, *God and Government-A Biblical and Historical Study* (Atlanta, GA: American Vision Press, 1982), p. 116. Peter G. Mode, *Sourcebook and Bibliographical Guide for American Church History* (Menasha, WI: George Banta Publishing Co., 1921), p. 133. David Barton, *The Myth of Separation* (Aledo, TX: WallBuilder Press, 1991), p. 89.
38 Constitution of the State of New York. 1777, *Article XXXVIII. Davis v. Beason*, 133 U.S. 333, 341-343, 348 (1890). David Barton, *The Myth of Separation* (Aledo, TX: WallBuilder Press, 1991), p. 68. Frances Newton Thorpe, ed., *Federal and State Constitutions, Colonial Charters, and Other Organic Laws of the States, Territories, and Colonies now or heretofore forming the United States*, 7 vols. (Washington: Government Printing Office, 1905; 1909; St. Clair Shores, MI: Scholarly Press, 1968). Edwin S. Gaustad, *Neither King nor Prelate - Religion and the New Nation*, 1776-1826 (Grand Rapids, MI: William B. Eerdmans Publishing Company, 1993), p. 168.
39 Constitution of the State of New York. 1846, in the Preamble. Frances Newton Thorpe, ed., *Federal and State Constitutions, Colonial Charters, and Other Organic Laws of the States, Territories, and Colonies now or heretofore forming the United States*, 7 vols. (Washington: Government Printing Office, 1905; 1909; St. Clair Shores, MI: Scholarly Press, 1968). Charles E. Rice, *The Supreme Court and Public Prayer* (New York: Fordham University Press, 1964), p. 173; "Hearings, Prayers in Public Schools and Other Matters," Committee on the Judiciary, U.S. Senate (87th Cong., 2nd Sess.), 1962, pp. 268 et seq. Benjamin Weiss, *God in American History: A Documentation of America's Religious Heritage* (Grand Rapids, MI: Zondervan, 1966), p. 155. Tim LaHaye, *Faith of Our Founding Fathers* (Brentwood, TN: Wolgemuth & Hyatt, Publishers, Inc., 1987), p. 93. Gary DeMar, *America's Christian History: The Untold Story* (Atlanta, GA: American Vision Publishers, Inc., 1993), p. 66. Gary DeMar, "Censoring America's Christian History" (Atlanta, GA: *The Biblical Worldview*, An American Vision Publication - American Vision, Inc., July 1990).
40 Chester County, New York. August 23, 1831. Alexis de Tocqueville, *The Republic of the United States of America and Its Political Institutions, Reviewed and Examined*, Henry Reeves, trans. (Garden City, NY: A.S. Barnes & Co., 1851), Vol. I, p. 334. David Barton, *The Myth of Separation* (Aledo, TX: WallBuilder Press, 1991), p. 81. Alexis de Tocqueville, *Democracy in America*, 2 vols. (New York: Alfred A. Knopf, [1834, 1840] 1960), Vol. 2, p. 306. Gary DeMar, *America's Christian History: The Untold Story* (Atlanta, GA: American Vision Publication, Inc., 1993), p. 69.
41 Supreme Court of New York. 1811, *The People v. Ruggles*, 8 Johns 545 (1811). David Barton, *The Myth of Separation* (Aledo, TX: WallBuilder Press, 1991), p. 55.
42 Supreme Court of New York. 1811, *The People v. Ruggles*, 8 Johns 545 (1811). David Barton, *The Myth of Separation* (Aledo, TX: WallBuilder Press, 1991), p. 55.
43 Supreme Court of New York. 1811, *The People v. Ruggles*, 8 Johns 545-547 (1811). *Church of the Holy Trinity v. United States*, 143 US 457, 458, 465-471, 36 L ed 226, Justice David Josiah Brewer. David Barton, *The Myth of Separation* (Aledo, TX: WallBuilder Press, 1991), pp. 47-51, 55-61. "Our Christian Heritage," *Letter from Plymouth Rock* (Marlborough, NH: The Plymouth Rock Foundation), p. 6. Gary DeMar, *America's Christian History: The Untold Story* (Atlanta, GA: American Vision Publishers, Inc., 1993), p. 63.
44 Supreme Court of New York. *Lindenmuller v. The People*, 33 Barbour, 561. Supreme Court Justice David Josiah Brewer, *The United States - Christian Nation* (Philadelphia: The John C. Winston Company, 1905, Supreme Court Collection). Catherine Millard, *The Rewriting of America's History* (Camp Hill, PA: Horizon House Publishers, 1991), p. 392.
45 Supreme Court of New York. 1958, *Baer v. Kolmorgen*, 181 N.Y.S. 2d. 230, 237 (Sup. Ct. N. Y. 1958). David Barton, *The Myth of Separation* (Aledo, TX: WallBuilder Press, 1991), p. 15.
46 Supreme Court of New York. December 30, 1993, in the Appellate Division case of *Alfonso v. Fernandez*. "What Are They Teaching in the Public Schools?" *The Phyllis Schlafly Report* (Alton, IL: Eagle Trust Fund, January 1994), Vol. 27, No. 6, pp. 3-4.
47 Robert Carter Nicholas. May 24, 1773, in a proposal for a Day of Prayer and Fasting in response to the British closing of the port at Boston. (H.B. Journal, 1773-76, 124). Douglas Southall Freeman, *George Washington*, 6 Vol. (NY: Charles Scribner's Sons, 1948-54), Vol. III, p. 350.
48 Reinhold Niebur. 1934, in *The Serenity Prayer*. John Bartlett, *Bartlett's Familiar Quotations* (Boston: Little, Brown and Company, 1855, 1980), p. 823.
49 Reinhold Niebur. 1949, in *Discerning the Signs of the Times*. John Bartlett, *Bartlett's Familiar Quotations* (Boston: Little, Brown and Company, 1855, 1980), p. 823.
50 Martin Niemoeller. John Bartlett, *Bartlett's Familiar Quotations* (Boston: Little, Brown and Company, 1855, 1980), p. 824.
51 Richard Milhous Nixon. January 20, 1969, Monday, in his Inaugural Address. *Department of State Bulletin*, February 10, 1969. *Inaugural Addresses of the Presidents - From George Washington 1789 to Richard Milhous Nixon 1969* (Washington, D.C.: United States Government Printing Office, 91st Congress, 1st Session, House Document 91-142, 1969), pp. 275-279. *The Annals of America*, 20 vols. (Chicago, IL: Encyclopedia Britannica, 1968, 1977), Vol. 19, pp. 8-12. Benjamin Weiss, *God in American History: A Documentation of America's Religious Heritage* (Grand Rapids, MI: Zondervan, 1966), p. 154. Willard Cantelon, *Money Master of the World* (Plainfield, NJ: Logos International, 1976), p. 122. J. Michael Sharman, J.D., *Faith of the Fathers* (Culpepper, Virginia: Victory Publishing, 1995), pp. 116-117.
52 North American Review. 1867. Stephen K. McDowell and Mark A. Beliles, *The Spirit of the Constitution*. David Barton, *The Myth of Separation* (Aledo, TX: WallBuilder Press, 1991), p. 136.
53 Colony of (North) Carolina. 1650, first permanent settlement; April 9, 1585, the Roanoke Settlement was begun, later to be called The Lost Colony; August 13, 1587, members of the colony converted an Indian named Manteo; August 18, 1587, the first child, Virginia Dare was born in America. *The World Book Encyclopedia*, 18 vols. (Chicago, IL: Field Enterprises, Inc., 1957; W.F. Quarrie and Company, 8 vols., 1917; World Book, Inc., 22 vols., 1989), Vol. 10, p. 4596.
54 Colony of (North) Carolina. 1653. *The World Book Encyclopedia*, 18 vols. (Chicago, IL: Field Enterprises, Inc., 1957; W.F. Quarrie and Company, 8 vols., 1917; World Book, Inc., 22 vols., 1989), Vol. 15, p. 7587; Vol. 12, p. 5732.
55 Colony of (North) Carolina. 1653, 1727. *The World Book Encyclopedia*, 18 vols. (Chicago, IL: Field Enterprises, Inc., 1957; W.F. Quarrie and Company, 8 vols., 1917; World Book, Inc., 22 vols., 1989), Vol. 12, p. 5732.

⁵⁶ **Charter of Carolina.** 1663, issued by King Charles II to Sir William Berkeley and the seven other lord proprietors, (initially granted by King Charles I to Sir Robert Heath in 1629). Hugh Talmage Lefler, ed., *North Carolina History* (Chapel Hill: Univ. of North Carolina Press, 1934, 1956), pp. 16, 26. David Barton, *The Myth of Separation* (Aledo, TX: WallBuilder Press, 1991), p. 86. Frances Newton Thorpe, ed., *Federal and State Constitutions, Colonial Charters, and Other Organic Laws of the States, Territories, and Colonies now or heretofore forming the United States,* 7 vols. (Washington: Government Printing Office, 1905; 1909; St. Clair Shores, MI: Scholarly Press, 1968), Vol. 5, p. 2743. Pat Robertson, *America's Dates With Destiny* (Nashville, TN: Thomas Nelson Publishers, 1986), p. 32.

⁵⁷ **Fundamental Constitutions of the Carolinas.** 1663, John Locke. *The World Book Encyclopedia,* 18 vols. (Chicago, IL: Field Enterprises, Inc., 1957; W.F. Quarrie and Company, 8 vols., 1917; World Book, Inc., 22 vols., 1989), Vol. 12, p. 5736; Vol. 15, p. 7591.

⁵⁸ **Fundamental Constitutions of the Carolinas.** 1663. Supreme Court Justice David Josiah Brewer, who served 1890-1910, in his work, *The United States - Christian Nation* (Philadelphia: The John C. Winston Company, 1905, Supreme Court Collection). Catherine Millard, *The Rewriting of America's History* (Camp Hill, PA: Horizon House Publishers, 1991), p. 389.

⁵⁹ **North Carolina, Mecklenburg County Resolutions.** May 20, 1775. Loraine Boettner, *The Reformed Doctrine of Predestination* (Philadelphia: Presbyterian and Reformed, 1972), pp. 387-388. John Eidsmoe, *Christianity and the Constitution - The Faith of Our Founding Fathers* (Grand Rapids, MI: Baker Book House, A Mott Media Book, 1987, 6th printing 1993), pp. 25-26. "Our Christian Heritage," *Letter from Plymouth Rock* (Marlborough, NH: The Plymouth Rock Foundation), p. 3. *America, Great Crises in Our History Told by Its Makers, A Library of Original Sources, Vol. III* (Chicago: Veterans of Foreign Wars, 1925), pp. 184-185. Stephen McDowell and Mark Beliles, "The Providential Perspective" (Charlottesville, VA: The Providence Foundation, P.O. Box 6759, Charlottesville, Va. 22906, January 1994), Vol. 9, No. 1, p. 2.

⁶⁰ **Constitution of the State of North Carolina.** 1776, Article XIX. Frances Newton Thorpe, ed., *Federal and State Constitutions, Colonial Charters, and Other Organic Laws of the States, Territories, and Colonies now or heretofore forming the United States,* 7 vols. (Washington: Government Printing Office, 1905; 1909; St. Clair Shores, MI: Scholarly Press, 1968), Vol. V, p. 2788. Allen Nevins, *The American States During and After the Revolution: 1770-1789* (New York: MacMillan, 1924), pp. 437-438. Edwin S. Gaustad, *Neither King nor Prelate - Religion and the New Nation, 1776-1826* (Grand Rapids, MI: William B. Eerdmans Publishing Company, 1993), p. 168. Anson Phelps Stokes and Leo Pfeffer, *Church and State in the United States* (NY: Harper and Row, Publishers, 1950, revised one-volume edition, 1964), p. 54. Tim LaHaye, *Faith of Our Founding Fathers* (Brentwood, TN: Wolgemuth & Hyatt, Publishers, Inc., 1987), p. 257.

⁶¹ **Constitution of the State of North Carolina.** 1776, Article XXXII. *The Constitutions of the Several Independent States of America, Published by Order of Congress* (Boston: Norman & Bowen, 1785) p. 138. *The Constitutions of All the United States According to the Latest Amendments* (Lexington, KY: Thomas T. Skillman, 1817), p. 224. Benjamin Franklin Morris, *The Christian Life and Character of the Civil Institutions of the United States* (Philadelphia, PA: L. Johnson & Co., 1863; George W. Childs, 1864), p. 233. Supreme Court Justice David Josiah Brewer, who served 1890-1910, in his work, *The United States - Christian Nation* (Philadelphia: The John C. Winston Company, 1905, Supreme Court Collection). Frances Newton Thorpe, ed., *Federal and State Constitutions, Colonial Charters, and Other Organic Laws of the States, Territories, and Colonies now or heretofore forming the United States,* 7 vols. (Washington: Government Printing Office, 1905; 1909; St. Clair Shores, MI: Scholarly Press, 1968). Gary DeMar, "Censoring America's Christian History" (Atlanta, GA: *The Biblical Worldview,* An American Vision Publication - American Vision, Inc., July 1990), p. 7. Catherine Millard, *The Rewriting of America's History* (Camp Hill, PA: Horizon House Publishers, 1991), p. 389. David Barton, *The Myth of Separation* (Aledo, TX: WallBuilder Press, 1991), p. 24. Gary DeMar, *America's Christian History: The Untold Story* (Atlanta, GA: American Vision Publishers, Inc., 1993), p. 68. David Barton, *Keys to Good Government,* p. 4.

⁶² **Constitution of the State of North Carolina.** 1835. Supreme Court Justice David Josiah Brewer, who served 1890-1910, in his work, *The United States - Christian Nation* (Philadelphia: The John C. Winston Company, 1905, Supreme Court Collection). Catherine Millard, *The Rewriting of America's History* (Camp Hill, PA: Horizon House Publishers, 1991), p. 389.

⁶³ **Constitution of the State of North Carolina.** 1868, Article 1, Section 1, Section 26; Article IV, Section 8; Article XXXIV (1776). Charles E. Rice, *The Supreme Court and Public Prayer* (New York: Fordham University Press, 1964), p. 173; "Hearings, Prayers in Public Schools and Other Matters," Committee on the Judiciary, U.S. Senate (87th Cong., 2nd Sess.), 1962, pp. 268 et seq. Tim LaHaye, *Faith of Our Founding Fathers* (Brentwood, TN: Wolgemuth & Hyatt, Publishers, Inc., 1987), p. 92. Supreme Court Justice David Josiah Brewer, who served 1890-1910, in his work, *The United States - Christian Nation* (Philadelphia: The John C. Winston Company, 1905, Supreme Court Collection). Catherine Millard, *The Rewriting of America's History* (Camp Hill, PA: Horizon House Publishers, 1991), p. 389. Frances Newton Thorpe, ed., *Federal and State Constitutions, Colonial Charters, and Other Organic Laws of the States, Territories, and Colonies now or heretofore forming the United States,* 7 vols. (Washington: Government Printing Office, 1905; 1909; St. Clair Shores, MI: Scholarly Press, 1968). Edwin S. Gaustad, *Neither King nor Prelate - Religion and the New Nation, 1776-1826* (Grand Rapids, MI: William B. Eerdmans Publishing Company, 1993), p. 169.

⁶⁴ **Constitution of the State of North Carolina.** 1868, Preamble. Charles E. Rice, *The Supreme Court and Public Prayer* (New York: Fordham University Press, 1964), p. 173; "Hearings, Prayers in Public Schools and Other Matters," Committee on the Judiciary, U.S. Senate (87th Cong., 2nd Sess.), 1962, pp. 268 et seq. Tim LaHaye, *Faith of Our Founding Fathers* (Brentwood, TN: Wolgemuth & Hyatt, Publishers, Inc., 1987), p. 92. Supreme Court Justice David Josiah Brewer, who served 1890-1910, in his work, *The United States - Christian Nation* (Philadelphia: The John C. Winston Company, 1905, Supreme Court Collection). Catherine Millard, *The Rewriting of America's History* (Camp Hill, PA: Horizon House Publishers, 1991), p. 389. Frances Newton Thorpe, ed., *Federal and State Constitutions, Colonial Charters, and Other Organic Laws of the States, Territories, and Colonies now or heretofore forming the United States,* 7 vols. (Washington: Government Printing Office, 1905; 1909; St. Clair Shores, MI: Scholarly Press, 1968). Edwin S. Gaustad, *Neither King nor Prelate - Religion and the New Nation, 1776-1826* (Grand Rapids, MI: William B. Eerdmans Publishing Company, 1993), p. 169.

⁶⁵ **Northwest Ordinance.** July 13, 1787, passed by the Continental Congress; July 21, 1789, passed by the United States Congress; August 4, 1789, signed by President Washington. *Section 13, 14; Article I, III.* Journal of Congress (ed. 1800) (early proposals of the bill) Vol. IX, pp. 109-110. *The Constitutions of the United States of America with the Latest Amendments* (Trenton: Moore & Lake, 1813), p. 364. *Revised Statutes of the United States relating to the District of Columbia and Post Roads...together with the Public Treaties in force on the first day of December 1873* (ed. 1878). *Life, Journal and Correspondence of Manasseh Cutler,* Vol. I, chap. 8. William MacDonald, *Select Documents Illustrative of the History of the United States, 1776-1861* (NY: Macmillan Company, 1897, 1898), p. 26. Frances Newton Thorpe, ed., *Federal and State Constitutions, Colonial Charters, and Other Organic Laws of the States, Territories, and Colonies now or heretofore forming the United States,* 7 vols. (Washington: Government Printing Office, 1905; 1909; St. Clair

Shores, MI: Scholarly Press, 1968), Vol. I, pp. 957-962. Poole, *North American Rev.*, (includes history of the act) CXXII: 229-65. *Article III of An Ordinance for the Government of the Territory of the United States, North-West of the River Ohio (Northwest Ordinance).* Henry Steele Commager, ed., *Documents of American History*, 2 vols. (NY: F.S. Crofts and Company, 1934; Appleton-Century-Crofts, Inc., 1948, 6th edition, 1958; Englewood Cliffs, NJ: Prentice Hall, Inc., 9th edition, 1973), p. 131. Paul M. Angle, ed., *By These Words* (NY: Rand McNally & Company, 1954), pp. 91-93. William Benton, *The Annals of America*, 20 vols. (Chicago, IL: Encyclopedia Britannica, 1968), Vol, III, pp. 194-195. Stephen McDowell and Mark Beliles, "The Providential Perspective" (Charlottesville, VA: The Providence Foundation, P.O. Box 6759, Charlottesville, Va. 22906, January 1994), Vol. 9, No. 1, p. 5. Lillian W. Kay, ed., *The Ground on Which We Stand - Basic Documents of American History* (NY: Franklin Watts., Inc, 1969), p. 38-39. Daniel L. Driesbach, *Real Threat and Mere Shadow - Religious Liberty and the First Amendment* (Westchester, IL: Crossway Books, 1987), Vol. I, pp. 427-428. Edwin S. Gaustad, *Neither King nor Prelate - Religion and the New Nation, 1776-1826* (Grand Rapids, MI: William B. Eerdmans Publishing Company, 1993), (complete text including drafts and proposals), pp. 153-158. David Barton, *The Myth of Separation* (Aledo, TX: WallBuilder Press, 1991), pp. 37-39. Tim LaHaye, *Faith of Our Founding Fathers* (Brentwood, TN: Wolgemuth & Hyatt, Publishers, Inc., 1987), p. 91. D.P. Diffine, Ph.D., *One Nation Under God - How Close a Separation?* (Searcy, Arkansas: Harding University, Belden Center for Private Enterprise Education, 6th edition, 1992), p. 3.

O

[1] **Daniel O'Connell.** Lewis C. Henry, *Best Quotations For All Occasions* (Greenwich, Conn.: Fawcett Publications, Inc., 1961), p. 179.

[2] **Flannery O'Connor.** 1957, in a talk at Notre Dame University. John Bartlett, *Bartlett's Familiar Quotations* (Boston: Little, Brown and Company, 1855, 1980), p. 905.

[3] **James Edward Oglethorpe.** 1732. *The World Book Encyclopedia*, 18 vols. (Chicago, IL: Field Enterprises, Inc., 1957; W.F. Quarrie and Company, 8 vols., 1917; World Book, Inc., 22 vols., 1989), Vol. 7, p. 2950; Vol. 12, p. 5857.

[4] **James Edward Oglethorpe.** 1732. Stephen K. McDowell and Mark A. Beliles, *America's Providential History* (Charlottesville, VA: Providence Press, 1988), p. 55. David Barton, *The Myth of Separation* (Aledo, TX: WallBuilder Press, 1991), p. 87.

[5] **James Edward Oglethorpe.** 1732. Stephen K. McDowell and Mark A. Beliles, *America's Providential History* (Charlottesville, VA: Providence Press, 1988), p. 55. David Barton, *The Myth of Separation* (Aledo, TX: WallBuilder Press, 1991), p. 87.

[6] **Constitution of the State of Ohio.** November 1, 1802, Article VIII, Section 3. *The Constitutions of All the United States According to the Latest Amendments* (Lexington, KY: Thomas T. Skillman, 1817), p. 343. David Barton, *The Myth of Separation*, (Aledo, TX: WallBuilder Press, 1991), p. 38. Congressional Records, April 30, 1802, c. 40,2 Stat. 289. Frances Newton Thorpe, ed., *Federal and State Constitutions, Colonial Charters, and Other Organic Laws of the States, Territories, and Colonies now or heretofore forming the United States*, 7 vols. (Washington: Government Printing Office, 1905; 1909; St. Clair Shores, MI: Scholarly Press, 1968), Vol. V., p. 2910. Rodney L. Mott and W.L. Hindman, eds., *The Constitutions of the States and the United States*, p. 1192. Anson Phelps Stokes and Leo Pfeffer, *Church and State in the United States* (NY: Harper and Row, Publishers, 1950, revised one-volume edition, 1964), p. 155.

[7] **Motto of the State of Ohio.** 1959, included in proclamation by Governor George V. Voinovich. Ken Waggoner, *United In Prayer* (Reston, VA: Intercessors For America Newsletter, May 1993), Vol. 20, No. 5, p. 1. Ohio State Income Tax Booklet, 1993, cover; courtesy of Karen Morgan.

[8] **State of Ohio.** February 18, 1992, the State of Ohio issued an Executive Proclamation declaring May 7, 1992, as "A Day of Prayer in Ohio," signed by Governor George V. Voinovich, in the Capitol City of Columbus. Mrs. James Dobson (Shirley), chairman, *The National Day of Prayer Information Packet* (Colorado Springs, CO: National Day of Prayer Tack Force, May 6, 1993).

[9] **State of Oklahoma, District Court for Tulsa County.** July 15, 1993, District Judge Robert J. Scott granting summary judgement for the defendants in the case of *Crowley, Gaines and Ries v. Tilton* (Case No. CJ-92-3279).

[10] **Old Deluder Satan Law.** 1647. *The Code of 1650, Being a Compilation of the Earliest Laws and Orders of the General Court of Connecticut* (Hartford: Silus Andrus, 1822), pp. 92-93. *Records of the Governor of the Massachusetts Bay in New England*, II:203. Henry Steele Commager, ed., *Documents of American History*, 2 vols. (NY: F.S. Crofts and Company, 1934; Appleton-Century-Crofts, Inc., 1948, 6th edition, 1958; Englewood Cliffs, NJ: Prentice Hall, Inc., 9th edition, 1973), Vol. I, p. 29. David Barton, *The Myth of Separation* (Aledo, TX: WallBuilder Press, 1991), p. 90. *The Laws and Liberties of Massachusetts*, 1648 (reprinted Cambridge: 1929), cited in *McCollum v. Board of Education*, 68 S.Ct. 461, 333 U.S. 203 (1948). John Eidsmoe, *Christianity and the Constitution - The Faith of Our Founding Fathers* (Grand Rapids, MI: Baker Book House, A Mott Media Book, 1987, 6th printing 1993), p. 28. *The Annals of America*, 20 vols. (Chicago, IL: Encyclopedia Britannica, 1968), Vol. I, p. 203. John Wilson Taylor, M.A., Ph.D., et al., *The Lincoln Library of Essential Information* (Buffalo, New York: The Frontier Press Company, 1935), p. 1623. D.P. Diffine, Ph.D., *One Nation Under God - How Close a Separation?* (Searcy, Arkansas: Harding University, Belden Center for Private Enterprise Education, 6th edition, 1992), p. 2.

[11] **Henry Opukahai'a.** In his memoirs. "Hawaii's Heroes of Faith" University of the Nations (Hawaii: Youth With a Mission Newsletter).

[12] **Henry Opukahai'a.** December 30, 1993, the State of Hawaii issued an Executive Proclamation declaring February 12 - 22, 1994, as "Christian Heritage Week," signed by Governor John Waihee, in the Capitol City of Honolulu. Courtesy of Bruce Barilla, Christian Heritage Week Ministry (P.O. Box 58, W.V. 24712; 304-384-7707, 304-384-9044 fax).

P

[1] **Robert Morris Page.** *The Evidence of God in an Expanding Universe* (New York: G.P. Putnam's Son's), p. 29. Willard Cantelon, *New Money or None?* (Plainfield, NJ: Logos International, 1979), p. 226.

[2] **Thomas Paine.** December 23, 1776, in *The American Crisis*, No. 1. John Bartlett, *Bartlett's Familiar Quotations* (Boston: Little, Brown and Company, 1855, 1980), p. 384. Robert Flood, *The Rebirth of America* (Philadelphia: Arthur S. DeMoss Foundation, 1986), p. 16. "*Common Sense*" *Thomas Paine - 1776* (Reston, VA: Intercessors For America, July/August 1993), Vol. 20, No. 7/8, p. 1.

[3] **Thomas Paine.** December 23, 1776. *The American Crisis.* "*Common Sense*" *Thomas Paine - 1776* (Reston, VA: Intercessors For America, July/August 1993), Vol. 20, No. 7/8, p. 1.

[4] **Thomas Paine.** December 23, 1776. *The American Crisis.* "*Common Sense*" *Thomas Paine - 1776* (Reston, VA: Intercessors For America, July/August 1993), Vol. 20, No. 7/8, p. 1.

Notes

[5] **Thomas Paine.** December 23, 1776. *The American Crisis. "Common Sense" Thomas Paine - 1776* (Reston, VA: Intercessors For America, July/August 1993), Vol. 20, No. 7/8, p. 1.

[6] **Thomas Paine.** Benjamin Hart, *Faith & Freedom - The Christian Roots of The American Liberty* (Dallas, TX: Lewis and Stanley, 1988, 1990), p. 309. Peter Marshall and David Manuel, *The Glory of America* (Bloomington, MN: Garborg's Heart'N Home, Inc., 1991), 1.29.

[7] **Thomas Paine.** *The World Book Encyclopedia,* 18 vols. (Chicago, IL: Field Enterprises, Inc., 1957; W.F. Quarrie and Company, 8 vols., 1917; World Book, Inc., 22 vols., 1989), Vol. 13, p. 6035.

[8] **Ambroise Pare'.** Favorite saying. John Bartlett, *Bartlett's Familiar Quotations* (Boston: Little, Brown and Company, 1855, 1980), p. 162.

[9] **Theodore Parker.** Tryon Edwards, D.D., *The New Dictionary of Thoughts - A Cyclopedia of Quotations* (Garden City, NY: Hanover House, 1852; revised and enlarged by C.H. Catrevas, Ralph Emerson Browns and Jonathan Edwards [descendent, along with Tryon, of Jonathan Edwards (1703-1758), president of Princeton], 1891; The Standard Book Company, 1955, 1963), p. 46.

[10] **Theodore Parker.** May 29, 1850, in *The American Idea.* John Bartlett, *Bartlett's Familiar Quotations* (Boston: Little, Brown and Company, 1855, 1980), p. 537.

[11] **Blaise Pascal.** 1670, in *Pensees,* No. 556. John Bartlett, *Bartlett's Familiar Quotations* (Boston: Little, Brown and Company, 1855, 1980), p. 300.

[12] **Blaise Pascal.** Wager of Pascal. Henry M. Morris, *Men of Science - Men of God* (El Cajon, CA: Master Books, Creation Life Publishers, Inc., 1990), pp. 15-16.

[13] **Blaise Pascal.** O.W. Wight, translator from the French language, *Thoughts, Letters, and Opuscules,* pp. 334-335. Stephen Abbott Northrop, D.D., *A Cloud of Witnesses* (Portland, OR: American Heritage Ministries, 1987; Mantle Ministries, 228 Still Ridge, Bulverde, Texas), pp. 352-353.

[14] **Blaise Pascal.** 1662, in a writing of his found in his effects after his death. John Bartlett, *Bartlett's Familiar Quotations* (Boston: Little, Brown and Company, 1855, 1980), p. 300.

[15] **Louis Pasteur.** John Hudson Tiner, *Louis Pasteur - Founder of Modern Medicine* (Milford, Michigan: Mott Media, Inc., 1990), p. 75.

[16] **Louis Pasteur.** Henry M. Morris, *Men of Science - Men of God* (El Cajon, CA: Master Books, Creation Life Publishers, Inc., 1990), pp. 60-62.

[17] **Louis Pasteur.** John Hudson Tiner, *Louis Pasteur - Founder of Modern Medicine* (Milford, Michigan: Mott Media, Inc., 1990), p. 63.

[18] **Louis Pasteur.** John Hudson Tiner, *Louis Pasteur - Founder of Modern Medicine* (Milford, Michigan: Mott Media, Inc., 1990), p. 90.

[19] **William Paterson.** Stephen K. McDowell and Mark A. Beliles, *America's Providential History* (Charlottesville, VA: Providence Press, 1988), p. 93. David Barton, *The Myth of Separation* (Aledo, TX: WallBuilder Press, 1991), p. 92.

[20] **William Paterson.** Stephen K. McDowell and Mark A. Beliles, *America's Providential History* (Charlottesville, VA: Providence Press, 1988), p. 93. David Barton, *The Myth of Separation* (Aledo, TX: WallBuilder Press, 1991), p. 92.

[21] **William Paterson.** Brantz Mayer, *Baltimore Past and Present,* 1729-1970 (Washington: Library of Congress, n.d.), p. 403. Tim LaHaye, *Faith of Our Founding Fathers* (Brentwood, TN: Wolgemuth & Hyatt, Publishers, Inc., 1987), pp. 173-174.

[22] **William Penn.** *The World Book Encyclopedia,* 18 vols. (Chicago, IL: Field Enterprises, Inc., 1957; W.F. Quarrie and Company, 8 vols., 1917; World Book, Inc., 22 vols., 1989), Vol. 13, pp. 6181-6183, 6192-6195. Catherine Millard, *A Children's Companion Guide to America's History* (Camp Hill, PA: Horizon House Publishers, 1993), p. 25.

[23] **William Penn.** *Treatise of the Religion of the Quakers.* Stephen Abbott Northrop, D.D., *A Cloud of Witnesses* (Portland, OR: American Heritage Ministries, 1987; Mantle Ministries, 228 Still Ridge, Bulverde, Texas), p. 355.

[24] **William Penn.** *The World Book Encyclopedia,* 18 vols. (Chicago, IL: Field Enterprises, Inc., 1957; W.F. Quarrie and Company, 8 vols., 1917; World Book, Inc., 22 vols., 1989), Vol. 13, pp. 6181-6183, 6192-6195.

[25] **William Penn.** No Cross, No Crown, 1668. Burton Stevenson, *The Home Book of Quotations* (New York: Dodd, Mead and Company, 1967), p. 267.

[26] **William Penn.** From his writing *No Cross, No Crown,* written while imprisoned in the Tower of London for 8 months. Thomas Pyrn Cope, ed., *Passages from the Life and Writings of William Penn* (Philadelphia: Friends Bookstore, 1882). Catherine Millard, *The Rewriting of America's History* (Camp Hill, PA: Horizon House Publishers, 1991) pp. 46-47.

[27] **William Penn.** *Chambers' Cyclopedia of English Literature,* Acme Edition, vol.III, p. 12. Stephen Abbott Northrop, D.D., *A Cloud of Witnesses* (Portland, OR: American Heritage Ministries, 1987; Mantle Ministries, 228 Still Ridge, Bulverde, Texas), p. 355.

[28] **William Penn.** *The World Book Encyclopedia,* 18 vols. (Chicago, IL: Field Enterprises, Inc., 1957; W.F. Quarrie and Company, 8 vols., 1917; World Book, Inc., 22 vols., 1989), Vol. 13, pp. 6181-6183, 6192-6195.

[29] **William Penn.** *Travels in Holland and Germany.* Stephen Abbott Northrop, D.D., *A Cloud of Witnesses* (Portland, OR: American Heritage Ministries, 1987; Mantle Ministries, 228 Still Ridge, Bulverde, Texas), p. 355.

[30] **William Penn.** *The World Book Encyclopedia,* 18 vols. (Chicago, IL: Field Enterprises, Inc., 1957; W.F. Quarrie and Company, 8 vols., 1917; World Book, Inc., 22 vols., 1989), Vol. 13, pp. 6181-6183, 6192-6195.

[31] **William Penn.** *The World Book Encyclopedia,* 18 vols. (Chicago, IL: Field Enterprises, Inc., 1957; W.F. Quarrie and Company, 8 vols., 1917; World Book, Inc., 22 vols., 1989), Vol. 13, pp. 6181-6183, 6192-6195.

[32] **William Penn.** January 1, 1681. Peter G. Mode, *Sourcebook and Bibliographical Guide for American Church History* (Menasha, WI: George Banta Publishing Co., 1921), p. 163. Thomas Clarkson, *Memoirs of the Private and Public Life of William Penn* (London: Longman, Hunt, Rees, Orme, & Brown, 1813), Vol. I, p. 287. David Barton, *The Myth of Separation* (Aledo, TX: WallBuilder Press, 1991), p. 89.

[33] **William Penn.** January 1, 1681. *Remember William Penn, 1644-1944, Tercentenary Memorial* (Harrisburg, PA: The Commonwealth of Pennsylvania and Pennsylvania Historical Commission, 1944). Thomas Clarkson, *Memoirs of the Private and Public Life of William Penn* (London: Longman, Hunt, Rees, Orme, & Brown, 1813), Vol. I, p. 280. David Barton, *The Myth of Separation* (Aledo, TX: WallBuilder Press, 1991), p. 89. Robert Flood, *The Rebirth of America* (Philadelphia: Arthur S. DeMoss Foundation, 1986), pp. 46-47.

[34] **William Penn.** *The World Book Encyclopedia,* 18 vols. (Chicago, IL: Field Enterprises, Inc., 1957; W.F. Quarrie and Company, 8 vols., 1917; World Book, Inc., 22 vols., 1989), Vol. 13, pp. 6181-6183, 6192-6195.

[35] **William Penn.** August 18, 1681, in his letter to the Indians before his arrival. Pennsylvania Historical Society Collection,

Philadelphia. Catherine Millard, *The Rewriting of America's History* (Camp Hill, PA: Horizon House Publishers, 1991) pp. 37-38.
[36] **William Penn.** April 25, 1682, in the preface of his *Frame of Government of Pennsylvania.* William Wistar Comfort, *William Penn and Our Liberties* (Published in the Penn Mutual's Centennial Year in honor of the man whose name the company adopted at its founding in the year 1847.) Philadelphia: The Penn Mutual Life Insurance Company, 1947, n.p. Benjamin Franklin Morris, *The Christian Life and Character of the Civil Institutions of the United States* (Philadelphia: George W. Childs, 1864), pp. 82-83. Thomas Clarkson, *Memoirs of the Private and Public Life of William Penn* (London: Longman, Hurst, Orme, & Grown, 1813), Vol. I, p. 303. Frances Newton Thorpe, ed., *Federal and State Constitutions, Colonial Charters, and Other Organic Laws of the States, Territories, and Colonies now or heretofore forming the United States,* 7 vols. (Washington: Government Printing Office, 1905; 1909; St. Clair Shores, MI: Scholarly Press, 1968), Vol. V, pp. 3052-3059. Charles E. Rice, *The Supreme Court and Public Prayer* (New York: Fordham University Press, 1964), pp. 163-164. *The Annals of America,* 20 vols. (Chicago, IL: Encyclopedia Britannica, 1968), Vol. I, pp. 265-267. Richard L. Perry, ed., *Sources of Our Liberties - Documentary Origins of Individual Liberties in the United States Constitution and Bill of Rights* (Chicago: American Bar Foundation, 1978; New York: 1952). Gary DeMar, *God and Government - A Biblical and Historical* Study (Atlanta, GA: American Vision Press, 1982), p. 115. Catherine Millard, *The Rewriting of America's History* (Camp Hill, PA: Horizon House Publishers, 1991) p. 44. David Barton, *The Myth of Separation* (Aledo, TX: WallBuilder Press, 1991), p. 248. Catherine Millard, *A Children's Companion Guide to America's History* (Camp Hill, PA: Horizon House Publishers, 1993), p. 29. Stephen McDowell and Mark Beliles, "The Providential Perspective" (Charlottesville, VA: The Providence Foundation, P.O. Box 6759, Charlottesville, Va. 22906, January 1994), Vol. 9, No. 1, p. 1.
[37] **William Penn.** *The World Book Encyclopedia,* 18 vols. (Chicago, IL: Field Enterprises, Inc., 1957; W.F. Quarrie and Company, 8 vols., 1917; World Book, Inc., 22 vols., 1989), Vol. 13, pp. 6181-6183, 6192-6195.
[38] **William Penn.** 1684. William Penn, *Prayer for Philadelphia* (Philadelphia, PA: Historical Society of Pennsylvania). Catherine Millard, *The Rewriting of America's History* (Camp Hill, PA: Horizon House Publishers, 1991), p. 57.
[39] **William Penn.** October 28, 1701, Charter of Privileges, granted by William Penn. Philosophical Society of Pennsylvania Collection, Philadelphia. Frances Newton Thorpe, ed., *Federal and State Constitutions, Colonial Charters, and Other Organic Laws of the States, Territories, and Colonies now or heretofore forming the United States,* 7 vols. (Washington: Government Printing Office, 1905; 1909; St. Clair Shores, MI: Scholarly Press, 1968), Vol. V, p. 3076 ff. Henry Steele Commager, ed., *Documents of American History,* 2 vols. (NY: F.S. Crofts and Company, 1934; Appleton-Century-Crofts, Inc., 1948, 6th edition, 1958; Englewood Cliffs, NJ: Prentice Hall, Inc., 9th edition, 1973), Vol. I, p. 40-41. Richard L. Perry, ed., *Sources of Our Liberties: Documentary Origins of Individual Liberties in the United States Constitution and Bill of Rights* (Chicago: American Bar Foundation, 1978; New York: 1952). Charles E. Rice, *The Supreme Court and Public Prayer* (New York: Fordham University Press, 1964), pp. 164-165. Rosalie J. Slater, *Teaching and Learning America's Christian History* (San Francisco: Foundation for American Christian Education, 1975), p. 202. Marshall Foster and Mary-Elaine Swanson, *The American Covenant - The Untold Story* (Roseburg, OR: Foundation for Christian Self-Government, 1981; Thousand Oaks, CA: The Mayflower Institute, 1983, 1992), p. 98. Catherine Millard, *The Rewriting of America's History* (Camp Hill, PA: Horizon House Publishers, 1991) p. 44. *Church of the Holy Trinity v. United States,* 143 US 457, 458, 465-471, 36 L ed 226, Justice David Josiah Brewer. David Barton, *The Myth of Separation* (Aledo, TX: WallBuilder Press, 1991), pp. 47-51. "Our Christian Heritage," *Letter from Plymouth Rock* (Marlborough, NH: The Plymouth Rock Foundation), p. 6.
[40] **William Penn.** October 28, 1701, Charter of Privileges, granted by William Penn. Philosophical Society of Pennsylvania Collection, Philadelphia. Frances Newton Thorpe, ed., *Federal and State Constitutions, Colonial Charters, and Other Organic Laws of the States, Territories, and Colonies now or heretofore forming the United States,* 7 vols. (Washington: Government Printing Office, 1905; 1909; St. Clair Shores, MI: Scholarly Press, 1968), Vol. V, p. 3076 ff. Henry Steele Commager, ed., *Documents of American History,* 2 vols. (NY: F.S. Crofts and Company, 1934; Appleton-Century-Crofts, Inc., 1948, 6th edition, 1958; Englewood Cliffs, NJ: Prentice Hall, Inc., 9th edition, 1973), Vol. I, p. 40-41. Richard L. Perry, ed., *Sources of Our Liberties: Documentary Origins of Individual Liberties in the United States Constitution and Bill of Rights* (Chicago: American Bar Foundation, 1978; New York: 1952). Charles E. Rice, *The Supreme Court and Public Prayer* (New York: Fordham University Press, 1964), pp. 164-165. Rosalie J. Slater, *Teaching and Learning America's Christian History* (San Francisco: Foundation for American Christian Education, 1975), p. 202. Marshall Foster and Mary-Elaine Swanson, *The American Covenant - The Untold Story* (Roseburg, OR: Foundation for Christian Self-Government, 1981; Thousand Oaks, CA: The Mayflower Institute, 1983, 1992), p. 98. Catherine Millard, *The Rewriting of America's History* (Camp Hill, PA: Horizon House Publishers, 1991) p. 44. *Church of the Holy Trinity v. United States,* 143 US 457, 458, 465-471, 36 L ed 226, Justice David Josiah Brewer. David Barton, *The Myth of Separation* (Aledo, TX: WallBuilder Press, 1991), pp. 47-51. "Our Christian Heritage," *Letter from Plymouth Rock* (Marlborough, NH: The Plymouth Rock Foundation), p. 6.
[41] **William Penn.** Stephen K. McDowell and Mark A. Beliles, *America's Providential History* (Charlottesville, VA: Providence Press, 1988), p. 62. Hildegarde Dolson, *William Penn: Quaker Hero* (NY: Random House, 1961), p. 155. David Barton, *The Myth of Separation* (Aledo, TX: WallBuilder Press, 1991), p. 89. D.P. Diffine, Ph.D., *One Nation Under God - How Close a Separation?* (Searcy, Arkansas: Harding University, Belden Center for Private Enterprise Education, 6th edition, 1992), p. 4. *The Annals of America,* 20 vols. (Chicago, IL: Encyclopedia Britannica, 1968), Vol. I, p. 189. Charles Fadiman, ed., *The American Treasury* (NY: Harper & Brothers, Publishers, 1955), p. 116.
[42] **William Penn.** Peter Marshall and David Manuel, *The Glory of America* (Bloomington, MN: Garborg's Heart'N Home, Inc., 1991), 10.14.
[43] **William Penn.** Original Bible in the Penn Mutual Archives Collection, Philadelphia. Catherine Millard, *The Rewriting of America's History* (Camp Hill, PA: Horizon House Publishers, 1991) p. 37. Catherine Millard, *A Children's Companion Guide to America's History* (Camp Hill, PA: Horizon House Publishers, 1993), p. 25.
[44] **William Penn.** In his sermon entitled, "A Summons or Call to Christendom - In an Earnest Expostulation with Her to Prepare for the Great and Notable Day of the Lord that is at the Door." Catherine Millard, *The Rewriting of America's History* (Camp Hill, PA: Horizon House Publishers, 1991) pp. 44-46.
[45] **William Penn.** In a letter to his wife and family. Thomas Pyrn, ed., *Passages from the Life and Writings of William Penn* (Philadelphia: Friends Bookstore, 1882). Catherine Millard, *The Rewriting of America's History* (Camp Hill, PA: Horizon House Publishers, 1991) pp. 47-49.
[46] **William Penn.** Verna M. Hall, *The Christian History of the Constitution of the United States of America* (San Francisco: Foundation for American Christian Education, 1966), p. 262A. George Bancroft, *Bancroft's History of the United States* (Boston: Little, Brown & Co., 1859), Vol. II, p. 385. Mason Locke Weems, *The Life of William Penn* (Philadelphia: Uriah Hunt, 1836), p. 121. David Barton, *The Myth of Separation* (Aledo, TX: WallBuilder Press, 1991), pp. 34, 89.
[47] **Charter of Pennsylvania.** 1681. Granted to William Penn by King Charles II. Frances Newton Thorpe, ed., *Federal and State*

Constitutions, Colonial Charters, and Other Organic Laws of the States, Territories, and Colonies now or heretofore forming the United States, 7 vols. (Washington: Government Printing Office, 1905; 1909; St. Clair Shores, MI: Scholarly Press, 1968), Vol. V, p. 2743. Pat Robertson, *America's Dates With Destiny* (Nashville, TN: Thomas Nelson Publishers, 1986), p. 32.

⁴⁸ **Fundamental Constitutions of Pennsylvania.** April 25, 1682, Article XXII, written by William Penn, in the First Frame of Government. Frances Newton Thorpe, ed., *Federal and State Constitutions, Colonial Charters, and Other Organic Laws of the States, Territories, and Colonies now or heretofore forming the United States,* 7 vols. (Washington: Government Printing Office, 1905; 1909; St. Clair Shores, MI: Scholarly Press, 1968), Vol. V, pp. 3052, 3059. *The Annals of America,* 20 vols. (Chicago, IL: Encyclopedia Britannica, 1968), Vol. 1, pp. 265, 2271. The Historical Society of Pennsylvania Collection, Philadelphia. Richard L. Perry, ed., *Sources of Our Liberties: Documentary Origins of Individual Liberties in the United States Constitution and Bill of Rights* (Chicago: American Bar Foundation, 1978; New York: 1952). Charles E. Rice, *The Supreme Court and Public Prayer* (New York: Fordham University Press, 1964), pp. 163-164. Catherine Millard, *The Rewriting of America's History* (Camp Hill, PA: Horizon House Publishers, 1991) pp. 41-44. Catherine Millard, *A Children's Companion Guide to America's History* (Camp Hill, PA: Horizon House Publishers, 1993), p. 29.

⁴⁹ **Great Law of Pennsylvania.** December 7, 1682. Benjamin Franklin Morris, *The Christian Life and Character of the Civil Institutions of the United States, Developed in the Official and Historical Annals of the Republic* (Philadelphia, PA: George W. Childs, 1864), p. 83. *Charter to William Penn..., and Duke of Yorke's Book of Laws. Remember William Penn, 1644-1944, Tercentenary Memorial* (Harrisburg, PA: The Commonwealth of Pennsylvania and Pennsylvania Historical Commission, 1944), p. 85-86. Gary DeMar, *God and Government - A Biblical and Historical Study* (Atlanta, GA: American Vision Press, 1982), p. 115. "Our Christian Heritage," *Letter from Plymouth Rock* (Marlborough, NH: The Plymouth Rock Foundation), p. 2. D.P. Diffine, Ph.D., *One Nation Under God - How Close a Separation?* (Searcy, Arkansas: Harding University, Belden Center for Private Enterprise Education, 6th edition, 1992), p. 4. Gary DeMar, *America's Christian History: The Untold Story* (Atlanta, GA: American Vision Publishers, Inc., 1993), p. 67. Gary DeMar, "God and the Constitution" (Atlanta, GA: *The Biblical Worldview,* An American Vision Publication - American Vision, Inc., December 1993), p. 9. 1682. *Charter of William Penn, and Laws of the Province of Pennsylvania, passed between the Years 1682 and 1700* (Harrisberg: 1870), pp. 16-18. Anson Phelps Stokes and Leo Pfeffer, *Church and State in the United States* (NY: Harper and Row, Publishers, 1950, revised one-volume edition, 1964) p. 19.

⁵⁰ **Charter of Privileges of Pennsylvania.** 1701, granted by William Penn. Philosophical Society of Pennsylvania Collection. Philadelphia. Catherine Millard, *The Rewriting of America's History* (Camp Hill, PA: Horizon House Publishers, 1991) p. 44. Catherine Millard, *A Children's Companion Guide to America's History* (Camp Hill, PA: Horizon House Publishers, 1993), p. 29.

⁵¹ **Charter of Privileges of Pennsylvania.** *Church of the Holy Trinity v. United States,* 143 US 457, 458, 465-471, 36 L ed 226, Justice David Josiah Brewer. David Barton, *The Myth of Separation* (Aledo, TX: WallBuilder Press, 1991), pp. 47-51. "Our Christian Heritage," *Letter from Plymouth Rock* (Marlborough, NH: The Plymouth Rock Foundation), p. 6.

⁵² **Constitution of the State of Pennsylvania.** 1776, in the Preamble. Charles E. Rice, *The Supreme Court and Public Prayer* (New York: Fordham University Press, 1964), p. 174; "Hearings, Prayers in Public Schools and Other Matters," Committee on the Judiciary, U.S. Senate (87th Cong., 2nd Sess.), 1962, pp. 268 et seq. Benjamin Weiss, *God in American History: A Documentation of America's Religious Heritage* (Grand Rapids, MI: Zondervan, 1966), p. 155. Gary DeMar, *America's Christian History: The Untold Story* (Atlanta, GA: American Vision Publishers, Inc., 1993), p. 65.

⁵³ **Constitution of the State of Pennsylvania.** 1776, Frame of Government, Section 10. S.E. Morison, ed., *Sources and Documents Illustrating the American Revolution 1764-1788 and the Formation of the Federal Constitution* (NY: Oxford University Press, 1923), p. 166. Benjamin Franklin Morris, *The Christian Life and Character of the Civil Institutions of the United States* (Philadelphia, PA: L. Johnson & Co., 1863; George W. Childs, 1864), p. 233. David Barton, *The Myth of Separation* (Aledo, TX: WallBuilder Press, 1991), pp. 23, 143.

⁵⁴ **Supreme Court of Pennsylvania.** 1815. *The Commonwealth v. Jesse Sharpless and others,* 2 Serg.& R. 91-92, 97, 101-104 (1815). David Barton, *The Myth of Separation* (Aledo, TX: WallBuilder Press, 1991), pp. 64-67.

⁵⁵ **Supreme Court of Pennsylvania.** 1815. *The Commonwealth v. Jesse Sharpless and others,* 2 Serg.& R. 91-92, 97, 101-104 (1815). David Barton, *The Myth of Separation* (Aledo, TX: WallBuilder Press, 1991), pp. 64-67.

⁵⁶ **Supreme Court of Pennsylvania.** 1815. *The Commonwealth v. Jesse Sharpless and others,* 2 Serg.& R. 91-92, 97, 101-104 (1815). David Barton, *The Myth of Separation* (Aledo, TX: WallBuilder Press, 1991), pp. 64-67.

⁵⁷ **Supreme Court of Pennsylvania.** 1817. *The Commonwealth v. Wolf,* 3 Serg.& R. 48, 50 (1817). David Barton, *The Myth of Separation* (Aledo, TX: WallBuilder Press, 1991), pp. 75-76.

⁵⁸ **Supreme Court of Pennsylvania.** 1824. *Updegraph v. The Commonwealth,* 11 Serg. & Rawle, 393-394, 398-399, 400-401, 402-407 (1824); 5 Binn. R. 555; of New York, 8 Johns. R. 291; of Connecticut, 2 Swift's System. 321; of Massachusetts, Dane's Ab. vol. 7, c. 219, a. 2, 19. *Church of the Holy Trinity v. United States,* 143 US 457, 458, 465-471, 36 L ed 226, Justice David Josiah Brewer. Vide Cooper on the Law of Libel, 59 and 114, et seq.; and generally, 1 Russ. on Cr. 217; 1 Hawk, c. 5; 1 Vent. 293; 3 Keb. 607; 1 Barn. & Cress. 26. S. C. 8 Eng. Com. Law R. 14; Barnard. 162; Fitsgib. 66; Roscoe, Cr. Ev. 524; 2 Str. 834; 3 Barn. & Ald. 161; S. C. 5 Eng Com. Law R. 249 Jeff. Rep. Appx. See 1 Cro. Jac. 421 Vent. 293; 3 Keb. 607; Cooke on Def. 74; 2 How. S. C. 11-ep. 127, 197 to 201. David Barton, *The Myth of Separation* (Aledo, TX: WallBuilder Press, 1991), pp. 47-51, 51-55. "Our Christian Heritage," *Letter from Plymouth Rock* (Marlborough, NH: The Plymouth Rock Foundation), p. 6.

⁵⁹ **Samuel Pepys.** March 22, 1660, in his *Diary.* John Bartlett, *Bartlett's Familiar Quotations* (Boston: Little, Brown and Company, 1855, 1980), p. 309.

⁶⁰ **Samuel Pepys.** February 23, 1667, in his *Diary.* John Bartlett, *Bartlett's Familiar Quotations* (Boston: Little, Brown and Company, 1855, 1980), p. 310.

⁶¹ **Samuel Pepys.** May 31, 1669, in the last entry of his *Diary.* John Bartlett, *Bartlett's Familiar Quotations* (Boston: Little, Brown and Company, 1855, 1980), p. 310.

⁶² **Matthew Calbraith Perry.** W.E. Griffs, Biography. Stephen Abbott Northrop, D.D., *A Cloud of Witnesses* (Portland, OR: American Heritage Ministries, 1987; Mantle Ministries, 228 Still Ridge, Bulverde, Texas), p. 350.

⁶³ **Matthew Calbraith Perry.** 1853. Stephen Abbott Northrop, D.D., *A Cloud of Witnesses* (Portland, OR: American Heritage Ministries, 1987; Mantle Ministries, 228 Still Ridge, Bulverde, Texas), p. 350.

⁶⁴ **Oliver Hazard Perry.** Tucker, *Poltroons,* pp. 331-332. Peter Marshall and David Manuel, *The Glory of America* (Bloomington, MN: Garborg's Heart'N Home, Inc., 1991), 9.10.

⁶⁵ **Oliver Hazard Perry.** Tucker, *Poltroons,* pp. 331-332. Morris and Woodress, eds., *Voices from America's Past,* Vol. I, p. 219. Peter Marshall and David Manuel, *The Glory of America* (Bloomington, MN: Garborg's Heart'N Home, Inc., 1991), 9.10.

⁶⁶ **Sir William Phipps.** *Lives of the Great Fathers of New England*, pp. 240-241. Stephen Abbott Northrop, D.D., *A Cloud of Witnesses* (Portland, OR: American Heritage Ministries, 1987; Mantle Ministries, 228 Still Ridge, Bulverde, Texas), pp. 359-360.

⁶⁷ **Franklin Pierce.** March 4, 1853, in his Inaugural Address delivered from the steps of the Capitol building. James D. Richardson (U.S. Representative from Tennessee), ed., *A Compilation of the Messages and Papers of the Presidents 1789-1897*, 10 vols. (Washington, D.C.: U.S. Government Printing Office, published by Authority of Congress, 1897, 1899; Washington, D.C.: Bureau of National Literature and Art, *1789-1902*, 11 vols., 1907, 1910), Vol. 5, pp. 197-203. Benjamin Franklin Morris, *The Christian Life and Character of the Civil Institutions of the United States* (Philadelphia: George W. Childs, 1864), p. 609. *Inaugural Addresses of the Presidents of the United States - From George Washington 1789 to Richard Milhous Nixon 1969* (Washington, D.C.: United States Government Printing Office; 91st Congress, 1st Session, House Document 91-142, 1969), pp. 103-109. Davis Newton Lott, *The Inaugural Addresses of the American Presidents* (NY: Holt, Rinehart and Winston, 1961), pp. 104, 107, 108. Charles E. Rice, *The Supreme Court and Public Prayer* (New York: Fordham University Press, 1964), pp. 183-184. Arthur Schlesinger, ed., *The Chief Executive* (NY: Chelsea House Publishers, 1965), pp. 113-114, 117, 118. Benjamin Weiss, *God in American History: A Documentation of America's Religious Heritage* (Grand Rapids, MI: Zondervan, 1966), p. 86. Willard Cantelon, *Money Master of the World* (Plainfield, NJ: Logos International, 1976), p. 120. J. Michael Sharman, J.D., *Faith of the Fathers* (Culpepper, Virginia: Victory Publishing, 1995), pp. 53-54.

⁶⁸ **Franklin Pierce.** December 5, 1853, in his First Annual Message to Congress. James D. Richardson (U.S. Representative from Tennessee), ed., *A Compilation of the Messages and Papers of the Presidents 1789-1897*, 10 vols. (Washington, D.C.: U.S. Government Printing Office, published by Authority of Congress, 1897, 1899; Washington, D.C.: Bureau of National Literature and Art, *1789-1902*, 11 vols., 1907, 1910), Vol. 5, pp. 207, 213. Benjamin Franklin Morris, *The Christian Life and Character of the Civil Institutions of the United States* (Philadelphia: George W. Childs, 1864), pp. 609-610. Stephen Abbott Northrop, D.D., *A Cloud of Witnesses* (Portland, OR: American Heritage Ministries, 1987; Mantle Ministries, 228 Still Ridge, Bulverde, Texas), p. 361.

⁶⁹ **Charles Cotesworth Pinckney.** Sir William Blackstone, *Commentaries on the Laws of England* (Philadelphia: J.B. Lippincott and Co., 1879), Vol. II, p. 59. David Barton, *The Myth of Separation* (Aledo, TX: WallBuilder Press, 1991), p. 52.

⁷⁰ **Charles Cotesworth Pinckney.** Sir William Blackstone, *Commentaries on the Laws of England* (Philadelphia: J.B. Lippincott and Co., 1879), Vol. I, p. 39. David Barton, *The Myth of Separation* (Aledo, TX: WallBuilder Press, 1991), p. 197.

⁷¹ **Charles Cotesworth Pinckney.** Article XXXVIII of the Constitution of South Carolina 1778. John J. McGrath, ed., *Church and State in American Law: Cases and Materials* (Milwaukee: The Bruce Publishing Co., 1962), p. 375. David Barton, *The Myth of Separation* (Aledo, TX: WallBuilder Press, 1991), p. 29.

⁷² **Charles Cotesworth Pinckney.** Tim LaHaye, *Faith of Our Founding Fathers* (Brentwood, TN: Wolgemuth & Hyatt, Publishers, Inc., 1987), p. 176.

⁷³ **Charles Cotesworth Pinckney.** Marvin R. Zahniser, *Charles Cotesworth Pinckney: Founding Father* (Chapel Hill: University of North Carolina Press, 1967), pp. 272-274. M.E. Bradford, *Religion & The Framers: The Biographical Evidence* (Marlborough, NH: Plymouth Rock Foundation, 1991), p. 6.

⁷⁴ **Charles Cotesworth Pinckney.** M.E. Bradford, *Religion & The Framers: The Biographical Evidence* (Marlborough, NH: Plymouth Rock Foundation, 1991), p. 6.

⁷⁵ **Charles Cotesworth Pinckney.** Francis Williams, *The Pinckneys of South Carolina* (New York: Harcourt, Brace, Jovanovich, 1978), p. 21. Tim LaHaye, *Faith of Our Founding Fathers* (Brentwood, TN: Wolgemuth & Hyatt, Publishers, Inc., 1987), pp. 176-177.

⁷⁶ **Charles Cotesworth Pinckney.** Alex Garden, *Eulogy of Charles Cotesworth Pinckney* (Charleston: Printed by A.E. Miller, 1825), pp. 42-43. Tim LaHaye, *Faith of Our Founding Fathers* (Brentwood, TN: Wolgemuth & Hyatt, Publishers, Inc., 1987), pp. 178-179.

⁷⁷ **Charles Cotesworth Pinckney.** *The World Book Encyclopedia*, 18 vols. (Chicago, IL: Field Enterprises, Inc., 1957; W.F. Quarrie and Company, 8 vols., 1917; World Book, Inc., 22 vols., 1989), Vol. 13, p. 6341.

⁷⁸ **Charter of the Plymouth Council.** "Our Christian Heritage," *Letter from Plymouth Rock* (Marlborough, NH: The Plymouth Rock Foundation), p. 1.

⁷⁹ **Edgar Allen Poe.** 1827, in *Tamerlane*, l. 177. John Bartlett, *Bartlett's Familiar Quotations* (Boston: Little, Brown and Company, 1855, 1980), p. 525.

⁸⁰ **James Knox Polk.** March 4, 1845, Tuesday, in his Inaugural Address. James D. Richardson (U.S. Representative from Tennessee), ed., *A Compilation of the Messages and Papers of the Presidents 1789-1897*, 10 vols. (Washington, D.C.: U.S. Government Printing Office, published by Authority of Congress, 1897, 1899; Washington, D.C.: Bureau of National Literature and Art, *1789-1902*, 11 vols., 1907, 1910), Vol. 4, pp. 373-382. Benjamin Franklin Morris, *The Christian Life and Character of the Civil Institutions of the United States* (Philadelphia: George W. Childs, 1864), p. 607. *Inaugural Addresses of the Presidents*, House Document #540, 1952, p. 90. *Inaugural Addresses of the Presidents of the United States - From George Washington 1789 to Richard Milhous Nixon 1969* (Washington, D.C.: United States Government Printing Office; 91st Congress, 1st Session, House Document 91-142, 1969), pp. 89-98. Arthur Schlesinger Jr., ed., *The Chief Executive* (NY: Chelsea House Publishers, 1965), p. 106. Charles E. Rice, *The Supreme Court and Public Prayer* (New York: Fordham University Press, 1964), pp. 182-183. Benjamin Weiss, *God in American History: A Documentation of America's Religious Heritage* (Grand Rapids, MI: Zondervan, 1966), p. 80. Willard Cantelon, *Money Master of the World* (Plainfield, NJ: Logos International, 1976), p. 120. Peter Marshall and David Manuel, *The Glory of America* (Bloomington, MN: Garborg's Heart 'N Home, Inc., 1991), 4.6. J. Michael Sharman, J.D., *Faith of the Fathers* (Culpepper, Virginia: Victory Publishing, 1995), pp. 47-48.

⁸¹ **James Knox Polk.** March 4, 1845, Tuesday, in his Inaugural Address. James D. Richardson (U.S. Representative from Tennessee), ed., *A Compilation of the Messages and Papers of the Presidents 1789-1897*, 10 vols. (Washington, D.C.: U.S. Government Printing Office, published by Authority of Congress, 1897, 1899; Washington, D.C.: Bureau of National Literature and Art, *1789-1902*, 11 vols., 1907, 1910), Vol. 4, pp. 373-382. Benjamin Franklin Morris, *The Christian Life and Character of the Civil Institutions of the United States* (Philadelphia: George W. Childs, 1864), p. 607. *Inaugural Addresses of the Presidents*, House Document #540, 1952, p. 90. *Inaugural Addresses of the Presidents of the United States - From George Washington 1789 to Richard Milhous Nixon 1969* (Washington, D.C.: United States Government Printing Office; 91st Congress, 1st Session, House Document 91-142, 1969), pp. 89-98. Arthur Schlesinger Jr., ed., *The Chief Executive* (NY: Chelsea House Publishers, 1965), p. 106. Charles E. Rice, *The Supreme Court and Public Prayer* (New York: Fordham University Press, 1964), pp. 182-183. Benjamin Weiss, *God in American History: A Documentation of America's Religious Heritage* (Grand Rapids, MI: Zondervan, 1966), p. 80. Willard Cantelon, *Money Master of the World* (Plainfield, NJ: Logos International, 1976), p. 120. Peter Marshall and David Manuel, *The Glory of America* (Bloomington, MN: Garborg's Heart 'N Home, Inc., 1991), 4.6. J. Michael Sharman, J.D., *Faith of the Fathers* (Culpepper, Virginia: Victory

Publishing, 1995), pp. 47-48.

[82] **Pope John Paul I.** September 3, 1978, in the homily of the mass celebrating his installation. John Bartlett, *Bartlett's Familiar Quotations* (Boston: Little, Brown and Company, 1855, 1980), p. 881.

[83] **Pope John Paul II.** August 12, 1993, at the Stapleton International Airport, Denver, Colorado. Kathy Lewis and Judith Lynn Howard, "Pope Blasts Abortion - Crowd exhorted to 'defend life'" (Dallas, TX: Dallas Morning News, Friday, August 13, 1993), p. 1A.

[84] **Pope John Paul II.** August 12, 1993, at Regis University, Denver, Colorado. Kathy Lewis and Judith Lynn Howard, "Pope Blasts Abortion - Crowd exhorted to 'defend life'" (Dallas, TX: Dallas Morning News, Friday, August 13, 1993), pp. 1A, 24A.

[85] **Pope John Paul II.** August 12, 1993, in an address at Regis University, Denver, Colorado. John Wheeler, "Pope Defends Unborn Life" (Chesapeake, VA: *Christian American*, September 1993), p. 10.

[86] **Pope John Paul II.** August 12, 1993, in an address at Regis University, Denver, Colorado. John Wheeler, "Pope Defends Unborn Life" (Chesapeake, VA: *Christian American*, September 1993), p. 10.

[87] **Pope John Paul II.** August 12, 1993, in an evening address at Denver's Mile High Stadium. John Wheeler, "Pope Defends Unborn Life" (Chesapeake, VA: *Christian American*, September 1993), p. 10.

[88] **Pope John Paul II.** August 14, 1993, addressing nearly a quarter of a million people during a Saturday night prayer vigil at Cherry Creek State Park, Colorado. John Wheeler, "Pope Defends Unborn Life" (Chesapeake, VA: *Christian American*, September 1993), p. 10.

[89] **Pope John Paul II.** August 15, 1993, speaking at the "World Youth Day" Mass, celebrated at Cherry Creek State Park, Colorado. Judith Lynn Howard, "Pontiff Caps U.S. Visit with Denver Mass" (Dallas, TX: Dallas Morning News, August 16, 1993), pp. 1A, 4A.

[90] **Pope John Paul II.** August 15, 1993, in his farewell address at the Stapleton International Airport, Denver, Colorado. Judith Lynn Howard, "Pontiff Caps U.S. Visit with Denver Mass" (Dallas, TX: Dallas Morning News, August 16, 1993), p. 1A.

[91] **Pope Leo XIII.** May 15, 1891, in his encyclical on the condition of labor, *Rerum Novarum.* John Bartlett, *Bartlett's Familiar Quotations* (Boston: Little, Brown and Company, 1855, 1980), p. 537. [James D. Richardson (U.S. Representative from Tennessee), ed., *A Compilation of the Messages and Papers of the Presidents 1789-1897,* 10 vols. (Washington, D.C.: U.S. Government Printing Office, published by Authority of Congress, 1897, 1899; Washington, D.C.: Bureau of National Literature and Art, *1789-1902,* 11 vols., 1907, 1910), Vol. 5, p. 492, February 25, 1858, in a Proclamation issued by President James Buchanan:

"Whereas satisfactory evidence has lately been received from the Government of His Holiness the Pope, through an official communication addressed by Cardinal Antonelli, his secretary of state, to the minister resident of the United States at Rome, under date of the 7th day of December, 1857, that no discriminating duties of tonnage or impost are imposed or levied in the ports of the Pontifical States upon vessels wholly belonging to citizens of the United States, or upon the produce, manufactures, or merchandise imported in the same from the United States or from any foreign country:

"Now, therefore, I, James Buchanan, President of the United States of America, do hereby declare and proclaim that the foreign discriminating duties of tonnage and impost within the United States are and shall be suspended and discontinued so far as respects the vessels of the subjects of His Holiness the Pope and the produce, manufactures, or merchandise imported into the United States in the same from the Pontifical States or from any of other country, the said suspension to take effect from the 7th day of December, 1857, above mentioned, and to continue so long as the reciprocal exemption of vessels belonging to citizens of the United States and their cargoes, as aforesaid, shall be continued and no longer. Given under my hand, at the city of Washington, the 25th day of February, A.D. 1858, and of the Independence of the United States the eighty-second. James Buchanan. By the President Lewis Cass, Secretary of State."

On June 7, 1827, in a Proclamation, President John Quincy Adams stated: "Whereas satisfactory evidence was given to the President of the United States on the 30th day of May last by Count Lucchesi, consul-general of His Holiness the Pope, that all foreign and discriminating duties of tonnage and impost within the dominions of His Holiness, so far as respected the vessels of the United States and the merchandise of their produce or manufacture imported in the same, were suspended and discontinued:

"Now, therefore, I, John Quincy Adams, President of the United States, conformably to the fourth section of the act of Congress aforesaid, do hereby proclaim and declare that the foreign discriminating duties of tonnage and impost within the United States are and shall be suspended and discontinued as far as respects the vessels of the subjects of His Holiness the Pope and the merchandise of the produce or manufacture of his dominions imported into the United States in the same, the said suspension to take effect from the 30th of May aforesaid and to continue so long as the reciprocal exemption of vessels belonging to citizens of the United States and merchandise as aforesaid therein laden shall be continued, and no longer." (Vol. II, p. 377.)]

[92] **Pope Pius XI.** Herbert V. Prochnow, *5100 Quotations for Speakers and Writers* (Grand Rapids, MI: Baker Book House, 1992), p. 478.

[93] **Pope Pius XI.** Herbert V. Prochnow, *5100 Quotations for Speakers and Writers* (Grand Rapids, MI: Baker Book House, 1992), p. 449.

[94] **Pope Pius XII.** September 1, 1944, in a radio broadcast. John Bartlett, *Bartlett's Familiar Quotations* (Boston: Little, Brown and Company, 1855, 1980), p. 757.

[95] **David Dixon Porter.** Stephen Abbott Northrop, D.D., *A Cloud of Witnesses* (Portland, OR: American Heritage Ministries, 1987; Mantle Ministries, 228 Still Ridge, Bulverde, Texas), p. 364.

[96] **John Pory.** July 30, 1629, in the House of Burgesses, Jamestown, Virginia. *Collections of the New-York Historical Society,* 2nd series, New York, 1857, Vol. III, Pt. 1, pp. 335-358: "Proceedings of the First Assembly of Virginia, 1619." *The Annals of America,* 20 vols. (Chicago, IL: Encyclopedia Britannica, 1968), Vol. I, pp. 40, 43, 45.

[97] **William Prescott.** 1774, in writing to the citizens on the occasion of the British blockade. George Bancroft, *History of the United States of America,* 6 vols. (Boston: Charles C. Little and James Brown, Third Edition, 1838), Vol. VII, p. 99. David Barton, *The Myth of Separation* (Aledo, TX: WallBuilder Press, 1992), p. 96. Lucille Johnston, *Celebrations of a Nation* (Arlington, VA: The Year of Thanksgiving Foundation, 1987), p. 76. Peter Marshall & David Manuel, *The Glory of America* (Bloomington, MN: Garborg's Heart 'N Home, 1991), 7.27.

[98] **Princeton University.** 1746. David Barton, *The Myth of Separation* (Aledo, TX: WallBuilder Press, 1991), p. 92.

[99] **Princeton University.** 1746. Stephen K. McDowell and Mark A. Beliles, *America's Providential History* (Charlottesville, VA: Providence Press, 1988), p. 93. David Barton, *The Myth of Separation* (Aledo, TX: WallBuilder Press, 1991), p. 92.

[100] **Princeton University.** 1746. Stephen K. McDowell and Mark A. Beliles, *America's Providential History* (Charlottesville, VA:

Providence Press, 1988), p. 93. David Barton, *The Myth of Separation* (Aledo, TX: WallBuilder Press, 1991), p. 92.
[101] **Samuel de Pufendorf.** Samuel de Pufendorf, *The Law of Nature and Nations.* Verna M. Hall, *The Christian History of the Constitution of the United States of America: Christian Self-Government with Union* (San Francisco: Foundation for American Christian Education, 1962, 1979), p. 279. John Eidsmoe,*Christianity and the Constitution - The Faith of Our Founding Fathers* (Grand Rapids, MI: Baker Book House, A Mott Media Book, 1987, 6th printing 1993), p. 65.

Q

[1] **Queen Elizabeth I.** Her answer on being asked concerning Christ's presence in the Sacrament. S. Clarke,*Marrow of Ecclesiastical History* [ed. 1675], pt. II, *Life of Queen Elizabeth.* John Bartlett, *Bartlett's Familiar Quotations* (Boston: Little, Brown and Company, 1855, 1980), p. 164. Burton Stevenson, *The Home Book of Quotations - Classical & Modern* (New York: Dodd, Mead & Company, 1967).
[2] **Queen Elizabeth I.** From Chamberlin, *Sayings of Queen Elizabeth.* John Bartlett, *Bartlett's Familiar Quotations* (Boston: Little, Brown and Company, 1855, 1980), p. 163.
[3] **Queen Elizabeth I.** 1601, in *The Golden Speech.* John Bartlett,*Bartlett's Familiar Quotations* (Boston: Little, Brown and Company, 1855, 1980), p. 164.
[4] **Queen Elizabeth I.** Speaking to her ladies regarding her epitaph. John Bartlett, *Bartlett's Familiar Quotations* (Boston: Little, Brown and Company, 1855, 1980), p. 164.
[5] **Queen Isabella.** 1490-1492, in her commission to Christopher Columbus. *Letter from Plymouth Rock* (Marlborough, NH: The Plymouth Rock Foundation), p. 1. *Church of the Holy Trinity v. U.S.,* 143 U.S. 465-468 (1892). David Barton,*The Myth of Separation* (Aledo, TX: WallBuilder Press, 1991), p. 48.
[6] **Queen Isabella.** In a letter from Queen Isabella to Pope Alexander VI. Cecil Jane, trans. & ed., *The Voyages of Christopher Columbus* (London: Argonaut Press, 1930), p. 146. Peter Marshall and David Manuel, *The Glory of America* (Bloomington, MN: Garborg's Heart'N Home, Inc., 1991), 10.11.
[7] **Queen Isabella.** February 15, 1493, included in correspondence from Columbus on his return trip from having discovered America, to their Highnesses, King Ferdinand and Queen Isabella of Spain, from on board the ship *Caravel* anchored off the Canary Islands, in a letter addressed to Luis de Sant Angel, Treasurer of Aragon and Chancellor of the Exchequer. J.M. Dickey, compiler, *Christopher Columbus and his Monument,* p. 321. Stephen Abbott Northrop, D.D., *A Cloud of Witnesses* (Portland, Oregon: American Heritage Ministries, 1987; Mantle Ministries, 228 Still Ridge, Bulverde, Texas), p. 95. Also in a translation by Professors Hart and Channing, *American History Leaflets.* Charles W. Eliot, LL.D., ed., *American Historical Documents 1000-1904* (New York: P.F. Collier & Son Company, *The Harvard Classics,* 1910), Vol. 43, pp. 22-28.
[8] **Queen Ka'ahumanu.** 1832, in her last words to Rev. Hiram Bingham. "Hawaii's heroes of the faith," (Hawaii: University of the Nations Newsletter, Youth With a Mission, 1993), p. 8.
[9] **Queen Ka'ahumanu.** Testimony of High Chiefess Kapiolani. "Hawaii's heroes of the faith," (Hawaii: University of the Nations Newsletter, Youth With a Mission, 1993), p. 8.
[10] **Queen Victoria.** Stephen Abbott Northrop, D.D.,*A Cloud of Witnesses* (Portland, Oregon: American Heritage Ministries, 1987; Mantle Ministries, 228 Still Ridge, Bulverde, Texas), p. 236.
[11] **Queen Victoria.** Henry H. Halley, *Halley's Bible Handbook* (Grand Rapids, MI: Zondervan Publishing House, 1927, 1965), p. 18.
[12] **Queen Victoria.** 1849, in a letter the Queen instructed the Earl of Chichester to write the African Chieftain, Sagbua. (*London Christian World,* July 1897). Editor Stead, *Review of Reviews,* (March 1897). Stephen Abbott Northrop, D.D., *A Cloud of Witnesses* (Portland, OR: American Heritage Ministries, 1987; Mantle Ministries, 228 Still Ridge, Bulverde, Texas), p. 476.
[13] **Josiah Quincy.** 1774, speaking in response to the closing of the Boston harbor by the British. John Bartlett, *Bartlett's Familiar Quotations* (Boston: Little, Brown and Company, 1863, 1980), p. 393. Peter Marshall and David Manuel, *The Glory of America* (Bloomington, MN: Garborg's Heart'N Home, Inc., 1991), 2.10.

R

[1] **Sir Walter Raleigh.** 1584. United States Supreme Court,*Church of the Holy Trinity v. U.S.,* 143 U.S 465-468 (1892), Justice David Josiah Brewer. David Barton, *The Myth of Separation* (Aledo, TX: WallBuilder Press, 1991), p. 49.
[2] **Sir Walter Raleigh.** 1618, in a poem left in his Bible which was found in the Gatehouse at Westminster after his death. John Bartlett, *Bartlett's Familiar Quotations* (Boston: Little, Brown and Company, 1855, 1980), p. 173.
[3] **Samuel Jackson Randall.** *Washington Papers.* Stephen Abbott Northrop, D.D., *A Cloud of Witnesses* (Portland, OR: American Heritage Ministries, 1987; Mantle Ministries, 228 Still Ridge, Bulverde, Texas), pp. 373-374.
[4] **Edmund Jennings Randolph.** June 28, 1787. James Madison, *Notes of Debates in the Federal Convention of 1787* (1787; reprinted NY: W.W.Norton & Co., 1987), pp. 210-211. David Barton, *The Myth of Separation* (Aledo, TX: WallBuilder Press, 1991), p. 109. Irving Brant, James Madison,*Father of the Constitution, 1787-1800* (New York: Bobbs-Merrill, 1950), Vol. III, p. 84. Tim LaHaye, *Faith of Our Founding Fathers* (Brentwood, TN: Wolgemuth & Hyatt, Publishers, Inc., 1987), p. 126.
[5] **Edmund Jennings Randolph.** Tim LaHaye, *Faith of Our Founding Fathers* (Brentwood, TN: Wolgemuth & Hyatt, Publishers, Inc., 1987), p. 57.
[6] **Edmund Jennings Randolph.** Benjamin Franklin Morris, *The Christian Life and Character of the Civil Institutions of the United States* (Philadelphia: George W. Childs, 1864), pp. 253-254. David Barton,*The Myth of Separation* (Aledo, TX: WallBuilder Press, 1991), p. 110.
[7] **John Ray.** John Ray,*The Wisdom of God Manifested in the Works of Creation.* Henry M. Morris,*Men of Science - Men of God* (El Cajon, CA: Master Books, Creation Life Publishers, Inc., 1990), pp. 17-18.
[8] **John Ray.** John Ray,*The Wisdom of God Manifested in the Works of Creation.* Henry M. Morris,*Men of Science - Men of God* (El Cajon, CA: Master Books, Creation Life Publishers, Inc., 1990), pp. 17-18.
[9] **George Read.** J.C. Judson, *A Biography of the Signers of the Declaration of Independence* (Philadelphia: Dobson & Thomas, 1839), p. 85. Tim LaHaye, *Faith of Our Founding Fathers* (Brentwood, TN: Wolgemuth & Hyatt, Publishers, Inc., 1987), pp. 179-180.
[10] **George Read.** R.P. Bristol, *The American Bibliography of Charles Evans, Vol. 14* (Portsmouth [1785] Broadside: LOC Microfilm Library, November 24, 1785), #01291, Reel 224. Tim LaHaye,*Faith of Our Founding Fathers* (Brentwood, TN: Wolgemuth & Hyatt, Publishers, Inc., 1987), p. 180.

[11] **George Read.** Martha J. Lamb, ed., *The Framers of the Constitution, A Magazine of American History, Vol. XIII* (New York: Historical Publishing Co., 1885), p. 326. Tim LaHaye, *Faith of Our Founding Fathers* (Brentwood, TN: Wolgemuth & Hyatt, Publishers, Inc., 1987), p. 179.

[12] **George Read.** 1776, Constitution of the State of Delaware, Article XXII. *The Constitutions of the Several Independent States of America - Published by Order of Congress* (Boston: Norman & Bowen, 1785), pp. 99-100. *Church of the Holy Trinity v. U.S.* 143 US 457, 469-470 (1892). Frances Newton Thorpe, ed., *Federal and State Constitutions, Colonial Charters, and Other Organic Laws of the States, Territories, and Colonies now or heretofore forming the United States*, 7 vols. (Washington: Government Printing Office, 1905; 1909; St. Clair Shores, MI: Scholarly Press, 1968), Vol. I, p. 142. M.E. Bradford, *A Worthy Company* (NH: Plymouth Rock Foundation, 1982), p. x. Tim LaHaye, *Faith of Our Founding Fathers* (Brentwood, TN: Wolgemuth & Hyatt, Publishers, Inc., 1987), pp. 180-181. Gary DeMar, "Censoring America's Christian History" (Atlanta, GA: *The Biblical Worldview*, An American Vision Publication - American Vision, Inc., July 1990), p. 7. "Our Christian Heritage," *Letter from Plymouth Rock* (Marlborough, NH: The Plymouth Rock Foundation), p. 3. Gary DeMar, *America's Christian History: The Untold Story* (Atlanta, GA: American Vision Publishers, Inc., 1993), pp. 67-68. David Barton, *The Myth of Separation* (Aledo, TX: WallBuilder Press, 1991), pp. 23, 33. David Barton, *Keys to Good Government* (Aledo, TX: WallBuilder Press, 1994), p. 3.

[13] **Ronald Wilson Reagan.** 1980. *Our Christian Heritage, Letter from Plymouth Rock* (Marlborough, NH: The Plymouth Rock Foundation), p. 7.

[14] **Ronald Wilson Reagan.** October 4, 1982, signed into law *Public Law 97-280*, as authorized and requested by a Joint Resolution of the Senate and House in the 97th Congress of the United States of America, held at the City of Washington. "Our Christian Heritage," *Letter from Plymouth Rock* (Marlborough, NH: The Plymouth Rock Foundation), p. 7. Public Law 97-280, 96 Stat. 1211. Gary DeMar, *America's Christian History: The Untold Story* (Atlanta, GA: American Vision Publishers, Inc., 1993), p. 53. John Eidsmoe, *Christianity and The Constitution - The Faith of Our Founding Fathers* (Grand Rapids, MI: Baker Book House, 1987), p. 355.

[15] **Ronald Wilson Reagan.** 1983, in *The Human Life Review*. Ronald Reagan, "Abortion and the Conscience of a Nation," (Nashville, TN: Thomas Nelson, Inc., 1984), p. 38.

[16] **Ronald Wilson Reagan.** January 25, 1984. *Proclaim Liberty* (Dallas, TX: Word of Faith), p. 3.

[17] **Ronald Wilson Reagan.** August 23, 1984 at an ecumenical prayer breakfast at the Reunion Arena in Dallas, on the occasion of the enactment of the Equal Access Bill of 1984. *The Speech That Shook The Nation* (Forerunner, December 1984), p. 12. David Barton, *The Myth of Separation* (Aledo, TX: WallBuilder Press, 1991), pp. 17, 249. Jeremiah O'Leary, "Reagan Declares that Faith Has Key Role in Political Life," *The Washington Times* (August 24, 1984). Walter Shapiro, "Politics and the Pulpit," *Newsweek* (September 17, 1984), p. 24. Nadine Strossen, "A Constitutional Analysis of the Equal Access Act's Standards Governing School Student's Religious Meetings," *Harvard Journal on Legislation*, Winter, 1987. p. 118. David R. Shepherd, *Ronald Reagan: In God We Trust* (Wheaton, IL: Tyndale House Publishers, Inc., 1984), p. 146.

[18] **Ronald Wilson Reagan.** January 25, 1988 in the Second Session of the One Hundredth Congress. *Public Law 100-307 - May 5, 1988*. Mrs. James Dobson (Shirley), chairman, *The National Day of Prayer Information Packet* (Colorado Springs, CO: National Day of Prayer Task Force, May 6, 1993).

[19] **Ronald Wilson Reagan.** Proclamation of the National Day of Prayer, 1988. Mrs. James Dobson (Shirley), chairman, *The National Day of Prayer Information Packet* (Colorado Springs, CO: National Day of Prayer Task Force, May 6, 1993).

[20] **Ronald Wilson Reagan.** McCollister, *Help*, p. 195. Peter Marshall and David Manuel, *The Glory of America* (Bloomington, MN: Garborg's Heart'N Home, Inc., 1991), 2.6.

[21] **Ronald Wilson Reagan.** Robert Flood, *The Rebirth of America* (Philadelphia: Arthur S. DeMoss Foundation, 1986), p. 97.

[22] **Ronald Wilson Reagan.** Robert Flood, *The Rebirth of America* (Philadelphia: Arthur S. DeMoss Foundation, 1986), p. 114.

[23] **William Hubbs Rehnquist.** 1985, *Wallace v. Jaffree*, 472 U.S. 38, 99. "Our Christian Heritage," *Letter from Plymouth Rock* (Marlborough, NH: The Plymouth Rock Foundation), p. 8.

[24] **Joseph Ernest Renan.** 1863, in *La Vie de Jesus*, introduction. John Bartlett, *Bartlett's Familiar Quotations* (Boston: Little, Brown and Company, 1855, 1980), p. 593.

[25] **Joseph Ernest Renan.** 1866, in *Les Apotres*. John Bartlett, *Bartlett's Familiar Quotations* (Boston: Little, Brown and Company, 1855, 1980), p. 593.

[26] **Charter of Rhode Island and Providence Plantations.** July 1663. Rhode Island Colonial Records, Vol, II, pp. 3-20, 1644. Ebenezer Hazard, *Historical Collection: Consisting of State Papers and other Authentic Documents - Intended as Materials for an History of the United States of America* (Philadelphia: T. Dobson, 1792), Vol. II, p. 612. Robert Flood, *The Rebirth of America* (Philadelphia: Arthur S. DeMoss Foundation, 1986), p. 31.

[27] **Charter of Rhode Island and Providence Plantations.** July 8, 1663, granted by King Charles II, in the 14th year of his reign, to Roger Williams, confirming the colonial patent of 1644; and continuing in effect until 1842. Rhode Island Colonial Records, Vol, II, pp. 3-20, 1644. Ebenezer Hazard, *Historical Collection: Consisting of State Papers and other Authentic Documents - Intended as Materials for an History of the United States of America* (Philadelphia: T. Dobson, 1792), Vol. II, p. 612. *The Constitutions of the Several Independent States of America* (Evans Collection, #17390). William McDonald, ed., *Documentary Source Book of American History, 1606-1889* (NY: The MacMillan Company, 1909), pp. 67-68. David Barton, *The Myth of Separation* (Aledo, TX: WallBuilder Press, 1991), p. 87. Richard Perry, ed., *Sources of Our Liberties: Documentary Origins of Individual Liberties in the United States Constitution and Bill of Rights* (Chicago: American Bar Foundation, 1978; New York: 1952), p. 169. Pat Robertson, *America's Dates With Destiny* (Nashville, TN: Thomas Nelson Publishers, 1986), p. 32. Stephen McDowell and Mark Beliles, "The Providential Perspective" (Charlottesville, VA: The Providence Foundation, P.O. Box 6759, Charlottesville, Va. 22906, January 1994), Vol. 9, No. 1, p. 6. Robert Flood, *The Rebirth of America* (Philadelphia: Arthur S. DeMoss Foundation, 1986), p. 31. Benjamin Franklin Morris *The Christian Life and Character of the Civil Institutions of the United States* (Philadelphia, PA: L. Johnson & Co., 1863; George W. Childs, 1864), p. 236.

[28] **Seal of the State of Rhode Island.** 1797, motto inscribed on seal. "A New Display of the United States" (Washington, D.C.: Library of Congress). Gary DeMar, *God and Government* (Atlanta, GA: American Vision Press, 1984), Vol. 2, p. 118. Mark A. Beliles and Stephen K. McDowell, *America's Providential History* (Charlottesville, Virginia: Providence Foundation, 1989, 1994), p. 87. Gary DeMar, *America's Christian History: The Untold Story* (Atlanta, GA: American Vision Publishers, Inc., 1993), p. 64.

[29] **Constitution of the State of Rhode Island.** 1842, Preamble; Article I, Section 3. Charles E. Rice, *The Supreme Court and Public Prayer* (New York: Fordham University Press, 1964), p. 174; "Hearings, Prayers in Public Schools and Other Matters," Committee on the Judiciary, U.S. Senate (87th Cong., 2nd Sess.), 1962, pp. 268 et seq. Benjamin Weiss, *God in American History:*

A Documentation of America's Religious Heritage (Grand Rapids, MI: Zondervan, 1966), p. 155. Tim LaHaye,*Faith of Our Founding Fathers* (Brentwood, TN: Wolgemuth & Hyatt, Publishers, Inc., 1987), p. 92. Gary DeMar,*America's Christian History: The Untold Story* (Atlanta, GA: American Vision Publishers, Inc., 1993), pp. 64-64. Charles E. Rice,*The Supreme Court and Public Prayer* (New York: Fordham University Press, 1964), p. 174; "Hearings, Prayers in Public Schools and Other Matters," Committee on the Judiciary, U.S. Senate (87th Cong., 2nd Sess.), 1962, pp. 268 et seq.

³⁰ **Richard Rich.** 1610, in his narrative poem *Newes from Virginia: The Flock Triumphant* recounting his voyage to Virginia with Captain Christopher Newport. John Bartlett, *Bartlett's Familiar Quotations* (Boston: Little, Brown and Company, 1855, 1980), p. 261.

³¹ **Edward Vernon "Eddie" Rickenbacker.** Jessie Clayton Adams, *More Than Money* (San Antonio, TX: The Naylor Company, 1953), p. 26. Courtesy of the personal library of Mike Gross.

³² **(Marion Gordon) Pat Robertson.** 1986, in his book entitled,*America's Dates with Destiny* (Nashville, TN: 1986), pp. 89-92. Tim LaHaye, *Faith of Our Founding Fathers* (Brentwood, TN: Wolgemuth & Hyatt, Publishers, Inc., 1987), p. 186-188.

³³ **John Robinson.** Verna H. Hall, *Christian History of the Constitution* (San Francisco: Foundation for American Christian Education, 1975), p. 200. Marshall Foster and Mary-Elaine Swanson, *The American Covenant - The Untold Story* (Roseburg, OR: Foundation for Christian Self-Government, 1981; Thousand Oaks, CA: The Mayflower Institute, 1983, 1992), p. 85.

³⁴ **John Robinson.** Robert Ashton, ed., *The Works of John Robinson, Pastor of the Pilgrim Fathers* (London: John Snow, 1851), Vol. 2, pp. 140-141. Marshall Foster and Mary-Elaine Swanson,*The American Covenant - The Untold Story* (Roseburg, OR: Foundation for Christian Self-Government, 1981; Thousand Oaks, CA: The Mayflower Institute, 1983, 1992), pp. 83-84.

³⁵ **John Robinson.** July 22, 1620, in a sermon to the Pilgrims as they departed Delft Haven for England aboard the "Speedwell." John Robinson, *Answer to a Letter inferring Publique Communion in the Parish Assemblies upon private with godly persons there.* Leyden, Holland, 1615. Library of Congress Rare Book Collection, Washington, D.C. Catherine Millard,*A Children's Companion Guide to America's History* (Camp Hill, PA: Horizon House Publishers, 1993), p. 17.

³⁶ **Carlos Peña Romulo.** General of the Philippines. *Proclaim Liberty* (Dallas, TX: Word of Faith), p. 13.

³⁷ **Franklin Delano Roosevelt.** March 4, 1933, in his First Inaugural Address. *Inaugural Addresses of the Presidents of the United States - From George Washington 1789 to Richard Milhous Nixon 1969* (Washington, D.C.: United States Government Printing Office; 91st Congress, 1st Session, House Document 91-142, 1969), pp. 235-239. Richard D. Heffner, *A Documentary History of the United States* (New York: The New American Library of World Literature, Inc., 1961), p. 270. Davis Newton Lott, *The Inaugural Addresses of the American Presidents* (NY: Holt, Rinehart and Winston, 1961), p. 234. Charles E. Rice,*The Supreme Court and Public Prayer* (New York: Fordham University Press, 1964), p. 191. Benjamin Weiss,*God in American History: A Documentation of America's Religious Heritage* (Grand Rapids, MI: Zondervan, 1966), pp. 137-138. John Bartlett, *Bartlett's Familiar Quotations* (Boston: Little, Brown and Company, 1855, 1980), p. 779. Lillian W. Kay, ed., *The Ground on Which We Stand - Basic Documents of American History* (NY: Franklin Watts., Inc, 1969), #257. Willard Cantelon, *Money Master of the World* (Plainfield, NJ: Logos International, 1976), p. 121. William Safire, ed., *Lend Me Your Ears - Great Speeches in History* (NY: W.W. Norton & Company 1992), p. 783. J. Michael Sharman, J.D., *Faith of the Fathers* (Culpepper, Virginia: Victory Publishing, 1995), p. 97.

³⁸ **Franklin Delano Roosevelt.** December 6, 1933, in his address to the Federal Council of Churches of Christ. John Bartlett, *Bartlett's Familiar Quotations* (Boston: Little, Brown and Company, 1855, 1980), p. 779.

³⁹ **Franklin Delano Roosevelt.** 1935, in a radio broadcast. Gabriel Sivan, *The Bible and Civilization* (New York: Quadrangle/The New York Times Book Co., 1973), p. 178. Gary DeMar, *America's Christian History: The Untold Story* (Atlanta, GA: American Vision Publishers, Inc., 1993), p. 60.

⁴⁰ **Franklin Delano Roosevelt.** January 20, 1937, in his Second Inaugural Address. *Inaugural Addresses of the Presidents of the United States - From George Washington 1789 to Richard Milhous Nixon 1969* (Washington, D.C.: United States Government Printing Office; 91st Congress, 1st Session, House Document 91-142, 1969), pp. 240-243. Charles E. Rice, *The Supreme Court and Public Prayer* (New York: Fordham University Press, 1964), p. 191. Benjamin Weiss, *God in American History: A Documentation of America's Religious Heritage* (Grand Rapids, MI: Zondervan, 1966), pp. 137-138. Davis Newton Lott, *The Inaugural Addresses of the American Presidents* (NY: Holt, Rinehart and Winston, 1961), p. 240. Willard Cantelon,*Money Master of the World* (Plainfield, NJ: Logos International, 1976), p. 121. J. Michael Sharman, J.D., *Faith of the Fathers* (Culpepper, Virginia: Victory Publishing, 1995), p. 98.

⁴¹ **Franklin Delano Roosevelt.** January 6, 1941, in his *Four Freedoms Speech* to Congress. Samuel I. Rosenman, ed., *The Public Papers of Franklin D. Roosevelt* (NY:1941) Vol. VI, p. 411. Paul M. Angle, ed., *By These Words* (NY: Rand McNally & Company, 1954), pp. 381-382. Richard D. Heffner, *A Documentary History of the United States* (New York: The New American Library of World Literature, Inc., 1961), pp. 282-289. *The Annals of America*, 20 vols. (Chicago, IL: Encyclopedia Britannica, 1968), Vol. 16, p. 456. Peter Marshall & David Manuel, *The Glory of America* (Bloomington, MN: Garborg's Heart 'N Home, 1991), 1.6.

⁴² **Franklin Delano Roosevelt.** January 20, 1941, Third Inaugural Address.*Inaugural Addresses of the Presidents of the United States - From George Washington 1789 to Richard Milhous Nixon 1969* (Washington, D.C.: United States Government Printing Office; 91st Congress, 1st Session, House Document 91-142, 1969), pp. 244-247. Charles E. Rice, *The Supreme Court and Public Prayer* (New York: Fordham University Press, 1964), p. 191. Benjamin Weiss, *God in American History: A Documentation of America's Religious Heritage* (Grand Rapids, MI: Zondervan, 1966), pp. 137-138. Willard Cantelon, *Money Master of the World* (Plainfield, NJ: Logos International, 1976), p. 121. J. Michael Sharman, J.D., *Faith of the Fathers* (Culpepper, Virginia: Victory Publishing, 1995), p. 99.

⁴³ **Franklin Delano Roosevelt.** January 25, 1941, in the prologue of a special World War II edition of the Gideons New Testament and Psalms, (KJV-1611), printed by National Bible Press, Philadelphia. The Gideons International, 202 South State Street, Chicago, Illinois.

⁴⁴ **Franklin Delano Roosevelt.** January 20, 1945, Saturday, in his Fourth Inaugural Address, delivered on the Portico of the White House. *Inaugural Addresses of the Presidents of the United States - From George Washington 1789 to Richard Milhous Nixon 1969* (Washington, D.C.: United States Government Printing Office; 91st Congress, 1st Session, House Document 91-142, 1969), pp. 248-249. Davis Newton Lott, *The Inaugural Addresses of the American Presidents* (NY: Holt, Rinehart and Winston, 1961), p. 247-248. Charles E. Rice, *The Supreme Court and Public Prayer* (New York: Fordham University Press, 1964), p. 191. Benjamin Weiss, *God in American History: A Documentation of America's Religious Heritage* (Grand Rapids, MI: Zondervan, 1966), pp. 137-138. Willard Cantelon,*Money Master of the World* (Plainfield, NJ: Logos International, 1976), p. 121.*Proclaim Liberty* (Dallas, TX: Word of Faith), p. 2. J. Michael Sharman, J.D., *Faith of the Fathers* (Culpepper, Virginia: Victory Publishing, 1995), p. 99.

⁴⁵ **Franklin Delano Roosevelt.** In a Mid-Atlantic Summit with Prime Minister Churchill. Larry Witham, "'Christian Nation' Now Fighting Words" (*The Washington Times*, November 23, 1992), p. Al. Gary DeMar, *The Biblical Worldview* (Atlanta, GA: An

American Vision Publication - American Vision, Inc., 1993), Vol. 9, No. 2, p. 12.

⁴⁶ Theodore Roosevelt. September 14, 1901, in a Proclamation of a National Day of Mourning and Prayer, issued at the occasion of President William McKinley's assassination. *A Compilation of the Messages and Papers of the Presidents* 20 vols. (New York: Bureau of National Literature, Inc., prepared under the direction of the Joint Committee on Printing, of the House and Senate, pursuant to an Act of the Fifty-Second Congress of the United States, 1893, 1923), Vol. XIII, p. 6639.

⁴⁷ Theodore Roosevelt. Tryon Edwards, D.D., *The New Dictionary of Thoughts - A Cyclopedia of Quotations* (Garden City, NY: Hanover House, 1852; revised and enlarged by C.H. Catrevas, Ralph Emerson Browns and Jonathan Edwards [descendent, along with Tryon, of Jonathan Edwards (1703-1758), president of Princeton], 1891; The Standard Book Company, 1955, 1963), p. 92.

⁴⁸ Theodore Roosevelt. Alfred Armand Montapert, *Distilled Wisdom* (Englewood Cliffs, NJ: Prentice Hall Inc., 1965), p. 36. Bob Cutshall, *More Light for the Day* (Minneapolis, MN: Northwestern Products, Inc., 1991), 2.17.

⁴⁹ Theodore Roosevelt. March 4, 1905, in his Second Inaugural Address. *A Compilation of the Messages and Papers of the Presidents* 20 vols. (New York: Bureau of National Literature, Inc., prepared under the direction of the Joint Committee on Printing, of the House and Senate, pursuant to an Act of the Fifty-Second Congress of the United States, 1893, 1923), Vol. XIV, pp. 6930-6932. *Inaugural Addresses of the Presidents of the United States - From George Washington 1789 to Richard Milhous Nixon 1969* (Washington, D.C.: United States Government Printing Office; 91st Congress, 1st Session, House Document 91-142, 1969), pp. 183-185. Davis Newton Lott, *The Inaugural Addresses of the American Presidents* (NY: Holt, Rinehart and Winston, 1961), p. 185. Charles E. Rice, *The Supreme Court and Public Prayer* (New York: Fordham University Press, 1964), p. 188. *Proclaim Liberty* (Dallas, TX: Word of Faith), p. 2. J. Michael Sharman, J.D., *Faith of the Fathers* (Culpepper, Virginia: Victory Publishing, 1995), p. 82.

⁵⁰ Theodore Roosevelt. 1909. Ferdinand C. Iglehart, *Theodore Roosevelt - The Man As I Knew Him* (A.L. Burt, 1919). "Our Christian Heritage," *Letter from Plymouth Rock* (Marlborough, NH: The Plymouth Rock Foundation), p. 6. Noah Brooks, *Men of Achievement: Statesmen* (NY: Charles Scribner's Sons, 1904), p. 317. George Grant, *Third Time Around* (Brentwood, TN: Wolgemuth & Hyatt, Inc., 1991) p. 118.

⁵¹ Theodore Roosevelt. 1909. Noah Brooks, *Men of Achievement - Statesmen* (NY: Charles Scribner's Sons, 1904), p. 317. George Grant, *Third Time Around* (Brentwood, TN: Wolgemuth & Hyatt, Inc., 1991), p. 118. George Grant, *The Quick and the Dead* (Wheaton, IL: Crossway, 1981), p. 134. John Eidsmoe, *Columbus & Cortez, Conquerors for Christ* (Green Forest, AR: New Leaf Press, 1992), pp. 296-297.

⁵² Theodore Roosevelt. 1910, in his message "The New Nationalism." Richard D. Heffner, *A Documentary History of the United States* (New York: The New American Library of World Literature, Inc., 1961), p. 225.

⁵³ Theodore Roosevelt. Charles E. Jones, *The Books You Read* (Harrisburg, PA: Executive Books, 1985), p. 117.

⁵⁴ Theodore Roosevelt. John McCollister, *So Help me God* (Bloomington, MN: Landmark Books, 1982), p. 79. Peter Marshall & David Manuel, *The Glory of America* (Bloomington, MN: Garborg's Heart 'N Home, 1991), 10.27.

⁵⁵ Theodore Roosevelt. June 17, 1912, in a speech at the Progressive Party Convention in Chicago. John Bartlett, *Bartlett's Familiar Quotations* (Boston: Little, Brown and Company, 1855, 1980), p. 687. David, L. Johnson, *Theodore Roosevelt: American Monarch* (Philadelphia: American History Sources, 1981), p. 103. George Grant, *Third Time Around* (Brentwood, TN: Wolgemuth & Hyatt, Inc., 1991) p. 182-183.

⁵⁶ Theodore Roosevelt. November 15, 1913, in a letter to Sir Edward Grey. John Bartlett, *Bartlett's Familiar Quotations* (Boston: Little, Brown and Company, 1855, 1980), p. 688.

⁵⁷ William Starke Rosecrans. His motto as a Union general in the Civil War. Jeffery Warren Scott, "Fighters of Faith" (Carol Stream, IL: Christian History, Issue 33-1992), Vol. XI, No. 1, p. 37.

⁵⁸ Jean Jacques Rousseau. *Emilius and Sophia* (English Edition, 1767), Vol. III, Book IV, pp. 136-139. Stephen Abbott Northrop, D.D., *A Cloud of Witnesses* (Portland, Oregon: American Heritage Ministries, 1987; Mantle Ministries, 228 Still Ridge, Bulverde, Texas), pp. 385-386. Frank Ballard, *The Miracles of Unbelief* (Edinburgh: T & T Lark), p. 251. Willard Cantelon, *New Money or None?* (Plainfield, NJ: Logos International, 1979), p. 247. Tryon Edwards, D.D., *The New Dictionary of Thoughts - A Cyclopedia of Quotations* (Garden City, NY: Hanover House, 1852; revised and enlarged by C.H. Catrevas, Ralph Emerson Browns and Jonathan Edwards [descendent, along with Tryon, of Jonathan Edwards (1703-1758), president of Princeton], 1891; The Standard Book Company, 1955, 1963), p. 47.

⁵⁹ Jean Jacques Rousseau. 1762, in his work *Emile; ou, De l'Education,* I. John Bartlett, *Bartlett's Familiar Quotations* (Boston: Little, Brown and Company, 1855, 1980), p. 358.

⁶⁰ Jean Jacques Rousseau. 1762, in his work *Emile; ou, De l'Education,* I. John Bartlett, *Bartlett's Familiar Quotations* (Boston: Little, Brown and Company, 1855, 1980), p. 358.

⁶¹ Jean Jacques Rousseau. 1762, in his work *Emile; ou, De l'Education,* V. John Bartlett, *Bartlett's Familiar Quotations* (Boston: Little, Brown and Company, 1855, 1980), p. 359.

⁶² Benjamin Rush. 1798. 1786, in "Thoughts upon the Mode of Education Proper in a Republic," published in *Early American Imprints.* Benjamin Rush, *Essays, Literary, Moral and Philosophical,* Philadelphia, 1798: "Of the Mode of Education Proper in a Republic." *The Annals of America,* 20 vols. (Chicago, IL: Encyclopedia Britannica, 1968), Vol. 4, pp. 28-29. Stephen McDowell and Mark Beliles, "The Providential Perspective" (Charlottesville, VA: The Providence Foundation, P.O. Box 6759, Charlottesville, Va. 22906, January 1994), Vol. 9, No. 1, p. 3. David Barton, *The WallBuilder Report* (Aledo, TX: WallBuilder, Summer 1993), p. 3.

⁶³ Benjamin Rush. *Essays, Literary, Moral, and Philosophical* (1798, 2nd edition, 1806). Stephen Abbott Northrop, D.D., *A Cloud of Witnesses* (Portland, OR: American Heritage Ministries, 1987; Mantle Ministries, 228 Still Ridge, Bulverde, Texas), p. 388.

⁶⁴ Benjamin Rush. David Ramsay, *An Eulogium upon Benjamin Rush, M.D.* (Philadelphia: Bradford and Inskeep, 1813), p. 103. David Barton, *Keys to Good Government* (Aledo, TX: WallBuilder Press, 1994), p. 24.

⁶⁵ Benjamin Rush. *American Medical Biography,* p. 45. Stephen Abbott Northrop, D.D., *A Cloud of Witnesses* (Portland, OR: American Heritage Ministries, 1987; Mantle Ministries, 228 Still Ridge, Bulverde, Texas), p. 388.

⁶⁶ John Ruskin. Henry H. Halley, *Halley's Bible Handbook* (Grand Rapids, MI: Zondervan Publishing House, 1927, 1965), p. 18.

⁶⁷ John Ruskin. Tryon Edwards, D.D., *The New Dictionary of Thoughts - A Cyclopedia of Quotations* (Garden City, NY: Hanover House, 1852; revised and enlarged by C.H. Catrevas, Ralph Emerson Browns and Jonathan Edwards [descendent, along with Tryon, of Jonathan Edwards (1703-1758), president of Princeton], 1891; The Standard Book Company, 1955, 1963), p. 47.

⁶⁸ John Ruskin. *Ruskin's Praeterita,* Vol. II. Stephen Abbott Northrop, D.D., *A Cloud of Witnesses* (Portland, OR: American Heritage Ministries, 1987; Mantle Ministries, 228 Still Ridge, Bulverde, Texas), p. 389.

⁶⁹ John Ruskin. *The Crown of Olives,* Preface. Stephen Abbott Northrop, D.D., *A Cloud of Witnesses* (Portland, OR: American

Heritage Ministries, 1987; Mantle Ministries, 228 Still Ridge, Bulverde, Texas), pp. 389-390.

[70] **John Ruskin.** *The Pall Mall Gazette.* Stephen Abbott Northrop, D.D., *A Cloud of Witnesses* (Portland, OR: American Heritage Ministries, 1987; Mantle Ministries, 228 Still Ridge, Bulverde, Texas), pp. 389-390.

[71] **Rutgers University.** Theodore Frelinghuysen. "Gallery - Thumbnail sketches of important leaders in the Pietist Movement," *Christian History* (Worcester, PA: Christian History Magazine, 1986), Vol. 5, No. 2, p. 15.

[72] **Rutgers University.** 1766. Stephen K. McDowell and Mark A. Beliles, *America's Providential History* (Charlottesville, VA: Providence Press, 1988), p. 93. David Barton, *The Myth of Separation* (Aledo, TX: WallBuilder Press, 1991), p. 92.

[73] **Samuel Rutherford.** Samuel Rutherford, *Lex, Rex, or The Law and the Prince*, 1644 (reprinted Harrisonburg, Virginia: Sprinkle Publications, 1982), pp. 1, 6-7. John Eidsmoe, *Christianity and the Constitution - The Faith of Our Founding Fathers* (Grand Rapids, MI: Baker Book House, A Mott Media Book, 1987, 6th printing 1993), p. 24.

[74] **Samuel Rutherford.** John W. Whitehead, *The Second American Revolution* (Elgin, IL: David C. Cook, 1982), pp. 30-32. Tim LaHaye, *Faith of Our Founding Fathers* (Brentwood, TN: Wolgemuth & Hyatt, Publishers, Inc., 1987), pp. 84-88. Gary DeMar, *God and Government-A Biblical and Historical Study* (Atlanta, GA: American Vision Press, 1982), p. 99.

S

[1] **Carl Sandburg.** Carroll E. Simcox, comp., *4400 Quotations for Christian Communicators* (Grand Rapids, MI: Baker Book House, 1991), p. 23.

[2] **George Santayana.** Lewis C. Henry, *Best Quotations For All Occasions* (Greenwich, Conn.: Fawcett Publications, Inc., 1961), p. 171.

[3] **George Santayana.** 1926, in *Dialogues in Limbo*, 1926. John Bartlett, *Bartlett's Familiar Quotations* (Boston: Little, Brown and Company, 1855, 1980), p. 704.

[4] **George Santayana.** 1931, *The Genteel Tradition at Bay.* John Bartlett, *Bartlett's Familiar Quotations* (Boston: Little, Brown and Company, 1855, 1980), p. 704.

[5] **Francis August Schaeffer.** Francis Schaeffer, *A Christian Manifesto*, pp. 101-104. Gary DeMar, *God and Government-A Biblical and Historical Study* (Atlanta, GA: American Vision Press, 1982), p. 99.

[6] **Francis August Schaeffer.** Francis Schaeffer, *A Christian Manifesto*, pp. 89-91. Gary DeMar, *God and Government-A Biblical and Historical Study* (Atlanta, GA: American Vision Press, 1982), p. 99.

[7] **Francis August Schaeffer.** Francis Schaeffer, *A Christian Manifesto* in *The Complete Works of Francis A. Schaeffer: A Christian Worldview*, 5 vols. (Wheaton, IL: Crossway Books, 1982), V:430. Gary DeMar, "The Lost Legacy of Francis A. Schaeffer" (Atlanta, GA: *The Biblical Worldview*, An American Vision Publication - American Vision, Inc., September 1992), Vol. 8, No. 9, p. 12.

[8] **Francis August Schaeffer.** Francis Schaeffer, *Escape from Reason* (1968) in *The Complete Works of Francis A. Schaeffer: A Christian Worldview*, 5 vols. (Wheaton, IL: Crossway Books, 1982), Vol. I, pp. 262-263. Gary DeMar, "The Lost Legacy of Francis A. Schaeffer" (Atlanta, GA: *The Biblical Worldview*, An American Vision Publication - American Vision, Inc., September 1992), Vol. 8, No. 9, p. 11.

[9] **H. Norman Schwarzkopf.** 1991, in an interview with David Frost. Peter Marshall and David Manuel, *The Glory of America* (Bloomington, MN: Garborg's Heart'N Home, Inc., 1991), 3.27.

[10] **H. Norman Schwarzkopf.** 1991, in an interview with David Frost. Peter Marshall and David Manuel, *The Glory of America* (Bloomington, MN: Garborg's Heart'N Home, Inc., 1991), 5.29.

[11] **Robert Falcon Scott.** March 29, 1912, Thursday, in his last entry in his journal before dying. John Bartlett, *Bartlett's Familiar Quotations* (Boston: Little, Brown and Company, 1855, 1980), p. 726.

[12] **Sir Walter Scott.** In chapter XII of *The Monastery*, 1920.

[13] **Sir Walter Scott.** *Allibone's Prose Quotations*, p. 74. Stephen Abbott Northrop, D.D., *A Cloud of Witnesses* (Portland, OR: American Heritage Ministries, 1987; Mantle Ministries, 228 Still Ridge, Bulverde, Texas), pp. 399-400.

[14] **Sir Walter Scott.** J.G. Lockhart, *Memoirs of the Life of Scott*, p. 729. Stephen Abbott Northrop, D.D., *A Cloud of Witnesses* (Portland, OR: American Heritage Ministries, 1987; Mantle Ministries, 228 Still Ridge, Bulverde, Texas), p. 399.

[15] **Edmund Hamilton Sears.** 1850, in *The Angel's Song*, st. I. John Bartlett, *Bartlett's Familiar Quotations* (Boston: Little, Brown and Company, 1855, 1980), p. 537.

[16] **William Henry Seward.** Tryon Edwards, D.D., *The New Dictionary of Thoughts - A Cyclopedia of Quotations* (Garden City, NY: Hanover House, 1852; revised and enlarged by C.H. Catrevas, Ralph Emerson Browns and Jonathan Edwards [descendent, along with Tryon, of Jonathan Edwards (1703-1758), president of Princeton], 1891; The Standard Book Company, 1955, 1963), p. 49. Henry H. Halley, *Halley's Bible Handbook* (Grand Rapids, MI: Zondervan Publishing House 1927, 1965), p. 18. George E. Baker. *Life of William Henry Seward.* Stephen Abbott Northrop, D.D., *A Cloud of Witnesses* (Portland, OR: American Heritage Ministries, 1987; Mantle Ministries, 228 Still Ridge, Bulverde, Texas), p. 404.

[17] **William Henry Seward.** In his oration entitled *The Destiny of America*. George E. Baker, *Life of William Henry Seward.* Stephen Abbott Northrop, D.D., *A Cloud of Witnesses* (Portland, OR: American Heritage Ministries, 1987; Mantle Ministries, 228 Still Ridge, Bulverde, Texas), p. 404.

[18] **William Henry Seward.** 1836, address as Vice-President of the American Bible Society. George E. Baker, *Life of William Henry Seward.* Stephen Abbott Northrop, D.D., *A Cloud of Witnesses* (Portland, OR: American Heritage Ministries, 1987; Mantle Ministries, 228 Still Ridge, Bulverde, Texas), p. 404. D.P. Diffine, Ph.D., *One Nation Under God - How Close a Separation?* (Searcy, Arkansas: Harding University, Belden Center for Private Enterprise Education, 6th edition, 1992), p. 11.

[19] **Horatio Seymour.** July 4, 1876, in an oration at Rome, NY., entitled *The Future of the Human Race.* Stephen Abbott Northrop, D.D., *A Cloud of Witnesses* (Portland, OR: American Heritage Ministries, 1987; Mantle Ministries, 228 Still Ridge, Bulverde, Texas), pp. 402-403.

[20] **William Shakespeare.** 1591, in *King Henry the Sixth*, Part II, act II, scene i, line 34. John Bartlett, *Bartlett's Familiar Quotations* (Boston: Little, Brown and Company, 1855, 1980), p. 185.

[21] **William Shakespeare.** 1591, in *King Henry the Sixth*, Part II, act II, scene i, line 66. John Bartlett, *Bartlett's Familiar Quotations* (Boston: Little, Brown and Company, 1855, 1980), p. 185.

[22] **William Shakespeare.** 1591, in *King Henry the Sixth*, Part II, act II, scene iii, line 55. John Bartlett, *Bartlett's Familiar Quotations* (Boston: Little, Brown and Company, 1855, 1980), p. 185.

[23] **William Shakespeare.** 1591, in *King Henry the Sixth*, Part III, act V, scene v, line 7. John Bartlett, *Bartlett's Familiar Quotations*

(Boston: Little, Brown and Company, 1855, 1980), p. 186.

[24] **William Shakespeare.** 1592-1593, in *King Richard the Third*, act I, scene iv, line 2. John Bartlett, *Bartlett's Familiar Quotations* (Boston: Little, Brown and Company, 1855, 1980), p. 187.

[25] **William Shakespeare.** *Richard the Third*, act I, scene 4. Stephen Abbott Northrop, D.D., *A Cloud of Witnesses* (Portland, Oregon: American Heritage Ministries, 1987; Mantle Ministries, 228 Still Ridge, Bulverde, Texas), p. 405.

[26] **William Shakespeare.** 1595-1596, in *King Richard the Second*, act IV, scene i, line 97. John Bartlett, *Bartlett's Familiar Quotations* (Boston: Little, Brown and Company, 1855, 1980), p. 193. Stephen Abbott Northrop, D.D., *A Cloud of Witnesses* (Portland, Oregon: American Heritage Ministries, 1987; Mantle Ministries, 228 Still Ridge, Bulverde, Texas), p. 406.

[27] **William Shakespeare.** 1595-1596, in *King Richard the Second*, act IV, scene i, line 170. John Bartlett, *Bartlett's Familiar Quotations* (Boston: Little, Brown and Company, 1855, 1980), p. 193.

[28] **William Shakespeare.** 1595-1596, in *King Richard the Second*, act IV, scene i, line 239. John Bartlett, *Bartlett's Familiar Quotations* (Boston: Little, Brown and Company, 1855, 1980), p. 193.

[29] **William Shakespeare.** 1596-1597, in *The Merchant of Venice*, act I, scene ii, line 59. John Bartlett, *Bartlett's Familiar Quotations* (Boston: Little, Brown and Company, 1855, 1980), p. 198.

[30] **William Shakespeare.** 1596-1597, in *The Merchant of Venice*, act I, scene iii, line 99. John Bartlett, *Bartlett's Familiar Quotations* (Boston: Little, Brown and Company, 1855, 1980), p. 198. Stephen Abbott Northrop, D.D., *A Cloud of Witnesses* (Portland, Oregon: American Heritage Ministries, 1987; Mantle Ministries, 228 Still Ridge, Bulverde, Texas), p. 405.

[31] **William Shakespeare.** 1596-1597, in *The Merchant of Venice*, in act IV, scene i, line 184. John Bartlett, *Bartlett's Familiar Quotations* (Boston: Little, Brown and Company, 1855, 1980), p. 200.

[32] **William Shakespeare.** 1598, in *I Henry IV*, Act i, sc.1, l. 18. Burton Stevenson, *The Home Book of Quotations* (New York: Dodd, Mead & Company, 1967), p. 264. Stephen Abbott Northrop, D.D., *A Cloud of Witnesses* (Portland, Oregon: American Heritage Ministries, 1987; Mantle Ministries, 228 Still Ridge, Bulverde, Texas), p. 406.

[33] **William Shakespeare.** 1598-1600, in *King Henry the Fifth*, act III, scene vi, line 181. John Bartlett, *Bartlett's Familiar Quotations* (Boston: Little, Brown and Company, 1855, 1980), p. 207.

[34] **William Shakespeare.** 1598-1600, in *King Henry the Fifth*, in act IV, scene i, line 309. John Bartlett, *Bartlett's Familiar Quotations* (Boston: Little, Brown and Company, 1855, 1980), p. 208.

[35] **William Shakespeare.** *Hamlet*, act I, scene I. Stephen Abbott Northrop, D.D., *A Cloud of Witnesses* (Portland, Oregon: American Heritage Ministries, 1987; Mantle Ministries, 228 Still Ridge, Bulverde, Texas), p. 405.

[36] **William Shakespeare.** 1600-1691 in *Hamlet*, act III, scene i, line 150. John Bartlett, *Bartlett's Familiar Quotations* (Boston: Little, Brown and Company, 1855, 1980), p. 221.

[37] **William Shakespeare.** 1600-1691 in *Hamlet*, act III, scene iv, line 149. John Bartlett, *Bartlett's Familiar Quotations* (Boston: Little, Brown and Company, 1855, 1980), p. 223.

[38] **William Shakespeare.** 1600-1691 in *Hamlet*, act V, scene i, line 84. John Bartlett, *Bartlett's Familiar Quotations* (Boston: Little, Brown and Company, 1855, 1980), p. 224.

[39] **William Shakespeare.** 1604-1605, in *Othello*, act I, scene i, line 108. John Bartlett, *Bartlett's Familiar Quotations* (Boston: Little, Brown and Company, 1855, 1980), p. 229.

[40] **William Shakespeare.** 1604-1605, in *Othello*, act II, scene iii, line 106. John Bartlett, *Bartlett's Familiar Quotations* (Boston: Little, Brown and Company, 1855, 1980), p. 230.

[41] **William Shakespeare.** 1604-1605, in *Othello*, act II, scene iii, line 293. John Bartlett, *Bartlett's Familiar Quotations* (Boston: Little, Brown and Company, 1855, 1980), p. 230.

[42] **William Shakespeare.** 1613, in *King Henry the Eighth*, act III, scene ii, line 456. John Bartlett, *Bartlett's Familiar Quotations* (Boston: Little, Brown and Company, 1855, 1980), p. 249.

[43] **William Shakespeare.** 1613, in *King Henry the Eighth*, act V, scene v, line 51. John Bartlett, *Bartlett's Familiar Quotations* (Boston: Little, Brown and Company, 1855, 1980), p. 249.

[44] **William Shakespeare.** *Bless Your Heart (series II)* (Eden Prairie, MN: Heartland Sampler, Inc., 1990), 7.20.

[45] **William Shakespeare.** 1616, first clause in his last will. Stephen Abbott Northrop, D.D., *A Cloud of Witnesses* (Portland, OR: American Heritage Ministries, 1987; Mantle Ministries, 228 Still Ridge, Bulverde, Texas), p. 405.

[46] **William Shakespeare.** 1616, lines carved on his tombstone, Holy Trinity Church, Stratford-on-Avon, England. *The World Book Encyclopedia*, 18 vols. (Chicago, IL: Field Enterprises, Inc., 1957; W.F. Quarrie and Company, 8 vols., 1917; World Book, Inc., 22 vols., 1989), Vol. 15, p. 7372.

[47] **John Sherman.** Stephen Abbott Northrop, D.D., *A Cloud of Witnesses* (Portland, OR: American Heritage Ministries, 1987; Mantle Ministries, 228 Still Ridge, Bulverde, Texas), p. 409.

[48] **Roger Sherman.** June 28, 1787. James Madison, *Notes of Debates in the Federal Convention of 1787* (1787; reprinted NY: W.W. Norton & Co., 1987), p. 210. David Barton, *The Myth of Separation* (Aledo, TX: WallBuilder Press, 1991), p. 109.

[49] **Roger Sherman.** Tim LaHaye, *Faith of Our Founding Fathers* (Brentwood, TN: Wolgemuth & Hyatt, Publishers, Inc., 1987), p. 58. Christopher Collier, *Roger Sherman's Connecticut* (Middleton, CT: Wesleyan University Press, 1971), p. 185. David Barton, *The Myth of Separation* (Aledo, TX: WallBuilder Press, 1991), p. 121.

[50] **Roger Sherman.** Lewis Henry Boutell, *The Life of Roger Sherman* (Chicago: A.C. McClure & Co., 1896), p. 213. Tim LaHaye, *Faith of Our Founding Fathers* (Brentwood, TN: Wolgemuth & Hyatt, Publishers, Inc., 1987), p. 137. Edwin Gaustad, *Faith of Our Fathers* (San Francisco: Harper & Row, 1987), p. 158. David Barton, *The Myth of Separation* (Aledo, TX: WallBuilder Press, 1991), p. 174.

[51] **Roger Sherman.** February 1776, in a directive for the embassy to Canada. Christopher Collier, *Roger Sherman's Connecticut* (Middletown, CT: Wesleyan University Press, 1979), p. 129. David Barton, *The Myth of Separation* (Aledo, TX: WallBuilder Press, 1991), pp. 35, 122. John Eidsmoe, *Christianity and The Constitution - The Faith of Our Founding Fathers* (Baker Book House, 1987), p. 325.

[52] **Roger Sherman.** *Annals of the Congress of the United States - First Congress - The Debates and Proceedings in the Congress of the United States with an Appendix Containing Important State Papers and Public Documents and All the Laws of a Public Nature - with a Copious Index, 1789-1791* 42 vols. (Washington, D.C.: Gales & Seaton, 1834-56), Vol. I, p. 914. David Barton, *The Myth of Separation* (Aledo, TX: WallBuilder Press, 1991), p. 114.

[53] **Roger Sherman.** Christopher Collier, *Roger Sherman's Connecticut* (Middleton, CT: Wesleyan University Press, 1971), p. 185. David Barton, *The Myth of Separation* (Aledo, TX: WallBuilder Press, 1991), p. 121.

[54] **Roger Sherman.** John Eidsmoe, *Constitution,* p. 321. Peter Marshall and David Manuel, *The Glory of America* (Bloomington, MN: Garborg's Heart'N Home, Inc., 1991), 8.23.

[55] **Roger Sherman.** Lewis Henry Boutell, *The Life of Roger Sherman* (Chicago: A.C. McClure & Co., 1896), p. 269. Tim LaHaye, *Faith of Our Founding Fathers* (Brentwood, TN: Wolgemuth & Hyatt, Publishers, Inc., 1987), pp. 135-136.

[56] **Roger Sherman.** Lewis Henry Boutell, *The Life of Roger Sherman* (Chicago: A.C. McClure & Co., 1896), pp. 272-273. Tim LaHaye, *Faith of Our Founding Fathers* (Brentwood, TN: Wolgemuth & Hyatt, Publishers, Inc., 1987), pp. 136-137.

[57] **Roger Sherman.** Charles Francis Adams (son of John Quincy Adams and grandson of John Adams), *Familiar Letters of John Adams with his wife Abigail Adams - during the Revolution* (NY: Hurd and Houghton, 1876), p. 251. Tim LaHaye, *Faith of Our Founding Fathers* (Brentwood, TN: Wolgemuth & Hyatt, Publishers, Inc., 1987), p. 134.

[58] **Roger Sherman.** Epitaph engraved on Roger Sherman's tomb, New Haven, CT. Tim LaHaye, *Faith of Our Founding Fathers* (Brentwood, TN: Wolgemuth & Hyatt, Publishers, Inc., 1987), p. 135.

[59] **Jonathan Shipley.** H. Niles, *Principles and Acts of the Revolution in America* (Baltimore: 1822), p. 164. Peter Marshall and David Manuel, *The Glory of America* (Bloomington, MN: Garborg's Heart'N Home, Inc., 1991), 1.64.

[60] **Edward Rowland Sill.** *The Fool's Prayer.* John Bartlett, *Bartlett's Familiar Quotations* (Boston: Little, Brown and Company, 1855, 1980), p. 646.

[61] **Benjamin Silliman.** Yale College faculty member. Henry M. Morris, *Men of Science - Men of God* (El Cajon, CA: Master Books, Creation Life Publishers, Inc., 1990), p. 39.

[62] **Benjamin Silliman.** G.P. Fisher, Vol. II of his life. Stephen Abbott Northrop, D.D., *A Cloud of Witnesses* (Portland, OR: American Heritage Ministries, 1987; Mantle Ministries, 228 Still Ridge, Bulverde, Texas), p. 411.

[63] **Benjamin Silliman.** June 13, 1855, in concluding a course of college lectures. G.P. Fisher, Vol. II of his life. Stephen Abbott Northrop, D.D., *A Cloud of Witnesses* (Portland, OR: American Heritage Ministries, 1987; Mantle Ministries, 228 Still Ridge, Bulverde, Texas), pp. 411-412.

[64] **Sir James Young Simpson.** Henry M. Morris, *Men of Science - Men of God* (El Cajon, CA: Master Books, A Division of Creation Life Publishers, Inc., 1988), p. 52.

[65] **Sir James Young Simpson.** Henry M. Morris, *Men of Science - Men of God* (El Cajon, CA: Master Books, A Division of Creation Life Publishers, Inc., 1988), p. 52.

[66] **Sir James Young Simpson.** James Macaulay, *Short Biographies for the People,* Vol. 7. Stephen Abbott Northrop, D.D., *A Cloud of Witnesses* (Portland, OR: American Heritage Ministries, 1987; Mantle Ministries, 228 Still Ridge, Bulverde, Texas), pp. 413-414.

[67] **Jedediah Strong Smith.** Smith, *Nation,* Vol. IV, p. 350. Peter Marshall and David Manuel, *The Glory of America* (Bloomington, MN: Garborg's Heart'N Home, Inc., 1991), 12.19.

[68] **Samuel Francis Smith.** 1823, writing patriotic hymn, *My Country 'Tis Of Thee. Patriotic Anthology,* p. 480. Peter Marshall and David Manuel, *The Glory of America* (Bloomington, MN: Garborg's Heart'N Home, Inc., 1991), 2.2. Hugo Frey, ed., *America Sings* (New York: Robbins Music Corporation, 1935), p. 104.

[69] **Samuel Francis Smith.** 1832, writing patriotic hymn, *My Country 'Tis Of Thee. Patriotic Anthology,* p. 480. Peter Marshall and David Manuel, *The Glory of America* (Bloomington, MN: Garborg's Heart'N Home, Inc., 1991), 2.2. Hugo Frey, ed., *America Sings* (New York: Robbins Music Corporation, 1935), p. 104. D.P. Diffine, Ph.D., *One Nation Under God - How Close a Separation?* (Searcy, Arkansas: Harding University, Belden Center for Private Enterprise Education, 6th edition, 1992), p. 11.

[70] **Sydney Smith.** 1855, *Lady Holland's Memoir,* Vol. I, chap. 6. John Bartlett, *Bartlett's Familiar Quotations* (Boston: Little, Brown and Company, 1855, 1980), p. 432.

[71] **Alexander Solzhenitsyn.** May 1983, in receiving the Templeton Prize for Progress in Religion. Marshall Foster and Mary-Elaine Swanson, *The American Covenant - The Untold Story* (Roseburg, OR: Foundation for Christian Self-Government, 1981; Thousand Oaks, CA: The Mayflower Institute, 1983, 1992), p. 164.

[72] **Alexander Solzhenitsyn.** Lloyd Billingsley, *The Generation that Knew Not Josef: A Critique of Marxism and the Religious Left* (Portland, OR: Multnomah Press, 1985), p. 24. Gary DeMar, *America's Christian History: The Untold Story* (Atlanta, GA: American Vision Publishers, Inc., 1993), p. 28.

[73] **Colony of (South) Carolina.** 1650, first permanent settlement; April 9, 1585, the Roanoke Settlement was begun, later to be called The Lost Colony; August 13, 1587, members of the colony converted an Indian named Manteo; August 18, 1587, the first child, Virginia Dare was born in America. *The World Book Encyclopedia,* 18 vols. (Chicago, IL: Field Enterprises, Inc., 1957; W.F. Quarrie and Company, 8 vols., 1917; World Book, Inc., 22 vols., 1989), Vol. 12, p. 5732; Vol. 10, p. 4596.

[74] **Colony of (South) Carolina.** 1653. *The World Book Encyclopedia,* 18 vols. (Chicago, IL: Field Enterprises, Inc., 1957; W.F. Quarrie and Company, 8 vols., 1917; World Book, Inc., 22 vols., 1989), Vol. 15, p. 7587; Vol. 12, p. 5732.

[75] **Colony of (South) Carolina.** August 13, 1587. Roanoke Settlement-The Lost Colony. *The World Book Encyclopedia,* 18 vols. (Chicago, IL: Field Enterprises, Inc., 1957; W.F. Quarrie and Company, 8 vols., 1917; World Book, Inc., 22 vols., 1989), Vol. 12, p. 5732.

[76] **Charter of Carolina.** 1663. *North Carolina History,* Hugh Talmage Lefler, ed., (Chapel Hill: Univ. of North Carolina Press, 1934, 1956), p. 16. David Barton, *The Myth of Separation* (Aledo, TX: WallBuilder Press, 1991), p. 86. Frances Newton Thorpe, ed., *Federal and State Constitutions, Colonial Charters, and Other Organic Laws of the States, Territories, and Colonies now or heretofore forming the United States,* 7 vols. (Washington: Government Printing Office, 1905; 1909; St. Clair Shores, MI: Scholarly Press, 1968), Vol. V, p. 2743. Pat Robertson, *America's Dates With Destiny* (Nashville, TN: Thomas Nelson Publishers, 1986), p. 32.

[77] **Fundamental Constitutions of the Carolinas.** 1663, John Locke. *The World Book Encyclopedia,* 18 vols. (Chicago, IL: Field Enterprises, Inc., 1957; W.F. Quarrie and Company, 8 vols., 1917; World Book, Inc., 22 vols., 1989), Vol. 12, p. 5736, Vol. 15, p. 7591.

[78] **Fundamental Constitutions of the Carolinas.** 1663. Supreme Court Justice David Josiah Brewer, who served 1890-1910, in his work, *The United States - Christian Nation* (Philadelphia: The John C. Winston Company, 1905, Supreme Court Collection). Catherine Millard, *The Rewriting of America's History* (Camp Hill, PA: Horizon House Publishers, 1991), p. 389.

[79] **Constitution of the State of South Carolina.** 1778, in the Preamble. Frances Newton Thorpe, ed., *Federal and State Constitutions, Colonial Charters, and Other Organic Laws of the States, Territories, and Colonies now or heretofore forming the United States,* 7 vols. (Washington: Government Printing Office, 1905; 1909; St. Clair Shores, MI: Scholarly Press, 1968). Charles E. Rice, *The Supreme Court and Public Prayer* (New York: Fordham University Press, 1964), pp. 174-175; "Hearings, Prayers in Public Schools and Other Matters," Committee on the Judiciary, U.S. Senate (87th Cong., 2nd Sess.), 1962, pp. 268 et seq. Benjamin Weiss, *God in*

Notes

American History: A Documentation of America's Religious Heritage (Grand Rapids, MI: Zondervan, 1966), p. 155. Gary DeMar, "Censoring America's Christian History" (Atlanta, GA: *The Biblical Worldview*, An American Vision Publication - American Vision, Inc., July 1990), p. 7. Gary DeMar,*America's Christian History: The Untold Story* (Atlanta, GA: American Vision Publishers, Inc., 1993), p. 66.

[80] **Constitution of the State of South Carolina.** 1778, Article III; Article XII; Article XXXVIII. Frances Newton Thorpe, ed.,*Federal and State Constitutions, Colonial Charters, and Other Organic Laws of the States, Territories, and Colonies now or heretofore forming the United States*, 7 vols. (Washington: Government Printing Office, 1905; 1909; St. Clair Shores, MI: Scholarly Press, 1968). Edwin S. Gaustad,*Neither King nor Prelate - Religion and the New Nation*, (Grand Rapids, MI: William B. Eerdmans Publishing Company, 1993), p. 170-171. Benjamin Franklin Morris, *The Christian Life and Character of the Civil Institutions of the United States* (Philadelphia, PA: L. Johnson & Co., 1863; George W. Childs, 1864), pp. 230-231. John J. McGrath, ed., *Church and State in American Law: Cases and Materials* (Milwaukee: The Bruce Publishing Co., 1962), p. 375. Anson Phelps Stokes and Leo Pfeffer, *Church and State in the United States* (NY: Harper and Row, Publishers, 1950, revised one-volume edition, 1964), p. 79. David Barton, *The Myth of Separation* (Aledo, TX: WallBuilder Press, 1991), p. 29.

[81] **Supreme Court of South Carolina.** 1846, *City of Charleston v. S.A. Benjamin*, 2 Strob. 508 (1846). David Barton, *The Myth of Separation* (Aledo, TX: WallBuilder Press, 1991), p. 73.

[82] **Supreme Court of South Carolina.** 1846, *City of Charleston v. S.A. Benjamin*, 2 Strob. 518-520 (1846). David Barton, *The Myth of Separation* (Aledo, TX: WallBuilder Press, 1991), p. 73.

[83] **Supreme Court of South Carolina.** 1846, *City of Charleston v. S.A. Benjamin*, 2 Strob. 521-524 (1846). David Barton, *The Myth of Separation* (Aledo, TX: WallBuilder Press, 1991), p. 73.

[84] **State of South Carolina.** November 20, 1994, the State of South Carolina issued an Executive Proclamation declaring November 20 - November 26, 1994, as "Christian Heritage Week," signed by Governor Carroll A. Campbell, Jr. A similar Proclamation was signed November 21, 1993. Courtesy of Bruce Barilla, Christian Heritage Week Ministry (P.O. Box 58, W.V. 24712; 304-384-7707, 304-384-9044 fax).

[85] **Motto of the State of South Dakota.** 1889. *The World Book Encyclopedia*, 18 vols. (Chicago, IL: Field Enterprises, Inc., 1957; W.F. Quarrie and Company, 8 vols., 1917; World Book, Inc., 22 vols., 1989), Vol. 15, p. 7601. John Wilson Taylor, M.A., Ph.D., et al., *The Lincoln Library of Essential Information* (Buffalo, New York: The Frontier Press Company, 1935), p. 2068. Charles Wallis, ed., *Our American Heritage* (NY: Harper & Row, Publishers, Inc., 1970), p. 30.

[86] **Robert Louis Stevenson.** In *Songs of Travel - If This Were Faith*. John Bartlett,*Bartlett's Familiar Quotations* (Boston: Little, Brown and Company, 1855, 1980), p. 669.

[87] **Robert Louis Stevenson.** 1889, in his work *The Master of Ballantrae - Mr. Mackellar's Journey*. John Bartlett, *Bartlett's Familiar Quotations* (Boston: Little, Brown and Company, 1855, 1980), p. 669.

[88] **Robert Louis Stevenson.** Among his manuscripts, written a few months before his death. Stephen Abbott Northrop, D.D., *A Cloud of Witnesses* (Portland, OR: American Heritage Ministries, 1987; Mantle Ministries, 228 Still Ridge, Bulverde, Texas), p. 430.

[89] **Robert Louis Stevenson.** His prayer engraved on the bronze memorial to him in St. Giles Cathedral, Edinburgh, Scotland. John Bartlett, *Bartlett's Familiar Quotations* (Boston: Little, Brown and Company, 1855, 1980), p. 669.

[90] **Ezra Stiles.** Verna M. Hall,*Christian History of the Constitution* (San Francisco: Foundation for American Christian Education, 1975), p. 382. Marshall Foster and Mary-Elaine Swanson,*The American Covenant - The Untold Story* (Roseburg, OR: Foundation for Christian Self-Government, 1981; Thousand Oaks, CA: The Mayflower Institute, 1983, 1992), p. 134.

[91] **Ezra Stiles.** May 8, 1783, in an election sermon, entitled "The United States elevated to Glory and Honor," delivered before the Governor and the General Assembly of the State of Connecticut. John Wingate Thornton, *The Pulpit of the American Revolution* (Gould & Lincoln, 1860). Stephen McDowell and Mark Beliles, "The Providential Perspective" (Charlottesville, VA: The Providence Foundation, P.O. Box 6759, Charlottesville, Va. 22906, January 1994), Vol. 9, No. 1, p. 7. John Wingate Thornton, *The Pulpit of the American Revolution* (Boston: D. Lothrop & Co., 1876). Perry Miller,*The Life of the Mind in America* (London: Victor Gallanz, 1966).

[92] **Ezra Stiles.** 1783, in an address before the Assembly of Connecticut. Robert Flood,*The Rebirth of America* (Philadelphia: Arthur S. DeMoss Foundation, 1986), p. 45.

[93] **Charles Milton Stine.** Henry M. Morris, *Men of Science - Men of God* (El Cajon, CA: Master Books, Creation Life Publishers, Inc., 1990), p. 83.

[94] **Richard Stockton.** In his *Last Will and Testament*. Edward J. Giddings, *American Christian Rulers*, p. 463. Stephen Abbott Northrop, D.D., *A Cloud of Witnesses* (Portland, OR: American Heritage Ministries, 1987; Mantle Ministries, 228 Still Ridge, Bulverde, Texas), pp. 431-432. D.P. Diffine, Ph.D., *One Nation Under God - How Close a Separation?* (Searcy, Arkansas: Harding University, Belden Center for Private Enterprise Education, 6th edition, 1992), p. 7.

[95] **Joseph Story.** 1829, in a speech made when he become a professor at Harvard. Perry Miller, *The Life of the Mind in America* (London: Victor Gallanz, 1966), p. 33. John Whitehead, *The Second American Revolution* (Wheaton, Illinois: Crossway Books, 1982), p. 197.

[96] **Joseph Story.** 1833. Joseph Story, *Commentaries on the Constitution, 1833* (reprinted NY: Da Capo Press, 1970), Vol. III, p. 726, Sec. 1868, and p. 727, Sec. 1869. Joseph Story,*A Familiar Exposition of the Constitution of the United States* (MA: Marsh, Capen Lyon, and Webb, 1840; reprinted Washington, D.C.; Regnery Gateway, 1986), p. 314, Sec. 441, p. 316, Sec. 444. David Barton,*The Myth of Separation* (Aledo, TX: WallBuilder Press, 1991), pp. 32, 79-80. "Our Christian Heritage," *Letter from Plymouth Rock* (Marlborough, NH: The Plymouth Rock Foundation), p. 5.

[97] **Joseph Story.** 1833. Joseph Story, *Commentaries on the Constitution, 1833* (reprinted NY: Da Capo Press, 1970), Vol. III, p. 726, Sec. 1868, and p. 727, Sec. 1869. Joseph Story,*A Familiar Exposition of the Constitution of the United States* (MA: Marsh, Capen Lyon, and Webb, 1840; reprinted Washington, D.C.; Regnery Gateway, 1986), p. 314, Sec. 441, p. 316, Sec. 444. David Barton,*The Myth of Separation* (Aledo, TX: WallBuilder Press, 1991), pp. 79-80. "Our Christian Heritage,"*Letter from Plymouth Rock* (Marlborough, NH: The Plymouth Rock Foundation), p. 5.

[98] **Joseph Story.** 1844. *Vidal v. Girard's Executors*, 43 U.S. 126, 132 (1844), pp. 198, 205-206. David Barton, *The Myth of Separation* (Aledo, TX: WallBuilder Press, 1991), pp. 62-63. William W. Story,*Life and Letters of Judge Story*, Vol. II, Chap. XII. Stephen Abbott Northrop, D.D., *A Cloud of Witnesses* (Portland, OR: American Heritage Ministries, 1987; Mantle Ministries, 228 Still Ridge, Bulverde, Texas), p. 434.

[99] **Joseph Story.** Judge Brevard Hand, in*Jaffree v. Board of School Commissioners of Mobile County*, 544 F. Supp. 1104 (S. D. Ala. 1983).

Russell Kirk, ed., *The Assault on Religion: Commentaries on the Decline of Religious Liberty* (Lanham, NY: University Press of America, 1986), p. 84. Gary DeMar, *America's Christian History: The Untold Story* (Atlanta, GA: American Vision Publishers, Inc., 1993), p. 113.

[100] **Joseph Story.** Tryon Edwards, D.D., *The New Dictionary of Thoughts - A Cyclopedia of Quotations* (Garden City, NY: Hanover House, 1852; revised and enlarged by C.H. Catrevas, Ralph Emerson Browns and Jonathan Edwards [descendent, along with Tryon, of Jonathan Edwards (1703-1758), president of Princeton], 1891; The Standard Book Company, 1955, 1963), p. 337.

[101] **Harriet Beecher Stowe.** Abraham Lincoln's greeting to her. *The World Book Encyclopedia*, 18 vols. (Chicago, IL: Field Enterprises, Inc., 1957; W.F. Quarrie and Company, 8 vols., 1917; World Book, Inc., 22 vols., 1989), Vol. 15, p. 7750.

[102] **Harriet Beecher Stowe.** 1852. Harriet Beecher Stowe, *Uncle Tom's Cabin* (1852), p. 458. Peter Marshall and David Manuel, *The Glory of America* (Bloomington, MN: Garborg's Heart 'N Home, Inc., 1991), 3.20.

[103] **William Strong.** Stephen Abbott Northrop, D.D., *A Cloud of Witnesses* (Portland, OR: American Heritage Ministries, 1987; Mantle Ministries, 228 Still Ridge, Bulverde, Texas), p. 433.

[104] **John Strutt, Lord Rayleigh.** Henry M. Morris, *Men of Science - Men of God* (El Cajon, CA: Master Books, Creation Life Publishers, Inc., 1990), pp. 78-79.

[105] **George Hay Stuart.** *The Presbyterian Church Throughout the World*, p. 578. Stephen Abbott Northrop, D.D., *A Cloud of Witnesses* (Portland, OR: American Heritage Ministries, 1987; Mantle Ministries, 228 Still Ridge, Bulverde, Texas), p. 437.

[106] **Charles Sumner.** E.C. Lester, *Life and Public Services of Charles Sumner*, pp. 321, 171. Stephen Abbott Northrop, D.D., *A Cloud of Witnesses* (Portland, OR: American Heritage Ministries, 1987; Mantle Ministries, 228 Still Ridge, Bulverde, Texas), p. 436.

[107] **William Ashley "Billy" Sunday.** Tryon Edwards, D.D., *The New Dictionary of Thoughts - A Cyclopedia of Quotations* (Garden City, NY: Hanover House, 1852; revised and enlarged by C.H. Catrevas, Ralph Emerson Browns and Jonathan Edwards [descendent, along with Tryon, of Jonathan Edwards (1703-1758), president of Princeton], 1891; The Standard Book Company, 1955, 1963), p. 93.

T

[1] **William Howard Taft.** March 4, 1909, in his Inaugural Address. *A Compilation of the Messages and Papers of the Presidents* 20 vols. (New York: Bureau of National Literature, Inc., prepared under the direction of the Joint Committee on Printing, of the House and Senate, pursuant to an Act of the Fifty-Second Congress of the United States, 1893, 1923), Vol. XV, p. 7379. *Inaugural Addresses of the Presidents of the United States - From George Washington 1789 to Richard Milhous Nixon 1969* (Washington, D.C.: United States Government Printing Office; 91st Congress, 1st Session, House Document 91-142, 1969), pp. 187-198. Charles E. Rice, *The Supreme Court and Public Prayer* (New York: Fordham University Press, 1964), pp. 188-189. Benjamin Weiss, *God in American History: A Documentation of America's Religious Heritage* (Grand Rapids, MI: Zondervan, 1966), p. 120. Willard Cantelon, *Money Master of the World* (Plainfield, NJ: Logos International, 1976), p. 121. Davis Newton Lott, *The Inaugural Addresses of the American Presidents* (NY: Holt, Rinehart and Winston, 1961), p. 197. J. Michael Sharman, J.D., *Faith of the Fathers* (Culpepper, Virginia: Victory Publishing, 1995), p. 84.

[2] **Nahum Tate.** 1700, in his *Christmas Hymn*, st. I. John Bartlett, *Bartlett's Familiar Quotations* (Boston: Little, Brown and Company, 1855, 1980), p. 317.

[3] **Zachary Taylor.** February 14, 1849, in a message sent to a delegation of ladies from Frankfurt, Kentucky, who had presented him with a beautifully bound Bible and a copy of the Constitution of the United States. *Frankfurt Commonwealth*, February 21, 1849. Stephen Abbott Northrop, D.D., *A Cloud of Witnesses* (Portland, OR: American Heritage Ministries, 1987; Mantle Ministries, 228 Still Ridge, Bulverde, Texas), p. 447-448. D.P. Diffine, Ph.D., *One Nation Under God - How Close a Separation?* (Searcy, Arkansas: Harding University, Belden Center for Private Enterprise Education, 6th edition, 1992), p. 8.

[4] **William Temple.** In *The Malvern Manifesto*. John Bartlett, *Bartlett's Familiar Quotations* (Boston: Little, Brown and Company, 1855, 1980), p. 775.

[5] **Constitution of the State of Tennessee.** 1796, Article VIII, Section II; Article XI, Section 3. *The Constitutions of All the United States According to the Latest Amendments* (Lexington, KY: Thomas T. Skillman, 1817), p. 287. David Barton, *The Myth of Separation* (Aledo, TX: WallBuilder Press, 1991), p. 33. *The Constitutions of the United States of America*, pp. 342, 344. Frances Newton Thorpe, ed., *Federal and State Constitutions, Colonial Charters, and Other Organic Laws of the States, Territories, and Colonies now or heretofore forming the United States*, 7 vols. (Washington: Government Printing Office, 1905; 1909; St. Clair Shores, MI: Scholarly Press, 1968). Edwin S. Gaustad, *Neither King nor Prelate - Religion and the New Nation, 1776-1826* (Grand Rapids, MI: William B. Eerdmans Publishing Company, 1993), pp. 172-173. Governor Ned McWherter and Secretary of State Riley C. Darnell, *Proclamation declaring Christian Heritage Week*, August 29 - September 4, 1993, signed June 21, 1993, in the Capitol City of Nashville. Courtesy of Bruce Barilla, Christian Heritage Week Ministry (P.O. Box 58, W.V. 24712; 304-384-7707, 304-384-9044 fax).

[6] **Supreme Court of Tennessee.** 1975. *Swann v. Pack*, 527 S.W. 2d 99, 101 (Sup. Ct. Tn. 1975). David Barton, *The Myth of Separation* (Aledo, TX: WallBuilder Press, 1991), p. 192.

[7] **Alfred, Lord Tennyson.** Henry H. Halley, *Halley's Bible Handbook* (Grand Rapids, MI: Zondervan Publishing House, 1927, 1965), p. 19.

[8] **Alfred, Lord Tennyson.** *Tennyson; A Memoir by Hallam Lord Tennyson*, Vol. II, pp. 457, 466. Stephen Abbott Northrop, D.D., *A Cloud of Witnesses* (Portland, OR: American Heritage Ministries, 1987; Mantle Ministries, 228 Still Ridge, Bulverde, Texas), p. 452.

[9] **Alfred, Lord Tennyson.** Queen Victoria of England commenting on *In Memoriam. Tennyson; A Memoir by Hallam Lord Tennyson*, Vol. II, pp. 457, 466. Stephen Abbott Northrop, D.D., *A Cloud of Witnesses* (Portland, OR: American Heritage Ministries, 1987; Mantle Ministries, 228 Still Ridge, Bulverde, Texas), p. 452.

[10] **Alfred, Lord Tennyson.** *In Memoriam. Sec. xxxvi.* Burton Stevenson, *The Home Book of Quotations* (New York: Dodd, Mead & Company, 1967), p. 264. Stephen Abbott Northrop, D.D., *A Cloud of Witnesses* (Portland, OR: American Heritage Ministries, 1987; Mantle Ministries, 228 Still Ridge, Bulverde, Texas), p. 451.

[11] **Alfred, Lord Tennyson.** *In Memoriam.* Stephen Abbott Northrop, D.D., *A Cloud of Witnesses* (Portland, OR: American Heritage Ministries, 1987; Mantle Ministries, 228 Still Ridge, Bulverde, Texas), p. 451.

[12] **Alfred, Lord Tennyson.** 1852, in the *Ode on the Death of the Duke of Wellington*, st. 9. John Bartlett, *Bartlett's Familiar Quotations* (Boston: Little, Brown and Company, 1855, 1980), p. 533.

Notes

[13] **Alfred, Lord Tennyson.** 1855, *Maud*, Part II, sec. iv, st. 3. Stephen Abbott Northrop, D.D., *A Cloud of Witnesses* (Portland, OR: American Heritage Ministries, 1987; Mantle Ministries, 228 Still Ridge, Bulverde, Texas), p. 451. John Bartlett, *Bartlett's Familiar Quotations* (Boston: Little, Brown and Company, 1855, 1980), p. 533.

[14] **Alfred, Lord Tennyson.** 1864, in *Enoch Arden*, line 222. John Bartlett, *Bartlett's Familiar Quotations* (Boston: Little, Brown and Company, 1855, 1980), p. 535.

[15] **Alfred, Lord Tennyson.** 1869, *The Higher Pantheism*, st. 6. John Bartlett, *Bartlett's Familiar Quotations* (Boston: Little, Brown and Company, 1855, 1980), p. 535. *Bless Your Heart (series II)* (Eden Prairie, MN: Heartland Sampler, Inc., 1990), 8.11.

[16] **Alfred, Lord Tennyson.** *In Grief.* Stephen Abbott Northrop, D.D., *A Cloud of Witnesses* (Portland, OR: American Heritage Ministries, 1987; Mantle Ministries, 228 Still Ridge, Bulverde, Texas), pp. 451-452.

[17] **Alfred, Lord Tennyson.** *Lazarus.* Stephen Abbott Northrop, D.D., *A Cloud of Witnesses* (Portland, OR: American Heritage Ministries, 1987; Mantle Ministries, 228 Still Ridge, Bulverde, Texas), p. 452.

[18] **Alfred, Lord Tennyson.** 1869, in *Flower in the Crannied Wall.* John Bartlett, *Bartlett's Familiar Quotations* (Boston: Little, Brown and Company, 1855, 1980), p. 535.

[19] **Alfred, Lord Tennyson.** 1859-1885, in *Idylls of the King, The Passing of Arthur*, line 9. John Bartlett, *Bartlett's Familiar Quotations* (Boston: Little, Brown and Company, 1855, 1980), p. 535.

[20] **Alfred, Lord Tennyson.** 1859-1885, in *Idylls of the King, The Passing of Arthur*, line 407. John Bartlett, *Bartlett's Familiar Quotations* (Boston: Little, Brown and Company, 1855, 1980), p. 535.

[21] **Alfred, Lord Tennyson.** 1889, in *Crossing the Bar*, st. 3. John Bartlett, *Bartlett's Familiar Quotations* (Boston: Little, Brown and Company, 1855, 1980), p. 535.

[22] **Mother Teresa of Calcutta.** Quoted from the documentary film, *Mother Teresa*. Carroll E. Simcox, comp., *4400 Quotations for Christian Communicators* (Grand Rapids, MI: Baker Book House, 1991), p. 373.

[23] **Mother Teresa of Calcutta.** Bob Cutshall, *More Light for the Day* (Minneapolis, MN: Northwestern Products, Inc., 1991), 3.3.

[24] **Mother Teresa of Calcutta.** *Bless Your Heart (series II)* (Eden Prairie, MN: Heartland Samplers, Inc., 1990), 2.19.

[25] **Mother Teresa of Calcutta.** *Bless Your Heart (series II)* (Eden Prairie, MN: Heartland Samplers, Inc., 1990), 6.2.

[26] **Mother Teresa of Calcutta.** *Bless Your Heart (series II)* (Eden Prairie, MN: Heartland Sampler, Inc., 1990), 10.15.

[27] **Mother Teresa of Calcutta.** February 3, 1994, at the National Prayer Breakfast, Washington, D.C. "National Prayer Breakfast - Mother Teresa Defends Life," *Christian American* (Chesapeake, VA: The Christian Coalition, March 1994), Vol. 5, No. 1, p. 29. "Mother Teresa Condemns Abortion At National Prayer Breakfast" *The Dallas/Fort Worth Heritage* (Dallas, TX: The Dallas/Fort Worth Heritage, March 1994), Vol. 2, No. 9, p. 6.

[28] **Texas Declaration of Independence.** March 2, 1836, in General Convention at the Town of Washington. Printed by Baker and Bordens, San Felipe de Austin. Historical Documents Company, (8 North Preston Street, Philadelphia, Pa. 19104), 1977.

[29] **Supreme Court of Texas** June 30, 1993, *Ex Parte: Reverend Keith Tucci.* Jay Alan Sekulow, "Chief Counsel's Report - For the year 1992-1993" (Virginia Beach, VA: The American Center for Law and Justice, 1993), p. 3.

[30] **Cal Thomas.** 1983. Cal Thomas, *Book Burning* (Westchester, IL: Crossway Books, 1983), p. 26. John Eidsmoe, *God & Caesar - Christian Faith & Political Action* (Westchester, IL: Crossway Books, a Division of Good News Publishers, 1984), p. 166.

[31] **Norman Mattoon Thomas.** November 27, 1965, in a speech before an antiwar protest in Washington, D.C. John Bartlett, *Bartlett's Familiar Quotations* (Boston: Little, Brown and Company, 1855, 1980), p. 787.

[32] **Leo Nikolaevich Tolstoi.** 1865-1869, in *War and Peace*, book XIV, chapter 18. John Bartlett, *Bartlett's Familiar Quotations* (Boston: Little, Brown and Company, 1855, 1980), p. 602.

[33] **Leo Nikolaevich Tolstoi.** In eulogizing the President Abraham Lincoln. William J. Johnson, *Abraham Lincoln, The Christian* (NY: The Abington Press, 1913), p. 187. Peter Marshall and David Manuel, *The Glory of America* (Bloomington, MN: Garborg's Heart 'N Home, Inc., 1991), 4.16.

[34] **Augustus Montague Toplady.** October 1775, published the hymn, *Rock of Ages*, in the *Gospel Magazine.* John Bartlett, *Bartlett's Familiar Quotations* (Boston: Little, Brown and Company, 1855, 1980), p. 386.

[35] **Harry S. Truman.** April 12, 1945, in his first address to Congress as President. Merle Miller, *Plain Speaking - An Oral Biography of Harry S. Truman* (Berkley, 1982). Charles E. Jones, *The Books You Read* (Harrisburg, PA: Executive Books, 1985), p. 197. Edmund Fuller and David E. Green, *God in the White House - The Faiths of American Presidents* (NY: Crown Publishers, Inc., 1968), p. 210.

[36] **Harry S. Truman.** Larry Witham, "'Christian Nation' Now Fighting Words" (*The Washington Times*, November 23, 1992), p. A1. Gary DeMar, *The Biblical Worldview* (Atlanta, GA: An American Vision Publication - American Vision, Inc., 1993), Vol. 9, No. 2, p. 12.

[37] **Harry S. Truman.** November 29, 1948, in a personal letter to Dr. Chaim Weizmann, President of the State of Israel. Harry S. Truman, *Memoirs by Harry S. Truman - Volume Two: Years of Trial and Hope* (Garden City, NY: Doubleday & Company, Inc., 1956), pp. 168-169.

[38] **Harry S. Truman.** January 20, 1949, in his Inaugural Address. Harry S. Truman, *Memoirs by Harry S. Truman - Volume Two: Years of Trial and Hope* (Garden City, NY: Doubleday & Company, Inc., 1956), pp. 226-227. *Inaugural Addresses of the Presidents of the United States - From George Washington 1789 to Richard Milhous Nixon 1969* (Washington, D.C.: United States Government Printing Office; 91st Congress, 1st Session, House Document 91-142, 1969), pp. 251-256. Davis Newton Lott, *The Inaugural Addresses of the American Presidents* (NY: Holt, Rinehart and Winston, 1961), pp. 251-255. Charles E. Rice, *The Supreme Court and Public Prayer* (New York: Fordham University Press, 1964), pp. 191-192. Lillian W. Kay, ed., *The Ground on Which We Stand - Basic Documents of American History* (NY: Franklin Watts., Inc, 1969), p. 275. Benjamin Weiss, *God in American History: A Documentation of America's Religious Heritage* (Grand Rapids, MI: Zondervan, 1966), p. 141. Willard Cantelon, *Money Master of the World* (Plainfield, NJ: Logos International, 1976), p. 121. *Proclaim Liberty* (Dallas, TX: Word of Faith), p. 2. J. Michael Sharman, J.D., *Faith of the Fathers* (Culpepper, Virginia: Victory Publishing, 1995), pp. 102-104.

[39] **Harry S. Truman.** 1950. Mrs. James Dobson (Shirley), chairman, *The National Day of Prayer Information Packet* (Colorado Springs, CO: National Day of Prayer Task Force, May 6, 1993).

[40] **Harry S. Truman.** Herbert V. Prochnow, *5100 Quotations for Speakers and Writers* (Grand Rapids, MI: Baker Book House, 1992), p. 502.

[41] **Harry S. Truman.** Herbert V. Prochnow, *5100 Quotations for Speakers and Writers* (Grand Rapids, MI: Baker Book House, 1992), p. 502.

[42] **Harry S. Truman.** February 15, 1950, at 10:05 a.m., in an address given to the Attorney General's Conference on Law Enforcement Problems in the Department of Justice Auditorium, Washington. DC.; organizations present included the

Department of Justice, the National Association of Attorneys, the United States Conference of Lawyers, and the National Institute of Municipal Law Officers. *Public Papers of the Presidents: Harry S. Truman, 1950 - Containing Public Messages, Speeches, and Statements of the President, January 1 to December 31, 1950* (Washington, DC: United States Government Printing Office, 1965), Item 37, p. 157. Steve C. Dawson,*God's Providence in America's History* (Rancho Cordova, CA: Steve Dawson, 1988), p. 13:1. David Barton, *The Myth of Separation* (Aledo, TX: WallBuilder Press, 1991), p. 260. Gary DeMar, *America's Christian History: The Untold Story* (Atlanta, GA: American Vision Publishers, Inc., 1993), p. 60.

⁴³ **Jonathan Trumbull.** 1773. Charles E. Kistler, *This Nation Under God* (Boston: Richard G. Badger, The Gorham Press, 1924), p. 56. Peter Marshall and David Manuel, *The Glory of America* (Bloomington, MN: Garborg's Heart'N Home, Inc., 1991), 2.16.

⁴⁴ **Jonathan Trumbull.** H. Niles, *Principles and Acts of the Revolution in America* (Baltimore: 1822), p. 198. Cushing Stout, *The New Heavens and New Earth* (NY: Harper and Row, 1974), p. 59. Peter Marshall and David Manuel,*The Glory of America* (Bloomington, MN: Garborg's Heart'N Home, Inc., 1991), 2.17.

⁴⁵ **Jonathan Trumbull.** April 19, 1775, as Governor of the Connecticut Colony proclaiming a day of fasting and prayer. Verna M. Hall, *The Christian History of the American Revolution* (San Francisco: Foundation for American Christian Education, 1976), p. 407. Peter Marshall and David Manuel, *The Glory of America* (Bloomington, MN: Garborg's Heart'N Home, Inc., 1991), 3.22. Marshall Foster and Mary-Elaine Swanson, *The American Covenant - The Untold Story* (Roseburg, OR: Foundation for Christian Self-Government, 1981; Thousand Oaks, CA: The Mayflower Institute, 1983, 1992), p. 120.

⁴⁶ **Jonathan Trumbull.** July 13, 1775, in a letter to General Washington. Verna M. Hall and Rosalie J. Slater, *The Christian History of the American Revolution - Consider and Ponder* (San Francisco, CA: Foundation for American Christian Education, 1976), p. 511. Peter Marshall and David Manuel, *The Glory of America* (Bloomington, MN: Garborg's Heart'N Home, Inc., 1991), 7.13. Jared Sparks, ed., *Correspondence of the American Revolution - being Letters of Eminent Men to George Washington from the time of his Taking Command of the Army to the End of his Presidency*, 4 vols. (Boston: Little, Brown and Co., 1853), Vol. I, pp. 2-3. Douglas Southall Freeman, *George Washington*, 6 vols. (NY: Charles Scribner's Sons, 1948-1954), Vol. III, pp. 503-504.

⁴⁷ **Jonathan Trumbull.** Isaac W. Stuart, *Life*. Stephen Abbott Northrop, D.D., *A Cloud of Witnesses* (Portland, Oregon: American Heritage Ministries, 1987; Mantle Ministries, 228 Still Ridge, Bulverde, Texas), p. 467. George Bancroft, *Bancroft's History of the United States* vols. I-X (Boston: Charles C. Little & James Brown, 3rd edition, 1838), Vol. IX, p. 79. Peter Marshall and David Manuel, *The Light and the Glory* (Old Tappan, NJ: Fleming H. Revell Company, 1977), p. 312.

⁴⁸ **Sojourner Truth.** Page Smith,*The Nation Comes of Age* (New York: McGraw-Hill Book Co., 1981), Vol. 4, p. 660. Peter Marshall and David Manuel, *The Glory of America* (Bloomington, MN: Garborg's Heart'N Home, Inc., 1991), 11.26.

⁴⁹ **Harriet Tubman.** Page Smith, *The Nation Comes of Age* (New York: McGraw-Hill Book Co., 1981), Vol. 4, pp. 658-659. Peter Marshall and David Manuel, *The Glory of America* (Bloomington, MN: Garborg's Heart'N Home, Inc., 1991), 3.10.

⁵⁰ **Harriet Tubman.** 1868, to her biographer, Sarah H. Bradford. John Bartlett,*Bartlett's Familiar Quotations* (Boston: Little, Brown and Company, 1855, 1980), p. 593.

⁵¹ **Mark Twain.** Henry and Dana Thomas, 1942. Charles E. Jones, *The Books You Read* (Harrisburg, PA: Executive Books, 1985), p. 133.

⁵² **Mark Twain.** *Innocents Abroad, or the New Pilgrim's Progress*, p. 492. Stephen Abbott Northrop, D.D., *A Cloud of Witnesses* (Portland, OR: American Heritage Ministries, 1987; Mantle Ministries, 228 Still Ridge, Bulverde, Texas), p. 88.

⁵³ **Mark Twain.** *Innocents Abroad, or the New Pilgrim's Progress*, pp. 499-502. Stephen Abbott Northrop, D.D., *A Cloud of Witnesses* (Portland, OR: American Heritage Ministries, 1987; Mantle Ministries, 228 Still Ridge, Bulverde, Texas), p. 88.

⁵⁴ **Mark Twain.** *Innocents Abroad, or the New Pilgrim's Progress*, p. 513. Stephen Abbott Northrop, D.D., *A Cloud of Witnesses* (Portland, OR: American Heritage Ministries, 1987; Mantle Ministries, 228 Still Ridge, Bulverde, Texas), pp. 88-89.

⁵⁵ **Mark Twain.** 1876, in *The Adventures of Tom Sawyer*, chapter 13. John Bartlett, *Bartlett's Familiar Quotations* (Boston: Little, Brown and Company, 1855, 1980), p. 622.

⁵⁶ **Mark Twain.** 1894, in *Pudd'nhead Wilson*. Lewis C. Henry, *Best Quotations For All Occasions* (Greenwich, CONN: Fawcett Publications, Inc., 1961), p. 8.

⁵⁷ **Mark Twain.** 1894, in *Pudd'nhead Wilson, Pudd'nhead Wilson's Calendar*, chapter 2. John Bartlett, *Bartlett's Familiar Quotations* (Boston: Little, Brown and Company, 1855, 1980), p. 624.

⁵⁸ **Mark Twain.** 1894, in *Pudd'nhead Wilson, Pudd'nhead Wilson's Calendar*, chapter 3. John Bartlett, *Bartlett's Familiar Quotations* (Boston: Little, Brown and Company, 1855, 1980), p. 624.

⁵⁹ **Mark Twain.** 1897, in *Pudd'nhead Wilson's New Calendar*, chapter 20. John Bartlett, *Bartlett's Familiar Quotations* (Boston: Little, Brown and Company, 1855, 1980), p. 625.

⁶⁰ **Mark Twain.** Attributed. John Bartlett, *Bartlett's Familiar Quotations* (Boston: Little, Brown and Company, 1855, 1980), p. 626.

⁶¹ **Mark Twain.** 1912, from Albert Bigelow Paine, *Mark Twain*. John Bartlett, *Bartlett's Familiar Quotations* (Boston: Little, Brown and Company, 1855, 1980), p. 626.

⁶² **Mark Twain.** 1940, from Bernard De Voto, *Mark Twain in Eruption*. John Bartlett, *Bartlett's Familiar Quotations* (Boston: Little, Brown and Company, 1855, 1980), p. 626.

⁶³ **John Tyndall.** In *Fragments of Science*, Vol. II, "Professor Virchow and Evolution." John Bartlett, *Bartlett's Familiar Quotations* (Boston: Little, Brown and Company, 1855, 1980), p. 580.

U

¹ **United States Supreme Court.** 1789, Robert Byrd, United States Senator from West Virginia, July 27, 1962, in a message delivered in Congress two days after the Supreme Court declared prayer in schools unconstitutional. Robert Flood, *The Rebirth of America* (Philadelphia: Arthur S. DeMoss Foundation, 1986), pp. 66-69. Gary DeMar, *America's Christian History: The Untold Story* (Atlanta, GA: American Vision Publishers, Inc., 1993), p. 54.

² **United States Supreme Court.** 1844, *Vidal v. Girard's Executors*, 43 U.S. 126, 132, 143, 152-153, 170, 175 (1844). David Barton, *The Myth of Separation* (Aledo, TX: WallBuilder Press, 1991), pp. 61-62.

³ **United States Supreme Court.** 1844,*Vidal v. Girard's Executors*, 43 U.S. 126, 132 (1844), pp. 198, 205-206. David Barton,*The Myth of Separation* (Aledo, TX: WallBuilder Press, 1991), pp. 62-63.

⁴ **United States Supreme Court.** 1892, Justice David Josiah Brewer, *Church of the Holy Trinity v. United States*, 143 US 457, 458, 465-471, 36 L ed 226. David Barton, *The Myth of Separation* (Aledo, TX: WallBuilder Press, 1991), pp. 47-51. "Our Christian Heritage," *Letter from Plymouth Rock* (Marlborough, NH: The Plymouth Rock Foundation), p. 6. Gary DeMar,*America's Christian*

History: The Untold Story (Atlanta, GA: American Vision Publishers, Inc., 1993), p. 63.

[5] **United States Supreme Court.** 1878, *Reynolds v. United States*, 98 U.S. 145, 165 (1878). David Barton, *The Myth of Separation* (Aledo, TX: WallBuilder Press, 1991), p. 72.

[6] **United States Supreme Court.** 1884, "Our Christian Heritage," *Letter from Plymouth Rock* (Marlborough, NH: The Plymouth Rock Foundation), p. 6.

[7] **United States Supreme Court.** 1885, *Murphy v. Ramsey & Others*, 144 U.S. 15, 45 (1885). David Barton, *The Myth of Separation* (Aledo, TX: WallBuilder Press, 1991), p. 71.

[8] **United States Supreme Court.** 1889, *Davis v. Beason*, 133 U.S. 333, 341-343, 348 (1890). David Barton, *The Myth of Separation* (Aledo, TX: WallBuilder Press, 1991), pp. 67-69. John Eidsmoe, *The Christian Legal Advisor* (Milford, MI: Mott Media, 1984), p. 150. Gary DeMar, *America's Christian History: The Untold Story* (Atlanta, GA: American Vision Publishers, Inc., 1993), pp. 68, 106.

[9] **United States Supreme Court.** 1890, *The Church of Jesus Christ of Latter Day Saints v. United States*, 136 U.S. 1 (1890). Gary DeMar, *America's Christian History: The Untold Story* (Atlanta, GA: American Vision Publishers, Inc., 1993), p. 68. [The following related quotations are taken from James D. Richardson (U.S. Representative from Tennessee), ed., *A Compilation of the Messages and Papers of the Presidents 1789-1897*, 10 vols. (Washington, D.C.: U.S. Government Printing Office, published by Authority of Congress, 1897, 1899; Washington, D.C.: Bureau of National Literature and Art, 1789-1902, 11 vols., 1907, 1910).

On January 4, 1896, President Grover Cleveland, in a Proclamation, stated: "Whereas said convention, so organized, did, by ordinance irrevocable without the consent of the United States and the people of said State, as required by said act, provide that perfect toleration of religious sentiment shall be secured and that no inhabitant of said State shall ever be molested in person or property on account of his or her mode of religious worship, but that polygamous or plural marriages are forever prohibited, and did also by said ordinance make the other various stipulations recited in section 3 of said act." (Vol. IX, p. 689).

On September 25, 1894, President Grover Cleveland issued a Proclamation: "Whereas Congress by a statute approved March 22, 1882, and by statutes in furtherance and amendment thereof defined the crimes of bigamy, polygamy, and unlawful cohabitation in the Territories and other places within the exclusive jurisdiction of the United States and prescribed a penalty for such crimes; and Whereas on or about the 6th day of October, 1890, the Church of the Latter-day Saints, commonly known as the Mormon Church, through its president issued a manifesto proclaiming the purpose of said church no longer to sanction the practice of polygamous marriages and calling upon all members and adherents of said church to obey the laws of the United States in reference to said subject-matter; and Whereas on the 4th day of January, A.D. 1893, Benjamin Harrison, then President of the United States, did declare and grant a full pardon and amnesty to certain offenders under said acts upon condition of future obedience to their requirements, as is fully set forth in said proclamation of amnesty and pardon; and Whereas upon the evidence now furnished me I am satisfied that the member and adherents of said church generally abstain from plural marriages and polygamous cohabitation and are now living in obedience to the laws, and that time has now arrived when the interests of public justice and morality will be promoted by granting of amnesty and pardon to all such offenders as have complied with the conditions of said proclamation, including such of said offenders as have been convicted under the provisions of said act: Now, therefore, I, Grover Cleveland, President of the United States, by virtue of the powers in me vested, do hereby declare and grant a full amnesty and pardon to all persons who have in violation of said acts committed either of the offenses of polygamy, bigamy, adultery, or unlawful cohabitation under the color of polygamous or plural marriage, or who, having been convicted of violations of said acts, are now suffering deprivation of civil rights in consequence of the same, excepting all persons who have not complied with the conditions contained in said executive proclamation of January 4, 1893. In witness whereof I have hereunto set my hand and caused the seal of the United States to be affixed. Done at the city of Washington, this 25th day of September, A.D. 1894, and of the Independence of the United States the one hundred and nineteenth. Grover Cleveland. By the President: W.Q. Gresham, Secretary of State." (Vol. IX, pp. 510-511).

On January 4, 1893, President Benjamin Harrison, in a Proclamation, stated: "Whereas Congress by statute approved March 22, 1882, and by statutes in furtherance and amendment thereof defined the crimes of bigamy, polygamy, and unlawful cohabitation in the Territories and other places within the exclusive jurisdiction of the United States and prescribed a penalty for such crimes; and Whereas on or about the 6th day of October, 1890, the Church of the Latter-day Saints, commonly known as the Mormon Church, through its president issued a manifesto proclaiming the purpose of said church no longer to sanction the practice of polygamous marriages and calling upon all members and adherents of said church to obey the laws of the United States in reference to said subject-matter; and Whereas it is represented that since the date of said declaration the members and adherents of said church have generally obeyed said laws and have abstained from plural marriages and polygamous cohabitation; and Whereas by a petition dated December 19, 1891, the officials of said church, pledging the membership thereof to a faithful obedience to the laws against plural marriage and unlawful cohabitation, have applied to me to grant amnesty for past offenses against said laws, which request a very large number of influential non-Mormons residing in the Territories have also strongly urged; and Whereas the Utah Commission in their report bearing date September 15, 1892, recommend that said petition be granted and said amnesty proclaimed, under proper conditions as to the future observance of the law, with a view to the encouragement of those now disposed to become law-abiding citizens; and Whereas during the past two years such amnesty has been granted to individual applicants in a very large number of cases, conditioned upon the faithful observance of the laws of the United States against unlawful cohabitation, and there are now pending many more such applications: Now, therefore, I, Benjamin Harrison, President of the United States, by virtue of the powers in me vested, do hereby declare and grant a full amnesty and pardon to all persons liable to the penalties of said act by reason of unlawful cohabitation under the color of polygamous or plural marriage who have since November 1, 1890, abstained from such unlawful cohabitation, but upon the express condition that they shall in the future faithfully obey the laws of the United States hereinbefore named and not otherwise. Those who shall fail to avail themselves of the clemency hereby offered will be vigorously prosecuted. In witness whereof I have hereunto set my hand and caused the seal of the United States to be affixed. Done at the city of Washington, this 4th day of January, A.D. 1893, and of the Independence of the United States the one hundred and seventeenth. Benj. Harrison. By the President: John W. Foster, Secretary of State." (Vol. IX, pp. 368-369).

On December 9, 1891, President Benjamin Harrison, in his Third Annual Message, stated: "The legislation of Congress for the repression of polygamy has, after years of resistance on the part of the Mormons, at last brought them to the conclusion that resistance is unprofitable and unavailing. The power of Congress over this subject should not be surrendered until we have satisfactory evidence that the people of the State to be created would exercise the exclusive power of the State over this subject in the same way. The question is not whether these people now obey the laws of Congress against polygamy, but rather would they make, enforce, and maintain such laws themselves if absolutely free to regulate the subject? We can not afford to experiment with this subject, for when a State in once constituted the act is final and any mistake irretrievable." (Vol. IX, p. 206).

On December 1, 1890, President Benjamin Harrison, in his Second Annual Message, stated: "The increasing numbers and influence of the non-Mormon population of Utah are observed with satisfaction. The recent letter of Wilford Woodruff, president of the Mormon Church, in which he advised his people to 'refrain from contracting any marriage forbidden by the laws of the land,' has attracted wide attention, and it is hoped that its influence will be highly beneficial in restraining infractions of the laws of the United States. But the fact should not be overlooked that the doctrine or belief of the church that polygamous marriages are rightful and supported by divine revelation remains unchanged. President Woodruff does not renounce the doctrine, but refrains from teaching it, and advises against the practice of it because the law is against it. Now, it is quite true that the law should not attempt to deal with faith or belief of anyone; but it is quite another thing, and the only safe thing, so to deal with the Territory of Utah as that those who believe polygamy to be rightful shall not have the power to make it lawful." (Vol. IX, p. 118).

On December 3, 1888, in his Fourth Annual Message, President Grover Cleveland stated: "It also appears from this report that though prior to March, 1885, there had been but 6 convictions in the Territories of Utah and Idaho under the laws of 1862 and 1882, punishing polygamy and unlawful cohabitation as crimes, there have been since that date nearly 600 convictions under these laws and the statutes of 1887; and the opinion is expressed that under such a firm and vigilant execution of these laws and the advance of ideas opposed to the forbidden practices, polygamy within the United States is virtually at an end." (Vol. 8, p. 794).

On December 8, 1885, in his First Annual Message to Congress, President Grover Cleveland stated: "In the Territory of Utah the law of the United States passed for suppression of polygamy has been energetically and faithfully executed during the past year, with measurably good results. A number of convictions have been secured for unlawful cohabitation, and in some cases pleas of guilty have been entered and a slight punishment imposed, upon a promise by the accused that they would not again offend against the law, nor advise, counsel, aid, or abet in any way its violation by others. The Utah commissioners express the opinion, based upon such information as they are able to obtain, that but few polygamous marriages have taken place in the Territory during the last year. They further report that while there can not be found upon the registration lists of voters the name of a man actually guilty of polygamy, and while none of that class are holding office, yet at the last election in the Territory all the officers elected, except in one county, were men who, though not actually living in the practice of polygamy, subscribe to the doctrine of polygamous marriages as a divine revelation and a law unto all higher and more binding upon the conscience than any human law, local or national. Thus is the strange spectacle presented of a community protected by a republican form of government, to which they owe allegiance, sustaining by their suffrages a principle and a belief which set at naught that obligation of absolute obedience to the law of the land which lies at the foundation of republican institutions. The strength, the perpetuity, and the destiny of the nation rest upon our homes, established by the law of God, guarded by parental care, regulated by parental authority, and sanctified by parental love. These are not the homes of polygamy. The mothers of our land, who rule the nation as they mold the characters and guide the actions of their sons, live according to God's holy ordinances, and each, secure and happy in the exclusive love of the father of her children, sheds the warm light of true womanhood, unperverted and unpolluted, upon all within her pure and wholesome family circle. These are not the cheerless, crushed, and unwomanly mothers of polygamy. The fathers of our families are the best citizens of the Republic. Wife and children are the sources of patriotism, and conjugal and parental affection beget devotion to the country. The man who, undefiled with plural marriage, is surrounded in his single home with his wife and children has a stake in the country which inspires him with respect for its laws and courage for its defense. These are not the fathers of polygamous families. There is no feature of this practice or system which sanctions it which is not opposed to all that is of value in our institutions. There should be no relaxation in the firm but just execution of the law now in operation, and I should be glad to approve such further discreet legislation as will rid the country of this blot upon its fair fame. Since the people upholding polygamy in our Territories are reenforced by immigration from other lands, I recommend that a law be passed to prevent the importation of Mormons into the country." (Vol. 8, pp. 361-362).

On March 4, 1885, in his First Inaugural Address, President Grover Cleveland stated: "The conscience of the people demands that the Indians within our boundaries shall be fairly and honestly treated as wards of the Government and their education and civilization promoted with a view to their ultimate citizenship, and that polygamy in the Territories, destructive of the family relation and offensive to the moral sense of the civilized world, shall be repressed." (Vol. 8, p. 302).

On December 1, 1884, in his Fourth Annual Message, President Chester A. Arthur stated: "The report of the Utah Commission will be read with interest. It discloses the results of recent legislation looking to the prevention and punishment of polygamy in that Territory. I still believe that if that abominable practice can be suppressed by law it can only be by the most radical legislation consistent with the restraints of the Constitution. I again recommend, therefore, that Congress assume absolute political control of the Territory of Utah and provide for the appointment of commissioners with such governmental powers as in its judgement may justly and wisely be put into their hands." (Vol. 8, p. 250).

On December 4, 1883, in his Third Annual Message, President Chester A. Arthur stated: "The Utah Commission has submitted to the Secretary of the Interior its second annual report. As a result of its labors in supervising the recent election in that Territory, pursuant to the act of March 22, 1882, it appears that persons by that act disqualified to the number of about 12,000, were excluded from the polls. This fact, however, affords little cause for congratulation, and I fear that it is far from indicating any real and substantial progress toward the extirpation of polygamy. All the members elect of the legislature are Mormons. There is grave reason to believe that they are in sympathy with the practices that this Government is seeking to suppress, and that its efforts in that regard will be more likely to encounter their opposition than to receive their encouragement and support. Even if this view should happily be erroneous, the law under which the commissioners have been acting should be made more effective by the incorporation of some such stringent amendments as they recommend, and as were included in bill No. 2238 on the Calendar of the Senate at its last session. I am convinced, however, that polygamy has become so strongly intrenched in the Territory of Utah that it is profitless to attack it with any but the stoutest weapons which constitutional legislation can fashion. I favor, therefore, the repeal of the act upon which the existing government depends, the assumption by the National Legislature of the entire political control of the Territory, and the establishment of a commission with such powers and duties as shall be delegated to it by law." (Vol. 8, p. 184).

On December 6, 1881, in his First Annual Message to Congress, President Chester A. Arthur stated: "For many years the Executive, in his annual message to Congress, has urged the necessity of stringent legislation for the suppression of polygamy in the Territories, and especially in the Territory of Utah. The existing statute for the punishment of this odious crime, so revolting to the moral and religious sense of Christendom, has been persistently and contemptuously violated ever since its enactment. Indeed, in spite of commendable efforts on the part of the authorities who represent the United States in that Territory, the law has in very rare instances been enforced, and, for a cause to which reference will presently be made, is practically a dead letter. The fact that adherents of the Mormon Church, which rests upon polygamy as its corner stone, have recently been peopling in large numbers Idaho, Arizona, and other of our Western Territories is well calculated to excite the liveliest interest and apprehension. It imposes upon Congress and the Executive the duty of arraying against this barbarous system all the power which under the Constitution and the law they can wield for its destruction. Reference has been already made to the obstacles which the United States officers have encountered in their efforts to punish violations of law. Prominent among these obstacles is the difficulty of procuring legal evidence sufficient to warrant a conviction even in the case of the most notorious offenders. Your attention is called to a recent opinion of the Supreme Court of the United States, explaining its judgement of reversal in the case of Miles, who had been convicted of bigamy in Utah. The court refers to the fact that the secrecy attending the celebration of marriages in that Territory makes the proof of polygamy very difficult, and the propriety is suggested of modifying the law of evidence which now makes a wife incompetent to testify against her husband. This suggestion is approved. I recommend also the passage of an act providing that in the Territories of the United States the fact that a woman has been married to a person charged with bigamy shall not disqualify her as a witness upon his trial for that offense. I further recommend legislation by which any person solemnizing a marriage in any of the Territories shall be required, under stringent penalties for neglect or refusal, to file a certificate of such marriage in the supreme court of the Territory. Doubtless Congress may devise other practicable measures for obviating the difficulties which have hitherto attended the efforts to suppress this iniquity. I assure you of my determined purpose to cooperate with you in any lawful and discreet measures which may be proposed to that end." (Vol. VIII, pp. 57-58).

On March 4, 1881, in his Inaugural Address, President James A. Garfield stated: "The Constitution guarantees absolute religious freedom. Congress is prohibited from making any law respecting an establishment of religion or prohibiting the free exercise thereof. The Territories of the United States are subject to the direct legislative authority of Congress, and hence the General Government is responsible for any violation of the Constitution in any of them. It is therefore a reproach to the Government that in the most populous of the Territories the constitutional guaranty is not enjoyed by the people and the authority of Congress is set at naught. The Mormon Church not only offends the moral sense of manhood by sanctioning polygamy, but prevents the administration of justice through ordinary instrumentalities of law. In my judgement it is the duty of Congress, while respecting to the uttermost the conscientious convictions and religious scruples of every citizen, to prohibit within its jurisdiction all criminal practices, especially of that class which destroys the family relations and endanger social order." (Vol. 8, p. 11).

On December 6, 1880, in his Fourth Annual Message to Congress, President Rutherford B. Hayes stated: "It is the recognized duty and purpose of the people of the United States to suppress polygamy where it now exists in our Territories and to prevent its extension. Faithful and zealous efforts have been made by the United States authorities in Utah to enforce the laws against it. Experience has shown that the legislation upon this subject, to be effective, requires extensive modification and amendment. The longer action is delayed the more difficult it will be to accomplish what is desired. Prompt and decided measures are necessary. The Mormon sectarian organization which upholds polygamy has the whole power of making and executing the local legislation of the Territory. By its control of the grand and petit juries it possesses large influence over the administration of justice. Exercising, as the heads of this sect do, the local power of the Territory, they are able to make effective their hostility to the law of Congress on the subject of polygamy, and, in fact, do prevent its enforcement. Polygamy will not be abolished if the enforcement of the law depends on those who practice and uphold the crime. It can only be suppressed by taking away the political power of the sect which encourages and sustains it. The power of Congress to enact suitable laws to protect the Territories is ample. It is not a case for halfway measures. The political power of the Mormon sect is increasing. It controls now one of our wealthiest and most populous Territories. It is extending steadily into other Territories. Wherever it goes it establishes polygamy and sectarian political power. The sanctity of marriage and the family relation are the corner stone of our American society and civilization. Religious liberty and the separation of church and state are among the elementary ideas of free institutions. To reestablish the interests and principles which polygamy and Mormonism have imperiled, and to fully reopen to intelligent and virtuous immigrants of all creeds that part of our domain which has been in a great degree closed to general immigration by intolerant and immoral institutions, it is recommended that the government of the Territory of Utah be reorganized. I recommend that Congress provide for the government of Utah by a governor and judges, or commissioners, appointed by the President and confirmed by the Senate - a government analogous to the provisional government established for the territory northwest of the Ohio by the ordinance of 1787. If, however, it is deemed best to continue the existing form of local government, I recommend that the right to vote, hold office, and sit on juries in the Territory of Utah be confined to those who neither practice nor uphold polygamy. If thorough measures are adopted, it is believed that within a few years the evils which now afflict Utah will be eradicated, and that this Territory will in good time become one of the most prosperous and attractive of the new States of the Union." (Vol. 7, pp. 605-606).

On December 1, 1879, in his Third Annual Message to Congress, President Rutherford B. Hayes stated: "The continued deliberate violation by a large number of prominent and influential citizens of the Territory of Utah of the laws of the United States for the prosecution and punishment of polygamy demands the attention of every department of the Government. This Territory has a population sufficient to entitle it to admission as a State, and the general interests of the nation, as well as the welfare of the citizens of the Territory, require its advance from the Territorial form of government to the responsibilities and privileges of a State. This important change will not, however, be approved by the country while the citizens of Utah in very considerable number uphold a practice which is condemned as a crime by the laws of all civilized communities throughout the world. The law for the suppression of this offense was enacted with great unanimity by Congress more than seventeen years ago, but has remained until recently a dead letter in the Territory of Utah, because of the peculiar difficulties attending its enforcement. The opinion widely prevailed among the citizens of Utah that the law was in contravention of the constitutional guaranty of religious freedom. This objection is now removed. The Supreme Court of the United States has decided the law to be within the legislative power of Congress and binding as a rule of action for all who reside within the Territories. There is no longer any reason for delay or hesitation in its enforcement. It should be firmly and effectively executed. If not sufficiently stringent in its provisions, it should be amended, and that this Territory may in aid of the purpose in view I recommend that more comprehensive and more searching methods for preventing as well as punishing this crime be provided. If necessary to secure obedience to the law, the enjoyment and exercise of the rights and priviledges of citizenship in the Territories of the United States may be withheld or withdrawn from those who violate or oppose the enforcement of the law on this subject."(Vol. 7, pp. 559-569).

On December 7, 1875, in his Seventh Annual Message to Congress, President Ulysses S. Grant stated: "In nearly every annual message that I have had the honor of transmitting to Congress I have called attention to the anomalous, not to say scandalous, condition of affairs existing in the Territory of Utah, and have asked for definite legislation to correct it. That polygamy should exist in a free, enlightened, and Christian country, without the power to punish so flagrant a crime against decency and morality, seems preposterous. True, there is no law to sustain this unnatural vice; but what is needed is a law to punish it as a crime, and at the same time to fix that status of the innocent children, the offspring of this system, and of the possibility innocent plural wives. But as an institution polygamy should be banished from the land....I deem of vital importance [to]....drive out licensed immorality, such as polygamy and the importation of women for illegitimate purposes."(Vol. 7, pp. 355-356).

On December 4, 1871, in his Third Annual Message to Congress, President Ulysses S. Grant stated: "In Utah there still remains a remnant of barbarism, repugnant to civilization, and to the laws of the United States. Territorial officers, however, have been found who are willing to perform their duty in a spirit of equity and with a due sense of the necessity of sustaining the majesty of the law. Neither polygamy nor any other violation of existing statutes will be permitted within the territory of the United States. It is not with the religion of the self-styled Saints that we are now dealing, but with their practices. They will be protected in the worship of God according to the dictates of their consciences, but they will not be permitted to violate the laws under the cloak of religion. It may be advisable for Congress to consider what, in the execution of the laws against polygamy, is to be the status of plural wives and their offspring. The propriety of Congress passing an enabling act authorizing the Territorial legislature of Utah to legitimize all children born prior to a time fixed in the act might be justified by its humanity to these innocent children."(Vol. 7, p. 151).

On December 6, 1858, in his Second Annual Message to Congress, President James Buchanan stated: "The present condition of the Territory of Utah, when contrasted with what it was one year ago, is a subject for congratulation. It was then in a state of open rebellion, and, cost what it might, the character of the Government required that this rebellion should be suppressed and the Mormons compelled to yield obedience to the Constitution and the laws. In order to accomplish this object, as I informed you in my last annual message, I appointed a new governor instead of Brigham Young, and other Federal officers to take the place of those who, consulting their personal safety, had found it necessary to withdraw from the Territory. To protect these civil officers, and to aid them, as a *posse comitatus*, in the execution of the laws in case of need, I ordered a detachment of the Army to accompany them to Utah. The necessity for adopting these measures in now demonstrated. On the 15th of September, 1857, Governor Young issued his proclamation, in the style of an independent sovereign, announcing his purpose to resist by force of arms the entry of the United States troops into our own Territory of Utah. By this he required all the forces in the Territory to 'hold themselves in readiness to march at a moment's notice to repel any and all such invasion,' and established martial law from its date throughout the Territory. These proved to be no idle threats. Forts Bridger and Supply were vacated and burnt down by the Mormons to deprive our troops of a shelter after their long and fatiguing march. Orders were issued by Daniel H. Wells, styling himself 'Lieutenant-General, Nauvoo Legion,' to stampede the animals of the United States troops on their march, to set fire to their trains, to burn the grass and the whole country before them and on their flanks, to keep them from sleeping by night surprises, and to blockade the road by felling trees and destroying the fords of rivers, etc. These orders were promptly and effectually obeyed. On the 4th of October, 1857, the Mormons captured and burned, on Green River, three of our supply trains, consisting of seventy-five wagons loaded with provisions and tents for the army, and carried away several hundred animals. This diminished the supply of provisions so materially that General Johnston was obliged to reduce the ration, and even with this precaution there was only sufficient left to subsist the troops until the 1st of June. Our little army behaved admirably in their encampment at Fort Bridger under these trying privations. In the midst of the mountains, in a dreary, unsettled, and inhospitable region, more than a thousand miles from home, they passed the severe and inclement winter without a murmur. They looked forward with confidence for relief from their country in due season, and in this they were not disappointed. The Secretary of War employed all his energies to forward them the necessary supplies and to muster and send such a military force to Utah as would render resistance on the part of the Mormons hopeless, and thus terminate the war without the effusion of blood. In his efforts he war efficiently sustained by Congress. They granted appropriations sufficient to cover the deficiency thus necessarily created, and also provided for raising two regiments of volunteers 'for the purpose of quelling disturbances in the Territory of Utah, for the protection of supply and emigrant trains, and the suppression of Indian hostilities on the frontiers.' Happily, there was no occasion to call these regiments into service. If there had been, I should have felt serious embarrassment in selecting them, so great war the number of our brave and patriotic citizens anxious to serve their country in this distant and apparently dangerous expedition. Thus it has ever been, and thus may it ever be. The wisdom and economy of sending sufficient reinforcements to Utah are established, not only by the event, but in the opinion of those who from their position and opportunities are the most capable of forming a correct judgement. General Johnston, the commander of the forces, in addressing the Secretary of War from Fort Bridger under date of October 18, 1857, expresses the opinion that 'unless a large force is sent here, from the nature of the country a protracted war on their [the Mormon's] part is inevitable.' This he considered necessary to terminate the war 'speedily and more economically than if attempted by insufficient means.' In the meantime it was my anxious desire that the Mormons should yield obedience to the Constitution and the laws without rendering it necessary to resort to military force. To aid in accomplishing this object, I deemed it advisable in April last to dispatch two distinguished citizens of the United States, Messrs. Powell and McCulloch, to Utah. They bore with them a proclamation addressed by myself to the inhabitants of Utah, dated on the 6th day of that month, warning them of their true condition and how hopeless it was on their part to persist in rebellion against the United States, and offering all those who should submit to the laws a full pardon for their past seditions and treasons. At the same time I assured those who should persist in rebellion against the United States that they must expect no further lenity, but look to be rigorously dealt with according to their deserts. The instructions to these agents, as well as a copy of the proclamation and their reports, are herewith submitted. It will be seen by their report of the 3d of July last that they have fully confirmed the opinion expressed by General Johnston in the previous October as to the necessity of sending reinforcements to Utah. In this they state that they 'are firmly impressed with the belief that the presence of the Army here and the large additional force that had been ordered to this Territory were the chief inducements that caused the Mormons to abandon the idea of resisting the authority of the United States. A less decisive policy would probably have resulted in a long, bloody, and expensive war.' These gentlemen conducted themselves to my entire satisfaction and rendered useful services in executing the humane intentions of the Government. It also affords me great satisfaction to state that Governor Cumming has performed his duty in an able and conciliatory manner and with the happiest effect. I can not in this connection refrain from mentioning the valuable services of Colonel Thomas L. Kane, who, from motives of pure benevolence and without any official character or pecuniary compensation, visited Utah during the last inclement winter for the purpose of contributing to the pacification of the Territory. I am happy to inform you that the governor and other civil officers of Utah are now performing their appropriate functions without resistance. The authority of the Constitution and the laws has been fully restored and peace prevails throughout the Territory." (Vol. 5, pp. 503-506).

On April 6, 1858, President James Buchanan issued the Proclamation: "Whereas the Territory of Utah was settled by certain emigrants from the States and from foreign countries who have for several years past manifested a spirit of insubordination to the Constitution and laws of the United States. The great mass of those settlers, acting under the influence of leaders to whom they seem to have surrendered their judgement, refuse to be controlled by any other authority. They have been often advised to obedience, and these friendly counsels have been answered with defiance. The officers of the Federal Government have been driven from the Territory for no offense but an effort to do their sworn duty; others have been prevented from going there by threats of assassination; judges have been violently interrupted in the performance of their functions, and the records of the courts have been seized and destroyed or concealed. Many other acts of unlawful violence have been perpetrated, and the right to repeat them has been openly claimed by the leading inhabitants, with at least the silent acquiescence of nearly all the others. Their hostility to the lawful government of the country has at length become so violent that no officer bearing a commission from the Chief Magistrate of the Union can enter the Territory or remain there with safety, and all those officers recently appointed have been unable to go to Salt Lake or anywhere else in Utah beyond the immediate power of the Army. Indeed, such is believed to be the condition to which a strange system of terrorism has brought the inhabitants of that region that no one among them could express an opinion favorable to this Government, or even propose to obey its laws, without exposing his life and property to peril. After carefully considering this state of affairs and maturely weighing the obligation I was under to see the laws faithfully executed, it seemed to me right and proper that I should make such use of the military force at my disposal as might be necessary to protect the Federal officers in going into the Territory of Utah and in performing their duties after arriving there. I accordingly ordered a detachment of the Army to march for the city of Salt Lake, or within reach of that place, and to act in case of need as a posse for the enforcement of the laws. But in the meantime the hatred of that misguided people for the just and legal authority of the Government had become so intense that they resolved to measure their military strength with that of the Union. They have organized an armed force far from contemptible in point of numbers and trained it, if not with skill, at least with great assiduity and perseverance. While the troops of the United States were on their march a train of baggage wagons, which happened to be unprotected, was attacked and destroyed by a portion of the Mormon forces and the provisions and stores with which the train was laden were wantonly burnt. In short, their present attitude is one of decided and unreserved enmity to the United States and to all their loyal citizens. Their determination to oppose the authority of the Government by military force has not only been expressed in words, but manifested in overt acts of the most unequivocal character. Fellow-citizens of Utah, this is rebellion against the Government to which you owe allegiance; it is levying war against the United States, and involves you in the guilt of treason. Persistence in it will bring you to condign punishment, to ruin, and to shame; for it is mere madness to suppose that with your limited resources you can successfully resist the force of this great and powerful nation. If you have calculated upon the forbearance of the United States, if you have permitted yourselves to suppose that this Government will fail to put forth its strength and bring you to submission, you have fallen into a grave mistake. You have settled upon territory which lies, geographically, in the heart of the Union. The land you live upon was purchased by the United States and paid for out of their Treasury; the proprietary right and title to it is in them, and not in you. Utah is bounded on every side by States and Territories whose people are true to the Union. It is absurd to believe that they will or can permit you to erect in their very midst a government of your own, not only independent of the authority which they all acknowledge, but hostile to them and their interests. Do not deceive yourselves nor try to mislead others by propagating the idea that this is a crusade against your religion. The Constitution and laws of this country can take no notice of your creed, whether it be true or false. That is a question between your god and yourselves, in which I disclaim all right to interfere. If you obey the laws, keep the peace, and respect the just rights of others, you will be perfectly secure, and may live one in your present faith or change it for another at your pleasure. Every intelligent man among you knows very well that this Government has never, directly or indirectly, sought to molest you in your worship, to control you in your ecclesiastical affairs, or even to influence you in your religious opinions. This rebellion is not merely a violation of your legal duty; it is without just cause, without reason, without excuse. You never made a complaint that was not listened to with patience; you never exhibited a real grievance that was not redressed as promptly as it could be. The laws and regulations enacted for your government by Congress have been equal and just, and their enforcement was manifestly necessary for your own welfare and happiness. You have never asked their repeal. They are similar in every material respect to the laws which have been passed for the other Territories of the Union, and which everywhere else (with one partial exception) have been cheerfully obeyed. No people ever lived who were freer from unnecessary legal restraints than you. Human wisdom never devised a political system which bestowed more blessings or imposed lighter burdens than the Government of the United States in its operation upon the Territories. But being anxious to save the effusion of blood and to avoid the indiscriminate punishment of a whole people for crimes of which it is not probable that all are equally guilty, I offer now a free and full pardon to all who will submit themselves to the just authority of the Federal Government. If you refuse to accept it, let the consequences fall upon your own heads. But I conjure you to pause deliberately and reflect well before you reject this tender of peace and good will. Now, therefore, I, James Buchanan, President of the United States, have thought proper to issue this my proclamation, enjoining upon all public officers in the Territory of Utah to be diligent and faithful, to the full extent of their power, in the execution of the laws; commanding all citizens of the United States in said Territory to aid and assist the officers in the performance of their duties; offering to the inhabitants of Utah who shall submit to the laws a free pardon for the seditions and treasons heretofore by them committed; warning those who shall persist, after notice of this proclamation, in the present rebellion against the United States that they must expect no further lenity, but look to be rigorously dealt with according to their deserts; and declaring that the military forces now in Utah and hereafter to be sent there will not be withdrawn until the inhabitants of that Territory shall manifest a proper sense of the duty which they owe to this Government. In testimony whereof I have hereunto set my hand and caused the seal of the United States to be affixed to these presents. Done at the city of Washington the 6th day of April, 1858, and of the Independence of the United States the eighty-second. James Buchanan, By the President: Lewis Cass, Secretary of State." (Vol. 5, pp. 493-495).

On December 8, 1857, in his First Annual Message to Congress, President James Buchanan stated: A Territorial government was established for Utah by act of Congress approved the 9th September, 1850, and the Constitution and laws of the United States were thereby extended over it 'so far as the same of any provisions thereof may be applicable.' This act provided for the appointment by the President, by and with the advice and consent of the Senate, of a governor (who was to be *ex officio* superintendent of Indian affairs), a secretary, three judges of the supreme court, a marshal, and a district attorney. Subsequent acts provided for the appointment of the officers necessary to extend our land and our Indian system over the Territory. Brigham Young was appointed the first governor on the 20th September, 1850, and has held the office ever since. Whilst Governor Young has been both governor and superintendent of Indian affairs throughout this period, he has been at the same time the head of the church called the Latter-day Saints, and professes to govern its members and dispose of their property by direct inspiration and authority from the Almighty. His power has been therefore, absolute over both church and state. The people of Utah almost exclusively belong to this church, and believing with a fanatical spirit that he is governor of the Territory by divine appointment, they obey his commands as if these were direct revelations from Heaven. If, therefore, he chooses that his government shall come into collision with the Government of the United States, the members of the Mormon Church will yield implicit obedience to his will. Unfortunately, existing facts leave but little doubt that such is his determination. Without entering upon a minute history of occurrences, it is sufficient to say that all the officers of the United States, judicial and executive, with the single exception of two Indian agents, have found it necessary for their own personal safety to withdraw from the Territory, and there no longer remains any government in Utah but the despotism of Brigham Young. This being the condition of affairs in the Territory, I could not mistake the path of duty. As Chief Executive Magistrate I was bound to restore the supremacy of the Constitution and laws within its limits. In order to effect this purpose, I appointed a new governor and other Federal officers for Utah and sent with them a military force for their protection and to aid as a *posse comitatus* in case of need in the execution of laws. With the religious opinions of the Mormons, as long as they remained mere opinions, however deplorable in themselves and revolting to the moral and religious sentiments of all Christendom, I had no right to interfere. Actions alone, when in violation of the Constitution and laws of the United States, become the legitimate subjects for the jurisdiction of the civil magistrate. My instructions to Governor Cummings have therefore been framed in strict accordance with these principles. At their date a hope was indulged that no necessity might exist for employing the military in restoring and maintaining the authority of the law, but this hope has now vanished. Governor Young has by proclamation declared his determination to maintain his power by force, and has already committed acts of hostility against the United States. Unless he should retrace his steps the Territory of Utah will be in a state of open rebellion. He has committed these acts of hostility notwithstanding Major Van Vliet, an officer of the Army, sent to Utah by the Commanding General to purchase provisions for the troops, had given him the strongest assurances of the peaceful intentions of the Government, and that the troops would only be employed as a *posse comitatus* when called on by the civil authority to aid in the execution of the laws. There is reason to believe that Governor Young has long contemplated this result. He knows that the continuance of his despotic power depends upon the exclusion of all settlers from the Territory except those who will acknowledge his divine mission and implicitly obey his will, and that an enlightened public opinion there would won prostrate institutions at war with the laws both of God and man. He has therefore for several years, in order to maintain his independence, been industriously employed in collecting and fabricating arms and munitions of way and in disciplining the Mormons for military service. As superintendent of Indian affairs he has had an opportunity of tampering with the Indian tribes and exciting their hostile feelings against the United States. This, according to out information, he has accomplished in regard to some of these tribes, while others have remained true to their allegiance and have communicated his intrigues to our Indian agents. He has laid in a store of provisions for three years, which in case of necessity, as he informed Major Van Vliet, he will conceal,'and then take to the mountains and bid defiance to all powers of the Government.' A great part of all this may be idle boasting but yet no wise government will lightly estimate the efforts which may be inspired by such frenzied fanaticism as exists among the Mormon in Utah. This is the first rebellion which has existed in our Territories, and humanity itself requires that we should put it down in such a manner that it shall be the last. To trifle with it would be to encourage it and to render it formidable. We ought to go there with such an imposing force as to convince these deluded people that resistance would he vain, and thus spare the effusion of blood. We can in this manner best convince them that we are their friends, not their enemies. In order to accomplish this object it will be necessary, according to the estimated of the War Department, to raise four additional regiments, and this I earnestly recommend to Congress. At the present moment of depression in the revenues of the country I am sorry to be obliged to recommend such a measure; but I feel confident of the support of Congress, cost what it may, in suppressing the insurrection and in restoring and maintaining the sovereignty of the constitution and laws over the Territory of Utah.' (Vol. 5, pp. 454456).]

[10] **United States Supreme Court.** February 29,1892, decided, January 7,1892, submitted. Justice David Josiah Brewer, *Church of the Holy Trinity v. United States,* 143 US 457-458, 465-471, 36 L ed 226. D.P. Diffine, Ph.D., *One Nation Under God - Have Close a Separation?* (Searcy, Arkansas: Harding University, Belden Center for Private Enterprise Education, 6th edition, 1992), p. 3.

[11] **United States Supreme Court.** 1892, *Church of the Holy Trinity v. U.S.,* 143 U.S. 457, 469 (1892). David Barton *The Myth of Separation* (Aledo, TX: WallBuilder Press, 1991), p. 247.

[12] **United States Supreme Court.** A commentary on the United States Supreme Court's decision on the case *Church of the Holy Trinity v. U.S.,* 143 U.S. (1892). Robert Flood, *The Rebirth of America* (Philadelphia: Arthur S. DeMoss Foundation, 1986), p. 21. "Our Christian Heritage" *Letter from Plymouth Rock* (Marlborough, NH: The Plymouth Rock Foundation), p. 6. D. James Kennedy, *What if Jesus Had Never Been Born?* (Nashville, TN: Thomas Nelson, Inc., 1994), p. 73. Tal Brooke, *America's Waning Light* (Chicago: Moody Press, 1994), pp. 20-21.

[13] **United States Supreme Court.** 1895, in the case of *Pollock v. Farmers' Loan and Trust Co.,* 157, U.S. 429, 574 (1895), declaring income tax unconstitutional. Harold M. Groves, University of Wisconsin, *Financing Government - Revised Edition* (New York: Henry Holt and Company, Inc., 1939,1945), p. 156. John Wilson Taylor, M.A., Ph.D., et al., *The Lincoln Library of Essential Information* (Buffalo, New York: The Frontier Press Company, 1935), p. 1491. *The World Book Encyclopedia* 18 vols. (Chicago, IL: Field Enterprises, Inc., 1957; W.F. Quarrie and Company, 8 vols., 1917; World Book, Inc., 22 vols., 1989), Vol. 9, p. 3681; Vol 14, p. 7095.

[14] **United States Supreme Court.** 1895, Chief Justice Melville W. Fuller, in the case of *Pollock v. Farmers' Loan and Trust Co.,* 157, U.S. 429, 574 (1895), declaring income tax unconstitutional. Harold M. Groves, University of Wisconsin, *Financing Government - Revised Edition* (New York: Henry Holt and Company, Inc., 1939, 1945), p. 156.

[15] **United States Supreme Court.** 1895, Justice Stephen J. Field, in the case of *Pollock v. Farmers' Loan and Trust Co., 157*, U.S. 429, 574 (1895), declaring income tax unconstitutional. Harold M. Groves, University of Wisconsin, Financing

Notes

Government - Revised Edition (New York: Henry Holt and Company, Inc., 1939, 1945), p. 156.

[16] **United States Supreme Court.** 1925, *Pierce v. Society of Sisters*, 268 U.S. 510 (1925). *Reed v. van Hoven*, 237 F.Supp. 48, 51 (W.D.Mich. 1965). David Barton, *The Myth of Separation* (Aledo, TX: WallBuilder Press, 1991), p. 192.

[17] **United States Supreme Court.** 1925, in the case of *Pierce v. Society of Sisters*, 268 U.S. 510. Michael Farris, *Home School Legal Defense Association Newsletter* (Paeonian Springs, VA: Home School Legal Defense Association, February 19, 1994), p. 1. David Barton, *The Myth of Separation* (Aledo, TX: WallBuilder Press, 1991), p. 192.

[18] **United States Supreme Court.** 1931, Justice George Sutherland, (reviewing the 1892 decision), *United States v. Macintosh*, 283 U.S. 605, 625 1931. David Barton, *The Myth of Separation* (Aledo, TX: WallBuilder Press, 1991), p. 76. "Our Christian Heritage," *Letter from Plymouth Rock* (Marlborough, NH: The Plymouth Rock Foundation), p. 6.

[19] **United States Supreme Court.** 1939, *Hague v. C.I.O.*, 307 U.S. 496, 515 (1939). Jay Sekulow, *Letter to Mayors* (Virginia Beach, VA: American Center for Law and Justice, November 17, 1992), p. 1.

[20] **United States Supreme Court.** 1948, Justice Frankfurter, *McCollum v. Board of Education*, 333 U.S. 203. John Eidsmoe, *God & Caesar - Christian Faith & Political Action* (Westchester, IL: Crossway Books, a Division of Good News Publishers, 1984), pp. 140-141.

[21] **United States Supreme Court.** 1952, Justice William O. Douglas,*Zorach v. Clauson*, 343 US 306 307 312-315 (1952). Dr. Ed Rowe, *The ACLU and America's Freedom* (Washington: Church League of America, 1984), pp. 20-21. Tim LaHaye, *Faith of Our Founding Fathers* (Brentwood, TN: Wolgemuth & Hyatt, Publishers, Inc., 1987), pp. 9-10. "Our Christian Heritage," *Letter from Plymouth Rock* (Marlborough, NH: The Plymouth Rock Foundation), p. 7. David Barton, *The Myth of Separation* (Aledo, TX: WallBuilder Press, 1991), p. 77. *The Capitol: A Pictorial History of the Capitol and of the Congress* (Washington, D.C.: U.S. Government Printing Office, 1979), p. 24. Gary DeMar, *America's Christian History: The Untold Story* (Atlanta, GA: American Vision Publishers, Inc., 1993), p. 105. Keith A. Fournier, *Religious Cleansing in the American Republic* (Washington, D.C.: Liberty, Life, and Family Publications, 1993), p. 33.

[22] **United States Supreme Court.** 1962, *Engel v. Vitale*, 1962 as quoted in *Stone v. Graham*, 449 U.S. 39, 46 (1980) and *Abington v. Schempp*, 374 U.S. 203, 212 (1963). David Barton, *The Myth of Separation* (Aledo, TX: WallBuilder Press, 1991), pp. 18, 152.

[23] **United States Supreme Court.** 1963,*Abington v. Schempp*, 374 U.S. 203, 212 (1963). David Barton,*The Myth of Separation* (Aledo, TX: WallBuilder Press, 1991), p. 152.

[24] **United States Supreme Court.** 1963, *Abington v. Schempp*. "Our Christian Heritage," *Letter from Plymouth Rock* (Marlborough, NH: The Plymouth Rock Foundation), p. 7.

[25] **United States Supreme Court.** 1963, in the case of *School District of Abington Township v. Schempp*, 374 U.S. 203, 212, 225, 83 S. Ct. 1560, 10 L. Ed. 2d 844 (1963), pp. 21, 71. Bill Gothard, *Applying Basic Principles-Supplementary Alumni Book* (Oak Brook, IL: Institute of Basic Youth Conflicts, 1984), p. 3.

[26] **United States Supreme Court.** 1963, in the case of *Abington School District v. Schempp*, 374 U.S. 203, 225, 232, 300-301 (1963); Associate Justice Tom Clark writing the Court's opinion; Justice William Joseph Brennan, Jr. concurring. John Whitehead, *The Rights of Religious Persons in Public Education*, pp. 183, 187, 191, 285. Jay Sekulow, *Letter to School Superintendents* (Virginia Beach, VA: American Center for Law and Justice, November 17, 1992), p. 1. *Religion in the Public School Curriculum - Questions and Answers* (available from the Christian Legal Society, P.O. Box 1492, Merrifield, Va. 22116.), pp. 1-2.

[27] **United States Supreme Court.** 1969, *Tinker v. Des Moines Independent School District*, 393 U.S. 503, 506, 512, 513 (1969). *Special Bulletin* (Virginia Beach, VA: American Center for Law and Justice, 1993), pt. I, Graduation Prayer.

[28] **United States Supreme Court.** 1969,*Tinker v. Des Moines Independent School District*,393 U.S. 503, 506, 512, 513 (1969). *Education Newsline* (Costa Mesa, CA: National Association of Christian Educators/Citizens for Excellence in Education, May/June 1993), p. 2.

[29] **United States Supreme Court.** 1973, *Anderson v. Salt Lake City Corp*, 475 F.2d 29, 33, 34 (10th Cir. 1973), cert. denied, 414 U.S. 879. David Barton, *The Myth of Separation* (Aledo, TX: WallBuilder Press, 1991), pp. 187-188.

[30] **United States Supreme Court.** 1980, *Stone v. Graham*, 449 U.S. 39, 46 (1980). David Barton, *The Myth of Separation* (Aledo, TX: WallBuilder Press, 1991), p. 18.

[31] **United States Supreme Court.** 1980, *Stone v. Graham*, 449 U.S. 39, 42 (1980). Jay Sekulow, *Letter to School Superintendents* (Virginia Beach, VA: American Center for Law and Justice, November 17, 1992), p. 1.

[32] **United States Supreme Court.** 1981, *Widmar v. Vincent*, 454 U.S. 263, 269 (1981). Jay Sekulow,*Letter to Mayors* (Virginia Beach, VA: American Center for Law and Justice, November 17, 1992), p. 1.

[33] **United States Supreme Court.** 1982,*Chambers v. Marsh*, 675 F.2d 228, 233 (8th Cir. 1982); review allowed, 463 U.S. 783 (1982), Chief Justice Warren Earl Burger. David Barton, *The Myth of Separation* (Aledo, TX: WallBuilder Press, 1991), p. 187.

[34] **United States Supreme Court.** 1982,*Chambers v. Marsh*, 675 F.2d 228, 234 (8th Cir. 1982); review allowed, 463 U.S. 783 (1982), Chief Justice Warren Earl Burger. David Barton, *The Myth of Separation* (Aledo, TX: WallBuilder Press, 1991), p. 187.

[35] **United States Supreme Court.** 1982,*Chambers v. Marsh*, 675 F. 2d 228, 233 (8th Cir. 1982); review allowed, 463 U.S. 783 (1982), Chief Justice Warren Earl Burger. "Our Christian Heritage," *Letter from Plymouth Rock* (Marlborough, NH: The Plymouth Rock Foundation), p. 7.

[36] **United States Supreme Court.** 1982,*Chambers v. Marsh*, 675 F. 2d 228, 233 (8th Cir. 1982); review allowed, 463 U.S. 783 (1982), Chief Justice Warren Earl Burger. Tracy Everbach, *Dallas Morning News*, March 16, 1993, pp. 1A, 8A.

[37] **United States Supreme Court.** 1982,*Chambers v. Marsh*, 675 F.2d 228, 233 (8th Cir. 1982); review allowed, 463 U.S. 783 (1982), Chief Justice Warren Earl Burger. Tracy Everbach, *Dallas Morning News*, March 16, 1993, pp. 1A, 8A.

[38] **United States Supreme Court.** 1983, *United States v. Grace*, 461 U.S. 171, 177 (1983). Jay Sekulow, *Letter to Mayors* (Virginia Beach, VA: American Center for Law and Justice, November 17, 1992), p. 1.

[39] **United States Supreme Court.** 1985, *Lynch v. Donnelly*, 465 U.S. 668, 669-670, 673 (1985), Chief Justice Warren Burger. David Barton, *The Myth of Separation* (Aledo, TX: WallBuilder Press, 1991), p. 189.

[40] **United States Supreme Court.** 1985, *Lynch v. Donnelly*, 465 U.S. 668, 669-670, 673 (1985), Chief Justice Warren Burger. David Barton,*The Myth of Separation* (Aledo, TX: WallBuilder Press, 1991), p. 189. Tracy Everbach,*Dallas Morning News*, March 16, 1993, pp. 1A, 8A. John Whitehead, *The Rights of Religious Persons in Public Education*, pp. 49, 52.

[41] **United States Supreme Court.** 1985, *Wallace v. Jaffree*, 472 U.S., 38, 99. "Our Christian Heritage," *Letter from Plymouth Rock* (Marlborough, NH: The Plymouth Rock Foundation), p. 8.

[42] **United States Supreme Court.** 1986, in the case of *Bowers v. Hardwick*, 478 U.S. 186, 92 L Ed 2d 140, 106 S. Ct. 2841, p. 149, (Chief Justice Warren E. Burger). Gary DeMar, *America's Christian History: The Untold Story* (Atlanta, GA: American Vision Publishers,

Inc., 1993), p. 68.
[43] **United States Supreme Court.** 1986, in the case of *Bowers v. Hardwick*, 478 U.S. 186, 92 L Ed 2d 140, 106 S. Ct. 2841, reh den (US) 92 L Ed 2d 779, 107 S. Ct. 29. pp. 147-148 (Chief Justice Warren E. Burger). Gary DeMar, *America's Christian History: The Untold Story* (Atlanta, GA: American Vision Publishers, Inc., 1993), pp. 102-103.
[44] **United States Supreme Court.** 1990, *Westside v. Mergens*. David Barton, *The WallBuilder Report* (Aledo, TX: WallBuilder, Inc., 1993), p. 3. The American Family Association Law Center, (AFA Law Center, P.O. Drawer 2440, Tupelo, MS. 38803), has compiled a "Students Bill of Rights" guaranteed by the United States Constitution:
    1. You have the right to meet with other Christian students on campus for prayer, Bible study, and worship. The First Amendment guarantees the right of freedom of association with others.
    2. You have the right to form and meet with Bible clubs and prayer groups on campus. The U.S. Supreme has held the federal Equal Access Act gives students the right to organize and participate in Bible clubs and prayer groups, just like any other club that is not related to curriculum.
    3. You have the right to share your Christian faith on campus. The First Amendment guarantees freedom of speech, which can not be prohibited on school grounds without significant justification.
    4. You have the right to wear Christian T-shirts or symbols to express your beliefs through your clothing, jewelry, buttons, etc.
    5. You have the right to carry your Bible, and read it during unassigned reading time, on campus.
    6. You have the right to publicize the gospel or hand out tracts on campus. First Amendment free speech rights include the right to hand out literature, use school bulletin boards, school newspapers, or other methods of communication available to students.
    7. You have the right to include religious themes or points of view relevant to school projects. Nothing in the Constitution prevents the mention of religion or religious beliefs in school. In fact, religion can be legitimately studied, if the school does not try to advocate a particular faith.
    8. You have the right to study and to observe Christmas and Easter holidays on campus. These have been held to be part of the culture and heritage of our country.
    9. You have the right to voluntarily participate in prayer at school. The only prayers which have been held unconstitutionally are those which are mandatory, and initiated by the school administration. Student-led, student-initiated prayers are allowed.
    10. You have the right not to participate in activities (or possibly classes) that conflict with sincerely held religious beliefs.
[45] **United States Supreme Court.** June 4, 1990, *Westside Community Schools v. Mergens*, 496, U.S. 226, 250 (1990). *Special Bulletin* (Virginia Beach, VA: American Center for Law and Justice, 1993), pt. I. Graduation Prayer.
[46] **United States Supreme Court.** June 4, 1990, Justice O'Connor, *Westside Community Board of Education v. Mergens*, 88-1597, part. III, p. 18, 496 U.S. 248, citing *McDaniel v. Paty*, 435 U.S. 618, 641 (1978) Justice Brennan concurring in judgment. Jay Sekulow, *Letter to Mayors* (Virginia, Beach, VA: American Center for Law and Justice, November 17, 1992), p. 1.
[47] **United States Supreme Court.** June 4, 1990, Justice O'Connor, *Westside Community Board of Education v. Mergens*, 88-1597, part. III, p. 18.
[48] **United States Supreme Court.** June 4, 1990, Justice Kennedy, Justice Scalia, *Westside Community Board of Education v. Mergens*, 88-1597-CONCUR, part II, p. 4.
[49] **United States Supreme Court.** 1992, *Lee v. Weisman*, 112 S.Ct. 2649 (1992). Dissenting opinion given by Justice Antonin Scalia, joined by Chief Justice William Rehnquist, Justice Byron White and Justice Clarence Thomas. Eugene H. Methvin, "Let Us Pray" (Pleasantville, NY: *Reader's Digest*, The Reader's Digest Association, Inc., November 1992), pp. 75-79.
[50] **United States Supreme Court.** 1992, *Lee v. Weisman*, 112 S. Ct. 2649 (1992). Dissenting opinion given by Justice Antonin Scalia, joined by Chief Justice William Rehnquist, Justice Byron White and Justice Clarence Thomas. Candy Berkebile, *One Hundred Years of the Pledge* (Washington, D.C.: Family Voice, Concerned Women for America, October 1992), p. 13.
[51] **United States Supreme Court.** 1993, Justice Scalia writing the majority decision in *Jayne Bray v. Alexandria Women's Health Clinic*. Jay Alan Sekulow, "Chief Counsel's Report - For the year 1992-1993" (Virginia Beach, VA: The American Center for Law and Justice, 1993), p. 1. [note: Norma McCorvey, known as "Jane Roe" in the 1973 Supreme Court *Roe vs. Wade* decision legalizing abortion, stated in an interview on ABC's *World News Tonight*, August 10, 1995:
    "I think abortion's wrong. I think what I did with *Roe vs. Wade* was wrong. I just have to be pro-life....I just totally lost it - I thought the playgrounds are empty because there's no children, they've all been aborted." In an interview with the Dallas radio station WBAP-AM (820), Norma McCorvey stated she plans to help women "save their babies...[and] won't be doing pro-choice stuff....I'm pro-life. I think I've always been pro-life. I just didn't know it."
    Norma McCorvey, who recently quit her job as a marketing director at the Dallas abortion clinic, A Choice for Women, converted to Christianity and was baptized in a Garland swimming pool on Tuesday, August 8, 1995, by Phillip "Flip" Benham, president of the national pro-life organization *Operation Rescue*. Norma McCorvey described how one day in January, when no one was in the clinic:
    "I went into the procedure room and laid down on the table. I must have laid there maybe for 10, maybe 15 minutes, trying to imagine what it would be like having an abortion...I broke down and cried." In referring to the pro-abortion leaders, Norma McCorvey stated: "I felt like they only cared about what I could do for them, not what they could do for me."
    Jeannine Lee and Masud Khan, "'Roe' litigant's about-face: 'I'm pro-life'" (*USA Today*, a division of Gannett Co. Inc., Friday, August 11, 1995), p. 3A. Gayle Reaves, Charles Ornstein, Jeff Mosier and Monica Soto, "'Jane Roe' says views on abortion changed - McCorvey quits job at women's clinic, is baptized by Operation Rescue chief," (Dallas, TX: *The Dallas Morning News*, Communications Center, Dallas, Texas, 75265, August 11, 1995) pp. 1A, 7A. In a "Sound Off!" column entitled, "'Jane Roe' Speaks," *Dallas/Fort Worth Heritage*, (January, 1996, Vol. 4, No. 7, p. 4, Norma McCorvey stated:
    "I have a few thoughts I'd like to share. First of all, thank you Heather Hadaway, my new sister in Christ, for taking up for me, (November 1995 "Sound Off!"). Please, let's get together sometime for a Coke and Bible readings. You're the greatest! Secondly, I'd like to thank the Christian community for all your support and understanding of a "new" child in Christ Jesus. Now, to the task at hand....My heart and brain tell me you need to find the Lord Jesus Christ and ask Him into your heart. So, here goes. Number one, Dick, I'm pro-life, clear across the board. I believe all abortions are wrong. This is part of my testimony. I've never had an abortion. I was just used and lied to. And when I came out and told the world that I was Jane Roe I was scared to death. My house was even filled with gunshot blasts some years ago. I was so scared I moved out of town. Secondly, the

relationship I have with Connie Gonzales today is still with love and also with sisterhood in Christ Jesus. We were best friends first...and Jesus has shown us both the true way to walk with Him and Him alone. So with these few thoughts to ponder, Dick, if you ever need a friend to talk to or a church to go to please let me know."]

[52] **United States Supreme Court.** June 7, 1993, *Lamb's Chapel v. Center Moriches.* Jay Sekulow, *Supreme Court Case Update* (Virginia Beach, VA: American Center for Law and Justice, 1993).

[53] **United States Supreme Court.** June 7, 1993, *Lambs Chapel v. Center Moriches Union Free School District.* Steve Fitschen, "ACLJ Wins Lamb's Chapel" (Chesapeake, VA: Christian American, July\August 1993), p. 19.

[54] **United States Supreme Court.** June 7, 1993, in the case of *Lamb's Chapel v. Center Moriches Union Free School District,* from the Official Transcript. Keith A. Fournier, *Religious Cleansing in the American Republic* (Washington, D.C.: Liberty, Life, and Family Publications, 1993), p. 3.

[55] **United States Supreme Court.** June 7, 1993, Justice White, *Lamb's Chapel v. Center Moriches Union Free School District,* in a 9-0 unanimous decision, overturning a ruling by the Second U.S. Circuit Court of Appeals. Jay Alan Sekulow, "Chief Counsel's Report - For the year 1992-1993" (Virginia Beach, VA: The American Center for Law and Justice, 1993), p. 1.

[56] **United States Supreme Court.** June 7, 1993, in the case of *Lamb's Chapel v. Center Moriches Union Free School District,* Justice Scalia in his concurring opinion. Keith A. Fournier, *Religious Cleansing in the American Republic* (Washington, D.C.: Liberty, Life, and Family Publication, 1993), p. 38.

[57] **United States Supreme Court.** June 7, 1993, *Jones v. Clear Creek School District,* upholding decision of the Fifth Circuit Court of Appeals. Jay Sekulow, *Supreme Court Case Update* (Virginia Beach, VA: American Center for Law and Justice, 1993). *Student Prayer Wins A Victory At The Supreme Court* (St.Paul, MN: The Wanderer, June 17, 1993), Vol. 124, No. 24, pp. 1, 8.

[58] **United States Supreme Court.** June 7, 1993, *Jones v. Clear Creek Independent School District,* 977 F. 2d 963, 972, (5th Cir. 1992), upheld by the Supreme Court. *Special Bulletin* (Virginia Beach, VA: American Center for Law and Justice, 1993), pt. I. Graduation Prayer.

[59] **United States Supreme Court.** June 7, 1993, *Jones v. Clear Creek Independent School District,* 977 F. 2d 963, 969, 972, (5th Cir. 1992), upheld by the Supreme Court; quoting from *Westside Community Schools v. Mergens,* 496, U.S. 226, 250 (1990). *Special Bulletin* (Virginia Beach, VA: American Center for Law and Justice, 1993), pt. I. Graduation Prayer. On June 26, 1995, the United States Supreme Court continued to permit student-led prayer at graduation ceremonies by lifting a temporary ban imposed on nine western states by the San Francisco-based 9th Circuit Court of Appeals. Samuel Harris, a student, had challenged Idaho's Grangeville High School's practice of allowing student-led prayer at graduation ceremonies, but the United States Supreme Court dismissed the case as moot, thereby allowing the practice of student-led graduation prayer to continue. Associated Press, "Ban lifted on student-led graduation prayers in Idaho case" (Dallas, TX: *The Dallas Morning News,* Communications Center, Dallas, Texas, 75265, June 27, 1995), p. 4A.

[60] **United States Court of Appeals - 6th Circuit.** 1992, in the case of *Americans United for Separation of Church and State v. City of Grand Rapids,* 980 F.2d 1538, 1555. Jay Alan Sekulow, *Letter to Mayors* (Virginia Beach, VA: The American Center for Law and Justice, November 19, 1993), p. 4.

[61] **United States Court of Appeals - 7th Circuit.** 1992. *Doe v. Small,* 964 F.2d 611, 618 (7th Cir. 1992). Jay Sekulow, *Letter to Mayors* (Virginia Beach, VA: American Center for Law and Justice, November 17, 1992), p. 1.

[62] **United States Court of Appeals - 7th Circuit.** May 17, 1993. *Walsh v. Boy Scouts of America.* USA Today, May 19, 1993. *National Reports* (Reston, VA: Intercessors For America, July/August 1993), Vol. 20, No.7/8, p. 8.

[63] **United States Court of Appeals - 7th Circuit.** May 17, 1993. *Walsh v. Boy Scouts of America. Appeals Court Panel Rules Boy Scouts Can Exclude Atheists* (Chicago: United Press International, May 18, 1993). *News Reporter* (White Springs, FL: People's Network, Inc., May 31, 1993), Vol. II, No. 9, p. 4.

[64] **United States Court of Appeals - 7th Circuit.** May 17, 1993. *Walsh v. Boy Scouts of America. Appeals Court Panel Rules Boy Scouts Can Exclude Atheists* (Chicago: United Press International, May 18, 1993). *News Reporter* (White Springs, FL: People's Network, Inc., May 31, 1993), Vol. II, No. 9, p. 4.

[65] **United States Court of Appeals - 8th Circuit.** 1980. *Florey v. Sioux Falls School District,* 619 F.2d 1311, 1314 (8th Cir. 1980). Jay Sekulow, *Letter to School Superintendents* (Virginia Beach, VA: American Center for Law and Justice, November 17, 1992), p. 1.

[66] **United States Court of Appeals - 9th Circuit.** 1993, in the case of *Kreisner v. City of San Diego,* 1 F.3d 775, 785. Jay Alan Sekulow, *Letter to Mayors* (Virginia Beach, VA: The American Center for Law and Justice, November 19, 1993), p. 3.

[67] **United States Court of Appeals - 10th Circuit.** July 12, 1993, *Cannon v. City and County of Denver,* in a unanimous decision. Jay Alan Sekulow, "Chief Counsel's Report - For the year 1992-1993" (Virginia Beach, VA: The American Center for Law and Justice, 1993), pp. 2-3.

[68] **United States Court Appeals - 11th Circuit.** October 18, 1993, in the case of *Chabad - Lubavitch of Georgia v. Miller,* No. 92-8008. Jay Alan Sekulow, *Letter to Mayors* (Virginia Beach, VA: The American Center for Law and Justice, November 19, 1993), p. 3.

[69] **United States District Court.** March 18, 1992, Western District of Texas - Austin Division. United States District Judge Sam Sparks, *Word of Faith World Outreach Center Church, Inc., a Church non-profit Texas corporation, Robert G. Tilton and Martha Phillips Tilton, Plaintiffs v. Dan Morales, in his official capacity as Attorney General of the State of Texas, Defendant,* Civil No. A-92-CA-089. See also: Supreme Court of Texas, No. D-3902, Robert "Bob" Tilton (individually and [sued as allegedly] D/B/A Robert Tilton Ministries, Word of Faith World Outreach Center Church, Inc. (a dissolved corporation), and Word of Faith World Outreach Center Church, et al.) v. The Honorable Eric V. Moye Judge, January 20, 1994, On Petition for Writ of Mandamus. Justice Spector delivered the opinion of the Court, in which all Justices join:
"The Relators in this mandamus proceeding complain of a trial court order requiring production of documents in response to two separate discovery requests. As both discovery requests, we conclude that the trial court abused its discretion in ordering production....We hold that the trial court abused its discretion by ordering production of the documents at issue....Accordingly, we conditionally grant mandamus relief. - Rose Spector, Justice. Opinion Delivered: February 2, 1994."

[70] **United States District Court.** July 1993, in the case of *Black v. City of Atlanta.* Pat Robertson, (Virginia Beach, VA: The American Center of Law and Justice, July 1993), pp. 1-2.

[71] **Constitution of the United Soviet Socialist Republic.** 1922-1991, Article 124. Gary Demar, *God and Government* (Atlanta: American Vision Press, 1982), p. 163. David Barton, *The Myth of Separation* (Aledo, TX: WallBuilder Press, 1991), p. 45.

[72] **Tomb of the Unknown Soldier.** November 11, 1932, inscription on back panel. Thomas Vorwerk, *The Unknown Soldier* (Springfield, MO: Pentecostal Evangel, June 28, 1992), p. 12.

V

[1] **Cesar Vallejo.** 1939, in *Poemas Humanos, Whatever May Be the Cause,* translated by Clayton Eshleman. John Bartlett, *Bartlett's Familiar Quotations* (Boston: Little, Brown and Company, 1855, 1980), p. 824.

[2] **Martin Van Buren.** March 4, 1837, Saturday, in his Inaugural Address. James D. Richardson (U.S. Representative from Tennessee), ed., *A Compilation of the Messages and Papers of the Presidents 1789-1897*, 10 vols. (Washington, D.C.: U.S. Government Printing Office, published by Authority of Congress, 1897, 1899; Washington, D.C.: Bureau of National Literature and Art, 1789-1902, 11 vols., 1907, 1910), Vol. III, pp. 313-320. Benjamin Franklin Morris, *The Christian Life and Character of the Civil Institutions of the United States* (Philadelphia: George W. Childs, 1864), p. 604. *Inaugural Addresses of the Presidents of the United States - From George Washington 1789 to Richard Milhous Nixon 1969* (Washington, D.C.: United States Government Printing Office; 91st Congress, 1st Session, House Document 91-142, 1969), pp. 61-69. Charles E. Rice, *The Supreme Court and Public Prayer* (New York: Fordham University Press, 1964), p. 182. Stephen Abbott Northrop, D.D., *A Cloud of Witnesses* (Portland, OR: American Heritage Ministries, 1987; Mantle Ministries, 228 Still Ridge, Bulverde, Texas), p. 473. J. Michael Sharman, J.D., *Faith of the Fathers* (Culpepper, Virginia: Victory Publishing, 1995), p. 41.

[3] **Martin Van Buren.** 1862, acknowledgement made during his last illness. Benjamin Franklin Morris, *The Christian Life and Character of the Civil Institutions of the United States* (Philadelphia: George W. Childs, 1864), p. 605. Stephen Abbott Northrop, D.D., *A Cloud of Witnesses* (Portland, OR: American Heritage Ministries, 1987; Mantle Ministries, 228 Still Ridge, Bulverde, Texas), p. 473.

[4] **Sir Henry Vane.** *Knight's England*, Vol. IV, Chapter XVI, p. 260. Stephen Abbott Northrop, D.D., *A Cloud of Witnesses* (Portland, OR: American Heritage Ministries, 1987; Mantle Ministries, 228 Still Ridge, Bulverde, Texas), p. 471.

[5] **Sir Henry Vane.** Jacob Sparks, *Library of American Biography*, p. 293. Stephen Abbott Northrop, D.D., *A Cloud of Witnesses* (Portland, OR: American Heritage Ministries, 1987; Mantle Ministries, 228 Still Ridge, Bulverde, Texas), p. 471.

[6] **Henry Vaughan.** 1655, in *Silex Scintillans, The Night*, line 25. John Bartlett, *Bartlett's Familiar Quotations* (Boston: Little, Brown and Company, 1855, 1980), p. 298.

[7] **Henry Vaughan.** 1655, in *Silex Scintillans, Peace*, st. I. John Bartlett, *Bartlett's Familiar Quotations* (Boston: Little, Brown and Company, 1855, 1980), p. 299.

[8] **William Henry Venable.** In *Johnny Appleseed*, st. 25. John Bartlett, *Bartlett's Familiar Quotations* (Boston: Little, Brown and Company, 1855, 1980), p. 765.

[9] **Constitution of the State of Vermont.** Edwin Gaustad, *Faith of Our Fathers* (San Francisco: Harper & Row, 1987), pp. 173-174. Anson Phelps Stokes, *Church and State in the United States* (NY: Harper & Brothers, 1950), Vol. I, p. 441. David Barton, *The Myth of Separation* (Aledo, TX: WallBuilder Press, 1991), p. 34. Frances Newton Thorpe, ed., *Federal and State Constitutions, Colonial Charters, and Other Organic Laws of the States, Territories, and Colonies now or heretofore forming the United States*, 7 vols. (Washington: Government Printing Office, 1905; 1909; St. Clair Shores, MI: Scholarly Press, 1968). Anson Phelp Stokes and Leo Pfeffer, *Church and State in the United States*, 3 vols. (NY: Harper & Brothers, 1950), Vol. I, p. 441.

[10] **Queen Victoria.** Stephen Abbott Northrop, D.D., *A Cloud of Witnesses* (Portland, OR: American Heritage Ministries, 1987; Mantle Ministries, 228 Still Ridge, Bulverde, Texas), p. 236.

[11] **Queen Victoria.** Henry H. Halley, *Halley's Bible Handbook* (Grand Rapids, MI: Zondervan Publishing House, 1927, 1965), p. 18.

[12] **Queen Victoria.** 1849, in a letter the Queen instructed the Earl of Chichester to write the African Chieftain, Sagbua. (*London Christian World*, July 1897). Editor Stead, *Review of Reviews*, (March 1897). Stephen Abbott Northrop, D.D., *A Cloud of Witnesses* (Portland, OR: American Heritage Ministries, 1987; Mantle Ministries, 228 Still Ridge, Bulverde, Texas), p. 476.

[13] **First Charter of Virginia.** 1606, granted by King James I. *Church of the Holy Trinity v. United States*, 143 US 457, 458, 465-471, 36 L ed 226, (1892), Justice David Josiah Brewer. Henry Steele Commager, ed., *Documents of American History*, 2 vols. (NY: F.S. Crofts and Company, 1934; Appleton-Century-Crofts, Inc., 1948, 6th edition, 1958; Englewood Cliffs, NJ: Prentice Hall, Inc., 9th edition, 1973), p. 8. Gary DeMar, *God and Government - A Biblical and Historical Study* (Atlanta, GA: American Vision Press, 1984), p. 127. "Our Christian Heritage," *Letter from Plymouth* (Marlborough, NH: The Plymouth Rock Foundation), pp. 1, 6. Robert Flood, *The Rebirth of America* (Philadelphia: Arthur S. DeMoss Foundation, 1986), p. 46. David Barton, *The Myth of Separation* (Aledo, TX: WallBuilder Press, 1991), pp. 84, 47-51. Catherine Millard, *The Rewriting of America's History* (Camp Hill, PA: Horizon House Publishers, 1991). Catherine Millard, *A Children's Companion Guide to America's History* (Camp Hill, PA: Horizon House Publishers, 1993), p. 7. Gary DeMar, *America's Christian History: The Untold Story* (Atlanta, GA: American Vision Publishers, Inc., 1993), p. 37.

[14] **Colony of Virginia.** 1607. Robert Flood, *The Rebirth of America* (Philadelphia: Arthur S. DeMoss Foundation, 1986), p. 46. (Historical Marker in front of the Cross at Cape Henry, Virginia quoted the 1607 settler's original words, "Set up a cross at Chesapeake Bay, and named that place Cape Henry.") Catherine Millard, *A Children's Companion Guide to America's History* (Camp Hill, PA: Horizon House Publishers, 1993), p. 7.

[15] **Colony of Virginia.** 1607. Inscription of original 1607 Settler's testimony engraved upon the bronze *Robert Hunt Memorial*, Jamestown Island, Virginia. Catherine Millard, *The Rewriting of America's History* (Camp Hill, PA: Horizon House Publishers, 1991), p. 308. Catherine Millard, *A Children's Companion Guide to America's History* (Camp Hill, PA: Horizon House Publishers, 1993), p. 9.

[16] **Second Charter of Virginia.** May 23, 1609. William McDonald, ed., *Documentary Source Book of American History, 1606-1889* (NY: The Macmillan Company, 1909), pp. 1-2. David Barton, *The Myth of Separation* (Aledo, TX: WallBuilder Press, 1991), p. 85. "Our Christian Heritage," *Letter From Plymouth Rock* (Marlborough, NH: The Plymouth Rock Foundation), p. 1.

[17] **Second Charter of Virginia.** May 23, 1609, granted by King James I. Ebenezer Hazard, *Historical Collection: Consisting of State Papers and other Authentic Documents: Intended as Materials for an History of the United States of America* (Philadelphia: T. Dobson, 1792), Vol. I, p. 72. Perley Poore, ed., *The Federal and State Constitutions, Colonial Charters, and Other Organic Laws of the United States* (Washington, 1877), Vol. II, p. 1893 ff. Henry Steele Commager, ed., *Documents of American History*, 2 vols. (NY: F.S. Crofts and Company, 1934; Appleton-Century-Crofts, Inc., 1948, 6th edition, 1958; Englewood Cliffs, NJ: Prentice Hall, Inc., 9th edition, 1973), Vol. I, pp. 10-11. David Barton, *The Myth of Separation* (Aledo, TX: WallBuilder Press, 1992), p. 85.

[18] **Colony of Virginia.** 1613, Pocahontas, the Indian princess, who was baptized into the Christian faith, receiving the Christian name Rebekah, and married to John Rolfe. The original painting of Pocahontas, *National Portrait Gallery*, Smithsonian Institution. Historic Marker within reconstructed interior of original church, Jamestown Island, Virginia. *The World Book*

Encyclopedia, 18 vols. (Chicago, IL: Field Enterprises, Inc., 1957; W.F. Quarrie and Company, 8 vols., 1917; World Book, Inc., 22 vols., 1989), Vol. 13, pp. 6434-6435. Catherine Millard, *A Children's Companion Guide to America's History* (Camp Hill, PA: Horizon House Publishers, 1993), p. 13.

[19] **Colony of Virginia.** July 30, 1619, at the first Representative Assembly at Jamestown, recorded by James Pory, secretary of the Colony. Marker outside original Church Tower, Jamestown Island, Virginia. Association for the Preservation of Virginia Antiquities. Catherine Millard, *The Rewriting of America's History* (Camp Hill, PA: Horizon House Publishers, 1991), pp. 309-310. Catherine Millard, *A Children's Companion Guide to America's History* (Camp Hill, PA: Horizon House Publishers, 1993), p. 11.

[20] **Colony of Virginia.** December 4, 1619, in the charter of the colonists who landed at Berkeley Hundred. Jim Dwyer, ed., "Strange Stories, Amazing Facts of America's Past" (Pleasantville, NY: *Reader's Digest*, The Reader's Digest Association, Inc., 1989), p. 189. Gary DeMar, *America's Christian History: The Untold Story* (Atlanta, GA: American Vision Publishers, Inc., 1993), p. 16.

[21] **Colony of Virginia.** March 22, 1622. Marker within reconstructed interior of original church, Jamestown Island, Virginia. Catherine Millard, *The Rewriting of America's History* (Camp Hill, PA: Horizon House Publishers, 1991), p. 311.

[22] **Colony of Virginia.** "Our Christian Heritage," *Letter from Plymouth Rock* (Marlborough, NH: The Plymouth Rock Foundation), p. 2.

[23] **Virginia Bill of Rights.** July 12, 1776; 1830; 1851; 1868; 1902; 1928, Bill of Rights, Article I, Section 16. Frances Newton Thorpe, ed., *Federal and State Constitutions, Colonial Charters, and Other Organic Laws of the States, Territories, and Colonies now or heretofore forming the United States*, 7 vols. (Washington: Government Printing Office, 1905; 1909; St. Clair Shores, MI: Scholarly Press, 1968), Vol. VII, p. 3814. Benjamin Franklin Morris, *The Christian Life and Character of the Civil Institutions of the United States* (Philadelphia, PA: L. Johnson & Co., 1863; George W. Childs, 1864), p. 232. Henry Steele Commager, ed., *Documents of American History*, 2 vols. (NY: F.S. Crofts and Company, 1934; Appleton-Century-Crofts, Inc., 1948, 6th edition, 1958; Englewood Cliffs, NJ: Prentice Hall, Inc., 9th edition, 1973), pp. 103-104. Charles Fadiman, ed., *The American Treasury* (NY: Harper & Brothers, Publishers, 1955), p. 121. Charles E. Rice, *The Supreme Court and Public Prayer* (New York: Fordham University Press, 1964), pp. 175-176; "Hearings, Prayers in Public Schools and Other Matters," Committee on the Judiciary, U.S. Senate (87th Cong., 2nd Sess.), 1962, pp. 268 et seq. *The Annals of America*, 20 vols. (Chicago, IL: Encyclopedia Britannica, 1968), Vol. 2, p. 433. Pat Robertson, *America's Dates with Destiny* (Nashville: Thomas Nelson Publishers, 1986), pp. 80-81. "Our Christian Heritage," *Letter form Plymouth Rock* (Marlborough, NH: The Plymouth Rock Foundation), p. 3. Catherine Millard, *The Rewriting of America's History* (Camp Hill, PA: Horizon House Publishers, 1991), p. 145. Stephen McDowell and Mark Beliles, "The Providential Perspective" (Charlottesville, VA: The Providence Foundation, P.O. Box 6759, Charlottesville, Va. 22906, January 1994), Vol. 9, No. 1, p. 2. Edwin S. Gaustad, *Neither King nor Prelate - Religion and the New Nation, 1776-1826* (Grand Rapids, MI: William B. Eerdmans Publishing Company, 1993), p. 174.

[24] **Virginia Statute of Religious Liberty.** January 16, 1786. H.A. Washington, ed., *The Writings of Thomas Jefferson - Being His Autobiography, Correspondence, Reports, Messages, Addresses, and Other Writings, Official and Private*, 9 vols. (NY: Derby & Jackson, 1859, Washington, 1853-1854. Vol. 8, Philadelphia, 1871), Vol. VIII, pp. 454-456. Benjamin Franklin Morris, *The Christian Life and Character of the Civil Institutions of the United States* (Philadelphia, PA: L. Johnson & Co., 1863; George W. Childs, 1864), p. 232. William Taylor Thom, *The Struggle for Religious Freedom in Virginia - The Baptists*, Johns Hopkins Studies in Historical and Political Science, Herbert B. Adams, ed., (Baltimore: Johns Hopkins, 1900), p. 79. *The Annals of America*, 20 vols. (Chicago, IL: Encyclopedia Britannica, 1968), Vol. 3, p. 53. Norman Cousins, *In God We Trust - The Religious Beliefs and Ideas of the American Founding Fathers* (NY: Harper & Brothers, 1958), p. 124. Pat Robertson, *America's Dates with Destiny* (Nashville: Thomas Nelson Publishers, 1986), p. 83. "Our Christian Heritage," *Letter from Plymouth Rock* (Marlborough, NH: The Plymouth Rock Foundation), p. 4. Stephen McDowell and Mark Beliles, "The Providential Perspective" (Charlottesville, VA: The Providence Foundation, P.O. Box 6759, Charlottesville, Va. 22906, January 1994), Vol. 9, No. 1, p. 2.

[25] **State of Virginia.** March 13, 1994, the State of Virginia issued an Executive Proclamation declaring March 13 - March 19, 1994, as "Christian Heritage Week," signed by Governor George Allen and the Secretary of State Betsy Davis Beamer. Courtesy of Bruce Barilla, Christian Heritage Week Ministry (P.O. Box 58, W.V. 24712; 304-384-7707, 304-384-9044 fax).

W

[1] **Wyandot Indian, William Walker.** 1833, in a letter to the *"Christian Advocate & Journal."* Huston Horn, *The Pioneers, The Old West.* (Alexandria, VA: Time'Life Books, 1974), p. 49. Peter Marshall and David Manuel, *The Glory of America* (Bloomington, MN: Garborg's Heart 'N Home, Inc., 1991), 4.23.

[2] **Lewis "Lew" Wallace.** February 2, 1893. "How I came to Write 'Ben Hur'" (Youth Companion). Stephen Abbott Northrop, D.D., *A Cloud of Witnesses* (Portland, Oregon: American Heritage Ministries, 1987; Mantle Ministries, 228 Still Ridge, Bulverde, Texas), pp. 480-481.

[3] **William Ross Wallace.** In *The Hand That Rules the World*, st. I. John Bartlett, *Bartlett's Familiar Quotations* (Boston: Little, Brown and Company, 1855, 1980), p. 573.

[4] **John Wanamaker.** Gordon MacClennon - Pastor of Bethany Presbyterian Church in Philadelphia, *Prayers of John Wanamaker.* Catherine Millard, *The Rewriting of America's History* (Camp Hill, PA: Horizon House Publishers, 1991), p. 276.

[5] **John Wanamaker.** Gordon MacClennon - Pastor of Bethany Presbyterian Church in Philadelphia, *Prayers of John Wanamaker.* Catherine Millard, *The Rewriting of America's History* (Camp Hill, PA: Horizon House Publishers, 1991), pp. 277-278.

[6] **John Wanamaker.** Tryon Edwards, D.D., *The New Dictionary of Thoughts - A Cyclopedia of Quotations* (Garden City, NY: Hanover House, 1852; revised and enlarged by C.H. Catrevas, Ralph Emerson Browns and Jonathan Edwards [descendent, along with Tryon, of Jonathan Edwards (1703-1758), president of Princeton], 1891; The Standard Book Company, 1955, 1963), p. 47.

[7] **John Wanamaker.** July 9-11, 1889, in an address at the Eighth Annual Conference of the Young People's Society of Christian Endeavor. Stephen Abbott Northrop, D.D., *A Cloud of Witnesses* (Portland, OR: American Heritage Ministries, 1987; Mantle Ministries, 228 Still Ridge, Bulverde, Texas), pp. 481-482.

[8] **Anna Bartlett Warner.** 1858, in *The Love of Jesus.* John Bartlett, *Bartlett's Familiar Quotations* (Boston: Little, Brown and Company, 1855, 1980), p. 599.

[9] **James Warren.** June 16, 1775, in a Resolution of the Provincial Congress of Massachusetts, James Warren, president. Copied from original, printed courtesy Essex Institute, Salem, Massachusetts. Verna M. Hall, *The Christian History of the American Revolution* (San Francisco, CA: Foundation For American Christian Education, 1976), p. 410.

[10] **Booker Taliaferro Washington.** Bob Cutshall, *More Light for the Day* (Minneapolis, MN: Northwestern Products, Inc., 1991), 1.20. Perry Tanksley, *To Love is to Give* (Jackson, Mississippi: Allgood Books, Box 1329; Parthenon Press, 201 8th Ave., South, Nashville, Tennessee, 1972), p. 43.

[11] **George Washington.** 1745. *110 Rules of Civility and Decent Behavior in Company and Conversation* (copied in his own handwriting at the age of 15) (Bedford, MA: Apple Books, 1988, distributed by The Globe Pequot Press, Chester, CT.), p. 30. Moncure D. Conway, *George Washington's Rules of Civility* (1890), pp. 178, 180. William J. Johnson, *George Washington - The Christian* (St. Paul, MN: William J. Johnson, Merriam Park, February 23, 1919; Nashville, TN: Abingdon Press, 1919; reprinted Milford, MI: Mott Media, 1976; reprinted Arlington Heights, IL: Christian Liberty Press, 502 West Euclid Avenue, Arlington Heights, Illinois, 60004, 1992), p. 20. Catherine Millard, *The Rewriting of America's History* (Camp Hill, PA: Horizon House Publishers, 1991), p. 60.

[12] **George Washington.** November 1753, in his parting words from his mother, Mrs. Mary Washington. John N. Norton, *Life of General Washington* (1870), p. 34. Marion Harland, *The Story of Mary Washington* (1892), p. 87. William J. Johnson, *George Washington - The Christian* (St. Paul, MN: William J. Johnson, Merriam Park, February 23, 1919; Nashville, TN: Abingdon Press, 1919; reprinted Milford, MI: Mott Media, 1976; reprinted Arlington Heights, IL: Christian Liberty Press, 502 West Euclid Avenue, Arlington Heights, Illinois, 60004, 1992), p. 36. Peter Marshall and David Manuel, *The Light and the Glory* (Old Tappan, NJ: Fleming H. Revell Company, 1977), p. 285.

[13] **George Washington.** July 18, 1755. George Washington, in a letter to his brother. Jared Sparks, ed., *The Writings of George Washington* 12 vols. (Boston: American Stationer's Company, 1837, NY: F. Andrew's, 1834-1847), Vol. II, p. 89. Joseph Banvard, *Tragic Scenes in the History of Maryland and the Old French War* (Boston: Gould and Lincoln, 1856), p. 153. *George Washington, Programs and Papers* (Washington: U.S. George Washington Bicentennial Commission, 1932), p. 33. William J. Johnson, *George Washington - The Christian* (St. Paul, MN: William J. Johnson, Merriam Park, February 23, 1919; Nashville, TN: Abingdon Press, 1919; reprinted Milford, MI: Mott Media, 1976; reprinted Arlington Heights, IL: Christian Liberty Press, 502 West Euclid Avenue, Arlington Heights, Illinois, 60004, 1992), p. 40. John F. Schroeder, ed., *Maxims of Washington* (Mt. Vernon: Mt. Vernon Ladies' Association, 1942), p. 275. Tim LaHaye, *Faith of Our Founding Fathers* (Brentwood, TN: Wolgemuth & Hyatt, Publishers, Inc., 1987), pp. 102-104. David Barton, *The Bulletproof George Washington* (Aledo, TX: WallBuilder Press, 1990), p. 47.

[14] **George Washington.** 1770. George Washington Parke Custis, *Recollections and Private Memoirs of Washington*, Benson J. Lossing, editor, (1860), p. 303; narrative, told by Dr. Craik to Mr. George Washington Parke Custis, first published in 1828. [Mr. George Washington Parke Custis (1781-1857), was the son of John Parke Custis, and the grandson of Daniel Parke and Martha Dandridge Custis. After Daniel Parke Custis' death, George Washington married Martha in 1759. After Martha's son, John Parke Custis, died November 5, 1781, of a violent case of campfever while serving as an aide-de-camp during the siege of Yorktown, George Washington, who had no children of his own, adopted the fatherless children, Eleanor Parke "Nellie" Custis and George Washington Parke Custis, as his own. They lived at Mount Vernon with George and Martha Washington as their children. Mr. George Washington Parke Custis, who was nineteen years old when George Washington died, lived to the age of 77 and is considered one of the most reliable authorities on George Washington's private life. He later built a mansion, which stands on the site of the present Arlington National Cemetery; and in 1831, his daughter, Mary Ann Randolph Custis, married a young West Point graduate, by the name of Robert E. Lee. Lee's father was the Revolutionary War hero, "Light-Horse Harry" Lee, who authored the famous epitaph of George Washington, "First in war, first in peace, first in the hearts of his countrymen."] William J. Johnson, *George Washington - The Christian* (St. Paul, MN: William J. Johnson, Merriam Park, February 23, 1919; Nashville, TN: Abingdon Press, 1919; reprinted Milford, MI: Mott Media, 1976; reprinted Arlington Heights, IL: Christian Liberty Press, 502 West Euclid Avenue, Arlington Heights, Illinois, 60004, 1992), pp. 41-42. Peter Marshall and David Manuel, *The Light and the Glory* (Old Tappan, NJ: Fleming H. Revell Company, 1977), p. 285-286. David Barton, *The Bulletproof George Washington* (Aledo, TX: WallBuilder, Inc., Winter, 1993), pp. 50-51. Denise Williamson, "Wilderness Fight" (Colorado Springs, CO: Focus on the Family Clubhouse, July 1994), p. 14; referencing the testimony of Billy Brown, who in 1825, at the age of 93 recounted the incident with a historian.

[15] **George Washington.** 1770. David Barton, *The Bulletproof George Washington* (Aledo, TX: WallBuilder, Inc., Winter, 1993), p. 49.

[16] **George Washington.** June 1, 1774, in an entry in his diary. E.C. M'guire, *The Religious Opinions and Character of Washington* (1836), p. 142. (E.C. M'Guire was the son-in-law of Mr. Robert Lewis, Washington's nephew and private secretary.) William J. Johnson, *George Washington - The Christian* (St. Paul, MN: William J. Johnson, Merriam Park, February 23, 1919; Nashville, TN: Abingdon Press, 1919; reprinted Milford, MI: Mott Media, 1976; reprinted Arlington Heights, IL: Christian Liberty Press, 502 West Euclid Avenue, Arlington Heights, Illinois, 60004, 1992), p. 62. John Eidsmoe, *Christianity and The Constitution - The Faith of Our Founding Fathers* (Baker Book House, 1987), p. 136. Catherine Millard, *The Rewriting of America's History* (Camp Hill, PA: Horizon House Publishers, 1991), p. 73.

[17] **George Washington.** July 4, 1775, in his General Orders from the Headquarters at Cambridge. Jared Sparks, ed., *The Writings of George Washington* 12 vols. (Boston: American Stationer's Company, 1837, NY: F. Andrew's, 1834-1847), Vol. III, p. 491. William J. Johnson, *George Washington - The Christian* (St. Paul, MN: William J. Johnson, Merriam Park, February 23, 1919; Nashville, TN: Abingdon Press, 1919; reprinted Milford, MI: Mott Media, 1976; reprinted Arlington Heights, IL: Christian Liberty Press, 502 West Euclid Avenue, Arlington Heights, Illinois, 60004, 1992), pp. 69-70. John Clement Fitzpatrick, ed., *The Writings of George Washington, from the Original Manuscript Sources 1749-1799*, 39 vols. (Washington, D.C.: United States Government Printing Office, 1931-1944), Vol. III, p. 309. William Barclay Allen, ed., *George Washington - A Collection* (Indianapolis: Liberty Classics, Liberty Fund, Inc., 7440 N. Shadeland, Indianapolis, Indiana 46250, 1988; based almost entirely on materials reproduced from *The Writings of George Washington from the original manuscript sources, 1745-1799*/John Clement Fitzpatrick, editor), pp. 42-43. Norman Cousins, *In God We Trust - The Religious Beliefs and Ideas of the American Founding Fathers* (NY: Harper & Brothers, 1958), p. 50. Peter Marshall and David Manuel, *The Light and the Glory* (Old Tappan, NJ: Fleming H. Revell Company, 1977), p. 289. Saxe Commins, ed., *The Basic Writings of George Washington* (NY: Random House, 1948), p. 122. *The American Vision - 360 Years Later* (Atlanta, GA: The American Vision, Inc., 1980), p. 10-11. John Eidsmoe, *Christianity and the Constitution - The Faith of Our Founding Fathers* (Grand Rapids, MI: Baker Book House, A Mott Media Book, 1987, 6th printing 1993), p. 116. Peter Marshall & David Manuel, *The Glory of America* (Bloomington, MN: Garborg's Heart 'N Home, 1991), p. 7.5.

[18] **George Washington.** July 20, 1775, in the general orders to the troops under his command. *Orderly Book*. Elizabeth Bryant Johnston, *George Washington, Day by Day* (1894), p. 107. William J. Johnson, *George Washington - The Christian* (St. Paul, MN: William J. Johnson, Merriam Park, February 23, 1919; Nashville, TN: Abingdon Press, 1919; reprinted Milford, MI: Mott Media,

Notes

1976; reprinted Arlington Heights, IL: Christian Liberty Press, 502 West Euclid Avenue, Arlington Heights, Illinois, 60004, 1992), pp. 69-70. Peter Marshall and David Manuel, *The Light and the Glory* (Old Tappan, NJ: Fleming H. Revell Company, 1977), p. 289. John Eidsmoe, *Christianity and the Constitution - The Faith of Our Founding Fathers* (Grand Rapids, MI: Baker Book House, A Mott Media Book, 1987, 6th printing 1993), p. 116.

[19] **George Washington.** Inscription on Washington's Cruisers. U.S. Marine Corps, *How to Respect & Display Our Flag* (Washington: U.S. Government Printing Office, 1977), pp. 11, 16.

[20] **George Washington.** July 2, 1776, from his Head Quarters in New York the General Orders were issued to his troops. Jared Sparks, ed., *The Writings of George Washington* 12 vols. (Boston: American Stationer's Company, 1837, NY: F. Andrew's, 1834-1847), Vol. III, p. 449. John Bartlett, *Bartlett's Familiar Quotations* (Boston: Little, Brown and Company, 1863, 1980), p. 379. William J. Johnson, *George Washington - The Christian* (St. Paul, MN: William J. Johnson, Merriam Park, February 23, 1919; Nashville, TN: Abingdon Press, 1919; reprinted Milford, MI: Mott Media, 1976; reprinted Arlington Heights, IL: Christian Liberty Press, 502 West Euclid Avenue, Arlington Heights, Illinois, 60004, 1992), p. 82. William Barclay Allen, ed., *George Washington - A Collection* (Indianapolis: Liberty Classics, Liberty Fund, Inc., 7440 N. Shadeland, Indianapolis, Indiana 46250, 1988; based almost entirely on materials reproduced from *The Writings of George Washington from the original manuscript sources, 1745-1799*/John Clement Fitzpatrick, editor), p. 71. John Clement Fitzpatrick, ed., *The Writings of George Washington, from the Original Manuscript Sources 1749-1799*, 39 vols. (Washington, D.C.: United States Government Printing Office, 1931-1944). Henry Steele Commager and Richard B. Morris, ed., *Spirit of '76* (New York: The Bobbs - Merrill Co., Inc., 1958), p. 32. Peter Marshall and David Manuel, *The Glory of America* (Bloomington, MN: Garborg's Heart'N Home, Inc., 1991), 11.18.

[21] **George Washington.** July 9, 1776; previously $20.00 a month, approved July 1775. *American Army Chaplaincy - A Brief History* (prepared in the Office of the Chief of Chaplains: 1946), p. 6. Anson Phelps Stokes and Leo Pfeffer, *Church and State in the United States* (NY: Harper and Row, Publishers, 1950, revised one-volume edition, 1964), p. 35. John Clement Fitzpatrick, ed., *The Writings of George Washington, from the Original Manuscript Sources 1749-1799*, 39 vols. (Washington, D.C.: United States Government Printing Office, 1931-1944), Vol. V, pp. 244-245. David Barton, *The Myth of Separation* (Aledo, TX: WallBuilder Press, 1991), p. 104. "Our Christian Heritage," *Letter from Plymouth Rock* (Marlborough, NH: The Plymouth Rock Foundation), p. 3.

[22] **George Washington.** July 9, 1776, order issued to the army in response to the reading of the Declaration of Independence by the Continental Congress. Jared Sparks, ed., *The Writings of George Washington* 12 vols. (Boston: American Stationer's Company, 1837; NY: F. Andrew's, 1834-1847), Vol. XII, p. 401, citing *Orderly Book*; also orders of August 3, 1776, in ibid., IV, 28 n. Abraham Lincoln quoted this order of Washington's on November 15, 1862, to have his troops maintain regular sabbath observances. Abraham Lincoln, *Letters and Addresses and Abraham Lincoln* (NY: Unit Book Publishing Co., 1907), p. 261. William J. Johnson, *George Washington - The Christian* (St. Paul, MN: William J. Johnson, Merriam Park, February 23, 1919; Nashville, TN: Abingdon Press, 1919; reprinted Milford, MI: Mott Media, 1976; reprinted Arlington Heights, IL: Christian Liberty Press, 502 West Euclid Avenue, Arlington Heights, Illinois, 60004, 1992), p. 83. John Clement Fitzpatrick, ed., *The Writings of George Washington, from the Original Manuscript Sources 1749-1799*, 39 vols. (Washington, D.C.: United States Government Printing Office, 1931-1944), Vol. V, p. 245. William Barclay Allen, ed., *George Washington - A Collection* (Indianapolis: Liberty Classics, Liberty Fund, Inc., 7440 N. Shadeland, Indianapolis, Indiana 46250, 1988; based almost entirely on materials reproduced from *The Writings of George Washington from the original manuscript sources, 1745-1799*/John Clement Fitzpatrick, editor), p. 73. John Clement Fitzpatrick, ed., *The Writings of George Washington, from the Original Manuscript Sources 1749-1799*, 39 vols. (Washington, D.C.: United States Government Printing Office, 1931-1944). John F. Schroeder, ed., *Maxims of Washington* (Mt. Vernon: Mt. Vernon Ladies' Association, 1942), p. 299. Saxe Commins, ed., *The Basic Writings of George Washington* (NY: Random House, 1948), p. 236. Anson Phelps Stokes and Leo Pfeffer, *Church and State in the United States* (NY: Harper and Row, Publishers, 1950, revised one-volume edition, 1964), p. 35. Norman Cousins, *In God We Trust - The Religious Beliefs and Ideas of the Founding Fathers* (NY: Harper & Brothers, 1958), p. 50. Paul F. Boller, Jr., *George Washington and Religion* (Dallas: Southern Methodist University Press, 1963), p. 69. Frank Donovan, *Mr. Jefferson's Declaration* (New York: Dodd Mead & Co., 1968), p. 192. A. James Reichley, *Religion in American Public Life* (Washington, D.C.: The Brookings Institute, 1985), p. 99. John Eidsmoe, *Christianity and The Constitution - The Faith of Our Founding Fathers* (Grand Rapids, MI: Baker Book House, A Mott Media Book, 1987, 6th printing 1993), pp. 120-121. Tim LaHaye, *Faith of Our Founding Fathers* (Brentwood, TN: Wolgemuth & Hyatt, Publishers, Inc., 1987), p. 108. David Barton, *The Myth of Separation* (Aledo, TX: WallBuilder Press, 1991), p. 98.

[23] **George Washington.** August 27, 1776. John Fiske, *The American Revolution*, 2 vols. (Boston and New York: Houghton, Mifflin & Co., 1898), Vol. I, p. 212. Marshall Foster and Mary-Elaine Swanson, *The American Covenant - The Untold Story* (Roseburg, OR: Foundation for Christian Self-Government, 1981; Thousand Oaks, CA: The Mayflower Institute, 1983, 1992), p. 41. Peter Marshall and David Manuel, *The Light and the Glory* (Old Tappan, NJ: Fleming H. Revell Company, 1977), pp. 312-316.

[24] **George Washington.** August 27, 1776. John Fiske, *The American Revolution*, 2 vols. (Boston and New York: Houghton, Mifflin & Co., 1898), Vol. I, p. 212. Marshall Foster and Mary-Elaine Swanson, *The American Covenant - The Untold Story* (Roseburg, OR: Foundation for Christian Self-Government, 1981; Thousand Oaks, CA: The Mayflower Institute, 1983, 1992), p. 41. George F. Scheer & Hugh F. Rankin, *Rebels and Redcoats* (New York: The World Publishing Co., 1957), p. 171. Peter Marshall and David Manuel, *The Light and the Glory* (Old Tappan, NJ: Fleming H. Revell Company, 1977), p. 315.

[25] **George Washington.** In a letter written from Valley Forge to John Banister, dated April 21, 1778. William Barclay Allen, ed., *George Washington - A Collection* (Indianapolis: Liberty Classics, Liberty Fund, Inc., 7440 N. Shadeland, Indianapolis, Indiana 46250, 1988; based almost entirely on materials reproduced from *The writings of George Washington from the original manuscript sources, 1745-1799*/John Clement Fitzpatrick, editor), p. 103. John Clement Fitzpatrick, ed., *The Writings of George Washington, from the Original Manuscript Sources 1749-1799*, 39 vols. (Washington, D.C.: United States Government Printing Office, 1931-1944). Douglas S. Freeman, *George Washington - A Biography* vols. I-VII (New York: Charles Scribner's Sons, 1948), Vol. IV, p. 621. Peter Marshall and David Manuel, *The Light and the Glory* (Old Tappan, NJ: Fleming H. Revell Company, 1977), p. 322.

[26] **George Washington.** Winter of 1777, *Washington's Prayer at Valley Forge* as observed by Isaac Potts, recounted by Ruth Anna Potts. William Herbert Burk, D.D., *The Washington Window in the Washington Memorial Chapel of Valley Forge*, p. 25. Catherine Millard, *The Rewriting of America's History* (Camp Hill, PA: Horizon House Publishers, 1991), pp. 73-74. William J. Johnson, *George Washington - The Christian* (St. Paul, MN: William J. Johnson, Merriam Park, February 23, 1919; Nashville, TN: Abingdon Press, 1919; reprinted Milford, MI: Mott Media, 1976; reprinted Arlington Heights, IL: Christian Liberty Press, 502 West Euclid Avenue, Arlington Heights, Illinois, 60004, 1992), pp. 102-107. Peter Marshall and David Manuel, *The Light and the Glory* (Old Tappan, NJ: Fleming H. Revell Company, 1977), p. 323. J.T. Headly, *The Illustrated Life of Washington*, pp. 307-308. Stephen Abbott Northrop, D.D., *A Cloud of Witnesses* (Portland, OR: American Heritage Ministries, 1987; Mantle Ministries, 228 Still

Ridge, Bulverde, Texas), pp. 487-488. Mason Locke Weems, *The Life of George Washington; with Curious Anecdotes, Equally Honourable to Himself, and Exemplary to His Young Countrymen* (Cambridge, Massachusetts: Belknap Press of Harvard University Press, 1800, 1809 edition; reprinted 1962), pp. 181-182: "In the winter of '77, while Washington, with the American army lay encamped at Valley Forge, a certain good old friend, of the respectable family and name of Potts, if I mistake not, had occasion to pass through the woods near headquarters. Treading his way along the venerable grove, suddenly he heard the sound of a human voice, which as he advanced increased on his ear, and at length became like the voice of one speaking much in earnest. As he approached the spot with a cautious step, whom should he behold, in a dark natural bower of ancient oak, but the commander in chief of the American armies on his knees at prayer! Motionless with surprise, friend Potts continued on the place till the general, having ended his devotions, arose, and with a countenance of angel serenity, retired to headquarters: friend Potts then went home, and on entering his parlour called out to his wife, 'Sarah, my dear! All's well! all's well! George Washington will yet prevail!' "'What's the matter, Isaac?' replied she; 'thee seems moved.' "'Well, if I seem moved, 'tis no more than what I am. I have this day seen what I never expected. Thee knows that I always thought the sword and the gospel utterly inconsistent; and that no man could be a soldier and a Christian at the same time. But George Washington has this day convinced me of my mistake.' "He then related what he had seen, and concluded with this prophetical remark - 'If George Washington be not a man of God, I am greatly deceived - and still more shall I be deceived if God does not, through him, work out a great salvation for America.'" Rev. E.C. M'Guire (son-in-law of Mr. Robert Lewis, the nephew and private secretary of Washington), *The Religious Opinions and Character of Washington* (1836), pp. 158-159: records that in 1832, Devault Beaver, who was 80 years old, claimed to have received the account directly from Isaac Potts; Dr. James Ross Snowden, whose father was Isaac Potts, gave a similar account; Benson J. Lossing also gave a confirming account; General Knox, Washington's associate at Valley Forge, mentioned that Washington frequently used a grove in the area for prayer. Theodore Wm. John Wylie, *Washington - A Christian* (1862), pp. 28-29. Benjamin J. Lossing, *The Pictorial Field-Book of the Revolution*, 2 vols. (1860), Vol. II, p. 130. John Eidsmoe, *Christianity and the Constitution - The Faith of Our Founding Fathers* (Grand Rapids, MI: Baker Book House, A Mott Media Book, 1987, 6th printing 1993), pp. 113-114. Peter Marshall & David Manuel, *The Glory of America* (Bloomington, MN: Garborg's Heart 'N Home, 1991), 3.1.

[27] **George Washington.** Theodore G. Tappert and John W. Doberstern, trans. and ed., Henry Melchior Muhlenberg, *The Notebook of a Colonial Clergyman* (Philadelphia: Fortress Press, 1975), p. 195. Peter Marshall and David Manuel, *The Light and the Glory* (Old Tappan, NJ: Fleming H. Revell Company, 1977), p. 323.

[28] **George Washington.** 1775, in a sermon by John Peter Muhlenberg on Ecclesiastes 3:1. *The World Book Encyclopedia*, 18 vols. (Chicago, IL: Field Enterprises, Inc., 1957; W.F. Quarrie and Company, 8 vols., 1917; World Book, Inc., 22 vols., 1989), Vol. 11, p. 5324. Peter Marshall and David Manuel, *The Glory of America* (Bloomington, MN: Garborg's Heart'N Home, Inc., 1991), 6.25.

[29] **George Washington.** John Joseph Stoudt, *Ordeal at Valley Forge* (Philadelphia: University of Pennsylvania, 1963), p. 146. Peter Marshall and David Manuel, *The Light and the Glory* (Old Tappan, NJ: Fleming H. Revell Company, 1977), p. 325.

[30] **George Washington.** March 10, 1778. *The Writings of George Washington - Bicentennial Edition* (March 1 through May 31, 1778, 11:83-84, published by the U.S. Government Printing Office, 1934. Howard Phillips, *The Howard Phillips Issues and Strategy Bulletin* (March 31, 1993, Vienna, Virginia 22182). Gary DeMar, *The Biblical Worldview* (Atlanta, GA: An American Vision Publication - American Vision, Inc., May 1993), Vol. 9, No. 5, p. 8. John Clement Fitzpatrick, ed., *The Writings of George Washington, from the Original Manuscript Sources 1749-1799*, 39 vols. (Washington, D.C.: United States Government Printing Office, 1931-1944), Vol. XI, p. 83-84.

[31] **George Washington.** May 2, 1778, orders issued to his troops at Valley Forge. George Washington, *General Orders* (Mount Vernon, VA: Archives of Mount Vernon). Henry Whiting, *Revolutionary Orders of General Washington, selected from MSS. of John Whiting* (1844), p. 74. Benson J. Lossing, *The Pictorial Field-Book of the Revolution* (1886), Vol. II, p. 140. John Clement Fitzpatrick, ed., *The Writings of George Washington, from the Original Manuscript Sources 1749-1799*, 39 vols. (Washington, D.C.: United States Government Printing Office, 1931-1944), Vol. XI, p. 343. William J. Johnson, *George Washington - The Christian* (St. Paul, MN: William J. Johnson, Merriam Park, February 23, 1919; Nashville, TN: Abingdon Press, 1919; reprinted Milford, MI: Mott Media, 1976; reprinted Arlington Heights, IL: Christian Liberty Press, 502 West Euclid Avenue, Arlington Heights, Illinois, 60004, 1992), p. 112. Norman Cousins, *In God We Trust - The Religious Beliefs and Ideas of the Founding Fathers* (NY: Harper & Brothers, 1958), p. 51. David Barton, *The Myth of Separation* (Aledo, TX: WallBuilder Press, 1991), p. 95. Peter Marshall & David Manuel, *The Glory of America* (Bloomington, MN: Garborg's Heart 'N Home, 1991), 9.5. Catherine Millard, *The Rewriting of America's History* (Camp Hill, PA: Horizon House Publishers, 1991), p. 60. D.P. Diffine, Ph.D., *One Nation Under God - How Close a Separation?* (Searcy, Arkansas: Harding University, Belden Center for Private Enterprise Education, 6th edition, 1992), p. 8.

[32] **George Washington.** May 5, 1778, orders issued from the headquarters at Valley Forge upon receiving intelligence that France had joined the War on the side of the Colonies. Henry Whiting, *Revolutionary Orders of General Washington, selected from MSS. of John Whiting* (1844), p. 77. William J. Johnson, *George Washington - The Christian* (St. Paul, MN: William J. Johnson, Merriam Park, February 23, 1919; Nashville, TN: Abingdon Press, 1919; reprinted Milford, MI: Mott Media, 1976; reprinted Arlington Heights, IL: Christian Liberty Press, 502 West Euclid Avenue, Arlington Heights, Illinois, 60004, 1992), pp. 112-113. Charles E. Kistler, *This Nation Under God* (Boston: Richard G. Badger, The Gorham Press, 1924), pp. 74-75. Peter Marshall and David Manuel, *The Light and the Glory* (Old Tappan, NJ: Fleming H. Revell Company, 1977), p. 326.

[33] **George Washington.** August 20, 1778, in a letter to Thomas Nelson in Virginia. Jared Sparks, ed., *The Writings of George Washington* 12 vols. (Boston: American Stationer's Company, 1837; NY: F. Andrew's, 1834-1847), Vol. VI, p. 36. William J. Johnson, *George Washington - The Christian* (St. Paul, MN: William J. Johnson, Merriam Park, February 23, 1919; Nashville, TN: Abingdon Press, 1919; reprinted Milford, MI: Mott Media, 1976; reprinted Arlington Heights, IL: Christian Liberty Press, 502 West Euclid Avenue, Arlington Heights, Illinois, 60004, 1992), pp. 119-120. John Clement Fitzpatrick, ed., *The Writings of George Washington, from the Original Manuscript Sources 1749-1799*, 39 vols. (Washington, D.C.: United States Government Printing Office, 1931-1944), Vol. XII, p. 343. Saxe Commins, ed., *The Basic Writings of George Washington* (NY: Random House, 1948), p. 332. Norman Cousins, *In God We Trust - The Religious Beliefs and Ideas of the American Founding Fathers* (NY: Harper & Brothers, 1958), p. 54. Paul F. Boller, Jr., *George Washington and Religion* (Dallas: Southern Methodist University, 1963), p. 106. Edmund Fuller, and David E. Green, *God in the White House - The Faiths of American Presidents* (NY: Crown Publishers, Inc., 1968), p. 14. John Eidsmoe, *Christianity and The Constitution - The Faith of Our Founding Fathers* (Baker Book House, 1987), p. 137. Catherine Millard, *The Rewriting of America's History* (Camp Hill, PA: Horizon House Publishers, 1991), p. 61. David Barton, *The Myth of Separation* (Aledo, TX: WallBuilder Press, 1991), p. 99. "Our Christian Heritage," *Letter from Plymouth Rock* (Marlborough, NH: The Plymouth Rock Foundation), p. 4. Peter Marshall and David Manuel, *The Light and the Glory* (Old Tappan, NJ: Fleming H.

Revell Company, 1977), p. 332.

34 George Washington. May 12, 1779, from his "Address to Delaware Chiefs Indian Chiefs," John Clement Fitzpatrick, ed., *The Writings of George Washington from the Original Manuscript Sources: 1749-1799*, 39 vols. (Washington, DC: Bureau of National Literature and Art, 1907), 1:64. John Clement Fitzpatrick, ed., *The Writings of George Washington, from the Original Manuscript Sources 1749-1799*, 39 vols. (Washington, D.C.: United States Government Printing Office, 1931-1944), Vol. XV, p. 55. William Barclay Allen, ed., *George Washington - A Collection* (Indianapolis: Liberty Classics, Liberty Fund, Inc., 7440 N. Shadeland, Indianapolis, Indiana 46250, 1988; based almost entirely on materials reproduced from *The Writings of George Washington from the original manuscript sources, 1745-1799/*John Clement Fitzpatrick, editor), pp. 132-133. Saxe Commins, ed., *The Basic Writings of George Washington* (NY: Random House, 1948), p. 356. Norman Cousins, *In God We Trust - The Religious Beliefs and Ideas of the American Founding Fathers* (NY: Harper & Brothers, 1958), p. 51. Paul F. Boller, Jr., *George Washington and Religion* (Dallas: Southern Methodist University Press, 1963), p. 68. John Eidsmoe, *Christianity and the Constitution - The Faith of Our Founding Fathers* (Grand Rapids, MI: Baker Book House, A Mott Media Book, 1987, 6th printing 1993), p. 120. David Barton, *The Myth of Separation* (Aledo, TX: WallBuilder Press, 1991), pp. 92, 158. Gary DeMar, *The Biblical Worldview* (Atlanta, GA: An American Vision Publication - American Vision, Inc., 1992), Vol. 8, No. 12, p. 8. Gary DeMar, *America's Christian History: The Untold Story* (Atlanta, GA: American Vision Publishers, Inc., 1993), p. 76. Stephen McDowell and Mark Beliles, "The Providential Perspective" (Charlottesville, VA: The Providence Foundation, P.O. Box 6759, Charlottesville, Va. 22906, January 1994), Vol. 9, No. 1, p. 8.

35 George Washington. June 1779, near his headquarters on the Hudson River, in a private prayer. E.C. M'guire, *The Religious Opinions and Character of Washington* (1836), pp. 162-167. (E.C. M'Guire was the son-in-law of Mr. Robert Lewis, Washington's nephew and private secretary.) William J. Johnson, *George Washington - The Christian* (St. Paul, MN: William J. Johnson, Merriam Park, February 23, 1919; Nashville, TN: Abingdon Press, 1919; reprinted Milford, MI: Mott Media, 1976; reprinted Arlington Heights, IL: Christian Liberty Press, 502 West Euclid Avenue, Arlington Heights, Illinois, 60004, 1992), pp. 126-127. Stephen Abbott Northrop, D.D., *A Cloud of Witnesses* (Portland, OR: American Heritage Ministries, 1987; Mantle Ministries, 228 Still Ridge, Bulverde, Texas), p. 484.

36 George Washington. June 1780. W.P. Breed, *Presbyterians and the Revolution* (Philadelphia: Presbyterian Board of Publication, 1876), pp. 80-82. Peter Marshall and David Manuel, *The Light and the Glory* (Old Tappan, NJ: Fleming H. Revell Company, 1977), p. 291. Milton Hadley, *Great Americans and Their Noble Deeds* (San Antonio, TX; Mantle Ministries, 1992, originally published 1901).

37 George Washington. September 26, 1780, Tuesday, in his General Orders from his headquarters in Orangetown. John Clement Fitzpatrick, ed., *The Writings of George Washington, from the Original Manuscript Sources 1749-1799*, 39 vols. (Washington, D.C.: United States Government Printing Office, 1931-1944), Vol. XX, pp. 94-95. Saxe Commins, ed., *The Basic Writings of George Washington* (NY: Random House, 1948), p. 410. Richard Wheeler, *Voices of 1776* (Greenwich: Fawcett Premier Book, 1972), p. 382. Peter Marshall and David Manuel, *The Light and the Glory* (Old Tappan, NJ: Fleming H. Revell Company, 1977), pp. 328-329. David Barton, *The Myth of Separation* (Aledo, TX: WallBuilder Press, 1991), p. 105.

38 George Washington. February 13, 1781, in a report from British Commander-in-Chief Henry Clinton. William Hosmer, *Remember our Bicentennial - 1781* (Foundation for Christian Self-Government Newsletter - June 1981), p. 5. Marshall Foster and Mary-Elaine Swanson, *The American Covenant - The Untold Story* (Roseburg, OR: Foundation for Christian Self-Government, 1981; Thousand Oaks, CA: The Mayflower Institute, 1983, 1992), p. 166.

39 George Washington. October 20, 1781, in an order to his troops after the capitulation of Yorktown. Horace W. Smith, *Orderly Book of the Siege of Yorktown* (1865), p, 47. William J. Johnson, *George Washington - The Christian* (St. Paul, MN: William J. Johnson, Merriam Park, February 23, 1919; Nashville, TN: Abingdon Press, 1919; reprinted Milford, MI: Mott Media, 1976; reprinted Arlington Heights, IL: Christian Liberty Press, 502 West Euclid Avenue, Arlington Heights, Illinois, 60004, 1992), p. 134. William Barclay Allen, ed., *George Washington - A Collection* (Indianapolis: Liberty Classics, Liberty Fund, Inc., 7440 N. Shadeland, Indianapolis, Indiana 46250, 1988; based almost entirely on materials reproduced from *The Writings of George Washington from the original manuscript sources, 1745-1799/*John Clement Fitzpatrick, editor), p. 198. John Clement Fitzpatrick, ed., *The Writings of George Washington, from the Original Manuscript Sources 1749-1799*, 39 vols. (Washington, D.C.: United States Government Printing Office, 1931-1944). Peter Marshall and David Manuel, *The Light and the Glory* (Old Tappan, NJ: Fleming H. Revell Company, 1977), p. 332.

40 George Washington. November 15, 1781, in a letter written from Mount Vernon to the President of the Continental Congress, Thomas McKean. John Clement Fitzpatrick, ed., *The Writings of George Washington, from the Original Manuscript Sources 1749-1799*, 39 vols. (Washington, D.C.: United States Government Printing Office, 1931-1944), Vol. 23, p. 343. William Hosmer, *Remember our Bicentennial - 1781* (Foundation for Christian Self-Government Newsletter - June 1981), p. 5. Marshall Foster and Mary-Elaine Swanson, *The American Covenant - The Untold Story* (Roseburg, OR: Foundation for Christian Self-Government, 1981; Thousand Oaks, CA: The Mayflower Institute, 1983, 1992), pp. 150, 167. Jared Sparks, ed., *The Writings of George Washington* 12 vols. (Boston: American Stationer's Company, 1837, NY: F. Andrew's, 1834-1847), ed., Vol. VIII, p. 207. William J. Johnson, *George Washington - The Christian* (St. Paul, MN: William J. Johnson, Merriam Park, February 23, 1919; Nashville, TN: Abingdon Press, 1919; reprinted Milford, MI: Mott Media, 1976; reprinted Arlington Heights, IL: Christian Liberty Press, 502 West Euclid Avenue, Arlington Heights, Illinois, 60004, 1992), pp. 133-136.

41 George Washington. June 14, 1783, in a "Circular Letter Addressed to the Governors of all the States on Disbanding the Army." *Old South Leaflets*, No. 51. Jared Sparks, ed., *The Writings of George Washington* 12 vols. (Boston: American Stationer's Company, 1837, NY: F. Andrew's, 1834-1847), Vol. VIII, pp. 440, 444, 452. Selim Peabody, ed., *American Patriotism: Speeches, Letters, and Other Papers Which Illustrate the Foundation, the Development, the Preservation of the United States of America* (NY: American Book Exchange, 1880), p. 142. William J. Johnson, *George Washington - The Christian* (St. Paul, MN: William J. Johnson, Merriam Park, February 23, 1919; Nashville, TN: Abingdon Press, 1919; reprinted Milford, MI: Mott Media, 1976; reprinted Arlington Heights, IL: Christian Liberty Press, 502 West Euclid Avenue, Arlington Heights, Illinois, 60004, 1992), pp. 139-141. John Clement Fitzpatrick, ed., *The Writings of George Washington, from the Original Manuscript Sources 1749-1799*, 39 vols. (Washington, D.C.: United States Government Printing Office, 1931-1944), Vol. 26, p. 483-496. William Barclay Allen, ed., *George Washington - A Collection* (Indianapolis: Liberty Classics, Liberty Fund, Inc., 7440 N. Shadeland, Indianapolis, Indiana 46250, 1988; based almost entirely on materials reproduced from *The Writings of George Washington from the original manuscript sources, 1745-1799/*John Clement Fitzpatrick, editor), pp. 240, 241, 249. Saxe Commins, ed., *The Basic Writings of George Washington* (NY: Random House, 1948), p. 493. Norman Cousins, *In God We Trust - The Religious Beliefs and Ideas of the American Founding Fathers*

(NY: Harper & Brothers, 1958), p. 55. *The Annals of America*, 20 vols. (Chicago, IL: Encyclopedia Britannica, 1968), Vol. 2, p. 60. David Barton, *The Myth of Separation* (Aledo, TX: WallBuilder Press, 1991), p. 99. D.P. Diffine, Ph.D., *One Nation Under God - How Close a Separation?* (Searcy, Arkansas: Harding University, Belden Center for Private Enterprise Education, 6th edition, 1992), p. 8. Stephen McDowell and Mark Beliles, "The Providential Perspective" (Charlottesville, VA: The Providence Foundation, P.O. Box 6759, Charlottesville, Va. 22906, January 1994), Vol. 9, No. 1, p. 4.

[42] **George Washington.** June 8, 1783, original source of prayer is the concluding paragraph in Washington's farewell circular letter sent to the governors of the thirteen states from his headquarters in Newburgh, New York. This version is used at Pohick Church, Fairfax County, Virginia, where Washington was a vestryman from 1762-1784. It also appears on a plaque in St. Paul's Chapel in New York City. Tim LaHaye, *Faith of Our Founding Fathers* (Brentwood, TN: Wolgemuth & Publishers, Inc., 1987), pp. xi-xii. John F. Schroeder, ed., *Maxims of Washington* (Mt. Vernon: Mt. Vernon Ladies' Associations, 1942), p. 299. Tim LaHaye, *Faith of Our Founding Fathers* (Brentwood, TN: Wolgemuth & Hyatt, Publishers, Inc., 1987), pp. 108-109.

[43] **George Washington.** December 23, 1783, from the Maryland Capitol at Annapolis, in an address to Congress regarding the official resignation of his military commission. Jared Sparks, ed., *The Writings of George Washington* 12 vols. (Boston: American Stationer's Company, 1837, NY: F. Andrew's, 1834-1847), Vol. VIII, p. 504-505. William Herbert Burk, D.D., *The Washington Window in the Washington Memorial Chapel of Valley Forge*, p. 27. William J. Johnson, *George Washington - The Christian* (St. Paul, MN: William J. Johnson, Merriam Park, February 23, 1919; Nashville, TN: Abingdon Press, 1919; reprinted Milford, MI: Mott Media, 1976; reprinted Arlington Heights, IL: Christian Liberty Press, 502 West Euclid Avenue, Arlington Heights, Illinois, 60004, 1992), pp. 144-145. William Barclay Allen, ed., *George Washington - A Collection* (Indianapolis: Liberty Classics, Liberty Fund, Inc., 7440 N. Shadeland, Indianapolis, Indiana 46250, 1988; based almost entirely on materials reproduced from *The Writings of George Washington from the original manuscript sources, 1745-1799* / John Clement Fitzpatrick, editor), pp. 272-273. John Clement Fitzpatrick, ed., *The Writings of George Washington, from the Original Manuscript Sources 1749-1799*, 39 vols. (Washington, D.C.: United States Government Printing Office, 1931-1944). John F. Schroeder, ed., *Maxims of Washington* (Mt. Vernon: Mt. Vernon Ladies' Association, 1942), pp. 280-281. Saxe Commins, ed., *The Basic Writings of George Washington* (NY: Random House, 1948), complete work, pp. 503-504. Tim LaHaye, *Faith of Our Founding Fathers* (Brentwood, TN: Wolgemuth & Hyatt, Publishers, Inc., 1987), p. 105. John Eidsmoe, *Christianity and the Constitution - The Faith of Our Founding Fathers* (Grand Rapids, MI: Baker Book House, A Mott Media Book, 1987, 6th printing 1993), p. 117. Catherine Millard, *The Rewriting of America's History* (Camp Hill, PA: Horizon House Publishers, 1991), p. 72.

[44] **George Washington.** May 25, 1787, in his opening remarks to the delegates of the Constitutional Convention. Elizabeth Bryant Johnston, *George Washington, Day by Day* (1894), p. 70. William J. Johnson, *George Washington - The Christian* (St. Paul, MN: William J. Johnson, Merriam Park, February 23, 1919; Nashville, TN: Abingdon Press, 1919; reprinted Milford, MI: Mott Media, 1976; reprinted Arlington Heights, IL: Christian Liberty Press, 502 West Euclid Avenue, Arlington Heights, Illinois, 60004, 1992), p. 152. Charles Fadiman, ed., *The American Treasury* (NY: Harper & Brothers, Publishers, 1955), p. 323. *The Annals of America*, 20 vols. (Chicago, IL: Encyclopedia Britannica, 1968), Vol. 3, p. 121. Marshall Foster and Mary-Elaine Swanson, *The American Covenant - The Untold Story* (Roseburg, OR: Foundation for Christian Self-Government, 1981; Thousand Oaks, CA: The Mayflower Institute, 1983, 1992), p. 42.

[45] **George Washington.** July 20, 1787, in a letter to Joseph Rakestraw. Original in the Archives of Mount Vernon, Virginia. John Clement Fitzpatrick, ed., *The Writings of George Washington, from the Original Manuscript Sources 1749-1799*, 39 vols. (Washington, D.C.: United States Government Printing Office, 1931-1944), Vol. 29, p. 250. Catherine Millard, *The Rewriting of America's History* (Camp Hill, PA: Horizon House Publishers, 1991), pp. 67-68. Catherine Millard, *A Children's Companion Guide to America's History* (Camp Hill, PA: Horizon House Publishers, 1993), p. 53.

[46] **George Washington.** June 29, 1788, in a letter written from Mount Vernon to Benjamin Lincoln. John Clement Fitzpatrick, ed., *The Writings of George Washington, from the Original Manuscript Sources 1749-1799*, 39 vols. (Washington, D.C.: United States Government Printing Office, 1931-1944), Vol. X, p. 11. William Barclay Allen, ed., *George Washington - A Collection* (Indianapolis: Liberty Classics, Liberty Fund, Inc., 7440 N. Shadeland, Indianapolis, Indiana 46250, 1988; based almost entirely on materials reproduced from *The Writings of George Washington from the original manuscript sources, 1745-1799* / John Clement Fitzpatrick, editor), pp. 403-404. Peter Marshall and David Manuel, *The Glory of America* (Bloomington, MN: Garborg's Heart'N Home, Inc., 1991), 6.30.

[47] **George Washington.** July 20, 1788, in a letter written from Mount Vernon to the Governor of Connecticut, Jonathan Trumbull. Jared Sparks, ed., *The Writings of George Washington* 12 vols. (Boston: American Stationer's Company, 1837; NY: F. Andrew's, 1834-1847), Vol. IX, p. 397. William J. Johnson, *George Washington - The Christian* (St. Paul, MN: William J. Johnson, Merriam Park, February 23, 1919; Nashville, TN: Abingdon Press, 1919; reprinted Milford, MI: Mott Media, 1976; reprinted Arlington Heights, IL: Christian Liberty Press, 502 West Euclid Avenue, Arlington Heights, Illinois, 60004, 1992), pp. 152-153. John Clement Fitzpatrick, ed., *The Writings of George Washington, from the Original Manuscript Sources 1749-1799*, 39 vols. (Washington, D.C.: United States Government Printing Office, 1931-1944), Vol. XXX, p. 21. William Barclay Allen, ed., *George Washington - A Collection* (Indianapolis: Liberty Classics, Liberty Fund, Inc., 7440 N. Shadeland, Indianapolis, Indiana 46250, 1988; based almost entirely on materials reproduced from *The Writings of George Washington from the original manuscript sources, 1745-1799* / John Clement Fitzpatrick, editor), p. 412. Peter Marshall and David Manuel, *The Glory of America* (Bloomington, MN: Garborg's Heart'N Home, Inc., 1991), 7.20.

[48] **George Washington.** October 1781, Mary Washington's response to the news of the war ending. Rosalie J. Slater, *Reflective Education: The Principle Approach* (San Francisco, CA: Principly Speaking, The Foundation for American Christian Education, November 1992), Vol. 2, No. 3, p. 2.

[49] **George Washington.** April 14, 1789, in his final visit with his mother, as recorded by George Washington's adopted son, George Washington Parke Custis. (George Washington Parke Custis was the son of John Parke Custis, who was the son of Mrs. Washington before her first husband died. He was adopted by George Washington at six months old when his father died shortly after Cornwallis' surrender at Yorktown. He lived at Mount Vernon with the Washingtons as their son. George Washington Parke Custis was nineteen years old when George Washington died, and then lived to the age of seventy-seven, 1857.) William Herbert Burk, D.D., *The Washington Window in the Washington Memorial Chapel of Valley Forge*, p. 36. Benson J. Lossing, *The Pictorial Field-Book of the Revolution*, 2 vols. (1860), Vol. II, p. 220. William J. Johnson, *George Washington - The Christian* (St. Paul, MN: William J. Johnson, Merriam Park, February 23, 1919; Nashville, TN: Abingdon Press, 1919; reprinted Milford, MI: Mott Media, 1976; reprinted Arlington Heights, IL: Christian Liberty Press, 502 West Euclid Avenue, Arlington Heights, Illinois, 60004, 1992), pp. 156-157. Catherine Millard, *The Rewriting of America's History* (Camp Hill, PA: Horizon House

Notes

Publishers, 1991), p. 71.
[50] **George Washington.** April 23, 1789, article in the newspaper, *Daily Advertiser*. Benjamin Franklin Morris, *The Christian Life and Character of the Civil Institutions of the United States* (Philadelphia: George W. Childs, 1864), p. 272. David Barton, *The Myth of Separation* (Aledo, TX: WallBuilder Press, 1991), p. 112.
[51] **George Washington.** April 27, 1789, prior to the Inauguration of President George Washington. *Annals of Congress*, 1789-1791 (Washington, D.C: Gales & Seaton, 1843), Vol. I, p. 25. David Barton, *The Myth of Separation* (Aledo, TX: WallBuilder Press, 1991), p. 112.
[52] **George Washington.** April 30, 1789, following President George Washington's Inauguration. *Annals of Congress*, 1789-1791 (Washington, D.C.: Gales & Seaton, 1843), Vol. I, p. 29. David Barton, *The Myth of Separation* (Aledo, TX: WallBuilder Press, 1991), p. 113.
[53] **George Washington.** April 30, 1789, in his Oath of Office and Inaugural Address. Charles W. Eliot, LL.D., ed., *American Historical Documents 1000-1904* (New York: P.F. Collier & Son Company,*The Harvard Classics*, 1910), Vol. 43, pp. 241-245. Charles E. Kistler, *This Nation under God* (Boston: Richard G. Badger, The Gorham Press, 1924), p. 97. William J. Johnson, *George Washington - The Christian* (St. Paul, MN: William J. Johnson, Merriam Park, February 23, 1919; Nashville, TN: Abingdon Press, 1919; reprinted Milford, MI: Mott Media, 1976; reprinted Arlington Heights, IL: Christian Liberty Press, 502 West Euclid Avenue, Arlington Heights, Illinois, 60004, 1992), pp. 161-162. Peter Marshall and David Manuel, *The Light and the Glory* (Old Tappan, NJ: Fleming H. Revell Company, 1977), p. 349. John W. Whitehead, *The Separation Illusion* (Milford, MI: Mott Media, 1977), p. 123. Deuteronomy 28. Gary DeMar, *God and Government* (Atlanta, GA: American Vision Press, 1984), p. 170. Tim LaHaye, *Faith of Our Founding Fathers* (Brentwood, TN: Wolgemuth & Hyatt, Publishers, Inc., 1987), pp. 63-64. Genesis 49:22-25a. Catherine Millard, *A Children's Companion Guide to America's History* (Camp Hill, PA: Horizon House Publishers, 1993), p. 47. John Eidsmoe, *Christianity and the Constitution - The Faith of Our Founding Fathers* (Baker Book House, 1987), p. 117. *The World Book Encyclopedia* 22 vols. (Chicago, IL: Field Enterprises Educational Corporation, 1976; Field Enterprises, Inc., 1957; W.F. Quarrie and Company, 8 vols., 1917), Vol. 21, p. 79. Edmund Fuller and David E. Green, *God in the White House - The Faiths of American Presidents* (NY: Crown Publishers, Inc., 1968), p. 15. Lucille Johnston, *Celebrations of a Nation* (Arlington, VA: The Year of Thanksgiving Foundation, 1987), p. 142. Pat Robertson, *America's Dates with Destiny* (Nashville: Thomas Nelson Publishers, 1986), p. 102.
[54] **George Washington.** April 30, 1789, Thursday, in his First Inaugural Address. National Archives, Original work and facsimile, (complete text), No. 22 (Washington: 1952). Jared Sparks, ed., *The Writings of George Washington* 12 vols. (Boston: American Stationer's Company, 1837, NY: F. Andrew's, 1834-1847), Vol. XII, pp. 2-5. James D. Richardson (U.S. Representative from Tennessee), ed., *A Compilation of the Messages and Papers of the Presidents 1789-1897*, 10 vols. (Washington, D.C.: U.S. Government Printing Office, published by Authority of Congress, 1897, 1899; Washington, D.C.: Bureau of National Literature and Art, 1789-1902, 11 vols., 1907, 1910), Vol. 1, pp. 52-53. *Inaugural Addresses of the Presidents of the United States - From George Washington 1789 to Richard Milhous Nixon 1969* (Washington, D.C.: United States Government Printing Office; 91st Congress, 1st Session, House Document 91-142, 1969), pp. 1-4. Charles W. Eliot, LL.D., ed.,*American Historical Documents 1000-1904* (New York: P.F. Collier & Son Company, *The Harvard Classics*, 1910), Vol. 43, pp. 241-245. William J. Johnson, *George Washington - The Christian* (St. Paul, MN: William J. Johnson, Merriam Park, February 23, 1919; Nashville, TN: Abingdon Press, 1919; reprinted Milford, MI: Mott Media, 1976; reprinted Arlington Heights, IL: Christian Liberty Press, 502 West Euclid Avenue, Arlington Heights, Illinois, 60004, 1992), pp. 161-162. John Clement Fitzpatrick, ed., *The Writings of George Washington, from the Original Manuscript Sources 1749-1799*, 39 vols. (Washington, D.C.: United States Government Printing Office, 1931-1944), Vol. 30, pp. 291-296. William Barclay Allen, ed., *George Washington - A Collection* (Indianapolis: Liberty Classics, Liberty Fund, Inc., 7440 N. Shadeland, Indianapolis, Indiana 46250, 1988; based almost entirely on materials reproduced from *The Writings of George Washington from the original manuscript sources, 1745-1799* / John Clement Fitzpatrick, editor), pp. 460-463. John F. Schroeder, ed., *Maxims of Washington* (Mt. Vernon: Mt. Vernon Ladies' Association, 1942), pp. 287-288. Saxe Commins, ed., *The Basic Writings of George Washington* (NY: Random House, 1948), complete work, pp. 599-602. Frederick C. Packard, Jr., ed., *Are You an American? - Great Americans Speak* (NY: Charles Scribner's Sons, 1951), pp. 14-18. Paul M. Angle, ed., *By These Words* (NY: Rand McNally & Company, 1954), pp. 128-131. Davis Newton Lott, *The Inaugural Addresses of the American Presidents* (NY: Holt, Rinehart and Winston, 1961), p. 3-5. Charles E. Rice,*The Supreme Court and Public Prayer* (New York: Fordham University Press, 1964), p. 177-178. Daniel Boorstin, Jr., ed.,*An American Primer* (Chicago: The University of Chicago Press, 1966), complete work, pp. 172-174. Henry Steele Commager, ed., *Documents of American History*, 2 vols. (NY: F.S. Crofts and Company, 1934; Appleton-Century-Crofts, Inc., 1948, 6th edition, 1958; Englewood Cliffs, NJ: Prentice Hall, Inc., 9th edition, 1973), Vol. I, pp. 152-154. Gary DeMar,*God and Government, A Biblical and Historical Study* (Atlanta, GA: American Vision Press, 1984), p. 127-28. Pat Robertson, *America's Dates With Destiny* (Nashville, TN: Thomas Nelson Publishers, 1986), p. 104. Tim LaHaye,*Faith of Our Founding Fathers* (Brentwood, TN: Wolgemuth & Hyatt, Publishers, Inc., 1987), pp. 63-64, 107. John Eidsmoe, *Christianity and the Constitution - The Faith of Our Founding Fathers* (Grand Rapids, MI: Baker Book House, A Mott Media Book, 1987, 6th printing 1993), pp. 117, 123. David Barton, *The Myth of Separation* (Aledo, TX: WallBuilder Press, 1991), p. 113. "Our Christian Heritage," *Letter from Plymouth Rock* (Marlborough, NH: The Plymouth Rock Foundation), p. 4. D.P. Diffine, Ph.D.,*One Nation Under God - How Close a Separation?* (Searcy, Arkansas: Harding University, Belden Center for Private Enterprise Education, 6th edition, 1992), p. 2. J. Michael Sharman, J.D., *Faith of the Fathers* (Culpepper, Virginia: Victory Publishing, 1995), pp. 18-19.
[55] **George Washington.** In a message to a gathering of Episcopal Church. Paul F. Boller, Jr., *George Washington and Religion* (Dallas: Southern Methodist University Press, 1963), pp. 163-194. John Eidsmoe, *Christianity and the Constitution - The Faith of Our Founding Fathers* (Grand Rapids, MI: Baker Book House, A Mott Media Book, 1987, 6th printing 1993), p. 121.
[56] **George Washington.** May 10, 1789, in addressing the General Committee of the United Baptist Churches of Virginia. Jared Sparks, ed., *The Writings of George Washington* 12 vols. (Boston: American Stationer's Company, 1837; NY: F. Andrew's, 1834-1847), Vol. XII, p. 154. Charles F. James, *Documentary History of the Struggle for Religious Liberty in Virginia* (1899, reprint, New York: Da Capo, 1971), p. 173. William J. Johnson,*George Washington - The Christian* (St. Paul, MN: William J. Johnson, Merriam Park, February 23, 1919; Nashville, TN: Abingdon Press, 1919; reprinted Milford, MI: Mott Media, 1976; reprinted Arlington Heights, IL: Christian Liberty Press, 502 West Euclid Avenue, Arlington Heights, Illinois, 60004, 1992), pp. 164-166. John Clement Fitzpatrick, ed.,*The Writings of George Washington, from the Original Manuscript Sources 1749-1799*, 39 vols. (Washington, D.C.: United States Government Printing Office, 1931-1944), Vol. XXX, p. 321 n. William Barclay Allen, ed., *George Washington - A Collection* (Indianapolis: Liberty Classics, Liberty Fund, Inc., 7440 N. Shadeland, Indianapolis, Indiana 46250, 1988; based almost entirely on materials reproduced from The writings of George Washington from the original manuscript sources, 1745-

1799/John Clement Fitzpatrick, editor), pp. 531-532. Saul Padover, ed., *The Washington Papers* (New York: Harper and Bros., 1955), pp. 410-411. Paul F. Boller, Jr., *George Washington and Religion* (Dallas: Southern Methodist University Press, 1963), pp. 169-170. Pat Robertson, *America's Dates With Destiny* (Nashville, TN: Thomas Nelson Publishers, 1986), pp. 111-112. John Eidsmoe, *Christianity and the Constitution - The Faith of Our Founding Fathers* (Grand Rapids, MI: Baker Book House, A Mott Media Book, 1987, 6th printing 1993), pp. 122, 124. Tim LaHaye, *Faith of Our Founding Fathers* (Brentwood, TN: Wolgemuth & Hyatt, Publishers, Inc., 1987), pp. 108-109. David Barton, *The Myth of Separation* (Aledo, TX: WallBuilder Press, 1991), pp. 113, 144.

[57] **George Washington.** May 29, 1789, in a letter to the Bishop of the Methodist Episcopal Church of New York. Jared Sparks, ed., *The Writings of George Washington* 12 vols. (Boston: American Stationer's Company, 1837; NY: F. Andrew's, 1834-1847), Vol. XII, p. 153. William J. Johnson, *George Washington - The Christian* (St. Paul, MN: William J. Johnson, Merriam Park, February 23, 1919; Nashville, TN: Abingdon Press, 1919; reprinted Milford, MI: Mott Media, 1976; reprinted Arlington Heights, IL: Christian Liberty Press, 502 West Euclid Avenue, Arlington Heights, Illinois, 60004, 1992), pp. 163-164. John F. Schroeder, ed., *Maxims of Washington* (Mt. Vernon: Mt. Vernon Ladies' Association, 1942), p. 302. Norman Cousins, *In God We Trust - The Religious Beliefs and Ideas of the Founding Fathers* (NY: Harper & Brothers, 1958), p. 59. Tim LaHaye, *Faith of Our Founding Fathers* (Brentwood, TN: Wolgemuth & Hyatt, Publishers, Inc., 1987), p. 108.

[58] **George Washington.** In writing to the Directors of the Society of the United Brethren for Propagating the Gospel among the Heathen. Jared Sparks, ed., *The Writings of George Washington* 12 vols. (Boston: American Stationer's Company, 1837; NY: F. Andrew's, 1834-1847), Vol. XII, p. 160. William J. Johnson, *George Washington - The Christian* (St. Paul, MN: William J. Johnson, Merriam Park, February 23, 1919; Nashville, TN: Abingdon Press, 1919; reprinted Milford, MI: Mott Media, 1976; reprinted Arlington Heights, IL: Christian Liberty Press, 502 West Euclid Avenue, Arlington Heights, Illinois, 60004, 1992), pp. 168-169. Paul F. Boller, Jr., *George Washington and Religion* (Dallas: Southern Methodist University Press, 1963), pp. 163-194. John Eidsmoe, *Christianity and the Constitution - The Faith of Our Founding Fathers* (Grand Rapids, MI: Baker Book House, A Mott Media Book, 1987, 6th printing 1993), p. 121.

[59] **George Washington.** October of 1789, in an address to the Quakers at their annual meeting for Pennsylvania, New Jersey, Delaware, and the western part of Virginia and Maryland. *Old South Leaflets.* William Barclay Allen, ed., *George Washington - A Collection* (Indianapolis: Liberty Classics, Liberty Fund, Inc., 7440 N. Shadeland, Indianapolis, Indiana 46250, 1988; based almost entirely on materials reproduced from *The Writings of George Washington from the original manuscript sources, 1745-1799/* John Clement Fitzpatrick, editor), pp. 533-534. John Clement Fitzpatrick, ed., *The Writings of George Washington, from the Original Manuscript Sources 1749-1799,* 39 vols. (Washington, D.C.: United States Government Printing Office, 1931-1944). Saul Padover, ed., *The Washington Papers* (New York: Harper and Bros., 1955), pp. 410-411. Paul F. Boller, Jr., *George Washington and Religion* (Dallas: Southern Methodist University Press, 1963), pp. 179-180. John Eidsmoe, *Christianity and the Constitution - The Faith of Our Founding Fathers* (Grand Rapids, MI: Baker Book House, A Mott Media Book, 1987, 6th printing 1993), p. 123. Tim LaHaye, *Faith of Our Founding Fathers* (Brentwood, TN: Wolgemuth & Hyatt, Publishers, Inc., 1987), pp. 108-109. Stephen McDowell and Mark Beliles, "The Providential Perspective" (Charlottesville, VA: The Providence Foundation, P.O. Box 6759, Charlottesville, Va. 22906, January 1994), Vol. 9, No. 1, p. 3.

[60] **George Washington.** October 3, 1789, from the city of New York, President issued a Proclamation of a National Day of Thanksgiving. Jared Sparks, ed., *The Writings of George Washington* 12 vols. (Boston: American Stationer's Company, 1837, NY: F. Andrew's, 1834-1847), Vol. XII, p. 119. James D. Richardson (U.S. Representative from Tennessee), ed., *A Compilation of the Messages and Papers of the Presidents 1789-1897,* 10 vols. (Washington, D.C.: U.S. Government Printing Office, published by Authority of Congress, 1897, 1899; Washington, D.C.: Bureau of National Literature and Art, *1789-1902,* 11 vols., 1907, 1910), Vol. 1, p. 64. William J. Johnson, *George Washington - The Christian* (St. Paul, MN: William J. Johnson, Merriam Park, February 23, 1919; Nashville, TN: Abingdon Press, 1919; reprinted Milford, MI: Mott Media, 1976; reprinted Arlington Heights, IL: Christian Liberty Press, 502 West Euclid Avenue, Arlington Heights, Illinois, 60004, 1992), pp. 172-174. William Barclay Allen, ed., *George Washington - A Collection* (Indianapolis: Liberty Classics, Liberty Fund, Inc., 7440 N. Shadeland, Indianapolis, Indiana 46250, 1988; based almost entirely on materials reproduced from *The Writings of George Washington from the original manuscript sources, 1745-1799/* John Clement Fitzpatrick, editor), pp. 534-353. John Clement Fitzpatrick, ed., *The Writings of George Washington, from the Original Manuscript Sources 1749-1799,* 39 vols. (Washington, D.C.: United States Government Printing Office, 1931-1944). John F. Schroeder, ed., *Maxims of Washington* (Mt. Vernon: Mt. Vernon Ladies' Association, 1942), pp. 275, 287. Anson Phelps Stokes and Leo Pfeffer, *Church and State in the United States,* 3 vols. (NY: Harper & Brothers, 1950), p. 87. Pat Robertson, *America's Dates with Destiny* (Nashville: Thomas Nelson Publishers, 1986), p. 112. Tim LaHaye, *Faith of Our Founding Fathers* (Brentwood, TN: Wolgemuth & Hyatt, Publishers, Inc., 1987), pp. 104-106. John Eidsmoe, *Christianity and the Constitution - The Faith of Our Founding Fathers* (Grand Rapids, MI: Baker Book House, A Mott Media Book, 1987, 6th printing 1993), p. 118. David Barton, *The Myth of Separation* (Aledo, TX: WallBuilder Press, 1991), p. 115. Gary DeMar, *The Biblical Worldview* (Atlanta, GA: An American Vision Publication - American Vision, Inc., 1992), Vol. 8, No. 12, p. 8. D.P. Diffine, Ph.D., *One Nation Under God - How Close a Separation?* (Searcy, Arkansas: Harding University, Belden Center for Private Enterprise Education, 6th edition, 1992), p. 9. Gary DeMar, *America's Christian History: The Untold Story* (Atlanta, GA: American Vision Publishers, Inc., 1993), pp. 76-77.

[61] **George Washington.** October 9, 1789, in a letter to the Synod of the Dutch Reformed Church in North America. *Old South Leaflets.* John Clement Fitzpatrick, ed., *The Writings of George Washington, from the Original Manuscript Sources 1749-1799,* 39 vols. (Washington, D.C.: United States Government Printing Office, 1931-1944), Vol. XXX, p. 432. Norman Cousins, *In God We Trust - The Religious Beliefs and Ideas of the American Founding Fathers* (NY: Harper & Brothers, 1958), p. 60. Paul F. Boller, Jr., *George Washington and Religion* (Dallas: Southern Methodist University Press, 1963), pp. 177-178. John Eidsmoe, *Christianity and the Constitution - The Faith of Our Founding Fathers* (Grand Rapids, MI: Baker Book House, A Mott Media Book, 1987, 6th printing 1993), p. 124. David Barton, *The Myth of Separation* (Aledo, TX: WallBuilder Press, 1991), pp. 113, 146, 246. Stephen McDowell and Mark Beliles, "The Providential Perspective" (Charlottesville, VA: The Providence Foundation, P.O. Box 6759, Charlottesville, Va. 22906, January 1994), Vol. 9, No. 1, p. 8.

[62] **George Washington.** March 15, 1790, in addressing the Roman Catholic Churches in America. Paul F. Boller, Jr., *George Washington and Religion* (Dallas: Southern Methodist University Press, 1963), pp. 163-194. John Eidsmoe, *Christianity and the Constitution - The Faith of Our Founding Fathers* (Grand Rapids, MI: Baker Book House, A Mott Media Book, 1987, 6th printing 1993), p. 121. William Barclay Allen, ed., *George Washington - A Collection* (Indianapolis: Liberty Classics, Liberty Fund, Inc., 7440 N. Shadeland, Indianapolis, Indiana 46250, 1988; based almost entirely on materials reproduced from *The Writings of George*

Washington from the original manuscript sources, 1745-1799/John Clement Fitzpatrick, editor), pp. 546-547. John Clement Fitzpatrick, ed., *The Writings of George Washington, from the Original Manuscript Sources 1749-1799*, 39 vols. (Washington, D.C.: United States Government Printing Office, 1931-1944).

[63] **George Washington** March 11, 1792, in a letter from Philadelphia to John Armstrong. Jared Sparks, ed., *The Writings of George Washington* 12 vols. (Boston: American Stationer's Company, 1837; NY: F. Andrew's, 1834-1847), Vol. X, p. 222. William J. Johnson, *George Washington - The Christian* (St. Paul, MN: William J. Johnson, Merriam Park, February 23, 1919; Nashville, TN: Abingdon Press, 1919; reprinted Milford, MI: Mott Media, 1976; reprinted Arlington Heights, IL: Christian Liberty Press, 502 West Euclid Avenue, Arlington Heights, Illinois, 60004, 1992), p. 210. John Clement Fitzpatrick, ed., *The Writings of George Washington, from the Original Manuscript Sources 1749-1799*, 39 vols. (Washington, D.C.: United States Government Printing Office, 1931-1944), Vol. XXXII, p. 2. David Barton, *The Myth of Separation* (Aledo, TX: WallBuilder Press, 1991), p. 114. "Our Christian Heritage," *Letter from Plymouth Rock* (Marlborough, NH: The Plymouth Rock Foundation), p. 4.

[64] **George Washington.** January 27, 1793, in a letter to the congregation of the New Church in Baltimore, Washington. Norman Cousins, *In God We Trust - The Religious Beliefs and Ideas of the Founding Fathers* (NY: Harper & Brothers, 1958), pp. 48, 62. John F. Schroeder, ed., *Maxims of Washington* (Mt. Vernon: Mt. Vernon Ladies' Association, 1942), pp. 301-302. Tim LaHaye, *Faith of Our Founding Fathers* (Brentwood, TN: Wolgemuth & Hyatt, Publishers, Inc., 1987), p. 110. Gary DeMar, *America's Christian History: The Untold Story* (Atlanta, GA: American Vision Publishers, Inc., 1993), p. 92.

[65] **George Washington.** In writing to the Hebrew Congregations of the city of Savannah, Georgia. William Barclay Allen, ed., *George Washington - A Collection* (Indianapolis: Liberty Classics, Liberty Fund, Inc., 7440 N. Shadeland, Indianapolis, Indiana 46250, 1988; based almost entirely on materials reproduced from *The Writings of George Washington from the original manuscript sources, 1745-1799*/John Clement Fitzpatrick, editor), p. 549. John Clement Fitzpatrick, ed., *The Writings of George Washington, from the Original Manuscript Sources 1749-1799*, 39 vols. (Washington, D.C.: United States Government Printing Office, 1931-1944). John F. Schroeder, ed., *Maxims of Washington* (Mt. Vernon: Mt. Vernon Ladies' Association, 1942), p. 303. Tim LaHaye, *Faith of Our Founding Fathers* (Brentwood, TN: Wolgemuth & Hyatt, Publishers, Inc., 1987), p. 109.

[66] **George Washington.** November 19, 1794, in his Sixth Annual Message to Congress. Journals of Senate and House, 3rd Congress, 2nd Session. Jared Sparks, ed., *The Writings of George Washington* 12 vols. (Boston: American Stationer's Company, 1837; NY: F. Andrew's, 1834-1847), Vol. XII, p. 54. James D. Richardson (U.S. Representative from Tennessee), ed., *A Compilation of the Messages and Papers of the Presidents 1789-1897*, 10 vols. (Washington, D.C.: U.S. Government Printing Office, published by Authority of Congress, 1897, 1899; Washington, D.C.: Bureau of National Literature and Art, 1789-1902, 11 vols., 1907, 1910), Vol. I, pp. 162-168. *American State Papers, Miscellaneous,* (complete text), Vol. I, p. 83-85. William MacDonald, *Select Documents Illustrative of the History of the United States, 1776-1861* (NY: Macmillan Company, 1897, 1898), p. 130. William J. Johnson, *George Washington - The Christian* (St. Paul, MN: William J. Johnson, Merriam Park, February 23, 1919; Nashville, TN: Abingdon Press, 1919; reprinted Milford, MI: Mott Media, 1976; reprinted Arlington Heights, IL: Christian Liberty Press, 502 West Euclid Avenue, Arlington Heights, Illinois, 60004, 1992), pp. 214-215. Saxe Commins, ed., *The Basic Writings of George Washington* (NY: Random House, 1948), p. 616. John F. Schroeder, ed., *Maxims of Washington* (Mt. Vernon: Mt. Vernon Ladies' Association, 1942), p. 281. Tim LaHaye, *Faith of Our Founding Fathers* (Brentwood, TN: Wolgemuth & Hyatt, Publishers, Inc., 1987), p. 105.

[67] **George Washington.** January 1, 1795, from Philadelphia, in a Proclamation of a National Day of Public Thanksgiving and Prayer. Jared Sparks, ed., *The Writings of George Washington* 12 vols. (Boston: American Stationer's Company, 1837; NY: F. Andrew's, 1834-1847), Vol. XII, pp. 132-134. James D. Richardson (U.S. Representative from Tennessee), ed., *A Compilation of the Messages and Papers of the Presidents 1789-1897*, 10 vols. (Washington, D.C.: U.S. Government Printing Office, published by Authority of Congress, 1897, 1899; Washington, D.C.: Bureau of National Literature and Art, 1789-1902, 11 vols., 1907, 1910), Vol. I, pp. 179-180. William J. Johnson, *George Washington - The Christian* (St. Paul, MN: William J. Johnson, Merriam Park, February 23, 1919; Nashville, TN: Abingdon Press, 1919; reprinted Milford, MI: Mott Media, 1976; reprinted Arlington Heights, IL: Christian Liberty Press, 502 West Euclid Avenue, Arlington Heights, Illinois, 60004, 1992), pp. 215-217. Catherine Millard, *The Rewriting of America's History* (Camp Hill, PA: Horizon House Publishers, 1991), pp. 61-62.

[68] **George Washington.** 1752, in his personal prayer book, entitled "Daily Sacrifice," consisting of 24 pages in his own handwriting. This book, along with remarkable items belonging to George Washington, Bushrod C. Washington (his nephew who became a U.S. Supreme Court Justice and vice-president of the American Sunday School Union), Lawrence Washington, Thomas B. Washington, and J.R.C. Lewis were sold at an auction in Philadelphia on April 21, 22, 23, 1891. Experts in Washington City, Philadelphia and New York are satisfied beyond all doubt that it is George Washington's own handwriting. J.M. Toner, *Washington's Barbados Journal, 1751-2.* W. Herbert Burk, *Washington's Prayers* (1907), pp. 13-95. William J. Johnson, *George Washington - The Christian* (St. Paul, MN: William J. Johnson, Merriam Park, February 23, 1919; Nashville, TN: Abingdon Press, 1919; reprinted Milford, MI: Mott Media, 1976; reprinted Arlington Heights, IL: Christian Liberty Press, 502 West Euclid Avenue, Arlington Heights, Illinois, 60004, 1992), pp. 23-36, 277. William Evarts Benjamin, *The Daily Sacrifice,* (New York). Stephen Abbott Northrop, D.D., *A Cloud of Witnesses* (Portland, OR: American Heritage Ministries, 1987; Mantle Ministries, 228 Still Ridge, Bulverde, Texas), pp. 484-487. W. Herbert Burk, B.D., *Washington's Prayers* (Norristown, PA: Published for the Benefit of the Washington Memorial Chapel, 1907), pp. 15, 87-95. Tim LaHaye, *Faith of Our Founding Fathers* (Brentwood, TN: Wolgemuth & Hyatt, Publishers, Inc., 1987), pp. 111-113. Peter Marshall and David Manuel, *The Light and the Glory* (Old Tappan, NJ: Fleming H. Revell Company, 1977), pp. 284-285. John Eidsmoe, *Christianity and the Constitution - The Faith of Our Founding Fathers* (Grand Rapids, MI: Baker Book House, A Mott Media Book, 1987, 6th printing 1993), pp. 130-131. Peter Marshall & David Manuel, *The Glory of America* (Bloomington, MN: Garborg's Heart 'N Home, 1991), 2.26.

[69] **George Washington.** 1752, in his personal prayer book, entitled "Daily Sacrifice," consisting of 24 pages in his own handwriting. W. Herbert Burk, B.D., *Washington's Prayers* (Norristown, PA: Published for the Benefit of the Washington Memorial Chapel, 1907), pp. 87-95. William J. Johnson, *George Washington - The Christian* (St. Paul, MN: William J. Johnson, Merriam Park, February 23, 1919; Nashville, TN: Abingdon Press, 1919; reprinted Milford, MI: Mott Media, 1976; reprinted Arlington Heights, IL: Christian Liberty Press, 502 West Euclid Avenue, Arlington Heights, Illinois, 60004, 1992), pp. 23-36. Peter Marshall and David Manuel, *The Light and the Glory* (Old Tappan, NJ: Fleming H. Revell Company, 1977), pp. 284-285. W. Herbert Burk, *Washington's Prayers* (1907), pp. 87-95. Tim LaHaye, *Faith of Our Founding Fathers* (Brentwood, TN: Wolgemuth & Hyatt, Publishers, Inc., 1987), pp. 111-113. John Eidsmoe, *Christianity and the Constitution - The Faith of Our Founding Fathers* (Grand Rapids, MI: Baker Book House, A Mott Media Book, 1987, 6th printing 1993), pp. 130-131.

[70] **George Washington.** 1752, in his personal prayer book, entitled "Daily Sacrifice," consisting of 24 pages in his own handwriting. W. Herbert Burk, B.D., *Washington's Prayers* (Norristown, PA: Published for the Benefit of the Washington

Memorial Chapel, 1907, pp. 87-95. Tim LaHaye, *Faith of Our Founding Fathers* (Brentwood, TN: Wolgemuth& Hyatt, Publishers, Inc., 1987), pp. 111-113.William J. Johnson, *George Washington -The Christian* (St. Paul, MN: William. Johnson, Merriam Park, February 23,1919; Nashville, TN: Abingdon Press, 1919, reprinted Milford, MI: Mott Media, 1976; reprinted Arlington Heights, IL: Christian Liberty Press, 502 West Euclid Avenue, Arlington Heights, Illinois, 60004, 1992), pp. 23-28. Peter Marshall and David Manuel, *The Light and the Glory* (Old Tappan, NJ: Fleming H. Revell Company, 1977), pp. 284-285.

[71] **George Washington**. 1752, in his personal prayer book, entitled "Daily Sacrifice," consisting of 24 pages in his own handwriting. W. Herbert Burk, B.D., *Washington's Prayers* (Norristown, PA: Published for the Benefit of the Washington Memorial Chapel, 1907), pp. 87-95. Tim LaHaye, *Faith of our Founding Fathers* (Brentwood, TN: Wolgemuth & Hyatt, Publishers, Inc., 1987), pp. 111-1 13. William J. Johnson, *George Washington - The Christian* (St. Paul, MN: William 1. Johnson, Merriam Park, February 23,1919; Nashville, TN: Abingdon Press, 1919; reprinted Milford, MI: Mott Media, 1976; reprinted Arlington Heights, IL: Christian Liberty Press, 502 West Euclid Avenue, Arlington Heights, Illinois, 60004;1992), pp. 23-28. Peter Marshall and David Manuel, *The Light and the Glory* (Old Tappan, NJ: Fleming H. Revell Company, 1977), pp. 284-285.

[72] **George Washington**. 1752, in his personal prayer book, entitled 'Daily Sacrifice," consisting of 24 pages in his own handwriting. W. Herbert Burk, B.D., *Washington's Prayers* (Norristown, PA: Published for the Benefit of the Washington Memorial Chapel, 1907), pp. 87-95. William J. Johnson, *George Washington - The Christian* (St. Paul, MN: William J. Johnson, Merriam Park, February 23,1919; Nashville, TN: Abingdon Press, 1919; reprinted Milford, MI: Mott Media, 1976; reprinted Arlington Heights, IL: Christian Liberty Press, 502 West Euclid Avenue, Arlington Heights, Illinois, 60004,1992), pp. 23-30.

[73] **George Washington**. 1752, in his personal prayer book, entitled "Daily Sacrifice," consisting of 24 pages in his own handwriting. W. Herbert Burk, B.D., *Washington's Prayers* (Norristown, PA: Published for the Benefit of the Washington Memorial Chapel, 1907), pp. 87-95. William J. Johnson, *George Washington - The Christian* (St. Paul MN: William J. Johnson, Merriam Park, February 23,1919; Nashville, TN: Abingdon Press, 1919; reprinted Milford, MI: Mott Media, 1976; reprinted Arlington Heights, IL: Christian Liberty Press, 502 West Euclid Avenue, Arlington Heights, Illinois, 60004,1992), pp. 23-35. Tim LaHaye, *Faith of Our Founding Fathers* (Brentwood, TN: Wolgemuth & Hyatt, Publishers, Inc., 1987), pp. 11 1-1 13.

[74] **George Washington**. 1752, in his personal prayer book, entitled "Daily Sacrifice," consisting of 24 pages in his own handwriting. W. Herbert Burk, B.D., *Washington's Prayers* (Norristown, PA: Published for the Benefit of the Washington Memorial Chapel, 1907), pp. 87-95. William J. Johnson, *George Washington - The Christian* (St. Paul, MN: William J. Johnson, Merriam Park, February 23, 1919; Nashville, TN: Abingdon Press, 1919; reprinted Milford, MI: Mott Media, 1976; reprinted Arlington Heights, IL: Christian Liberty Press, 502 West Euclid Avenue, Arlington Heights, Illinois, 60004,1992), pp. 23-35. Tim LaHaye, *Faith of our Founding Fathers* (Brentwood, TN: Wolgemuth & Hyatt, Publishers, Inc., 1987), pp. 111-113.

[75] **George Washington**. Attributed. Henry Halley, *Halley's Bible Handbook* (Grand Rapids, MI: Zondervan, 1927,1965), p. 18. Gary DeMar, *America's Christian History: The Untold Story* (Atlanta, GA: American Vision, Publishers, Inc., 1993), p. 58.

[76] **George Washington**. James K. Paulding, *A Life of Washington*, 2 vols. (1836), Vol. H, p. 208. William J. Johnson, *George Washington - The Christian* (St. Paul, MN: William J. Johnson, Merriam Park, February 23,1919; Nashville, TN: Abingdon Press, 1919; reprinted Milford, MI: Mott Media, 1976, reprinted Arlington Heights, IL: Christian Liberty Press, 502 West Euclid Avenue, Arlington Heights, Illinois, 60004,1992), pp. 263-264. John F. Schroeder, ed., *Maxims of Washington* (Mt. Vernon: Mt. Vernon Ladies' Association, 1942), p. 275. James K. Paulding, *Life of Washington* (1935). Stephen McDowell and Mark Beliles, "The Providential Perspective" (Charlottesville, VA: The Providence Foundation, P.O. Box 6759, Charlottesville, Va. 22906, January 1994), Vol. 9, No. 1, p. 1.

[77] **George Washington**. John F. Schroeder, ed., *Maxims of Washington* (Mt. Vernon: Mt. Vernon Ladies' Association, 1942), p. 275. Tim LaHaye, *Faith of our Founding Fathers* (Brentwood, TN: Wolgemuth & Hyatt, Publishers, Inc., 1987), p. 104.

[78] **George Washington**. John F. Schroeder, ed., *Maxims of Washington* (Mt. Vernon: Mt. Vernon Ladies' Association, 1942), pp. 280-281. Tim LaHaye, *Faith of our Founding Fathers* (Brentwood, TN: Wolgemuth & Hyatt, Publishers, Inc., 1987, p. 105.

[79] **George Washington**. September 9,1786, from Mount Vernon in a letter to John F. Mercer. William S. Baker, *Washington after the Revolution, 1784-1799* (1897), p. 62. William J. Johnson, *George Washington - The Christian* (St. Paul, MN: William J. Johnson, Merriam Park, February 23, 1919; Nashville, TN: Abingdon Press, 1919; reprinted Milford, MI: Mott Media, 1976; reprinted Arlington Heights, IL: Christian Liberty Press, 502 West Euclid Avenue, Arlington Heights, Illinois, 60004, 1992), p. 151.

[80] **George Washington**. September 19,1796, in his Farewell Address. *Address of George Washington, President of the United States, and Late Commander in Chief of the American Army. To the People of the United States, Preparatory to His Declination*. Published in *the American Daily Advertiser*, Philadelphia, September, 1796. Jared Sparks, ed., *The Writings of George Washington* 12 vols. (Boston: American Stationer's Company, 1837, NY: F. Andrew's, 1834-1847), Vol. XII, pp. 227-228. James D. Richardson (U.S. Representative from Tennessee), ed., *A Compilation of the Messages and Papers of the Presidents 1789-1897*, 10 vols. (Washington, D.C.: U.S. Government Printing Office, published by Authority of Congress, 1897, 1899; Washington, D.C.: Bureau of National Literature and Art, 1789-1902, 11 vols., 1907, 1910), Vol. 1, pp. 205-216, 220. William J. Johnson, *George Washington - The Christian* (St. Paul, MN: William J. Johnson, Merriam Park, February 23, 1919; Nashville, TN: Abingdon Press, 1919; reprinted Milford, MI: Mott Media, 1976; reprinted Arlington Heights, IL: Christian Liberty Press, 502 West Euclid Avenue, Arlington Heights, Illinois, 60004, 1992), pp. 217-219. John Clement Fitzpatrick, ed., *The Writings of George Washington, from the Original Manuscript Sources 1749-1799,39* vols. (Washington, D.C.: United States Government Printing Office, 1931-1944), Vol. 35, p. 229. Henry Steele Commager, ed., *Documents of American History*, 2 vols. (NY: F.S. Crofts and Company, 1934; Appleton-Century-Crofts, Inc., 1948, 6th edition, 1958, Englewood Cliffs, NJ: Prentice Hall, Inc., 9th edition, 1973), Vol. 1, pp. 169-173. William Barclay Allen, ed., *George Washington - A Collection* (Indianapolis: Liberty Classics, Liberty Fund, Inc., 7440 N. Shadeland, Indianapolis, Indiana 46250, 1988, based almost entirely on materials reproduced from *The Writings of George Washington from the original manuscript sources, 1745-1799* John Clement Fitzpatrick, editor), pp. 512-527. Charles W. Eliot, LL.D., ed., *American Historical Documents 1000-1904* (New York, P.F. Collier & Son Company, *The Harvard Classics*, 1910), Vol. 43, pp. 250-266. John F. Schroeder, ed., *Maxims of Washington* (Mt. Vernon: Mt. Vernon Ladies' Association, 1942), pp. 286-287. Saxe Commins, ed., *The Basic Writings of George Washington* (NY: Random House, 1948), complete work, pp. 636-W. Frederick C. Packard, Jr., ed., *Are You an American? - Great Americans Speak* (NY: Charles Scribner's Sons, 1951), p. 2. Paul M. Angle, ed., *By These Words* (NY: Rand McNally & Company, 1954), pp. 138; 145, 146. Richard D. Heffner, A *Documentary History of the United States* (New York: The

New American Library of World Literature, Inc., 1961), pp. 60-67. Daniel Boorstin, Jr., ed., *An American Primer* (Chicago: The University of Chicago Press, 1966), complete work, pp. 197-207. Lillian W. Kay, ed., *The Ground on Which We Stand - Basic Documents of American History* (NY: Franklin Watts., Inc, 1969), pp. 123-125. John Eidsmoe, *God and Caesar* (Westchester, IL: Crossway Books, 1984), p. 22. John Eidsmoe, *Christianity and the Constitution - The Faith of Our Founding Fathers* (Grand Rapids, MI: Baker Book House, A Mott Media Book, 1987, 6th printing 1993), p. 119. Tim LaHaye, *Faith of Our Founding Fathers* (Brentwood, TN: Wolgemuth & Hyatt, Inc., 1987), pp. 91, 105-106. Ronald Reid, ed., *Three Centuries of American Rhetorical Discourse - An Anthology and a Review* (Prospect Heights, IL: Waveland Press, Inc., 1988), pp. 187-201. David Barton, *The Myth of Separation* (Aledo, TX: WallBuilder Press, 1991), pp. 115-116, 124. William Safire, ed., *Lend Me Your Ears - Great Speeches in History* (NY: W.W. Norton & Company 1992), p. 359-365. D.P. Diffine, Ph.D., *One Nation Under God - How Close a Separation?* (Searcy, Arkansas: Harding University, 6th edition, Belden Center for Private Enterprise Education, 1992), p. 9. Rush H. Limbaugh III, *See, I Told You So* (New York, NY: reprinted by permission of Pocket Books, a division of Simon & Schuster Inc., 1993), pp. 73-76. Stephen McDowell and Mark Beliles, "The Providential Perspective" (Charlottesville, VA: The Providence Foundation, P.O. Box 6759, Charlottesville, Va. 22906, January 1994), Vol. 9, No. 1, p. 4.

[81] George Washington. September 19, 1796, in his Farewell Address, published in the *American Daily Advertiser*, Philadelphia, September, 1796. James D. Richardson (U.S. Representative from Tennessee), ed., *A Compilation of the Messages and Papers of the Presidents 1789-1897*, 10 vols. (Washington, D.C.: U.S. Government Printing Office, published by Authority of Congress, 1897, 1899; Washington, D.C.: Bureau of National Literature and Art, *1789-1902*, 11 vols., 1907, 1910), Vol. 1, p. 213-224, September 17, 1796. John Clement Fitzpatrick, ed., *The Writings of George Washington, from the Original Manuscript Sources 1749-1799*, 39 vols. (Washington, D.C.: United States Government Printing Office, 1931-1944), Vol. 35, p. 229. William Barclay Allen, ed., *George Washington - A Collection* (Indianapolis: Liberty Classics, Liberty Fund, Inc., 7440 N. Shadeland, Indianapolis, Indiana 46250, 1988; based almost entirely on materials reproduced from *The Writings of George Washington from the original manuscript sources, 1745-1799*/John Clement Fitzpatrick, editor), pp. 512-527. Charles W. Eliot, LL.D., ed., *American Historical Documents 1000-1904* (New York: P.F. Collier & Son Company, *The Harvard Classics*, 1910), Vol. 43, pp. 250-266. Tim LaHaye, *Faith of Our Founding Fathers* (Brentwood, TN: Wolgemuth & Hyatt, Inc., 1987), p. 91. David Barton, *The Myth of Separation* (Aledo, TX: WallBuilder Press, 1991), p. 124.

[82] George Washington. December 7, 1796, Wednesday, in his Eighth Annual Message to Congress. Jared Sparks, ed., *The Writings of George Washington* 12 vols. (Boston: American Stationer's Company, 1837; NY: F. Andrew's, 1834-1847), Vol. XII, pp. 65, 74. James D. Richardson (U.S. Representative from Tennessee), ed., *A Compilation of the Messages and Papers of the Presidents 1789-1897*, 10 vols. (Washington, D.C.: U.S. Government Printing Office, published by Authority of Congress, 1897, 1899; Washington, D.C.: Bureau of National Literature and Art, *1789-1902*, 11 vols., 1907, 1910), Vol. I, pp. 199-204. William Barclay Allen, ed., *George Washington - A Collection* (Indianapolis: Liberty Classics, Liberty Fund, Inc., 7440 N. Shadeland, Indianapolis, Indiana 46250, 1988; based almost entirely on materials reproduced from *The Writings of George Washington from the original manuscript sources, 1745-1799*/John Clement Fitzpatrick, editor), pp. 505-512. John Clement Fitzpatrick, ed., *The Writings of George Washington, from the Original Manuscript Sources 1749-1799*, 39 vols. (Washington, D.C.: United States Government Printing Office, 1931-1944). William J. Johnson, *George Washington - The Christian* (St. Paul, MN: William J. Johnson, Merriam Park, February 23, 1919; Nashville, TN: Abingdon Press, 1919; reprinted Milford, MI: Mott Media, 1976; reprinted Arlington Heights, IL: Christian Liberty Press, 502 West Euclid Avenue, Arlington Heights, Illinois, 60004, 1992), pp. 220-221. John F. Schroeder, ed., *Maxims of Washington* (Mt. Vernon: Mt. Vernon Ladies' Association, 1942), pp. 280-281. Saxe Commins, ed., *The Basic Writings of George Washington* (NY: Random House, 1948), p. 645. Tim LaHaye, *Faith of Our Founding Fathers* (Brentwood, TN: Wolgemuth & Hyatt, Publishers, Inc., 1987), p. 105.

[83] George Washington. May 30, 1799, in a letter from Mount Vernon to Reverend William White. Original letter in Archives vault of Christ Church, Christ Church, Philadelphia. Catherine Millard, *A Children's Companion Guide to America's History* (Camp Hill, PA: Horizon House Publishers, 1993), p. 49.

[84] George Washington. July 3, 1799, recommendation written on the inside page of George Washington's copy of Reverend Mason Locke Weems, D.D., *The Immortal Mentor; or Man's unerring Guide to a Healthy, Wealthy, and Happy Life* (1796). Library of Congress Rare Book Collection, Washington, D.C. Catherine Millard, *A Children's Companion Guide to America's History* (Camp Hill, PA: Horizon House Publishers, 1993), p. 51.

[85] George Washington. *Last Will and Testament*. Original in Fairfax County Courthouse, Fairfax, Virginia. William Barclay Allen, ed., *George Washington - A Collection* (Indianapolis: Liberty Classics, Liberty Fund, Inc., 7440 N. Shadeland, Indianapolis, Indiana 46250, 1988; based almost entirely on materials reproduced from *The Writings of George Washington from the original manuscript sources, 1745-1799*/John Clement Fitzpatrick, editor), pp. 667-679. John Clement Fitzpatrick, ed., *The Writings of George Washington, from the Original Manuscript Sources 1749-1799*, 39 vols. (Washington, D.C.: United States Government Printing Office, 1931-1944). Catherine Millard, *A Children's Companion Guide to America's History* (Camp Hill, PA: Horizon House Publishers, 1993), p. 53.

[86] George Washington. December 29, 1799, comments in a service by the Reverend John Thorton Kirkland, minister of the New South Church, Boston, Massachusetts. *Eulogies and Orations on the Life and Death of George Washington* (1800), p. 292. William J. Johnson, *George Washington - The Christian* (St. Paul, MN: William J. Johnson, Merriam Park, February 23, 1919; Nashville, TN: Abingdon Press, 1919; reprinted Milford, MI: Mott Media, 1976; reprinted Arlington Heights, IL: Christian Liberty Press, 502 West Euclid Avenue, Arlington Heights, Illinois, 60004, 1992), pp. 252-253. John F. Schroeder, ed., *Maxims of Washington* (Mt. Vernon: Mt. Vernon Ladies' Association, 1942), p. 274. Tim LaHaye, *Faith of Our Founding Fathers* (Brentwood, TN: Wolgemuth & Hyatt, Publishers, Inc., 1987), p. 102.

[87] George Washington. John Marshall, *The Life of George Washington* Abridged Edition, 2 vols. (1832; first edition in 5 vols. 1804-7), Vol. II, p. 445. (John Marshall was chosen by the Washington family to write the biography of George Washington.) William J. Johnson, *George Washington - The Christian* (St. Paul, MN: William J. Johnson, Merriam Park, February 23, 1919; Nashville, TN: Abingdon Press, 1919; reprinted Milford, MI: Mott Media, 1976; reprinted Arlington Heights, IL: Christian Liberty Press, 502 West Euclid Avenue, Arlington Heights, Illinois, 60004, 1992), p. 260. John F. Schroeder, ed., *Maxims of Washington* (Mt. Vernon: Mt. Vernon Ladies' Association, 1942), p. 274. Tim LaHaye, *Faith of Our Founding Fathers* (Brentwood, TN: Wolgemuth & Hyatt, Publishers, Inc., 1987), p. 102.

[88] George Washington. William White, *Washington's Writing*, as quoted by John F. Schroeder, ed., *Maxims of Washington* (Mt. Vernon: Mt. Vernon Ladies' Association, 1942), p. 406. Jared Sparks, ed., *The Writings of George Washington* 12 vols. (Boston: American Stationer's Company, 1837; NY: F. Andrew's, 1834-1847), Vol. XII, p. 407. William J. Johnson, *George Washington - The*

Notes

Christian (St. Paul, MN: William J. Johnson, Merriam Park, February 23, 1919; Nashville, TN: Abingdon Press, 1919; reprinted Milford, MI: Mott Media, 1976; reprinted Arlington Heights, IL: Christian Liberty Press, 502 West Euclid Avenue, Arlington Heights, Illinois, 60004, 1992), pp. 245-246. Tim LaHaye, *Faith of Our Founding Fathers* (Brentwood, TN: Wolgemuth & Hyatt, Publishers, Inc., 1987), p. 103.

[89] **George Washington.** July 11, 1802, inscription that his adopted son, George Washington Parke Custis, wrote in George Washington's Bible at the occasion of its donation to the Pohick Church in Truro Parish. Catherine Millard, *The Rewriting of America's History* (Camp Hill, PA: Horizon House Publishers, 1991), p. 64.

[90] **George Washington.** Paul F. Boller, Jr., *George Washington & Religion* (Dallas: Southern Methodist University, 1963), p. 27. A. James Reichley, *Religion in American Public Life* (Washington, D.C.: The Brookings Institution, 1985), p. 94. Pat Robertson, *America's Dates With Destiny* (Nashville, TN: Thomas Nelson Publishers, 1986), p. 108.

[91] **George Washington.** Inscription engraved above Washington's tomb, from John 11:25-26. Catherine Millard, *A Children's Companion Guide to America's History* (Camp Hill, PA: Horizon House Publishers, 1993), p. 53.

[92] **George Washington.** Washington Monument, Washington, District of Columbia. Willard Cantelon,*Money Master of the World* (Plainfield, NJ: Logos International, 1976), p. 135-136. Robert Byrd, *United States Senator from West Virginia*, July 27, 1962. in a message delivered in Congress two days after the Supreme Court declared prayer in schools unconstitutional. Robert Flood, *The Rebirth of America* (Philadelphia: Arthur S. DeMoss Foundation, 1986), pp. 66-69. D.P. Diffine, Ph.D., *One Nation Under God - How Close a Separation?* (Searcy, Arkansas: Harding University, Belden Center for Private Enterprise Education, 6th edition, 1992), p. 3.

[93] **Isaac Watts.** John W. Whitehead, *The Second American Revolution* (Elgin, IL: David C.Cook Publishing Co., 1982), p. 100. Quoting from J.O. Wilson,*Public Schools of Washington* (Washington, D.C.: Columbia Historical Society, 1897), Vol. 1, p. 5. David Barton, *The Myth of Separation* (Aledo, TX: WallBuilder Press, 1991), pp. 130, 175.

[94] **Isaac Watts.** Burton Stevenson, *The Home Book of Quotations* (New York: Dodd, Mead, & Co., 1967), p. 158.

[95] **Isaac Watts.** Burton Stevenson, *The Home Book of Quotations* (New York: Dodd, Mead, & Co., 1967), p. 158.

[96] **Isaac Watts.** Burton Stevenson, *The Home Book of Quotations* (New York: Dodd, Mead, & Co., 1967), p. 158.

[97] **Isaac Watts.** 1707, in *Hymns and Spiritual Songs.*

[98] **Isaac Watts.** 1719, in *Psalm 90*, st. I. John Bartlett,*Bartlett's Familiar Quotations* (Boston: Little, Brown and Company, 1855, 1980), p. 328.

[99] **Francis Wayland.** Tryon Edwards, D.D.,*The New Dictionary of Thoughts - A Cyclopedia of Quotations* (Garden City, NY: Hanover House, 1852; revised and enlarged by C.H. Catrevas, Ralph Emerson Browns and Jonathan Edwards [descendent, along with Tryon, of Jonathan Edwards (1703-1758), president of Princeton], 1891; The Standard Book Company, 1955, 1963), p. 47.

[100] **Daniel Webster.** Benjamin Franklin Morris,*The Christian Life and Character of the Civil Institutions of the United States of America* (Philadelphia: George W. Childs, 1864), p. 270. Henry H. Halley, *Halley's Bible Handbook* (Grand Rapids, MI: Zondervan Publishing House, 1927, 1965), p. 18. Alfred Armand Montapert, *Distilled Wisdom* (Englewood Cliffs, NJ: Prentice Hall, Inc., 1965), p. 37. D.P. Diffine, Ph.D., *One Nation Under God - How Close a Separation?* (Searcy, Arkansas: Harding University, Belden Center for Private Enterprise Education, 6th edition, 1992), p. 13. Stephen McDowell and Mark Beliles, "The Providential Perspective" (Charlottesville, VA: The Providence Foundation, P.O. Box 6759, Charlottesville, Va. 22906, January 1994), Vol. 9, No. 1, p. 7.

[101] **Daniel Webster.** December 22, 1820. *The Works of Daniel Webster* (Boston: Little, Brown and Company, 1853), Vol. I, pp. 22-44. David Barton,*The Myth of Separation* (Aledo, TX: WallBuilder Press, 1991), p. 134. Gary DeMar,*God and Government, A Biblical and Historical Study* (Atlanta, GA: American Vision Press, 1984), p. xiii. *The Rebirth of America* (Philadelphia: Published by the Arthur S. DeMoss Foundation, 1986), p. 29. Burton Stevenson, *The Home Book of Quotations* (New York: Dodd, Mead and Company, 1967), p. 266. John Bartlett, *Bartlett's Familiar Quotations* (Boston: Little, Brown and Company, 1855, 1980), p. 450. Charles Fadiman, ed., *The American Treasury* (NY: Harper & Brothers, Publishers, 1955), p. 695. John Warwick Montgomery, *The Law Above the Law* (Minneapolis: Bethany House Publishers, 1975), p. 37. D. James Kennedy,*Defending the First Amendment* (Fort Lauderdale, FL: Coral Ridge Ministries, 1993), p. 29.

[102] **Daniel Webster.** December 22, 1820, in an oration at Plymouth, Massachusetts. Daniel Webster, *The Works of Daniel Webster* (Boston: Little, Brown and Company, 1853), Vol. I, p. 22. Robert Myers, *Celebrations - The National Experience* (NY: Harcourt, Brace & World, Inc., second edition, 1963, 1968), p. 279. Charles Fadiman, ed., *The American Treasury* (NY: Harper & Brothers, Publishers, 1955), p. 695. John Warwick Montgomery, *The Law Above the Law* (Minneapolis: Bethany House Publishers, 1975), p. 37. D. James Kennedy,*Defending the First Amendment* (Fort Lauderdale, FL: Coral Ridge Ministries, 1993), p. 29. David Barton, *The Myth of Separation* (Aledo, TX: WallBuilder Press, 1991), p. 134. D.P. Diffine, Ph.D., *One Nation Under God - How Close a Separation?* (Searcy, Arkansas: Harding University, Belden Center for Private Enterprise Education, 6th edition, 1992), p. 10. John Warwick Montgomery, *The Law Above the Law* (Minneapolis: Bethany House Publishers, 1975), p. 37.

[103] **Daniel Webster.** *The Works of Daniel Webster* (Boston: Little, Brown and Company, 1853), Vol. I, p. 48. David Barton,*The Myth of Separation* (Aledo, TX: WallBuilder Press, 1991), p. 134. "Our Christian Heritage," *Letter from Plymouth Rock* (Marlborough, NH: The Plymouth Rock Foundation), p. 5. Walker Lewis, ed., *Speak for Yourself, Daniel: A Life of Webster in His Own Words* (Boston: Houghton Mifflin Co., 1969), p. 86. Peter Marshall and David Manuel, *The Glory of America* (Bloomington, MN: Garborg's Heart'N Home, Inc., 1991), 12.22. Marshall Foster and Mary-Elaine Swanson,*The American Covenant - The Untold Story* (Roseburg, OR: Foundation for Christian Self-Government, 1981; Thousand Oaks, CA: The Mayflower Institute, 1983, 1992), p. 158. Stephen McDowell and Mark Beliles, "The Providential Perspective" (Charlottesville, VA: The Providence Foundation, P.O. Box 6759, Charlottesville, Va. 22906, January 1994), Vol. 9, No. 1, p. 8. D.P. Diffine, Ph.D.,*One Nation Under God - How Close a Separation?* (Searcy, Arkansas: Harding University, Belden Center for Private Enterprise Education, 6th edition, 1992), p. 10. Charles Fadiman, ed., *The American Treasury* (NY: Harper & Brothers, Publishers, 1955), p. 695. John Warwick Montgomery, *The Law Above the Law* (Minneapolis: Bethany House Publishers, 1975), p. 37. D. James Kennedy,*Defending the First Amendment* (Fort Lauderdale, FL: Coral Ridge Ministries, 1993), p. 29.

[104] **Daniel Webster.** June 17, 1825, in an address on Laying the Cornerstone of the Bunker Hill Monument. John Bartlett,*Bartlett's Familiar Quotations* (Boston: Little, Brown and Company, 1855, 1980), p. 450.

[105] **Daniel Webster.** 1825, in an address at the laying of the cornerstone of the Bunker Hill Monument in Charlestown, Massachusetts. Lewis Walker, ed., *Speak for Yourself, Daniel: A Life of Webster in His Own Words* (Boston: Houghton Mifflin Co., 1969), p. 123. Peter Marshall and David Manuel, *The Glory of America* (Bloomington, MN: Garborg's Heart'N Home, Inc., 1991), 6.18. David Josiah Brewer, *World's Best Orations* (St. Louis: F.P. Kaiser, 1901), complete speech, Vol. 10, pp. 3828-3846. William

America's God and Country Encyclopedia of Quotations   831

Notes

Safire, ed., *Lend Me Your Ears - Great Speeches in History* (NY: W.W. Norton & Company 1992), pp. 43-44. Ronald Reid, ed., *Three Centuries of American Rhetorical Discourse - An Anthology and a Review* (Prospect Heights, IL: Waveland Press, Inc., 1988), p. 208 ff.

[106] **Daniel Webster.** August 2, 1826, in a discourse commemorating Adams and Jefferson at Faneuil Hall, Boston. John Bartlett, *Bartlett's Familiar Quotation* (Boston: Little, Brown and Company, 1855, 1980), p. 450.

[107] **Daniel Webster.** January 26, 1830, in his second speech on Foote's Resolution. John Bartlett, *Bartlett's Familiar Quotations* (Boston: Little, Brown and Company, 1855, 1980), p. 450.

[108] **Daniel Webster.** Walker Lewis, ed., *Speak for Yourself - Daniel: A Life of Webster in His Own Words* (Boston: Houghton Mifflin Co., 1969), p. 205. Peter Marshall and David Manuel, *The Glory of America* (Bloomington, MN: Garborg's Heart'N Home, Inc., 1991), 1.26.

[109] **Daniel Webster.** April 6, 1830, in presenting argument on the murder of Captain White. John Bartlett, *Bartlett's Familiar Quotations* (Boston: Little, Brown and Company, 1855, 1980), p. 451.

[110] **Daniel Webster.** June 3, 1834, in a speech. John Bartlett, *Bartlett's Familiar Quotations* (Boston: Little, Brown and Company, 1855, 1980), p. 451.

[111] **Daniel Webster.** 1837. Verna M. Hall, *The Christian History of the Constitution of the United States of America* (San Francisco: Foundation for American Christian Education, 1975), p. 33. Peter Marshall and David Manuel, *The Glory of America* (Bloomington, MN: Garborg's Heart'N Home, Inc., 1991), 4.29.

[112] **Daniel Webster.** June 17, 1843, in an address celebrating the completion of the Bunker Hill Monument, Charleston, Massachusetts. Burton Stevenson, *The Home Book of Quotations - Classical & Modern* (New York: Dodd, Mead and Company, 1967), p. 158. Peter Marshall and David Manuel, *The Glory of America* (Bloomington, MN: Garborg's Heart'N Home, Inc., 1991), 8.8. Stephen Abbott Northrop, D.D., *A Cloud of Witnesses* (Portland, OR: American Heritage Ministries, 1987; Mantle Ministries, 228 Still Ridge, Bulverde, Texas), p. 491. D.P. Diffine, Ph.D., *One Nation Under God - How Close a Separation?* (Searcy, Arkansas: Harding University, Belden Center for Private Enterprise Education, 6th edition, 1992), p. 12. Stephen McDowell and Mark Beliles, "The Providential Perspective" (Charlottesville, VA: The Providence Foundation, P.O. Box 6759, Charlottesville, Va. 22906, January 1994), Vol. 9, No. 1, p. 8.

[113] **Daniel Webster.** June 17, 1843, in a speech at the Bunker Hill Monument, Charleston, Massachusetts. John Bartlett, *Bartlett's Familiar Quotations* (Boston: Little, Brown and Company, 1855, 1980), p. 451.

[114] **Daniel Webster.** Peter Marshall and David Manuel, *The Glory of America* (Bloomington, MN: Garborg's Heart'N Home, Inc., 1991), 12.7. D.P. Diffine, Ph.D., *One Nation Under God - How Close a Separation?* (Searcy, Arkansas: Harding University, Belden Center for Private Enterprise Education, 6th edition, 1992), p. 12.

[115] **Daniel Webster.** "The Voices of America's Heritage," *Torch* (Dallas, TX: Texas Eagle Forum, February 1994), Vol. 1, No. 7, p. 4.

[116] **Daniel Webster.** Peter Harvey, *Reminiscences and Anecdotes of Daniel Webster* (Boston: Little, Brown & Co. 1890), pp. 393-394. Peter Marshall and David Manuel, *The Glory of America* (Bloomington, MN: Garborg's Heart'N Home, Inc., 1991), 1.16.

[117] **Daniel Webster.** Tryon Edwards, D.D.,*The New Dictionary of Thoughts - A Cyclopedia of Quotations* (Garden City, NY: Hanover House, 1852; revised and enlarged by C.H. Catrevas, Ralph Emerson Browns and Jonathan Edwards [descendent, along with Tryon, of Jonathan Edwards (1703-1758), president of Princeton], 1891; The Standard Book Company, 1955, 1963), p. 46.

[118] **Daniel Webster.** Walker Lewis, *Speak for Yourself, Daniel: A Life of Webster in His Own Words* (Boston: Houghton Mifflin Co., 1969), p. 418. Peter Marshall and David Manuel, *The Glory of America* (Bloomington, MN: Garborg's Heart'N Home, Inc., 1991), 8.2.

[119] **Daniel Webster.** Tryon Edwards, D.D.,*The New Dictionary of Thoughts - A Cyclopedia of Quotations* (Garden City, NY: Hanover House, 1852; revised and enlarged by C.H. Catrevas, Ralph Emerson Browns and Jonathan Edwards [descendent, along with Tryon, of Jonathan Edwards (1703-1758), president of Princeton], 1891; The Standard Book Company, 1955, 1963), p. 49. Charles Lanman, *Private Life of Daniel Webster*, p. 104. Stephen Abbott Northrop, D.D., *A Cloud of Witnesses* (Portland, OR: American Heritage Ministries, 1987; Mantle Ministries, 228 Still Ridge, Bulverde, Texas), p. 491.

[120] **Daniel Webster.** Charles Lanman, *Private Life of Daniel Webster*, pp. 104, 106-107. Stephen Abbott Northrop, D.D., *A Cloud of Witnesses* (Portland, OR: American Heritage Ministries, 1987; Mantle Ministries, 228 Still Ridge, Bulverde, Texas), pp. 491-493.

[121] **Daniel Webster.** 1851. Robert Flood, *The Rebirth of America* (Philadelphia: Arthur S. DeMoss Foundation, 1986), p. 21. *The Works of Daniel Webster* (Boston: Little, Brown and Company, 1853), Vol. II, p. 615, July 4, 1851. David Barton, *The Myth of Separation* (Aledo, TX: WallBuilder Press, 1991), p. 247.

[122] **Daniel Webster.** Tim LaHaye, *Faith of Our Founding Fathers* (Brentwood, TN: Wolgemuth & Hyatt, Publishers, Inc., 1987), p. 199. "The most important thought I ever had was that of my individual responsibility to God." *Bless Your Heart (series II)* (Eden Prairie, MN: Heartland Sampler, Inc., 1990), 8.28.

[123] **Daniel Webster.** B.F. Tefft, *Webster and His Master - Pieces* Vol. I & II (New York: Macmillan, 1923), p. 453. Peter Marshall and David Manuel, *The Glory of America* (Bloomington, MN: Garborg's Heart'N Home, Inc., 1991), 10.24. Samuel M. Smucker, *Life, Speeches, and Memorials of Daniel Webster*, chap. XII. Stephen Abbott Northrop, D.D., *A Cloud of Witnesses* (Portland, OR: American Heritage Ministries, 1987; Mantle Ministries, 228 Still Ridge, Bulverde, Texas), p. 493. Tryon Edwards, D.D., *The New Dictionary of Thoughts - A Cyclopedia of Quotations* (Garden City, NY: Hanover House, 1852; revised and enlarged by C.H. Catrevas, Ralph Emerson Browns and Jonathan Edwards [descendent, along with Tryon, of Jonathan Edwards (1703-1758), president of Princeton], 1891; The Standard Book Company, 1955, 1963), pp. 48, 226.

[124] **Daniel Webster.** Samuel M. Smucker, *Life, Speeches, and Memorials of Daniel Webster*, chap. XII. Stephen Abbott Northrop, D.D., *A Cloud of Witnesses* (Portland, OR: American Heritage Ministries, 1987; Mantle Ministries, 228 Still Ridge, Bulverde, Texas), p. 493.

[125] **Daniel Webster.** October 24, 1852. Sarah K. Bolton, *Famous American Statesmen*, p. 228. Stephen Abbott Northrop, D.D., *A Cloud of Witnesses* (Portland, OR: American Heritage Ministries, 1987; Mantle Ministries, 228 Still Ridge, Bulverde, Texas), p. 493.

[126] **Daniel Webster.** October 24, 1852. Sarah K. Bolton, *Famous American Statesmen*, p. 228. Stephen Abbott Northrop, D.D., *A Cloud of Witnesses* (Portland, OR: American Heritage Ministries, 1987; Mantle Ministries, 228 Still Ridge, Bulverde, Texas), pp. 493-494.

[127] **Daniel Webster.** October 24, 1852. Sarah K. Bolton, *Famous American Statesmen*, p. 228. Stephen Abbott Northrop, D.D., *A*

Cloud of Witnesses (Portland, OR: American Heritage Ministries, 1987; Mantle Ministries, 228 Still Ridge, Bulverde, Texas), p. 494.

[128] **Daniel Webster.** December 14, 1852, Senator Lewis Cass delivering the Eulogy Address of Daniel Webster in the United States Senate. Stephen Abbott Northrop, D.D., *A Cloud of Witnesses* (Portland, Oregon: American Heritage Ministries, 1987; Mantle Ministries, 228 Still Ridge, Bulverde, Texas), p. Introduction.

[129] **Noah Webster.** 1828, in the preface to his *American Dictionary of the English Language* (reprinted San Francisco: Foundation for American Christian Education, 1967), Preface, p. 22. David Barton, *The Myth of Separation* (Aledo, TX: WallBuilder Press, 1991), p. 126.

[130] **Noah Webster.** 1790, in a dedication page to Ezra Stiles, President of Yale College. Noah Webster, *American Spelling Book - Containing an easy Standard of Pronunciation. Being the first part of a Grammatical Institute of the English Language,* (1790), p. 2. Catherine Millard, *The Rewriting of America's History* (Camp Hill, PA: Horizon House Publishers, 1991), p. 158.

[131] **Noah Webster.** "Our Christian Heritage," *Letter from Plymouth Rock* (Marlborough, NH: The Plymouth Rock Foundation), p. 5.

[132] **Noah Webster.** "Our Christian Heritage," *Letter from Plymouth Rock* (Marlborough, NH: The Plymouth Rock Foundation), p. 5.

[133] **Noah Webster.** Verna M. Hall and Rosalie J. Slater,*The Bible and the Constitution of the United States* (San Francisco: Foundation for American Christian Education, 1983), p. 27. Tim LaHaye, *Faith of Our Founding Fathers* (Brentwood, TN: Wolgemuth & Hyatt, Publishers, Inc., 1987), pp. 76-78.

[134] **Noah Webster.** 1823, in his *Letters to a Young Gentleman Commencing His Education to which is subjoined to a Brief The History of the United States* (New Haven: Howe & Spalding, 1823; Durrie & Peck, 1832), pp. 18-19, letter 1. Stephen McDowell and Mark Beliles, "The Providential Perspective" (Charlottesville, VA: The Providence Foundation, P.O. Box 6759, Charlottesville, Va. 22906, January 1994), Vol. 9, No. 1, p. 6. David Barton, *The WallBuilder Report* (Aledo, TX: WallBuilder, Summer 1993), pp. 2-3. David Barton, *Keys to Good Government* (Aledo, TX: WallBuilder Press, 1994), p. 14.

[135] **Noah Webster.** 1828, in the preface to his *American Dictionary of the English Language* (reprinted San Francisco: Foundation for American Christian Education, 1967), Preface, p. 12. David Barton, *The Myth of Separation* (Aledo, TX: WallBuilder Press, 1991), pp. 126, 251. Peter Marshall & David Manuel, *From Sea to Shinning Sea* (Old Tappan, NJ: Fleming H. Revell Company, 1986), p. 412. D.P. Diffine, Ph.D.,*One Nation Under God - How Close a Separation?* (Searcy, Arkansas: Harding University, Belden Center for Private Enterprise Education, 6th edition, 1992), p. 10.

[136] **Noah Webster.** *An American Dictionary of the English Language - with pronouncing vocabularies of Scripture, classical and geographical names* (New Haven), preface. Catherine Millard,*The Rewriting of America's History* (Camp Hill, PA: Horizon House Publishers, 1991), p. 154. *Noah Webster's First Edition of an American Dictionary of the English Language* (San Francisco, CA: Foundation for American Christian Education, 1980), p. 12. Peter Marshall and David Manuel, *From Sea to Shining Sea* (Old Tappan, N.J.: Fleming H. Revell Company, 1986), p. 412.

[137] **Noah Webster.** 1828, *American Dictionary of the English Language 1828* (reprinted San Francisco: Foundation for American Christian Education, 1967). David Barton, *The Myth of Separation* (Aledo, TX: WallBuilder Press, 1991), p. 127.

[138] **Noah Webster.** 1828. *Webster's Dictionary.* Marshall Foster and Mary-Elaine Swanson, *The American Covenant - The Untold Story* (Roseburg, OR: Foundation for Christian Self-Government, 1981; Thousand Oaks, CA: The Mayflower Institute, 1983, 1992), p. 108.

[139] **Noah Webster.** 1828. *Webster's Dictionary.* Marshall Foster and Mary-Elaine Swanson, *The American Covenant - The Untold Story* (Roseburg, OR: Foundation for Christian Self-Government, 1981; Thousand Oaks, CA: The Mayflower Institute, 1983, 1992), p. 30.

[140] **Noah Webster.** *History of the United States,* p. 307. Peter Marshall and David Manuel,*The Glory of America* (Bloomington, MN: Garborg's Heart'N Home, Inc., 1991), 6.24. Stephen K. McDowell and Mark A. Beliles, *America's Providential History* (Charlottesville, VA: Providence Press, 1988), p. 6. David Barton, *The Myth of Separation* (Aledo, TX: WallBuilder Press, 1991), p. 127. D.P. Diffine, Ph.D.,*One Nation Under God - How Close a Separation?* (Searcy, Arkansas: Harding University, Belden Center for Private Enterprise Education, 6th edition, 1992), p. 10.

[141] **Noah Webster.** 1832. *History of the United States* (New Haven: Durrie & Peck, 1832), pp. 273-274, paragraph 578. David Barton, *The Myth of Separation* (Aledo, TX: WallBuilder Press, 1991), p. 125. "Our Christian Heritage," *Letter from Plymouth Rock* (Marlborough, NH: The Plymouth Rock Foundation), p. 5. Verna M. Hall, *The Christian History of the American Revolution* (San Francisco: Foundation for American Christian Education, 1976), p. 255. Peter Marshall and David Manuel,*The Glory of America* (Bloomington, MN: Garborg's Heart'N Home, Inc., 1991), 1.22. Stephen McDowell and Mark Beliles, "The Providential Perspective" (Charlottesville, VA: The Providence Foundation, P.O. Box 6759, Charlottesville, Va. 22906, January 1994), Vol. 9, No. 1, p. 6.

[142] **Noah Webster.** 1832. *The History of the United States* (New Haven: Durrie & Peck, 1832), p. 309, paragraph 53. David Barton, *The Myth of Separation* (Aledo, TX: Wallbuilder Press, 1991), pp. 125, 150, 249. Gary DeMar, *God and Government, A Biblical and Historical Study* (Atlanta, GA: American Vision Press, 1984), p. 4. "Our Christian Heritage," *Letter from Plymouth Rock* (Marlborough, NH: The Plymouth Rock Foundation), p. 5. Noah Webster,*The American Dictionary of the English Language* (NY: S. Converse, 1828; reprinted, San Francisco: Foundation for American Christian Education, facsimile edition, 1967), preface, p. 22. Gary DeMar,*God and Government - A Biblical and Historical Study* (Atlanta: American Vision Press, 1982), p. 4. Robert Flood, *The Rebirth of America* (The Arthur S. DeMoss Foundation, 1986), p. 33. David Barton, *America - To Pray or Not to Pray* (Aledo, Texas: WallBuilder Press, 1991), pp. 14, 44.

[143] **Noah Webster.** 1832. *History of the United States* (New Haven: Durrie & Peck, 1832), pp. 307-308, paragraph 49. Stephen McDowell and Mark Beliles, "The Providential Perspective" (Charlottesville, VA: The Providence Foundation, P.O. Box 6759, Charlottesville, Va. 22906, January 1994), Vol. 9, No. 1, p. 6. David Barton,*The Myth of Separation* (Aledo, TX: WallBuilder Press, 1991), p. 265-266.

[144] **Noah Webster.** 1832, in "Advice to the Young,"*History of the United States* (New Haven: Durrie & Peck, 1833), pp. v-vi.Stephen McDowell and Mark Beliles, "The Providential Perspective" (Charlottesville, VA: The Providence Foundation, P.O. Box 6759, Charlottesville, Va. 22906, January 1994), Vol. 9, No. 1, pp. 3-5. David Barton, "The WallBuilder Report" (Aledo, TX: WallBuilder Press, Fall 1993), p. 4.

[145] **Noah Webster.** 1833. Noah Webster, *Common Version of the Holy Bible, containing the Old and New Testament, with Amendments of the Language* (1833), preface. Catherine Millard,*The Rewriting of America's History* (Camp Hill, PA: Horizon House Publishers,

Notes

1991), p. 160. Verna M. Hall, *The Christian History of the American Revolution-Consider and Ponder* (San Francisco: Foundation for American Christian Education, 1976), p. 21. David Barton, *The Myth of Separation* (Aledo, TX: WallBuilder Press, 1991), pp. 127, 254. Peter Marshall and David Manuel, *The Glory of America* (Bloomington, MN: Garborg's Heart'N Home, Inc., 1991), 2.9. Stephen McDowell and Mark Beliles, "The Providential Perspective" (Charlottesville, VA: The Providence Foundation, P.O. Box 6759, Charlottesville, Va. 22906, January 1994), Vol. 9, No. 1, p. 1.

[146] **Noah Webster.** 1848. Noah Webster, *Dictionary* (1848), preface. Catherine Millard, *The Rewriting of America's History* (Camp Hill, PA: Horizon House Publishers, 1991), p. 157.

[147] **Noah Webster.** H.R. Warfel, *Noah Webster, Schoolmaster to America* (New York: Octagon Press, 1966), pp. 181-182. Tim LaHaye, *Faith of Our Founding Fathers* (Brentwood, TN: Wolgemuth & Hyatt, Publishers, Inc., 1987), pp. 76-77.

[148] **Noah Webster.** Noah Webster, *The History of the United States* (New Haven: Durrie & Peck, 1832), p. 6. David Barton, *The Myth of Separation* (Aledo, TX: WallBuilder Press, 1991), p. 246.

[149] **Noah Webster.** Bob Cutshall, *More Light for the Day* (Minneapolis, MN: Northwestern Products, Inc., 1991), 7.11.

[150] **Noah Webster.** 1843. *Memoir of Noah Webster, Webster's Unabridged Dictionary.* Stephen Abbott Northrop, D.D., *A Cloud of Witnesses* (Portland, OR: American Heritage Ministries, 1987; Mantle Ministries, 228 Still Ridge, Bulverde, Texas), p. 495.

[151] **Charles Wesley.** 1739, in *Hymns and Sacred Poems, Christ, the Lord, Is Risen Today.* John Bartlett, *Bartlett's Familiar Quotations* (Boston: Little, Brown and Company, 1855, 1980), p. 350.

[152] **Charles Wesley.** *In Temptation.* Burton Stevenson, *The Home Book of Quotations* (New York: Dodd, Mead & Company, 1967), p. 264.

[153] **Charles Wesley.** 1742, in *Gentle Jesus, Meek and Mild.* John Bartlett, *Bartlett's Familiar Quotations* (Boston: Little, Brown and Company, 1855, 1980), p. 350.

[154] **Charles Wesley.** 1749, in *Soldiers of Christ, Arise.* John Bartlett, *Bartlett's Familiar Quotations* (Boston: Little, Brown and Company, 1855, 1980), p. 350.

[155] **Charles Wesley.** 1753, *Hark the Herald Angels Sing.* John Bartlett, *Bartlett's Familiar Quotations* (Boston: Little, Brown and Company, 1855, 1980), p. 350. Herbert V. Prochnow, *5100 Quotations for Speakers and Writers* (Grand Rapids, MI: Baker Book House, 1992), p. 519.

[156] **John Wesley.** Stephen K. McDowell and Mark A. Beliles, *America's Providential History* (Charlottesville, VA: Providence Press, 1988), p. 55. David Barton, *The Myth of Separation* (Aledo, TX: WallBuilder Press, 1991), p. 87.

[157] **John Wesley.** May 24, 1738, Wednesday. *John Wesley's Journal* (Curnock). "From the Journal" (Carol Stream, IL: Christian History), Vol. II, No. I, pp. 30-32.

[158] **John Wesley.** June 11, 1739, in his *Journal.* John Bartlett, *Bartlett's Familiar Quotations* (Boston: Little, Brown and Company, 1855, 1980), p. 346.

[159] **John Wesley.** February 12, 1772, in his *Journal.* John Bartlett, *Bartlett's Familiar Quotations* (Boston: Little, Brown and Company, 1855, 1980), p. 346.

[160] **John Wesley.** In his *Rule.* John Bartlett, *Bartlett's Familiar Quotations* (Boston: Little, Brown and Company, 1855, 1980), p. 346.

[161] **Samuel West.** 1776, speaking in Boston. John Wingate Thornton, *The Pulpit of the American Revolution* (Boston: D. Lothrop & Co., 1876), p. 311. Peter Marshall and David Manuel, *The Light and the Glory* (Old Tappan, NJ: Fleming H. Revell Company, 1977), pp. 296-297.

[162] **George Whitefield.** 1733, spoken at his conversion. John Pollock, *George Whitefield and the Great Awakening* (Garden City, NY: Doubleday and Co., 1972), p. 19. Peter Marshall and David Manuel, *The Glory of America* (Bloomington, MN: Garborg's Heart'N Home, Inc., 1991), 12.16.

[163] **George Whitefield.** J.L. Packer, *The Startling Puritan* (Carol Stream, IL: Christian History), Vol. XII, No. 2, Issue 38, p. 40.

[164] **George Whitefield.** J.I. Packer, *The Startling Puritan* (Carol Stream, IL: Christian History), Vol. XII, No. 2, Issue 38, p. 39.

[165] **George Whitefield.** In a letter from Sarah Edwards to her brother. Pollock, *Whitefield*, p. 164. Peter Marshall and David Manuel, *The Glory of America* (Bloomington, MN: Garborg's Heart'N Home, Inc., 1991), 12.17.

[166] **George Whitefield.** Benjamin Franklin, *The Autobiography of Benjamin Franklin* (New York: Books,Inc., 1791), p. 146. Tim LaHaye, *Faith of Our Founding Fathers* (Brentwood, TN: Wolgemuth & Hyatt, Publishers, Inc., 1987), p. 116. Pollock, *Whitefield*, p. 117.

[167] **George Whitefield.** 1752, in a letter to Benjamin Franklin. Frank Lambert, *The Religious Odd Couple* (Carol Stream, IL: Christian History), Vol. XII, No. 2, Issue 38, p. 31.

[168] **George Whitefield.** 1764, in ending a letter from Benjamin Franklin. Frank Lambert, *The Religious Odd Couple* (Carol Stream, IL: Christian History), Vol. XII, No. 2, Issue 38, p. 31.

[169] **George Whitefield.** 1769, in his last surviving letter to Benjamin Franklin. Frank Lambert, *The Religious Odd Couple* (Carol Stream, IL: Christian History), Vol. XII, No. 2, Issue 38, p. 31-32.

[170] **George Whitefield.** In the last letter from Benjamin Franklin. Frank Lambert, *The Religious Odd Couple* (Carol Stream, IL: Christian History), Vol. XII, No. 2, Issue 38, p. 31.

[171] **George Whitefield.** 1770, spoken at his death. John Pollock, *George Whitefield and the Great Awakening* (Garden City, NY: Doubleday and Co., 1972), p. 19. Peter Marshall and David Manuel, *The Glory of America* (Bloomington, MN: Garborg's Heart'N Home, Inc., 1991), 12.16.

[172] **Alfred North Whitehead.** 1925, in *Science and the Modern World*, chapter 12. John Bartlett, *Bartlett's Familiar Quotations* (Boston: Little, Brown and Company, 1855, 1980), p. 697.

[173] **William Whiting.** 1860, wrote *The Hymn of the U.S. Navy, Eternal Father, Strong to Save*, st. I. John Bartlett, *Bartlett's Familiar Quotations* (Boston: Little, Brown and Company, 1855, 1980), pp. 596-597.

[174] **Marcus Whitman.** July 3, 1923, in a speech by President Warren Gamaliel Harding about the Oregon Trail given at Meacham, Oregon. "Harding, Warren Gamaliel; A Government Document," Washington, D.C.: Government Printing Office, 1923. *A Compilation of the Messages and Papers of the Presidents* 20 vols. (New York: Bureau of National Literature, Inc., prepared under the direction of the Joint Committee on Printing, of the House and Senate, pursuant to an Act of the Fifty-Second Congress of the United States, 1893, 1923), Vol. XVIII, pp. 9299-9303. Catherine Millard, *The Rewriting of America's History* (Camp Hill, PA: Horizon House Publishers, 1991), pp. 208-211.

[175] **Walt Whitman.** 1855-1892, in *Leaves of Grass, Starting from Paumanok.* John Bartlett, *Bartlett's Familiar Quotations* (Boston: Little, Brown and Company, 1855, 1980), p. 574.

[176] **John Greenleaf Whittier.** Samuel T. Pickard, *Life and Letters of John Greenleaf Whittier*, pp. 264, 265. Stephen Abbott Northrop,

D.D., *A Cloud of Witnesses* (Portland, OR: American Heritage Ministries, 1987; Mantle Ministries, 228 Still Ridge, Bulverde, Texas), pp. 501-502. Peter Marshall and David Manuel, *The Glory of America* (Bloomington, MN: Garborg's Heart 'N Home, Inc., 1991), 4.22.

[177] **John Greenleaf Whittier.** 1876, in his poem *Centennial Hymn. Patriotic Anthology*, p. 395. Peter Marshall and David Manuel, *The Glory of America* (Bloomington, MN: Garborg's Heart'N Home, Inc., 1991), 12.14-15.

[178] **John Greenleaf Whittier.** Samuel T. Pickard, *Life and Letters of John Greenleaf Whittier*, pp. 264, 265. Stephen Abbott Northrop, D.D., *A Cloud of Witnesses* (Portland, OR: American Heritage Ministries, 1987; Mantle Ministries, 228 Still Ridge, Bulverde, Texas), pp. 501-502.

[179] **John Greenleaf Whittier.** Samuel T. Pickard, *Life and Letters of John Greenleaf Whittier*, pp. 264, 265. Stephen Abbott Northrop, D.D., *A Cloud of Witnesses* (Portland, OR: American Heritage Ministries, 1987; Mantle Ministries, 228 Still Ridge, Bulverde, Texas), pp. 501-502.

[180] **Oscar Fingal O'Flahertie Wills Wilde.** 1898, in the *Ballad of Reading Gaol*, Pt. V, st. 14. John Bartlett, *Bartlett's Familiar Quotations* (Boston: Little, Brown and Company, 1855, 1980), p. 676.

[181] **Emma Willard.** *The World Book Encyclopedia*, 18 vols. (Chicago, IL: Field Enterprises, Inc., 1957; W.F. Quarrie and Company, 8 vols., 1917; World Book, Inc., 22 vols., 1989), Vol. 18, p. 8776.

[182] **Emma Willard.** 1843. Emma Willard, *History of the United States*. Rosalie J. Slater, *Teaching and Learning America's Christian History* (San Francisco: Foundation for American Christian Education, 1980), p. 83. Stephen McDowell and Mark Beliles, "The Providential Perspective" (Charlottesville, VA: The Providence Foundation, P.O. Box 6759, Charlottesville, Va. 22906, January 1994), Vol. 9, No. 1, p. 3. David Barton, *The Myth of Separation* (Aledo, TX: WallBuilder Press, 1991), p. 135. Peter Marshall and David Manuel, *The Glory of America* (Bloomington, MN: Garborg's Heart'N Home, Inc., 1991), 9.23.

[183] **Emma Willard.** *Morals for the Young: or, Good Principles Instilling Wisdom.* Carole G. Adams, *Education for a Christian Republic* (San Francisco, CA: The American Christian Prompter, 1993), Vol. 4, No. 2, p. 4.

[184] **William I.** 1584, his last words after being shot. John Bartlett, *Bartlett's Familiar Quotations* (Boston: Little, Brown and Company, 1855, 1980), p. 166.

[185] **College of William and Mary.** Mary R.M. Goodwin, *Wren Building Interpretative Research Report*, College of William and Mary, Williamsburg, Virginia, p. 7. Catherine Millard, *A Children's Companion Guide to America's History* (Camp Hill, PA: Horizon House Publishers, 1993), p. 33.

[186] **College of William and Mary.** 1692. Original Charter of the College of William and Mary, Williamsburg, Virginia. Rare Book Collection, Swem Library. John Fiske, *The Beginnings of New England* (Boston: Houghton, Mifflin & Co., 1898), pp. 127-128, 136. Russ Walton, *Biblical Principles of Importance to Godly Christians* (NH: Plymouth Rock Foundation, 1984), p. 356. David Barton, *The Myth of Separation* (Aledo, TX: WallBuilder Press, 1991), p. 91. Catherine Millard, *The Rewriting of America's History* (Camp Hill, PA: Horizon House Publishers, 1991), p. 292.

[187] **George Williams.** Young Men's Christian Association. Stephen Abbott Northrop, D.D., *A Cloud of Witnesses* (Portland, OR: American Heritage Ministries, 1987; Mantle Ministries, 228 Still Ridge, Bulverde, Texas), p. 508.

[188] **Roger Williams.** *The World Book Encyclopedia*, 18 vols. (Chicago, IL: Field Enterprises, Inc., 1957; W.F. Quarrie and Company, 8 vols., 1917; World Book, Inc., 22 vols., 1989), Vol. 14, p. 6931.

[189] **Roger Williams.** Charter of Rhode Island, Granted July 1663 by King Charles II. William McDonald, ed., *Documentary Source Book of American History 1606-1889* (NY: The MacMillan Company, 1909), pp. 67-68. David Barton, *The Myth of Separation* (Aledo, TX: WallBuilder Press, 1991), p. 87.

[190] **Roger Williams.** *The World Book Encyclopedia*, 18 vols. (Chicago, IL: Field Enterprises, Inc., 1957; W.F. Quarrie and Company, 8 vols., 1917; World Book, Inc., 22 vols., 1989), Vol. 18, pp. 8780-8781. Lynn R. Buzzard and Samuel Ericsson, *The Battle for Religious Liberty* (Elgin, IL: David C. Cook, 1982), p. 51.

[191] **Roger Williams.** Lynn R. Buzzard and Samuel Ericsson, *The Battle for Religious Liberty* (Elgin, IL: David C. Cook, 1982), p. 51. John Eidsmoe, *Christianity and the Constitution - The Faith of Our Founding Fathers* (Grand Rapids, MI: Baker Book House, A Mott Media Book, 1987, 6th printing 1993), pp. 215, 243. David Barton, *The Myth of Separation* (Aledo, TX: WallBuilder Press, 1991), p. 42.

[192] **Roger Williams.** January 9, 1872, Senator Henry Bowen Anthony delivers the Eulogy of Roger Williams in Congress. Stephen Abbott Northrop, D.D., *A Cloud of Witnesses* (Portland, Oregon: American Heritage Ministries, 1987; Mantle Ministries, 228 Still Ridge, Bulverde, Texas), p. 16.

[193] **Hugh Williamson.** John Neal, *Trinity College Historical Society Papers, Series 13* (New York: AMS Press, 1915), pp. 62-63. Tim LaHaye, *Faith of Our Founding Fathers* (Brentwood, TN: Wolgemuth & Hyatt, Publishers, Inc., 1987), p. 182.

[194] **Hugh Williamson.** John Neal, *Trinity College Historical Society Papers, Series 13* (New York: AMS Press, 1915), pp. 62-63. Tim LaHaye, *Faith of Our Founding Fathers* (Brentwood, TN: Wolgemuth & Hyatt, Publishers, Inc., 1987), p. 182.

[195] **Hugh Williamson.** Tim LaHaye, *Faith of Our Founding Fathers* (Brentwood, TN: Wolgemuth & Hyatt, Publishers, Inc., 1987), p. 183.

[196] **Henry Wilson.** Stephen Abbott Northrop, D.D., *A Cloud of Witnesses* (Portland, Oregon: American Heritage Ministries, 1987; Mantle Ministries, 228 Still Ridge, Bulverde, Texas), preface. Peter Marshall and David Manuel, *The Glory of America* (Bloomington, MN: Garborg's Heart'N Home, Inc., 1991), 8.1.

[197] **Henry Wilson.** 1866, at Natick, Massachusetts to the Young Men's Christian Association. Thomas Russell, *Life of Henry Wilson*. Stephen Abbott Northrop, D.D., *A Cloud of Witnesses* (Portland, Oregon: American Heritage Ministries, 1987; Mantle Ministries, 228 Still Ridge, Bulverde, Texas), pp. 509-510. Peter Marshall and David Manuel, *The Glory of America* (Bloomington, MN: Garborg's Heart'N Home, Inc., 1991), 12.23.

[198] **James Wilson.** *Updegraph v. The Commonwealth*, 11 Serg, & R. 393, 403 (1824). David Barton, *The Myth of Separation* (Aledo, TX: WallBuilder Press, 1991), pp. 78-79.

[199] **(Thomas) Woodrow Wilson.** March 4, 1913 in his Inaugural Address. *A Compilation of the Messages and Papers of the Presidents* 20 vols. (New York: Bureau of National Literature, Inc., prepared under the direction of the Joint Committee on Printing, of the House and Senate, pursuant to an Act of the Fifty-Second Congress of the United States, 1893, 1923), Vol. XVI, p. 7871. *Inaugural Addresses of the Presidents of the United States - From George Washington 1789 to Richard Milhous Nixon 1969* (Washington, D.C.: United States Government Printing Office; 91st Congress, 1st Session, House Document 91-142, 1969), pp. 199-202. Ray Stannard Baker and William E. Dodd, eds., *The Public Papers of Woodrow Wilson* (New York and London, 1926), Vol. IV, p. 414. Paul M. Angle, *By These Words* (NY: Rand McNally & Company, 1954), p. 318. Davis Newton Lott, *The Inaugural Addresses of*

the American Presidents (NY: Holt, Rinehart and Winston, 1961), p. 201. Charles E. Rice, *The Supreme Court and Public Prayer* (New York: Fordham University Press, 1964), p. 189. Benjamin Weiss, *God in American History: A Documentation of America's Religious Heritage* (Grand Rapids, MI: Zondervan, 1966), p. 125. Thomas A. Baily, *The American Pageant - A History of the Republic* (Lexington, MA: D.C. Heath and Company, 1971), p. 729. Willard Cantelon, *Money Master of the World* (Plainfield, NJ: Logos International, 1976), p. 125. Ronald Reid, ed., *Three Centuries of American Rhetorical Discourse - An Anthology and a Review* (Prospect Heights, IL: Waveland Press, Inc., 1988), p. 638. J. Michael Sharman, J.D., *Faith of the Fathers* (Culpepper, Virginia: Victory Publishing, 1995), p. 86.

²⁰⁰ **(Thomas) Woodrow Wilson.** Alfred Armand Montapert, *Distilled Wisdom* (Englewood Cliffs, NJ: Prentice Hall, Inc., 1965), p. 36. Tryon Edwards, D.D., *The New Dictionary of Thoughts - A Cyclopedia of Quotations* (Garden City, NY: Hanover House, 1852; revised and enlarged by C.H. Catrevas, Ralph Emerson Browns and Jonathan Edwards [descendent, along with Tryon, of Jonathan Edwards (1703-1758), president of Princeton], 1891; The Standard Book Company, 1955, 1963), p. 47. Charles E. Jones, *The Books You Read* (Harrisburg, PA: Executive Books, 1985), p. 117. George Herbert Walker Bush, February 22, 1990, at the request of Congress, Senate Joint Resolution 164, in a Presidential Proclamation declaring 1990 the *International Year of Bible Reading*. Courtesy of Bruce Barilla, Christian Heritage Week Ministry (P.O. Box 58, W.V. 24712; 304-384-7707, 304-384-9044 fax). D.P. Diffine, Ph.D., *One Nation Under God - How Close a Separation?* (Searcy, Arkansas: Harding University, Belden Center for Private Enterprise Education, 6th edition, 1992), p. 16.

²⁰¹ **(Thomas) Woodrow Wilson.** *Bless Your Heart (series II)* (Eden Prairie, MN: Heartland Sampler, Inc., 1990), 9.8.

²⁰² **(Thomas) Woodrow Wilson.** July 4, 1913, in a message delivered at Gettysburg, Pennsylvania. *A Compilation of the Messages and Papers of the Presidents* 20 vols. (New York: Bureau of National Literature, Inc., prepared under the direction of the Joint Committee on Printing, of the House and Senate, pursuant to an Act of the Fifty-Second Congress of the United States, 1893, 1923), Vol. XVI, pp. 7883-7884. Christine F. Hart, *One Nation Under God* (NJ: American Tract Society, reprinted by Gospel Tract Society, Inc., Independence, Mo.), p. 3. D.P. Diffine, Ph.D., *One Nation Under God - How Close a Separation?* (Searcy, Arkansas: Harding University, Belden Center for Private Enterprise Education, 6th edition, 1992), p. 16. [see also: President Woodrow Wilson, November 5, 1915, in an address celebrating the fiftieth Anniversary of the Manhattan Club, at the Biltmore Hotel, New York. *A Compilation of the Messages and Papers of the Presidents* 20 vols. (New York: Bureau of National Literature, Inc., prepared under the direction of the Joint Committee on Printing, of the House and Senate, pursuant to an Act of the Fifty-Second Congress of the United States, 1893, 1923), Vol. XVI, p. 8087.]

²⁰³ **(Thomas) Woodrow Wilson.** 1911, in a remark at a Denver rally. Robert Flood, *The Rebirth of America* (Philadelphia: The Arthur S. DeMoss Foundation, 1986), pp. 12, 37. Steve C. Dawson, *God's Providence in America's History* (Rancho Cordova, CA: Steve C. Dawson, 1988), p. 11:7. David Barton, *The Myth of Separation* (Aledo, TX: WallBuilder Press, 1991), p. 261. Peter Marshall and David Manuel, *The Glory of America* (Bloomington, MN: Garborg's Heart'N Home, Inc., 1991), 2.3. Gary DeMar, *America's Christian History: The Untold Story* (Atlanta, GA: American Vision Publishers, Inc., 1993), pp. 60, 121. "Our Christian Heritage," *Letter from Plymouth Rock* (Marlborough, NH: The Plymouth Rock Foundation), p. 6. Alan R. Crippen II, "Reel Politics - Ideals with Illusions" (Colorado Springs, CO: Focus on the Family Citizen Magazine, August 21, 1995), Vol. 9, No. 8, p. 5.

²⁰⁴ **(Thomas) Woodrow Wilson.** Robert Flood, *The Rebirth of America* (Philadelphia: The Arthur S. DeMoss Foundation, 1986), p. 131.

²⁰⁵ **(Thomas) Woodrow Wilson.** Gary DeMar, *America's Christian History: The Untold Story* (Atlanta, GA: American Vision Publishers, Inc., 1993), p. 60.

²⁰⁶ **(Thomas) Woodrow Wilson.** March 5, 1917, Monday, in his Second Inaugural Address, delivered on the front portico of the Capitol. *A Compilation of the Messages and Papers of the Presidents* 20 vols. (New York: Bureau of National Literature, Inc., prepared under the direction of the Joint Committee on Printing, of the House and Senate, pursuant to an Act of the Fifty-Second Congress of the United States, 1893, 1923), Vol. XVII, pp. 8221-8223. *Inaugural Addresses of the Presidents of the United States - From George Washington 1789 to Richard Milhous Nixon 1969* (Washington, D.C.: United States Government Printing Office; 91st Congress, 1st Session, House Document 91-142, 1969), pp. 203-206. Frederick C. Packard, Jr., ed., *Are You an American? - Great Americans Speak* (NY: Charles Scribner's Sons, 1951), p. 86. Davis Newton Lott, *The Inaugural Addresses of the American Presidents* (NY: Holt, Rinehart and Winston, 1961), p. 20. Charles E. Rice, *The Supreme Court and Public Prayer* (New York: Fordham University Press, 1964), p. 189. Benjamin Weiss, *God in American History: A Documentation of America's Religious Heritage* (Grand Rapids, MI: Zondervan, 1966), p. 125. Lillian W.Kay, ed., *The Ground on Which We Stand - Basic Documents of American History* (NY: Franklin Watts, Inc, 1969), p. 254. Willard Cantelon, *Money Master of the World* (Plainfield, NJ: Logos International, 1976), p. 125. *Proclaim Liberty* (Dallas, TX: Word of Faith), p. 2. William Safire, ed., *Lend Me Your Ears - Great Speeches in History* (NY: W.W. Norton & Company, 1992), p. 117. J. Michael Sharman, *Faith of the Fathers* (Culpepper, Virginia: Victory Publishing, 1995), p. 87.

²⁰⁷ **(Thomas) Woodrow Wilson.** 1917, in his *War Message* to Congress. *A Compilation of the Messages and Papers of the Presidents* 20 vols. (New York: Bureau of National Literature, Inc., prepared under the direction of the Joint Committee on Printing, of the House and Senate, pursuant to an Act of the Fifty-Second Congress of the United States, 1893, 1923), Vol. XVII, p. 8233. Richard D. Heffner, *A Documentary History of the United States* (New York: The New American Library of World Literature, Inc., 1961), p. 243. John Bartlett, *Bartlett's Familiar Quotations* (Boston: Little, Brown and Company, 1855, 1980), p. 682. Frederick C. Packard, Jr., ed., *Are You an American? - Great Americans Speak* (NY: Charles Scribner's Sons, 1951), p. 86. Lillian W.Kay, ed., *The Ground on Which We Stand - Basic Documents of American History* (NY: Franklin Watts, Inc, 1969), p. 254. William Safire, ed., *Lend Me Your Ears - Great Speeches in History* (NY: W.W. Norton & Company, 1992), p. 117.

²⁰⁸ **(Thomas) Woodrow Wilson.** Herbert V. Prochnow, *5100 Quotations for Speakers and Writers* (Grand Rapids, MI: Baker Book House, 1992), p. 499.

²⁰⁹ **Edward Winslow.** *Young's Chronicles*, p. 350. Peter Marshall and David Manuel, *The Glory of America* (Bloomington, MN: Garborg's Heart'N Home, Inc., 1991), 10.18.

²¹⁰ **John Winthrop.** May 15, 1629, in a letter to his wife. *Appleton's Cyclopedia of American Biography*, Vol. VI. Stephen Abbott Northrop, D.D., *A Cloud of Witnesses* (Portland, OR: American Heritage Ministries, 1987; Mantle Ministries, 228 Still Ridge, Bulverde, Texas), p. 516.

²¹¹ **John Winthrop.** Peter Marshall and David Manuel, *The Light and the Glory* (Old Tappan, NJ: Fleming H. Revell Company, 1977), p. 148.

²¹² **John Winthrop.** 1630, "A Model of Christian Charity." *Winthrop Papers, 1623-1630* (Boston: Massachusetts Historical Society, 1931), Vol. II, pp. 292-295. John Bartlett, *Bartlett's Familiar Quotations* (Boston: Little, Brown and Company, 1855, 1980), p. 264. Perry Miller and Thomas H. Johnson, *The Puritans: A Sourcebook of Their Writings*, Vol. I (New York: Harper & Row, 1938, 1963),

pp. 195-199. John Eidsmoe, *Christianity and the Constitution - The Faith of Our Founding Fathers* (Grand Rapids, MI: Baker Book House, A Mott Media Book, 1987, 6th printing 1993), pp. 29-30. Peter Marshall and David Manuel, *The Light and the Glory* (Old Tappan, NJ: Fleming H. Revell Company, 1977), pp. 161-162. Francis W. Coker, ed., *Democracy, Liberty, and Property: Readings in the American Political Tradition* (NY: The Macmillan Co., 1942), pp. 18-20. David Barton, *The Myth of Separation* (Aledo, TX: WallBuilder Press, 1991), pp. 85-86. Marshall Foster and Mary-Elaine Swanson, *The American Covenant - The Untold Story* (Roseburg, OR: Foundation for Christian Self-Government, 1981; Thousand Oaks, CA: The Mayflower Institute, 1983, 1992), p. 80. Mark A. Noll, et al., eds., *Eerdmans' Handbook to Christianity in America* (Grand Rapids, MI: William B. Eerdmans Publishing Company, 1983), p. 38. Gary DeMar, *America's Christian History: The Untold Story* (Atlanta, GA: American Vision Publishers, Inc., 1993), p. 5. Stephen McDowell and Mark Beliles, "The Providential Perspective" (Charlottesville, VA: The Providence Foundation, P.O. Box 6759, Charlottesville, Va. 22906, January 1994), Vol. 9, No. 1, p. 2. *The Annals of America*, 20 vols. (Chicago, IL: Encyclopedia Britannica, 1968), Vol. I, pp. 109-115. Charles H. Lippy, et al., *Christianity Comes to the Americas, 1492-1776* (NY: Paragon House, 1989), p. 265.

[213] **John Winthrop.** 1598-1628, writing in his Journal. *The Winthrop Papers* (Boston: Massachusetts Historical Society, 1929), Vol. I, pp. 196, 201.

[214] **John Winthrop.** *Winthrop Papers*, Vol. II, pp. 292-295. Peter Marshall and David Manuel, *The Glory of America* (Bloomington, MN: Garborg's Heart'N Home, Inc., 1991), 3.26.

[215] **John Winthrop.** 1645. Charles Hurd, ed., *A Treasury of Great American Speeches* (NY: Hawthorne Books, 1959), p. 18.

[216] **John Winthrop.** May 19, 1643, in the Constitution of the New England Confederation. Benjamin Franklin Morris, *The Christian Life and Character of the Civil Institutions of the United States* (Philadelphia, PA: L. Johnson & Co., 1863; George W. Childs, 1864), p. 56. William McDonald, ed., *Documentary Source Book of American History 1606-1889* (NY: The Macmillan Company, 1909), p. 46. Henry Steele Commager, ed., *Documents of American History*, 2 vols. (NY: F.S. Crofts and Company, 1934; Appleton-Century-Crofts, Inc., 1948, 6th edition, 1958; Englewood Cliffs, NJ: Prentice Hall, Inc., 9th edition, 1973), p. 26. Gary DeMar, *God and Government* (Atlanta, GA: American Vision Press, 1984), p. 112. "Our Christian Heritage," *Letter from Plymouth Rock* (Marlborough, NH: The Plymouth Rock Foundation), p. 2. David Barton, *The Myth of Separation* (Aledo, TX: WallBuilder Press, 1991), p. 88.

[217] **Robert Charles Winthrop.** May 28, 1849, in an address, entitled "Either by the Bible or the Bayonet," at the Annual Meeting of the Massachusetts Bible Society in Boston. *Addresses and Speeches on Various Occasions* (Boston: Little, Brown & Company, 1852), p. 172. Benjamin Franklin Morris, *The Christian Life and Character of the Civil Institutions of the United States* (Philadelphia, PA: L. Johnson & Co., 1863; George W. Childs, 1864), pp. 227-228. Stephen McDowell and Mark Beliles, "The Providential Perspective" (Charlottesville, VA: The Providence Foundation, P.O. Box 6759, Charlottesville, Va. 22906, January 1994), Vol. 9, No. 1, p. 1. Verna M. Hall, *The Christian History of the American Revolution* (San Francisco: Foundation for American Christian Education, 1976), p. 20. Marshall Foster and Mary-Elaine Swanson, *The American Covenant - The Untold Story* (Roseburg, OR: Foundation for Christian Self-Government, 1981; Thousand Oaks, CA: The Mayflower Institute, 1983, 1992), p. 7. Gary DeMar, *America's Christian History: The Untold Story* (Atlanta, GA: American Vision Publishers, Inc., 1993), p. 58. David Barton, *The Myth of Separation* (Aledo, TX: WallBuilder Press, 1992) p. 254. John Whitehead, *The Separation Illusion* (Milford, Michigan: Mott Media, 1977), p. 90.

[218] **Robert Charles Winthrop.** Stephen Abbott Northrop, D.D., *A Cloud of Witnesses* (Portland, OR: American Heritage Ministries, 1987; Mantle Ministries, 228 Still Ridge, Bulverde, Texas), p. 518. Verna M. Hall, *The Christian History of the American Revolution* (San Charlottesville, VA: Providence Press, 1988), p. 20, quoting from Robert Winthrop, *Addresses and Speeches on Various Occasions* (Boston, 1852), Vols. I, II, from his "Either by the Bible or the Bayonet." David Barton, *The Myth of Separation* (Aledo, TX: WallBuilder Press, 1991), p. 254.

[219] **Robert Charles Winthrop.** 1866, in addressing the American Bible Society in New York on its jubilee. *The Jubilee of the American Bible Society, New York*, 20c. Verna M. Hall, *The Christian History of the American Revolution* (San Francisco: Foundation for American Christian Education, 1976), p. xxv.

[220] **John Witherspoon.** 1768-1794. Martha Lou Lemmon Stohlman, *John Witherspoon: Parson, Politician, Patriot* (Philadelphia: Westminster Press, 1897), p. 172. Varnum Lansing Collins, *President Witherspoon* (New York: Arno Press and *The New York Times*, 1969), II:229. M.E. Bradford, *A Worthy Company* (Marlborough, New Hampshire: Plymouth Rock Foundation, 1982). John Eidsmoe, *Christianity and the Constitution - The Faith of Our Founding Fathers* (Grand Rapids, MI: Baker Book House, A Mott Media Book, 1987, 6th printing 1993), pp. 83, 87. John Eidsmoe, *Christianity and the Constitution - The Faith of Our Founding Fathers* (Grand Rapids, MI: Baker Book House, A Mott Media Book, 1987, 6th printing 1993), p. 83. Stephen K. McDowell and Mark A. Beliles, *America's Providential History* (Charlottesville, VA: Providence Press, 1988), p. 100. David Barton, *The Myth of Separation* (Aledo, TX: WallBuilder Press, 1991), pp. 92-93.

[221] **John Witherspoon.** 1746, Princeton University. Stephen K. McDowell and Mark A. Beliles, *America's Providential History* (Charlottesville, VA: Providence Press, 1988), p. 93. David Barton, *The Myth of Separation* (Aledo, TX: WallBuilder Press, 1991), p. 92.

[222] **John Witherspoon.** 1746, Princeton University. David Barton, *The Myth of Separation* (Aledo, TX: WallBuilder Press, 1991), p. 92.

[223] **John Witherspoon.** 1746, Princeton University. Stephen K. McDowell and Mark A. Beliles, *America's Providential History* (Charlottesville, VA: Providence Press, 1988), p. 93. David Barton, *The Myth of Separation* (Aledo, TX: WallBuilder Press, 1991), p. 92.

[224] **John Witherspoon.** May 17, 1776, in his sermon entitled, "The Dominion of Providence over the Passions of Men." Varnum Lansing Collins, *President Witherspoon* (New York: Arno Press and *The New York Times*, 1969), I:197-98. John Eidsmoe, *Christianity and the Constitution - The Faith of Our Founding Fathers* (Grand Rapids, MI: Baker Book House, A Mott Media Book, 1987, 6th printing 1993), p. 85. *The Works of the Rev. John Witherspoon* (Philadelphia, William W. Woodward, 1802), Vol. III, p. 46. David Barton, *The Myth of Separation* (Aledo, TX: WallBuilder Press, 1991), pp. 117, 146, 245. Stephen McDowell and Mark Beliles, "The Providential Perspective" (Charlottesville, VA: The Providence Foundation, P.O. Box 6759, Charlottesville, Va. 22906, January 1994), Vol. 9, No. 1, p. 7. William Safire, ed., *Lend Me Your Ears - Great Speeches in History* (NY: W.W. Norton & Company 1992), p. 430. Rosalie Slater, *Teaching and Learning America's Christian Heritage* (San Francisco: Foundation for American Christian Education, American Revolution Bicentennial Edition, 1975), p. 249.

[225] **John Witherspoon.** May 17, 1776, in his sermon entitled, "The Dominion of Providence over the Passions of Men" delivered at The College of New Jersey (Princeton). Varnum Lansing Collins, *President Witherspoon* (New York: Arno Press and *The New*

York Times, 1969), I:197-98. John Eidsmoe,*Christianity and the Constitution - The Faith of Our Founding Fathers* (Grand Rapids, MI: Baker Book House, A Mott Media Book, 1987, 6th printing 1993), p. 85. William W. Woodward, *The Works of the Rev. John Witherspoon* (Philadelphia: 1802), Vol. III, p. 46. David Barton, *The Myth of Separation* (Aledo, TX: WallBuilder Press, 1991), pp. 118, 247. Peter Marshall and David Manuel, *The Light and the Glory* (Old Tappan, NJ: Fleming H. Revell Company, 1977), p. 296. Stephen McDowell and Mark Beliles, "The Providential Perspective" (Charlottesville, VA: The Providence Foundation, P.O. Box 6759, Charlottesville, Va. 22906, January 1994), Vol. 9, No. 1, p. 7. David Barton, *Keys to Good Government* (Aledo, TX: WallBuilder Press, 1994) p. 10. William Safire, ed., *Lend Me Your Ears - Great Speeches in History* (NY: W.W. Norton & Company 1992), p. 429.

[226] **John Witherspoon.** Edward Frank Humphrey, *Nationalism and Religion* (Boston: Chipman Law Publishing Co., 1924), p. 85. Peter Marshall and David Manuel, *The Glory of America* (Bloomington, MN: Garborg's Heart'N Home, Inc., 1991), 2.5.

[227] **John Witherspoon.** Martha Lou Lemmon Stohlman, *John Witherspoon: Parson, Politician, Patriot* (Philadelphia: Westminster Press, 1897), p. 129. John Eidsmoe,*Christianity and the Constitution - The Faith of Our Founding Fathers* (Grand Rapids, MI: Baker Book House, A Mott Media Book, 1987, 6th printing 1993), p. 86.

[228] **John Witherspoon.** John Eidsmoe,*Christianity and the Constitution - The Faith of Our Founding Fathers* (Grand Rapids, MI: Baker Book House, A Mott Media Book, 1987, 6th printing 1993), p. 87.

[229] **John Witherspoon.** John Adams. Roger Schultz, "Covenanting in America: The Political Theology of John Witherspoon," Master's Thesis, Trinity Evangelical Divinity School, Deerfield, Illinois, 1985, p. 149. John Eidsmoe, *Christianity and the Constitution - The Faith of Our Founding Fathers* (Grand Rapids, MI: Baker Book House, A Mott Media Book, 1987, 6th printing 1993), p. 92.

[230] **William Wordsworth.** *Trust in the Saviour.* Stephen Abbott Northrop, D.D., *A Cloud of Witnesses* (Portland, OR: American Heritage Ministries, 1987; Mantle Ministries, 228 Still Ridge, Bulverde, Texas), pp. 521-522.

[231] **William Wordsworth.** *Hymn for the Boatman.* Stephen Abbott Northrop, D.D., *A Cloud of Witnesses* (Portland, OR: American Heritage Ministries, 1987; Mantle Ministries, 228 Still Ridge, Bulverde, Texas), pp. 521-522.

[232] **William Wordsworth.** *Translation of the Bible.* Stephen Abbott Northrop, D.D., *A Cloud of Witnesses* (Portland, OR: American Heritage Ministries, 1987; Mantle Ministries, 228 Still Ridge, Bulverde, Texas), pp. 521-522.

[233] **Rev. Richard Wurmbrand.** *Richard Wurmbrand Letters* (Pomona, CA: Cross Publications, Inc., 1967), p. 9. John Eidsmoe,*God & Caesar - Christian Faith & Political Action* (Westchester, IL: Crossway Books, a Division of Good News Publishers, 1984), pp. 215-226.

[234] **John Wycliffe.** General Prologue of the *Wycliffe Translation of the Bible,* 1384. John Bartlett, *Bartlett's Familiar Quotations* (Boston: Little, Brown and Company, 1863, 1955), p. 1021.

[235] **George Wythe.** Tim LaHaye, *Faith of Our Founding Fathers* (Brentwood, TN: Wolgemuth & Hyatt, Publishers, Inc., 1987), p. 249.

[236] **George Wythe.** Christopher Collier,*Roger Sherman's Connecticut* (Middletown, CT: Wesleyan University Press, 1979), p. 129. David Barton, *The Myth of Separation* (Aledo, TX: WallBuilder Press, 1991), p. 249.

Y

[1] **Yale College.** 1701, in an act by the General Court. David A. Lockmiller, *Scholars on Parade: Colleges, Universities, Costumes and Degrees* (New York: MacMillan, 1969), p. 70. Pat Robertson, *America's Dates With Destiny* (Nashville, TN: Thomas Nelson Publishers, 1986), p. 46.

[2] **Yale College.** 1701. Peter G. Mode,*Sourcebook and Bibliographical Guide for American Church History* (Menasha, WI: George Banta Publishing Co., 1921), p. 109. John Elliot, *New England First Fruits,* 1643. David Barton, *The Myth of Separation* (Aledo, TX: WallBuilder Press, 1991), p. 91. Peter G. Mode, ed., *Sourcebook and Bibliographical Guide for American Church History* (Menasha, WI: G. Banta Publishing Company, 1920, p. 109. Pat Robertson, *America's Dates With Destiny* (Nashville, TN: Thomas Nelson Publishers, 1986), p. 45.

[3] **Yale College.** 1701. Peter G. Mode, ed.,*Sourcebook and Bibliographical Guide for American Church History* (Menasha, WI: G. Banta Publishing Company, 1920, pp. 109-110. Pat Robertson, *America's Dates With Destiny* (Nashville, TN: Thomas Nelson Publishers, 1986), pp. 45-46. Franklin B. Dexter, ed., *Documentary History of Yale University* (NY: Amo Press & The New York Times, 1969), p. 32.

[4] **Yale College.** 1701. Richard Hofstader and Wilson Smith, eds., *American Higher Education: A Documentary History* (Chicago, IL: University of Chicago Press, 1961), 1:49. Gary DeMar, *America's Christian History: The Untold Story* (Atlanta, GA: American Vision Publishers, Inc., 1993), p. 43.

[5] **Yale College.** 1701. Stephen K. McDowell and Mark A. Beliles,*America's Providential History* (Charlottesville, VA: Providence Press, 1988), p. 92. David Barton, *The Myth of Separation* (Aledo, TX: WallBuilder Press, 1991), p. 91.

[6] **Yale College.** 1701, as stated by the founders. William C. Ringenberg, *The Christian College: A History of Protestant Higher Education in America* (Grand Rapids, MI: William B. Eerdmans Publishing Company, 1984), p. 38. Gary DeMar, *America's Christian History: The Untold Story* (Atlanta, GA: American Vision Publishers, Inc., 1993), p. 42.

[7] **Yale College.** 1745, in the Yale Charter. Quoted in Richard Hofstader and Wilson Smith, eds., *American Higher Education: A Documentary History* (Chicago, IL: University of Chicago Press, 1961), 1:49. Gary DeMar,*America's Christian History: The Untold Story* (Atlanta, GA: American Vision Publishers, Inc., 1993), pp. 43-44.

[8] **Yale College.** In a writing of Yale faculty member Benjamin Silliman. Henry M. Morris, *Men of Science - Men of God* (El Cajon, CA: Master Books, Creation Life Publishers, Inc., 1990), p. 39.

[9] **Year of the Bible.** 1983, passed as Public Law 97-280, 96 Stat. 1211 by a Joint Resolution of the Senate and House in the 97th Congress of the United States of America. October 4, 1982. Gary DeMar, *America's Christian History: The Untold Story* (Atlanta, GA: American Vision Publishers, Inc., 1993), p. 53. John Eidsmoe, *Christianity and The Constitution - The Faith of Our Founding Fathers* (Grand Rapids, MI: Baker Book House, 1987), p. 355.

[10] **William Butler Yeats.** 1899, in *The Wind Among the Reeds, Into the Twilight.* John Bartlett,*Bartlett's Familiar Quotations* (Boston: Little, Brown and Company, 1855, 1980), p. 713.

[11] **William Butler Yeats.** 1928, in *The Tower, Two Songs from a Play,* II, st. I. John Bartlett, *Bartlett's Familiar Quotations* (Boston: Little, Brown and Company, 1855, 1980), p. 715.

[12] **William Butler Yeats.** 1933, in *The Winding Stair and Other Poems, For Anne Gregory,* st. 3. John Bartlett, *Bartlett's Familiar Quotations* (Boston: Little, Brown and Company, 1855, 1980), p. 716.

Topical Index

626, 638, 644, 650, 683

Charters (Colonial, Colleges, etc.), **33, 34, 35, 71, 90, 91,** 369, 418, 419, 424, 434, 435, 466, 472, 481, 490, 498, 499, 502, 503, 514, 532, 533, 567, 599, 600, 617, 622, 624, 625, 626, 627, 692, 694, 708

Chemist, 93, 231, 493, 562, 572

Child, 21, 27, 85, 86, 90, 93, 183, 208, 210, 215, 332, 363, 404, 410, 441, 448, 452, 459, 480, 509, 512, 537, 544, 565, 567, 585, 586, 601, 610, 630, 632, 665, 681, 685

Christian (Character), 237, 352, 439, 442, 444, 454, 455, 643, 669

Christian (Commonwealth), 181, 227

Christian (Faith), 32, 65, 71, 90, 91, 99, 116, 119, 189, 262, 279, 282, 417, 424, 435, 455, 525, 544, 567, 599, 600, 626, 693, 694

Christian (Forbearance), 289, 412, 423, 628

Christian (Ideas), 321, 480

Christian (Liberty), 62, 101, 202, 280, 324, 421, 422, 455, 497, 503

Christian (Liberality), 444

Christian (Morality), 3, 8, 10, 11, 12, 16, 19, 32, 33, 72, 85, 101, 106, 153, 158, 165, 167, 204, 205, 206, 222, 243, 246, 251, 280, 317, 320, 325, 333, 348, 392, 398, 401, 421, 430, 437, 439, 451, 454, 455, 465, 474, 477, 478, 483, 485, 486, 487, 507, 508, 540, 548, 574, 595, 596, 598, 600, 601, 611, 661, 669, 671, 675, 676, 679, 707

Christian (Nation), 28, 71, 237, 318, 320, 352, 455, 589, 600, 601, 697

Christian (People), 169, 255, 258, 265, 318, 347, 348, 353, 424, 453, 476, 477, 507, 559, 599, 600, 602, 677, 706

Christian (Religion), 10, 13, 28, 35, 36, 61, 71, 72, 98, 101, 102, 118, 132, 166, 192, 204, 211, 232, 237, 258, 269, 274, 280, 311, 324, 347, 348, 399, 417, 418, 419, 420, 421, 422, 429, 431, 433, 439, 445, 453, 454, 476, 477, 502, 503, 506, 514, 519, 572, 596, 599, 601, 623, 624, 626, 669, 677, 678, 708

Christian (Republic), 431, 696

Christmas, 81, 119, 126, 207, 218, 244, 465, 571, 579, 607, 613, 667, 682

Church (Supported), 169, 179, 293, 303, 327, 421, 430, 537, 548, 573, 569, 602, 688, 702, 707, 708

Churches, 51, 62, 72, 93, 179, 191, 195, 205, 216, 228, 245, 280, 282, 303, 325, 342, 365, 425, 437, 448, 46, 500, 530, 531, 537, 540, 601, 622, 653, 654, 684, 688, 700, 708

Citizen 568

Commodore, 44, 403, 509

Composer, 31, 43, 277, 285, 458

Compromiser, 107

Comptroller, 223

Concentration of Power (admonition to America), 308, 329, 375, 540, 662, 698

Congregational, 7, 55, 136, 160, 409, 426, 431, 436, 560, 707

Congress, (Acts in support of religion), 33, 41, 46, 47, 48, 81, 85, 136, 137, 138, 139, 143, 145, 146, 147, 148, 149, 150, 151, 153, 154, 155, 156, 157, 158, 159, 160, 161, 163, 165, 166, 167, 168, 170, 171, 172, 173, 174, 175, 176, 185, 194, 217, 237, 271, 297, 315, 316, 326, 328, 338, 339, 340, 365, 366, 367, 393, 418, 541, 606, 626, 638, 644, 650, 683

Constitution (re.), 8, 10, 23, 65, 81, 83, 150, 163, 165, 205, 248, 296, 301, 310, 323, 325, 326, 327, 328, 330, 331, 348, 373, 374, 378, 381, 397, 436, 443, 454, 476, 478, 480, 498, 508, 535, 618, 654, 656, 660, 661, 671, 672, 678

Constitution (U.S.), 149-163, 168-170, 175, 180, 182, 219, 233, 235, 273, 274, 473, 479, 507, 528, 569, 598, 603, 606, 607, 609, 611, 612, 653, 675

Constitutions (State), 4, 22, 38, 39, 41, 76, 91, 177, 178, 179, 203, 261, 287, 288, 295, 303, 307, 317, 345, 349, 410, 420, 421, 422, 429, 430, 432, 451, 455, 465, 466, 469, 472, 475, 476, 481, 482, 483, 486, 502, 504, 506, 507, 511, 527, 533, 543, 568, 580, 586, 623, 627, 684, 701

Country, 2, 4, 6, 7, 8, 15, 16, 23, 39, 40, 41, 63, 65, 72, 81, 83, 86, 87, 91, 100, 105, 112, 118, 123, 136, 139, 146, 164, 172, 181, 184, 187, 197, 204, 205, 206, 213, 224, 235, 243, 247, 259, 271, 288, 290, 308, 319, 323, 325, 327, 329, 332, 334, 337, 338, 346, 348, 351, 352, 364, 366, 372, 376, 377, 379, 384, 385, 391, 401, 416, 419, 423, 424, 439, 440, 446, 462, 475, 477, 481, 486, 498, 502, 506, 507, 508, 512, 513, 514, 515, 528, 537, 538, 552, 565, 566, 568, 572, 574, 575, 585, 586, 590, 591, 594, 596, 598, 600, 606, 607, 609, 615, 619, 621, 623, 635, 639, 641, 642, 647, 648, 649, 654, 656, 657, 659, 660, 662, 668, 669, 671, 672, 676, 679, 684, 686, 688, 696, 704

Creator, 17, 18, 24, 52, 53, 69, 71, 74, 82, 84, 86, 95, 118, 130, 143, 185, 199, 200, 204, 229, 240, 250, 251, 274, 288, 301, 309, 318, 322, 332, 337, 338, 344, 345, 350, 410, 411, 423, 424, 429, 432, 462, 490, 493, 500, 503, 504, 516, 542, 557, 572, 589, 597, 600, 623, 627, 659, 678

Crime, 5, 6, 51, 83, 112, 162, 209, 218, 243, 254, 296, 342, 379, 403, 431, 432, 505, 516, 564, 593, 598, 608, 644, 678

Crisis, 59, 75, 106, 150, 157, 248, 489, 516, 558, 586, 652

D

Debase, 61, 513, 598
Dedication, 45, 107, 173, 226, 259, 282, 386, 496, 529, 537, 662, 669, 676, 698
Denominations, 25, 35, 87, 90, 101, 139, 153, 160, 169, 180, 205, 216, 247, 265, 276, 324, 336, 358, 359, 375, 419, 420, 422, 428, 429, 432, 469, 470, 481, 482, 497, 499, 512, 559, 567, 568, 574, 634, 655, 682, 706

E

Educators, 33, 36, 39, 48, 214, 222, 230, 234, 322, 439, 456, 457, 478, 634, 675, 691, 697, 702, 708
Effeminacy, 13
Electrician, 26
Episcopal, 7, 53, 70, 75, 90, 136, 274, 287, 310, 329, 331, 436, 481, 567, 635
Equality (Religious), 204, 289, 310, 376, 410, 411, 419, 420, 421, 422, 429, 469, 503, 568, 626, 627, 628
Euthanasia, 515
Evangelical, 32, 75, 93, 112, 114, 264, 268, 329, 338, 494, 512, 570, 577, 583, 671, 682, 684
Evolution, 61, 69, 198, 300, 366, 368, 493, 594, 702

F

Family, 3, 5, 24, 54, 61, 63, 80, 83, 90, 101, 125, 178, 179, 181, 215, 216, 217, 224, 245, 253, 268, 272, 273, 290, 298, 301, 309, 312, 364, 411, 423, 426, 440, 462, 474, 481, 488, 494, 496, 513, 517, 518, 531, 552, 567, 591, 597, 598, 613, 656, 657, 658, 659, 663, 686
Fasting, 132, 133, 544, 699
Fasting, Day of, 11, 58, 64, 139, 140, 141, 170, 171, 240, 260, 261, 275, 276, 322, 339, 359, 365, 378, 383, 384, 395, 401, 427, 428, 428, 437, 470, 590, 591, 703
First Amendment, 25, 26, 81, 153, 158, 159, 160, 161, 168, 219, 235, 325, 373, 432, 532, 559, 573, 574, 598, 603, 604, 605, 606, 607, 608, 611, 612, 615, 616, 617

G

Geographer, 456
Geologist, 198, 562
God (In God We Trust), 85, 100, 172, 173, 174, 175, 392, 530, 666
God (under God), 36, 43, 45, 58, 86, 173, 174, 175, 226, 240, 377, 386, 393, 466, 482, 524, 529, 538, 548, 571, 639, 659, 707, 708
God (Country), 6, 83, 86, 91, 100, 105, 206, 224, 235, 259, 288, 323, 352, 364, 379, 384, 391, 401, 424, 439, 440, 462, 475, 481, 486, 498, 502, 512, 513, 528, 538, 552, 568, 586, 594, 609, 641, 647, 649, 657, 669, 696, 704
God (God and Country), 100, 288, 323, 513, 528, 538, 647, 704
God (The Name of God), 20, 49, 55, 65, 72, 113, 119, 128, 137, 149, 183, 190, 193, 204, 221, 251, 252, 281, 283, 328, 334, 337, 352, 361, 428, 429, 431, 435, 468, 509, 542, 557, 601, 631, 632, 658, 659, 663
Godliness, 37, 62, 280, 337, 360, 392, 433, 458, 471, 500, 513, 533, 536, 685, 708
God's Word, 64, 73, 113, 178, 190, 524, 624, 641, 676, 708

H

Hebrew, 12, 17, 18, 64, 67, 79, 88, 113, 199, 209, 269, 333, 488, 655
History (repeat of), 547
Holy Spirit, 11, 28, 32, 39, 41, 43, 76, 101, 113, 118, 127, 128, 147, 202, 203, 214, 232, 255, 293, 336, 340, 365, 367, 495, 497, 528, 544, 560, 590, 647, 658, 674, 690, 693, 730
Holy Word, 77, 78, 119, 175, 232, 278, 286, 528, 533, 657, 677, 693, 708, 709
Huguenot, 90, 236, 320, 415, 481, 567
Hydrographer, 434

I

Immorality, 202, 234, 353, 505, 570, 596, 704
Immortality, 14, 50, 115, 183, 206, 218, 243, 250, 277, 286, 312, 313, 314, 337, 349, 391, 446, 561, 576, 582, 663, 671, 673, 674, 702
Inventors, 73, 231, 239, 255, 269, 296, 326, 331, 344, 357, 366, 395, 456, 457, 489, 491, 563, 594, 678

J

Jerusalem, 75, 128, 209, 210, 391, 399, 404, 465, 536, 552, 553, 593
Jesus Christ (referred by Artists, Authors, Historians, Musicians, Philosophers, Poets, etc,), 27, 31, 79, 89, 109, 110, 202, 207, 208, 209, 210, 211, 263, 264, 278, 299, 342, 345, 362, 368, 398, 400, 449, 459, 447, 532, 542, 550, 553, 554, 555, 557, 581, 582, 583, 588, 593, 622, 629, 630, 632, 633, 666, 678, 681, 682, 689, 690, 691, 704, 705
Jesus Christ (referred by Businessmen, Producers), 37, 111, 631, 632, 709
Jesus Christ (referred by Clergymen, Missionaries, Religious Leaders, etc.), 42, 43, 104, 221, 224, 293, 345, 405, 418, 437, 515, 516, 576, 584, 585, 641, 666, 681, 682, 683, 685, 687, 693, 699, 700, 701, 703, 705
Jesus Christ (referred by Educators,

271, 278, 281, 286, 298, 300, 312, 321,
347, 350, 371, 375, 383, 385, 395, 397,
399, 403, 404, 425, 437, 440, 443, 446,
447, 448, 450, 468, 473, 476, 488, 492,
495, 499, 504, 506, 507, 512, 518, 528,
529, 542, 550, 551, 554, 559, 560, 564,
570, 588, 618, 623, 663, 666, 668, 672,
676, 676, 677, 678, 679, 689, 691, 695,
698, 708, 709
Separation, 25, 81, 158, 159, 160, 161, 169,
170, 204, 205, 219, 324, 325, 328, 331,
348, 422, 432, 476, 477, 478, 532, 573,
574, 598, 603, 606, 607, 612, 617, 618,
653, 693, 694
Signers, 4, 33, 38, 41, 53, 69, 75, 101, 144,
153, 180, 199, 211, 273, 279, 322, 326,
337, 352, 354, 357, 362, 394, 442, 494,
511, 527, 543, 572, 694, 702, 706
Slavery, 5, 15, 20, 29, 39, 42, 43, 55, 56, 66,
77, 87, 90, 93, 98, 100, 104, 106, 107,
214, 219, 220, 234, 258, 265, 266, 288,
297, 298, 319, 320, 321, 333, 353, 363,
364, 374, 375, 377, 380, 381, 382, 389,
390, 422, 423, 468, 474, 481, 491, 512,
529, 567, 571, 572, 573, 576, 577, 591,
592, 634, 639, 663, 678, 683, 689, 695
Sodomy, 124, 184, 188, 190, 467, 608, 644
Soldiers, 46, 47, 56, 60, 98, 134, 146, 161,
183, 186, 187, 189, 193, 264, 291, 297,
315, 328, 339, 357, 365, 366, 387, 404,
427, 442, 447, 460, 511, 538, 555, 559,
576, 619, 634, 635, 638, 639, 640, 641,
642, 643, 644, 675, 681, 688, 703
Spiritual, 28, 45, 87, 111, 112, 125, 130,
174, 192, 216, 226, 227, 264, 273, 296,
298, 343, 401, 405, 407, 462, 474, 502,
528, 531, 537, 603, 655, 667, 672, 697,
698, 705
Students, 1, 176, 216, 257, 281, 324, 340,
373, 447, 448, 452, 472, 473, 478, 479,
488, 494, 530, 550, 562, 565, 601, 604,
608, 609, 610, 611, 612, 613, 636, 703,
707, 708, 709
Surgeon, 44, 241, 343, 394, 490, 543, 695
Surveyor, 75, 558, 634
Supreme Being, 3, 10, 11, 25, 35, 36, 37,
52, 53, 54, 55, 75, 108, 109, 156, 213,
219, 237, 240, 247, 251, 268, 277, 279,
308, 327, 369, 377, 412, 419, 420, 429,
430, 432, 451, 462, 482, 511, 514, 581,
603, 621, 652, 660, 668, 677
Supreme Court (re. Separation), 88, 581,
587, 599, 602, 603, 604, 605, 606, 607,
608, 609, 611, 612, 614

T
Teacher, 14, 32, 111, 125, 196, 227, 256,
262, 349, 368, 373, 430, 439, 442, 473,
478, 479, 496, 574, 604, 617, 680, 688
Thanksgiving, 20, 252, 299, 300, 658, 659,
696

Thanksgiving, Day of, 66, 67, 146, 147,
148, 164, 163, 165, 172, 175, 219, 236,
276, 277, 303, 322, 358, 362, 385, 388,
390, 401, 430, 469, 470, 559, 603, 627,
646, 654, 655, 656
Truth, 4, 11, 27, 28, 32, 36, 47, 49, 53, 71,
72, 77, 107, 131, 137, 150, 151, 171, 177,
191, 192, 196, 197, 211, 221, 230, 248,
254, 259, 267, 269, 269, 270, 272, 274,
281, 282, 288, 292, 298, 317, 320, 324,
345, 375, 383, 384, 398, 404, 411, 414,
415, 417, 418, 429, 433, 441, 450, 462,
466, 467, 474, 482, 492, 496, 497, 506,
509, 515, 532, 547, 552, 554, 588, 591,
597, 600, 601, 633, 655, 658, 667, 671,
673, 676, 677, 689, 691, 701, 708
Tutor, 281, 343, 363, 635

U
Unborn, 301, 516, 517, 532, 586, 637, 639

V
Virtue, 3, 6, 7, 8, 9, 10, 12, 13, 19, 23, 24,
34, 64, 83, 123, 136, 147, 152, 153, 165,
170, 171, 206, 240, 242, 243, 244, 246,
247, 250, 252, 253, 275, 277, 289, 308,
323, 342, 348, 358, 359, 381, 384, 403,
424, 430, 449, 454, 462, 471, 472, 477,
493, 498, 499, 501, 512, 513, 526, 530,
543, 543, 551, 561, 570, 608, 611, 613,
641, 648, 654, 660, 661, 662, 664, 701

W
Wills, 24, 33, 49, 211, 290, 313, 319, 424,
557, 572, 663, 674
Women, 19, 77, 103, 106, 113, 123, 124,
125, 188, 189, 203, 205, 209, 215, 223,
234, 290, 296, 298, 299, 444, 493, 501,
504, 506, 518, 519, 537, 540, 570, 585,
597, 598, 614, 632, 691
Word of God, 16, 32, 52, 71, 78, 99, 107,
119, 110, 175, 177, 196, 214, 225, 228,
232, 267, 269, 270, 278, 286, 342, 352,
365, 404, 405, 412, 433, 440, 468, 490,
495, 523, 528, 536, 548, 563, 575, 600,
602, 671, 675, 690, 693, 696, 697, 698,
702, 709

Y
YMCA (Young Men's Christian
Association), 94, 234, 693, 696
Youth, 23, 34, 49, 74, 78, 111, 132, 182,
240, 247, 264, 277, 365, 404, 411, 417,
439, 440, 467, 496, 499, 500, 501, 504,
505, 516, 517, 525, 527, 561, 563, 565,
574, 596, 627, 629, 636, 644, 675, 679,
680, 692, 693, 707